Philip Henry Gosse is known chiefly as the ɛ
Edmund's memoir, *Father and Son*. Douglas V
has shown that Edmund grossly misrepresen..... ....
Philip as he really was, an immensely popular writer on natural history
and a devoted member of the Christian Brethren. Between 1846 and
1857 Gosse published as many as twenty-five separate books on science
and religion. Meticulous research has enabled Douglas Wertheimer to
write a riveting account of Gosse's contributions to both fields and his
persistent efforts to reconcile them.

DAVID BEBBINGTON, Emeritus Professor of History,
University of Stirling

Douglas Wertheimer's meticulous study restores Philip Henry Gosse
to his rightful place as a leading Victorian naturalist and popularizer
of science. Although excluded from the post-Darwinian scientific
community by his religious views, his technical publications on natural
history were praised by eminent zoologists such as E. Ray Lankester.
Nor—as historians now recognize—were his religious views a barrier
to success in arousing public interest in nature, including his role as a
founder of the aquarium craze that swept the mid-Victorian world.

PETER J. BOWLER, Professor emeritus of the History of Science,
Queen's University Belfast

Philip Henry Gosse was one of the most important scientists and one
of the most creative religious thinkers of the nineteenth century. More
than most, he attempted to combine the conclusions of these fields of
knowledge that, many of his contemporaries feared, were slowly drifting
apart. But his views, both in science and religion, were eccentric – and
sometimes, perhaps, heterodox. This outstanding new book is the
definitive account of Gosse's life and work. Based on extensive archival
research, it offers the most detailed reading of Gosse's many kinds of
writing, and reveals his extraordinary achievement.

CRAWFORD GRIBBEN, Professor of early modern British history,
Queen's University Belfast

Like a forgotten fossil vertebrate, stashed at the back of a dusty drawer,
the life of Philip Henry Gosse was never correctly articulated until
Douglas Wertheimer became fascinated with his oddly nonconforming
world. By excavating Gosse's literary remains, dissecting, tweezering and

toothcombing obscure papers and rare tracts, Wertheimer reconstructs and reanimates the hidden body of Gosse's scientific work. It is a labour worthy of Gosse's own filigree studies in natural history, the achievement of decades from which, like the Victorian discovery of dinosaurs, science reappears unexpectedly to open up exotic new environments.

JAMES MOORE, Darwin biographer and historian of
'religion and science'

Fifty years ago, Wertheimer was not satisfied with just a 'glimpse of the wonderful' world of Philip Gosse, let alone the travesty of a story with which Philip's son deceived the world about his father. In the intervening years Wertheimer has made it his business to get remorselessly familiar with Philip Gosse's world, — Methodism in Newfoundland, the thrill of microscopic discovery, the Bible study circle in Hackney, the insect life of Jamaica, the complexity of marine life on the sea shore, the mysteries of Brethren eschatology — each one a subject in its own right. They place Gosse's *Omphalos* in its full context.

TIMOTHY C. F. STUNT, author of *From Awakening to Secession:
Radical Evangelicals in Switzerland and Britain 1815–35* (2000),
Ph.D. (Cantab)

STUDIES IN BRETHREN HISTORY
SUBSIDIA

PHILIP HENRY GOSSE

A Biography

PHILIP HENRY GOSSE

A Biography

DOUGLAS WERTHEIMER

STUDIES IN BRETHREN HISTORY
SUBSIDIA

BAHN
Brethren Archivists
& Historians Network

2024

First published 2024 by Brethren Archivists and Historians Network
1/1, 99 Wilton Street, Glasgow G20 6RD, UK

29 28 27 26 25 24   8 7 6 5 4 3 2 1

British Library Cataloguing in Publication Data
A catalogue record of this book is available from the British Library

ISBN 978-1-7391283-2-6 (paperback)
ISBN 978-1-7391283-3-3 (hardback PPC)
ISBN 978-1-7391283-4-0 (hardback cloth bound)

Cover design and typesetting by projectluz.com

Printed and bound by Bookvault, Peterbororugh, PE2 6XD, UK

Cover image (detail): P. H. Gosse in his prime,
photographed in 1855 by Maull and Polyblank, London
NPG P120(51) © National Portrait Gallery, London
Used by permission.

For Gila

My beloved life partner

Series Preface

Brethren of all branches are a small but significant component of evangelical Christianity. Having their origins in Britain and Ireland in the 1830s, there are now congregations of Open Brethren in maybe 160 countries in the world, a tribute to the missionary zeal of the movement. No exact statistics are available, but probably today, based on the 141 countries for which figures are available, there are at least 40,500 congregations worldwide, attended on any Sunday by about 3.6 million adults and children. The influence of the Brethren on evangelicalism has been significant through their ecclesiology, distinctive eschatological interpretations, their principle that Christian workers can and should 'live by faith', and the significant influence that individuals nurtured in the Brethren have had in other Christian groupings and parachurch bodies.

From the beginning, the Brethren have had a strong strain of academic scholarship and this flourished again in the decades following the Second World War. The Brethren Archivists and Historians Network (BAHN) is heir to this. Its main manifestations are an annual publication (*Brethren Historical Review*) and a biennial International Brethren History Conference (IBHC). Studies in Brethren History aims to make readily accessible the product of the conferences, as well as other scholarly works on subjects related to the movement's history, practice, and thought. Volumes are published as material becomes available and voluntary editorial resources and money permit.

Membership of BAHN is open to anyone with a significant interest in the history of the Brethren movement in all its manifestations. More details are available on the website (www.brethrenhistory.org).

Contents

Abbreviations   xiii

List of Illustrations   xv

Preface   xvii

PART ONE   FOUNDATIONS (1810-1846)

ONE   Hackney and Bloomsbury   3

TWO   A Dorset Boyhood   14

THREE   The Wonder Years   33

FOUR   Those Gorgeous Scenes   97

PART TWO   'HOW GREAT ARE YOUR WORKS' (1846-1875)

FIVE   'The Open Eye'   159

SIX   One Family, One Song   245

SEVEN   'Is It Not Possible—I Do Not Ask For More'   275

EIGHT   'Blossomed Beauties', the Royal Society, and Protest   332

NINE   The 'Sure Word of Prophecy'   390

PART THREE   FATHER AND SON (1857-1875)

TEN   Born for Immortality   439

ELEVEN   'You are My Joy & Crown'   475

PART FOUR   LAST YEARS (1875-1888)

TWELVE   As Age Lengthens Its Shadow   537

THIRTEEN   Afterwards   602

APPENDIX

P. H. Gosse, 'Fairy: A Recollection' [1877]   615

Select Bibliography   635
Acknowledgments   663
Illustration sources   665
Index   667

Abbreviations

AMNH	*Annals and Magazine of Natural History*
BAHNR	*Brethren Archivists and Historians Network Review*
BHR	*Brethren Historical Review*
BMNH	British Museum (Natural History)
Boase	Frederic Boase, *Modern English Biography*
CBRF	Christian Brethren Research Fellowship
Charteris	Evan Charteris, *The Life and Letters of Sir Edmund Gosse* (1931)
Corr. Bk.	P. H. Gosse, Correspondence Book (MS)
CUL	Cambridge University Library
DCB	*Dictionary of Canadian Biography*
DEB	*Dictionary of Evangelical Biography 1730-1860*
DNB	*Dictionary of National Biography*
DNCJ	*Dictionary of Nineteenth-Century Journalism in Great Britain and Ireland*
DSB	*Dictionary of Scientific Biography*
EG	Emily Gosse
EWG	Edmund William Gosse
Father and Son	Edmund Gosse, *Father and Son* (1st impression, 1907)
Freeman & Wertheimer-EG	R. B. Freeman and Douglas Wertheimer, 'Emily Gosse: A Bibliography', *Brethren Historical Review* 17 (2021), 24-77
Freeman & Wertheimer-PHG	R. B. Freeman and Douglas Wertheimer, *P. H. Gosse: A Bibliography* (1980)
GLC	Minutes of the General Literature & Education Committee, SPCK
GT	Gosse Tracts (referring to the tract number in P. H. Gosse and Emily Gosse, *Narrative Tracts* ([1864]))

Hudson & Gosse	C[harles]. T[homas]. Hudson, *The Rotifera; or Wheel-Animalcules*. Assisted by P. H. Gosse (2 vols. London: Longmans, Green, and Co., 1886)
'Jamaica Journal'	P. H. Gosse, 'A Voyage to and Residence in Jamaica: from 1844 to 1846' (Institute of Jamaica, National Library of Jamaica)
JRMS	*Journal of the Royal Microscopical Society*
JTVI	*Journal of the Transactions of the Victoria Institute*
LeBL	Leeds University, Brotherton Library, Brotherton Collection
Life	Edmund Gosse, *The Life of Philip Henry Gosse, F.R.S.* (1890)
NG	Nellie Gosse
ODNB	*Oxford Dictionary of National Biography*
OED	*Oxford English Dictionary*
PHG	Philip Henry Gosse
'Reminiscences'	P. H. Gosse, 'Anecdotes and Reminiscences of My Life' (MS, 2 vols., CUL Add. 7016-7)
Sandhurst Catalogue	*Catalogue of Furniture and Effects, Valuable Books, and Orchids* [belonging to P. H. and Eliza Gosse] ([1900]) [CUL]
SPCK	Society for Promoting Christian Knowledge (London)
Testimony of Prophecy	P. H. Gosse, Ἡ Μαρτυρία τῆζ Προφητείαζ (the Greek title is translated in *Sandhurst Catalogue*, item #455, as The Testimony of Prophecy) (MS)
Wellesley Index	*Wellesley Index to Victorian Periodicals, 1824-1900*
Wertheimer, *Identification*	D. Wertheimer, 'The Identification of Some Characters and Incidents in Gosse's "Father and Son"', *Notes and Queries* n.s. XXIII (January 1976), 4-11
Wertheimer, 'Son and Father'	D. Wertheimer, 'A Son and His Father: Edmund Gosse's Comments and Portraits, 1875-1910', *Nineteenth-Century Prose* 48 (Spring/Fall 2021), 45-92

List of Illustrations

Illustrations are located between pages 244 and 245. For source identifications, see page 665.

1	Father and son
2	Christian naturalist
3	Emily Gosse
4	Eliza Gosse
5	Pioneer Newfoundland entomologist
6	First record of butterflies
7	Father of Jamaican ornithology
8	Father of Jamaican herpetology
9	Orchid lover
10	Microscopic 'builder' rotifer
11	Father of the Aquarium
12	Fantastical microscopic animal
13	Aquarium occupant
14-15	Scenes of sea anemones
16	The most beautiful

Preface

PHILIP HENRY GOSSE (1810-1888) WAS ONE OF THE CHIEF FIGURES among Brethren[1] (British evangelical Christians frequently referred to by the misnomer 'Plymouth Brethren'). For forty-five years, starting from close to the dawning days of the movement, he communed, corresponded with, and debated, Brethren—known in his lifetime as 'Open Brethren'[2]—and other Christians. He advanced his religious outlook with 'tongue & pen',[3] lecturing, evangelising, teaching, preaching, baptising, and watching for the Second Advent. He helped spread the movement across the world; he was an ardent student of prophecy; for three decades he was a shepherd to those under his religious guidance. His religious (and religion-related) writings consisted of six books, eight pamphlets, sixty-nine articles, 104 entries in a Bible dictionary, and six evangelistic tracts. The Victorian preacher C. H. Spurgeon was among those who recognized him for his 'profound reverence for the Word of the Lord.'[4]

As a naturalist, Gosse was a pioneer, innovator, and entrepreneur—renowned as an observer, writer and illustrator; peerless as a populariser; and the publisher on an author's-risk basis of nine of his most important works.[5] He did this lacking independent wealth or the support of any public or scientific body. His vision of the animate world spanned creatures detectable only to the microscopic eye to those soaring in the sky. He spent two decades in the field in Newfoundland, Canada, Alabama, Jamaica, and Britain. He was the first to systematically investigate and record the entomology of Newfoundland,[6] the first to

---

1. 'Philip Henry Gosse, F.R.S.', in Henry Pickering (comp.), *Chief Men Among the Brethren* (Glasgow: Pickering & Inglis, [1918]), 228-232. I am grateful to the late G. C. D. Howley, editor of *The Witness*, who kindly lent me his copy of this rare volume in 1974.

2. Neil Dickson, '"Exclusive" and "Open": A Footnote', *Brethren Historical Review* [hereafter *BHR*] 19 (2023), 82-90.

3. Philip Henry Gosse [hereafter PHG]-Edmund William Gosse [hereafter EWG], 11 Mar. 1872 (Cambridge University Library [hereafter CUL] Add. 7041, 51).

4. *Sword and the Trowel* XXI (May 1885), 236.

5. R. B. Freeman and Douglas Wertheimer, *Philip Henry Gosse: A Bibliography* (Folkestone, Kent: Dawson Publishing, 1980), 6 [hereafter Freeman & Wertheimer-PHG].

6. Carl H. Lindroth, *The Carabid Beetles of Newfoundland* (Entomologiska Sällskapet i Lund

devote a study exclusively to the natural history of Canada,[7] and the first experienced naturalist to live in Alabama (producing a book known as 'an Alabama classic').[8] He is the 'Father of Jamaican Ornithology',[9] the 'Father of Jamaican Herpetology' (amphibians and reptiles), and the Father of 'many other aspects of Jamaican biology',[10] whose 'two monumental works'[11] on that island have not been superseded.[12] The Gosse Bird Club in Jamaica began publishing a *Broadsheet* in 1963,[13] Gosse Nature Guides began appearing in Alabama in 2010, and a meeting of the London-based international Society for the History of Natural History marked the bi-centenary of his birth.

In Britain, Gosse transformed the 'almost universally neglected' field of marine zoology into 'the most popular in the whole range of science.'[14] As the first one to use the word 'aquarium' in its present sense, and the pre-eminent proponent for the aquarium movement, he is the 'Father of the Aquarium'.[15] When he was 50, he completed eight years of research on British sea anemones (invertebrate marine animals related to corals), establishing him as the 'first adequate monographer' of the group.[16] He was '*il riverito autore ... Il capo di tutti per merito e carattere*' ('the revered author ... the leader of all by merit and character'),[17] about

[Entomological Society of Lund, Sweden], Opuscula Entomologica Supplementum XII, 1955), 7.

7. V. R. Vickery and D. K. McE. Kevan, *A Monograph of the Orthopteroid Insects of Canada and Adjacent Regions* (Ste. Anne de Bellevue, Quebec: Lyman Entomological Museum and Research Laboratory, Memoir No. 13, 1983), I: 39.

8. Harvey H. Jackson III, 'Introduction' to PHG, *Letters from Alabama, (U.S.)* (Tuscaloosa: University of Alabama Press, annotated edition, 1993), 21.

9. D. B. Stewart, 'Philip Henry Gosse', *Gosse Bird Club, Broadsheet* No. 11 (Sept. 1968), 2.

10. Ernest E. Williams, 'Over 300 Years of Collecting in the Caribbean', in Brian I. Crother (ed.), *Caribbean Amphibians and Reptiles* (San Diego: Academic Press, 1999), 75.

11. C. B. Lewis and C. Swabey, 'The Study of Natural History in Jamaica', in Members of the Natural History Society of Jamaica, *Glimpses of Jamaican Natural History* (Kingston: Institute of Jamaica, 2ed. 1949), II: 8.

12. Catherine Levy, 'Gosse's Sojourn in "Glorious Jamaica"', *BirdLife Jamaica Broadsheet* No. 92 (Sept. 2010), 15.

13. Catherine Levy, 'Gosse Bird Club', *BirdLife Jamaica Broadsheet* No. 98 (Sept. 2013), 14-18. In 1998, the Gosse Bird Club became BirdLife Jamaica, indicating an alliance with BirdLife International (*BirdLife Jamaica Broadsheet* No. 71 (Sept. 1998), 12).

14. *London Quarterly Review* VIII (Apr. 1857), 290. On the author, see below, 277 fn.10.

15. W. A. Lloyd, 'The Aquarium', *Popular Recreator* (London: Cassell, Petter & Galpin, 2vols. in 1, n.d. [1873-4]), I: 126.

16. H. J. Fleure, 'Alfred Cort Haddon, 1855-1940', *Obituary Notices of Fellows of the Royal Society* III (Jan. 1941), 451; 'the first detailed investigation of the group': Freeman & Wertheimer-PHG, 67.

17. Angelo Andres, *Fauna und Flora des Golfes von Neapel.[Vol.] IX. Monographie: Die Actinien* [*Fauna and Flora of the Gulf of Naples and the adjacent Sea Sections. [Vol.] IX.*

whom it was said that 'no keener observer of marine organisms ever lived.'[18] Few other works could match the 'care and conscientiousness' of *Actinologia Britannica*,[19] while he 'stands alone and unrivalled in the extremely difficult art of drawing objects of zoology.'[20] Nearly thirty years later he co-authored and co-illustrated a three-volume study on Rotifera (microscopic aquatic animals). It was then 'the most complete and exhaustive history of the Rotifera in any language',[21] with drawings of 'extreme minuteness, accuracy, and beauty ... [which] have never been equalled in this particular department, and never exceeded in any line of investigation.'[22] A twentieth century zoologist lamented: 'to draw like Gosse is no longer given to mortal man.'[23] On the subject of Rotifera Gosse was in a class by himself (*'facile princeps'*),[24] and in general the 'G.O.M. [Grand Old Man] of aquatic zoology.'[25] His scientific bibliography is substantial: thirty-two book titles (some multi-volume or multi-edition), ten pamphlets, and over 152 serial articles (some multi-part). He was an inveterate wordsmith, and the current edition of the *Oxford English Dictionary* lists Gosse among its 'Top 1,000 sources'.[26]

Infusing his strictly scientific researches and appealingly written, high-quality popular natural history studies with his religious worldview was a consistent practice throughout his life. All three characteristics were neatly noted in an English West Country weekly:

> Multitudes of books have been written lately to guide the young naturalist
> in his quest, but among them all the works of Mr. Gosse, a pious and

Monograph: The Actinia] (Leipzig: Wilhelm Engelmann, 1884), 68.

18. Edward Heron-Allen, 'On Beauty, Design, and Purpose in the Foraminifera', *Nature* 95 (5 Aug. 1915), 634.

19. Review of *Actinologia Britannica*, *Annals and Magazine of Natural History* [hereafter *AMNH*] ser. 3, VI (1860), 372.

20. Review of *Actinologia Britannica*, *Literary Gazette* n.s. IV (7 Apr. 1860), 427.

21. *Journal of the Quekett Microscopical Club*, ser. 2, IV (1890), 86.

22. 'Living Specks', *Pall Mall Gazette* (30 Nov. 1886), 5.

23. D['Arcy] W[entworth] T[hompson], 'The Fauna of the Seaside', *Nature* 144 (16 Dec. 1939), 998.

24. C. T. Hudson, *The Rotifera; or Wheel-Animalcules, both British and Foreign. Supplement. Assisted by P. H. Gosse* (London: Longmans, Green, and Co., 1889), vi [hereafter Hudson & Gosse *Supplement*].

25. H. G. S. Wright, 'Philip Henry Gosse's Microscope', *The Microscope* IX (Jan.-Feb. 1953), 113.

26. As of July 2021. PHG is referred to in *Oxford English Dictionary* [hereafter *OED*] 3ed as a 'zoologist and religious writer', but of the 494 quotations from his texts, all but a few are from natural-history-related works. *OED* did not consult his serial contributions nor his religious works.

able naturalist, maintain a deserved pre-eminence, as at once clear and
beautiful in style, accurate in scientific statement, and truly healthful
and pious in the spirit with which they are imbued.[27]

He was a practitioner of non-Darwinian science who twice challenged
the evolutionary theory on scientific grounds. He logically contested the
assumptions of uniformitarian geologists and urged Christians to avoid
adopting their conclusions as destructive of religious faith.

I realise that nearly all of those reading the preceding paragraphs
will consider them hyperbole and astonishingly wrong-headed. Their
objection: This is not the P. H. Gosse with whom they are familiar. The
man they recognise was a fundamentalist fanatic, a father with an 'almost
insane religious mania' who raised his son in 'narrowness' and 'ugliness'
in a home devoid of 'culture, beauty, urbanity, graciousness'.[28] He was a
'mediocre naturalist',[29] an 'honest hodman of science'[30] no more notable

Reasoned and analytical in his approach to life's issues, having
determined a course of action or thought he remained inflexible in
pursuing it. He was honest and upright in conduct. He was a dutiful
son, a devoted brother, a loving husband, a doting (if over-protective
and controlling) father, and an attentive grandfather.

---

27. *Wells Journal* (Wells, Somerset) (29 Aug. 1857), 4.

28. Virginia Woolf, 'Edmund Gosse', *Fortnightly* 135 (1931), 767.

29. This off-hand characterization by the late Charles Coulston Gillispie in *Genesis and Geology* (New York: Harper Torchbooks, 1951, 1959), 239, shows how even a highly esteemed historian of science could be influenced by EWG's work. Gillispie gave no indication that he was familiar with PHG's scientific studies. There were no plans to include PHG among the 5,000 individuals covered in the *Dictionary of Scientific Biography,* for which Gillispie was the Editor in Chief (letter, Marshall De Bruhl–D. Wertheimer, 1 Oct. 1971).

30. EWG claimed in *Father and Son*, 1907, 136 (without offering a source) that T. H. Huxley classified his father as an 'honest hodman of science.' The phrase was intended to contrast PHG— an unrivalled 'collector of facts and marshaller of observations'—with 'others whose horizons were wider than his could be' who 'pursue those purely intellectual [scientific] surveys for which [PHG] had no species of aptitude.' The hodman characterization is absent from Edmund Gosse, *The Life of Philip Henry Gosse, F.R.S.* (London: Kegan Paul, Trench, Trübner & Co., Ltd., 1890) [hereafter *Life*], which appeared while Huxley was alive (he died in 1895). It seems reasonable to speculate that EWG created the phrase and attributed it to Huxley. In an undated letter from J. D. Hooker to Francis Darwin, Hooker wrote of Charles Darwin that 'he would never allow a depreciatory remark to pass unchallenged on the poorest class of scientific workers, provided that their work was honest, and good of its kind. I have always regarded it as one of the finest traits of his character,—this generous appreciation of the hod-men of science, and of their labours' (Francis Darwin (ed.), *The Life and Letters of Charles Darwin* (London: John Murray, 1887), I: 347). The condescending phrase was used as a unifying idea in a generally excellent article by Frederic R. Ross, who accepted as accurate the dismissive terminology as applied to PHG (Ross, 'Philip Gosse's *Omphalos*, Edmund Gosse's *Father and Son*, and Darwin's Theory of Natural

than a bricklayer at the pyramids, a researcher who only described 'several' new species of marine animals,[31] an anti-Darwinian who challenged the great naturalist with a preposterous, universally ridiculed production entitled *Omphalos*. He has been called a misogynist,[32] a plagiarist,[33] a racist and colonialist-enabler[34] who imposed European influence on Jamaica,[35] a 'witness to different visibilities of justice and injustice ... in the natural world,'[36] a scientist whose work (when viewed in 'Gothic contexts') involves 'crossing boundaries, with potentially transgressive consequences',[37] who emphasised 'the beauty of the sea-creatures, often accompanied by a sense of sexual innuendo' and whose *Actinologia Britannica* contains 'more than a hint ... of forbidden sexual

Selection', *Isis* 68 (Mar. 1977), 85). 'Huxley's cynical description of Gosse as "an honest hodman of science" may have seemed apt' at the time, wrote zoologist D. B. Stewart (1916-2006). 'Today we can see him as one of the first zoologists to penetrate beyond morphology and taxonomy into the field of animal behavior' (D. B. Stewart, 'Philip Henry Gosse—Part 2', *Gosse Bird Club Broadsheet No. 6* (Mar. 1969), 6).

31. Michael Boulter, *Bloomsbury Scientists. Science and Art in the Wake of Darwin* (London: UCL Press, 2017), 132.

32. Barbara T. Gates, *Kindred Nature: Victorian and Edwardian Women Embrace the Living World* (Chicago: University of Chicago Press, 1998), 74; Barbara T. Gates, 'Those Who Drew and Those Who Wrote. Women and Victorian Popular Science Illustrations', in Ann Shteir and Bernard Lightman, eds., *Figuring It Out: Science, Gender, and Visual Culture* (Hanover, NH: Dartmouth College Press, 2006), 193. Gates' claims are rebutted in Freeman & Wertheimer-EG, 27-28fn. 7, who describe them as 'detached from the facts'.

33. Rebecca Stott, *Theatres of Glass: The Woman Who Brought the Sea to the City* (London: Short Books, 2003), 113.

34. Emily Senior, '"Glimpses of the Wonderful": The Jamaican Origins of the Aquarium', *Atlantic Studies* (2021), 10-11, 20.

35. Suzanne Davis has criticised PHG for writing 'Papers' which 'document the fine game Jamaican birds provided for plantation owners, overseers, visitors and slaves' (Davis, 'Food for Thought *or* Birdseed!' *Gosse Bird Club Broadsheet* no. 66 (Mar. 1996), 16). On PHG's test of the culinary qualities of birds: PHG, 'A Voyage to and Residence in Jamaica, from 1844 to 1846', MS, National Library of Jamaica (Kingston) [hereafter 'Jamaica Journal'] (e.g., 23 July 1845; 15 June 1846); many citations in PHG, *Birds of Jamaica. Assisted by Richard Hill* (London: John Van Voorst, 1847) [hereafter *Birds of Jamaica*], 362-3, 394 (citing Robinson), 414 ('The [pelican] flesh is eaten by some of the negroes'). On Davis' presentism (including the fact that there were no slaves in Jamaica during PHG's time): Charlotte Goodbody, 'In Defence of Philip Gosse', *Gosse Bird Club Broadsheet* no. 67 (Sept. 1996), 2.

36. Sue Edney, 'Philip Henry Gosse, Newfoundland, and the Unveiling of Wonders', in Dewey W. Hall (ed.), *Victorian Ecocriticism: The Politics of Place and Early Environmental Justice* (Lanham, Maryland: Lexington Books, 2017), 142.

37. Sue Edney, 'At Home with Miniature Sea-Monsters: Philip Henry Gosse, Charles Kingsley, and "The Great Unknown"', in Ruth Heholt and Melissa Edmundson (eds.), *Gothic Animals: Uncanny Otherness and the Animal With-Out* ([S. I.]: Palgrave Macmillan, 2020), 142.

pleasures',[38] a subverter of 'traditional ideas of Victorian masculinity',[39] even a figure in the emerging 'gay sensibility' of his son.[40] He embodies the pathetic features of the stereotypical Victorian man, husband, father, Christian, and scientist.

How is it possible that two such contrasting images of one individual exist? The answer might seem, but is not, complex. It consists of just two words: Edmund Gosse. The established view of P. H. Gosse is drawn from the biographical and autobiographical writings of his son. His *Life of Philip Henry Gosse, F.R.S.* (1890) was a conventional Victorian biography. *Father and Son* (1907), a memoir of 'becoming',[41] dramatized how Edmund overcame obstacles to emerge from his constricting background to build a life for himself. So successful was he in that task that his story has been regarded as among the most impactful narratives explaining the modern world.[42] In the process, Edmund's father was straight-jacketed by the portrayals of the great littérateur, whose approach (in the poet's words) was to

> Damn with faint praise, assent with civil leer,
> And without sneering, teach the rest to sneer.[43]

Following from this, one would anticipate that any new biography of Philip Gosse would start by contesting the validity of Edmund Gosse's writings on him. Yet there is no need to do so. That argument has already been settled. In 2021, I documented for the first time how recollections by Edmund Gosse of his childhood appearing during a thirty-five-year period are 'riddled with error, distortion, contradictions, unwarranted claims, misrepresentation, abuse of the written record, and unfamiliarity with the subject.'[44] What this means is that, with some exceptions,

38. Christiana Payne, *Where the Sea Meets the Land: Artists on the Coast in Nineteenth-Century Britain* (Bristol: Sansom & Co., 2007), 119.

39. Agnes Arnold-Foster, 'Gender and Pain in Nineteenth-Century Cancer Care', *Gender & History* 32 (Mar. 2020), 13-29.

40. Martin Goodman, 'Nature Vs Naturalist: Paths Diverging and Converging in Edmund Gosse's *Father and Son*', *Life Writing* 11 (2014), 85-101.

41. Vivian Gornick, *The Situation and the Story: The Art of Personal Narrative* (New York: Farrar, Straus and Giroux, 2001), 108.

42. Fred Eastman, *Books that have shaped The World* (Chicago: American Library Association, 1937), 28.

43. Alexander Pope, *Epistle to Dr. Arbuthnot* (1735), referenced in W. R. Le Fanu, *Book Collector* IV (1955), 334.

44. Douglas Wertheimer, 'A Son and His Father: Edmund Gosse's Comments and Portraits, 1875-1910', *Nineteenth-Century Prose* 48 (Spring/Fall 2021), 45-92.

every previous account of Philip Gosse—large or small—and most of the assumptions about him, are unreliable in detail and warped in form. They are structures erected upon a faulty foundation. What this also means is that an opportunity exists to publish a comprehensive and dispassionate treatment of Philip Gosse—his life, and his work in religion and science. That is what I attempt here, and this is the first study to do so.

Readers will benefit from knowing that this is both an old and a new study. Howso? It's old in that its first iteration was completed as a 1977 doctoral dissertation. Breaking new ground, that unpublished research—based on manuscripts in over two dozen archives and over half a dozen private collections in Britain, Canada, Jamaica, and the United States, as well as research in historic newspapers and other primary sources—was the first assessment of Gosse's life and career which was not by his son or based upon his son's accounts. Together with a path-breaking, exhaustive Gosse bibliography which I wrote with R. B. Freeman, it became the go-to source mined by subsequent Gosse biographers for their published books.

This biography is new because during the past several years I have rethought, re-investigated, updated, expanded, and rewritten my earlier work. In the world of computer software, it would be like going from version 1.0 to 3.1. The result is the entirely new perspective on P. H. Gosse which I introduce at the outset. Among the important topics newly treated here are the background to Gosse's 'wonder year' at the age of 22; the record of his role in spreading the Brethren movement to Jamaica; a detailed examination, in context, of his Second Advent thought; the pioneering nature of his career as a man of science in entomology, ornithology, natural history in general, and his wide-ranging strategy in popularising marine natural history specifically; his attitude to the science of his day and its relationship to his religious beliefs, including dispensing with myths surrounding the *Omphalos* episode; his treatment by the elite of Victorian science as a 'creationist whipping boy',[45] and their boycott of his work; and a new perspective on his fraught relationship with his son.

When I first began to write about Gosse, I considered my personal background irrelevant. It wasn't that I was unaware that it could influence my research, it was that I intended (to the best of my ability) to be fair-

---

45. The phrase is Nicolaas A. Rupke's, referring to his rehabilitation of the biologist Richard Owen in his *Richard Owen: Biology without Darwin* (Chicago: University of Chicago Press, 1994, revised ed., 2009), [xi].

minded, and wanted to be judged on the merits of what I produced. I still think that attitude was not wrong, but a word on the subject may strike today's readers as germane.

In 1913, in the author's preface to the first volume of his *History of the English People in the Nineteenth Century*, the great French historian Élie Halévy acknowledged an audaciousness in his effort:

> A Frenchman, I am undertaking a history of England. I am attempting the study of a people to whom I am foreign alike by birth and by education. Despite copious reading, visits to London and the provinces, and frequent intercourse with different circles of English society, I have nevertheless been obligated to learn with great difficulty, and in a manner which would seem necessarily artificial, a multitude of things which even an uneducated Englishman knows, so to speak, by instinct. I fully realize all this. ... In short, because I am French my knowledge of English life is, indeed, more external than would have been the case were I a native Englishman, but on the other hand, for that very reason it is perhaps more objective.[46]

Halévy, of course, was far from unique in writing from an outsider status. The Frenchman Alexis de Tocqueville wrote *Democracy in America*, the Protestant historian David Wyman *The Abandonment of the Jews*, the Catholic historian Paul Johnson *A History of the Jews*, the British-born Jewish scholar Bernard Lewis was the foremost historian of Islam and the Middle East, and so forth.

I fit in with this group in undertaking this study of a British Evangelical Christian naturalist. Neither by nationality nor religious background nor profession can I claim any of the primary characteristics which featured in Gosse's life. A Jew born in America and educated as an historian in America, Israel, and Canada, I have affiliated all of my adult life with what is commonly termed 'modern Orthodox Judaism'. Like Halévy, in studying Gosse I have struggled to understand concepts and practices which are self-evident to many. Like Halévy, I believe that my outsider status, far from presenting an insurmountable disadvantage, can have its advantages. Outsiders are not likely to have scores to settle or an agenda to promote. If the goal is fairness and understanding achieved through

46. Élie Halévy, *A History of the English People in the Nineteenth Century* (London: Ernest Benn Ltd, 1913, 1964), I: xii-xiii.

careful investigation, the outsider can stand apart and may see things not previously detected from within. That's a point noted long ago by the British Ambassador to the United States James Bryce in his study of the *American Commonwealth*.[47] It is also embedded in an observation about human nature by the late Jonathan Sacks. 'We see more clearly than others what is lacking in our lives,' wrote Sacks,

> while others see more clearly than we do the blessings we have. We complain, while others wonder what we are complaining about when we have so much to be thankful for.[48]

47. James Bryce, *The American Commonwealth* (New York: The Macmillan Co., 1910), I: 7-8.
48. Jonathan Sacks, *I Believe. A Weekly Reading of the Jewish Bible* (Jerusalem: Maggid Books, 2022), 98.

PART I

1810-1846

Foundations

CHAPTER ONE

1843

Hackney and Bloomsbury

-I-

ONE SUMMER EVENING IN 1843,[1] several young men and one woman sat around a table in Hackney, then three miles north of London. They were not Chartists or Anti-Corn Law leaguers, Owenites, Fourierists, or freethinkers; they were not meeting to discuss any of the social or political issues of the day. They might have been considered radicals, had they been better known and understood.[2] Part

1. The date is given (without a source citation) as 9 July 1843 in Robert Boyd, *Emily Gosse: A Life of Faith and Works* (Inverness: Olivet Books, 2004), 37. In an earlier reconstruction of events, Boyd dated the Bible reading to May or June 1843 (Boyd, 'Bibliographical: Philip Henry Gosse, 1810-1888', *CBRF Broadsheet* No. 2 (Mar.-Apr. 1969), 4-5). By July 1843 PHG knew Matthew Habershon (PHG-Nadir Baxter, 22 July 1843, a copy of the letter is in 'Testimony of Prophecy'), and Habershon was associated with Brethren at around that time (PHG-EWG, 1 Mar. 1867, CUL Add. 7018,3).

In *The Life of Philip Henry Gosse, F.R.S.* (London: Kegan Paul, Trench, Trübner & Co., 1890), 378fn., by Edmund William Gosse, EWG contradicted his father's claim that he first associated with Brethren in London in 1843. EWG moved the encounter from 1843 (the year *before* PHG left for natural history pursuits in Jamaica) to April 1847 (the year *after* he returned from there). EWG's chronology has been disproven, and the implications of the contradiction explained, in D. Wertheimer, 'The Truth About 1843, and Why It's Important: Gosse, Brethren, Jamaica and the Scorpion', *BHR* 18 (2022), 15-63. This disputed dating is only one example of why EWG is an unreliable witness in all of his writings about his father. The Hebrew proverb is *kabdeihu v'chashdeihu* (כבדהו וחשדהו), i.e., 'respect him and suspect him' (or more colloquially, 'Trust. But verify'). My principle in this book concerning EWG has been 'distrust unless verified'—not sometimes or frequently, but always.

2. In Britain, a description at that time of 'Plymouth Brethren', for example, misidentifies the Anglican Robert Hawker (1753-1827), of Plymouth, as its originator (James Hews Bransby, *Evans's Sketch of the Various Denominations of the Christian World, and of Atheism, Deism, Mahometanism, &c.* (London: Longman & Co., 18th edition, 1841), 305). Early members of Brethren at Plymouth did, however, come from Hawker's congregation (Tim Grass, *Gathering*

of an emerging, unstructured impulse, they proposed nothing less than a toppling of the Christian religious order, not by force but by example. The 10 people (chiefly from the Hackney neighborhood) who met in the dining room at William Berger's house in Well Street were there to discuss eternal problems. The topic for that evening's Scripture Reading was the seventeenth verse of Romans 1, 'For therein is the righteousness of God revealed from faith to faith: as it is written, "The just shall live by faith."'[3]

The most prominent figure there was 29-year-old William Thomas Berger (1814-1899),[4] one of five sons of Samuel Berger, the Younger (d. 1855), of Homerton, a wealthy colour and starch manufacturer.[5] William had been brought up in an Anglican household which was hardly very 'serious' in matters of religion, but at an evening party in 1833, when he was 19, a contemporary introduced into the conversation the subject of religion. Suddenly overcome by the girl's evident sincerity and her joyful belief in a personal Saviour, Berger withdrew to the drawing-room to 'hide his tears of thankfulness' at receiving 'the Lord Jesus as his Saviour'. From then his progress was steady. Two years later his brother, Samuel Berger, Jr. (1811-1848), wrote in his diary:

> My brothers Thomas and William [Thomas] are also going forward. It is, indeed, cause of thanksgiving, when I look back at a short time ago when neither of them would at all agree with me in anything I could say on the subject of religion, and now how different is the case.[6]

to His Name. The Story of Open Brethren in Britain and Ireland. (Milton Keynes: Paternoster, 2006), 34). Confusion about Brethren and their origins was not limited to Britain: Wertheimer, 'The Truth About 1843', 36-7.

3. The general account which I give here of the Scripture Reading follows PHG, 'Anecdotes and Reminiscences of My Life' [hereafter 'Reminiscences'], vol. II: 250-7 (CUL Add. 7017), this section having been reprinted in EWG, *Life* as Appendix II: 375-8; and apparent allusions to this event by James Van Sommer, *Lay Service: Its Nurseries and its Spheres* (London: John F. Shaw & Co., [?1881]).

4. W.T. Berger contributed to the business with a patent for improvements in the manufacture of starch, described in the *Hereford Journal* (16 Feb. 1842), 4; the patent was contested, London *Standard* (27 June 1842), 4. He died on 9 Jan. 1899, age 84, in Cannes, where he lived for many years (London *Morning Post*, 12 Jan. 1899, 1).

5. Thomas B. Berger, *A Century & a Half of the House of Berger* (London: Waterlow & Sons, Ltd., 1910), 25, 40. Samuel Berger left an estate of £160,000 (Probate, Public Record Office: Chancery Lane—not £250,000 as in *House of Berger*, 41), and was said to have been a keen fisherman: (anon), *Affection's Tribute to the Memory of Samuel Berger, Esq., Jun., of Homerton, Middlesex; with a Short Account of his Brother, Mr. Thomas Berger* (London: Printed for the author, 1853), 29 (about W. T. Berger's brothers, but including mentions of him).

6. *Affection's Tribute*, 52.

In later years, as a landowner and manufacturer of patent rice starch, W. T. Berger became an important benefactor of missionaries in China, and his 'Saint Hill' country home, at East Grinstead, Sussex, was a familiar meeting place for people in those circles. He was, indeed, the 'nursing Father' of the China Inland Mission (CIM), which was begun by James Hudson Taylor in 1865.[7]

His wife, Mary (1814 or 1815-1877), also present that evening, was the 'nursing Mother' of the CIM. She was born a Van Sommer, and until recent years had lived with her family at 2 Chatham Place, Hackney. She and William Berger married on 4 April 1843, and she was recalled as 'a very sweet, simple Christian lady, very lowly and very loving,' while together they were 'indeed true yokefellows, of one heart and soul.'[8] Mary Berger worked closely with her husband throughout her life, the couple remaining childless.

To the extent that there were two relatives of the Bergers' present, the meeting had the air of a family gathering. Mary's brother, James Van Sommer (1822-1901), was then a law student working as secretary at the London Stock Exchange, and at 21 likely the youngest person at

7. Biographical details about W. T. Berger: B. B[roomhall]., 'In Memoriam—William Thomas Berger', *China's Millions* n.s. VII (Feb. 1899), 18-20, and Mrs Jenny Berger (his second wife), 'The Late Mr. W. T. Berger', *China's Millions* n.s. VII (Mar. 1899), 47; *Affection's Tribute*; and Berger, *A Century & a Half of the House of Berger*. For his Anglican background and conversion: Berger's *Wages of Sin & Everlasting Punishment* (London: Elliott Stock, 1886), p. [1], and Dr & Mrs Howard Taylor, *Hudson Taylor and the China Inland Mission* (London: Morgan & Scott, 1918), 25. The remark about the lack of seriousness of his parent's household is based on the fact that Samuel Berger Jr. says he gave his brother Thomas a Bible (*Affection's Tribute*, 28), and 'I feel it to be my duty now [17 Dec. 1834] (by God's help) to introduce religious subjects of conversation at home, but am ashamed how much I fail in this' (*Affection's Tribute*, 49).

The extract from Samuel Berger Jr's diary is quoted from *Affection's Tribute*, 52 (dated 8 Apr. 1835); for his profession as landowner and patent rice starch manufacturer: *1851 Census Returns for Hackney*, Enumeration District 3, p. 24, and *1871 Census Returns for East Grinstead (Sussex)*, Enumeration District 4, p. 5. Berger was then director of Samuel Berger & Co., St. Leonard Street, Bromley, Middlesex, which he inherited from his father, who died in 1855; for the will of Samuel Berger the elder, of Upper Homerton, colour manufacturer, see Public Record Office, London; and the *Post Office London Directory, 1871*, p. 1777, for the firm of Samuel Berger. For the characterisation of William and Mary Berger as nursing father and mother of the CIM, see B[roomhall]., *China's Millions*, as cited, 18.

Berger was introduced to J. H. Taylor by George Pearse (J. Hudson Taylor, 'The Late Mr. Geo. Pearse', *China's Millions* n.s. X (Sept. 1902), [117]).

8. For Mary Berger: *1841 Census Returns for Hackney*, Enumeration District 10, p. 25, where she is listed as living with her family in Hackney at 2, Chatham Place; *1871 Census Returns* (RG 10/1058, Enumeration District 4) gives her age as 56; for the date of their marriage on 4 Apr. 1843: Robert Boyd, 'Philip Henry Gosse, 1810-1888', *CBRF Broadsheet*, no.2 (Mar.-Apr. 1969), 4. The description of her is by Philip Gosse, in 'Reminiscences', as cited (*Life*, 376).

the table.[9] He would become an ardent supporter of missionary activity (editing the *Missionary Reporter* from 1853-8), and the author of some practical pamphlets on religious subjects. Decades later, in recalling the early Scripture readings, he said that they were 'very valuable, and [they] left [their] mark long after [their] cessation.'[10]

A cousin of William's, Capel Berrow Berger (1809 or 1810-82),[11] a cashier, was also present (he was probably employed by the firm in which his father and William's father were partners). He had entered Harrow in September 1823, and left three years later; but he apparently did not experience a religious conversion until around 1835. While at one point maintaining an interest in landscape painting (in which he was said to excel), he also was in 1854 on the committee of the Evangelical Tract Association, to which W. T. Berger belonged. In 1860 he and his brother Lewis became partners in the firm of Lewis Berger & Sons, Ltd.[12]

Another member of the Evangelical Tract Association was George Pearse (1815-1902), a 28-year-old clerk, eventually a stock-jobber at (and then a member of) the London Stock Exchange.[13] Pearse, like Berger

9. Van Sommer is listed as Secretary in London *Morning* Post, 2 Dec. 1842, 3.

10. The authoritative work on James Van Sommer is by Timothy C. F. Stunt, 'James Van Sommer, an Undenominational Christian and Man of Prayer', *Journal of CBRF* No. 16 (Aug. 1967), 2-8. The remark by Van Sommer about the meetings is from Van Sommer, *Lay Service*, 29. He is listed in the *1841 Census Returns for Hackney* with his sister Mary; see also W. T. Stunt, 'James Van Sommer: Missionary Enthusiast', *Echoes Quarterly Review* IX (Oct.-Dec. 1957), 18-23, and [James Van Sommer], *Records of the Van Sommer Family* (Bath: The Ralph Allen Press, 1945); he died 7 Apr. 1901, age 78 (*Surrey Mirror*, 12 Apr. 1901, 1; London *Daily Telegraph*, 30 Apr. 1901, 5). James Van Sommer is not to be confused with James Van Sommer (d. 1851; London *Morning Post*, 8 Feb. 1851, 8), Secretary of the Stock Exchange in London (*Morning Post*, 2 Dec. 1842, 3).

11. He was 72 at his death on 1 Jan. 1882: *Pall Mall Gazette* (5 Jan. 1872), 10; Will proved, *Newcastle Weekly Courant* (1 Dec. 1882), 5.

12. For Capel B. Berger: *1841 Census Returns for Hackney*, Enumeration District 6, pp. 28-9, where a Capel Berger (with a son by the same name, *viz*, Capel Henry Berger, 1839-68, see London *Era*, 5 July 1868, 15) is given as aged 30, a cashier. In the *1851 Census Returns for Hackney*, Enumeration District 6, p. 10, he is listed as 42, landed proprietor; also his wife, previously given as Cordellia (also spelled 'Cordelia', London *Times*, 12 July 1883, 14) is now Caroline. 'Cordelia' was C. B. Berger's widow (*Newcastle Weekly Courant*, 1 Dec. 1882, 5). See *Harrow School Register 1800-1911*, eds. M. G. Dauglish & P. G. Stephenson (London: Longmans, Green, & Co., 3rd ed., 1911), 107; *Affection's Tribute*, 51, for his relations to William and Thomas Berger in 1835; and the *House of Berger*, 41, 48, 62-3. He is given as a member of the committee of the Evangelical Tract Association in the *Missionary Reporter* No. 9 (Mar. 1854), 118, along with W. T. Berger, G. Pearse, E. Spencer, and Henry Heath, and a donor to the Anglo-Oriental Society for the Suppression of the Opium Trade (London *Friend of China* III (June 1878), 178; (Mar. 1879), 302).

13. Willy Normann Heggoy, 'Fifty Years of Evangelical Missionary Movement in North Africa, 1881-1931' (Hartford Seminary Foundation, PhD dissertation, 1960), 22-36. The *1841 Census*

and Van Sommer, was to devote his life to missionary and evangelical causes. In the early 1850s he was secretary of the Chinese Evangelization Society, editor of the *Chinese Missionary Recorder*,[14] and he may also have edited the earliest of the undenominational missionary publications, *The Gleaner in the Missionary Field*. From 1851 he encouraged J. Hudson Taylor to do mission work in China, and it was in 1865 at Pearse's home in Brighton that Taylor 'surrendered to God' and formed the CIM (for that reason, Pearse liked to refer to himself as the 'grandfather' of the CIM).[15] In 1865 Pearse was secretary of the South London Mission, in the following year secretary to the Foreign Evangelist Society, and in 1868 a referee for the East London Christian Mission (whose head was William Booth, founder of the Salvation Army). After many years of working for gospel efforts Pearse served as a missionary first in France and Italy during 1868-73, and then with his wife Charlotte as the first missionaries to the Kabyle people (a Berber ethnic group) in Setif, Algeria, from 1880.[16]

Three others present—Edward Spencer, also to be on the committee of the Evangelical Tract Association, Edward Hanson, and Martin Stapley[17]—made their contribution to that evening's discussion. As the

Returns for Hackney gives an address for a George Pearse as Brook Place.

14. J. Hudson Taylor, 'The Late Mr. Geo. Pearse', *China's Millions* n.s. X (Sept. 1902), [117].

15. J. Hudson Taylor, 'The Late Mr. Geo. Pearse', *China's Millions* n.s. X (Sept. 1902), [117].

16. Edward H. Glenny, *The Gospel in North Africa. Part II. Mission Work in North Africa* (London: Percy Lund, Humphries & Co., Ltd., 1900), 135-9; E[dward] H. G[lenny]., 'The Late Mr. George Pearse', London *North Africa: The Monthly Record of the North Africa Mission* no. 168 (Aug. 1902), 85-7 (I am grateful to Robert Boyd for bringing this obituary to my attention). Pearse was a founder of the *Illustrated Missionary News*; for the conjecture of his editing the *Gleaner*, see *Hudson Taylor in Early Years*, 90fn., which is accepted by Stunt, 'James Van Sommer'. For his activities as a missionary and with missionary societies, see *The Revival*, 1867-73, *passim* (R. C. Morgan was 'very sympathetic' to Pearse in the *Christian*: Glenny, *The Gospel in North Africa*, 139, 141). There are pictures of him in *North Africa*, *op.cit.*, 85; one with his wife Charlotte distributing tracts in Algeria in the *Christian Herald and Signs of Our Times* (17 Nov. 1880), 272-3; and images of him and his wife in Glenny, *The Gospel in North Africa*, 6, 136. Pearse, H. Grattan Guinness, and others, founded in 1881 the North African Mission ('A Moorish Mosque', New York *Christian Herald and Signs of Our Times*, 9 Feb. 1888, 93; J. Edwin Orr, *The Fervent Prayer*. Chicago: Moody Press, 1974, 139; Heggoy, *Fifty Years of Evangelical Missionary Movement*, 23-4). For his connection with the Howards and J. Hudson Taylor: Gerald T. West, *From Friends to Brethren: The Howards of Tottenham—Quakers, Brethren, and Evangelicals* (Troon: Brethren Archivists and Historians Network, 2016), 16-17.

In spite of the fact that George Pearse's surname is sometimes spelled 'Pearce' (even in West, *From Friends to Brethren*, *passim*) he is not to be confused with the Baptist George Pearce of India (Thomas Evans, *A Brief Sketch of the Life & Labours of … G. Pearce*, Calcutta, 1888). Moreover, his name is not found in G. G. Pearse, *The Pedigree of the Family of Pearse* (London: Printed privately, 1897). See *1841 Census Returns for Hackney*, Enumeration District 6, p. 2, and *1861 Census Returns for Kensington, London*, Enumeration District 23, p. 42.

17. I could not find Spencer, Hanson or Stapley listed in the *1841 Census Returns for Hackney*.

meeting commenced, it soon settled into the familiar format: reading round, then prayer, followed by meditation on the selected passage expressed aloud, and, finally, instruction and exhortation.[18]

There was, however, something special about that night: a new member, Philip Henry Gosse, was introduced. Gosse, 33, who had been operating a school for three years, was then living at Woodbine Cottage, Hackney. He had never been a missionary, did not belong to any of the common evangelical associations, did not even know of the Hackney circle until a contemporary and fellow Methodist, Samuel Berger, Jr., a Class-Leader and Society-Steward in the 8th London Circuit,[19] told him about it. Berger was an influential member in the Hackney Methodist Society who was recognized for his catholicity in religious matters—'He loved good men of every name and denomination, acknowledging his Saviour's image wherever he saw it.'[20] It was natural that he would introduce his friend Gosse to his brother William, and that's how Gosse ended up at the evening reading.

For Gosse, the meeting was a turning point in his life—never to be forgotten, its teachings never to be abandoned. His association with this band of believers introduced him to a movement founded only some fifteen years earlier in Dublin and reaching Hackney in 1841, just two years before his introduction to it.[21] Decrying sectarian Christian division and striving to avoid it in the future, they met simply as believers. They called themselves 'Christian Brethren', 'Brethren in Christ',[22] or

Somewhat later, their addresses were: Edward T. Spencer (12 St. Thomas's Square, Mare Street); Hanson (2 Paragon, Paradise Fields); and Stapley (1 Homerton Terrace). As a member of the Evangelical Tract Association, Edward Spencer's address is given in the *Missionary Reporter* (sometime after July 1853) as 2 Pembury Road, Hackney (Forrest, '"The Missionary Reporter"', *CBRF Journal*, 34). I have seen a letter from an E. Hanson on revival services in Halifax in *The Revival* X (21 Apr. 1864), 25, and there are also a number of letters to 'Hanson' in PHG's Correspondence Book [hereafter Corr. Bk.] (see, for example, Apr. 27, May 28, 1869).

18. This description of the Hackney Scripture reading mirrors the format of Open Brethren practices from the earliest days of the movement: Massimo Introvigne, *The Plymouth Brethren* (Oxford: Oxford University Press, 2018), 40, describing the meetings of George Müller and Henry Craik in Bristol in 1832.

19. Obituary notice, *Wesleyan-Methodist Magazine* n.s. 4, IV (July 1848), 800.

20. *Affection's Tribute*, 151.

21. Grass, *Gathering to His Name*, 53.

22. 'Interesting meetings have been held in the Royal Assembly-rooms, Great George-street ... by a number of excellent people known by the name of the Plymouth brethren, for discussing various important questions. The leading features of these people are, that they wish to unite real Christians of every name and denomination under the simple epithet of "Brethren in Christ"' ('The Plymouth Brethren', *Liverpool Mercury*, 18 Nov. 1843, 8). For a discussion of the name, Donald Harman Akenson, *Exporting the Rapture: John Nelson Darby and the Victorian Conquest of*

simply 'Christians' or 'Brethren' (although they were commonly referred to by outsiders from their earliest days, and since, by the misnomer 'Plymouth Brethren').[23] Gosse was a born Christian and in his early 20s had undergone a conversionary experience. Yet he witnessed many things which were new to him that night: the close and minute scrutiny of Scripture, the method of exegesis, and the great respect for the Word, which could be referred to by almost all those present in the Greek original. This type of Scripture (or 'conversational') reading event exemplified a truth for Brethren: the Bible was nothing less than the 'heartbeat' of their movement. Precisely expressing their methodological approach to that book, such gatherings became 'the most influential' of the approaches to Bible study in the late Victorian era, spreading from Britain into the Protestant world in America.[24]

One topic from that evening fixed itself in Gosse's memory: the subject of the Heavenly Citizenship. 'Because I am a Christian, surely I am not less an Englishman!' he said. But Hanson, at whom he looked as he spoke, shook his head. In the view of Brethren, Gosse learned, the possession of a citizenship in heaven precluded a serious involvement in a citizenship on earth. Just before the meeting closed, Gosse exclaimed: 'I have learned a great truth tonight!'[25]

North American Evangelicalism (New York: Oxford University Press, 2018), 29.

23. The earliest reference I have seen to the use of the term 'Plymouth Brethren' (also the earliest recorded use in the *OED* 3ed.) is to the number of 'Plymouth Brethren' (50) in Hereford in 1838 (*Hereford Times*, 31 Mar. 1838, 4).

They were also pejoratively referred to at that time as 'Darbyites': Edinburgh *Caledonian Mercury* (7 Mar. 1836), 4; 'Catholic Institute of Great Britain', London *Chartist* (9 June 1839), 3: 'There was a period when the Catholic clergy, watching over the integrity of that faith ... were very cautious in allowing an indiscriminate reading of the Scriptures. This was a period when there was a mania amongst men to pick out a religion for themselves. ... There might be a Fitz-Wygram—one of the new sects in Devonshire—(Laughter)—or a Darbyite here and there—but they were only one or two out of millions, and there was now no danger of Catholics running after the one or the other—(Laughter)'. The *OED* 2ed. cites the earliest usage of 'Darbyite' as 1884, 'Darbyism', 1876.

Other names by which Brethren have been known include (in the West Indies in the 1870s) 'Slimites' or 'Slimite Brethren', after B. T. Slim, an associate and promoter there of Darby (Wertheimer, 'The Truth About 1843', 61). One newspaper's taxonomy was '1, Darbyites; 2, Newtonites; and 3, Müllerites' (*Irish Christian Advocate* [*Achill Missionary Herald*], 1 Nov. 1873, 551). The best history of the terms used is Dickson, '"Exclusive" and "Open"', 82-90.

24. B. M. Pietsch, *Dispensational Modernism* (Oxford: University Press, 2015), 100-1. I am grateful to Neil Dickson for bringing this work to my attention.

25. For PHG's address at Woodbine Cottage: 'Reminiscences', II: 246. For the remark on Samuel Berger: *Affection's Tribute*, 151. The Administration of Samuel Berger's estate is at the Public Record Office, London, and the obituary notice of him in the *Wesleyan-Methodist Magazine* ser. 4, vol. IV (July 1848), 800. PHG's participation in the group is from 'Reminiscences', II:

-II-

At about the same date, only a mile-and-a-half away at the British Museum in Bloomsbury, another group of men met informally and irregularly in Room IV. Here a visitor might see, neatly displayed in the Table Cases, 'jaw-bearing' and 'suctorial' insects, wingless and winged 'annulose animals' (the term was employed for the Arthropods generally), and numerous species of butterflies. The general collection of the Insect Room, however, was not in the cases but in cabinets, and 'such studious and curious persons who are desirous to see the Museum' needed first to obtain a ticket[26] from the Keeper of the Zoological Collection, John Edward Gray (1800-1875).[27] Admission was on Tuesdays and Thursdays only.

Gray had joined the Museum as an assistant in 1824. He became Keeper in 1840, and during the next thirty-five years of his distinguished career organized the Zoology Department on modern scientific lines.[28] He was fortunate in being assisted by an able staff. Among these were his brother George Gray (1808-1872), the author of *Genera of Birds* (3 folio vol., 1844-9), who devoted himself to the ornithological section; Dr William Baird (1803-1872), a broadly knowledgeable zoologist who wrote on the lower orders of Crustacea and helped organize the conchological collection; Adam White (1817-1879), who was responsible

250-57. *The Christian* states about these meetings that 'Forty years afterwards [PHG] alludes in one of his letters to "those happy evenings", and adds, "those conversations are burned in on my memory."' (21 Sept. 1888, p. 886).

On the heavenly citizenship: PHG, 'The Breaking of the Day', *The Christian* I (23 June 1870), 273: 'I take no side in politics; I am neither Whig nor Tory: my citizenship, my *politeuma*, is in heaven'; W. B. Neatby, *A History of the Plymouth Brethren* (London: Hodder and Stoughton, 1901), 271; and the valuable overview by Elisabeth Wilson, 'Your Citizenship in Heaven: Brethren Attitudes to Authority and Government', *BAHNR* 2 (2003), 75-90. PHG's view of politics curiously translated to his son, who was said to have had no interest in it (George Saintsbury, 'Some Memories of Edmund Gosse', *London Mercury* XVIII (July 1928), 265).

26. Robert Cowtan, *Memories of the British Museum* (London: Richard Bentley and Son, 1872), 304.

27. The description of the Insect Room at about this time is from (anon), *Synopsis of the Contents of the British Museum* (London: G. Woodfall & Son, 44th ed., 1842), 151-56. PHG mentioned his visits to the Insect Room in 'Reminiscences', II: 258-9, and PHG-J.O. Westwood, 8 June 1881 (CUL Add. 7313, 369).

28. On Gray: among other notices *Annals and Magazine of Natural History* [hereafter *AMNH*], ser. 4, vol. XV (Apr. 1875), 284-5; *Athenaeum* (13 Mar. 1875), 363; G. S. B[oulger]., *DNB*, vol. VIII (1890), 453; Cowtan, *Memories of the British Museum*, 354-5; Lovell Reeve (ed.), *Portraits of Men of Eminence in Literature, Science, and Art, with Biographical Memoirs* (London: Lovell Reeve & Co., 1863), I: 112-118; and Edward Miller, *That Noble Cabinet. A History of the British Museum* (London: Andre Deutsch, 1973), 233.

during the years 1835-42 for the arrangement of the greater part of the insect collection in all orders, and who specialised in Coleoptera; and Edward Doubleday (1811-1849), the Quaker entomologist who, in 1842, commenced what was probably the first systematic arrangement of the butterfly collection.[29]

It was these men of science—which later included J. O. Westwood (1805-1893),[30] the distinguished author of *An Introduction to the Modern Classification of Insects* (2 vols., 1839-40)—that Philip Gosse encountered on his not infrequent visits to the Insect Room. One might think that this was an extraordinary achievement for someone like Gosse—not independently wealthy, a member of no British scientific society, affiliated with no university and not college educated—to gain access to this group of naturalists. But Gosse was no novice when it came to the direct study of the Book of Nature. As early as 1832, while a clerk in a mercantile house in far-off Newfoundland, he had enthusiastically commenced his insect studies, and butterflies especially were his 'first love' in natural history.[31] Like his friend Doubleday, who had recently returned to England after nearly two years of collecting in America, Gosse had already had field experience in Newfoundland, Canada, and Alabama. His visits to the British Museum had begun within months of his return to England from Alabama in 1839,[32] and now—as the author of the *Canadian Naturalist* (1840)—he took his place among naturalists such as those in the Insect Room, who could readily and comfortably deal with more than one chapter of the Great Book. But at this point in his career, before he turned his attention to marine zoology, it was the help with entomology, ornithology, and botany which must have proven of greatest value.

29. On Baird, G. R. Gray, White, and Doubleday: in general, *DNB*, and (many authors), *The History of the Collections Contained in the Natural History Departments of the British Museum* (London: Printed by order of the Trustees, 1906), vol. II: 551-601. For Baird: *Proc. Royal Society* 20 (1871-2), xxiii-xxiv; for White: *Journal of Botany* n.s. 8 (Mar. 1879), 96; and for Doubleday: *Proc. Linnean Society* 2 (1850), 84-7, and *Annual Monitor* n.s. IX (1851), 20 (obituaries of members of the Society of Friends). There is a letter PHG-Doubleday for 16 July 1845 (LeBL). *Life*, 171, 233, says that PHG used to visit Doubleday's Epping home at this time.

30. On Westwood: PHG-Westwood, 8 June 1881 (CUL Add. 7313, 369); *DNB*, *ODNB*; *Zoologist* ser. 3, vol. XVII (Mar. 1893), 99-101; and Lovell Reeve (ed.), *Portraits of Men of Eminence in Literature, Science, and Art, with Biographical Memoirs* (London: Lovell Reeve & Co., 1864), II: 96-102.

31. PHG-W. H. Edwards, 25 Apr. 1882 (Department of Archives and History, State of West Virginia).

32. PHG-EWG, 16 Nov. 1872 (CUL Add. 7041, 55).

Gosse found here, too, men such as Baird and White who saw in nature 'glimpses of the wonderful', and were as attached as he was to the natural theology tradition.[33] White, moreover, whom Gosse had known since 1839 as a fellow Christian and who called on the Gosse household for many years to come, wrote in defence of the plenary inspiration of the Bible.[34] It seems fair to assume that a very definite intellectual atmosphere characterized this group—a Christian one,[35] to be sure, and also one which, when Darwin's theory of evolution appeared, would influence not only Gosse but also J. E. Gray, Westwood, and White in taking an antagonistic stance to it.[36]

Gosse's immediate basis for visiting the Insect Room was that he was engaged on what became an *Introduction to Zoology*. In May 1843, the Society for Promoting Christian Knowledge had commissioned that work, and so on Wednesday and Saturday afternoons he spent his time doing research and writing in the Reading Room of the British Museum.[37] Perhaps it was on the appointed Tuesdays and Thursdays that he was in Room IV.

-III-

In the years after 1843, P. H. Gosse's life was dominated by the magnetic

33. Baird, White and PHG all wrote for Revd James Hamilton's monthly periodical *Excelsior: Helps to Progress in Religion, Science, and Literature*. See also [PHG], *Glimpses of the Wonderful* (1845), a juvenile Christmas annual.

34. Arachnophilus (identified in the British Library *Catalogue* as Adam White), *A Contribution Towards an Argument for the Plenary Inspiration of Scripture, Derived from the Minute Historical Accuracy of the Scriptures of the Old Testament, as Proved by Certain Ancient Egyptian and Assyrian Remains Preserved in the British Museum* (London: Samuel Bagster & Sons, 1851). On White's friendship with PHG: PHG's letter (27 Apr. 1854) in (various contributors), *Testimonials in Favour of Mr. Adam White, During Twenty-five Years Assistant in the Zoological Department, British Museum* (Edinburgh: Thomas Constable, 1865), 11, and the Diary of Emily Gosse for 1854 (under Feb. 13, Apr. 27), at LeBL.

35. 'Mr. [Robert] Cowtan [a catalogue transcriber at the British Museum] one-day came to me when I was consulting some work of valuable plates in one of the private halls, & introduced himself very kindly, out of respect for my character, he said. He seemed a Christian man' (PHG-EWG, 16 Nov. 1872, CUL Add. 7041, 55).

36. For Gray's antagonism to Darwin: Charles Darwin-J.D. Hooker, 14 Dec. [1859], in Francis Darwin (ed.), *The Life and Letters of Charles Darwin* (London: John Murray, 1887), II: 243); for Westwood's opposition: his letter in the *Gardener's Chronicle* (11 Feb. 1860), 122; for White: his *Heads and Tales* (London: James Nisbet & Co., 1870), 9-10, and esp. White's copy of the book at the British Museum (Natural History).

37. *Minutes of the Committee of General Literature and Education of the SPCK* [hereafter GLC], Feb. 3, May 5, 18, 1843; 'Reminiscences', II: 258. Between 1848-54, PHG wrote a series of works on natural history for the SPCK which were planned to serve as manuals to the collection at the British Museum (PHG, *Natural History, Birds*, 1849, p. iv).

forces represented by the Hackney Brethren and the Bloomsbury naturalists. From the one pole, he drew his religious ideals: the place of sin and redemption, the iron-clad faith in One Book, the believer's outlook, the conception of Christian ministry, the importance of evangelistic effort, and the teaching of the Sure-Word of Prophecy. From the other, he drew stimulus for his scientific field work, encouragement for his early popular and learned natural history studies, and a familiarity with the work of disciplined, cabinet scientists. From both he benefitted across the years from friendships formed.

This interpretation of a life requires a clarifying note. Hackney and Bloomsbury were separate but interwoven features of one life. The afternoon devoted to science and the evening to religion, yet all part of the same day. Recall the biblical Joseph's insight: he insisted that 'the two dreams of Pharaoh are one and the same' (Gen. 41: 25). *That* was Gosse. As his friend, R. C. Morgan, the founder and editor of *The Christian*, explained: 'Is it possible to separate such a man's work into two parts, and to say, this is secular and scientific, and this is religious?' His observation as one who knew Gosse was: 'We think not. ... His chief glory, indeed, is that he so combined science with religion that we cannot detect where the one ends and the other begins, so beautifully are they woven together in his works.'[38]

---

38. [R. C. Morgan], 'Mr. Philip Henry Gosse, F.R.S., The Christian Naturalist', *The Christian* (21 Sept. 1888), 886.

CHAPTER TWO

1810-1827

A Dorset Boyhood

-I-

P HILIP HENRY[1] GOSSE WAS THE SECOND of the four children of Thomas and Hannah Gosse. His first name was probably after Hannah's father, but whether his middle name (he was the only one of the offspring to have one) was after Thomas' father, his mother's father, or his older brother (who died eight months after Philip was born) is unknown. By a curious coincidence the Henry Gosse (1754-1810) who was Thomas' brother spent his youth as a clerk in a merchant's counting-house in Newfoundland, and went to the West Indies—like the future bearer of the name.[2]

Philip's father, Thomas, was descended on his paternal side from the Gosses of Ringwood. That pleasant rural town, situated on the River Avon close to the west end of the New Forest, near Southampton, in Hampshire, had once been known for its knitted gloves ('Ringwoods').[3]

1. John P. Hodges, 'Mode of address of the nineteenth-century naturalist P. H. Gosse', *Annals of Natural History* 38 (Apr. 2011), 172-174, correctly notes that to 'family and friends' PHG could be referred to by his middle name alone. However he was most frequently known as 'P. H. Gosse' and signed his name that way, even when writing his wife, son or brothers. Since the author of this work is neither family nor friend, PHG is referred to in these pages as he was known to the public: by his full or last name, or by his forename alone when required for clarity.

2. For these details about Henry Gosse and the Gosse family: Thomas Gosse's unpublished 'Memoirs' (seen in the Family Collection). Unless otherwise stated, information on Thomas is from this source. Fayette Gosse, *The Gosses: An Anglo-Australian Family* (Canberra, Australia: Brian Clouston, 1981) is a valuable source.

3. Findlay Muirhead (ed.), *The Blue Guides: England* (London: Macmillan & Co. Ltd., 1920), 96.

Thomas' grandfather, Henry (d. 1777), and his father, William (1714-1784), had both been in the woollen trade. So much is known for certain about the Gosse ancestry, and it is possible that the family itself could trace its origins to Huguenots of Bordeaux.[4] On his maternal side was, as has been mentioned, another Henry, of the Corbins of Newfoundland, who were tanners. When William Gosse and Elizabeth Corbin (1723-1788) were married, in 1741 or 1742, the woollen trade was still flourishing, and the £3,000 dowry which Elizabeth—'the beauty of Ringwood'—brought to the union allowed the family to live comfortably. In due course the mechanisation of the trade left William Gosse behind, and he died with little remaining for his 10 children (two additional ones had died in or before infancy).

Thomas (1765-1844) was the second youngest member of the family. His parents, early recognising his propensity for drawing, sent him off at the age of 12 to study the subject at Honiton, Devon. Here he also learned the elements of Latin, and two years later, in 1779, his father took him up to London to enroll him at the Royal Academy. In spite of a letter of introduction to Edward Penny (1714-1791), the Academy's first professor of painting, Penny attempted to persuade William Gosse to find another profession for his son. The father was not to be put off, and Thomas remained at the Academy until William died in 1784.

The death of the head of the family meant that Elizabeth had to leave the Ringwood mansion and that Thomas had to earn a living. Between 1784 and 1803 he studied mezzotinting and tried marketing his works. He was a good engraver[5] but the public interest in prints was declining, and the trade unprofitable. He left London in 1803, and for nearly forty years lived as an itinerant miniature portrait painter on ivory.[6] He also fancied himself a poet and author,[7] a profession in which he was 'even

4. Evan Charteris, *The Life and Letters of Sir Edmund Gosse* (London: William Heinemann Ltd., 1931), 511. *Life*, 2, claims that the Gosse family had lived in Ringwood as cloth manufacturers since the reign of Charles II.

5. Raymond Lister, 'Thomas Gosse: Miniaturist and Diarist', *The Connoisseur* CXXXII (Dec. 1953), 158, and Raymond Lister, *Thomas Gosse: A Biographical Sketch of an Itinerant Miniature Painter of the Early Nineteenth Century* (Linton, Cambridge: Golden Head Press, 1953). Evelyn Hardy's unpublished typescript, *The Limner: Being the Life of Thomas Gosse 1765-1844* (2vols, undated [?1938], about 62,000 words; Johnstone Collection) was of little use for the present work.

6. For a published list of his 1803-34 travels (based on 'Memoirs'): Lister, *Thomas Gosse*, 17-22.

7. Thomas Gosse was eminently unsuccessful as a writer, though he pursued the avocation from at least 1822 ('Memoirs'). He produced tales, dialogues, allegories, and poems, 'all intended to illustrate & enforce what he called 'the best things'; but all in the quaintest style & most obsolete

less successful' than as a miniaturist, his grandson observed, 'but not less persistent.'[8]

The impact on Thomas of his childhood environment is evident throughout his life. His intense love of the countryside reflected his upbringing in pastoral Ringwood; his desire to attain wealth mirrored the decline in the family's economic fortunes; the disruption of the Ringwood household and the scattering of the Gosses to many parts of southern England, and to Newfoundland, created a sense of rootlessness. Travelling about earning a living suited him in more than one way: it also allowed him to escape his own unhappy marriage.

Both the great religious awakening begun by the Wesleys and Whitefield in 1739, and the Evangelical Revival in the Church of England later in the century, passed the Gosse parents by without effecting any noticeable change in their religious outlook. The mighty efforts of the evangelicals in particular to reform the morals of society and redefine religious belief came too late for them (William Wilberforce, the Evangelical leader, was not converted until 1785, the year after William Gosse died). And yet, evangelicals believed that there was no way of knowing when or under what circumstances the gnawing pangs of a guilty sinner might begin to be felt. It was thus not surprising that children brought up in a morally upright family like that of the Gosses—even though they were not so strict as to forbid playing cards, and for money!—should eventually yield to a higher calling.

phraseology. John Bunyan was manifestly his model, both in prose & verse' ('Reminiscences', I: 35). It is unsurprising that he was unable to get published, given his rambling and prolix style. Surviving TG MSS (seen in the Family Collection) include TG, 'Hebrew Memoirs; Meant to Elucidate, in Sacred Writ, the Story of the Early Descendants of the Holy Patriarchs, in Canaan' (n.d., but paper has an 1837 watermark), an attempt to elucidate obscurities or difficulties from the 'Inspired Narratives' while 'blending ... entertainment with religious improvement' (p. [iii]); TG, 'Lectures, on the Earliest Times: With the View to an Illustration of the Poem, on the Baleful Attempt to Repossess Paradise' (n.d., but 1839 watermark) is some 400,000 words—longer than the book the reader holds in hand. It is interesting to note that in this work TG adhered to the 'interval' or 'restitution' theory of the history of the earth, according to which the earth had a history of 6,000 years, while at the same time admitting that a 'former System of creation has existed even for myriads of ages before the six days' operations of divine Omnipotence, recorded in the opening of the Bible; and ere 'the evening and the morning', in the present edition of creation, 'were the first day." (p. 68, also pp. 61-66) For the future rejection by PHG of this commonly held view, see below, pp. 289, 308-9. Other unpublished works of Thomas are mentioned in *Life*, 14, 189-90. On the 150th anniversary of Thomas' birth, his grandson, EWG, introduced (and probably silently edited) 'Fragments of the Autobiography of Thomas Gosse', *Burlington Magazine* XXVII (July 1915), 141-50.

8. EWG, 'Fragments of the Autobiography of Thomas Gosse', 141.

The first of the Gosse children to succumb to the Revival spirit appears to have been Susan Gosse (1750-1829),[9] who had become 'decidedly serious in religion' when she came to London in 1782 as the governess of a school. Susan (married to Dr Thomas Bell and the mother of zoologist Thomas Bell, FRS) had several years earlier been the first to give her brother Thomas drawing lessons, and thirty-five years later Philip would consult her for information on natural history. Around 1787 Thomas too had become religious, 'formally so at least' (as he said in his *Memoirs)*, and certainly on at least one occasion he attended the Tottenham Court Road Chapel in London of the famed Methodist leader, George Whitefield. Yet his ultimate direction was unclear: he still attended Unitarian chapels, both in London and (before that) at Ringwood.

At that time, Thomas was a 'temperance and water-drinker' and a vegetarian. He thought he was too much in the grasp of 'The World'. He barely gave a thought to religion, had read very little of the New Testament or the Hebrew Bible, was unschooled in the meaning of Scripture faith, was not convinced of his sinful state, and felt no need for a Redeemer. Then the unexpected moment: 'my Effectual Calling from on high ... A day for ever memorable it truly was: for what I then was given to experience has been following me from time to time ever since; & will anon go with me, to my rejoicing & comfort, into eternity.'

> In the evening of the never-to-be-forgotten twenty-second of July [1790], a Thursday evening; I was walking after tea, in one & another of the streets of London. All at once, I was under a supernatural conviction of my own lost & undone condition by nature. This conviction of my sinfulness was by the Spirit of Truth; & this was the first of those lessons which he teaches us, in the Work of Grace. The Law in his hand was like the rod in the hand of a schoolmaster, it was to drive me to Christ. ... Thus did I ... begin to pray; yet not so much with utterance of words, (I being in the public street,) as with importunate earnest aspiration, under that impression of my sinfulness & non-conformity to God's Law & image, & with the view to speedy deliverance. ... For my own part, as I still prayed on,—while walking in Chancery Lane on that remarkable evening,—all at once that whole sensation of my depravity dropt away.
>
> At that very instant, heaven was opened to me. ... I saw with heaven-anointed eyes 'the Lord of Righteousness.' The Father shewed me the

---

9. Gosse, *The Gosses: An Anglo-Australian Family*, genealogical table following p. 215.

Son, by a supernatural revelation. ... thus was I now brought out of the world & into the Church. ...

I was moved with a reverential love to God, & with a brotherly philanthropy to mankind. And thus was Christ realized as Holiness to sanctify me, as well as Righteousness to justify me. ... And as for me; I seemed a new creature; parting with my own debased & sinful nature, and getting out of it into a new & holy & heavenly nature. For the blood of the Atonement was applied, & was benignly cleansing me from all sin.[10]

Thomas had passed through stages leading to an evangelical conversion (over the centuries, the 'morphology of conversion' has been variously described).[11] 'Impressions' of his guilty nature were quickly transformed into conviction of sin; conviction was followed by conversion, and conversion by regeneration.[12] When Thomas returned to his rooms that evening, he opened his New Testament and turned to the Apostle Paul with new eyes. He told his brother Henry (with whom he was then living) about his new life and he changed his conduct. There were inevitably times of decline in his spiritual health, yet the rebirth stuck. That was what counted, 'the *reality*, not *degree*, of faith & grace.'[13]

Later that summer, Thomas began to associate with another believer, probably went to Whitefield's Chapel again, and began to attend the ministry of John Newton (1725-1807), at St. Mary Woolnoth, in the very heart of the City, opposite the Bank. This was the same John Newton who acknowledged his infidelity as a youth, had been an African slave-trader, had undergone a remarkable spiritual revolution, become a leader of the Evangelical Revival and brought William Wilberforce, Hannah More, and others to 'serious' religion. When Thomas's sister Sarah (1762-1813), later Mrs George Kemp, came up to London in September 1791, she took him to Newton—the former 'African blasphemer'—and (according

10. TG, 'Memoirs'. In the nine-page 'Fragments of the Autobiography of Thomas Gosse', EWG ignored TG's record of 'religious experiences and pietistic observations' (p. 150).

11. D. Bruce Hindmarsh, *The Evangelical Conversion Narrative: Spiritual Autobiographies in Early Modern England* (Oxford: Oxford University Press, 2005), 37. I am grateful to Neil Dickson for bringing this to my attention.

12. This is the general way Thomas described the experience in a tract (submitted for publication to, but rejected by, the Religious Tract Society) entitled 'Why Am I a Christian?' (n.d., postmarked 27 January 1843; seen in the Johnstone Collection). The notion of a conventional order of conversion was described by R. J. Helmstadter, 'Evangelical Conversion' (paper read at the Annual Meeting of the Canadian Historical Association, 7 June 1975), 10ff.

13. Thomas Gosse, 'Why Am I a Christian?'. Emphasis in the original.

to Thomas's *Memoirs*) Newton spoke to them 'of his former state of unregeneracy, when carrying on the slave-trade on the coast of Guinea, & how profane he then was.'

In June 1792 Thomas began to read some of the classic evangelical works. He had previously enjoyed the minor Greek poets, especially Theocritus, whose love of pastoral nature had pleased him. Now it was Isaac Watts' *Psalms and Hymns*, and a three-volume edition of James Hervey's *Meditations* and *Dialogues Between Theron and Aspasio* which drew his attention.

Thomas continued to enjoy spiritual health for many years after this, but the constant travels which began in 1803 had an ill effect. He wrote in his *Memoirs* that by 1806 he was in a state of 'religious declension & desertion'. That lasted for a few years, until he had another vision restoring him to his former state. Meanwhile, in 1807, during a visit to Worcester to make miniature portraits, he met Hannah Best (1780-1860), a domestic servant some fifteen years younger than the 42-year-old Thomas. She was the fourth of five children of Philip and Sarah Best, of Titton Brook, near Stourport in Worcestershire. Her father was a shepherd and the peasant proprietor of a cottage. Hannah was attractive, faithful, frugal, industrious, and more than a little superstitious.[14] Shortly after Thomas and Hannah were married, in the Parish Church of St. Nicholas, Worcester, on 15 June 1807,[15] they began the first of their many wanderings, from Titton Brook to Worcester to Bristol. Here they attended Hope Chapel, where 'the Word was preached in purity'. Thomas, in order to supplement the meagre income from the portraits which he took, gave drawing lessons at two local schools. Their first child, William (1808-1893) was born on 24 April 1808.

After about a year and a half at Bristol, in a number of hired lodgings, Thomas had exhausted his business, and they returned again to Worcester at the beginning of 1810. Their second child, Philip Henry, the subject of these pages, was born here in their lodgings in the High Street over Garner's, the shoemaker, on 6 April 1810. They were soon once again on the road, moving to Coventry and then to Leicester before the end

14. Biographical information on Hannah Best is from 'Reminiscences', I: 33-4, 57-60.

15. Thomas Gosse signed his surname 'Goss' on his marriage certificate (copy at CUL Adv. c. 82.5, 7), a variant spelling which he used ('Reminiscences', I: 32). Their eldest son, William, marked their wedding anniversary, taking note of what would have been their 50th anniversary (WG's Diary under 15 June 1857).

of the year; in May 1812 they were in Poole, Dorset, joining three of Thomas's married sisters (Bell, Kemp, and Wills). There they finally settled. Elizabeth (1813-1840) was born, followed by their last child, Thomas (1816-1898).

-II-

Almost everything that we know about Philip Gosse's childhood and youth is from what he has told us. Looking back from the vantage point of 1868, when he began to write an autobiography which remained unfinished and unpublished, it was natural that his 'Anecdotes and Reminiscences of My Life' should attempt to trace, to an extent, the factors which made him what he became. In recounting the events of his early years, Gosse no doubt gave some events an emphasis and direction that at the time may not have existed, or were unperceived. The 'Reminiscences', however, impress one as an attempt to record faithfully and accurately, and this purpose we may all the more assume from the character of the writer.[16]

Philip's childhood seems to have been much like that of any boy living in similar circumstances in the Poole of the early nineteenth century. All of this seaport town of about 6,000 inhabitants (when the Gosses arrived) was a playground for its youthful citizens. Philip was as quick as anyone to run in and around the bulwarks of the moored boats and brigs, to watch shrimp in local pools, or to associate with the many colourful characters of the place: Bridle the town-crier, old Hurdle the postman, or the half-witted fellow known as 'Tip-it-in-here-man'. Poole quay, as he recalled,

> with its shipping & sailors; their songs, & cries of "heave with a will, yoho!"; the busy merchants bustling to & fro; fishermen & boatmen, & hoy-men in their sou'westers, guernsey frocks, & loose trowsers; countrymen, young bumpkins in smocks, seeking to be shipped as "youngsters" for Newfoundland; rows of casks redolent of train oil; Doball the gauger moving among them, rod in hand; customs-officers & tide waiters taking notes; piles of salt fish landing; packages of dry goods being shipped; coal cargoes discharging; dogs in scores; idle boys,

---

16. An edited version of PHG's 'Reminiscences', vol. II only (CUL Add. 7017), begun in 1869 and left unfinished at his death in 1888, was published with annotations by Ronald Rompkey, 'Philip Henry Gosse's Account of his Years in Newfoundland, 1827-35', *Newfoundland Studies* 6 (1990), 210-266.

larking about, or mounting the rigging ... all this makes a lively picture in
my memory, while the church bells, a full peal of 8 are ringing merrily.[17]

Probably at the beginning of 1813, Thomas settled his wife and children
at No.1, Skinner Street, better known as Meeting Lane (the Independent
Meeting house was on the street, just opposite the Gosses' home).[18]
Thomas then left Poole in search of commissions, returning only a few
times a year. He would send, just as irregularly, money to support the
family, never exceeding £100 in any year. Hannah had to take in lodgers
as a supplement.[19]

Both of these aspects of the Gosse household—the constant separation
of the parents, and their impecunious state—left an impact on the
children. Although Hannah did the best she could to bring them up 'in
reputable subgentility, always clean & neat in person ... sufficiently clad,
& sufficiently fed, & a good education furnished to us all,'[20] they were
well aware of their low social standing. The consciousness of that fact,
moreover, was enforced by Thomas's sisters, who looked down from
a position of wealth and had disapproved of Thomas's marriage to a
common domestic servant.[21] Thus it was that Philip, from early childhood,

> had a peculiarly deep sense of the shame of poverty, and of consequent
> ignorance of etiquette. This made me shy in company, & has left quite
> evident traces even to my present. Even now, with fashionable people,
> I never can feel quite at ease: unless learning, & intellect manifestly
> preponderate. I hence acquired an awkward shyness in boyhood, which
> I never got rid of.[22]

Thomas's sisters disapproved of his marriage to Hannah for social
reasons, and perhaps they also recognised that the match itself was
unsatisfactory. No happily married husband devoted to his family will
voluntarily exile himself for most of his life from those he loves, yet that
is precisely what Thomas did. His son was not deceived about the reason.
'My earliest recollections of Father,' Philip wrote,

17. 'Reminiscences', I: 1-14, p. 14. Vol. I of the 'Reminiscences', was sent to Thomas Gosse
to read on 14 Aug. 1869 (Corr. Bk. annotation).
18. 'Reminiscences', I: 122-4.
19. 'Reminiscences', I: 70-1.
20. 'Reminiscences', I: 70.
21. 'Reminiscences', I: 122.
22. 'Reminiscences', I: 148.

are of a tall & thin man, of dark hair & complexion, with an expression peculiarly grave, & even sad, rarely relaxing into a smile. He was thoughtful & silent, uncommunicative & inward, remarkably simple & unacquainted with the world's way, notwithstanding his life of constant travel; living almost wholly in an imaginary world of his own creating; upright & guileless as a child; very meek he was by natural temperament; easily led, easily imposed upon, yet ever unsuspecting. His roving life, preventing the forming of any deep-seated friendships, & the rarity of his presence in his family at home, where I suppose he did not pass one-tenth of his time, precluding the possibility of his taking much tender interest in his children's proceedings, helped to deepen & settle that habit of his mind, which looked inward rather than outward for its enjoyments, & ever more & more fed upon itself. To this was added the utter want of sympathy between him & my Mother;—she totally ignorant of book-learning, yet clever, practical, shrewd, self-reliant, fertile in resources, cautious in yielding her confidence, affectionate, demonstrative, warm in temper, fond of ruling & qualified for it, peremptory, living wholly in the outward, with neither the power nor the inclination for much introspection;—the wonder is, that my Father could ever see in her that which prompted the desire to make her his wife, rather than that married life found so little in common between them. The determination was sudden, the courtship short: she was a very handsome woman; & I suspect Father was attracted by her beauty ... I know she was not at all attracted towards him; but the counsels of her friend & mistress, whom she greatly respected, induced her to consent, as to a match which seemed a good one. ... [Philip's mother had] been brought to a sense of her lost condition as a sinner. And I do not doubt that in this aspect, the marriage was very helpful to Mother's own salvation, & the godly upbringing of her children. It is observable, that throughout life, amid the many occasions of disagreement, & the ever widening alienation between them, my Mother invariably retained the highest estimation of Father's faith & holiness. Since I have been grown up Mother has told me that with all his peculiarities & defects, which were offensive to her, she had never seen any thing in his conduct, inconsistent with the character of a Christian.[23]

In spite of this situation, a sense of warmth was not absent from this

23. 'Reminiscences', I: 32-5.

effectively single-parent family. Philip recalled that 'When I was a very tiny boy, my love for Mother was very ardent.'[24]

Philip's formal education began shortly after the move to Poole. Ma'am Sly, 'who taught A B C to babies', was his teacher in 1813, and shortly thereafter he attended Ma'am Drew's dame school, returning around 1815 to the parlour of their Skinner Street residence and the care of their landlady, Mrs Josiah Brown.[25] When she ceased taking in students, Philip, then eight years old, joined his brother William at Charles Sells' day-school, reputedly the best in town, and here he remained for four years.[26]

Unsurprisingly, the most important education which he received at this time came as the result of his own curiosity. Philip was introspective, like his father, with few close friends other than brother William and John Hammond Brown (d. 1827).[27] Although he played at scourge-tops, peg-tops, humming-tops, marbles, and other street games with his friends, he enjoyed even more spending time with John Brown. Neither required any other friend: 'We sat side by side at [Sells'] school, walked to & fro with the arm of one round the other's neck, & out of school hours were nearly always together.'[28] During their spare time, they played on the rocking-horse and with the toys and chemicals in John's room, or pored over the natural history plates in two encyclopedias, the *Pantologia* and *Encyclopaedia Parenthesis* (the name Philip gave to the *Encyclopaedia Perthensis*). It was these two works, as well as the association with Aunt Susan Bell and cousin Thomas Salter, which Philip recalled as factors which aroused his love for natural history.[29]

24. 'Reminiscences', I: 64.

25. 'Reminiscences', I: 142; PHG, 'A Country Day-School Seventy Years Ago', *Longman's Magazine* XIII (Mar. 1889), 512. J. S. Udal mined the *Longman's* article for 'Dorsetshire Children's Games, Etc.', *Folk-Lore Journal* VII (1889), 234-6, 252-7; see also T. Gosse, 'Memoirs'. It is not clear whether the *Longman's* article, with its headnote description by EWG, was actually a separate PHG memoir or, more likely, a version of 'Reminiscences', I:142-235 edited by EWG (D. Wertheimer, 'Some Hardy Notes on Dorset Words and Customs', *Notes and Queries* n.s.21 (Jan. 1974), 26).

26. PHG, 'Country Day-school'. PHG thought that there were never more than 30 students at a time at Sells school, but William was able to list 71 who had come and gone between 1818-21 ('Reminiscences', I: 181-85).

27. 'Reminiscences', I: 239.

28. 'Reminiscences', I: 176, and PHG, 'Country Day-school', 513-7.

29. 'My love for natural history was very early awakened', PHG wrote, referring to the reading of the encyclopedias. That must have been around 1817, as PHG remembered seeing the former work at the home of his Uncle John Gosse, who didn't return to Poole from Newfoundland until that year. The second edition of *Pantologia* appeared in 24 vols., illustrated (1816), and

Reading was an integral part of this self-education. He was a quick reader with bookish tastes. 'I can recal [*sic*] myself, when a very tiny boy, stretched at full length on my belly on the hearthrug before the parlour fire, reading with eager delight some childish book; & this as an ordinary habit.'[30] By the age of 13 he had already devoured a fair amount, having calculated that he had read some fifty books—juvenile writings, romances, histories and natural histories, poetry and hymns, and a variety of religious works.[31] Moreover, Gosse claimed that much of this literature left a lasting impression upon him—a credible claim in light of his remarkably retentive memory. Such might be expected of a child who was encouraged by his mother to learn chapters of the Bible, hymns, and catechisms by heart, and who could memorize entire chapters of Scripture before the age of eight, 'and this with great ease.'[32] Mary Sherwood's *The History of Little Henry and His Bearer* (1814), which Gosse borrowed from John Brown, 'was a wonderful favourite. It was decidedly helpful in preparing my mind for its after decision in religious matters. Long after I became a man, I could not read parts of this story without tears.'[33] Grace Kennedy's *Anna Ross, a Story for Children* (1824), 'had a very beneficent effect, making me feel my sinfulness, & the need of a new heart.'[34] To her immensely popular *Father Clement. A Roman Catholic Story* (1823), 'I probably owe very much of the strong dislike to Popery, wh. has grown with years.'[35] Thomas Scott's

Encyclopaedia Perthensis in 12vols.(1813). Susan Bell and Thomas Salter were prepared to help William and Philip and John Brown identify strange specimens they found, and the former showed the brothers how to keep sea anemones alive in a dish of sea-water ('Reminiscences', I: 153-5).

30. 'Reminiscences', I: 61, 149. PHG remarked that 'This habit & this power [of memorizing] have been of vital advantage to me in my labour as a minister of Christ; as I have acquired a grasp of the letter of Scripture which is possessed by few' (ibid, 149-50).

31. 'Reminiscences', I: 210; 345-62, which contains a list of all the works PHG recalled reading between 1813-21. Some of the books read by 1824 (others are mentioned in this paragraph) include John Gay's *Fables* (ser. 2, 1738); John Aikin & Mrs Barbauld's *Evenings at Home* (6vols., 1795) and Barbauld's *Hymns in Prose for Children* ([1775?]); Samuel Johnson's *Rasselas* (1759); Goldsmith's school histories of England, Rome, and Greece; J. Macloc's *New, Complete, and Universal Natural History* (1813), Mrs Barbauld's Isaac Watts' *Divine & Moral Songs for Children* (1720); Hervey's *Theron and Aspasio* and *Meditations* (both from his father's library); Maria Edgeworth's *Continuation of Early Lessons* (2vols., 1814); and Grace Kennedy's novels (including *The Decision*, 1821 and *Profession is Not Principle*, 1822).

32. 'Reminiscences', I: 152.

33. 'Reminiscences', I: 153.

34. 'Reminiscences', I: 365.

35. 'Reminiscences', I: 354. The unfavourable depiction of Catholicism in this book was controversial (see the entry on the Scottish writer Grace Kennedy in *DNB*) and influential. The

Commentary (1788-92) on the Bible, the famous work of the Evangelical who succeeded John Newton at Olney and which Philip found in his father's library, 'I studied with much interest, even in childhood, & not without important advantage. His Notes on the Apocalypse & on Daniel laid the foundation of my subsequent study of unfulfilled Prophecy, & with the single exception that he did not see the personal coming & premillennial reign of the Lord Jesus, there is very little in his views to which I can except even now [Dec. 1868].' Besides the lasting impressions which these works made, there was Isaac Watts' *Psalms and Hymns* which his mother gave him and which 'has accompanied me in all my wanderings since'; Edward Young's didactic 10,000-line blank verse poem, *Night Thoughts on Life, Death, and Immortality* (1742-45), 'which I took with me to Newfoundland. I knew long passages of this by rote'; Wordsworth's *Lyrical Ballads*, 'a great delight'; collections of poetry through which he became acquainted with Dryden, Spenser, Milton, Pope, Blair, Prior, Shenstone, and others; and *A Complete Natural History ... of Upwards of 300 Animals*, 'a great favourite with us.'[36]

In 1822 Philip's happy circle of friends was broken up. At the end of March, William (who was about to turn 14) left for Carbonear, Newfoundland, to work as a clerk in his uncle John Gosse's firm (Gosse, Pack, & Fryer).[37] The parting of brothers and friends was a sad one:

> William's last act was to tie a comforter round my throat, just as I was leaving the ship; and this mark of brotherly care would bring tears to my eyes for months afterwards, whenever I thought of it. In fact I turned the recollection to useful account; for whenever I felt an inclination to merriment at unseasonable times, as when at meetings for instance,

work was in print for over 50 years (advertisement, *Athenaeum*, 27 July 1878, 123). Edward Denny, an early Brethren, was supposed to have been 'brought under conviction of sin by reading an Irish story, "Father Clement," and soon confessed his Lord' (Hy. Pickering (comp.), *Chief Men Among the Brethren* (London: Pickering & Inglis Ltd, 2nd ed., 1931, 1968), 45). PHG associated Catholicism with anti-Semitism (PHG, 'History of the Jews', 1851, Family Collection copy only, p. 388: 'It is curious to observe how intimately [during the Middle Ages] the persecutions of the miserable Children of Israel were connected with the idolatries and lying wonders of Popery').

36. 'Reminiscences', I: 354-5; the quotations in this paragraph are all from this source, 353-5. I am grateful to R. B. Freeman for identifying for me [?T. Boreman's] *A Complete Natural History ...* (1730, many later editions, including 1813).

37. The company was known by different names at different times and places. In England: Fryer, Gosse, and Pack; in Newfoundland: Pack, Gosse, and Fryer ('Notices', *The Star and Conception Bay Journal*, 25 Nov. 1835, 2; 'Pack, Robert', *DCB* VIII). PHG consistently referred to the business as 'Gosse, Pack & Fryer' (e.g., 'Reminiscences', II: 59, etc.). In 1842 W. R. Fryer left what had been W. R. and J. Fryer, J. Gosse, and R. Pack (London *Examiner*, 10 Sept. 1842, 590).

and wished to restrain it, I had but to recal the image of William tying my comforter, & all sense of the ludicrous, all tendency to risibility, wd. cease in an instant.[38]

Then John Brown left Sells' to attend the Revd R. Keynes' school in the neighbouring town of Blandford, and another companion was lost. Philip had admired Sells as a teacher, and learned a fair amount at his school (he especially enjoyed geography), but the Gosses' financial situation was a constant worry. Studies had to be continued under cheaper tuition elsewhere.[39]

The time which Philip spent at John Hosier's in Cinnamon Lane was not particularly productive. His handwriting remained a wretched scrawl, even though Hosier specialised in instruction in writing and ciphering (arithmetic). His first attempt at painting (around 1823) was inspired by his father's miniaturist style.[40] A Wesleyan, Hosier used to tell students 'how he had lain across a table all night on one occasion, weeping in agony on account of his sins.' Afterwards, there was his repertory of stale jokes.[41]

An opportunity soon came to acquire a classical education. With William earning a living in Carbonear, and Thomas Jr. doing the same at a grocer's in Poole, Philip became '"cock of the walk"' in the family, and a determination was made to further his intellectual development.[42] Henry F. Lance (d. 1852)[43] opened a new day and boarding school in Blandford, and in January 1823 Philip and some other boys from Poole set off for the school. 'As night came,' Philip wrote later,

> we boys, who had never been from home before, except for short holiday making, began to feel our desolateness, & to think of mothers. Green, who slept with me, was careful to inform me, on going to bed, that he suffered under a weakness of the eyes, wh[ich] often made them water at night. I fear that others of us caught the same disorder that night.[44]

The main emphasis at Lance's school was Latin and, towards the end,

---

38. 'Reminiscences', I: 235. On Pack, Gosse, and Fryer, see see 'Pack, Robert', *DCB* VIII.
39. 'Reminiscences', I: 206, 234.
40. 'Reminiscences', I: 89, 238.
41. 'Reminiscences', I: 232; PHG, 'Country Day-school', 524.
42. 'Reminiscences', I: 237-8, 244, 284.
43. 'Deaths', Sherborne, Dorset *Western Flying Post* (23 Mar. 1852), 3. Lance died at the age of 50.
44. 'Reminiscences', I: 245. It appears that when PHG first went to Blandford, there were 8 other boys (p. 275).

Greek. Both subjects were of particular interest to Philip then,[45] and of great value in later years in both his scientific and religious writings. Moreover, they suited his personality. The study of Latin especially helps to train and encourage one to think logically, even if it seems also to make the mind impatient of usages which follow a different pattern from the Latin one. Philip had learned some Latin from his father in 1818[46] and his grasp of the subject was superior to that of his classmates. Lance recognised this by making him his only junior assistant.[47] But what that assistant learned had to come largely through his own efforts, for the 20-something Lance, 'tall, foppish, wearing his hair frizzed straight up from his head on all sides',[48] did not encourage this shy and timid boy to seek help. Indeed, Lance—Henry 'Fitzherbert' Lance, to give him his full due, the middle name being an addition to make the whole sound genteel—was a harsh tyrant. 'His common expression, when one had made a blunder in translation, was "O you fool-ass!" usually accompanied by a sound box on the ear. The little boys he was in the habit of lifting bodily from the ground by one of the ears, catching the lad a box on the ear, as he let him drop.'[49]

Some of the other subjects taught included Euclid, ciphering, and elocution, and Gosse's favorites, English grammar and composition. Already he could express his thoughts with ease, he recalled, but

> My great difficulty was to find thoughts, not to express them. I recollect that when I chose to take as my Theme, "The Attributes of God", it seemed as if I could say a good deal that was telling; but when I began to write, I was painfully struck to observe how few thoughts presented themselves for recording.[50]

He also volunteered to draw and colour animals and birds, 'work in which I delighted.'[51]

For awhile, Philip enjoyed being one of the boys at school. He went with the others on Sundays to the Revd Mr Keynes' Independent Meeting.[52] He

45. 'Reminiscences', I: 249, 292.
46. 'Reminiscences', I: 54.
47. 'Reminiscences', I: 284.
48. 'Reminiscences', I: 258.
49. 'Reminiscences', I: 253.
50. 'Reminiscences', I: 293.
51. 'Reminiscences', I: 284.
52. 'Reminiscences', I: 269-70.

had his nicknames, too—'Goose' from Poole days, 'Philip the Fair' from Sells', 'Gos-hawk' or 'Skuff' at Blandford. From the habit of stooping his shoulders while walking, Lance called him 'Old Slouch'.[53]

Philip gradually came to miss more and more the companionship of close friends which he had at Sells' school. 'I was bookish, inward, craving after affection, little caring for mere romps, or fun,' he recalled. He thought Lance disliked him,[54] and when, in January 1824, Lance discovered that some of the boys planned to run away from Blandford and return home, it was Gosse who was accused of having been the ringleader (unfairly, he claimed). He was expelled the next month.[55]

For slightly more than a year, Philip was back at Hosier's school, until June 1825 when, at the age of 15, he obtained through the intervention of some family friends a position as a junior clerk at the Poole counting-house of Messrs. George Garland and Sons. The salary of £20 per year seemed low, though it was likely appropriate for a position which only required the copying of the partners' daily correspondence into a letterbook.[56] Gosse was left with plenty of time for reading. In a bookcase at Garland's he found Fielding's *Joseph Andrews*, the first novel he had come across,[57] and Byron's *Lara*, the reading of which 'was an era to me; for it was the dawning of Poetry on my imagination.' He was, as has been mentioned, already acquainted with some poets, and now 'It appeared as if I had acquired a new sense.'[58] The Scotsman Robert Pollok's *The Course of Time* (1827), a best-seller,[59] was the work of a different sort of poet than Byron,[60] and the impact was, to the mature Gosse, not nearly as favourable: 'The knowledge of unfulfilled Prophecy which I

---

53. 'Reminiscences', I: 183-4, 94; PHG, 'Country Day-school', 521.

54. 'Reminiscences', I: 280-1.

55. 'Reminiscences', I: 287-90, 296; the account of this expulsion was not mentioned in *Life*, 23.

56. 'Reminiscences', I: 306-7.

57. 'Reminiscences', I: 312.

58. 'Reminiscences', I: 310.

59. Pollok's *Course of Time* is said to have sold 12,000 copies in the first 18 months after publication, and 78,000 to 1869: Richard D. Altick, *The English Common Reader. A Social History of the Mass Reading Public 1800-1900* (Chicago: University of Chicago Press, 1957, 1967), 387.

60. Robert Pollok (1798-1827), *The Course of Time. A Poem in Ten Books* (Edinburgh: Wm. Blackwood) had reached a fourth edition within a year (*Athenaeum*, 7 May 1828, 445, 446) and eventually appeared in 50 American editions (Le Roy Edwin Froom, *The Prophetic Faith of Our Fathers* (Washington, D.C.: Review and Herald, 1954), IV,130 and 130fn.41); Crawford Gribben, 'Scottish Romanticism, Evangelicalism and Robert Pollok's *The Course of Time* (1827)', *Romanticism* 21 (2015), 26.

had imbibed from Scott was warped & distorted by Pollok's millennial views, which are, indeed, those of the dissenting bodies generally. So that when fifteen years after, I began to study [Matthew] Habershon, & other pre-millennarian [sic] writers, the whole subject appeared novel.'[61] Gosse also apparently read at this time Paley's *Natural Theology* (1802), Thomas Dick's *Christian Philosopher* (1823), and *Don Quixote*.[62]

In 1826, under the influence of all of this literary activity, Philip copied out a report dealing with a mouse said to be attracted to the playing of music. He sent it to the *Youth's Magazine* (a London miscellany which described itself as the first of its type to combine 'Evangelical instruction with useful information',[63] to which the Gosse family subscribed). The item was published in July under the pseudonym Φιλιπ [*Greek*, Philip]— the first of more than 230 articles in over forty-seven different serials issued from his pen during the remaining sixty-two years of his life.[64] Also notable: with one effort, Philip had managed to publish more than his father, who had been vainly attempting for a number of years to get some of his epic poetry and biblical narratives into print.

John Brown had returned from Blandford just as Philip was entering Garland's firm. Once again the two pursued their previous activities, playing, reading, and drawing together while adding to their zoological knowledge.[65] Yet there was an important difference now: both were 'under spiritual concern feeling after Him, though very darkly.'[66]

According to Gosse's record of his 'Religious Impressions', set down in 1869 at the end of the first volume of his 'Reminiscences', throughout his youth he was drawn towards an evangelical conversion much like his father experienced in 1790. 'I cannot recal [sic] the thoughts & feelings of a time so early as that I did not know that I was not by nature fit for heaven,' he observed,

61. 'Reminiscences', I: 360. By 'millennial views' PHG here presumably meant 'postmillennial'. The two terms could be interchangeable.

62. 'Reminiscences', I: 348.

63. Jonathan R. Topham, 'Periodicals and the Making of Reading Audiences for Science in Early Nineteenth-Century Britain: The *Youth's Magazine*, 1828-37', in Louise Henson, et. al., *Culture and Science in the Nineteenth-Century Media* (Aldershot: Ashgate Publishing, 2004), 60.

64. Φιλιπ [Greek, Philip = PHG], 'The Mouse a Lover of Music', *Youth's Magazine* n.s. XI (July 1826), 239-40. PHG states he copied the anecdote ('Reminiscences', I:314-15), which *Life*, 28, changed to 'composed' (Freeman & Wertheimer-PHG, 107, 103). For the base tabulation of publications: Freeman & Wertheimer-PHG and some additions by other writers.

65. 'Reminiscences', I: 323.

66. 'Reminiscences', I: 370.

& that I must become converted, give myself to God, have a new heart, be born again, before I could enter into the kingdom. Dim as were my notions of how this was to be effected, still I knew this much; & it was one of the inestimable blessings of my parentage, & early surroundings, that I *did* know it. So that from earliest childhood, the paramount claims of God upon my heart & life, were acknowledged at least, *in foro conscientiae*,[67] if not conceded. The atmosphere in which we lived, the chapel services, the vestry prayer-meeting, the week-night meetings, the Sunday-school, the hymns, the catechisms, the godly periodicals & other books, the morning & evening family reading & prayer, parental examples, the profession of all our honoured friends,—all these things aided in infixing & in deepening salutary spiritual impressions in the mind of a child naturally thoughtful.[68]

Ever since Philip was 3-years old his father, when in Poole, had sat under the Revd Thomas Durant (1776 or 1777-1849),[69] at the Independent (also known as the Congregational) Meeting, and his mother later followed. The Gosse children were used to attending a chapel which could hold between 1,200-1,500 people by 1824, and William had sung in the choir for a few years.[70] During all the time that Philip was in Poole, Durant was his minister and his associations were with the Independents. Philip felt that this connection, together with the spiritual inheritance from his parents, had a manifest tendency for good. Like William Friend Durant (1803-1821), the minister's son, Philip had been taught Paley's proofs for God's existence, and was acquainted with the primary truths of revelation: the fallen condition of man and grace for recovery from sin. Undoubtedly something of the tenor of William Durant's upbringing was also present in Philip's. As Durant claimed, William 'never saw gloom in us; and he soon learned that religion was at once the inspirer and the guardian of our happiness.'[71]

It was a sermon by Durant which made a memorable impact on Philip.

67. Latin: morally though not necessarily legally.
68. 'Reminiscences', I: 364-5. Emphasis in the original.
69. Durant had been the minister at Poole Congregational church since about 1801 ('Death of the Rev. Thomas Durant', *Leeds Mercury*, 8 Dec. 1849, 7). He died 1 Dec. 1849 (*Jackson's Oxford Journal*, 8 Dec. 1849, 3).
70. 'Reminiscences', I: 12, 16, and TG, 'Memoirs'.
71. T. Durant, *Memoirs and Select Remains of an Only Son Who Died November 27th, 1821, in His Nineteenth Year; While a Student in the University of Glasgow* (Poole: J. Lankester, 2vols., 1822), I: 19-20, and pp. iii-iv, 23.

Around 1824, he preached from Mark 12: 34, 'Thou are not far from the Kingdom of God.' Durant 'took occasion to show, very forcibly, that one might be, by light, knowledge, morality, service, &c. *'not far from* the Kingdom', & yet not be *in* it, & never reach it!'[72]

Religious and spiritual yearnings became more frequent while Philip was at Garland's. He remembered feeling a 'powerful emotion of heavenward aspiration' one day while on an errand. On another occasion a Unitarian minister, lending him some of the works of the Unitarian Lant Carpenter (1780-1840), tried unsuccessfully 'to overthrow my faith in the Deity of Christ.'[73] And in the beginning of 1826, he had a dream:

> The world was all passing away, the day of doom was come, I was the last man: I was called to the bar of God, & found wanting. But a special mercy arrested judgment; the Almighty Judge informed me that I should have a respite of 50 years, to be to me a new probation. Immediately I descended to the earth, which I found void of inhabitants & in utter darkness. At that moment I was in terror.
>
> Though I could not help seeing that in much of the detail of this dream there was absurdity & incongruity too manifest to allow me to look on it as a Divine revelation, yet it took a strong hold on my imagination. I did, in spite of reason, view it as a possible intimation that I had 50 years to live. And as, from Scott's Commentary, I had been taught to expect the Millennium to begin in 1866, it was a comfort to me to think that, living thus 10 years into that period of blessing, I must of course have been converted to God at its commencement.[74]

These religious tendencies, and the discussions with John Brown, were soon to be cut short. In October 1826 Philip was released by his employer George Garland, who needed to find employment for a nephew.[75] Odd jobs were found for a time, until the following spring, when the ever-faithful John Brown obtained a clerkship for Philip in the counting-house of Messrs Harrison, Slade & Co.—2,300 miles away in Carbonear, Newfoundland. With the position of Poole as a principal trading partner with Newfoundland, Quebec, and other parts of America in oil, fish, and

72. 'Reminiscences', I: 365. Emphasis in the original.

73. 'Reminiscences', I: 366-7.

74. 'Reminiscences', I: pp. 367-8. PHG thought that the dream may have been connected with his reading of Thomas Campbell's poem, 'The Last Man' (1823).

75. 'Reminiscences', I: 338.

timber;[76] with the historic link of the Gosse family with Newfoundland; and with the example of brother William five years earlier, the job was a natural one for Philip. The terms were for five or six years of service, free board and lodging, and £20 per annum. One trip back to England was allowed at the firm's expense. 'I had dreaded expatriation,' Philip recalled, but the agreement was signed.[77]

On 22 April 1827, days after turning 17, Philip boarded the brig *Carbonear*. From on deck he could watch his family and Dorset boyhood receding from view. He carried with him a copy of the popular evangelical work *Scripture Help* (1816; 21ed., 1853), by Edward Bickersteth (1786-1850),[78] a parting gift from John Brown.[79]

76. PHG, 'On Poole', in *Themes … at Blandford*; Gertrude E. Gunn, *The Political History of Newfoundland 1832-1864* (Toronto: University of Toronto Press, 1966), 12.

77. 'Reminiscences', I: 342-3.

78. It was not until 1832 that Bickersteth adopted historicist premillennialist views (Martin Spence, *Heaven on Earth. Reimagining Time and Eternity in Nineteenth-Century British Evangelicalism* (Eugene, Oregon: Pickwick Publications), 2015, 56), to which PHG also adhered.

79. 'Reminiscences', I: 359; II: 1.

CHAPTER THREE

1827-1839

The Wonder Years

-I-

T HE COUNTRY TO WHICH PHILIP GOSSE WAS NOW TRAVELLING was the first of the British overseas dominions to be discovered. At some 300 miles wide by 270 miles, Newfoundland is the sixteenth largest island in the world. Yet in 1821 its inhospitable interior was still virtually all *terra incognita*. Its size could only be estimated,[1] and even two decades later one writer claimed there was 'utter ignorance' about the colony in virtually all sectors of English society. Seventy per cent of a population of 60,000 was nestled around the three major bays (Conception, Trinity, and Bonavista) or in the vicinity of the principal port, St. John's.[2]

Englishmen who had been to Newfoundland were divided in their opinion about it. A geologist who spent some eighteen months there said the place was known 'only by its dogs.'[3] A writer in *Fraser's Magazine*,

1. William Charles St. John, *A Catechism of the History of Newfoundland, from the Earliest Accounts to the Close of the Year 1834, For the Use of Schools* (St. John's: J. M'Coubrey, Printer, 1835), 47; Beckles Willson, 'Newfoundland', *Encyclopaedia Britannica* (11th ed., 1910-11), XIX: 482; R. Gordon Moyles, *'Complaints is Many and Various, but the Odd Divil Likes It': Nineteenth Century Views of Newfoundland* (Toronto: Peter Martin Associates, 1975), 155.

2. This calculation is based upon the figures given in 'Population of Newfoundland. 1827-8', *Carbonear Star, and Conception Bay Journal*, 1 May 1833, 71. Another source estimates the total population as 80,000 people in 1834, and 98,000 in 1845: W. C. St. John, *Catechism of the History of Newfoundland* (Boston: George C. Rand, revised edition, 1855), 49, 52.

3. J. B. Jukes, *Excursions in and about Newfoundland, during the years 1839 and 1840* (London: John Murray, 1842), I: vi. PHG owned a copy of this work (*Sandhurst Catalogue*, item #612). English unfamiliarity with 'the most ancient American possession of the Crown' was long a subject of regret (Sir Cavendish Boyle, 'Newfoundland, the Ancient Colony', *Proceedings of the Royal Colonial Institute* XXXV, 1903-4, 378-9).

the oft-quoted London monthly, was dissatisfied with the quality of life. A Newfoundland village, for instance, usually consisted of

> A few low wooden huts perched here and there among the rocks, with a rude path of communication between them; a small, plain church, also of wood; and a building, generally of more pretension, surmounted by a small cross, the Roman Catholic chapel; such are its component parts. No flowers; no gardens, save here and there a patch of potatoes; no parsonage, for a clergyman comes from a distance to perform divine service on a Sunday. ... Their talk is of seals and cod-fish, of *hauling* and *jigging*; and their jargon generally betrays an Irish origin. All this is little cheerful, but there is a sadness induced by the silence of Nature in the scenery of Newfoundland, that none that have not felt it can understand.[4]

To other Englishmen, the country did have its attractions. Merchants could accumulate great fortunes from the two chief fisheries of the Island (cod and seal), and this is precisely what Gosse's relatives—George Kemp (1756-1845)[5] and James Kemp (1770-1836),[6] and John Gosse (1767-1834)[7]—had done. Fishing, furthermore, required fishermen as well as merchants, and Ireland's poor were quick to fill the need, even if the seasonal wages of a good fisherman might amount only to £25.[8] One estimate is that 24,000 Irish came to the colony between 1811-30.[9]

Now it was precisely the confluence of fishermen and merchants which gave Newfoundland the unhappy social and political environment which it had when Gosse arrived. There were only two classes whom the merchants supplied: the smaller one of merchants and their agents, and

4. [anon], 'A Day's Excursion in Newfoundland', *Fraser's Magazine* XXXII (Dec. 1845), 740-2, p. 740. The author is unidentified in the *Wellesley Index*. Emphasis in the original.

5. George Edward Kemp, *Kemps of Ollantigh and Kemps of Poole* (Seattle, Washington: McKay Printing Co., 1939), 29.

6. Kemp, *Kemps of Ollantigh and Kemps of Poole*, 23.

7. John Gosse death notice, Southampton *Hampshire Advertiser* (12 July 1834), 3; Philip Tocque, *Newfoundland: As It Was, and As It Is In 1877* (Toronto: John B. Magurn, 1878), 118. The Kemps are said to have each returned to England with £30,000 ($150,000: Philip Tocque, 'When I Was a Boy', St. John's, Newfoundland *Evening Telegram*, 15 Feb. 1897, [3]; James Murphy, *Murphy's Old Carbonear*. St. John's, Newfoundland: James Murphy, 1916, 2); *Encyclopedia of Newfoundland and Labrador* II: 574-5. The Kemp counting-house closed in 1837 (Joseph Peters, 'Obituary [of George Apsey]', Halifax, Nova Scotia *Provincial Wesleyan* XXI, 10 Nov. 1869, [2]. The obituary was written by Peters, whom PHG knew, and submitted to the newspaper by his friend John Prince).

8. St. John, *History of Newfoundland*, 52 (the estimate appears to refer to the cod-fishery season, from mid-June to mid-October each year).

9. Gunn, *Political History of Newfoundland*, 9.

the more numerous one of fishermen. The relationship was one of master to serf, and the serf was often bound into inexorable indebtedness.[10] The situation was exacerbated, moreover, by the fact that most of the former, and half of the latter, were Protestants, while the remaining fishermen-debtors were Roman Catholics, chiefly southern Irish. While Catholics (30,928) only slightly outnumbered Protestants (28,212) in 1827, the two groups tended to segregate around different areas, giving still more encouragement to their mutual hostility. The 'Irish problem' had thus been exported, as one historian has remarked, and become an Imperial one:

> In Ireland the Irish had known defeat and coercion, plantation and
> union, eviction and famine; they had suffered the absence of landlords
> and the presence of agents; they had resented the privileges of an alien
> church and the restrictions on national industry. In Newfoundland they
> found the English still their masters in industry and government, still
> their betters in wealth and status; they faced monopolistic suppliers
> and ruthless agents, high prices and perpetuating debts, curtailed credit
> and recurrent famine; they saw the English church established in effect,
> if not in fact, and their livelihood limited by English concessions to
> the French. In Ireland they had met arrogance with defiance and had
> looked to their demagogues as spokesmen and to their clergy as guides;
> in Newfoundland, too, they resorted to the intimidation of Protestants
> and relied upon the leadership of democrats and priests.[11]

On the voyage over, Philip Gosse brought all of the trappings and intellectual baggage of the Old World, little suspecting what he would find in the New: 'the very quaintness of the costume in which I had been sent from the parental nest told what a yokel I was,' he recalled. 'A surtout coat of snuff-brown hue, reaching to my ankles ... enveloped my sturdy body ... while my intellectual region rejoiced in the protection of a white hat (forsooth!) somewhat battered in sides and crown, and manifestly the worse for wear.'[12] Bickersteth's *Scripture Help* he read carefully, '& found

10. G. G. Findlay and W. W. Holdsworth, *The History of the Wesleyan Methodist Missionary Society* (London: Epworth Press, 1921), I: 261fn.2.

11. Gunn, *Newfoundland*, 182, and for the information in this paragraph, pp. 5-8, 206. Calvin Hollett, 'A People Reaching for Ecstasy: The Growth of Methodism in Newfoundland, 1774-1874' (Memorial University, PhD dissertation, 2008), 244-5, questions whether in 1827 Irish Catholics actually predominated in Conception Bay.

12. 'Reminiscences', II: 19-20.

instructive & profitable'. He also obeyed his mother's directive to read the Bible daily. With no chance to carry this out in private, the habit attracted the attention of his shipmate, Luke Thomas, who advised him "'to get rid of that sort of thing, as that wouldn't do for Newfoundland." However, I persevered.'[13] By keeping a journal intended for home consumption, and in commencing a work in which he illustrated quadrupeds, he soon found his time fully occupied, and hardly missed home.[14] It was during his involvement in the latter project that 'I suddenly found the power of stippling,' which creates tones in images resulting in a half-tone effect.[15] 'The art seemed to come to me without effort, quite suddenly.'[16]

After an unusually long trip of forty-six days, Gosse landed at Carbonear on 7 June 1827. Having expected to find desolation, he was pleased to see that the town was a substantial place. A favourable impression was no doubt encouraged by his brother William, who had come to Newfoundland in 1822[17] and greeted him upon his arrival. He provided him with an etiquette code to familiarize him with the new environment.[18]

The principal buildings in Carbonear, the second largest town on the island (less than half the size of Poole), were the churches and chapels, and mercantile houses. The Anglican Church was supported by the merchants, clerks, and some of the English working class, but Catholics and Methodists had larger establishments.[19] The Wesleyan Methodist chapel had been built in 1821, and was the largest Methodist meeting in Newfoundland.[20] Of the counting-houses, Thomas Chancey & Co. was the smallest. It was exceeded in size by two equally large outfitters: Slade, Elson, and Company, and Pack, Gosse, and Fryer.[21] For many years John

---

13. 'Reminiscences', II: 11.

14. 'Reminiscences', II: 2.

15. Michael Twyman, *A History of chromolithography: printed colour for all* (London: The British Library, 2013), 82, 262, 681.

16. 'Reminiscences', II: 5.

17. 'Reminiscences', I: 95-6; 'Gosse, William', *Encyclopedia of Newfoundland and Labrador* II:576.

18. 'Reminiscences', II: 12-15; 'a remarkable day—as this day 30 years ago—I welcomed Henry on his first arrival in Nfld.—(June 7 1827.) at Carbonear' (WG's Diary under 7 June 1857).

19. Carbonear had 1,279 Catholics and 1,248 Protestants; St. John's and Quidvidi had 8,841 Catholics and 3,262 Protestants (*Carbonear Star*, 1 May 1833, 71).

20. Philip Tocque, *Wandering Thoughts, or Solitary Hours* (London: Thomas Richardson and Son, 1846), 367; 'Reminiscences', II: 31. In 1846, the Methodist chapel had a capacity of 1,500.

21. This was the ranking, according to PHG, in 1827 ('Reminiscences', II: 59). Subsequently Pack, Gosse and Fryer was the largest (Keith Matthews appears to suggest that during 1820-58

Gosse, a partner in the latter merchant trading firm, was 'a pillar of the Methodist cause' not just in Carbonear but throughout the island.[22]

Just as Gosse was settling into his job at Slade's firm, the resident partner, John Elson (1774 or 1775-1840),[23] a Unitarian,[24] left Carbonear for a visit to England, and William Gosse followed at about the same time. The absence of these two made Philip more dependent upon the establishment's four clerks for friendship. It must have been at about this time that he heard that his school-mate John Brown had died of consumption. The news had virtually no impact: 'It was true, in more than one sense, that I had migrated to "The New World."'[25]

The companion who now took his place in Gosse's affections was William Charles St. John (1806-1873).[26] Nicknamed the 'Newfoundland Poet'[27] and the 'Philosopher of Newfoundland', St. John was said to know 'something of everything.'[28] 'Charley' was born in Harbour Grace and descended from Protestants from the south of Ireland, 'a youth of manly height, with features of the Grecian type':

> I saw in him a new type of character; he was a fair sample of the Irish
> youth at his best, when undebased by Popery. Sarcastic and keen, ready
> in reply, unabashed, prompt to throw back a Rowland [*sic*] for every
> Oliver, full of fun and frolic, as ready at a practical as at a verbal joke,

Pack, Gosse, and Fryer was the largest: 'Pack, Robert', *DCB* VIII). I do not know when Harrison, Slade, and Co. became Slade, Elson, and Co. There is a reference to 'Messrs. Slade, Elson, Harrison & Co., of Carbonear' (T. W. Fyles, obituary notice of PHG, *Canadian Entomologist* XXI (Jan. 1889), 17), but in 1833 the name appeared without 'Harrison': *Carbonear Star*, 4 Sept. 1833, 143. For the characterization of Slade, Elson, and Co.: 'Prescott, Sir Henry', *DCB* X.

22. Findlay and Holdsworth, *History of the Wesleyan Methodist Missionary Society* I: 269.

23. Portsmouth *Hampshire* Telegraph, 4 May 1840, 4; *Book of Newfoundland* VI: 424.

24. 'Reminiscences', II: 26, 44.

25. 'Reminiscences', II: 74-5.

26. St. John's death date is incorrectly given as Feb. 21, 1872 (instead of Feb. 21, 1873) in Edward Stephens Clark, *The American Genealogical Record* (San Francisco: Jos. Winterburn Co., 1892), I: 50; for the correct date, 'Death of a Newspaper Man', *Boston Evening* Transcript, 24 Feb. 1873, 1; and 'Deaths', Boston *Massachusetts Ploughman & New England Journal of Agriculture*, 1 Mar. 1873, 2.

27. A miniature portrait of St. John by William Gosse in Aug. 1841, is so entitled (seen in the Family Collection, stuck in WG's copy of St. John's *History of Newfoundland*). St. John started the *Conception Bay Herald* (Philip Tocque, 'The Fin-Backed Whale', St. John's, Newfoundland *Evening Telegram*, 8 Feb. 1897, [4]), apparently in 1842 (*Book of Newfoundland* VI: 426). He is described as 'Late U.S. Vice-Consul for the Bay of Conception', in the Boston 'Revised Edition' of his *Catechism of the History of Newfoundland* (1855). St. John's newspaper career is cited in Maudie Whelan, 'Journalism in Newfoundland: A Beginning History' (Carleton University, Master of Journalism, 1993), 1.

28. Philip Tocque, 'The Fin-Backed Whale', *Evening Telegram*, [4].

possessing a strong perception of the ludicrous side of everything,
cool and self-possessed, already a well-furnished man of the world,
St. John presented as great a contrast as can well be imagined to
me. I was thoroughly a greenhorn; fresh from my Puritan home and
companionships; utterly ignorant of the world; raw, awkward, and
unsophisticated; simple in countenance as unsuspicious in mind ... the
idea of a witticism or repartee, made hot on the occasion, had never
entered my noodle ... Intellectually I think we were pretty much on a
par. We were both readers, but possibly I had read more books than he;
I had learned Latin at school, he French; my slight knowledge of natural
history was balanced by his acquaintance with chemistry ... But then he
was a poet; at least, he had the art of versification ...

And Gosse added, surely with some exaggeration, that 'Whatever of
humour or wit in conversation I possess, whatever of logical precision
of thought; whatever of readiness of speech, or power in debate; I largely
owe to those years of companionship.'[29]

Outside of the fishing seasons, Gosse's chores at the counting-house
were not arduous. During March and April he was kept busy outfitting
the seal-fishery fleets, and then tallying their catch; in June and October
he did the same for the cod trade.[30] This left plenty of spare time for the
clerks, whose main task during the rest of the year was the copying of
letters and ledgers. They attended numerous parties (Gosse bemoaned
the fact that because of the '"Puritan prejudices" of my parents' he had
not learned how to dance),[31] and the clerks formed youthful attachments
with the local girls. Not Gosse, though. He kept his affection for Jane, one
of Elson's daughters, so closely guarded a secret that even she did not
know of it. Once, while escorting her home, 'we walked for full half a mile,
and not a word—literally, not a single word—broke the awful silence!'[32]

Gosse was more at ease when talk turned to intellectual matters.
Reading, debating, and writing followed. He had early discovered that
Carbonear had a book club, whose president and librarian was John
Elson. Gosse delved into the novels of Bulwer-Lytton, Walter Scott,

29. 'Reminiscences', II: 18-24.
30. For details of the routine of work, see 'Reminiscences', II: 58-91, 182-3 (long sections of
which are quoted in *Life*, 47-52, 57-9, 76); PHG, *Introduction to Zoology* ([1844]), I: 110-5, on
the seal-fishery; and Gunn, *Political History of Newfoundland*, 5-6.
31. 'Reminiscences', II: 52-7.
32. 'Reminiscences', II: 57.

and Disraeli, finding those of James Fenimore Cooper and the Banim brothers' *Tales, by the O'Hara Family* 'prime favourites'.[33] Turning to discussion, he then would debate 'every imaginable subject' with St. John, 'so that the Counting house was an arena of constant mental gladiatorship between us two.'[34] They talked of God, 'as the schoolmen had done long before us', and the meaning of time. With a Captain Andrews they argued about the truth of the Scriptures, the dispute revolving around Job's question (6: 6), 'Is there any taste in the white of an egg?' The captain argued in the affirmative, meaning that the Bible must be fictional; Gosse countered that eggs are insipid, upholding the text; St. John maintained that Job's question was rhetorical.[35] A novel about 'Edwin something, 'a youth about 18', who 'dropped a tear over the ship's side' as he left his native country' was begun by Gosse at St. John's insistence. Its author knew it was far from inspired.[36]

During Gosse's first few years at Carbonear, his life continued to be marked by this mixture of intellectual probing and humdrum office duties. It was a stressless existence, and also lacked direction. Variety punctuated the pattern in August 1828, when Gosse was sent to a branch of Slade, Elson, and Co. in St. Mary's, about sixty miles south of Carbonear. His five months there were ones of dreary isolation from friends and books. Only two events gave the period any redeeming value: his four-day overland trek back to Carbonear, and the reading in a newspaper of excerpts of the Revd George Croly's tragedy, *Salathiel* (1827). That work had been wildly popular since its appearance in London, and Gosse found on his return to Elson's that his comrades 'were all open-mouthed' about it. He soon read the whole work, '& was delighted with its grandeur & scriptural eloquence.' It also whetted his interest in prophetic studies.[37]

The remainder of the year 1829 continued in this fashion: more

33. On the book club: 'Reminiscences', II: 31-2; Marjorie M. Doyle and Patrick O'Flaherty, 'Tocque, Philip', *DCB* XII; and P. Tocque, *Newfoundland*, 119, and on his readings, 'Reminiscences', II: 77-8. Philip recalled having once been so immersed in a novel that when he completed it, 'it was some minutes before I could at all recall where I was, or my circumstances.' On another occasion, he read two of the three volumes of a novel at a single sitting (ibid.).

34. 'Reminiscences', II: 24.

35. 'Reminiscences', II: 79n.

36. 'Reminiscences', II: 80-1.

37. On the popularity of *Salathiel*: 'Hymn-Books and Hymn Writers', *Wesleyan Times*, 4 Jan. 1864, 7, and 'Reminiscences', II: 102, 113. *Salathiel* was among the 'Better [not Best] Sellers' in the United States for 1828 (Frank Luther Mott, *Golden Multitudes: The Story of Best Sellers in the United States* (New York: Macmillan, 1947), 317). PHG's residence at St. Mary's is described in 'Reminiscences', II: 92-111.

debating and more work. In June 1830, St. John married Elizabeth Susanna Comer (the sister of William S. Comer, editor of the *Conception Bay Mercury*) and quit Elson's in the autumn of the next year to open a wine-importing business in nearby Harbour Grace.[38] Before St. John left, however, he witnessed the early phase of a religious crisis in his own—and Gosse's—life.

At the beginning of 1830, Gosse was on the cusp of turning 20 and had been in Newfoundland for nearly three years. His daily activities had fallen into a pattern, while his religious condition, of concern to him before he left Poole, had turned dormant. True, he had told St. John that he fancied that one day he would own a home on a piece of wooded land near Carbonear, and that a place of worship—under his ministry—was part of that dream. Like many dreams, basic details were absent. What kind of a minister would he be? He was not inclined towards Methodism, he 'despised & ridiculed' Wesley's hymns, and had instead turned to Isaac Watts (an Independent) or the Anglican liturgy.[39] Gosse's religious feelings were confused, and it was in that state of uncertainty that a drama unfolded which changed the direction of his life.

The first missionary to establish Methodism in Newfoundland settled at Conception Bay in 1765.[40] The Irish minister found he had come to a place virtually without a Christian presence. His theology and his preaching struggled to find acceptance,[41] and financing the effort was a persistent problem. That meant that the Newfoundland District, run by the Missionary Committee in London, was resented as an ongoing drain

38. Advertisement in the *Conception Bay Mercury* III, 30 Dec. 1831, [p. 3]: 'W. C. St. John Has for Sale, A few Dozen Madeira Wine, Of the very best quality. Harbour Grace, Dec. 23, 1831'; on the wedding: 'Reminiscences', II: 123. By April 1834, when St. John nearly died of scarlet fever, he had three children ('Reminiscences', II: 195-6).

Pat Byrne confuses St. John with his son, Charles Henry St. John (1831-1925), a published Boston poet and assistant editor of *Zion's Herald* (Byrne, 'Folk Tradition, Literature, and a Society in Transition: Newfoundland'. Memorial University of Newfoundland, PhD dissertation, 1994), 216fn.112, 518; see *Delaware Tribune*, 18 Apr. 1867, 4; 'Charles H. St. John, 95, Editor and Author, Dead', *Boston Globe*, 22 Apr. 1925, 24; 'Death of a Newspaper Man [William Charles St. John]', *Boston Evening Transcript*, 24 Feb. 1873, 1). *Encyclopedia of Newfoundland and Labrador* V (1994), 25, misstates C. H. St. John's date of birth. C. H. St. John's first book of poetry (*Poems* (Boston: A. Williams and Co., 1859)) was dedicated: 'To Philip Henry Gosse, Esq., F.R.S., F.L.S., &c. As a tribute from one whom he caressed in childhood, and in token of family associations and personal respect'.

39. 'Reminiscences', II: 148-9.

40. T. Watson Smith, *History of the Methodist Church within the territories embraced in the late conference of Eastern British America* (Halifax: Methodist Book Room, 1877), I: 45-6.

41. Parsons, 'Origin and Growth of Newfoundland Methodism', 15-19.

on central office resources.[42] Yet by the end of the century the movement was firmly established.[43] What brought about the change? What was it that led to a religious revival—a 'Great Awakening'[44]—in Carbonear from 1830-32?[45] It was the leadership of Wesleyan Methodist missionaries from Britain: 'In answer to prayer the Spirit was poured out, and many were brought to God.'[46] That's the official account, and it makes sense. It is just not accurate, argues Calvin Hollett, who has built the case that it was a populist spiritual movement that turned the tide: 'the preachers of Methodism were the people themselves as they sang and shared their spirituality with their friends and neighbors.'[47]

When Gosse arrived at Carbonear in 1827, most Methodist members in Conception Bay were in the north. From St. John's to Carbonear there was a total of 301 members;[48] in Carbonear in the winter of 1829, all of the members could sit in a single pew.[49] That was historic Methodism. Then an 'indigenous popular movement' arose in the colony, in which Methodist missionaries played a secondary role.[50] Remarkably, the ignition of the revival has a date: Easter Sunday, 11 April 1830. It also has a name: George Apsey.[51]

The English-born George Apsey (1798-1869) typified the populist story to such an extent that his life transformation was long celebrated among Newfoundland Methodists. Apsey had been a clerk since he was a teenager in 1812 at George & James Kemp & Co. in Brigus and later Carbonear.[52] Known to pursue 'a careless pleasure seeking life'[53] during his first three decades, he was 'jovial, profane, licentious ... Hot & irascible'. He would extract a kiss from a girl when the opportunity

42. Parsons, 'Origin and Growth of Newfoundland Methodism', 87.

43. Parsons, 'Origin and Growth of Newfoundland Methodism', 46.

44. Hollett, 'A People Reaching for Ecstasy', 286.

45. Hollett, 'A People Reaching for Ecstasy', 235.

46. Thomas M'Cullagh, 'Memoir of the Rev. John Haigh, Sometime Missionary in Newfoundland', *Wesleyan-Methodist Magazine* ser. 5, VII (Apr. 1861), 300.

47. Hollett, 'A People Reaching for Ecstasy', 229.

48. The numbers are for 1828: Hollett, 'A People Reaching for Ecstasy', 231.

49. Smith, *History of the Methodist Church* II: 169-170.

50. Hollett, 'A People Reaching for Ecstasy', 238.

51. In his excellent work, Hollett, 'A People Reaching for Ecstasy', 233-6, offers a slightly different interpretation of the sequence of events. Dwelling on the importance of Apsey, he does not specifically cite him as the first convert. The account of Smith, *History of the Methodist Church* II: 170, is not as clear as one would like on this point, but he appears to outline events as I here present them.

52. Peters, 'Obituary [of George Apsey]', *Provincial Wesleyan*, [2].

53. Peters, 'Obituary [of George Apsey]', *Provincial Wesleyan*, [2].

presented itself.[54] Though he was at a different counting-house than Gosse and was a dozen years older than him, the two knew each other. "You son of a bitch!" he had once called out to Gosse, after an encounter which annoyed him.[55]

Apsey's conversion was not the work of a day. It began in 1828, when signs of a 'mighty revolution' in Apsey's heart became evident. Inexplicably, he was struck with 'a vivid apprehension of sudden death and eternal perdition.' He drew back from committing suicide.[56] On Candlemas Day, February 2, 1830 (a holiday celebrated by Wesleyans though not at Elson's), Apsey could no longer control himself. That morning he had, as usual, gone to work at Pack, Gosse, and Fryer (formerly the Kemp firm), where he held a senior position. Rising up unexpectedly, 'the peace of God flowed in upon his heart'. It was a 'red-letter day'[57] for him when, in Gosse's words, Apsey 'burst into the office' at Elson's '& astonished us all by narrating, in his rapid inconsequential style, that he had just been in to Mr. Elson to ask permission to shut up the store, & go down to Meeting.' Elson granted the request.

Dumbfounded, the clerks wondered: What could possibly have induced the Apsey they had known to want to go to a Wesleyan meeting, of all places? Apsey 'made no secret of his change,' Gosse said: 'he was deeply & soundly converted to God.'[58] After sharing his feelings with his friends, a few months later at the Easter Sunday service of the Revd John Haigh, Apsey publicly 'unbosomed his whole soul'. He 'cried out in bitterness of spirit,'[59] revealing his 'wretched state of mind as a sinner.'[60]

Haigh (1795-1859) had come to Newfoundland as a Wesleyan minister at the age of 21.[61] He was witness to the revival in religion in Carbonear[62] as it went from a 'nominal, church-attending Methodist area to that of a religion of experience and passion.'[63] He took Apsey into his mission

54. 'Reminiscences', II: 128-9; see pp. 52-7.
55. 'Reminiscences', II: 126.
56. Peters, 'Obituary [of George Apsey]', *Provincial Wesleyan*, [2].
57. Smith, *History of the Methodist Church* II: 170.
58. 'Reminiscences', II: 127-8.
59. First quotation, Peters, 'Obituary [of George Apsey]', *Provincial Wesleyan*, [2]; second quotation: Smith, *History of the Methodist Church* II:170.
60. Peters, 'Obituary [of George Apsey]', *Provincial Wesleyan*, [2].
61. M'Cullagh, 'Memoir of the Rev. John Haigh', 296.
62. William Wilson, *Newfoundland and its Missionaries* (Cambridge, Mass.: Dakin & Metcalf, 1866), 240.
63. Hollett, 'A People Reaching for Ecstasy', 237, 233.

house and followed his 'progress in Divine things.' On 2 May, Apsey finally 'found peace and deliverance.' One friend, Joseph Peters, described that moment in lyrical terms: it represented a 'glorious transition from despair to hope, from darkness to light, from death to life, from hell to heaven.'[64] Junior counting-house clerk Samuel W. Sprague added another appreciation: 'I have often thought of his conversion as being as remarkable as any in the Bible.'[65] Exclaimed Gosse, rhetorically: 'Was Saul then among the prophets?'[66]—a proverb describing a sudden change in a person's character, based on the spirit of God infusing Saul when he became Israel's king. Though Apsey referred to himself as Haigh's 'son in the Gospel,'[67] the minister acknowledged that what was underway in Carbonear had more to do with the 'considerable abilities' of the young converts 'in the salvation of sinners' than it did with his own missionary efforts.[68] Apsey was 'the first-born child of the revival'[69] in Carbonear.

Surprisingly, the new direction in Apsey's life had little immediate impact on his friends. 'My conscience, indeed, was not at rest' at the time, Gosse conceded, yet he sensed no urgent crisis. St. John, with whom he discussed Apsey's transformation, felt the same way.[70] The matter faded from attention. Gosse turned to an enthusiasm for poetry, which now gripped him.

In October 1830, Gosse selected his favourite verse and copied rhythmical lines into volumes of what he called *Gems*.[71] Simultaneously, he began to compose his own poems. He started with the 'Song to Poland'

64. Peters, 'Obituary [of George Apsey]', *Provincial Wesleyan*, [2].

65. Smith, *History of the Methodist Church* II: 171.

66. Smith, *History of the Methodist Church* II: 171. The saying is taken from 1 Sam. 10: 11-23 and 19: 24.

67. For Apsey's work at Messrs. Kemps: Peters, 'Obituary [of George Apsey]', *Provincial Wesleyan*, [2]; for his conversion: letter from Apsey dated 12 Mar. 1860, quoted in M'Cullagh, 'Memoir of the Rev. John Haigh', 300; Smith, *History of the Methodist Church* II:170.

68. Hollett, 'A People Reaching for Ecstasy', 234.

69. This was the way Apsey referred to himself (Smith, *History of the Methodist Church* II:170).

70. 'Reminiscences', II: 130.

71. 'Gems, Collected by P. H. Gosse. "Orient Pearls at Random Strung. —" Newfoundland. Octr. 1830' (seen in the Family Collection) contains 99 poems in 180 unnumbered pages. Among the poets represented were Thomas Campbell, Croly, Mrs Hemans, Shelley, Coleridge, Wordsworth, Byron, Mrs Barbauld, James Montgomery, and Jewsbury. The last poem was dated 31 Dec. 1834. A second volume, begun in Jan. 1835, is referred to in a letter from EWG-PHG (13 Jan. 1868; CUL Add. 7018, 42), but it has not been traced. The poems in the first volume reflect its compiler's youthful and religious feelings; they deal with death, love, eternity, and melancholy and dramatic themes. See also 'Reminiscences', II: 139.

in a notebook entitled *Sprigs of Laurel*, and added a few scriptural and other lyrics. That was as far as he got: 'My genius lay not in poesy.'[72] In the next year, he made an Aeolian harp and (though he apparently was unable to play it) a violin. That winter he and several friends (including St. John and brother William) formed a debating society, thought to be the first literary-scientific institution of its kind on the island. By January 1832 the Society had twenty members, and met every Saturday at the 'grandiloquently' named Gilmour's Academy.[73] The next month saw Gosse addressing the question of whether the British Government ought to free West Indian slaves without compensating the slave-owners for their loss.[74]

For some two-and-a-half years Gosse had been occupied with this-and-that, until the aimlessness ended. It was 1832—the first great Reform Bill was passed in Britain and representative government granted to Newfoundland. It was the wonder year, the *annus mirabilis*, of Philip Gosse. 'A year now opens which must ever remain the most memorable of my life', Gosse said:

> It is notable for several respects. I visited my native country, & my parents, after five years' absence. I commenced in it that serious & decisive devotion to scientific Natural History, which has given the bent to my whole life. Above all, it was in this year that I first definitely and solemnly yielded myself to God; and began that course heavenward,

72. The 'Song to Poland', which PHG says was dated 22 Apr. 1831, was perhaps inspired by Thomas Campbell's *Poland: A Poem* (1831). The notebook has not been traced; 'Reminiscences', II: 141.

73. 'ACADEMY.—A term grandiloquently applied even to the most insignificant village school. A writer in *Putnam's Magazine* sarcastically remarks that 'schools no longer exist in the towns and villages; academies and colleges supplant them" (John S. Farmer, *Americanisms, Old & New. A Dictionary of Words, Phrases and Colloquialisms Peculiar to the United States, British America, the West Indies, &c., &c.* (London: Thomas Poulter & Sons, 1889), 4).

74. I have been unable to confirm PHG's claim of priority for this Debating Society ('Reminiscences', II: 142). It may be relevant to note that 'Several benefit Societies, called "Fishermen's and Sharemen's Associations" and "Mechanic Societies"', were established in Newfoundland in 1830 (St. John, *History of Newfoundland*, 36). Between 21 Jan.- 21 May 1832, PHG kept copious notes of the proceedings of the Society; these have not been traced. The reference to his own oration, in which 'I had treated the subject sentimentally, totally disregarding the truth and reason of the matter, & merely striving after high sentiment, eloquent bursts of indignation, pathetic appeals, harmonious cadences, & well balanced sentences' is from 'Reminiscences', II: 160-1. On Gilmour's Academy, see below, 45 and fn.80, and Ruby Louise Gough, 'An Historical Study of Science Education in Newfoundland' (Boston University School of Education, Ed.D. dissertation, 1972), 39-40; on Gilmour, *Encyclopedia of Newfoundland and Labrador* I: 347.

wh[ich] though with many deviations and many haltings and many falls,
I have been enabled to pursue, on the whole steadfastly, until now [*c*.
1869]. In 1832 I became a New Creature in Christ Jesus.[75]

By this time, the new group of clerks at Elson's had been together
for two years (St. John and John Durell had left). Samuel W. Sprague
(1814-1893)[76] and D. E. Gilmour had joined Gosse, Apsey, and Luke
Thomas. Yet it mattered not that Sprague (a nephew of John Elson[77]
from Exmouth, England[78] who was only 13 when he became a clerk in
Newfoundland)[79] and Thomas had attended Haigh's chapel with Gosse.[80]
It mattered not that in the time since Apsey's announcement, no one else
at Pack, Gosse, and Fryer had experienced 'God's grace'.[81] These were
background factors, but not the source moving Gosse from conviction
to conversion.

The spark came, rather, from a letter which reached Gosse in June.
His sister Elizabeth was seriously ill in Poole, and it was her wish to see
her brothers one more time. As Gosse analysed it years later, it was the
likelihood that death was about to remove a beloved family member that
ignited a profound transformation in his life:

> I dearly loved my sister; & the probability that I should not see her alive
> affected me keenly. I immediately remembered the resource of God: that
> "He is a very present help in trouble;—that He commands his people
> to cast all their burdens on Him." I thought of this, & would have gone
> to Him; but then I felt that I was not one of his people; that He was not
> *my* God, for I had never accepted Him. I made up therefore my mind at
> once; I immediately, solemnly, deliberately, and uprightly, took God for
> my God, & yielded myself to be his servant and worshipper. I put away
> my idols from my heart, so far as I knew them, & set myself to live godly.

75. 'Reminiscences', II: 159.
76. On Sprague, 'Gone Hence', Fredericton *Herald* (27 May 1893), 3; Robert Wilson, *Methodism in The Maritime Provinces* (Halifax: S. F. Huestis, 1893), 53.
77. Marjorie M. Doyle, 'A Biography of Philip Tocque (1814-1899)' (Memorial University of Newfoundland, MA thesis, 1986), 14).
78. 'Gone Hence', Fredericton *Herald* (27 May 1893), 3; Smith, *History of the Methodist Church* II:172.
79. Hollett, 'A People Reaching for Ecstasy', 236.
80. 'Reminiscences', II: 126, 132. Gilmour also ran an Academy for boys and, by 1833, for girls (*Carbonear Star*, 3 July 1833, p. 107). At that time, Gilmour was editor of the *Carbonear Star*, which he had just founded.
81. 'Reminiscences', II: 128.

In all this there was no distinct recognition of Christ; no conspicuous sense of guilt, or sorrow for sin, or dread of the wrath of God: no prominent thought of the need of a covering, a hiding-place, a refuge, a Righteousness other than my own: no acceptance of Christ crucified for me; no thought of substitution.

This was not the aspect under which the Gospel had been habitually put before me. No doubt I knew of these aspects doctrinally, & latently they were in my mind. If I had been asked, "How can guilty sinners be accepted with God?" I could doubtless have answered,—"Through Christ having died, the just for the unjust." I had with me Bickersteth's "Scripture Help", which is clear on these points, though not diffuse: I had been used to read from my early Childhood, not task-wise but for my own pleasure, Scott's Commentary, Hervey's Works, Grace Kennedy's Tales, Mrs. Sherwood's Tales, Jane Taylor's writings, and others in the Youths' Magazine: I was familiar with the Assembly's Catechism, & Watt's Hymns, besides many of Toplady's, Cowper's, Hart's, & Wesley's,—used in Dobell's Selection; so that I am sure I must have been theoretically acquainted with Gospel Truth.

Nevertheless, my prominent thought was legal. I wanted the Almighty to be my Friend; to go to Him in my need; I knew He required me to be holy; He had said, "My son, give me thy heart!"—I closed with Him; not hypocritically, but sincerely; intending henceforth to live a new, a holy, life; to please & serve God. I knew nothing of my own weakness, or of the power of sin. My experience had much of the character of Rom. vii.;—but it was, beyond doubt, the work of the Spirit of God. I cannot say I was born again yet: but a work was commenced which was preparatory to, & which culminated in, regeneration. I at once came to God, with much confidence, as a Hearer of prayer, and He graciously honoured my faith, imperfect as it was.[82]

Gosse immediately took the letter from home and showed it to Elson, who agreed that he should be on the next ship to Poole. Apsey, whom he told of his new religious commitment, 'rejoiced over me'.[83]

The conversion experience of the Carbonear clerks was typical of evangelicals during Victorian times in at least two ways. Firstly, there was the role which death (or the fear of it) played for Apsey, Gosse and

82. 'Reminiscences', II: 159. Emphasis in the original.
83. 'Reminiscences', II: 169.

Tocque.[84] Only preaching the Gospel may have had an equal impact in bringing about conversions, according to a study of 317 testimonies in Leeds from 1833-48.[85] Then there was the average age of the clerks (22.7) at their conversion: from Tocque (16), Lush (18), Sprague (20), and Gosse (22) to St. John (28) and Apsey (32).[86] Though the Carbonear sampling is admittedly small, it is not far out of range with the results of another study of the average conversion age of 20.5 brought about through Brethren and other evangelistic agencies in Scotland between 1859-1869.[87] Whether or not it was more common for men to be bachelors or married at the time of their conversion is unknown. In Carbonear, all but one of the men was a bachelor.[88]

Gosse celebrated the *moment* of his rebirth throughout his life, and looking back from our perspective of almost centuries makes it evident that this *moment* was a source of strength for him. Firstly, Apsey served as the model. In 'becoming the Lord's', he encouraged a group of counting-house workers—Gosse, Sprague,[89] Thomas Newell,[90] St. John, and William Fuller Lush (1816-1892)[91]—to do likewise. The men

84. Tocque joined the Carbonear Methodist Society in 1830. That was also the year that his father died, though the conversion may have preceded that event (Doyle, 'A Biography of Philip Tocque', 9).

85. Helmstadter, 'Evangelical Conversion', 16; on the role of the spectre of death in conversion, Hindmarsh, *Evangelical Conversion Narrative*, 256.

86. I have found birth dates and conversion years for these six clerks or friends of PHG, but not both sets of data for John Bemister, John Durell, G. E. Jaques, or Thomas Newell.

87. Neil T. R. Dickson, 'The History of the Open Brethren in Scotland 1838-1999' (University of Stirling, PhD dissertation, 2000), 97-8, 18fn.87. Dr Dickson's study draws on 8,285 obituary notices in *The Witness* (1907-78), a Brethren publication, which provide conversion information. He tabulated the average age of conversion and age at which individuals came into Brethren fellowship from 1860-1923 (Table 3.1).

88. Those who are known to have married after their conversion: Apsey, on 24 Dec. 1833 (*Star and Conception Bay Journal*, 1 Jan. 1834, 5); Tocque, on 11 Dec. 1838 (Doyle, 'A Biography of Philip Tocque', 16); Jaques was already a Wesleyan friend of PHG's when he married on 21 Feb, 1833 (*Liverpool Mercury*, 22 Feb. 1833, 8; 'Reminiscences', II: 177); PHG in 1848. Those who were married before they underwent conversion: Newell around 1824 (Mary Newell obituary, *Star and Conception Bay Journal*, 11 May 1836, 3).

89. In 1838, Sprague began to serve in the Methodist ministry in Newfoundland (Wilson, *Methodism in The Maritime Provinces*, 53; Charles Lench, *The History of the Rise and Progress of Methodism on the Western Bay Circuit* ([?St. John's, Newfoundland]: Barnes & Co., [?1912]), 8).

90. PHG did not provide a first name, but Thomas Newell was the bookkeeper at Slade, Elson & Co. (Doyle, 'A Biography of Philip Tocque', 13). For 'Thomas Newell' in association with PHG: the advertisement in the *Carbonear Star and Conception Bay Journal* (17 July 1833), 115. Newell's conversion occurred after 1835, when PHG had left for Canada (PHG-G. Apsey, 1868, quoted in Smith, *History of the Methodist Church* II: 171).

91. Lush (1 Apr. 1816-11 Apr. 1892): born Wiltshire, England, married Sarah McMichael, 4 children (https://www.ancestry.com/genealogy/records/william-fuller-lush-24-bhxh6b),

at Elson's were special; there was no similar following at Pack, Gosse, and Fryer, the other main counting-house in Carbonear where Apsey had previously emerged from a dissolute life. Secondly, Apsey set the outward-looking attitude. In autumn 1834, Gosse convinced Sprague and Lush to 'yield themselves to God'. Ultimately Sprague became a regular Wesleyan minister, and he said to Gosse: 'You may consider me ... as your 'own son in the gospel'.'[92] Thirdly, Apsey's conversion was both life-changing and life-lasting.[93] So was that of Gosse. Lush appears unusual in that he 'relapsed', but Sprague, too, 'persevered; never went back at all'.[94] In these three ways, Gosse's religious conviction was fortified throughout his life by the memory of how he had been reborn as a Christian to spread the holy word, from a mighty foundation which provided a supportive environment. That was the work of George Apsey.

Thus the first aspect to Gosse's *annus mirabilis*. A month earlier, there had been another transformative point in time. Attending an auction of books from the collection of a Wesleyan minister in Carbonear on May 5, Gosse purchased the 1798 edition of *Essays on the Microscope* by George Adams, junior (1750-1795).[95] Adams had been part of his father's business, at which mathematical instruments were manufactured for King George III. The large, 724-page quarto volume, enhanced by 32 lovely folio plates, was a bargain at 10s. (it originally sold for £1.8s.).[96] Gosse marveled at the apparently serendipitous event:

> I cannot conclude ... without noticing the superintending Providence, that, without our forethought, often causes the most important events of our life to originate in some trifling & apparently accidental

accessed 12/22/2022.

92. 'Reminiscences', II: 199.

93. Peters, 'Obituary [of George Apsey]', *Provincial Wesleyan*, [2].

94. 'Reminiscences', II: 199.

95. George Adams, *Essays on the Microscope; Containing a Practical Description of the Most Improved Microscopes; a General History of Insects, their Transformations, Peculiar Habits, and Oeconomy; An Account of the Various Species, and Singular Properties, of the Hydrae and Corticellae; a Description of Three Hundred and Eighty-three Animalcula: With a Concise Catalogue of Interesting Objects: A View of the Organization of Timber, and the Configuration of Salts, When Under the Microscope.* Illustrated with 32 folio plates (London: Dillon and Keating, 1787, 2nd edition, 1798, 'with considerable additions and improvements', by Frederick Kanmacher, F.L.S.). PHG had an unstated edition of the work in his library (*Sandhurst Catalogue*, item #315).

96. Advertisement, London *Times* (2 Jan. 1798), 2. In 1839, the Kanmacher edition was still selling in Britain for £1.1s (advertisement, 'Cheap, Second-Hand Books', *Bristol Mercury*, 26 Jan. 1839, 2).

circumstance;—to be, like our own huge globe,— "hung upon nothing"!
After years only can decide how much of that happiness wh. chequers my
earthly existence, may have depended on the laying out of ten-shillings
at a Book-sale.[97]

To this point in Gosse's life, his interest in natural history had been
diffuse, if eager. Adams' counsel was precisely the type of inspiration
and instruction which he required: 'it just condensed and focussed the
wandering rays of science that were kindling in my mind.' Suddenly
his energy in collecting insects was unbounded, but where to start?
Beauty was to be his guide, as 'I proposed to include the more handsome
Butterflies and Moths & the larger Beetles, of which poor barren
Newfoundland yielded a poor store indeed.' Having 'commenced as an
entomologist in earnest,'[98] he returned to the parlour window of the
counting-house and retrieved a giant wood wasp (Gosse called it a female
Sirex gigas)—which he had discarded three years previously. It became
his collection's nucleus.[99] Gosse could also look to his friend St. John as
one who shared this new enthusiasm.[100]

Certainly *Essays on the Microscope* confirmed Gosse's previous
readings about the justification for the study of nature. In Adams, he read
about 'DIVINE WISDOM in the creation', and how 'the farther our researches
are carried, the more striking proofs of it every where abound.'[101] The
rational faculty is properly employed in studying 'the works of that
glorious Being,' an exercise which produces 'a great deal of pleasure'
by revealing the 'exuberant and overflowing goodness of the SUPREME
BEING.'[102] The 'true philosopher' studies nature's 'noblest productions,'
and the smallest of works is not ignored. They, too, 'are perfect in their
kind, and carry about them as strong marks of infinite wisdom, power,
and beneficence as the greatest.'[103] This is something that even the
atheist cannot contest, a theme which Adams alluded to in other works

---

97. 'Reminiscences', II: 162. Ellipsis in original.
98. 'Reminiscences', II: 163-4.
99. 'Reminiscences', II: 121.
100. J. B. Jukes, *Excursions in and about Newfoundland* II: 192.
101. Adams, *Essays on the Microscope*, 2ed., 167.
102. Adams, *Essays on the Microscope*, 2ed., chap. V.
103. Adams, *Essays on the Microscope*, 2ed., 172; Marjorie H. Nicolson, *The Microscope and English Imagination* (Northampton, Mass.: Smith College Studies in Modern Languages XVI, 1935), 64-5.

he published following the excesses of post-Revolutionary France.[104] Adams's statements were well within the natural theology tradition, and were nothing new to Gosse.

Adams' emphasis on insects thus had a prompt impact on Gosse, though there is no indication that he realized the significance of *Essays on the Microscope* to entomological science. Since the mid-1700s a shift had occurred in France in the teleological argument for God's existence, as illustrative examples of proportion, regularity, and design in the biological world came to replace those hitherto drawn from the Newtonian world-machine.[105] In Europe, entomology was gaining a respectable place among the zoological sciences.[106] In Britain, the acceptance of entomology as a valid specialization appears to have been more erratic.[107] In the early 1820s, the study of insects could still be mocked. Writing in the *Edinburgh Review*, one of Britain's leading quarterlies then at the height of its circulation, a reviewer acknowledged:

> ... we must own, that we are by no means convinced that the study of insects is the very best thing in the world to form the understanding and elevate the mind. That the habit of looking for microscopic differences or analogies among the legs or antennae of gnats and spiders, will render a person extremely acute in such matters, we have no manner of doubt: but how the quick perception of such differences among resemblances, or the reverse, is to lead to that general intellectual eminence which constitutes an able lawyer, a discerning judge, a great general, a sagacious physician, a painter, an orator, or even an exciseman, we are really at a loss to conjecture.[108]

104. John R. Millburn, *Adams of Fleet Street, Instrument Makers to King George III* (London: Routledge, 2000), 246.

105. Aram Vartanian, 'Trembley's Polyp, La Mettrie, and Eighteenth-Century French Materialism', *Journal of the History of Ideas* XI (June 1950), 267-8. David Allen suggests that in the early 1800s the study of insects in Britain had an appeal to the industrial middle class in offering an aesthetic interaction with nature not provided by pursuits like shell-collecting (David E. Allen, *The Naturalist in Britain: A Social History* (London: Allen Lane, 1976), 100-6).

106. W. Conner Sorensen, *Brethren of the Net: American Entomology, 1840-1880* (Tuscaloosa: University of Alabama Press, 1995), 4.

107. William Charles Kimler, 'One Hundred Years of Mimicry: History of an Evolutionary Exemplar' (Cornell University, PhD dissertation, 1983), 11.

108. 'History of Insects', *Edinburgh Review* 37 (June 1822), 122. The article is a review of Kirby and Spence, *Introduction to Entomology* (2vols., 1818). *Wellesley Index* I: 463, gives the author as 'Possibly Henry Brougham [1778-1868]', the British statesman. On the *Edinburgh*'s circulation: Alvar Ellegård, *The Readership of the Periodical Press in Mid-Victorian Britain* (Vol. LXIII. Göteborg: Göteborgs Universitets Arsskrift, 1957), 27.

Works such as *Essays on the Microscope* aimed to put entomological investigations on a sounder footing by correcting the errors of past microscopists.[109] The 1798 update by Frederick Kanmacher (the edition purchased by Gosse) was, like Adams's original 1787 edition, well-received in the London press.[110] Though it was a substantially derivative work, it was cutting edge, remaining a standard work into the 1830s, when improvements in microscope instrumentation reduced its utility.[111]

Gosse's claim that his book purchase was 'one of the main pivots'[112] in his career as a man of science thus seems justified. It confirmed his ideas about the value of entomological work and helped him to understand what it meant to be an entomologist. Yet let us here pose a thought experiment: What might have happened had Gosse purchased, instead of Adams, one of the contemporary volumes of William Kirby and William Spence's *Introduction to Entomology; or Elements of the Natural History of Insects* (London, 4 vols., 1815-26; 7ed., 1 vol., 1856, reprinted to 1876)?[113] The question is entirely plausible. Gosse, having just turned 22, might well have been among those 'listless and transient schoolboy' collectors[114] who fell under the sway of this first popular work in English on the subject.[115] But there was a huge difference between Adams's well-regarded work and the volumes of 'Kirby and Spence' (as they were known). The latter was the 'seminal' Victorian entomological text,[116] the 'most learned and elaborate "Introduction to Entomology" ever written'[117] which attained 'world-wide' fame.[118] From the perspective of half-a-century after its first volume appeared, Kirby and Spence was

109. George Adams, *Essays on the Microscope* (London: Robert Hindmarsh, 1ed., 1787), x.

110. Reviews of the first edition of Adams' *Essays on the Microscope* in *Critical Review* 65 (Jan. 1788), 40-6 and *Monthly Review* 78 (Mar. 1788), 227-31; second (Kanmacher) edition, 1798: *Monthly Review* n.s.26 (June 1798), 199-202; *British Critic* XII (July 1798), 49-59; and *Critical Review* ser.2 XXIII (Aug. 1798), 397-9.

111. Millburn, *Adams of Fleet Street*, 217.

112. 'Reminiscences', II: 163.

113. R. B. Freeman, *British Natural History Books, 1495-1900. A Handlist* (Folkestone, Kent: Dawson Publishing, 1980), 201. PHG had a 1-vol. edition of this work (Sandhurst Catalogue, item #288), suggesting it was printed between 1856-76 (assuming he did not have a random volume).

114. Allen, *Naturalist in Britain*, 102.

115. E. O. Essig, *A History of Entomology* (New York: Macmillan Co., 1931), 671.

116. Sheila T. Wille, 'Governing Insects in Britain and the Empire, 1691-1816' (University of Chicago, PhD dissertation, 2014), 7.

117. *Zoologist* XIV (1856), 4982. It is not entirely clear if the writer (presumably the editor Edward Newman) was here referring to *Introduction to Entomology* vols. 3-4 only, or (more likely) the entire work.

118. *Gardeners' Chronicle*, 4 Nov. 1871, 1437.

pronounced 'the most interesting work upon the natural history of insects which has ever appeared in any language.'[119] Would Gosse's scientific path have been changed had he acquired that 'immortal' work?[120]

The answer is, probably not—simultaneously confirming Gosse's reflection and making an important statement about entomological studies at that time. As William Charles Kimler has pointed out in his valuable study, Kirby and Spence boosted the prestige of entomology and expanded its scope. Significantly, the authors provided *hints* and seeming *suggestions* for *new* areas of research, but there was no 'coherent explanation linking them causally'.[121] This is not a criticism of the work. It is a reflection of the dominance at the time of natural theology in working from the concept of the fixity of species to explain design, adaptation, variation, utility, parallelism, analogies, and affinities in the natural world. It was not until 1859 that an alternate causal explanation would be proposed which could replace natural theology's teleological explanation for the existence of a Creator: Darwin's theory of evolution by natural selection. This is the scientific environment to which Gosse was introduced, and from which he never deviated.

Meanwhile, before Gosse could make much headway in entomological pursuits he was off to Poole on 10th July. He arrived there on 6th August, on the way recording (nearly four decades later) the rare sighting of a beluga whale.[122] He found his sister Elizabeth recovering. So with that burden removed, he reverted to his new passion. Armed with pill-boxes and assisted by his brother Tom, he set-out at four the next morning

> ready for the capture of any unlucky insect desirous to experience the benefit of early rising. ... How often have I recalled that delightful morning! I was brimful of happiness. The beautiful & luxuriant hedgerows, the mossy gnarled oaks; the towering elms; the verdant fields; the fragrant flowers; the pretty warbling birds; the blue sky & bright sun; the dancing butterflies;—above all, the unwonted freedom from a load of anxiety;—altogether, it seemed to my enchanted senses,

119. *Gardeners' Chronicle*, 13 Oct. 1866, 974.
120. W. L. Distant, 'Biological Suggestions. Mimicry', *Zoologist* ser. 4, III (1899), 464.
121. Kimler, 'One Hundred Years of Mimicry', 19-44.
122. The description of the beluga was not published until 1869. A meticulous accounting of this event and PHG's description of it is given by R. B. Williams, 'Another Published Letter by Philip Henry Gosse: A Beluga in the English Channel', *Archives of Natural History* 41, Apr. 2014, 170-2. Williams writes that PHG's 'sighting may have been the first verifiable record of a beluga off the south coast of England, and is perhaps still unique' (p. 171).

just come from drear[y] Newfoundland, like Paradise. How I love to recal [*sic*] every little incident connected with that excursion! the poor brown Cranefly, the first English insect I caught; then our crossing the ditch at the top of the lane; the little grey Moth under the oaks at [the] end of the last field; our return through the first field where the Satyridae were sporting on the sunny bank; the great fat Musca in Heckfordfield hedge, which I in my ignorance called a Bombylius, & the consequent display of entomological lore manifested all that day by [my brother] Tom, in the frequent repetition of the sounding words—'Bombylius Bee-fly'.[123]

Shortly after Gosse arrived in Poole, William and his father Thomas followed. It was the first time in a decade that the family was united. Philip attended the Independent Meeting again with his parents, and spoke with the Revd Thomas Durant. He was disappointed that no one thought to inquire about his inner life, nor knew of the change which had occurred. Durant was pleased when Gosse cited the words 'My Kingdom is not of this world' from John 18: 36, yet he regretted that the minister did not venture to ask 'whether I had personally embraced that kingdom.' The change *had* occurred. It *was* real. That's why Gosse was delighted when Apsey, in a letter to him received in Poole, called him 'by the sweet title "Brother in Christ."'[124]

Time passed quickly, and the family circle was again broken after six weeks, when Gosse left for Carbonear. He reached Newfoundland on 1st November, bearing with him the warm recollections of his entomological excursions in Poole, his botanical rambles with his cousin (the botanist Thomas Bell Salter, 1814-58), and his newly-acquired entomological friend, Samuel Harrison (who had promised to exchange specimens with him).[125]

-II-

With a life now inspired by two new factors, Gosse viewed Newfoundland under a new lens. It was a place to explore, and a place in which to

123. 'Reminiscences', II: 170-2.

124. PHG-G. Apsey, 1868, quoted in Smith, *History of the Methodist Church*, II:171. In 'Reminiscences', II:169, PHG described Apsey's 'long loving godly letter' to him, 'beginning: "Dear Sir, & Brother, I trust, in Christ."'

125. 'Reminiscences', II: 172-77. Salter was the author of *A Short Account of the Botany of Poole* (1839), cited in James Britten and George S. Boulger, *A Biographical Index of Deceased British and Irish Botanists* (London: Taylor and Francis, 2nd ed., 1931), 267.

develop. He began to enter careful scientific observations in journals, while extracts from his meteorological record were published in the *Conception Bay Mercury* and later in the *Carbonear Star*.[126]

A scientific novice such as Gosse would have greatly benefitted from professional help, if only he could have found it on the island. But Newfoundland possessed no men of science, no scientific institutions, and no cabinet collections; science education in the schools was a half century away.[127] To naturalists of the day, Newfoundland and Labrador were unfamiliar territory when, in 1766, the English botanist Joseph Banks (1743-1820) spent nearly five months there collecting specimens of mainly plants and birds, and some insects.[128] His was the first wide-ranging effort to document scientifically what he collected, yet he never published anything about his trip.[129] Some of the work of the three artists whom he enlisted to provide a pictorial record of his findings was subsequently used by others, though their drawings were not always from living specimens[130] (an example of the counter-trend was the illustrated volume of 'Wild Flowers and Fruits of Newfoundland from Nature' by Philip's brother William, composed around 1830, accompanied by useful descriptions).[131] The well-known view that science does not develop in a society which lacks a leisured, middle-class—or an upper-class of patrons—has relevance here. For it will be recalled that at this time Newfoundland comprised only two classes, and, not surprisingly, their members were mainly interested in their immediate concerns.

126. These reports appeared from the end of 1832 until he left Newfoundland in 1835 (Freeman & Wertheimer-PHG, 107-8). The only known issue of the *Conception Bay Mercury*, a weekly, is for 16 Dec. 1831 (Whelan, 'Journalism in Newfoundland', 13).

127. Gough, 'An Historical Study of Science Education in Newfoundland', 46.

128. Banks apparently collected many insects, but most lack locality labels (Averil M. Lysaght, *Joseph Banks in Newfoundland and Labrador, 1766. His Diary, Manuscripts and Collections* (Berkeley: University of California Press, 1971), 129, 166fn.103, 291-2, 404-5).

129. Lysaght, *Joseph Banks*, 9, 36, 40.

130. Lysaght, *Joseph Banks*, 101-7.

131. William Gosse's unpublished volume was seen in the Family Collection. It is described by Raymond Lister as a 'brilliant ... book of *trompe l'oeil* water-colour studies' (Lister, *British Romantic Art*. London: G. Bell & Sons, 1973, 152). On at least one occasion while in London, he brought it to Mrs Morgan's while EWG was staying there (William Gosse, Diary, under 14 Mar. 1857). What is probably WG's sketchbook of scenes and buildings in Newfoundland, from c. 1841, is at the T. B. Browning Collection at the Newfoundland Provincial Archives (P6[A]1). It was exhibited, along with a painting by PHG, in St. John's in 1931 ('Gosse Sketches on Exhibit at M.U. Col. "Open House" Days', St. John's, Newfoundland *Daily News*, 9 July 1931, 3). J. Russell Harper has confused the careers and lives of WG and PHG in his entries for them in *Early Painters and Engravers in Canada* (Toronto: University of Toronto Press, 1970), 131.

Even with its deficiencies, Gosse's entomological efforts established his place as the pioneer in Newfoundland who provided the first records of the island's butterflies[132] and was the first to systematically investigate and record the entomology of that island.[133] For students of Lepidoptera in Newfoundland (as well as Jamaica) Gosse's work in those two regions is important to our own day.[134] Not knowing where to start, Gosse commenced, as we have seen, by collecting every insect that came his way:

> for identification, I had but the terse, highly-condensed, intensely technical generic characters from Linnaeus's Systema Naturae, in the article "Entomology" in Tegg's "London Encyclopaedia" ... These characters I copied out, & have still: they were of great value: I studied them most intently; was often puzzled, discouraged, but ever returned to the attack. I made many mistakes, which were gradually corrected. Experience taught me many things; the want of books cast me more upon nature; & so I struggled on, constantly increasing my acquaintance with the Divine handiwork, & laying a solid foundation for book-knowledge, whenever it might fall in my path.[135]
>
> The leading forms of that great Class were familiarized to me in a way that they never could have been if I had merely learned their names from coloured engravings, or from the oral information of some learned friend; and what was of far greater value,—I acquired the habit of comparing structure with structure, of marking minute differences

132. Richard Holland, 'Notes on Newfoundland Butterflies', *Journal of The Lepidopterists' Society* 23 (1969), 33; Harry Krogerus, 'Investigations on the Lepidoptera of Newfoundland. [Vol.] I. Macrolepidoptera', *Acta Zoologica Fennica 82* (1954), 5. PHG's observations at Carbonear, Newfoundland date to 1832-35, but were not published until 1883, when W.H. Edwards sent them as 'Notes on Butterflies Obtained at Carbonear Island, Newfoundland, 1832-1835. By P.H. Gosse' to the *Canadian Entomologist* XV (Mar. 1883), 44-51. Edwards provided an introduction to the article ('Newfoundland Butterflies, Collected by P. H. Gosse', 43-44), which included excerpts from a letter from PHG-W.H. Edwards, 25 Apr. 1882 (State of West Virginia, Dept. of Archives and History). Edwards also referred to the 'excellent colored figures of many Coleoptera, Hemiptera, Orthoptera, Diptera, Hymenoptera, and Heterocerous Lepidoptera' (p. 43). See also PHG-W.H. Edwards, 30 May 1882 (State of West Virginia, Dept. of Archives and History).

133. Carl H. Lindroth, *The Carabid Beetles of Newfoundland*, 7; F. A. Bruton, 'Pioneer Entomologist [PHG] of Newfoundland', St. John's, Newfoundland, *Evening Telegram*, 16 Dec. 1927, 22; 'The Entomology of Newfoundland. Philip H. Gosse's Book Of Insects Of Newfoundland Acknowledged By Royal Society. A Discovery', St. John's, Newfoundland *Daily News* (6 Jan. 1930), 6; Douglas Wertheimer, 'Gosse, Philip Henry', *DCB* XI: 364.

134. F. Martin Brown-D. Wertheimer, 2 Dec. 1972 (Brown and Bernard Heineman co-authored *Jamaica and its Butterflies* (London: E. W. Classey, 1972)).

135. 'Reminiscences', II: 194-5.

of form, and became in some measure accustomed to that precision of language, without which descriptive Natural History could not exist.[136]

By noting every fact which appeared to be of importance, Gosse thus took steps to become 'not merely a collector of insects ... but a *scientific naturalist*'.[137]

Meanwhile, Gosse had found it necessary to begin to recover the momentum in religious affairs which he had lost while in Poole. Although some people viewed the study of God's works, in the natural theology tradition, as leading one to the Creator as surely as a study of his word, this was not Gosse's opinion. The pursuit of natural history might make the mind reflect on design in the universe and on the Divine Craftsman, but 'it should never be forgotten that we must not rest in the creature, but be led up to the Creator; and not only perceive His hand, but fear Him, trust in Him, and love Him.'[138] One could not look to a study of God's works, then, to answer that momentous question, How can a sinner be saved? That was the issue which occupied Gosse's inner thoughts at the time, and entomological excursions could only be a distraction. The enthusiasm for science was 'not favourable to heavenliness of mind; though, on the other hand, it did materially, both now and subsequently, fortify me against many of the more ordinary & more virulent forms of temptation.'[139]

Reconsidering his former reservations about Methodism, and uninterested in the Roman Catholic and Anglican forms of worship as either unappealing or unfamiliar to him, Gosse had joined the Methodist Society in Carbonear as soon as he could. He entered Apsey's class, and began to read the theological works of John and Charles Wesley, 'whence the Divine scheme of salvation through Christ became known to me. ... I learned to lean on the atoning work of Christ, on his Blood shed for me, as the ground on which I could meet God.'[140] He followed the Methodist

136. PHG, *A Manual of Marine Zoology for the British Isles* (London: John Van Voorst, Part I, 1855), Preface.

137. 'Reminiscences', II: 175, emphasis in the original; for a parallel statement, see PHG-W. H. Edwards, 25 Apr. 1882 (State of West Virginia, Department of Archives & History).

138. PHG, *The Canadian Naturalist. A Series of Conversations on the Natural History of Lower Canada* (London: John Van Voorst, 1840), 360.

139. 'Reminiscences', II: 176. That PHG's corpus of marine zoology work exemplifies only one understanding of Paley's natural theology is a point made by Jonathan Smith in 'Philip Gosse and the Varieties of Natural Theology', in Linda Woodhead (ed.), *Reinventing Christianity: 19th Century Contexts* (London: Routledge, 2001, 2019), 251-262.

140. 'Reminiscences', II: 177-9. At that time, Philip Tocque was memorizing Wesley's sermons (Doyle, 'A Biography of Philip Tocque', 10).

discipline of fasting once a week and, to encourage concentration, prayed aloud in his room.

By the spring of 1833, Gosse had completed the terms of his indenture at the counting-house. With nowhere else to go, and in the midst of such exciting self-discovery, he decided to stay on. The collecting of insects was carried out assiduously, whether on the mainland or, with Andrew Elson (one of John Elson's sons), on Carbonear Island, in Conception Bay; by the end of the year, he had 388 species.[141] Even people in the town were on the look-out for unusual specimens. The acquisition of insects led naturally to the depiction of them with pen and pencil. On May 25, in describing the transformation of a lacewing fly, Gosse first became conscious of his skill in 'word-painting'.[142]

During the summer, he began to take the portraits of these creatures, entering them into a volume which he entitled *Entomologia Terrae Novae*. Among the 232 coloured figures in the over-sixty-page volume are thirteen butterflies, forty-three moths, and three dozen beetles. Most of these were drawn to scale, and others magnified with the aid of two lenses which he had brought from Poole. In one respect, these illustrations unsurprisingly reflected Gosse's insufficient entomological knowledge: a number of the names given to his sitters are inaccurate. Nonetheless, some of the insects which he drew (in the diurnal lepidoptera, for instance) were not again described until nearly fifty years later. And the drawings themselves, painstakingly made and attaining an unusually high level of scientific accuracy, were considered by Gosse himself, half a century later, to be 'in no wise inferior to any that I have executed in later years.' The work—continued until he left Newfoundland in June 1835[143]—was an important achievement in his early career. Although the volume has remained unpublished, Gosse's beautiful drawings have been admired by later generations of entomologists.[144] Newfoundlanders

141. 'Reminiscences', II: 187; an entry from an 1833 entomological journal (cited in *Life*, 81) indicates that he had taken 102 species of Coleoptera; 29 of Hemiptera; 70 of Lepidoptera (15 butterflies, 55 moths); Neuroptera, 43; Hymenoptera, 69; and Diptera, 75.

142. 'Reminiscences', II: 186; the passage is quoted in *Life*, 77-8.

143. D. K. McE. Kevan believed that the work was probably completed in 1836 (cited in R. B. Williams, 'More Fragments on Gosse Illustrations', *Society for the History of Natural History Newsletter* no. 23 (1984), 8).

144. PHG's MS *Entomologia Terrae Novae* is now in the Canadian Museum of Nature in Ottawa. In 1929, while still in the Family Collection, it was taken to the Department of Entomology at the British Museum (Natural History), and there the illustrations—which 'evoked the admiration of the experts'—were given proper scientific names (F. A. Bruton, 'Philip Henry

have looked back on his modest place in their history with pride, citing his scientific career launched there as an example of 'a Newfoundland genius'[145] who persisted in the face of obstacles.[146]

This year was an equally active one for Gosse amongst his Wesleyan friends. Religion at the time in Carbonear, in the words of Gosse's acquaintance Philip Tocque, was 'of the most primitive type—plain, practical preaching. No obscuring of the truth of the Word of God by learned exegesis, but every precept and injunction was allowed its full force.'[147] Around this time, Gosse, Sprague, and Fuller (a new clerk in the counting-house) joined the chapel's choir, with William Gosse playing violin; Gosse also began to participate in the public prayer-meetings.[148] Switching from Apsey's Class to that of the newly-married local businessman George Edward Jaques (1807 or 1808-91),[149] Gosse

Gosse's Entomology of Newfoundland', *Entomological News* XLI (Feb. 1930), 34-7). Upon his return to England in 1839, Gosse showed the volume to Andrew Melly (1802-1851), the collector of Coleoptera, who praised it highly ('Reminiscences', II: 188). In 1882, PHG expressed his appraisal of the MS to the American entomologist W. H. Edwards (PHG-W. H. Edwards, 17 Feb. 1882. State of West Virginia, Department of Archives and History), and subsequently sent it to him. Edwards identified a few of the insects, and in returning the book cited its 'excellent coloured figures' (Edwards, 'Newfoundland Butterflies Collected by P. H. Gosse', *Canadian Entomologist*, 43). Three illustrations were published from this MS in 1980 and 1983 (R. B. Williams, 'More fragments on Gosse illustrations', *Society for the History of Natural History Newsletter* no. 23 (1984), 8, and the same author's 'Yet more on Gosse illustrations', *SHNHN* no. 24 (1985), 8). The work was digitized in 2017 and is available at the Biodiversity Heritage Library website. The late Newfoundland Premier Joey Smallwood referred to 'a very notable book on one aspect' of Newfoundland written by PHG, which he termed among 'the dozen greatest works written' about the province. Perhaps this mystifying reference was to this unpublished work (Lysaght, *Joseph Banks*, 7). For the view that the MS 'has no scientific value', see the exchange between Alfred Van Peteghem, 'T. W. Fyles on P. H. Gosse', *Canadian Notes & Queries*, no. 12 (Nov. 1973), 7; D. Wertheimer, *CN&Q* no. 13 (June 1974), 6-7; and Audrey E. Dawe, *CN&Q* no. 14 (Nov. 1974), 4.

EWG's assertion that his father made a ruler at this time which, 'in contempt of all modern improvements, he continued to use until the year of his death', is untrue. PHG wrote 'I still possess it', not that he used it (*Life*, 80; 'Reminiscences', II: 188b).

145. 'A Newfoundland Genius', New York *Evening Post* (22 Nov. 1870), 1, is about PHG: 'Let no one imagine, writes our St. Johns correspondent, that because Newfoundland is behind in the race for material prosperity her children are deficient in intellectual gifts. ... In proof that I am not romancing, take the following case in point. There is now living in London a distinguished naturalist whose fame is world-wide, by name Philip Henry Gosse .... He was born in Carbonear ... and in very humble circumstances. ... He now holds a foremost place among England's sons of science.' Provincial premier Joey Smallwood wrote that 'it is not every small island that has a Philip Henry Gosse or Averil Lysaght' (Lysaght, *Joseph Banks*, 7).

146. Tocque, *Kaleidoscope Echoes*, 15-16.

147. Philip Tocque, 'When I Was a Boy', St. John's, Newfoundland *Evening* Telegram, 15 Feb. 1897, [3]. Tocque did not work at Slade's until 1835 (Doyle, 'A Biography of Philip Tocque', 14).

148. 'Reminiscences', II: 148, 180, 196.

149. Jaques died on 12 July 1891, 'aged 84 years': Revd Thomas W. Fyles, 'A Visit to the Canadian Haunts of the Late Philip Henry Gosse', *Twenty-third Annual Report of the*

soon formed a fast friendship with this couple of 'decided Christians' which had the effect of gradually separating him more and more from the companionship of the unconverted: 'it was a marked commencement of that course of decided separateness from the world, wh. I have sought to maintain ever since.'[150] From around 1833, Gosse was persuaded to become a local preacher for the Wesleyans. Together with Jaques, the 'saintly and popular Local Preacher'[151] and class leader[152] Apsey, and the Carbonear-native Philip Tocque (1814-1899),[153] he every Sunday visited Otterbury, a hamlet less than 10 miles north of Carbonear. Gosse also became friends with another Carbonear native and Wesleyan, John Bemister (1815-1892), a clerk who worked at Pack, Gosse, and Fryer, in Carbonear.[154]

Though said to be a 'talented local preacher',[155] from Gosse's perspective, speaking before twenty or thirty 'illiterate, simple, confiding' people was a severe test. He found it much more difficult to handle than the occasional taunt which he received because of his religious beliefs:[156]

Entomological Society of Ontario (1892), 27.

150. 'Reminiscences', II: 177-8.

151. Findlay and Holdsworth, *History of the Wesleyan Methodist Missionary Society* I: 343.

152. Hollett, 'A People Reaching for Ecstasy', 235.

153. Philip Tocque joined the Methodist Society at Carbonear when he was 16 (Tocque, 'When I Was a Boy', St. John's, Newfoundland *Evening* Telegram, 15 Feb. 1897, [3]; Hollett, 'A People Reaching for Ecstasy', 234), having come from the Church of England. As a Methodist local preacher he visited small towns outside of Carbonear: Freshwater, Perry's Cove, Mosquito, and Otterbury. Tocque was joined by PHG, Samuel W. Sprague, George Apsey and Alfred Parsons (Doyle, 'A Biography of Philip Tocque', 9-10); Parsons was an area businessman around 1825 (Charles Lench, *The Story of Methodism in Bonavista And the Settlements visited by the Early Preachers* (Publisher not identified: 1919), 144). Tocque is, however, listed in C. V. Forster Bliss (ed.), *The Clerical Guide and Churchman's Directory. An Annual Register for the Clergy and Laity of the Anglican Church in British North America. 1877* (Ottawa: J. Durie & Son, 2ed., 1877), 373. Tocque joined Slade, Elson and Co., the same company at which PHG worked, in 1835 (Doyle, 'A Biography of Philip Tocque', 14). In 1840, Tocque unsuccessfully applied to join the Methodist Missionary Society in London ('Tocque, Philip', *Encyclopedia of Newfoundland and Labrador* (1994), V: 395).

154. PHG-John Bemister, 21 Dec. 1871 (Corr. Bk.). PHG and Bemister knew each other around 1831, 'when I was a clerk in Elson's office, & you were one in Pack's'. Philip Tocque was an early friend of Bemister's (Tocque, letter to the editor, 'When I Was a Boy', St. John's, Newfoundland *Evening Telegram*, 15 Feb. 1897, 3). In 1861, Bemister was Newfoundland's Receiver General, among other government positions he later held: 'Bemister, John', *Encyclopedia of Newfoundland and Labrador* (1981), I:174; Gunn, *Political History of Newfoundland*, 159, 199-202, 204; *DCB* X: 778; *Waterford News* (Ireland), 26 May 1865, 3; Bemister obituary notice in *Vancouver Daily World*, 28 Dec. 1892, 2.

155. Lench, *History of the Rise and Progress of Methodism*, 8.

156. To the amusement of others, around this time one of the local captains ridiculed PHG's religious views. 'I was kept in meekness & in peace; comforted by the vivid presentation to my

> I suffered from mauvaise honte to an extreme which was ludicrous,
> yet very painful. I recollect with vivid distinctness, how I used to feel
> as if my whole subject was an absolute black [*sic*] before my mind: I
> could not see two words ahead of what I was uttering; what I *had* said
> instantly disappeared from my view; & thus it habitually seemed as if
> every moment I must utterly break down.[157]

The open confession of Christ as Saviour was made in other ways, too.
Gosse wrote to his brother Tom, to St. John, Samuel Harrison, and Tom
Salter, 'as one not ashamed of Him.' He felt that a perception of the
importance of unfulfilled prophecy may be found in his poem on 'The
Restoration of Israel' (composed in 1833 under the influence of Croly's
Salathiel).[158]

In those letters to St. John and friends in Poole written between 1832-4,
the claims of entomology vied with those of God. They were characterised
by 'the commingling, or rather the alternating, of the serious and the
jocose, which has ever marked my character.'[159] During 1834, Gosse
acquired his first insect cabinet; during one of his many excursions with
Andrew Elson in July, obtained a black swallowtail butterfly, his 'first
cabinet specimen';[160] and was sent other specimens by his brother Tom
and by Sam Harrison. He continued to make excursions with Andrew
Elson, increased the number of scientific books in his collection, and
filled his journals with his observations, some of which were published
years later.[161]

At the same time, he was increasingly in the company of the Jaqueses,
and an active Wesleyan. In the autumn of this year, Sprague and Fuller,
after a conversation with him, made a commitment to become serious

mind of Acts v. 41, "Rejoicing that they were counted worthy to suffer shame for his name." I
accepted it as a real honour' ('Reminiscences', II: 184).

157. 'Reminiscences', II: 180-1, 184-5. Emphasis in the original.

158. 'Reminiscences', II: 185, 183.

159. 'Reminiscences', II: 185.

160. PHG, 'Notes on Butterflies Obtained at Carbonear Island, Newfoundland, 1832[1834]-
1835', *Canadian Entomologist*, 44-5.

161. 'Reminiscences', II: 194, 188, 200. From Poole, he was sent two books: James Rennie's
Alphabet of Insects for the Use of Beginners (1832) and his *A Conspectus of the Butterflies and
Moths Found in Britain* (1832). In the autumn of 1834 he purchased a treatise on structural
botany (SPCK) and Alexander Wilson and Charles Lucien Bonaparte's *American Ornithology*,
ed. By Robert Jameson (4vols., 1831). For the excursions with A[ndrew] E[lson], and for the
excerpts from his scientific journals: PHG, 'Notes on Butterflies Obtained at Carbonear Island,
Newfoundland, 1832[1834]-1835', *Canadian Entomologist*, 44-51, and PHG, 'The Y-shaped
Organ of Papilio Larvae', *Hardwicke's Science-Gossip* VIII (1 Oct. 1871), 224.

Christians, but while Fuller 'relapsed, and remained careless,' Sprague
'persevered; never went back at all,' in 1838 became one of the two first
Newfoundlanders to join the ministry,[162] and served fifty-four years in the
ministry of the Methodist Church.[163] Sprague owed that development as 'a
passionate Methodist'[164] to Gosse (as Gosse noted, 'The first God ever gave
me!').[165] Indeed, ever since Apsey's conversion, nearly all of the clerks at
Elson's had taken the same step towards rebirth.[166] And somewhat before
this, in April 1834, St. John, who was amongst the reborn, nearly died
of scarlet fever. 'I hastened to see him,' Gosse recalled,

> & as I stood by his bed-side, his face attenuated by illness, his beard
> unshaved for many days,—[it] struck me so painfully that I burst into
> uncontrollable weeping. I however read to him,—from the Scriptures, &
> from Wesley's Hymns; & sought to point him upwards. He anticipated
> death, & commended his wife and three infant children to my care, which
> I solemnly promised. He recovered, however ...[167]

Since those memorable months in May and June of 1832, then, Gosse
had been immersed in personal concerns. But a public matter had been
gradually forcing itself upon his attention, becoming more discomfiting
each year. Although the general elections in Newfoundland in the autumn
of 1832 following hard upon the granting of representative government
to the colony had aroused little excitement other than in the capital, St.
John's,[168] tension was already mounting between the Irish Catholics and
English Protestants. Three decades of disorder were to follow the events
of 1832, for the 'Irish Popish party' (the pejorative label is Gosse's) 'stirred
by demagogues, & more privately by their priests had been striving to get
a monopoly of power. Party spirit ran high: Protestants went in mortal

162. Findlay and Holdsworth, *History of the Wesleyan Methodist Missionary Society*, I:
343; Smith, *History of the Methodist Church* II: 172.

163. Fredericton *Herald*, 27 May 1893, 3; Wilson, *Methodism in The Maritime Provinces*, 53.

164. Hollett, 'A People Reaching for Ecstasy', 363.

165. 'Reminiscences', II: 199. PHG's personal influence on Sprague is repeated in Lench,
History of the Rise and Progress of Methodism, 8; Sprague was also apparently influenced by
Apsey in his 'change of heart' (Hollett, 'A People Reaching for Ecstasy', 236).

166. Besides Apsey and Sprague, who became Wesleyan ministers, also undergoing a
conversion were St. John, William F. Lush, and Newell (two new clerks). Philip Tocque, who
joined the counting-house at some time, became an Anglican minister ('Reminiscences', II: 129).
Apsey remained a Methodist to his death at age 71 on 30 Apr. 1869 (Peters, 'Obituary [of George
Apsey]', *Provincial Wesleyan*, [2]; 'Reminiscences', II: 128).

167. 'Reminiscences', II: 195-6.

168. Gunn, *Political History of Newfoundland*, 14.

fear; for the Irish vastly outnumbered us, & everywhere dark threatening glances and muttering words beset us.'[169]

This comment reflects Gosse's life-long animosity towards Catholics (one observer has called him 'a terrible bigot'),[170] his anxiety over the role of the Roman Catholic pulpit in inciting its followers to mob violence,[171] and the apparently sincerely-expressed feeling that the English were in the minority. Yet the English were not in the minority; Carbonear, as we have seen, was typical of Newfoundland as a whole in being equally populated by the two groups (St. Mary's, which Gosse had visited in 1828-9, did have nearly 600 Catholics versus seventeen Protestants).[172]

While the facts were wrong, Gosse knew from a single instance that the fear was real. Not long after he had arrived in Newfoundland, he had been asked how he found the country, and—not suspecting that an Irishman, Moore, was present—he had impertinently replied, 'I see little in it, but dogs and Irishmen.'

I had but given expression to a deep feeling, which every one in the company felt much more than I could yet do;—Moore, certainly not least. For Moore was an Ulster Protestant, whose antagonism to the papist[173] Irish was even stronger than ours. It was not exactly Irishmen, but Papists, that really constituted the anti-English party in Newfoundland; & whose rancour & insolence was soon to grow, under priestly teaching, to formidable dimensions. Already there existed in the Protestants of the Island, far more oppressively felt than openly expressed, an habitual dread of the papist Irish as a class; & an habitual caution in conversation, to avoid any unguarded expression, which might be laid hold of by their

169. 'Reminiscences', II: 191.

170. Linda Little, 'Plebeian Collective Action in Harbour Grace and Carbonear, Newfoundland, 1830-1840' (Memorial University of Newfoundland, MA thesis, 1984), 29.

171. For instances of such activities (e.g., of Bishop Fleming), see Gunn, *Political History of Newfoundland*, chap. 2; also Moyles, *Nineteenth Century Views of Newfoundland*, 84-5, and D. W. Prowse, *A History of Newfoundland from the English, Colonial, and Foreign Records* (London: Macmillan and Co., 1895), 439fn.4.

172. *Carbonear Star and Conception Bay Mercury* (1 May, 1833), 71.

173. The term 'Papist' was reputedly applied early in Catholic history to denote 'their leading tenet—the infallibility and supremacy of the Pope (in the Latin *Papa*, signifying father)', but 'They, however, [now] considering it a title of reproach, the term Roman Catholic has been substituted by courtesy' (James Aikman (ed.), *Evans' Sketch of the Denominations of the Christian World* (Edinburgh: Peter Brown, 1794, corrected and enlarged from the 7ed., 1837), 158 and 158fn.). PHG distinguished between the terms 'Papacy' and 'Popery': 'Papacy means the status or condition of the Pope. ... the Papal doctrine, = Popery' (PHG-EWG, 12 July 1875 (CUL Add. 7019,16).

jealous enmity. It was very largely this dread that impelled me to forsake Newfoundland, as a residence, in 1835; & I recollect saying to my friends the Jaqueses, that 'when we got to Canada, we might climb to the top of the tallest tree in the forest, and shout 'Irishman!' at the top of our voice, without fear.'[174]

Most contemporary observers blamed 'unscrupulous [Catholic] priests' for inciting the Catholic laity for political purposes.[175] The concern about uncontrolled violence may also have been behind the support Gosse gave to a petition at a public meeting complaining about the failure of Carbonear police in the 'maintaining [of] public order, the prevention of crime, or the protection of life and property.'[176]

It was not only the Irish issue which made Gosse look elsewhere for a home. He was making little money at the counting-house (when he left, he was earning £50 per annum, although during his first six years he averaged only slightly more than £20), and the fishing trade was falling into a depression.[177] Moreover Jaques, whose mercantile business was failing, had towards the end of 1834 heard 'some very flaming accounts of the fertility of the regions around Lake Huron, & of the certainty of success being attained in agriculture by emigrants settling there.'[178] Gosse, unable to bear the thought of being separated from his friends, wrote his family in Poole in December 1834 of the bright future in Canada, and invited them to join him in a few years. To his brother Tom he held out a special attraction: that 'We would have all things common; we could entomologize together in the noble forest, and, in the peaceful and happy pursuits of agriculture, forget the toils and anxieties of commerce.' He expected him, at least, to come immediately, and bring with him all the English insects he could: 'I have learned to stuff birds, and there are beauties in Canada. We could make a nice museum.'[179]

---

174. 'Reminiscences', II: 43-4.

175. Little, 'Plebeian Collective Action in Harbour Grace and Carbonear, Newfoundland, 1830-1840', 30.

176. *Carbonear Star and Conception Bay* Mercury, 17 July 1833, 115.

177. PHG could not remember exactly what his salary had been (board and lodging were included). As we have already seen, he spoke of an annual income of £20. According to another estimation, he earned £10 in 1827 with increments of £5 per annum through 1831 (when he was paid £30). In 1832, this jumped to £40 ('Reminiscences', II: 68, and see p. 216).

178. 'Reminiscences', II: 200-1; at the end of 1832, Jaques had dissolved a partnership and gone off on his own (*Carbonear Star*, 6 Feb. 1833, 23).

179. PHG-Tom Gosse, 1 Dec. 1834 (cited in *Life*, 86-7).

With the exception of Tom, however, the family was not enthusiastic. Philip's father, in fact, wrote William (still in the employ of Pack, Gosse, and Fryer, in Carbonear, but soon to be sent to one of the firm's branches, at Bay Roberts)[180] that 'Your condition appears indeed no better than exile,' and that he had heard of clerks in England making £200 a year. Thomas told him, too, of his plan to start a family magazine—a similar venture, so he said, had earned its proprietor a fortune in another part of the country—and if it proved successful, Philip and William were welcome to join. It 'will enable you to live no longer in exile from your kindred & friends & Country.'[181]

The possibility that Philip might set aside one dream for another was never, however, seriously entertained. It was not more money that he wanted: it was more insects. Of all the reasons which motivated him to leave Newfoundland, the one which was 'unconfessed & never even uttered, yet stronger than all', was entomological greed:

> I had pretty well exhausted Entomology in Newfoundland; it was a cold barren unproductive region: I longed to try a new field. One of the numerous works which we read on Canada this autumn;—for we eagerly devoured every thing we could find,—was a gossiping pleasant book by a lady, in which she described enthusiastically & with much detail, though not scientifically, the insects & familiar flowers of Upper Canada. The descriptions were so attractive as to fire my imagination; & thenceforth the time seemed long till I could wield my butterfly-net in the Canadian forest.[182]

180. For William's residence at the latter location, see Elizabeth Gosse-WG, 5 Oct. 1835 (LeBL), and at the former, see fn. below.

181. Thomas Gosse-William Gosse (at Carbonear), 16 Mar. 1835 (LeBL). At least one specimen number of the uninspiring *The Bee and Blossom Magazine* appeared (price one penny), probably around September 1835 (CUL Adv. c.82.5, 19). According to Thomas's letter, it was to provide children with a liberal education, 'what the more independent people & gentry have been till now monopolizing'.

182. 'Reminiscences', II: 201-2. PHG correctly described the contents of *The Backwoods of Canada. Being Letters from the Wife of an Emigrant Officer, Illustrative of the Domestic Economy of British America*, published anonymously in London. The work, by Catharine Parr Traill (1802-1899), was intended for the use of the potential 'female emigrant' to the country (p. 1). *The Backwoods of Canada* was published in London in parts, the first one appearing in 1835 ('This day is published', advertisement, London *Morning Post*, 31 Dec. 1835, 1). In book form, it is dated 1836 and was early reviewed in the *Athenaeum* (20 Feb. 1836), 138-9. I have not seen that the book was serialised prior to publication, which (if so) would mean that PHG misdated his reading of it at least by several months.

Evening after evening was now spent with the Jaqueses, planning the move to the British colony of Upper Canada (the present-day Canadian province of Ontario).[183] By the middle of 1835, they were ready to leave, the cruel attack by a gang of Catholics upon the Congregationalist editor and co-founder of the St. John's *Public Ledger*, Henry David Winton (1793-1855), in May, giving their decision an added impetus, as if one were needed.[184] Gosse told Elson that he would be quitting, and he was surprised and disappointed to see that it made no impact. Perhaps it was partially his own fault, for not having heeded the advice of John Brown's father to make himself an indispensable figure in the counting-house. Elson, however, as he later discovered, 'never liked the man' (Gosse believed that Elson's Unitarian faith made him unsympathetic to 'personal religion').[185]

It would have been a sad note upon which to end his eight-year residence in Newfoundland, but it proved only a passing cloud. Gosse hoped for much in the future; he had already gained much from the past, owing his early training as a Christian and as a naturalist to those years in Newfoundland. That memory, four swallow-tail chrysalids, some caterpillars and eggs, and a long-sought-after specimen of the yellow swallow-tail butterfly were what he took with him on board the boat to Upper Canada on 25 June 1835.[186]

---

183. The term 'Upper Canada' was used from 1791-1841, then 'Canada West' until 1867, after which it assumed its present name of Ontario (David J. Bercuson and J.L. Granatstein, *The Collins Dictionary of Canadian History 1867 to the Present* (Toronto: Collins, 1988), 210).

184. Winton was well-known for his denunciations of the Roman Catholic clergy for their alleged interference in political issues. Leaving Carbonear on horseback on the afternoon of 19 May 1835, Winton was attacked by five men who cut off both his ears and part of one of his cheeks. A reward of £200, and later £1,500, was offered. The perpetrators were neither caught nor revealed and their identity remains 'a mystery' (Patrick O'Flaherty, 'Winton, Henry David', *DCB* VIII (1985)). According to William Gosse, one of those involved was the surgeon Dr Molloy ('Reminiscences', II: 192). For accounts of the attack, see Smith, *History of the Methodist Church* II:177; Charles Pedley, *The History of Newfoundland* (London: Longman, Green, Longman, Roberts, & Green, 1863), 391-7; Tocque, *Newfoundland: As It Was, and As It Is In 1877*, 35; Hollett, 'A People Reaching for Ecstasy', 156.

Some of the establishment at St. Mary's of Slade, Elson, & Co., was also destroyed by the local Catholics in this year: Gunn, *Political History of Newfoundland*, 26-7; Prowse, *History of Newfoundland*, 436 and fn. 2; Moyles, *Nineteenth Century Views of Newfoundland*, 104-5; and *Newspaper Cuttings Consisting Principally of Proclamations Relating to Newfoundland* [from Newfoundland papers], Packet #2, clipping from an unspecified paper, 26 May 1835 (British Library, Department of Printed Books, 8155.ee.6).

185. For John Brown's father's advice: PHG-EWG, 5 Feb. 1867 (CUL Add. 7041, 5), 'Reminiscences', II: 204.

186. PHG, 'Notes on Butterflies Obtained at Carbonear Island, Newfoundland, 1832[1834]-

-III-

'Hope has, all my life, been strong in me,' Gosse once observed.[187] In one way, it was fortunate that he possessed this trait, for the attitude helped him to persevere in times of personal difficulty, and to look beyond the despair of the moment. Yet there was a disadvantage, too. Rosy expectations need often to be tempered by realism. In moving to Canada, enthusiasm had overcome caution.

It is not surprising that Gosse would be looking to leave Newfoundland. Among his fellow clerks, John Durell had left in 1829;[188] in 1831, as previously mentioned, W. C. St. John departed Carbonear for Harbour Grace and Luke Thomas returned to England;[189] with the mercantile business of his close friends the Jaques failing at the close of the summer 1834,[190] they were 'turning their eyes towards Upper Canada'.[191] Philip Tocque began to seek work outside Carbonear in 1840.

With so many leaving, why didn't Gosse return to England? After all, he invariably referred to time away from family and home as periods of 'exile', and he had gloried so much in the natural variety and richness of Poole when he had visited there in 1832. Or an equally good question: If not England, than why not Boston? From 1850-1900 Boston and environs was the most popular destination for Newfoundlanders no longer able to navigate the difficult economic climate the island was facing in the 1840s.[192] Between 1846 and 1859 some 3,000 of them departed for Boston and environs.[193] They included the native-born like Tocque (in 1849),[194] who

1835', *Canadian Entomologist*, 47, and 'Reminiscences', II: 206.

187. 'Reminiscences', II: 212.

188. 'Reminiscences', II: 102.

189. 'Reminiscences', II: 146.

190. Advertisement, 'Sale by Auction. To-morrow, The 28th Inst. At 11 o'Clock, at Carbonear, at the shop lately occupied by Mr George E. Jaques, Insolvent, All the remaining Stock in Trade, of the said George E. Jaques, for the benefit of his Creditors', *Carbonear Star and Conception Bay Journal*, 27 Aug. 1834, 3.

191. 'Reminiscences', II: 200.

192. Doyle and O'Flaherty', Tocque, Philip', *DCB* XII:1060. From 1850-1900 Boston and environs was also the most popular destination for those from the Maritimes seeking economic improvement (Alan Alexander Brookes, 'The Exodus: Migration from the Maritime Provinces to Boston during the Second Half of the Nineteenth Century' (University of New Brunswick, PhD dissertation, 1978), ii, 253-253a).

193. Edward-Vincent Chafe, 'A New Life on 'Uncle Sam's Farm:' Newfoundlanders in Massachusetts, 1846-1859' (Memorial University of Newfoundland, MA thesis, 1982), v.

194. Philip Tocque, *A Peep at Uncle Sam's Farm* (Boston: Charles H. Peirce and Co., 1851), 1; Doyle, 'A Biography of Philip Tocque', 44.

became an Anglican minister and 'a great historian',[195] and St. John (in 1854),[196] a successful journalist in Boston.[197] Lush moved to Philadelphia.[198]

In his 'Reminiscences', Gosse gives three different reasons for his action. Firstly, 'the land where I go, is exceeding[ly] fertile & productive,' he had written in reference to Lower Canada, '& *with little more than half the toil necessary on an English farm*, will yield not only the necessaries, but the luxuries of life.' With about three-quarters of the £100 which he took with him from Newfoundland, he had estimated that he could live through the first year, and that profits would soon flow from the investment.[199] Secondly, even granting that the religious life in this obscure colony might be poor, might he not benefit from the company of the Jaqueses, fellow Wesleyans? And finally (and above all), there were the insects: Was it not possible that they would be even more numerous in this relatively unexplored land than in England? At home he would be just another neophyte man of science, whereas in Canada he had the opportunity to become a scientific explorer and discoverer.

No sooner had this trio—or, perhaps, quartet: Ann Jaques (1808-1891)[200] was either pregnant or had just given birth to a daughter[201]—

195. Murphy, *Murphy's Old Carbonear*, 8. Tocque is also referred to as 'Newfoundland's first man of letters' ('Tocque, Philip', *Encyclopedia of Newfoundland and Labrador* (1994), V: 395).

196. Clark, *American Genealogical Record*, I: 50. In Boston, St. John was publisher and proprietor of the *Anglo-Saxon Weekly News*, the *Albion* ('Death of a Newspaper Man', *Boston Evening Transcript*, 24 Feb. 1873, 1; Chafe, 'A New Life on "Uncle Sam's Farm"', 85), *Zion's Herald*, a Methodist Episcopal publication (Lench, *History of the Rise and Progress of Methodism*, 8), and *International Journal* (the last two are cited in 'St. John, William Charles', *Encyclopedia of Newfoundland and Labrador* V (1994), 26). PHG maintained a sporadic correspondence with St. John until at least 1872 (Corr. Bk.).

197. Philip Tocque refers to St. John without naming him, and judged him to be successful: P. Tocque, '(Nothing Succeeds Like Success)', in Annie S. W. Tocque (ed.), *Kaleidoscope Echoes, being Historical, Philosophical, Scientific, and Theological Sketches, from the Miscellaneous Writings of the Rev. Philip Tocque, A.M.* (Toronto: Hunter, Rose Co., Ltd., 1895), 16.

198. Philadelphia *American Sentinel*, 12 Apr. 1838, 2 (giving his address as 27 Sansom St.).

199. 'Reminiscences', II: 202-3. Emphasis in the original. Judging from calculations made at about this time, PHG's figures appear about 50% too low. For example, in one guide book the cost of an acre of land in Lower Canada was put at £1 sterling and the cost of clearing that land, £2 an acre; a log house could be constructed for about £20. If, as they proposed, 100 acres were bought and 20 cleared, the cost (with the log house) would be £160. PHG's figures (for Upper Canada, where the prices were probably higher) were: 10s. to buy an acre, and 30s. to clear it; £7 to build a log house, equalling (on the same basis) £87. To this sum, he had added £20 for livestock, and half that for expenses. See [anon], *Canada, Nova Scotia, New Brunswick, Newfoundland, etc. With the History, Present State, and Prospects of Those Colonies, in Regard to Emigration* (London: Cradock and Co., 1843), 57.

200. Ann (*née* Heap) Jaques, 2 Jan. 1808-30 Dec. 1891 (death notice, Montreal *Gazette*, 4 Jan. 1892, 4). Her name is sometimes spelled 'Anne'.

201. The daughter's name was Alice (mentioned in a letter, PHG-EWG, 2 May 1868, CUL

arrived in Quebec City, than they made a detour from their plan to proceed to the London district of Upper Canada. People told them that their prospects would be better in Lower Canada (the present-day Canadian province of Quebec),[202] and that they should at least have a look at a partially cleared farm which had come up for sale. Gosse, having already provided for his insects as soon as they arrived in Quebec,[203] was amenable to the plan, and they set out in an open carriage on 19 July 1835.

Compton, in the County of Sherbrooke in the Eastern Townships of Quebec, was their final destination. The village itself, directly south of Quebec City, 110 miles east of Montreal and about twenty miles north of the Vermont border of the United States, had a population of some 1,200 people, and contained a Protestant chapel, a school, two shopkeepers, the same number of taverns, and seven saw mills. Populated largely by New Englanders since the days of its first settlement in 1793,[204] the area had early gained a reputation as a 'liquor resort', and the first ministers (American Methodists) to serve the area had met with much opposition, viewing it, on their part, as a moral wasteland.[205] In spite of the crisp, cold, and harsh weather—frost being not uncommon in the spring or early autumn—and the consequent starvation which had been a fact of life for the earliest settlers, the general area had the reputation of being rich agriculturally. Yet the difficulty of sending grain to market forced the settlers to accommodate their use of the land to more profitable sources of income. As the trades established in the village indicate, those sources included the rearing of livestock, dairy farming, and the lumber industry.[206]

Add.7041,20). Their son, the shipping agent also named George Edward Jaques, was born 26 June 1842 (Wm. Cochrane, ed:, *Canadian Album. Men of Canada; or, Success by Example* (Brantford, Ontario: Bradley, Garretson & Co., 1894), III: 472).

202. The term 'Upper Canada' was used from 1791-1841, then 'Canada East' until 1867, after which it assumed its present name of 'Quebec' (Bercuson and Granatstein, *Collins Dictionary of Canadian History*, 121).

203. PHG, scientific journal (this untraced MS is cited in *Life*, 90).

204. Françoise Noël Smith, 'The Establishment of Religious Communities in the Eastern Townships of Lower Canada, 1799 to 1851' (McGill University, MA thesis, 1976), 14.

205. Leonard Stewart Channell, *History of Compton County and Sketches of the Eastern Townships, District of St. Francis, and Sherbrooke County* (Cookshire, Quebec: Published by L. S. Channell, 1896), 166-7, 189 (the estimated population is for 1830); C. M. Day, *History of the Eastern Townships, Province of Quebec, Dominion of Canada, Civil and Descriptive* (Montreal: John Lovell, 1869), 209-11, and John Carroll, *Cyclopaedia of Methodism in Canada* (Toronto: Methodist Book and Publishing House 1881), 193.

206. Channell, *History of Compton County*, 166; *Canada, Nova Scotia, New Brunswick, Newfoundland, etc.*, 58; Day, *History of the Eastern Townships*, 388-9.

The farm which they went to see was more than a mile north of Compton village, not far from two saw mills (Bradley's Brook and Smith's Mill) and Tilden's tavern, in the area which has since become Waterville village.[207] Situated in lovely country, and 'containing hill and dale, hard and soft wood, and streams of water,' the lot itself was 110 acres, of which forty-five had already been cleared. With a downpayment of £50, and an equal amount in two annual installments, the land could be purchased. After a little hesitation, it was taken and became theirs on August 7.[208] 'The country, cultivated & well-peopled, in the height of its summer beauty, was charming,' Gosse later related. He had already seen a Canadian lynx in the museum of the Literary and Historical Society of Quebec, which may well have impressed him more than any description in a book. Then there was

> the profusion of fine butterflies, & other insects [on the farm], which of course I could not stop to catch, altogether dazzled my imagination; so that the important matter of selecting a scene of residence and occupation *for life* (so far as I knew),—had no hold on my serious thought. Like a child, I felt and acted, as if butterfly-catching had been the great business of life.[209]

Having purchased the property, they travelled back to Quebec City to collect their belongings, returning to the farm later in August. The western portion of sixty acres, containing a log-hut, maple-sugary, apple orchard, and four tons of hay, was taken by Gosse; the remainder (a barn and a 30 x 24-foot log house, in which they all lived) went to the Jaqueses.[210] Although by the time they had settled themselves the agricultural season was already far advanced, Gosse did get some work done, ploughing a field of about six acres, clearing away stones, logs, and bushes, and planning for the next year's activity. Because of the expense required to raise livestock, Gosse had decided to attempt to make a living

207. Channell, *History of Compton County*, 184-5; Thomas W. Fyles, 'A Visit to the Canadian Haunts of the Late Philip Henry Gosse', *Twenty-third Annual Report of the Entomological Society of Ontario* (1892), 23-4.

208. The property was conveyed from Benjamin Pomroy to PHG on that date (J. I. Little, 'The Naturalist's Landscape: Philip Henry Gosse in the Eastern Townships, 1835-38', *Journal of Eastern Townships Studies* 20, (Spring 2002), 68fn.15).

209. PHG-Dr Molloy, 4 Nov. 1835, as quoted in *Life*, 92, 94; 'Reminiscences', II: 207 (emphasis in the original); PHG, *Canadian Naturalist*, 41 (with illustration of the lynx).

210. 'Reminiscences', II: 207-8; for the size of the house: Fyles, 'Visit to the Canadian Haunts', 23. PHG paid the Jaqueses 10s. per week for room and board ('Reminiscences', II: 128).

farming land which, it is clear, was not very rich. At the time, he could only envisage a farm with eight acres of grass, four of pasture, three each of wheat, oats, and potatoes, two of turnips, and one each of peas and perhaps buckwheat.[211]

   During the first months, the wave of optimism upon which they had departed from Newfoundland buoyed them up. The work was '*hard*, but not *severe*', and certainly preferable to working behind a desk at Slade's; the neighbours, though 'Yankees' with manners 'too forward and intruding for our English notions' were, nonetheless, not all disagreeable; Gosse had obtained employment for the winter as a teacher in a government school, for £3 per month.

   As for the insects: Gosse was happy to find that there were many new species which he had not seen in Newfoundland to enrich his cabinet, and his work was not so demanding as to prohibit collecting excursions after work. While in Quebec, too, he had met some members of the Literary and Historical Society, and he soon sent them some of his duplicate specimens. Canada, he wrote, 'holds out a charming field of exploration in all branches of natural history.'[212]

   It was in this first winter of 1835-6 that Gosse assembled his scientific journals from Newfoundland and composed his first book, 'The Entomology of Newfoundland'. The manuscript for the work (which disappeared after Gosse's death) was to serve as a companion to the illustrated *Entomologia Terrae Novae*. Written in the stereotyped style of natural history books of the time, it apparently contained anecdotes and descriptions of scenery around Carbonear, besides the scientific observations themselves. Excerpts from the journals (if not the book itself) were subsequently published, but Gosse knew that while it was valuable it was taxonomically deficient.[213]

   By March 1836 Gosse had probably completed his first winter of teaching, and with his horse and cow could look forward to the first full

   211. PHG-Dr Molloy, as cited (*Life*, 92-3); on the decision to farm rather than raise livestock: Fyles, 'Visit to the Canadian Haunts', 24-5 ('I have often wondered what he intended to do with his acres of turnips ... without storage for the preservation of the produce, or stock to consume it, or any available market — for his neighbours would grow what they wanted of such like crops for themselves'). On the difficulties of keeping cattle, see PHG, *Canadian Naturalist*, 107.

   212. PHG-Dr Molloy, as cited (*Life*, 93-4); PHG, *Canadian Naturalist*, 231.

   213. 'Reminiscences', II: 218; for the disappearance of the manuscript, EWG-Dr Philip H.G. Gosse, 27 Nov. 1926 (stuck-in the volume of the *Entomologia Terrae Novae*). It appears likely that the *Entomology* was sold along with other manuscripts in the auction of the contents of the Gosses' Devonshire home in 1900 (*Sandhurst Catalogue*, p. 22).

season of work. 'It seems almost a contradiction in terms, for a naturalist to be in low spirits', he once observed: 'everything he sees tends to enrapture and delight him.'[214] The spring especially, a time of renewal, is an exciting period for the naturalist, but not then. Gosse and the Jaqueses could not avoid feeling depressed by the arduous, demanding, unproductive labour. Ann Jaques, who had been brought up in a genteel home, with a new-born baby was now left to care for the house herself, unable to afford a servant. Her husband and Gosse worked separately at their own plots, with only the occasional assistance from agricultural labourers, who were scarce in the Eastern Townships.[215] Ploughing the fields, hauling stones, removing logs, raking leaves, sowing, reaping, winnowing, clearing the land in June for the next year's crops—all of this having to be done almost entirely alone—it is little wonder that they

> found the drudgery of the farm work very different from what it had seemed, as we looked at it through the halo of romance. Our hands blistered with the axe and the plough; our backs ached with the unwonted toil; no intellectual companions brightened our evening hours; our neighbours,—few & far between,—were all low sordid Yankees, sharp & mean; we saw no books, save those we had brought with us.[216]

They now realised that they had been misled by glowing accounts and their own wishful thinking. They were young, ardent, and resilient; Gosse's letters home were still sanguine.[217] Whether life would have been any better had they proceeded as planned to Upper Canada was hard to tell, and at any rate it was too late. Fortunately for Gosse he had his scientific interests, which gradually became, 'from the mere salt, the condiment, of life, almost its very pabulum.' Often in the summer, after a hard day's work, he would pick up his insect net and go off into field

214. PHG, *Canadian Naturalist*, 226.

215. 'Reminiscences', II: 208; PHG, *Canadian Naturalist*, 111.

216. 'Reminiscences', II: 208-9; a full account of these agricultural activities may be found in 'The Farm Journal of P. H. Gosse from the Season of 1837' [19 Sept. 1836-25 Dec. 1837] (Public Archives of Canada, M.G. 24 I 63).

217. PHG, *Canadian Naturalist*, 109; 'Reminiscences', II: 212. In the *Canadian Naturalist*, PHG wrote: 'I think that emigrant makes a very unfortunate choice, who fixes on the eastern townships of Lower Canada as his place of residence. From what I have heard from many sources, I believe that Upper Canada offers an incomparably greater advantage to the settler' (p. 111). But in 'Reminiscences', II: 211, composed many decades later, he thought that no advantage would have been gained by going there.

and forest 'pursuing the Sphinges & Moths, totally forgetful of fatigue.'[218]
Observers thought he was unstable, and began to speak of him as *'that
crazy Englishman who goes about picking up bugs.'*[219] Recognition was
given to his pursuits, however, when in the spring of 1836 he was elected
a Corresponding Member of the Literary and Historical Society of Quebec
(founded 1824) and then of the Natural History Society of Montreal
(founded 1827). Notwithstanding the lack of stature of the societies in
this far-off country, it nonetheless was gratifying to Gosse, and he sent
papers to each.[220]

As late as June 1836 he was still writing enthusiastically about the
country, hiding the truth to family members back home. At the end of
September, Gosse and Jaques divided their common property. The cart,
harness, drag, and harrow went to Jaques, and the plough, sled, chain,
and another implement to Gosse. By 12 October there was heavy snow,
then intense cold. With the end of the season fast approaching, Gosse
once again sought to supplement his income by teaching over the winter.
In the last week of November, he was instructing the son of one of his
neighbours at 3s. per week; on 12 December, he left Compton farm for
nearby Ascot, where he kept the Bullard School for £3.5s. per month,
including board. Here he remained until 4 March of the following year.[221]

The next season began with new problems. Gosse needed help to
prepare his wheat for sale, but had a hard time finding it; he tried, vainly,
on his own to clear logs from the field. He travelled to Lennoxville and
Sherbrooke (thirteen miles from the farm) to sell wheat, barley, and
hayseed, but no one was interested in the first two, and he was offered

218. 'Reminiscences', II: 209.

219. Remark of a Major Logee in 1864, quoted in Fyles, 'Visit to the Canadian Haunts', 23
(emphasis in the original). Another man told Fyles in 1892 that he remembered seeing PHG on
one of his excursions, and that his outfit made a marked impression on him: he wore clean linen,
and was dressed in rough frieze cloth (ibid., 24).

220. 'Reminiscences', II: 211. On December 13, 1836, Philip submitted an article on
'*Lepidoptera Comptoniensa*' to the Montreal Society (this may well have been the same article
published as a 'List of Butterflies Taken at Compton, in Lower Canada', *Entomologist* I (July
1841), 137-9). The two papers sent to Quebec were 'Observations on the Seasons in Newfoundland
and This Country' and 'Meteorological Tables, Kept at Carbonear in Conception Bay, on the
East Coast of Newfoundland, in the Year 1833, 1834, and Part of 1835' (see *Transactions of the
Literary and Historical Society of Quebec*, ser. 1, vol. III (1837), 403; in 'Reminiscences', PHG
gave these articles slightly different titles). None of these articles were published by the societies,
and a 1972 inquiry to the Literary and Historical Society of Quebec indicated that the disposition
of PHG's submissions remains unknown.

221. PHG-Thomas Gosse, 11 June 1836 (cited in *Life*, 98-9); PHG, *Farm Journal*, under 23
Sept.; 12, 19, 25 Oct.; 25, 28 Nov.; 6, 10, 12 Dec. 1836; and 4 Mar. 1837.

only a pittance for the last. Nonetheless, he had to live, and having on the former occasion sold nothing, he decided to return to Sherbrooke to sell the hayseed. On the way, the wagon wheels shattered. That caused a delay of several days. He borrowed a neighbour's saw one day. He had to return it on the next. He borrowed another. It broke.[222]

They had now been at Compton for nearly two years, during which time no one in Poole knew of their true situation. He had been constantly urging his brother Tom to come to Canada, and he finally did, arriving on 12 May 1837. Having been a shopman to a grocer in Poole, Tom (who had just turned 21), brought with him some practical skills, besides £10 in cash (a meagre if immediately useful sum), and a selection of seeds and plants from home. After a few days, he was set to work, milking the cow, churning butter, planting and harvesting, fertilizing the fields, and, of course, hunting for insects. It was a poor affair: 'hard labour did not suit him; we had frequent quarrels; the Jaqueses did not like him: and so, after about four months, he became thoroughly disgusted, & determined to make his way, in spite of shame, back to Poole.'[223]

'Failure' was all too painfully writ large over Gosse's experiment as a farmer, and he acknowledged the fact. In July, even before Tom left, he had advertised his portion of the farm—with a 'garden of rare exotic flowers'—for sale. Yet people knew that, with or without the botanical attraction, it was poor land, and by mid-September only one person had expressed any interest in purchasing it. Just before Tom left, he had killed their cow, and Gosse later sold the mare; in October, he was picking apples, many of which were frozen on the tree; during the next two months he was confined with rheumatism.[224] 'Could any employment be obtained at home?' he wrote his sister Elizabeth in November. 'I am tired of more than ten years' exile, far from friends & kindred. I have been thinking that I might do well by establishing a school in Poole. ... Is there any opening?'[225] There was not. There is a note of desperation in the request, for he had not enjoyed his past two winters as a teacher,

222. PHG, *Farm Journal*, under 23, 27 Mar.; 1, 3, 13, 21 Apr.; 4, 5 May, 1837.
223. 'Reminiscences', II: 212; PHG, *Farm Journal*, 12 May-29 Sept. 1837 (the period of Tom's visit).
224. 'Reminiscences', II: 213; PHG, *Farm Journal*, 20 Sept. [1837] ('showed Dickson the farm').
225. PHG-Elizabeth Gosse, 4 Nov. 1837, as quoted in 'Reminiscences', II: 214-5.

and was just then arranging to take the Compton school (at a lower salary than before).[226] But it was the only qualification he had.

However inadequate Gosse was as a farmer, and may have been as a teacher, he was becoming a most discerning naturalist. 'Dear father,' said one of the characters in his first published book, 'I already love the study of natural history; I scarcely know a greater delight than to bury myself in the woods, and watch the habits of the birds and insects, or inquire into the hidden causes of the phenomenon which present themselves to my observation.'[227] He kept meticulous scientific journals which long remained of value to him.[228]

After five years of accumulating data, and one attempt at book making, Gosse determined to bring his observations together into a general work on Canadian natural history. 'The whole plan of the work occurred to me, & was at once sketched in my mind, one day as I was walking up to Tilden's,' he wrote of *The Canadian Naturalist*, published in 1840:

> It was a lovely spring day, the 11th of May, 1837, the day before my brother arrived. I had a large amount of material already in my entomological journal, and thenceforward I kept my eyes always wide open for every other branch of Natural History. It was Sir H. Davy's *Salmonia; or Days of Fly-Fishing* [1828], which work, however, I knew only by quotations,—that formed my model for the dialogue, as it seemed to warrant my adopting that style.[229]

Gosse's scientific investigations in Newfoundland were pioneering, but observers had studied aspects of the Canadian scene before him. More than 300 years prior to his arrival in Canada, Jesuit missionaries had reported on the country's natural history, and after the seventeenth century a knowledge of the Canadian fauna was slowly being increased by the efforts of foreign travellers and, eventually, of residents themselves.[230] The value and precision of this early work varies, with notable

226. He was paid $12 per month at Compton School, which, at the exchange rate at the time of $5 to £1 sterling, comes to £2.8s. To take the Bullard School in the previous winter, he had been paid £3.5s. (PHG, *Farm Journal*, 12 Dec. 1837). When Fyles returned to Compton in 1892, he met a lady who remembered PHG: 'I went to school to [sic] him', she remarked. 'He couldn't teach school any, to suit this country' (Fyles, 'Visit to the Canadian Haunts', 23).

227. PHG, *Canadian Naturalist*, 21.

228. 'Reminiscences', II:190 (I believe this passage was written around 1869).

229. 'Reminiscences', II: 219.

230. Trevor H. Levere and Richard A. Jarrell (eds.), *A Curious Field-Book: Science & Society in Canadian History* (Toronto: Oxford University Press, 1974), 3-11.

achievements coming by the first quarter of the nineteenth century. The well-known expedition under Sir John Franklin in 1825-6, for example, which explored a vast area north of Fort William on Lake Superior, had resulted in the four-volume *Fauna Boreali-Americana* (1829-1837) of Sir John Richardson. In entomology in particular the advances had been less thorough. The first sustained notice of the colony's insects dates to 1824, and even then it was of the most general type, and comprised only one chapter in an emigrant's accounts of his travels.[231] A step forward came with the fourth volume of the *Fauna Boreali-Americana*, compiled by the Englishman William Kirby (1759-1850), devoted entirely to entomology. Most of the 447 insect species were here described for the first time. The books of American entomologists, such as Thomas Say (1787-1834), the 'father of American entomology',[232] were also often relevant to the understanding of the Canadian scene.[233]

The publication and reception of the *Canadian Naturalist* will be considered later, but its contribution to Canadian science deserves mention here. Gosse harboured no illusions about his limited acquaintance with natural history as a whole, or his lack of systematic knowledge. He necessarily wrote for a popular rather than a learned audience. Yet by taking as his motto the statement of the great English naturalist Gilbert White, that 'Every kingdom, every province, should have its own monographer' (reproduced on the title-page of the book), he unquestionably provided a valuable service. He brought together a great deal of accurate and original information about the flora and fauna of the Eastern Townships, confining his contribution not to

231. C. J. S. Bethune (1838-1932), 'The Rise and Progress of Entomology in Canada', *Transactions of the Royal Society of Canada* (1898, Section IV), 155-65, which also briefly discusses the Franklin expedition and Edward Allen Talbot's *Five Years' Residence in the Canadas* (2vols., 1824). See also Harry B. Weiss, *The Pioneer Century of American Entomology* (New Jersey: Published by the Author, 1936), 287-9, and Elaine Theberge, 'The Untrodden Earth: Early Nature Writing in Canada', *Nature Canada* III (Apr.-June 1974), 30-6. Other early 19th Century works which touched on entomology or aspects of Canada's natural history include (besides Talbot): Adam Fergusson, *Practical Notes Made During a Tour in Canada* (1833); C. P. Traill, *Backwoods of Canada* (1836); and Anna Jameson, *Winter Studies and Summer Rambles in Canada* (3vols., 1838). These three studies were mainly concerned with Upper Canada.

232. Judith Magee, *The Art and Science of William Bartram* (University Park, PA: Pennsylvania State University Press, 2007), 180; Essig, *A History of Entomology*, 751.

233. Thomas Say's classic *American Entomology* (3vols., 1824-8, plus a Glossary, 1825) is cited in PHG's *Canadian Naturalist*, 199, indicating that he knew of it before he returned to London in 1839.

taxonomy but to ecology—habits, seasonal appearances, food, and transformations.[234]

As for entomological studies in Canada, Gosse was 'a pioneer in the wilderness'.[235] No meeting of entomologists would occur in the country until 1862 (with incorporation and funding of an entomological society not coming until 1871),[236] no specifically entomological journal until 1868.[237] Unsurprisingly, the number of insects described in the *Canadian Naturalist* was not great: twenty-six butterflies, forty-three moths, and a variety from other orders, yet 'very many original observations' appeared throughout the book.[238] For some, the *Canadian Naturalist* was their 'first companion and interpreter of Canadian country life,'[239] while 'many Canadian entomologists of note received their first lessons, and learned the names of some of our common butterflies and moths.'[240] The work

---

234. Wertheimer, 'Gosse, Philip Henry', *DCB* XI: 364; D. Wertheimer, 'Gosse, Philip Henry', *Canadian Encyclopedia* (Edmonton: Hurtig Publishers, 2ed., 1988), II: 913 (and 1ed. (1985), I: 753).

235. Bethune, 'The Rise and Progress of Entomology in Canada', 156.

236. Bethune, 'The Rise and Progress of Entomology in Canada', 159-60; T.W. Fyles, 'The Rise in Public Estimation of the Science of Entomology', *Forty-Third Annual Report of the Entomological Society of Ontario, 1912*, (1913), 42; Osborn, *Fragments of Entomological History*, I: 122.

237. Osborn, *Brief History of Entomology*, 146.

238. Samuel H. Scudder, 'Bibliographical Record', *Psyche* III (Oct.-Dec. 1881), 281. For Scudder's index to PHG's notes on butterflies cited in *Canadian Naturalist*, with brief notes and updated synonymy: 'Gosse's Observations on the Butterflies of North America', Cambridge, MA, *Psyche* III (July-Sept. 1881), 245-7.

239. 'Editor's Table', Montréal *Dominion Illustrated* (4 May 1889), 279.

240. C. J. S. Bethune, 'The Rise and Progress of Entomology in Canada', 156. Fyles (1832-1921; Gilbert, *Compendium*, 131; *Vancouver Daily World*, 11 Aug. 1921, 11), who recalled being 'fairly carried away' when he first read the *Canadian Naturalist*, believed the entomological portions of the book were the 'weakest' (Fyles, 'A Visit to the Canadian Haunts of the Late Philip Henry Gosse', 22, 29). He did not mention that opinion in later instances in which he wrote on PHG (see 'Select Bibliography', below). Fyles' assessment contrasts with most entomologists' opinions, including that of the leading American entomologist Samuel H. Scudder, who found PHG's *Canadian Naturalist* and *Letters from Alabama* 'full of original observations', and included an index to them (Scudder, 'Gosse's Observations on the Butterflies of North America', *Psyche*, 245-7). *Canadian Naturalist* is also quoted in Scudder's *The Butterflies of the Eastern United States and Canada, with Special Reference to New England* (Cambridge [Mass.]: Published by the Author, 3vols., 1889), vols. I-II; and by William H. Edwards, *The Butterflies of North America* (Boston: Houghton, Mifflin and Co., 3 series, 1888-97), vol. III. For other uses of PHG's book: William Stewart M. d'Urban, 'Description of a Canadian Butterfly, and Some Remarks on the Genus Papilio', *Canadian Naturalist and Geologist* III (Dec. 1858), 417-8; L'Abbe L. Provancher, 'Naturalistes Canadiens', *Le Naturaliste Canadien* V (Feb. 1873), 130; and W. E. Ricker, René Malouin, Peter Harper, and H. H. Ross, 'Distribution of Quebec Stoneflies (Plecoptera)', *La Naturaliste Canadien* 95 (1968), 1086-7.

was sold in Canada as late as 1862,[241] and Gosse's friend W. C. St. John did what he could to promote it in Newfoundland.[242] It remained for over a century 'the most authoritative work' on the flora and fauna in that area.[243] Thus Gosse's achievement: the *Canadian Naturalist* was the first work devoted solely to Canadian natural history.[244]

In the last few weeks of 1837, while Gosse was preparing to take over the school in Compton for the winter, he witnessed 'stormy politics and martial alarms',[245] just as he had in his last days in Newfoundland. This time it was not the Irish problem which produced the menacing clouds, but overlapping rebellions (with different causes) in Upper and Lower Canada. In the latter situation, there was a fear that American forces would intervene in the unrest.[246] In the county of Sherbrooke units loyal to the government were formed. Gosse was not amongst those volunteers who did repulse the attack of Americans from Vermont,[247] but in November 1838 he was called as a witness in a criminal case. A band of counterfeiters and thieves, who had made Tilden's tavern their rendezvous, robbed an elderly couple, Witcher, who lived near Compton village, of $3,000. Some of the gang managed to escape to the United States, but Adolphus Barker was captured, and the case of Witcher vs. Barker was held in Lennoxville on 14 November. Gosse's role in the trial is not known, but he may have helped to convict Barker,

241. The *Canadian Naturalist* was sold in Montreal (*Montreal Gazette*, 9 Jan. 1841, 1), for 15s.6d. (the English price was 12s.) and in Boston (*Boston Post*, 4 Nov. 1841, 3, no price stated). T. W. Fyles purchased a copy in Montreal in 1862 (Fyles, 'The Rise in Public Estimation of the Science of Entomology', 42).

242. St. John may have been the author of the notice in the *Star and Newfoundland Advocate* (27 May 1840). He said he was 'charmed with [PHG's] performance; it does him infinite credit in every sense of the word' (St. John-William Gosse, 4 June 1840, seen in the Family Collection).

243. William O. Raymond (1880-1970), 'Philip Henry Gosse and *The Canadian Naturalist*', *Trans. Royal Society of Canada*, ser. 3, vol. 45, sect. II (June 1951), 45, 52, 58. Raymond was a professor of English at Bishop's University, Lennoxville, Quebec.

244. V. R. Vickery and D. K. McE. Kevan, *A Monograph of the Orthopteroid Insects of Canada and Adjacent Regions* I: 39. *The Canadian Naturalist* 'was the first accurate treatise on Canadian natural history in its broad sense' (Mary Quayle Innis, 'Philip Henry Gosse in Canada', *Dalhousie Review* XVII (1937), 59).

245. PHG, *Canadian Naturalist*, [vii].

246. P. A. Buckner, 'Rebellions of 1837', *Canadian Encyclopedia* (Edmonton: Hurtig Publishers, 1985, 2ed., 1988), III, 1831-33; Thomas Low Nichols, *Forty Years of American Life 1821-1861* (New York: Stackpole Sons, 1937), 367-8; Fyles, 'A Visit to the Canadian Haunts of the Late Philip Henry Gosse', 26-7, gives a detailed account of fighting around Compton.

247. See Fyles, 'Visit to the Canadian Haunts', 26; and Channell, *History of Compton County*, 31.

who was condemned to death (the sentence was later commuted to life in prison).[248]

By the time that Gosse's third and final term as a schoolmaster had come to an end in the spring of 1838, he had sold his farm and was ready to leave Canada. Having understood from his sister Elizabeth that there were no opportunities for him in Poole, he wrote his former companion at Elson's, William F. Lush (who now lived in Philadelphia) to inquire about opportunities for 'persons of education' in Georgia and South Carolina. Although Gosse does not mention the fact, it may be that he knew that those two US states were popular with naturalists. Six decades earlier, the American William Bartram (1739-1823) had famously spent four years there, having been preceded by the Englishman Mark Catesby (1683-1749).[249] At any rate, Gosse left Canada on 22 March 1838 headed for Philadelphia, being driven to Burlington, Vermont, by the friend with whom he had shared such high hopes, George Jaques.[250]

To Jaques, who later left Compton and moved some fifty miles west to Cowansville, the Canadian experiment must have been unrewarding. But he, after all, was not a naturalist like his friend Gosse; he did not know how to 'solace himself by ... simple but enchanting [natural history] studies, amidst the fatigues of labour, and the stormy politics and martial alarms of the times.'[251] Nonetheless, the favourable circumstances for the study of entomology and natural history which the residence in Canada afforded Gosse cannot be allowed to mask the disappointment he and the Jaqueses endured. When Gosse left Newfoundland, he had money and friends; now, three years later, at the age of 28, his £100 had dwindled to £26, and he had made no new lasting acquaintances.[252]

Finally, recall that Gosse had gone to Canada not only as a naturalist but as a Christian. He had shown no growth in that sphere, either.

248. Fyles conjectured that the case of Witcher v Barker (Fyles, 'Visit to the Canadian Haunts', 25-6) may have been the one referred to obliquely in *Life*, 103. The entry in *Farm Journal* for 14 November 1837, confirms that Fyles was right ('I attended court at Lennoxville by summons, as witness in case Witcher v. Barker.').

249. Catesby's focus was on botany, but part of his *Natural History of Carolina, Florida, and the Bahama Islands* (1731-47) was devoted to entomology (George Frederick Frick, 'Mark Catesby, Naturalist, 1683-1749.' (University of Illinois, PhD dissertation, 1957), 150-1). Lesser known naturalists are discussed in Samuel Wood Geiser, 'Naturalists of the Frontier. [Part] X. Notes on Scientists of the First Frontier', *Southwest Review* 18 (Oct. 1932), 50-86.

250. PHG-W. F. Lush, 5 Feb. 1838, as cited in 'Reminiscences', II: 215.

251. PHG, *Canadian Naturalist*, [vii].

252. 'Reminiscences', II: 215. PHG remained in contact with George and Ann Jaques long after he left Canada.

Religion appears, in fact, to have assumed a secondary importance. 'All this time,' he acknowledged,

> my spiritual life was at a very low ebb. Sunday services (Methodist) in the village of Compton ... were very occasional & irregular, & though now & then some vagrant would address his "b'loved bruthring" in one or other of the neighbouring school houses, it was of the meanest Yankee type, wretchedly poor in matter & in manner. After a while, Mr. Jaques or I would undertake the supply at Compton chapel, on a Sunday morning, & always reading one of Wesley's published sermons, never attempting *extempore*. And we tried to institute a Sunday School, but with slight success. In the winter evenings, prayer-meetings were held in the houses of two or three neighbours who were professors of religion, in which I bore a formal part. One of these was a very worthy consistent old man, named Spafford, a Baptist, whom I greatly respected, but dreaded. Whenever he met me, he would presently ask, "How do you enjoy your mind?" In my consciously barren, backslidden condition, this question was my terror; for I durst not lie, & I knew not how to answer without shame. In summer, when I did not go to the village, I often roamed in the high maple woods, *observing*, for conscience was sufficiently alive to prevent my formal *collecting*,—on the Sunday morning.
>
> There was a Wesleyan minister[253] whom we occasionally saw, Rev. Mr. Rain,[254] & a congregational minister, Rev. O. Pearson,[255] resident at the neighbouring village of Charleston, [Hatley]—both of whom were amiable, excellent, unassuming, intelligent men, whose friendship we possessed and truly valued. But I rarely met either.
>
> My own deadness was not wholly without exception. The word would sometimes prick, sometimes refresh me. I heard occasionally from my young friends Sprague & W. F. Lush ... Both spoke of their

253. Methodist preaching in Eaton dated to 1805, but with a gap in service until 1836. 'For seven years [c. 1838-45] no sound of the gospel was heard from a Methodist [in that region] unless it might have been from a passer-by' (Channell, *History of Compton County*, 71-2).

254. Presumably this was the Revd John Raine (d. 1844), a Wesleyan missionary who was a class-leader soon after his conversion at the age of 16. He was later a local preacher in Montreal ('Death of the Rev. John Raine', *Montreal Gazette*, 9 Sept. 1844, 2) and in the Compton area (Carroll, *Cyclopaedia of Methodism in Canada*, 128). He died aged 40 (*Montreal Gazette*) or aged 41 (Carroll, *Cyclopaedia*, 128).

255. The name is given as 'O. Pearsons' in Channell, *History of Compton County*, 74. The Congregational church in Eaton Township, adjacent to Compton Township, had been founded in November 1835 with 19 members (ibid.).

religious experience in terms which stirred up my own soul to fresh zeal
& resolution; soon, alas! to relapse into coldness again ...[256]

-IV-

'Human society that is not congenial is a greater bore than a total want
of it, but nature is always congenial, and always conversible.'[257] Gosse's
remark succinctly summarizes two notable aspects of the seven-and-
a-half months he spent in Alabama. We have already seen that Gosse
held the 'Yankee' character in low esteem, and this opinion—reinforced
by what he saw of that 'domestic institution,' slavery—was to confirm
his feelings of isolation and solitude. Gosse was, moreover, apparently
overwhelmed by a sense of depression, notwithstanding his hopeful
personality: cursed by the soil, he had become a 'fugitive and a wanderer',
uncertain as to what he was doing or where he was going.

Having reached Burlington, Vermont, Gosse headed south on the first
available stage-coach. He was forced to leave behind the insect-filled
cabinet which he had acquired in 1834, and on the way lost a purse with
$7 in it. He arrived in Philadelphia on 26 March 1838. To Gosse, the
Quaker City was 'agreeable' with 'a genteel and respectable middle-class';
others spoke more highly of it, characterizing it as the 'Athens of America,
the very fountain-head of American intellect.'[258] Here he lodged at the
boarding-house of his friend William Lush, then a clerk in the American
Colonization Society.[259]

Gosse had about $120 with him, and was in no hurry to seek
employment. Some of the time he spent talking with Lush's friends who,
impressed with his articulateness, asked if the guest was not a minister.[260]

---

256. 'Reminiscences', II: 220-2. Emphasis in the original.

257. PHG, *Letters from Alabama, (U.S.) Chiefly Relating to Natural History* (London:
Morgan and Chase, 1859), 100; 'Reminiscences', II: 232.

258. Lambert A. Wilmer, describing Philadelphia's reputation around 1826 (Wilmer,
*Our Press Gang, or, A Complete Exposition of the Corruptions and Crimes of the American
Newspapers* (Philadelphia: J. T. Lloyd, 1859), 18); PHG, *Letters from Alabama*, 2.

259. 'Reminiscences', II: 225-7.

260. *Life*, 113, misrepresented PHG's description in claiming that PHG was unable to
participate with Lush's associates in their 'gaiety of conversation' because of 'his fluent gravity
in monologue and lack of capacity for small-talk'. PHG only wrote that they took note of his
articulateness ('Reminiscences', II: 225-7). They likely did so because Lush had a speech defect
(see the advertisement 'Institution for the Cure of Impediments of Speech', Philadelphia *American
Sentinel*, 12 Apr. 1838, 2, which includes a testimonial signed 'Wm. F. Lush, 27 Sansom st. Phila':
'For a period of more than twelve years, I was a very great stammerer').

On Sundays, he and Lush attended the Dutch Reformed Church.[261] His dominant concern, however, was scientific, and he must have heard he was in a country which was 'a treasure house for the naturalist ... Teeming with specimens of plant and animal life unknown in Europe.'[262] The founding period of the United States of America was then within living memory, and one of the *desiderata* of the country's leadership was the mapping out of the New World's natural history.[263] Pioneers had set out to do that, and in Philadelphia investigators from that generation had favoured natural history (especially botany) over mathematics or astronomy to such a degree as to make it fashionable.[264] By the 1820s an American scientific establishment was emerging[265] as that first generation—with whose works Gosse was familiar—was vanishing. As previously mentioned, Gosse owned and found valuable an edition of *American Ornithology* (9 vols., 1808-1814), by Alexander Wilson (1766-1813),[266] and likewise cited the 'venerable naturalist',[267] explorer, botanist and ornithologist William Bartram, and (for Canada) Thomas Say (1787-1834).[268] Those Americans influenced by this earlier generation of naturalists—the 'urbane' field-naturalist and illustrator of *American Ornithology*, Titian Ramsay Peale (1799-1885); the ornithologist and author of the first major American botanical study, Thomas Nuttall (1786-1859), and the paleontologist Timothy Abbott Conrad (1803-1877)—were now all active. Gosse met Peale, Nuttall and Conrad; he had, in other words, journeyed to America at a propitious time for a naturalist.

It was the Englishman's desire to search out the haunts of Alexander Wilson, the 'father of American ornithology',[269] which eventually led him to the Philadelphia Museum on Chestnut Street. There he met Titian Peale, the museum's curator and the field naturalist who had failed, in

261. 'Reminiscences', II: 227-9.

262. Whitfield J. Bell, Jr., 'Science and Humanity in Philadelphia 1775-1790' (University of Pennsylvania, PhD dissertation, 1947), 167.

263. Magee, *Art and Science of William Bartram*, 1-2.

264. Bell, 'Science and Humanity in Philadelphia', 167.

265. John C. Greene, 'American Sciences Comes of Age, 1780-1820', *Journal of American History* 55 (June 1968), 41; Magee, *Art and Science of William Bartram*, 2.

266. PHG, *Letters from Alabama*, 2-6.

267. PHG, *An Introduction to Zoology* (London: SPCK, [1844]), I: 353-4; 'Bartram, William', *DSB* I (2008), 488-90.

268. Say's work is cited in PHG's *Canadian Naturalist*, 199 but not in *Letters from Alabama*; 'Say, Thomas', *DSB* XII (2008), 132-4.

269. Magee, *Art and Science of William Bartram*, 159. Wilson was responsible for acquiring subscribers to this work.

1833, to find a market for his book *Lepidoptera Americana*.[270] Peale showed him some of his entomological drawings.[271] He 'received me with a deferent courtesy,' Gosse recalled, 'which took me somewhat by surprise. American science had scarcely yet learned to stand alone; & I could see a very modest deference to an English savant, even though so wholly unknown to fame as myself; & certainly I assumed no bunkum airs.'[272] The perceived attention Gosse received may have been influenced by the fact that at the time, British visitors to the United States were not common (numbers increased after 1848, when relations between the two countries improved),[273] and few were serious naturalists.

The meeting with Peale was followed by an introduction to Nuttall. Gosse discussed ornithological issues with both men,[274] and he may have been particularly fascinated with Nuttall's description of bird songs in that author's *Manual of the Ornithology of the United States and Canada* (1832).[275] Nuttall in turn took him to a soirée at the Academy of Natural Sciences (founded in 1812), the earliest institution in America devoted to the natural sciences.[276] It was the first time that Gosse—though a Corresponding Member of two Canadian scientific organizations—had been in the company of devoted and knowledgeable naturalists.

In truth, his scientific modus operandi matched the orientation of most of his American counterparts. Like them, religion infused his work as he studied nature through the lens of the natural theology tradition. The Quaker faith had long predominated amongst the Philadelphia

270. Dolores M. Gall, 'Titian Ramsay Peale: An American Naturalist and Lithographer', *Yale University Art Gallery Bulletin* 38 (Winter 1983), 8. Peale's work on lepidoptera was admired by J. O. Westwood (Ellery E. Foutch, 'Arresting Beauty: The Perfectionist Impulse of Peale's Butterflies, Heade's Hummingbirds, Blaschka's Flowers, and Sandow's Body' (University of Pennsylvania, PhD dissertation, 2011), 37fn.59). As previously indicated, PHG was friendly with Westwood in London from around 1843. On Peale's butterfly illustrations: Foutch, *Arresting Beauty*, 14-92.

271. Peale was one of the illustrators of Thomas Say's *American Entomology* (Magee, *Art and Science of William Bartram*, 186), with which PHG was familiar; 'Peale, Titian Ramsay', *DSB* X (2008), 439-40.

272. 'Reminiscences', II: 228.

273. Royce Gordon Shingleton, 'Rural Life in the Old South: the British Travelers' Image, 1820-1860' (Florida State University, PhD dissertation, 1971), 5-6.

274. PHG, *Canadian Naturalist*, 92.

275. 'Reminiscences', II: 229; 'Nuttall, Thomas', *DSB* X (2008), 163-5. In future years, PHG would regularly comment on songs of birds (*Popular British Ornithology*, 30-34, 37-40; *Naturalist's Sojourn in Jamaica*, 154-5, 166-72; *Birds of Jamaica*, 188), occasionally with musical notations (*Birds of Jamaica*, 206-7); Charles Darwin-PHG, 22, 28 Sept. 1856 (cited in *Life*, 266-7).

276. Magee, *Art and Science of William Bartram*, 181, 183.

scientists, and even though their attitude to the Bible was not that of Gosse, they too shared the belief that the study of nature revealed God's handiwork.[277] Like the best of them, Gosse was an autodidact and all-in-one field collector, identifier, and classifier;[278] like them, there was an aesthetic appeal to natural history which called for artistic skill on the part of the investigator in rendering its wonders; like them, he would (in the near future) begin to create and cultivate networks of natural history contacts.[279] Like some of them, too, he was a 'scientific-entrepreneur' lacking institutional or governmental backing, serving as his own promoter and salesman.[280] This was the view then: for many in the English-speaking world, scientific activity was a gentleman's pursuit, a 'high-minded labour of love'.[281] The duty of a 'man of science' was to expand human knowledge generally, not turn it into a business. Only later in the century did the word 'scientist' emerge (a neologism dating to 1834)[282] to denote a specialist who moved beyond the traits of that time towards a new attitude to the study of science.

Perhaps it was amongst this group to which Gosse was introduced that he encountered the naturalist who suggested to him his next course of action. Timothy Abbott Conrad (1803-1877) had recently published a work on the *Eocene Fossils of Claiborne, With ... a Geological Map of Alabama* (1835),[283] and he recommended that Southern state as a

277. Bell, 'Science and Humanity in Philadelphia', 174. Bartram, Conrad, and Say were Quakers; Peale's third wife was a Quaker.

278. Other examples of this were Alexander Wilson and Thomas Say (John C. Greene, *American Science in the Age of Jefferson* (Ames, IA: Iowa State University Press, 1984), 310).

279. Nathan Reingold (ed.), *Science in Nineteenth-Century America. A Documentary History* (London: Macmillan, 1966), 29-30.

280. John Fothergill was the patron of William Bartram for *Travels through North & South Carolina*, and William Maclure was the patron of Thomas Say for *American Entomology* (Magee, *Art and Science of William Bartram*, 87-8, 189).

281. David Philip Miller, 'The story of "*Scientist*: the Story of a Word"', *Annals of Science* 74 (2017), 257.

282. Sydney Ross, "*Scientist:* The Story of a Word"', *Annals of Science* XVIII (June 1962), 65-85; J. T. Merz, *A History of European Thought in the Nineteenth Century* (London: William Blackwood & Sons, 1896), I: 23, postil 42 and 90-91fn1. PHG, like others of his day—Babbage, Darwin, Faraday, Huxley—did not use the word 'scientist' in his books. PHG's preferred term was 'man of science', which appears in his works from at least 1849 (*Natural History of Birds*) to 1876 (*Romance of Natural History*, first series, USA published). After that, he used the rare synonym 'scient' (PHG-James Fantone, 14 Oct. 1881, Corr. Bk. and PHG-Arthur Doncaster, 2 Jan. 1882, CUL Add.7313, 470-1; PHG, *The Mysteries of God* (London: Hodder and Stoughton, 1884), 260, 303; in *OED*, 3ed., the earliest use of the word 'scient' in print is given as 1854).

283. Harry Edgar Wheeler, 'Timothy Abbott Conrad, with Particular Reference to His Work in Alabama One Hundred Years Ago', *Bulletins of American Paleontology* XXIII (2 Sept. 1935),

worthwhile place to explore. The possibility of pursuing entomological and ecological studies in a warm climate was another attraction, as was Conrad's letter of introduction to a friend at Claiborne. So Gosse abandoned his original plan of travelling to Georgia or South Carolina and detoured to Alabama, a state with a population of some 590,756 people (fifty-seven per cent of whom were White)[284] which had only joined the Union as its twenty-second state in 1819.[285] He left Philadelphia on 18 April.[286]

-V-

The journey to the 'Cotton State' took one month and was not a pleasant one—a premonition of things to come. The skipper and crew—'churlish, vulgar, illiterate'—made the life of the Englishman, whom they taunted, uncomfortable, and 'every night I was compelled to hear, as I lay in my wretched berth, the interchange of obscene narratives between the skipper and his mate.' Foulness surrounded the passenger. In a passage evoking Dickens' *Our Mutual Friend*, Gosse described how

> Dirt, dirt, was the rule everywhere; dirt in the cabin, dirt in the caboose, dirt in the water-cask; dirt doubly begrimed on the table-cloth, on the cups and glasses, the dishes and plates that served the food; while the boy who filled the double office of cook and waiter, was the very impersonation of dirt. The only resource was to eat with as little thought as possible, to see as little as possible, and to be upon deck as much of the time as possible ...[287]

A sense of depression followed Gosse from sea to land. Having been deposited at Mobile on 14 May, he found himself with little money[288] and no friends in a totally alien environment. Many years later he reflected upon the paradox of being at once alone and yet not alone:

63-4; 'Conrad, Timothy Abbott', *DSB* III (2008), 391-3.

284. US Census for 1840, cited in Thomas McAdory Owen, 'Population', *History of Alabama and Dictionary of Alabama Biography* (Chicago: S. J. Clarke Publishing, 1921), II: 1134. Alabama's population had increased 91% in 10 years, with 335,185 Whites and 255,571 Blacks.

285. Marion Elias Lazenby, *History of Methodism in Alabama and West Florida* ([?Nashville, TN]: North Alabama Conference and Alabama-West Florida Conference of the Methodist Church, 1960), 77.

286. 'Reminiscences', II: 230; PHG, *Letters from Alabama*, 4.

287. PHG, *Letters from Alabama*, 8.

288. PHG, MS diary of the voyage from Philadelphia to Mobile, as cited in *Life*, 121. The diary has not been traced.

There is no solitude like that which is felt by him who walks the streets of a busy city in which he is a total stranger. Crowds of human beings pass by, each possessed of the thoughts, feelings, and affections of a man; yet not one stretches out the hand of friendship, not one bestows a nod of acquaintance, not one gives so much as a glance of recognition. In the gloom of the forest, in the silence of the wilderness, far from human abodes, my heart leaps for joy; there I am not lonely, though alone; there hundreds of objects meet my gaze, with which I have long been accustomed to hold sweet communion.[289]

'King Cotton' ruled in antebellum Mobile, then the second-largest cotton exporting centre in the United States during a period of prosperity for its 13,000 inhabitants.[290] But that fact had no relevance to Gosse. What turned the moment sunny was the opportunity to explore the forests around Mobile, where he was in his element. He was 'almost bewildered' by the sight of '[l]arge and gorgeously coloured insects.' No sooner was one collecting-box filled 'than it had to be emptied, and the former captive rejected for a more tempting prize, until at length I resolved to cease capturing, and content myself with admiring.'[291]

On the same day that Gosse arrived at Mobile he caught a high-pressure steamer up the winding Alabama River headed for Claiborne in Alabama's mountainous Black Belt. During the slow, leisurely trip he enjoyed standing on deck and observing what he could of the wildlife.[292] As luck would have it, Gosse met Reuben Saffold (1788-1847), a pioneer citizen of Alabama and one of the state's first Chief Justices, and showed him the letter of introduction from Timothy Conrad. Coincidentally, Saffold was looking for a schoolmaster for the children of the west-central part of Alabama in which he lived (Dallas County, north-east of Claiborne). He persuaded Gosse to fill the gap. So Gosse remained on the steamer until King's Landing, then made his way to Saffold's home, finally reaching Pleasant Hill, the site of the school, at the end of May.[293]

For about the next six months Gosse spent his time in this remote little

289. PHG, 'Letters from Alabama.—No. II', *Home Friend* n.s. 2 (Feb. 1855), 141; PHG, *Letters from Alabama*, 25.

290. Alan Smith Thompson, 'Mobile, Alabama, 1850-1861: Economic, Political, Physical, and Population Characteristics' (University of Alabama, PhD dissertation, 1979), 39, 14, 50.

291. PHG, *Letters from Alabama*, 27.

292. PHG, 'Notes on a Voyage up the Alabama River', *Zoologist* II (1844), 703-9.

293. 'Reminiscences', II: 231-2. On Saffold: *Appletons' Cyclopaedia of American Biography* V (1894), 366; [T. W.] *Herringshaw's National Library of American Biography* V (1914), 91-2;

village. Teaching Greek and other subjects to about a dozen pupils,[294] little light filtered into the rude log cabin in the romantic clearing in the forest which served as a school. It seems doubtful that much knowledge was transmitted, either. The boys, Gosse said, were 'real young hunters, who handle the long rifle with more ease and dexterity than the goose-quill, and who are incomparably more at home in '"twisting a rabbit", or "treeing a 'possum", than in conjugating a verb.'[295]

Since his Newfoundland days Gosse was accustomed to rising early in the morning to tour the natural scene, and now he was up at 6 ready for breakfast. With butterfly-net in hand, he then left for the school house (some two to three miles from Pleasant Hill), observing and collecting until 8 a.m., when classes started. The intense heat of the afternoons prevented further outdoor activity, allowing him time to arrange his specimens, write, or paint insects and flowers. After school ended at 5 p.m., he spent the next two hours leisurely returning home.[296]

In following this routine, Gosse accumulated a wealth of information in his field-books. In entomology—the subject which he would study most intently in Alabama[297]—he provided '"peeps through Nature's keyhole at her recondite mysteries;—"passages in the life of a spider;"—"unpublished memoirs of a beetle;"—"notes of the domestic economy of a fly".'[298] He apparently did not find Thomas Say's work useful in Alabama as he had in Canada, leaving him nowhere else to turn but nature itself. It was not until 1849 that entomology was taught at an American college and 1859 that the first American entomological society was founded,[299] while the teaching of applied entomology dates to 1872.[300]

and Owen, *History of Alabama and Dictionary of Alabama Biography* III: 326 and IV, 1488. In *Life*, 126, EWG mistakenly refers to Pleasant Hill as 'Mount Pleasant'.

294. PHG, *Letters from Alabama*, 43, and for teaching of Greek, 'Reminiscences', II: 231-2. *Life* does not mention the number of students; in two newspaper accounts full of other inaccuracies the digits are transposed to give 21 students ('View of Pioneer Days at Pleasant Hill Given in Letter [*sic*] of English Naturalist', *Selma Times-Journal*, 2 Nov. 1927, and Peter A. Brannon, 'Through the Years: Gosse, The Naturalist', *Montgomery Advertiser*, 9 Aug. 1931, 6).

295. PHG, *Letters from Alabama*, 44, also 108-9; PHG, 'Notes on the Dirt-daubers, North American Insects Belonging to the Wasp Tribe', *Zoologist* II (1844), 582; and PHG, 'Description of a Bee-tree', *Zoologist* II: 607 (the page numbers for this article are given incorrectly in Freeman & Wertheimer-PHG, 108).

296. PHG, *Letters from Alabama*, 45-59, 192-3; and for Newfoundland, PHG, *The Romance of Natural History* (London: James Nisbet and Co., 1860), 13-16.

297. PHG, *Letters from Alabama*, v-vi.

298. PHG, *Letters from Alabama*, 134.

299. Instruction was at Cornell University; the Entomological Society of Philadelphia was the first of its kind in America (Essig, *History of Entomology*, 575, 595).

300. L. O. Howard, *A History of Applied Entomology (Somewhat Anecdotal)* (Washington,

As in Newfoundland, he also kept an illustrated record of his findings. He titled the work *Entomologia Alabamensis*, a quarto volume eventually containing 233 coloured insect figures, 'the delightful amusement of these seven months' in Alabama.[301] Despite what an art historian called its 'brilliance', the work remained unpublished.[302] Until, that is, some 175 years after its composition, when scholars retrieved it and gave it a lavish treatment with appropriate scientific apparatus. They called it 'magnificent'[303] and 'a masterpiece of scientific art ... [with] superb illustrations, both scientifically and artistically.'[304]

In Canada, Gosse had confined himself to 'the smiling face of Nature';[305] in the United States, he expanded his field of vision to include observations on social customs mainly in Alabama, even instances of what to him were peculiar English language usages ('A "Possum, Sir, is not a critter, but a varmint"').[306] For the first time in his life Gosse had seen, in the area of King's Landing, Black slaves working in the fields.

Many British visitors to the American South in the antebellum period

D.C.: Smithsonian Miscellaneous Collections, 28 Nov. 1930), vol. 84: 72-4. The teaching of applied entomology dates to around 1872 (p. 70).

301. 'Reminiscences', II: 233. PHG also compiled 'Insects of Jamaica, 1 vol.' (*Sandhurst Catalogue*, item #466). Its disposition is unknown.

302. Lister, *British Romantic Art*, 152.

303. Gary R. Mullen and Taylor D. Littleton (eds.), Philip Henry Gosse, *Letters from Alabama* (Tuscaloosa: University of Alabama Press, 2013), 12. Of the 233 figures, 38 are Lepidoptera (p. 24).

304. Gary R. Mullen and Taylor D. Littleton (eds.), *Philip Henry Gosse: Science and Art in Letters from Alabama and* Entomologia Alabamensis (Tuscaloosa: University of Alabama Press, 2010), 8, 27. The authors provide a valuable appreciation of PHG's artistry in an introduction which otherwise suffers from an unfamiliarity with the manuscript and primary and secondary literature on him. Their praise for PHG's skill is unbounded. PHG's scientific illustrations were 'true works of art' and 'remain unmatched as the finest scientific illustrations of invertebrates in the nineteenth century' (pp. 8, 25-7).

The MS *Entomologia Alabamensis*, annotated by PHG, was in the Family Collection until 1992, when it was loaned—and in 2007, donated—to the British Library by Jennifer Gosse. In 1974, while in the Gosse family collection, R. B. Freeman had it photographed in colour. At his initiative, 19 experts from the Department of Entomology at the British Museum (Natural History) and two from the US Department of Agriculture gave modern names to as many of the insects as possible described in PHG's *Letters* and *Entomologia*. The result was 'An Annotated Index to Insects Mentioned in *Letters from Alabama* (1859) by P. H. Gosse', compiled by dipterist K. G. V. Smith of BMNH (typescript, [1974], 17pp.). Mullen and Littleton, who were the first to actually publish a reproduction of the MS, were either unaware of, or failed to acknowledge, the Freeman effort.

305. PHG, *Canadian Naturalist*, [vii].

306. PHG, *Letters from Alabama*, 110, 234. The negative characterisation of an opossum as a 'varmint' is also cited in PHG, *Natural History. Mammalia* (1848), 253 and fn.; Farmer, *Americanisms, Old & New*, 182; and Clarence Gohdes (ed.), 'Hunting in the Old South: Original Narratives of the Hunters', *Georgia Review* 19 (Fall 1965), 355-9.

did not find slavery objectionable,[307] including the geologist Charles Lyell.[308] Gosse was repelled by it. That seems to be the reason why there are few references (at least in Gosse's surviving writings) to residents in or around Pleasant Hill (even to Buddy Bohannon,[309] at whose home he resided). 'Poor wretches!' Gosse exclaimed, 'whose lot is harder than that of their brute companions in labour!'[310] He personally witnessed some of the savagery against slaves and heard of instances of their starvation and of slave-hunting parties. An immediate result was that he quickly realized he had to be circumspect in expressing his true feelings about his surroundings. As a non-southerner, he was known for several months as 'the stranger'[311] and was looked upon with suspicion; as an Englishman, he felt the 'hatred to England' which was common in the Northern, and less so in the Southern, states.[312] He knew that his trunk and letters were surreptitiously opened in order to determine, Gosse believed, if he was writing about the 'peculiar institution' of slavery.[313]

Gosse concluded that the cheap estimation in which life was held was a reflection of the slave system itself, which 'helps to brutalize the character, by familiarizing the mind with the infliction of human suffering.'[314] The true brutes were the masters, not the slaves. The 'institution is doomed,'

307. Shingleton, 'Rural Life in the Old South', 307.

308. Charles Lyell considered slavery 'a beneficent institution': Spencer Harris Reed, 'British Travelers in the United States 1835-1870' (American University, PhD dissertation, 1931), 99-102, 109; Max Berger, 'American Slavery as Seen by British Visitors', *Journal of Negro History* 30 (April 1945), 194; James Moore, 'Darwin's progress and the problem of slavery', *Progress in Human Geography* 34 (2010), 565-573.

309. PHG rendered the name as 'Bohanan', perhaps an alternate spelling: 'Gosse, Philip Henry', in Thomas McAdory Owen, *History of Alabama and Dictionary of Alabama Biography*, III: 684; and PHG, *Letters from Alabama Chiefly Relating to Natural History*, eds. Gary R. Mullen and Taylor D. Littleton, 3.

310. PHG, *Letters from Alabama*, 40.

311. PHG, *Letters from Alabama*, 228.

312. Thomas Low Nichols (1815-1901), an American who wrote a pre-Civil War account of America aimed at a British audience, described American dislike for England in virtually the same words as PHG. He claimed that the 'hatred' was more common among Northerners, who bordered Canada, and had a large Irish population 'who participate in, if they do not increase, the anti-English feelings there' (Nichols, *Forty Years of American Life* (London: John Maxwell and Co., 1864), I: 57). Nichols considerably expanded on the subject in an 1874 revised edition of the work (Nichols, *Forty Years of American Life 1821-1861*, Chap. 38, 'Hatred to England', 360-9); PHG, *Letters from Alabama*, 153 and 153fn.

313. 'Reminiscences', II: 232.

314. PHG, *Letters from Alabama*, 40, 153fn., 228, 250-55. One reviewer of *Letters from Alabama* felt that, in light of the violent tendencies there, PHG's decision not to write extensively about 'the institution of slavery' displayed 'sound discretion' (*Literary Gazette*, 8 Oct. 1859, 351).

he correctly predicted. 'Its end approaches surely, perhaps swiftly. Its fall ... can hardly be other than a terrible convulsion.'[315]

For an unknown reason, Gosse did not publish a record of his residence in America until fifteen years after he had left the country. The work which he offered to the SPCK in London at the end of 1854 was rejected, though it was serialised in its monthly *Home Friend* in 1855.[316] Four years later it appeared as *Letters from Alabama*, under the Morgan and Chase imprint. Other British travellers to the Southern States before 1860 had left their accounts of American institutions and customs, including some who had passed through Alabama;[317] other naturalists, as mentioned, had also provided glimpses of that area and Alabama's natural history[318] (including William Bartram, who during a brief period in 1775 became the first knowledgeable naturalist there).[319] All of these men were on their way to somewhere else. Gosse, on the other hand, was the first experienced naturalist to live in Alabama and write about its natural history.[320]

His natural history harvest—numerous species of plants (189 species), insects (94), marine fish (14), birds (59), mammals (21), and reptiles and amphibians (15)[321]—was small in comparison to what he would collect a few years later in Jamaica. But scattered throughout *Letters from Alabama* are 'very many original observations on insects.'[322] They exceeded in scientific value the observations of the few travellers and men of science who had preceded him to the state. Likewise his many references in *Letters* to Alabamian society make it 'one of the most interesting commentaries on the ante bellum South.'[323]

Taken together, *Letters from Alabama* is 'unparalleled in its detailed evocations of the natural history and cultural conditions of frontier

315. PHG, *Letters from Alabama*, 255.

316. Freeman & Wertheimer-PHG, 65-7, 114.

317. Shingleton, 'Rural Life in the Old South', 5-6.

318. L. J. Davenport, 'From Cro-Magnon to Kral: A History of Botany in Alabama', *Journal of the Botanical Research Institute of Texas* IX (30 Nov. 2015), 397-431.

319. Davenport, 'From Cro-Magnon to Kral', 400.

320. Davenport, 'From Cro-Magnon to Kral', 404. Davenport uses the phrase 'trained naturalist' in reference to both Bartram and PHG, by which he presumably meant 'experienced naturalist'.

321. The tabulation is by the editors Mullen and Littleton, in 'Introduction' to PHG, *Letters from Alabama*, 4, which provides a valuable list of this activity.

322. Samuel H. Scudder, 'Bibliographical Record', 281.

323. Joseph Ewan, 'The Scientist on the Frontier', in John Francis McDermott (ed.), *Research Opportunities in American Cultural History* ([Lexington:] University of Kentucky Press, 1961), 94.

Alabama,'[324] 'the most complete contribution to the natural history of our local field. Not only is it an authority on that subject but folk customs and kindred observations are carefully noted.'[325] To this day, admirers consider Gosse a 'hero' and his book 'the first (and, to our minds, the very best) early scientific work from our state.'[326] *Letters from Alabama* is known as 'an Alabama classic.'[327]

-VI-

During Gosse's period of isolation in Pleasant Hill, there was little formal support for his religious outlook (Pleasant Hill had only been visited by its first Methodist preacher in 1818),[328] so he looked to nature for sustenance. After all, observation and description were aspects of the celebration of the Creator and the recognition of the designing hand, and once in the forest God's workshop became at the same time His Temple. 'To walk in the forest alone is a high gratification,' Gosse explained:

> The perfect stillness and utter solitude, unbroken, commonly, by even ordinary woodland sounds and sights, tranquillize and sober the mind; the gloom has a solemn effect, for there is no light but what penetrates through the green leaves far above our head. ... The devout spirit is drawn upward in such a scene, which imagination presently turns into

324. Review of PHG, *Letters from Alabama*, in *Southeastern Naturalist* XII (2013), B8.

325. Peter A. Brannon, 'Through the Years: Gosse, The Naturalist', *Selma Times-Journal*; George Fremault, 'Customs And Appearance Of Mobile Century Ago Described In Book Written By English Naturalist. "Letters From Alabama" By Philip Henry Grosse [*sic*] Is Authoritative Volume On State in 1839', *Mobile Press-Register*, 9 June 1946: this article refers, though I know not with what authority, to some birds mentioned in *Letters* which have since become extinct; *Letters from Alabama*, pp. [v]-vi; and for some references to early visitors to Alabama, H. Taylor Rankin and D. E. Davis, 'Woody Vegetation in the Black Belt Prairie of Montgomery County, Alabama, in 1845-46', *Ecology* LII (Summer 1971), 716-9. Two excellent editions of this book have been published in the Library of Alabama Classics: a photo-reproduction with an introduction by Harvey H. Jackson III (Tuscaloosa: University of Alabama Press, 1993), and a beautifully produced edition in which the type is re-set which includes a taxonomic list of plants and animals cited by PHG, edited by Gary R. Mullen and Taylor D. Littleton (as cited).

326. L. J. Davenport, 'In the Footsteps of Gosse', *Alabama Heritage* Issue 98 (Fall 2010), 51. Davenport was a member of the Birmingham Audubon Society, for whom 'Gosse is our hero.' In the spring of 2010, 'fifty devoted disciples of a mighty man' gathered in Selma, Alabama. 'Our procession filed south to the end of Broad Street and across the Edmund Pettus Bridge and gazed down at the Alabama River flowing below. Then on with our pilgrimage, following in the footsteps of ... MLK? No, PHG: Philip Henry Gosse.' (p. 51). See also Davenport, 'From Cro-Magnon to Kral', 404.

327. Harvey H. Jackson III, 'Introduction' to PHG, *Letters from Alabama*, 21.

328. Anson West, *A History of Methodism in Alabama* (Nashville, TN: Printed for the Author, 1893), 154, 211.

a magnificent temple, whose far distant roof is borne on uncounted columns; and indeed it is a glorious temple, one worthy of the Hand that reared it.[329]

The plan worked sufficiently to again spark a religious rejuvenation reminiscent of the one he experienced in Newfoundland in 1832. At the beginning of September 1838, Gosse underwent 'a great spiritual revival & restoration, which was like a new conversion,' he recalled: 'I strove long & hard for the grace of perfect Sanctification, as taught in Wesleyan doctrine.[330] Though I did not attain any such permanent condition, yet then, & for the remainder of the year, I enjoyed much enlargement of heart, much nearness to God, & an unwavering confidence in His love & favour.'[331]

The train of events which followed this new *annus mirabilis* suggests that Gosse wavered about his next step.[332] Was it time to return home? Should he remain in Alabama? His instinct was to leave: after just three months at Pleasant Hill, that's what he was already thinking, due to the slave system, 'so enormous an evil'.[333] Against that was the pioneer naturalist's impulse, with fantasies of unimagined opportunities in Alabama's 'rich and almost virgin field for the pursuit of natural history.'[334] Then, before 1 December, his term at the school ended. For some unknown reason he was let go and replaced by another schoolmaster.[335] Without employment, the severe headaches (said to have put him in a near comatose state) may have had a doubly harsh impact. Also encouraging his exodus: that fall, entries in his scientific journals had become increasingly brief. Realistically, maybe there was less to record than he had anticipated.[336] Overall the path seemed clear for

329. PHG, *Letters from Alabama*, 118.

330. The term 'Christian perfectionism' was coined by John Wesley: Mark Ackerman, 'Wesleyan Sanctification and its Influence on the Assemblies of God' (Regent University, MA thesis, 2011), 2.

331. 'Reminiscences', II: 233.

332. Excerpts from a PHG diary appear in *Life*, 145. In 'Reminiscences', II: 233, PHG wrote: 'The condition of my inward life, through the remaining months [in Alabama], I have recorded, with much careful introspection, in a MS. Diary, still among my papers'. He also refers to a diary he kept of his 1839 return voyage from Mobile, Alabama to Liverpool ('Reminiscences', II: 235). I believe the Alabama section of 'Reminiscences', was written probably around 1874. The disposition of these diaries is unknown.

333. PHG, *Letters from Alabama*, 255.

334. PHG, *Letters from Alabama*, 255.

335. PHG diary entry for Dec. 1, 1838, cited in *Life*, 145.

336. PHG, *Letters from Alabama*, 286; *Life*, 143-4, gives a different explanation.

a return to England, where he was confident he could become a travelling preacher for the Wesleyans.[337]

At some point in early December, he hesitated. Suddenly serving as a Methodist minister in Alabama became an option, even the will of God.[338] That Gosse should follow this train of thought was unsurprising, given that the religious outlook in Alabama was familiar to him. The Methodism he had encountered in Newfoundland was English; while he was in Canada, it was a mixture of British and American elements.[339] In America in the early nineteenth century preserving traditional Methodist practice and doctrine was favoured, with modifications for frontier life. The custom of a 'Quarterly Meeting', for example, an activity mandated by John Wesley, was maintained.[340] During these meetings—supervised in America by the powerful 'presiding elders'—circuit leaders would convene with itinerant preachers. A distinctive and controversial theological development was the emphasis on sanctification,[341] the achievement of 'Christian perfection' or 'perfect love'[342] (the 'perfect Sanctification' which Gosse mentioned as being appealing). John Wesley had mooted the possibility of attaining during one's lifetime spiritual perfection through increasing holiness—an idea horrifying to many Christians who could not reconcile its seemingly voluntary aspect with the concept of man's innate sin. Yet some American Methodist theologians suggested it was achievable, even instantaneously.[343]

Besides Gosse's evident familiarity with the American Methodist outlook, in Alabama there was work to be done. It was only in 1808,[344] three decades before his time, that Methodists had established a formal

337. 'Reminiscences', II: 233.

338. PHG diary entry for Dec. 16, 1838, cited in *Life*, 145.

339. Smith, 'Establishment of Religious Communities in the Eastern Townships of Lower Canada', 104, 96-105.

340. Michael Kenneth Turner, '"Redeeming the Time": The Making of Early American Methodism' (Vanderbilt University, PhD dissertation, 2009), 70.

341. Turner, '"Redeeming the Time"', 223.

342. David W. Bebbington, *The Dominance of Evangelicalism: The Age of Spurgeon and Moody* (Downers Grove, IL: InterVarsity Press, 2005), 153.

343. Turner, '"Redeeming the Time"', 223-4; Jonathan David Burnham, 'The Controversial Relationship Between Benjamin Wills Newton and John Nelson Darby' (University of Oxford, DPhil dissertation, 1999), 159.

344. West, *History of Methodism in Alabama*, 38, 598. The meeting at which the first appointed Methodist missionary took place was held from 27 Dec. 1807 to 2 Jan. 1808. That likely explains why some writers date the formal Methodist presence to 1807, e.g. Lazenby, *History of Methodism in Alabama and West Florida*, 24-5; both dates are given in Thomas McAdory Owen, *History of Alabama and Dictionary of Alabama Biography* II: 979.

presence in Alabama; only since the end of 1822 that Pleasant Hill, in Dallas County, began to be served by the Methodist Cedar Creek Circuit;[345] only since 1830 that they established the first college in the state;[346] and only in 1837 when, in Selma, the first Methodist Society and the first Methodist Church were organized.[347] In the 1830s, the various Methodist groups in Alabama had over 12,000 adherents (which included Blacks and Native Americans) served by over sixty-five itinerant ministers and an unknown number of local preachers.[348] From its initiation, the Cedar Creek Circuit itself covered 'unoccupied territory' where 'Indians were fishing in the river while we [Methodists] were preaching and praying; the bears were ravaging the corn-fields, and the wolves and tigers were howling and screaming in the woods in the neighborhood.' The movement as a whole was expanding and there was 'a pleasing hope ... of seeing the desert blossom as the rose.' Even while soliciting funds for the Alabama Conference Missionary Society (auxiliary to the Missionary Society of the Methodist Episcopal Church), the complaint in 1834 was that 'The missionary field enlarges greatly in all the south and west; but we lack men. The length and breadth of a vast frontier lie open before us—but where are the laborers?'[349]

It was Ebenezer Hearn (1794-1862)—the veteran Alabama-born Methodist minister who had been the first itinerant Methodist preacher in Pleasant Hill in 1818[350]—who apparently persuaded Gosse to serve as a minister in Alabama.[351] Hearn had been appointed to the Cedar Creek Circuit in 1835 and followed this as Presiding Elder of another Methodist district.[352] Perhaps it was under Hearn's influence that Gosse had decided to attend the Fourth Quarterly Meeting of the Methodist

345. Lazenby, *History of Methodism in Alabama and West Florida*, 113; West, *History of Methodism in Alabama*, 211.

346. Owen, *History of Alabama and Dictionary of Alabama Biography* II: 837.

347. West, *History of Methodism in Alabama*, 535; Lazenby, *History of Methodism in Alabama and West Florida*, 229.

348. Owen, *History of Alabama and Dictionary of Alabama Biography* II: 980 (the figures are as of the end of 1832).

349. 'Missionary Drafts', Cincinnati *Western Christian* Advocate, 6 Feb. 1835, 16.

350. West, *History of Methodism in Alabama*, 145.

351. Another influence was 'Brother Noseworthy' (PHG diary entry for Dec. 16, cited in *Life*, 145), whom I have been unable to further identify.

352. The name usually appears as 'Hearn'. In *Life*, 145, EWG rendered it 'Hearne', apparently based on a PHG diary entry for 16 Dec. 1838. 'Hearne' was an infrequent contemporary spelling. On Hearn: Owen, *History of Alabama and Dictionary of Alabama Biography* III: 782; there is an image of 'Hearne' in ibid., I: [257].

Society for Selma and Valley Creek Station at the Methodist Church in Selma (a town with an 1840 population of 1,053,[353] 16.5 miles northeast of Pleasant Hill). It began on 21 December.[354] One can only speculate as to whether or not it was like similar meetings at that time, which were characterized by 'raucous enthusiasm'[355] from a clergy said to be contemptuous of 'book-learning'.[356]

If Gosse had indeed committed to go to Selma in response to Hearn's urging, that career-path was short-lived. Already the day before the meeting Gosse noted he was 'on the point of returning to England.'[357] And he remained undeterred in his decision following the Quarterly Meeting. 'I have had some profitable seasons,' he said about the event, 'though I find too much of a narrow bigotry with all.'[358]

We do not know what inner thoughts ultimately led Gosse to settle on a course of action, but on December 29 he assembled his boxes and cabinets, said goodbye to the Saffolds, and booked passage on a steamer bound for Mobile. He continued his observations of Alabamian society on his passage down the Alabama River, leaving a unique ethno-musical record of a local work song (or sea shanty).[359] Arriving at Mobile on the last day of the year to find the battered insect-cabinet from Canada, he waited in the city until January 6, 1839, when he left for Liverpool on the *Isaac Newton*.[360]

353. Of the total, 431 were White and 622 non-White (Lazenby, *History of Methodism in Alabama and West Florida*, 229).

354. Advertisements, *Selma Free Press* (1 Dec. 1838), 3; Columbus, Mississippi *Southern Argus*,12 Dec. 1838, 3. According to Turner, '"Redeeming the Time"', 70-1, quarterly meetings were initially for a single day (normally a Tuesday), but later started on a Friday or Saturday and lasted many days (21 Dec. 1838 was a Friday).

355. Turner, '"Redeeming the Time"', 97, 71. 'Throughout much of the eighteenth and nineteenth centuries, Methodism was intimately associated with enthusiastic worship services. People thought of Methodists as shouting from the pews, echoing approbation to the preachers in the pulpit, waving arms and handkerchiefs, crying, praying aloud and unbidden, even breaking spontaneously into song. This association was not unfounded' (Turner, 65).

356. Nichols, *Forty Years of American Life 1821-1861*, 230. Nichols said that from his memory, Presbyterians and orthodox Congregationalists were known for their educated clergy.

357. 'Being on the point of returning to England' (PHG, *Letters from Alabama*, 299: Letter XVIII, dated Dec. 20).

358. PHG diary entry for 25 Dec. 1838, cited in *Life*, 146.

359. R. B. Williams, 'Philip Henry Gosse at Mobile, Alabama: his unique record of a sea shanty', *Archives of Natural History* 35 (2008), 360-3.

360. 'Reminiscences', II: 234; *Letters from Alabama*, 303, 299; 'Mobile, [Alabama], Jan. 5', South Carolina *Charleston Daily Courier*, 9 Jan. 1839, 2.

-VII-

'As a matter of fact,' Edmund Gosse observed with much truth, '... the rolling stone returned to England, after an exile of eleven years, with practically no moss whatever on its surface.'[361] The £22.10s. in cash which he carried with him was somewhat less than the sum with which he had left Canada; nor could the birds, fur skins, or most of his insect collection (which he sold to Andrew Melly) have markedly added to that sum.[362]

On the other hand, the stone had changed in a manner which could not be measured in physical terms. For one thing, on the *Isaac Newton* Gosse completed the manuscript for *The Canadian Naturalist*, the first book he published; for another, he continued to expound the Word. 'On Sundays,' he recalled, 'the Captain, though he professed infidel sentiments, allowed me to gather the crew to the quarter-deck, & to preach Christ to them in my poor manner; I know not with what result.'[363]

In later years, Gosse occasionally referred to his sojourn in Newfoundland and Canada[364] with some warmth, and maintained contact with several of his friends from those days.[365] He never spoke of his experiences in America in that way. It took him two decades before he wrote about American slavery,[366] and when he did—just before the outbreak of the American Civil War—he detailed what he knew and left no doubt about what he thought. 'I had had personal opportunities

361. *Life*, 148.

362. 'Reminiscences', II: 234-5. The small amount does not imply that PHG was not paid well for teaching; it appears that he was (*Letters from Alabama*, 43, 255).

363. 'Reminiscences', II: 235.

364. PHG, *Canadian Naturalist*, [vii]; PHG–John Bemister, 21 Dec. 1871 (Corr. Bk.).

365. 'I hear from my old friend W. C. St. John at Boston, now & then: he sent me a cutting from a paper cont[ainin]g a very interesting Memoir of Apsey, by J. B. Peters [Peters, 'Obituary', *Provincial Wesleyan*, (2)]. My brother William is still hale & hearty ... He sees Mrs. Ayles (Lavinia Pack) occasionally. I hear frequently from Mr. Jaques in Canada; occasionally from S.W. Sprague in N[ew] Brunswick; &, a year or two ago, from Phil[ip] Tocque, a clergyman in Canada. Not long ago I had occasion for a little friendly corresp[onden]ce with W. B. Bugden, who lives at Lyndhurst' (PHG–John Bemister, 21 Dec. 1871, Corr. Bk.). There are no letters listed in Corr. Bk. to and from Bugden before 1872. PHG's 'Bugden' appears to be not the Revd Wilbert B. Bugden of Newfoundland (Lench, *Story of Methodism in Bonavista*, 154-5, 193-4) but the farmer William Beale Bugden of Lyndhurst (Southampton *Hampshire Advertiser*, 6 July 1870, 3 and 30 Dec. 1871, 4).

366. PHG included an extensive critique of the American institution of slavery in the book form of *Letters from Alabama* (Letter XII, 250-255), using words which had not appeared in the serial form (compare Letter XII, *Home Friend* III, Dec. 1855, 548-50). The textual differences may have been due to self-censorship or (more likely) were the result of editorial intervention on the part of the SPCK, the publisher of *Home Friend* (Freeman & Wertheimer-PHG, 66). *Life*,142, is an inaccurate transcription of *Letters from Alabama*, 253.

of witnessing the horrors of Southern American slavery,' he wrote in 1860, witnessing 'cruelties … practiced on their fellow-man, for no crime worse than the colour of his skin.'[367] He might have felt similarly about the treatment of Indian tribes at the time, but he seems not to have encountered (and does not mention) the dozen native tribes once resident in Alabama.[368] Evangelical Christian missionary activity among the tribes dates to the beginning of the nineteenth century,[369] and the US Government programme to move Indians west of the Mississippi River along the 'Trail of Tears' was well underway by the time Gosse arrived in Alabama.

His sympathies, Gosse told his son in referring to the US Civil War, 'are not Southern, but anti-American: I hoped that the war might break up that vast insolent republican Empire which aims to domineer over the whole world, & is so relentlessly, bitterly, unreasonably hostile to England.'[370] Once, in speaking of the Welsh-born explorer H. M. Stanley (who at times maintained an American affiliation), he said 'I dislike [him] exceedingly: his meanness, his egotism, his jealousy of England, make him a typical American, as do also his energy, his fertility of resource, his courage, & other *good* qualities.'[371]

On 15 February 1839, the *Isaac Newton* landed at Liverpool. Gosse was happy to be back in 'the dear home to which, in all my wanderings, my heart ever turns.'[372] He was 17 when he left Poole for Newfoundland and was nearly 30 when he returned home from Alabama. His future life path was arguably more unclear on his return than it had been on his departure.

367. PHG, 'The Negro Slave', *Gosse's Gospel Tracts* no. 25 [1860], printed in book form in EG and PHG, *Narrative Tracts* (London: Morgan and Chase, [1864]). For the date and attribution, see Freeman & Wertheimer-PHG, 98-99; Freeman & Wertheimer-EG, 57.

368. Lazenby, *History of Methodism in Alabama and West Florida*, 27; West, *A History of Methodism in Alabama*, 20, 27.

369. James William Moffitt, 'A History of Early Baptist Missions among the Five Civilized Tribes' (University of Oklahoma, PhD dissertation, 1946), 1.

370. PHG-EWG, 11 May 1869 (CUL Add. 7041, 25).

371. PHG-EWG, 16 Nov. 1872 (CUL Add. 7041, 55). Emphasis in the original.

372. PHG, *Letters from Alabama*, 305.

CHAPTER FOUR

1839-1846

Those Gorgeous Scenes

-I-

A TEACHER OF PAINTING? A CURATOR AT A MUSEUM? A Methodist travelling minister? What would Gosse do, now that he was in Liverpool? The first idea was Gosse's; the second was suggested by William Clarke, with whom he stayed (he was the brother-in-law of Gosse's Canadian friend Ann Jaques); the third was an idea which had percolated in his mind while yet in Alabama and could be explored in Liverpool thanks to Ann Jaques' brother, George Heap, a local Wesleyan Methodist preacher there.

Nothing came of the first idea, and the second was not appealing. 'I should fear that I should be thrown into situations in which I might find it difficult to keep that purity of intention which I value more than life,' Gosse told Clarke about the museum position, 'and likewise, that my opportunities of being useful to my fellow-men, especially to their souls, would be much curtailed.'[1] Nor was the reality of becoming a preacher what he'd imagined it would be. George Heap took him to a village meeting, where Gosse preached. He later recalled that 'The large & fine Wesleyan Chapels of Liverpool, the fashionable attire of the audience, & the studied refinement of the discourses,—were all thoroughly out of keeping with my fresh & ardent devotional feelings. I mourned over the degeneracy of Methodism.'[2]

---

1. Letters, PHG-William Clarke, 4 Mar. 1839 (CUL Adv.c.82.5,11) and 25 Apr. 1839 ('Reminiscences', II: 237-9; also quoted in *Life*, 151-53, with transcription errors).
2. 'Reminiscences', II: 239-40, 236, 242.

After nearly two weeks with the Clarkes, Gosse headed south by train to London, for the first time passing through 'the queen of cities, the emporium of the world.' By 1 March he was once again united in Wimborne in Dorset with his brother Tom, a grocer, and their mother, who was living with him.[3]

During his three months in Wimborne, Gosse revived the idea of attending to the spiritual welfare of his neighbours. He worshipped at the same Methodist chapel which his brother Tom attended, served as a local preacher in Wimborne and in the surrounding area, and filled in as minister at the local Independent meeting.[4] When the time came, however, to apply to the Methodist Conference as a travelling preacher, he was rejected as too old for the regular ministry. That didn't bother Gosse, who had again cooled to the idea.[5] Perhaps, as he later thought, the loss of 'freshness and fervor' had been connected with his affection for a Wesleyan woman named Amelia Button, 'an accomplished, pious, and winning lady, older than I, and much pitted with small pox.' Without a permanent job, however, there was no way he could be a successful suitor. On 7 June, he set off for London.[6]

It is fair to speculate that leaving Wimborne was related to Amelia Button, but there may have been a more obvious motive. For more than four months Gosse had carried with him his account of his experiences as a naturalist in Canada, and it was time to see if it was publishable. He turned to his first cousin, Thomas Bell, FRS (1792-1880), then professor of zoology at King's College, London (later President of the Linnean Society) and a dental surgeon at Guy's Hospital. Bell was impressed with the effort, and showed it to the London publisher John Van Voorst (1804-1898). The first title Van Voorst had issued, in 1834, already revealed his focus on illustrated natural history works,[7] and Bell's *History of the British Quadrupeds* (1837) and *History of British Reptiles* (1839) were on the Van Voorst list. 'I like the book,' Van Voorst told Gosse. He offered him £100 for the copyright and £5 for his drawings on wood to be used as illustrations.[8] It was the beginning of a business and personal

3. 'Reminiscences', II: 240; PHG-William Clarke, 4 Mar. 1839 (CUL Adv. c. 82.5, 11).
4. 'Reminiscences', II: 241.
5. 'Reminiscences', II: 242-3.
6. 'Reminiscences', II: pp. 241-43 (*Life*, 154).
7. R. B. Williams, 'John Van Voorst: patron publisher of Victorian natural history', *The Private Library* ser. 4, I (Spring 1988), 5-12.
8. 'Reminiscences', II: 244, says that Van Voorst paid £100 for the copyright and £5 for PHG

friendship which lasted nearly 50 years; it was a most welcome addition to Gosse's finances. At the time, however, it was apparently only a dimly perceived signal that Gosse—who, in dedicating the work to Bell, styled himself on the book's title page as 'Cor. Mem. of the Nat. Hist. Soc. of Montreal, and of the Lit. and Hist. Soc. of Quebec'—had struck upon a lifetime profession.

A shadow was soon cast over this good news. Concurrent with his attempt to get his manuscript published, Gosse wrote to his sister Elizabeth in Sherborne to find out whether she thought he could get a job by giving drawing lessons there to children of wealthy families.[9] Apparently she was doubtful. Then Bell used his influence at the Bank of England to find a clerkship for him. Once again, Gosse was too old.[10] He introduced himself to a fellow Wesleyan, George Loddiges (1784-1846), a partner in the leading orchid nursery in Europe, who recommended that he move to cheaper lodgings in the suburbs and try to find employment teaching flower painting in ladies' schools. With no other options, Gosse moved to No.1, Retreat Cottages, Hackney (where the air is 'salubrious and healthy'),[11] conducting family worship at the home of Hester Neal, a Christian woman as old as his mother. 'Now, day after day,' as he later recalled, 'I trudged wearily through the streets, with my portfolio under my arm, seeking to show my drawings of flowers and insects.' He had minimal success.[12]

Gosse filled his plentiful spare time by frequenting the British Museum to study the animals, and there began his long-term friendship with Adam White, an assistant in the Insect Room.[13] He also cultivated his

drawings on wood; *Life*, 157, which deviates markedly from PHG's account, says Van Voorst paid PHG 100 guineas for the book and does not mention the illustrations. *Canadian Naturalist* was dedicated to Thomas Bell 'By his grateful relative, The Author'.

9. Fragment of a letter, PHG-Elizabeth Green, 15 June 1839 (cited in *Life*, 156). Elizabeth died in Sherborne on 26 July 1840 (WG's Diary, under July 26, 1857).

10. 'Reminiscences', II: 244.

11. *Turner's Directory for 1847, Containing an Alphabetical List of the Inhabitants of Hackney, Clapton, Stoke Newington, &c., &c., &c.,* ... (Hackney: Caleb Turner, 1847), 19.

12. 'Reminiscences', II: 245. For Loddiges, also *Proc. Linnean Society* I (Sept. 1847), 334-5. For Hester Neal (or Neale), who was 56 in June 1841: *1841 Census Returns for Hackney*, Enumeration District 9, p. 2. At that time, the household at Retreat Cottages was comprised of PHG, Neal, Sarah Kemp (aged 45), and Susan Warner (aged 79). PHG had previously lived in cheap lodgings in Drury Lane kept by a Methodist, and later took a sleeping room in Farringdon Street ('Reminiscences', II: 243. The description of this episode in *Life*, 155, is an imaginary retelling unrelated to what PHG wrote).

13. 'Reminiscences', II: 245; letter from PHG, 27 Apr. 1854, printed in [various authors], *Testimonials in Favour of Mr. Adam White*, 11 ('I have had the pleasure of an intimate

acquaintance with Loddiges, with whom he shared many interests.[14] Finally, though apparently too old for the regular ministry, from at least October 1839, he served as a Wesleyan Methodist Class-Leader and local preacher in the First London Circuit.[15]

Throughout 1840 there was more uncertainty about his life direction. While the *Canadian Naturalist*, published by Van Voorst on 29 February 1840, was well received,[16] only a ripple of activity (in the shape of a brief list of Canadian butterflies by Gosse in *The Entomologist*) followed that small wave.[17] A few months later, Gosse heard that Amelia Button had

acquaintance with Mr. Adam White during the last fifteen years, and entertain the highest esteem for him as a Gentleman and as a Christian').

14. Loddiges had large collections of orchids, palms, and humming-birds, drew illustrations for the Botanical Cabinet (which he edited), and was much interested in microscopical studies. Around this time, PHG was present at a 'nocturnal soiree' called by Loddiges to witness the expanding of a beautiful tropical orchid ([PHG], *Wanderings Through the Conservatories at Kew* (London: SPCK, [1856],) 281).

15. PHG's name is not listed in 'The Stations of the Preachers for 1839-40' (*Wesleyan-Methodist Magazine* ser. 3, XVIII, Sept. 1839, 740) or 'The Stations of the Wesleyan-Methodist Ministers' for 1840-1 or 1841-2 (*Wesleyan-Methodist Magazine* ser. 3, XIX, Sept. 1840, 753; XX, Sept. 1841, 745, see 1056), but he is listed in the 'First London Circuit Wesleyan Methodist Preachers' Plan. [Oct. 6] 1839-[Jan. 12] 1840', and [Apr. 11 -Aug. 29] 1841 (I am grateful to Mrs Jeannette Harkin, Assistant Archivist of the Methodist Archives and Research Centre, London, for providing me with a copy of that document). PHG kept 'A MS. book of skeleton Sermons, preached by me in the Chaples [*sic*] around London, from 1839 to 1842', which showed 'how very poor & crude my theology was at that time'. The book has not been traced. Around 1842 PHG succeeded in converting a young artisan of Homerton shortly before his death ('Reminiscences', II: 250).

16. The *Canadian Naturalist* was announced as forthcoming in *The Athenaeum* (30 Nov. 1839), 908, but according to 'Reminiscences', II: 244, it was published on 29 Feb. 1840. It was fairly extensively reviewed (and unanimously commended)—in the general press (*Literary Gazette*, 14 Mar. 1840, 167; *Spectator* XIII (14 Mar.), 256-7; *Monthly Review* I, (Apr.), 581-9; *New Monthly Magazine* LVIII (Apr., 575-6); *The Atlas*, 4 Apr., 220; *Tait's Edinburgh Magazine* VII (May), 338-9; *Westminster Review* XXXIV (June), 248-9 [author not identified in *Wellesley Index* III]; *Athenaeum*, 3 Apr. 1841, 260);—foreign news publications (*Colonial Magazine* I (Mar. 1840), 513; *United Service Gazette*, #376 (21 Mar.), 6; *Asiatic Journal* n.s. XXXII (May), 71);— and in religious serials (*Church of England Quarterly Review* VII (Apr. 1840), 513; *Christian Remembrancer* XXII (Apr.), 211-12; *Congregational Magazine* n.s. IV (Dec.), 871-2). There were then few specialist scientific reviews, and Edward Newman wrote the only known scientific notice (*The Entomologist* I (Apr. 1841), 81-88).

Several reviews compared the *Canadian Naturalist* to Gilbert White's *Natural History of Selborne*, applauded the quality and accuracy of the engravings, its instructive nature, pleasant style (though three reviewers complained that the dialogue was deficient), the freshness of the observations, its usefulness to emigrants, and the variety of subjects treated. The *Christian Remembrancer* and *Congregational Magazine* noted the pious attitude of the author, Edward Newman said the work contained accurate observations and was useful to entomologists interested in geographical distribution, and *The Athenaeum* hoped that Gosse 'will be induced to continue his researches on the natural peculiarities of his native country.'

17. PHG, 'List of Butterflies Taken at Compton, in Lower Canada', *Entomologist* I (July 1841), 137-9; Freeman & Wertheimer-PHG, 19-20.

chosen another suitor. He thought of returning to America or going to the West Indies, where he calculated he could easily earn more than £200 a year and gather material for a new book.[18] Instead, relying upon his youthful experiences at Lance and Sells' schools, and teaching jobs in Canada and Alabama,[19] around September 1840 he improved his knowledge of Greek and took over a school in London Lane with three pupils. At the end of the month, the 'Classical and Commercial School for Young Gentlemen' was opened.[20]

Gosse was a school master for the next three years, giving instruction in (among other subjects) grammar, composition, writing, bookkeeping, arithmetic, the Bible, Greek and Latin. Meeting with moderate success, he had fifteen students by 1842, when the school was apparently transferred to his mother's new home at Woodbine Cottage, Hackney.[21]

-II-

Recall that the *annus mirabilis* of Philip Gosse took place in Carbonear, Newfoundland, in 1832. In 1838 in Alabama, he experienced another, if lesser, religious revival. Now in London, two other events occurred which were nearly as momentous.

There was nothing extraordinary about the theology of the 32-year-old Gosse. He had been raised as an Independent (that is, a Congregationalist)[22] and nourished on many of the classical evangelical works in a spiritually oriented environment. In the language of the day, he recognized his own sinfulness and the need for a new heart. He was an eager exponent of the plenary inspiration of the Bible, appreciating the Two Book perspective of natural theology. In practice he was heavenly minded, with the chapel playing its role in daily life. Like many Dissenters, he had a deep, even obsessive, animosity towards Catholicism[23] (Protestants, including

18. 'Reminiscences', II: 242; *Life*, 164.

19. PHG-James [Green], 4 Sept. 1840 (CUL Adv. c. 82.5, 14), and the schedule of classes (Adv. c. 82.5, 13).

20. 'Reminiscences', II: 246; and PHG's announcement of the opening of the 'Academy' (copies at LeBL and CUL Adv. c. 82.5, 11).

21. 'Reminiscences', II: 247-8. PHG moved to Woodbine Cottage around June 1841.

22. J. Burns (ed.), *Evans' Sketch of the Denominations of the Christian World* (London: Thomas Allman, 1794, new edition, 1851), 173: 'The Independents, or Congregationalists ... deny not only the subordination of the clergy, but also all dependency on other assemblies.'

23. In describing a jellyfish in *Tenby*, PHG interjected a note about 'Papal cruelty' (PHG, *Tenby*, 176; he was chastised for this in the *Saturday Review*, 10 May 1856, 38). 'The Brethren retained the deeply rooted anti-Catholicism of their radical evangelical background' (Neil T. R. Dickson, '"The Church Itself is God's Clergy": The Principles and Practices of the Brethren',

Brethren, viewed Catholicism as 'the massive and glowering evil of Christendom').[24]

During his North American sojourn, Gosse had largely turned away from the Independent and Anglican worlds and come under the influence of Wesleyan Methodism (whether of the British, American, or Canadian variety, as previously noted). Religion, to be true, must be personal. God is *my* God, *my* Saviour, because Christ died for *my* sins. Gosse had also followed the Methodist concern for evangelism and the conversion of souls (while maintaining a proper separation from the world). In becoming a Methodist he had entered into the heart and backbone of the Evangelical movement.

Before 1842, millenarianism[25] (the belief that the second advent of Christ will precede a thousand-year period of blessedness) was not a major concern in Gosse's theology. It is true that, in the Independent tradition, he had read works on unfulfilled prophecy. He knew Scott's popular *Commentary* (1788-92),[26] Croly's *Salathiel* (1828)[27]—'one of the most splendid productions among works of fiction that the age has brought forth'[28]—and Pollok's standard historicist interpretation in *Course of Time* (1827).[29] But he had no clear conviction or position on the subject until mid-1842:

> A great crisis in my spiritual life was approaching; for the Holy Ghost
> was about to unfold to me the hope of the personal Advent of the Lord
> Jesus, of which hitherto I had not the slightest conception. Two of the

in Deryck W. Lovegrove (ed.), *The Rise of the Laity in Evangelical Protestantism* (London: Routledge, 2002), 217); David W. Bebbington, *Evangelicalism in Modern Britain: A History from the 1730s to the 1980s* (London: Routledge, 1989, 2005), 101-2; Pietsch, *Dispensational Modernism*, 67. Catholic prejudice extended to British Protestant students of prophecy at least from the time of Isaac Newton (William H. Austin, 'Newton on Science and Religion', *Journal of the History of Ideas* xxxi (Oct.-Dec. 1970), 523). Newton was an historicist pre-millennialist (Froom, *Prophetic Faith* II:658-669, 786-7).

24. Akenson, *Exporting the Rapture*, 283.

25. During the 19th Century, 'millenarian' could be considered a synonym for 'premillennialist' (Ernest R. Sandeen, *The Roots of Fundamentalism. British and American Millenarianism 1800-1930* (Chicago: University of Chicago Press, 1970), 5fn. 3).

26. Scott's work was the 'most popular and widely quoted of early nineteenth-century Bible commentators' (Froom, *Prophetic Faith* IV,120).

27. Croly, *Salathiel: A Story of the Past, the Present, and the Future* (London: Colburn, 1828, 3vols.), by the Anglican Revd George Croly (1780-1860), was originally published anonymously. It deals with the legend of the Wandering Jew (review, *Literary Gazette*, 8 Mar. 1828, [145]).

28. Review in *The Athenaeum*, 18 Apr. 1828, 386.

29. Froom, *Prophetic Faith* IV: 120.

most valued of my pupils [at his Academy] were Edward and Theodore Habershon;[30] the elder of whom, Edward, a thoughtful and very amiable youth of fifteen, had already secured a large place in my affections. He had occasionally spoken to me of his father, Matthew Habershon, as an author, and had suggested that I might feel interested in his works on Sacred Prophecy. But I had never heard of them or him; and Edward's words met with little response. One day, however, Mr. Habershon sent for my acceptance, his *Dissertation on the Prophetic Scriptures*, second edition [1840].[31] It was in June, 1842, when days were at the longest. I began to read it after my pupils were dismissed in the afternoon, sat in the garden eagerly devouring the pages, and actually finishing the work (of four hundred octavo pages) before darkness set-in. When I closed the book, I knew not where I was; I had become so wholly absorbed in the great subjects, that some minutes elapsed before I could recal [sic] my surroundings, before the new world of my consciousness did 'fade into the light of common day.'[32]

Of the Restoration of the Jews, I had received some dim inkling already, perhaps from Croly's *Salathiel*: but of the destruction of the Papacy, the end of Gentilism, the kingdom of God, the Resurrection and Rapture of the Church at the Personal Descent of the Lord, and the imminency of this,—all came on me that evening like a flash of lightning. My heart drank it in with joy: I found no shrinking from the nearness of Jesus. It was indeed a Revelation to a spirit prepared to accept it. I immediately began a practice, which I have pursued uninterruptedly for forty-six years, of constantly praying that I may be one of the favoured saints who shall never taste of death, but be alive and remain until the coming of the Lord, to be "clothed-upon with my house which is from heaven."[33]

30. 'But the Appendix [to EWG's *Life*] startled me—to think that *my* Mr. Habershon—Theodore—should have been a pupil of your father's; how I did love him at our Sunday School, in Peel Grove [London]. He was a friend indeed to many, tho' apparently, he lost his footing, afterwards' (M. A. Chaplin-EWG, 28 Nov. 1920, CUL Add. 7041,80).

31. The first edition of Habershon's *A Dissertation on the Prophetic Scriptures, Chiefly Those of a Chronological Character; Shewing Their Aspect on the Present Times, and on the Destinies of the Jewish Nation* (London, 1834) was entitled for the second edition *An Historical Dissertation on the Prophetic Scriptures of the Old Testament* (London: James Nisbet and Co., 1840).

32. William Wordsworth, 'Ode: Intimations of Immortality from Recollections of Early Childhood' (1807).

33. 'Reminiscences', II: 250-53 (quoted, with slight errors, in *Life*, 375-6), citing 2 Corinthians 5: 2 (KJV).

Many Christians have intentionally avoided the subject of unfulfilled prophecy by pointing to Jesus' warning against those who attempt 'to know the times or the seasons' (Acts 1: 6-7). Many others have not, perhaps a reflection (among other things) of the fact that one-third of the Bible (by one estimate) consists of prophecy.[34] Gosse's introduction to the subject came during an eruption of interest in millenarianism in Britain, and forced him to make choices which affected the direction of his life.

Calculators of the end of days had existed in ancient Israel prior to the first century BC; they drew on several apocryphal works, as well as that *locus classicus* of Jewish prophetic writings, the Book of Daniel.[35] When Jesus came to Galilee, a new period of speculation began, lasting until the third or fourth centuries AD. Like their Jewish brethren, and influenced by their hermeneutics, these early Christians expected a speedy advent of the millennium: the Christian text was the Book of Revelation. Even during this period, however, certain Church Fathers interpreted the visions of Daniel and John as referring to unfulfilled events which would have a future *literal*—rather than *symbolic*—realization. Thus one of the main schools of interpretation—the futurist—was already visible in outline.

A new period of crisis in church history, the Protestant Reformation, ushered in a second era of prophetic concern. After 1517, it was natural that Martin Luther should turn both away from, and against, Rome, and indeed for many students of prophecy, the Antichrist or 'Man of sin' of Revelation became identified with the papacy itself.[36] So arose the Protestant historical (also referred to as the 'presentist' or 'historicist') school, which claimed

34. H. Grattan Guinness, *The Approaching End of the Age Viewed in the Light of History, Prophecy, and Science* (London: Hodder and Stoughton, 1878), xi.

35. On this subject, see the monumental history of Le Roy Edwin Froom, *The Prophetic Faith of Our Fathers. The Historical Development of Prophetic Interpretation* (Washington, D.C.: Review and Herald Publishing Association, 4vols., 1946-54); F. Roy Coad's excellent *Prophetic Developments, with Particular Reference to the Early Brethren Movement*, CBRF Occasional Paper no.2 (1966); Sandeen's important reinterpretation of *The Roots of Fundamentalism*, chap. 1; Edward Bishop Elliott's classic *Horae Apocalypticae; or, A Commentary on the Apocalypse, Critical and Historical; Including also an Examination of the Chief Prophecies of Daniel* (London: Seeley, Jackson, and Halliday, 1844, 5th ed., 'carefully revised, corrected, enlarged, and improved throughout', 4vols., 1862), IV, 275-609; Abba Hillel Silver, *A History of Messianic Speculation in Israel* (Boston: Beacon Press, 1927, 1959), chap. I; a concise statement is in Bebbington, *Evangelicalism in Modern Britain*, 85-6; Robert Kieran Whalen, 'Millenarianism and Millennialism in America, 1790-1880' (State University of New York at Stony Brook, PhD dissertation, 1971), chap. 1.

36. The Pope 'has often since the Reformation been denounced by the highest authorities of the Church of England as "The Man of Sin"' ('Signs of the Times', *Christian* 15 Dec. 1870), 585, citing the *Record*, a Church of England serial.

that Daniel and the Apocalypse spoke of events which were not *in the future* but *had occurred and were still to occur*, events which could be precisely calculated by proper and careful interpretation. The study of the past and a knowledge of mathematics were now the keys unlocking a new understanding of the imminence of the millennium.

No sooner had this historicist school been initiated than a reaction set in as part of the Counter-Reformation. Resisting the equation of the Antichrist with the papacy, two Jesuits of the sixteenth century proposed different prophetic principles. One (Francisco Ribera) revived the futurist scheme, whereby the Antichrist was viewed as a single individual, not as a line of succession; another (Luis de Alcázar) founded the preterist school, according to which the prophecies in Revelation had already been fulfilled during the first years of the Christian era. By the eighteenth century, historicism had fallen into disfavour, further weakened by Daniel Whitby (1638–1726), an English Protestant who postponed the second advent from before the commencement of the millennium (called premillennialism) to its close (postmillennialism).

The stage was now set for the third period of prophetic exegesis, in the nineteenth century. The larger issues in interpretation were still the same: Did the futurist, the historicist, or the preterist school of thought represent the most accurate reading of Revelation? Would the millennial period described in Revelation 20 be signalled by a personal return of the Lord to earth prior to its commencement (premillennialism), or begin without that presence, which would be postponed until the close of the thousand years (postmillennialism)? The finer points of this abstruse controversy also remained: Who was the Antichrist? The impure Whore? The saints? What did the ten horns, or the Little Horn, or the fourth beast of Daniel, represent? Were the seals opened, the trumpets sounded, or the vials poured out? What of the prophetic periods, the 'seven times', 'time, times, and a half', 1290, 1335, 2300 'days', the seventy weeks, or 'a time no longer'? Was a biblical 'day' literally twenty-four hours, or symbolic of a year?

These problems vexed expositors. Then came the upheaval of the French Revolution. To the prophecy-attuned mind, it was nothing less than a sensation. Christians now 'turned to the apocalyptic writings of Scripture, in the hope of making sense of the chaos of their surroundings.'[37] As

37. Stunt, *From Awakening to Secession*, 21.

they witnessed daily events, many students of prophecy were convinced that the events chronicled in the books of Daniel and Revelation were unfolding before their eyes. Consider: Had it not been foretold in Daniel 7: 25 that a Man of Sin—*i.e.*, the Antichrist—would reign for 'a' time, times, and a half'? Was a 'time' not equal to 360 years, and thus three-and-a-half 'times' was 1,260 years? Had not the Pope been recognized as the head of the Church in 533 AD? Had not Rome been liberated from the Goths in 538? And (in the technical jargon of the times) this *terminus a quo* (i.e., the earliest possible date) being granted, was not 1798—*the very year in which Napoleon expelled the Pope from Rome*—precisely 1,260 years after 538 AD?

Coincidence? Could be. Yet these calculations seemed so remarkable as to make that view improbable. The result was that new life was breathed into the historicist school. Attention now passed to the historical fulfillment of the 2,300 year-days of Daniel 8: 14, after which the 'sanctuary shall be cleansed'. Calculators saw signs pointing to 1843-47 as (in their usage) the *terminus ad quem* (i.e., the latest possible date) of this period. A rush of eschatological activity was unleashed. During the first four decades of the nineteenth century, scores of books were written, conferences held, associations formed, and periodicals founded. There was movement away from the postmillennialist outlook (which had been absorbed by Protestants) back to premillennialism. And as the return of the Jews to Palestine and Christ's premillennial advent were, according to the sure word of prophecy, inextricably linked, there was a new desire to see that prophecy fulfilled.

Coincidental with this excitement among historicists was the weakening of their support, from within and from without. In 1826 the futurist interpretation found acceptance among some Protestants, later including J. H. Newman and the Oxford Movement (that attempt to 'unprotestantize the Church of England').[38] Preterism was given a new dignity by rationalist Protestants. Even during historicism's high-water mark, Catholics and Protestants were turning to futurist, preterist,[39] and even postmillennialist alternatives, as a natural defence against, or as an expression of disgust with, the date-fixing of the historicist premillennialists.

38. E. B. Elliott, *Horae Apocalypticae*, IV: 555. The *Horae* was written to refute futurism.
39. By at least 1866, preterism had 'few, if any, adherents in this country' (PHG, *The Revelation: How Is It To Be Interpreted?*, London: Morgan and Chase, 1866, 3).

It is against this backdrop that Gosse's reading of Habershon in June 1842 needs to be placed. At that time, Gosse knew little about the long history of conflicting prophetic exposition. However, through the expositor Scott he gained familiarity with standard historicist positions: the equation of the Little Horn with the papacy, and the belief that the termination of the 2,300 days was not distant. Scott, nonetheless, was a postmillennialist.[40] From Croly, Gosse read how the final catastrophe was at hand, the events of the French Revolution had been foretold, futurism was attempting to penetrate into the Protestant camp and 'Popery' was the corruption of Christianity.[41] And in Pollok, who was also a postmillennialist, he read of the redemption and the true Church.[42]

Thus Gosse's choice: Align with the futurist premillennialist school— which was gaining more and more adherents in Britain—or with the historicist one, which expected the time of the end sometime between 1843 and 1847 (and was, though he could not have known it, at the zenith of its influence)? The timing of the second advent was not an issue to him, because both schools were predominantly premillennialist. The reading of Habershon, with its anti-Catholic bias, likely added justification for a position to which Gosse was already inclined.

Gosse has told us that he knew nothing about Matthew Habershon when he encountered him. Too bad; the author's career would certainly have had its appeal. An architect by profession, Habershon (1789-1852), of Bonner's Hall, near Hackney, worked for the London Society for Promoting Christianity Amongst Jews (LSPCJ, founded in 1809).[43] For him, prophetic studies and architectural work were intertwined in two ways. The first concerned Catholicism. In his prophetic books, Habershon combatted Catholicism as 'anti-scriptural' and a source of 'corruption and impurity'.[44] He also pursued that outlook in his architectural books[45]

---

40. Froom, *Prophetic Faith* III: 347-50; IV: 394-5.

41. Froom, *Prophetic Faith* III: 544-48, 744-5; IV: 129-30.

42. Froom, *Prophetic Faith* IV, 130-33; Robert Pollok, *The Course of Time: A Poem* (1st ed, 1827; 23ed, Edinburgh: William Blackwood and Sons, 1860), Book V, 112- 47.

43. Mark Crinson, 'Victorian architects and the Near East: Studies in colonial architecture, architectural theory and orientalism, 1840-1870' (University of Pennsylvania, PhD dissertation, 1989), 93.

44. Habershon, *An Historical Dissertation on the Prophetic Scriptures* (2nd edition, 1840), 225.

45. Matthew Habershon, *The Ancient Half-Timbered Houses of England* (London: John Weale, 1836), xvii-xxviii; Nikolaus Pevsner, *Some Architectural Writers of the Nineteenth Century* (Oxford: Clarendon Press, 1972), 109.

and projects, in both of which he opposed the Gothic architecture of his contemporary, Augustus Pugin (1812-1852). The Englishman Pugin was a convert to Catholicism, and he used his architectural designs to promote his faith.[46] In addition, for Habershon prophecy and architecture crossed paths concerning teachings about Jews. In Habershon's *Dissertation on the Prophetic Scriptures* (1st edition, 1834)—which he abridged (1835), issued in a second (1840) and apparently third edition (1842), and epitomised (1841)[47]—he predicted (as previously mentioned) that the advent was at hand. One of the required signs heralding the end days was the restoration of Jews to their ancient homeland. Habershon asked: 'When shall this period of wonders take place?'[48] He answered: 1843 or 1844. That happened to precisely synchronize with another required sign of the times: the end of 'Mahometanism and Popery'.[49]

In a brief but unanticipated sequence of events, with a single experience Habershon now combined opposition to Catholicism, belief in an imminent Second Advent, and support for the return of Jews to their homeland. In November 1842—just months after Gosse had read Habershon's *Historical Dissertation*—the LSPCJ sent architect Habershon to the Ottoman Empire-controlled Palestine. His mission: Reverse the plan to build a church in Jerusalem based on *Roman Catholic* design elements and insert an *Anglican* church in its place. A church had first been mooted in 1835, stopped in 1837 (Islamic law prohibited a new church building in Jerusalem), and illegally restarted following the Second Syrian War of 1841 (which resulted in renewed Ottoman control of Palestine). It turned out that the LSPCJ architect working on the church was a Pugin acolyte. He was fired in 1842 and replaced by Habershon. If all went well, the building (which became known as

46. Sam McKinstry and Neil Dickson, 'Elusive Exclusive? John Murray Robertson (1844-1901), Architect, Dundee', *BHR* 18 (2022), 93; Crinson, 'Victorian architects and the Near East', 121.

47. For the later issues of Habershon's book, see the British Library *Catalogue*. The pamphlet entitled *Two Remarkable Signs of the Times* (1842) is described in its subtitle as ... *an Appendix to the Third Edition of 'A Dissertation ...' Lately Published*, but there seems to be no record of this third edition. On Habershon's prophetic views: Froom, *Prophetic Faith* III: 632-9, 744-5; IV: 404-5; 'Habershon, M. Esq.', in [Joshua William Brooks], *A Dictionary of Writers on the Prophecies, with the Titles and Occasional Description of Their Works* (London: Simpkin, Marshall and Co., 1835), xxxvi.

48. Habershon, *Historical Dissertation on the Prophetic Scriptures* (2nd edition, 1840), 112, 85.

49. Habershon, *Historical Dissertation on the Prophetic Scriptures* (2nd edition, 1840), 301-2.

Christ Church) would establish a Protestant presence in Jerusalem. Its purpose: to serve as a centre where Jews returning to Palestine could be converted to Christianity.[50]

No sooner had Habershon arrived in Jerusalem than the project was stopped by the Ottoman authorities in January 1843. Nonetheless, Habershon managed to present his own church plans in place of the previous ones. Habershon's church, the oldest Anglican one in the Middle East,[51] was finally opened in 1849.

Though the day had been saved, Habershon was unable to proceed as planned, and returned from Jerusalem to London. There he met Gosse (who by then was familiar with his *Historical Dissertation*) by no later than July 1843.[52] Gosse found that the two also shared a common religious practice: likely by around that time, Habershon joined Gosse at Brethren meetings in Hackney.[53]

The immediate result of Gosse's reading of Habershon's *Dissertation*, and later contact with him, is that a whole constellation of new ideas was put into his head. Gosse was at once and forever converted to historical premillennialism; he became a warrior against futurism;[54] he focussed on Jewish history; and he was confirmed in his anti-Catholic bias.[55] To the end of his life, the 'subject of Chronology, as bearing on the Hope of the Lord's Appearing,' remained a favourite study with him. Along the way, there were 'many disappointments,' Gosse admitted, 'but I do cling to it.'[56]

With these new principles around which to organize his worldview, Gosse began devoting time to a study of prophecy. Early in the spring of 1843, while still conducting his school in Hackney, he visited the Reading Room of the British Museum on Wednesday and Saturday afternoons to examine works on prophecy. One result was 'The Testimony of Prophecy' (Gosse gave it the Greek title Ἡ Μαρτυρία τῆζ Προφητείαζ), a guide which

50. This paragraph is based on Crinson, 'Victorian architects and the Near East', 98-128.

51. 'Church Missions to Jews', Jerusalem *Palestine Bulletin* (10 Nov. 1926), 3.

52. That July, Habershon was the conduit for a message to PHG from Nadir Baxter (PHG-Nadir Baxter, 22 July 1843, a copy of the letter is in PHG, 'Testimony of Prophecy').

53. PHG-EWG, 1 Mar. 1867 (CUL Add. 7018,3): 'The dear Misses Habershon I knew some 20 years ago; and their dear Father was a very valued friend;—the author of some works on Prophecy. They used to break bread at Hackney, where I first met your own loved Mamma, in 1843.'

54. Among many examples is PHG's critique of the Darbyite dispensationalist William Kelly (1821-1906), of London (PHG, '"The Saints" of the Revelation', *London Monthly Review* II (May 1857), 467-70 and Kelly's reply, pp. 552-3); on Kelly: Sandeen, *Roots of Fundamentalism*, 85.

55. 'Reminiscences', II: 254 (*Life*, 376).

56. PHG-James Pascoe, 5 Mar. 1881 (CUL Add. 7313, 318-19).

he prepared to all scriptural passages on unfulfilled prophecy, cited in full with his commentary, and arranged in chronological order under subject headings.[57] The collection, he hoped, would impress those who doubted or hesitated 'of the number, the force, & the clearness of those illustrious predictions, which have written the history of approaching events, as if with a sunbeam on the sky.'[58] In sketching a scenario of future events as foretold in the Bible, Gosse also gave expression to his hermeneutical principles. The word of God could not be self-contradictory; 'Heaven & earth may pass away, but one jot or one tittle of his words shall in no wise pass away, till all are fulfilled'; the 'plain & literal signification' of words is to be preferred; and

> *in general* nothing more is necessary to understand *the meaning* of the word of God, than that of any other book: viz. acquaintance with the ordinary acceptation of language, a freedom from prepossession, a child-like disposition to receive truth however strange it may seem, & (in proportion to the importance of the subject) a dependence on the Holy Spirit for this assistance in distinguishing truth from error.[59]

From some remarks on 'Synchronology' (the word emerged at the time

57. 'Reminiscences', II: 258-9. PHG cut out relevant passages from two Bibles and pasted them into one manuscript book, later copying out 'The Testimony of Prophecy' in a fair copy into another book. In February 1973, Geoffrey Barrow, of Bromley, Kent, informed me that he possessed what turned out to include the Preface to PHG's proposed work on prophecy. Barrow, who was connected with the antiquarian book trade, had in 1962 retrieved the MS from the London antiquarian book dealer Quaritch's before it was thrown out (Barrow-D. Wertheimer, 18 June; 4 Aug. 1972). Containing material from 1843-50, Barrow kindly lent it to me. This small 4to volume of 95 leaves contains autograph copies of letters, memoranda, and some subsequently published materials, covering 1843 to 5 October 1850. The table of contents is: 'Grant of the Land [Palestine]; Promises of a Termination to the Captivity; Restoration of Israel; Assault of the Nations; Coming of Christ; First Resurrection; Rapture of the Living; Overthrow of Rome; Descent of Christ; The Judgment; Overthrow of the Invading Army; Execution of the Sentence upon the Nations; Punishment of Satan and his Giants; Descent of the New Jerusalem; Restoration of the National Institutions; The Glory and A Visible Glory; National Supremacy of Israel; Establishment of the Kingdom, and Assumption of the Throne; Co-reign of the Saints; Triumphal Odes; Holiness of Israel; Conversion of the Gentiles; General Description of Prosperity; Deliverance of the Animals.'
58. PHG, 'Testimony of Prophecy', Preface.
59. PHG, 'Testimony of Prophecy', 59, 1, 86, and Preface. Emphasis in the original. Futurists and historicists of the early 19th Century shared a literal interpretation of the Bible (Sandeen, *Roots of Fundamentalism*, 5-7, 20-2, and chap. V; and Sandeen, 'Towards a Historical Interpretation of the Origins of Fundamentalism', *Church History* XXXVI (Mar. 1967), 69-70). Historicists felt (unlike Futurists) that there were prophetic utterances which had been (or could be expected to be) fulfilled symbolically.

to describe a combined or comparative secular and religious chronology),[60] we know that Gosse had been fully persuaded by Habershon that the very year in which he was writing—1843—or at most the next, would witness the second coming.[61] Though Gosse felt his prophetic investigations were valuable, he decided against separately publishing the 'Testimony of Prophecy', and left it in manuscript.[62] Instead, he wrote an article on 'The Signs of the Times', in which he presented the evidence for looking for 'the coming of the Lord, at this particular period.'[63] That essay appeared in July 1843 in Charlotte Elizabeth's *Christian Lady's Magazine*,[64] which Gosse considered 'the only Periodical wh[ich] in these times of darkness points to the coming day'.[65] Elizabeth was strongly opposed to 'Popery' and, like Gosse, held premillennialist prophetic views.[66] Besides its religious articles, the *Magazine* included instructive pieces for a middle-class female readership on science, history, and education.[67]

It is possible that Gosse was now being drawn into a small circle of

60. PHG, 'Testimony of Prophecy', 92. The word 'synchronology' was newly in use, with *OED* 2ed. recording the word in 1736 and a second usage a century later by Charles Crosthwaite, *Synchronology: Being a Treatise on the History, Chronology, and Mythology of the Ancient Egyptians, Greeks, and Phoenicians, and the Harmony between the Chronology of those Nations and that of the Holy Scriptures* (Cambridge: University Press, 1839).

61. Habershon believed that the prophetic period of 'seven times' would terminate in 1843, the 391 years in 1844, and the 2,300 year-days in 1843-44. However, the 1,335 years would extend to 1867. Various other expositors looked to 1843-47 as the final date: tables in Froom, *Prophetic Faith* III: 744-5, and esp. IV, 404-5. Apparently in 1844, Habershon gave PHG his *Historical Exposition of the Prophecies of the Revelation of St. John* (2nd ed., 2vols., 1844): 'This also is a work of great value; though, as increasing study made me more critical, I found numerous matters of detail to which exceptions might be taken; and though his confidently anticipated dates were not realized, as, indeed, those of none others are yet; the grand outline of interpretation of Divine prophecy given is beyond dispute' ('Reminiscences', II: 254; *Life*, 376). Early Brethren leader Percy F. Hall (1801-1884) predicted the second advent's occurrence on 19 Mar. 1844 or 'April next', in a lecture in Worcester ('The Pre-Millennial Advent', *Hereford Journal*, 13 Mar. 1844, 4).

62. 'Reminiscences', II: 259.

63. Holograph copy of a letter, PHG-Editor of *The Christian Lady's Magazine* [Charlotte Elizabeth], n.d. [after 13 May 1843, before 1 July 1843] (PHG, 'Testimony of Prophecy').

64. There is an autograph draft in 'Testimony of Prophecy' of PHG's 'The Signs of the Times', *Christian Lady's Magazine* XX (July 1843), 49-57.

65. PHG-Editor of the *Christian Lady's Magazine*, undated [after 13 May and before 1 July 1843].

66. Charlotte Elizabeth Tonna's (1790-1846) Protestant views were well-known and shared by her husband, L. H. J. Tonna, who edited the *Christian Annotator* (for which PHG wrote). 'Popery was to her a hideous reality, not merely a nominal distinction, and, under whatever name it might seek to hide, she unsparingly denounced it' ('Hymnbooks and Hymn-writers', *Wesleyan Times*, 22 Feb. 1864, 123). For Charlotte Tonna's premillennialist outlook: Froom, *Prophetic Faith* III: 640-5.

67. Monica Correa Fryckstedt, 'Charlotte Elizabeth Tonna & *The Christian Lady's Magazine*', *Victorian Periodicals Review* XIV (Summer 1981), 43.

Protestant premillennialist anti-Catholics, of which Habershon and Charlotte Elizabeth were members. Nadir Baxter (d. 1848), a friend of Habershon's, was another. Though details of Baxter's life are sketchy, he was known as the 'Universal Secretary' because of his involvement in a multitude of evangelical organizations.[68] He also promoted the cause of the restoration of the Jews to Palestine;[69] supported the printing press of the Revd A. R. C. Dallas (1791-1869), an Irish anti-Tractarian foe of futurism;[70] and did 'conscientiously believe' that the Oxford Movement was 'the most fatal evil against true Christianity that has yet appeared.'[71] Late in July, Baxter contacted Gosse through Habershon to ask for permission to reissue 'The Signs of the Times' in tract form. A few months later Gosse sent Baxter a new version of the essay, which he felt more artfully presented the material. He told Baxter that he was thinking of publishing it on his own as an eight-page tract. Nothing apparently came of either idea.[72] Meanwhile and more significantly, Gosse was all the while finding a place in another, quite different, circle of friends.

This was the second crucial event in Gosse's *annus mirabilis* of 1843. For some time prior to his reading of Habershon, Gosse had casually known a fellow Methodist, Class-Leader Samuel Berger, Jr., then living in

68. One of the Protestant Party [pseud.], *Random Recollections of Exeter Hall, In 1834-1837* (London: James Nisbet, 1838), 177.

69. The £1,000 which he left in his will 'in evidence of Christian faith towards the political restoration of the Jews to Jerusalem and to their own land' was legally voided (H.S.Q. Henriques, *The Jews and the English Law* (Oxford: University Press, 1908), 25-6).

70. For Dallas: [Mrs A. R. C. Dallas], *Incidents in the Life and Ministry of the Rev. Alex. R. C. Dallas, A.M.* (London: James Nisbet & Co., 1871), 281, 293-4, 298, 308, 316-8; *DEB* I:68-9. On Dallas' historic premillennialism: Spence, *Heaven on Earth*, 84. According to Boyd, *Emily Gosse*, 26, EG came in contact with Dallas when she was about 11-years-old.

71. Baxter died 'in his 55th year' on 23 January 1848 ('Births, Marriages, and Deaths', London *Observer*, 30 Jan. 1848, 8); his dates of birth and death are given imprecisely in *DEB* I: 68-9, where the entry on Robert Dudley Baxter, his father, is helpful. He was connected for a time with the Clapham Sect (Ford K. Brown, *Fathers of the Victorians* (Cambridge: University Press, 1961), 390fn.). From Baxter's fascinating will (Public Record Office, Chancery Lane), we learn that he left £2,000 to 33 evangelical societies; £1,000 to support the Jewish return 'to their own land'; £500 to the Anglican Bishopric in Jerusalem; his MSS on the Jews and prophecy to Habershon; £200 to the Revd A. R. C. Dallas for his printing press (which issued anti-Tractarian works); and £1,000 towards the purchase of an advowson for the son of his cousin, on the condition that the son 'do disavow—*ex animo*—by the grace & teaching of the Holy Spirit the published and known views and doctrines of the Reverend Messieurs Pusey Newman Keble and others of the Oxford Tractarian party'. Baxter's will was contested ('Habershon *v.* Yardon', London *Times*, 11 June 1849, 8).

72. PHG-N. Baxter, 22 July, 21 November 1843, in PHG, 'Testimony of Prophecy' (holograph copies of letters). I have not seen any reference to such a tract in PHG's corpus.

Hackney.[73] His wife, Ann (d. 1852),[74] was already the author of religious materials, including a pamphlet and perhaps some tracts. Sometime after June 1842 the Bergers asked Gosse to assist her in the preparation of a new work.[75] The frequent visits with these amiable and 'earnest believers' led to a deepening friendship. Said Berger one day: 'I wish you could know my brother Will: you would be much interested in each other!' Soon the two met: 'I was charmed with William Thomas Berger: his meekness, his exceeding love and grace—the manifest image of Christ in him—drew to him my whole heart; and then began a mutual esteem and friendship, which no cloud has ever shadowed from that day to this [1888].'[76]

Although Samuel Jr. and William Berger had been born into a wealthy Anglican family in the colour and starch manufacturing business, it was under Samuel Jr.'s influence that his brothers were gradually converted to 'truer' forms of religion (as previously mentioned). Samuel was the first to make the break in deciding to become a Methodist, and gradually he guided his brothers, and then his cousin Capel B. Berger, in that general direction.[77] William Berger had already travelled a considerable distance in the evangelical world when he was introduced to Gosse. By that time, however, he was not a Methodist. When Gosse visited William Berger's home after the latter's marriage in April 1843, he discovered believers in Hackney who were quite unlike any Christians he had ever encountered.[78]

The Hackney group was part of a movement only recognized on the British religious landscape in 1838,[79] though by then it had been

73. 'Berger' and 'Goss' are listed in the 'First London Circuit Wesleyan Methodist Preachers' Plan. [Oct. 6] 1839-[Jan. 12] 1840', where Berger's residence is given as Water Lane, Homerton.

74. 'Died', *Cheltenham Looker-on* (4 Sept. 1852), 13. Ann Berger was 56.

75. *Affection's Tribute*, 127, 141-4; 'Reminiscences', II: 254 (*Life*, 376). I have not been able to identify Ann Berger's writings.

76. 'Reminiscences', II: 254-5 (*Life*, 377).

77. *Affection's Tribute*, 10-12, 47-52, 78.

78. 'Reminiscences', II: 255; and for the date of the visit, Boyd, 'Bibliographical: Philip Henry Gosse, 1810-1888'.

79. In a wonderful insight, Donald Harman Akenson finds 'no profit in looking for a precise starting point' of the Brethren and suggests instead the significance of various moments between 1829-38 'when the proto-Brethren broke out of their chrysalis and became an organized assembly that was visible to outsiders and ... acted in a manner that indicated a continuing institutional existence' (Akenson, *Exporting the Rapture*, 61fn. 10). Akenson considers the Brethren conference at the Gloucester Hotel in Clifton on 3 July 1838 as marking 'a solid date for asserting that the Brethren in the British Isles were extant as a separate, identifiable, and continuing organization' (p. 92). Newspaper reports which I have seen from 1838-9 referencing for the first time 'Plymouth Brethren' buttress Akenson's argument (see *Hereford Times*, 31 Mar. 1838, 4; 14 Apr. 1838, 4; 29 Dec. 1838, 3; 8 June 1839, 2; 'The Plymouth Brethren', *Eclectic Review* n.s. IV (May 1839), 571-90).

growing and shaping its identify for roughly a decade.[80] There is something satisfying in the fact that even today, historians can't agree on a precise start for the movement (the range is from 1825-1838). After all, Brethren never viewed themselves as innovators. On the contrary: while most early figures considered themselves primitivists (that is, they wished to imitate the primitive church but not restore it)[81] and others

80. Neatby's claim that 'The origins of Brethrenism are not perhaps particularly obscure; at all events, the materials for elucidating them are fairly copious' (*History of the Plymouth Brethren*, 3) may have seemed satisfactory in 1901, but not to anyone today. There is still no consensus among historians on assigning a specific founding date to the Brethren, with a range from around 1825 to 1838. Neil Summerton provides a valuable overview: Summerton, *"I thanked the Lord and asked for more": George Müller's Life and Work* (Glasgow: Brethren Archivists and Historians Network, 2022),63-6. Peter L. Embley (one of those who point to a Dublin meeting in November 1829 as the first gathering of Brethren) makes the point that initially the founders did not intend to start a new movement (Embley, 'Origins and Early Development of the Plymouth Brethren' (Cambridge University, PhD dissertation, 1966), 58; Embley, The Early Development of the Plymouth Brethren', in Bryan R. Wilson (ed.), *Patterns of Sectarianism* (London: Heinemann, 1967), 213; this same point is made in 'The Plymouth Brethren', *Church Quarterly Review* VIII (Apr. 1879), 195-6).

FOUNDING IN 1825: Frederick F. Bruce gives the Brethren's founding as 'around the year 1825, although the Brethren commonly insist that their roots are really in the apostolic age' (*Who Are the Brethren?* (London & Glasgow: Pickering & Inglis Ltd, Witness Booklet no.1, 1962), 7); H. A. Ironside 'in Ireland in the year 1825' (*A Historical Sketch of the Brethren Movement* (Grand Rapids, Michigan: Zondervan, 1942), 8); 'The earliest incontrovertible record of any gathering which later became associated with the Brethren dates to 1825' (West, *From Friends to Brethren*, 126).

FOUNDING IN 1826-7: Napoleon Noel in 1826 (Noel, *The History of the Brethren*, ed. by William F. Knapp. (Denver, Colorado: W.F. Knapp, 1936), I: 19); Owen Chadwick 'in Dublin from 1827' (*The Victorian Church* (London: Adam & Charles Black, 1966), Part I: 38fn.1).

FOUNDING IN 1829-31: Among those who point specifically to the 1829 date are (besides Embley) Neil T. R. Dickson (the 'late 1820s', in Dickson, 'History of the Open Brethren', 2) and more recently 'around 1830' (Dickson, 'Hunter Beattie (1876-1951): A Conscientious Objector at the Margins', *Scottish Church History* 50, 2021, 147); and Paul Richard Wilkinson, 'John Nelson Darby and the Origins of Christian Zionism' (University of Manchester, PhD dissertation, 2006), 136. T. C. F. Stunt argues that the 'Plymouth Brethren, as such, really only begin to develop a meaningful identity in late 1831' (Stunt, 'Trinity College, John Darby and the Powerscourt Milieu', in Joshua Searle, Kenneth G.C. Newport (eds.), *Beyond the End: The Future of Millennial Studies* (Sheffield: Sheffield Phoenix Press), 2012, 63).

What follows here is based upon Tim Grass, *Gathering to His Name*; Harold H. Rowdon, *The Origins of the Brethren, 1825-1850* (London: Pickering & Inglis Ltd, 1967); Embley, 'Origins and Early Development' and Embley, 'The Early Development of the Plymouth Brethren', 213-43; F. Roy Coad, *A History of the Brethren Movement. Its Origins, its Worldwide Development and its Significance for the Present Day* (London: Paternoster Press, 1968), and his *Prophetic Developments*, as cited; Neatby, *History of the Plymouth Brethren*; Sandeen's *Roots of Fundamentalism*; 'Brethren, The (or Plymouth Brethren)', *Encyclopaedia Britannica* (Edinburgh: Adam and Charles Black, 8th ed., 1854), V: 316. The explanation of the origins and name of the Brethren in *Life*, 213, is uninformed.

81. James Patrick Callahan, 'Primitivist Piety: The ecclesiology of the early Plymouth Brethren' (Marquette University, PhD dissertation, 1994), 237-56. I am grateful to Neil Dickson

were 'restorationists' (they thought it possible to restore the apostolic Christian church),[82] both agreed that church history had been 'confused, divided, complicated, and corrupt'.[83] The only option was a separation from it and a return to the 'simplicity of Christian union'.[84] Their chosen name—annoyingly indefinite to many yet to themselves a solemn sign of authenticity and Christian unity—reflected their goals. Not this-or-that hyphenated-Christian, just plain 'Christian'. Not partisan Christians of parties and politics, just 'Brethren' devoted to harmony and walking on a common path. What they wanted was to take the Apostolic pattern of life as revealed in the New Testament and use it as a model for Christian life in Victorian Britain. And they were convinced this was necessary because they found the institutionalized religious forms of the day—the use of a formal liturgy, ordained ministry, administrative machinery, and so forth—to be lamentable incrustations that 'quenched the Spirit'. Moreover, although the invisible church was really one, in the earthly world it was palpably divided. To Brethren, Christian communion had to be both pure (*i.e.*, resembling the Apostolic practices) and catholic (*i.e.*, non-sectarian) to be true. These conditions could be met by making adherence to what they considered vital Christian truths the sole criterion for attendance at the Lord's Supper.

Notwithstanding their restorationist goal, the Brethren had not proclaimed this outlook in a vacuum. They had their eighteenth-century British ideological precursors (Glasites, Walkerites,[85] and Kellyites). Historically, their context lay not with these groups but with the religious radicals of the 1830s who seceded from the British religious establishment. The Irvingites and Oxford Tractarians, like the

---

for bringing this work (in its 1996 published form) to my attention.

82. The label is Louis Billington's: 'The Churches of Christ in Britain: A Study in Nineteenth-Century Sectarianism', *Journal of Religious History* VIII (June 1974), 21; for the same idea, David J. Beattie, *Brethren: The Story of a Great Recovery* (Kilmarnock: John Ritchie Ltd., [1939]), 5. Bryan Wilson uses the term 'introversionist' to define the 'Exclusive' Brethren's attitude to the question of personal salvation, but he does not categorize the Open Brethren, with whom PHG was aligned. They would, however, probably be considered 'conversionists'. See Wilson's *Religious Sects. A Sociological Study* (London: Weidenfeld and Nicolson, 1970), 36-41; Wilson, *Patterns of Sectarianism*, 22-45; and the informative review of the latter by T. C. F. Stunt, *CBRF Journal* no. 19 (1969), 35-9.

83. Callahan, 'Primitivist Piety', 73.

84. Callahan, 'Primitivist Piety', 74 and chap. 3.

85. T. C. F. Stunt has effectively questioned the long-held claim that John Walker (1768-1833) and his followers were precursors, or a subsection, of the Brethren (Stunt, 'Trinity College, John Darby and the Powerscourt Milieu', 50-53).

founders of the Brethren, shared a revulsion against what they viewed as the degeneracy of the Established religious order. To look ahead they needed to look back, with the New Testament as their model. These ingredients—together with a deep concern with the study of prophecy and an emphasis on the personal and experimental nature of Christian belief—resulted in a Brethren perspective unique in its time not for its doctrine but for its practice.

It was to Dublin in the 1820s that Brethrenism traced its immediate origins. Here, three small independent meetings took place, consisting of dissatisfied Dissenters, Churchmen, or a mixture of the two. The main emphasis was on the preference for invertebrate ecclesiastical organization, while neither an ordained ministry nor a formal liturgy were deemed requisites for Christian practice. In these early days, a clergyman of the Church of Ireland, John Nelson Darby (1800-1882), joined the embryonic movement and became one of its best-known, most creative, most hard-driving and prickly leaders.

From Ireland the Brethren expanded to three foci in south-west England. The first and largest of these began at Plymouth around 1831 and provided the group with its popular (though misleading) moniker 'Plymouth Brethren'.[86] Under the leadership of Benjamin Wills Newton (1807-1899), and with the assistance of Darby and his stalwart, George Vicesimus Wigram (1807-1879), and others, the meeting soon prospered. A little later, assemblies were begun at Bristol and Barnstaple, both of which were influenced by the Dissenting character of the leading figures there.

As the Brethren expanded, their chief characteristics—which outsiders frequently decried as amorphous—became evident. In their early years, as one historian has put it, Brethren 'had no agreed creed' and their 'one organizational premise was that the Brethren were not an organization.'[87] Yet one can deduce tendencies, and from those tendencies characteristics which helped to define who they intended to be. In eschewing a central organisation, an influential role was left for leading personalities in the

86. 'In the first place, the little that is popularly known, or supposed to be known about them, turns out on inquiry to be quite wrong, and the very name a misnomer ... The title appears to have originated in an idea that the sect originated in Plymouth, whereas the principal source was near Dublin' (Charles Maurice Davies, 'The Plymouth Brethren', in C. M. Davies, *Unorthodox London: or Phases of Religious Life in the Metropolis* (London: Tinsley Brothers, 2nd ed., 1874), 175-6). The nomenclature is succinctly examined in Akenson, *Exporting the Rapture*, 29-30.

87. Akenson, *Exporting the Rapture*, 95; Grass, *Gathering to His Name*, 3.

various assemblies. These personalities—predominantly aristocratic in background—had come from the Established Church, Dissent, and the Society of Friends (Quakers). They were individuals unhappy with the status quo. During the first two decades, the movement was given cohesion—in Britain and overseas—by the itinerant ministry of Darby.[88]

Other aspects of the Brethren world-view were related to the concern with prophecy. It has been said that 'Brethrenism is the child of the study of unfulfilled prophecy, and of the expectation of the immediate return of the Saviour.'[89] Historians consider this an exaggeration, though not without a core of truth.[90] Certainly the Powerscourt Conferences for the study of biblical prophecy, which took place in Ireland between 1831-36 and were attended by many early Brethren, were an important stimulus for the progress of the movement.[91] It was here that the conflicting views of Darby and Newton on the subject were first evident, and that Darby adopted futurist views, and the Brethren as a whole, premillennialism.[92] This premillennialist perspective, which involved the belief in an 'any moment' advent, made many Brethren (especially Darby and his followers) pessimistic in their attitude towards political or social change, and inhibited their involvement in the secular world. Simultaneously, it provided a motivation for spreading the word: no time could be wasted in bringing souls to salvation since the Lord's coming was at hand. The Brethren revival, occurring during a period of increasing speculation about the end of days, was prone to being influenced by these ideas.

When Gosse became aware of the existence of the Brethren, they numbered about 6,000.[93] Not a great deal is known about the London-area assemblies, but at least three of them (and likely more) had been founded by 1838. The meeting at Rawstorne Street in Camden Town, apparently initiated by Wigram, was one of the first in London, perhaps

88. Embley, 'Origins and Early Development', 104; for an example of Darby's overseas influence, Wertheimer, 'The Truth About 1843', 38, 43-44, 55-6.

89. Neatby, *History of Plymouth Brethren*, 339, 38.

90. Embley, 'Origins and Early Development', 94; Coad, *Prophetic Developments*, 19; on the place of prophecy in general, Rowdon, *Origins*, 50, 301-2.

91. On the Conferences: Grass, *Gathering to His Name*, 26-29; Rowdon, *Origins*, 86-96; Coad, *Brethren Movement*, 108-10; Sandeen, *Roots*, 34-38; Froom, *Prophetic Faith* IV: 1223-4; Burnham, 'The Controversial Relationship Between Benjamin Wills Newton and John Nelson Darby', 121-139.

92. On prophecy as the basis of the Newton-Darby split: Sandeen, *Roots*, 30-40, 61-9; Rowdon, *Origins*, 231ff, and 252fn. 5; Coad, *Brethren Movement*, 129-36; Embley, 'Origins and Early Development', 156-66, does not emphasize this factor.

93. Embley, 'Origins and Early Development', 156.

dating to 1833.[94] John Eliot Howard (1807-1883), the ex-Quaker quinologist, had founded another, which he transferred to Brook Street, Tottenham, in 1838 (by 1842 there were eighty-eight people in communion). An assembly in Little Portland Street, near Oxford Circus, began functioning in 1836.[95]

There is uncertainty about when the Hackney group began and its precise links with the other assemblies in London or elsewhere in 1843. That its members were aware of the other meetings in London is certain; that they were aware of Brethren activity in the colonies is also certain;[96] that there was a connection with the Devonshire groups seems likely (it came through William Berger, who at least by 1846 appears to have known Newton).[97]

Philip Gosse's introduction to the Brethren was thus the result of two fortuitous events in 1843: his reading of Habershon on prophecy, and his friendship with Samuel, Jr. (and then William) Berger. The important place which prophecy occupied in Brethren thought made the former a sound preparation for 'the perception, and then reception, of what are known as "Brethren's principles." And this,' as Gosse later wrote, 'though there was no definite or sensible connection between the two movements in my mind.'[98]

What, then, was the profile of these Brethren from Hackney, with whom Gosse met at his first Scripture reading in the summer of 1843? Though much remains unknown about their backgrounds, in a number of ways they were typical of those attracted to Brethrenism in its early years.[99] The ten for whom we have biographical data averaged 29 years of

94. Occasionally newspapers described the 'Rawston Street meeting-house, near the City Road' ('Plymouth Brethren', Dundee *Courier and Argus*, 5 Nov. 1844, 1).

95. Gerald West, 'The Early Development of Brethren Assemblies in London', *Christian Brethren Review* no. 41 (1990), 69-70; Grass, *Gathering to His Name*, 53-4; Rowdon, *Origins*, 161-3; Coad, *Brethren Movement*, 74-6 (on p. 304, Wigram is said to have started a 'church in London' by about 1833, see G. West, 'Early Developments', 68).

96. While PHG was in Jamaica (1844-46), he corresponded with W. T. Berger and Mary Berger (his wife), and George Pearse, though what they wrote remains unknown: Wertheimer, 'The Truth About 1843', 15-63.

97. Rowdon, *Origins*, 249, 256fn.109.

98. 'Reminiscences', II: 254 (*Life*, 376); PHG-Rev. W. E. Jellicoe, 5 Apr. 1881 (CUL Add. 7313, 332).

99. D. W. Bebbington, 'The Place of the Brethren Movement in International Evangelicalism', in Neil T. R. Dickson and Tim Grass (eds.), *The Growth of the Brethren Movement: National and International Experiences. Essays in Honour of Harold H. Rowdon* (Bletchley, Milton Keynes: Paternoster, 2006), 251.

age.[100] They were learned: they knew their Greek and could mine the Bible they revered by consulting it in that language. On the other hand, unlike Brethren leaders in several other assemblies, they were not products of the university,[101] wealthy (with the exception of William Berger, a businessman),[102] or of high social rank.[103] A mixture of former Anglicans with, probably, a preponderance of those of Dissenting origin, they resembled in their religious backgrounds more the Brethren leadership in Bristol and Barnstaple than that in Dublin or Plymouth. Like the former group, they also emphasized mission work along with prophetic study.[104] And in practice they adhered to the idea of 'liberty of ministry,' allowing the 'energy of the Holy Spirit' to guide their free discussions—just as they understood had been the case in New Testament times.[105]

The discovery of the group at Hackney, with whom forty to fifty others met at Ellis' Room in London every Lord's Day to 'break bread',[106] led Gosse to an acquaintance with other Brethren. That included Charles Frearson Hargrove (1792-1869), who had joined the movement in 1835.[107] In supporting limitations on 'liberty of ministry', Hargrove's position

100. Approximate ages of Hackney members in 1843: C. B. Berger, 35; Mary Berger, 29; W.T. Berger, 29; PHG, 33; Pearse, 28; James Van Sommer, 21. Average age: 29.

101. Grass, *Gathering to His Name*, 62.

102. C.B. Berger and G. Pearse then had clerical-type positions, PHG was an educator and Van Sommer was a law student.

103. Grass, *Gathering to His Name*, 86-8; Embley, *Origins*, 100.

104. T. C. F. Stunt, 'James Van Sommer'; Coad, *Brethren Movement*, 155; Neatby, *History of Plymouth Brethren*, 330.

105. 'Reminiscences', II: 255-7 (*Life*, 377-8).

106. 'The term 'Breaking of Bread' came into general use among the Brethren, and the unusual term serves to draw attention to the distinctive character of its celebration' (Rowdon, *Origins*, 299fn.190). For example, PHG-Hannah Gosse [his mother], 29 Dec. 1844 (LeBL): 'Mr Coleman who when I arrived was lying at the very point of death, has been very graciously restored so as to break bread with us today [Dec. 29].' It was distinctive enough as a synonym for a communion service not involving ordained clergy to be worthy of comment by observers ([Caroline Frances Cornwallis (ed.)], *Christian Sects in the Nineteenth Century in a Series of Letters to a Lady* (London: William Pickering, 1846), 85). The term had occasionally been used earlier by Baptists (Thomas Armitage, *A History of the Baptists; Traced by their Vital Principles and Practices, from the Time of our Lord and Saviour Jesus Christ to the Present* (New York: Bryan, Taylor & Co., revised, 1890), 381, 697, 753). The only 19th Century usage of the phrase cited in the *OED* (3ed., Mar. 2022, Phrases P1) has nothing to do with Brethren.

107. Hargrove 'was one of the very first that I knew among "brethren" in 1843, & I always greatly valued his searching ministry, & loved his person' (PHG-EWG, 8 February 1869, CUL Add. 7041, 23); Neatby, *History of Plymouth Brethren*, 116 fn.1; and Embley, in *Patterns of Sectarianism*, 222-3. It is not clear where PHG met him; in the late 1840s, Hargrove led an assembly in Gower Street (Rowdon, *Origins*, 163).

drew the ire of J. N. Darby.[108] Matthew Habershon,[109] as mentioned, entered into fellowship at Hackney, and probably also in 1843, Gosse met John B. Bateman (the printer and publisher), and John and Robert Howard, of the Tottenham assembly. At least by early December (after Gosse had moved to a new residence, No. 73, Gloucester Place, in Kentish Town),[110] Gosse attended a Brethren meeting in Camden Town. This was certainly the one at Rawstorne Street. Here his father Thomas (who now lived with Philip and his mother) also broke bread.[111] It appears to have been at Rawstorne Street that Gosse met Darby and Wigram.[112] Another person whom Gosse encountered among the Brethren at Hackney, a 37-old blue-stocking and apparently a relative of the Loddiges, was Emily Bowes. They would marry five years later.[113]

Shortly after Gosse had aligned himself with the Brethren he terminated his association with the Methodists.[114] This break with his past was not, however, followed by a repudiation of his scientific interests. While the pursuit of several purely mundane professions, especially those regarded as of a 'worldly' nature, were frowned upon by many Brethren, the study of nature—as science in general—was not proscribed.[115] How could it be? In mid-Victorian England, the pious researcher found God in his Book as well as in his created work.

So while Gosse was reading prophetic texts, and absorbing Brethren ideas, he was simultaneously continuing his natural history studies. The visits to the British Museum in the spring of 1843 were not confined to an examination of the testimony of prophecy in the Reading Room. Through his influential cousin Thomas Bell, and on the recommendation of Van

108. Neatby, *History of Plymouth Brethren*, 116fn.1; he did not otherwise side with Darby (Grass, *Gathering to His Name*, 82).

109. PHG-EWG, 1 Mar. 1867 (CUL Add. 7018, 3).

110. For the move to Kentish Town: PHG-Nadir Baxter, 21 November 1843 (PHG, 'Testimony of Prophecy').

111. Thomas Gosse: PHG's postscript to TG's 'Memoirs'.

112. For Bateman, the Howards, Darby, and Wigram: PHG-Rev. W. E. Jellicoe, 5 Apr. 1881 (Add. 7313, 332). Darby is known to have visited Rawstorne Street in August 1843 (Rowdon, *Origins*, 162; Coad, *Brethren Movement*, 89).

113. PHG-EWG, 1 Mar. 1867 (CUL Add. 7018, 3), and PHG-William Gosse, 21 October 1848 (CUL Adv. c. 82.5, 29): '... for the past seven or eight years [Emily had been] in communion with us who break bread simply at Hackney.' For the suggestion about the Bowes' relationship to the Loddigeses: William R. Power-Philip H. G. Gosse, 29 December 1928 (CUL Add. 7032, 109).

114. 'Reminiscences', II: 257, reads: 'It was not long before I formally severed my connection with the Wesleyan Society'. This was changed in *Life*, 378 to: 'I had already formally severed my connection ...' [by 1847]; but see also *Life*, 169.

115. Neatby, *History of Plymouth Brethren*, 271; *Life*, 214.

Voorst, the Society for Promoting Christian Knowledge had offered in February to publish an introductory zoology text by Gosse.[116] Not knowing enough general zoology, Gosse hesitated to undertake the task, 'but my cousin was encouraging ... & I entered upon it with zeal, pursuing it with much zest and interest.'[117]

Perhaps it was as a result of his friendship with the entomologist Adam White that Gosse began to visit at this time as well the Museum's Insect Room. Here in Bloomsbury he became acquainted with a group of men quite different from those at Hackney. Somewhat older than his Brethren friends (their average age was 35), the brothers John E. Gray and George R. Gray (the former Keeper of the Zoological Department at the British Museum, the latter a zoologist), the zoologist William Baird (known for sharing his expertise with others),[118] and the entomologists Edward Doubleday, J. O. Westwood, and White, had all done taxonomic work, in addition to other research. And a number of them adhered to the natural theology tradition with which Gosse was in full sympathy.

The contact with these men of science brought Gosse to the attention of others. Edward Newman (1801-1876), the editor of *The Entomologist* (and later other natural history publications),[119] he had apparently known since the appearance of Newman's review of the *Canadian Naturalist* in that publication in 1841. He was also acquainted with W. W. Saunders, FLS (1809-1879), the former President of the Entomological Society; J. S. Bowerbank, FRS (1797-1877), the microscopist and authority on sponges, who was known for his helpfulness to young naturalists and whom Gosse considered the highest authority 'for aught that concerns marine zoology';[120] J. W. Whymper (1813-1903), the wood-engraver who had worked on illustrations for Gosse's early books; and probably David W. Mitchell, FLS (1813-1859), who had provided the plates for George Gray's *Genera of Birds* (1844). And Edward Doubleday, with whom Gosse had entomologized in Epping Forest, soon introduced him

116. Freeman & Wertheimer-PHG, 21.
117. 'Reminiscences', II: 258.
118. Obituary, 'Dr. Baird', *Athenaeum*, 3 Feb. 1872, 148.
119. Susan Sheets-Pyenson, 'Low Scientific Culture in London and Paris, 1820-1875' (University of Pennsylvania, PhD dissertation, 1976), 208-210; Matthew Wale, '"The Sympathy of a Crowd": Periodicals and the Practices of Natural History in Nineteenth-Century Britain' (University of Leicester, PhD dissertation, 2018), 38-9.
120. PHG, *Tenby*, 2.

to Hugh Cuming (1791-1865), the shell collector and dealer, and to Sir William Jackson Hooker (1785-1865), the Director of Kew Gardens.[121]

-III-

All the while Gosse's third occupation—as a school master—was becoming increasingly tenuous. By the end of 1843 attendance at the Academy had declined from fifteen pupils the year before to only six.[122] The opportunity to write *An Introduction to Zoology* (2 vols., 1844) for the SPCK and get paid £170.10s. for it and the drawings he supplied,[123] encouraged Gosse to take another momentous step in his life. In December 1843, 'I at length determined to give up my school, & to look to literature for a livelihood.'[124]

There were immediate indications that the momentous decision was a wise one, and Gosse entered into it with his usual energy. Between the end of February and the autumn of 1844, he published four entomological articles based on his Alabamian researches in Newman's *Zoologist*, and remunerative engagements followed. In May, he submitted a proposal to the SPCK for a work on *The Ocean*, which was accepted two months later (that added £120 to his pocket). Sometime before November, he completed a Christmas annual for children, entitled *Glimpses of the Wonderful*.[125]

These three works—the *Introduction to Zoology* (2 vols., 1844), *The Ocean* (1845), and *Glimpses of the Wonderful* (1845), together with his serial writings and the *Canadian Naturalist*—gained Gosse modest attention in the scientific world. And this, in spite of the fact that, with

121. All of the above, except Mitchell, have *DNB* entries. For Bowerbank, Cuming, J. D. Hooker, W. J. Hooker, see Lovell Reeve (ed.), *Portraits of Men of Eminence in Literature, Science, and Art, with Biographical Memoirs* (London: Lovell Reeve & Co., 1863-4), vols. I-II; for Mitchell: Boase II: 902, and for Bowerbank: Lloyd C. Sanders (ed.), *Celebrities of the Century* (London: Cassell & Co., revised ed., 1890), 161. For PHG's friendship with these naturalists: *Life*, 167-8, 171-3, 178, 211, 223, 244; Saunders and Bowerbank are mentioned in PHG, 'Testimony of Prophecy', and PHG's 'Jamaica Journal' records letters from Whymper (12 July 1845) and 'Mitchell' (2 August 1845).

122. 'Reminiscences', II: 257 (*Life*, 169, incorrectly gives 8 as the number of students); 'Jamaica Journal', Preface.

123. Freeman & Wertheimer-PHG, 21. *Life*, 170, does not mention payment for the drawings.

124. 'Reminiscences', II: 259.

125. Freeman & Wertheimer-PHG, 20-5. PHG's name did not appear on the book's title page, and as a consequence Freeman & Wertheimer-PHG referred to *Glimpses of the Wonderful* as an anonymous work (p. 25). Strictly speaking that is correct, but *Glimpses* is described as 'edited by P. H. Gosse, square, 5s. cl. gilt' in a 'List of New Books' in *The Athenaeum*, 2 Nov. 1844, 999. The copy of this work at Cambridge is inscribed in PHG's holograph to his brother William, undated; the copy seen in the Family Collection is inscribed PHG-EG, 1 Nov. 1848.

the exception of the articles and the *Canadian Naturalist*, they were not original contributions to knowledge, nor were they noticed in the British press.[126] The *Introduction to Zoology* bore the defects which the author recognized, including some embarrassing inaccuracies.[127] *The Ocean* included personal experiences and illustrations by Gosse and was among the most successful books he ever wrote. Popular and well-received in England and America,[128] like his *Introduction* it was derivative. *Glimpses of the Wonderful*—that is, of the wonders of man and of God—expresses Gosse's belief in the unification and harmonization of science and religion. The world, he observed, contains examples of great human achievements, 'but if these excite our wonder, how much more wonderful, beyond our utmost thought, is the power and wisdom of God!' All of God's works are perfect; all have a use, though through ignorance we may not immediately perceive it; the warfare present in nature is the result of man's sin, through which 'death came into the world'; we should praise the Creator whose works we study; and the most astonishing wonder of all, the wonder of wonders, is that 'the great and glorious God ... so loved poor wretched sinners, as to give His beloved Son for them!' And God, finally, should be properly worshipped by 'drawing near to him in heart, through the blood of his dear Son; and this can be done as well in a barn, or in the field, or in the street, as in the finest house. I speak of this because it is important: it is of little value to know all science and learning if you have mistaken thoughts of God, and of what is real and true worship.'[129]

Even with their shortcomings, Gosse's first scientific books showed promise. They were the results of a totally self-taught man of science who had experience in the field in Newfoundland, Canada, and Alabama. His scientific friends noted his fluent and pleasant writing style, his accuracy as an observer, his unusual abilities as an illustrator, and his reverent

126. The exception to this is *Glimpses of the Wonderful*, which was given slight if favourable notice by *The Athenaeum*, 14 Feb. 1846, 173; *Nonconformist*, 2 Dec. 1846, 809; and the *Literary Gazette*, 12 Dec. 1846, 1048.

127. Freeman & Wertheimer-PHG, 20-1.

128. PHG's *Ocean* was still available from the SPCK in 1902 (Supplement to *Nature*, 4 Sept. 1902, iv), and in the USA (where it appeared under the imprint of at least five publishers) until at least 1874 (reviewed in *Lutheran Observer*, 10 July 1874, 5, under the title *Wonders of the Great Deep*). Freeman & Wertheimer-PHG, 22-25, gives the latest dated edition as 1874.

129. [P. H. Gosse], *Christmas Annual. Glimpses of the Wonderful* (London: Harvey and Darton, 1845), 26 (and for the other quotations, 26, 69-70, 90-91, 109-110, 126, 156).

stance. Having now gained book knowledge in London, it was time for him to move to the next level.

That was the thought of his friend, Edward Doubleday, early in 1844. 'Gosse, you would do well as an insect collector in the Tropics,' he said. First to be considered was Demerara (part of present-day Guyana in South America), but then Jamaica was chosen. Little was known about the natural history of what was (after Cuba and Hispaniola) the third largest of the Caribbean islands, in spite of the few treatises written on it and the not infrequent visits there by Europeans.[130] To set Jamaica in context for English readers, one writer described it as about forty miles wide and 150 long—considerably smaller than the county of Yorkshire.[131] Nonetheless Gosse felt it was a great idea, and 'eagerly jumped at the proposal'. He began to read up on Jamaica, and to compile a list of objects to collect (among them orchids, butterflies, and hummingbirds). Soon he was packing his chests and trunks with the requisites of the naturalist: his Cuvier, dredge, towing net, traps, iron tools, nails and hooks, pressboards, bottles, pens and paper, cord, blacking, awls, scissors, and (for the sun and heat) hat and umbrella. Bibles and tracts were included.[132]

Everyone who knows about Gosse is aware that he went on a natural history mission to Jamaica. We have only learned recently, however—over 130 years after the first description of Gosse's time there—that he was on a spiritual one as well, the continuation of his encounter with Brethren in Hackney in 1843. Even though he was never a missionary, Gosse had been imbued with Brethren ideas and was about to spread them across the globe. His plan was to connect with John Coleman in Jamaica, the first-ever Brethren member on the island, while remaining in contact with his Brethren friends back home.[133]

---

130. PHG, 'Jamaica Journal', Preface; 'Reminiscences', II: 260; *AMNH* ser. 2, IX (Jan. 1852), 50.

131. Review of *Birds of Jamaica*, in London *Eclectic Review* n.s. XXII (Oct. 1847), 399.

132. For PHG's reading and a detailed inventory of the contents of his containers: PHG, 'Testimony of Prophecy'. Works consulted at his home included: Edward Long's *History of Jamaica* (3vols., 1774); Thomas Dancer, *Medical Assistant, or Jamaica Practice of Physic* (1801); James Macfadyen, *Flora of Jamaica* (vol. 1, 1837); Charles Lucien Bonaparte's *Ornithology*; Thomas Gage, *The English American, His Travail by Sea and Land* (1648); and 'Audubon' (*viz.*, Audubon) and others.

133. As previously noted, EWG wreaked havoc with his father's biography when, in *Life*, he contradicted his recollection that he had first associated with Brethren in 1843, *before* he left for Jamaica. Instead, EWG asserted that the encounter did not occur until 1847, the year *after* PHG returned from Jamaica. The longstanding chronology dispute was finally settled by D. Wertheimer, 'The Truth About 1843', 15-63. Every study written prior to that article which chronicles PHG's life from 1843-6 is either inaccurate, incomplete, or both.

On October 18, 1844, with £50 in hand, Gosse joined the ship *Caroline* at Gravesend, and headed for Jamaica two days later.[134] The thirty-four-year-old had already agreed to send the occasional article to Edward Newman, editor of the *Entomologist* and *Zoologist* (two publications which he had founded and recently combined).[135] In the autumn, Gosse settled his parents at No. 37, The Oval, Hackney Road. And now he looked forward to an adventure in Jamaica—the land 'abounding in springs'[136]— which 'appeared delightful.'[137]

-IV-

One of the characteristics of his time, Gosse mused, was that it was 'an age of rapid and universal travelling.'[138] Travel, with its uncertainty and insecurity, was appealing to him. There was the excitement generated by that 'romance of the unknown' which is 'One of the greatest pleasures of the out-of-door naturalist ... He makes his excursions not knowing what he may meet with; and, if disappointed of what he had pictured to himself, he is pretty sure to be surprised with something or other of interest that he had not anticipated.'[139] In viewing his journeys this way, reward had followed risk when Gosse went to Newfoundland in 1827, Canada in 1835, and Alabama in 1838. He had experienced religious tension in one, political discontent in another, and a racial divide in a third. Having arrived after the emancipation of slaves in Jamaica, the 'Queen of the Antilles',[140] for the first time in his life outside of England, he was in a land largely free from strife. Still, he had little idea of what he would find, no committed subscribers to buy what he collected,[141] not even a pre-selected base of operations.

134. PHG, *Naturalist's Sojourn in Jamaica*, 1.

135. *Zoologist* V (1847), 1808.

136. Thus the derivation of the name 'Jamaica' in Richard Hill, *A Week at Port-Royal* (Montego-Bay: Cornwall Chronicle Office, 1855), 17.

137. 'Reminiscences', II: 260; PHG, 'Jamaica Journal', Preface; *Zoologist* V (1847), 1808; T. Gosse [the father]-William Gosse, 4 Nov. 1844 (CUL Adv. c. 82.5, 17); and PHG's postscript to TG's 'Memoirs'.

138. PHG, 'The Signs of the Times', *Christian Lady's Magazine*, 56.

139. PHG, *Romance of Natural History* (1860), 271 *et seq*; PHG, 'A Day in the Woods of Jamaica', *Good Words* III (Apr. 1862), 235; PHG, *The Aquarium* (London: John Van Voorst, 1854), 129; PHG, *A Naturalist's Sojourn in Jamaica* (London: Longman, Brown, Green, and Longmans, 1851), 49-50.

140. [Walter Hark and Augustus Westphal], *The Breaking of the Dawn: Or, Moravian Work in Jamaica 1754-1904* (Belfast: Wm. Strain & Sons, [1904]), 1.

141. In *DNB* XXII: 258, EWG incorrectly states that PHG was commissioned as a collector

The general spirit of Gosse's Jamaica venture thus evokes comparison with his North American ones. The outbound voyage was also reminiscent of previous Atlantic crossings, only now the impact of Brethren ideas, and new scientific knowledge, is evident. A contemporary of Gosse's who headed across the ocean for the West Indies reported that the trip 'does not afford many incidents'.[142] So true for one inattentive to life's opportunities, so untrue for one attuned to the creation around him who reaches out to others to accompany him on the path to salvation.

On the ship to Newfoundland, Gosse had brought with him Bickersteth's *Scripture Help*, the popular evangelical reading guide. Now he studied with 'great edification' *On Worship: Or, Jewish and Christian Worship Contrasted*, by the early Brethren leader J. L. Harris (1793-1877).[143] The private Bible readings done on the way to Newfoundland, or the simple preaching of Christ on the return from Alabama, were replaced by more pointed exercises. At every turn, Gosse communicated the outlook and language of the Brethren.

Brethren opposed a human priesthood[144]—Gosse spent most of one morning talking with fellow travellers, including Gustavus Henry Plessing (d. 1863),[145] a German missionary for the Church of the United

by the British Museum. He went on his own responsibility (PHG-W. W. Saunders, 8 Aug. 1846 in PHG, 'Testimony of Prophecy').

142. Edward Bean Underhill, *The West Indies: Their Social and Religious Condition* (London: Jackson, Walford, and Hodder, 1862), 3.

143. PHG, 'Jamaica Journal', 20 Oct, 16 Dec. 1844. PHG may not have known that 'J. L. H.'—that is how he identifies the author of *On Worship* in 'Jamaica Journal'—was Harris. Harris's book is not listed under his name in the British Museum *Catalogue*, but there is a copy of J. L. H[arris]., *On Worship: Or, Jewish and Christian Worship Contrasted* (London: W. H. Broom, n.d.) at the British Library with an accession date of 30 July 1870. The book appears to have first been published by W. H. Broom in 1844 (Broom issued Brethren works: Ehlert, *Brethren Writers*, 74). *On Worship* is cited as by Harris in Pickering, *Chief Men Among the Brethren*, 2ed., 19. PHG and Harris were speakers at Freemasons' Hall in London in 1864, and the two corresponded in the 1870s and later (Corr. Bk.). On Harris: *DEB* I: 523. Though initially a follower of Darby, it appears that Harris later associated with Open Brethren (T. C. F. Stunt, 'New Source Materials for the Open Brethren in the 1850s', *BHR* 18 (2022), 64).

144. Thus PHG's reference to praying 'without "administration"' ('Jamaica Journal' 5 July [1845]). During the 'mid-1830s, open communion and liberty of ministry had become unmistakable elements in the [Plymouth] Brethren's rallying cry' (Timothy C. F. Stunt, 'From Wandsworth to British Guiana: The Strong Family Saga', in T.C.F. Stunt, *The Elusive Quest of the Spiritual Malcontent. Some Early Nineteenth-Century Ecclesiastical Mavericks* (Eugene, OR: Wipf & Stock, 2015), 192; Bruce, *Who Are the Brethren?*, 7). In the view of the Bridgetown, Barbados *Times* (6 Sept. 1873), 3, distinctive characteristics of Brethren were that they were 'a quiet and growing, though unobtrusive sect. They are self-supporting, recognize no human priest, and receive no money from the state'.

145. *Periodical Accounts Relating to the Missions of the Church of the United Brethren,*

Brethren (known as Moravian Brethren), on the impropriety of a formal ministry (Moravians maintained a Church liturgy and ordered ministry—bishops, presbyters, deacons).[146] He even chastised the ship's captain, William Deane,[147] for 'making himself a Priest' when, on a Sunday, he read the liturgy. Brethren emphasized the importance of the atoning 'Blood of Jesus'[148] as proclaimed in the Gospel of John (1 John 1: 7) and promoted the acceptance of the 'Free Gift' of salvation,[149] ideas which Gosse put before those he met. Gosse's vocabulary reflected the Brethren outlook. In his journal, he used keywords such as 'Saints'[150] (i.e., fellow Brethren), 'breaking bread' (holding a weekly Lord's-Day Communion service) and the honorifics 'Brother' or 'Sister'.[151] Gosse also spoke of widely accepted evangelical principles. He called passengers to recognize 'the worthlessness & even abomination of outward worship, while the heart is not reconciled to God' and of the resurrection, 'the grand truth of the Gospel'. He scolded crew members about their use of 'blasphemous & filthy conversation'. He admitted to making little progress in that area, but he did have his successes. A carpenter, listening to Gosse's appeal, subsequently declared that 'the few poor words just spoken had made

Established Among the Heathen (London: For the Brethren's Society, XVII, 1844), 146 [hereafter *Periodical Accounts*]. On Plessing: Wertheimer, 'The Truth About 1843', 24fn.83.

146. Augustus C. Thompson, *Moravian Missions* (London: Hodder and Stoughton, 1883), 8-17; J. E. Hutton, 'Moravian Brethren', *Encyclopaedia Britannica* (11ed., 1911), XVIII: 818-19; Bryan Wilson labels the Moravians a 'conversionist' sect (like the Open Brethren, see Wilson, *Religious Sects*, 93).

147. PHG gives his name as 'W. Deane' in 'Jamaica Journal'. In 1850, 'William Deane' (presumably the same person) commanded the Apolline, which sailed from Jamaica to London (Montego Bay, Jamaica *Cornwall Chronicle and County Gazette*, 11 Jan. 1850, 7).

148. 'The two cardinal points of Plymouth Brethren belief were, firstly, that the saving blood of Jesus was the only means of access to Heaven; good works, charity, humility and cheerfulness got no one anywhere without it; so that it followed automatically that these virtues were thought little of by those who *were* saved; and, secondly, that the Scriptures should be followed implicitly and exclusively' (Patricia Beer, *Mrs Beer's House* (London: Macmillan, 1968), 9). Beer's comment draws attention to the importance of this doctrine for Brethren (though it was not distinctive to them as evangelicals), yet in so doing she misstates the general attitude of Brethren to good works. They were valued but not as an end to salvation. For a succinct statement: EG, 'The Pilgrim to St. Patrick's Well', in PHG and EG, *Narrative Tracts*, tract no. 31. This leaflet was published between Nov. 1855-Dec. 1856: Freeman & Wertheimer-EG, 54).

149. The concept of a 'free gift' featured frequently in EG's tracts: EG, *The Young Guardsman of the Alma* (GT7); *The Consumptive Deathbed* (GT17); *Is Christ Willing?* (GT18); *The Dying Postman* (GT39); *The Cure for Cholera* (GT50); also GT1-4, 15, and others.

150. '... "saints", as Brethren, true to their biblical primitivism, habitually called their members' (Dickson, 'Hunter Beattie', 146). See, for example, PHG's 'Jamaica Journal' entry for 11 May 1845: 'Rode to Shrewsbury to meet the Saints to break bread in the name of Jesus.'

151. The use of the words 'brother' or 'sister' are characteristic, but of course not unique, to Brethren.

the matter more open than he had before seen it'. On two occasions, when forced to remain below because of seasickness, Gosse meditated on 'the grace of God in Jesus,' being 'uncomfortable in body, but happy in Jesus.'[152]

Gosse's enhanced scientific knowledge was put to use on the *Caroline*. During his previous years abroad, he was a student of nature; now, he was a developing man of science. As we have seen, before leaving England in 1844 he had authored (within a five-and-a-half-year period) his first four natural history books (five volumes in all) and published (besides three incidental items) six articles in scientific journals and one on prophetic studies.[153] During the Atlantic crossing, he spotted a rare cetacean, and made notes on it and flying fish which were later published.[154] Previously, his illustrations of natural objects seen crossing the ocean had been from memory. Now he had the latest marine biology tools: the towing net (to capture planktonic organisms at the water's surface) and the dredge (for sub-surface catches), both of which he apparently tried out for the first time. Animals were thus captured and pictured, observed and preserved (in rum).[155]

On 4 December 1844, after being at sea for seven weeks, the Blue Mountains of Jamaica came into view. It was a sight which, Gosse declared, 'I never can forget,' for his mind was 'full of Columbus'.[156] His anticipation was not only about discovering and describing natural history finds of untold marvels. He was also recording his thoughts about Brethren whom he was about to meet on the island, even as 'my affections were much drawn out towards the beloved Saints at home,' he wrote in reference to his Hackney friends on the Sunday before landing.[157]

On the night before disembarking at Savannah-le-Mar (the main town

---

152. 'Jamaica Journal' 24 and 27 Oct. 1844.

153. For this output: Freeman & Wertheimer-PHG. PHG's books were: *Canadian Naturalist* (1840); *An Introduction to Zoology* (2vols., 1844, preface dated Apr. 1844); *The Ocean* (1845; the SPCK ordered a preview sample of the work on 17 May 1844; it was accepted for publication on 5 July 1844); *Glimpses of the Wonderful* (1845), preface dated Oct. 1844); his serial publications appeared in the *Entomologist*, *Zoologist*, and *Christian Lady's Magazine*.

154. PHG, 'Note on a Species of *Delphinorhynchus*', *Zoologist* IV (1846), 1527-8; PHG, 'Flying Fish', *Hardwicke's Science-Gossip* III (1 Aug. 1867), 184.

155. For the equipment: David Elliston Allen, *Naturalist in Britain*, 129-30; on PHG's use of it: 'Jamaica Journal', 5, 12-13, 16, 22 Nov. 1844 *et passim*; also 25 Oct. 1844), and PHG, *Naturalist's Sojourn in Jamaica*, 6ff.

156. PHG, *Naturalist's Sojourn in Jamaica*, 17, 19; PHG, 'Jamaica Journal', 4 Dec. 1844.

157. PHG, 'Jamaica Journal', 16 Dec. [1844].

of Westmoreland parish),[158] he confided in his journal: 'I slept scarcely an hour, my thoughts being much exercised in meeting the dear Saints.'[159] During the morning of 19 December, they passed Parker's Bay (where Gosse understood the Brethren leader John Coleman lived) and then set anchor at Bluefields Harbor. Gosse went directly to the Post Office to retrieve letters from George Pearse and William T. Berger,[160] Hackney Brethren, as well as his brothers Tom and William. Then he made contact with the Jamaica Brethren Aaron De Leon[161] and Forrest.[162] Gosse was unable to contain himself: 'The joy of being once more with beloved Saints overcame me even to weeping, so that I was some [time?] before I was composed.'[163]

From them Gosse learned two things: firstly, that Coleman now lived not at Parker's Bay, but at Bluefields; and secondly, that John Coleman was at death's door. Gosse saw the situation firsthand when he reached Bluefields, less than ten miles east on the southwest side of the Island, about a quarter mile from the seashore.[164] It was 21 December 1844, marking exactly nine weeks since he had begun his journey.[165] He rented two rooms[166] from Coleman and his wife, Anna Elizabeth Coleman (d. 1866),[167] both of whom were older than him. He remained there for the next eighteen months.

That Gosse had expected to find the Colemans at Parker's Bay is not a superfluous detail. Why so? Because John Coleman (d. 1861), the first of

158. At the time, the name was variously spelled and hyphenated, including Savannah-la-Mar, Savanna-la-Mar, Savana-la-Mar, and Savannah la Mer.

159. PHG, 'Jamaica Journal', 19 Dec. [1844].

160. At least 10 letters from Berger (William or his wife Mary) are cited in 'Jamaica Journal' 1844-46, only a few from Pearse during that time.

161. With one exception, PHG wrote the surname 'Deleon'. Aaron De Leon was a Jew who converted to Christianity, a 'free coloured' and a merchant: Wertheimer, 'The Truth About 1843', 56-8.

162. Forrest's first name is unknown. He was associated with Brethren in Jamaica at least from the time of PHG's arrival there: Wertheimer, 'The Truth About 1843', 58.

163. PHG, 'Jamaica Journal', 19[=18] Dec. 1844). The journal entry is dated Wednesday, December 19, [1844], but that Wednesday was the 18th. PHG lost track of the dates and corrected some of them for early December. I could not interpret the bracketed word in the quotation. See also PHG, *Naturalist's Sojourn*, 39: 'Kind friends were waiting for me on the beach, and the hospitable roof of Bluefields soon received me'.

164. PHG, 'On the Insects of Jamaica', *AMNH* ser.2, I (Jan. 1848), 110-1.

165. PHG, 'Jamaica Journal', 21 Dec. 1844.

166. PHG-Hannah Gosse, 29 Dec. 1844 (LeBL). The rent was 28s./week; in Canada, he had paid 10s./week for room and board ('Reminiscences', II: 208).

167. Anna Coleman died in 1866, aged 70 (*Periodical Accounts* XXVI (1866), 88).

Brethren in Jamaica, had a previous evangelical Christian life.[168] While living in Leominster, Herefordshire, he had committed to Moravian Brethren when he was about 20. Before long, his faith clouded over. Moving to Dublin, his religious views were crystallized on reading the then newly published *Unconditional Freeness of the Gospel* (Edinburgh, 1828), by Thomas Erskine (1788-1870). Following that, Coleman returned to the Moravians and was inspired to evangelize for the movement.

At the time, Moravians were recognized as 'the most successful missionaries in the world'[169] in part because in their dictionary, 'Christian' and 'missionary' were synonyms.[170] Moravian missionaries went where none had gone before and few dared to follow. In 1754[171] they became the first Protestant missionaries in Jamaica,[172] and growth had been rapid in the early nineteenth century. Having been selected by a committee whose members 'prayed over each person' to determine if they displayed the proper character traits,[173] Coleman was first stationed in Antigua in 1829, followed by Demerara-Essequibo and the Barbados.[174] In February 1838,[175] the Colemans established the Moravian mission station called

168. Coleman is an important part of PHG's story as well as of the expansion of Brethren outside Britain. The details of his Brethren connection, including with Darby and Wigram, were first revealed in Wertheimer, 'The Truth About 1843', 28-33, 55, with non-Brethren biographical information from W. R. Vines, 'Biographical Notice' of John Coleman, in John Coleman, *"The Time of the End;" or, Prophecy Unfolded* (London: Wertheim, Macintosh, & Hunt, 2ed., 1862), iii-xii. Coleman died 'in his 64th year' or 'aged 64'.

169. William Brown, *The History of the Propagation of Christianity among the Heathen since the Reformation* (London: Longman, Hurst, Rees, Orme, & Brown, 1814), II: 219 and William Brown, *The History of the Christian Missions of the Sixteenth, Seventeenth, Eighteenth, and Nineteenth Centuries* (London: Thomas Baker, 3rd ed., 1864), II: 34; Froom, *Prophetic Faith* II: 697-8.

170. Randall L. Downs, 'The Influence of the Moravian Missions Movement on Baptist Global Missions' (Mid-America Baptist Theological Seminary, PhD dissertation, 2018), 146.

171. Thompson, *Moravian Missions*, 96.

172. Downs, 'Influence of the Moravian Missions Movement', 146; Kelly R. Elliott, "Chosen Race": Baptist Missions and Mission Churches in the East and West Indies, 1795-1875' (Florida State University, PhD dissertation, 2010), 1.

173. Downs, 'Influence of the Moravian Missions Movement', 68-71.

174. The places and dates in this paragraph are from Vines, *'The Time of the End."* Material cited to me by C. W. Schooling, *in litts.*, Archivist at the Moravian Church House in London, give different dates for Coleman's missionary work: in Antigua (from Feb. 1834); Georgetown, Demerara (from July 1835); and the Barbadoes until Jan. 1838. See also [Walter Mark], *Retrospect of the History of the Mission of the Brethren's Church in Jamaica, for the Past Hundred Years* (London: William Tyler. [?1854]), 30 (the author was identified for me as Walter Mark [*sic*] by C. W. Schooling).

175. *Periodical Accounts* XV (1839), 26.

New Hope, 'charmingly situated on the seashore'[176] not far from Parker's Bay, Jamaica.

There were signs the committee had chosen well in sending out Coleman. In an evaluation of his work in Jamaica, he was said to demonstrate 'a considerable amount of energy and earnestness.'[177] Yet notwithstanding the committee's approval, and Coleman's varied experience, the stars were not aligned. For an unknown reason, in 1841 Coleman left the Moravian Church and joined the Brethren. Not surprisingly, it was a step which caused 'no little embarrassment to the Mission.'[178]

That Gosse knew that Coleman once had been at Parker's Bay explains his previously-cited casual journal reference, yet it raises related questions. How did Gosse know about Coleman? Why didn't he know that Coleman had moved to Bluefields after leaving Moravians? And how did Coleman become aligned with the Brethren in the first place?[179] We can do no more than speculate about any of these questions.[180] The third one, nonetheless, presents us with a remarkable insight into the historical expansion of the Brethren movement. It tells us that Brethren ideas had, with amazing rapidity, spread across the globe from their Irish and English origins.[181] The movement was only some dozen years old, recognized as a Dissenting group for a mere three years,[182] surrounded by rumour,[183]

---

176. [Hark and Westphal], *Breaking of the Dawn*, 122.

177. [Hark and Westphal], *Breaking of the Dawn*, 80.

178. [Hark and Westphal], *Breaking of the Dawn*, 80. I am indebted to C. W. Schooling for first bringing Coleman's Plymouth Brethren connection to my attention (*in litts.*, 1974-75).

179. In the case of Coleman, we do know that at least from 1842, G.V. Wigram, the lieutenant of the 'roving preacher' J. N. Darby, sent him money (G.V. Wigram-J.N. Darby, postmark 18 August 1842, in *Letters of J. N. Darby: Supplement. Correspondence with G. V. Wigram. Volume 1: 1838-1855* (Chessington [England]: Bible and Gospel Trust, 2019, repr. 2021), 46). The question of how Coleman came to associate with Brethren is discussed in Wertheimer, 'The Truth About 1843', 39-45.

180. Wertheimer, 'The Truth About 1843', 39-44.

181. Dickson, 'Hunter Beattie', 147; Grass, *Gathering to His Name*, 3.

182. In 1836, the 'new sect of Christians' was called 'Darbyites' (Edinburgh *Caledonian Mercury*, 7 Mar. 1836, 4). The earliest newspaper mentions of 'Plymouth Brethren' which I have seen (also the earliest recorded use in *OED*, 3ed.) are in 1838 (*Hereford Times*, 14 Apr. 1838, 4; 29 Dec. 1838, 3; and 8 June 1839, 2; 'The Plymouth Brethren', London *Eclectic Review* n.s. IV (May 1839), 571-590).

183. A Trinidad newspaper, commenting on the controversial evangelistic work of the Scots minister and physician Robert Reid Kalley (1809-1888) in Madeira, neutrally identified him as belonging to Plymouth Brethren (*Trinidad Standard*, 5 Nov. 1846, 3), although the connection appears questionable (Michael Presbyter Testa, 'The Apostle of Madeira [Kalley], Part II: Portuguese Protestants in the Americas', *Journal of Presbyterian History* 42, (Dec. 1964), 256, 267 and 267fn.80). Kalley is mentioned in two tracts by EG (published by Feb. 1855 and no later than Dec. 1856: Freeman & Wertheimer-EG, entries 15, 30). In 1880 Kalley and his wife visited

and little understood[184] when—in 1841—Coleman joined it in Jamaica. That was the very same year that Brethrenism had been introduced to Hackney, two years before Gosse himself came upon it and eight years after it had reached London.[185]

Coleman did not remain with the Brethren in Jamaica for long. In 1848, he inexplicably resumed fellowship with Moravian Brethren.[186] Four years later he and his wife returned to England, where he wrote *Prophecy Unfolded*. That volume expressed prophetic views—dispensationalist, pre-tribulationist, futurist premillennialism—precisely aligned with the thought of the Brethren leader J. N. Darby,[187] though Darby's name is nowhere to be found in its pages. Whether or not it was the Darby-Wigram alliance that drew Coleman into the Brethren orbit, Coleman and Gosse later fell out of favour with them.[188]

Regardless of these known unknowns, Gosse connected with an established community of believers. Already active there in gospel work were Coleman and his associates—De Leon, Forrest, E. Grimley (d. 1847)[189]—and some five dozen 'Negro men and women'.[190] As mentioned,

PHG at Sandhurst (PHG-James Fanstone, 4 Oct. 1880, CUL Add. 7313,194-5).

184. 'Captain [Percy F.] Hall was the founder of the Dissenters included under this name [Plymouth Brethren] in this city; they consist chiefly of seceders from the church of St. Peter's; they have made a most rapid progress for the time they have been established—about six months' (letter to the editor from Pietatis Amicus [pseud.], 'Who is the Enemy of the Church?', *Hereford Times*, 14 Apr. 1838, 4).

185. Grass, *Gathering to His Name*, 53; West, 'The Early Development of Brethren Assemblies in London', 68, 75.

186. *Periodical Accounts* XVIII (1846), 393.

187. Wertheimer, 'The Truth About 1843', 30-1. Coleman, *Prophecy Unfolded; or, Eternal Redemption: with Providential Agencies, the Second Advent of the Lord Jesus Christ, the Restoration of Israel, &c.* (London: J. B. Bateman, 1861), 111, 123, 130-1, 242. PHG held opposing prophetic views, which he had described prior to going to Jamaica: PHG, 'Signs of the Times', *Christian Lady's Magazine*, 49-57.

188. In the extant correspondence, Darby and Wigram did not hide their dissatisfaction with PHG, Coleman and other Brethren in Jamaica. Wigram was told that Coleman had taught the 'non-eternity system' and that PHG was aware of this 'error' (Wigram-Darby, 9 Nov. 1855, in *Letters of Darby, Supplement 1*, 431). On the 'non-eternity system': Grass, *Gathering to His Name*, 294, and *passim* (I am grateful to Dr Neil Dickson for help on this subject); on their dissatisfaction: Wertheimer, 'The Truth About 1843', 47 fn.202.

189. On Grimley: Wertheimer, 'The Truth About 1843', 58-9, and *passim*.

190. PHG only notes that there were a 'considerable number' of 'Negro men and women' present during his first Sunday at Bluefields ('Jamaica Journal', 23 Dec. 1844). In an obituary notice, however, written by PHG's friend R. C. Morgan, the figures above are cited: 'John Coleman, who with his wife had gathered round them a little church of some fifty or sixty members, mostly negroes. Here [PHG] found sympathetic friends, and a field for ministerial labour' ('Mr. Philip Henry Gosse, F.R.S.', *The Christian*, 21 Sept. 1888, 886, partially reprinted in *The Christian Herald and Signs of Our Times*, 26 Sept. 1888, 172). I have been unable to confirm these numbers,

Coleman was close to death when Gosse arrived at Bluefields, likely afflicted by one of those diseases which made Jamaica a dangerous missionary field.[191] During Gosse's first Sunday there, Brother E. Grimley supervised the breaking of bread as Coleman lay sick.[192] Gosse, who spoke 'on our nighness to God' before the assembly, did not protest at the form or content of the service, only at its six-hour length.[193] By the end of 1844, Coleman had sufficiently recovered to 'break bread' with his guest.[194]

The Great House in which the Colemans resided was on what had once been a sugar estate. As soon as Gosse had a chance, he explored the now-decayed plantation and environs. Situated in about ten acres of open land, Bluefields stood at the foot of the Blue Mountains, and was only a few hundred yards from the seashore. A small stream with cascades and rapids was near the House. In the past it had served to turn a mill wheel, and was now a convenient bathing place.[195] As it turned out, the area was an excellent headquarters for the naturalist.[196]

Coleman and Gosse maintained contact and proper relations, even if an absence of Coleman's name from Gosse's journal suggests a lack of close fellowship, perhaps related to differences over prophetic interpretation or other matters. Gosse's scientific work was centred in Bluefields House, though not his religious activities (or, 'Higher engagements than those connected with Natural History,' as Gosse put it).[197] He spent about a third of his Sundays with a little meeting at (or near) Content cottage, fifteen miles to the east of Bluefields, high up in the Luana Mountains, and an equal number of weekends at the residence of Aaron De Leon and

but coming from Morgan they would likely be accurate.

191. J. H. Buchner, *The Moravians in Jamaica* (London: Longman, Brown, & Co., 1854), 12-13; [Walter Mark], *Retrospect of the History of the Mission*, 6. Buchner himself had been a missionary in Jamaica from 1844. During a six-month period in 1843, the superintendent of the Moravian Jamaican missions and three other missionaries died, leaving the Moravians 'sorely thinned' ([Hark and Westphal], *Breaking of the Dawn*, 85-7).

192. PHG, 'Jamaica Journal', Sunday [=22 Dec. 1844].

193. The service was, in its form and length, typical of Moravian worship in Jamaica: Buchner, *Moravians in Jamaica*, 158-9.

194. PHG-Hannah Gosse, 29 Dec. 1844 (LeBL).

195. In the 1970s, the eight bedrooms of Bluefields, 'closely associated with the English naturalist, Philip Henry Grosse [sic]', were available to vacationers for overnight stay (Landt and Lisl Dennis, 'The Good Life. Great Houses Open to Guests in Jamaica', *Chicago Tribune*, 18 June 1972, sec. 6, p.12).

196. PHG, 'Jamaica Journal', 22 [=21] Dec. 1844; PHG, 'On the Insects of Jamaica', *AMNH* ser. 2, I (Jan. 1848), 110-111; PHG-Hannah Gosse, 29 Dec. 1844 (LeBL); PHG, *Naturalist's Sojourn in Jamaica*, frontispiece and pp. 39, 62-6, 80.

197. PHG, *Naturalist's Sojourn in Jamaica*, 86.

his wife, Helen De Leon. When Gosse was at Phoenix Park (the De Leons' home),[198] he would drive into Savannah-le-Mar on Sunday mornings with the De Leons and their children, and a Mrs Sturridge, to break bread at a Mrs Sweet's (Mrs Sturridge worshipped at a local Wesleyan chapel). 'Oh yes,' Gosse later wrote, 'I recal [sic] those days very often, with much affection.'[199]

Through Coleman, Gosse was introduced to the English-born William W. Tydeman (1824-1898), whom he baptized in 1846. Years after leaving Jamaica, evangelizing in Port-au-Prince, Haiti, working as a watchmaker in New York City, and receiving financial support from the Wigram-Darby duo, Tydeman (who remained in touch with Gosse) surfaced in Knoxville, Tennessee, as a wealthy, well-respected homoeopathic physician, affiliated with the local Episcopal church.[200] Also in 1846 Gosse met William Hume, the earliest Baptist missionary in Jamaica. Arriving in the island in January 1841,[201] he affiliated with the Brethren in 1846[202] (almost certainly meeting Gosse in that year).[203]

-V-

When Gosse arrived in Jamaica, the island's total population was 377,433, divided in three classes: whites (4.2%); 'coloured' (18.1%); and

198. On Content cottage, in the parish of St. Elizabeth: PHG, 'Jamaica Journal', esp. 9 Jan., 1-2 Mar. 1845; PHG, 'On the Insects of Jamaica', *AMNH* ser. 2, I (Jan. 1848), 113-5, and its continuation, *AMNH* I (Apr. 1848), 268; *Naturalist's Sojourn in Jamaica*, 86, 93, says he went there every other week, which appears to be not quite correct. Content may have been the residence of a Mr Rankin. Two miles down the mountain was Shrewsbury, certainly the site of some, or maybe all, of the meetings. Grimley was the one to first take Gosse here ('Jamaica Journal' 1 Mar. 1845). On Phoenix Park, in the parish of Westmoreland: 'Jamaica Journal', 25 January 1845 (Analysis), and *passim*; PHG, *Birds of Jamaica*, 92; and *Naturalist's Sojourn in Jamaica*, 155.

199. PHG-Mrs Sturridge, 16 Oct. 1880 (CUL Add. 7313,211).

200. Tydeman baptism at Coulter Spring: PHG, 'Jamaica Journal' and *Analysis*, 8 June 1846. During 1877, PHG's Corr. Bk. records letters to and from 'Tydeman' (the entry for 1 July 1877 identifies the correspondent as 'W. W. Tydeman'). Wigram sent him money in 1867: Wertheimer, 'The Truth About 1843', 62-3, *passim*.

201. John Clarke, *Memorials of Baptist Missionaries in Jamaica, including A Sketch of the Labours of Early Religious Instructors* (London: Yates & Alexander, 1869), 186, ix; Edward Bean Underhill, *Life of James Mursell Phillippo, Missionary in Jamaica* (London: Yates & Alexander, 1881), 73-4; John Clarke, W. Dendy, and J. M. Phillippo, *The Voice of Jubilee: A Narrative of the Baptist Mission, Jamaica* (London: John Snow, 1865), 121.

202. 'About 1846 he adopted the views of the Plymouth Brethren, and in a short time his connection with the [Baptist] Mission ceased' (Clarke, *Memorials of Baptist Missionaries in Jamaica*, 186).

203. Wertheimer, 'The Truth About 1843', 59-60, *passim*.

Blacks (77.7%).[204] Some 33,000 people lived in Kingston, the colony's largest city.[205] Jamaica had been a slave country. The superficial tranquility of the 'masters' hid the 'untold misery' of the slaves, who were viewed 'with the utmost contempt.' Those enchained were even taught—though not by missionaries, who vocally opposed the system— that 'Christ had died for white men only, whilst black people had been created by the devil.'[206] At the end of 1831, the campaign to abolish slavery in the British Empire was well underway when a slave revolt in Jamaica erupted and was suppressed. At the time, Gosse was aware of what was taking place. Nearly 2,400 miles away at the Debating Society in Carbonear, Newfoundland, some twenty members turned out on Saturday night, 25 February, 1832, to hear him argue the question: 'Is the British Government bound in justice to emancipate the Slaves in the West Indies immediately, without affording remuneration to the Planters?'[207] Slave holders did receive payment in 1837, and in the following year slavery was abolished throughout the British colonies.

Gosse is not known to have ever commented on the aftermath of slavery in Jamaica. Indeed, he seemed oblivious to racial issues there altogether, unlike his experience in Alabama. Besides knowing of Jamaican slavery from his Newfoundland days, he had also read the colonial administrator Edward Long's *History of Jamaica*, a justification of slavery[208] by one who (in today's parlance) voiced a 'radical racialist philosophy'.[209] Of the people Gosse encountered in Jamaica whose background might have elicited a comment from him about their race—Aaron De Leon;

204. Census returns, reported in 'West Indies and South America', *The Newspaper* (monthly section included with *Gardeners' Chronicle*), 16 Nov. 1844, [n.p.].

205. Underhill, *The West Indies*, 190 (figure for 1844).

206. For the quotations in these two sentences: ([Hark and Westphal], *Breaking of the Dawn*, 3-4.

207. PHG does not indicate whether he spoke in favour or against the proposition, but he recalled being extremely pleased with his memorized oration. Upon hearing the opposing statement of his friend W. C. St. John, however, he realized he had 'treated the subject sentimentally, totally disregarding the truth and reason of the matter, and merely striving after high sentiment, eloquent bursts of indignation, pathetic appeals, harmonious cadences, & well balanced sentences' ('Reminiscences', II: 160-1).

208. Howard Johnson, 'Introduction: Edward Long, Historian of Jamaica', in Edward Long, *The History of Jamaica, or, General Survey of the antient and modern state of the island: with reflections on its situation, settlements, in habitants, climate, products, commerce, laws, and government* (Montreal: McGill-Queen's, 2002), I: vi.

209. Carra Glatt, 'Of Monkeys and Men: The Genesis of a Fabricated Racial Experiment in Edward Long's *History of Jamaica*', *ANQ: A Quarterly Journal of Short Articles, Notes and Reviews* 34 (2021), 129.

Gosse's assistant, Sam Campbell; or the naturalist Richard Hill (discussed below)—it was only Campbell whom Gosse described as a 'negro'.[210] Gosse said nothing about the racial traits of De Leon (whom others referred to as 'a respectable gentleman of colour'[211] or 'of dark hue, with thick-set curly hair'[212]) or Richard Hill (variously known as a Negro, mulatto,[213] quadroon,[214] 'brown Jamaican'[215] or Anglo-Indian[216]).

Free from social and political distractions, Gosse was able to concentrate all his energies on natural history collecting. When he left for the Caribbean the pursuit of the beautiful was constantly on his mind. He was expecting to find Jamaica's forests filled with beautiful butterflies, elegant humming-birds, magnificent orchids.[217] He recognized he had

210. PHG, *Birds of Jamaica*, 36fn.; PHG, *Naturalist's Sojourn in Jamaica*, 62.

211. Brown, *History of the Christian Missions* II:83-4. I have conjectured that De Leon, a Jew who converted to Christianity, may have been of Sephardic Jewish descent (Wertheimer, 'The Truth About 1843', 57 fn.242).

212. Sarah E. Fox (ed.), *Edwin Octavius Tregelles: Civil Engineer and Minister of the Gospel* (London: Hodder and Stoughton, 1892), 246. Along these lines, it seems curious that PHG, with his wide-ranging interest in Jewish history, did not note that several people he knew—Jamaican residents De Leon and J. L. Lewin, and Dr Michael M. A. H. Laseron (who examined EG for cancer in London)—were born Jews who converted to Christianity. Perhaps he was unaware of the backgrounds of De Leon or Lewin, though likely he was familiar with Laseron (Wertheimer, 'The Truth About 1843', 57, 60). For comparison, Edwin Tregelles specifically identified the three converted Jews he met in Jamaica (Fox, *Edwin Tregelles*, 241, 246, 289).

213. E. O. Tregelles, who met Hill, called him 'a man of colour' (Fox, *Tregelles*, 220). William A. Griffey wrote that Hill was 'the first Negro in the western hemisphere, as far as is known, to make a worthwhile contribution to scientific knowledge' (Griffey, 'A Bibliography of Richard Hill: Negro, Scholar, Scientist. Native of Spanish Town, Jamaica', *American Book Collector* II (Oct. 1932), 220). Frank Cundall disagreed: 'To call him [Hill] a negro is misleading, to an Englishman at all events! Half his blood was English; of the remainder, half was probably negro and half East Indian' (Cundall, 'A Supplementary Bibliography of Richard Hill', *American Book Collector* III (Jan. 1933), 46-8). From a description of Hill by John Bigelow it appears likely he was a mulatto (Bigelow, *Jamaica in 1850*. New York: George P. Putnam, 1851, 24-5); that is the term used in Adrian Desmond and James Moore, *Darwin's Sacred Cause: How a Hatred of Slavery Shaped Darwin's Views on Human Evolution* (Boston: Houghton Mifflin Harcourt, 2009), 348. On Hill: [Frank Cundall], 'Richard Hill', *Journal of the Institute of Jamaica* II (July 1896), 223-30, which was the basis for Cundall's other article in *Journal of Negro History* V (Jan. 1920), 37-44. There is no entry on Hill in the *Oxford Companion to Black British History* (2007).

214. Richard Hill was said to be a quadroon, defined as "the offspring ... of the Caucasian and the mulatto" ('The "Colored People" of the West Indies', *New-York Tribune*, 29 May 1866, 5).

215. Emily Sessions, 'Anti-Picturesque Landscapes, Entangled Fauna, and Interracial Collaboration in Post-Emancipation Jamaica in the Work of Philip Henry Gosse and Richard Hill', *Terrae Incognitae* 53 (2021), 41.

216. Thus the characterisation by Marlene Manderson-Jones, cited in Monica Shuler, 'Coloured Civil Servants in Post-Emancipation Jamaica: Two Case Studies', *Caribbean Quarterly* 30, Sept.-Dec. 1984, 95fn. 5.

217. PHG, *Romance of Natural History* (1860), 16; (2nd series, 1861), 302; *Naturalist's Sojourn*, 94; 'On the Insects of Jamaica', *AMNH* ser. 1, I (Jan. 1848), 110.

his work cut out for him, because (as the *Annual Magazine of Natural History* noted) 'There are perhaps few parts of the world of whose natural productions we know less than those of our own West Indian Colonies.'[218]

The initial wave of travellers and natural history investigators to Jamaica had joined Sir Hans Sloane (1660-1753) on a fifteen-month trip between 1687-89. Sloane, whose collections helped to launch the British Museum, was the first of the island's butterfly collectors.[219] He also gathered plants, birds, insects, and mammals, bringing back to England a great deal that was new.[220] Around the 1750s, three contemporaries supplemented Sloane's efforts. Patrick Browne (?1720-90) wrote largely (though not exclusively) on botany,[221] Anthony Robinson (d. 1768) on all natural history fields, and Edward Long (1734-1813) drew, without acknowledgement, from Sloane, Browne, and Robinson, making additions of obscure origin.[222] Then, after a period of quiescence, researchers again returned to Jamaica during the first forty years of the nineteenth century, interested primarily in shells and plants.[223]

Considered generally, the natural history investigations up to this time were random and problematic. For example, the one who collected specimens and the one who identified and described them, were often different people who never met.[224] The notes of Sloane were 'full of

---

218. *AMNH* ser. 2, IX (1852), 50.

219. Brown and Heineman, *Jamaica and its Butterflies*, 8.

220. Hans Sloane, *A Voyage to the Islands of Madera, Barbados, Nieves, S. Christophers and Jamaica, with the Natural History ... of the Last of Those Islands* (London, 2vols. fol., 1707, 1725); *Catalogus Plantarum quae in Insula Jamaica* (1696); Brown and Heineman, *Jamaica and its Butterflies*, 8-10; C. Swabey, 'The Study of Natural History in Jamaica', *Natural History Notes of the Natural History Society of Jamaica* I (Apr. 1941), 2-3; C. B. Lewis and C. Swabey, 'The Study of Natural History in Jamaica', in Members of the Natural History Society of Jamaica, *Glimpses of Jamaican Natural History* (Kingston, Jamaica: Institute of Jamaica, 2ed., 1949), II: 7-13; Ian Foster, 'Sir Hans Sloane and Birds', *BirdLife Jamaica Broadsheet* No. 95 (Mar. 2012), 14-17.

221. P. Browne, *The Civil and Natural History of Jamaica* (London, 1756), Pt. II: 67-490; on the printing history of the book: E. C. Nelson, 'Patrick Browne's *The civil and natural history of Jamaica* (1756, 1789)', *Archives of Natural History* 24 (1997), 327-336.

222. E. Long, *History of Jamaica* (3vols., 1774); Long, Brown: *ODNB*; Robinson: T. D. A. Cockerell, 'A Little Known Jamaican Naturalist, Dr. Anthony Robinson', *American Naturalist* XXVIII (Sept. 1894), 775-80, and D. B. Stewart, 'An Eighteenth Century Bird Club (Dr. Anthony Robinson and His Friends)', *Gosse Bird Club, Broadsheet* No. 13 (Sept. 1969), 8-10.

223. Those included in the former: Edward Chitty (1804-1863) and C. B. Adams (1814-1853); in the latter: James Macfadyen (1800-1850) and William Purdie (d. 1857). Richard Hill is discussed later.

224. Williams, 'Over 300 Years of Collecting in the Caribbean', 13.

confusion and error,' and published accounts were of uneven quality.[225] Excluding Robinson's observations and drawings (which remained in MS), the general natural histories of the area were unreliable, with only botany and conchology on anything like a stable footing by Gosse's time. Previous work in herpetology was of little scientific value,[226] entomology remained a largely uncultivated field, and ornithological publications prior to 1847—that is, the year in which Gosse's *Birds of Jamaica* appeared—were not worth mentioning (with a few exceptions).[227] Against this background it is possible to empathize with the difficulty Gosse had in reconciling what he read as a naturalist to what he saw in the wild: 'Books puzzle me incomparably more than nature.'[228]

Oblivious to time and devoted to place, Gosse pursued his research as he had done in Newfoundland, Canada, and Alabama: with care, energy, thoroughness, determination and ingenuity. He began the moment he touched Jamaican soil and gathered his first specimens.[229] On 1 January 1845, he hired a 17-year-old 'negro lad', Samuel Campbell (1827-1892), who became his full-time, paid assistant at $4 per month.[230] '[B]y God's blessing I have obtained several valuable things,' Gosse wrote his mother in high spirits after less than ten days at Bluefields:

> I work very hard at collecting, but you will be glad to hear that I find no
> weariness in it, but great delight. I usually rise about daylight, & take my
> rounds in the woods or on the seashore till about 10 which is the hour
> for breakfast, but I take a bit before starting. Then the middle of the
> day is occupied indoors, cleaning shells, or setting insects, or preparing

225. These are PHG's evaluations. On Sloane: PHG, 'On the Habits of Mabouya agilis', *Proc. Zoo. Soc. London*, Part 16 (1848), 61-2; 'Description of a New Genus and Six New Species of Saurian Reptiles', *AMNH* ser. 2, VI (Nov. 1850), 347; *Birds of Jamaica*, 128; on Robinson: *Birds of Jamaica*, 20fn; *Naturalist's Sojourn in Jamaica*, 348, *passim*. Browne was hardly ever mentioned by PHG (PHG, *Natural History. Reptiles*, 104-6). Excerpts from Robinson's MSS. had appeared in Long's book.

226. W. Gardner Lynn and Chapman Grant, 'The Herpetology of Jamaica', *Bulletin of the Institute of Jamaica, Science Series*, No. 1 (1940), 6, 29, 63.

227. Alfred and Edward Newton, 'List of the Birds of Jamaica', in *The Handbook of Jamaica for 1881: Comprising Historical and Statistical Information; together with Essays on Economic Plants and Other Subjects Connected with the Island* (Kingston: Government Printing Establishment, 1881), 103; Jean Anker, *Bird Books and Bird Art* (Copenhagen: Levin & Munksgaard, 1938), 21, 197.

228. PHG-[Richard Hill], 9 Jan. 1846 (PHG, 'Testimony of Prophecy').

229. PHG, 'Jamaica Journal', 4 Dec. 1844.

230. For the salary, PHG, 'Jamaica Journal', 1 Jan. 1845; *Naturalist's Sojourn*, 62, and for a 'tribute of affection' for his 'great service to me', *Birds of Jamaica*, 36fn.

plants; & sometimes in the latter part of the afternoon if I have time, I take another walk.[231]

Gosse discovered from the start that his expectation of finding fine insects in Jamaica—'large and gaily-coloured beetles, I supposed, would be crawling on almost every shrub, gorgeous butterflies be filling the air, moths be swarming about the forest-edges at night, and caterpillars be beaten from every bush'[232]—would not be realized.[233] He therefore turned his attention to assembling orchids, plants, and seashore objects for his first consignment to his agent, Hugh Cuming. One day's work alone yielded 400 plant specimens,[234] and by the end of January 1845 he was contemplating a large illustrated work on the native Orchideae.[235] After a few more months he was trying to domesticate hummingbirds, Sam having brought him three of the long-tailed variety (*Trochilus polytmus*), 'One of the very loveliest of birds, not of Jamaica only, but of the whole world.'[236] He was disappointed by his failure to bring any of them back to England alive.[237]

Not a day now went by (except for Sundays) during which Gosse was not at work.[238] So unbounded was his enthusiasm that even the assiduous and keen-eyed Sam was unable to do enough. Gosse hired Thomas Clement and James Richard Blythe as assistants; De Leon and Forrest, even children, even a cat,[239] brought him specimens. His helpers

231. PHG-Hannah Gosse, 29 Dec. 1844, with 2 Jan. 1845 postscript (LeBL); on Campbell: *Birds of Jamaica*, 36fn, and J. E. Duerden, 'Philip Henry Gosse, F.R.S.', *Journal of the Institute of Jamaica* II (1899), 578. For a detailed description of his work habits: *Naturalist's Sojourn*, 235-9. PHG's father, Thomas, died on 26 Nov. 1844, but he did not hear of it until January ('Jamaica Journal' 18 Jan. 1845); Thomas Gosse-William Gosse, [10 or 12 Nov.] 1844 (CUL Adv. c. 82.5, 18).

232. PHG, 'On the Insects of Jamaica', *AMNH* ser.2, I (Jan. 1848), 110.

233. PHG, 'Jamaica Journal', 9 Dec. 1844; 30 Apr. 1845; PHG-Edward Doubleday, 16 July 1845 (LeBL); PHG-W. W. Saunders, 8 Aug. 1846 (PHG, 'Testimony of Prophecy'); PHG, *Naturalist's Sojourn in Jamaica*, 94.

234. PHG, 'Jamaica Journal', 10 Jan. 1845.

235. PHG, 'Jamaica Journal', 31 Jan. 1845.

236. PHG, 'Jamaica Journal', 22-3 Mar. 1845; PHG, 'A Day in the Woods of Jamaica', *Good Words* III (Apr. 1862), 239; PHG, *Natural History. Birds* (London: SPCK, 1849), 67. The male and female are figured in PHG, *Illustrations of the Birds of Jamaica* (London: John Van Voorst, 1849), plates XIX-XX.

237. PHG, *Birds of Jamaica*, 112-27; *Naturalist's Sojourn in Jamaica*, 48-9; Donald Culross Peattie (ed.), *A Gathering of Birds. An Anthology of the Best Ornithological Prose* (New York: Dodd, Mead & Company, 1939), 205-17; Brown and Heineman, *Jamaica and Its Butterflies*, 11.

238. PHG-Hugh Cuming, 18 June (with 3 July postscript), 1845 (LeBL).

239. 'The Cat brought in to her kittens a beautiful Ground Lizard, & then a Scink, both of which were transferred to me' (PHG, 'Jamaica Journal', 16 Apr. 1845).

were not always helpful. That was the case when 'A little urchin came to my door ... exposing two of the most common butterflies, both so rubbed as to be utterly transparent, & one with but a single pair of wings, & with all sincerity inquired, "Do you want to buy any batts?"' [sic][240]

In order to collect most effectively, Gosse utilised and improved upon various standard scientific implements. For plants he had his vasculum, presses, and Wardian cases (to ship them back alive); for insects, a net with a twenty-foot handle; for mammals, a specially adapted springe.[241] Nothing could require too much effort to capture or to gather. He stripped and jumped into water up to his neck to get corals; spent nearly four hours fruitlessly trying to trap some hummingbirds; relentlessly pursued a snake which escaped in his study, crawled out the window, and even when put in spirits 'continued to twine about very briskly';[242] and with Sam pursued a single bird,

> which sat on a projecting high branch, & which fluttered at the report [of Gosse's rifle] but did not fly. I fired at it & it fell over, but held fast by one foot. I fired three times more in succession, evidently hitting it, with large shot; but could not deprive it of life, nor cause it to relinquish its hold. We then after much throwing of stones, thought of cutting down the tree, which having borrowed an axe, Sam & I succeeded in doing, though a hard Manchioneel. [sic] The bird fell with the falling tree, but no sooner had it touched the sea, than it sprang up & flew to a great distance seaward.[243]

Once the search of land and seashore had ended, and the objects were safely in the work room, the task of the scientific describer began. That's when Gosse made ecological notes, cleaned, measured, weighed, drew,[244] dissected, examined (under a microscope), skinned, stuffed, and preserved his finds. After accumulating a sufficient amount of material, a shipment was prepared. These were important, not only because Gosse

240. PHG, 'Jamaica Journal', 16 Apr. 1845, also recorded in *Naturalist's Sojourn in Jamaica*, 163). The locals called butterflies 'bats' and bats 'rat-bats'.

241. PHG, *Romance of Natural History* (1860), 272; 'Jamaica Journal', 1, 5 May 1846, Analysis; 18 Mar. 1845; 30 October 1845.

242. PHG, 'Jamaica Journal', 23 Jan. 1845; 21 Mar. 1845.

243. PHG, 'Jamaica Journal', 3 Sept. 1845.

244. I saw the volume of unpublished drawings, entitled 'Jamaica Studies' (1844-46), while it was in the Family Collection.

was supporting his mother, but also because the expenses in Jamaica were greater than anticipated.[245]

Sometimes problems arose with a consignment: birds or plants were spoiled by mould, the items arrived in poor order,[246] or were misattributed.[247] Included in Gosse's list of things that could go wrong was his relationship with Hugh Cuming, his natural history dealer in London. Gosse had selected him on the recommendation of his friend Edward Doubleday at the British Museum, but 'though upright, [Cuming] was a churl' who 'never showed me any interest or sympathy.' Courteous reports sent to him, inquiries for guidelines as to the most saleable items on the markets, even pleas to be paid ('I am reduced to my last Pound!') were all unanswered.[248] Nearly four decades later, Gosse bemoaned his choice. 'I have never ceased to regret that I had not the privilege of knowing *you*, when, in 1844-1846, I made my own collections in Jamaica,'[249] he wrote Samuel Stevens (1817-1899), who had acted as agent for H. W. Bates and A. R. Wallace. In the end, however, Gosse seems to have been fairly satisfied with the seven consignments which he made.[250]

In August 1845, Gosse decided to re-orient his collecting. Until then

245. PHG-Hannah Gosse, 29 Dec. 1844 (as cited). His rent, for example, was 28s. per week, whereas in Canada it had been 10s. for room and board, as previously noted.

246. *Life*, 191, incorrectly claimed that all the shipments arrived in good condition: PHG, 'Jamaica Journal', 2 Aug. 1845, PHG-Hugh Cuming, 3 Oct. 1845; 27 Jan. 1846 (both LeBL); and for spoilage, 'Jamaica Journal', 25 Mar., 30 May, 9 Sept. 1845.

247. The British Museum's J. E. Gray incorrectly stated that PHG was the source of a seal in its collections: J. A. Allen, *History of North American Pinnipeds: A Monograph of the Walruses, Sea-lions, Sea-bears and Seals of North America* (Washington, D.C.: Government Printing Office, 1880), 720fn.

248. PHG-A. E. Hodgson, 23 Mar. 1880 (CUL Add. 7313, 63-4); PHG-Samuel Stevens, 30 Mar. 1880 (CUL Add. 7313, 74); L. C. Biggs, 14 Apr. 1880 (CUL Add. 7313, 80-1); PHG-Hugh Cuming, 3 Jan., 12 Feb., 23 Apr., 18 June 1845 (all LeBL). Complaints against Cuming, the 'Prince of Shell Collectors', were common (S. Peter Dance, *Shell Collecting. An Illustrated History* (Berkeley: University of California Press, 1966), 162-5). His unique shell collection and 'on balance, beneficial' contribution to systematic zoology and botany is noted in S. Peter Dance, 'Hugh Cuming (1791-1865) Prince of Collectors', *Journal of the Society for the Bibliography of Natural History* IX (1980), 477-501. Cuming's 12.5% commission charged to PHG amounted to £57 (PHG, 'Jamaica Journal', 18 Dec. 1845; and the 'Summary' on the last page of the MS). For comparison, H.W. Bates calculated he paid a 25% commission for his efforts in South America (consisting of 20% to his London agent Samuel Stevens and 5%, miscellaneous). On Bates' commission: Edward Clodd, 'Memoir', in H. W. Bates, *The Naturalist on the River Amazons. With a Memoir of the Author by Edward Clodd* (London: John Murray, 1892), xxvi.

249. PHG-Samuel Stevens, 30 Mar. 1880 (CUL Add. 7313, 74). Emphasis in the original. D. B. Baker, 'Alfred Russel Wallace's record of his consignments to Samuel Stevens, 1854-1861', *Zoologische Mededelingen* 75 (2001), 305-6.

250. The first shipment left Jamaica 17 Feb. 1845, the last accompanied him when he returned to England.

he had been regularly gathering insects, reptiles, fishes, and mammals; orchids from January to March; landshells and palm seed to May; birds casually and at all times. Perhaps it was partially his fear that his trip would fail because of the paucity of insects[251] that ultimately encouraged him to make ornithology the chief focus of his attention during the remainder of his stay. Initially he had preferred to strangle birds rather than club them to death.[252] At the end of July he bought and used for the first time (Gosse's term was 'hanselled') a gun, soon was proficient enough to bring down two birds with a single shot, and wrote Cuming that 'You may if you please mention to Mr. D[oubleday]. that I am collecting notes of the habits &c of our Birds, wh[ich] I exp[ec]t will be suff[icien]tly interesting to lay before the public.'[253]

It was in connection with this ornithological work that Gosse was introduced to Richard Hill (1795-1872), of Spanish Town. As mentioned, before arriving in Jamaica Gosse had known of the scientific researches of foreign visitors there, yet nothing of the efforts of Hill, the island's first resident naturalist and ornithologist.[254] Of mixed race, Hill was born at Montego Bay[255] and lived for nearly two decades in England before returning to Jamaica in 1818. While abroad, he had received part of his education at Selina Lady Huntingdon's college, this association with Calvinist Methodism probably having confirmed him in his life-long Low Church beliefs. His activities in the anti-slavery movement brought him to England again between 1827 and around 1832, where he met the leading Evangelical advocates of that cause. From that year Hill never again left the British colony, pursuing what turned out to be a

251. PHG-Edward Doubleday, 16 July 1845 (LeBL). The insects he sent to H. Cuming in London, however, 'sold well' (PHG, 'Jamaica Journal', 18 Dec. 1845).

252. PHG, *Birds of Jamaica*, 46. Field glasses (binoculars) were available in England from the mid-1850s for military use (advertisement, London *Morning Post*, 17 Feb. 1854, 1), but appear to have been used for bird-watching at a much later date (T. A. C., 'A Country Diary', London *Guardian*, 5 Nov. 1913, 14, appealed to those 'who are interested in birds to use the field glasses rather than the gun'.)

253. PHG, 'Jamaica Journal', 18, 25[=26] June, Analysis; 23 July, esp. 30, 1845; PHG had first used a gun in Canada (*Life*, 99); for his proficiency with it: 'Jamaica Journal', 20 Aug. 1845; PHG-Hugh Cuming, 2 Sept. 1845 (LeBL).

254. Anna Maria Hendriks, 'Richard Hill, 1795-1872', *Gosse Bird Club Broadsheet* No. 65 (Sept. 1995), 2. Hill was considered 'a man of almost European reputation, being well known as the author of the Ornithology of Jamaica, together with Mr. Goose [sic]' (*St. Christopher Advertiser and Weekly Intelligencer*, 5 Feb. 1861, 1).

255. Frank Cundall, and all others, claims that Hill was born at Montego Bay, Jamaica (Cundall, *Journal of Negro History*, 37), but Marlene Manderson-Jones states he was not born in Jamaica (cited in Shuler, 'Coloured Civil Servants in Post-Emancipation Jamaica, 95fn. 5).

brief career as a member of the Jamaica House of Assembly. Among other things, Hill was a passionate abolitionist and advocate for workers' rights who was subjected to the threat of physical violence for his views.[256] For much of his life he held a lucrative position as a stipendiary magistrate,[257] allowing him in his leisure to pursue (from at least 1833) natural history studies. By 1845 he had already published a number of articles on local birds and fish.[258]

It would seem likely that it was Aaron De Leon or J. L. Lewin[259] who first urged Gosse to contact Hill, both of whom knew him.[260] And when Gosse did write Hill at the end of October 1845, he was pleased to learn that, as the author of the *Canadian Naturalist*, his name was already known to the Jamaican.[261] At once the correspondence assumed a cordial tone: 'May I not write to you with the privileged freedom of an old friend,' Gosse inquired, 'rather than the formality of a new acquaintance?' The younger naturalist, having only recently commenced ornithological studies in earnest, felt obliged to point out that 'you must not give me credit for more than I know, wh[ich] is not much.'[262] Hill, he understood, was basically concerned with 'philosophic generalization, the investigation of the relations of beings to each other, & to inanimate matter,' while

> ... what I delight in, [is] the minute details of habits, the *biography* of animals; such as proceeds from the pleasant pen of [W. J.] Broderip & others. ... I willingly admit the inferiority of my humbler path to yours; yet still it is a pleas[an]t I may say a fasc[inatin]g one, & suits my capacity;—I the more thankfully receive the results of yr. investigations,

256. Marlene Manderson-Jones, 'Two Chapters from the Life of Richard Hill' (typescript, Department of History, University of West Indies, n.d. [?1975]), 52-3, 38.

257. Hill's annual salary was £500 (Bigelow, *Jamaica in 1850*, 24-5).

258. About two dozen items by Richard Hill on meteorological and natural history subjects are listed for 1833-1844 in two bibliographies: William A. Griffey, 'A Bibliography of Richard Hill: Negro, Scholar, Scientist. Native of Spanish Town, Jamaica', *American Book Collector* II (Oct. 1932), 220-24 and the more comprehensive work by Frank Cundall, 'A Supplementary Bibliography of Richard Hill', *American Book Collector* III (Jan. 1933), 46-8.

259. On Lewin, a Jewish convert to Christianity: Wertheimer, 'The Truth About 1843', 60.

260. PHG-[Richard Hill], 20 Dec. 1845 (PHG, 'Testimony of Prophecy'); Clarke, Dendy, and Phillippo, *Voice of Jubilee*, 84; for the connection of De Leon and Lewin with Hill: Wertheimer, 'The Truth About 1843', 60.

261. PHG first wrote Hill on 31 Oct. or Nov. 1 (PHG, 'Jamaica Journal', 31 Oct. 1845), with the reply, 6 Nov. 1845 (*Life*, 194-6).

262. PHG-[Richard Hill], 13 Nov. 1845 (PHG, 'Testimony of Prophecy').

for I think I can appreciate them, & follow the reasoning when presented to me, tho' incompetent to originate it.[263]

During the next few months, Hill supplied Gosse with lists of local birds, identifications of species, accurate sketches, and other information and assistance. 'It seems absurd contin[uin]g to repeat the same expressions,' Gosse wrote in February 1846, '& yet every comm[unicatio]n of yrs. demands fresh, & I may say, increased, thanks.'[264] Eager to talk to Hill, to see his collection of drawings, and to visit the Blue Mountains,[265] Gosse travelled to Spanish Town at the beginning of March 1846, and the two finally met.[266]

Gosse had only once before ventured far from the Content-Bluefields-Savannah-le-Mar region, having spent a few days in October 1845 at Montego Bay.[267] Previously he had found the flora and fauna of Bluefields Ridge, Content, the Belmont estate, and Sabito Bottom so rich that he was not motivated to leave Westmoreland or St. Elizabeth parishes.[268] And when he did venture to the parish of St. James, he realised that his decision to concentrate his work in the south had been wise.

Going to Spanish Town and nearby Kingston was a different matter, with its own immediate rewards. Gosse was absent from Bluefields for nearly three weeks (4-23 March), and while he did meet some local naturalists (including the Glasgow-born botanist James Macfadyen in Kingston, who had been active nearly twenty years earlier),[269] and go on an excursion to Highgate, atop of the Liguanae Mountains (for some reason he never reached the Blue Mountains), his chief ornithological accomplishments on that trip were done indoors and not in the field. For

263. PHG-[Richard Hill], 4 Dec. 1845 (PHG, 'Testimony of Prophecy'). Emphasis in the original.

264. PHG-[Richard Hill], 21 Feb. 1846; see also 20 Dec. 1845, 9 Jan. 1846 (all PHG, 'Testimony of Prophecy').

265. PHG-[Richard Hill], 24 Jan. 1846 (PHG, 'Testimony of Prophecy'); 'Jamaica Journal', 23 Feb. 1846.

266. PHG, 'Jamaica Journal', 6 March 1846

267. PHG, 'Jamaica Journal', 22-24 Oct. 1845; *Naturalist's Sojourn in Jamaica*, 252.

268. PHG, *Birds of Jamaica*, 99-100; *Naturalist's Sojourn in Jamaica*, 96; PHG, 'Insects of Jamaica', *AMNH* ser. 1, I (Jan. 1848), 109-115; Phoenix Park was not a good hunting ground (*Naturalist's Sojourn*, 155, 217, 252).

269. PHG, 'Jamaica Journal', 18 Mar. 1846; 'Dr. James M'Fadyen, Jamaica', St. John's *Antigua Weekly Register* (18 Feb. 1851), 3; Frank Cundall, *Biographical Annals of Jamaica* (Kingston: Institute of Jamaica, 1904), 30; Britten and Boulger, *Biographical Index of Deceased British and Irish Botanists*, 198; *Glasgow Herald* (27 Dec. 1850), 4.

Richard Hill, that 'truly amiable man'[270] whose 'scientific attainments are equaled [*sic*] only by his urbane manners, and truly estimable character,'[271] took Gosse to Kingston to visit the Jamaica Society for the Encouragement of Agriculture and Other Arts and Sciences (of which Hill was then vice-president). There Gosse viewed the botanical and ornithological drawings and MSS of Anthony Robinson. Gosse several times studied this material before leaving the West Indies, and found it 'executed with an elaborate accuracy worthy of a period of science far advanced of that in which he lived.'[272] Of similar value to Gosse were Hill's own notes and 'large collection of most magnificent drawings of birds.'[273] Between 13-17 March the two men completed a revised list of Jamaican birds, identifying about 184 species.[274]

Though scientific interests dominated Gosse's relationship with Hill, evidence suggests that they shared an evangelical perspective as well. Gosse spoke of Hill's 'excellencies as a man of science, as a gentleman, and as a Christian,'[275] and a pamphlet by Hill on biblical criticism[276] calls to mind Gosse's publication on that subject (as discussed later). Based on a letter from Gosse to Hill, one can speculate that the two may have shared prophetic concerns.[277]

Gosse decided, for an unknown reason, to wind up his affairs in the tropics at the beginning of 1846,[278] but his collecting at Bluefields continued for three months. At the end of May he said goodbye to the De Leons at Phoenix Park, to the Saints at Shrewsbury (who 'commended me to the Grace of God'),[279] and to the 'dear Colemans' at Bluefields.

---

270. PHG, 'Jamaica Journal', 5 Mar. 1846. Hill made a good impression on others as well. Edwin Tregelles, the Quaker, in meeting him in Kingston on 3 Aug. 1844, described Hill as 'highly cultivated, intelligent and pleasing: we have met him repeatedly, and I have never been five minutes in his company without instruction' (Fox, *Tregelles*, 220).

271. PHG, *Naturalist's Sojourn*, 11fn.

272. PHG, *Birds of Jamaica*, 20fn.

273. PHG, 'Jamaica Journal', 6 Mar. 1846; *Naturalist's Sojourn*, 492.

274. PHG, 'Jamaica Journal', 17 Mar. 1846.

275. PHG, *Naturalist's Sojourn*, xi.

276. R. Hill, *The Books of Moses, How Say You, True or Not True? Being a Consideration of the Critical Objections in Dr. Colenso's Review of the Books of Moses and Joshua* (Kingston, Jamaica: James Gall, 1863). Citing this 90-page pamphlet, Desmond and Moore, *Darwin's Sacred Cause*, 314, say that Hill and Gosse 'shared a narrow biblical view'.

277. A copy of a letter (PHG-R. Hill, 5 Oct. 1850, Corr. Bk.) consists of an outline of topics discussed, including the words 'List of plants for names - Prophecy &c.'

278. PHG-Hugh Cuming, 27 Jan. 1846 (LeBL).

279. PHG, 'Jamaica Journal', 28 May 1846, and Analysis.

Leaving there on 19 June, 'I took the last glance at a place where I have spent so many pleasant months.'[280]

For three more weeks Gosse awaited the departure of the *Avon* for England, travelling between Spanish Town and Kingston, visiting and comparing notes with Hill, studying the Robinson MSS, 'searching the Scriptures & discoursing concerning the will of God as to the position of his church, the evil of divisions, & the Lord's coming' with a Dr Fairbanks, even attempting to convince a Revd Mr Sterne of his 'false position.'[281]

The return voyage to England took four weeks. Though sick much of that time, he did not suspend evangelistic efforts. He distributed tracts in English, French, and Spanish to passengers and crew, and he spoke on salvation to the captain—a shrewd man, Gosse thought, yet 'no more capable of understanding "God's way", than a stone.'[282] When the *Avon* stopped at the island of St. Thomas, Gosse entomologized, called at the Moravian mission, and met the local English rabbi, Moses Nathan Nathan (1807-1883).[283] Landing at Southampton on 5 August 1846 still feeling unwell,[284] he travelled the next day to London. There he re-united with his mother and the twenty live birds which he had brought with him.

-VI-

Philip Gosse was 'a man in love with Jamaica.'[285] For no other foreign place did he have such fond memories; his eighteen months there seemed to him 'like a midsummer night's dream.'[286] Joy in his work, the absence of distractions, growth in the religious sphere, basically sound health[287]— these elements provide the backdrop for his classic Jamaican natural history works.

He came to Jamaica with his tools and, to make taxonomic distinctions, a minimally helpful copy of Cuvier. When not in the field he had to rely

280. PHG, 'Jamaica Journal', 19 June 1846.

281. For the last two, PHG, 'Jamaica Journal', 28 June, 2 July 1846. The last meeting with Richard Hill was on 27 June. On 5 July, he and Fairbanks' 'Saints' 'broke bread, for the first time, without "administration"'.

282. PHG, 'Jamaica Journal', 18 July 1846.

283. PHG, 'Jamaica Journal', 15 July 1846. Nathan was a student of the Jewish mystical tradition known as the *Kabbalah* (obituary in the *Athenaeum*, 26 May 1883, 670).

284. PHG-W. W. Saunders, 8 Aug. 1846 (PHG, 'Testimony of Prophecy').

285. F. J. du Quesnay, 'Philip Henry Gosse—"A Man in Love with Jamaica"', Jamaican *Daily Gleaner* (20 July 1965).

286. PHG, 'A Day in the Woods of Jamaica', 235.

287. He does not appear to have been at all sick until July 1845 (PHG, 'Jamaica Journal', 3 July, 7 Aug., 22 Dec. 1845; 23 Jan. 1846).

on others—Richard Hill and Robinson's notes and drawings, and (as in Alabama) the bird descriptions of Wilson and Audubon.[288] He and and his assistants collected the respectable total of 21,200 specimens: 1,510 birds, more than 3,000 shells, about 7,800 insects, 5,000 dried plants and about 800 living orchids, 102 reptiles, 94 fish, as well as nests and eggs, sponges, Crustacea, bulbs, ferns, seeds, and blocks of wood.[289] While the comparison is not precise, H. W. Bates collected a total of 14,712 *species* of vertebrates and invertebrates during eleven years in the Amazon region (8,000 of which he thought were new to science),[290] and 7,553 insect specimens.[291] A. R. Wallace collected 110,000 insect specimens during roughly eight years in the Malay Archipelago.[292] Gosse's seven consignments were purchased by well-known botanists,[293] ornithologists,[294] entomologists,[295] other men of science,[296] and scientific

288. For the use of Robinson's drawings: PHG, *Illustrations of the Birds of Jamaica*, in Freeman & Wertheimer-PHG, 34; for Wilson and Audubon: May Jeffrey-Smith, 'Gosse's Observations on Jamaican Birds—Some Further Observations on Warblers', *Natural History Notes of the Natural History Society of Jamaica* IV (Jan. 1951), 207. Audubon is considered 'one of the greatest artists of birds, famous for his double elephant volumes of life-size portraits of American birds published between 1827 and 1838 ... Audubon's drawings tower over Wilson's, who was never an accomplished artist' (Magee, *Art and Science of William Bartram*, 173). Though both Audubon and Wilson were familiar with birds in their natural habit and were 'excellent observers of nature', their claim that their ornithological drawings were done from life was not 'absolutely true' (Magee, 174,179). 'These men were more than natural scientists; they were also artists and poets' (p. 179).
289. PHG, *Naturalist's Sojourn in Jamaica*, 493fn.; for a detailed breakdown: 'Shipments' and 'Sales' at the back of PHG's 'Jamaica Journal'.
290. H. W. Bates, *The Naturalist on the River Amazons* (London: John Murray, 1863), I:v. One reviewer of Bates' book was 'utterly astonished' at that collecting result ('Bibliographical Notices', *AMNH* ser.3, XII (Nov. 1863), 391).
291. After leaving South America in 1851, Bates had taken 7,553 specimens of insects (Clodd, 'Memoir', in H.W. Bates, *Naturalist on the River Amazons*, xxvi).
292. Baker, 'Alfred Russel Wallace's record of his consignments to Samuel Stevens', 254. Wallace's main collecting focus was on insects.
293. At the back of the 'Jamaica Journal' is a detailed analysis of the purchasers of PHG's specimens. Botanical specimens were purchased by R. J. Shuttleworth, Robert Brown, and Loddiges.
294. Purchasers of ornithological specimens included Edward Doubleday, D. W. Mitchell, the 13th Earl of Derby (who placed his birds in his menagerie at Knowsley Hall: PHG-C. R. Rowe, 29 Apr. 1881, CUL Add. 7313, 350), Johann Friedrich von Brandt, T. C. Eyton, John Gould, Viscount B. L. du Bus, William Yarrell, and Richard Owen.
295. Purchasers of entomological specimens included W. W. Saunders, Andrew Melly, and W. C. Hewitson.
296. Thomas Bell purchased Crustacea specimens, J. S. Bowerbank, Poriphera (PHG, 'Jamaica Journal').

institutions in Britain, Europe and Russia.[297] Some published work cited his collecting.[298]

For his efforts, Gosse grossed on average a solid £1 per day (in round numbers, £577 for his 577 days collecting in Jamaica, leaving him with a net £488 after expenses and funds dispersal). Put another way, Gosse took in about £385 p.a. For a rough comparison, H. W. Bates' 'total savings' for eleven years in South America amounted to less than £800, or some £73 p.a.[299] While away from home, Gosse provided £25 to his mother.[300] In other words, from a financial standpoint, he had succeeded wonderfully.

More notably, Gosse's time in Jamaica was a scientific triumph. He was just the third of the early butterfly collectors there, but unlike his predecessors he had 'superb powers of observation'.[301] Some creatures he identified in printed works remained undescribed for half-a-century.[302] Some behaviour—describing the flight patterns of various butterfly species, for example—'were unparalleled contributions ... and some of the earliest studies published' in that field.[303] He was the only collector for nearly a century to make a concerted effort to list, and provide an account of, the island's reptiles.[304] He was the first to describe the methods of commercial fishing (useful data for ichthyological studies);[305] his Jamaica books are a source for linguists;[306] in the view of an art historian, the

297. Among scientific institutional purchasers were museums in Newcastle, Strasburg, Berlin, Vienna, and St. Petersburg; Royal Botanic Society, London; and the British Museum, which bought many of the holotypes of birds, bats, and mammals (*History of the Collections contained in the Natural History Departments of the British Museum* (London: British Museum, 1906), II: 34, 250, 373). The British Museum also had the first pick of the Lepidoptera (PHG-A. E. Hodgson, 25 Feb. 1880, CUL Add. 7313, 38).

298. For instances of published work using his materials: PHG, *Birds of Jamaica*, 187, 207, 399; *Naturalist's Sojourn*, 145; and Louis Pfeiffer, 'Descriptions ... of New Species of Land-Shells from Jamaica, Collected by Mr. Gosse', *Proc. Zool. Soc.* Part 13 (1845), 137-8. Pfeiffer was a friend of Cuming's.

299. Clodd, 'Memoir', in H.W. Bates, *Naturalist on the River Amazons*, lxiv. Presumably by 'total savings' Bates meant net profit.

300. 'Summary', last page of PHG, 'Jamaica Journal, Analysis'.

301. Brown and Heineman, *Jamaica and its Butterflies*, 10.

302. In 1845 PHG found (and later described) a worm not seen again until 1892 (J. E. Duerden, 'Abundance of Peripatus in Jamaica', *Nature* 63 (7 Mar. 1901), 440-1).

303. Jacqueline Y. Miller, 'Presidential Address, 1990: The Age of Discovery—Lepidoptera in the West Indies', *Journal of the Lepidopterists' Society* 45 (1991), 8-9.

304. Lynn and Grant, 'The Herpetology of Jamaica', 63.

305. David K. Caldwell, 'Marine and Freshwater Fishes of Jamaica', *Bulletin of the Institute of Jamaica*, Science Series no. 17 (1966), 11; PHG, *Naturalist's Sojourn in Jamaica*, 205-211.

306. F. G. Cassidy and R. B. Lepage, *Dictionary of Jamaican English* (Cambridge: University Press, 1967), xxiii.

illustrations he made for those works,[307] mainly done *in situ*, created what were then 'new types of illustration, both of landscape and of natural history specimens'.[308]

These are worthy details, yet it is Gosse's trilogy of books written following his return to London—*Birds of Jamaica* (1847), *Illustrations of the Birds of Jamaica* (1849), and *Naturalist's Sojourn in Jamaica* (1851)—which account for his reputation as the 'Father of Jamaican Ornithology',[309] the 'Father of Jamaican Herpetology',[310] and the Father of 'many other aspects of Jamaican biology.'[311] Of the three volumes, *Illustrations of the Birds of Jamaica*, the first of nine books Gosse published on an author's risk basis, was issued in such small numbers (perhaps three dozen copies) as to have little impact, and resulted in a small loss. The fifty-two beautiful lithographs were drawn on the stone and coloured by Gosse himself.[312]

In terms of the advance in ornithological knowledge, the achievement of *Birds of Jamaica*, explained British zoologist P. L. Sclater (1829-1913), was that it 'let in a flood of light upon a subject previously left almost in the dark since the days of Sir Hans Sloane [1660-1753].'[313] Before

307. PHG documents his time spent drawing and illustrating in 'Jamaica Journal Analysis': e.g., 'Sketch of Bl[uefiel]ds River (20 June 1845); 'Sketch of Bl[uefiel]ds House' (21 June 1845); 'I sketched 7 species' (3 Oct. 1845); 'Painted' (1 June 1846); 'Notes & sketches' (16 June 1846); on his way to Jamaica, PHG did paintings of Colias [a butterfly] ('Jamaica Journal', 31 Oct. 1844) and humming birds (25 Oct. 1844), even while he was sick.

308. Sessions, 'Anti-Picturesque Landscapes, Entangled Fauna, and Interracial Collaboration', 45-6.

309. Stewart, 'Philip Henry Gosse', *Gosse Bird Club, Broadsheet*, 2.

310. For a PHG herpetological illustration not published during his lifetime, see the several articles beginning with Geoffrey Lapage, 'Draughtsmanship in Zoological Work', *Endeavour* VIII (Apr. 1949), 70-79; Garth Underwood, 'Notes on a hitherto unpublished Gosse illustration of Jamaican herpetology', *Natural History Notes of the Natural History Society of Jamaica* IV (Mar. 1949), 46-48; 'Corrections and Comments', *NHNNHSJ* (1949), 66; Editor, 'Gosse's Illustrations of Jamaican Reptiles and Amphibia', *NHNNHSJ* (1949), 102-3; Keith Murray, 'Gosse's Herpetological Bibliography', *Herpetologica* V (1949), 128 (for complete descriptions and an additional item, see Freeman & Wertheimer-PHG, 'Reptiles' in index).

311. Ronald I. Crombie, 'Jamaica', in Brian I. Crother (ed.), *Caribbean Amphibians and Reptiles* (San Diego: Academic Press, 1999), 75.

312. Freeman & Wertheimer-PHG, 32-36, provides the only complete publishing history for this expensive work, which sold for 36s. *Illustrations of the Birds of Jamaica* was alone in PHG's Jamaica trilogy for failing to be reviewed. I have found only a single advertisement ('List of New Books', *Birmingham Journal*, 28 July 1849, 3, apparently a listing for the coloured plate edition, see Freeman & Wertheimer-PHG, item 39). Freeman & Wertheimer-PHG, 34, describe the colour quality as 'high throughout', and the drawings of humming birds 'superb'. Sixteen plates (eight in colour) from PHG's *Illustrations of the Birds of Jamaica* (1849) are reproduced in D. B. Stewart (ed.), *Gosse's Jamaica 1844-45* (Kingston, Jamaica: Institute of Jamaica Publications, 1984).

313. P. L. Sclater, 'Revised List of the Birds of Jamaica', in *Handbook of Jamaica for 1910*

Gosse, men of science had collected specimens,[314] leaving much to be desired when it came to describing what they found. For sure Gosse was a collector, but he went beyond that: he was 'a keen observer, and a most fluent and yet unaffected describer.'[315] Explained the Jamaican educator R. G. Taylor:

> His industry was amazing. He collected and prepared skins; he studied the courting, nesting and feeding habits of birds (a line of research requiring an immense amount of time and patience); he investigated the composition and materials of nests; he analysed the contents of stomachs, and he measured and weighed with enormous industry. His results were recorded with an accuracy and a vividness of style that makes his great work "The Birds of Jamaica," published in 1847, not only a reliable but also an indispensable guide to the modern student, even now a hundred years after it was written.[316]

Birds of Jamaica was 'far ahead of its time', said British evolutionary biologist David Lack (1910-73), and established itself as 'one of the best bird books on any part of the world for at least half a century.'[317]

There was also a literary aspect to the work. *Birds of Jamaica* continued a rule of thumb: starting with the *Canadian Naturalist*, Gosse's books were nearly always widely praised in the press. In this case, readers found an ornithological account accessible to a popular audience. That Gosse could do this came as a bit of a surprise, since English reviewers thought they were encountering a peripatetic writer, one day in Canada, the next in Jamaica. They did not realise that in the seven-year period since the publication of the *Canadian Naturalist*, Gosse had been honing his skills with three books and seven scientific articles. His seeming disappearance from the public eye after the *Canadian Naturalist* was due to the fact that the SPCK, the publisher of two of his books, did not send out review copies (the third book was formally anonymous). Nonetheless, though

(Kingston: Institute of Jamaica, 1910), 1.

314. Catherine Levy, 'History of Ornithology in the Caribbean', *Ornithologia Neotropical* 19, Supplement (2008), 418.

315. Peattie, *Gathering of Birds*, 206.

316. R. G. Taylor, 'Gosse's Observation[s] on Jamaican Birds', *Natural History Notes of the Natural History Society of Jamaica*, IV (Nov. 1950), 178.

317. David Lack, *Island Biology, Illustrated by the Land Birds of Jamaica* (Berkeley: University of California Press, 1976), 8.

the *Canadian Naturalist* sold slowly,[318] those who read it appreciated what they had before them. No higher praise could have been given to *Birds of Jamaica* than the comparison (by eight of its fifteen identified reviewers) to Gilbert White's eighteenth century classic, *The Natural History of Selborne*. In modern times, one observer noted how Gosse, living during the 'Golden Age' of nature writing in England, composed with 'charm and vivacity',[319] while another commented that the 'beauty of his prose borders on poetry.'[320]

These scientific and literary qualities have made *Birds of Jamaica* the 'ornithological classic of the English-speaking Caribbean.'[321] In the twenty-first century, it has 'still not been superseded completely' as a valuable source for ornithologists and conservationists.[322]

The third volume in Gosse's Jamaica trilogy, *A Naturalist's Sojourn in Jamaica*, was contemplated at the same time that Gosse was working on his illustrated bird volume, but was rejected by the SPCK.[323] When it appeared, Edward Forbes, the prominent zoologist and paleontologist, called it 'by far the best delineation' of any of the tropic islands in the Western hemisphere—'and this is no mean praise.'[324]

Jamaicans have never forgotten Gosse.[325] Taken together, *Birds of Jamaica* and *A Naturalist's Sojourn* are authoritative studies,[326] 'marvels

318. *Canadian Naturalist* was still advertised for sale by Gurney & Jackson's (successors to the original publisher, Van Voorst) in 1895 (*Athenaeum*, 15 June 1895, 757), with all remaining copies sold in 1911 (Freeman & Wertheimer-PHG, 26).

319. E. D. H. Johnson (ed.), *The Poetry of Earth. A Collection of English Nature Writings from Gilbert White of Selborne to Richard Jefferies* (New York: Atheneum, 1966, 1974), vii, 269.

320. Catherine Levy, 'Gosse's Sojourn in 'Glorious Jamaica'', *BirdLife Jamaica Broadsheet* no. 92 (Sept. 2010), 15.

321. D. B. Stewart (ed.), *Gosse's Jamaica 1844-45*, v.

322. Catherine Levy, 'Gosse's Sojourn in "Glorious Jamaica"', 15.

323. *Life*, 225, states *Naturalist's Sojourn in Jamaica* was composed in 1850, ignoring the SPCK's rejection of PHG's proposal to publish such a work in 1848 (Freeman & Wertheimer-PHG, 41).

324. [Edward Forbes], review of *Naturalist's Sojourn* in London *Literary* Gazette, 25 Oct. 1851, 715 (reprinted as 'The Naturalist Abroad and at Home', in *Literary Papers by the late Professor Edward Forbes, F.R.S., Selected from his writings in The Literary Gazette'* (London: Lovell Reeve, 1855), 278ff.). According to *Life*, 227, *Sojourn* was published on Oct. 17, though the date of Oct. 21 is given in an advertisement (London *Morning Post*, 13 Oct. 1851, 1: 'On Tuesday, October 21, will be published ...').

325. 'Considerations of the Classic Character of Bluefields' led the Institute of Jamaica to establish a small temporary marine laboratory there in the 1890s. In 1963, the Gosse Bird Club was founded in Jamaica. Besides the articles already cited, see also Anna Black, 'Naturalist with Most Delicate and Accurate Perception', Jamaican *Sunday Gleaner* (30 July 1961).

326. Alfred Newton, 'Ornithology', *Encyclopaedia Britannica* (9th ed., 1885), XVIII: 16; *History of the Collections ... of the British Museum* (1906), 373.

of West Indian natural history, lyrical as well as informative,' which are 'still the best general sources of information'[327] on that island. They mark an achievement which 'remains unsurpassed.'[328] The former is one of Gosse's most significant scientific works, 'perhaps the most enduring of them all',[329] and the latter one of his 'finest books, showing his powers as a field naturalist, and is still of value today.'[330]

Natural history was one area in which Gosse made his mark. It was also in Jamaica, close to the dawn of Brethrenism, that Gosse further developed as a Christian. He extended his ties with the movement from London to the West Indies where (as mentioned) he associated with John Coleman, the pioneer Brethren individual on the island. As the second Brethren figure to come there,[331] Gosse knew and communed with local Brethren and their friends. He evangelized. He taught. He preached. He baptized.[332]

He also watched. Recall that for Gosse, the year in which he set off for the Caribbean—1844—was not just another calendrical milestone. From the long day in June 1842 when, in a single sitting, he 'devoured' all 407 pages of Matthew Habershon's *Historical Dissertation on the Prophetic Scriptures,* Gosse had become a new man committed to the historicist premillennialist mode of prophetic interpretation. The 'time of the end', Habershon had declared, *might be so near*—'so near as to happen in the year 1844'.[333] Before leaving England, Gosse publicly proclaimed his 'desire to awaken and to promote the spirit of Christian watchfulness, and to confirm the faith of believers' that the signs of the times announced that 'The Lord is at hand!'[334] Once in Jamaica, Gosse not only 'taught

327. C. B. Lewis and C. Swabey, 'The Study of Natural History in Jamaica', 8.

328. Ian Thomson, *The Dead Yard: A Story of Modern Jamaica* (New York: Nation Books, 2009), 310-1.

329. Freeman & Wertheimer-PHG, 25.

330. Freeman & Wertheimer-PHG, 40.

331. Benjamin T. Slim (d. 1894), who is said to have founded the first Brethren meeting in Barbados in 1862, promoted J. N. Darby there from at least 1870, and became its leading figure. Prior to this, Slim is said to have associated with Brethren in Jamaica in 1843. There is, however, no documentary evidence to support that claim (Wertheimer, 'The Truth About 1843', 60-62).

332. For these activities, see e.g., PHG, 'Jamaica Journal', 20, [23], 25, 29 Dec. 1844; 9 Mar. 1845; 28 June, 2 July 1845; Tydeman's baptism, 8 June 1846.

333. Matthew Habershon, *An Historical Dissertation on the Prophetic Scriptures of the Old Testament, Chiefly Those of a Chronological Character* (London: James Nisbet and Co., 2ed., 1840), 330.

334. PHG, "The Signs of the Times," *Christian Lady's Magazine* XX (July 1843), 50-1. The article is dated Hackney, 13 May 1843.

and preached', he also declared his Second Advent expectations[335] (a core concern of Brethren).[336]

Finally, historians have previously observed how the absence of a central authority during the opening moments of the emerging Brethren movement in Britain set the stage for the 'influence of personalities'.[337] Small, loosely-associated yet often closely-knit circles of Brethren played a key role in the spread of their ideas. Sometimes the result was cooperation and concord; sometimes competition and discord.

The example of Jamaica provides a case study of how this British dynamic was replicated abroad.[338] From the formative days of Brethrenism in Jamaica, personalities and circles were also touching and even overlapping. During Gosse's time there, one Brethren outlook was promoted by Darby and Wigram (the formidable Brethren apostles) among Coleman, William Hume, William W. Tydeman, and De Leon; another manifested itself in the circle of Berger-Pearse-Gosse (later identified with Open Brethren). Though never a missionary, after committing himself to Brethren in 1843 Gosse helped to spread their gospel across the world. Simultaneously, from at least 1842 John Coleman in Jamaica was in touch with, and received financial assistance from, Darby-Wigram; from at least 1845, the duo were in contact with E. Grimley,[339]and from at least the 1850s with other Jamaica Brethren– William Hume, William W. Tydeman, De Leon and Gosse.

A fog conceals the activities of these two circles, making it difficult to discern the nature of their interaction. What we do know, however, suggests disharmony between them—as there was between Brethren in Britain, beginning in 1845. Grimley was the informant for Darby and Wigram, and surviving letters indicate that those leaders did not much like what they saw of Jamaica Brethren. Grimley told them of heretical

---

335. From PHG, 'Jamaica Journal': 29 Oct., 24 Nov. 1844: PHG was 'meditating on the Resurrection of Jesus'; 25 Dec. 1844: speaks to the 'Saints' on Thessalonians I-II (see PHG, '2 Thessalonians ii.4,' *Christian Annotator*, 9 Dec. 1854, 342; PHG, '2 Thessalonians ii.8,' *Christian Annotator*, 3 Mar. 1855, 72); 9 Mar. 1845: speaks on coming judgement from 2 Peter II (see PHG, 'The Breaking of the Day. – XXIV,' *The Christian*, 1 Sept. 1870, 394); 28 June 1846: speaks on 'Lord's coming'.

336. Rowdon (*Origins*, 187, 215fn.16) notes that Second Advent expectation was the 'most distinctive mark of Brethren missionary work,' though not unique to Brethren.

337. Embley, *Origins*, 105-6; Grass, *Gathering to His Name*, 49-50.

338. The following two paragraphs are based on Wertheimer, 'The Truth About 1843', 43-45 and Appendix, which first suggested the nature, and impact, of this 'influence of personalities' in Jamaica.

339. Wertheimer, 'The Truth About 1843', 43fn. 177.

teaching by Coleman being tolerated by Gosse, while Hume and De Leon had likewise 'shown the spirit of heresy'. Though Tydeman was baptized by Gosse (as previously mentioned), he later came under the influence of Darby and Wigram, receiving financial aid from them after leaving Jamaica and later abandoning Brethren for 'Universalism'.

-VII-

After leaving the Caribbean, Gosse maintained his interest in the natural history of Jamaica and was occasionally contacted on scientific matters.[340] Above all, he was fond of recalling the spiritual thrill of Jamaica. Just a few years after he had left, while sitting down at his desk 'here in the suburbs of London', he felt at a loss to describe the 'kind of paradisiacal association' which he had with 'lovely Jamaica':

> ... how shall I transfer these impressions to my readers? I can name some of the prominent objects that helped to make up the picture ... and by some short description, or a few well-selected epithets, may communicate a certain definiteness to those objects; but the picture itself, the thousand things that cannot be enumerated, birds, insects, flowers, trees, the tone of the whole, the sunlight, the suffused sky, the balmy atmosphere, the variety of the foliage, the massive light and shadow, the dark, deep openings in the forest, all new, rich, and strange ... all this I cannot hope to convey.[341]

Ten years after writing these words, he seemed to allude to the West Indies again: 'I have gazed on some very lovely prospects,' he wrote, 'bathed perhaps in the last rays of the evening sun, till my soul seemed to struggle with a very peculiar undefinable sensation, as if longing for

---

340. Seven letters from the Englishman William Osburn (d. 1860) to PHG on Jamaican natural history were forwarded by PHG to the *Zoologist*, where they were published (vols. 17-18, 1859-1860). Though almost nothing has previously been known about Osburn, he spent two years in Jamaica, dying there at the age of 29 ('Deaths', Chester *Cheshire Observer*, 24 Mar. 1860, 7; *Proceedings of the Scientific Meetings of the Zoological Society of London*, 1865, 61; K. E. Ingram, 'W. Osburn, Naturalist—His Journal & His Letters', *Jamaican Historical Review* II (1978), 33-37). On at least one occasion, PHG asked Richard Hill to send him Jamaican orchids (PHG-R. Hill, 15 Nov. 1862, National Library of Jamaica). PHG provided notes about Jamaican lightning-bugs for Charles Frederick Holder, *Living Lights. A Popular Account of Phosphorescent Animals and Vegetables* (London: Sampson Low, Marston, Searle, and Rivington, 1887), 50-2.

341. PHG, *Naturalist's Sojourn in Jamaica*, 49-50.

a power to enjoy, which I was conscious I did not possess, and which found relief only in tears.'[342]

To Gosse, the glory of nature was only significant because in it were images of the glory of God. He could study nature because he found *'God appearing in the creatures ...* without Him they are but carcases [*sic*], deformed, useless, vain, insignificant, and very nothings.'[343] Gosse detected in what he called the 'gem of the Caribbean Sea' a hint of what the 'new earth' might be like during Jesus' millennial kingdom.

A fantasy: Having just turned 52, Gosse was convinced he would never again return 'in this body' to Jamaica, yet he couldn't help thinking:

> How I should delight to transport myself in a moment, as by an electric telegraph, to the summit of Bluefields Peak, or to the sombre glooms of Rotherwood, or to the sunny glades of the Kepp, and spend just one long day in re-exploring there! ... those sweet ties that advertisers strangely call "encumbrances" have clustered round me, and grey hairs are peeping out of my head and beard, and mere locomotion has not the charm that it once had; but I sometimes think that, when the Lord Jesus, bringing in the times of restitution of all things, shall clothe this sin-pressed globe with far more than pristine glory and loveliness, and I have put on the resurrection body, fashioned in his likeness, to whose incorruptible, immortal powers time and space will be as nothing, one of the myriad joys reserved for me may be the looking again upon those gorgeous scenes of beauty, which, even as I have already seen them, are so little marred by the sin of man, and retain so much of Paradise,—the mountain-woods of glorious Jamaica.[344]

342. PHG, *Romance of Natural History* (2nd series, 1861, 343; 1st series, 175-9).
343. PHG, *Birds of Jamaica*, 444. Emphasis in the original (citing Richard Baxter).
344. PHG, 'A Day in the Woods of Jamaica', 235.

PART II

1846-1875

'How Great are Your Works'

CHAPTER FIVE

1846-1857

'The Open Eye'

O Lord, how manifold are thy works!
In wisdom hast thou made them all:
the earth is full of thy riches.
　　Psalms 104: 24[1]

My object is to become to my readers an humble guide to
this fountain of delight [Nature]. I would take you with
me, gentle stranger, and ask your companionship in a few
of those investigations which I find so fascinating that
a summer's day is only too brief for their enjoyment. Let
me lift the veil from some of those beings, of whose very
existence you are probably unaware, and show you beauties
that you have never suspected or imagined.
　　[P. H. Gosse], *Sea-side Pleasures* (1853).

-I-

*H*OW DID HE DO IT? P. H. Gosse did not let up after he completed
his intense natural history field work in Jamaica. During the
twelve years from 1846-1857 now under review, he produced
twenty-five book titles (twenty-seven volumes in all) on scientific
and religious topics, totalling some 9,700 pages. Of the twenty-seven

---

1. Quoted in [PHG], *Wanderings through the Conservatories at Kew* (London: SPCK,
[1856]), title page, using the King James Version.

volumes, eighteen contained illustrations from his hand, and several were pioneering and trend-setting, receiving enormous popular attention not equalled before or since, and an enduring reputation for its author; others earned him scientific honour and election to the prestigious Royal Society of London; some titles were reprinted or appeared in more than one edition during this period, a few were largely derivative efforts and one was a pot-boiler. Nearly all were unanimously praised, and all received positive assessments in the press. Gosse also wrote eighty-three articles (eleven were anywhere from 2-to-30 parts) printed in 925 pages, at least ten of which contained his illustrations.[2] Did we mention that Gosse lectured (indoors and outdoors) on marine zoology at no fewer than nine different locations in London, the provinces, and Scotland, and at least once on prophecy; that he undertook field research in Britain and collected thousands of marine specimens, preached, took a notable place in the Brethren community, married, and had a son? To chronicle this breathtaking activity within the confines of a chapter is difficult; to properly set it in context seems impossible. The wonder is that a single person could find the time and energy to do in a decade what most of us fail to accomplish in a lifetime.

When Gosse returned from Jamaica, he settled, as mentioned, with his mother at 16 Richmond Terrace, Queen's Road, in Dalston.[3] The illness which had troubled him during the Atlantic voyage seems not to have lasted long, as he set about fulfilling his desire to earn a living by his pen and pencil. One would imagine that it would have been a simple matter for him to resume his London activities where he had left off in 1844. Yet there is a reason that (as Thomas Wolfe proclaims in the title of his novel) *You Can't Go Home Again*—you've changed and they've changed. In Gosse's case, besides his own personal development, the worlds of Hackney and Bloomsbury had been buffeted by tradewinds. Controversies had erupted in both camps which were to have their affect on adherents.

Firstly, there was Richard Chambers' anonymous *Vestiges of the Natural History of Creation*, which appeared in October 1844 (the same month Gosse sailed for the West Indies). In many ways an amateurish

2. This information is derived from Freeman & Wertheimer-PHG.
3. EWG-William R. Power, 22 January 1918 (typescript copy of a letter, Department of Archives, Shoreditch District Library, London; Bagust Collection XI:100); for PHG's address: *Turner's Directory for 1847* (Hackney: Caleb Turner, 1847), 136.

production, the *Vestiges'* crude espousal of an evolutionary theory was nonetheless a sensation, condemned by men of science and theologians.[4]

Secondly, between April 1845 and 1848 Brethren were riven by disagreement. Leader fought leader as J. N. Darby attacked B. W. Newton of Plymouth for (among other things) denying 'liberty of ministry', purportedly promulgating false ideas about the humanity of Christ, and allegedly adhering to erroneous prophetical ideas. Later, George Müller and Henry Craik of Bristol came in for condemnation by Darby for advocating independency rather than centralization in church organization. These conflicts eventually touched all Brethren, sundering their dreams of Christian unity and their union into two main factions: 'Exclusive' (Darby's followers) and 'Open'. W. T. Berger of Hackney (who was involved in the upheaval from the spring of 1846), and the Howard brothers of Tottenham (excommunicated by Darby in 1849), took the side of the Open Brethren,[5] whose '*de facto*' founders, in the view of a recent scholar, were Müller and Craik.[6] It is not unreasonable to speculate that Gosse may have experienced Brethren discord while he was in Jamaica, with subtle competition pitting the Wigram-Darby circle against that of the Hackney Brethren (represented by Gosse) for domination.[7] Whether or not that was so, once returned to England Gosse had to struggle with new developments in his scientific and religious life, even if his antagonism to the theory of evolution and his sympathy for the Open Brethren were both evident from the outset.

In the fall of 1846, meanwhile, Gosse was occupied with his own agenda. He was anxious to make use of his Jamaica materials, and during the next five years he sold specimens to Sir William Jardine, Richard Owen of the Natural History Departments of the British Museum in Bloomsbury, and others.[8] In September he began to revise his field notes

4. James A. Secord, *Victorian Sensation. The Extraordinary Publication, Reception, and Secret Authorship of 'Vestiges of the Natural History of Creation'* (Chicago: University of Chicago Press, 2000).

5. On Berger: Rowdon, *Origins*, 249, 256 fn. 109; on John and Robert Howard: West, *From Friends to Brethren*, 15, 238; Embley, 'Origins and Early Development', 193-4; and on the various controversies with Darby and the great Brethren schism of 1848-9: Grass, *Gathering to His Name*, 63-83; Akenson, *Exporting the Rapture*; Rowdon, *Origins*, chaps. 9-11; Coad, *Brethren Movement*, chaps, 9-10; Embley, 'Origins and Early Development', chap. 4.

6. Summerton, *'I thanked the Lord and asked for more': George Müller's Life and Work*, 32-3.

7. Wertheimer, 'The Truth About 1843', 44.

8. PHG-W. Jardine, 10 Aug. 1848 (PHG, 'Testimony of Prophecy'); PHG-R. Owen, 18 Oct. 1850 (Owen Correspondence, BMNH, XIII: 209); PHG-W. J. Hooker, 12 Mar. 1851 (Kew, *English*

for a monograph on the birds of Jamaica;[9] in 1847-48 four papers on reptiles and mammals appeared in the *Proceedings of the Zoological Society of London*, a series of seven articles on Jamaican insects in the *Annals and Magazine of Natural History*, and an illustrated atlas of Jamaican ornithology. He also started a volume detailing his general natural history experiences in the island.[10]

As previously mentioned, all of these works are of high scientific quality. As a result, Gosse's research was beginning to attract the attention of other men of science—including naturalists Charles Darwin, Edwin Lankester, and W. J. Broderip; the comparative anatomist Richard Owen; the zoologist Edward Forbes; ornithologist William Jardine; and the botanist George Luxford.[11] He was less well-known to the public. That was because while Gosse's first publisher, John Van Voorst, sent out copies of the *Canadian Naturalist* for press review, his second (and main) one, the Society for Promoting Christian Knowledge, did not.[12]

Letters, 1851, XXXI: 179); and for type-specimens sold to the British Museum in 1848: Charles P. Alexander, 'The Craneflies of Jamaica', *Bulletin of the Institute of Jamaica*, Science Series No. 14 (1964), 5, 48, and Oldfield Thomas, 'On Indigenous Muridae in the West Indies; with the Description of a New Mexican Oryzomys', *AMNH* ser. 7, I (Feb. 1898), 176-7.

9. After *Birds of Jamaica* was published, PHG realized he had omitted from the book two of the birds which he depicted in *Illustrations of the Birds of Jamaica* (PHG, 'Description of two new birds from Jamaica', *AMNH* ser. 2, III (Apr. 1849), 257-9).

10. The MS journal for the *Birds of Jamaica* (1847) is at Cambridge (entitled 'MS. Zoology of Jamaica. 1846', Add. 7040); PHG, 'Brief Notes on the Habits of *Noctilio mastivus*'; 'On the Habits of *Ameiva dorsalis*'; 'On the Habits of *Mabouya agilis*'; 'On the Habits of *Cyclura lophoma*, an Iguaniform Lizard', all *Proceedings of the Zoological Society*, Parts 15-16 (1847-8), 105-10, 24-27, 59-62, 99-104; 'On the Insects of Jamaica', *AMNH* ser. 2, vols. I-II (Jan., Mar.-May, July, Sept.-Oct. 1848); PHG, *Illustrations of the Birds of Jamaica*, contains 52 coloured lithographs; PHG, *Naturalist's Sojourn in Jamaica*; Freeman & Wertheimer-PHG; *Life*, 211, 218-19.

11. The ornithologist William Jardine recommended that Darwin read PHG's *Birds of Jamaica* (Darwin Papers, CUL 119: 'Books Read/Books to be Read', under the latter); Darwin annotated his copy of *Naturalist's Sojourn in Jamaica* (Frederick Burkhardt and Sydney Smith (eds.), *The Correspondence of Charles Darwin. Volume 5: 1851-1855* (Cambridge: Cambridge University Press, 1989), 489fn.7); Richard Owen privately praised *Naturalist's Sojourn* (copy of a letter, Owen-'Mamma [Hannah] Troutbeck', 29 Nov. 1851, CUL Add. c. 82.5, 42), as did the invertebrate zoologist Edward Forbes in an anonymous review in the *Literary Gazette* (25 Oct. 1851), 715-17 (repr. as 'The Naturalist Abroad and at Home', in *Literary Papers by the late Professor Edward Forbes, F.R.S., Selected from his writings in 'The Literary Gazette'*, 278ff.). Positive reviews of *Naturalist's Sojourn* appeared by [Edwin Lankester], *Athenaeum*, 19 Feb. 1848, 183-5; *Fraser's Magazine* XLV (Apr. 1852), 379-98 (probably the lawyer and naturalist W. J. Broderip: *Wellesley Index* II: 415); and *Westminster Review* XLVII (July 1847), 308-28 (Walter Houghton informed me, *in. litt.*, that this was almost certainly by George Luxford).

12. This claim in *Life*, 229, appears confirmed by my own failure to find reviews of SPCK works in England (an exception: two brief 1851 press notes on *Text-book of Zoology for Schools*). In the United States, PHG's works were widely reviewed between 1844-1903 (D. Wertheimer, 'P. H. Gosse's Scientific Reception in America', unpublished MS, 2023).

The consistent praise which Gosse now received in the press for his *Naturalist's Sojourn in Jamaica*, under the imprint of Longmans, was thus something altogether new for him.[13]

That positive reception frequently rested as much on Gosse's view of the proper way to study nature as it did on his pleasant and fluent style and evocative and meticulously accurate descriptions. Twenty years earlier, the naturalist W. J. Broderip (1789-1859) had complained that 'Few have turned their thoughts to the minutiae of animal habits with such devotion' as the famed Gilbert White of Selborne, or the American ornithologist Alexander Wilson. Investigators, he asserted, 'feel that it is beneath us to be biographers of "rats and mice and such small deer"', and preferred classifying in the museum to studying in the field.[14] Broderip was amongst the best in his time at that craft,[15] and in his Jamaican works Gosse took Broderip's call to heart. 'What should we think,' he wrote in *A Naturalist's Sojourn in Jamaica*,

> if the world were to collect from Egypt the tens of thousands of mummies that are said to be entombed in the mighty catacombs of that country, and having placed them in museums should appoint learned men minutely to measure their differing features and limbs, to describe their appearance with exactitude, and to depict their portraits in all the leathery blackness of their physiognomy; then to give each a name, and

13. *Life*, 229, incorrectly states that *Naturalist's Sojourn in Jamaica* was the first of PHG's books to receive substantial public attention. All of the reviews of these two works which I have seen were favourable. On *Birds*, see: *Spectator* XX (15 May 1847), 471-2; *Literary Gazette* (5 June 1847), 411-12; *Guardian* (23 June 1847), 396; *Church of England Quarterly Review* XXII (July 1847) 239-41; *Christian Remembrancer* XIV (July 1847), 219-20; *The Atlas* (10 July 1847), 474-5; *The Critic* n.s. VI (10, 17 July 1847), 26-8, 40-2; *Gardeners' Chronicle* (17 July 1847), 470-1; *Gentleman's Magazine* n.s. XXVIII (Aug. 1847), 161-4; *Eclectic Review* n.s. XXII (Oct. 1847), 399-416; *Chambers' Journal* IX (1 Apr. 1848), 210-212; *Tait's Edinburgh Magazine* n.s. XVI (Aug. 1849), 543-4; extensive excerpts appeared in *Zoologist* V (1847), 1808-20, and *Edinburgh New Philosophical Journal* XLIII (1847), 90-4. *Life*, 212, incorrectly states that reviewers complained that the book lacked illustrations: only the *Guardian* and *Christian Remembrancer* did so, and the latter added: 'but really Mr. Gosse is himself a literary Bewick.'

On *a Naturalist's Sojourn in Jamaica* (besides reviews previously cited), see also: *Spectator* XXIV (25 Oct. 1851), 1024-6; *London Medical Gazette* n.s. XIII (31 Oct. 1851), 763; *John Bull* XXXI (8 Nov. 1851), 719; *The Critic* n.s. X (15 Nov. 1851), 535-7; *AMNH* ser. 2, IX (Jan. 1852), 50-4; *Gardeners' Chronicle* (3 Jan. 1852), 6-7; *Kidd's Own Journal* I (10 Jan. 1852),19-20; *Zoologist* XI (1853), 3850-57, 3865-70; *Chambers' Journal* V (12 July 1856), 30-1.

14. W. J. Broderip, 'On the Utility of Preserving Facts Relative to the Habits of Animals, with Additions to Two Memoirs in "White's Natural History of Selborne"', *Zoological Journal* II (Apr. 1825), 14-17. 'But mice and rats and such small deer': Shakespeare, *King Lear*.

15. 'Few naturalists have more graphically described the habits of animals' (G. C. B[oase]., 'Broderip, William John', *DNB* VI, 1886, 377).

record the whole in a book;—what should we think if the world would call this Egyptian *History*?

It is manifest that there is not an iota of History [here] ... For History is the record of the actions of men, their relations to other men, the circumstances in which they acted, their characters, the influence of their lives upon society, their connexion with the times preceding and following their own, and other points of interest, not one of which could be gathered from a description of their dead and preserved bodies, though ever so exact and minute. *Natural History*, which investigates and records the condition of living things, or things in a state of nature; if animals, of *living* animals:—which tells of their "sayings and doings," their varied notes and utterances, songs and cries; their actions, in ease and under the pressure of circumstances; their affections and passions, towards their young, towards each other, towards other animals, towards men: their various arts and devices, to protect their progeny, to procure food, to escape from their enemies, to defend themselves from attacks; their ingenious resources for concealment; their stratagems to overcome their victims; their modes of bringing forth, of feeding, and of training, their offspring; the relations of their structure to their wants and habits; the countries in which they dwell; their connexion with the inanimate world around them, mountain or plain, forest or field, barren heath or bushy dell, open savanna or wild hidden glen, river, lake, or sea:—this would be indeed *zoology*, *i.e.*, the science of living creatures. And if we have their portraits, let us have them drawn from the life, while the bright eyes are glancing, and the flexible features express the emotions of the mind within, and the hues, so often fleeting and evanescent, exist in their unchanged reality, and the attitudes are full of the elegance and grace that free, wild nature assumes.[16]

Nearly all of the reviewers of *Naturalist's Sojourn* agreed with the thought in this passage (the *Athenaeum* quite reasonably saw it as a critique of the British Museum's Keeper of the Zoological Department, John Edward Gray, then perhaps the supreme example of a closet-naturalist).[17] Some, however, were angered by Gosse's words. The *Gardeners' Chronicle* took it as 'an attack upon science, which is

---

16. PHG, *Naturalist's Sojourn in Jamaica*, vi-vii. Emphasis in the original.

17. [W.J. Broderip], *Athenaeum* (8 Nov. 1851), 1172; Williams, 'Over 300 Years of Collecting in the Caribbean', 18.

nei[t]her just nor in good taste,'[18] an opinion supported by the *Annals and Magazine of Natural History*.[19] Yet this attitude, which perceives the naturalist as a biographer first and then as a systematist, guided Gosse in virtually all his scientific writings. Much later in the century, the approach became more popular, as the appearance of English terms to designate it—ecology (1859), bionomics (1888), and ethology (1897)—indicates.[20]

While his Jamaican experiences were much on Gosse's mind in the first several years after 1846—in the winter of that year he even apparently considered another collecting trip to the Azores[21]—he was simultaneously busy with non-scientific ventures. He renewed his connection with the SPCK by suggesting a work on the antiquities of ancient Egypt 'for very plain people' which would in part illustrate the background of the Old Testament, and they asked him to compose another on Jews. H. H. Milman's *History of the Jews* (3 vols., 1829; 2ed, 1830), then the best-known such study in English, had not been followed by a similar effort.[22] Unlike the liberal Milman, Dean of St. Paul's, whose *History* had invited controversy due to its critical historicist viewpoint,[23] Gosse proposed to deal with the subject in the light of the 'sure word of prophecy'.[24]

While working on these religion-related studies in 1847, at his cousin Thomas Bell's request ('I owe so much of my success to his unvarying kindness')[25] Gosse began to write five guides to the British Museum natural history collections, to include his own woodcuts. Four were

18. *Gardeners' Chronicle* (3 Jan. 1852), 6.

19. *AMNH* ser. 2, IX (Jan. 1852), 50-4.

20. For these terms: *OED*, 1ed., and D. E. Allen, *Naturalist in Britain*, 201, 238, 180.

21. On a small sheet of paper pasted into 'Testimony of Prophecy' are some notes—not in PHG's holograph, perhaps in that of EG—concerning a potential trip. *Life*, 210, appears to cite information from this document, dating it to an apparent unrealized 1846 idea of PHG's to collect natural history objects for the British Museum in the Azores. Additional information about the small sheet is in D. Wertheimer, 'The Truth About 1843', 42fn.176.

22. 'Dean Milman's History of the Jews', London *Reader* (23 May 1863), 496. Hannah Adams (London, 1818) and [James A. Huie] (Edinburgh, 1840) also authored histories of the Jews; for the dearth of such works: 'The Patriarchs of the West, and the Princes of the Captivity', *Christian Remembrancer* XLII (July 1862), 50-1.

23. James Robert Thrane, 'The Rise of Higher Criticism in England, 1800-1870' (Columbia University, PhD dissertation, 1956), 214, 205-239.

24. On PHG, *The Monuments of Ancient Egypt* (1847): PHG-Rev. J. Evans, of SPCK, 26 Oct. 1846; and on that and PHG, *History of the Jews* (1851): the letter to the same person, 20 June 1848 (both in PHG, 'Testimony of Prophecy'). Freeman & Wertheimer-PHG treat the difficulties in publishing PHG's *History of the Jews*.

25. PHG-EWG, 11 June 1877 (CUL Add. 7019, 22). For PHG, *Introduction to Zoology* as well as PHG, *Natural History. Mammalia*, 'the sheets are submitted to Mr. Bell's supervision' (PHG-William Gosse, 19 Nov. 1847, CUL Adv.c.82.5,22).

published by the SPCK in quick succession: *Natural History. Mammalia* (1848), *Natural History. Birds* (1849), *Natural History. Reptiles* (1850), and *Natural History. Fishes* (1851). With the exception of the more sophisticated *Natural History. Mollusca*, in 1854, the books were largely derivative.[26] The quality of the series may have been affected by its possibly coming in response to the mid-century controversy between the British government under Lord John Russell (which had a monopoly on subsidising school books in Ireland) and independent London publishers.[27] Along these lines was another SPCK work, Gosse's *A Text-book of Zoology for Schools* (1851). There were few such works at the time and Gosse's volume was largely unoriginal.[28] The *Literary Gazette* drew attention to the fact that the SPCK work had a title strikingly similar to one on the government's approved list—Robert Patterson's *Introduction to Zoology for the Use of Schools* (1849).[29] In 1850, the SPCK suggested that Gosse supervise the preparation of additional scientific studies.[30]

On 16 September 1848, Gosse started a work for a new publisher, an ornithological calendar for young people with his illustrations. The 20 high-quality colour plates were drawn and lithographed by Gosse from specimens at the British Museum.[31] The book was finished on 21 November—that is, ten weeks later—and appeared for the Christmas trade.[32] This event is doubly notable. It is a demonstration of Philip's fluid and natural writing style, for in order to complete the 320 letterpress pages of *Popular British Ornithology* he had to average the equivalent of five printed pages a day. In addition, Gosse began the book the day

26. PHG-William Gosse, 19 Nov. 1847 (CUL Add. c. 82.5, 22); Freeman & Wertheimer-PHG, 29-30.

27. 'Our Weekly Gossip', *Athenaeum* (12 Apr. 1851), 407-8.

28. Freeman & Wertheimer-PHG, 39-40.

29. A review of *On the Publication of School Books by Government at the Public Expense* in *Literary Gazette* (19 Apr. 1851), 280-1, makes this point.

30. GLC, 17 May 1850.

31. Freeman & Wertheimer-PHG, 32. PHG's *Popular British Ornithology* (London: Reeve, Benham, and Reeve, 1849) was well received: *Spectator* XXII (20 Jan. 1849), 66; *Literary Gazette* (27 Jan. 1849), 55; London *Morning Chronicle* (31 Jan. 1849), 6; *Mirror* V (Feb. 1849), 159-60; *John Bull* XXIX (24 Mar. 1849), 183; *Tait's Edinburgh Magazine* XVI (Aug. 1849), 544; *Notes & Queries* ser. 1, V (21 Feb. 1852), 190.

32. The inscription in the Family Copy of the book reads: 'commenced on Sept. 16th and finished Nov. 21st 1848'. Freeman & Wertheimer-PHG, 32, following *Life*, 221, dates the publication to February 1849, which seems improbable. There was an advertisement for the book noting it would be available 'in December' in the London *Spectator* (18 Nov. 1848), 1122, and another states 'Just ready' in the London *Examiner* (9 Dec. 1848), 799, and *Spectator* (16 Dec. 1848), 1217. The earliest review I've seen is in the London *Spectator* (20 Jan. 1849), 66.

before his formal declaration of love to Emily Bowes, and completed the
work a day (or two) before their marriage.

-II-

Recall that Emily, who had been in fellowship at Hackney from 1841,
had first met Philip in 1843. Emily had come to Brethren from a
different direction than Gosse. Both of her Anglican parents—William
Bowes (1771-1850), the son of William Bowes (1734-1805), and Hannah
Troutbeck (1768-1851), the daughter of the Revd John Troutbeck—were
born in Boston.[33] They settled long enough in London for Emily to be
born at 74 Great Portland Street, Marylebone, on 10 November 1806.[34]
In the next year, the family moved to Dôlymelynllyn, near Dolgelly,
Merionethshire, North Wales, where William and Hannah had two
other children, Edmund Elford Bowes (1808-1877)[35] and Arthur Bowes
(1813-before 1870).[36] Around 1814, Emily's father lost all his property,
they were reduced to poverty and forced to move from place to place in
the south of England.[37]

The penury, instability, and insecurity of Emily's upbringing stayed
with her all her life. Deeply fearful of being cast out and left alone, she
yearned from her early years to feel wanted. She confessed to her diary
that to gain friends, 'I have also concealed my own opinion & pretended
to adopt that of those I wished to please.' She was comforted in believing
that a watchful eye preserved her from small mishaps, yet death was

33. James H. Stark, *The Loyalists of Massachusetts and the Other Side of the American Revolution* (Boston: Salem Press Co., 1910), 224.

34. In works published in 1890, EWG gives his mother's date of birth as 9 November ('Gosse, Emily', *DNB* xxii, 258) and 10 November (*Life*, 215). The correct date is 10 November: Freeman & Wertheimer-EG, 26fn.2. On the Bowes family: 'Pedigree of Bowes of Boston, (New-England) North-America', n.d., apparently in PHG's holograph (CUL Adv. c. 82.5, 24); EWG-[Oliver Wendell] Holmes, 1 Sept. 1888, in Paul F. Mattheisen and Michael Millgate (eds.), *Transatlantic Dialogue: Selected American Correspondence of Edmund Gosse* (Austin: University of Texas Press, 1965), 210-11; *Life*, 215-6. According to Cyril Davenport, EWG 'told me his mother was of low extraction & her brother was a private soldier in the army—His father married a second time and his mother-in-law left him a fortune' (CD-Evan Charteris, 21 [?August] 1929, CUL Add. 7027,82). Though not directly responding to this comment, EWG's half-truths are unraveled in Boyd, *Emily Gosse*, chap. 2.

35. Death notice, London *Standard* (29 Jan. 1877), 1.

36. On Edmund Elford Bowes and Arthur Bowes: D. Wertheimer, 'The Identification of Some Characters and Incidents in Gosse's "Father and Son"', *Notes and Queries* n.s. XXIII (January 1976), 4-11 [hereafter Wertheimer, *Identification*], 10.

37. Information and quotations on EG are (unless otherwise indicated) from 'Recollections of Emily Bowes 1835'.

on her mind.[38] She was self-critical, alluding to 'many instances in my younger days when I have even dishonestly eaten in private what I know wd. not have been given me.' Before she turned 30, she wrote that 'I am ever fearing poverty, destitution, starvation, even in the midst of friends & affluence.' She was isolated from her own parents. 'I can remember,' she stated in the same place, 'when out of spirits finding great comfort from the text when my father & my mother forsake me[: the Lord taketh me up. Psalm 27: 10].'

Immediately after leaving North Wales, the Boweses lived in and near Exmouth (1814-7). With the assistance of friends, and a £25 annuity from her godfather, Jonathan Elford (1776-1823), 'for and towards her maintenance and education',[39] Emily was able to avoid being a financial burden to her parents. She attended local schools, learned French and perhaps German, and supervised a Sunday school. Teaching there was 'the greatest pleasure of my life.'[40]

Emily enjoyed reading the Bible,[41] knew portions of it by heart, loved clergymen and the Lord's Day, and at school had a reputation for being religious. 'I cannot recollect the time when I did not love religion', she said. Nonetheless she was not satisfied: 'The great & worst defect in my religious education was that I was never fully impressed with the utter depravity & helplessness of my nature, with the efficacy of the Atonement, of the new birth, & the work of the Spirit.' When or if Emily underwent a distinct evangelical conversionary moment is not known; but the message of William Law's impactful *Serious Call to a Devout and Holy Life* (1728), which she read, was heeded: 'I set apart a corner of my room for reading &

38. There are a number of poems on that subject in E[mily]. B[owes]., *Hymns and Sacred Poems* (Bath: A. E. Binns, 2ed., 1832) and E[mily]. B[owes]., *Hymns and Sacred Poems. Second Series* (Bath: A.E. Binns, 1834).

39. The original annuity is at CUL (Add. 7035/II/20). A large Oxford Bible (1807), seen in the Family Collection, bears the inscription: 'This Bible, originally the property of Jonathan Elford, Esq., was by him presented to his 'god-daughter', Emily Bowes, on the 7th of Apr., 1814. ...' His date of death is noted in pencil; for his date of birth: Boyd, *Emily Gosse*, 17fn.10.

40. 'Recollections of Emily Bowes 1835', p. [26].

41. Of the Bible, she wrote in *Hymns and Sacred Poems. Second Series* (Bath: A. E. Binns, 1834), 31:

'Twas in childhood my delight,
'Neath my pillow laid at night,
From its page my task I said,
In it to my parents read,
Thence I learnt in early youth,
To revere the God of truth.

prayer,' and she thus became confirmed in her 'preference for evangelical religion as far as I knew the difference.'

Her stay in Exmouth was apparently followed by a brief one in Warwick, and in 1819 the family returned to London. By now Emily had at least a rudimentary knowledge of several languages (French, German, Latin, and Greek),[42] and four years later, at the age of 17, she turned these to good account in leaving home to become a governess to the Revd John Hawkins of Compton, near Farringdon, Berkshire.[43]

For some fourteen years Emily cared for this young clergyman's family, which eventually numbered twelve children. Towards the end of this period, when her brother Edmund matriculated at Cambridge (1835), she assisted him financially.[44] She also devoted time to literary activity. In childhood she had enjoyed story-telling, and later had written some hymns, but the former activity was considered sinful and the latter products destroyed.[45] Now, however, inventiveness and poetry were combined for a legitimate purpose: the composition in 1831, and then publication, of two series of *Hymns and Sacred Poems*.[46]

Emily was reading the hymns and poetry of Charlotte Elizabeth, the reverends H. F. Lyte, John Moultrie, and other celebrated Christian

---

42. And perhaps then (or apparently later) EG studied Hebrew as well: E[dmund]. G[osse]., 'Gosse, Emily', *DNB* xxii (1890), 258 ('a fair Greek and a good Hebrew scholar'), and Edmund C. Stedman, 'Some London Poets [on Edmund Gosse]', *Harper's New Monthly Magazine* LXVI (May 1882), 887: 'His mother was ... a Greek and Hebrew scholar, and her son still possesses her manuscript comments on the Book of Daniel, of which both the English and Hebrew text are beautiful specimens of calligraphy.' Of course half of Daniel is in Aramaic and half in Hebrew. Robert Boyd's claim that a footnote in EG's *Abraham and His Children* (1855) reflects a knowledge of Hebrew is unpersuasive (Boyd, *Emily Gosse*, 30fn.3, incorrectly citing *Abraham and His Children*, 157 should be p.137fn).

43. Copy of a letter, [Emily Bowes]-Sarah Stoddard, 16 Sept. 1841 (CUL Adv. c. 82.5, 25); the biographical information about EG below is from here. According to an annotation on the letter by PHG, Sarah Stoddard was EG's cousin living in Roxbury, Massachusetts. Sarah Stoddard was presumably related to Mary Stoddard (d. 1774), the second wife of EG's grandfather William Bowes (1734-1805), whom Mary Stoddard married in 1769 (Stark, *Loyalists of Massachusetts*, 224). In Emily's letter to Stoddard, PHG has written in pencil 'Rev. I. Hawkins' above the words 'as a governess in a Clergymans [sic] family' and added in square brackets 'Compton, nr. Farringdon, Berks.' next to the words 'in a little country village'. According to Boyd, *Emily Gosse*, 26-7, this was the Revd John C. C. P. Hawkins (1793-1871), the curate of Compton Beauchamp.

44. Anna Shipton, *'Tell Jesus.' Recollections of Emily Gosse* (London: Morgan and Chase, [1863]), 68; *Life*, 216.

45. 'Recollections of Emily Bowes 1835', pp. [16, 23].

46. For a history of *Hymns and Sacred Poems:* Freeman & Wertheimer-EG, 38-40.

authors,[47] and her own volumes testified to the presence of a confirmed evangelical conscience. Since Emily knew that Christ

> ... hast shed thy blood for me;
> This, of all thy gifts the best,
> Crowns and sanctifies the rest.[48]

she desired nothing more than to serve her master:

> Use my tongue, my hands, my feet,
> Use my heart while that shall beat,
> Use my purse, its gold is thine,
> Use whatever else is mine.[49]

And to do that, she asked 'Help ... to understand, / All that scripture does command':

> Help me meekly to receive,
> All a christian should believe;
> Day by day increase my faith,
> In whate'er the Bible saith.
>
> Lord, thy prophecies unfold,
> Till the future I behold,
> And by faith thy glories view,
> Ever bright and ever new!
>
> Thou wilt come, as comes a thief,
> Chase our sloth and unbelief,
> May we, hourly watch and pray,
> And be waiting for thy day.[50]

Other notes made at the time provide further instances of conviction.[51] She felt the need for separation from 'the vain pleasures & pomps of this world', considered the purpose of education 'To train & prepare the soul for its eternal destiny', and knew the importance of watching for the second coming. Her devotion to prophecy probably dates from this time, and her adherence to the historical school of interpretation appears to have led her to place special importance on the years 1866-7.[52]

---

47. 'Recollections of Emily Bowes 1835'.
48. EB, 'Thanksgiving', *Hymns and Sacred Poems* (1832), 50.
49. EB, 'Self-Devotion', *Hymns and Sacred Poems* (1834), 35.
50. EB, 'I Say Unto All—Watch', *Hymns and Sacred Poems* (1832), 52-3.
51. 'Recollections of Emily Bowes 1835'.
52. PHG, *A Memorial of the Last Days on Earth of Emily Gosse* (London: James Nisbet

In the spring of 1838, Emily left Compton for a similar position with the family of the late Revd Sir Christopher Musgrave (d. 1834), at Brighton.[53] As soon as her brother Edmund completed his BA at Cambridge in 1841, however, she returned to London, where she resided with her parents and her other brother Arthur, at Brook Street, Upper Clapton.[54] It was apparently sometime during the next few years that Emily spent time 'in endeared intimacy' at Plymouth with Hannah Newton (1798-1846), the first wife of B. W. Newton, and was enthralled 'by the beautiful and elaborate system and bold assertions of that eminent teacher.'[55]

It was in 1841 that Emily came in contact in Hackney with 'a collection of Christians who meet as such out of all the different Sects, and *are* endeavouring to revive the brotherly love of the early Christians.'[56] Brethren assemblies, as has been already noticed above, had spread to London in 1833, reaching Hackney in 1841.[57] Two years later Emily met Philip Gosse[58]—a person like her of intellectual and literary abilities, inward and thoughtful, who shared her evangelical orientation and devotion to prophecy. The friendship continued for several years and 'ripened into love', until Philip was convinced 'we have His smile' on marriage.[59] Emily was no less gratified that, once united, she would fulfill the role of a wife 'most calculated to strengthen' her husband's faith by

---

& Co., 1857), 54, states she had been a 'diligent student' for more than 25 years (*viz.*, before 1832). Her 'Notebook' (n.d., seen in the Family Collection) has 14 pages of notes on prophetic chronology, some of those apparently taken from writings of T. R. Birks (and thus post-1843), focus on these dates.

53. In [Emily Bowes]-Sarah Stoddard, 16 Sept. 1841, the name is rendered 'Sir Charles Musgrave'. According to Boyd, *Emily Gosse*, 32-3, it was the Revd Sir Christopher John Musgrave, who died at the age of 36.

54. [Emily Bowes]-Sarah Stoddard, 16 Sept. 1841, and *1841 Census Returns for Hackney*, Enumeration District 4, p. 29. Emily is not listed, possibly indicating that she did not arrive until after 6 June 1841, when the census took place.

55. PHG, *Memorial*, 55. Robert Boyd initially set Emily's time with Newton to the period 1841-45 (Boyd-Wertheimer, 7 June 1976), later settling on 1843-44 (Boyd, *Emily Gosse*, 47). Hannah Abbott, a Quaker by upbringing, married Newton in Mar. 1832 and died on 18 May 1846 (Akenson, *Exporting the Rapture*, 228). Newton left Plymouth in 1847 (Stunt, *From Awakening to Secession*, 388). Boyd, *Emily Gosse*, 46, gives her birth as 1798, without citing a source.

56. [Emily Bowes]-Sarah Stoddard, 16 Sept. 1841 (CUL Adv. c. 82.5, 25). Emphasis in the original.

57. Gerald West, 'The Early Development of Brethren Assemblies in London', 68, 75.

58. PHG-EWG, 1 Mar. 1867 (CUL Add. 7018,3): '… at Hackney, where I first met your own loved Mamma, in 1843'.

59. PHG-William Gosse, 21 Oct. 1848 (CUL Adv. c. 82.5, 29), for the two quotations.

bringing up children 'after a godly sort'.[60] On 23 November 1848,[61] the two were married by Robert Howard at Brook Street Chapel, Tottenham, in the presence of Emily's brothers Arthur and Edmund, cousin Mrs Ann Morgan, and some friends. 'I have a wife who is in every way worthy of being honoured & loved, who is in every way a help meet for me,' Philip told his brother William, 'all our Christian friends ... seemed to think our union peculiarly happy & suitable.'[62]

Emily had just turned 42, and Philip was 38. Theirs was a tender relationship motivated by a love for the word and bound-up in devotion to the Word. It is telling that the gifts they gave each other before and after they married included copies of their own books. They were inscribed by Philip to Emily from 'her affectionate lover', to 'my sweetest and best beloved', 'my darling', 'my cherished & beloved wife'—all with 'the true love of her affectionate husband'. In return, he received a copy of Emily's published poems 'from his affectionate Emily'.[63]

From Tottenham the Gosses returned to Philip's home in Kingsland (since around mid-March 1848 he and his mother had been living at 13 Trafalgar Terrace, Mortimer Road, De Beauvoir Square).[64] Here they spent their few weeks' honeymoon in solitude, Hannah having gone to

---

60. Emily Gosse, *Abraham and his Children: or Parental Duties Illustrated by Scriptural Examples* (London: Nisbet & Co., 1855), 141.

61. Their date of marriage is given as 22 November in all prior studies of PHG (e.g., *Life*, 218, 220; D. L. Wertheimer, 'Philip Henry Gosse: Science and Revelation in the Crucible'. University of Toronto, PhD dissertation, 1977, 170 [hereafter D.L. Wertheimer, 'Philip Henry Gosse']; Freeman & Wertheimer-PHG, 32; Freeman & Wertheimer-EG, 27; Boyd, 'Gosse, Emily', *DEB* I, 1995, 460; Boyd and Rowdon, *ODNB* (2004); Boyd, *Emily Gosse*, 2004, 38). Additional support for that date comes from 'Pedigree of Bowes of Boston, (New-England) North-America' [n.d. but not before Jan. 1851] (CUL Adv.c.82.5,24), which appears to be in PHG's holograph, and the copy of PHG's *Popular British Ornithology* (seen in the Family Collection) which states it was completed on 21 November, pointing to a marriage the next day.

The only source for 23 Nov. is PHG's letter to his brother William, dated 25 Dec. 1848 (CUL Adv.c.82.5,30): 'We were married at Tottenham at the Chapel, where Brethren worship, on the 23rd, November'. This same sentence is cited in Boyd, *Emily Gosse*, 48, where he transcribed the date as '22nd November', though on p. 49 Boyd gave the date as 23 November. I have opted for the 23 November date because it was cited in close proximity to the actual event. I am grateful to Louise Clarke, Superintendent of the Manuscripts Reading Room at Cambridge, for confirming the accuracy of my transcription of PHG's 25 Dec. letter (e-mail, 30 May 2023).

62. PHG-William Gosse, 25 Dec. 1848 (CUL Adv. c. 82.5, 30), and see a manuscript note in the Gosse Papers, Miscellaneous MSS & Typescripts (LeBL).

63. All of these works were seen in the Family Collection. In order of year of inscription, they are: 1848 (PHG, *Introduction to Zoology*; *Monuments of Ancient Egypt*; *Natural History. Mammalia*; *Popular British Ornithology*) and 1852 (*Naturalist's Sojourn in Jamaica*); from Emily: 1848 (*Hymns and Sacred Poems*).

64. For the address: PHG-William Gosse, 3 Mar. 1848 (Family Collection).

stay with a cousin. Though they did not know how the mother would get along with the new daughter-in-law when she would return to live with them, the newlyweds assumed those buoyant expectations which couples evince in starting a new life. Long after those weeks had elapsed, Gosse spoke to his brother of their honeymoon as 'not over yet, & we intend to keep it up for an indefinite period: in fact, its termination has been adjourned, (by mutual consent) 'sine die'. It is a very sweet thing, dear William, to love & to be loved.'[65]

During the three years following the wedding, Philip continued his scientific labours non-stop. Besides those projects already mentioned on which he was working, the SPCK offered to pay Gosse £100 for an elementary textbook on zoology for children. This he agreed to do, and the project was under way in March 1849.[66] By that month, he had published ten volumes and more than that many articles; was acquainted with many of England's leading naturalists;[67] and now was about to receive formal recognition for his contributions to science. Gosse was the author of several natural works, his nomination form noted, and 'a Gentleman conversant with many branches of natural science, particularly Zoology.' On the initiative of his friends Adam White and Edward Doubleday, he was elected an Associate of the Linnean Society on 20 March 1849.[68] Later that year, Bowerbank gained for him membership in the Microscopical Society.[69]

---

65. PHG-William Gosse, 3 May 1849 (CUL Adv. c. 82.5, 27).

66. PHG-Rev. J. Evans, 24 Mar. 1849, PHG-Thomas Bell, same day (both in PHG, 'Testimony of Prophecy'); *Life*, 221; Freeman & Wertheimer-PHG, 40. *A Text-book of Zoology for Schools* appeared in 1851.

67. Besides those people already mentioned above, he also knew personally John J. Bennett, the Secretary of the Linnean Society; Edward Forster, the botanist; George Newport, the entomologist; J. T. Quekett, the microscopist (*Life*, 223); and G. R. Waterhouse of the Natural History Museum (PHG, *Naturalist's Sojourn in Jamaica*, 443fn.). All of these men have entries in the *DNB*; the first three signed Philip's recommendation for admission into the Linnean Society (see fn. below).

68. 'As to the matter of [my] ALS-ship it was arranged long ago, *without my knowledge*, by Edward Doubleday & Adam White, on my return from Jamaica' (PHG-J. D. Hooker, 19 Dec. 1861, Kew, *English Letters*, 87/70. Emphasis in the original). PHG's election was proposed on 16 Jan. 1849 by T. Bell, E. Doubleday, A. White, W. Baird, John J. Bennett, Edward Forster, George Newport, and John Gould (Linnean Society *Certificates of Fellows, Foreign Members & Associates 1846-56*), and confirmed on 20 Mar. 1849 (*Gardeners' Chronicle*, 24 Mar. 1849, 183). The nomination proposal for PHG cited his *Canadian Naturalist, Introduction to Zoology, Birds of Jamaica* '& other works on Zoology'.

69. According to *Life*,223, PHG was elected a member of the Microscopical Society on 14 Nov. 1849, at Bowerbank's 'proposition'. The Society did meet on that date and Bowerbank was in the chair, but I have not seen that at that meeting members were elected (*Zoologist* VII (1849),

It was not long before Emily's time was fully occupied. After a difficult and painful labour, Emily and Philip's only child was born at home at noon on 21 September 1849.[70] At first, the infant uttered no sound, leading the attending physician to fear that convulsions might terminate the life of the newborn. Soon, however, Edmund William Gosse showed signs of life, developing normally thereafter. After her recovery from the delivery, Emily went to the Room at Hackney. There 'Mr. Balfour prayed for us & for our child that he may be the Lord's.'[71]

It is sobering to find that notwithstanding the changes in attitudes towards child-rearing from generation to generation, familiar parental challenges and concerns endure. Parents have to decide how, when, and what to feed the infant; how to prevent spoiling; how to adjust to the time-consuming process of changing and diapering. There are the seemingly inevitable disagreements with in-laws and between parents, and the issues which only proud parents could think worthwhile documenting in minute detail for posterity—the change in hair colour, the first smile, the first laugh, the first occasion on which objects and non-parents are noticed, the first time outside, the first steps ('I took my rule & measured the distance, & found it six feet!'),[72] the reaction to strangers, allowing one's treasure to be cared for by others, and the never-ending dispute about who the child looks like (some said Arthur, Emily said her husband). All these little issues swirled around the advent

2636). PHG signed himself 'F.M.S.' in his letter on 'The Diseased Wheat', London Standard, 18 Oct. 1850, 6. He was elected a member of the Microscopical Society Council at the 12 Feb. 1851 meeting (*Zoologist* IX (1851), 3097; *Life*, 223, 230). On 9 Feb. 1887, PHG was named an Honorary Fellow of the Royal Microscopical Society (*Journal of the Royal Microscopical Society* ser. 2, VII (Apr. 1887), 355). RMS elected a maximum of 50 Honorary Fellows 'consisting of persons eminent in Microscopical or Biological Science' (*JRMS* p. [iii]).

70. PHG-William Gosse, 21 Sept. 1849 (CUL Add. 7027, 2b); EG, Diary for 1849 [with subsequent additions for 1851, 1854-5] (LeBL) [hereafter EG, Diary. This is distinct from EG's Diary for [Jan. 1-Apr. 27,] 1854, which is hereafter cited as Diary for 1854]; *Father and Son*, 1907, 7. All of the information below, unless otherwise indicated, is from EG's Diary. Wertheimer, *Identification*, 9-10, analyses the citation in *Father and Son*, 1907, 7, of PHG's alleged entry in his diary the day EWG was born: 'E. delivered of a son. Received green swallow from Jamaica'. The bird is figured in PHG, *Illustrations of the Birds of Jamaica*, plate XII. On this bird, see David Marshall, 'The Jamaican Golden Swallow is Now Probably Extinct', *BirdLife Jamaica Broadsheet* no. 99 (Mar. 2014), 21-24.

71. EG, Diary (under 4 Nov. 1849).

72. PHG-EG, 2 Aug. 1850 (CUL Adv. c. 82.5, 36). EWG was 10½ months old when PHG measured his achievement. All of the concerns mentioned in the paragraph were recorded in EG's Diary.

of Emily and Philip's precious child, as they have to good parents from time immemorial.

To these, Emily added worries peculiar to a mid-Victorian evangelical home. It was a common belief (later rejected by her) that 'the child who in infancy manifests grace will die in infancy.'[73] She was prepared for tragedy: 'only if it please the Lord to take him I do trust we may be spared seeing him suffer in lingering illness, & much pain. But in this as in all things His will is better than what we can choose.'[74] From her own experiences as a governess, she had formulated notions as to how to rear a child into godliness. The training must begin at birth; the child's will must be subservient to the parents', even if that meant not sparing the rod at six months; the parents should teach the child themselves, not relying on a surrogate; they should set a good example ('Let them see that we love not the world; let them see that we fear not to be poor and despised for Christ's sake; that we esteem the reproach of Christ greater riches than the treasures of Egypt'); and it should be known that the parents daily pray for the child in secret, so that

> he who, in addition to the rest, can look back to his early infancy, and can remember hearing his father and his mother pray for him, and with him, and that day after day, and year after year, is not likely in future life to be a prayerless man. The little hands soon learn to clasp together, and the little lips to lisp prayers and praises.[75]

Parents learn that nuance and patience are part of the best of child-rearing plans. Disappointment is inevitable. Too much discipline may fail, for 'obedience that is not voluntary, and submission that is enforced by restraint and fear only, is not likely to be of long continuance.' Too high expectations may mislead, since 'children are the creatures of imitation.'[76] The appearance of religious conversion may be no more than that. That first winter Emily devoted herself entirely to caring for Edmund, and learned some of these lessons. It was an experience made easier when Hannah Gosse, never very happy at Trafalgar Terrace, left them in the middle of November.[77]

73. EG, *Abraham and his Children*, xvi-xvii.
74. EG, Diary (under 4 Nov. 1849).
75. EG, *Abraham and his Children*, 69-70; and for the discussion of these guidelines, the same source, pp. 159-60, 168-92; 160-2; 67-8.
76. EG, *Abraham and his Children*, 193, 218.
77. EG, Diary (under 4 Nov. 1849), and also under 25 Nov. 1849. With Hannah gone they

-III-

In June 1849, Philip Gosse bought himself a microscope.[78] It certainly wasn't something new to him—as previously mentioned, he was familiar with the capabilities of the instrument since his days in Newfoundland, when he purchased Kanmacher's edition of Adams' *Essays on the Microscope*. Nor was it new for others. Microscopy was gaining the attention of men of science and the general public in London by the early 1830s,[79] and Gosse's interest in the subject could have been enhanced by his acquaintance with knowledgeable microscopists like Bowerbank, Newman, the Quekett brothers,[80] or T. H. Huxley (who bought himself an expensive microscope in 1846 for £13).[81] We don't know how Gosse came to make the purchase or how much it cost, though what he did with it is not in question. He went to a nearby pond and took some water samples, and 'looking with ignorant but interested curiosity' at them through his microscope he was 'charmed with the varied forms and sprightly motions of the strange creatures'. He immediately decided to turn his scientific eye on their activities, concentrating on Rotifera.[82]

Findings followed. His first paper on Rotifera was read before the Microscopical Society of London in January 1850, with a second read in March 1850 and a third published in July.[83] In October, his advice as a microscopist was sought to determine whether a sample of diseased wheat was being infected by Rotifera (he even managed in his reply to

started looking for a new home in Hackney, not only because the rent was now too high, but also in order to be closer to the Brethren Room and to Emily's mother.

78. *Life*, 222.

79. R. Tanner Hewlett, 'One Hundred Years of Microscopy: The Royal Microscopical Society', *Nature* 144 (18 Nov. 1939), 850-2.

80. *Life*, 223, states that at this time he corresponded with John Quekett (1815-1861); PHG already knew Bowerbank, Forbes, and Huxley.

81. Isobel Armstrong, 'The Microscope: Mediations of the Sub-visible World', in Roger Luckhurst and Josephine McDonagh (eds.), *Transactions and Encounters: Science and Culture in the 19th Century* (Manchester: Manchester University Press, 2002), 30.

82. PHG, 'Contributions to the History of the Rotifera, or Wheel Animalcules. I. The Crown Animalcule (*Stephanoceros Eichhornii*)', *Popular Science Review* I (Oct. 1861), 26.

83. PHG, 'On the architectural instincts of *Melicerta ringens*, an animal of the Class Rotifera', *Trans. Micro. Soc.* ser. 1, III (Mar. 1851), 58-64, read at the 16 Jan. 1850 meeting (*Gardeners' Chronicle*, 19 Jan. 1850, 39); PHG, 'On the anatomy of *Notommata aurita*, an animal of the Class Rotifera', *Trans. Micro. Soc.* ser. 1, III (Mar. 1851), 93-104; PHG, 'Description of *Asplanchna priodonta*, an animal of the Class Rotifera', *AMNH* ser. 2, VI (July 1850), 18-24 (this was actually the first of PHG's *published* articles on Rotifera, his one on *Melicerta ringens* read before, but appearing after, it).

refer to Adams' *Essays on the Microscope*).[84] In July 1851, he compiled an ambitious catalogue of British Rotifera.[85]

Gosse was fascinated with the strange new world of Rotifera[86] (*Latin*, 'wheel-bearers', reflecting the wheel-like image produced by rotating cilia at the head of the animal). 'So elegant are their outlines,' he wrote,

> so brilliantly translucent their texture, so complex and yet so patent their organisation, so curious their locomotive wheels, so unique their apparatus for mastication, so graceful, so vigorous, so fleet, and so marked with apparent intelligence their movements, so various their forms and types of structure, so readily attainable for study in almost every locality, and at all seasons of the year: that, as fact after fact and detail after detail of organisation and habit revealed itself to me, I often wondered that scarcely anyone seemed to know anything about them.[87]

They were not as unknown to men of science as Gosse suspected. Rotifera had been the object of curiosity since the late seventeenth century when, with the aid of the microscope (invented about 1608), their existence was discovered.[88] During that century the Dutchman Antoni van Leeuwenhoek,[89] the Frenchman Louis Joblot, the Englishmen Henry

84. PHG letter dated Oct. 12, 1850, published in 'The Diseased Wheat', London *Standard* (18 Oct. 1850), 6.

85. PHG, 'A catalogue of the Rotifera found in Britain; with descriptions of five new genera and thirty-two new species', *AMNH* ser. 3, VIII (Sept. 1851), 197-203.

86. Today's nomenclatorial rules favour the group being called 'Rotifera' (Cuvier, 18th Century) and not 'Rotatoria' (Ehrenberg, 19th Century): Claudia Ricci, 'Rotifera or Rotatoria?', *Hydrobiologia* 104 (1983), 1.

87. PHG, 'Contributions to the History of the Rotifera', *Popular Science Review* I (Oct. 1861), 27.

88. The information which follows on the history of rotiferan studies is, unless otherwise indicated, drawn from: Paul Marais de Beauchamp, 'Recherches sur les Rotifères. Les formations tégumentaires et l'appareil digestif', *Archives de Zoologie Expérimentale et Générale*, 4e ser., X (25 Jan. 1909), 7-18; C. T. Hudson and PHG, *The Rotifera* (London: Longmans, Green, and Co., 2vols., 1886), I: 15-22; *Natural History Review* n.s. I (1861), 121-26; Mary Pickard Winsor, 'Issues in the Classification of Radiates, 1830-1860' (Yale University, PhD dissertation, 1971), chaps. 1-2, 4-5; and entries on Ehrenberg and Dujardin in *DSB*.

89. Rotifera research dates to the Dutch naturalist von Leeuwenhoek in 1676 (David Mark Welch, 'Evidence for the Evolution of Bdelloid Rotifers Without Sexual Reproduction or Genetic Exchange' (Harvard University, PhD dissertation, 1999), 1-4); 'Leeuwenhoek, Antoni van', *DSB* VIII, 2008, 127. Others, incorrectly, date the discovery to 1687 (Diego Fontaneto and Willem H. De Smet, 'Rotifera', in Andreas Schmidt-Rhaesa (ed.), *Handbook of Zoology. Gastrotricha, Cycloneuralia and Gnathifera. Volume 3: Gastrotricha and Gnathifera* (Berlin: De Gruyter, 2015), 217) or 1696 (C[harles]. T[homas]. Hudson, *The Rotifera; or Wheel-Animalcules*. Assisted by H. Gosse (2vols. London: Longmans, Green, and Co., 1886) [hereafter Hudson & Gosse] I: 15, crediting the Revd John Harris of Winchelsea).

Baker and John Harris, and the Prussian J. C. Eichhorn had all published observations on the heterogeneous class of uni- and multicellular plants and animals known as 'infusoria' (a word coined in 1763 to refer to—besides rotifers—diatoms, desmids, rhizopods, vorticella, and some worms).[90] In the posthumous *Animalcula Infusoria Fluviatilia et Marina* (1786) of the Dane, O. F. Müller, a classification was first attempted. Parts of it, however, caused 'greater confusion than ever,'[91] and it was eventually superseded most notably by Cuvier (1817), who made the infusoria one of the five classes of the *embranchement* ('branches' or 'phyla') known as 'radial animals'. Cuvier's system, not based upon any thorough inspection of the animalcules, reflected his belief in a 'great chain of being' stretching in uniform gradations from the lowest forms to the highest.

Around 1830, a second period of rotiferan studies was initiated when the Prussian savant Christian Gottfried Ehrenberg (1795-1876), with remarkable patience and industry, turned his attention to the infusoria.[92] After finding a suitable microscope, he challenged Cuvier's assertion that the 'radiates' were not complex creatures (sea anemones and jellyfish were among the animals included in the now obsolete classificatory system of Radiata). Ehrenberg maintained that even the single-celled animals (no less than all others) possessed nervous, vascular, muscular, digestive, and sexual organs, and so were complete animals. This thesis he presented in lectures and in communications to the Berlin Academy, and above all in his monumental *Die Infusionsthierchen als Vollkommene Organismen* (*The Infusion Animalcules as Complete Organisms*) (Leipzig, 1838), an imposing monograph of 550 folio pages with descriptions in Latin, German, and French and an atlas of sixty-four beautifully coloured copperplates.

The 'noble volumes'[93] of *Die Infusionsthierchen* 'swallowed up as it

---

90. Frederick B. Churchill, 'The Guts of the Matter. Infusoria from Ehrenberg to Bütschli: 1838-1876', *Journal of the History of Biology* 22 (Summer 1989), 189fn. 1.

91. F. J. Cole, *The History of Protozoology* (London: University of London Press, 1926), 18.

92. On the historic development of rotiferan studies: De Beauchamp, 'Recherches sur les Rotifères', 8-18, and H. G. Bronn's *Klassen und Ordnungen des Tierreichs* [*Classes and Orders of the Animal Kingdom*], reviewed in *Nature* 129 (21 May 1932), 743-4. For an estimate of Ehrenberg (which Ehrenberg himself may have written): *A Dictionary of Contemporary Biography: A Handbook of the Peerage of Rank, Worth, and Intellect* (London: Richard Griffin, 1861), 148-9 (the original is at British Library, Add. MSS. 28, 510, f. 15).

93. PHG, 'On the Anatomy of *Notommata aurita*', 93.

were the very memory of all [its] predecessors,'[94] and for the next half-century this work and its classification set the standard by which all other studies were measured. Ehrenberg's precise observations, and his acquaintance with the habits of the subjects treated were, for the most part, exceptional. Yet at the same time, in his drive to reveal complexity he was led to depict organs which 'existed only in his imagination,'[95] while he fell into numerous and sometimes serious errors which were either observational or rooted in the outmoded microscope which he used.[96] Ehrenberg did not help his reputation by denying his shortcomings.[97]

These defects detracted from his mighty achievements and made Ehrenberg something of a joke among some naturalists (though not Gosse, who defended the 'gigantic labours of the Prussian microscopist').[98] In 1841, Félix Dujardin (1801-1860), who had been relentlessly ridiculed in *Die Infusionsthierchen*, published his *Histoire Naturelle des Zoophytes: Infusoires*, a polemic response to Ehrenberg.

94. Hudson & Gosse, I: 20.

95. PHG, 'On the Structure, Functions, and Homologies of the Manducatory Organs in the Class Rotifera', *Philosophical Transactions of the Royal Society* CXLVI (1857), 420. The MS for this work was completed by 20 Dec. 1854 (Royal Society, PT.53.1), and it was read before the Society in February and March 1855.

96. Ehrenberg's assumption that the so-called stomachs he noted in Rotifera 'were part of a visceral system is one of the strangest and most unfortunate mistakes ever made by a highly competent observer' (Cole, *The History of Protozoology*, 22). 'An enormous number [of 'Infusorial Animalcules'] were discovered and described by Ehrenberg, who, according to his own statement, did all his work with a microscope which he bought in Paris for thirty francs. We may observe that if this be true, it would partly account for the extraordinary mistakes of that indefatigable observer' (report of a lecture by Edwin Lankester at the Birmingham and Midland Institute, 23 Apr. 1855, in *Birmingham Journal*, 28 Apr. 1855, 7). See also and 'C. J.', 'Ehrenberg and His Microscopes', *Notes & Queries* ser. 2, I (5 Apr. 1856), 277-8.

97. Cole, *The History of Protozoology*, 23.

98. See, e.g., [?G. H. Lewes], *The Leader* (23 Oct. 1852), 1020-1; the remarks of T. H. Huxley (Cole, *The History of Protozoology*, 23) and Huxley as quoted by Charles Darwin (*The Autobiography of Charles Darwin*, ed. by Nora Barlow. New York: W. W. Norton & Co., 1969, 106-7). PHG's estimate: 'It is the fashion to deprecate and decry Ehrenberg. I have no sympathy with those who, taking their stand upon the ground which he has cleared with incredible labour and genius, can assume airs of pity or contempt when they discern inconsistencies or defects in his system. Many years' study of the Rotifera has enabled me in some measure to appreciate the gigantic labours of the Prussian microscopist, and to compare them with those of his successors and critics. ... looking at microscopic zoology as it was when Ehrenberg took it up, and as it was when he laid it down, I think it not too much to say that he stands in the foremost ranks of the scientific army, side by side with such names as Aristotle, Linnaeus, and Cuvier, and that his *Die Infusionsthierchen* is a monument to his fame, *aere perennius*, and such as few indeed have been able to erect' (PHG, 'The Natural History of the Hairybacked Animalcules (Chaetonotidae)', *Intellectual Observer* V (July 1864), 389 fn.). PHG's Latin citation signifying an immortal work is from Horace.

While inferior to the Prussian as an observer, he nonetheless improved upon his classification.[99] Seven years later, the Englishman Thomas Brightwell (1787-1868) disproved Ehrenberg's claim that the Rotifera were all hermaphrodites, when he found and depicted male specimens.[100] Bit-by-bit, the German's edifice was diminished.

Although Gosse may have recalled that Chapter VIII of Kanmacher's edition of Adams' *Essays on the Microscope* was devoted to 'Animalcula Infusoria,'[101] he had no difficulty in acquainting himself with the latest Continental researches. Gosse had studied German,[102] Latin,[103] Greek,[104] and French,[105] and if he needed help with German, he could turn to Emily.[106] Besides, a summary of Ehrenberg's work was available in Andrew Pritchard's *Natural History of Animalcules* (1st ed., 1834; 2nd, 1841; 3rd, 1852; last, 1861).[107] As we shall see, it would be nearly a half-century before Pritchard's research would be replaced by the 'classic monograph' of Hudson and Gosse.[108]

Meanwhile it was about a dozen years after the appearance of

99. Cole, *The History of Protozoology*, 24-6.

100. C. Wesenberg-Lund, 'Contributions to the Biology of the Rotifera', *Memoires de l'Academie Royales des Sciences et des Lettres de Danemark*, Section des Sciences, ser. 8, IV (1923), 192. In 1855, Brightwell sent rotifers to PHG: PHG, *Infusoria.4* (seen in the R. B. Freeman Collection), 132.

101. Adams used the term 'animalculum' to refer to all creatures invisible to the naked eye (Adams, *Essays on the Microscope*, 415).

102. *Life*, 224, incorrectly states that PHG 'was not acquainted' with German. On his way to Jamaica in 1844 PHG wrote that 'I have begun to study German' ('Jamaica Journal', 9 Nov. 1844), perhaps in order to better communicate with Moravian Brethren missionaries from Germany like Gustavus Henry Plessing (d. 1863). Plessing spent nearly a year in Fulneck, Yorkshire, improving his English before going to Jamaica on the same voyage as PHG (*Periodical Accounts* XVI, 1841, 542).

103. 'Reminiscences', I: 249 (he acquired a 'good fundamental knowledge' at Blandford School: 'Reminiscences', I:292).

104. 'Reminiscences', I: 255. He just began Greek when he left the school. PHG owned a copy of August Heinrich Matthiae's *Copious Greek Grammar* [trans. from German, 5ed., 1837] (*Sandhurst Catalogue*, item #615), two Greek Lexicons (#607) and a Greek concordance (#561).

105. PHG's facility in French may date to later years: PHG-Alfred Wailly, 18 Mar. 1881 (CUL Add. 7313, 322-3).

106. Perhaps for dramatic affect, *Life*, 224, claims that Emily translated Ehrenberg's work into English. EWG's statement reads as incomplete or exaggerated. A full translation would have been a dubious and redundant exercise, since PHG was able to read Ehrenberg's descriptions in Latin or German, and perhaps the ones in French as well (PHG-Alfred Wailly, 18 Mar. 1881, CUL Add. 7313,322-3, where PHG mentions he can read French).

107. PHG owned a copy of Dujardin's and Pritchard's works on infusoria, the editions are not stated (*Sandhurst Catalogue*, item #384).

108. Charles G. Hussey, 'An Historical Survey of the Collection and Study of Rotifers in Britain', *Hydrobiologia* 73 (1980), 237.

Ehrenberg's *Die Infusionsthierchen* that Gosse began acquainting himself with this new field. The former collector in the tropics found that he could readily transfer those skills to this microcosm. He gathered specimens of Rotifera from all over London: from ponds in Samuel Berger's residence in Hackney, and those near Walthamstow (sent by Edmund Bowes),[109] from the Serpentine in Hyde Park, from pools in Hampstead Heath, from a reservoir in Trafalgar Square, from the lake in front of Kensington Palace, and from the Black Sea at Wandsworth. With his microscope, Gosse reduced himself to an unseen observer of their life and work, recording everything in journals. In order to highlight the digestive organs of the Rotifera, Gosse fed them carmine (as Ehrenberg had),[110] and developed a means of manipulating them on slides.[111]

A few weeks after his own son was born, Philip witnessed the birth of a rotifer; he searched for male specimens, and watched them in coition.[112] Upon seeing what was perhaps a parasitic rotifer inside *Volvox globator*, he wrote:

> The structure in *h* is obscure, but I drew it as it appeared, not choosing
> to add anything I did not perceive. The difficulty of drawing, or even of
> defining by the eye, complex organs of a hyaline transparency, one within
> another, all in motion, while the active animal is every moment liable
> more or less to alter its position,—is exceedingly great, & can only be
> done after much observation, or by the happy fortune of the moment.[113]

And on another occasion, witnessing two subjects inhabiting the same space, he mused: 'brethren living in one house in amity'[114] —an undoubted allusion to the Brethren controversies of 1845-48.

Gosse's initial foray into the microscopic world of Rotifera was not

---

109. PHG named the Rotifer *Asplanchna Bowesii*, discovered by Edmund E. Bowes in 1849 in ponds in Walthamstow (today part of greater London), 'in honour of the esteemed relative to whom I owe my acquaintance with it' (PHG, 'Description of *Asplanchna priodonta*', 23).

110. For the use of carmine: PHG, *The Infusoria of Britain* (vols. 2-3, 1849, with later additions: BMNH, Zoological Library), II: 20; for EWG's misunderstanding of his father's use of carmine: *Father and Son*, 1907, 169-174; for the record of his researches: the two volumes of *Infusoria of Britain*, plus vol. IV, entitled *Infusoria.4* (seen in the R. B. Freeman Collection), and vol. V, *Rotifera.V.* (BMNH, Zoological Library).

111. PHG, *The Infusoria of Britain*, II: 49 (entry for 2 May 1850).

112. For the first: PHG, *The Infusoria of Britain* II: 49, 89 (3 Nov. [1849]); for the second, *Infusoria.4*, p. 39 (3 May 1850); and the last, *Infusoria.4*, p. 58 (11 May 1850).

113. PHG, *The Infusoria of Britain* II: 41-2 (8 Oct. [1849]).

114. PHG, *The Infusoria of Britain* II: 48 (15 Oct. [1849]).

inconsequential. In two of his studies, he extended the researches of Brightwell and others, further revealing the existence of species with separate males[115] and adding to the existing knowledge of the structure and habits of Rotifera.[116] Three others were faunal records, in which new species and genera were described;[117] another five essentially anatomical and biographical;[118] and the remainder systematic, together with a general natural history of the class.[119] A common comment on Gosse's drawings of Rotifera was that 'as might be expected, they are far superior to any others.'[120]

More specifically, Gosse's first Rotifera article—on *Melicerta ringens*, which is today called *Floscularia ringens* (Linnaeus, 1758)—deals with an animal about 1000 micrometres (written technically as ≤1000 μm) in total length, or 0.0393701 inches (a human hair is about 100 micrometres in diameter). Nearly fifty years after it was presented, the microscopist W. H. Dallinger remarked on 'the beautiful results obtained by the insight and patient researches of Gosse [which were] confirmed and enriched by scores of subsequent observers.'[121] Gosse was the first to describe the

115. PHG, 'Description of *Asplanchna priodonta*', 18-24; 'On the Dioecious Character of the Rotifera', *Phil. Trans. of the Royal Society*, CXLVII (Mar. 1858), 313-26 (received 19 Feb. 1856, read Mar. and Apr.); and see on this, Wesenberg-Lund, 'Contributions to the Biology of the Rotifera', 192.

116. Referee's report by Arthur Farre, 'On the Dioecious Character of the Rotifera' (Royal Society RR.3.114). PHG's article did not benefit from Farre's recommendation that it be published. Farre mislaid his report and did not send it to the Royal Society until after PHG's article appeared (Farre-G.G. Stokes, 11 Sept. 1858, RR.3.113). Farre was president of the Microscopical Society of London in 1851 when PHG was elected to its Council.

117. PHG, 'A Catalogue of Rotifera Found in Britain; with Descriptions of Five New Genera and Thirty-two New Species', *AMNH* ser. 2, VIII (Sept. 1851), 197-203; 'A Rotifer New to Britain—(*Cephalosiphon Limnias*)', *Intellectual Observer* I (Feb. 1862), 49-53, and the discussion following, pp. 53-57, 234; '*Dinocharis Collinsii*; A Rotiferon New to Science', ibid., X (Nov. 1866), 269-72.

118. PHG, 'On the Architectural Instincts of *Melicerta ringens*, an Animal of the Class Rotifera'; 'On the Anatomy of *Notommata aurita*, an Animal of the Class Rotifera' (on this, see Hudson & Gosse, I: 21); 'On the *Notommata parasita* (Ehrenb.), a Rotiferous Animal Inhabiting the Spheres of *Volvox globator*', all in *Transactions of the Microscopical Society*, ser. 1, III (1851-52): each paper was read in 1850; 'On the Structure, Functions, Habits, and Development of *Melicerta ringens*', *Quarterly Journal of Microscopical Science* I (Jan. 1853), 71-6; and PHG's manducatory organs paper.

119. PHG, 'On the Zoological Position of *Dysteria*', *Quarterly Journal of Microscopical Science*, n.s. V (Apr. 1857), 138-41; 'Contributions to the History of the Rotifera, or Wheel Animalcules', *Popular Science Review* I-II (Oct. 1861-July 1863), in 4 parts.

120. Henry J. Slack, 'Voracity of the Asplanchna, and its Stomach Currents', *Intellectual Observer* V (Apr. 1864), 182fn.: '... Mr. Gosse has allowed me to see his collection of drawings of these creatures [*Asplanchna*], and, as might be expected, they are far superior to any others.'

121. W. H. Dallinger, 'Note on Melicerta ringens', *Scientific American* 73 (10 Aug. 1895), 91

manner in which this rotifer built its surrounding tube, pellet by pellet (not described in greater detail for 100 years).[122] Gosse's 1851 'Catalogue of Rotifera Found in Britain', listing 108 species, was a major contribution in identifying species.[123]

In filling files with data and illustrations, Gosse was inevitably led into characteristic actions. He measured what he observed against Ehrenberg's descriptions, and detected errors. That led him to think about Ehrenberg's system for grouping species, because 'the artificial character of Ehr.'s arrangement continually strikes me.'[124] But Cuvier's classification—which Gosse had dutifully followed in his earlier zoological work—was not better. What to do? In truth, not much. Rotifera have been in existence for millions of years,[125] yet owing to a lack of any paleontological record they have been related over the years to many different groups. Their precise location in the invertebrate world could not be definitely established in Gosse's time, nor is there agreement to our day on the evolutionary (phylogenetic) position of Rotifers.[126]

In general, in mid-Victorian England the majority felt that the Rotifera were allied to the Annelida (segmented worms). The minority view was shared by Gosse, who in 1854 concluded that their true affinity lay with the Arthropoda[127] (invertebrates which form the largest phylum in the

(reprinted from *Science-Gossip*). The reference was to PHG's three papers published 1851-61 (Freeman & Wertheimer-PHG, items 201, 217, 310).

122. Diego Fontaneto, Giulio Melone and Robert L. Wallace, 'Morphology of *Floscularia ringens* (Rotifera, Monogononta) from egg to adult', *Invertebrate Biology* 122 (Summer 2003), 231.

123. Hussey, 'An Historical Survey of the Collection and Study of Rotifers in Britain', 237-8. Hussey calculated that PHG's single article identifying 108 species constituted nearly half of the 230 species known in 1886.

124. PHG, *The Infusoria of Britain* III: 21, 23 (14 Nov. [1849], and for the quotation, *Infusoria*.4., 1 (2 Apr. 1850); 'I have arranged them [the Rotifera] on the system of Professor Ehrenberg; not that I think his classification natural, but because none more convenient has been published' (PHG, 'A Catalogue of Rotifera found in Britain', 197); also *Rotifera.V*: 16: 'Thus I once more proved the trustworthiness of the great Prussian zoologist, in describing species' (under 5 Apr. 1887).

125. Bdelloids (a class of Rotifera known colloquially in PHG's time as 'creepers') have been found in amber dating to 35-40 million years ago (Welch, 'Evidence for the Evolution of Bdelloid Rotifers', 1-10).

126. Robert L. Wallace, Terry W. Snell, and Hilary A. Smith, 'Phylum Rotifera', in James H. Thorp and D. Christopher (eds.), *Thorp and Covich's freshwater invertebrates. Volume 1, Ecology and general biology* (Amsterdam: Elsevier/Academic Press, 4th ed., 2015), 230.

127. This was also the view of C. T. Hudson: 'Is Pedalion a Rotifera?' *Monthly Microscopical Journal* VIII (1 Nov. 1872), 214; 'On the Classification and Affinities of the Rotifera', *Report of the Forty-fifth Meeting of the British Association ... Bristol* (London: John Murray, 1876), 161-2.

animal kingdom), and within that not to Crustacea (primarily aquatic animals) but to insects.[128] Gosse first laid out his systematic ideas about the Rotifera in his 1855 Royal Society memoir 'On the Structure, Functions, and Homologies of the Manducatory Organs in the Class Rotifera'.[129] A modern assessment ranks that paper 'amongst the best' of all of his scientific serial studies.[130] No one prior to Gosse had properly delineated the complex masticating (or biting and chewing) apparatus of Rotifera;[131] and now, having already created a nomenclature,[132] he reduced the various forms to a common type. This was a 'remarkable' effort.[133] Huxley called it an 'excellent memoir,'[134] and another reader said the paper, with its 'new and original observations, constitutes an important addition to our present knowledge of the structure of Rotifera, and is rendered the more valuable on account of the number and extreme accuracy of the illustrations.'[135] In his referee's report recommending Gosse's Rotifera study for publication by the Royal Society, physiologist W. B. Carpenter (1813-1885) explained why descriptive, non-theoretically-centered science based on accurate and original research—the type of science Gosse enjoyed doing all his life—is important:

> Although the Paper [by Gosse] is full of minute details, yet I am not able to say that any of these are superfluous. They have obviously been observed with great care, and recorded with conscientious accuracy;

128. PHG, 'On the Structure, Functions, and Homologies of the Manducatory Organs in the Class Rotifera', 447. In enclosing some of his papers on Rotifera (including this one) in a letter to Ferdinand Grut (1820-1891), librarian at the Entomological Society in London, PHG wrote: '... I have laboured to show [in these reports] that the affinities of the Rotifera are with the Insecta' (PHG-Grut, 15 Oct. 1880, CUL Add. 7313,209).

129. PHG's MS (dated 20 Dec. 1854) was received at the Royal Society of London in Jan. 1855 and read in Feb. and Mar., but not published until Feb. 1857 in the *Philosophical Transactions ... for 1856* (Freeman & Wertheimer-PHG,116).

130. Freeman & Wertheimer-PHG, 9.

131. W. B. Carpenter, referee's report on the 'Manducatory organs' paper (Royal Society, RR.3.116).

132. Some of PHG's neologisms (mastax, malleus, manubrium) are cited in the *OED* (1st edition); others which have *OED* entries in which he has priority (incus, trophi), do not mention him.

133. Henry J. Slack, 'Pleasant Hours with the Microscope', *Knowledge* IX (1 June 1886), 246.

134. T. H. Huxley, 'On Dysteria; a new genus of infusoria', *Quarterly Journal of Microscopical Science* n.s. V (Jan. 1857), 82. PHG returned Huxley's compliment, referring to Huxley's 'excellent memoir' in PHG, 'On the zoological position of Dysteria', *Quarterly Journal of Microscopical Science* n.s. V (Apr. 1857), 138.

135. Referee's report of Arthur Farre, dated 11 Aug. 1855, at Royal Society (RR.3.115).

and they all seem necessary links in the chain of proof, by which his
conclusions are sustained.

All the higher generalisations in Natural History and Physiology,
must be based (if they are to have any permanent value) upon accurate
and comprehensive *studies* of this kind; and whether they relate to the
entire organization of a single species, or to the comparative organization
of some single apparatus in a great number, such studies appear to me
to [be] equally deserving of a place among the records of Science.[136]

Over fifty years later, the French zoologist de Beauchamp referred to this
'masterful study' ('l'étude magistrale'), 'a model of comparative anatomy
which can not be better compared than to the famous work of [Marie
Jules-César Lelorgne de] Savigny on the mouthparts of insects, and to
which almost nothing is to be changed after fifty years.'[137]

Not surprisingly, opinions were divided over Gosse's success in solving
this classificatory puzzle, with the whole question remaining a free-for-
all.[138] Gosse and Huxley agreed that, contrary to Cuvier, the Rotifera had
no connection with radiate animals.[139] At the same time, in 1851 Huxley
had asserted that the Rotifera were 'permanent forms of Echinoderm
larvae'. To accommodate his solution he created an arrangement in
which Rotifera belonged to the Annuloida, a division of the sub-kingdom
Annulosa (crustacea and other invertebrates).[140] It may be that Gosse was

136. W. B. Carpenter, referee's report on 'Manducatory organs' (Royal Society RR.3.116,
dated 30 Jan. 1856). Emphasis in the original.

137. De Beauchamp, 'Recherches sur les Rotifères', 12; also pp. 176-8. The reference is to the
comparative morphologist Marie Jules-César Savigny, *Mémoires sur les Animaux san Vertèbres*
(1816), q.v. Winsor, 'Issues in the Classification of Radiates', 31.

138. *Natural History Review* n.s. I (1861), 124-5, and Pritchard were unconvinced (J. T.
Arlidge, W. Archer, A. Pritchard, J. Ralfs, and W. C. Williamson (eds.), *A History of Infusoria*
(London: Whittaker & Co., 3rd ed., 1852), 473-4); W. B. Carpenter's report on the manducatory
organs paper indicated PHG had shown 'strong reasons' for his view (Royal Society, RR.3.116);
H. J. Slack, *Marvels of Pond-life; or, a Year's Microscopic Recreations among the Polyps,
Infusoria, Rotifers, Water-bears, and Polyzoa* (London: Groombridge and Sons, 1861), 35-6,
states the opposing views without comment.

139. In June 1850, when some of PHG's drawings were exhibited by Adam White at a meeting
of the Linnean Society, it was stated that PHG felt that the Rotifera had no connection with
the radiates (*General Minute Book No. 6* (1844-50), 5 (18 June 1850); reprinted with minor
changes, in *AMNH* ser. 2, VII (May 1851), 424); Huxley, '*Lacinularia socialis*. A Contribution to
the Anatomy and Physiology of the Rotifera', *Trans. Micro. Society* n.s. I (1853), 19 (the paper
was read 31 Dec. 1851).

140. Huxley, '*Lacinularia socialis*', 19; and for the disagreement about *Dysteria*: PHG, 'On
the Zoological Position of *Dysteria*', *Quarterly Journal of Microscopical Science* n.s. V (Apr.
1857), 138-41; Winsor, 'Issues in the Classification of Radiates', 146-54; the classificatory dispute
is discussed in the entry on 'Rotifera' in Charles Knight (ed.), *The English Cyclopaedia. Natural*

led to his view because of his sustained study of insects, just as Huxley was concerned to discern an ideal type of larva. Neither Huxley's nor Gosse's arrangement received ultimate support.

-IV-

The impact of Gosse's research on Rotifera was that it brought his vision down from the birds in the air and the 'rats and mice and such small deer' on earth to the microscopic creatures of the marine world. We can track the transition in three of his general natural history works. Only five per cent of his *Introduction to Zoology* (1844) was devoted to Rotifera and other radiates, but eighteen per cent of his *Text-book of Zoology* (begun 1849, published 1851) and thirty-four per cent of his *Life in its Lower, Intermediate, and Higher Forms* (serialized, 1853-56, published 1857).

Notwithstanding his achievements in this area, an obsession with Rotifera is no way for an independent researcher to earn a living. That explains why, as he was pursuing Rotifera, he also published *Sacred Streams* (among his more successful works)[141] and *Assyria*, on the world's first empire.[142] Gosse needed to do such work, since his income from writing never exceeded £160 a year between 1846-51.[143] He took virtually no time off;[144] and though the portion of an inheritance of £9,000 which Emily received in 1850 was helpful, much of it was lost in a bad investment.[145]

History. Volume IV (London: Bradbury and Evans, 1856), col. 626.

141. PHG's *Sacred Streams: the Ancient and Modern History of the Rivers of the Bible* (1850) appeared in London and New York editions to 1883 (Freeman & Wertheimer-PHG, 36-38).

142. PHG's *Assyria: Her Manners and Customs, Arts and Arts; Restored from her Monuments* (1852) appeared in only one edition (Freeman & Wertheimer-PHG, 44-45). Dismissed at the time as a derivative potboiler connecting recent archaeological findings with the Bible (review, *Athenaeum*, 21 Aug. 1852, 887-8), years later it was cited for its useful information (two articles by Mary Eliza Rogers, *Art-Journal* n.s. VII (1868), 42, 207).

143. For his income as £160 in 1849: PHG-EWG, 1 Sept. 1879 (CUL Add. 7018, 32).

144. *Life*, 233.

145. For the sum of the legacy: Robert Boyd, '"Father and Son"—A New Look', *The Witness* (July 1975), 265; for the date, *Life*, 225. As early as 1852 PHG had invested in mines (PHG-William Gosse, 2 Jan. 1852: CUL Adv. c. 82.5, 46), and probably early in 1854 purchased shares in Castle Dinas, in St. Columb, Cornwall. In December 1853, the extraordinary discovery of gold at Castle Dinas was announced, and the shares shot up in value from 2s.6d. to 37s.6d. Thomas Gosse (who ever-after was considered a black sheep in the family) was involved from the beginning in getting PHG to invest, but it was later revealed that the precious metal was non-existent. PHG, EG, and Edmund Bowes and Arthur Bowes, lost about £2,500 (PHG-W. Gosse, 29 Sept. 1854; CUL Adv. c. 82.5, 47). When PHG left London in 1857, he had £1,000 or £1,500, 'the wreck of what was left by your own Mother's Aunt' (PHG-EWG, 22 Feb. 1870, CUL Add. 7041, 33). For Castle Dinas: esp. *The Mining Journal* XXIII (16 Jan., 3, 24 Dec. 1853) 16, 756-7, 811; and XXIV

Perhaps fears of never being able to escape this pressured existence induced Gosse in November 1850 to briefly toy with the idea of again returning to the Caribbean area.[146] Twelve months later, headaches brought on a severe illness which lasted several weeks. He was exhausted from his punishing research and writing schedule, and his doctor urged him to leave London to recuperate. 'Now where shall it be?', Philip recalled thinking: 'Leamington —Tonbridge Wells — Clifton? No, none of these; since I must go, it shall be to the sea-shore; I shall take my microscope with me, and get among the shells and nudibranchs, the sea-anemones and the corallines. What part so promising as the lovely garden of England, fair Devonshire?'[147]

On 27 January 1852, the Gosses ('wife, self, and little naturalist in petticoats')[148] left London for St. Marychurch,[149] on the south coast of Devonshire, that village having been recommended as an ideal one for their purposes. Gosse brought with him a small compound microscope and a shelf of books, including T. Rymer Jones' *General Outline of the Animal Kingdom* (1841); Edward Forbes' *History of British Starfishes* (1841) and *Monograph of the British Naked-eyed Medusae* (1848); George Johnston's standard histories of British zoophytes (1838; 2nd ed., 1847), sponges (1842), and *Introduction to Conchology* (1850); William Yarrell's histories of British fishes (1836; 2nd ed., 1841) and birds (1837-43; 2nd ed., 1845); Joshua Alder and Albany Hancock's *Monograph of the British Nudibranchiate Mollusca* (2 vols, 1845-55); William Swainson's *Treatise on Malacology* (1840); R. E. Grant's *Outlines of Comparative Anatomy* (1841); Richard Owen's *Lectures on Comparative Anatomy* (1843); and W. H. Harvey's 'beautiful' *Sea-side Book* (1849).[150] That such weighty baggage was necessary is not without significance.

For the next three months the Gosses remained in South Devon, but because Philip had not recovered his former stamina, his researches fell

(6 May, 10 June, 2, 9, 23 Sept., 4 Nov. 1854), 288, 375, 587, 596, 632, 739.

146. *Life*, 227. I do not know whether EWG's claim that PHG contemplated a trip to the Virgin Islands and Tortuga (both in the Caribbean) in Nov. 1850 is related to his unrealised idea (previously mentioned) to go to the Azores in 1846 (*Life*, 210).

147. PHG, *A Naturalist's Rambles on the Devonshire Coast* (London: John Van Voorst, 1853), 2; EG-W. Gosse, 2 Jan. 1852 (CUL Adv. c. 82.5, 46).

148. PHG, *Naturalist's Rambles*, 3.

149. PHG invariably referred to it as 'Marychurch'. An alternative spelling is 'Mary Church', usually preceded by 'St.'

150. PHG, *Naturalist's Rambles*, 5.

short of expectations.[151] At the end of April they moved to Ilfracombe, on the north Devon coast, where they passed six months in communion with nature and a small Brethren gathering.[152]

While in Devon, Philip's scientific attitude once again evoked the energetic and optimistic outlook he had adopted in Jamaica. He studied the organization and habits of all sorts of invertebrates (among them sea anemones, medusae, sponges, polypes, and molluscs); he placed whatever he could under the microscope; he experimented with everything, burning corals, famously eating sea anemones,[153] smashing, killing, pulling apart various animals; he tried to keep sea creatures alive in an artificial environment; he minutely described in all its diversity the population of a two inch square piece of slate rock. All of this he recorded in journals, and where his pen failed him, he took up his pencil to illustrate what he saw.[154]

Gosse conducted himself at the seashore as though he were an explorer in darkest Africa. In truth, that is what he was. Others had come before, and had hewed out small paths through the jungle.[155] We have already seen how the development of the microscope drew attention to the smaller invertebrates in the eighteenth century, and this interest was furthered in Britain by John Ellis' study of corals (1775) and William Pennant's *British Zoology* (vol. IV, 1777). Yet in the 1700s the seashore and its inhabitants remained largely unexamined by naturalists: the British thought of it in terms of its medicinal value, the popular attraction of natural history in mid-century was focused on botany, and to a lesser extent on entomology,

---

151. PHG, *Naturalist's Rambles*, 100.

152. PHG, *Naturalist's Rambles*, 103fn.; PHG-EG, 15 Apr. 1852 (CUL Adv. c. 82.5, 44), and another letter, 'Friday morning' [from internal evidence, 16 Apr. 1852] (Adv. c. 82.5, 43), in which the Brethren gathering is mentioned; for their address in 1857 as 53 Fore Street: G. Tugwell, ed., *North Devon Handbook* (London: Simpkin, Marshall & Co., [1857]), 38.

153. On eating sea anemones: PHG, *Naturalist's Rambles*, 150-3; PHG, *Actinologia Britannica*, 169. 'The late Mr. Gosse used to relate how once upon a time he cooked and ate a sea-anemone. In the days of my youth, fired with a strong emulation to imitate my masters in science, I went and did likewise. The experiment was not a success. The anemone was tough, and it wanted a nice *Sauce Hollandaise*' (Andrew Wilson, 'Science Jottings. Oysters', *Illustrated London News*, 27 Oct. 1888, 494).

154. For these activities: PHG, *Naturalist's Rambles*, e.g., 202-8, 40-1.

155. Relevant works (others are cited below) are: J. E. Smith, 'A History of the Study of Invertebrates', in J. E. Smith, J. D. Earthy, G. Chapman, R. B. Clark, D. Nichols, *The Invertebrate Panorama* (London: Weidenfeld and Nicolson, 1971), 6-24; C. M. Yonge, *The Sea Shore* (London: Collins, 1949, 1972), chap. 2; Yonge, 'Victorians by the Sea Shore', *History Today* XXV (Sept. 1975), 602-9; W. P. Jones, 'The Vogue of Natural History in England, 1750-1770', *Annals of Science* II (15 July 1937), 345-52; Allen, *Naturalist in Britain*, chaps. 4-6.

ornithology, and conchology. The celebrated 10th edition of Linnaeus' *Systema Naturae* (1758) listed only ten known microscopic animals, out of a total of 4,000 identified in its pages.

During the first four decades of the nineteenth century, much was done to fill out the inevitable deficiencies in Linnaeus' catalogue. Contributions came from two directions: from university (or scientific institution-based) zoologists, such as Henri Milne-Edwards in Paris, J. L. S. Steenstrup in Copenhagen, Johannes von Müller in Bonn, Ehrenberg in Berlin, Louis Agassiz in Switzerland (and, later, the United States), J. D. Dana (from 1850 in the United States), T. H. Huxley in London, and Edward Forbes (London and Edinburgh); and from talented naturalists of various professions, including Alder, Bowerbank, J. G. Dalyell, George Johnston, Hancock, and Gosse. A small number of investigators did so in the belief that marine invertebrates might prove relevant to an understanding of the origin of life[156] (the first volume of Darwin's monograph on living barnacles, *Cirripedia*, appeared in 1851). By 1850, zoophytes had become the most studied of all the divisions of the animal kingdom.[157]

In Britain the focus on the study of marine life was encouraged by the coalescence of a number of scientific and extra-scientific factors.[158] New tools were introduced for the man of science: the microscope went down in price and up in quality;[159] the towing net (perfected by J. V. Thompson after 1816) and the dredge were introduced for the natural history collector. After the 1830s, the steam-driven printing press contributed to cheaper newspapers, periodicals and books, enhanced by illustrations rendered by lithographic means. Railways boosted daily newspaper circulation by providing distribution to locales distant from London,[160] and unintentionally created a demand for cheap literature for the traveller. The reduction in paper, advertising and stamp duties—the so-called 'taxes on knowledge'—helped to create an era of democratic journalism and fuel the growth of a popular press.[161] The expansion of

156. Silvia Granata, *The Victorian aquarium. Literary discussions on nature, culture, and science* (Manchester: Manchester University Press, 2021), 18-19.

157. C. Th. von Siebold and H. Stannius, *Comparative Anatomy*. Translated from the German, and ed. with notes & additions, by Waldo I. Burnett (London: Trübner & Co., vol. 1, 1854), 34.

158. Allen, *Naturalist in Britain*, 128-30, 96-8, 138, 76-82.

159. For the importance of the microscope: *Brighton Gazette* (30 June 1853), 7; *Quarterly Journal of Microscopical Science* n.s. II (1854), 47; *The Leader* (2 Aug. 1856), 735.

160. Philip S. Bagwell, *The Transport Revolution* (London: Routledge, 1974, 1988), 117-118.

161. Joel H. Wiener, *The War of the Unstamped: The Movement to Repeal the British Newspaper Tax, 1830-1836* (Ithaca: Cornell University Press, 1969), xi.

the British railway system eventually made the coasts more accessible[162] (including for round-trip daily excursions by workers).[163] The town of Torquay celebrated in 1848 when it was linked by rail to London, and the number of residents at seaside resorts quadrupled in the first half of the century.[164] From around 1840, the vastness of the ocean became less mysterious and more socially appealing[165] (Gosse's *Ocean* was the only book on the subject when it appeared in 1845).[166]

Finally, the prevailing mid-Victorian ethos favoured a new engagement with the seaside. Hitherto the 'excitements of the beach' with its 'physical pleasure, flirtation and voyeurism'[167] had prevailed; now the evangelical and utilitarian outlook found a new purpose for the visitor to the seashore. One went there not for a 'vacation'—that word, denoting a private holiday, was not used until the 1870s (and the verb until the 1890s)[168]—but to

162. The expansion of the railway system in the 1840s is not infrequently proposed as a factor in the aquarium craze, in carrying people to the seashore (Philip F. Rehbock 'The Victorian Aquarium in Ecological and Social Perspective', in Mary Sears and Daniel Merriman, eds., *Oceanography: The Past*. New York: Springer-Verlag, 1980, 533). It seems, however, that the impact of railways was to bring wider attention to seashore life *after* the heyday of the aquarium craze (that is, post-1860). The examples cited in John F. Travis, *The Rise of the Devon Seaside Resorts 1750-1900* (Exeter: University of Exeter Press, 1993), 168-9, though starting with PHG, are otherwise from the 1860s. I did not find Rehbock's claim reflected in the serials of the period. The *Literary Gazette* said that 'cheap excursion trains offered by the railway company will doubtless induce many' to participate in PHG's seashore classes (30 June 1855, 412), though it is unclear who would be taking the 'cheap' trains. The fare structure was persistently high for the working and middle classes (John R. Kellett, *The Impact of Railways on Victorian Cities* (London: Routledge & Kegan Paul, 1969), 87-99). Moreover, every indication is that PHG's seashore classes were not attended by large numbers. By 1864, W. R. Hughes, who knew PHG, affirmed that the 'impetus which the writings of Mr. Gosse and other modern authors ... has given to excursionists interested in Marine Natural History, who take their annual fortnight's holiday at the sea side, to ransack every available part of the coast for specimens, has well-nigh exhausted every British locality' (Hughes, 'Notes on the Aquarian Zoology of Aberystwith', *Zoologist* XXII (1864), 9337). The discussion of the subject between an uncle and his niece in 1866 would seem to point to the railway's impact coming post-aquarium mania:
    "Oh, uncle, I wish all boys and girls could see the wonders of the sea."
    "I wish so too, Nell. But although they cannot go now, they may all be able to see them when they grow up to be men and women, thanks to railroads" ('Chats by the Sea. No.V.—Sea-Flowers', *Christian World* X, 24 Aug. 1866, 517-18).

163. Michael Walzer, *Spheres of Justice: A Defense of Pluralism and Equality* (New York: Basic Books, 1983), 190.

164. Bagwell, *Transport Revolution*, 116.

165. Helen Margaret Rozwadowski, 'Fathoming the Ocean: Discovery and Exploration of the Deep Sea, 1840-1880' (University of Pennsylvania, PhD dissertation, 1996), 2.

166. Freeman & Wertheimer-PHG, 22; Joel W. Hedgpeth, 'Fishers of the Murex', *Isis* 37 (May 1947), 26-7.

167. Payne, *Where the Sea Meets the Land*, 97.

168. Walzer, *Spheres of Justice*, 190.

contemplate the wonders of Creation and experience the salubrious value of its environment.[169]

In other words, there was an existing framework for a new appreciation of the seashore before Gosse's attention was drawn to it in 1852. In addition, a popular seashore literature already existed to extol the intellectual virtues of the study of nature. There was Mary Roberts' *Seaside Companion* (1835); Elizabeth Anne Allom's *Sea-side Pleasures: or, a Peep at Miss Eldon's Happy Pupils* (1845); Mary Matilda Howard's *Ocean Flowers and Their Teachings* (1846); Anne Pratt's *Chapters on the Common Things of the Sea-side* (1850); and most notably, W. H. Harvey's important *Sea-side Book* (1849; 4th ed., 1857).

-V-

All of this being the case, what was it that marked Gosse's work as the dawn of a new era in the history of the seashore?

It was chiefly the invention of the aquarium which revolutionised popular attitudes towards marine fauna. Over the years, there has never been a shortage of claimants to whom this discovery has been attributed. Indeed, there are plentiful references to artificial environments for fish and plants in Roman, Mexican, and Chinese literature.[170] In those times, however, the 'piscinae', 'vivaria', or 'Dragon-containers' (as they were variously termed) were constructed largely to breed, and only occasionally to observe, their inhabitants. It was not until the eighteenth century that one finds these environments being employed for scientific purposes.

In truth, it is improper to grant the honour of discovery to any claimant who lived before a knowledge of the principle upon which aquaria are constructed was unveiled: namely, that animals and plants rely upon each other for their existence, the former giving off the carbon dioxide which plants require, and the latter supplying animals with the necessary oxygen.[171] Hence the development of the aquarium is linked with a

169. Travis, *Rise of the Devon Seaside Resorts*, 167-9.
170. A thorough analysis of the aquarium movement is provided in Matthew Goodrum, 'The British Sea-Side Studies, 1820-1860: Marine Invertebrates, the Practice of Natural History, and the Depiction of Life in the Sea' (Indiana University, PhD dissertation, 1997). A valuable brief survey is Hans Frey, 'Geschichte der Aquarienkunde', in *Das Aquarium von A bis Z* (Leipzig: Neumann Verlag, 1959), 272-6.
171. Though this is a long-held belief, aquariums do not technically succeed due to a plant-animal life balance: James W. Atz, 'The Myth of the Balanced Aquarium', *Natural History* (American Museum of Natural History) 58 (Feb. 1949), 72-7, 96.

chemical problem, the determination of the existence and nature of oxygen by Priestley and Lavoisier in the eighteenth century.

At the hands of N. B. Ward (1791-1868), a London surgeon, the matter took on a botanical character. In the 1830s he came to realise that ferns might be grown and transported alive in closed glass containers (so-called 'Wardian cases'). Ward was initially interested in the subject because he hoped that his investigations would be adopted by philanthropists to improve the condition of the poor by protecting them from disease, but in the meanwhile he extended his research and built a freshwater aquarium in 1841. His successful effort, however, remained unpublicized until 1854.[172]

Meanwhile a number of naturalists began independently carrying out experiments with the same end in mind.[173] The most important of these were the efforts of the chemist Robert Warington (1807-1867), begun in 1849, and Gosse (from around the same year); and by 'the father of our marine invertebrate zoology,'[174] George Johnston (1797-1855), from around 1842.[175] The possibility of disseminating their findings was given

172. Stephen H. Ward, *On Wardian Cases for Plants, and Their Applications* (London: John Van Voorst, 1854), 23, and N. B. Ward, *On the Growth of Plants in Closely Glazed Cases* (London: John Van Voorst, 1842), esp. Chap. V. On 'the beneficial influences on the labouring men of being enabled thus to cultivate a garden of choice plants in his otherwise cheerless room': 'Royal Institution', London *Morning Chronicle* (20 Mar. 1854), 9.

173. E.g., Anna Thynne (1806-1866) in 1846 (S. H. Ward, *On Wardian Cases*, p.ii; J. E. Taylor, *The Aquarium*. London: Hardwicke & Bogue, 1876, 13fn.; W. A. Lloyd, 'Aquaria', Bath *Field*, 12 May 1877, 573); Edwin Lankester in 1849 (Lankester, *The Aquavivarium, Fresh and Marine* (London: Robert Hardwicke, 1856), 10); C. S. Harris in 1850 (Harris, 'On the Marine Vivarium', *AMNH* ser. 2, XV (Feb. 1855), 131-4); Shirley Hibberd in 1851 (Hibberd, *Rustic Adornments for Homes of Taste* (London: Groombridge & Sons, 1856), 11); and W. A. Lloyd in 1853 (Bernard H. Becker, *Official Handbook to the Royal Aquarium ... With a Description of the Aquarium by W. A. Lloyd* (London: Charles Dickens & Evans, 1876), 99).

174. PHG, 'Notes on some new or little-known Marine Animals', *AMNH* ser. 2, XVI (July 1855), 35, referring to *Othonia johnstoni* (PHG-P.W. Maclagan, 6 May 1855, American Philosophical Society Library).

175. For Warington (whose name is frequently misspelled 'Warrington'): 'Notice of Observations on the Adjustment of the Relations Between the Animal and Vegetable Kingdoms, by Which the Vital Functions of Both are Permanently Maintained', *Quarterly Journal of the Chemical Society of London* III (1851), 52-4; 'On the Aquarium', a lecture delivered at the Royal Institution, 27 Mar. 1857, printed in *Notices of the Proceedings at the Meetings of the Members of the Royal Institution* II (Nov. 1856-July 1857), 403-8; 'The Aquatic Plant Case, or Parlour Aquarium', *Gardener's Magazine of Botany* n.s., Part I (Jan. 1852), 5-7; 'On Preserving the Balance Between Vegetable and Animal Organisms in Sea Water', *Report of the Twenty-third Meeting of the British Association ... in September 1853* (London: John Murray, 1854), 72, &c.; for Gosse's earliest experiments (with fresh-water Rotifera): PHG, 'On Keeping Marine Animals and Plants Alive in Unchanged Sea-water', *AMNH* ser. 2, X (Oct. 1852), 263-8, *Naturalist's Rambles*, 228-34 and Appendix; and for Johnston: PHG, *The Aquarium* (London: John Van Voorst, 1854), 7-8.

an unanticipated boost by the repeal by Robert Peel's government of the excise duties on plate glass in 1845 (the so-called 'Window tax'),[176] which meant that it was economically feasible to think of constructing cheap glass enclosures for widespread distribution.[177]

In other words, the aquarium idea was very much 'in the air' while Gosse was in Devon, though he did not then realise that he had been anticipated by others and could not have known that non-scientific factors would broaden the appeal of his enthusiasm. Attempting to designate a single individual as *the* inventor of the aquarium is a fruitless exercise, but whether one assigns that innovation to Johnston,[178] Ward,[179] Warington,[180] Gosse, Thynne,[181] or the independent efforts of naturalists,

176. 'The Window Duties', *Birmingham Journal* (1 Mar. 1845), 3; on the background to the tax: Élie Halévy, *A History of the English People in the Nineteenth Century: Victorian Years* (London: Ernest Benn Ltd, 1961), IV: 100.

177. Allen, *Naturalist in Britain*, 137; see also [probably W. J. Broderip: *Wellesley Index* II: 425, item 3253], *Fraser's Magazine* 50 (Aug. 1854), 190, which referred to the period as 'The Crystal Age'.

178. PHG 'assigned the honour of the first accomplishment' of the actual formation of a marine aquarium to Johnston (PHG, *The Aquarium*, 1854, 7).

179. Edwin Lankester described Ward as 'the first introducer of the fresh water aquarium and the suggester of the marine' ('Aquaria', *Newcastle Journal*, 2 Oct. 1858, 7), and Allen credits Ward with being the 'true inventor of the aquarium' (Allen, *Naturalist in Britain*, 132-7). W. A. Lloyd called Ward 'the earliest recorded person who *intentionally* arranged together certain animals and plants in water', adding that 'this gentleman [Ward] and this lady [Thynne] are the two first known persons who, keeping a chemical law in view, deliberately and purposely set about attaining means for its fulfilment in an aquarium' (Lloyd, 'Aquaria: Their Present, Past, and Future', *Popular Science Review* XV (July 1876), 256-7, emphasis in the original).

180. PHG and Warington both published articles dated Sept. 10, 1852 on the sea-water aquarium in the Oct. 1852 issue of *AMNH*. Nonetheless PHG noted he was not jealous of Warington's achievement but congratulated him on it: 'I rejoice to see that your success has far exceeded mine' (PHG-Warington, 1 Oct. 1852, reproduced in W. H. Brock, 'The Warington-Gosse Aquarium Controversy: Two Unrecorded letters', *Archives of Natural History* 18 (1991), 179). Hamlin affirms Warington's priority as inventor (Christopher Hamlin, 'Robert Warington and the Moral Economy of the Aquarium', *Journal of the History of Biology* 19 (Spring 1986), 131).

181. Rebecca Stott has made a weak argument for Anna Thynne's priority (Stott, *Theatres of Glass: The Woman Who Brought the Sea to the City*. London: Short Books, 2003). PHG wrote that Thynne 'succeeded in maintaining a self-supporting Aquarium' with observations 'of the highest interest in a physiological view', but not that she should be credited with the invention of the aquarium (PHG, *Aquarium*, 1856, 2ed., 7fn.). Stott restates S. H. Ward's 1841 view that Thynne 'established the first balanced marine aquarium in London' (108-9; Ward, cited in PHG, *Aquarium*, 1856, 7fn.), but she inflates Thynne's importance in arguing that she 'invented the marine aquarium ... And this invention and its commercial application would in turn lead to one of the most eccentric of Victorian crazes ... few naturalists at mid-century ... had begun to study and record the behavior of living marine animals in a near-natural environment. It simply had not been possible before Anna brought the sea to the city' (21-2). In order to make her case, Stott smears PHG with conjecture, innuendo, and error. She writes that PHG *may* have met Thynne in London in 1849, he *may* have seen her tanks, and he *may* then have pursued his aquarium

horticulturists, and chemists,[182] it was unquestionably Gosse whose name stands above all others as the 'Father of the Aquarium'.[183] 'Fancy a book on Aquaria in which the name of Gosse is not once mentioned!' an astonished *Athenaeum* reviewer exclaimed in 1856.[184] Before Gosse, the zoologist T. Rymer Jones reminded his readers, the idea of establishing 'a miniature sea' in the great British capital metropolis 'appeared utterly wild and visionary':

> Various and daring were the projects that were suggested on all hands; but they all turned out to be futile or impracticable when brought to the test of execution, and all successively sank into oblivion. Some proposed to lay pipes from Brighton to London, and, by the erection of water-works at the sea-side, to cause fountains to play from basins stored with marine products—others were for chartering steam-boats for the express purpose of supplying, at an enormous expense, the pure salt water of the ocean. ... at length, the most sanguine began to despair of ever seeing the object realized.
>
> It was just at this period, when every one had convinced himself that, however desirable, the establishment of a marine vivarium in London

studies, all the while intentionally failing to acknowledge her (113). No evidence is presented in support of these speculations. Stott's case is not helped by her factual inaccuracies about PHG (113-14), the most egregious of which is her statement that since Thynne was a woman, it is 'not surprising' (140) that PHG flagrantly took partial credit for her article in *AMNH* (ser. 3, III (June 1859), 449). This is unwarranted. Stott describes Thynne's article as 'listed as co-authored' by PHG (140), indicating that she had apparently not actually seen the article. It was PHG who submitted Thynne's notes to *AMNH* for publication, and contrary to Stott, the paper is titled: 'On the Increase of Madrepores. By Mrs. Thynne. With Notes by P. H. Gosse, F.R.S.' (Freeman & Wertheimer-PHG, item 295). A balanced critique of Stott's statements is given by Silvia Granata, *Victorian aquarium*, 20-1.

182. PHG's cousin, Susan Bell (1750-1829), has been put forward as the 'first person to preserve invertebrate animals alive in aquaria of sea-water' (EWG, 'Fragments of the Autobiography of Thomas Gosse', 141fn. 1). So has her son, Thomas Bell, who is said to have 'isolated in basins and glasses little seas full of Actineae [sic] and Sponges and Polyps, for purposes of zoological observation' in the 1820s ('Thomas Bell, F.R.S., etc.' *Portraits of Men of Eminence in Literature, Science and Art*. London: Alfred William Bennett, 1865, III: 8). Philip F. Rehbock reviews the unfolding of the 'aquarium movement' in 'The Victorian Aquarium in Ecological and Social Perspective', in Mary Sears and Daniel Merriman (eds.), *Oceanography: The Past* (New York: Springer-Verlag, 1980), 522-39.

183. W. A. Lloyd, 'The Aquarium', *Popular Recreator* (London: Cassell, Petter & Galpin, 2vols. in 1, n.d. [1873-4]), I: 126.

184. The remark concluded a disapproving review of James Bishop, et. al., *Brief Instructions for the Management of the Aquarium*, which the anonymous reviewer (Thomas Bell, PHG's cousin) condemned as nothing more than a promotional work for aquarium suppliers (*Athenaeum*, 30 Aug. 1856, 1085).

was an impossibility, that a gentleman appeared who, by a touch of genius, loosed the Gordian knot. He at once dispensed with pipes, and water-works, and steam-boats, and gave us what we now behold in many a drawing-room—the wonders of the deep displayed to our eyes ... The gentleman who accomplished all this, we need hardly say, was Mr. Gosse ...[185]

Gosse and the aquarium are inseparable. Why so? The aquarium perfectly matched Gosse's experience and talents as a naturalist. His skill, knowledge, entrepreneurship, and motivation were unmatched by any of his predecessors or contemporaries.[186] He had spent nearly nine years as a field naturalist in Newfoundland, Canada, Alabama, and Jamaica focussing on entomology, ornithology, and general natural history before turning his attention to the seashore. He knew how to use the towing net, dredge, and Wardian cases. He had a biographical and ecological bent as a researcher. His skills as a word-painter allowed him to take advantage of a cheap press, and the introduction of colour lithography into printing provided a medium in which he could display his talent as an illustrator. He had experience in book publishing, and by 1854 had produced fifteen natural history books and thirty-one articles in natural history journals (some multi-part, not including books and serial contributions on other subjects).

Men of science admired Gosse's work. 'I have never seen the author Mr. Gosse, that I know of; although we have corresponded,' said Richard Owen, the anatomist and paleontologist, after reading Gosse's *Naturalist's Sojourn*. 'He is a very true observer & a very beautiful describer of what he sees.'[187] Edward Forbes, the co-author of the four-volume *History of the Mollusca*, wrote Gosse: 'I can assure you, that a letter from one I esteem so highly & from whose writings I have derived very great pleasure, is valued by me as a favour.'[188] As mentioned, Gosse's

185. [T. Rymer Jones], 'The Aquarium', *Saturday Review* I (22 Dec. 1855), 135 (for the author identification: Merle Mowbray Bevington, *The Saturday Review 1855-1868* (New York: Columbia University Press, 1941), 356).

186. 'To both Mr. Warrington [sic] and Mr. Gosse the credit of having discovered the Aquarium may fairly be given, and to the works of the last mentioned naturalist may be attributed the rapid spread of knowledge in connection with its improvement and more universal application, which has recently taken place' (*Natural History Review* IV (1857), 100).

187. R. Owen-'Mamma [Hannah] Troutbeck', 29 Nov. 1851 (CUL Adv.c.82.5,42).

188. Edward Forbes-PHG, 2 Apr. 1852 (Institute of Geological Sciences, London; see *Society for the Bibliography of Natural History Newsletter*, no. 3 (Aug. 1979), 12-13).

colleagues recognized his achievements by electing him an Associate of the Linnean Society, Fellow of the Microscopical Society, and later to the Royal and Entomological societies. And newspaper critics, in an unceasing outpouring, recognized his books as the gold standard in the field.[189] Said one publication: 'Multitudes of books have been written lately to guide the young naturalist in his quest, but among them all the works of Mr. Gosse, a pious and able naturalist, maintain a deserved pre-eminence, as at once clear and beautiful in style, accurate in scientific statement, and truly healthful and pious in the spirit with which they are imbued.'[190] Decades later, assessing the history of aquaria, another naturalist noted: 'The most marked epoch in the history of the marine aquarium ... undoubtedly took place when Mr. Philip Henry Gosse's most charming books made their appearance. ... Never before had the common objects of the seaside found a historian at once so charming and so accurate.'[191]

Those who knew Gosse likewise held him in esteem. W. A. Lloyd hung his portrait in his office at the Crystal Palace Aquarium in Hyde Park, telling a visitor about Gosse's 'wonderful knowledge of sea creatures'.[192] An experienced aquarium owner referred to his attempt to convert a novice to 'a disciple of Saint Gosse', meaning: the one who understood 'the true principles of aquarianism'.[193] On the lecture circuit, he was 'Professor Gosse'[194] the 'eminent naturalist',[195] 'able and devout ... known to the world'.[196] At his seashore classes he was the 'hero, whose locks our enthusiasm had silvered in our dreams' who drew around him 'a circle of admirers of nature's charms, before whose eyes he daily unfolds

---

189. Judith Hamera, *Parlor Ponds: The Cultural Work of the American Home Aquarium 1850-1970* (Ann Arbor: University of Michigan, 2012), 51; Granata, *Victorian aquarium*, 38 (referring to PHG's *Aquarium*).

190. *Wells Journal* (Wells, Somerset) (29 Aug. 1857), 4.

191. J. E. Taylor, *The Aquarium*, 14. Silvia Granata has lately echoed this view of PHG as 'the one who really made [the marine aquarium] popular ... who turned domestic tank keeping into a proper craze' (Granata, *Victorian aquarium*, 22, 23).

192. W. H. Chesson, *Eliza Brightwen: The Life and Thoughts of a Naturalist* (London: T. Fisher Unwin, 1909), 93, describing a visit by Brightwen to Lloyd on 11 Nov. 1871. In private, Lloyd was critical of PHG's ability to maintain an aquarium (Fernando E. Vega, 'A recently discovered manuscript by William Alford Lloyd on the growth of seaweeds in aquaria', *Archives of Natural History* 39 (2012), 349-51).

193. Samuel Highley, 'Marine Aquaria', *Athenaeum*, 10 Mar. 1860, 342.

194. 'Marine Zoology', Scotland *Fife Herald* (5 Mar. 1857), 3.

195. E.g., Newcastle-upon-Tyne *Newcastle Journal* (7 Feb. 1857), 5.

196. *North Devon Journal* (26 July 1855), 8 (the newspaper misprinted 'world' as 'word').

the chart of wisdom.' So engaged were his students in their teacher's instruction, the *Tenby Observer* light-heartedly wrote, that 'the most enthusiastic sleep on beds of mussels, with nothing to shield them from the inclemency of the weather but the mantles of the inhabitants.'[197] Summed up one newspaper: Gosse's renown placed him alongside 'some of the greatest minds the world has produced,' men known for their 'patient industry, unceasing labours, and brilliant genius.' Gosse had a place in this stellar pantheon of the scientific elite, right between Darwin and Huxley:

> Copernicus, Galileo, Newton, Herschel, Adams, Leverrier, Lyall, Owen, Darwin, Gosse, Tyndall, and Huxley, are now household words in many an obscure but thoughtful family circle, and thousands of artisans and labourers, unknown to fame, after the toils of the day are over, sit down to peruse the great principles that have been published by the philosophers whose names have just been enumerated.[198]

In contrast to Gosse, neither Ward nor Johnston ever wrote a separate article or treatise on the aquarium. The chemist Warington—who later maintained that he was the originator of the idea (and was likely jealous of the attention Gosse received as the propagandist for the aquarium)[199]—admitted that he was 'most ignorant on the subject of natural history'.[200] When the aquarium businessman W. A. Lloyd—'that enterprising devotee to the wants of naturalists and amateurs'[201]—first became interested in the aquarium he had 'never seen, and was not so presumptuous as even to hope to see' the sea.[202] In 1876, when Lloyd for the first time personally collected marine specimens, he did so with Gosse.[203]

---

197. Editorial, *Tenby Observer* IV (12 Sept. 1856), n.p.

198. 'Juvenile Museums', Newcastle-upon-Tyne *Newcastle Journal* (28 Oct. 1867), 2. 'Lyall' was a typo for the Scottish geologist, Charles Lyell.

199. Brock, 'Warington-Gosse Aquarium Controversy', 182.

200. For these remarks: Warington, 'On the Aquarium', 403, and 'Observations on the Natural History of the Water-Snail and Fish Kept in a Confined and Limited Portion of Water', *AMNH* ser. 2, X (Oct. 1852), 273.

201. G. H. Lewes, *Sea-side Studies at Ilfracombe, Tenby, the Scilly Isles, & Jersey* (Edinburgh & London: William Blackwood and Sons, 1858), 103 (curiously, this comment does not appear in the 1860, 2ed., of the book).

202. W.A. Lloyd, 'The Aquarium', *Popular Recreator* (London: Cassell, Petter & Galpin, 2vols. in 1, n.d. [1873-4]), I: 128.

203. Bob Alexander, 'William Alford Lloyd, 1824-1880', http://parlouraquariums.org.uk/ [2012], [p. 22].

-VI-

The immediate attraction which the aquarium held for Gosse was two-fold. It could bring seldomly seen animals and plants into the home, making the glass vases containing mimic seas 'a desirable ornament in the parlour or drawing-room.' More significantly, it would be an invaluable aid to the marine zoologist, furnishing him with 'much insight into the functions and habits of these creatures, into their embryology, metamorphoses and other peculiarities.'[204] Another observer, looking back to these years, cited this as signalling the moment when zoologists 'were no longer content to be mere cataloguers of species. ... They were eager to learn the living structure of animals and plants, and to trace them from the germ to full growth.'[205]

Gosse began to turn his aquarium knowledge into an action campaign as soon as his family returned to London from Ilfracombe in November 1852.[206] He contacted Warington, and supplied him with sea animals;[207] he hired a fabricator to produce parlour aquaria;[208] and he discovered that his acquaintance, D. W. Mitchell, the Secretary of the Zoological Gardens in Regent's Park, was apparently already planning to establish a public aquarium. Mitchell had been fascinated with an aquarium seen at J. S. Bowerbank's, which, in turn, was the result of Bowerbank's contact with Nathaniel Ward.[209] In December, Gosse transferred some zoophytes and annelids taken in Ilfracombe to the newly-erected 'Fish House' in Regent's Park. He was then hired to collect more specimens in 1853.[210]

Initially, Mitchell was content to construct a fresh-water aquarium containing fish, but soon decided to attempt a marine aquarium. By January the project was well under way, and on 21 May 1853, the first public aquarium in the world (actually, six separate tanks) was formally opened for view.[211] A week later, Gosse's record of his nine months in

204. PHG, 'On Keeping Marine Animals and Plants Alive in Unchanged Seawater', 264-5.

205. [Proposal to found a British Zoological Station], London *Standard* (9 Oct. 1883), 4.

206. *Life*, 243-4; they lived at 16 Hampton Terrace, Camden Town.

207. PHG, 'On Artificial Sea Water', *AMNH* ser. 2, XV (Jan. 1855), 17; Warington, 'On Preserving the Balance Between the Animal and Vegetable Organisms in Sea Water', *AMNH* ser. 2, XII (Nov. 1853), 321.

208. PHG, *Naturalist's Rambles*, 441.

209. S. H. Ward, *On Wardian Cases*, 23.

210. PHG, *The Aquarium*, 3-4.

211. [Edwin Lankester], 'Zoological Gardens, Regent's Park', *Athenaeum* (22 Jan., 28 May 1853), 110-111, 647. The first marine aquarium at Regent's Park was a significant enough event for officials to mark its centenary ('Celebrations at the Zoo', London *Times*, 7 Apr. 1953, 8).

Devonshire was advertised for sale as *A Naturalist's Rambles on the Devonshire Coast*.[212] In it he wrote about fulfilling his 'cherished scheme for the conservation of marine animals and plants in a living state' in what he referred to both as 'marine vivaria' and an 'aquarium'. An appendix increased the public's awareness of the Regent's Park project.[213] The work itself, the first in his celebrated seashore trilogy, received more reviews than any other book he wrote.[214]

With the *Devonshire Coast*, a new genre in marine natural history writings was initiated, one which fully appealed to both the scientific and non-scientific reader. The former could find accurate discussions of issues of immediate concern: the alternation of generations in polypes and medusae, the embryological development of these and of the polyzoa; discoveries of new sea animals, and of the offensive and defensive apparatus of the sea anemones. The latter could read enticing descriptions of natural scenery, antiquities, and sites, and narratives of Devonshire legends, all infused with a healthy moral tone.[215] And for the enjoyment and instruction of both classes Gosse added twelve coloured and sixteen plain lithographed plates, which he drew on the stone and 'constitute in themselves a beautiful work of art.'[216]

'Everything that had life in it on the sea-shore had an interest for

212. Publisher's advertisement for *Naturalist's Rambles*, 'This Day is Published', London *Standard* (27 May 1853), 1; Freeman & Wertheimer-PHG, 46; *Life*, 245.

213. PHG, *Naturalist's Rambles*, 228-34, 439-41. The book increased awareness of the Regent's Park Fish House: *The Naturalist* III (1853), 230; *Gardeners' Chronicle* (23 July 1853), 470; *Literary Gazette* (3 Sept. 1853), 855; [probably W. J. Broderip: *Wellesley Index* II: 421, item 3140], 'The Naturalist in Devonshire', *Fraser's Magazine* XLVIII (Oct. 1853), 388-9; [Edwin Lankester], *The Athenaeum* (15 Oct. 1853), 1217; 'A Naturalist at the Sea-side', *Leisure Hour* (9 Feb. 1854), 90.

214. I have found 29 reviews of *Naturalist's Rambles*, as against 27 for the *Aquarium*, 23 for *Tenby*, and 26 for *Omphalos*. How many books PHG sent out to serials for review is not known. Notwithstanding the obvious differences, it would appear that the number of serials which reviewed *Naturalist's Rambles* compares favourably with Darwin's *Origin of Species* (1859). *Naturalist's Rambles* had a print run for the first (and only) edition of 1,500 copies (Freeman & Wertheimer-PHG, 45); *Origin* had a print run for the first edition of 1,250, and 41 review copies were sent out (Freeman, *Darwin*, 2ed., 75).

215. For comments on its healthy moral tone: *Naturalist* III (1853), 231; *Literary Gazette* (3 Sept. 1853), 855-8; *Christian Remembrancer* XXVI (July 1853), 261; *Atlas* (9 July 1853), 451; *Brighton Gazette* (30 June 1853), 7; *English Churchman* XI (11 Aug. 1853), 693; *Natural History Review* III (1856), 29.

216. *Brighton Gazette* (30 June 1853), 7. Some of the drawings, together with ones from other PHG books, were used in J. Reay Greene's *A Manual of the Sub-Kingdom Coelenterata* (London: Longman, Green, Longman, and Roberts, 1861), ix, and *passim* (see R. B. Williams' excellent analysis, 'Yet more on Gosse illustrations', *Society for the History of Natural History Newsletter* no. 24 (1985), 7-8).

him,' the *Athenaeum* noted.[217] *The Globe* expressed the consensus of the newspaper press reviewers:

> Mr. Gosse is not a dry systematiser; on the contrary he communicates knowledge in a mode peculiarly attractive—with precision enough to satisfy the most learned, and an eloquence enough to excite the most apathetic. He has the artist's eye for the perception of beauty in all its multiform phases—the poet's soul to feel its influence—and the "ready writer's pen" to pour forth his own emotions, and to wake their echoes in other breasts. His "pen pictures" of the scenery in North Devon are such charming morceaux that we could wish they had occupied a larger space in the volume; while over all his descriptions, whether of animate or inanimate nature, is breathed a spirit of piety so pure and fervent— he has so married science to religion (untoward couple as some have thought them), that we rise from his pages better, it may be hoped, as well as wiser than before.[218]

Fraser's Magazine urged readers to pause before contemplating another holiday on the Continent. Instead, 'Take Mr. Gosse's book in your hand, and turn your face towards Devon, with its green uplands, sparkling streams, rich flower-enamelled valleys, and the lovely living gardens of its translucent, dark-blue sea.'[219]

Meanwhile, as the first stages of the aquarium movement were commencing, the Gosses were in Weymouth, Dorset. For eight months in 1853 (April-December) he was dredging and trawling, sending 4,000 marine animals to Regent's Park by the end of July.[220] When, at this time, a quarrel with Mitchell at the Zoological Gardens resulted in his ceasing to supply him, he transferred his catches to the short-lived aquarium at the Surrey Zoological Gardens at the Crystal Palace.[221] Recognizing that many of the animals which passed under his eye were new to science,

217. *Athenaeum* (15 Oct. 1853), 1218.
218. *The Globe* (14 July 1853), front page.
219. 'The Naturalist in Devonshire', *Fraser's Magazine* XLVIII (Oct. 1853), 400.
220. PHG-C. Kingsley, 28 July 1853 (LeBL); PHG, 'Notes on Some New or Little-known Marine Animals', *AMNH* ser. 2, XII (Aug. 1853), 124.
221. 'Royal Surrey Zoological Gardens ... Exhibition of the Marine Aquarium, a collection of sea and fresh water fish alive, in five large glass tanks, the Mollusca, Zoophytes, and Crustacea, procured expressly by P.H. Gosse, Esq., the eminent naturalist' (London *Daily News*, 1 Sept. 1853, p. 4, advertisement appearing underneath another for the Zoological Gardens at Regent's Park); W. A. Lloyd, *A Guide Book to the Marine Aquarium of the Crystal Palace Aquarium Company (Limited)* (London: R. K. Burt & Co., 1872), 5 (on the Surrey Zoological Gardens); *Life*, 248-250.

Gosse now began to publish descriptions of them in the *Annals and Magazine of Natural History*. The anonymous *Sea-side Pleasures* (one chapter of which has been attributed to Emily) appeared before September.[222] The public's delight with the aquarium was spreading, and the Revd Charles Kingsley became an early acolyte. In 1853 he initiated a correspondence with Gosse, offering to collect for him in Clovelly, Torbay, and elsewhere.[223]

Returning again to London, Gosse started serializing his last general natural history survey, *Life in its Lower, Intermediate and Higher Forms* (issued in book form in 1857),[224] began gathering materials for a monograph on sea anemones,[225] constructed an 'Actiniarium',[226] maintained six well-stocked aquaria,[227] and became the first person to cultivate the beautiful red seaweeds (Rhodosperms) in an aquarium.[228] Shortly after this, he utilised an analysis of sea-water to create a formula for manufacturing it which met the needs of those unable to afford the expense or inconvenience of importing the liquid from the coast.[229] In spite of some doubts about its effectiveness,[230] Gosse's formula was extensively quoted and its practical usefulness confirmed.[231] One experienced aquarist

222. For PHG's 'Notes on Some New or Little-known Marine Animals', see *AMNH* ser. 2, XII, XVI (1853, 1855); for *Sea-Side Pleasures:* Freeman & Wertheimer-PHG.

223. PHG-CK correspondence is at LeBL (1853-8), Corr. Bk. preserves the dates of later letters, and other letters are at CUL.

224. PHG's *Life in its lower, intermediate and higher forms* was serialized in *Excelsior*, 1853-4 (Freeman & Wertheimer-PHG, index).

225. PHG-C. Kingsley, 9 Jan. 1854 (LeBL).

226. PHG-C. Kingsley, 24 Apr. 1854 (LeBL).

227. PHG-C. Kingsley, 30 May 1854 (LeBL).

228. PHG, 'On the Growth of Sea-Weeds', *AMNH* ser. 2, XIII (June 1854), 488-91; PHG-C. Kingsley, 15 Apr. 1854 (LeBL).

229. PHG, 'On Manufactured Sea-Water for the Aquarium', *AMNH* ser. 2, XIV (July 1854), 65-7; PHG, 'On Artificial Sea Water'.

230. For remarks about the alleged inaccuracy of PHG's formula: G. Wilson, 'On the Artificial Preparation of Sea-water for Marine Vivaria', *Report of the Twenty-fourth Meeting of the British Association ... in September 1854* (London: John Murray, 1855), 76; G. Wilson, 'On the Artificial Preparation of Sea Water for the Aquarium', *Edinburgh New Philosophical Journal* n.s. I (Jan. 1855), 129-32; *Natural History Review* II (1855), 3, 10. Robert Warington in particular was angered by PHG's above-cited July 1854 paper (Warington, 'On Artificial Sea Water', *AMNH* ser. 2, XIV (Dec. 1854), 419-21). Warington claimed PHG had announced an 'erroneous formula' after having first 'consulted' with him on the subject. PHG's pointed response was that his 'erroneous formula' actually worked, and that he had not 'consulted' with Warington, who was 'most thoroughly mistaken' if he believed that 'I obtained from him one atom of information previously unknown to me' (PHG, 'on Artificial Sea Water', 17). A recent comment on the dispute concludes that 'Warington was jealous of Gosse's success in a field in which he had made the major scientific breakthrough' (Brock, 'Warington-Gosse Aquarium Controversy', 182).

231. Among other confirmations was one from W. A. Lloyd (*Athenaeum*, 15 Nov. 1854, 1401).

recalled seeing a dealer, with two family members, carrying gallons of water from shore to home to refresh his stock. 'I pointed out to him how he might save himself this great and unnecessary toil,'

> And on showing him my own Aquaria, which were in beautiful condition, I could hardly persuade him, after he had admired the brilliancy of the water, tasted its freshness, and extolled the expanded Sabella, that the water had not been changed for four months; but though he admitted the advantage that would accrue by following the system I employed, in a few days I saw him engaged at his old work: it was evident I had failed to convert him to the true principles of aquarianism, or succeeded in making him a disciple of Saint Gosse.[232]

All the while Philip was also going over the notes made at Weymouth in preparation for the publication of another seashore work, which had once tentatively been titled 'The Aquarium: a Biography of Marine Animals'.[233] Recall that biography was Gosse's obsession—though not the Victorian double-decker *Life and Letters* variety, inclined to reticence and uninterested in facts, selective and abbreviated in its 'kit-kat' portraits. Gosse preferred to chronicle the activities of the animate world in full: the development, interactions, social and economic habits, quarrels and violence of the animals, even conjectures about intellectual, and comments on sexual,[234] matters.

When *The Aquarium: An Unveiling of the Wonders of the Deep Sea* appeared by June 1854 (well-timed for the advent of the seashore

---

232. Samuel Highley, 'Marine Aquaria', *Athenaeum*, 10 Mar. 1860, 342.

233. PHG-C. Kingsley, 23 December 1853 (LeBL). *Life*, 251, makes the claim—unconfirmed and apparently incorrect—that the work was originally titled *The Mimic Sea* until ready for the press (Freeman & Wertheimer-PHG, 47).

234. PHG handled sex in nature for descriptive purposes and as a morphological tool, and did so frankly and directly, not euphemistically and without any apparent subconscious expression. He wrote about the sex characteristics of Rotifera; he named, described, and illustrated the penis in Lepidoptera (PHG, 'On the Dioecious Character of the Rotifera', *Phil. Trans. Royal Society*, 1858; 'On the clasping-organs ancillary to generation in certain groups of the Lepidoptera', Linnean Soc. *Transactions*, 1883). In his Jamaica journal, PHG made fun of an amateur collector who brought him a male and female boa, and who, 'in pointing out the difference of the sex, had no other word to indicate it, than "this is a *woman!*" (PHG, 'Jamaica Journal', 16 Apr. [1845]). In commenting on the unsatisfactory comparative morphological treatment of copulation in the animal kingdom in a 1977 scientific work, reviewer Joel W. Hedgpeth said: 'That most devout of Victorian Christians, P. H. Gosse, wrote and illustrated a splendid monograph on the genitalia of butterflies ... the beautifully illustrated facts were laid before all. It is a pity that this [current] author did not follow Gosse's noble precedent' (Hedgpeth, *Quarterly Review of Biology* 54 (Sept. 1979), 328).

season),[235] Gosse reaped more fulsome praise. His purpose was to show people how to make their own household aquaria, and to provide an example of the positive benefits for science which would accrue from a sustained study of living animals. His enthusiasm for the subject was as unbounded as it was infectious. *The Aquarium* may well be the best of his seashore monographs.

Blackwood's Magazine warned its readers to keep the book out of the reach of youngsters, 'for if it once gets a lodgment in drawing-room or school-room, we may safely trust to every boy and girl of spirit that there will be very little peace in that devoted household till it has made an attempt at an Aquarium.'[236] The aquarium was considered by the same writer as 'the most wonderful little microcosm ever presented to the bigger world,' while the *New Monthly Magazine*, passing over the names of all previous contenders for the honour of the origination of the aquarium, declined to quibble: 'Gosse is, *par eminence*, the historian of those strange creatures which inhabit our shores and dwell on our rock-bound coasts. ... Nothing can equal its popularity just now; and for that result we are entirely indebted to this amiable, pious, and indefatigable observer and collector.'[237] The *Gardeners' Chronicle* concurred—coincidentally, the reviewer even used some of the same terminology and thoughts:

> Mr. Gosse is indefatigable. ... It is superfluous to say that the author's whole heart is in his subject, and that in acquaintance with marine animals he is excelled by no one. When we add to these qualifications an agreeable, gossiping style, enough has been said to show why he is so popular. The resident at the seaside can know no tedium, with a work like this on the table, a good coast at his feet, and a glass vessel of sea water in which the curious animals that Mr. Gosse loves to describe can be kept alive for a few days.[238]

What attracted the most attention to the *Aquarium*, however, was its inclusion of six colour plates from Gosse's original water colours,[239]

235. Advertisement, 'Just Published', *Exeter Flying Post* (15 June 1854), 5; Freeman & Wertheimer-PHG, 48.
236. [Margaret Oliphant], 'Modern Light Literature—Science', *Blackwood's Magazine* LXXVIII (Aug. 1855), 220-3.
237. *New Monthly Magazine* CII (Sept. 1854), 117.
238. *Gardeners' Chronicle* (1 July 1854), 422.
239. PHG has been charged with failing to recognize his wife's contribution as an illustrator.

chromolithographed by the London firm M. and N. Hanhart.[240] If it is fair to argue that printing—and printing in colour—aided the growth of science in that both allowed for 'more or less identical images' to be produced in quantity,[241] then Gosse's skill in using relatively new printing techniques had an added importance.

In our day of instant and effortlessly created high-quality digital images, it is difficult to appreciate the demanding skill level and expense which constituted the revolution of colour printing of some 200 years

Life, 341, states that the 'submarine landscapes in many of these last examples' (referring to images in PHG's *Year at the Shore*, 1865) 'were put in by Mrs. Gosse, who had been in early life a pupil of Cotman.' Relying upon this source, nearly a century later scientist and bookseller S. Peter Dance wrote: 'The responsibility for the submarine scenery rested with Mrs Gosse, who had been a student of the landscape painter John Sell Cotman; her assistance is nowhere acknowledged by [P. H.] Gosse' (S. P. Dance, *The Art of Natural History: Animal Illustrators and their Work* (Woodstock, NY: Overlook Press, 1978), 200; it is unclear if Dance was referring to PHG's *Year at the Shore* or *Actinologia Britannica*). Twenty years later, Barbara T. Gates, a professor of English and women's studies, citing Dance's overstatement of what EWG had asserted, turned the reputed omission into a grievance:

> 'Emily Bowes Gosse ... executed all of the underwater landscapes for *The Aquarium* (1854)... This book bears the subtitle *An Unveiling of the Wonders of the Deep Sea*, a designation that clearly points to the importance of its illustrations. ... Emily Gosse's illustrations are both more dramatic and more accessible to the uninitiated than are Philip Gosse's accompanying words. She is the real unveiler for the public. ... although the sale of books like *The Aquarium* was in large part dependent upon the quality of their pictures ... Emily Gosse's contributions went unacknowledged by her husband' (B.T. Gates, *Kindred Nature: Victorian and Edwardian Women Embrace the Living World* (Chicago: University of Chicago Press, 1998), 74).

Gates continued this attack in another article, 'Those Who Drew and Those Who Wrote. Women and Victorian Popular Science Illustrations', in Ann Shteir and Bernard Lightman (eds.), *Figuring It Out: Science, Gender, and Visual Culture* (Hanover, NH: Dartmouth College Press, 2006), 193. There she stated that EG 'rendered beautiful artwork for the chromolithographs that graced science popularizations by her husband' in 'anonymity', receiving no 'picture-credits', thus constituting a 'binary [which] mirrors gender politics' in making pictures inferior to text. Several others have adopted her analysis (e.g., Mareike Vennen, *Das Aquarium. Praktiken, Techniken und Medien der Wissensproduktion (1840-1910)*. Göttingen: Wallstein Verlag, 2018, 87; Sara Albuquerque and Luciana Martins, 'Place, gender and the making of natural history: Hannah im Thurn in British Guiana, 1895-1897', *Journal of Historical Geography* 62 (2018), 12; Stephen E. Hunt, '"Free, Bold, Joyous": The Love of Seaweed in Margaret Gatty and Other Mid-Victorian Writers', *Environment and History* 11 (Feb. 2005), 13).

Notwithstanding Gates' persistence and the repetition by other researchers of her criticism of PHG, her allegation is detached from the facts. Contrary to her contention, the 'Mrs. Gosse' to whom EWG referred in *Life* was not Emily Gosse but Eliza (*née* Brightwen) Gosse, the *second* Mrs P. H. Gosse. The claim that PHG did not acknowledge the original work of others—including Emily Gosse—is without merit. For more details: Freeman & Wertheimer-EG, 26-7fn7.

240. Freeman & Wertheimer-PHG, 5.

241. This is the argument suggested in Twyman, *History of chromolithography*, 63; Jonathan Smith appears to come close to making the same point (Smith, *Charles Darwin and Victorian Visual Culture* (Cambridge: Cambridge University Press, 2006), 31).

ago. Commercial chromolithography (colour printing) had first appeared
in England in the 1830s, capturing the archeological discoveries of the
day.[242] The pioneer and innovative British colour lithographer Charles
Joseph Hullmandel (1789-1850), was followed in the 1840s by, among
others, the Hanharts, the most successful English firm in the field. As
far as natural history works were concerned, they had hitherto included
(if at all illustrated) black and white wood cuts. Colour printing was a
revelation. The Hanharts produced lithographs for eight plates in Gosse's
Naturalist's Sojourn in Jamaica (1851),[243] while the firm of Hullmandel
and Walton printed in colour Gosse's lithographic plates (drawn on the
stone by Gosse himself) for the *Naturalist's Rambles on the Devonshire
Coast* (1853). It was not until the Great Exhibition in London of 1851 that
colour printing in general attracted major public attention.[244]

By the time the *Aquarium* appeared in 1854, chromolithography had
made 'surprising advances' in England.[245] The Hanharts had produced
their first colour-printed book in 1842; the first use of colour printing in
popular journalism in England occurred in the *Illustrated London News*
in 1855.[246] As works containing chromolithographs of seashore creatures,
the *Naturalist's Rambles* and *Aquarium* are landmark publications. The
latter achieved something never before attempted: marine animals shown
in colour *in situ*, or as they might appear in a drawing-room aquarium.[247]
As a measure of the moment, one need only refer to a London publisher
who, in the same year the *Aquarium* appeared, thought it worthwhile
to draw attention to the fact that *one* of its scientific books contained a
single chromolithograph.[248] Gosse's *six* chromolithographs, from his

242. Twyman, *History of chromolithography*, 91.
243. Freeman & Wertheimer-PHG, 41; Christine E. Jackson, 'M. & N. Hanhart: printers
of natural history plates, 1830-1903', *Archives of Natural History* 26 (1999), 291; Twyman,
History of chromolithography, 136. The claim in Boase III: 332, that the firm of George Rowney
& Co. was, in 1857, the first English publisher to produce chromolithographs, is incorrect (the
firm specialized in chromolithographed watercolours from around 1853; Twyman, *History of
chromolithography*, 175-6).
244. Twyman, *History of chromolithography*, 125.
245. Robert Hunt, 'Lithography, and Other Novelties in Printing', London *Art-Journal* n.s.
VI (1 Jan. 1854), 2.
246. Charles Hasler, 'Mid-nineteenth-century Colour Printing', *Penrose Annual* 45 (1951), 67.
247. Freeman & Wertheimer-PHG, 5. Chromolithographed bird illustrations credited to the
Hanharts appeared in 1853 (Twyman, *History of chromolithography*, 161).
248. Lionel S. Beale, *The Microscope, its Applications to Clinical Medicine* (London: Samuel
Highley, 1854), advertised in the *Literary Gazette* (27 May 1854), 501.

original watercolours, produced a near-unrestrained outpouring of praise crossing class and religion.[249]

Start with religious publications like the *Church of England Quarterly Review*, a moderate High Church serial. 'Of the beautiful illustrations ... we cannot speak in sufficiently high terms of praise; the grace of form and delicacy of outline, the richness of tint, and infinite variety of position and arrangement.'[250] Declared the *English Churchman*, a High Church weekly: 'The letter-press is illustrated by some exceedingly well executed plates in coloured lithography ... which will astonish many persons.'[251] The *Christian Remembrancer*, a monthly with an evangelical appeal, said the plates were 'of ravishing beauty—quite miracles of the art of tinted lithography,' and added: 'We know that this is high praise: but we cannot speak with less moderation on the subject.'[252] Newspapers with a middle-to-upper-class readership like the daily *Globe* or *John Bull* (a good-quality conservative literary weekly) added their encomiums. The former commented on the 'singular beauty, both of design and execution, of the plates'[253] and the latter noted that the illustrations were of the 'most admirable character, beautifully printed in colours.'[254] The must-read *Athenaeum*, the literary and scientific weekly, lauded the 'faithful and beautiful representations'.[255] The *Brighton Gazette* said they were 'exquisite.'[256] *The Atlas*, a general and literary Liberal weekly, concurred:

> The coloured engravings are the most beautiful applications of chromolithography to natural history illustration that we have seen, and are not only scientifically correct, but from their admirable grouping, possess great merit as works of art. They are, in fact, transcripts of Aquarium scenery, and of the views which can to some extent be

249. The descriptions of the publications follow (if included) two works by Ellegård: *The Readership of the Periodical Press in Mid-Victorian Britain* and *Darwin and the General Reader. The Reception of Darwin's Theory of Evolution in the British Periodical Press, 1859-1872* (Göteborg: Göteborgs Universitets Arsskrift, Vol. LXIV, 1958).

250. *Church of England Quarterly Review* n.s. II (Oct. 1854), 440; *DNCJ*, 118.

251. *English Churchman* XII (6 July 1854), 635; Ellegård, *Readership of the Periodical Press*, 25.

252. *Christian Remembrancer* XXVIII (July 1854), 259-60; Ellegård, *Readership of the Periodical Press*, 30.

253. *The Globe* (22 June 1854), 1; *DNCJ*, 252; Ellegård, *Readership of the Periodical Press*, 18.

254. *John Bull* XXXIV (8 July 1854), 426; *DNCJ*, 321-2; Ellegård, *Readership of the Periodical Press*, 19.

255. [Edwin Lankester], *Athenaeum* (19 Aug. 1854), 1017; *DNCJ*, 26-8; Ellegård, *Readership of the Periodical Press*, 22.

256. *Brighton Gazette* (22 June 1854), 3.

observed among the thickly-peopled rocks beneath the translucent water on the shores of Cornwall and North Devon. ... These plates are so novel and so beautiful, that we hardly know which to prefer, but perhaps No.6, representing a miniature cavern, with the quaint and graceful Esop [sic] prawn in front, the bunch of sea-weed called ladies' tresses springing from the rock, and that wonderful little zoophyte, the *Lucernaria auricula*, which looks like a living fire-work hanging against the dark stone, is most deserving of admiration.[257]

Nor should it be thought that such remarks from 175 years ago are extravagant. One twenty-first century art historian noted that many of the mid-Victorian seaside handbooks 'are beautifully illustrated, particularly those by Gosse,'[258] and another has considered Gosse a 'true Romantic' whose illustrations 'have that particularization, that minute accuracy of representation, that sense of communion with Nature, which may be seen also in the work of George Stubbs and Thomas Bewick.'[259] As a group, zoologists after Gosse concur. Edwin Ray Lankester (the son of Edwin Lankester, who was known during his lifetime, and referred to here, as Ray Lankester) so admired Gosse's 'beautiful coloured pictures' that in 1915 he used one of them for the frontispiece of his *Diversions of a Naturalist*,[260] even though he himself was known for his artistic ability.[261] Another zoologist called Gosse's illustrations 'among the finest of their kind ever produced.'[262] A third mused: 'to draw like Gosse is no longer given to mortal man.'[263]

257. *The Atlas* (22 July 1854), 564; for the description of *The Atlas*: C[harles]. Mitchell's *Newspaper Press Directory* (London: C. Mitchell and Co., 1856), 19.

258. Payne, *Where the Sea Meets the Land*, 117.

259. Raymond Lister, *British Romantic Art*, 30; also pp. 143-4. Sacheverell Sitwell's pretentious remarks do not hide his ignorance of his subject (Sitwell, 'The Illustrations of Philip Henry Gosse', in Peter Stageman, *A Bibliography of the First Editions of Philip Henry Gosse, F.R.S.* (Cambridge: Golden Head Press, Ltd., 1955), 7-16. The proofs for this book, including some correspondence related to it which documents Sitwell's unfamiliarity with PHG's work, is at LeBL, donated by Raymond Lister).

260. The 'Plumose Anemone' appears as 'A Corner in a Marine Aquarium, Painted by Philip Henry Gosse, F.R.S.' in Ray Lankester, *Diversions of a Naturalist* (London: Methuen & Co. Ltd., 1915), frontispiece and p. 83. A century after PHG, the Plumose Anemone was described as the 'noblest, the most beautiful of all sea-anemones', and the one scientifically studied more than any other (Maurice Burton, 'The Noblest Sea-Anemone', *Illustrated London News*, 22 Aug. 1953, 282).

261. Edwin S. Goodrich, 'The Scientific Work of Edwin Ray Lankester', *Quarterly Journal of Microscopical Science* ser. 2 (1931), 363, 364, 367.

262. Yonge, 'Victorians by the Sea Shore', 604.

263. D['Arcy] W[entworth] T[hompson], 'The Fauna of the Seaside', *Nature* 144 (16 Dec. 1939), 998.

Gosse was the one who gave the word 'aquarium' its modern signification,[264] and the outbreak in England of aquaromania dates to his *Naturalist's Rambles* and *Aquarium*. Aquaromania surpassed in importance all other contemporary British 'manias'—for ferns (pteridomania), porcelain jars (potichomania), or Berlin work.[265] In 1854, the *Athenaeum* observed, an aquarium was 'now almost a domestic institution.'[266]

Within and without Britain, Gosse was credited for his role. A French

264. The *OED* (1st and 2ed., as of this writing the entry is unrevised for the 3ed.) gives an incomplete history of the words 'aquarium' and 'aquavivarium'. Without explaining the term 'aquarium', PHG twice used it in its modern sense in his *Naturalist's Rambles*, 189 (the work was available as early as Jan. 1853, Freeman & Wertheimer-PHG, 46): 'Mr. Robert Warington ... has now (Dec. 1852) at his residence in London a marine aquarium, with living Algae and Sea-anemones in a healthy condition' (p. 234) and 'All who have seen this aquarium' (p. 441)—a reference to the 'large glass tank, filled with sea-water ... and stocked with marine plant and animals so as to resemble one of those charming tide-pools'. PHG also used 'aquarium' in that work in connection with aquatic plants. In 1854, PHG famously explained his adoption of the word in his *Aquarium*, 256-7 (the book was available in May 1854: Freeman & Wertheimer-PHG, 48).

In June 1853, Charles Knight was the first to use the word 'aquavivarium' (Lankester, *Aquavivarium*, 12-13; see also 'The *Aquavivarium*, as it is proposed to call the collection of marine and fresh-water animals in the Regent's-park', *Illustrated London News*, 23 July 1853, 37).

The Latin word *aquarium* had been used in Roman times to designate a cattle-trough, and later (by botanists) to describe tanks in which aquatic plants were grown (advertisement for the *Horticultural Magazine* in *Illustrated London News*, 28 Mar. 1846, 215; 'Mr. Groom's Exhibition of Tulips', *Illustrated London News*, 31 May 1851, 479, and PHG, *Aquarium*, 256; this is the sense in which the word is used by Warington in *Gardener's Magazine of Botany* n.s., Part I (Jan. 1852), 7, and the title under the woodcut).

When the Regent's Park aquarium was opened in 1853, it was indiscriminately referred to as the 'Fish House', 'Aquatic Vivarium' (*Illustrated London News*, 28 May 1853, 420), 'Aquarium', or 'Marine Vivarium' (*The Zoological Gardens; A Description of the Gardens and Menageries of the Zoological Society. A Handbook for Visitors* (London: H. G. Clarke & Co., n.d. [but with British Library stamp of 21 Sept. 1853]). For some time, 'Vivarium', 'Aquavivarium', or 'Marine vivarium' were also used, all of which yielded to 'aquarium'.

Concerning the history of word usage, W. A. Lloyd wrote: '... I think that the word 'aquarium' used in its present sense, was first employed by Mr. Henry Philip Gosse [*sic*], in his book entitled "The Aquarium", published in April, 1854 ... Mr. R. Warrington, [*sic*] Mrs. Thynne, and other early experimenters, never used it before 1854; and the aquarium in Regent's Park has always been from the beginning officially termed 'The Fish-House" (Lloyd, 'The Aquarium', *Popular Recreator* I (1873), 126).

265. For the first, see *OED* (citing Kingsley, *Glaucus*); for the second and third, *Wells Journal* (Wells, Somerset) (29 Aug. 1857), 4, and W. R. Hughes, *On the Principles and Management of the Marine Aquarium* (Birmingham: Cornish Brothers, 1875), 4 (first read as a paper before the Birmingham Natural History and Microscopical Society, 27 Jan. 1874). Berlin wool work was a form of needlepoint.

266. *Athenaeum*, 18 Nov. 1854, 1401. See also 'Forty or fifty years ago, when 'nature study' was still unthought of in the schools, the admirable writings of the late Charles Kingsley and P. H. Gosse and others directed attention to the marvels of the beach. For a brief space 'collecting' was as fashionable as golf is today, and every house of any pretensions boasted an aquarium' ('Summer in Sark', London *Times*, 3 Aug. 1909, 15).

man of letters termed the aquarium 'an unprecedented popular success in England, the primary cause of this infatuation with the things of sea, which extended for a time to all the inhabitants of the United Kingdom. ... After reading Mr. Gosse's book, everyone wanted to have an aquarium to verify his assertions and repeat his experiments.'[267] Similarly, an American promoter noted how, after Gosse had 'perfected all the labors of his predecessors' and the public gained access to aquaria,

> An AQUARIUM-mania seized upon the public mind. The AQUARIUM was on everybody's lip. The AQUARIUM rang in everybody's ear. Morning, noon, and night, it was nothing but the AQUARIUM. Books innumerable were written upon it. Lectures, without end, were delivered in elucidation of it. The gardens of the Zoölogical Society, in Regent's Park, groaned with the crowd; and the AQUARIUM-house therein sweltered beneath the multitudes that suffered martyrdom, every day, to contemplate the cause of the sensation.[268]

In truth as these remarks suggest, the aquarium movement was too powerful to be confined to one country. It was a sign of a cutting-edge society, a matter of national pride, a tribute to advanced scientific knowledge. Battle lines were drawn. The rush was on to view, imitate, acquire, and build.

First came the argument about priority. The German zoologist Emil Adolf Rossmässler (1806-1867) said he could have 'hit himself' ('an die Stirn schlagen mögen')[269] for not having realised how the aquarium movement could impact the educational field until he read Gosse's *Aquarium*. Yet in *Das Süsswasser-Aquarium* (*The Freshwater Aquarium*), he proceeded inexplicably to ignore the work of English naturalists, crediting the invention instead to Europeans—Swammerdam, Leeuwenhoek, Réaumur, Trembley, and others (albeit as 'unintentional inventors').[270] To which a less-than-pleased writer in the London

267. Hippolyte Bout de Charlemont, 'Notes pour server a l'histoire des aquariums', *Bulletin Mensuel de la Société Nationale d'Acclimatation de France* ser. 4, vol 3 (Jan. 1886), 34-5 ('... un ouvrage qui obtint en Angleterre un succès de popularité sans précédent, et qui fut la cause première de cet engouement pour les choses de la mer, qui s'étendit pendant un moment à tous les habitants du Royaume-Uni. ... Après avoir lu le livre de M. Gosse, tout le monde voulut posséder un aquarium pour verifier ses assertions et répéter ses experiences').

268. Henry D. Butler, *The Family Aquarium; or, Aqua Vivarium* (New York: Dick & Fitzgerald, [1858]), 15. Small-caps in the original.

269. E. A. Rossmässler, 'Der See im Glase', Leipzig *Die Gartenlaube* III ([?20 Sept.] 1855), 252.

270. E.A. Rossmässler, *Das Süsswasser-Aquarium. Eine Anleitung zur Herstellung und*

Saturday Review responded: 'Begging [the] pardon of Herr Rossmässler's ignorance, these men were nothing of the kind. ... Naturalists, at all times, as well as boys and girls, have placed animals and plants in tumblers of water, in order that they might watch them. But a tumbler of water containing organic beings is not an aquarium, any more than a tramway is a railroad.'[271] Meanwhile Rossmässler, who had abandoned theology for science, in his 1855 article in *Die Gartenlaube* (*The Gazebo*), the widely read weekly magazine published in Leipzig for middle-class families,[272] became the founder of the aquarium movement in Germany[273] and the first to promote aquariums for the German home.[274]

Acting with more grace, a French writer nodded to the work of English naturalists yet observed that, *en vérité*, it was 'one of our nationals'—the naturalist Charles des Moulins (1798-1875)—who was 'the first to identify and make known' one of the key principles of aquarium science.[275]

It wasn't only that nations were eager to *claim* priority for discovering this marvel. Everyone *wanted* and *needed* an aquarium, and it seemed as if everyone actually *had* one. P. T. Barnum, working with D. W. Mitchell at the Zoological Gardens, brought the first aquarium to America in 1856,[276]

Pflege desselben (Leipzig: Hermann Mendelssohn, 1857), 1. This was Rossmässler's most successful work, appearing in five 'editions' by 1892 (Andreas W. Daum, 'Science, Politics, and Religion: Humboldtian Thinking and the Transformations of Civil Society in Germany, 1830-1870', *Osiris* ser. 2, XVII (2002), 126). Curiously, England is acknowledged as 'the birthplace of the marine-aquarium' in 'Wie er= und behält man den Ocean auf dem Tische, oder das Marine=Aquarium', *Die Gartenlaube* III ([?20 Sept.] 1855), 503.

271. 'The Aquarium in Germany', *Saturday Review* IX (12 Dec. 1857), 540. The reviewer concluded that Rossmässler 'appears to us a very stupid gentleman' (p. 541). Rossmässler claimed that his book received approving reviews (Rossmässler, *Mein Leben und Streben im Verkehr mit der Natur und dem Volke*. Hannover: Carl Rümpler, 1874, 283).

272. Bernd Brunner, *The Ocean at Home. An Illustrated History of the Aquarium* (New York: Princeton Architectural Press, 2005), 60, incorrectly claims that Rossmässler was a co-founder of *Die Gartenlaube*. Rossmässler was, however, close to the founder, Ernst Keil (Chase Richards, 'Pages of Progress: German Liberalism and the Popular Press after 1848' (University of Pennsylvania, PhD dissertation, 2013), 164). On *Gartenlaube*, see also Kirsten Belgum, *Popularizing the Nation: Audience, Representation, and the Production of Identity in* Die Gartenlaube, *1853-1900* (Lincoln: University of Nebraska Press, 1998), xiv, xxv.

273. Frey, *Das Aquarium van A bis Z*, 274-5; also (anon), 'Wie er= und behält man den Ocean auf dem Tische, oder das Marine=Aquarium'.

274. Andreas W. Daum, 'Science, Politics, and Religion, 126; Daum, 'Rossmässler, Emil Adolf', *Neue Deutsche Biographie* XXII (2005), 96; 'Rossmaessler (Emil Adolf)', in J. M. Wheeler, *A Biographical Dictionary of Freethinkers* (London: Progressive Publishing Company, 1889), 284.

275. Hippolyte Bout de Charlemont, 'Notes pour server a l'histoire des aquariums', 33-4; Kathleen Kete, *The Beast in the Boudoir: Petkeeping in Nineteenth-Century Paris* (Berkeley: University of California Press, 1994), 58.

276. John Rickards Betts, 'P. T. Barnum and the Popularization of Natural History', *Journal*

where it enjoyed popularity in the following decades.[277] In words befitting the modest showman, the 'GRAND AQUARIA at the AMERICAN (BARNUM'S) MUSEUM, New York' were described as 'beyond dispute, the largest, most costly, most complete, and most elegant production of the kind on the face of the globe!'[278] Not for long. An aquarium followed in Paris five years later,[279] while in Germany the Zoological Society in Hamburg announced the construction of a new aquarium in 1863 under the guidance of W. A. Lloyd—'at least three times as large as any in existence.'[280]

Meanwhile in England, the number of visitors to the Regent's Park Zoo increased significantly in 1854. It was 'the most attractive spot' there,[281] especially among the working classes.[282] The novelist George Eliot, the geologist Charles Lyell, and others took an early opportunity to witness the wonders of the seashore there;[283] Charles Kingsley wrote a book on the subject after reviewing the *Devonshire Coast* and *Aquarium* (his work is discussed later in the chapter); Charles Darwin, when he met

of the History of Ideas XX, 1959, 355-7; Butler, *Family Aquarium*, 15-17; a useful but frequently unreliable account of the aquarium movement in America is in Brunner, *Ocean at Home*, 68-77.

277. Rebecca Duffy, *The Age of Aquaria: The Aquarium Pursuit and Personal Fish-Keeping, 1850-1920* (University of Delaware, MA thesis, 2018), 135-6. Brunner mistakenly predates aquaromania in the United States to 1854, when PHG's *Aquarium* was reviewed in *Littell's Living Age* (Brunner, *Ocean at Home*, 68). Likewise Hamera, in referring to the *Littell's* review, claims 'There are an extraordinary number of American reviews' of *Aquarium* (*Parlor Ponds*, 237fn. 21). This is incorrect. The reviews cited by these investigators are not original works in USA serials but reprints from English ones. Secondly, PHG's *Aquarium* received far less attention in USA newspapers than did other works by him, such as *Romance of Natural History* (1860), *Evenings at the Microscope* (1859), *Life in its Lower, Intermediate, and Higher Forms* (1857), or the *Ocean* (1845). Thirdly, unlike other books by PHG which appeared in America before and after 1854, no USA edition of the *Aquarium* was ever published (likely related to the difficulty of reproducing the coloured illustrations). Serious attention was not given to the *Aquarium* in America until 1858, at the time that two books on the subject appeared there.

278. Butler, *Family Aquarium*, 16. Small caps in the original. Butler and John Greenwood, Jr., had bought the American Museum collection from Barnum in 1855 (P. T. Barnum, *Struggles and Triumphs: or, Forty Years' Recollections. Author's Edition* (Buffalo, NY: Warren, Johnson & Co., 1869,1873), 408).

279. The Paris aquarium opened at the Jardin d'acclimatation in 1861 (Sophie Lachapelle and Heena Mistry, 'From the Waters of the Empire to the Tanks of Paris: The Creation and Early Years of the Aquarium Tropical, Palais de la Porte Dorée', *Journal of the History of Biology* 47 (Spring 2014), 2).

280. *Illustrated London News*, 4 Apr. 1863, 383.

281. Review, 'Gosse's Aquarium', London *Spectator* 27 (24 June 1854), 681.

282. [Andrew Wynter], 'The Zoological Gardens', *Quarterly Review* XCVIII (Dec. 1855), 232, 248.

283. George Eliot-Mrs Bray, [13 June 1853], in Gordon Haight (ed.), *George Eliot Letters* (New Haven: Yale University Press, 1954), II: 103; journal of Sir Charles J. F. Bunbury, 8 May 1853, in Frances J. Bunbury (ed.), *Life, Letters and Journals of Sir Charles J. F. Bunbury, Bart* (London: Printed for private circulation, 1894), II: 530.

Gosse for what may have been the first and only time,[284] informed a
correspondent that 'he told me that he had now the *same* several sea-
animals & algae living & breeding for 13 months in the *same* <u>artificially</u>
made sea water! Does not this tempt you? it almost tempts me to set
up a marine vivarium.'[285] The graphic artist George Cruikshank, in his
etching on 'Passing Events, or The Tail of the Comet of 1853,' in which he
illustrated the main occurrences of that year, gave a prominent place to
the Regent's Park 'vivarium'.[286] An 'Invitation to the Aquarium' appeared
in rhyme in 1856,[287] and a serio-comic song entitled 'The Aquarium
Mania' was performed in London in 1858.[288]

-VII-

For two months in 1854 (June 22-August 18) the Gosse family was in
Tenby, Wales. Possibly at one point, the nearly five-year-old Edmund
Gosse provided guidance to some Brethren contemporaries (two daughters
of the Soltau family and students at a school of William Hake) during a
seaside excursion.[289] In 1855, a month and a half (20 March-*c.* 13 May)

284. *Life*, 256, claims that 'my father was that evening [20 Mar. 1855] presented for the first
time' to Darwin, who was at the Linnean while PHG read his paper on *Peachia hastata* (Freeman
& Wertheimer-PHG, 115). *Father and Son* did not repeat the claim. Charles Kingsley told his
wife that he went to the 2 May 1854 meeting of the Linnean Society in London to meet PHG,
and while there also met Darwin (CK-his wife [Frances E. Grenfell Kingsley], [s.d.] May 1854,
in [Frances E. Grenfell Kingsley] (ed.), *Charles Kingsley: His Letters and Memories of His Life*
(London: C. Kegan Paul & Co., 1878), I: 427). Kingsley does not indicate whether he introduced
PHG to Darwin. Little business was conducted at that meeting (*Gardeners' Chronicle*, [6] May
1854, 287). Darwin had been elected a Fellow of the Linnean Society at their 7 Mar. meeting
(*Athenaeum*, 18 Mar. 1854, 345; *Gardeners' Chronicle*, 18 Mar. 1854, 166).

285. Darwin-J. S. Henslow, 26 Mar. [1855], in Frederick Burkhardt and Sydney Smith (eds.),
The Correspondence of Charles Darwin. Volume 5: 1851-1855 (Cambridge: Cambridge University
Press, 1989), 489fn.7; also Darwin Correspondence Project, Letter no. 1655). Emphasis in the
original. Though the meaning is unaffected, the transcription is not quite accurate in Nora Barlow
(ed.), *Darwin and Henslow. The Growth of an Idea. Letters 1831-1860* (London: John Murray,
1967), 173-4). Cf.: 'As the Aquarium is now almost a domestic institution, some of our readers
will be glad to hear that they can make their own salt water artificially' (*The Athenaeum*, 18
Nov. 1854, 1401).

286. I saw a copy of this etching at the Victoria & Albert Museum, Prints and Drawings
Section (no reference number).

287. 'Invitation to the Aquarium', *Punch* 31 (13 Dec. 1856), 231: 'Oh come with me, / And
you shall see / My beautiful Aquarium; / Or if that word / You call absurd, / We'll say, instead,
Vivarium'.

288. Silvia Granata, *Victorian aquarium*, 1.

289. Mildred Cable and Francesca French, *A Woman Who Laughed. Henrietta Soltau
who Laughed at Impossibilities and Cried: 'It Shall be Done'* (London: China Inland Mission,
1934), 41-2. This activity appears to me to have taken place in 1854 or 1855, but it is unclear
where. Timothy Stunt has written (*in. litt.*, 26 Jan. 2023) that the dates are uncertain because

was spent at Weymouth, and then July to 6 September, at Ilfracombe. Here Gosse lectured on the invertebrate fauna, and conducted the first of his outdoor 'Marine Natural History' classes for men and women.[290] He continued to publish scientific articles and issued *A Handbook to the Marine Aquarium* (1855), an inexpensive and useful guide 'in clear and simple language'[291] to the construction of parlour aquaria.[292]

Then came *A Manual of Marine Zoology* (2 vols, 1855-6), a groundbreaking, comprehensive list of British marine animals.[293] No one was in a better position to write such a work: no one had handled more aquarium creatures than Gosse,[294] and no one knew more about marine zoology than he did.[295] The *Manual* did away with the necessity of carrying a shelf of books to the seashore as Gosse had done in 1852,

Cable and French conflated time spent by the Soltaus at Exmouth and at Bideford. William Hake (1795-1890) and Henry W. Soltau were associates of Robert C. Chapman, the prominent Brethren figure. PHG's correspondence with Soltau and Chapman, and perhaps Hake, is listed in Corr. Bk.

290. For the lecture, see *North Devon Journal* (26 July 1855), 8; for the classes: advertisement, *Bath Chronicle* (28 June 1855), 2; 'Topics of the Week', *Literary Gazette* (30 June 1855), 412; *Life*, 257. The classes were also mentioned by Charles Kingsley in the first edition of *Glaucus*. There Kingsley wrote that 'he has often regretted that no naturalist has established shore-lectures at some watering places ... This want, however, bids fair to be supplied at last. The most pious and most learned naturalist, Mr. Gosse, whose works will be so often quoted in these pages, purposes, it is understood, to establish this summer a regular shore-class, probably at Weymouth' (Kingsley, *Glaucus* (Cambridge: Macmillan & Co., 1855), 51). The same remark appears in the second edition, also published in 1855. PHG subsequently asked Kingsley to advertise the classes, and apparently he requested an update (only the letters from Kingsley are extant: CK-PHG, 13 May 1856, LeBL). The third edition of *Glaucus* thus states: 'That pious and learned naturalist, Mr. Gosse ... has now established summer shore-classes. Tenby is his post for this summer' (*Glaucus* (Cambridge: Macmillan and Co., 3ed., 1858), 48). The remark is not present in the fifth edition of 1873.

291. [T. Rymer Jones], 'The Aquarium', *Saturday Review* I (22 Dec. 1855), 135.

292. For reviews of the *Handbook to the Marine Aquarium*: *Spectator* XXVIII (10 Nov. 1855), 1167; *Notes & Queries* ser. 1, XII (17 Nov. 1855), 396; *Gardeners' Chronicle* (22 Dec. 1855), 838-9; [T. Bell], *Athenaeum*, 29 Dec. 1855, 1531; *Natural History Review* III (1856), 29; *Quarterly J. Micro. Sci.* n.s. IV (1856), 147-9; *New Quarterly Review* V (1856), 78; *Zoologist* XIV (Jan. 1856), 4933-4; *English Churchman* XIV (10 Jan. 1856), 35; *AMNH* ser. 2, XVIII (Feb. 1856), 197-8; *Christian Remembrancer* LIII (Apr. 1856), 499; *Dublin University Magazine* XLVIII (Sept. 1856), 353-62.

293. Review of *Manual of Marine Zoology*, Part I: *AMNH* ser. 2, XVI (Oct. 1855), 277; *Spectator* (1 Sept. 1855), 911; Freeman & Wertheimer-PHG, 4.

294. W. A. Lloyd, cited in John T. Carrington, 'Aquarium Notes', *Zoologist* ser. 2, XI (Aug. 1876), 5038.

295. Thus *Zoologist* XIV (1856), 5343; *AMNH* ser. 2, XVIII (Aug. 1856), 162; *Gardeners' Chronicle* (1 July 1854), 422; *Monthly Magazine* CII (Sept. 1854), 117, *Excelsior* V (Apr. 1856), 360; *Athenaeum*, 19 Aug. 1854, 1017.

thus giving 'such an impetus to shore-collecting'[296] and making it the forerunner of modern lists.[297]

While the *Manual* is usually overlooked in discussions of Gosse's corpus of natural history writings, for a work of science its reputation has been notably enduring. On the appearance of Part I, the reviewer in the *Gardeners' Chronicle* said that 'We can recommend it as a capital seaside companion.'[298] When Part II followed, the *Natural History Review* was effusive: it is 'the most useful work that has been for a long time, if ever, published.'[299] Two years later, T. Rymer Jones, Professor of Natural History in King's College London, called it 'indispensable to the sea-side visitor'.[300] In 1881 it was still 'invaluable to the student of our marine fauna,'[301] and over eighty years after its first appearance, the Scottish zoologist D'Arcy Wentworth Thompson (1860-1948) noted that the *Manual's* 'two little green volumes ... were used and loved by many.' The nearly 700 woodcuts drawn by Gosse, often from living specimens— 'the best part of the book' in Thompson's opinion—were 'only thumb-nail sketches' but 'every one is unmistakable.'[302]

In 1856, there were second editions of the *Aquarium* and *Handbook*, joining a shelf-full of other Gosses. In that year alone, SPCK was

296. 'Fresh-Water Zoology', London *Spectator*, Supplement, 26 June 1897, 891, recalling the situation 'nearly forty years ago'.

297. Freeman & Wertheimer-PHG, 51-2. For reviews of the *Manual of Marine Zoology*: *Zoologist* XIII-XIV (Nov. 1855, Dec. 1856), 4885-89, 5339-40; *Natural History Review* II, IV (1855, 1857), 94-8, 90-2; [two articles by W. S. Dallas, per *Wellesley Index* III: 625, item 1461; p. 626, item 1487 in] *Westminster Review* n.s. IX, XI (Apr. 1856, Jan. 1857), 604-5, 280-1 (Dallas' latter review is misidentified as by T. H. Huxley in Paul White, 'Cross-cultural encounters: the co-production of science and literature in mid-Victorian periodicals', in Roger Luckhurst and Josephine McDonagh (eds.), *Transactions and Encounters: Science and Culture in the 19th Century* (Manchester: Manchester University Press, 2002), 94fn.41. The error is repeated in Paul White, *Thomas Huxley: Making the 'Man of Science'* (Cambridge: University Press, 2003), 184 and Granata, *Victorian aquarium*, 134); *Literary Gazette* (1 Sept. 1855, 25 Oct. 1856), 553, 829; *John Bull* XXXV, XXXVI (15 Sept. 1855, 1 Nov. 1856), 589, 699; *Spectator* XXVIII-XXIX (1 Sept. 1855, 1 Nov. 1856), 911, 1159; *Christian Remembrancer* XXX (Dec. 1855), 518; *Leader* (3 Jan. 1857), 18.

298. *Gardeners' Chronicle* (1 Sept. 1855), 583.

299. Review of PHG's *Tenby*, *Manual* (Part II), and *Life in its Lower, Intermediate, and Higher Forms*, in *Natural History Review* IV (1857), 91.

300. Thomas Rymer Jones, *The Aquarian Naturalist. A Manual for the Sea-side* (London: John Van Voorst, 1858), 440.

301. John T. Carrington and Edward Lovett, 'Notes and Observations on British Stalk-eyed Crustacea', *Zoologist* ser. 3, V (May 1881), 198.

302. D. W. T[hompson]., 'The Fauna of the Seaside', *Nature* 144 (16 Dec. 1939), 997-8. Eight woodcuts from the *Manual of Marine Zoology* were used in 1915 by the zoologist Ray Lankester in *Diversions of a Naturalist*.

advertising for sale on a single day 12 distinct Gosse titles[303]—and that was not even all of the works by him available. The latest was *Tenby: A Sea-side Holiday*, the final volume in Gosse's seashore trilogy. "En iterum!" ['Once again!'], the *Athenaeum* said in its review of *Tenby*: 'Here we have another issue of that fertile pen of Mr. Gosse, and another of his delightful sea-side books.'[304] Proclaimed the *Zoologist*: 'Mr. Gosse is beyond all comparison the most voluminous writer on Natural History among the present generation of men: his powers are as inexhaustible as his subject. Volume follows volume with a rapidity that is marvellous; and the last has always the rare merit of appearing the best.'[305]

With his 'pleasant style' which 'doth not delight in long Latinised words,' Gosse is the '"eyes" to those of us who have no eyes for many of the wonders of the deep.'[306] A notice of a meeting of the Teignmouth Useful Knowledge Society urged 'All lovers of natural history who visit the sea coast, should purchase Mr. Gosse's elegant sea-side work.'[307] That Gosse was the first to popularise the 'special features' of Tenby remained part of local lore for decades.[308]

Let me sum up the factors considered so far which made Gosse a phenomenon as a natural history populariser. He had the field experience and the skill to speak with authority on many facets of the natural world. His scientific writings earned him the respect of his peers. His amiable literary persona drew people to his side as he vividly and accurately pictured what he saw, with pen and pencil. He was unabashed in expressing his feelings about the natural world, his awe and wonder as a Christian. His enthusiasm resonated. He was a reliable guide, a wholesome religious counsellor and a trusted mentor in the classroom of the Creator. It is why (in the assessment of the *Saturday Review* years

303. *Aris's Birmingham Gazette* (29 Dec. 1856), 1. The 12 titles advertised in that issue were: *Ancient Egypt, Monuments of* [1847]; *Assyria: Her Manners and Customs* [1852]; *Fishes (Families and Orders of), Tabular View* [canvas and roller editions, 1856]; *History of the Jews* [1851]; *Natural History: Mammalia* [1848]; *Birds* [1849]; *Fishes* [1851]; *Reptiles* [1850]; *Mollusca* [1854]; *Ocean* [1845]; *Wanderings through the Conservatories at Kew* [1856]; *Introduction to Zoology* [2vols., 1844]. In the same advertisement, eight natural history books by the Revd C. A. Johns are for sale.

304. [T. Bell], *Athenaeum*, 31 May 1856, 681.

305. *Zoologist* XIV (1856), 5343.

306. 'Literature', *Birmingham Journal*, 11 June 1856, 2.

307. 'Teignmouth Useful Knowledge Society', *Woolmer's Exeter and Plymouth Gazette*, 14 Apr. 1855, 4.

308. 'Birmingham Naturalists at Tenby', *Tenby Observer*, 17 June 1886, 5.

later) Gosse stands 'absolutely companionless among those who have popularized scientific subjects.'[309]

By gaining the trust of his readers in these ways, Gosse was proposing for consideration a worldview for mid-Victorians which lay outside of the industrial, commercial life which predominated, away from class strife, political jostling, empire building, even mundane religious concerns or divisions. It was not a revolutionary view, but it carried the authority of a seasoned man of science challenging others to think in a new way about how they experienced the world around them and specifically the shore which surrounded their island gem.

Prior to the Gossean era, the seashore was the place where one went for a change of air or for physical recreation.[310] Gosse had a different agenda. To him, the marine shore was not a backdrop to be traversed in going from one place to another. It was a world to be valued in-and-of itself. That's because it contained a world of remarkable creatures, different from our terrestrial experience yet not less striking. A seashore encounter added meaning to life—if only one adopted Gosse's teaching about the value of the 'open eye'. 'When I see gentlemen at a beautiful marine village,' Gosse wrote in his delightful treatise, *Sea-side Pleasures* (1853),

> lounging by the hour together in the news-room, and young ladies sitting about the rocks novel-reading, and others of both sexes wandering to and fro with listless and vacant countenances, I cannot help saying within myself, 'You have outstayed the pleasure for which you came here, and for any peculiar gratification which you get from the sea you might as well be back in the towns or cities whence you came.'

Instead, Gosse proposed this richer way of looking at the natural world:

> What if I were to open before you resources that you could never exhaust in the longest life; a fund of intellectual delight that would never satiate; pursuits so enchanting that the more you followed them the more single and ardent would be your love for them; so excellent that they would elevate as well as entertain the mind; that leave no moral or mental defilement; that strengthen rather than enervate both mind and body?

---

309. *Saturday Review* LXXI (3 Jan. 1891), 17.

310. *The Leader*, 13 Feb. 1858, 159; *AMNH* ser. 2, XII (Sept. 1853), 197; [Margaret Oliphant, *Wellesley Index* I: 100, item 3407], *Blackwood's Magazine* LXXVIII (Aug. 1855), 217-8; *New Monthly Magazine* XCIX (Nov. 1853), 298.

Does such promise seem extravagant? Believe me, it is no more than may be fulfilled. I am writing not from the report of others, not what I have read in musty books, but what I have felt and proved in many years' experience. The pursuits of which I speak have been my delight from early youth onward, and they have not abated one jot of their freshness; nay, they are more enchanting than the first day I followed them.

... The whole difference between one who sees in the external world of Nature a paradise, and one to whom it is a barren desert, consists in the open eye. When once the attention has been awakened to the perception in detail, of the wonderful beauty and fitness, the endless variety of structure and form, the curious contrivances, relations, modifications, and compensations, that are manifested in God's marvellous works, a well of pleasure has been unsealed that is never closed again. It is as if a new face had been put on everything, whereas the change is only in the beholder. ...[311]

Victorians took Gosse's message seriously, and while aquaromania lasted they approached the coasts with an 'open eye'. Popular and scientific works displaced the novel as fashionable reading material for a seaside holiday,[312] for a young lady in London 'Mr. MITCHELL's Vivarium' is 'The pleasantest refuge I know,'[313] and the eccentrically dressed naturalist roaming the shores with his array of jars became respectable.[314] According to *Punch*, the most common object seen at the seashore were bipeds—bending over, net in hand, collecting seaweeds and other objects.[315] The *Saturday Review* even claimed that in the home of many a country parson or village surgeon, W. H. Harvey's *Sea-side Book* and Gosse's *Aquarium* 'rank in the family estimation next after the Bible and Shakespeare.'[316]

In a modest way, the British artistic community also translated into their work this new appreciation of the seashore. 'Babbacombe Bay, Devon' by watercolour painter George Price Boyce (1826-1897),[317] and

311. [PHG], *Seaside Pleasures* (London: SPCK, 1853), 6-8. This work had been serialised in 1852 with PHG's name but issued anonymously in book form (Freeman & Wertheimer-PHG, 46-7).

312. [W. S. Dallas, per *Wellesley Index* III: 625, item 1461] in *Westminster Review* XLII (July 1856), 238-9, and *The Leader*, 13 Feb. 1858, 159.

313. 'A Young Lady's Lament', *Punch* XXX (14 June 1856), 243.

314. See, e.g., the cartoon by J[ohn] L[eech] in *Punch* XXXV (21 Aug. 1858), 76.

315. *Punch* XXXV (21 Aug. 1858), 76.

316. 'Popular Books of Natural History', *Saturday Review*, 29 Oct. 1859, 521.

317. 'Babbacombe Bay' was exhibited in London in 1854 (London *Daily News*, 13 Mar. 1854, 2).

'Anstey's Cove,' by landscape painter John William Inchbold (1830-1888), were both apparently begun shortly after the appearance of Gosse's *Devonshire Coast* in 1853, and their locations—including the canvases done in Ilfracombe as early as 1853 by George Robert Lewis (1782-1871)[318]—were inspired by it.[319] The sculptor Henry Weekes (1807-1888) exhibited at the Royal Academy in 1854 a statue of 'The Young Naturalist' (a semi-nude girl collecting shells by the seashore),[320] while 'Ramsgate Sands, Life at the Sea-side' (1854), by William Powell Frith (1819-1909), famously displayed 'an epitome of an English bathing-place,'[321] thus celebrating the Victorian seaside.[322] 'Pegwell Bay, Kent: A Recollection of October 5th, 1858' (exhibited in 1860 and now in the Tate), by William Dyce (1806-1864), was a 'veritable transcript of nature' showing seashells 'with a distinctness sufficient to satisfy even a conchologist.'[323] The painting suggests that, in the year after *Omphalos*,[324] an artist known for producing 'Sacred Art'[325] believed that religion and science could co-exist.[326] British artists of the 1850s and 1860s emphasised in their work geology and astronomy over natural history, yet allowed trends and thoughts of the day to give enhanced significance to their landscapes.[327]

-VIII-

In mid-Victorian Britain, men of inherited wealth like Bowerbank or Darwin could respectably pursue scientific studies; for others, the thought that one should or could earn a living from science was suspect.[328] A

318. Payne, *Where the Sea Meets the Land*, 127.

319. Payne, *Where the Sea Meets the Land*, 128. PHG's *Devonshire Coast* appeared in May 1853.

320. *Athenaeum*, 27 May 1854, 656; London *Art-Journal*, 1 June 1854, 172.

321. 'Private View of the Royal Academy', *Spectator*, 29 Apr. 1854, 462.

322. Marcia Pointon, 'A study of William Dyce's *Pegwell Bay: A Recollection of October 5th, 1858*', *Art History* I (Mar. 1978), 102; Payne, *Where the Sea Meets the Land*, 118.

323. *Lloyd's Weekly Newspaper*, 27 May 1860, 8; see Edinburgh *Caledonian Mercury*, 17 Feb. 1865, 2.

324. Jonathan P. Ribner, 'John Ruskin, Philip Henry Gosse, William Dyce, and the Contemplation of Time at Mid-century', *British Art Journal* XVIII (Winter 2017/2018), 74. Ribner associates *Omphalos* with 'Pegwell Bay', but does not assert a causative relation.

325. James Dafforne, 'British Artists: Their Style and Character, with Engraved Illustrations. No. LI. William Dyce, R.A.', *Art-Journal* (1 Oct. 1860), 293.

326. Payne, *Where the Sea Meets the Land*, 120-1.

327. Payne, *Where the Sea Meets the Land*, 125ff.

328. Jim Endersby, 'A Life More Ordinary: The Dull Life but Interesting Times of Joseph Dalton Hooker', *Journal of the History of Biology* 44 (Winter 2011), 628-9.

lucky few naturalists were appointed to one of the rare university posts or positions in a scientific institution. Others, as T. H. Huxley pointed out in March 1851, had to be prepared for a harsh truth: 'To attempt to live by any scientific pursuit is a farce. Nothing but what is absolutely practical will go down in England. A man of science may earn great distinction, but not bread. He will get invitations to all sorts of dinners and conversationes, but not enough income to pay his cab fare.'[329] In the case of Gosse, his singularity—no wealth, no influencers—was acknowledged. 'Mr. Gosse is perhaps, the only man in this country who makes natural history his profession,' observed *The Critic*, a London literary weekly, 'and dares to go alone, unsupported by any public establishment or scientific society.'[330]

Thus are we driven back to the question which stands at the opening of this chapter: *How did he do it?* Only now, we mean: How was it that— lacking in advantages which others had—Gosse was able to become a phenomenon as a natural history populariser?

Let us first consider Gosse's book publishing (no data has been found on income from his serial writing). He began in a conventional way, by selling the copyright to the publisher. As previously mentioned, John Van Voorst paid him £105 for the text and illustrations for his first work, the *Canadian Naturalist*. During 1844-56, the SPCK paid him at least £860.10s. for fourteen works,[331] the £170.10s. for the copyright and illustrations to the two-volume *Introduction to Zoology* (1844) being the most he received during those years from the SPCK for any title.[332] A turning point came at the end of 1843, when (as previously mentioned) Gosse determined to earn a living by writing.[333] In order to maximize his income, he positioned himself to arrange to publish his books on a profit-sharing (also known as author's-risk) agreement.[334] Returning to Van Voorst, Gosse issued *Illustrations of the Birds of Jamaica* (1848-9),

329. Huxley, cited in Leonard Huxley (ed.), *Life and Letters of Thomas Henry Huxley* (London: Macmillan and Co., 1903), I: 96.

330. *The Critic* (24 Mar. 1860), 364. Hamera makes a technically correct, but context-lacking and easily misconstrued, observation that PHG 'was not a professional man of science' (Hamera, *Parlor Ponds*, 55).

331. GLC, 1843-56, *passim*.

332. The information from this paragraph is from 'Account of P.H.G.'s Works to the end of 1867[-1869]' (CUL Adv. c. 82.5, 77), in PHG's holograph, and GLC, 1843-56.

333. 'Reminiscences', II: 259.

334. PHG's author's risk strategy was first analysed in Freeman & Wertheimer-PHG, 6-7, 19, on which this is based.

with plates which he drew on the stone and coloured. Every copy sold at a loss. His arrangement with Longman, also based in London, was for 1,000 copies of *A Naturalist's Sojourn in Jamaica* (1851). The book remained in print until 1865. No record has been traced tabulating its profit-loss status.

With that start, a prudent author could not be blamed for discarding the profit-sharing strategy. It was less common than the outright sale of copyright in mid-Victorian Britain until the 1850s,[335] and besides, the coloured plates and letterpress of Gosse's books made them pricey. One newspaper casually referred to him as 'the well known author of those valuable and expensive works.'[336] In its analysis of *Tenby*, the *Church of England Quarterly Review*, after applauding Gosse for being a 'popular instructor' in science—'we scarcely know of anyone so felicitous as our author'—and writing of Gosse's 'luminous descriptions, and exquisite pictorial illustrations' which were 'so full of interesting information … so genial in their tone, and, above all, so sound in their moral and religious teaching,' bemoaned the cost factor:

> … we only regret that his books are published at such a price as to place them out of the reach of many. In their present form of publication it would, perhaps, be scarcely safe to venture upon a cheaper issue; but it may be well for the publishers to consider whether they might not be reproduced in some less expensive form, with advantage to himself, to the author, and certainly to the public at large. *Such* a teacher ought to have as wide a stage as possible to lecture from: and we ask this for him in the name of science, of morality, and, above all, in the name of Christianity.[337]

335. Bernard Lightman, *Victorian Popularizers of Science: Designing Nature for New Audiences* (Chicago: University of Chicago Press, 2007), 175fn.23.

336. 'Philip Henry Gosse, Esq. and William Thompson, Esq. the Naturalists', Southampton *Hampshire Advertiser* (24 Nov. 1855), 7. The word 'expensive' was also used in a review of the London edition of the *Aquarium* in the *Canadian Naturalist and Geologist* n.s.III (Feb. 1858), 75, and in the Boston *Atlantic Monthly* II (July 1858), 255. In Boston it sold for 'between four and five dollars', whereas the *Common Objects of the Seashore*, by J. G. Woods, cost 25 cents.

337. Review of *Tenby* in *Church of England Quarterly Review* n.s. VI (July 1856), 225. Emphasis in the original. While *Tenby* was considered expensive, reviewers were impressed with the low price of each of the 12 parts of PHG's *Actinologia Britannica*, which were issued over a nearly two-year period, each part selling for 1s.6d. 'For cheapness we know of no rival' (*Belfast News-Letter*, 16 Sept. 1858, 3), and for similar comments: *Natural History Review* V (1858), 103; London *Critic* XVII (31 July 1858), 434; London *Atlas*, 8 Aug. 1858, 5; and London *Globe*, 26 Aug. 1858, [1].

Now there was merit to the suggestion that perhaps Gosse's books could be produced in a less expensive form. *Naturalist's Rambles* (1853) had twelve coloured and sixteen plain lithograph plates, and sold for £1.1s.; *Aquarium* (1854), with six coloured chromolithographs and six plain plates, for 17s.; and *Tenby* (1856), with twenty coloured and four plain lithographs, for 21s.[338] In contrast, other publishers of similar works gave the public low-cost fare. The first and second editions of Kingsley's *Glaucus* (1855), with the same plain frontispiece illustration, were each available for 3s.6d.[339] J. G. Wood's *Common Objects of the Country* and *Common Objects of the Sea Shore* (both 1858) each sold for 1s., illustrated (and in a uniform, cloth gilt binding with coloured illustrations, at 3s.6d.[340]; with gilt edges, 4s.[341]).

Nonetheless, Gosse continued with the profit-sharing approach. Why? The reason appears to have been that he had confidence in the popular appeal of his writings and illustrations, and this would be the best way for him to earn the most. It was a risky move.

What happened was that *Naturalist's Sojourn* was followed by *Naturalist's Rambles on the Devonshire Coast* (1853), the first of his sea-shore books based entirely on his own observations.[342] Gosse had succeeded in negotiating a fifty-seven per cent share in a division of net profits—higher than the more common 33-to-50 per cent range[343]—and over sixteen years he made £592 on *Naturalist's Rambles*.[344] From the two editions of *The Aquarium* (1854, 1856)—the second work in his sea-shore trilogy—Gosse made at least £818 (nearly equalling all the SPCK payments to him), and from the third work, *Tenby* (1856), at least £360. The *Handbook to the Marine Aquarium* (1855) brought Gosse at least £189, and the *Manual of Marine Zoology* (2 vols., 1855-56) at least £251.

338. Freeman & Wertheimer-PHG, s.v. the separate titles.

339. 'List of New Books', *Literary Gazette* (26 May 1855), 329; publisher's advertisement, *Athenaeum*, 15 Sept. 1855, 1067.

340. Publisher's advertisement, *Athenaeum*, 12 June 1858, 742.

341. Publisher's advertisement, *Athenaeum*, 27 Mar. 1858), 392.

342. Between the publication of *Naturalist's Sojourn in Jamaica* (1851) and *Naturalist's Rambles* (1853) three SPCK published books by PHG appeared: in 1851, *Natural History. Fishes*; *History of the Jews*; and in 1852, *Assyria*. SPCK records are unclear as to how much he was paid for each title, but they were all accepted for publication prior to the appearance of *Naturalist's Sojourn* in October 1851 (Freeman & Wertheimer-PHG, 40-6).

343. Lightman, *Victorian Popularizers of Science*, 175fn.23.

344. Freeman & Wertheimer-PHG, 6, 45, 47, 51, 53, 68.

Gosse may only have broken even on two subsequent works—*Omphalos* (1857) and *Actinologia Britannica* (1860).[345]

By keeping his eye on profitability rather than high sales or low cost, Gosse aimed to support his family through literary activity when so many fell short. Three examples illustrate his business acumen. Charles Kingsley's *Glaucus* was issued by Macmillan in London in five editions between 1855-73. From four of those editions, Kingsley earned a total of £400.[346] G. H. Lewes's *Sea-side Studies* (1858) was serialised, translated into German, and released in two editions. Lewes was paid a total of £230.2s.[347] J. G. Wood (1827-1889), a popular natural history writer, is said to have published over seventy books (not all scientific).[348] According to his son, a notoriously unreliable witness, he sold the copyright for *Common Objects of the Country* and *Common Objects of the Sea Shore* (both 1857) to Routledge 'for merely a small sum'.[349] For the former title, Routledge records state he received £40.[350] For his numerous other works, Wood's publisher Longmans benefited far more than he did.[351] When Wood died four decades after *Common Objects*, his widow and six children were 'absolutely destitute'. A public appeal ensued, and within a short time, £1,300 was raised for the family.[352]

Today we have access to data unavailable to Victorians which allows us to understand how Gosse, as an entrepreneur, found a way successfully to set his writings before the public. Because he was the leading figure in his field, with books widely reviewed and wildly praised, the assumption

345. Freeman & Wertheimer-PHG, s.v. the separate titles.

346. Macmillan Archives, British Library (Add. MSS. 54911, 51,65,82). For *Glaucus'* 4th edition, Kingsley received £125 for an unknown quantity printed (Add. MSS. 54911, 90). I did not see publishing information for the 5th edition of 1873. Freeman & Wertheimer-PHG, 7, inadvertently omitted income to Kingsley from the 4ed. At the same time that Kingsley was dabbling in natural history, his historical novel *Westward Ho!* (1855-61, 4 editions, 12,000 copies printed) brought Kingsley £1,050 (Macmillan Archives, British Library, Add. MSS. 54911, 47,83,76,95).

347. Freeman & Wertheimer-PHG, 7.

348. J. G. Wood in *ODNB*. Freeman, *British Natural History Books*, 373-5, describes 44 titles.

349. Theodore Wood, *The Rev. J. G. Wood: His Life and Work* (New York: Cassell Publishing, 1890), 61-2.

350. Lightman, *Victorian Popularizers of Science*, 175 and fn.22. Wood, *Rev. J. G. Wood*, 62, claimed his father was paid £30 for both of the 1857 titles. One writer calculated that Wood would have earned £416 had he been paid one penny for each volume sold (*The Spectator*, Supplement, 19 Nov. 1910, 833).

351. Andrea Kennedy, 'The Beauty of Victorian Beasts: Illustrations in the Reverend J. G. Wood's *Homes without hands*', *Archives of natural history* 40 (2013), 197.

352. 'The Late Rev. J. G. Wood. An Appeal', London *Daily News*, 9 Mar. 1889, 6; 'The Late Rev. J. G. Wood at Home', London *Pall Mall Gazette*, 27 Mar. 1889, 3.

has been that they were were published in large quantities and 'sold very well'.[353] 'So far as marine studies are concerned, the aquarian will in all probability make for the Devonshire coast,' the *London Quarterly Review* observed in 1857. 'Everybody goes to the Devonshire coast, because everybody reads Mr. Gosse's beautiful books.'[354] An appealing explanation, but not true. By the standards of our day or his day, in a country of some 29 million people[355] Gosse's books were neither printed in large numbers nor scooped up by readers.

No more than 4,000 copies of any Gosse work was ever printed in Britain.[356] The *Devonshire Coast* and *Tenby* were each published in one edition only, each of 1,500 copies; there were 3,500 combined copies printed of the two editions of the *Aquarium* (1,500 and 2,000, respectively); 2,000 of the *Manual of Marine Zoology*; and 3,000 of the two editions of the *Handbook to the Marine Aquarium*.[357] Each of these works was profitable, but they sold slowly. Copies of the *Canadian Naturalist* were still available twenty-seven years after publication.[358] It took about sixteen years for the *Devonshire Coast* to sell out. By that time (1869), many copies of the other works remained unsold: *Tenby*, about one-third of the total copies printed; *Aquarium*, about thirty per cent; *Manual of Marine Zoology*, about thirty-three per cent; and *Handbook*, fifty per cent.[359]

In terms of number of copies printed, Gosse's books take their place respectably alongside some natural history works of his time (for context,

353. In reference to PHG's *Aquarium*, the words 'sold very well' are used by Dance, *Art of Natural History*, 197, and Granata, *The Victorian aquarium*, 23. Stageman, *A Bibliography of the First Editions of Philip Henry Gosse*, 19, says the book sold 'like wildfire'.

354. [P. H. Gosse, per *Wellesley Index* IV: 385, item 148, but on the questionable identification, see below, 277 fn.10], *London Quarterly Review* VIII (Apr. 1857), 87.

355. The Census of the United Kingdom for 1861 gave a population of 29,334,788 (*Annual Register ... of the Year 1861* (1862), 367).

356. In the United States, 25 PHG works were available for sale to 1903, and between 1845-1902 at least 21 book publishers there printed PHG titles. Given the state of international copyright in the USA prior to 1891, there is no reason to assume (and there is no evidence to suggest) that PHG received any royalties (D. Wertheimer, 'P. H. Gosse's Scientific Reception in America', unpublished MS). '*Three-fourths of all the books* printed in America are reprints of English works. As there is no international copyright law or treaty, *these books* cost nothing to their American publishers' (Nichols, *Forty Years of American Life*, I: 340). Emphasis in the original.

357. 'Account of P.H.G.'s Works to the end of 1867[-1869]', as cited.

358. John Van Voorst-PHG, 18 Nov. 1867, quoted in PHG-[James Hubbert], 27 Nov. 1867 (Blacker-Wood Library of Zoology and Ornithology, McGill University).

359. Freeman & Wertheimer-PHG, 45, 47, 51, 52, 53.

it may not be irrelevant that in America around 1865, the average book sale was 1,500 copies).[360] William Blackwood, the publisher of G. H. Lewes's *Sea-side Studies* (1858), ordered 1,250 copies for its first edition.[361] John Murray had the same number of copies printed for the first edition of Charles Darwin's *Origin of Species* (1859), with the second through fifth editions totalling 8,500 copies.[362] The first six editions of Kirby and Spence's classic *Introduction to Entomology* (1815-43) were said to have exceeded a press run of 3,000 copies.[363]

At the same time, the print run for Gosse's books was easily overshadowed by other natural history works. Within two years of its first appearance, 6,750 copies of three editions of Kingsley's *Glaucus* were printed.[364] J. G. Wood's *Common Objects of the Country* (1858) performed better. Two editions of the book appeared within a year, totalling 9,000 copies; within four decades, a total of 86,000 copies had been printed.[365]

360. John Tebbel, *A History of Book Publishing in the United States* (New York: R.R. Bowker, 1972), I: 390.

361. Haight, *George Eliot Letters* II: 432; 800 of the 1,250 copies had been pre-subscribed (ibid., II: 434, 438). In March 1864 Blackwood wrote that 'the sale I am sorry to say [of the 2ed. of *Sea-Side Studies*] seems past' (ibid., IV: 137).

362. R. B. Freeman, *The Works of Charles Darwin: An Annotated Bibliographical Handlist* (Folkestone, Kent: Dawson, 2nd ed., 1977), 75ff). The figures for these editions of *Origin of Species* were: 2nd, 1860, 3,000 copies printed; 3rd, 1861, 2,000; 4th, 1866, 1,500; 5th, 1869, 2,000.

363. *Natural History Review* III (1856), 51.

364. Macmillan Archives, British Library (Add. MSS. 54911, 51, 65,82).

365. Lightman, *Victorian Popularizers of Science*, 174-5. Wood, *Rev. J. G. Wood*, 61, claimed *Common Objects of the Country* 'took the public completely by storm. A first edition of one hundred thousand copies was prepared, and at the end of a single week not a copy was to be procured!' (p. 61). A number of writers have repeated this fantastical contention: John Upton, *Three Great Naturalists* (London: Pilgrim Press, [1910]), 151; Nicola Gauld, "What is Meant by this System?' Charles Darwin and the Visual Re-ordering of Nature', in Diana Donald and Jane Munro (eds.), *Endless Forms: Charles Darwin, Natural Science and the Visual Arts* (New Haven: Yale University Press, 2009), 128, who calls Wood 'one of the most renowned popularisers of Victorian natural history', p. 128; Kete, *The Beast in the Boudoir*, 60. That the figure was reduced to 10,000 'within the first week' in the entry on Wood in the *Dictionary of Nineteenth-Century British Scientists* IV,2194, does not make it more palatable. After having survived in historical fairyland for over a century, Bernard Lightman (*Popularizers of Science*, 174-5) and Aileen Fyfe confirmed, upon searching the publisher Routledge's archives, that Wood's publication figures were far lower than promoted by his son (A. Fyfe, 'Natural History and the Victorian Tourist: From Landscapes to Rock-Pools', in David N. Livingstone and Charles W. J. Withers (eds.), *Geographies of Nineteenth-Century Science* (Chicago: University of Chicago Press, 2011), 398fn81.). In America around 1865, science books could apparently sell in large number. L. Agassiz and A. A. Gould's *Zoology* (1848), are said to have sold 25,000 copies, and A. H. Guyot's *Earth and Man* (1849), 19,000 copies (Tebbel, *History of Book Publishing in the United States* I: 390).

Another contributing factor to the Gosse phenomenon is found in newspaper and press marketing (Victorian newspapers give a far better insight into public opinion than book publishing).[366] Gosse's seashore works were praised and quoted in the press in its various forms. Reviewers liked them. Readers liked them. But there were two factors which could circumscribe his influence. He could not expect a huge following when his books were expensive and were not available in large numbers. Moreover, while reviews draw attention to a book, Gosse had no control over if, when or where the reviews might appear. Enter newspaper and periodical press advertising, the publisher's way to encourage the name recognition of one of its authors.

Recall that the SPCK did not send out review copies of Gosse's books. That did not, however, prevent that publisher (or others) from *advertising* them. During the annual holiday seasons from 1854-60, the SPCK was placing newspaper advertisements listing Gosse titles for sale. In 1854, the SPCK was advertising in a single listing eleven distinct Gosse titles;[367] in 1855 (also on a single day), eleven distinct Gosse titles;[368] in 1856, on a single day twelve distinct Gosse titles;[369] and in 1858, the SPCK was selling nine of Gosse's natural history titles at the same time.[370] Meanwhile in 1857, four publishers were simultaneously marketing ten distinct Gosse

366. Alvar Ellegård, 'Public Opinion and the Press: Reactions to Darwinism', *Journal of the History of Ideas* XIX (1958), 383.

367. London *Times* (22 Nov. 1854), 3. The 11 titles were: *Ancient Egypt, Monuments of* [1847]; *Assyria: her Manners and Customs* [1852]; *History of the Jews* [1851]; *Natural History: Mammalia* [1848]; *Birds* [1849]; *Fishes* [1851]; *Reptiles* [1850]; *Mollusca* [1854]; *Sea-side Pleasure[s]* [1853]; *Text-book of Zoology* [*for Schools*, 1851]; *Zoology, an Introduction to* [2vols., 1844].

368. *Birmingham Journal Supplement*, 8 Dec. 1855, 12. The 11 titles were: *Ancient Egypt, Monuments of* [1847]; *Assyria: her Manners and Customs* [1852]; *History of the Jews* [1851]; *Natural History: Mammalia* [1848]; *Birds* [1849]; *Fishes* [1851]; *Reptiles* [1850]; *Mollusca* [1854]; *Ocean* [1845]; *Text-book of Zoology* [*for Schools*, 1851]; *Zoology, an Introduction to* [2vols., 1844].

369. *Aris's Birmingham Gazette*, 29 Dec. 1856, 1. The 12 titles were: *Ancient Egypt, Monuments of* [1847]; *Assyria: her Manners and Customs* [1852]; *Fishes (Families and Orders of), Tabular View* [canvas and roller editions, 1856]; *History of the Jews* [1851]; *Natural History: Mammalia* [1848]; *Birds* [1849]; *Fishes* [1851]; *Reptiles* [1850]; *Mollusca* [1854]; *Ocean* [1845]; *Wanderings through the Conservatories at Kew* [1856]; *Introduction to Zoology* [2vols., 1844]. In the same advertisement, 8 natural history books by Revd C. A. Johns are for sale.

370. 'Society for Promoting Christian Knowledge. Books Suitable for Christmas and New Year's Presents', *The Athenaeum*, 11 Dec. 1858, 746 (also 9 SPCK books in *Southampton Hampshire Advertiser*, 11 Dec. 1858, 4). The titles by PHG were: *Natural History Birds* (... *Reptiles. Mammalia. Fishes. Mollusca*); *Text-book of Zoology*; *Ocean*; *Evenings at the Microscope* ('Nearly ready'); and *Wanderings through the Conservatories at Kew*.

natural history titles;[371] in 1859, there were eight Van Voorst titles in a single newspaper advertisement,[372] while Mudie's Select Library carried nine of his natural history titles in 1859[373] and in 1860, seven.[374] Thus could aquaromania be promoted in yet another manner by a seemingly omnipresent Gosse.

-IX-

The story of the Gosse phenomenon is not complete in describing Gosse's acumen in book publishing and the boost to his name given by publishers' advertising. More help was received in spreading the message.

There were, firstly, manufacturers and suppliers throughout Britain who catered to the public's desire to form parlour aquaria. England 'has been Gosse-ified, whole families at a time,' *The Atlas* reported: 'everybody keeps a vivarium, and fills it with sea anemonies [*sic*] and sea-snails.'[375] These suppliers had sprung up suddenly to meet the demand, and between 1854-7 there were at least twenty of them in England and Scotland (nearly all were in London).[376] The *Literary Gazette*, recalling the rise of the aquarium movement, noted that

> It was almost as though we went to bed one night innocent of anything but a dim suspicion of having heard of some crotchet of that kind, or having seen some glass tanks at the Zoological Gardens, and rose to find every naturalist's shop, half the fishing-tackle houses, and all the filtered water and ginger-pop establishments, displaying elegant assortments

371. PHG titles from Van Voorst: *Tenby*; *Manual of Marine Zoology* (2vols.); *Naturalist's Rambles on the Devonshire Coast*; *Aquarium*; *Canadian Naturalist*; and *Birds of Jamaica* ('Books Published by Mr. Van Voorst', *Saturday Review*, 10 Oct. 1857, 334); Lovell Reeve: *Popular British Ornithology* (*Literary Gazette*, 10 Oct. 1857, 963); SPCK: *The Ocean* and *Wanderings through the Conservatories at Kew* (*Literary Gazette*, 28 Nov. 1857, 1150); James Nisbet & Co.: *Life* (*Literary Gazette*, 28 Nov. 1857, 1152).

372. London *Times*, 28 May 1859, 12. The Van Voorst works were: *Birds of Jamaica*; *Omphalos*; *Handbook to the Marine Aquarium* (2ed.); *Manual of Marine Zoology* (Pts. 1-2); *Naturalist's Rambles on the Devonshire Coast*; *Aquarium*; *Canadian Naturalist*; and *Tenby*.

373. *Catalogue of New and Standard Works, in Circulation at Mudie's Select Library* (London: Charles Edward Mudie, [Jan. 1860]), 63. The titles were: *Popular British Ornithology*; *Tenby*; *Aquarium*; *Life*; *Naturalist's Sojourn in Jamaica*; *Naturalist's Rambles*; *Omphalos*; *Letters from Alabama*.

374. John Van Voorst: *History of the British Sea-anemones*; *Naturalist's Rambles on the Devonshire Coast*; *Aquarium* (2ed); *Handbook to the Marine Aquarium* (2ed); *Manual of Marine Zoology* (2vols); *Tenby*; and *Omphalos* (London *Examiner*, 25 Aug. 1860, 544).

375. *The Atlas*, 25 October 1856, 683.

376. Yonge, in 'Victorians by the Sea Shore', 609, claims that there were 100 dealers. I have only found the number cited.

of living, swimming fishes ... whilst more than half the centre drawing-room windows in the most fashionable parts of the town appeared furnished with an ornamental chest of plate glass, with a shingly, rocky, weedy bottom, and numerous silvery fishes, and other marine animals of strange shapes, floating in the water above. ... The world had become suddenly alive to the fact that in order to observe the habits of the water-dwellers, it was no longer necessary to lie for hours on your stomach by the side of some clear deep stream.[377]

From these establishments one could purchase all the requisites for the marine or fresh-water aquarium: the animals and plants, containers of all sizes and shapes, even sea water crystals. Among the dealers, none was better known than William Alford Lloyd (1824-1880),[378] whom Gosse for a time supplied and with whom he corresponded.[379] In his Aquarium Warehouse at 19, 20, & 20A Portland Road, near Regent's Park, Lloyd kept in stock (in 1857) 15,000 specimens, and had a 600 and a 700 gallon seawater cistern.[380] His useful[381] *List, with Descriptions, Illustrations, and Prices, of Whatever Relates to Aquaria* (1858) contained more than 120 pages, with an 1860 supplement adding forty more.

Nor was there any shortage, secondly, of popular writers of seashore works imitating Gosse. Writers on the aquarium, observed the *Literary Gazette*, were as 'plentiful as blackberries.'[382] A 'special literature' had been launched which was 'so exhaustive that no small space in the British Museum Library is occupied with the gaudy covered and sumptuously illustrated books' on aquaria.[383] Some of these popularisers composed handbooks of varying quality to the marine or fresh-water aquarium (Gosse did not deal with the latter subject, perhaps because

377. *Literary Gazette* n.s. I (21 Aug. 1858), 235.
378. Information on Lloyd's date and place of birth varies. According to a biographical notice by Edward Newman, who knew Lloyd and who was assisted by him in writing his review of the history of the aquarium for the *Zoologist*, Lloyd was born 8 Aug. 1828 in London (*Zoologist* ser. 2, VIII, Nov. 1873, 3747). Ray Ingle's 'Who Was ... William Alford Lloyd?' (*Biologist* 60, 2013, 24), cites Bob Alexander's authoritative 'William Alford Lloyd'. Alexander found baptismal records dating Lloyd's birth to 8 Aug. 1824.
379. PHG-Lloyd letters, 1856-8, are at Edinburgh University Library (La. II.425/22).
380. [P. H. Gosse, per *Wellesley Index* IV, p. 385, item 148] in *London Quarterly Review* VIII (Apr. 1857), 76-7; for the size of the tanks, W. A. Lloyd-C. W. Peach, 24 June 1858 (Institute of Geological Sciences, London, 1/527).
381. Thus the review by [Edwin Lankester], *Athenaeum* (12 Feb. 1859), 221-2.
382. *Literary Gazette* n.s. V (8 Sept. 1860), 179.
383. [Proposal to found a British Zoological Station], London *Standard*, 9 Oct. 1883, 4.

its creatures were not as diverse or beautiful as marine ones). Among them were Francis S. Merton's *Handbook to the [fresh-water] Aquarium* (1856), James Bishop's (ed.), *Handbook of Plain Instructions for the Construction and Management of Fresh-water Aquaria* ([1856]), Shirley Hibberd's *Book of the Marine Aquarium* (1856) and *Book of the Fresh-Water Aquarium* (1856), and R. M. Stark's *Marine Aquarium* (1857). The best of them was *The Aquavivarium, Fresh and Marine* (1856), by Edwin Lankester (1814-74).[384]

Mimics of Gosse's seashore trilogy, even his illustrations, were sometimes superficial, sometimes scientifically uninformed, and sometimes both.[385] Reviewers did not hesitate to point to the crudities of *Popular History of the Aquarium* (1857), by George Brettingham Sowerby (1812-1884). The author was a talented illustrator, yet his 'good-for-nothing book'[386] was largely a mixture of inaccurate observations and selections from Bell, Baird, Forbes, Gosse, Harvey, and others. The *Ocean Gardens* and *River Gardens* (both 1857), from the pen and pencil of the 'exceptional designer'[387] and prolific illustrator H. Noel Humphreys (1810-1879), were not of a higher quality.[388] Notwithstanding his highly reputable entomological drawings[389] and chromolithographed giftbooks,[390] the *Athenaeum* considered his *River Gardens* illustrations 'almost useless'.[391] And in spite of the 'astounding claim'[392] of the Revd J. G. Wood's biographer that 'he was the first to popularize natural history,' his *Common Objects of the Sea Shore* (1857), illustrated by Sowerby,

384. This is both a personal and contemporary opinion ([T. Bell], *Athenaeum*, 22 Nov. 1856, 1430).

385. This point is made in *AMNH* ser. 2, XX (Aug. 1857), 138-40; *London Quarterly Review* VIII (July 1857), 541-2; London *Art-Journal* n.s. III (1 July 1857), 232; *Natural History Review* IV (1857), 100-6.

386. *Natural History Review* IV (1857), 103; 'a respectable but not a very valuable addition' to Aquarian literature' (*Saturday Review*, 11 July 1857, 44).

387. Simon Houfe, *The Dictionary of 19th Century British Book Illustrators and Caricaturists* (Woodbridge, Suffolk: Antique Collectors' Club Ltd., 1978, revised ed., 1996), 20. It is noteworthy that as an illustrator and author, Henry Noel Humphreys' skill 'did not bring him affluence'; he died intestate, worth less than £800 (Engen *Dictionary of Victorian Wood Engravers*, 1985, 131).

388. Humphreys' *Ocean Gardens* and *River Gardens* are filled with 'erroneous notions and unscientific explanations of vital phenomena' (*Natural History Review* IV (1857), 106).

389. J. O. Westwood, 'Henry Noel Humphreys', *Academy*, 21 June 1879, 550.

390. Twyman, *History of chromolithography*, 153-6.

391. [John Doran], *Athenaeum*, 6 June 1857, 719-20. On Doran: Leslie A. Marchand, *The Athenaeum. A Mirror of Victorian Culture* (Chapel Hill: University of North Carolina Press, 1941), 82.

392. [F. Jeffrey Bell], review of T. Wood's *Rev. J. G. Wood* in *Athenaeum*, 3 May 1890, 569.

while able[393] and extremely successful from a sales viewpoint, lacked an original and investigative spirit and contained a number of errors.[394] This well-known and prolific natural history writer with exaggerated book sales, 'was held in higher esteem by the general public, who bought his books largely, than by naturalists.'[395] A modern assessment places Wood among the 'less deeply knowledgeable' who was 'content to travel in shallower waters.'[396]

It was the proliferation of these sorts of low-quality volumes which caused critics to bemoan the mania. The *Natural History Review* decried the opportunism of 'certain obscure and ill informed persons,' who, 'taking advantage of the ignorance of the public, on a subject almost entirely new,' were posing as experts on the aquarium.[397] In a two sentence review of one such work, the *Athenaeum* remarked that 'the highest compliment we can pay it is to say that it is less full of errors than most of the popular books on the aquarium.'[398] The *London Quarterly Review* was sarcastic:

> Opening one of the 'popular' manuals at random, we learn that the frond of a certain genus is 'coriaceous, orbicular, pezizaeform', and rather think we should know it at a glance; another is characterized as 'pectinatopinnate', and a third as 'gelatinoso-carnose.' But we are a little puzzled by the 'cruciate tetraspores, which are vertically placed

393. [John Doran], *Athenaeum*, 20 June 1857, 786; London *Critic* (15 July 1857), 322.

394. 'The author is a clergyman, and, of course, writes with tolerable fluency; but he tells us nothing that is not far better told in other books. Errors, as we have seen, his work contains' (*Natural History Review* IV (1857), 104).

395. Thus the obituary notice, *Athenaeum*, 9 Mar. 1889, 316 (by the 'Editor', *viz.*, Norman MacColl). For the Revd Theodore Wood's claim that his father's 'great distinction was that of being the pioneer in the work of popularising natural history, and presenting it to the general public in the form of an alluring and deeply interesting study', see Wood, *Rev J. G. Wood*, 125. In its write-up of this biography, the *Saturday Review* stated: 'Mr. J. G. Wood, a versatile writer and pleasant naturalist, was nothing of what his son fancies that he sees him by the light of filial piety; that he was essentially secondary, and without initiative of any kind; and that, so far from imitating no one, all he wrote ... was written in following of some more original or more enterprising naturalist. Even as a popularizer, he was neither the first nor in the first rank ... the first systematic popularizer of general natural history was P. H. Gosse, whose *Canadian Naturalist* was published when J. G. Wood was a child, and more than half of whose popular volumes had illustrated the various sections of zoology before Wood had printed a page' (19 Apr. 1890, 479). For a review of all four of these works, see *Natural History Review* IV (1857), 100-6.

396. D. E. Allen, 'Natural history and social history', *Journal for the Bibliography of Natural History* VII (June 1976), 516.

397. *Natural History Review* IV (1857), 100-101.

398. Review of F. S. Merton, *Handbook to the Aquarium* (*Athenaeum*, 14 Nov. 1857, 1422).

among the filaments of the periphery, in sub-defined sori;' and are fairly beaten by the 'favellidia, sub-solitary near the apex of the ramuli, affixed to the base of the whorled ramelli, and covered by them, containing, within a hyaline membranaceous perispore, a subglobose mass of minute spores.' The sentence resembles a rebus, in which we recognise one or two simple words, as 'and' or 'in,' but surrounded by incomprehensible hieroglyphics. We are sincerely rejoiced to see that some of the more recent writers are breaking through these trammels, and making use of intelligible language.[399]

Not all of the popular seashore works were, naturally, of this character. W. H. Harvey's excellent *Sea-side Book*, already mentioned, had a deserved success, as did T. Rymer Jones' *Aquarian Naturalist* (1858). Shirley Hibberd's *Rustic Adornments for Homes of Taste, and Recreations for Town Folk, in the Study and Imitation of Nature* (1856), well written and modest in its scientific discussions, is an important work for the cultural historian. The volumes of the Revd Charles Kingsley and G. H. Lewes require special treatment, not only because of their contemporary acclaim, but as examples of the different approaches to, and uses made of, the seashore.

As we have seen, Kingsley (1819-1875) was one of the earliest to be touched by the seashore mania. In an active correspondence with Gosse between 1853-6, he followed every step of that naturalist's career, even aiding him by sending collected animals. While Kingsley's interest in natural history dated from 1845, and he maintained more than a dilettantish interest in the subject,[400] it was the reading of Gosse's works which brought about his conversion. 'Your books have done me *spiritual* good,' he told Gosse in 1856,

for they have humbled me, & taught me that I must not pretend to be a naturalist but simply look on & admire the work wh[ich] you & your compeers are doing.—No. When I glanced my eye merely over your division of the Actiniae, at the end of your 'Tenby' I felt how great God's world was, & how small I was; & that any man who pretends to know even one corner of the Lord's world thoroughly must devote his whole

399. [P.H. Gosse, per *Wellesley Index* IV: 385, item 148; for the questionable identification, see below, 277 fn.10], *London Quarterly Review* VIII (Apr. 1857), 78.

400. Mary Wheat Hanawalt, 'Charles Kingsley and Science', *Studies in Philology* XXXIV (Oct. 1937), 592.

mind & life to it, & not fancy that he can pry into the doings of the Spirit, while he is frittering away his time on half-a-dozen other hobbies— Indeed, you have all but frightened me away from physical science, by making me feel—(though not for the first time) how vast it is.[401]

And in a letter the next day, Kingsley continued by alluding to the underlying yet profound sympathy which he felt the two shared. 'I am glad, too, to find you so thorough a Protestant,' he wrote. 'I fancy that you & I should agree there as well as we do on sea-beasts.'[402]

In light of Kingsley's career, his controversy with the Roman Catholic convert and later Cardinal, J. H. Newman, his association with Christian Socialism, and his union of the physical and spiritual in 'muscular Christianity,' it is not surprising that his only seashore work should differ markedly from Gosse's. The highly popular *Glaucus: or, the Wonders of the Shore* (1855; 5th ed., 1873), initially appeared as a laudatory analysis of the *Devonshire Coast, Aquarium*, and other works, in the *North British Review* (1854).[403] *Glaucus* is an example of imitation as a form of praise: in style and format the work was a fair mimic of Gosse's two seashore books, with its coloured plates (not executed, apparently, after or by Kingsley), animadversions on various topics, and excursions (not always well directed) as a scientific observer.[404] Kingsley's purpose was to encourage the enjoyment of his subject, and he did so not so much by making contributions to knowledge, but by claiming that the ideal type of naturalist is the ideal type of man: one who combines Godliness and manliness.[405]

A different sort of seashore work, the philosophical treatment of 'the complex facts of life,' is represented by *Sea-side Studies at Ilfracombe, Tenby, the Scilly Isles, and Jersey* (1858; 2nd ed., 1860), by the English philosopher and writer George Henry Lewes. Lewes (1817-1878) had been interested in science since boyhood, and had developed a philosophical

401. CK-PHG, 12 May 1856 (LeBL). Emphasis in the original.

402. CK-PHG, 13 May 1856 (LeBL).

403. [Charles Kingsley], 'The Wonders of the Shore', *North British Review* XXII (Nov. 1854), 1-56.

404. *Natural History Review* III-IV (1855-7), 5-9, 43-4. A more positive view is *Gardeners' Chronicle* n.s. I (1 Aug. 1855), 244: 'We have never enjoyed a sea-side book so much'.

405. C. Kingsley, *Glaucus; or, the Wonders of the Shore* (Cambridge: Macmillan & Co., 1855), 40-3. Kingsley sent PHG a copy of an 1855 printing of the book signed 'From the Author' (R. J. Lister, *A Catalogue of a Portion of the Library of Edmund Gosse* (London: Ballantyne Press, Privately Printed, 1893), 92).

rather than experimental knowledge of it.[406] Though he admitted that his knowledge was 'mainly of this despised second-hand kind,'[407] Lewes reacted to T. H. Huxley's 1854 disparaging characterisation of him as a mere 'book scientist'[408] by going down to Devon and Wales with George Eliot in 1856 to gain some first-hand acquaintance with marine animals. As his letters of the time indicate, Lewes was eager 'to create a stir among the naturalists,'[409] but he first had to overcome his inexperience and ignorance in recognizing what he was searching for. Once he had done that to his satisfaction, and spent more time in 1857 in the Scilly Isles and Jersey, he serialised his findings in *Blackwood's Magazine*, later collecting them into a book.

Sea-side Studies, a work intended for the novice and the naturalist, is an instance of how quickly one can exchange the garb of the student for the gown of the professor. Though admitting his deficient background in invertebrate zoology, Lewes did not hesitate to pronounce upon some of the most frequently mooted questions in anatomy and physiology. Some of these points will be considered later; in the meantime, it is sufficient to point out that Lewes did not relate his investigations (as did Kingsley and Gosse) to natural theology, or to muscular Christianity, or to sinful man, the Fall, or the Redemption. Nature, he believed, had a deeper significance: it 'brings us into closer presence of the great mysteries of life; and while quickening our sense of the infinite marvels which surround the simplest object, teaches us many and pregnant lessons which may help us through our daily needs':[410]

> We may consider Life itself as an ever-increasing identification with Nature. ... What we call growth, is it not a perpetual absorption of Nature, the identification of the individual with the universal? And may we not in speculative moods consider Death as the grand impatience of the soul to free itself from the circle of individual activity,—the yearning of the creature to be united with the Creator?[411]

406. Anna Theresa Kitchel, *George Lewes and George Eliot. A Review of Records* (New York: John Day Co., 1933), 167; Gordon S. Haight, *George Eliot. A Biography* (Oxford: Clarendon Press, 1968, 1969), 196. PHG owned a copy of Lewes' book (*Sandhurst Catalogue*, item #299).

407. [G. H. Lewes], 'Recent Natural History Books', *Blackwood's Magazine* LXXXIX (Mar. 1861), 334.

408. Haight, *George Eliot*, 136, 196; Haight, *George Eliot Letters* II: 132.

409. Haight, *George Eliot Letters* II: 281, 338, 361.

410. Lewes, *Sea-side Studies*, 1858, 396.

411. Lewes, *Sea-side Studies*, 1858, 218-9.

Another, surely, was to enforce our belief in a *scala naturae* of increasing complexity from crystal to plant to animal to man. Man must never forget his 'high calling' and 'high estate.'[412]

-X-

We began to account for the Gosse phenomenon in relation to the aquarium movement by noting his years of experience as a field naturalist, his investigative, descriptive and artistic powers and peerless knowledge of marine life which earned him admiration as a man of science, the appeal of his 'open eye' approach to the natural world, his devout Christian melding of science and religion, the remarkably consistent and effusive praise from the press for his many publications, the success of his entrepreneurial book-publishing strategy, the promotion of his name via newspaper advertising which enhanced his many scientific activities, and the endorsement of, and support for, aquaromania and the seashore by fabricators, suppliers, imitators, amateurs, opportunists, promoters, nationalists, artists and scientists. There remains one factor to consider: Gosse's experience as a natural history lecturer.[413]

Gosse started his lecturing career with out-of-doors marine natural history classes in Ilfracombe in July 1855.[414] Recall that by that time, he had experience speaking and teaching in Newfoundland, Canada, Alabama, Jamaica, and London, making it unsurprising that one of the attendees would characterise him as that 'amiable and excellent gentleman, and accomplished naturalist.'[415] No detailed reports have

412. Lewes, *Sea-side Studies*, 1858, 264.

413. The information and analysis presented here, unless otherwise stated, is based upon D. Wertheimer, 'On the Battlefield of Science and Revelation: P. H. Gosse as a Lecturer, 1855-1870' (unpublished MS, 2022).

414. *Life*, 245, states: 'In February of that year [1853] Philip Gosse was asked to lecture. He had never attempted such a thing, but he said he would willingly make a few remarks about sponges, the siliceous skeletons of which he was studying at that moment in correspondence with Bowerbank. He accompanied the lecture with some large drawings in chalk on the blackboard, and the success of the experiment, which was novel at that time, was such, that he adopted lecturing as a branch of his professional labours, and became a very popular lecturer during the next four or five years.' As stated above, natural history lectures were not novel in 1853, and PHG's scientific lectures continued until 1861. PHG's earliest documented natural history lecture—likely the one EWG claimed took place in 1853—was a talk on sponges illustrated with coloured drawings, in 1855 (Wertheimer, 'On the Battlefield of Science and Revelation').

415. Mrs S. C. Hall [Anna Maria Hall, 1800-1881], 'A New Pleasure. The Marine Aquarium', London *Art-Journal* n.s.II (1 May 1856), 147fn., referring to the Ilfracombe classes.

been traced for those classes,[416] but judging from a Gosse talk at the Shaftesbury Institute in London that October,[417] his second outdoor classes in 1856 at Tenby,[418] and a lecture by him at the end of 1856 at the Islington Literary and Scientific Society in London,[419] they appear to have been of a descriptive type.

Gosse's outdoor classes were likely novel, though not his public natural history lecturing (contrary to what has been claimed).[420] Naturalists such as T. Rymer Jones,[421] Thomas Hincks,[422] George Johnston[423] and Thomas Huxley[424] preceded him, while Edwin Lankester,[425] J.S. Bowerbank,[426] and the populariser J. G. Wood[427] were among his lecture hall contemporaries.

Public lecturing had only just gained respectability in Britain in the 1850s (thanks to the example in the area of fiction of Charles Dickens, Samuel Smiles, and others),[428] but being paid for lecturing remained for many a questionable category to the end of that decade.[429] There were exceptions: at his top rate, the novelist W. M. Thackeray could earn fifty guineas or 'nearly a guinea a minute' for one lecture in 1857, with a series

---

416. The classes were announced in the *Bath Chronicle*, 28 June 1855, 2; *Literary Gazette*, under 'Topics of the Week', 30 June 1855, 412; *Birmingham Journal*, 4 July 1855, 2; *North Devon Journal*, 26 July 1855, 8; *Life*, 257. I do not know how many attended PHG's outdoor lectures, though the number was small ('Marine Natural History Class', advertisement in PHG, *Tenby*, 1856, 400). In 1855, Anna Shipton accompanied two women from London to the lectures (Shipton, '*Tell Jesus.*', [1863], 2-5), and the prolific writer Mrs S. C. Hall apparently attended one series by herself (Hall, 'A New Pleasure. The Marine Aquarium', 147fn.).

417. Shaftesbury Institute 1855 flyer: CUL Adv.c.82.5, [84b]. No local paper of the Islington area exists for 1855, and I did not find coverage of PHG's lectures in other London newspapers.

418. *Tenby Observer* IV (5 Sept. 1856), n.p.

419. Advertisement, London *Daily News* (3 Nov. 1856), 1.

420. *Life*, 341-2, 245.

421. For example, 'Lectures on Natural History', Kendal *Westmorland Gazette*, 3 Aug. 1839, 3.

422. For example, 'Exeter Literary Society. Lectures on Zoophytes', Exeter *Western Times*, 14 Nov. 1846, 6.

423. For his lecturing, including in 1851: James Hardy (ed.), *Selections from the Correspondence of Dr George Johnston* (Edinburgh: David Douglas, 1892), 440, 467, 497.

424. Huxley gave his first-ever lecture in April 1852 at the Royal Institution 'On Animal Individuality' (Huxley (ed.), *Life and Letters of Thomas Henry Huxley* I: 142-3).

425. For an 1855 example: 'Literature, Science, and Art', *Birmingham Journal*, 4 July 1855, 2.

426. For an 1856 example: *Tenby Observer* IV (12 Sept. 1856), n.p., Editorial.

427. Wood's first lecture was on insects in 1856 insects (*Jackson's Oxford Journal*, 15 Mar. 1856, 5). Theodore Wood, *The Rev. J. G. Wood*, 128, gives the date of the lecture but was unable to provide the topic.

428. Janette Lisa Martin, 'Popular Political Oratory and Itinerant Lecturing in Yorkshire and the North East in the Age of Chartism, 1837-60' (University of York, PhD dissertation, 2010), 249.

429. *The Literary and Educational Year Book for 1859* (London: Kent and Co., [1859]) included both a 'List of Paid Lecturers' (pp. 96-102) and 'List of Gratuitous Lecturers' (pp. 102-11).

discounted to between thirty and forty guineas each appearance.[430] A science lecturer was another matter. For not more than eight lectures at the Royal Botanic Society of London in 1854, Edwin Lankester was paid five guineas per lecture,[431] a rate which applied as well twenty-five years later to J. G. Wood.[432] Towards the end of the century an in-demand science lecturer could charge as much as £40 per event and earn £600 per year.[433] Someone like Gosse was paid for his efforts, though at only a fraction of these rates.[434]

And yet Gosse's timing was fortuitous. His lecturing years came during the voluntary movement to improve adult education in Britain. While literacy rates were beginning to climb in England by around 1850, reading for many working people remained a challenge.[435] The entertaining lecturer allowed one to benefit from an oral presentation of the latest natural history developments for those for whom a Gosse book was too expensive and reading it too difficult. It has been argued that while the mechanics' institutes (the most striking of these efforts), which were established in many cities in the first half of the nineteenth century, were mainly unsuccessful in instructing the working classes, they were impactful for the middle class.[436] Nonetheless there was a growing conviction at the time, if more in theory than practice, that a knowledge of science was important for all. The Birmingham and Midland Institute

430. [W. F. Pollock], *Personal Remembrances of Sir Frederick Pollock* (London: Macmillan and Co., 1887), II: 57; *DNB* (Thackeray). At least some literary society's considered Thackeray's fee onerous and his lectures on *The Four Georges* 'calculated to bring the kingly name into contempt' and 'certainly grossly slanderous' (*Newcastle Journal*, 7 Feb. 1857, 5).

431. Mary P. English, *Victorian Values. The Life and Times of Dr. Edwin Lankester M.D., F.R.S.* (Bristol: Biopress Ltd, 1990), 56.

432. The typical fee for a J. G. Wood lecture, apparently around 1879, was five guineas (Lightman, *Victorian Popularizers*, 178).

433. This was the case with the astronomer Robert S. Ball (1840-1913): Lightman, *Victorian Popularizers*, 402.

434. 'A Young Naturalist' claimed in a letter that PHG had charged 100 guineas per month for his marine natural history classes, which met daily. The writer complained: 'This is *rather* too much' ('Marine Zoology and Botany', Newcastle-upon-Tyne *Daily Chronicle*, 18 June 1860, 2). Judging from the general description of PHG's 1855 lectures at Ilfracombe ('Marine Natural History Class', in PHG, *Tenby*, following p. 400), each session was about two hours, meeting 'almost every day for a month'. Assuming that the class met 6 days per week for 2 hours x 4 weeks = 48 hours for 100 guineas (not including equipment provided, which included aquaria, microscope, pocket lens, and dredging equipment).

435. Martin, 'Popular Political Oratory and Itinerant Lecturing', 256.

436. J. F. C. Harrison, *Learning and Living 1790-1960: A Study in the History of the English Adult Education Movement* (London: Routledge and Kegan Paul, 1961), 57-61.

was just one example of an organization whose goal was 'the promotion of science and art amongst the middle and working classes.'[437]

That Gosse could bring his artistic skills to the circuit and combine them with his authoritative knowledge of the subject and his speaking ability, though not unique, was unusual.[438] An unknown number[439]— perhaps all—of Gosse's lectures included his own drawings, and some[440]— perhaps all—were drawings in colour. For comparison, the illustrations for virtually all of George Johnston's scientific works, including for his lectures, were by his wife, Catherine.[441] Charles Darwin wrote extensively but never lectured and was not an illustrator.[442] J. G. Wood was a prolific author and (after Gosse's time) is said to have lectured widely, but was no illustrator.[443] '[S]uccess in this field requires a rare combination of gifts,' including an ability to describe the subject in non-technical and readily understandable terms, commented a later observer. Alas, he continued, 'Huxley, the younger [Francis] Buckland, Gosse, and Hugh Miller are gone, and few follow in their steps.'[444]

From July 1855 to February 1861 Gosse delivered at least twenty-eight public natural history lectures at nineteen venues in England, Scotland and Wales (about half consisted of a series of talks).[445] He spoke before

437. 'Birmingham and Midland Institute', *Illustrated London News*, 24 Nov. 1855, [page unknown].

438. T. H. Huxley was 'an admirable draughtsman, and his blackboard illustrations were always a great feature of his lectures' (Leonard Huxley, *Life-stories of Famous Men. Thomas Henry Huxley: A Character Sketch* (London: Watts & Co., 1920), 46, 87). Edwin Lankester illustrated his talks (*Birmingham Journal*, 13 Feb. 1856, 2), but it is not known who made them.

439. For example, Edinburgh *Caledonian Mercury*, 28 Feb. 1857, p. [2]; *Yorkshire Gazette*, 19 Feb. 1859, 7.

440. For example, Edinburgh *Caledonian Mercury*, 3 Oct. 1856, 2.

441. Peter Davis, 'George Johnston (1797-1855) of Berwick upon Tweed and the Pioneers of Marine Biology in North-east England', *Archives of Natural History* 22 (1995), 352; James Hardy (ed.), *Selections from the Correspondence of Dr George Johnston* (Edinburgh: David Douglas, 1892), 125 and *passim*; ODNB.

442. Donald and Munro (eds.), *Endless Forms*, 10, 243.

443. Wood, *J. G. Wood*, 156. Pages 157-8: 'He had, indeed, something of the peculiar art of the scene-painter ... This aptitude for drawing was quite a natural gift, for my father never had a drawing-lesson in his life, and was entirely his own pupil. ...But he never pretended to be an artist, and, indeed, always disclaimed the title, saying that he could show what he wanted to show by a rough drawing, but that anything in the shape of a finished sketch was altogether beyond his powers'.

444. Letter to the editor, H. Neville Hutchinson, 'Popular Science Lectures on Natural History', *Nature* 106 (27 Jan. 1921), 694.

445. PHG was to give four lectures for the Literary and Philosophical Society of Newcastle-upon-Tyne in February-March 1857 (*Newcastle Journal*, 7 Feb. 1857, 5). His lectures are cited in two works which do not specify the lecture dates: 'Marine Zoology (four), by Mr. P. H. Gosse', in

mechanics' institutes and 'Literary' and 'Philosophical' societies on his speciality areas of marine zoology and the aquarium. It is true that a talk on lower marine animals was no match for one from the popular novelist Thackeray[446] or the notorious dancer and adventuress Lola Montez.[447] Yet from every available indication, Gosse's performance at the podium was stellar. As the Liverpool *Daily Post* put it, 'Mr. Gosse's skill as a lecturer is not in the least inferior to his reputation as a writer on "Marine Zoology." He is wonderful in both.'[448] Or as the *Birmingham Journal* stated:

> We have often referred in these columns to his many and valuable popular contributions to natural history ... but we we did not expect so interesting and admirable a lecture as we heard on Monday night [March 23]. Mr. Gosse has the reading and observation which make "a full man," as Bacon says, and the writing which makes "a ready man," and consequently his lecture was clear, graphic, and instructive, and was listened to with great interest by all. The coloured drawings by which the lecture was illustrated, were excellent; and those who missed the first lecture will do well to repair their loss by attending all the rest.[449]

Lecturing was part of Gosse's effort to spread knowledge of the subject throughout the United Kingdom, and he had the talent to do it well.

A different explanation for Gosse's relatively brief career as a lecturer is that while he was ideally positioned to take advantage of, and to promote, aquaromania and marine zoology, he slid into the activity because he needed the money.[450] There is a point to this explanation. Gosse's income was dependent upon his work. He had no independent resources, no

---

Some Account of the Lectures Hitherto Delivered in Connection with the Literary and Philosophy Society of Newcastle-upon-Tyne (Newcastle-on-Tyne: John Bell & Co., 1882), 31, and Robert Spence Watson, *The History of the Literary and Philosophical Society of Newcastle-upon-Tyne* (London: Walter Scott, 1897), 249, 348. I have only found information for the 5 March lecture, which is described as the second one (Newcastle-upon-Tyne *Newcastle Journal*, 7 Feb. 1857, 5).

446. PHG had to postpone one of his lectures at the Literary and Philosophical Society of Newcastle-upon-Tyne to avoid conflict with one by Thackeray (*Newcastle Journal*, 7 Feb. 1857, 5).

447. *Dundee, Perth and Cupar Advertiser*, 8 Feb. 1859, [2]: 'The only thing to be regretted in connection with Mr Gosse's lectures is, that they should have been attended by comparatively small audiences. It is certainly far from creditable to the town of Dundee that about a thousand people will pay two shillings each to see and hear Lola Montez, while such lectures as those of Mr Gosse, which may be heard for as many pence, are attended by so few.' Lola Montez was the stage name of Marie Dolores Eliza Rosanna Gilbert (1818-1861): *DNB*.

448. Liverpool *Daily* Post, 15 Feb. 1859, 5.

449. *Birmingham* Journal, 25 Mar. 1857, 4.

450. *Father and Son*, 1907, 83-4.

employer to pay him a salary, no family members who could assist him financially. He could earn money by lecturing, and while doing so could promote sales of his books.[451] Lecturing would not be onerous because of his personal knowledge and the eleven seashore titles he could draw on, published from 1855-61.[452] An added bonus was that while travelling around the country, Gosse could also search for new sea creatures at 'the most prolific parts of the British shores,—the coast of Dorset, South and North Devon, and South Wales,' while 'many zealous scientific friends' were assisting him by sending him for further study animals for his aquaria 'from the Channel Isles to the Shetlands'.[453] This work was most notably summed up by Gosse in his landmark volume on sea anemones (discussed below in Chapter 8). Field studies in Newfoundland, Canada, Alabama, and Jamaica were now supplemented by eight years of research throughout Great Britain.

Lecturing unquestionably helped Gosse earn a living, but the economic motivation falls short of fully accounting for his decision to lecture. Although none of Gosse's lecture notes have survived, we know what he said because newspaper reports give us the transcripts. Thanks to innovations in shorthand, they provide lengthier summaries of events and quotes from speakers than had hitherto been feasible.[454] Two themes stand out in Gosse's lectures from 1857-61.

The first one concerns his emphasis on the natural theology tradition's argument of design. In Gosse's lectures in Birmingham 'On Lower Marine Animals' in March 1857, for example, his theme was crafted to resonate for residents of an industrial city. They knew about the relationship between form and function in their lives, so they could appreciate that it also operated elsewhere:[455]

---

451. An advertisement in the *Tenby Observer* listed five PHG works (5 Sept. 1856); another advertisement (3 July 1857, 2), five works plus his *British Ornithology*.

452. PHG's works published between 1855-61 were: *Handbook to the Marine Aquarium* (1855); *Manual of Marine Zoology* (2vols., 1855-6); *Wanderings through the Conservatives at Kew* (1856); *Tenby* (1856); *Omphalos* (1857); *Life in its lower, intermediate, and higher forms: or, manifestations of the divine wisdom in the natural history of animals* (1857); *Evenings at the Microscope* (1859); *Letters from Alabama* (1859); *Actinologia Britannica* (1860); *Romance of Natural History* (1860); and a new edition of *The Ocean* (1860).

453. PHG, *Actinologia Britannica*, vi.

454. Martin, 'Popular Political Oratory and Itinerant Lecturing', 121.

455. PHG apparently commuted from Birmingham to London during the lectures. He sent a Referee's Report to the Royal Society on 24 Mar. 1857, dated from 58 Huntingdon St., Islington (Royal Society, RR.3.182).

The connexion was most intimate; and though from the number of organs [in invertebrates] we might expect confusion, the utmost harmony prevailed; the same as a manufactory in which there were a large number of cranks, and pulleys, and wheels, and bands, everything to the inexperienced eye seemed in the greatest disorder, but the machinist saw the use of them all and knew that they all contributed to the design in hand. Every animal might indeed be called a complex and elaborate manufactory, in which was the most perfect adaptation of means to ends—a contrivance of the most perfect kind—for it was a divine contrivance.[456]

Gosse's point was that animal species were wonderfully adapted to their environment.

They were created that way, fixed from the moment of creation. The more one studies animate life, he argued, the more ineluctably one sees that fact—even where one might least expect it, even in the minutest of details, even in the lowest forms of life, even in the *mundus invisibilis* (invisible world) only discoverable by use of a microscope. That was the Creator's plan. The man of science does no more than reveal the architectural details, so to say, in order to help us to understand the Creator's overall goal. Gosse had learned that lesson decades earlier from Adams' *Essays on the Microscope* ('the more we inquire into the works of nature, the more fully are we satisfied of their divine origin')[457] and frequently repeated it in his works.[458]

Gosse's second theme had to do with the religious implication of the study of nature. There was 'a very prevalent tendency in scientific men,' Gosse believed, 'to suppose that their peculiar pursuits had the effect of leading them to God, and capacitating them for His presence hereafter.'[459] Not so: 'there could be no scientific way to heaven.'[460] Initially hesitant

---

456. *Birmingham Daily Press*, 25 Mar. 1857, 3; for other reports of the lectures in 1857: *Birmingham Mercury*, 4 Apr., 6, and the advertisement of 21 Mar., 8; *Birmingham Journal*, 28 Mar., 8, and 1 Apr., 2, and the advertisement of 21 Mar., 8; *Birmingham Daily Press*, 31 Mar., 3, and the advertisement of 23 Mar., 2; and *Aris's Birmingham Gazette*, 30 Mar. Interestingly enough, the thread capsules in sea anemones were used as one of the examples in a lecture on divine contrivances.

457. Adams, *Essays on the Microscope* (Kanmacher 2ed.), 711.

458. For example, P.H.G[osse]., 'The Fowls of the Air', *Weekly Visitor* III (8 May 1852), 298: 'You know that God often appeals to his created works as proofs of his greatness and wisdom.'

459. 'Lectures by Mr. Gosse', *Sheffield Independent*, Supplement (19 Feb. 1859), 10.

460. *Yorkshire Gazette* (19 Feb. 1859), 7.

to speak on the subject publicly, Gosse began to talk about it in early 1859.[461] At the conclusion of his second lecture at the Watt Institution in Dundee on 'Some Remarkable Examples of Divine Contrivances in the Structure of the Lowest Animals', 'he warned his hearers that, wonderful as are these illustrations of Divine wisdom and power in nature, man as a sinner cannot approach God through the works of nature. To make such an attempt was to fall into Cain's error and crime of offering the fruits of the ground instead of the blood of the Lamb.'[462]

As far as is known, Gosse gave only a single natural history lecture in 1860, with his one in 1861 being his last known appearance at the scientific podium. One reasonably wonders why he gave up the activity. Was it due to the appearance of Darwin's *Origin of Species* on 24 November 1859?[463] It's easy to think so. Gosse's zero-sum perspective was that God's creation of the world was either perfect, or it was not.[464] If it *was* perfect, to maintain that animate life gradually adapted to its environment made no sense. If it was *not* perfect, creation by a Creator and the very notion of a perfect Creator (as well as belief in sinful man, a redeemer, life eternal, and so forth) also made no sense—which to Gosse made no sense. This was not an incidental point: the relationship of supernatural design to Darwin's naturalistic theory stood at the heart of the public debate over evolution, with Darwin arguing that a Designer was not required to achieve a scientifically accurate understanding of the development of life on earth.[465] Natural selection to him was a preferable explanation.

One might think that Gosse would give up the design argument after Darwin made the case that it was no longer a necessary tool for an understanding of the natural world. One would be wrong. Neither before Darwin nor after him did Gosse fail to affirm the idea of a perfect Creator

461. PHG had previously defined his position on the topic, and did not deviate from it. Thus *Aquarium*, 1854, 205-6: 'Some of the attributes of the Creator, indeed, may be deduced from his works, and man is held responsible for the deduction. But if this be attained, it will go but a little way towards that acquaintance with God, which will set a man "at peace", and to communicate which is the object of the Divine Revelation. A man may be a most learned and complete expounder of the truths of natural theology, and yet be pitiably blind on the all-important subject of a Sinner's justification with God.'

462. 'Watt Institution Lectures', *Dundee and Perth Saturday Post*, 5 Feb. 1859, [3].

463. Freeman, *Darwin*, 2ed., 75.

464. On this point: Kimler, 'One Hundred Years of Mimicry', 42-3.

465. Alvar Ellegård, 'The Darwinian Theory and the Argument from Design', *Lychnos* (1956), 173.

creating a perfect creation. The world was 'a grand whole,' Gosse had written in 1844, 'so perfect, so beautifully consistent, that none but an All-wise Mind could have contrived, none but an Almighty Hand could have created.'[466] Or, as he wrote in 1863, 'Are not all His works perfect? The answer must be that they are.'[467]

A more prosaic explanation is available to account for Gosse ending his scientific lecturing. In December 1860, after the death of Emily, he had married his second wife, Eliza Brightwen.[468] Three years later, John Brightwen, an uncle, died,[469] and left Eliza with what amounted to a substantial annual income of £400 during her lifetime.[470] Gosse had 'legal control of it, [though] morally & honourably, I always consider [it] hers.'[471] Nonetheless, the pressure to achieve an income which had hovered over Gosse's life had ended.

-XI-

The high-water mark of the popular aquarium movement in Britain, to which all these factors made their contribution, lasted from 1853 to 1860— emerging with the Regent's Park vivarium and *Naturalist's Rambles on the Devonshire Coast* of May 1853, and framed by two of Gosse's works, the *Aquarium* (1854) and *Actinologia Britannica* (1860).[472] After this,

---

466. PHG, *Introduction to Zoology* I: v.

467. PHG, 'Contributions to the History of the Rotifera, or Wheel-Animalcules. Part IV. The Flexible Creepers (Notommatina)', *Popular Science Review* II (July 1863), 475.

468. London *Daily News*, 29 Dec. 1860, 7.

469. 'Deaths', London *Daily News*, 24 May 1864, 7. John Brightwen, who was a banker with Gurneys, Birkbeck, and Brightwens (*Ipswich Journal*, 19 Feb. 1859, 3), died at the age of 81.

470. PHG-EWG, 22 Feb. 1870 (CUL Add. 7041,33); 'Legacy of John Brightwen to his Niece Eliza Gosse' (CUL Adv.c.82.5,70); *Life*, 359.

471. PHG-EWG, 22 Feb. 1870 (CUL Add. 7041,33). Emphasis in the original. *Life*, 359.

472. Edward Newman (*Zoologist* ser. 2, VIII, Sept. 1873, 3661) divided the aquarium movement into three periods: 1830-40 (Utilitarian); 1840-60 (Literary, poetic, fashionable); and post-1860 (Commercial). There is consensus that dwindling popular interest in aquaria dates to the early 1860s. The anonymous author of 'Marine Aquarium. With Tidal Arrangements' introduces the article by stating that 'The so-called 'mania' for aquaria may have passed away' (*Intellectual Observer* III, May 1863, 245). W. A. Lloyd consistently cited about 1862 as the time of the 'almost entire abandonment by the general public' of interest in small domestic aquaria (Lloyd, cited in *Athenaeum*, 5 Feb. 1876, 203). He begins the aquarium movement in May 1853, with the opening of the first public aquarium in the world in the gardens of the Zoological Society of London: '... it originated by far the greater part of the popular movement in the cultivation of Aquaria in Britain and elsewhere, and which prevailed as a kind of mania from 1854 to 1860, reaching its highest pitch in the last-named year, and then declining till it almost ceased to exist in its domestic aspect in 1862' (Lloyd, *A Guide Book to the Marine Aquarium of the Crystal Palace Aquarium Company*, 1872, 5).

the decline was precipitate among the general public,[473] a result of the wedding of 'fashion and science'. Popular movements come and go; and while it is possible to give some idea of why certain ones rise and have a sustained life, it is difficult to account for their decline. For a time, the aquarium and seashore held an attraction and meaning for many Victorians; when these wore out, they gave it up.[474] In the next fifty-five years, only two guides to the British seashore appeared.[475]

Naturalists continued to find the aquarium an indispensable tool. It was, after all, 'the most effective aid to the investigations of [marine] natural history which the present age has produced'.[476] In their hands it underwent a metamorphosis during the next two decades. Initially their focus switched in the 1860s from the littoral to the deep-sea fauna, resulting in the famous circumnavigation of the globe in search of deep-sea life made by the *Challenger* expedition (1872-6). Then, in the early 1870s, at the instigation of the German zoologist, Anton Dohrn (1840-1909), a marine biological station was opened at Naples, and sixteen years later, in 1888, one at Plymouth. Even before that time, as W. A. Lloyd complained, naturalists were no longer using the Crystal Palace aquarium.[477]

During 1852 to 1856 Gosse was busy with the aquarium and related research: on Rotifera, sea anemones, and popular scientific work for the SPCK. Second editions of three books were published: both *Popular British Ornithology*[478] and *Sacred Streams*[479] were hardly altered,

473. *Athenaeum*, 6 July 1857, 719.

474. Of course the aquarium as an educational and entertaining tool continued to the present day. For a Victorian example, see (anon), *The Boy's Own Book: A Complete Encyclopaedia of Sports and Pastimes, Athletic, Scientific, and Recreative* (London: Crosby Lockwood and Son, new ed., 1889), 430-33.

475. *Zoologist* ser.4, XVIII (15 May 1914), 198-9, referencing Edward Step's *By the Deep Sea: A Popular Introduction to the Wild Life of the British Shores* (1896), which included illustrations by PHG, and G. A. and C. L. Boulenger's *Animal Life by the Sea-shore* (1914).

476. 'An Aquarium for Manchester', *Manchester Weekly Times*, 6 Apr. 1872, 6.

477. W. A. Lloyd, *Nature* XVII (20 Dec. 1877), 143-4; for the connection of the aquarium with oceanography and marine biological stations: Henry Scherren, *The Zoological Society of London* (London: Cassell and Co., 1905), 108; Albert E. Gunther, *A Century of Zoology at the British Museum through the Lives of Two Keepers 1815-1914* (London: Dawsons, 1975), 385-99; Allen, *Naturalist in Britain*, 207-12; and for the subsequent dispute between coastal and city marine biologists: Wesenberg-Lund, 'Contributions to the Biology of the Rotifera', 212-3.

478. Freeman & Wertheimer-PHG, 32. *The Rambler*, Feb. 1854, 202, a Catholic monthly, praised the 2ed. of *Popular British Ornithology* in a backhanded manner, commending the plates, writing, and the author's avoidance of 'mawkish religionism' and 'that bitter spirit of Protestantism' which it discerned in PHG's *Naturalist's Rambles*.

479. Freeman & Wertheimer-PHG, 37-8. The 2ed. of *Sacred Streams*, which was titled *The*

though *The Aquarium* was revised and enlarged.[480] He serialized his Alabamian journals in the SPCK's *Home Friend* (twelve parts, 1855; published as a book, 1859), and (in the same journal) his *Wanderings Through the Conservatories at Kew* (seven parts, 1855-6; published as a book, 1856).[481] He was a featured contributor of religious articles for the *Weekly Visitor and Christian Family Reader* (1852-53), edited by Robert Bickersteth (1816-1884), future Bishop of Ripon,[482] and wrote thirty largely exegetical notes for the highly regarded weekly, *Christian Annotator; or, Notes and Queries on Scriptural Subjects*, edited by the 'ultra-protestant' L. H. J. Tonna (1812-1857).[483]

-XII-

In September 1856 Gosse conducted his second annual marine natural history class, this time at Tenby. The event was well-publicized,[484] and eagerly awaited. 'Last week we announced the arrival of a well-known friend of Tenby, Mr. Gosse,' the *Tenby Observer* stated in an editorial:

> It was a sight which went to our hearts to see the hero, whose locks our enthusiasm had silvered in our dreams, descend the side of the vessel. In his right hand he bore a basket, (pardon the vulgar term,) an emblem of himself, being full of all things curious; and so he was borne to shore. We understand Mr. Gosse has been very successful in drawing around

Ancient and Modern History of the Rivers of the Bible, may have been prompted by a dispute with the publisher about the book's title. The book was advertised in 1853 (London *Daily News*, 23 Dec. 1853, 8), but appears not to have been published until 1854 (review, *Bath Chronicle*, 29 June 1854, 4).

480. Freeman & Wertheimer-PHG, 48-9. The only review I've seen of the 2ed. of the *Aquarium* appeared in the Boston *Atlantic Monthly* II (July 1858), 253-255.

481. A segment of *Wanderings through the Conservatories at Kew* also appeared anonymously as a single 'very pleasing account' (London *Morning Chronicle*, 7 Aug. 1849, 3) in *Fraser's Magazine* XL (Aug. 1849), 127-35.

482. PHG was featured as a *Weekly Visitor* contributor (with the Revds J. Cumming, T. R. Birks, and Thomas Lathbury) in an advertisement in the *Illustrated London News* 20 (19 June 1852), 500 (where Bickersteth is listed as editor; Boase I: 270, lists him as editor only for 1851).

483. For a favourable view of *Christian Annotator* see: *Quarterly Journal of Prophecy* XVI (Jan. 1864), 98-9. According to *Christian Annotator* contributor William Kelly, a J. N. Darby supporter, Darby 'did not care for' the *Christian Annotator* (Heyman Wreford, *Memories of the Life and Last Days of William Kelly* (London: T. Weston, 1906), 74). The *Christian Annotator* ceased with Tonna's death, when its circulation was about 1,500 (28 Mar. 1857, 96). For the characterisation of Tonna, *DNB*.

484. The classes were advertised in *Manual of Marine Zoology* and *Tenby* (both 1856).

him a circle of admirers of nature's charms, before whose eyes he daily unfolds the chart of wisdom.[485]

While at Tenby, the Gosses customarily broke bread with a half dozen Brethren.[486] Prior to leaving for London on 2 October, Philip reported, the Brethren 'gathered together to commend us to the Lord's care.' Little did those few realize how much that attention was needed. Emily had lately been diagnosed with breast cancer. Everyone knew what that meant: 'no malady [is] so dreadful in its character and fatal in its results,' read a newspaper advertisement at the time.[487] Enveloped by this affectionate display,

> They received the tidings with simple, but most true-hearted sympathy; and the prayers which one after another of the little company, with many tears, sent up to God for us both, were something to be treasured up in my memory as long as I remain in the body, as I am sure they are treasured up in the memory of Jesus, to be brought out unto praise and honour and glory at his appearing.[488]

Gosse likewise mentioned the development to Frederic D. Dyster (d. 1893),[489] a physician who went dredging with him at Tenby. Dyster was a contemporary whom Gosse called 'my valued friend and fellow-labourer in marine zoology.'[490]

'I hope you got home well and without damage to Mrs. Gosse,' Dyster wrote. 'We shall be anxious to hear about you.'[491]

---

485. *Tenby Observer*, 12 Sept. 1856, no pagination.

486. PHG, *Memorial*, 26-7.

487. Advertisement, 'Free Cancer Hospital', *Illustrated London News* XIX (13 Dec. 1851), 702. Over 170 years later, though breast cancer is no longer a sentence of death it is the most common cancer in women in the United States (Brianna Abbott, 'Breast-Cancer Treatment Rethought', *The Wall Street Journal*, 16 Feb. 2023, A7) and worldwide, and is increasing in most countries (Edoardo Colzani, 'Health Outcomes of Women with Breast Cancer', Karolinska Institutet, Stockholm, PhD dissertation, 2014, 1).

488. PHG, *Memorial*, 27.

489. F. D. Dyster-PHG, 7 Oct. 1856, letter loosely stuck in *Infusoria.4* (seen in the R. B. Freeman Collection). Dyster's first name was sometimes spelled 'Frederick'. An M. D. and a J. P., Dyster was elected a Fellow of the Linnean Society in 1854 (London *Morning Chronicle*, 25 Mar. 1854, 9). When he died at the age of 83 in 1893, he was called 'one of Tenby's best known residents' ('Death of Dr. Dyster, of Tenby', Cardiff *Western Mail*, 6 Mar. 1893, 5; London *Guardian*, 15 Mar. 1893, 13; London *Commercial Gazette*, 31 May 1893, 21).

490. PHG, *Tenby*, 135.

491. F. D. Dyster-PHG, 7 Oct. 1856 (R. B. Freeman Collection). In a second latter (undated, but a follow-up to 7 Oct. 1856), Dyster added: '… I trust dear Mrs. Gosse is going on satisfactorily.'

1. FATHER AND SON: This photo, dated by Edmund Gosse to 1857, would likely have been taken some time after his mother's death in London on 10 Feb. 1857. It served as the frontispiece in all editions of *Father and Son*, including the first one (which was formally anonymous).

2. CHRISTIAN NATURALIST: A line-drawing of 'Mr. Philip Henry Gosse, F.R.S., The Christian Naturalist' (1888).

3. EMILY GOSSE: Prior to her death in 1857, only two portraits existed of Gosse's first wife: one of Emily as a child and this one, as a young girl. William Gosse used deathbed photos of her as the basis for a third portrait. An attempt in 1856 to have her photographed by Maull and Polyblank in London was unsuccessful.

4. ELIZA GOSSE: Gosse married Eliza Brightwen in December 1860 (undated photo). She was bequeathed an annual income of £400 by an uncle, who died in 1864, easing the Gosses' financial situation. Gosse said Eliza was 'in no sense unfit to pair with my sainted Emily'.

5. PIONEER NEWFOUNDLAND ENTOMOLOGIST: During his years in the British colony,
Gosse became 'not merely a collector of insects ... but a *scientific naturalist*'.
He was the first to systematically investigate and record the entomology
of the island. Above: Drawings of the beetle *Aphodius fimetarius* (to size
and magnified).

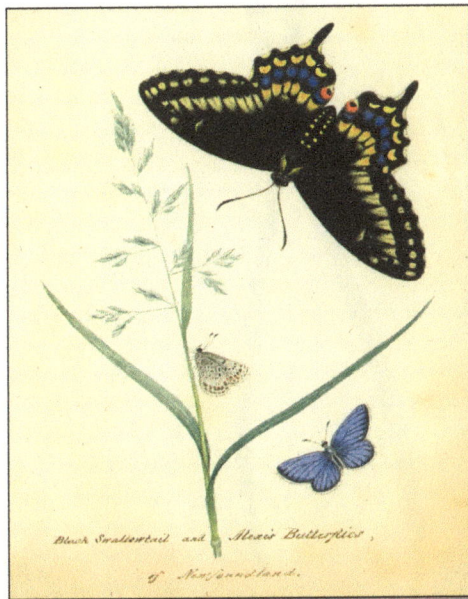

6. FIRST RECORD OF BUTTERFLIES: Gosse was the first to provide a record of the
butterflies of Newfoundland. His *Entomology of Newfoundland* (1835-6), now
lost, was supplemented by the illustrative volume *Entomologia Terrae Novae*
(completed ?1836) and other articles by him.

One of his drawings is of the Black Swallowtail (*Papilio polyxenes*, cropped
image above), which was his first 'cabinet specimen' (taken at Carbonear
Island on 25 July 1834). The scientific value of Gosse's illustrations was
enhanced by his inclusion of the host environment of the insects.

Plate XIX

7. FATHER OF JAMAICAN ORNITHOLOGY: Gosse, known as the 'Father of Jamaican Ornithology', domesticated hummingbirds there. He called *Trochilus polytmus* (above) 'one of the very loveliest of birds, not of Jamaica only, but of the whole world.' This figure, from his *Illustrations of the Birds of Jamaica*, was like the others in the book drawn on the stone and coloured by him.

8. FATHER OF JAMAICAN HERPETOLOGY: Gosse was not the first to study the amphibians and reptiles of Jamaica, but previous work in the area was of little scientific value. His groundbreaking observations about them, in *Naturalist's Sojourn in Jamaica* (1851) and in scientific articles and elsewhere, made him the 'Father of Jamaican Herpetology'.

Above: Gosse's tinted illustration of a large boa (*Chilabothrus inornatus*, left) and 'Venus' lizard (*Dactyloa Edwardsii=Anolis garmani* Stejneger) was, like others in *Naturalist's Sojourn*, drawn on the stone by Gosse and printed by the London firm of M. & N. Hanhart.

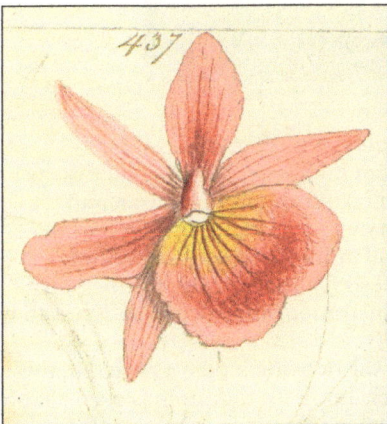

9. ORCHID LOVER: Prior to leaving England for Jamaica in 1844, Gosse read up on the natural history of the island. His 'Referenda for Jamaica' consisted of 'Rough Sketches of Plants & Animals to help in Identification'. He was not disappointed in his hope that he would find magnificent orchids there, but his plan to illustrate a work on Jamaican Orchideae was never realized.

Gosse included a drawing of *Broughtonia sanguinea* (at left), an orchid native to Jamaica, in his 'Referenda'. He wrote in his *Naturalist's Sojourn in Jamaica* that he found the 'elegant' plant 'growing in profuse luxuriance'.

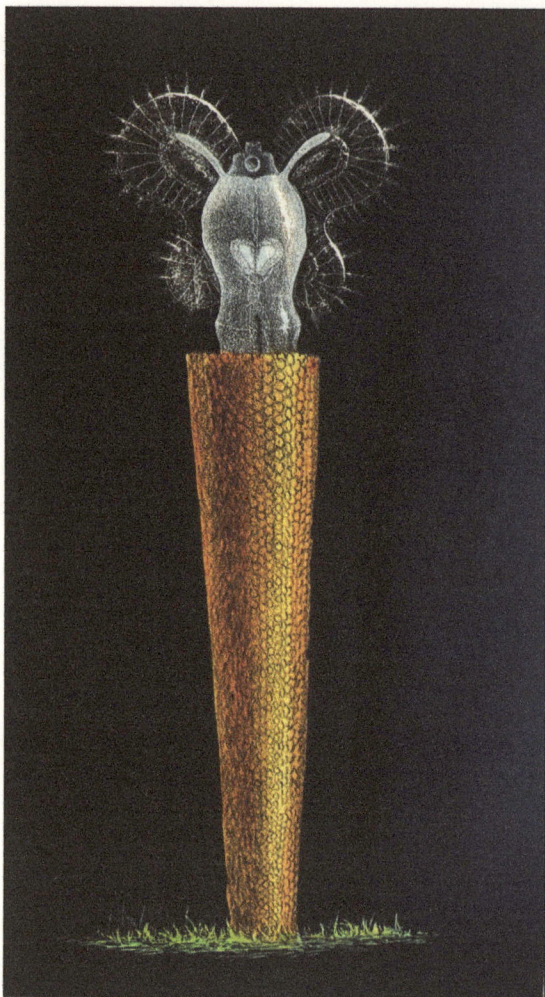

10. Microscopic 'builder' rotifer: Gosse's study of Rotifera (microscopic aquatic animals) spanned four decades, from his acquisition of a microscope in 1849 to the posthumously published joint supplement to Hudson and Gosse's *Rotifera* in 1889. His first research on the subject, on *Melicerta ringens* ('The builder animalcule'), was read at the Microscopical Society of London in 1850. Gosse was the first to describe the manner in which this rotifer built its surrounding tube (Gosse illustration, above), not undertaken in greater detail for a century.

This minute creature 'is not larger than the dot which puts a period to this sentence,' Gosse said. 'Surely the soul which animates this atom is even a more wonderful example of Divine power than the inanimate mass of the planet of Jupiter'.

11. FATHER OF THE AQUARIUM: When a name was required to describe the device which brought the seashore into British homes, Gosse came up with the word 'aquarium'. He first used it in its modern signification in 1853 (and fully explained his reason for the choice of the term in the following year in his book *The Aquarium*).

Gosse included a fanciful illustration of 'The Fountain Aquarium' in the book (the drawing reappeared in 1855 in one of the earliest articles in Germany on the subject). Within a few years, tanks were being widely sold in inventive shapes, in particular by W. Alford Lloyd, who patented improvements in 1858.

12. FANTASTICAL MICROSCOPIC ANIMAL: At a meeting of the Linnean Society of London in 1856, Gosse described a microscopic aquatic animal which he named *Lar sabellarum*, Gosse (currently known as *Proboscidactyla stellata* (Forbes)). His illustration, subsequently published in the society's *Transactions*, was so fantastical that its accuracy was regarded with scepticism and 'polite suspicion'. It was confirmed as accurate in 1872.

P.H. Gosse. del.   Hanhart. Chromo lith.

THE ANCIENT WRASSE

13. AQUARIUM OCCUPANT: 'The Ancient Wrasse' is one of six colour plates (here slightly cropped) from Gosse's *Aquarium* (1854), reproduced from his original watercolours as chromolithographs by M. and N. Hanhart. At the time, colour printing was a revelation, and this book (together with his *Devonshire Coast* and *Tenby*), in locating marine animals in colour *in situ*, were landmark publications which received rave reviews.

Gosse called the six-inch-long fish pictured above–whose 'splendour' rivals 'the most richly-tinted denizens of the tropical seas'–among the easiest to keep in an aquarium. It is shown 'lurking under a projecting ledge of rock, a situation it loves to haunt, under the shadow of the branching tufts of sea-weeds, from which it picks its insect food.'

14-15. SCENES OF SEA ANEMONES: As had been the case earlier with Gosse's seashore trilogy, reviewers were passionate about his landmark study of sea anemones. They lauded *Actinologia Britannica's* contribution to science, the 'care and conscientiousness with which it has been got up', and its chromolithographs, which set him 'alone and unrivalled in the extremely difficult art' of producing illustrations both scientifically accurate and aesthetically pleasing.

In 1863, when the German glassworker Leopold Blaschka was commissioned to create anatomicallly accurate glass models of marine invertebrates, he turned to these illustrations by Gosse.

The illustration is labelled "P.H. Gosse, del." (lower left), "Hanhart, Chromo lith." (lower right), and titled "THE PLUMOSE ANEMONE &c."

16. 'THE MOST BEAUTIFUL': A century after this drawing by Gosse appeared as a chromolithograph in *The Aquarium*, the 'Plumose anemone' was called the 'noblest, the most beautiful of all sea-anemones'.

CHAPTER SIX

1856-1857

One Family, One Song

-I-

T HE HARD LUMP IN EMILY'S LEFT BREAST had first been noticed by her at the end of April.[1] Her husband thought she was only 'slightly' alarmed. Perhaps so—she had, after all, enjoyed a life notably free of illness.[2] Or maybe it was not how she felt but how she outwardly presented herself. Whatever the case, it only took the suggestion of her friend, Mary Stacey (1792-1876)—an ex-Quaker who had joined Brethren (from 1851 she was acquainted with George Pearse, Philip Gosse's friend)[3]—to set her on a path towards obtaining the assessments of physicians.[4] Stacey, a single woman considerably older than Emily, was known as a 'significant member' of the Brook Street assembly at Tottenham from 1838.[5]

The first to be visited was Michael M. A. H. Laseron (1819-1894),[6] a

---

1. PHG, *Memorial*, 1. PHG's account is unclear as to when precisely the first consultation occurred. *Life*, 262, gives the date as 1 May 1856; *Father and Son*, 1907, 59, states that it was 'in the beginning of May'.

2. So EG told Anna Shipton (Shipton, *"Tell Jesus."*, 41); also PHG, *Memorial*, 60.

3. J. Hudson Taylor, 'The Late Mr. Geo. Pearse', *China's Millions* n.s. X (Sept. 1902), [117].

4. PHG, *Memorial*, 5.

5. For Stacey's dates: West, *From Friends to Brethren*, 257; for her alignment with Brethren: West, 19fn. 150, 235, 238; as a 'significant member': T.C.F. Stunt, 'Early Brethren and the Society of Friends', *CBRF Occasional Paper* No. 3 (1970), 21. She died 'aged 84': *Pall Mall Gazette*, 13 May 1876, 5; London *Morning Post*, 15 May 1876, 7, and London *Standard*, 15 May 1876), 1.

6. The sole source for the physician's name is PHG, *Memorial*, 5, where he is referred to only as 'Dr. Laseron'. Wertheimer, *Identification*, 6, was the first to suggest that this was the Revd Edward Laseron (d. prior to 1872; *Pall Mall Gazette*, 14 Aug. 1872, 3), a missionary to the Jews in India and elsewhere (this identification was adopted by Boyd, *Emily Gosse*, 55, and all others).

European-trained doctor aligned with Open Brethren.[7] Like a number of other Brethren, he was familiar with homoeopathy.[8] Laseron was a Jew who converted to Christianity, and had founded evangelical societies in suburban London, including the Orphan Home (dating to 1856)[9] and Deaconesses' House, a nurse training institute for women.[10] Stacey attended the session with Laseron and heard his diagnosis: the growth was cancerous.[11]

The next day the Gosses, in their methodical manner, sought a second opinion. They turned to a relative of Philip's, the London physician Henry Hyde Salter (1823-1871), who had, coincidentally, been elected a Fellow of the Royal Society at the same 1856 meeting as Gosse.[12] Salter got them an appointment with James Paget (1814-1899), whom Philip named

---

The identification was, however, confused and incorrect, as Edward Laseron was not a physician. There was a contemporary Laseron who was a physician: Michael Maximilian Augustus Henry Laseron (referred to in contemporary newspapers as 'Dr. M. Laseron', the middle names are sometimes rendered 'August Heinrich'). See John Dunlop, *Memories of Gospel Triumphs Among the Jews during the Victorian Era* (London: S.W. Partridge & Co., 1894), 336-40; A. Bernstein, *Some Jewish Witnesses for Christ* (London: Operative Jewish Converts' Institution, 1909), 325-6; death notices, London *Daily Telegraph* (3 May 1894), 1, and *Lancet* (5 May 1894), 1169.

Laseron's philosophy was similar to George Müller's reliance on 'living by faith' (Timothy Larsen, '"Living by faith": A short history of Brethren practice', *BAHNR* 1/2 (1997-8), 67-102), but with a self-proclaimed difference: Laseron did not hesitate to approach potential wealthy donors for support ('The Edmonton Orphan Home', London *Daily News*, 4 Nov. 1871, 5). Laseron described his prayerful conduct in the pamphlet *Narrative of the Origin and Progress of the Edmonton and Tottenham Ragged School*, which was ridiculed in a *Literary Gazette* review (6 Oct. 1860, 275). The *Literary Gazette* subsequently apologized for the piece ('Dr. Laseron's Edmonton and Tottenham Ragged School', 17 Nov. 1860, 419).

Müller's *Narrative* (1837-1856) of how he had 'demonstrated the viability of "living by faith"' is examined in Summerton, *'I thanked the Lord, and asked for more': George Müller's Life and Work*, Chap. 5 and index. It became famous (Alan Thomas Terlep, 'Inventing the Rapture: The Formation of American Dispensationalism' (University of Chicago, PhD dissertation, 2010), 240) and was imitated (Lenz, '"Strengthening the Faith of the Children of God"', 356). Müller was preceded in following this precept, however, by A. N. Groves (Larsen, '"Living by faith"', 73).

7. Massimo Introvigne, *The Plymouth Brethren* (Oxford: Oxford University Press, 2018), 2.

8. T. C. F. Stunt, 'Homoeopathy and Brethren', *The Witness* 103 (Apr. 1973), 127-8; Grass, *Gathering to His Name*, 257.

9. 'The Edmonton Orphan Home', London *Daily News* (4 Nov. 1871), 5; J. Clifford and J. Colebrook, 'The Bright Side of London: Or, Visits to the Centres of Christian Work. No. V.—The Orphan Home at Tottenham', London *General Baptist Magazine* n.s.76 (June 1874), 215.

10. C. Golder, *History of the Deaconess Movement in the Christian Church* (Cincinnati: Jennings and Pye, 1903), 184-5.

11. PHG, *Memorial*, 5-6.

12. [Charles Richard Weld], 'Our Weekly Gossip', *Athenaeum*, 14 June 1856, 747; PHG-William Gosse, 10 Nov. 1856 (CUL Adv.c.82.5, 52); PHG, *Memorial*, 6. Salter was a son of PHG's cousin Elizabeth, who was the daughter of his aunt Susan (Wertheimer, *Identification*, 6); Gosse, *The Gosses*, 38.

the 'first authority on cancer in London.'[13] As a surgeon, it was said of him that he 'has perhaps never been surpassed.'[14] For Paget, Emily's case was typical: she was in that 45-50 year-old age-bracket of women who most frequently had breast cancer.[15] In spite of the fact that Salter and Paget both agreed that the best plan was to pursue an unappealing option—immediate excision of the growth—Salter proposed yet another consultation.[16] Before that happened, Emily wrote to her friend Anna Shipton (in a reference to her husband): 'Pray for H[enry].'[17]

This third doctor was an American, Jesse Weldon Fell (1819-1890),[18] who had come to England in 1855 claiming to be in possession of 'an entirely original mode of treating the disease of Cancer in all its various forms.'[19] Fell's novel treatment consisted of a paste which he claimed to have co-developed in America in 1847, modifying a Native American treatment for cancer.[20] The advantage of his new therapy was that it was described as non-surgical and painless. These claims were of enormous significance.

At the time, Philip said that Emily's 'nervous system ... was peculiarly sensitive to pain.'[21] Decades later, Edmund Gosse misinterpreted his father's remark as an explanation. Edmund wrote that his mother had

13. PHG, *Memorial*, 6. Boase VI: 342: 'the leading surgeon in London from 1861'. Paget was an Anglican.

14. F. W. Tunnicliffe, 'Sir James Paget, Bart, F.R.S.', *Nature* 61 (11 Jan. 1900), 256; *ODNB*. A decade after this, when PHG was concerned that EWG (then in London) might have tetanus, he recommended that he see Paget (PHG-EWG, 26 Dec. 1868, CUL Add. 7018, 25).

15. James Paget, *Lectures on Tumours, delivered at the Royal College of Surgeons of England* (London: Longman, Brown, Green, and Longmans, 1853), 324.

16. PHG, *Memorial*, 6.

17. Shipton, *"Tell Jesus."*, 33-4.

18. The doctor who treated Emily for her cancer is referred to as 'Dr. F—' throughout PHG's *Memorial*, and as 'a certain American' in *Life*, 263. On the basis of an annotation in a secondhand copy of *Life*, a friend of Philip H. G. Gosse (PHG's grandson) suggested to him that 'Dr. F—' was 'Pattison, a Quack' (letter of 19 Dec. 1936, CUL Adv.c.82.5,49). While the description of Pattison was accurate, he was not the doctor in question. In August 1973 I examined EWG's copy of *Life*, then in the Family Collection. 'Dr Fell' is written in EWG's holograph next to the words 'The doctor lived in Pimlico' (*Life*, 263). Jesse Weldon Fell was first named and described as the one who treated EG in Wertheimer, *Identification*, 6-7.

19. M. F. Ashley Montagu and W. J. Musick, 'A Yankee Doctor in England in 1859', *Bulletin of the History of Medicine* XIII (Feb. 1943), 219; J. Weldon Fell, *A Treatise on Cancer, and Its Treatment* (London: John Churchill, 1857), v.

20. Fell's paste consisted of bloodroot (*Sanguinaria canadensis*) and zinc chloride (Lauren Fravor and Amor Khachemoune, 'Dermatologic uses of bloodroot: a review and reappraisal', *International Journal of Dermatology* 60, 2021, 1071-2). The authors conclude: '... bloodroot in any form is not recommended for human use' (p. 1074).

21. PHG, *Memorial*, 35, 60.

an 'excessive dread of physical pain' which explained why she 'shrank' from surgery and turned to Fell.[22] But even if Emily had been 'peculiarly sensitive to pain,' there could not have been anything 'excessive' about her sense of dread. General anaesthesia had only been introduced in England in 1846, and was not in frequent use ten years later.[23] Prior to that time, a mastectomy was performed quickly in a noisy, unsanitary environment, with no pain killer stronger than alcohol. For the female patient, the shocking description by novelist Fanny Burney of her own mastectomy in 1811 bore witness to an experience which to this day reads as searingly painful and unimaginably horrifying.[24]

In an 1852 study of 235 breast cancer operations, James Paget tabulated that 'not less' than ten per cent of the women died *during* the operation;[25] in general, almost half died not long *after* the operation, from infection (sepsis).[26] In another Paget study, in the sixth year following surgery, 77.75 per cent of the women were dead, compared to 76.57 per cent of women who had not undergone surgery.[27] No wonder that many surgeons at the time believed the treatment was 'considerably worse than the disease itself due to the intense pain that the women had during and after surgery.'[28] Summing up these facts in 1853, Paget offered a nuanced assessment. Dismiss the thought that the operation could provide a complete cure, he cautioned: 'I will not say that such a thing is impossible; but it is so highly improbable, that a hope of its occurring in any single case cannot be reasonably entertained.' And confront this ultimate question: Is it probable 'that the operation will add to the length or comfort of life, enough to justify the incurring this risk from its own consequences'?[29] Paget's answer: Possibly yes. Possibly no.

Notwithstanding the many questions about cancer in mid-Victorian

22. *Life*, 262-3; *Father and Son*, 1907, 62.

23. G. H. Sakorafas and M. Safioleas, 'Breast cancer surgery: an historical narrative. Part II. 18th and 19th centuries', *European Journal of Cancer* XIX (Jan. 2010), 18.

24. Burney's experience is retold in many places: Joyce Hemlow (ed.), *Fanny Burney. Selected Letters and Journals* (Oxford, 1986), 135-138; Sakorafas and Safioleas, 'Breast cancer surgery', 18-19; Birgit Whitman, 'Breast Cancer: Patient Narratives and Treatment Methods' (University of Glasgow, PhD dissertation, 2004), 46-67.

25. James Paget, *Lectures on Tumours*, 351; Paget, 'On the Average Duration of Life in Patients with Scirrhous Cancer of the Breast', *The Lancet* I (19 Jan. 1856), 63.

26. Sakorafas and Safioleas, 'Breast cancer surgery', 12, 19.

27. Paget, 'On the Average Duration of Life in Patients with Scirrhous Cancer of the Breast', 62.

28. Sakorafas and Safioleas, 'Breast cancer surgery', 18.

29. Paget, *Lectures on Tumours*, 350-1.

Britain, attention was increasingly being given to treatment. The establishment in London in 1851 of the Cancer Hospital for the poor pointed to that development.[30] At the same time, because solutions remained indeterminate, an opportunity presented itself for those preying on the hopeful. Dr Fell was only one of those who wrote (or lectured) on cancer treatment, recommended ointments or pills, or promised a groundbreaking therapy. Other competitors included John Pattison, M.D., who said he was originally from Scotland. His surgical education, he claimed, was in the United States, where he had practised for a decade. He described his treatment as effective half of the time without use of 'the knife'.[31] In 1852, he moved to England 'to offer it to the Profession,'[32] but the Middlesex Hospital in London declined to accept his generosity because he would not reveal details of the treatment.[33] Another curer was the London surgeon and homoeopathist Dr William Batchelour (d. 1878),[34] a member of the Royal College of Surgeons.[35] He employed a 'certain preparation' which worked on the nervous system 'internally and externally'.[36] Pain was 'immediately relieved'.[37] It was no less than 'one of the most astounding discoveries of our age,' he averred.[38]

How to choose? The Gosses again turned to Hyde Salter. Though Pattison had been denied access to the Middlesex Hospital in 1852, Fell was approved four years later.[39] He had agreed to reveal details of his

30. 'Cancer Hospital', *Illustrated London News* XXIX (16 Aug. 1856), 161.

31. John Pattison, *Cancer: Its True Nature, Treatment, & Cure. Illustrated by Cases* (London: Charles Westerton, 1855), 5-8; T. Spencer Wells, *Cancer Cures and Cancer Curers* (London: John Churchill, 1860), *passim*.

32. Advertisement, 'Important Medical Discovery', *Glasgow Herald* (17 Dec. 1852), 8.

33. *Report of the Surgical Staff of the Middlesex Hospital, to the Weekly Board and Governors, upon the Treatment of Cancerous Diseases in the Hospital, on the Plan Introduced by Dr. Fell* (London: John Churchill, 1857), 7. Montagu and Musick, 'A Yankee Doctor in England in 1859', 217fn1., attribute the authorship of the *Report* to Fell. This seems unlikely, given the title of the work and its criticism of some of Fell's cures (e.g., pp. 49-50).

34. 'Deaths', *Pall Mall Gazette* (16 Nov. 1878), 5.

35. Advertisement, *Halifax Courier* (2 June 1855), 2.

36. William Batchelour, *The Curableness of Cancer: with Reports of Cases and Testimonials* (London: J. H. Bailliere, 1854), 18-21. In 1856, Batchelour issued a widely-advertised, 'Just published' work 'on his new and successful system of treatment for cancer, whereby pain is immediately relieved' (*Nottinghamshire Guardian*, 10 Jan. 1856, 7; *Leeds Intelligencer*, 16 Feb. 1856, 2; *Hull Packet*, 7 Mar. 1856, 2).

37. Advertisements, *Nottinghamshire Guardian* (10 Jan. 1856), 7; *Leeds Intelligencer* (16 Feb. 1856), 2.

38. Advertisement, 'Extraordinary Discovery.—A Certain Cure for Cancer, &c.', London *Era* (18 Sept. 1853), 16.

39. *Report of the Surgical Staff of the Middlesex Hospital*, 7-9. *The Athenaeum* was one of

cancer cure in exchange for the opportunity to undertake clinical trials at the hospital. The surgical staff reported that Fell's treatment was 'in entire accordance with known principles of surgery, is ingenious, safe, and easy of application by well-instructed surgeons.'[40] After Dr Fell had been at Middlesex for five months, however, the assessment became more nuanced, if not confusing. On the one hand, 'the new plan of treatment is not superior to that by the knife.'[41] On the other, Fell's therapy is 'a clear advance upon the past, and may not only be itself improved, but may be the way to more extended blessings upon a class of the community now signally distressed.'[42] Fell had allowed interested parties to observe him treating patients. Over 100 did so, including Hyde Salter.[43] Salter's final recommendation: Proceed with Dr Fell.

The Gosses visited Fell themselves. He told them of his 'secret medicament'. He asserted the 'painlessness of the treatment'. He provided them with testimonials. He showed them pictures. He reported an eighty per cent success rate. They prayed.[44] And so, 'trusting that He would care for us according to his word—a word that cannot lie,' and with Fell's assurances of a positive outcome, husband and wife 'perfectly agreed' to try his remedy. On 12 May, Emily began a thrice-weekly treatment at Fell's office in Pimlico. It was a 'wearisome' trip, but she was initially buoyed up with hope.[45] Fell applied a few types of ointment to her breast. There was pain. He exuded confidence. He encouraged her to make the September trip to Tenby with her family, previously described.[46]

When the Gosses returned from Wales to London in October, the extractive process continued. There seemed good reason to think that the cancerous tumour would not prove fatal. In informing his brother William of Emily's cancer, Philip referred *en passant* to the most important scientific honour he ever received: his election as a Fellow of the Royal Society. His qualifications for the prestigious recognition were deemed to be his technical article on the manducatory organs in Rotifera (published in the society's *Philosophical Transactions*), several of his

those critical of the hospital for accepting Fell (26 Dec. 1857, 1623).

40. *Report of the Surgical Staff of the Middlesex Hospital*, 10.
41. *Report of the Surgical Staff of the Middlesex Hospital*, 45.
42. *Report of the Surgical Staff of the Middlesex Hospital*, 47.
43. Fell, *Treatise on Cancer*, vi.
44. PHG, *Memorial*, 6-13.
45. Shipton, *"Tell Jesus."*, 41.
46. PHG, *Memorial*, 6-15, 19.

natural history works, 'and many other works in Zoology.' He was listed as the 'Inventor or Improver' of the aquarium, and cited for his research 'particularly [in] microscopic Zoology.'[47] At age 46, he was somewhat older than the median age of 42 for new Fellows.[48] The voting took place on 5 June 1856, beginning at 4 o'clock. Out of 39 proposed candidates, Gosse was one of fifteen selected, he told his brother,

> & that in a very complimentary way; being the first time my name was proposed; tho' most candidates have to wait over one season at least, & some cannot gain the honour after many trials. It was all done for me, without my taking any personal part in it. My recommendation was very handsomely worded, & was signed by Professor [Thomas] Bell, Prof. [Richard] Owen, Prof. [T. H.] Huxley, & several other names of the highest eminence. There is only one election in the year, & the number of admissions is limited to 15 annually, but there are always double that number of candidates. ...
>
> But what would all this be worth, if I were not a member of another Royal Society, even of that Society of Kings & Priests, for whom Jesus died? This is the true honour, to be an heir of God, & a joint-heir with Christ; & this, through grace, has long been mine. Is it yours, dear William?[49]

-II-

Once there was a widespread belief that 'to be a good wife and mother

---

47. PHG was proposed on 18 Feb. 1856: 'Certificate of a Candidate for Election', Royal Society *Certificates* IX (1840-60), 373. The books by PHG specifically listed under 'Qualifications' were *Naturalist's Rambles*; *Canadian Naturalist*; *Birds of Jamaica*; *Naturalist's Sojourn in Jamaica*; and *Aquarium*.

48. A. V. Hill, 'Age of Election to the Royal Society', *Notes and Records of the Royal Society of London* II (Apr. 1939), 71; A. V. Hill, 'Age of Election to the Royal Society', *Notes and Records of the Royal Society of London* XI (Jan. 1954), 14.

49. PHG-William Gosse, 10 November 1856 (CUL Adv. c. 82.5, 52). PHG had been recommended for election from general knowledge by the Revd James Booth (1806-1878), the mathematician and educator; and from personal knowledge by the zoologist and paleontologist George Busk; marine zoologist J. Gwyn Jeffreys; paleontologist S. P. Pratt, and the scientific editor and librarian E. W. Brayley (besides Bell, Owen and Huxley).

The names of the 15 elected candidates are given in Royal Society *Certificates* IX (1840-60), 373, and printed in [Charles Richard Weld], 'Our Weekly Gossip', *Athenaeum*, 14 June 1856, 747; on Weld: Marchand, *Athenaeum*, 224; and *Proceedings of the Royal Society of London* VIII (1857), 143. The election was noted in *Woolmer's Exeter and Plymouth Gazette* (31 May 1856), 3. In 1868, *Trewman's Exeter Flying Post* reported that 16 Fellows of the Royal Society (PHG among them) lived in Devon at that time (12 Feb. 1868, 5).

is the great earthly business of woman, and if she fails here she fails totally.'[50] It was long before women's liberation, and in those days it was considered useful, proper, and meritorious for women to forge a career in the home. Emily Gosse lived in such a period of history, and thus not surprisingly we find that during the five years after Edmund was born, she devoted nearly all of her time to him and to her husband. The two occupations were based, however, upon an intellectual framework which did not exclude, as we shall see, the assumption of a third one, in which a woman might develop her own talents.

Though the evangelicals with whom the Gosses were associated had only one citizenship, the heavenly, attention necessarily had to be focussed on the earthly life. No one could reach the former without passing through the tribulations and seductions of the latter. The peculiar task of the mother was thus to set her offspring on a heavenly path from which, it was hoped, the child would not deviate; that of the wife was to give encouragement to the godly conduct of her husband.

These were exactly the roles which Emily set out to fill. Having 'given [Edmund] to the Lord' at birth,[51] she was careful that his physical and spiritual health should be protected, and that his diet should be not 'raw apples' but readily digested and wholesome foods.[52] Before Edmund's tastes were definitely formed, she brought him up not on 'nursery rhymes and other Trash', but on 'God's Word and hymns, with good principles, and, above all, with good examples.' No time could be lost, for a child might die at any moment, and then it would be too late.[53]

As Edmund grew, Emily discovered that propounding an educational philosophy was one thing, putting it into practice another. When 'Willy' (as they affectionately called him) was five and could read, she taught him a biblical verse every morning. The lesson was not freely imbibed. He was 'self willed—often says what is not true,' and was not infrequently 'perverse & fretful,' Emily wrote in her diary. Moreover, Emily didn't have enough servants to help her,[54] so she was forced to persevere in

50. EG, *Abraham and his Children*, 73.

51. EG, Diary (under 4 Nov. 1849).

52. EG, 'Letters from the Nursery', *Mother's Friend* VI (Sept.-Oct. 1853), 173, 189; 'A Page for Young Mothers. The Raw Apple', *Mother's Friend* VII (Jan. 1854), 15-16.

53. EG, 'A Page for Young Mothers. More Raw Apples', *Mother's Friend* VII (Feb. 1854), 28-30; 'A Lesson on Prayer', *Mother's Friend* VII (Sept. 1854), 178.

54. For these see EG, Diary (under 13 Dec. 1854, and 27 Aug. 1851); also EG, Diary for 1854 (under Feb. 12, 15).

her exercise of a proper control over her child.[55] She sought 'Scriptural grounds for believing that he is saved,'[56] and soon sensed that her efforts were succeeding. Edmund confessed that 'I love Jesus,'[57] and once, after she had prayed with him, he said to her:

> "Mamma, I've been thinking of something. This world & heaven are like a house, & God & Christ are like the people to whom the house belongs. We are like the things in the house that want to be put to rights, & the wicked people are like the dust that must be swept away."
>
> "Who told you that story Willy?"
>
> "Nobody I thought of it, will it do? it is right, isn't it? Don't you think so? You said when you were praying you hoped Christ would soon come & put us all to rights.["][58]

Not long after Edmund turned 6, Emily wrote a friend that *yes*, it seemed that her son 'was indeed a child of God.'[59]

Emily's relations with her husband were, of course, of a different nature. The couple had a close spiritual bond, with time set aside to pray together,[60] which Emily hoped to augment: 'O bless us together. May we have more communion. May we love thy word & prayer more. ... May our thoughts be more heavenly. May we avoid all foolish talking, & things not becoming saints. May we grow in grace.'[61]

Emily and Philip also had a close spatial bond: during their married life they were never apart for more than a few days.[62] Emily admired her husband, and desired all things which were for his good. As we have seen, she partook as far as she could in Philip's scientific work. She helped him to categorise marine animals sent to them on consignment,[63] encouraged him in his work ('Thank you my darling for your account of the pretty

55. EG, 'The Delicate and Industrious Young Mother', *Mother's Friend* VII (June-July 1854), 110-1, 129-31; 'I Don't Want to be Naughty', *Mother's Friend* IX (Feb. 1856), 34-5; 'Early Control', *Mother's Friend* XI (Jan. 1858), 14-16.

56. EG, Diary (under 10 Nov. 1849).

57. EG, *The Two Tenants*, in PHG and EG, *Narrative Tracts*, No. 56. This tract was published between 10 Feb.-May 1857 (Freeman & Wertheimer-EG, 56).

58. EG, Diary (under 19 Feb. 1855).

59. EG-Anna Shipton, Jan. 1856 (cited in Anna Shipton, *"Tell Jesus."*, 30).

60. PHG-EG, 2 Aug. 1850 (CUL Adv.c.82.5,36); EG-PHG, undated (but filed near an envelope dated 2 July 1850) (CUL Adv.c.82.5,32).

61. EG, Diary (under 30 June 1850).

62. PHG, *Memorial*, 19.

63. PHG-Charles Kingsley, 2 Feb. 1854 (LeBL).

little rotifer[.] I am so glad you have found a new one'),[64] and jointly authored some magazine articles with him.[65]

Additionally, Emily joined in fellowship with Philip among Brethren in London. From at least 1848 she knew George and Charlotte Pearse, and William and Mary Berger,[66] and perhaps from that time John and Robert Howard, and others, at Tottenham.[67] She attended Ellis' Room in Hackney, and probably another unidentified meeting at Clapham, where Philip preached in 1849.[68] Apparently sometime between 1850-4 the Hackney Room was transferred to St. Thomas' Rooms, St. Thomas's Road, Hackney,[69] where the Gosses joined Henry Heath (1815-1900) and R. C. Morgan (1827-1908), both of whom had come up to London in 1848, as well as James Wright,[70] T. Kyffin Freeman, Pearse, Berger, and others.[71] In 1856 yet another location was found, when William Berger purchased the lease of Providence Chapel, Paragon Road, Hackney. Robert Chapman (1803-1902) and Henry Dyer (1821-96), two chief Brethren, occasionally ministered there.[72] By the time Philip left London in 1857, he was active not only at Hackney and Tottenham, but also at assemblies in Henrietta and Collier Streets.[73]

64. EG-PHG, undated [but apparently 2 June 1850] (CUL Adv. c. 82.5, 31).

65. The co-authored articles appeared in 1852 (Freeman & Wertheimer-EG, 60).

66. PHG-EG, 20 Sept. 1848 (CUL Adv. c. 82.5, 26).

67. In 1851, J. Hudson Taylor recalled being with the Robert Howards, who lived in Bruce Grove, Tottenham, 'then a charming and peaceful village, with its colony of members of the Society of Friends' (M[arshall]. B[roomhall]., 'In Loving Memory of Mr. Theodore Howard', *China's Millions* n.s. XXII (Apr. 1914), 51).

68. EG, Diary (under 25 Nov. [1849]).

69. G. West, 'Early Developments', 75, notes that the Hackney group was in existence by 1851, moved by 1854 to St. Thomas's Room and a year later to Paragon Road Chapel.

70. James Ireland Wright of Bristol (1795-1842), initially a Quaker and later Brethren, was the father of James Wright of Bristol (1826-1905), also among Brethren: Arthur T. Pierson, *James Wright of Bristol* (London: James Nisbet & Co., Ltd., 1906), 157-8; Stunt, 'Early Brethren and the Society of Friends', No.3 (1970), 20; West, *From Friends to Brethren*, 258, and *passim*.

71. For these people, events, and associations: M. A. Chaplin-EWG, 28 Nov. 1920 (CUL Add. 7041, 80); (anon), 'Paragon Hall, Hackney, London, 1850-1954', *The Witness* LXXXIV (Dec. 1954), 238; Pierson, *James Wright of Bristol*, 47-8; obituary notice of R. C. Morgan in *The Christian* (5 Nov. 1908), 1447; obituary notice of PHG, *The Christian* (21 Sept. 1888), 887; J. W. Forrest, '"The Missionary Reporter"', *CBRF Journal*, no. 21 (1971), 42fn.20; G. West, 'Early Developments', 75; Rowdon, *Origins*, 163.

72. Beattie, *Brethren. The Story of a Great Recovery*, 80; 'The Late Robert Chapman of Barnstaple', London *North Africa: The Monthly Record of the North Africa Mission* no. 168 (Aug. 1902), 88-9; Ironside, *Historical Sketch*, 162.

73. EWG, Diary for 1857 (under May 31, July 4-5, 12, 19, LeBL). The entry for July 19 reads: 'Papa preached at Collie [*sic*] St', which is presumably Collier Street, for which see William Townsend, *Church & Dissent* (Lewes: Printed at the Sussex Express, [1880]), 29-31. G. West, 'Early Developments', does not mention Henrietta or Collier street sites.

For his part, in private Philip's love was open and impassioned, as strikingly exemplified in two letters from him, written 15 and 16 April 1852. He was in Ilfracombe, she was not far away at St. Marychurch. 'My best beloved Emily,' he began the first letter. He proceeded to describe his trip to that point, adding:

> I have just been reading the 1st Psalm. May our experience, my own beloved, be that of the Godly man, the blessed man there described;— may we delight in the Law of the Lord, & may we bring forth fruit to God in our season. ... O my sweet beloved one, my helper, my comforter, my joy, my love. I wished I could just now throw my arms round your neck & kiss your dear mouth. And kiss my sweet little Willy's sweet little mouth too. ... O my darling imagine that this paper embodies a thousand kisses & a thousand wishes of affection for your own sweet self. ... Farewell for the present, my dearest, remember me much in prayer. The Lord be with you & comfort you ... [signed] Your most affectionate husband ...[74]

'My sweetest Love,' began concluding remarks to a long letter the next day from Philip, in which the word 'love' (or a form of it) appears seven times:

> I have just got your kind, dear & most welcome letter from the Post ... Many thanks for all the love that fills your letter. I do love you more dearly than ever. What a blank wd. the fairest scenes on earth be without your dear presence! ... Now farewell; many kisses & prayers attend you both, my own gentle, beloved wife, & my dear little darling boy. The Lord bless & keep you ... Ever your own faithful, affectionate, devoted, longing lover & husband ... [P.S.] You may be sure I shall devour & kiss your letter many times between this & tomorrow morning.[75]

While caring for others, Emily never forgot her own condition. Indeed, that was to be expected from one who 'habitually walked with an exercised conscience.'[76] Those notebooks and diaries of hers which have survived contain frequent assessments of her spiritual health. In July 1851 Emily observed that 'I am too much taken of with earthly things. I find little time for reading the word, & none for private prayer & meditation.' And a month later, she added: 'Am too apt to blame others for my deadness. ...

74. PHG-EG, 15 Apr. 1852 (CUL Adv.c.82.5,44).
75. PHG-EG, [16 Apr. 1852] (CUL Adv.c.82.5,43).
76. PHG, *Memorial*, 63.

Keep me from evil speaking & harsh judgments, give me zeal, charity
faith, love, devotional habits, self command. May I not be irritable.'[77]
She acted in all matters in the belief that 'God is a hearer of prayer; that
the object of prayer is to receive—what "ye ask in prayer believing, ye
shall receive."'[78]

This solicitude for the small circle of self, husband, and child, gradually
broadened until her energies were concentrated on Christians at large.
Emily began by working in 1851 for the Irish Society (founded 1816),
one of the numerous evangelical organizations intended to 'save' the
Irish from Catholicism.[79] She published four articles on education in
1853-4 in the newly founded *Mother's Friend: A Monthly Magazine, To
Aid and Encourage Those Mothers who Have Little Time to Read, and
Little Money to Spend on Books*, and a well-received book on the same
topic, *Abraham and His Children*, in 1855.[80] At the beginning of 1853
she corresponded with George Müller (1805-1898), of orphan school
fame,[81] later read one of the parts of his *Narrative of Some of the Lord's
Dealings with George Müller*,[82] and passed it on to her friend Anna
Shipton (1815-1901).[83] When Emily's brother Edmund had a stroke in
1855, she unsuccessfully tried to point his thoughts heavenward.[84]

During the last five years of her life, Emily was an evangelist in person
and in print, handing out her own tracts on the railway or omnibus, city
streets or seashore beaches.[85] She began in 1852 with a weekly series
of articles examining, in the Christian typological tradition, portions
of Genesis and Exodus (the series was partly written by her, mostly by

77. EG, Diary, (under July 21, Aug. 27, 1851). Capitalization as in the original.

78. EG, 'A Lesson on Prayer', *Mother's Friend* VII (Sept. 1854), 178, citing Matthew 21:22.

79. EG, Diary (under 24 [Mar.] 1851); on the Irish Society: Brown, *Fathers of the Victorians*, 336, 342.

80. For the brief, though favourable, reviews: *Christian Annotator* I (17 Mar. 1855), 88; *Christian Weekly News*, 13 Mar. 1855, 172; *British Messenger* I (Apr. 1855), 4; *Mother's Friend* VIII (Apr. 1855), 80; *Wells Journal*, 14 Apr. 1855, 4; and *Evangelical Magazine* n.s. XXXIII (June 1855), 338.

81. EG, Diary *for 1854* (under Jan. 23).

82. The complicated bibliographical history of Müller's *Narrative*, published between 1837-1886, is reviewed in Summerton, *'I thanked the Lord and asked for more': George Müller's Life and Work*, 3fn.11.

83. Anna Shipton, *"Tell Jesus."*, 22. Shipton was deeply impressed by the book, with which she had been unfamiliar.

84. EG, Diary (under May 12, 1855).

85. This paragraph is based on, and adds to, Freeman & Wertheimer-EG, 29-35, 46-7; Shipton, *"Tell Jesus."*, 8-9, 42.

Philip).[86] Altogether she published thirty articles during her lifetime, with ten more appearing posthumously in a total of ten different evangelical serials. Simultaneously, she discovered her true literary *métier*: not as a poet or parenting counselor or popular natural history/travel writer, but as an author of religious tracts.

It may well have been Emily's friendship with the Hackney Brethren which led her to use her talents in a way which brought her to public notice. Around 1853, C. B. Berger, Henry Heath, Edward Spencer, George Pearse (Secretary), and William Berger (Treasurer), formed the Evangelical Tract Association. Their aim was to print and circulate gospel tracts to Christians in the immediate area, provided by the Association or by other organisations (such as the successful Religious Tract Society). These were to appeal to the unconverted, and were to be '*narrative* tracts of a decidedly evangelical tone—not omitting this important point—the application of truth *to the heart and conscience*, and not simply the didactic statements which are so common.'[87] Emily began in 1853 by distributing the tracts of others.[88] By March 1854, Emily's first tract, *The Railway Lamp*, was published by the Evangelical Tract Association, and others soon poured out.[89]

Setting aside the characterisation of the Holy Scriptures as the aggregation of only so many separate tracts, the tract industry antedated the mid-Victorian period by about a century, being a product of the Evangelical revival and educational reform movements of the mid-eighteenth century.[90] In 1745, John Wesley had founded an inexpensive publication house, but the modern tract period commenced with that well-known Evangelical Hannah More, whose Cheap Repository Tracts (1794-98)[91] was so successful that it drew numerous imitators. The

86. [P. H. Gosse and Emily Gosse], 'The Master-key', London *Weekly Visitor and Christian Family Reader* III-IV (13 Mar.—5 Nov. 1852). Later that year one of the essays which appeared as 'Sea-side pleasures' in the SPCK publication *Home Friend* is attributed to her in *Life*, 242; Freeman & Wertheimer-EG, 40, 60.

87. (anon), 'Evangelical Tract Association', *Missionary Reporter* I (Mar. 1854), 117-18. Emphasis in the original.

88. EG, Diary for 1849-55 (under Dec. 13, 1854).

89. *Missionary Reporter* I (Mar. 1854),117-18; also (Sept. 1854), 181; Freeman & Wertheimer-EG, 29-35, 45-58.

90. Louis James, *Fiction for the Working Man 1830-1850* (London: Oxford University Press, 1963), 114-28; 'Our Religious Societies', *Christian Work*, 1 Nov. 1865, 495-501, and (1 Feb. 1866), 55-63; Henry Mayhew, *London Labour and the London Poor* (London: George Woodfall and Son, 1851), I: 21, 241-2, 289, 308; 'Tract', *Encyclopaedia Britannica* (11th ed., 1910-11), XXVII: 117-18.

91. On More and the Cheap Repository Tracts: Brown, *Fathers of the Victorians*, 135-55.

non-denominational Religious Tract Society (founded 1799) was the first of these;[92] and by the 1850s there were the Christian Tract Society (Unitarian, 1819), Wesleyan Methodist Tract Society (1822), Friends' Tract Association (1828), Catholic Institute (1838), Baptist Tract Society (1841), Baptist Evangelical Society (1845), Weekly Tract Society for the Religious Instruction of the Labouring Classes (1847), Stirling Tract Enterprise (1848), and Congregational Tract Society (1852). There was also a host of book publishers in 'The Row' (Paternoster Row) in London, who likewise later joined the specialists, including Nisbet; Houlston and Stoneman; Partridge; Jackson and Walford; Groom; and Hatchard, Seeley, and Mackintosh.

All of this led to the observation by the *British and Foreign Evangelical Review* that 'One of the most distinguishing features of the religion of the present time is the distribution of tracts. This century has been the Tract Century.'[93] Tract societies and publishers thrived, with their goal being not capital gain but elevated morality.[94] Here was not only a popular way of 'directing the sinner to the Saviour,'[95] but one in which men and women could participate.[96] Tracts were addressed to virtually everyone virtually everywhere virtually on every topic: to the unconverted and the converted, to those would could or could not read, to infidels, Deists, soldiers, servants, children, railway workers and travellers, prostitutes, theatre goers, 'Papists', workers, the urban or non-urban dweller, hospitals, asylums, penitentiaries, reformatories, ragged schools, and young men's associations.[97] They dealt with all sorts of topics: household and sanitary reform, premillennialism, drunkenness, Sabbath-breaking, revivals, death scenes, and biographies of noted Christians. They appeared in numerous forms: conversational, didactic, narrative, scriptural, historical. They were inserted in letters,[98] distributed by

92. RTS archives have provided material for important studies like Joseph Stubenrauch's 'Silent Preachers in the Age of Ingenuity: Faith, Commerce, and Religious Tracts in Early Nineteenth-Century Britain', *Church History* 80 (Sept. 2011), 547-574.

93. 'Christian Female Authorship', *British and Foreign Evangelical Review* XVIII (Apr. 1869), 239.

94. Joseph Stubenrauch, 'Silent Preachers in the Age of Ingenuity, 555-60.

95. 'Distribution of Religious Tracts', London *Wesleyan-Methodist Magazine* ser. 3, XVII (Apr. 1838), 289.

96. 'There cannot be any person but has, at one time or another, the opportunity presented to him or her of tract distribution—not, it may be, systematically and at set times and places; but casually and at all times' (*British Messenger*, 1 Jan. 1872, 11).

97. London *Bookseller*, 31 May 1867, 357, referring to SPCK books and tracts.

98. PHG enclosed tracts with his correspondence throughout his life. In 1855, for example,

costermongers (street hawkers) and at special depots, even by 'Malays, Hindoos, and Negros. ... Mahometans, or worshippers of Bramah!'[99] They were sold in bulk or given away free of charge, thrown out windows, strewn along the seashore, left in omnibuses, given to criminals about to be hanged. They appeared as hand-bills, in 1, 2, 4, 8, 12, 16, or 20 pages, in 12, 32, or 48 mo. size.

Their sales were remarkable. Edmund Gosse must have thought he was citing an impressive statistic in repeating the claim that 'not less than half a million copies' of his mother's gospel tracts were distributed. In another place, he went even higher, estimating that her *Young Guardsman of the Alma* (pre-Feb. 1855) alone achieved that distribution.[100] The *British and Foreign Evangelical Review* believed that in Britain and the United States by 1869 tracts had been 'circulated by the million.'[101] Impressive claims, indeed—just not high enough. The actual figures are stunning. Four million copies of the 1809 tract *The Dairyman's Daughter*, by the Revd Legh Richmond (1772-1827), were circulated by 1828 in nineteen languages,[102] and twice that number by the end of that century.[103] The Anglican Bishop J. C. Ryle (1816-1900), 'Prince of Tract-Writers',[104] began writing tracts in 1843 and published over 200 of them, aimed principally at middle-class church-goers.[105] *Living or Dead?* sold more than 100,000 copies in a year, and by 1897, 12 million of 'Ryle's Tracts' had been bought (including translations into twelve languages).[106]

he concluded a letter to Philip W. Maclagan, the son-in-law of the recently-deceased George Johnston: 'May I take the liberty, through you as a relation, of expressing my kindly sympathies with Dear Mrs. Johnston in her bereavement. ... Mrs. Gosse begs Mrs. Johnston's kind acceptance of a packet of *her own* Gospel Tracts' (PHG-Maclagan, 6 Nov. 1855, American Philosophical Society Library. This letter is cited in Freeman & Wertheimer-EG, 47fn.88, where it is erroneously described as PHG-William Gosse. Emphasis in the original).

99. H. Mayhew, *London Labour and the London Poor* I: 242.

100. *Life*, 260; *Father and Son*, 1907, 34. On this subject in general, see Freeman & Wertheimer-PHG, 95-8; Freeman & Wertheimer-EG, 30-1.

101. 'Christian Female Authorship', *British and Foreign Evangelical Review*, 239.

102. T. S. Grimshawe, *A Memoir of the Rev. Legh Richmond, A.M.* (London: R.B. Seeley and W. Burnside, 3rd edition, 1828), 298; letter from Benjamin Carvosso, '"The Dairyman's Daughter"', *Wesleyan-Methodist Magazine* ser. 3, XVII (Feb. 1838), 102.

103. Kyle B. Roberts, 'Locating Popular Religion in the Evangelical Tract: The Roots and Routes of "The Dairyman's Daughter"', *Early American Studies* IV (Spring 2006), 236.

104. 'Bishop Ryle, the Prince of Tract Writers' (Stirling: Drummond's Tract Depot, Biographical Series No. 2, 1890).

105. 'John Charles Ryle, D.D. Lord Bishop of Liverpool', in *'The Christian' Portrait Gallery, containing over One Hundred Life-like Illustrations: with Biographic Sketches* (London: Morgan and Scott, [1889]), 320.

106. Bennett Wade Rogers, 'John Charles Ryle: An Intellectual Biography' (Southern Baptist

Within months of launching a 'Tracts for Ireland' series in 1853 written
by himself, the Revd Thomas Millar (d. 1858) of Lurgan, Ireland, had
paid for the free distribution of 500,000 tracts, exhausting his personal
resources.[107] An appeal for new funds reached the United States,[108] and
when the Revival took place in 1859, his tract series was said to have
paved the way for that renewal.[109] In its first ten years, the Weekly Tract
Society distributed 11,218,701 tracts;[110] the Stirling Tract Enterprise of
Peter Drummond circulated over 46 million tracts from its founding
in 1848 to 1881;[111] not to be outdone, between 1834-49, the RTS issued
more than 60 million.[112] Then there was Henry Bewley (1814-1876), the
founder of the Dublin Tract Society. During the course of a lifetime he
issued nearly 500 million tracts in English, French, German, Italian,
Spanish and other languages. They were printed at his sole expense.[113]

What was the purpose of all this activity? Some tracts, such as those
of Hannah More or ones written during years of political and social
agitation, were intended to tamp down revolutionary enthusiasm among
the poor,[114] and others had similar (if implicit) goals. But probably the
majority aimed to spread the gospel message, knowing that one had

Theological Seminary, PhD dissertation, 2015), 59-60; G. R. Balleine, *A History of the Evangelical
Party in the Church of England* (London: Longmans, Green, and Co., 1909), 278.

107. 'Tracts for Ireland', Chicago *Christian Advocate and Journal* (Nov. 24, 1853), 186; A.
Albert Campbell, *Irish Presbyterian Magazines, Past and Present. A Bibliography* (Belfast:
Hugh Greer, 1919), 5.

108. 'Tracts for Ireland', *New York Observer and Chronicle* (Nov. 17, 1853), 362.

109. William Gibson, *The Year of Grace: A History of the Ulster Revival of 1859* (Edinburgh:
Andrew Elliot, 1860), 260. Millar died in a railway crash ('The Late Rev. Thomas Millar', *Belfast
News-Letter*, 12 May 1858, 2).

110. 'The Weekly Tract Society for the Religious Instruction of the Labouring Classes',
Illustrated London News XXX (9 May 1857), 425; 'The Weekly Tract Society', *Wells Journal*
(Wells, Somerset) (9 May 1857), 7.

111. *British Messenger* (Feb. 1882), 32. Drummond's Tract Depository has been called 'the
foremost agency in the production and circulation' of religious tracts (L. E. Elliott-Binns, *Religion
in the Victorian Era*. London: Lutterworth Press, 1936, 3rd impression, 1964, 349). By 1898,
the Enterprise had issued 470 million *publications*, 'more than 24,000 copies a day during 50
years, or, in a ten hours' day, 40 copies a minute for the 50 years' ('Jubilee of the Stirling Tract
Enterprise', Dundee *Evening Telegraph*, 12 Oct. 1898, 2).

112. From 1799-1849 the Religious Tract Society issued nearly half a billion tracts and other
publications, and 33 million publications a year by the 1860s (Joseph Stubenrauch, '"Pleasing
Testimony": Plebeian Readers' Voices in the Tract Magazine', *Victorian Periodicals Review* 52
(Spring 2019), 126).

113. 'Mr. Henry Bewley, of Dublin', *Sunday at Home* XXIII (Oct. 21, 1876), 684 (taken from *The
Christian* obituary. Bewley was 'A "Friend" by birth, and to some extent a "Plymouth Brother" by
conviction"); also Henry Pickering (comp.), *Chief Men Among the Brethren* (London: Pickering
& Inglis, 1918, 1931, 1968), 146.

114. Brown, *Fathers of the Victorians*, 133-55, esp. p. 151.

to be enlightened before the truth became evident. The purpose of an effective tract was educational, in that it 'condenses into a small space great verities, solemn marriages, affectionate invitations, startling and appropriate facts and anecdotes, and brings prominently before the reader, Gethsemane and Calvary, life and death, blessing and cursing, and the retributions of a coming eternity.'[115]

The record of success was mixed. Henry Mayhew (1812-1887), the London investigative journalist, reported that there were poor folk who scoffed at the idea 'of giving people reading before you've taught them to read,' though certain evangelists, whom they praised, did read to them, visit their sick, and give them food.[116] From the point of view of this movement, however, success was not measured in numbers. One true conversion after numerous failed attempts was a triumph over Satan. Who knew when that might occur? Stories of seemingly fortuitous incidents demonstrating the value of tracts were not uncommon. One magazine reported this tale: A disbeliever was given a tract, which he tore up and threw away. In the process, a fragment stuck to his coat. He looked and saw 'God' on one side and 'Eternity' on the other. 'He tried drinking, he tried gambling, to drive those words from his mind, but it was no use; they haunted him wherever he went, and he never had any comfort until he became a Christian.'[117] Another story (known to be true) went this way: A 15-year-old boy was looking through his father's library for a book to read. He spotted a gospel tract, and thought to himself, 'There will be an interesting story at the commencement, and a sermon or moral at the end; I will take the former, and leave the latter for those who like it.' The writing was more engrossing than expected, and he read the whole tract. Through it, and his mother's prayers, he was converted. The boy was James Hudson Taylor, the famous missionary to China.[118]

From the start, most of the tract writers were men and ministers,[119] but Hannah More set an example which was increasingly followed in the decades after her death in 1833. Women evangelists stepped forward

---

115. 'Our Religious Societies', *Christian Work*, 1 Nov. 1865, 496.

116. H. Mayhew, *London Labour and the London Poor* I: 21.

117. (anon), 'The Value of Tracts', *The Evangelist* n.s. II (1868), 91-2.

118. James Hudson Taylor, 'A Retrospect', *China's Millions* XI (May 1886), 53-55; the story is repeated in 'Rev. J. Hudson Taylor', in *'The Christian' Portrait Gallery*, 367-9.

119. This appears to have been the case in the first half of the 19th Century in America (F. Allen Briggs, 'Didactic Literature in America 1825-1850.' Indiana University, PhD dissertation, 1954, 151).

to claim a role not less significant than men.[120] 'It has been said, if the first Reform Bill [of 1832] denied [women] votes, it gave them pens,' noted the *British and Foreign Evangelical Review* in 1869. And although some women used their talents in 'frivolous, and even, alas! in corrupting literature ... the evil has [been] met with the suitable counteractive of "women professing godliness, adorning themselves with the good works' of consecrated and Christianised authorship".'[121]

One of the two notable mid-Victorian female contributors in this field referred to by the *British and Foreign Evangelical Review* was Margaret Fraser Barbour (1823-1892),[122] the Scottish author and poet known as 'Mrs. Barbour of Bonskeid.'[123] A member of the evangelical Free Church in Scotland, she wrote the initially anonymous books *The Way Home* (1856), about the death of her four-and-five-year-old sons in a railway accident, and its sequel, *The Irish Orphan in a Scottish Home* (1866). She was also known as the author of *The Child of the Kingdom* (1862), *The Soul Gatherer* (1863), and 12-page tracts such as 'Who is this King of Glory?', 'Golden Vials Filled', 'Called to the Marriage',[124] and other illustrated tracts.[125]

There was a second notable woman—her name was Emily Gosse.[126] She was a published educational theorist and a poet who stands next to hymn-writer Frances Bevan (1827-1909) as the most prolific of nineteenth century Brethren female writers.[127] Gosse had a special facility as a writer of tracts. In speaking with people and listening to their stories, she took her pen and adopted the tract format to convey gospel truths succinctly,

120. Beth Dickson, 'To Encourage Historians of the Christian Brethren: A Meditation', in Neil T. R. Dickson and Tim Grass, eds., *The Growth of the Brethren Movement: National and International Experiences. Essays in Honour of Harold H. Rowdon* (Bletchley, Milton Keynes: Paternoster, 2006), 29.

121. 'Christian Female Authorship', *British and Foreign Evangelical Review*, 225, 245. The textual citation is to 1 Timothy 2: 10.

122. 'The Late Mrs Barbour of Bonskeid', *Perthshire Advertiser*, 8 Feb. 1892, 3.

123. Robert Ford, *The Harp of Perthshire. A Collection of Songs, Ballads, and other Poetical Pieces Chiefly by Local Authors* (Paisley: Alexander Gardner, 1893), 436-7; William Marshall, *Historic Scenes in Perthshire* (Edinburgh: William Oliphant & Co., 1880), 417-18; Dickson, 'History of the Open Brethren', 50.

124. All tracts were available from Drummond's Tract Depot (*British Messenger*: 1 Feb. 1870, 24; 1 July 1870, 84; 1 Feb. 1872, 24; Jan. 1873, 12). I have not seen any of these tracts.

125. Advertisement, *The Christian*, 13 Apr. 1882, 4.

126. 'Christian Female Authorship', *British and Foreign Evangelical Review*, 239.

127. Neil T. R. Dickson-Wertheimer, 31 Aug. 2021; Dickson, 'Bevan [*née* Shuttleworth], (Emma) Frances', *ODNB*.

directly and dramatically. It became 'her favourite employment,'[128] and the public was responsive. In 1855 she learned that at least two people had been converted by reading her tracts[129] and that tens of thousands of them would be circulated.[130] During her lifetime thirty-one of her tracts were published, and Philip issued thirty-two posthumous ones, for a total of sixty-three.[131]

Emily Gosse's connection with the Evangelical Tract Association in 1854 was accompanied, simultaneously, by similar efforts for others. She composed a series of tracts for the Weekly Tract Society (Philip Gosse spoke in favour of the group's work at its anniversary meeting after her death),[132] and some for the Religious Tract Society, Stirling Tract Enterprise, and Millar of Lurgan's 'Tracts for Ireland'. At least one of her tracts was published in French, and others appeared in Paris in *Archives du Christianisme au dix-neuvième Siècle*, the leading evangelical journal of Frédéric Monod (1794-1863). In this year, too, she began to submit tracts to evangelical periodicals: to Peter Drummond's *British Messenger*; the *Christian Weekly News*; *The British Flag: or, Soldiers' and Sailors Journal*; the Religious Tract Society's *Monthly Messenger*, and several others. It was not long before it was recognized that tracts had inevitably to appear in periodicals, for 'It is more novel, more varied, more attractive to different classes at once, and more likely to find its way among the prejudiced.'[133]

Unlike Hannah More's tracts, Emily's were directed solely towards the salvation of souls, most particularly those of the poor. She had experienced their lot, and could speak to their hearts. Moreover, having an 'eminently practical' character, the ability to put others at ease and to speak in a language which they could understand,[134] she did not talk down to them or avoid earthly subjects. 'Her own purse-strings were

---

128. PHG, *Memorial*, 14-15.

129. PHG, *Memorial*, 3.

130. EG, Diary (under 10 Nov. 1855).

131. Freeman & Wertheimer-EG, 32.

132. The ninth anniversary meeting took place at Exeter Hall on 7 May 1857 ('The Weekly Tract Society for the Religious Instruction of the Labouring Classes', *Illustrated London News* XXX, 9 May 1857, 425); also *Wells Journal* (Wells, Somerset), 9 May 1857, 7.

133. G. H. Davis, 'Tracts—Their Production and Distribution', *The Revival* V (5 Oct. 1861), 109-10.

134. PHG, *Memorial*, 39, 24-5, 21; Shipton, *"Tell Jesus."*, 10.

always very loosely tied,' Philip attested, 'but, not satisfied with this, she was diligent and successful in appealing to the bounty of others.'[135]

The message which Emily imparted to simple people was itself simple, an elaboration in different guises of six often-quoted texts. She began with the innate and unavoidably sinful nature of man, inherited from Adam, and then turned to John 3: 3: 'Except a man be born again, he cannot see the kingdom of God.' But how does one gain a new life? One cannot save oneself;[136] it is not enough to do good deeds, or to live a moral and upright life.[137] There is only one 'Pass Ticket'[138] to eternity, and yet 'there is not a man upon earth rich enough to purchase' it.[139] The wise and the wealthy have no priority over the poor, uncouth, and ignorant:[140] they all stand in the same queue. When all come to the window, each has only to witness that he believes.[141] Believes what? 'That Christ Jesus came into the world to save sinners' (1 Timothy 1: 15); 'Believe on the Lord Jesus Christ, and thou shalt be saved, and thy house' (Acts 16: 31). The ticket, in other words, costs nothing; it is free for the asking, if sincerely requested. Once one recognizes one's sinfulness, and that (in the verse which Emily delighted to quote)[142] 'the blood of Jesus Christ his Son cleanseth us from all sin' (1 John 1: 7), then one 'hath everlasting life, and shall not come into condemnation; but is passed from death unto life' (John 5: 24).

Then, and only then, can one expect merciful treatment from God.[143] The decision must be made immediately: 'The time is short. The work is great. The labourers are few. The enemy is busy. Opportunities soon pass away for ever.'[144] Once one believes, one may 'tremble on the Rock, [but] the Rock does not tremble under' him or her.[145] That is, one need not fear being unworthy of being saved, for the Word promises the contrary: 'him that cometh to me I will in no wise cast out' (John 6: 37).

In carrying this gospel message, Emily was always careful to use

---

135. PHG, *Memorial*, 40.
136. EG, *The Pilgrim to St. Patrick's Well* (GT31).
137. EG, *The Christian Soldier* (GT5), *The King and the Prince* (GT34), and others.
138. EG, *The Pass Ticket* (GT32).
139. EG, *The Railway Ticket* (GT1).
140. EG, *The King's Daughter* (GT48); *The Bathing Woman and her Visitor* (GT54).
141. EG, *The Two Maniacs* (GT10); *The Scattered Tracts* (GT42).
142. PHG, *Memorial*, 26, 38-9fn.
143. EG, *The Suicide* (GT16).
144. EG, *The Faithful Nurse* (GT14).
145. EG, *The Old Soldier's Widow* (GT24).

episodes which were meaningful to her audience. They were, on the whole, true to life because derived from it.[146] The metaphors and images, too, struck home to English people in an industrial society. And if one could not read them, one could be read to.[147] Over and over again, Emily had to emphasize that there was actually something outside of the cash-nexus society, an utterly free gift.[148] While the Crimean War was being fought, she addressed tracts to soldiers and sailors; death and sickness, constant facts of life, were turned to account; drunkenness, the attachment to Mammon, the 'errors' of the 'Papists', were denounced. The railway age provided another image, while the new rage for the seashore was the backdrop of yet further lessons. And all the while, in relating conversion experiences, Emily urged others to make haste and look to life eternal.

That Emily's tracts accomplished their goal is borne out not only by their high circulation, which was a sign that they were long-standing favourites in the evangelical world (this was especially so after they were taken over by Morgan and Chase, publishers of *The Revival*).[149] Ever since Emily had begun to work in this genre she had hoped that they would be the source of conversions and inspiration to the Saints. As she wrote in her diary:

> Be a lamp to the feet of those who read.
> Be the Good Physician to their souls.
> Teach them that the Blood of J. cleanseth one.
> May they look unto thee & be saved.
> May the prodigal arise & return to thee.
> May they accept thy freely given righteousness.
> May they cry the Lord remember me.
> In thee may the dead be made alive.
> May they be ready for thy coming.
> May the sick & dying find life & healing.[150]

It was not long after her first tracts appeared that she began to get feedback on them. Before the end of 1855, she heard that her tracts had

---

146. PHG, *Memorial*, 15; *The Two Maniacs* (GT10) is an example of an unrealistic story.

147. EG, *The Power of the Word* (GT30).

148. EG, *The Young Guardsman of the Alma* (GT7); *The Consumptive Deathbed* (GT17), *Is Christ Willing?* (GT18), *The Cure for Cholera* (GT50); also GT1-4, 15, and others.

149. Freeman & Wertheimer-PHG, 95-8; and for favourable notices of the Gosse tracts: *Bible-Reader's Journal* No. 10 (1 Oct. 1859), 232, and *Wesleyan Times* (cited in *The Revival* X (4 Feb. 1864), 80).

150. EG, Diary (under 13 Dec. 1854; and for the quotation, under 21 Feb. 1855).

produced not only the two conversions previously mentioned, but three others had followed after personal appeals to young people.[151] A man called 'Badger Joe', a former badger-baiter and cock-fighter, was given a 'new life' after reading *Thomas Winter's Stray Sheep*;[152] another was saved by *The Eleventh Hour*, a tract which had been given out three years earlier;[153] Anna Shipton, the noted evangelical writer, was led to accept Jesus as her personal Saviour after first meeting Emily at Ilfracombe in the summer of 1855.[154] Recall that Emily herself was an industrious distributor of her own tracts, which were said to be 'far superior to almost any.'[155] Emily's tracts were used at mothers' meetings and Sunday schools,[156] given away with copies of *The Revival*, Richard Weaver's and the Blackdown tracts, or similar evangelistic works.[157]

Ten years after Emily died, Morgan and Chase reported that there was still a constant demand for her tracts.[158] Over the years, thirteen different publishers issued her individual tracts, some (as mentioned) appeared in French translation and at least one in America (in 1901).[159] From 1859-65, 7 million of her tracts were distributed by Morgan and Chase alone,[160] and they remained in print until at least 1893.[161] In 1864 they were brought together in a single volume which achieved circulation

151. PHG, *Memorial*, 3; Shipton, *"Tell Jesus."*, 30. An 1861 advertisement for the Gosse *Gospel Narrative Tracts* noted: 'These Tracts have been blessed to the conversion of many persons' (R. C. Morgan, *The Life of Richard Weaver, the Converted Collier*. London: Morgan and Chase, 1861, ads at back of book). It is not known if that reference is separate from, or included in, other similar statements.

152. 'Death of Man Converted by Emily Gosse's "Stray Sheep"', *The Revival* X (18 Feb. 1864), 101.

153. W. J. Lewis, 'Gospel Narrative Tracts', *The Revival* VIII (26 Mar. 1863), 155.

154. Shipton, *"Tell Jesus."*, 2, 5ff.

155. This remark was made by 'A lady who is largely occupied in the Lord's work, in Paris', and appears on the paper cover copy, back cover, of the first edition of Shipton's *"Tell Jesus."* ([1863]).

156. Lewis, 'Gospel Narrative Tracts', 155.

157. 'On Tract Distributing', *The Revival* XIII (5 Oct. 1865), 207; *Revival* XIII (17 Aug. 1865), 108. Gosse tracts were among the recommended tracts to be distributed by a proposed fund offering grants for that purpose ('Fund for the Supply of Tracts', *The Christian*, 28 Mar. 1872, 12).

158. *The Revival* XVI (10 Oct. 1867), 571.

159. Freeman & Wertheimer-EG, 63.

160. *Christian Work*, 1 Feb. 1866, 63. *Life*, 260, and *Father and Son*, 1907, 34, give incorrect information for EG's tract circulation: Freeman & Wertheimer-PHG, 97, and Freeman & Wertheimer-EG, 33, 48.

161. *The Christian* (6 July 1893), 31.

in England, Canada, and the United States.[162] It was still being sold in 1882.[163]

-III-

It is possible that Emily may have attained the reputation of J. C. Ryle as a composer of tracts had she not noticed that small lump in her breast in April 1856 which was diagnosed as cancer. 'How very happy we are!' she had often remarked to her husband before then: 'surely this cannot last!'[164]

Having returned from Tenby to London in October 1856, Emily resumed her treatment at Dr Fell's, moving to Pimlico next to his office with her son. During the previous month, she had applied the prescribed ointment. It made her ill and produced 'intense aching', leading to a time of 'much suffering'.[165] Recognizing that after five months not much had been achieved, on October 11 Dr Fell opted for excision of the tumour. This is how Philip described what happened:

> The whole surface of the left breast, an area of four inches in diameter, was wetted with nitric acid ... The smart was very trying, and continued for several hours augmenting; the effect being to blister and destroy the whole skin, exactly as if a severe burn had taken place.
>
> On the succeeding day, the doctor proceeded to incise the tumour, in order that it might be penetrated by the peculiar medicament which he used for its separation. With the scalpel he drew, on the surface of the new exposed flesh, a series of parallel scratches, about half an inch apart, reaching from top to bottom. When these were made, a plaister of a purple mucilaginous substance was spread over the whole. The next day, on renewing this plaister, the scalpel was passed again along the scratches, deepening them a very little; and a fresh plaister was applied. By the daily repetition of this operation, the scratches were in a few days deepened into long parallel cuts or scores, into which narrow strips of linen rag, covered with purple mucilage, were pressed ... Every

162. PHG and EG, *Narrative Tracts*, [1864]) and later editions (the tracts in volume form are described in Freeman & Wertheimer-PHG, 74-77, and Freeman & Wertheimer-EG, 41-46). PHG had a single copy in his library (*Sandhurst Catalogue*, item #473).

163. Advertisement, *The Christian*, 22 June 1882, 31; Freeman & Wertheimer-EG, 43.

164. EG as quoted in PHG, *Memorial*, 5.

165. PHG, *Memorial*, 20.

day these strips of rags were renewed, and the scores were made deeper and deeper.

The effect of this application was very distressing. In about an hour after its renewal every morning, the breast began to be the seat of an aching, piercing pain, under which my beloved sufferer was fain to wander up and down her narrow room, leaning now and then her head upon the mantel-piece or against the wall, unable from the agony to lie, sit, or stand. ... suffering never *ceased* from the beginning of the operation, till her spirit was freed from the worn-out body.

... The only sleep she obtained ... was induced by opiates.[166] We were very reluctant to use them, but Dr. F— urged them upon my beloved as absolutely necessary ...

When the incisions had reached the depth of about an inch and a quarter, the operator announced that he had reached the bottom of the cancer. He now scored no more, but applied a "girdle," or annular plaister, around the line where the killed tumour adjoined the living flesh ... It was nearly four weeks after the removal of the skin that the "girdle" was first put on, and two weeks more before the tumour came away. ... At length, on Sunday, the 23d of November, to our delight, the great insensible tumour fell out of its cavity, hanging only by a slender fleshy thread, which presently yielded, and the breast was relieved of its load ...

There it lay on the table, a hard and solid block of black substance ... And then on the breast of my beloved sufferer was the corresponding cavity, raw and partly lined with pus, but presenting an apparently healthy appearance. ... This was the point to which our hopes had been directed for six weeks past ...[167]

But Fell soon found more cancerous tissue. It, too, required extraction, and the painful process was repeated again during four more weeks of 'grinding, wearing agony.' During that time, among all her 'sighs and moans', Philip 'never heard her utter a single murmuring word; not an expression, not a look, that intimated a doubt of the loving-kindness of the Lord.' Given the circumstances, one would understand Emily suspending her evangelistic labours—it's just, that's not what she did.

166. The use of opiates 'to assuage their pains [*sic*] and procure sleep' was not unusual among Dr Fell's patients (*Report of the Surgical Staff of the Middlesex Hospital*, 34).
167. PHG, *Memorial*, 28-34. Emphasis in the original.

Even in Dr Fell's crowded waiting room, she moved like a 'ministering angel' among her fellow-sufferers, strangers all, with her 'kind winning smile,' as she offered them 'one of her own Gospel Tracts.' Some were scornful; some responsive; for yet other patients, who were not only ill but poor, she tried to ameliorate their physical circumstances with her own money, or that of others.[168]

On Monday, 22 December, after the second tumour had been sloughed off, Fell met with Emily. Philip was not present when Emily got the report, but noted what happened:

> [Dr Fell said:] "Mrs. Gosse, I'm very sorry for this. I shall have to take out another piece under the arm."
>
> [Emily's] heart sank at this announcement, but she replied, "And what then, Doctor?"
>
> "Then I must treat this other part on the inner side of the breast."
>
> "But how do you account for this spreading of the disease beyond the part you have all along been dealing with?"
>
> "Oh, 'tis in your blood."[169]

Emily declined to contemplate a third or fourth process. To husband and wife, it was obvious that Fell's 'secret medicament' was not working.

Philip spoke 'most gratefully' of the 'personal kindness and attention to my beloved sufferer' of the physician whom he designated 'Dr. F—'.[170] His blunt opinion, however, was that notwithstanding those intentions, Fell's cure probably hastened his wife's death.[171] Others were less forgiving. In a lecture delivered in London at the time, Thomas Spencer Wells (1818-1897), who later served as surgeon to Queen Victoria, referred to Fell as '*Docteur Noir*'. The *Memorial of the Last Days on Earth of Emily Gosse*, wrote Wells, was a 'harrowing narrative of useless torture.'[172] Similarly Emily Gosse's 'melancholy case', a medical journal remarked, showed

---

168. PHG, *Memorial*, 37-9.

169. PHG, *Memorial*, 44-5, where these words are in a single paragraph. They are formatted here as a dialogue, without changing the words.

170. PHG, *Memorial*, 46.

171. PHG, *Memorial*, 46fn., 10, 12. That the surgical treatment was preferable to Fell's therapy was also the judgment of *The Lancet*, 13 June 1857, 606-7.

172. The lecture by T. Spencer Wells delivered on 8 July 1857 was published under his name as *Cancer Cures and Cancer Curers* (London: John Churchill, 1860). For these remarks, see pp. [2], 55. In reviewing *Cancer Cures*, the *Leicestershire Mercury*, 28 July 1860, 2, referring specifically to *Memorial*, observed: 'Some of the cases given are truly harrowing in their details.'

'the baselessness of this man's pretensions, as a painless and effectual cancer-curer.'[173]

Did Dr Fell deserve his reputation as a charlatan? In his self-promoting conduct, he was certainly his own worst enemy.[174] His claims were bogus: there was no unique cure, no Native-American cancer treatment, no knifeless therapy and no painless procedure. He initially lied about the chemical formula of his medicament. In fact, Fell's zinc-chloride paste therapy had been used in chemosurgery to treat accessible tumors since 1824, and continued thereafter. Ironically the composition of Fell's paste was identical to one used 100 years later by the American skin cancer researcher and surgeon Frederic E. Mohs (1910-2002), even if it was not a 'direct anticipation' of his method.

Facing a grim future, the couple now 'committed the matter to our sympathising Lord in prayer.'[175] No earthly act could intercede to save Emily from an immediate future of agony—they knew that. Yet they were not less convinced that a heavenly state of mind promised a way through the present into the redemptive future. All his life Philip lived by the motto *nil desperandum*[176]—*Do not despair!* A person of faith is never alone. What Emily was enduring was part of a plan, of that the couple had no doubt. What that plan was, they had no knowledge. They could only trust. And so Emily returned to 58 Huntingdon Street in Islington at the end of December to be cared for by the homoeopathic physician, John Epps (1805-1869), an acquaintance of early Brethren, including G. V. Wigram.[177] Epps held out no possibility of a removal of the disease. All he could do was try to temper the pain. Emily's paroxysms of coughing continued.[178] In the words of Anna Shipton, 'No hope of recovery was held forth, but no probability of a speedy decease was anticipated.'[179]

It had now become, as Philip recalled,

---

173. Review of T. Spencer Wells, *On Cancer Cures and Cancer Curers*, in W. H. Ranking and C. B. Radcliffe (eds.), *The Half-Yearly Abstract of the Medical Sciences* XXXI (Jan.-June 1860), 327.

174. This paragraph is based on Charles DePaolo, 'Frederic E. Mohs, MD, and the history of zinc chloride', *Clinics in Dermatology* 36 (2018), 568-575, which places Dr Fell in a medical tradition spanning the early 19th Century to Frederic Mohs.

175. PHG, *Memorial*, 46.

176. Cited by PHG, 'Contributions to the History of the Rotifera, or Wheel Animalcules. II. The Floscules (*Floscularia*)', *Popular Science Review* I (Jan. 1862), 160; 'Reminiscences', II: 212.

177. Wertheimer, *Identification*, 7.

178. PHG, *Memorial*, 50-1.

179. Shipton, *"Tell Jesus."*, 76.

evident to us both, that the severance of that happy union, which, without a single interruption of its peace and love, had been vouchsafed to us for the last eight years, was an event not very far from us. We looked it in the face; we well knew no blessing, no strength, was to be gained by concealing it from ourselves or from each other, and we talked of it freely. To me the prospect was dark indeed; but to her death had no terrors. Our dear child she was able to leave in the hands of that loving Lord, for whom she had trained him from earliest infancy, and to whose tender care she now, in the confidence of faith, committed him; but her loving heart deeply tasted the bitterness of the cup which she saw I should soon have to drink. It was but a day or two before her departure that she said with peculiar emphasis, dwelling on each precious word, now embalmed in my inmost heart: "I love *you*,—better than on my wedding-day—better than when I was taken ill—better than when I came home from Pimlico."

At another time she said, "My beloved Henry, gladly would I remain, if such were the Lord's will, and be your companion for the rest of your pilgrimage!"[180]

Once back at Islington, the worst of the pain had ended. It never disappeared. Yet she did not turn from her evangelistic work: 'Travelling one day by rail, I had provided a good supply of tracts, and gave them round,' she wrote in one of her posthumously published tracts.[181] Nor was there any reduction in her enjoyment of prophetic studies. Philip read to her the Revd E. B. Elliott's Warburton Lectures, which had appeared several months earlier.[182] In it, the famed author of *Horae Apocalypticae* [*Hours with the Apocalypse*] attempted to prove the correctness of the historical school of prophecy's identification of Rome with the Antichrist.[183] Other than the Bible, it was Emily's last book.[184]

180. PHG, *Memorial*, 52-3. Emphasis in the original.

181. EG, 'The Sceptical Traveller', *Narrative Tracts*, no. 59. This tract was part of the Gosse 'Gospel Narrative Tracts' series, and was published posthumously by PHG in 1861 as an individual leaflet and then in 1864 in collected book form (Freeman & Wertheimer-EG, 58).

182. Elliott published a volume of Warburton (also rendered 'Warburtonian') Lectures for 1849-51 (*Manchester Courier*, 10 Dec. 1853, 2) and one for 1849-53 ('List of New Works', London *Christian Annotator* III, 1 Mar. 1856, 87). Presumably it was the latter edition which PHG read to Emily (*Memorial*, 57).

183. E. B. Elliott, *Warburtonian Lectures, preached in Lincoln's-Inn Chapel, in the Winters from 1849 to 1853* (reviewed in London *Literary Churchman* II (9 Aug. 1856), 316-18). Froom incorrectly refers to this as Elliott's final work on prophecy (Froom, *Prophetic Faith* III: 717).

184. PHG, *Memorial*, 57-73, *passim*.

Meanwhile with no family to turn to for financial support, no salary from a job, no steady source of income, Philip had committed in the previous November to lecturing on the aquarium at the nearby Islington Literary and Scientific Society.[185] Whether or not he did so is not known.

On Saturday, 7 February aware of what was before her, Emily spoke of the past of which she was a part and the future which would unfold without her. With Philip, she reviewed their married life and 'the principles by which we have striven to walk'; she 'expressed her wishes concerning Willy,'[186] to whom she gave the large Oxford Bible which she had received from Jonathan Elford.[187] What earthly service was left? With a servant at her bedside and a pile of tracts and copies of the *British Messenger* on the table, they folded and addressed them for distribution, just as she had been doing before, and ignored the end.[188]

At her bedside, Philip hovered over his wife. He was preparing to return his beloved 'into the hand of Him, who for a season had lent her to me, and who now reclaimed his loan.'[189] For some time, Philip had been recording Emily's dying words. He continued doing so to the very last moment:

> After a while, she said, "I shall walk with Him in white. Won't you take your lamb, & walk with me?" The last sentence she repeated two or three times, as she saw that I did not readily catch her meaning; but I believe she alluded to Willy, or else to herself, for "My lamb!" was one of the terms of endearment which I had habitually used to her, especially in these her last sufferings. Her speech was now so thick that a great deal was unintelligible; only a sentence now & then could be made out.[190]
>
> Presently she said;—"'Tis a pleasant way:—more pleasant than when I could not pray for what would make you unhappy:"—meaning doubtless her departure.

185. Advertisement, London *Daily News*, 3 Nov. 1856, 1.

186. PHG, *Memorial*, 68.

187. CUL Add. 7035/II/20. Death-bed visits by children of evangelical families were used for edification, repentance and/or conversion (Henry D. Rack, 'Evangelical Endings: Death-Beds in Evangelical Biography', *Bulletin of the John Rylands University Library*, 74 (1992), 50).

188. PHG, *Memorial*, 73.

189. PHG, *Memorial*, 76.

190. I have demonstrated elsewhere that 'Documents fortify the case that Edmund's account [in *Father and* Son] of the deathbed scene is fiction' (Wertheimer, *Son and Father*, 61-63).

She looked on us hanging over her, & said two or three times,—"One family", & then added "One song." "One family; one song."[191]

About ¼ to 11 [p.m. on 9 February], I spoke of the freeness of gospel grace, which she had proclaimed so fully in her Tracts; when she said, "I see it."

"See what, love?" I asked.

"I see the freeness of gospel grace that I have set before others; but in extreme weakness;—extreme weakness of body."

... About 11 she got into a heavy doze, breathing laboriously with opened mouth. I lay down for three quarters of an hour, the girls still hanging over her. When I got up, they told me she had not uttered a word except once, "Papa!" The breathing was feebler, with less of phlegm. She again breathed, "Papa!" which was the last word she uttered. Her eyes became fixed, & she was evidently unconscious, till exactly at 1 [a.m., 10 February], she breathed a long expiration, & ceased. I laid her dear head, wh. for an hour had been on my arm, on the pillow, closed her eyes; and kneeling around the bed gave thanks amidst sobs & tears, for her peaceful release.[192]

Emily Gosse died on 10 February 1857.[193] Three days later she was buried in Abney Park cemetery in Hackney: 'they took up the body and buried it, and went and told Jesus.'[194] Some fifteen years earlier, leading Brethren had purchased a section of the cemetery,[195] and perhaps the

---

191. In EG, 'A Happy Family', *Gosse's Gospel Tract* no. 521 (published posthumously in 1861, and in book form in 1864; Freeman & Wertheimer-EG, 45, 58, 64), the description of a family converted to true belief is described. Being part of such a family also means accepting the invitation of 'the King of Glory to become His son and heir'.

192. 'Dying Words of my Emily', a sheet of paper in PHG's holograph (CUL Adv. c. 82.5, 53). All of these words appear, usually verbatim but sometimes with minor though significant changes (as the first one below), in *Memorial*. Others are quoted, usually misleadingly, in *Father and Son*.

193. The date is incorrectly given as 9 February in *Life*, 270; EWG, 'Gosse, Emily', *DNB* XXII (1890), 258; Anna Shipton, *"Tell Jesus."*, 86; Stageman, *Bibliography of the First Editions of Philip Henry Gosse*, 2, and other works which rely on those sources. The correct date is 10 February (letter, R. Boyd-D. Wertheimer, 9 Nov. 1973; photograph of the tombstone in Boyd, *Emily Gosse*, 62; Freeman & Wertheimer-EG, 37fn.59). Obituary or death notices for EG in *Bath Express*, 14 Feb. 1857, 5; *Islington Gazette*, 14 Feb. 1857, 1; *Clifton Chronicle*, 18 Feb. 1857; *British Messenger*, Mar. 1857, 23.

194. Matthew 14:12, cited in Shipton, *"Tell Jesus."*, 85.

195. Rowdon, *Origins*, 162. Among other Brethren (or once-affiliated Brethren) known to have been buried there are Matthew Habershon, the architect and student of prophecy (*DNB*); Robert Howard (who had married Philip and Emily) (*A Brief Record of the Last Days of Robert Howard* (Printed for private circulation, 1871), 22); Michael Laseron (Dunlop, *Gospel Triumphs Among the Jews*, 340); and Samuel Morley (*DNB*).

Gosses made use of it. Her 7-year-old son's recollection was that she had been laid to rest in the cemetery's 'remotest corner'.[196] During a visit there half-a-century ago as these words are being written, I followed that description but could not locate the spot. The late Robert Boyd did. Proceeding along Little Elm Walk—but not close to any corner—the independent Brethren researcher and biographer of Emily reached the nearly five-foot-high headstone. It proclaims: 'The Dust of Emily Gosse ... awaits here the morning of the FIRST RESURRECTION.'[197]

Four months after Emily's death, Dr Fell's 100-page *Treatise on Cancer, and Its Treatment* appeared in London under the prestigious imprint of the medical publisher John Churchill.[198] A ninth edition of his *Cancer and External Tumours: Their Treatment Without the Knife* was advertised for sale in 1878.[199]

196. *Life*, 270.
197. So reads, in part, the inscription on her tombstone (Boyd, *Emily Gosse*, 62, 63fn.19).
198. 'Ready next week', *Illustrated London News* XXX (30 May 1857), 526.
199. London *Daily* Telegraph, 24 May 1878, 4.

CHAPTER SEVEN

1857

'Is It Not Possible—
I Do Not Ask For More'

-I-

MONDAY, FEBRUARY 16, 1857: 'WENT INTO MOURNING.' Those were the words William Gosse entered in his diary concerning his 'departed sister Emily,' about whom he had first heard one week earlier. A few days later William received four photographs of Emily from his brother, with the request that they be used as the basis for a portrait.[1] Only two images of Emily existed at that time: one was in the possession of a distant relation in America, the other dated from childhood.[2] Philip had tried to obtain up-to-date images of Emily after her breast cancer diagnosis in the summer of 1856, when they went to Maull and Polyblank in London, not far from the Monument to the Great Fire. The 'eminent photographers' were in the process of publishing *Photographic Portraits of Living Celebrities*, having just issued images for Professor Richard Owen and the Right Hon. T. B. Macaulay.[3] The Gosses waited there several hours to no avail, and then left.

'This was a subject of regret to her,' Philip recalled, 'for our little boy's sake; she would have liked him to possess some means of keeping in remembrance his mother's features; she knew they could never fade

1. William Gosse, Diary (under 19 Feb. 1857).
2. The latter portrait, taken c. 1831, was seen in the Family Collection. It was reproduced in the Folio Society edition of *Father and Son* (London, 1972), and Boyd, *Emily Gosse*.
3. Advertisements, London *Daily News* (31 May 1856, 8; 11 July 1856, 8).

from my memory.'[4] Thus Philip ended up commissioning photographs of Emily several days before she died. 'The circumstances were almost as unfavourable as they well could be,' he acknowledged, 'yet the resemblances produced, especially the first of two photographs, are to me beyond all price.' By early April, William's work was completed.[5]

Hardly a moment was available for Philip to recover from the shock. Here was the conundrum: because Emily and Philip were 'never parted, in life or death,'[6] he was now alone, yet not alone. And more: 'Himself Hath Done It.' The words from this anonymous hymn had been selected by Philip as the epigraph to his memoir of Emily to confirm that, yes, in another sense too, though alone, he could never be alone:

> "Himself hath done it."—Yes, although severe
> May seem the stroke, and bitter be the cup,
> 'Tis his own hand that holds it, and I know
> He'll give me grace to drink it meekly up. ...
>
> "Himself hath done it."—Then I fain would say,
> "Thy will in all things evermore be done;"
> E'en though that will remove whom best I love,
> While Jesus lives, I cannot be alone.[7]

-II-

Ten days after the burial of his wife, Philip was lecturing in Edinburgh. For Victorian widowers, a month (including a week of isolation for the family) was a common length of time for mourning.[8] Every circumstance is different. Gosse needed to supplement his income while preserving savings of £1,000 or £1,500,[9] and it may have been at this time that Gosse

---

4. PHG, *Memorial*, 66-7.

5. PHG, *Memorial*, 67. Two of the photographs mentioned are at Cambridge (CUL Adv. c. 82.5, 50-1).

6. 2 Samuel 1: 23.

7. PHG, *Memorial*, 81-2. PHG may well not have known the identity of the anonymous English hymn writer, Christina Forsyth (1825-1859). See John Julian, *A Dictionary of Hymnology: Setting forth the Origin and History of Christian Hymns of all Ages and Nations* (London: John Murray, revised ed., 1907), 199, 382, and C[hristina]. F[orsyth]., *Hymns* (London: Wertheim, Macintosh, and Hunt, 1858), 1-2. The hymn was in print from at least 1855 (Sutton-in-Ashfield, Nottinghamshire *Original Methodists' Record* II (Jan. 1855), 282), and has continued to be unattributed (as in Boyd, *Emily Gosse*, 65-7).

8. Judith Flanders, *Inside the Victorian Home: A Portrait of Domestic Life in Victorian England* (New York: W.W. Norton & Co., 2004), 377.

9. PHG-EWG, 22 February 1870 (CUL Add. 7041, 33).

published his first article in the *London Quarterly Review*.[10] Moreover, he had accepted invitations the previous autumn[11] to deliver natural history lectures in Scotland, the North of England, and the Midland counties.[12] The lectures Gosse was to have given at the Literary and Philosophical Society of Newcastle-upon-Tyne in February were postponed to March 'In consequence of a Domestic Bereavement,' advised a newspaper advertisement.[13] While his father was away, Edmund stayed with a cousin, Anne Morgan (b. 1811), of Clifton.[14] Mrs Morgan had come to

10. *Wellesley Index* IV,385, and index, attributes four *London Quarterly Review* articles appearing between Apr. 1857–Jan. 1865 to PHG (none of these are cited in Freeman & Wertheimer-PHG). *Wellesley Index* cites *LQR* ser. 2, XVI, Apr. 1891, 26 as its source: '... contributing articles to the pages of this Review, with whose editor, five-and-twenty years ago, he had some friendly acquaintance.' The editor might have been J. H. Rigg (1821-1909), a sub-editor at the publication during those years (*Wellesley Index* IV,378-9). Rigg, a President of the Wesleyan Conference, was (like PHG) a member of the Victoria Institute (*JTVI* 41, 1909, 3). Two of the articles attributed to PHG ('Marine Aquarium—Sea Anemones', *LQR* VIII, Apr. 1857; 'The Aquarian Naturalist', *LQR* XII, Apr. 1859) are questionable. They spell Robert Warington's name 'Warrington', a common misspelling at the time but one *not* made by PHG. In addition, the latter article uses the word 'aquariist', which does not appear in any known PHG MS or in any of his published books (the word does appear several times in T. Rymer Jones' *Aquarian Naturalist*, 1858. *OED* 2ed. gives the first usage of 'aquariist' as 1893).

11. The four lectures at the Edinburgh Philosophical Institution were announced in the Edinburgh *Caledonian Mercury* (3 Oct. 1856, 3), and the ones at the Paisley Artizans' Institution in the *Paisley Herald and Renfrewshire Advertiser* (13 Dec. 1856, 4).

12. How PHG selected the sites of his lectures; where he stayed during them; or whether while delivering those lectures he communed with Brethren, are among the questions I have been unable to answer regarding these lectures. No information exists concerning the first issue. All that I have seen concerning the second is an envelope addressed to him in an unknown hand to 'Miss Preston, 6 South Nelson St., Edinburgh', where he was then lecturing (EWG-PHG, 27 Feb. 1857, CUL Add. 7027, 20a & 20b). I have no information on Miss Preston. Finally, given that PHG had sought out Brethren ever since his first contact with them in 1843—in Jamaica, London, Ilfracombe (1852), Tenby (possibly in 1854 and certainly in 1856, as mentioned), and later at St. Marychurch/Torquay—did he also associate with Brethren during his lecturing travels? According to Dr Neil Dickson, 'The pivot date for the Brethren in Scotland is 1859, the year of evangelical revivals' (Dickson-Wertheimer, 15 Mar. 2022). Yet Dr Dickson acknowledges the possibility of a Brethren presence prior to that year. See the case of Richard Alexander of Edinburgh, imprisoned in 1854 for refusing to take an oath at trial because of his Brethren beliefs (Glasgow *North British Daily Mail*, 19 Jan. 1854, 4; *Glasgow Herald*, 20 Jan. 1854, 6). Also, in 1866, the forger John Henry Greatrex was thought to have moved to Glasgow in an indeterminate 'several years ago'. He was said to have been 'an active member' of the Brethren there ('How Greatrex Was Apprehended. His Career in New York', *Glasgow Herald*, 18 Dec. 1866, 2).

13. Advertisement, *Newcastle Journal* (14 Feb. 1857), 1. It's possible that the postponement also coincided with lecturing at the same institution by Thackeray (*Newcastle Journal*, 7 Feb. 1857, 5).

14. William Gosse, Diary (under 23 February); Wertheimer, *Identification*, 8. The name is spelled 'Ann' in Gosse, *The Gosses: An Anglo-Australian Family*, 57, and 'The Gosse Family' genealogy at the back of the book. Ann Morgan (b. 1811) is not to be confused with Ann Morgan (1841-1907). The former was Ann *née* Gosse, married to John Morgan; the latter was Ann *née* Morgan, married to Alex Waugh.

London, unsolicited, to nurse Emily during her last days. Into her heart 'the Lord put a desire to come up to London, leaving her large family,' Philip later wrote, providing 'affectionate, self-denying services, both before and since the departure of my Emily, [which] eternity only can repay.'[15]

The series of four evening lectures which Gosse gave at the Philosophical Institution, Queen Street Hall in Edinburgh, on 23 and 27 February,[16] and 3 and 6 March,[17] were all in his specialty, 'The Marine Zoology of the British Islands.' Dealing with the subject in the same manner which he first adopted in 1853 lectures, and able to utilise his hot-off-the-press popular survey of the animal kingdom,[18] Gosse dealt in turn with the structure, ecology, and reproductive systems in zoophytes and starfish, Annelida and Crustacea, and cuttlefish (then considered the highest type of invertebrate animals). His illustrative diagrams (many of which were drawn from the microscope) gave his talks their Gossean hallmark, so that these 'homely illustrations ... made what would have been otherwise a dry and uninteresting subject to the larger portion of his auditory, popular and attractive.'[19] The series was well attended, and at its conclusion a reporter for a local newspaper commented: 'Mr. Gosse has invested these lectures with a singular charm, owing to the original and popular manner in which he has treated this department of natural history; and they cannot fail to add to the well-established

15. PHG, *Memorial*, 59-60.

16. Edinburgh *Caledonian Mercury* (25 Feb. 1857), p. [3]; Edinburgh *Daily Express* (28 Feb. 1857), p. [2]. Due to a scheduling conflict, PHG's planned lecture for Feb. 23 was postponed to Mar. 5, according to the *Newcastle Journal* (7 Feb. 1857), 5.

17. Edinburgh *Daily Express*, 4 Mar. 1857), p. [2]; Edinburgh *Witness*, 7 Mar. 1857, p.[2].

18. PHG's *Life in its Lower, Intermediate, and Higher Forms* (1857) appeared in January: advertisement, 'This day', *Essex County* Standard, 7 Jan. 1857, 1, and reviews in the *Literary Gazette*, Jan. 31: Freeman & Wertheimer-PHG, 56-7) and London *Reynold's Newspaper*, 1 Feb. 1857, 2. On the 1853 lectures: *Life*, 245.

D. E. Allen has written that at an unknown time, PHG (together with Richard Owen and Charles Kingsley) provided natural history lessons for the Royal children at the invitation of Albert, the Prince Consort (Allen, *Naturalist in Britain*, 88). When queried, Allen was unable to recall the source for his claim (Allen-Wertheimer, Feb. 16, 1980), though he repeated it, verbatim, in the second edition of his book (Princeton, 1994, 78). Owen did give four, 45-minute-long lectures to the Royal children at Buckingham Palace on 23 Apr. 1860, but there is no mention of PHG (who then would have been living in St. Marychurch) or Kingsley (Revd Richard Owen, *The Life of Richard Owen* (London: John Murray, 1894), II: 98-100). Nicolaas A. Rupke mentions Owen's instruction without adding any new details (Rupke, *Richard Owen*, revised edition, 2009, 33). Kingsley by himself gave private history lessons to one of Albert's sons in 1861 ([Kingsley] ed., *Charles Kingsley* II:125-6).

19. *Caledonian Mercury* (28 Feb. 1857), p. [2].

reputation which he has already earned for himself as a writer upon marine zoology.'[20]

However charming and pleasant Gosse's lectures were to his audience, in private he reflected upon a different matter. 'I cannot tell you how much I love you,' he wrote to his son shortly after reaching Edinburgh:

> I seem to love you better than ever, now that I have had to be separated from you. And now that beloved Mamma is gone to be with Jesus, you are all that is left to me.
>
> I pray much for you: that the Lord will make you a real believer. Your sins can be washed away, only by the precious blood of Jesus; and you can only get that, by believing on Him with your heart; — by giving your heart to Him. O remember all the words of dearest Mamma, how she read to you, and taught you, and prayed for you.

'Do not think of self,' he added, 'but try to make others happy; and then you are sure to be happy'—just as Philip was doing in Edinburgh. And 'Do not forget prayer, and do not forget to remind the Lord of his promise. Pray for me too. ...'[21]

On the same day as this letter was written, William Gosse went to visit the Morgans. He saw Edmund, whom he judged to be 'very happy'.[22] Perhaps he was, in a juvenile way. For in spite of what Edmund's cousins thought of as a remarkable precociousness, he joined in with them in childish games and antics.[23] It was, as Edmund later mused, 'a blessed interval in my strenuous childhood.'[24] One day he played with a puzzle and was shown his uncle's beautiful photographic-like watercolours of the wildflowers of Newfoundland.[25] Another day, he wrote his father about a trip to the Zoological Gardens, not forgetting to mention that 'I think of dear Mamma very often.'[26] Soon Philip completed his first course

---

20. *The Witness*, 7 Mar. 1857, p. [2]. Besides the references just cited, the lectures were also reported in the following Edinburgh papers for 1857: *Caledonian Mercury*, 25 Feb., p. [3]; *Daily Express*, 28 Feb., p. [2], 4 Mar., p. [2], 7 Mar., p. [2]); *The Scotsman*, 25 Feb., p. [3], 4 Mar., p. [3]); and *The Witness*, 28 Feb., p. 1.

21. PHG-EWG, 24 Feb. 1857 (CUL Adv. c. 82.5, 54; an imperfect version is printed in Charteris, pp. 5-6).

22. William Gosse, Diary (under 24 Feb. 1857).

23. Arthur Waugh, *One Man's Road. Being a Picture of Life in a Passing Generation* (London: Chapman and Hall, 1931), 14. Waugh's maternal grandmother was a Gosse.

24. *Father and Son*, 1907, 86.

25. William Gosse, Diary (under 3 Mar. 1857).

26. EWG-PHG, 27 Feb. 1857 (CUL Add. 7027, 20b). The letter is written in another hand,

of lectures, and on 19 March, Anne Morgan brought Edmund to London to await his father's return the next day.[27]

Father and son were together for only a few days when Gosse resumed his whirlwind round of popular talks: at least fourteen marine zoology lectures, seven towns (many in the Edinburgh environs), five weeks. After Edinburgh on 24 February,[28] it was Kirkcaldy on 26 February,[29] back to Edinburgh on 27 February,[30] the Artizans' Institution in Paisley on 2 March[31] (where he was commended for 'rendering intelligible, Darwin's theory of the formation of the coral reefs and island, which he illustrated by a diagram'),[32] Edinburgh on 3 March,[33] Newcastle-upon-Tyne on 5 March,[34] back to Edinburgh on 6 March,[35] Newcastle-upon-Tyne on 9 and 10 March, Birmingham and Midland Institute on 12 March,[36] Leven (Fife) on 15 March,[37] Newcastle-upon-Tyne on 17 March, then back to Birmingham on 23 and 30 March.[38]

After the final lecture at Birmingham, Gosse appears to have spent the remainder of the spring and summer in London.[39] He remained as busy as ever, corresponding with J. D. Hooker and with W. A. Lloyd. Darwin asked him to carry out an experiment on molluscs (in a letter to Gosse, the great naturalist felt compelled to tell him of his 'indifferent' health,

---

perhaps that of Mrs Morgan.

27. William Gosse, Diary (19-20 Mar. 1857). PHG had returned from Newcastle-on-Tyne, where he had delivered four lectures in February and March (*Newcastle Journal*, 7 Feb. 1857, 5).

28. Edinburgh *Caledonian Mercury*, 25 Feb. 1857), p. [3].

29. Cupar, Scotland *Fife Herald and Kinross, Strathearn, and Clackmannan Advertiser*, 5 Mar. 1857, 3.

30. Edinburgh *Daily Express*, 28 Feb. 1857, p. [2].

31. *Paisley Herald and Renfrewshire Advertiser*, 7 Mar. 1857, 1, gives the lecture date as 'Monday' [i.e., Mar. 2]; on p.4 of the same issue, the date is 'Friday evening last', i.e., 6 Mar., or (perhaps) 27 Feb., which would appear incorrect.

32. 'Paisley Artizans' Institution. Mr Gosse's Lecture', *Paisley Herald and Renfrewshire Advertiser*, 7 Mar. 1857), 4.

33. Edinburgh *Scotsman*, 4 Mar. 1857, p. [3].

34. PHG, 'the eminent naturalist', was engaged to give four lectures in Newcastle in February and March (*Newcastle Journal*, 7 Feb. 1857, 5; 14 Feb. 1857, 1), but I have only found information on the second one. In this calculation, I am assuming he did give the four lectures.

35. Edinburgh *Daily Express*, 7 Mar. 1857), p. [2] (initially advertised for 2 Mar.: *Caledonian Mercury*, 13 Dec. 1856, 5).

36. Advertisement, *Paisley Herald*, 7 Mar. 1857, 4.

37. *Fife Herald and Kinross, Strathearn, and Clackmannan Advertiser*, 19 Mar. 1857, 3. Leven is a seaside town in Fife.

38. *Birmingham Journal*, 28 Mar. 1857, 8; *Birmingham Mercury*, 4 Apr. 1857, 6.

39. *Life*, 274, states that in the spring and summer PHG did 'a good deal of lecturing', but does not say how much, where, or when.

while making no inquiry about Gosse's life).[40] Moreover, he was able to spend some time with his son, walking along the Regent's Canal to watch the ducks, and reading with him the Epistle to the Hebrews and Book of Revelation.[41] On 5 May, perhaps on the suggestion of a friend, a governess was employed, Sarah Andrews. Years later, the motherless child recalled that Miss Andrews, who he thought was about 45 years old, was a 'somewhat grotesque personage' but 'thoroughly good and honest', and at least adequately suited to the position.[42]

Also in May, Gosse completed *A Memorial of the Last Days on Earth of Emily Gosse*, which appeared in the next month and today is the rarest of all of his books.[43] To those more comfortable with traditional biographical conventions—like Edmund Gosse, who in adult life was known as a master literary biographer—the 'harrowing details of these last weeks are given with too faithful and self-torturing minuteness' and the descriptions seem 'so harsh, so minute, so vivid'.[44] With the passage of time, that judgment lacks insight. Painful as is the subject, Philip Gosse's careful recounting of his wife's horrific suffering has made it an important historic document still quoted to this day.[45] Judging it from

40. PHG-J. D. Hooker, 8 Apr. 1857 (Kew, *English Letters*, XXXVII: 212); PHG-W. A. Lloyd, 28 Feb. 1857; 12, 31 Mar. 1857 (Edinburgh, La. 11.425/22); Darwin-PHG, 27 Apr. [1857] (LeBL; the year is added in PHG's holograph; printed with some errors in *Life*, 268-9).

41. *Father and Son*, 1907, 96, 102.

42. *Father and Son*, 1907, 107-8, where she was given the pseudonym 'Miss Marks'. Marks was first identified as Sarah Andrews by Wertheimer, *Identification*, 8; for the date of employment, EWG, Diary for 1857.

43. After PHG's death, there was a single copy of *Memorial* in his library (*Sandhurst Catalogue*, item #473). I saw the copy in the Family Collection, and the one at Cambridge. The book is described in Freeman & Wertheimer-PHG, 58-9. A bibliographical search spanning four decades turned up only five copies of this work, making it the rarest of PHG's books (Wertheimer, 'Son and Father', 58). William Gosse recorded receiving a copy of *Memorial* on 7 June (WG, Diary, Family Collection).

44. *Life*, 270, 273.

45. PHG's *Memorial* has been cited and excerpted for its documentation of the pain endured by cancer patients: Spencer Wells, *Cancer Cures and Cancer Curers* (London: John Churchill, 1860), 47-55; 'Cancer Cures', *British Medical Journal*, 23 Mar. 1907, 705; Frank Ellis, 'Cancer: A Memoir', *Areté*, no. 7 (Winter 2001), 69-87 (reviewed by James Fenton, 'Turgenev's Banana', *The New York Review of Books*, 13 Feb. 2003). Agnes Arnold-Forster provides a novel and generally sound appreciation of *Memorial* until she attempts to situate it in the 21st century. Whatever 'traditional ideas of Victorian masculinity and scientific detachment' existed, PHG certainly never attempted to fill them. Few things could have been further from his mind than the thought that the 'affective rhetoric and compassion' which he used in *Memorial* 'would resonate with a particular version of nineteenth-century masculinity' (A. Arnold-Foster, 'Gender and Pain in Nineteenth-Century Cancer Care', *Gender & History* 32 (Mar. 2020), 25-6). Many examples from his writings demonstrate that PHG was not one to withhold the expression of emotions (Appendix, 'Fairy: A Recollection', *infra*).

a literary perspective, a recent critic called it 'an exceptional piece of writing and a good test of literary ability.'[46]

But the memoir was not crafted as a biographical work or to detail a dreadful experience. In the evangelical tradition, the closing moments of one's earthly experience were a test of the strength of one's faith, a summation of all that the Christian life represented, a sign to those who lived on. And working on that premise, the medium became completely subservient to the message: 'do let us remember,' an earlier writer in this genre urged, 'the use of such afflictions.'[47] That's why one reviewer at the time described Gosse's *Memorial* as a 'deeply interesting glimpse of a very lovely and useful Christian,'[48] and how it came to be used in more successful and well-known accounts of her life by Anna Shipton (1863) and Edmund Gosse (1907).[49]

-III-

Some time during the spring, Gosse was apparently offered the resident professorship of natural history at a newly projected school.[50] Centered

46. Craig Raine (ed.), 'A death in the family', London *Times*, 22 May 2003, features section, 24 (the article consists of selections from *Memorial*).

47. Marianne Thornton, describing the last days of her parents in 1815, in an untitled notebook at Cambridge (CUL Add. 7674/1/T). For deathbed scene literature: Hindmarsh, *Evangelical Conversion Narrative*, 256-9; Brown, *Fathers of the Victorians*, 457-61. A work written in heart-rending detail similar to PHG's *Memorial* is by the Revd Thomas Durant, *Memoirs and Select Remains of an Only Son Who Died November 27th, 1821, in His Nineteenth Year; While a Student in the University of Glasgow* (Poole: J. Lankester, 2vols., 1822). Durant's life was filled with tragedy. His first wife died at the age of 46 (Portsmouth *Hampshire Telegraph*, 25 May 1818, 4); his son, William Friend Durant, died aged 19 in 1821 (*Jackson's Oxford Journal*, 15 Dec. 1821, 3); Thomas Durant married again in 1822 (Portsmouth *Hampshire Telegraph*, 30 Sept. 1822, 3); another son, also named William Friend, died at the age of 23 (*Bath Chronicle*, 28 May 1846, 3).

48. *Mother's Friend* X (July 1857), 160. Portions of PHG's *Memorial* were reprinted in 'Biography. Mrs. Gosse', London *Christian's Penny Magazine* XIX, 1864, 50-53.

49. PHG's *Memorial* was used in part in Anna Shipton's *"Tell Jesus."* (London: Morgan & Chase, [1863]). That work ran through 61 impressions by 1911 and 310,000 copies in England, and was still in print there in 1931. It was circulated in Australia and Canada, with an American edition in print until at least 1916, and translated into Dutch (1869), German (1873), French (1875), and Swedish (1901). The book was favourably reviewed in evangelical publications in Britain and the United States. For the background to its composition: A. Shipton, *The Upper Springs and the Nether Springs* (London: James Nisbet & Co., 1882), 17-24. The only bibliography of the work is Freeman & Wertheimer-EG, 63-77. Wertheimer, 'A Son and his Father', 58ff, documented for the first time how *Memorial* was used (without attribution) in EWG's *Father and Son*, 1907.

50. The fact that the sole source for PHG's connection with Gnoll College is *Life*, 274, raises the compulsory doubts about EWG's statements about his father which can not be independently corroborated. EWG's brief discussion gets the timing and the stated facts largely correct, and PHG would have merited being a candidate for Gnoll. PHG's interest in the position is peculiar, in that after leaving the employ of the Carbonear, Newfoundland counting-house of Slade, Elson & Co.

in the Gnoll mansion, in a little-known area in the Vale of Neath, near Swansea, South Wales,[51] Gnoll College was the brainchild of the Devon-born Trelawney William Saunders (1821-1910). At the time, Saunders was the map curator at the Royal Geographical Society in London; in his earlier years he had worked for Samuel Bagster & Sons, the Bible publishers, and been associated with Brethren in Plymouth.[52] Later, he became an English geographical authority.[53] The goal of the institution was to offer a three-year program to some 200 young men aged about 18 which would be 'Universal, Scientific, and Practical'—that is, open to all, concentrating on the sciences and their practical industrial application.[54] Heralded in April 1857 with the beginning of a heavy advertising campaign[55] and then a nearly 100-page statement of the school's *Principles*, Gnoll was to open in October.[56] Gosse would likely have been enticed: the beautiful locale of the college was already familiar to him;[57] Dissenters were welcomed; the natural history of the area was varied and rich; and perhaps above all, the liberal salary of £500 per annum meant that his economic circumstances would be eased.[58]

As a 'national institution adapted to the wants of the age,' Gnoll College sheds an interesting light on the development of science education in mid-Victorian England. As a result of the Great Exhibition of 1851, a number of mining and industrial institutions had been founded, including the Government School of Mines and Sciences Applied to the Arts, which aimed at harmonising the study of pure and applied science;

in 1835, he never again worked for anyone. The analysis here is new, and contains information not previously published.

51. 'Some, perhaps, even of our Welsh readers, and many of our English ones,—will not know, where Gnoll is': 'Gnoll College—in South Wales', *North Wales Chronicle*, 4 July 1857, 12. A colorized image of Gnoll and the Neath serves as the frontispiece to *The Principles of Collegiate Education Discussed and Elucidated, in a Description of Gnoll College, Vale of Neath, South Wales: A National Institution Adapted to the Wants of the Age* (London: Edward Stanford, 1857).

52. Stunt, *Elusive Quest of the Spiritual Malcontent*, 280-1.

53. John Bolton, 'Obituary. Trelawney William Saunders', *Geographical Journal* 36 (Sept. 1910), 364. Although Saunders was never a member of the Victoria Institute (like PHG), he did deliver a paper before it (*JTVI* XVII (1883), 15ff.).

54. *Principles of Collegiate Education*, 6.

55. Advertisement, London *Daily News*, 3 Apr. 1857, 1.

56. Advertisements, London *Times*, 12 June 1857, 4; London *Era*, 14 June 1857, 16.

57. PHG had passed through the area on his way to Tenby in June 1854: PHG, *Tenby*, 4.

58. For general details: [anon], *The Principles of Collegiate Education Discussed*. The work received favourable newspaper attention: *Literary Gazette*, 6 June 1857, 542, the issue of 11 Apr., p. 354; London *Weekly Dispatch*, 14 June 1857, 6; *Monmouthshire Merlin*, 20 June 1857, 2; *Derby Mercury*, 24 June 1857, 6; London *Morning Chronicle*, 24 Sept. 1857, 4.

the Birmingham and Midland Institute of Industrial Education, intended for the working classes; and Owen's College, Manchester, affiliated with the University of London.[59] Universities in France and Germany had already recognised science as a distinct faculty in which degrees were conferred, but this was not the case at British universities.[60] These new schools—though poorly attended and ill-supported—were meant to fill that gap.

Beginning under favourable auspices with a long list of local supporters including Connop Thirlwall (Bishop of St. David's) and William Daniel Conybeare (Dean of Llandaff), Gnoll immediately gathered general support as a national institution.[61] 'This is the most comprehensive scheme of instruction which has ever yet been established in this country,' observed one area newspaper.[62] 'If the proprietors of Gnoll College succeed,' as the London *Atlas* noted, 'and of this we have no doubt, they will justly be ranked among the greatest public benefactors of the nineteenth century.'[63]

Events appeared to move quickly. Although the names of the prospective staff to fill the seven professorships had intentionally not been revealed in the prospectus,[64] the prestigious list of mainly Cambridge and Oxford-affiliated scholars slowly leaked out[65] and were fully advertised by September[66] (Gosse is said to have accepted the Chair of Natural History

59. D. S. L. Cardwell, *The Organisation of Science in England* (London: Heinemann Educational Books, 1957, 1972), 87-92. The brief notice by Cardwell of Gnoll College is not completely accurate. For the Birmingham and Midland Institute, see also W. Matthieu Williams, 'The Birmingham and Midland Institute. Some Egotistical Reminiscences', *Knowledge* I (4 Nov. 1881), 16-17.

60. 'Science and the Universities', *Athenaeum*, 18 July 1857, 910-11; and for an earlier critique of 'Natural History Education' at Oxford and Cambridge: *Literary Gazette*, 16 June 1855, 378-9.

61. *Principles of Collegiate Education*, 79-80, lists 56 local supporters.

62. 'Gnoll College, Vale of Neath', *Cardiff and Merthyr Guardian*, 27 June 1857, 8.

63. 'Gnoll College', *The Atlas*, 18 July 1857, 480.

64. Advertisements for the seven professorships in Mathematics; Mechanics; Physics, Chemistry; Natural History; Human History; and Design appeared as early as Apr. 1857 (London *Daily News*, 3 April 1857, 1), and in a flurry during June (London *Morning Chronicle*, 9 June, 1; London *Times*, 12 June, 4; London *Era*, 14 June, 16).

65. For A. Bath Power (Professor of Physics): 'Ecclesiastical and Collegiate Preferments and Appointments', *Western Flying Post*, 25 Aug. 1857, 6; 'Ecclesiastical Intelligence', *North Wales Chronicle*, 29 Aug. 1857, 5; for Arthur Cayley (Mathematics): 'Ecclesiastical Intelligence', *Welshman*, 25 Sept. 1857, 6 and Cardwell, *Organisation of Science*, 91; for C. B. Wollaston (Mechanics): 'Gnoll College', *Journal of the Society of Arts*, 18 Sept. 1857, 596; for Andrew Wilson (Human History): 'Ecclesiastical Intelligence', *Welshman*, 25 Sept. 1857, 6; 'Cardiff and Its Neighborhood', *Cardiff and Merthyr Guardian*, 26 Sept. 1857, 5.

66. On September 19, 1857: *Carnarvon and Denbigh Herald* (p. 7); *Hampshire Telegraph*

in June).[67] A month before the school was to open, Gnoll's organizers announced that they were about to incorporate the institution as the Western University of Great Britain.[68]

Behind the scenes, a problem emerged when the primary funder announced he had experienced 'an unforeseen change in his circumstances.'[69] Edmund Gosse claimed that by 1 September his father believed the project would 'come to nothing,' and he therefore looked to move to the Torquay area.[70] That scenario is improbable. When names of the seven professors were finally announced, it was Thomas Spencer Cobbold (1828-1886), Lecturer on Botany at St. Mary's Hospital in London, who was named to occupy the Chair of Natural History.[71] It seems unlikely Gosse could have known Gnoll College had failed by 1 September. Its opening was initially postponed and not publicly abandoned until the end of November,[72] with hopes for its revival well into the next year.[73] Those who had projected it claimed that only one objection had been made—'the plan is too complete to be carried into action'[74]—and others cited additional flaws.[75]

Whatever the case may have been, and whether or not Philip Gosse was actually involved, with no other opportunities in sight, weary of life in London, and recalling the pleasant months spent in St. Marychurch near

(p. 3); *Manchester Courier* (p. 5); Edinburgh *Caledonian Mercury* (p. 1); London *Morning Chronicle* (p. 1).

67. *Life*, 274.

68. 'Gnoll College', *Journal of the Society of Arts* (18 Sept. 1857), 596; advertisement, London *Morning Chronicle* (24 Sept. 1857), 1; *Welshman* (16 Oct. 1857), 6.

69. Lewis C. Hertslet and Trelawney Saunders, 'Statement of Facts concerning the proposed establishment of Gnoll College' (dated 29 Oct. 1857), printed in 'Gnoll College, Neath', *Cardiff and Merthyr Guardian*, 5 Dec. 1857, 7. Trelawney Saunders took 'the failure of this scheme ... very much to heart' (Bolton, 'Obituary. Trelawney William Saunders', 364).

70. *Life*, 274. EWG maintained that PHG received an 'offer' from Gnoll for the professorship position. According to the 'Statement of Facts' and newspaper advertisements, the process was open to public competition and 'between 200 and 300 candidates appeared for the various chairs'.

71. *Hampshire Telegraph*, 19 Sept. 1857, 3.

72. 'The Gnoll College scheme has just been abandoned as abruptly as it was ushered into the world start[l]ingly': 'Gnoll College', *Monmouthshire Merlin*, 28 Nov. 1857, 8; *Cambridge Independent Press*, 28 Nov. 1857, 4.

73. J. E. D. Rodgers' letter to the London *Times*: 'I would also state that I am not now lecturer on chymistry [sic] at the St. George's School of Medicine, having resigned that appointment last year upon being elected to the Professor's chair in the proposed Gnoll College' (15 April 1858, 9).

74. *Principles of Collegiate Education*, 48.

75. The plan 'proved a complete abortion' because of the expense and 'its too exclusively scientific character' (Thomas Nicholas, *Middle and High Schools, and a University for Wales* (London: Jackson, Walford, and Hodder, n.d. [1863]), 11fn.).

Torquay in 1852, Gosse set out for Devonshire on 1 September to find a new home.[76] Three days later he returned to London, having selected for their residence 'Sandhurst,' just in from St. Marychurch Road.[77]

Arrangements were immediately made to settle affairs in London. Books were packed; visitors called to say goodbye, including Edmund's maternal uncles Arthur and Edmund Bowes, Mary Stacey, and William and Mary Berger; the Meeting was attended for the last time on the 20th. (Little could Edmund have realised that in ten years he would again meet both Stacey and the Bergers.) Two days later the Gosses left Islington with their cook Susan Mears (d. 1878).[78] On 25 September 1857, they settled at Sandhurst.[79]

A notable incident occurred just before boarding the train for St. Marychurch. '[W]ent to the terminus to day at ½ past 2,' William Gosse jotted down in his diary on 23 September, '& had a 10 minutes chat with Henry in the train on his way to Mary church where he intends residing having given up London ... Henry has got a work on geology in the press displaying in a new light—the present theory of the established antiquity of the world[']s age.' An announcement was sent to the press a month later,[80] and a 'This day is published' advertisement in the London *Times* explained: 'In this work the author aims to overthrow the received conclusions of geologists as to the remote antiquity of the earth, by the enunciation and illustration of a grand physical law, hitherto unrecognized—the law of Prochronism in organic creation.'[81]

76. Based upon his reading of *Father and Son*, V. S. Pritchett speculated that the 'Flight to Devonshire was a flight from the society of equals who would challenge [PHG's] faith every day, into a society of rustics who could be guaranteed to swallow everything he said' (V. S. Pritchett, 'Books in General', *New Statesman and Nation* XXVIII (9 Dec. 1944), 391). Judging from the events leading to PHG's move to St. Marychurch as described here, Pritchett's remark is thought-provoking but not congruent with what happened.

77. For the dates in Devon: EWG, Diary (LeBL). PHG states explicitly that he 'purchased Sandhurst' (PHG-EWG, 22 Feb. 1870, CUL Add. 7041, 33), but it is unclear when he did so. According to the account of his personal estate drawn up after his death, he held Sandhurst on a 99 year lease 'from Mids[umme]r 1856 [*sic*] at [a] yearly rent of £6.15.0 valued [in 1888] at £800' (CUL Add. 7041, 68). I have not seen any reference to PHG having been in that area in 1856. EWG's Diary (1 Sept. 1857) clearly states that 'Papa went to seek for a house', and William Gosse's Diary (under 22 Sept. 1857) refers to PHG 'having taken a house for a permanent residence at Mary Church'.

78. On Susan Mears: EWG-NG, n.d. [?1898] (CUL Add. 7023, 64); for her death by or in 1878, see Corr. Bk. entry for Feb. 5, 1878: 'Spencer (late Susan Mears)'; Wertheimer, *Identification*, 9; *Father and Son*, 1907, 161.

79. EWG, Diary.

80. The earliest notice I've seen for the book is in the *Birmingham Journal*, 21 Oct. 1857, 4.

81. London *Times* (11 Nov. 1857), 13. The statement 'This day is published' is naturally not

In the midst of all Gosse's other worries, he had found time to write his twenty-eighth book.

-IV-

Gosse's attitude towards the relationship between the Scriptures and science was evident to readers of all but the most purely descriptive of his scientific works. As an adherent to the natural theology tradition, he sought out instances of design in nature pointing to the Designer. He followed the orthodox lead of the two great taxonomists, Linnaeus and Cuvier, in considering species as 'distinct forms which are believed to have proceeded direct from the creating Hand of God, and on which was impressed a certain individuality, destined to pass down through all succeeding generations, without loss and without confusion.'[82] The Lamarckian (or transmutationist) view of species Gosse dismissed as 'unphilosophical' and 'derogatory to God's honour ... animals being in an equal degree perfect in their kind, equally formed by consummate wisdom, incapable of improvement.'[83] He felt similarly about the popular (but vague and error-ridden) evolutionary theory found in the *Vestiges of the Natural History of Creation*, the anonymously published work whose author did not appear on the title-page for four decades.[84] 'Coolly bowing aside His authority,' Gosse said of *Vestiges*, 'this writer has hatched a scheme, by which the immediate ancestor of Adam was a Chimpanzee, and his remote ancestor a Maggot!'[85]

Gosse's assumptions that species were at once divinely derived and immutable were shared by most naturalists at the time.[86] Yet concurrently there were geologists and biologists who claimed that the earth's organic and inorganic features could best be understood by examining only naturalistic causes. These scientists found no need to

to be taken literally, the same wording having been used in London publications on 6 and 7 November. In the previous month, an advertisement in the *Athenaeum*, 10 Oct. 1857, 1274, stated: 'Nearly ready'. William Gosse's diary for 1857 records that he received a copy of the book on 3 November (Freeman & Wertheimer-PHG, 60).

82. PHG, *An Introduction to Zoology* (London: SPCK, [1844]), I: xv.

83. PHG, *The Ocean* (London: SPCK, 1845), 101.

84. Robert Chambers's name appeared in the 12ed. of 1884 (Freeman, *British Natural History Books*, 83).

85. PHG, *Omphalos*, 27.

86. [Edwin Lankester], *The Athenaeum*, 21 Nov. 1857, 1482; see also *Natural History Review* V (Jan. 1858), 55; *London Quarterly Review*, Apr. 1858, 267; and Shirley Hibberd, 'The Genesis of Organic Forms', *Recreative Science* II (Jan. 1861), 269, 277.

consider miraculous occurrences or reveal supposed divine contrivances. Until Darwin presented a massive amount of evidence in support of an evolutionary theory in biology in the *Origin of Species* in 1859, however, the most serious conflict between science and the Bible resulted from the discoveries in the inorganic world. The geological researches of James Hutton and Charles Lyell led them to maintain that the earth must have existed for longer than the 6,000 years which, according to the traditional understanding, the Book of Genesis allowed.

There is a vast literature attempting to resolve this difficulty.[87] Some defenders of the traditional faith chose simply to ignore the geologists' findings. As one Methodist writer cavalierly put it, 'Gneiss, mica-schist, and clay-slate, red sandstone and lime, millstone grit and coal, may follow one another in any order they please and may bear incontestable evidence of the lapse of ages; and yet, we cannot accept such testimony in positive opposition to the Holy Bible.'[88]

More common were those who adhered to the clever compromise of the Scottish Divine, Thomas Chalmers (1780-1847), or a variety of it which was favoured for many years by scriptural geologists.[89] According to Chalmers' interval or 'restitution' theory, the Bible did not establish the antiquity of the globe, and it was thus possible that the aeons of time required by geologists took place between the actual creation in the first verse of Genesis and the chaotic state of the second. In other words, after the earth had been the scene of life for many ages it may have been destroyed, and new life emerged out of the old in a creative process

---

87. For a useful summary of these attempts: PHG, *Omphalos*, 8-29, and for an analysis: Milton Millhauser, 'The Scriptural Geologists: An Episode in the History of Opinion', *Osiris* XI (1954), 65-86, and F. C. Haber, *The Age of the World: Moses to Darwin* (Baltimore: Johns Hopkins Press, 1959), 187-264.

88. *Wesleyan Times* X (22 Feb. 1858), 115.

89. Haber, *Age of the World*, 203, and Millhauser, 'The Scriptural Geologists', 76, 81. It would appear that Chalmers' interpretation was adopted by Brethren leader J. N. Darby. In 'What has the Bible Taught? and What has Geology Proved? or, A Second Dialogue on Essays & Reviews', Darby (without displaying any great acquaintance with geological research) made the common distinction between geological facts and inferences, and found the Mosaic account more certain than any geological system. He felt that it was literally true, but since the Bible was not meant to teach science, 'There is nothing to conciliate. ... Scripture ... is totally silent as to [the facts of geology], but leaves a gap [between Genesis I-II] which may have been filled by millions of years when we were not' (p. 146). Darby believed that the important question 'between us and the rationalists is ...whether [the Bible's] contents are God's thoughts or man's thoughts' (p. 144). [Darby], *Dialogues on the Essays and Reviews, by One Who Values Christianity for Its Own Sake, and Believes in it as a Revelation from God* (London: W. H. Broom, 1862), Part I: 115-50, esp. pp. 131, 136-7, 142-6.

lasting only six days. When geologists discovered an inextricable link between the pre-Adamite fauna and that of their own time, new schemes and modifications were presented. Perhaps the most notable of these was *The Testimony of the Rocks* (1857) by the popular Scottish geologist Hugh Miller (1802-1856), in which the biblical 'day' was construed metaphorically, signifying a long period which could be brought into congruence with the geological record.[90]

Gosse was acquainted with this apologetic literature, and may once have been favourably disposed to, or adopted, Chalmers' theory.[91] Sympathising with the motives which had led Christians to tackle the geological problem, and nonetheless finding their solutions unsatisfactory, in 1857 Gosse presented his own solution. He called it *Omphalos: An Attempt to Untie the Geological Knot*,[92] and illustrated it with his own woodcuts.[93]

In *Omphalos*, Gosse imagined a 'High Court of Inquiry' which was adjudicating claims about the age of the earth. The imposing testimony of one Witness (geologists) for an immeasurably vast antiquity[94] had been heard, and the Judges (the general public) had favoured it. But there was another Witness (Scriptures) putting forth the claim for a far shorter history[95] who asked that the case be reopened prior to the court's verdict. Noting that geologists draw their conclusions from '*circumstantial* evidence'—they infer an ancient existence of life based on discovered fossils, but they have no '*direct* testimony' of that life since 'no one actually saw the living *Pterodactyle* flying about'[96]—Gosse instead proposed a way of looking at the issue which would leave geological research in place while allowing it to be harmonised with 'the simple literal sense of the words of God.'[97]

To achieve this end, Gosse took a logical approach. Start with the

---

90. For assertions that people at the time generally favoured this long chronology: [Edwin Lankester], *Athenaeum*, 28 Nov. 1857, 1482; *Critic*, 15 May 1858, 224; *The Record*, 19 Mar. 1858), 4; *North British Review* XXVIII (Feb. 1858), 276; and *Guardian*, 24 Mar. 1858, 246.

91. PHG, *Canadian Naturalist*, 18fn.

92. PHG, *Omphalos: An Attempt to Untie the Geological Knot* (London: John Van Voorst, 1858), 29; for a history of the book's publication: Freeman & Wertheimer-PHG, 59-61.

93. Five of the 56 text woodcuts were signed by PHG (Freeman & Wertheimer-PHG, 61).

94. PHG called this the 'Macro-chronology' (*macro* meaning 'large' in Greek).

95. PHG called this the 'Brachy-chronology' (*brachy* being a borrowing from Greek and Latin for 'short').

96. PHG, *Omphalos*, 103-4. Emphasis in the original.

97. PHG, *Omphalos*, 4-5.

assumptions (or postulates) that at some point matter had come into existence (and was not eternal) and that species were unchanged throughout time (and had not evolved one from the other).[98] Add to that the observation that as far as the animal and vegetable world are concerned, it is not possible to locate a life-cycle beginning or end. In a moth there is the 'pupa, larva, egg, moth, pupa, larva, egg, moth, &c. &c.'[99]; in a plant, there is seed, germination, growth, adult plant, seed, etc. Each stage of life presupposes a previous one. From this it follows that when creation of life-matter occurred, it had to represent 'the sudden bursting into a circle.' Since that was so, the life forms thus appearing at the moment of creation provided evidence of a past existence which— though logically deduced—were *unreal*.[100] Although the basic argument of *Omphalos* was admittedly not original,[101] Gosse's development of this hitherto unrecognized 'grand physical law' was more sophisticated than that of any predecessor. Here was the 'Law of Prochronism in Creation', or as more descriptively known, 'creation with appearance of age.'[102]

When the act of creation of life-matter occurred, time was divided into two categories. Gosse referred to those animals and plants which commenced their existence at the creation and necessarily bore evidence of a previous existence which was *unreal*, as having a prochronic existence (that is, before earthly time began). The remainder of organic life, which came into existence after the creation and also bore evidence of a previous existence which was *real*, he labelled diachronic (because it occurred in actual earthly time).[103] This meant that when Adam, the first human, was created, he displayed a navel (Greek, *omphalos*),[104]

98. PHG, *Omphalos*, 110-12.

99. PHG, *Omphalos*, 119.

100. PHG, *Omphalos*, 123-4.

101. PHG, *Omphalos*, vi-vii, acknowledging indebtedness to an anonymous tract and to Granville Penn's *The Mineral and Mosaical Geologies* (1822). For other parallels, with George Bugg and Chateaubriand, see Haber, *Age of the World*, 212-3, 248; and J. L. Borges, 'The Creation and P. H. Gosse' [1941], in *Other Inquisitions 1937-1952*, trans. by Ruth L. C. Simms (New York: Washington Square Press, 1966), 25.

102. This is the phrase used by Thomas Allen McIver, 'Creationism: Intellectual Origins, Cultural Context, and Theoretical Diversity' (University of California Los Angeles, PhD dissertation, 1989), 461.

103. PHG, *Omphalos*, 124-5. The words 'prochronic' and 'diachronic' were PHG neologisms (*OED* 3ed. cites PHG's *Creation*, without realizing that this was a printing of PHG's *Omphalos*; Freeman & Wertheimer-PHG, 59-60).

104. 'More's famous question, "Had Adam a Navel?" suggested the title to my volume' (PHG-L. C. Biggs, 30 April 1881, CUL Add. 7313, 356). PHG refers to Sir Thomas Browne's *Pseudodoxia Epidemica* (1646) in *Omphalos*, 289fn., and the epigraph to *Omphalos* cites Aristotle (in the

even though he had never been born. The tricky part was that there was no palpable physical difference between the prochronically and diachronically created individual.

To complete his analysis, Gosse wondered whether the Law of Prochronism could be extended from the organic to the inorganic world. It was necessary for this to be done to successfully 'untie the geological knot,' yet Gosse was not sure that the two worlds operated in the same cyclical pattern. Nonetheless he believed it was *possible* that this was so.[105] If the earth (like the animal and vegetable life on it) also had a prochronic existence, then the creation of the inorganic world also involved a 'sudden bursting into a circle' and left marks (*i.e.*, fossils) which testified to a previous history which was *unreal*. Then the argument for a six-day creation of the earth was at least *tenable*. So long as geologists kept the Law of Prochronism in mind, genesis and geology would no longer be in conflict.

Gosse correctly anticipated that there would be critics who would say that to claim that the world was 'created with fossil skeletons in its crust,—skeletons of animals that never really existed,' was to make of God a '*Deus quidam deceptor*',[106] accusing the Creator 'with forming objects whose sole purpose was to deceive us.'[107] Not so, he countered. Fossils had to be situated in the rocks, 'not to puzzle the philosopher, but because they are inseparable from the condition of the world at the selected moment of irruption into its history; because they constitute its condition; they make it what it is.'[108]

-V-

No work by Gosse has been more closely tied to his name and career than *Omphalos*. None has been more misunderstood. Past confusion can be clarified, however, by starting with why, what and how questions. Why did Gosse write *Omphalos* when he did? What was his purpose in directing his attention to geology and its relationship to

original Greek): 'All animals, or all such as have a navel, grow by the navel'. Borges states that PHG's Law of Prochronism was anticipated by an 1802 work by Chateaubriand (Borges, 'The Creation and P. H. Gosse', 25).

105. PHG, *Omphalos*, 335-345.

106. PHG, *Natural History Review* V (July 1858), 132; PHG, *Geology or God: Which? A Supplement to "Omphalos."* (London: Morgan & Chase, 1866), 12.

107. PHG, *Omphalos*, 347.

108. PHG, *Omphalos*, 352-3.

religion? How was the book received? Hovering over these three issues are the previously unquestioned scenarios promoted by Edmund Gosse.

Starting from the beginning, it seems odd that Gosse would have waited until 1857 to 'untie the geological knot'. His views on religion, science, and their connection were no secret and had remained virtually unchanged over the years. Moreover, he said he came across the kernel of the argument which he developed in *Omphalos* in a tract which he had seen in London around 1845.[109]

Gosse's timing remains inexplicable, but given its consistency with his previous positions it is not a critical part of the *Omphalos* picture.[110] Yet it is necessary to rebut the explanations by his biographer son. Not long after the death of his father, Edmund twice wrote on the subject. In an 1890 letter in the London *Spectator*, he defended *Omphalos*, stating that its argument was 'not absolutely insane.'[111] Appearing at precisely the same time was his *Life of Philip Henry Gosse*, in which he added detail not cited in the letter. After Emily Gosse died, Edmund wrote, his father's mind was 'morbid, and his nerves unstrung,' he was in a state of 'exhaustion and of irritation' and he believed he 'must needs break a lance with the windmills of the geologists.'[112] *Omphalos* was the result. Two decades later, Edmund revisited the subject in *Father and Son*, retracting his previous comment that the argument was 'not absolutely insane' and now characterizing the book as 'fanatical.'[113] He repeated his claim of a temporary 'dislocation of [his father's] intellectual system,'[114] and then inserted this new and startling revelation: Philip Gosse had been privately approached by J. D. Hooker and Charles Darwin 'after meetings of the Royal Society in the summer of 1857.' He was, according to this account, among a select number of naturalists who (at the suggestion

---

109. PHG, *Omphalos*, vi.

110. The sequence of events might have been that PHG began *Omphalos* not long after his *Memorial* of EG was published, at the beginning of June 1857. If PHG wrote *Omphalos* with the same speed that he had written *Popular British Ornithology*—that is, as previously mentioned, five printed pages per day—he would have started the 376-page *Omphalos* around the beginning of July and the book would have been in the press at the end of September (even though the preface is dated from Marychurch in October, PHG told William Gosse at the London train station that it was already 'in the press', as mentioned). This suggests the chronological picture, but not the rationale behind the book's timing.

111. EWG, 'The Late Mr. P. H. Gosse and Geology', *Spectator*, 25 Oct. 1890, 559. Most of this letter appears verbatim in *Life*, 277-8.

112. *Life*, 273, 275, 277.

113. *Father and Son*, 1907, 121.

114. *Father and Son*, 1907, 134.

of geologist Charles Lyell) were told of Darwin's theory before it was formally released, and probed for their reaction to it. Edmund wrote:

> ... every instinct in [Gosse's] intelligence went out at first to greet the new light. It had hardly done so, when a recollection of the opening chapter of Genesis checked it at the outset. He consulted with [W. B.] Carpenter, a great investigator ... They both determined, on various grounds to have nothing to do with the terrible theory [of evolution], but to hold steadily to the law of the fixity of species.[115]

In other words, Philip's response to this private revelation of Darwin's theory of evolution by natural selection was *Omphalos*.

This latter scenario, as has effectively been argued by Frederic R. Ross, is full of difficulties.[116] While an approach by evolution advocates is conceivable,[117] it could not have occurred as described. It's not only that *Omphalos* is about uniformitarian geology and not evolution, or that Gosse never favoured Darwin's theory, or that 1857 was not (as Edmund wrote) 'the great moment in the history of thought' when Darwin 'was preparing to throw a flood of light' on human knowledge.[118] It is that his characterization of the naturalists purportedly involved is a misrepresentation of their views at that time. To add to Ross's previously published case, although the botanist J. D. Hooker knew of Darwin's work,[119] it seems odd that he would have purportedly acted as a proponent of Darwin's theory in the summer of 1857, since for scientific reasons

---

115. *Father and Son*, 1907, 118-119.

116. Frederic R. Ross challenged the narrative in an excellent, detailed paper (Ross, 'Philip Gosse's *Omphalos*, Edmund Gosse's *Father and Son*, and Darwin's Theory of Natural Selection', *Isis* 68 (Mar. 1977), 85-96. Ross's paper was received at *Isis* in March 1974). Wertheimer, unaware of Ross's research, independently came to the same conclusion in 'Philip Henry Gosse', chap. 5 (accepted as a PhD dissertation on June 29, 1977). Letters, Wertheimer-Ross, 17 Aug. 1977; Ross-Wertheimer, 26 Aug. 1977. There is no known confirmation that PHG met Hooker or Darwin in 1857, and overwhelming negative evidence suggests that the alleged 1857 meeting was an invention by EWG. The treatment in this chapter is new, and uses a great deal of material never before considered.

117. In the summer of 1857, for example, the American botanist Asa Gray 'entered the little circle of initiates' that were told in writing of Darwin's evolution theory (including Charles Lyell and J. D. Hooker): Darwin-Gray, July 20, 1857, in A. Hunter Dupree, *Asa Gray 1818-1888* (New York: Atheneum, 1959, 1968), 244-7; Ross, 'Philip Gosse's *Omphalos*', 90fn. 21.

118. *Father and Son*, 1907, 117ff.

119. Derek Partridge, 'Further details concerning the Darwin-Wallace presentation to the Linnean Society in 1858, including its submission on 1 July, not 30 June', *Journal of Natural History* 50 (2016), 1039.

he was unconvinced that species had evolved,[120] did not commit to being a Darwinian until the autumn of 1858,[121] and publicly opposed evolution until after the *Origins* was published in 1859.[122] Nor would the physiologist W. B. Carpenter—a Unitarian who had been part of the London intellectual and scientific establishment from the mid-1840s[123]—have joined Gosse in 1857 to argue for the 'fixity of species'. Their world views were starkly distinct. Carpenter had praised the *Vestiges of the Natural History of Creation* in an 1844 review, was suspected of holding transmutationist and pantheistic ideas several years before 1859,[124] and at one point was even asked to revise the *Vestiges*.[125] His reviews of the *Origin* show him to have believed in the plasticity of species and the harmony of religion and science.[126]

While an explanation for the timing of the publication of *Omphalos* remains elusive, it is possible to speculate on what drew Gosse—who was not a geologist and never claimed to be one—to devote a nearly 400-page book to that subject. Again, the reason was not that the 'pet craze of the moment was the reconciliation of Genesis with geology,' as Edmund Gosse said,[127] drawing attention to books published immediately prior to *Omphalos* while breezily ignoring a vast literature on the subject stretching back decades or (if considered more generally) centuries. What uniformitarian geologists like Charles Lyell had done was to upend the Victorian religious world's view of time.[128] Instead of the commonly-accepted six days of creation and the relatively short chronology of Genesis, uniformitarians put forward a long, gradually unfolding chronology without a role for a creator. Charles Darwin's evolutionary theory came after this shock, but he himself drew the linkage between the short chronology and a denial of species evolution. 'Why, it may be

120. Turrill, *Joseph Dalton Hooker*, 87, 91.

121. Richard Donald Bellon, 'Joseph Hooker and the Progress of Botany, 1845-1865' (University of Washington, PhD dissertation, 2000), 254-5. Bellon dates the conversion to three months after the Darwin-Wallace joint paper before the Linnean Society of July 1858 (end of Sept. 1858).

122. Bellon, 'Joseph Hooker', 205.

123. Shannon Dina Delorme, 'The Unitarian Physiologist: Science and Religion in the Life and Work of William Benjamin Carpenter (1813-1885)' (University of Oxford, DPhil dissertation, 2016), 6, 75-6.

124. Delorme, 'The Unitarian Physiologist', 154, 159, 254.

125. Secord, *Victorian Sensation*, 243.

126. Delorme, 'The Unitarian Physiologist', 169-171.

127. *Life*, 277.

128. Pietsch, *Dispensational Modernism*, 129-133.

asked, have all the most eminent living naturalists and geologists rejected this view of the mutability of species?' wondered Darwin at the end of the *Origins of Species*. His reply: 'The belief that species were unchanging throughout time was almost unavoidable as long as the history of the world was thought to be of short duration.'[129] That is why to someone with Gosse's outlook, the geologists' claim of a lengthy age for the earth was intolerable and somehow had to be rebutted.

-VI-

Previously published accounts dealing with *Omphalos*—without a single known exception—have uncritically, persistently, even loudly adopted Edmund's description of how *Omphalos* was received by the British public.[130] 'Never was a book cast upon the waters with greater anticipation of success than was this curious, this obstinate, this fanatical volume,' Edmund wrote, speaking with certitude about the inner thoughts of his father when he was an eight-year-old child. 'He offered it, with a glowing gesture, to atheists and Christians alike. ... But, alas! atheists and Christians alike looked at it and laughed, and threw it away.'[131] Yet as the philosopher Ludwig Wittgenstein observed, repeating a claim with certainty is irrelevant to the certainty of the claim.[132] Recovering the historical record on *Omphalos* is a tedious process, yet it can be done by reading the reaction in the press to the book[133] and Gosse's own words. In order to be successful it is necessary to listen to what was said, try to recapture what was thought, and avoid projecting one's biases and

---

129. Charles Darwin, *On the Origin of Species by Means of Natural Selection* (London: John Murray, 1859), 480-1.

130. Even Frederic R. Ross, an insightful writer on *Omphalos*, repeated EWG's words without challenging them, citing only four reviews of the book (Ross, 'Philip Gosse's *Omphalos*', 87, 93 and fn.29). Among works in which *Omphalos* makes a negative appearance are A. M. Davies, *Evolution and its Modern Critics* (London: Thomas Murby & Co., 1937), 6; and Martin Gardner, *Fads and Fallacies in the Name of Science* (New York: Dover Publications, Inc., 1957), 124-6; and novels by John Fowles, *The French Lieutenant's Woman* (St. Albans, Herts.: Panther Books Ltd., 1973), 141fn.; H. G. Wells, *All Aboard for Ararat* (London: Secker & Warburg, 1940), 11; and Ann Lingard, *Seaside Pleasures* (Workington, Cumbria: Littoralis Press, 2003).

131. *Father and Son*, 1907, 121-2, 124.

132. These are my words summarizing Lorraine Code's paraphrase of Wittgenstein's *On Certainty* (Lorraine Code, '*Father and Son*: A Case Study in Epistemic Responsibility', *Monist* 66 (Apr. 1983), 280-1).

133. Unless otherwise stated, characterizations of the various serials are from Ellegård, *The Readership of the Periodical Press*, and Ellegård, *Darwin and the General Reader*, Appendix II.

feelings. The result dispenses with the myths surrounding *Omphalos*, its goal and reception.

There are several indications that Gosse had high expectations for his book. His self-assured, reasoned prose reflects that. He also said as much in *Omphalos*, in hoping that the book would gain serious attention and even acceptance among the 'thousands of thinking persons' who have been 'silenced but not convinced' with past efforts to reconcile 'Scriptural statements and Geological deductions.'[134] In addition, the fact that he ordered 4,000 copies of the book to be printed—a larger number than for any other work which he published on a profit-sharing basis except *Actinologia Britannica*, issued in the same quantity— confirms this (considered from a cost viewpoint, however, the print run was not extreme).[135] Finally, Gosse could confidently anticipate a positive reception for the work for two reasons: the press had rendered virtually unqualified and unstinting praise for every one of his previous publications, and at the beginning of 1857 it had highly rated Hugh Miller's posthumously published *Testimony of the Rocks*[136] (a work dealing with the same subject as *Omphalos*). Gosse might also have anticipated similar treatment for his book.

Nonetheless, *Omphalos* did not meet expectations. It was one of the three most frequently reviewed of his books,[137] and no other work by him received so many unfavourable notices.[138] It gained notable attention

134. PHG, *Omphalos*, vii-viii.

135. Freeman & Wertheimer-PHG, 68. The large printing reflects PHG's business acumen as well as his over-confidence. It cost him about as much to print 4,000 copies of *Omphalos* (£326) as it did 1,500 of the *Naturalist's Rambles* (£329) or 2,000 of *A Manual of Marine Zoology* (£318) (CUL Adv.c.82.5,77).

136. I have found that *Testimony of the Rocks* and *Omphalos* were both reviewed by at least these same 12 publications: *Athenaeum*; *Atlas*; *Birmingham Journal*; *British Messenger*; *Christian Remembrancer*; *Critic*; *Gardeners' Chronicle*; *Literary Gazette*; *Natural History Review*; *North British Review*; *Saturday Review*; and *Westminster Review*. With the exception of the *Saturday Review*, 25 Apr. 1857, 381-2, and *Westminster Review*, n.s.XII (July 1857), 176-85 [the author is unidentified in *Wellesley Index* IV], all notices of *Testimony* were positive. In the *Athenaeum*, Edwin Lankester anonymously reviewed *Testimony* (positively) and *Omphalos* (negatively).

137. PHG's *Naturalist's Rambles on the Devonshire Coast* (29 reviews) and *Aquarium* (27) were the first and second most frequently-reviewed of his works, followed by *Omphalos*. I have located 26 reviews of *Omphalos* in various British serials for 1857-61. For comparison, I found 26 reviews of Hugh Miller's *Testimony of the Rocks* (1857), 1857-8, though there were certainly more. Ellegård cites 41 reviews of *Origin of Species* during 1859-61 (Ellegård, *Darwin and the General Reader*, 25fn.6).

138. PHG's *Romance of Natural History*, second series (1861) was given a number of negative notices; *Mysteries of God* (1884) received several.

from 'real Christians' and the world of science, but little support from either. The book sold slowly from the start and may have ended up a financial loss, or only just broken even.[139] That being said, Edmund Gosse's claim that Victorians 'looked at [*Omphalos*] and laughed, and threw it away', would be valid if wishful thinking were a substitute for an inquiry into the facts.

On the face of it, Edmund Gosse's descriptions do not ring true because one anticipates that *Omphalos* would have been taken seriously in the British press. Recall that at the time, Gosse's view that species had not changed from the time of creation 'was not yet unorthodox,' as it became in the years after *Origin*.[140] Not less important, as the high-quality weekly newspaper *The Atlas* put it, in its review of *Omphalos*, was that 'Mr. Gosse is a man of great scientific attainments, and has done much to advance our knowledge in natural history.'[141] Close to half of the *Omphalos* reviewers I have identified echoed that sentiment, and even those who wrote of the 'worthlessness' of his argument or its 'hair-splitting philosophy'[142] invariably did so after lengthy analyses and the presentation of the author's case with long, excerpted quotes from the book. An unfavourable notice in the literary weekly *Saturday Review*, for example, consumed some 3,000 words spanning three printed pages.[143] Regardless of their final assessment, a number of reviewers characterized Gosse's prochronic argument as 'ingenious', a word still used about it to this day.[144]

Not surprisingly, *Omphalos* found its most sympathetic audience in the religious arena, where assessments ranged from partial to total support

139. Freeman & Wertheimer-PHG, 6, 60.

140. Turrill, *Joseph Dalton Hooker*, 95.

141. *Atlas*, 21 Nov. 1857, 766. For similar comments on PHG's stature: London *John Bull*, 21 Nov. 1857, 747; London *Daily News*, 15 Dec. 1857, 2; 'Science', *Westminster Review* n.s. XIII (Jan. 1858), 260-5 [by W.S. Dallas, *Wellesley Index* III: 627]; *British Messenger*, Jan. 1858, 103; *North British Review* XXVIII (Feb. 1858), 275; *Wesleyan Times* X (22 Feb. 1858), 115; *Guardian*, 24 Mar. 1858, 246; *British Quarterly Review* XXVII (Apr. 1858), 557; Shirley Hibberd, 'The Genesis of Organic Forms', *Recreative Science* II (Jan. 1861), 269.

142. *Atlas*, 21 Nov. 1857, 766.

143. London *Saturday Review*, 12 Dec. 1857, 534-6.

144. London *Literary Gazette*, 21 Nov. 1857, 1111; *St. James's Chronicle*, 26 Nov. 1857, 1; *British Messenger*, Jan. 1858, 103; *Sword and the Trowel* XXI (May 1885), 236; J. W. Dawson, *Archaia; or, Studies of the Cosmogony and Natural History of the Hebrew Scriptures* (Montreal: B. Dawson & Son, 1860), 203 fn., 334fn. Modern authors who have called the theory 'ingenious' include Borges, 'The Creation and P. H. Gosse' [1941], 24; Haber, *Age of the World*, 246; and Ron Roizen, 'The Rejection of "Omphalos": A Note on Shifts in the Intellectual Hierarchy of Mid-Nineteenth Century Britain', *Journal for the Scientific Study of Religion* 21 (Dec. 1982), 365.

(occasionally in the same article) to antipathy. Methodist publications were favourable. For the weekly *Wesleyan Times*, Gosse 'gives a very strong probable argument, that skeletons and all else were created as they are found ... Mr. Gosse's views bring the science of geology and the Revealed Word into direct accordance; and his argument appeals to common-sense. The Christian public owe him their warmest thanks for this treatise.'[145] The Methodist *London Review* found the work 'interesting', by which it meant that Gosse's 'clear and unanswerable' assertion of the separate creation of animate life (and thus defence of a literal reading of the Bible) was praiseworthy. His solution of geological issues, however, was unsatisfying.[146] The evangelical *St. James's Chronicle* newspaper called Gosse's argument 'important', qualifying the word by adding that 'Scripture ought [not] to dictate laws to science.'[147] The sizable circulation, monthly evangelical *British Messenger*[148] stated that 'Whether you agree with his views or not, you will find every page of his book stocked with interesting matter; and you will rise from the reading of it with the circle of your thoughts considerably widened, and your conceptions of the littleness of man and the greatness of God more vivid, definite, and influential.' Nonetheless the *Messenger* (which had published a number of Emily Gosse's writings) wondered why Gosse had rejected the day-period scheme of geologist Hugh Miller.[149] The *Guardian*, a largely High Church weekly newspaper with no appeal to evangelicals, thought Gosse's idea 'too grotesque to bear serious consideration. Mr. Gosse has written a pretty and instructive book, but he has not untied the geological knot.'[150] The *British Quarterly Review*, appealing to evangelical Dissenters,[151] said that the 'eminent naturalist' here appears as 'a fanciful theorist, bearing in his hand a book which, had it been published anonymously, we should almost have been inclined

---

145. *Wesleyan Times* X (22 Feb. 1858), 115.

146. *London Review* X (Apr. 1858), 267-8. In 1858 the publication founded as the *London Quarterly Review* was known as the *London Review* (*Wellesley Index* IV, 371; *DNCJ*, 376).

147. London *St. James's Chronicle*, 26 Nov. 1857, 1.

148. *British Messenger* circulation was 75,000 copies in 1856 (*Christian Weekly News*, 12 Feb. 1856, 348).

149. *British Messenger* No. 59 (Jan. 1858), 103.

150. *Guardian*, 24 Mar. 1858, 246.

151. *British Quarterly Review* XXVII (Apr. 1858), 557-60 [author not identified in *Wellesley Index* IV, 147]; on the characterization of *BQR*: 'The Projected British Quarterly Review', *Sheffield and Rotherham Independent*, 10 Aug. 1844, 3.

to regard as an elaborate *jeu d'esprit*.'[152] In a five-sentence-long review of *Omphalos* (the shortest known), the *Christian Remembrancer*, a monthly appealing to conservative, High Churchmen, noted that 'Mr. Gosse is at home with the sea-anemones. In these fields of disquisition we desire abler apologists.'[153]

Countering the varied coverage in the religious press was that of the literary (and largely secular) weeklies. With the exception of *John Bull*, a good-quality conservative literary weekly known as the 'favourite organ of the gentleman of England'[154]—'this very remarkable book is worthy of the author's fame, and calculated to make a stirring effect in the regions of scientific inquiry'[155]—they were savage in their treatment. The politically Liberal *Atlas* said it was a 'hair-splitting philosophy,'[156] the *Literary Gazette* a 'clever paradox,'[157] the *Saturday Review*'s vicious tirade covered one-and-a-half pages,[158] the *Athenaeum* said the book was based on 'an absurd assumption,'[159] the *Critic* called it another example of the 'many eccentricities of genius,'[160] the *Spectator* said the book's 'absurd' argument is 'one of the most fallacious, and the logic the most imperfect, of almost anything we have met with in the reasoning way,'[161] and the *Gardeners' Chronicle* termed prochronism an 'hallucination.'[162]

Nor were the monthlies and quarterlies any kinder. Writing anonymously in the *Westminster Review*, the natural history author and translator W. S. Dallas (1824-1890), an early Darwin supporter,[163] called the Law of Prochronism 'too monstrous for belief,' and referred to 'Mr.

---

152. *British Quarterly Review* XXVII (Apr. 1858), 557.

153. *Christian Remembrancer* XXXV (Jan. 1858), 249; *DNCJ*, 115-16. Later that year, the same publication gave a lengthy review to three works on this topic, including Miller's *Testimony*, with which it mainly (though not entirely) agreed (*Christian Remembrancer* XXXVI (Oct. 1858), 263-290).

154. *Mitchell's Newspaper Press Directory 1864*, 19.

155. London *John Bull*, 21 Nov. 1857, 747.

156. London *Atlas*, 21 Nov. 1857, 766; *Mitchell's Newspaper Press Directory 1856*, 19.

157. London *Literary Gazette*, 21 Nov. 1857, 1111, 1113.

158. *Saturday Review*, 12 Dec. 1857, 534-6.

159. [Edwin Lankester], *Athenaeum*, 28 Nov. 1857, 1483.

160. *Critic* XVII (15 May 1858), 224.

161. 'Gosse's Omphalos', *Spectator*, 30 Jan. 1858, 124.

162. *Gardeners' Chronicle*, 9 Jan. 1858, 23.

163. Dallas translated from the German Fritz Müller's *Facts and Arguments for Darwin* (London: John Murray, 1869). Müller supported Darwin's evolution theory by natural selection (John Lubbock, *Academy*, 9 Oct. 1869, 14).

Gosse and his disciples,—if he has any.'[164] The *North British Review*, once reflecting the evangelical wing of the Free Church of Scotland but by 1857 asserting a secular orientation whose reviews rivalled in quality those in the *Edinburgh* and *Quarterly*,[165] snidely remarked that not much could be expected from 'a scientific treatise based on a thought in a Plymouth Brother tract.'[166] The reviewer regretted that 'the writer of the "Manual of Marine Zoology" should also be the author of "Omphalos."'[167]

Only four scientific publications noticed the book.[168] In *Recreative Science*, a monthly covering natural history subjects in a 'popular style,'[169] Shirley Hibberd (1825-1890), an anti-Darwinian, labelled Gosse's prochronism a 'visionary scheme', without explaining what he meant.[170] The high-quality *Natural History Review*, founded by E. Perceval Wright and printed in Dublin, which at the time was generally opposed to Darwin's theory but later became an advocate for it,[171] not only provided the best analysis of the book printed anywhere (as discussed later), but devoted the most space to it.[172]

Rounding out the picture of press coverage were notices from London and provincial newspapers. The politically Liberal London *Daily News*,[173] and two weeklies—the *Leicester Journal*[174] and *Hereford Journal*[175]—were reticent in expressing an opinion.[176] Not the weekly liberal *Manchester Examiner*, which termed the book among the 'important issues of the year.'[177] The twice-weekly *Birmingham Journal* said people like Gosse

164. [W. S. Dallas, *Wellesley Index* III: 627], 'Science', *Westminster Review* n.s. XIII (Jan. 1858), 263, 265.

165. *DNCJ*, 457.

166. *North British Review* XXVIII (Feb. 1858), 275 (the writer is not identified in *Wellesley Index* I: 682); *DNCJ*, 457.

167. *North British Review* XXVIII (Feb. 1858), 280.

168. *Gardeners' Chronicle* has been mentioned previously, and *Geologist* is cited in the text below.

169. *The Critic*, 5 Jan. 1861, 21.

170. Shirley Hibberd, 'The Genesis of Organic Forms', *Recreative Science* II (Jan. 1861), 277. Hibberd's anti-Darwinian outlook is evident in this review.

171. Miguel DeArce, 'The natural history review (1854-1865)', *Archives of Natural History* 39 (2012), 253-69; 'Natural History Review', *DNCJ*, 441.

172. *Natural History Review* V (Jan. 1858), 55-60.

173. London *Daily News*, 15 Dec. 1857, 2.

174. 'The Last Attempt to Untie the Geological Knot', *Leicester Journal*, 22 Jan. 1858, 6.

175. 'Geology and the Bible', *Hereford Journal*, 9 Dec. 1857, 5.

176. The *Daily News* and *Leicester Journal* gave quotations from *Omphalos*; the *Hereford Journal* cited the *Athenaeum* review, but not its conclusions.

177. *Manchester Examiner*, cited in the New York *Asmonean*, 5 Feb. 1858, 134-5. I was unable to locate the original review. *DNCJ*, 395.

'waste their energies and degrade their powers in endeavouring to reconcile what no thoughtful mind finds any difficulty in harmonising.'[178]

Omphalos was a response to the research of uniformitarian geologists, and Gosse said he was extending an olive branch to geologists by acknowledging their 'calculations are sound on the recognised premises' even if the law of prochronism 'disturbs' their conclusions about the antiquity of the earth.[179] The British geological community, still developing an identity and *modus operandi* as a scientific discipline, was not amused. It also was not prepared to ignore Gosse, apparently because it could not. Joseph E. Portlock (1794-1864), President of the Geological Society of London, devoted considerable attention to countering *Omphalos* in his Anniversary Address of 19 February 1858 after having heard a colleague declare the book's thesis 'indisputable'. Gosse showed 'ingenuity' in his reasoning and his natural history descriptions could be valuable in 'exciting a taste' for the subject, Portlock said, yet 'I regret that he should have thought it necessary to assist geologists over a difficulty which to them has no existence.'[180] Portlock's Irish counterpart, the Revd Samuel Haughton (1821-1897), the President of the Geological Society of Dublin, declined to support his colleague's analysis of *Omphalos*, or that of other geologists who 'have shown more temper than logic, and more zeal than discretion.' But before offering his own assessment in his annual address of 8 February 1859 Haughton did say that *Omphalos* was a 'remarkable book which has given rise to much discussion, both outside and inside geological circles.'[181]

The context of the analysis by Haughton sounds shocking today. On 1 July 1858, Charles Darwin and Alfred Russel Wallace famously had their independently formulated natural selection theory presented at a special meeting of the Linnean Society of London. As it turned out, Haughton was the first to offer a public assessment of those papers seven months later, during his 1859 Dublin address.[182] He rejected them. Haughton

178. *Birmingham Journal*, 25 Nov. 1857, 2. The *Journal* expressed the same sentiment in a previous notice (21 Oct. 1857, 4).

179. PHG, *Omphalos*, vi.

180. Joseph E. Portlock, *Address delivered at the Anniversary Meeting of the Geological Society of London, On the 19th of February, 1858* (London: Taylor and Francis, 1858), 149-51.

181. All quotations in this paragraph related to PHG are from Samuel Haughton, *Annual Address delivered before the Geological Society of Dublin, February 8, 1859* (Dublin: M. H. Gill, 1859), 21-2.

182. Peter J. Bowler, 'In Retrospect. Charles Darwin and his Dublin critics: Samuel Haughton and William Henry Harvey', *Proceedings of the Royal Irish Academy* 109C (2009), 412.

explained that he was commenting on the Linnean Society papers because of their 'important' bearing on geology. But in truth, Haughton said, the 'speculation of Messrs. Darwin and Wallace' merited no more than a 'passing notice ... If it means what it says, it is a truism; if it means anything more, it is contrary to fact.'

It is not relevant here whether or not Haughton's critique was justified in light of what was read at the Linnean.[183] What is important is that following Haughton's dismissive words on Darwin and Wallace, he turned his attention to *Omphalos*. Unlike the Darwin and Wallace papers, Haughton said that Gosse had authored a 'remarkable book.' Unlike the Linnean Society meeting—which Haughton did not describe as resulting in controversy—*Omphalos*, he said, had generated considerable debate. Nonetheless, Haughton was unimpressed. 'Mr. Gosse's book is, in truth, an attack on the foundations of human knowledge, and, therefore, to be regarded rather as a metaphysical than a geological speculation,' he said. The proper response was to leave Gosse alone in his 'barren logical field.'

Other geologists took up, and cast down, *Omphalos*. The *Geologist*, edited by Samuel Joseph Mackie (1823-1902), a 'fierce critic' of critics of Darwin's *Origin of Species*,[184] found *Omphalos* 'a little book worthy of Mr. Gosse in its appearance and address, but very unworthy of Mr. Gosse, and indeed of anybody else, in its doctrine.'[185] It contains 'wild and hypothetical speculations, alike derogatory to the intellect of man, and to the power and wisdom of God.'[186] The Canadian J. W. Dawson, whose own reconciliation of science and geology, *Archaia*, would appear in 1860, anticipated that the 'excellent author' of the 'ingenious but eccentric theory' would eventually view it 'as a modern instance of that barren, metaphysical speculation, which, in a by-gone time, was applied to nature, instead of patient, inductive inquiry.'[187] William Pengelly (1812-

---

183. In a carefully researched and argued paper, Derek Partridge rebuts the dominant narrative of what happened at the 1858 Linnean Society. Like Samuel Haughton, Thomas Bell (then President of the Linnean Society) dismissed the event in his May 1859 presidential address to the Linnean Society: 'The year which has passed, has not, indeed, been marked by any of those striking discoveries which at once revolutionize ... the department of science on which they bear'. Bell's words have been consistently mocked, but they were not (in Partridge's analysis) 'so shockingly misguided, if at all misguided' (Partridge, 'The Famous Linnean Society Meeting: From Old Errors to New Insights', *Biological Journal of the Linnean Society* 137 (2022), 556-567).

184. Eric F. Freeman, 'The Founders of the Geologists' Association II: The Mysterious Mr Mackie', *Proceedings of the Geologists' Association* 107 (1996), 88-9.

185. *Geologist* I (May 1858), 214.

186. *Geologist* I (May 1858), 216.

187. Dawson, *Archaia*, 203 fn., 334fn. The comments on PHG do not appear in what was

1894), of Torquay, an early convert to Darwin's theory[188] who knew Gosse, dismissed the prochronic theory as unworthy of refutation.[189] In 1859, the comparative anatomist and paleontologist Richard Owen, in the entry on paleontology for the *Encyclopaedia Britannica*, without naming Gosse referred to him as one who,

> cognisant of the wonderful structures of the extinct Devonian fishes— of the evidence of design and adaptation in their structures ... would deliberately reject the conclusions which healthy human reason must, as its Creator has constituted it, draw from such evidences of His operation. There are now individuals, one at least, who prefer to try to make it be believed ... that the geological evidences of superposition, successive stratification, and upheaval were, equally with palaeontological evidences, an elaborate design to deceive and not instruct! Surely, on such an hypothesis, the workmanship must be that of the father of lies, not of the Author of Truth, and the imaginer of such [an] hypothesis must be a Manichean at heart.[190]

Similarly Charles Darwin had *Omphalos* in mind in the conclusion to the *Origin of Species*. Do those who maintain that species are Divinely derived 'really believe that at innumerable periods in the earth's history certain elemental atoms have been commanded suddenly to flash into living tissues?' Darwin wondered. He added: 'Were all the infinitely numerous kinds of animals and plants created as eggs or seed, or as full grown? and in the case of mammals, were they created bearing the false marks of nourishment from the mother's womb?'[191]

Many publicly objected to the Law of Prochronism, and some few (like the scriptural geologist William Ker in an 1864 sermon) spoke positively about it.[192] Charles Kingsley, Gosse's former admirer and fellow

a new edition of this work, published in London and New York as *The Origin of the World According to Revelation and Science* (1877).

188. A. R. Hunt, 'Some Personal Reminiscences of the [Torquay Natural History] Society', *Torquay Directory*, 31 Oct. 1894, 6.

189. William Pengelly, 'On the Devonian Age of the World', *Geologist* IV (Aug. 1861), 334. In this printed version of Pengelly's lectures delivered before the Royal Institution, *Omphalos* is only briefly mentioned. The fuller verdict on the book is given in the report on Pengelly's talk in the *Torquay Directory*, 22 May 1861, 5.

190. Richard Owen, 'Palaeontology', *Encyclopaedia Britannica* (Edinburgh: Adam and Charles Black, 8ed., 1859), XVII: 91-176, esp. pp. 124-5.

191. Darwin, *On the Origin of Species*, 1859, 480-3.

192. William Ker, *The Bible versus Geologists; or, Creation in Six Days, and the Deluge*

natural history enthusiast, is the only known example of a critic whose disappointment was privately shared. 'For 25 years,' Kingsley wrote Gosse in 1858, 'I have read no book which has so staggered & puzzled me.'[193] He concluded that Gosse's Law of Prochronism meant that 'God has written on the rocks one enormous and superfluous lie for all mankind,' making it so dangerous that 'I would not for a thousand pounds put your book into my children's hands.' Gosse's polite response to the points in Kingsley's letter did not seem to have an immediate, or possibly any, impact.[194] Kingsley had committed to Gosse that he would not review the book, but two months before the *Origin of Species* appeared in 1859 he publicized his private feelings in the fourth edition of *Glaucus*. 'It is with real pain that I have seen my friend Mr. Gosse ... make a step in the direction of obscurantism,' Kingsley wrote, 'which I can only call desperate.'[195] Several years later, when Gosse sought Kingsley's assistance in finding a job for his son Edmund, Kingsley privately expressed a new view. 'The more I differed from your conclusions in Omphalos,' he wrote, 'the more I admired the moral courage & conscientiousness which dared to say what it thought at such a time, & on such a matter, & I shall always look on you with thorough respect.'[196] Whatever Kingsley may have actually thought about Gosse, he was publicly aligning himself with the 'young guard of science'—Huxley, Darwin, Lockyer, and others.[197]

Universal: A Sermon Preached in the Parish Church of Tipton, Staffordshire, Apr. 17, 1864. With Addenda and Notes. Dedicated to the Working Men of the District (London: Simpkin, Marshall & Co., 1865), 27-35 (although indebtedness to PHG is clear, the author did not acknowledge him).

193. Charles Kingsley-PHG. 4 May 1858 (LeBL). This letter is printed *in extenso* in *Life*, 280-3, but with a few omissions, errors of punctuation, and misreadings (such as p. 280, 'microchronology' for 'macrochronology', and p. 281, 'instruction' for 'induction').

194. PHG- C. Kingsley, 20 May 1858 (CUL Add. c. 82.5, 60). The surviving letter is a copy made by Sarah Andrews with the concluding paragraph in PHG's holograph. *Life* printed Kingsley's letter but not PHG's reply.

195. Kingsley's *Glaucus* (London: Macmillan & Co., 4ed., 1859), 14-15fn. Kingsley did not explicitly mention the *Deus quidam deceptor* accusation. The 5th ed. of *Glaucus* (1873) excludes any direct mention of the subject; it does retain complimentary words about PHG's books (p. 214). *Glaucus* review: London *Daily News*, 21 Sept. 1859, 2.

196. Kingsley-PHG, 31 Oct. 1865 (CUL Add. 7027, 50).

197. Hanawalt, 'Charles Kingsley and Science', 591, notes Kingsley's associations with Huxley and Darwin. Kingsley was a friend of Norman Lockyer, the founder of *Nature* (Melinda Clare Baldwin, '*Nature* and the Making of a Scientific Community, 1869-1939' (Princeton University, PhD dissertation, 2010), 45). In 1869, Lockyer listed Kingsley among 'eminent Scientific men' who had been approved as writers for the weekly (*Nature* I (11 Nov. 1869), 66-7).

-VII-

Having examined Gosse's timing in publishing *Omphalos*; the reason he chose to write about geology specifically and to attempt to harmonize it with Scripture; and the reception of the book in Victorian periodicals and the scientific community, it remains to raise an audacious question.

Recall that Edmund Gosse claimed that his father wrote *Omphalos* because he was depressed after his Emily's death, and though inclined to support Darwin's theory lashed out against it with a 'fanatical' gesture. Though Edmund was closer to his subject than we are today, this was neither a sincere nor an informed explanation. An answer must be sought elsewhere. Is it possible, at this distance in time, to penetrate P. H. Gosse's deepest, innermost thoughts to understand what he was trying to achieve in untying the geological knot? Surprisingly, it is.

It has been said that Gosse was someone whose goal was 'to defend his science on religious grounds.'[198] But he never sought to do that because he didn't need to. His science was perfectly good. It was non-Darwinian—*i.e.*, did not depend upon the evolution theory—but it did not need to in order to be significant work. The late American evolutionary biologist Stephen Jay Gould understood that—Gosse was 'the finest descriptive naturalist of his day'—but like other writers on *Omphalos*, got carried away in his dismissal of what he called 'such spectacular nonsense'. Gould said that with *Omphalos*, 'Gosse sealed his fate and placed himself outside the pale of science.'[199] He did nothing of the sort.

Gosse published five natural history works in the four years after the appearance of *Omphalos*: in 1859, *Evenings at the Microscope* and *Letters from Alabama*; in 1860, *Actinologia Britannica* and *Romance of*

198. Jonathan Smith, 'Philip Gosse and the Varieties of Natural Theology', in Linda Woodhead (ed.), *Reinventing Christianity: 19th Century Contexts* (London: Routledge, 2001, 2019), 261. This essay contains a number of errors in dating; improperly assumes the accuracy of EWG's statements about his father's scientific work; stereotypes Brethren religious views in assuming there was a single outlook ('beliefs and exegetical practices of ... the Plymouth Brethren', p. 254); deals solely with PHG's zoological works to the exclusion of his ornithological and Lepidoptera studies; does not cite a single one of PHG's religious writings; and minimizes the scientific impact of the aquarium movement.

199. Stephen Jay Gould, 'Adam's Navel', American Museum of Natural History *Natural History* 93 (June 1984), 6, 8, 14. Many others have expressed a similar judgment: Virginia Richter, 'The Best Story of the World: Theology, Geology, and Philip Henry Gosse's *Omphalos*', in Rens Bod, Jaap Maat, Thijs Weststijn (eds.), *The Making of the Humanities. Volume III: The Modern Humanities* (Amsterdam University Press, 2014), 75; Stuart Mathieson, 'The Victoria Institute 1865-1932: A Case Study in the Relationship between Science and Religion' (Queen's University Belfast, PhD dissertation, 2018), 73.

Natural History; and in 1861, the second series of *Romance of Natural History*. An examination of forty-one critiques of these works in twenty-two different British publications[200]—half of them had also reviewed *Omphalos*—demonstrates that *Omphalos* was only mentioned or alluded to in four of the reviews.[201] Overall, the reviews were positive. Only one of the reviews was decidedly negative,[202] and three alluded cryptically to *Omphalos*.

And more: Charles Darwin is known to have written Gosse three letters between 1856-57 on species variation and distribution, including a request that Gosse conduct an experiment on molluscs. After *Omphalos* appeared, he wrote at least three more, in reply to Gosse's inquiries on orchids.[203] If, as Gould claims, Gosse had really 'placed himself outside the pale of science', and if (as he additionally claims) in *Omphalos* Gosse had fallen into a 'deep error ... in his failure to recognize' the 'essential character of scientific reasoning,'[204] why did Darwin not know that?

And yet more: in the United States, where a number of Gosse's books were republished, advertised for sale, or reviewed during his lifetime, *Omphalos* was a non-event. It was neither republished nor reviewed (though it was promoted).[205] But when Edmund Gosse lectured in

200. The serials examined for their reviews of the five PHG books were: *Atlas*; *Blackwood's Edinburgh Magazine*; *British and Foreign Evangelical Review*; *British Quarterly Review*; *Critic*; *Daily News* (London); *Ecclesiastic*; *Eclectic Review*; *Gardeners' Chronicle*; *Gentleman's Magazine*; *Guardian* (London); *John Bull*; *Leader*; *Leisure Hour*; *Literary Gazette*; *Natural History Review*; *Nonconformist*; *Quarterly Journal of Science*; *Saturday Review*; *Spectator*; *St. James's Chronicle*; *Westminster Review*.

201. In two of the five PHG books published after *Omphalos* to 1861, PHG explicitly mentioned either prochronism (*Romance* 1st series, 364fn.) or *Omphalos* (*Romance* 2nd series, 2fn).

202. Review of *Romance of Natural History*, 2nd series, in *Literary Gazette* n.s. VII (23 Nov. 1861), 489-91.

203. The *Darwin Correspondence Project* identified six letters of Darwin-PHG, and four letters of PHG-Darwin, written from 1856-64.

204. Gould, 'Adam's Navel', 14.

205. D. Wertheimer, 'P. H. Gosse's Scientific Reception in America' (unpublished MS). *Omphalos* and *Geology or God: Which?* were not totally ignored. [R. L. Dabney], 'Geology and the Bible', *Southern Presbyterian Review* (Columbia, South Carolina) XIV (July 1861), §4-5 (256-274), does not explicitly cite PHG or *Omphalos*, but for the connection see 'The Caution against Anti-Christian Science Criticised by Dr. Woodrow', in C. R. Vaughan (ed.), *Discussions by Robert L. Dabney, D.D., LL.D.* (Richmond, Virginia: Presbyterian Committee, 1892), III: 170. A reviewer designated as 'B.' in 'Blackwood's Magazine, for July', Boston *Christian Register*, 7 Aug. 1874, 4, correctly detected support for the prochronic argument in [William G. Hamley, Wellesley I: 143], 'Modern scepticism and its fruit', *Blackwood's Edinburgh Magazine* 118 (July 1875), 113-24. In his discussion of contemporary science, Hamley (an army officer) wrote: 'Those traces of organs and members which are of no use to the animal which bears them, do not of

America in 1884-85, he told his father that '*you* are admired here.'[206] What he meant was that Edmund and his wife, Nellie (who accompanied him), had encountered notable American scientists (opponents as well as supporters of Darwin) who admired Philip's non-Darwinian scientific studies.[207] Those scientists—the marine ichthyologist Alexander Agassiz, the naturalist and Smithsonian Institution curator Spencer F. Baird, the microscopist Frederick Barnard, the botanist Asa Gray, and the paleontologist Joseph Leidy—had not placed Gosse 'outside the pale of science'. To the contrary: they wanted to have their greetings conveyed to him.[208]

In summary: Notwithstanding the general failure of *Omphalos* in the British press and its disregard in America, there was virtually no fallout of note from that work concerning the public's high regard for Gosse the naturalist (even by individual scientists such as Darwin). How could there have been, when *Evenings at the Microscope, Letters from Alabama*, and *Actinologia Britannica* were all incontrovertible contributions to science? Rather what happened—as we shall see later in examining the reception of Gosse's research on clasping-organs in male butterflies and Hudson & Gosse's three-volume *Rotifera*—was that many in the British elite, practitioners of scientific naturalism, remained obsessed with *Omphalos* and boycotted Gosse's work because of it.

What Gosse wanted to do in *Omphalos* was not to protect his science, which was at any event secondary to his life. *It was to find a way to maintain his religious beliefs, with logical integrity and to his satisfaction.* He had been born into a religious family and had always been

necessity argue that the animal's ancestors were once in another stage of existence where such parts were required' (p. 119).

206. EWG-'My beloved Parents', 12 Dec. 1884 (CUL Add. 7018,80). Emphasis in the original.

207. Evolution opponents: Agassiz (*American National Biography*) and Barnard (Windsor Hall Roberts, 'The Reaction of the American Protestant Churches to the Darwinian Philosophy 1860—1900' (University of Chicago, PhD dissertation, 1936), 18; Barnard joined the Victoria Institute in 1887); supporters: Leidy (*American National Biography*) and Baird (*DSB*. Baird was familiar with the birds of Jamaica from specimens sent to him from there in the 1860s: Richard C. Banks and Robert Hole, Jr., 'W.T. March's Birds Collected in Jamaica', *Gosse Bird Club Broadsheet* No. 60, March 1993, 7-9). Asa Gray was an advocate for Darwin's theory, but believed that natural selection was compatible with the religious worldview (Dupree, *Asa Gray*, 296, 375; *American National Biography*; Ellegård, *Darwin and the General Reader*, 137).

208. EWG-PHG, 7 Jan. 1885 (CUL Add.7018,81); Nellie Gosse-'My dearest Mother' [Eliza Gosse], 12 Jan. 1885 (CUL Add. 7018,82); Robert L. Peters and David G. Halliburton (eds.), *Edmund Gosse, America. The Diary of a Visit, Winter 1884-1885*, in *English Literature in Transition: 1880-1920*, Special Series, No. 2 (1966); Wertheimer, 'A Son and his Father', 5, 31fn.32.

a devout Christian. His experience of an evangelical conversion when he was 22, surrounded by friends, had given him a new life, followed ten years later by his considered and thoughtful communion with Brethren, which gave that life a new direction. From the one, he gained life-long peer support; from the other, a meaningful and purposeful existence. Gosse's belief system was not 'blind faith,' as Lorraine Code intuited. It was the stance 'of a person who strives constantly to achieve intellectual and moral virtue. This is someone who sets rigorously high standards for himself in his relation to the world ... someone who places a high value upon intellectual integrity.'[209]

Gosse approached his religion through analysis and logic. At one point, concluding his defence of his position on various theological issues, he observed that 'The evidence, cumulative as it is, does not consist of my own speculations; I make no dogmatic assertions. It is exclusively inspired teaching, and inevitable logical deduction therefrom.'[210] Referring to a proposed article for the Victoria Institute submitted to him to referee, he said that he did 'not at all' accept the writer's outlook, but 'as a hypothesis legitimately arguable; &, as I considered, soberly & reverently propounded,' he recommended it.[211]

His belief system was based upon the conviction that the Bible was the Divine Word, and by definition could not be flawed. Yet inevitably a matter surfaces which suggests—or seems to lead to, or appears to force, on the preponderance of evidence—the ineluctable conclusion that the Divine Word is incomplete or erroneous or misguided or impossible or self-contradictory. What then? Some informed scientists modified their understanding of the Bible to accommodate the new situation. That was not Gosse. He maintained his position regardless of what others did, leading one observer to remark: 'We know of no one eminent in science,

---

209. Code, *'Father and Son*: A Case Study in Epistemic Responsibility', 268-269. Notwithstanding the author's understandable adoption of EWG's portrayals of his father, which mars her account and has led so many others astray, Code's essay is the most penetrating on the subject. The Canadian proponent of evolution Grant Allen (1848-99) told EWG that PHG was 'a most fascinating personality ... I have never cared ... for the great organisations; it is the man who, in religious thought or in science, strikes out a line for himself that appeals to my sympathies' (Allen-EWG, 7 July 1896, in Edward Clodd, *Grant Allen: A Memoir* (London: Grant Richards, 1900), 136).

210. PHG, *The Humanity of the Son of God: According to Scripture* (Printed for Private Circulation only, 1886), 32.

211. PHG-J.E. Howard, 27 June 1881 (CUL Add.7313,388). Howard was at the time a Victoria Institute Vice-President.

(excepting Mr. Gosse, and he is a zoologist) who has maintained the old faith concerning the cosmogony of Genesis.'[212] The way he did this was to rely on the same mode of reasoning throughout his life: *Give me the possibility—that is all I want—that the difficulty can be overcome*, and my understanding of my faith remains intact.[213] Statements in the Bible are perfect, accurate, certain, and literally true because they are the word of God. But scientific or other investigations—no matter how well intended, how carefully or thoroughly undertaken, how brilliantly argued, how widely accepted or how seemingly overwhelmingly or even inescapably persuasive—are still, at the end of the day, the conclusions of imperfect humans and susceptible to error. For Gosse, there was no question as to which path to follow.

This mode of thinking is already evident from the time of Gosse's earliest introduction to Brethren, when he was in his early thirties. In a notebook in which he placed copies of letters, memoranda, and various clippings and studies on prophetic subjects, Gosse jotted down this comment: 'Those who object to the literal fulfilment of these [Scripture] predictions,' he wrote, including the prophet Isaiah's words that in the future, 'the wolf and the lamb shall feed together' (KJV),

> on the ground that every part of the organization of an animal is adapted to its habits & appetites, & that it would be a physical impossibility for a lion to digest vegetable food, forget that the domestic Cat & the Dog, typical carnivora, are pledges & earnests even in the present state, of the possibility which is thus denied. It may be replied that these animals are in an unnatural condition, that the whole organization, the eye, the teeth, the talons, the flexible spine, the strong limbs, the hard bones, the firm muscles,—are thrown away. I grant this, in its full extent, still these examples *prove the possibility, (& this is all we want)* of subsisting in a state for which their whole organization is unadapted.[214]

212. Alexander Ferrie Kemp, reviewing J. W. Dawson's *Archaia*, in *Canadian Naturalist & Geologist* IV (Dec. 1859), 472. The Scottish-born Kemp (1822-1884) was active as a Presbyterian minister in Canada ('The Late Dr. A. F. Kemp', Montreal *Gazette*, 13 May 1884, 7; Kingston, Ontario *Weekly British Whig*, 8 May 1884, 4).

213. Conversely, PHG opposed arguments if they did not even meet the standard of being *possible*. Citing a critique of him by the Darbyite dispensationalist William Kelly, PHG wrote: 'I ask, is such an interpretation true? Is it probable? May I be forgiven for adding, is it possible?' (PHG, *The Revelation*, 36). On Kelly: Sandeen, *Roots of Fundamentalism*, 85.

214. PHG, 'Testimony of Prophecy', 86. Emphasis added. These words (up until 'I grant this, in its full extent') appear verbatim in PHG, *Mysteries of God* (1884), 289.

The same logical strategy is on view some two decades later, in writing about geology:

> The inspired Word distinctly states that animals and plants were created in full adult vigour:—great whales; moving creatures with life; winged fowl; cattle; creeping things; every plant of the field "before it was in the earth;" and every herb "before it grew." Therefore I am sure these objects bore evidences of prochronic development. Since this *was* the case with organic creation, it *may have been* the case with inorganic,—the world itself. Geologists say that this is altogether improbable. What of that? Is it *possible?* If they cannot deny the possibility, then the ground is cut from beneath their feet. Against the *certainty* of a short chronology, affirmed by the Holy Ghost, they bring the *probability* of a long one. I have sought to show that the Word of God absolutely compels me to the short chronology: I have sought to show that physical phenomena do not absolutely compel me to the long one.[215]

And a decade after this, in referring to the challenge of biblical criticism and Bishop Colenso, Gosse explained:

> I grant to the full, and support with both my hands, the need of uprightness in such inquiries, that Dr. Colenso so strenuously contends for. Will a man lie for God? Yet, having accepted, *on other grounds*, the fact of revelation, and that the Pentateuch is an integral part of the divinely-inspired Word, I come *assuming* that, being of God, it is true; I will yield one iota of it only when absolutely compelled to do so. I require the objector to give absolute proof of the *non*. It will not do to say, as is so constantly said, "I do not see how." Perhaps you do not; perhaps *we* do not; but is this proof of the *non?* We stand on testimony: at least you must *drive* us out; we are not going to retire at the mere gleam of weapons.[216]

It is the application of this approach—'Is it not possible—I do not ask for more'[217]—which explains why Gosse wrote *Omphalos*. Demonstrating to himself the logical feasibility of this (the Law of Prochronism) allowed

---

215. PHG, *Geology or God: Which?*, 12. Emphasis in the original.
216. PHG, 'The High Numbers of the Pentateuch: Are they Trustworthy?', *JTVI* V (Dec. 1871), 354. Emphasis in the original.
217. PHG, *Omphalos*, 345.

him to maintain that (his belief system). And, as previously noted, Gosse hoped that others would also find this analysis helpful.

Some have wished that Gosse—like numerous others of his time, naturalists or not—had been more flexible in his religious thinking. He might have rejected the notion of a conflict of science and religion by affirming that the former is 'declarative but never normative .... Science is about nature, after all, not about duties.'[218] He might have made the boundaries of religion and science 'fuzzy rather than solid,' Lorraine Code writes,[219] or abandoned his belief in the plenary inspiration of the Bible[220] or his conviction that Scripture does not teach science.[221] Gosse might have been spared an 'epistemological crisis' through these methods.

Perhaps he could have. Perhaps he should have. But, from Gosse's vantage, what for? He knew that grand scientific theories and findings, though initially heralded, could be (and had been determined to be) mistaken. The hugely popular *Vestiges of the Natural History of Creation* (1844) taught a crude 'transmutation' or evolution theory which never gained traction. Likewise the search by evolutionists for the source of all life in the late 1860s was short-lived. T. H. Huxley and others were convinced they could explain the origin of life by 'abiogenesis'—no Creator necessary. The theory was that life had emerged spontaneously from inorganic matter, and Huxley was convinced that a sample of primitive protoplasm had been dredged from the bottom of the sea. He even gave the living slime a name—*Bathybius haeckelii*, after fellow Darwinian Ernst Haeckel. But later, Huxley became *unconvinced*, changing his mind when *Bathybius* turned out to be not animal but mineral (Haeckel long clung to the original interpretation).[222]

Given such examples, might not Gosse have suspected that Darwin's theory could well suffer a similar burst of short-term notoriety?

218. Charles Coulston Gillispie, *The Edge of Objectivity* (Princeton: Princeton University Press, 1960), 350-1.

219. Code, '*Father and Son*: A Case Study in Epistemic Responsibility', 271.

220. Thrane, 'The Rise of Higher Criticism in England, 1800—1870', 272.

221. Though he did not explicitly mention *Omphalos*, the British psychiatrist Henry Maudsley (1835-1918) respected PHG's 'mature deliberation' on the subject of religion and science, criticising those 'who, without a particle of that moderation which a little knowledge would impart', place 'science in apparent antagonism to religion' (H. Maudsley, 'The Correlation of Mental and Physical Force; or, Man a Part of Nature', *Journal of Mental Science* VI (Oct. 1859), 53, 56).

222. Philip F. Rehbock, 'Huxley, Haeckel, and the Oceanographers: The Case of *Bathybius haeckelii*', *Isis* 66 (Dec. 1975), 506.

-VIII-

It was the failure of *Omphalos* to gain the significant following anticipated by Gosse which lead him 'to be angry with God,' Edmund Gosse tells us.[223] Facts disprove this fantasy. Gosse never gave up on the Creator. Gosse never stopped supporting the Law of Prochronism. That's what we learn from the historical record.

It was just a few months after the appearance of *Omphalos* that Gosse began to confront his critics. In January 1858 the *Natural History Review* carried a perceptive analysis of the book, perhaps written by E. Perceval Wright,[224] the director of the Dublin University Museum whom Gosse considered a friend.[225] 'We have no hesitation,' the review began, in a passage excerpted in advertisements for the work,[226]

> in pronouncing this book to be the most important and best written that has yet appeared on the very interesting question with which it deals. We believe the logic of the book to be unanswerable, its postulates true, its laws fairly deduced, and the whole considered as a play of metaphysical subtlety, absolutely complete; and yet, we venture to predict that its conclusion will not be accepted as probable by one in ten thousand readers.[227]

Omphalos could be compared to the Irish philosopher George Berkeley's *Three Dialogues Between Hylas and Philonous* (1713) and the French author Bernard de Fontenelle's *Entretiens sur la Pluralité des Mondes* (1786), the reviewer said, principally in the 'felt unreality' of the arguments:

> The admirable manner in which Berkeley draws his reader on, step by step, until at length he compels him, to his astonishment, to deny

---

223. *Father and Son*, 1907, 124.

224. *Natural History Review* V (Jan. 1858), 55-60. My conjecture is based upon a paragraph in a review of *Life* by 'E.P.W.' (*Nature*, XLIII, 30 Apr. 1891, 605) which repeats in parallel language and often with the exact words the characterisation of *Omphalos* in the *NHR*. Wright founded the *NHR* in 1854 and was editor until 1866 (DeArce, 'The natural history review (1854-1865)', 253-269). In 1858, Wright was a lecturer in Zoology at Trinity College, Dublin (Henry H. Dixon, 'Edward Perceval Wright', *Irish Naturalist* XIX (Apr. 1910), 61).

225. PHG, *Actinologia Britannica*, 64. Wright knew PHG and corresponded with him (e.g., Corr. Bk. 1877).

226. For example, the advertisement in the London *Globe*, 20 March 1858, 1, omitted the phrase 'and yet, we venture to predict that its conclusion will not be accepted as probable by one in ten thousand readers.'

227. *Natural History Review* V (Jan. 1858), 55.

the existence of an external world, finds a parallel in the process by which Mr. Gosse leads his readers to the conclusion that the fossils and other proofs of past duration, imbedded in the crust of the globe, are prochronic and not historic; that they were placed there by the Creator, in accordance with a plan or law, of which there are numerous examples in the organic world; and are by no means to be considered as having ever really, i.e. actually, existed.[228]

In an examination spanning six pages, the 'simple logic' of Gosse's position was thoughtfully dissected, with the conclusion that *Omphalos* contained 'idle speculations, fit only to please a philosopher in his hours of relaxation, but hardly worthy of the serious attention of any earnest man, whether scientific or not.'[229]

A few months later, the *Natural History Review* printed an entirely different critique, by the English geologist J. Beete Jukes (1811-1869).[230] It was one of the few instances in which the quarterly carried an opposing view.[231] Coincidentally, Jukes (like Gosse) had also spent time in Newfoundland, having undertaken a geological survey of the colony in 1839-40. Jukes, a supporter of Darwin's theory,[232] was startled to find that the *Review* had praised the book's logic, which he called (in a five-page letter) of 'the most flimsy character.'[233]

In Gosse's rejoinder (in the next issue of the *Review*),[234] he largely ignored Jukes' remarks, preferring instead to supplement his treatise with what he considered an important new argument.[235] It made no sense, Gosse said, to maintain that the natural world could be suffused with suffering and death when the world God had created was declared 'very good'. He felt that for Christians there was only one way to account for the

228. *Natural History Review* V (Jan. 1858), 55-6.
229. *Natural History Review* V (Jan. 1858), 59.
230. 'Correspondence', *Natural History Review* V (Apr. 1858), 106-110; *DSB* VII (2008), 185-6.
231. DeArce, 'The natural history review', 255. The PHG-Jukes exchange was reported in the *Salisbury and Winchester Journal*, 4 Dec. 1858, 3.
232. J. Beete Jukes, *The Student's Manual of Geology* (Edinburgh: Adam and Charles Black, 1857, 2ed. 1862), 416-420; Bowler, 'In Retrospect: Charles Darwin and his Dublin critics', 409.
233. 'Correspondence', *Natural History Review* V (Apr. 1858), 106.
234. *Natural History Review* V (July 1858), 126-32.
235. The British rationalist Edward Clodd (1840-1930), citing *Omphalos* as 'perhaps, the strangest specimen of human ingenuity' in attempting to reconcile Genesis and geology, also recognized that the challenge to the authority of Scripture went beyond the issue of a six-day creation (Edward Clodd, *Pioneers of Evolution from Thales to Huxley, with an Intermediate Chapter on the Causes of Arrest of the Movement* (London: Watts & Co., [?1896], 1903), 49).

state of the natural world of the time, in terms of the 'covenant theology' of Adam's 'Federal Headship'.[236] According to this theology, the suffering of present-day man was connected with the sin of Adam in the Garden of Eden. When Adam was created, God had entered into a covenant of life with him and his posterity on the condition that Adam would be perfectly obedient to his Creator. But this he failed to do, and when the human head of creation fell from grace by having sinned, creation fell with him, resulting in the appearance of the phenomenon of death for all creatures. Gosse believed, however, that there had never been any intention to allow the Divine plan to lapse. A new head—the Son of God—had all along been waiting to replace the fallen Adam. This was 'the great end for which all things were originally made. From all eternity, in the Divine prescience, "ALL things were made for" Christ.'[237] And in such a manner both the Fall and the Resurrection were inextricably bound together.

To Gosse's mind, the 'federal connexion of Creation with Humanity' offered Christians 'an impregnable position, which they might have defended against all assailants.'[238] Having ignored the argument in the past, however, they were unable to properly react to geologists who

> assure us that Creation—material creation, animals and plants on this very earth of ours—existed millions of ages before the headship of Man commenced. Nay, more; that Creation went on *in ruin*, for these countless periods; that vanity, suffering, pain, rapine, and death, was the undeviating rule. Nay, more; that there was an indefinite succession of universal ruins; that creation succeeded creation, fauna after fauna, race after race, through those doleful ages,—every one of which, without a solitary exception, fell into ruin; nay, *never knew anything else but ruin.* Shall Christians have such thoughts of God as this?[239]

To accept such deductions would be 'to dethrone the Lord Christ as Head of Creation, and to give the lie to the Revelation of God.'[240] And thus the

236. A brief exposition is given in F. F. Bruce, *Answers to Questions* (Exeter: Paternoster Press, 1972), 205-6; for other statements by PHG on this subject: *Naturalist's Rambles*, 208; *The Aquarium*, 176; *Natural History Review* V (July 1858), 127-8; *Geology or God: Which?*, 5-10; 'Adam's Federal Headship', *The Christian* (18 Oct. 1883), 743.

237. *Natural History Review* V (July 1858), 128; see also [PHG], *Glimpses of the Wonderful*, 109-10.

238. *Natural History Review* V (July 1858), 127.

239. *Natural History Review* V (July 1858), 128. Emphasis in the original.

240. *Natural History Review* V (July 1858), 132.

'geological conclusion of the continuance of species from a pre-human into the human era, is absolutely irreconcilable with the fact asserted by the Holy Spirit,—that creature-suffering is the consequence of imputed sin. It must, therefore, be pronounced false.'[241]

In the next issue of the *Natural History Review*, the editors discussed the letters of Jukes and Gosse. They found them both unconvincing. They thought that Jukes had failed to assault successfully Gosse's impregnable logic, and that Gosse had not proven that death had entered into the world through sin, 'an unscriptural and improbable' new principle.[242]

In later years, Gosse wrote and spoke about the danger for Christians in accepting the findings of geologists. In the second series of *The Romance of Natural History* (1861), he stressed the importance of the Law of Prochronism.[243] On 10 May 1864, attending a conference in London on the 'Sure Word of Prophecy,' he addressed the geological issue at one session on 'The Lord and King.' *Essays and Reviews* (1860), Gosse said, was based upon the assumption that 'God made this creation as miserable as it is.' He did not mention those who raised the possibility that the human species had evolved from a state of barbarism—Huxley or the early Lubbock or the cautious Lyell, or maybe even Darwin himself at that time—though he might have. 'Can we believe that the blessed God made creation like that?' Gosse asked. 'I cannot believe it. No, no; I believe that God made everything "very good"'. He thus issued an appeal to believing Christians:

> You will be told that there is irrefragable evidence to the contrary [of Bible statements]. There are strong facts, plausible facts, I know; but remember that the conclusions of geology are but man's inferences from certain facts. This I know, I cannot receive geological conclusions, and receive my Bible. I must give up one or the other. I am told I need not hold the 1st and 5th of Genesis. People, really Christian people, are saying very widely, that our belief in the Lord Jesus is not touched by the truth or falsehood of the Mosaic chronology, that it would not at all affect our salvation to reject it. Would it not? It would sap the very foundation of the Bible. ...

241. PHG, *Mysteries of God*, 256.
242. 'The Omphalos Controversy', *Natural History Review* V (Oct. 1858), 184-88.
243. PHG, *The Romance of Natural History* (London: James Nisbet, 1861), chapter I, 'The Extinct'.

I do solemnly and most tenderly appeal to the young, to whom the honour of Jesus is dear. I appeal to you, dear young friends, because it is to you that science, falsely so called, is mainly making its appeals; and I do beseech you, oh! think what you do. Weigh well what you do, before you give your faith to the conclusions of man. ...

Suppose I cannot see how these difficulties may be answered; shall I trust my God with a difficulty? Shall I trust Him for my eternal salvation, and hesitate in a matter that appeals to sense, or rather man's inferences from sensuous phenomena? "Let God be true, and every man a liar."[244] If one comes to me with facts which, *he says*, prove that man has lived upon the earth for millions of years, that the six days' creation had no existence, that an universal deluge in human history is a fable; if he says, "Here are facts; how will you get over these?" I fall back upon the word of the unlying God. I may possibly see a clue which would guide me through all the difficulties—I think I *have* such a clue—but that is not the point.[245]

In 1866, Gosse re-issued his *Natural History Review* letter as a 16-page pamphlet and titled it *Geology or God: Which? A Supplement to "Omphalos"*.[246] In this way he intended to emphasize the message found in his 1864 talk: Accept geology or accept God. It is a zero-sum choice.

Though *Geology or God* remained in print in Britain until at least 1877, it was barely noticed in the press there[247] or the United States.[248]

---

244. Romans 3:4.

245. *Report of Three Days' Meetings for Prayer, and Addresses on the "Sure Word of Prophecy," Held in Freemasons' Hall, May 9th, 10th, & 12th, 1864* (London: William Yapp, [1864]), 58-60. I am grateful to Mr. G. C. D. Howley, editor of *The Witness*, for kindly allowing me to borrow his copy of this rare pamphlet in 1973. Emphasis in the original.

246. In a review of *Life*, E. P. W[right] referred to PHG's intention to publish a supplement to *Omphalos*, but stated that it never appeared (*Nature*, XLIII (30 Apr. 1891), 605). In 1980, Freeman & Wertheimer-PHG claimed that such a supplement had indeed been published as *Geology or God: Which?* Although they failed to locate a copy (there had been one in the library of the Victoria Institute in London, *JTVI* IX (1876), 438), they gave it a bibliographical entry on the basis of newspaper advertisements and other information. They believed it 'likely' that it was 'a reprint, or an extension, of Gosse's original [*Natural History Review*] letter of 1858.' (pp. 81-2). In 2011, Wertheimer traced a copy of *Geology or God* to the John Rylands Library at the University of Manchester. The pamphlet turned out to be as anticipated (a modest amount of new material at p. 5fn, insertions at pp. 10, 13, and extracts from *Omphalos*, 14-15).

247. An exception was the positive review in *Achill Missionary Herald* 36 (1 Sept. 1870), 528-9. 'A. Layman', the pseudonymous author of *Conversations on the Creation: Chapters on Genesis and Evolution* (London: Sunday School Union, [?1881]), claimed that according to *Omphalos*, God 'has or can have deceived us in the strata' (p. 30).

248. *Geology or God* was favourably noticed in a New York newspaper (which I have been

It was one of the 'little brochures' which Gosse would include in letters to correspondents from at least 1870 to at least 1881.[249] Meanwhile *Omphalos* itself remained an extremely slow seller, with the price steeply reduced from 10s.6d. in 1857 to 3s.6d. in 1868.[250] By 1869, only 600 copies of *Omphalos* had been sold, and the book's printer wanted their warehouse cleared of the 3,400 remaining copies. That apparently prompted Gosse to change the title to *Creation* (*Omphalos*) in the hopes of boosting sales.[251] *Omphalos* remained for sale through the London publisher Van Voorst. Most of the copies appear to have been auctioned in 1873. By the autumn of 1874 the copyright passed to Reeves & Turner, who were selling it for 1s. 6d.[252]

From time to time after this, Gosse expressed his unwavering support of the theory of prochronism in published[253] and private letters.[254] 'I

unable to identify). PHG's approach was opposed in two publications: James Kerr, "Geology or God: Which?' Both', Philadelphia *Our Monthly: A Magazine of Religion and Literature* VII (Apr. 1873), 314-16 (a Presbyterian serial: Frank Luther Mott, *A History of American Magazines 1865-1885* (Cambridge: Harvard University Press, 1938), III: 74), where PHG's name is not mentioned in the notice; and A Layman, 'Conversations on Creation', Meadville, Pennsylvania *The Chautauquan* I (Jan. 1881), 170-3 (official publication of the Chautauqua Literary and Scientific Circle, an educational group: Mott, *History of American Magazines* III: 544-7), where PHG's name is mentioned.

249. Information drawn from Corr. Bk., where the entries are occasionally annotated by PHG (letter to 'Williams', 23 Mar. 1874, 'with Geol. + Proph. Times' or a letter to 'Morris' of 4 Sept. 1877: '+G. or G.'); PHG-Louis C. Biggs, 30 Apr. 1881 (CUL Add. 7313,356) says he is including in the letter *Geology or God*; PHG-E.B. Elliott, 5 Mar. 1870, notes he is sending 'little brochures' by PHG: '*Geol. or God*; *Revelation*; *6000 yrs*; [Great] Trib[ulation].' (letter in Corr. Bk.).

250. Advertisement, *Newcastle Courant*, 17 Jan. 1868, 4.

251. Freeman & Wertheimer-PHG, 59. The earliest listing of *Omphalos* under the title '*Creation* (*Omphalos*)' which I have seen is in William Wesley Bookseller's *Natural History and Scientific Book Circular*, no. 1 (July 1874), 19, where it was selling for 4s.6d. (published price: 10s. 6d.). However Freeman & Wertheimer-PHG, as cited, date the printing of the *Creation* (*Omphalos*) title-page edition of *Omphalos* to 'before 1869', regardless of the fact that the cancel title leaf for *Creation* is dated 1857. There was only the one (1857) printing of *Omphalos*, with the *Creation* (*Omphalos*) version using the same sheets with a cancel title leaf on the stub.

252. Freeman & Wertheimer-PHG, 60 (PHG calculated that if the 3,400 copies were sold for 7s. each the total would come to about £100, allowing him to 'clear costs, or nearly'). For the auction sale in 1873: *Athenaeum*, 3 May 1873, 555, and 17 May 1873, 619 (selling 3,000 copies at 6s. each) and London *Daily News*, 19 May 1873, 7. Corr. Bk. registers a letter, PHG-Van Voorst, 7 May 1872, annotated 'Omphalos'.

253. *English Mechanic* XV (24 May 1872), 255; *Glasgow News*, 11 Sept. 1874, 2.

254. PHG acknowledged an advance copy of Samuel Kinns' *Moses and Geology; or, the Harmony of the Bible with Science* (1882) by pointing out that the author had overlooked the important question 'of Death, & Federal Headship'. PHG sent him a copy of *Geology or God*, where he addresses the subject (PHG-S. Kinns, 21 Oct. 1881, CUL Add. 7313, 426). See also PHG-Alfred Russel Wallace, 10 Feb. 1880 (CUL Add. 7313, 31; original at the Linnean Society of London), and W. A. Lloyd-C. W. Peach, 22 Feb. 1858 (Institute of Geological Sciences, Museum

believe the argument to be logically impregnable,' he said in an 1874 letter. 'Granting my postulates, I have never yet seen any attempt to answer it,' Gosse said.[255] Occasionally he would be consulted about the geological question. In an 1880 letter to a fellow believer, Mrs Henry Oliver of Canada, Gosse showed how to buttress the Omphalotic point of view by taking the Resurrection as a fact:

> Does your friend believe this? believe it, I mean, as impregnable, indubitable? If so, then, mark the chain of links that hang on this. If Jesus was raised, then He was Son of God: then His every testimony was God's testimony; His every word was truth and no lie. But He constantly cited the Hebrew Scriptures as being the Words of God, written by men "in the Spirit" (Matt. xxii. 29, 31, 43); quoted from the first chapter of Genesis (Matt. xix.4, 5.) and on through the Law & the Prophets, abundantly; always appealing as to an irrefragable authority; "Have ye not read—?"
>
> On one occasion (John x.32-36), arguing with keen, spiteful disputants, he cited a brief verse from a brief psalm, as conclusive: and (mark this!) He spoke of "*the Scripture*" as one indivisible integer; making this weighty comment, "— the Scripture *cannot be broken!*"
>
> This is enough for me. He who is "declared to be Son of God with power, by the resurrection from the dead," has abundantly & unmistakably avouched the Scripture, as an entirety, to be "the Words of God" (see John vii, viii, *passim*) which "*cannot be broken.*" Errors in human transcribers, of course, there may be: these may be easily allowed for: but the great facts testified I must accept implicitly, until I am convinced that God *did not* raise Jesus from the dead.[256]

Four years before Gosse died, this defence was among those employed

of Geology, London, 1/527). PHG sent a copy of *Omphalos* to 'Mrs. [Fanny E.] Guinness' in 1882 (Corr. Bk., Dec. 28, 1882).

255. PHG-'C.', 10 Sept. 1874, published in *Glasgow News*, 11 Sept. 1874, 2 (with response by 'J. W.', 15 Sept. 1874, 7: 'for I confess I never met with a theory of Creation so dishonouring to God as the one in question'); *English Mechanic* XV (24 May 1872), 255 (and the reply by 'A Fellow of the Royal Astronomical Society', ibid., 31 May 1872, 274: '"Accepting my postulates", says Mr. Gosse. Exactly: Accept the postulate that 5 - 3 = 19, and see whether I will not deduce results before which "The Glorious Metric System" shall pale and dwarf into utter insignificance').

256. PHG-Mrs Henry Oliver, 14 Mar. 1880 (CUL Add. 7313, 51-2). Emphasis in the original.

in his *Mysteries of God* (1884).[257] It did not receive greater affirmation in 1884 than it had in 1857.[258]

Though the Law of Prochronism met Gosse's religious needs, many who came across it at the time, or in later years, remained convinced that the conflict could be otherwise managed. Some followed the editor of the *Natural History Review* who (as previously noted) recognized its 'unanswerable' logic while nonetheless noting that it failed the reality test. The British philosopher Bertrand Russell (1872-1970), without explicitly mentioning *Omphalos*, in 1921 dismissed this 'sceptical hypothesis,' which he called 'logically tenable, but uninteresting.'[259] He returned to this 'curious attempt to save orthodoxy in the field of biology' nearly fifteen years later:

> There is no logical possibility of *proving* that this theory [of Prochronism] is untrue. ... We may have all come into existence five minutes ago, provided with ready-made memories, with holes in our socks and hair that needed cutting. But although this is a logical possibility, nobody can believe it; and Gosse found, to his bitter disappointment, that nobody could believe his logically admirable reconciliation of theology with the data of science.[260]

The Canadian philosopher Lorraine Code, after observing that Gosse showed a 'complete absence of self-criticism,' put it more elegantly and insightfully: 'creationist fervour becomes an attitude which it is possible to respect, if not share, understand, if not respect.'[261]

The opinions of philosophers notwithstanding, there is an improbable postscript to the Law of Prochronism. *Omphalos* has been reborn. A century after its publication, many creationists—opponents of evolution

257. PHG, *Mysteries of God*, Chapters XX ('Science versus Revelation. I. Creation.') and XXI ('Science versus Revelation. II. Death.'), 233-60.

258. 'His theory of Geology, which would account for the existence of fossils, is exceedingly ingenious, but we do not think that it is more than *that*: it has too much the appearance of a fallacy ever to pass current as truth. That it has not been disproved is by no means remarkable, for it occurs to many minds that it is too improbable to need disproving. Still, for our part, we mean to ponder it in our heart, for we know well that many a great truth has at its first appearance been judged to be an absurdity' (presumably [C. H. Spurgeon] review of *Mysteries of God* in *Sword and the Trowel* XXI (May 1885), 236).

259. Bertrand Russell, *The Analysis of Mind* (London: George Allen & Unwin Ltd., 1921), 159-60.

260. Bertrand Russell, *Religion & Science* (New York: Oxford University Press, 1935, 1966), 69-70.

261. Code, '*Father and Son*: A Case Study in Epistemic Responsibility', 269, 278.

who favour a literalist biblical interpretation, believe in biblical inerrancy and a supernatural creation by God, among other ideas—have turned to the principle of 'creation with appearance of age' (also called the 'young Earth theory')[262] to resolve the apparent science-religion conflict. They frequently cite Gosse. The 'grand physical law' announced by Gosse 'allows you to have your cake and eat it too,' wrote James Jauncey in *Science Returns to God* (1961). Writing in 1964 in *Creation Revealed*, Frederick A. Filby called *Omphalos* 'that masterpiece of logic and literature.'[263]

-IX-

Geology was not the only science testing Gosse's understanding of Scripture. There was Darwin's evolution theory (relying on many of the same premises and much of the same evidence as used by geologists), and there was the challenge to the Divine origin of Scripture from scholars promoting a literary critique of its texts (also relying on projecting current modes of thinking into the past in a focus on the Bible's historical development). No sooner had the Law of Prochronism settled one controversy for Gosse than evolution and biblical criticism opened up two others.

Initially, Gosse had little concrete to say about Darwin's theory. This reflected the irrelevancy of his scientific studies to the evolutionary theory. Gosse's opportunities to study the effects of geographical isolation on species were never as great as those of Wallace, Darwin, Bates, or others.[264] The evolutionary history of sea anemones is to this day a matter of controversy. And even had Gosse wished to investigate the past transformations of the Rotifera he could not have done so, since no paleontological record has survived: rotiferan 'phylogeny must remain a matter of speculation.'[265]

---

262. Michaelis Michael, 'Philip Henry Gosse and the Geological Knot', in *Evolution by Natural Selection: Confidence, Evidence and the Gap* (Boca Raton, FL: CRC Press, 2016), 124.

263. The information in this postscript is from McIver, 'Creationism: Intellectual Origins,' esp. 464-73 (for the cited remarks, pp. 470-1). PHG's law of prochronism was the inspiration for the 22-minute experimental film by Pablo Martin Weber, *Homenaje a la Obra de P. H. Gosse [Tribute to the Work of P.H. Gosse]* (Universidad Nacional de Córdoba, 2020). The film includes colour images of sea anemones by PHG, but otherwise has a difficult-to-discern connection to him.

264. A. J. Cain (1921-99) expressed the same view in a MS. draft of 'The Omphalotic Argument in the Early Nineteenth Century: Penn and Gosse', which he kindly lent to me in 1972.

265. For the former, see T. A. Stephenson, *The British Sea Anemones* (London: Printed for the

As already noted, Gosse had met Darwin, corresponded with him, and was familiar with at least some of his work. He was 'a perfectly dependable naturalist,'[266] Gosse observed, who did 'admirable work.'[267] His evolution theory was another matter. Gosse's earliest allusion to it is in the *Romance of Natural History* (1860), published a year after Darwin's *Origin of Species*. There Gosse quotes from the *Origin*,[268] adding in a footnote: 'I am very far, indeed, from accepting Mr. Darwin's theory

Ray Society, 1928), I: 102-6; for the latter, W. T. C[alman], 'Rotifera', *Encyclopaedia Britannica* (Chicago: University of Chicago Press, 1946), XIX: 577, and Harry K. Harring, 'Synopsis of the Rotatoria', *Bulletin of the United States National Museum* LXXXI (1913), 9.

266. PHG, *A Year at the Shore* (London: Alexander Strahan, 1865), 145. PHG not infrequently quoted from Darwin's books and owned some of them, e.g., *Various contrivances by which British and foreign orchids are fertilised* (1862), and *Voyage of Researches* (1839), popularly known as the *Voyage of the Beagle* (*Sandhurst Catalogue* item #338, listed there as 'Darwin's Naturalist's Voyage'. Assuming the listing follows the title of the book as printed on its spine, the edition would either have been of 1845 or 1860, the former reading 'Naturalist's Voyage' and the latter 'Naturalist's Voyage round the world'; see Freeman, *Darwin*, 2ed., 32).

Darwin likewise owned PHG's books. The ornithologist William Jardine recommended that he read PHG's *Birds of Jamaica* (Darwin Papers, CUL 119: 'Books Read/Books to be Read', under the latter). Darwin's annotated copy of *Naturalist's Sojourn in Jamaica* is at CUL (Frederick Burkhardt and Sydney Smith (eds.), *The Correspondence of Charles Darwin. Volume 5: 1851-1855* (Cambridge: Cambridge University Press, 1989), 489fn.7). In a letter to the naturalist H. W. Bates, Darwin wrote: 'I was a *little* disappointed in [Alfred Russel] Wallace's book on the Amazon [*Travels on the Amazon and Rio Negro*, 1853]; hardly facts enough. On [the] other hand, in Gosse's book [*Naturalist's Sojourn*] there is not reasoning enough to my taste' (Darwin-Bates, 3 Dec. [1861], in Francis Darwin (ed.), *The Life and Letters of Charles Darwin* (London: John Murray, 1887), II: 380. Emphasis in the original). Darwin also had a copy of PHG's *Letters from Alabama* in publisher's cloth, 'probably a present from PHG', according to R. B. Freeman (Freeman-Wertheimer, Nov. 9 and Dec. 18, 1972; the book is at CUL). Darwin quotes from it in *The Variation of Animals and Plants under Domestication* (London: John Murray, 1868), II: 42)

In light of PHG's harsh critique of the science of his day, and his praise for Darwin's work both before and after the 1859 publication of *Origin of Species*, I believe Smith is mistaken in asserting that in 1865 PHG 'damns Darwin with the faintly praising epithet of "a perfectly dependable naturalist"' (Smith, 'Philip Gosse and the Varieties of Natural Theology', 258). PHG invariably spoke directly and not sarcastically or condescendingly. His characterization is a bold, respectful, and honest way of saying that, notwithstanding PHG's critique of Darwin's theory, he was not about to line up behind other anti-evolutionists who asserted that Darwin was not a reliable naturalist. The *Illustrated London News* (25 Feb. 1865, 194) humorously commented: "a perfectly *dependable* naturalist, Mr. Charles Darwin;' ... [suggesting] an unpleasant connection between Mr. Darwin and the gallows.'

267. PHG, *Evenings at the Microscope* (1874 ed.), 156fn., referring to Darwin's 1862 book on orchids (the 1874 edition of *Evenings at the Microscope* is the same as the first edition of 1859, except for the addition of footnotes such as this one; Freeman & Wertheimer-PHG, 62). Likewise PHG's *Manual of Marine Zoology* I (1855), 167 (where he refers to Darwin's 'admirable' *Monograph of the Sub-class Cirripedia*, 1851, 1854) and PHG's *Tenby* (1856), where he characterizes that monograph as 'that monument of research and acumen' (p. 118).

268. PHG, *Romance of Natural History* (1860), 79-81.

to the extent to which he pushes it, completely trampling on Revelation as it does;[269] but I think there is a *measure* of truth in it.'[270]

What does '*measure* of truth' mean? Some say: It means Gosse did not actually oppose Darwin's ideas.[271] That, of course, is not so. Gosse's thought appears to be similar to that expressed by many serious men of science in their initial reaction to Darwin. They recognized Darwin's 'profound knowledge'[272] and the 'remarkably concise and readable'[273] character of the *Origin of Species*, yet still opposed it.[274] That is how the Quaker naturalist Edward Newman, editor of the *Zoologist* who did not support the evolution theory, responded just after Gosse's remark appeared. He may even have had Gosse's statement in mind, since he used Gosse's 'measure of truth' phrase:

> Revelation must either be accepted or rejected by us *in toto:* there is no middle course. It is not to be pruned and docked according to our fancy and supposed experience, and then its mutilated remains honoured out of a conventional sense of propriety. ... The fresh conviction we have received from the perusal of 'The Origin of Species' is that there is a measure of truth in Mr. Darwin's deductions, that genealogical relationship between species is here and there true to a limited extent ...[275]

In the next year, Gosse obliquely criticised the evolutionary theory in the second series of the *Romance of Natural History* (1861). This work, which followed the pattern of his earlier writings in highlighting the wonders of creation, was mainly intended to examine the evidence pro and con of a number of phenomena in natural history which had been

269. 'It is given as the solemn condemnation of the polished nations of antiquity, that 'when they knew God [viz. in the works of His creation] [sic] they glorified Him not as God' (Rom. i.21). It was not that men were lacking among them who, as now, in their measure, studied and admired the works of Nature, so called, *but no praise, no glory, accrued to God from their studies*' (PHG, *The Aquarium*, 1854, 46. Emphasis in the original).

270. PHG, *Romance of Natural History* (1860), 81fn. Emphasis in the original. PHG left this statement unchanged and unexplained in later editions of the book.

271. EWG claims his father wanted to accept Darwin's theory (*Father and Son*, 1907, 119). Following that lead, Christoph Irmscher writes that PHG was 'too good an empiricist' not to do so, and that *Omphalos* was his 'most ambitious attempt' to distance himself from evolutionary ideas (Irmscher, 'Nature Laughs at Our Systems: Philip Henry Gosse's *The Canadian Naturalist*', *Canadian Literature* no. 170-1 (Autumn/Winter 2001), 79).

272. Edward Newman, 'Preface', Zoologist XIX (1861).

273. Edward Newman, review of *Origin of Species* (and other works), *Zoologist* XIX (1861), 7611.

274. *Zoologist* XIX (1861), 7611.

275. *Zoologist* XIX (1861), 7610, 7611

generally considered of dubious reality. Perhaps, Gosse argued, mermaids do not exist, swallows do not hibernate, animals do not mesmerize their victims, toads are not actually found immured in stones—but at least give these claims a fair hearing. It is too simplistic, he wrote, to 'set aside every phenomenon which I cannot explain, with the common resource,— "Pooh! pooh! there must be some mistake!" Rather would I say, "There must still be some ignorance in me."'[276]

In Gosse's chapter on 'The Extinct', prochronism and evolution came into direct contact for the first time. Darwin's theory was not actually mentioned, but its existence as a cause in Gosse's mind may be fairly deduced from its effects—the issues Gosse raised. Is competition through natural selection the cause of extinction in species? Must one admit that the earth has had an incomparably vast history (as demonstrated in Charles Lyell's uniformitarian geology)? These are questions which Darwin asked, and answered in the affirmative.[277] Gosse, as we know, looked elsewhere for solutions. Species, he asserted, are the same today as they were in the aeons past: they grow 'not by alteration of their specific characters, but by replacement of species by species.'[278] What appear as new species are not new; they might have ceased to exist because they had reached the allotted duration assigned to them by the Creator, but they were then succeeded by new creations.[279] And concerning the argument that 'the former changes of the earth's surface' are best explained 'by reference to causes now in operation,' Gosse said that was an assumption for which 'we have not a tittle of proof.'[280] Thus Gosse, in accordance with 'that prochronic hypothesis, by which alone, as I conceive, the facts revealed by geological investigation can be reconciled with the unerring statements of Scripture,'[281] thought that the world actually came into

276. PHG, *Romance of Natural History* (1861), 97; also PHG-T. Digby Pigott, 27 May 1863 (R. B. Freeman Collection).

277. Darwin, *On the Origin of Species*, 1859, 110, 282.

278. PHG, *Omphalos*, 95.

279. PHG, *Romance of Natural History* (1861), pp. 1-2, 89-90; cf. Darwin, *Origin of Species*: 'The whole subject of the extinction of species has been involved in the most gratuitous mystery. Some authors have even supposed that as the individual has a definite length of life, so have species a definite duration' (p. 318). Darwin concluded: 'natural selection, if it be a true principle, [will] banish the belief of the continued creation of new organic beings, or of any great modification in their structure.' (pp. 95-6)

280. PHG, *Romance of Natural History* (1861), 47; Charles Lyell, *Principles of Geology; Being an Attempt to Explain the Former Changes of the Earth's Surface by Reference to Causes Now in Operation* (London, 3vols. 1830-33).

281. PHG, *Romance of Natural History* (1861), 3.

existence during the Tertiary Era, and that the many fossil mammalia hitherto assumed to be of great antiquity had a synchronic existence with man.[282]

Gosse's aim of fairly treating evidence of reputable witnesses on behalf of doubtful occurrences met with a mixed reception. His continued adherence to prochronism, as well as his covert comments on Darwin, were not favourably noticed by any periodical.[283]

-X-

During the first half of the nineteenth century, historical biblical criticism—whose origins as an independent discipline can be dated to the late seventeenth century[284]—had gained a foothold in Britain, though largely confined to the Continent.[285] Also referred to as 'Higher Criticism', it was at its most controversial in the 'Documentary Hypothesis' on the sources and composition of the Pentateuch. A storm of protest followed the publication in England of the best-selling *Essays and Reviews* in 1860[286] and the first part of the hot-selling *Pentateuch and the Book of Joshua Critically Examined* (beginning in 1862), by J. W. Colenso (1814-1883).[287] The work of the Anglican Bishop of Natal in South Africa

---

282. PHG, *Romance of Natural History* (1861), 48-9.

283. *The Critic* (n.s. XXIV (8 Feb. 1862), p. 144) expressed a view shared even by many of those who praised *Romance of Natural History* (1861) in writing that 'At other times [PHG] has shown himself a sensible and pleasant companion in sea-side rambles, and a clever writer on recent marine zoology, and we are disappointed and shocked to find him casting aside the sobriety proper to a teacher of truth, and risking his well-earned reputation to become a chronicler of the marvellous, a retailer of absurdities, and a special pleader for tales which are only "fit for the marines."' For other generally unfavourable notices of the second series of *Romance*: [J. R. Leifchild], *Athenaeum* (7 Dec. 1861), 769-70; [G. H. Lewes: *Wellesley Index* I: 115], *Blackwood's Magazine* XCI (Apr. 1862), 444-6; *British Quarterly Review* XXXV (Apr. 1862), 508-9; *Gardeners' Chronicle* (21 Dec. 1861), 1117-18. For generally favourable ones: *Eclectic Review* n.s. II (Mar. 1862), 285; *Gentleman's Magazine* n.s. XII (Apr. 1862), 487; *Literary Gazette* n.s. VII (23 Nov. 1861), 489-91; Edward Newman (signed), *Zoologist* XX (1862), 7865-70.

284. Thrane, 'The Rise of Higher Criticism in England, 1800-1870', 53.

285. Thrane, 'The Rise of Higher Criticism in England, 1800-1870', 1, 314; Scott Gerard Prinster, 'Reading the Bible Scientifically: Science and the Rise of Modern Biblical Criticism in the Nineteenth- and Twentieth-Century United States' (University of Wisconsin-Madison, PhD dissertation, 2021), 154-5; Pietsch, *Dispensational Modernism*, 83-7; N. Merrill Distad, *Guessing at Truth: The Life of Julius Charles Hare (1795-1855)* (Shepherdstown, WV: Patmos Press, 1979), 81-92.

286. *Essays and Reviews* is said to have sold 20,000 copies in the first two years following publication: Altick, *The English Common Reader*, 390.

287. The first edition of the first part of *The Pentateuch and the Book of Joshua Critically Examined* was announced for October 29, 1862 (London *Daily News*, 20 Oct. 1862, 8) and apparently issued on October 28 (London *Morning Post*, 29 Oct. 1862, 3). It is said to have sold

was the 'first thoroughgoing, indigenous attempt' at biblical criticism in Britain.[288] Quantitatively considered, the response to *Essays and Reviews* in both the general[289] and the religious[290] British periodical press exceeded that for Darwin's *Origin*. The fear—shared by the traditionally religious, including students of prophecy[291]—was that the new scientific literary mode of investigating the Bible would have a toxic impact on belief. First *Origin* and then *Essays*: 'The intellectual crisis of Victorian faith,' as Josef Altholz neatly put it, 'was a tale of two books.'[292]

On 5 June 1871, Gosse's only paper dealing with biblical criticism was read before the Victoria Institute of London.[293] The society had been established on 24 May 1865 by James Reddie (1820-1871), a civil servant, with the aim to investigate 'fully and impartially the most important questions of Philosophy and Science, but more especially those that bear upon the great truths revealed in Holy Scripture, with the view of defending these truths against "the opposition of Science, falsely so called"'.[294]

Gosse was a founding vice-president of the Institute, encouraged family and friends to join,[295] and remained actively involved for the rest

8,000 copies in the first three weeks of November 1862 (Delorme, 'The Unitarian Physiologist: Science and Religion in the Life and Work of William Benjamin Carpenter (1813-1885)', 102).

288. Timothy Larsen, 'Bishop Colenso and his Critics: The Strange Emergence of Biblical Criticism in Victorian Britain', *Scottish Journal of Theology* 50 (Nov. 1997), 435.

289. Ellegård, *Darwin and the General Reader*, 106.

290. Josef L. Altholz, 'Early Periodical Responses to Essays and Reviews', *Victorian Periodicals Review* 19 (Summer 1986), 54.

291. Sears, 'The Interpretation of Prophecy and Expectations of the End in Britain', 131-3.

292. Josef L. Altholz, 'A Tale of Two Controversies: Darwinism in the Debate over "Essays and Reviews"', *Church History* 63 (Mar. 1994), 50.

293. PHG's 'The High Numbers of the Pentateuch: Are They Trustworthy?' first appeared in *JTVI* V (Dec. 1871), 349-77, and was published separately in 1871 by Wyman & Sons with re-numbered pages; Freeman & Wertheimer-PHG, 85.

294. A Member [James Reddie], *Scientia Scientiarum. Being Some Account of the Origin and Objects of the Victoria Institute, or Philosophical Society of Great Britain* (London: Robert Hardwicke, 3rd thousand, 1866), 5 (reprinted in *JTVI* I, 1866-67, 9).

295. PHG family relations who joined the Victoria Institute: PHG's brother-in-law from his second marriage, George Brightwen (1820-1883), husband of Eliza *née* Elder (joined 1871; *JTVI* V (1871), 418); PHG's sister-in-law Lucy Geldart (d. 1897, joined 1872; *JTVI* VI (1873), 436); EWG (joined 31 Oct. 1873, *JTVI* VII (1874), 402). Friends: James T. Gwyther (d. ?1885, joined 1880); newspaper editor and publisher R. C. Morgan (1827-1908, joined 1877). People with whom he corresponded: chemist J. H. Gladstone (1827-1902; member, 1866-1902); Futurist prophetic expositor Robert Govett (1813-1901; member 1880-1901). Though I have not seen evidence that PHG knew the chemist George Warington (1840-1874; member 1866-69), he did correspond with his father. Warington was the second son of the chemist Robert Warington who, as noted, was one of the earliest inventors of the aquarium ('Mr. George Warington', London *Daily News*, 18 Apr. 1874, 6).

of his life.[296] He was one of the few Brethren to affiliate with the society.[297] Under Reddie's leadership the Institute was primarily evangelical in outlook, overwhelmingly anti-Darwinian,[298] with meetings attended by 'potent, grave, and reverend signors.'[299] Initially, it had some difficulty in attracting members, especially from scientific circles, but in later years it was more successful in both arenas. Notable men of science who joined came from geology, paleontology, chemistry, mathematics, biology, marine zoology, natural history, entomology, botany, microscopy, horticulture, and pathology.[300] The Victoria Institute's influence spread throughout the English-speaking world and beyond.[301]

While Victoria Institute members were united for one purpose, disagreements were inevitable on how to achieve it. In Gosse's case, he had provided a few comments on papers read at the Institute but, in spite

296. PHG was a contributor to the Institute's library (*JTVI* VI (1873), 468). He also had a 21-volume run of *JTVI* in his library (*Sandhurst Catalogue*, item #404). The first volume is dated 1867, the twenty-first, 1888.

297. From 1865-1919, the following Brethren (besides PHG) joined the Victoria Institute: John Eliot Howard (1807-1883); Robert Anderson (1841-1918); David Anderson-Berry (1862-1926); J. G. Halliday (1822-1917); and A. T. Schofield (1846-1929). On these individuals: Pickering, *Chief Men*, 2ed.

298. At a 15 Apr. 1912 meeting of the Victoria Institute, botanist George Henslow claimed he had been an exception: 'I unwisely, it appears, assumed that after more than forty years *all* members of the Victoria Institute would have come to accept evolution; but my critics reproduce, almost *verbatim*, what I received, as the only evolutionist present in 1868, when on the Council of the Institute' (*JTVI* XLIV, 273-4. Emphasis in the original). Henslow actually became a member on 5 Apr. 1869 (*JTVI* IV (1870), 163). On Henslow: Stuart Mathieson, *Evangelicals and the Philosophy of Science: The Victoria Institute, 1865-1939* (London: Routledge, 2020), 58-9.

299. Charles Maurice Davies, *Heterodox London: or, Phases of Free Thought in the Metropolis* (London: Tinsley Bros., 1874), II: 333. The meeting was held in April 1874.

300. Geology (J.W. Dawson, Canada; James Dwight Dana and Arnold Guyot, USA; Peter Cormac Sutherland, Scotland); paleontology (Joachim Barrande, Austria); chemistry (J.H. Gladstone, J.E. Howard and George Warington, all UK; Louis Pasteur, France); mathematics (G.G. Stokes, UK); biology (Henry Alleyne Nicholson, UK); marine zoology (Alexander Agassiz, USA); natural history (H.B. Tristram and J.G. Wood, UK); entomology (T.V. Wollaston, UK); botany (George Henslow, UK); microscopy (Lionel S. Beale and W.H. Dallinger, UK); horticulture (James Bateman, UK); and pathology (Rudolf Virchow, Germany).

301. Doug Wertheimer, 'The Victoria Institute, 1865-1919: A Study in Collective Biography Meant as an Introduction to the Conflict of Science and Religion After Darwin' (University of Toronto, unpublished Master's Essay, 1971). This computer-assisted prosopographical study remains the only analysis of the Victoria Institute's entire membership of 3,390 from 1865-1919 (a selective study of the Institute's membership at four intervals from 1866-1926 is provided by Mathieson, 'The Victoria Institute 1865-1932', chap. 2). See also Timothy C. F. Stunt, 'The Victoria Institute: The First Hundred Years', *Faith and Thought: Journal of the Victoria Institute* 94 (1965), 162-81. The reason why James Clerk Maxwell (1831-1879), the Scottish Christian physicist, declined a 12 Mar. 1875 invitation to join the Institute is provided by Jerrold L. McNatt, 'James Clerk Maxwell's Refusal to Join the Victoria Institute', *Perspectives on Science and Christian Faith* 56 (Sept. 2004), 204-15.

of being 'repeatedly solicited to contribute a paper,' had not complied until the June submission. In doing so, he encountered a number of annoyances.[302] One anonymous referee of the paper questioned Gosse's presentation; the paper was said to be too long; unauthorised alterations were made to Gosse's manuscript after it had gone into proof stage; when it was finally ready for presentation, it had not been distributed before the meeting, as was customary. Gosse threatened to quit the Institute unless the issues were resolved.[303]

Gosse's essay came in response to a paper by the Revd Robinson Thornton (1824-1906), the Anglican headmaster of the Royal Medical Benevolent College, Epsom (later Archdeacon of Middlesex), who was a founding Council member of the Institute.[304] It was Thornton's fourth paper before the Institute, following ones on philology and aspects of scepticism. Given that Colenso was known as 'the very embodiment of Scriptural scepticism' and had published the first five parts of his *Pentateuch and Book of Joshua* by 1865, Thornton realised that a paper 'On the Numerical System of the Old Testament' would seem 'somewhat anomalous' at the Victoria Institute.[305] Indeed it was, especially since Thornton sought to balance an explicit denial of support for Colenso with a conviction that some of the numerical figures in the Pentateuch just did not add up.[306]

As anticipated, Thornton's reading of his paper at the Institute's 7 February 1870 meeting did leave many members feeling uneasy. As one put it, it was 'much as a small detachment of an army feels which, cautiously advancing in to meet a *known foe* in front, suddenly finds a *supposed friend* attacking them in flank [sic].'[307] The reaction deploring Thornton's article came over a year later, with rebuttals by the Revd

302. PHG's letters were read on 6 March and 1 May 1871 (*JTVI* VI:180-1 and 258-59); on his submission: PHG-Capt. F. W. H. Petrie, Secretary to the Institute, 6 May 1871 (Corr. Bk.).

303. See the following copies of letters for 1871, all in Corr. Bk.: PHG-Capt. F. W. H. Petrie, Secretary to the Institute, 6, 12 May and 6, 8, 21 June; PHG-Thornton, 19 June 1871.

304. *Crockford's Clerical Directory* VI (1872), 849; 'Death of an Archdeacon', London *Daily Mirror*, 17 Apr. 1906, 4; 'Dr. Robinson Thornton', London *Times*, 17 Apr. 1906, 4.

305. Robinson Thornton, 'On the Numerical System of the Old Testament', *JTVI* V (1871), 105.

306. Thornton, 'On the Numerical System of the Old Testament', 105-20.

307. Remark of Dr James Alexander Fraser (d. 1886), 19 June 1871, in *JTVI* V (1871), 407. Emphasis in the original.

Henry Moule (1801-1880), a leader of the Evangelical wing of the Church of England,[308] and Gosse.

When Gosse's paper was read at the Victoria Institute, he was already familiar with the 'Neology, or Higher Criticism' of the Bible and with the 'notorious *Essays and Reviews.*' He believed that 'an appalling multitude' of Anglican and Dissenting ministers were 'suffused' with its teaching, and that among the 'leading scientific men of England ... it has now become quite the usual thing to treat the notion of a personal creating and sustaining God with proud contempt.'[309] Thornton's arguments, Gosse maintained in 'The High Numbers of the Pentateuch: Are They Trustworthy?', *'if they are severely logical*, must inevitably lead to the rejection of inspiration.'[310]

Gosse knew that he was not equipped with the linguistic tools to address documentary issues raised by Colenso or others. Gosse had nothing new to say about the if, when, or by whom the Bible might have been edited, so instead (as he explained in a letter to his son) his attention was given to 'an adduction of such arguments as a mere student of the English Bible can bring to meet certain attacks ... against the *probability* of the high numbers.'[311] To defeat Bishop Colenso's argument, and whatever support Thornton gave him, Gosse was following the same logical analysis and the same reasoning as we have seen him use in *Omphalos* in responding to the geologists. It was as if he had written a pamphlet entitled *The Bible or the Bishop: Which?* They both can't be true.

Gosse dealt with two issues raised in Thornton's paper. The first was what he termed the *'cheval de bataille* [hobby horse] of the impugners of the Sacred Text':[312] Was it true—as the Book of Exodus stated—that 600,000 male Israelites left Egypt? Or maybe it was true—as Bishop Colenso stated—that evidence in the Pentateuch itself made such high numbers an impossibility? Gosse attempted to show that since the Book

308. Henry Moule, 'Israel in Egypt: The Period of their Sojourn and their Numbers at the Exodus and in the Wilderness', *JTVI* V (1871), 378-93. Moule then served a labouring-class parish in Fordington, near Dorchester, and was the inventor of the dry-earth closet system. He was engaged in a 'prolonged and exciting controversy with Bishop Colenso' ('Death of the Rev. Henry Moule', Yeovil *Western Gazette*, 6 Feb. 1880, 8; London *Daily News*, 4 Feb. 1880, 6; *Crockford's Clerical Directory* VII, 1874, 621; *ODNB*; *DEB*). Moule was present at the meeting; PHG was not, though apparently EWG was (CUL Add. 7041, 47).

309. PHG, 'The Breaking of the Day', *The Christian* I (23 June 1870), 274.

310. PHG, 'The High Numbers of the Pentateuch', 349. Emphasis in the original.

311. PHG-EWG, 11 May 1871 (CUL Add. 7041, 47). Emphasis in the original.

312. PHG, 'The High Numbers of the Pentateuch', 355.

of Exodus was not the only evidence for the vast size of Israel in leaving Egypt, that the high numbers were integral to the biblical narrative, and so 'truly given'[313] and probable. They could not be accounted for by claiming them to be a variant reading (or *lectio varia*).[314]

But how could Jacob have immigrated to Egypt with a household of seventy people (as claimed by the Book of Exodus), only to leave there perhaps some four generations later for the Land of Israel with a nation of over 600,000? In Colenso's view, this represented an inconceivable rate of fecundity. Gosse, however, with the same evidence attempted to demonstrate the possibility of such an increase, based upon a different (though he felt, warranted) rate of population increase.

Gosse realized that others might still prefer Colenso's interpretation. Channeling the omphalotic argument, he concluded:

> But, I submit, this is to lose sight of the true issue. It is enough for us, the defenders, to give a possible, a tenable interpretation, which being accepted, the narrative shall be consistent. It is for the opponent to show that there is *no possible* interpretation, on which the narrative can be true. If he has not done, if he cannot do, this, he has done nothing. Here is the venerable Record, bearing its witness: we must assume its truth, until it is *proved* false. It will not do to say, 'If we take a certain passage in a certain prescribed sense, it is false,' unless he can compel us to admit that sense; unless he can absolutely drive us from every other; unless he can prove no other tenable. Let us only be able to suggest another sense of the given words, which is maintainable: it may not be necessarily the true one, but it affords an escape from his dilemma, and his argument is absolutely harmless.[315]

In the discussion which followed Gosse's paper, as with his initial submission of it to the Council of the Institute, opinions were mixed as to the necessity of maintaining the plenary inspiration of the biblical text. In spite of minor objections, however, Gosse's view was the one accepted by most of the speakers.[316] Meanwhile Gosse learned after the Institute

313. PHG, 'The High Numbers of the Pentateuch', 360.
314. PHG, 'The High Numbers of the Pentateuch', 355, 362.
315. PHG, 'The High Numbers of the Pentateuch', 371-2. Emphasis in the original.
316. *JTVI* V (1871), 394-411 (discussion of papers at the meeting of 19 June); report on the meeting in *Illustrated London News* 58 (24 June 1871), 607. The major objector to PHG's paper was the Revd C. A. Row (1816-1896), a Member of Council and later Prebendary of St. Paul's, who felt that the fact of revelation could be accepted even if errors were acknowledged to exist in

meeting that he had insulted Thornton, who declined to respond to a letter of apology from him.[317]

The Victoria Institute programme drew press attention,[318] and two months after Gosse's paper was read, excerpts of his 'able and exhaustive examination' were published over two issues of the *Christian*, the well-known evangelical weekly. There Gosse's 'manifest victory' over the '"great swelling words"[319] of unbelief' appeared under the headlines 'The Literal Accuracy of the Books of Moses' and 'The Number of Israel'.[320]

-XI-

In 1858, the *Leeds Intelligencer* had occasion to muse about a naturalist who had been before the public for nearly two decades. 'Mr. Gosse's name revives a host of pleasant recollections,' a reviewer said:

> There are few readers who have not spent many happy hours in his companionship, either amid the gorgeous tropical vegetation of Jamaica, or the somber pine woods of Canada, or the green winding lanes of our own beautiful Devonshire. He has done more to diffuse a taste for his favourite studies than all the writers who preceded him; and has popularized the science of zoology, just as Hugh Miller popularised geology. Mr. Gosse's style is easy, natural, almost conversational at times, but its main characteristic is clearness, which is, unfortunately, a rare peculiarity among scientific writers. ... here and there some novel fact, connected with animal life, is turned to good account, and serves as an illustration of those higher truths which it is too much the fashion to hide away altogether.[321]

Scriptures. See also the comments of the Revd John James (1806-1886). Approval of the paper was expressed by Charles Graham, T. W. Masterman, J. A. Fraser, and Charles Brooke (*JTVI*, meeting of 19 June 1871, 394-411). Decades later, F. F. Bruce called PHG's piece 'a sledgehammer of a reply' (Stunt, 'The Victoria Institute', 164-5fn1).

317. PHG-R. Thornton, 19 June 1871 (Corr. Bk.). This is a copy of the letter, on which PHG added a note in red ink: 'NB. No notice was ever taken of this letter, by Dr. Th[ornton].' In his conciliatory letter to Thornton, PHG wrote: 'I am by nature & by long habit, a keen disputant; & such an one is very apt, in eager arg[umen]t, to press his antag[onis]t with unseemly ardour, approach[in]g to ferocity.'

318. Various versions of the same report appeared in the London *Daily News*, 21 June 1871, 3; London *Standard*, 22 June 1871, 2; *Coventry Standard*, 23 June 1871, 2; and the *Belfast News-Letter*, 24 June 1871, 4. Report on the meeting in *Illustrated London News* 58 (24 June 1871), 607; the papers by PHG and Moule were cited in the London *Weekly Dispatch*, 25 June 1871, 7.

319. Epistle of Jude 16.

320. *The Christian*, 10, 17 Aug. 1871, 385-6, 398-9.

321. 'Literature', *Leeds Intelligencer*, 27 Feb. 1858, 3.

These well-chosen words were a faithful depiction of the past, less and less relevant as the decade of the 1850s waned. Uniformitarian geology, Darwinian evolution, and biblical criticism were to come to the fore in the next decade, and Gosse's naturalist's past helped him little in those new areas. Convinced that his evangelical theology demanded the rejection of these approaches, Gosse found a personal way to stave off the challenge of geology and biblical criticism with his *Is it not possible—I do not ask for more*' reasoning. The British community, so empirically oriented and so accustomed to reasoning by analogy when seeking evidences of design in the world,[322] was not prepared to forsake those approaches for a conceivably impregnable logical solution.

Yet Gosse was not done. The challenge of Darwin's theory remained. Though fed-up with the science of the day, he seized on two opportunities to test pillars of the theory. Perhaps he could weaken them. Perhaps he could even cause the structure to collapse. That's what he was going to try to do. Scientifically.

---

322. Ellegård, 'The Darwinian Theory and the Argument from Design', 173-92.

CHAPTER EIGHT

1857-1865

'Blossomed Beauties',
the Royal Society, and Protest

-I-

I N SEPTEMBER 1857, WHEN THE GOSSES moved to Sandhurst, the village of St. Marychurch and town of Torquay were two distinct places with little intercommunication, although they were separated by less than a two-mile country walk through fields and markets.[1] Much of the attractiveness of the locale was due to the mild, salubrious climate, which was influential in transforming what had been a fishing hamlet at the turn of the century into the 'Queen of Watering Places', the 'Montpellier of England', as Torquay was known. With its seaport, bathing places, and picturesque location around the three sides of the Torbay harbour, this market town soon became a popular winter residence, and was visited by famous literary figures throughout the nineteenth century. During the fifteen-year period before Gosse's arrival, the number of dwellings had more than doubled, so that by 1857 the population was about 14,000 out

---

1. H. Terry, 'Old Torquay as I Knew It', *Transactions and Proceedings of the Torquay Natural History Society* VIII (1938-9), 87-8, referring to the situation *c.* 1866. The discussion of the two places is based upon: William White, *History, Gazetteer, and Directory of Devonshire* (Sheffield: Robert Leader, 1850), 437, 444-7; *Post Office Directory of Devonshire and Cornwall* (London: Kelly and Co., 1856); Charles Mitchell, *The Newspaper Press Directory ... 1857* (London: C. Mitchell & Co., 1857), 64; 'List of Residents and Visitors', supplement to *The Torquay Directory and South Devon Journal* (14 Oct. 1857, and other dates); J. T. White, *The History of Torquay* (Torquay: Torquay Directory Office, 1878), 327; Revd J. Charteris Johnston, '"Literary" Torquay', *Report and Transactions of the Devonshire Association* L (1918), 293-322; and Revd F. S. Edmonds, *Chronicles of St. Mary Church* (Torquay: Charles G. Jowitt, 1925), 58-9.

of season, or 20,000 in season. There were, as well, a profusion of hotels and boarding-houses, libraries, reading-rooms, and shops, churches and chapels for all persuasions, schools, and the customary Bible, missionary, temperance, and charitable institutions. In little more than five hours, one could be whisked by railroad from the soot and grime of London's Paddington Station to a Torquay free from fogs and protected against cold winds.

St. Marychurch, too, had been influenced by the growth of its neighbour, its population increasing in ten years by fifty per cent, to 3,200 in 1861. But while it had a modest number of bathing machines and marine cottages for the visitor, its primary asset was its natural beauty. An easy half hour's walk would bring one to the shore, or (in following a winding path) to the rock pools of Petit Tor, to Meadfoot beach, to the view of the bay from Daddy Hole Plain, or the romantic Anstey's Cove. Nearby lay numerous 'valleys'—Babbacombe and the Down, Oddicombe, Maidencombe, and Watcombe.

As previously noted, Gosse was familiar with St. Marychurch since 1852 when, with his microscope, he went to the seashore to be among 'the shells and nudibranchs, the sea-anemones and the corallines.'[2] That's what again figured prominently in his move there five years later.[3] His first action when settled at Sandhurst, however, was not to go down to the shore (he had dislocated his knee several times since late July,[4] making the negotiation of the steep ridges and pools a difficult matter). On Sunday, 27 September, two days after he settled at Sandhurst, Philip limped to the Brethren's Room in St. Marychurch on Sarah Andrews' arm, accompanied by Edmund.[5] There were, apparently, a dozen or so

2. PHG, *Naturalist's Rambles*, 2.

3. PHG-[Secretary of the Poole Literary Institution], 12 Mar. 1858 (Wellcome Historical Medical Library); PHG, *Naturalist's Rambles*, 68. PHG also took note of the botany of the area: see the letter, PHG-[Rev. R. H. Barnes], 6 Oct. 1864, published in 'History of St. Mary Church', Supplement to the *Exeter and Plymouth Gazette* (2 Nov. 1866), 10 (this item is not listed in Freeman & Wertheimer-PHG).

4. EWG's Diary for 1857 (under July 25, 28; August, 10; Sept. 7), and PHG-[W. A. Lloyd?], 12 Oct. 1857 (Edinburgh University Library La.II.425/22).

5. PHG-EWG, 17 Sept. 1877 (CUL Add. 7018, 75). In EWG's Diary, Sarah Andrews noted that on Sunday, October 11, they 'Went to meeting for the first time in Mary Church'. I do not know what she meant. PHG commemorated 27 September 1857 as the anniversary date (thus PHG-EWG, 20 Sept. 1882, CUL Add. 7018,36: 'Twenty-five years ago, next Wednesday [=Sept. 27], I, and you [EWG], and Miss Andrews walked down to the Public Room:—and I began that pastoral intercourse with the simple Church of God in this village').

present,[6] including Anne Hannaford (b. 1821/2), Thomas Lear, and Annie Taylor.[7]

At that time, the only Brethren assembly in St. Marychurch was at the 'Parish Room' on Park Street, founded several years earlier.[8] The Brethren presence in Torquay, however, was contemporaneous with the origins of the movement. In the 1830s, leading Brethren such as Craik and Müller had visited the town,[9] and from 1838 John Parnell (later the 2nd Lord Congleton) was accustomed to make the Teignmouth-Torquay-Newton Abbot circuit on the Lord's Day.[10] The first Brethren meeting, at the Christian Assembly Room, was opened by the former Anglican John Vivian in October 1834,[11] but it was probably not until the arrival of Leonard Strong (1797-1874) around 1848 or 1849[12] that the Brethren community began to noticeably increase. He soon gained a reputation as 'a humble consistent, and devout minister of Christ,'[13] associating with Open Brethren.[14]

For more than twenty years Strong had successfully ministered among the plantation slaves in Demerara (formerly British Guiana, now Guyana, South America).[15] Born into an Anglican household, he had entered the

6. 'There were about a dozen or so believers meeting here [in 1857], in the simple name of Jesus, to which the Word was ministered casually, irregularly, from Torquay or New[ton Abbot]' (PHG-George Pearse, 19 June 1881; CUL Add. 7313, 380-1). Part of this letter is reproduced, with some significant errors, by Eliza Gosse, in *Life*, 364, 367-8. The present transfer copy was uninterpretable to the naked eye when I saw it, but I was able to get a fairly good transcription with the aid of an ultra-violet lamp at Cambridge University Library.

7. PHG-EWG, 20 Sept. 1882 (CUL Add. 7018, 36). Anne Hannaford was one of the sisters referred to in *Father and Son* under the pseudonym 'Burmington'. In 1871 she was a dress-maker living on Park Street (Wertheimer, *Identification*, 5). By March 1858 attendance at the meetings had increased to between 30-40 people (*Life*, 354).

8. Beattie, *Brethren*, 65. Many years later, PHG called it the 'Public Room' (PHG-EWG, 20 Sept. 1882, CUL Add. 7018, 36). Beattie does not identify the location of this Room, but according to the *Torquay Directory* (14 Oct. 1857, Supplement), the only Brethren assembly at the time was on Park Street. EWG's account of the origins of the St. Marychurch Room was imaginary (*Father and Son*, 1907, 140-1).

9. Coad, *Brethren Movement*, 38, and Rowdon, *Origins*, 118-19.

10. Beattie, *Brethren*, 60.

11. Grass, *Gathering to His Name*, 42; Beattie, *Brethren*, 63; Coad, *Brethren Movement*, 304.

12. Stunt, 'Strong, Leonard', *DEB* II: 1066.

13. 'Torquay', Exeter *Western Times* (9 Sept. 1854), 7.

14. T. C. F. Stunt, 'New Source Materials for the Open Brethren in the 1850s', 67, 71

15. On Strong: Stunt, *CBR* (1983), 95-105; Stunt, 'From Wandsworth to British Guiana', 175-195; Pickering, *Chief Men*, 2ed., 22-3; Rowdon, *Origins*, 185-6; Coad, *Brethren Movement*, 197; Beattie, *Brethren*, 65-7; W. T. Stunt, et. al., *Turning the World Upside Down*, 25, 241-3; Strong's Will at Somerset House; and the *1861 Census Returns for Torquay*, Enumeration District 8, which indicates that his daughter Catherine (aged 10), was born at St. Marychurch (*i.e.*, in 1850 or 1851).

Navy at the age of 12 and saw action in French and American wars. In 1823 he went up to Oxford without taking a degree, and was for awhile a curate at Ross-on-Wye. But he turned to missionary work, and shortly after arriving in Demerara in February 1827, found himself confronted by planters who disliked his work and threatened to kill him. After being transferred to another parish,[16] he eventually gave up those efforts, and began meetings at Georgetown which resembled Brethren ones at Dublin and Plymouth, although he was unaware of those activities. During the first two and a half years he gained nearly 100 converts,[17] and he soon was given support by Brethren in Europe. After leaving Demerara, he returned to England and began to write religious and biographical tracts, and other works.[18]

In the early 1850s, Devon had already become (as it has remained) the stronghold of rural Brethrenism, especially of the Open section.[19] The Religious Census of 1851 listed six meetings with 201 worshippers at nearby Newton Abbot, and thirty congregants at Totnes.[20] The Room in Bitton Street, Teignmouth, which had been erected around 1810, could hold 250 people.[21] It may well have been at the time that the number of believers at Torquay was only 'a few'[22] or approximately the same as at Totnes, but in either case the situation changed.[23] In September

16. Strong was instituted to the rectory of St. Matthew on 17 Sept. 1829 (West Indies *Saint Christopher Gazette*, 6 Nov. 1829, [2]).

17. Leonard Strong in the *Missionary Reporter* (July 1853), 5-7.

18. The essays by Timothy Stunt on Leonard Strong, as cited, are authoritative. See also Wertheimer, *Identification*, 9, and Strong, *Gospel Reminiscences in the West Indies: Old Narquois, the Negro Driver*; *The Condemned Negro; or, Man's Victim, God's Chosen*; and *A Brief and Simple Record of the Lord's Gracious Work Among the Indians of British Guiana, by his Servant John Meyer, During Four Years and a Half* (all s.d., but before 1851). Strong was the author of some tracts published by 'J. B. Bateman, Christian and Anti-Popery Depot' (*The Revival*, 14 Jan. 1860, 16), and contributed articles to *The Sword and Trowel, Missionary Reporter, Rainbow*, and the *Voice Upon the Mountains*.

19. Embley, 'Origins and Early Development', 125.

20. Embley, 'Origins and Early Development', 129.

21. *Torquay, Newton Abbot, and District Directory, with Paignton, Totnes, Teignmouth and Dawlish, and the Intermediate Villages* (Torquay: Wells & Manton, 1887), 176.

22. 'I have been labouring all my life in a remote country amongst blacks and slaves, and since my return I have been labouring in a remote place amongst a few saints' (Leonard Strong, speaking at Freemasons' Hall in London on Thursday, 12 May 1864 (quoted in *Report of Three Days' Meetings for Prayer and Addresses on the "Sure Word of Prophecy,"* 124). According to an unclear statement by David Cresswell in *The Revival* (29 Dec. 1860), 204, 'The number altogether, whom we know to be converted in this place [Torquay], is about forty.' I do not know whether this refers solely to Strong's ministry, or only to 'believers' as against attendants.

23. The Christian Assembly Room had remained in existence, apparently on Lower Union Street, until Strong arrived (Beattie, *Brethren*, 65, and *Torquay Directory*, 14 Oct. 1857,

1854, Strong opened a 'neat and unostentatious building'[24] known as the Brethren's Room[25] (or Christian Brethren's Room)[26] on Warren Road. It had a seating capacity of 500.[27] As Strong weekly engaged in open-air preaching 'to large and attentive audiences',[28] the meeting prospered and the Parish Room was begun at St. Marychurch. This was the small group which Gosse joined.

The advent of intellectual and religiously experienced leaders such as Strong and Gosse was impactful. Within less than a month after Gosse's first visit to the Parish Room, he was speaking before the meetings,[29] and he came to assume a ministry which he held for the rest of his life. This work was all the more important because even by 1860, in spite of a number of untiring gospel preachers in the area[30] and after the impact of the period of revivalism in 1859-60 was beginning to be felt throughout the country, the complaint was heard that 'The people [of Devon] are perishing for lack of *earnest ministry:* the preaching we have is too much like an essay, it lacks earnestness and vitality.' Nonetheless,

> There is a very gracious work going on under the ministry of Mr. P. H. Gosse in this place. Several souls have been converted, and there is an earnest awakening among several others. The writer was led during this week to converse with a young man whom he had known in his unconverted state, and he said, with tears rolling down his face, "I shall have to bless God through eternity that I was ever brought to hear Mr. Gosse preach." And he said there was seldom a service in which good was not done. The writer wishes that fifty such men were raised up to go into the dark benighted parts of the south of Devon.[31]

Supplement, which lists two Brethren Rooms in Torquay, one on Lower Union Street and another on Warren Road).

24. Exeter *Western Times* (9 Sept. 1854), 7.

25. Exeter *Western Times* (8 Sept. 1855), 7. It was apparently also known as the 'Christian Brethren's Room'.

26. Exeter *Western Times* (2 May 1882), 5.

27. J. T. White, *History of Torquay*, 327, and 'Criticus' [Clayton Walker], *The Churches and Chapels of Torquay* (Torquay: MacKenzie & MacDonald, [1905]), 25. The latter work describes a visit to the Warren Road Room at the turn of the century.

28. Exeter *Western* Times, 8 Sept. 1855, 7.

29. On Sunday, 18 October, 1857, PHG spoke on baptism (on his views on the subject, see for example *Sacred Streams* (1850), 222-3), and the following week on the history of Naaman (2 Kings v. 1); Edmund's Diary for 1857, under those dates.

30. *The Revival*, 3 Nov. 1860, 140. One of those mentioned was J. E. Gladstone, 'a zealous preacher of Christ', who is referred to later in this chapter.

31. Both quotations are from the letter of 'F.M.' in *The Revival*, 29 Oct. 1860, 126. Emphasis in the original.

With the increase in worshippers at St. Marychurch larger quarters were soon required. On 9 July 1860, Brethren held their first meeting in the new chapel on Fore Street. It included a school room, which (like the chapel) had been built at Gosse's expense.[32]

-II-

Gosse's move to Sandhurst represented a new chapter in his engagement with Brethren, so it is useful to summarize that involvement to that date.

Ever since his introduction to Brethren at Hackney in 1843, he had remained committed to Brethren ideas as he knew them. As previously mentioned, he knew many early Brethren, was involved with its early assemblies and helped to spread the movement across the world to Jamaica. In so doing, he remained in touch with Brethren in Hackney. When Gosse returned to England in 1846, he sought out Brethren worship sites in London and chose a wife who had (like himself) freely come to Brethren. They raised their only child in congruence with a Brethren outlook and educated him in part at a school run by Brethren. They associated with Brethren individuals, and during their travels as a family sought out worship with Brethren believers.[33] Gosse spoke and wrote using Brethren terminology,[34] like them adopted an intense devotion to prophetic studies, and published religious and natural history works of interest and appeal to them. He was publicly referred to during his lifetime as being affiliated with 'Plymouth Brethren', and with rare exception was the 'sole pastor and conductor of all meetings'[35] at the 'Church of God' in Marychurch during his years there. 'Settled ministers' were not unusual among early Brethren.[36]

As we shall see in Chapter 10, Gosse made sure to situate his son in London among Brethren and his second wife was familiar with Brethren ideas before he met her. He corresponded with, and debated, what came

32. This fact is mentioned, *en passant*, in Smith, *History of the Methodist Church* II: 173; *Life*, 356, and *Father and Son*, 1907, 219-20. The *Torquay Directory* continued to list the Brethren Room as at Park Street until 27 Mar. 1861 (p. 7), and did not register the change of address until 15 May 1861 (p. 7).

33. Associating with Brethren: e.g., Ilfracombe, 1852 (PHG-EG, 16 Apr. 1852, CUL Adv.c.82.5,43); Tenby, possibly 1854 and certainly 1856 (PHG, *Memorial*, 26-7).

34. The terminology is described in Wertheimer, 'The Truth About 1843', 33-6.

35. Gosse, 'Reminiscences of My Husband from 1860 to 1888' (*Life*, 364).

36. Harold H. Rowdon, 'The Early Brethren and the Ministry of the Word', *CBRF Journal* (1967), 11.

to be known as 'Open Brethren'.[37] Three decades after his death, his life details were included among a select group of forty-six other British 'leaders'[38] in the movement, in Henry Pickering's *Chief Men among the Brethren*, the first Brethren biographical dictionary.

Notwithstanding this record of Brethren association (which admittedly has been undefined until now), there has been confusion about Gosse's relationship with the movement.[39] In part, this is a reflection of a lack of familiarity with Brethren history: less dogmatic and credal at the outset, attitudes hardened in the 1840s which led to the division into 'Exclusive' (Darbyite) and 'Open' Brethren. Where did Gosse stand once the movement split apart? Unquestionably with the Open faction. When he wrote his son in 1868 that he did not identify with Brethren 'as a distinctive body of Christians', looking within the movement itself he meant that he valued the non-sectarian vision of the earliest Brethren years, and not Darbyite Brethren with whom, as he told his son, 'the less you have to do the better.'[40] Looking beyond 'Open Brethren', Gosse was expressing his irenic outlook. As he explained to a correspondent: 'I do not emphasize "particular views." These are *comparatively* of little importance. The "great gulf" is not between Baptist & Friend [Quakers];— but between dead in sins & alive to God; between saved in Christ & exposed to the wrath of God. O my dear friend, never mind particular views, till this vital question is settled.'[41] Additionally although not

37. PHG's association with those who were for various lengths of time associated with Open Brethren was extensive and long-lasting. From 1843: J. B. Bateman, Emily Bowes, C. F. Hargrove, J. E. Howard, Robert Howard, R. C. Morgan, and G. V. Wigram. Among Open Brethren known to have had contact with PHG are (from at least 1856-64): Earl of Cavan, J. M. Code, Henry Dyer, J. Hambleton, Andrew Jukes, M. M. A. H. Laseron, W. Lincoln, H. H. Snell, H. W. Soltau, Mary Stacey, and W. H. G. Wellesley. From at least 1869-88, PHG's Corr. Bk. indicates he corresponded with (among others): T. J. Barnardo, Wm. H. Bennet, Edwin H. Bennett, Robert Chapman, J. L. Harris, George Müller, Robert Nelson, George Pearse, Lord Radstock, L. Strong, and William Yapp.

38. Pickering (comp.), *Chief Men Among the Brethren*, [1918], Preface.

39. The incorrect claim that PHG was not aligned with Brethren was made by EWG: 'In middle life he had connected himself with the Plymouth Brethren, principally, no doubt, because of their lack of systematic organization, their repudiation of all traditional authority, their belief that the Bible is the infallible and sufficient guide. But he soon lost confidence in the Plymouth Brethren also, and for the last thirty years of his life he was really unconnected with any Christian body whatever' (*Life*, 330). Peter L. Embley, relying on EWG's portraits of his father, wrote that PHG 'parted company with Brethren, mainly it seems over the matter of "liberty of ministry"' (Embley, 'Origins and Early Development', 216).

40. PHG-EWG, 22 Feb. 1868 (CUL Add. 7041, 13).

41. PHG-Arthur Doncaster, 1 Dec. 1881 (CUL Add. 7313,449). Emphasis in original, square brackets added.

intentionally, when Gosse denied that he was engaged with "'brethren"...
as a distinctive body of Christians',[42] he was making a revelatory, counter-
intuitive, declaration. One scholar has explained why: 'the denial that one
is, or can be, "Brethren" is still considered by some a mark of genuine
Brethrenism.'[43]

Finally, Gosse's differences with other Brethren—'especially in
the interpretation of Prophecy,[44] & in views of ministry'[45]—were not
determinative. Brethren did not have then, and do not have to this
day, a single playbook. 'The dogmas taught and generally held by those
Christians who are distinctively known as "Brethren,"' as Gosse observed,
'are not, so far as I am aware, clearly laid down in any authoritative
document.'[46]

-III-

With his knee healed, on 16 October 1857, Gosse headed for the large
cavernous pools on the north side of Petit Tor.[47] Nearly six years had
passed since he had first been there. He wondered: What would it be like?
And he discovered: 'The shore was as if I had left it but yesterday.'[48] But
the experience was not the same. 'It was with a mournful gratification,'
Gosse wrote in a journal, 'that I looked on the familiar scene remembering
my loved companion then, who now gazes on brighter scenes'.[49]

As we have already seen, when Gosse first commenced his studies of sea
anemones in 1852, zoophytes were only just beginning to gain sustained
attention as a field of study.[50] Since that time, two main factors were

42. PHG-EWG, 3 Mar. 1868 (CUL Add. 7041, 14).

43. West, From Friends to Brethren, 241. West points to the example of J. E. Howard. Though
he was among Open Brethren, Howard denied it: 'I cannot pledge myself to any brethren but
the sect which were called Christians first at Antioch' (West, From Friends to Brethren, 241).

44. In his prophetic mode of interpretation, PHG was an historicist. Brethren who adopted
the futurist interpretation followed J. N. Darby (for Darby as a Futurist, Spence, Heaven on
Earth, 49).

45. PHG-EWG, 3 Mar. 1868 (CUL Add. 7041, 14).

46. PHG, Humanity of the Son of God (1886), 3-4.

47. EWG Diary for 1857 (under 8-10, 13, 15-16, 19, 21 October).

48. PHG, Actinologia Britannica, 69-70. Emphasis in the original.

49. PHG, The Aquarium (MS notes, 1854-76) (LeBL). There is only the one entry for 1857,
which is almost identical—except for this sentence—to the printed version (PHG, Actinologia
Britannica, 69-70).

50. Henri Milne-Edwards, Histoire Naturelle des Coralliaires, ou Polypes Proprement Dits
(Paris: A la Librairie Encyclopédique de Roret, 1857), I: xxxiii. PHG owned and referred to this
3vol. work (Sandhurst Catalogue, item#305),

responsible for the increasing interest in the field in England: Gosse's own numerous writings in periodicals and books on anemones, and the popularization of the aquarium. Actiniae naturally took their place as the most prominent ornaments in aquaria, and to supply this new demand for them, the coasts were searched. The result was that many new species and genera were discovered,[51] local lists were compiled,[52] and the habits and habitats of these creatures became better known. All of this enthusiasm, guided by the investigations of many naturalists, helped to lay the ground-work for Gosse's comprehensive monograph.

Gosse had first announced a 'Proposed Work on the British Sea-Anemones' in an advertisement at the back of *Tenby* (which appeared by April 1856).[53] There he sought the cooperation of individuals living on the British and Irish coasts. They were urged to send him, through the post, specimens of uncommon species, and he described the way in which this should be done. For the first time in his career, he was now doing fieldwork in Britain—only unlike his experiences in Newfoundland, Canada, Alabama and Jamaica, numerous assistants were aiding him.

Before Gosse's volume appeared, two writers completed studies of zoophytes for neophytes, while a third one was addressed to a scientific audience. The anonymous *Sea Anemones; or, Tanks and Their Inhabitants* (1856) was a handy, inexpensive guide to everything from the identification of commonly-found species to five pages on how to construct and manage an aquarium.[54] The Revd George Tugwell (1830-1910), the curate of Ilfracombe who had seen the invading seashore hordes rampaging over his back yard, supplied the amateur rambler with *A Manual of the Sea-anemones Commonly Found on the English*

51. E. W. H. Holdsworth, three articles in the *Proceedings of the Zoological Society*: 'Descriptions of a New Sea Anemone' (1855), 85-6; 'Description of Two New Species of Actinia, from the South Coast of Devon' (1855), 235-7; 'Description of a New Species of Actinia from the Devonshire Coast' (1855), 172; T. S. Wright, 'On Two New Actinias from Arran', *Proceedings of the Physical Society of Edinburgh* I (1856), 70-2; and E. P. Wright, [notes on *Bunodes* (=*Tealia*) *Greenii*], *Natural History Review* V (1858), 264.

52. J. Alder, 'A Catalogue of the Zoophytes of Northumberland and Durham', *Trans. Tyneside Naturalists' Field Club* III (1856), 93-162; J. Reay Greene, 'Observations on the Distribution of [Irish] Actinoida', *Natural History Review* V (1858), 35-7; E. P. Wright, 'Notes on Irish Actinidae', *Natural History Review* VI (1859), 113-25.

53. Review, *Excelsior* V (Apr. 1856), 360.

54. *Sea Anemones* (London: Hamilton, Adams, and Co., 1856, 44 pp.) sold for 1s.6d. in 1859, and appeared in a new edition by Spencer Thomson in 1860. It was favourably noticed in *The Critic* n.s. XV (1 Apr. 1856), 173. Freeman, *British Natural History Books*, item 3338, gives the publisher in 1856 as Simpkin.

Coast (1856). It was praised for its chromolithographed plates by the draughtsman (and falconer) William Brodrick (1814-1888),[55] but it did not pretend to be a scientific treatise. Indeed, the 'scientific value [of the descriptions] is *nil*,' as one reviewer wrote.[56] Gosse himself was critical of Tugwell's distinction between species and varieties.[57]

Although the *Histoire Naturelle des Coralliaires* (1857-1860) of the great French zoologist Henri Milne-Edwards (1800-1885) was not as well-known in Britain as one might have expected,[58] it contained in its identification of new systematic characters improvements over the classification of previous works.[59] A number of these distinguishing characters were also used by Gosse in a different manner, and in spite of the fact that Gosse was mentioned several times in the book, Milne-Edwards (an anti-evolutionist)[60] never wrote of his English colleague's work with any enthusiasm. Perhaps Milne-Edwards was aware that while Gosse was impressed with the Frenchman's 'immense research, labour,

55. On Brodrick: Boase IV, 503 and 'The Late William Brodrick', *Zoologist* ser. 3, XIII (Apr. 1889), 139-142. For reviews of Tugwell's book: *The Leader*, 25 Oct. 1856, 1024-5 [by G. H. Lewes; see Haight, *George Eliot Letters* II: 243fn.8]; *Examiner*, 1 Nov. 1856, 692; *Critic* n.s. XV (15 Nov. 1856), 535; *Saturday Review* II (15 Nov. 1856), 647 [by G. H. Lewes per Haight, *George Eliot Letters* II: 243fn.8 and not by M. E. Grant Duff, see Bevington, *The Saturday Review*, 348]; and *Zoologist* XIV (1856), 5340-3 (signed 'Philactinia'). *The Atlas*, 25 Oct. 1856, did not think the illustrations as good as in most Van Voorst publications. For other favourable comments on the book in general: *Spectator*, 18 Oct. 1856, 1110, and *London Quarterly Review* XV (Apr. 1857), 76-92.

56. [Thomas Bell], *The Athenaeum* (22 Nov. 1856), 1430. The book was not reviewed by *AMNH*, *NHR*, or *Quarterly Journal of the Microscopical Society*.

57. 'What is a species?' Tugwell gave a commonly accepted definition: 'a collection of individuals, whose present form has been perpetuated without change since the creation.' (p. 116). But in attempting to indicate how we recognize one, he claimed that 'colour is the distinctive mark of a variety, and form and habit that of a species' (p. 94; he made the same distinction in his anonymous 'Science by the Seaside', *Fraser's Magazine* LIV, Sept. 1856, 259; see *Wellesley Index* II: 433). PHG pointed out that 'In many instances colour is not only specific, but even generic' (*Actinologia Britannica*, 50).

58. I have not seen any review of the work in the general British press, and it went unnoticed in some scientific periodicals which did examine PHG's work, such as the *Zoologist*, *Natural History Review*, *Annals and Magazine of Natural History*, and *Athenaeum*.

59. Some of these systematic characters were of doubtful value. For example, Milne-Edwards emphasized the systematic value of the pedal disk in certain species and of the marginal spherules. But he also founded two new groups—'Actinines vulgaires' and 'Actinines verruqueuses'—on the basis of the nature of the anemone's body, 'which is in itself unimportant and in no case clearly marked.' For this and another criticism: Richard Hertwig, 'Report on the Actiniaria Dredged by H.M.S. Challenger during the Years 1873-1876', *Report of the Scientific Results of the Voyage of H.M.S. Challenger, Zoology* (London: H. M. Stationery Office, 1882), VI:17.

60. J. T. Merz, *A History of European Thought in the Nineteenth Century* (London: William Blackwood & Sons, 1903), II: 322fn.1; Alberto Mario Simonetta, *Short History of Biology from the Origins to the 20th Century* (Firenze: Firenza University Press, 2003), 405.

and patience,' he nonetheless saw in the *Histoire Naturelle* 'the produce of the museum and the closet, not ... the aquarium and the shore. ... the distribution of the species into genera and families appears so full of manifest error to one personally familiar with the animals in a living state, that I have not attempted to follow his arrangement.'[61]

During the winter months of 1857, as the weather made visits to the shore infrequent,[62] Gosse was able to concentrate on the letterpress and illustrations for his sea anemone work. On 10 December he gave the originals for two plates to the engraver, William Dickes (1815-1892), an expert in colour printing.[63] Gosse asked his friend W. A. Lloyd to allow Dickes to study the anemones in his aquaria in order to become familiar with the living animals.[64] Three months later the first of the twelve bi-monthly parts of *Actinologia Britannica* appeared.[65] Gosse realized that there were disadvantages to issuing the monograph in this way[66]—it was, after all, not a novel, and earlier classificatory errors could not be easily emended if found faulty—yet the advantages were evident. The latest information could be incorporated; the continuous issuance of parts would keep alive the enthusiasm and contributions of his correspondents; and (it was no doubt hoped) the cheap price of 1s.6d. for thirty-two pages of letterpress and one coloured lithograph would put it within the reach of everyman's pocket.

Throughout 1858 Gosse pursued his subjects in all parts of the Kingdom, either in person or through one of his agents. He searched the tide-pools of the St. Marychurch area (accompanied by his son), especially those at Petit Tor, and if he found his prey located in a not readily accessible area, he would 'fairly strip', jump into even breast high water, and detach them with his hammer or cold chisel. They were then

61. PHG, *Actinologia Britannica*, vi. Both Milne-Edwards' and PHG's classifications are given in the article on 'Zoophytes' in the eighth edition of the *Encyclopaedia Britannica* (1860), XXI: 1004. According to Hertwig, 'Report on the Actiniaria' (p. 18), later naturalists sometimes followed Milne-Edwards more closely, and other times PHG. James Yate Johnson, for example, followed Gosse's nomenclature for the genera ('Notes on the Sea-anemones of Madeira, with Descriptions of New Species', *Proceedings of the Zoological Society of London* (1861), 298).

62. PHG-[W. A. Lloyd?], 18 Dec. 1857 (Edinburgh).

63. 'Dickes, William', *DNCJ*, 167.

64. PHG-[W. A. Lloyd?], 10 Dec. 1857 (Edinburgh).

65. Though 1 Mar. 1858 was the announced date of publication for Part I of *Actinologia Britannica* (*Birmingham Daily Post*, 7 Dec. 1857, 1), and is the date given by Freeman & Wertheimer-PHG, 69, it actually appeared slightly earlier. See the review of Part I in the *Leeds Intelligencer*, 27 Feb. 1858, 3.

66. PHG, *Actinologia Britannica*, vii.

brought home, and he waited for them to resume their normal state while spread-out in shallow pans, when the observation and recording of their habits would commence.[67] Frequently, he went dredging off Berry Head, Torbay, sometimes with Charles Kingsley and Edmund as partners,[68] and on one occasion went on an excursion down the Dart with the Torquay geologist William Pengelly, perhaps looking for anemones.[69] F. H. West, of Leeds, and the Revd Walter Gregor[70] of Macduff, near Banff in Scotland, were constant suppliers of specimens; while lecturing in Montrose in Angus, Gosse identified a new species of coral in the collection of James Cunningham Howden;[71] he asked C. W. Peach to look out for the northern forms; boxes and canisters came from Frederick Dyster and many others, drawings from C. P. Cocks, Peach, and Joshua Alder. During the whole period the postman brought Gosse a voluminous correspondence of over 400 letters.[72]

Lecturing provided Gosse with yet another opportunity to increase his finds, as well as his funds. In April he spoke at Exeter Hall in London, in October in Teignmouth, and in December before the Torquay Natural History Society (at the latter two he spoke on marine zoology).[73] In

67. PHG, *Actinologia Britannica*, 137, 345; *Father and Son*, 1907, 158-160. W. R. Hughes (1830-1899), the Treasurer of Birmingham, bibliophile, and F.L.S. (1865), provides another description of his collecting habits: W[illiam]. R[ichard].H[ughes]., 'Philip Henry Gosse, F.R.S.', *Midland Naturalist* XI (1888), 301.

68. PHG, *Actinologia Britannica*, 203; *Life*, 289.

69. The trip occurred on 11 November 1857. In *Actinologia Britannica*, 23, PHG records one specimen for the Dart, so that he may have mixed pleasure and profit on the trip. See Hester Pengelly (ed.), *A Memoir of William Pengelly, Torquay, F.R.S., Geologist, with a Selection of his Correspondence* (London: John Murray, 1897), 73.

70. *Gregoria fenestrate* Gosse was named by PHG after Gregor (Scotland *Elgin and Morayshire Courier*, 19 Nov. 1858, 3); see PHG, *Actinologia Britannica*, 145-7. The World Register of Marine Species regards the taxon details as valid today.

71. PHG, *Actinologia Britannica*, 320. Howden (d. 1897, aet. 67) was Physician Superintendent at Sunnyside Royal Lunatic Asylum for 40 years ('Death of Dr. Howden, Montrose', *Dundee Courier*, 18 Aug. 1897, 4; London *Daily News*, 21 Aug. 1897, 1) and for 5 years, vice-president of the Montrose Natural History and Antiquarian Society, where PHG lectured on Feb. 1, 1859 (*Montrose, Arbroath, & Brechin Review*, 28 Jan. 1859, 1, and *Montrose Standard*, 28 Jan. 1859, 1).

72. PHG, *Actinologia Britannica*, vi, 96, 207; PHG-Peach, 15 Mar., 3 June 1858 (Institute of Geological Sciences, London, 1/527); J. Alder-PHG, Jan. 6, 1859 (CUL Adv. c. 82.5, 62); L. J. P. Gaskin, 'On a Collection of Original Sketches and Drawings of British Sea-anemones and Corals by Philip Henry Gosse, and his Correspondents, 1839-1861, in the Library of the Horniman Museum', *J. Soc. Bibl. Nat. Hist.* I (July 1937), 65-7. There is an index to the letters Gosse received in a notebook with a dual title (*Anemones* and *Actinologia*) in the Zoology Library of the British Museum (Natural History) (89/o/G), but few of the letters have been traced.

73. For his lecture at Exeter Hall on the evening of 6 Apr. 1858, per Sarah Andrews-PHG, 5 Apr., and PHG-EWG, 7 Apr. (CUL Adv. c. 82.5, 58-9). In Dec. 1857 he had been asked to lecture

January 1859 he addressed the Torquay Mechanics' Institute[74] on one
of his favourite topics—Divine contrivances in the structure of the lower
animals—and during February lectured in Scotland before the Montrose
Natural History Society and the Watt Institution in Dundee, and then
at the Leeds Mechanics' Institute, on the same subject.[75] Montrose,
he wrote home, 'is said to be pretty good for zoology.'[76] These lectures
were, as usual, accompanied by Gosse's coloured diagrams, and added
to his reputation as 'a first-rate lecturer, familiar, off-hand, witty, and
amusing, with a rare power of setting his subject in a clear light before
his audience.'[77]

One might think that these projects would be sufficient to keep
even the most industrious person fully occupied. Gosse could
handle it all, and more. During 1858 he was continuously supplying
W. A. Lloyd's Aquarium Warehouse, and Lloyd's business was so
successful that he had to twice increase his premises.[78] At about this
time he was writing reviews for the London *Literary Gazette* and
articles for the Nonconformist monthly *Eclectic Review*.[79] In March

before the Y.M.C.A. in London for the coming March, but he excused himself by saying that he had
no prospects of coming to the city (PHG-W. E. Shipton, 20 Dec. 1857, William R. Perkins Library,
Duke University). I have been unable to find any report of Gosse's speech in five local papers,
and as it was not one of the well-known Exeter Hall Lectures, it was not printed in that series.

The three lectures at Teignmouth between October 22-31 were apparently on general marine
zoology, and reported as 'well attended and well delivered, and met with universal applause from
all who heard them. Mr. Gosse's talents tell their own tale' (*Teignmouth Gazette*, 1 Nov. 1858,
p. 2; *Torquay Directory*, 3 Nov., p. 5). The lecture at the Torquay Natural History Society on
December 20 was also on that subject (*Torquay Directory* and *Torquay Chronicle*, 21 Dec.).

74. Before the Torquay Mechanics' Institute he delivered the same set of lectures which he
gave at Birmingham on January 12 and 19, 1859 (*Torquay Directory*).

75. For the lecture at Montrose on February 1: *Montrose, Arbroath, and Brechin Review*,
28 Jan., p. 1; 4 Feb., p. 4, 1859; and *Montrose Standard*, 4 Feb. 1859, 4; for those in Dundee on
2 and 4 Feb: *Dundee and Perth Saturday Post*, 5 Feb., 3; *Dundee, Perth and Cupar Advertiser*,
8 Feb., 2; *Dundee Courier*, 9 Feb., 2; for Leeds: *Leeds Intelligencer*, 5 Feb. 1859, 5.

76. PHG-EWG, 1 Feb. 1859 (CUL Add. 7027, 30).

77. *Dundee Courier*, 9 Feb. 1859, 2. 'Perhaps no one has done more to popularize the science
of natural history than Mr. Gosse, and our readers will find him as entertaining a companion in
the lecture-room as in his own pleasant pages' (*Leeds Intelligencer*, 5 Feb. 1859, 5).

78. PHG-[W. A. Lloyd], 7 August 1858 (Edinburgh); PHG-Lloyd, 1 Feb. 1858, cited in the
bookseller Dr M. E. Korn's *List 173, Natural History* (London, [December 1972]), item 177); and
Lloyd-C. W. Peach, 24 June 1858 (Institute of Geological Sciences, London, 1/527), noting that
he is adding a 600 gallon sea-water cistern to the 700 gallon one which had proved insufficient
to meet the demand.

79. PHG-EWG, 26 Apr. 1872 (CUL Add. 7041,53); Mary Ruth Hiller, 'The Eclectic Review,
1805-1868', *Victorian Periodicals Review* 27 (Fall 1994), 179-283. John B. Paton (1830-1911),
editor of the *Eclectic Review*, published two, multi-part PHG articles in 1859, and rejected
another in 1860 (PHG PHG-Paton, 8 Aug. 1860, Wellcome Historical Medical Library). The

1859,[80] the SPCK published his *Evenings at the Microscope; or, Researches among the minuter organs and forms of animal life* for a popular audience. The illustrations were almost entirely done by the author drawing on the wood 'direct from the microscope'—a dramatic improvement over Adams' *Essays on the Microscope*, whose copper engraved plates, several steps removed from the actual microscopic images, Gosse had studied a quarter-century earlier in Newfoundland.[81]

The microscope was so much part of Gosse's psyche that it is unsurprising that this book was one of his most successful. In England, it went through four editions during his lifetime[82] and was widely reviewed; in America, the first edition text was reprinted by D. Appleton and two other publishers after his death, remaining in print until 1905. It received the second most reviews of any of his books there.[83] In 1890 it was considered one of the seven best works on microscopy.[84]

By the time *Evenings at the Microscope* was issued—Gosse had proposed it to the SPCK in the previous year—interest in the microscope had increased and become as widespread as that of the telescope, leading the instrument to be 'universally recognised as the indispensable companion of every true naturalist.'[85] As one newspaper impressively remarked, 'atoms have competed with planets for the wonder and

rejected article may have later appeared in the *Intellectual Observer:* Freeman & Wertheimer-PHG, items #284, 292, and 322. For the identification of anonymous *Literary Review* items, see above, 277 fn.10. PHG did not enjoy being a critic, and warned EWG against devoting his life to criticism in his 26 Apr. 1872 letter (emphasis in the original):

> It begets a habit of cynicism; our book-critics are generally *snarlers, carpers*; & almost universally dishonest, giving out their oracles, on the slightest possible examination of the books they criticise. I found this when I was engaged for a while on the Literary Gazette, & Eclectic Review. The ordinary mode was, (& doubtless is,) to skim the book (I refer chiefly to books of science) enough to select some striking or leading portion, perhaps by help of the preface or index, & retail it in the critique, not as the author's discovery, but as what the critic knows, & with which he tests the book; this is the main body of the article. A few words of scant praise; & a little ridicule if possible on something or other, often enough distorted or misunderstood, finishes off.

80. Advertisement, 'Now ready', London *Examiner* (5 Mar. 1859), 19; review, London *Literary Gazette* (19 Mar. 1859), 379.

81. Millburn, *Adams of Fleet Street*, 211.

82. Freeman & Wertheimer-PHG, 62.

83. This is based on D. Wertheimer, 'P. H. Gosse's Scientific Reception in America' (unpublished MS).

84. 'Scientific Reading. A List of the Best Works on Many Technical Subjects [from the *Indianapolis News*]', *St. Louis Daily Globe-Democrat*, Jan. 11, 1890, 6.

85. *Natural History Review* II (1855), 28.

admiration of mankind.'[86] Not all of the early works were useful,[87] but numerous publications were appearing[88]—among them technical treatments by John Quekett (1848), Lionel S. Beale (1854), and William B. Carpenter (1856),[89] and popular ones by Jabez Hogg (1854), Edwin Lankester (1859),[90] J. G. Wood (1861), William Houghton (1872), and others.[91]

'All that Mr. Gosse has hitherto done in the way of authorship has been well done,' observed the London *Art-Journal*, and *Evenings at the Microscope*, 'the latest of his works, affords no exception to the rule.'[92] Besides 'strengthening religious principles', a reviewer in the London *Literary Gazette* said,

> ... the researches of Mr. Gosse among the minuter organs and forms of animal life ... constitute in themselves a large field of original observation. He has been an observer *de novo*, and sets down what he has seen himself. The results of his investigations may be accepted as authoritative. But, while faithfully communicating results, he has relieved the technical necessities of the case by the charms of a colloquial and familiar style. He modestly describes the volume as but a gleaning;

86. Review of *Life in its Lower, Intermediate, and Higher Forms*, in *Wells Journal* (Wells, Somerset), 29 Aug. 1857, 4.

87. Of Jabez Hogg's *Microscope: Its History, Construction, and Application*, the *Gardeners' Chronicle* wrote: 'Mr. Hogg has compiled with very little skill a thick 8vo volume, and has illustrated it with a great number of cuts—he says 500—of which we can only say, that while some are good, others are not such as will prove either attractive or instructive' (1 July 1854, 423). *Microscope* was belittled as 'a work for the *million*' in *Natural History Review* II (1855), 36. The book nonetheless reached a 15ed. in 1898 and was still in print in 1911 (Freeman, *British Natural History Books*, 170).

88. Laura Forsberg, *Worlds Beyond: Miniatures and Victorian Fiction* (New Haven: Yale University Press, 2021), 83-106.

89. Carpenter's *Microscope* went through eight editions in England by 1891, and a 1901 'enlarged and revised' edition of 1,181 pages was called a 'classic work' (review in Ecological Society of America *Plant World* V, May 1902, 99); Freeman, *British Natural History Books*, 79.

90. Because the title-page of the first edition of Edwin Lankester's *Half-Hours with the Microscope* (1859) omitted his name but included that of the illustrator, Tuffen West, all of the reviews of the work I have seen attribute the book to West (e.g., reviews of 5 Feb. 1859 in *Literary Gazette*, 186, and London *Spectator*, 161; *Athenaeum*, 5 Mar. 1859, 319). The second edition (1860) corrected the error. Though no authority is cited, *Half-Hours with the Microscope* is said to have sold 7,000 copies by 1863, with a fifth and last edition, 1905 (English, *Victorian Values. The Life and Times of Dr. Edwin Lankester*, 130). Freeman & Wertheimer-PHG did not have publication figures for any editions of PHG's *Evenings at the Microscope*.

91. Freeman, *British Natural History Books*, 423, provides a subject index to books on 'Microscopy'.

92. Review of PHG, *Evenings at the Microscope*, in *Art-Journal* n.s. V (1 May 1859), 160.

but we find he has left little of that ample fund of Zoology untouched which can be brought under the control of the microscope.[93]

In the next month, having revised some of his old papers and journals, *Letters from Alabama* appeared. Though exhibiting the same qualities which had made Gosse's other works appealing, one reviewer thought it would have greater success in America than in England.[94] Tension between Northern and Southern States at the time may have contributed to the book being virtually ignored by reviewers there.[95]

In 1858-9, twenty-six papers by him (largely on natural history, with some religious pieces) were published in various periodicals.

-IV-

With the completion of the text of *Actinologia Britannica* in June 1859,[96] Gosse's trips to the shore became infrequent.[97] It was not, however, until six months later, in December 1859 or January 1860,[98] that he could write *finis* to the labour of eight years. It had been undertaken '*con amore*', and was sent forth 'as one more tribute humbly offered to the glory of the Triune God, "who is wonderful in counsel, and excellent in working."'[99]

Taking as his domain the sea anemones and corals of the class Anthozoa,[100] Gosse wanted his work to be accessible to the student (perhaps explaining the large print run). It was the first detailed investigation of

93. Review of PHG, *Evenings at the Microscope* in *Literary Gazette*, 19 Mar. 1859, 379.

94. 'Popular Books on Natural History', *Saturday Review*, 29 Oct. 1859, 521-2. Favourable English reviews appeared (among other places) in *Spectator*, 3 Sept. 1859, 907-9 and *Literary Gazette*, 8 Oct. 1859, 350-1. J. R. Leifchild, who frequently reviewed science works for the *Athenaeum* (including Darwin's *Origin* and *Descent of Man*), also critiqued several of PHG's works, generally unfavourably. Most of his piece on *Letters from Alabama*, 3 Sept. 1859, 304, was devoted to decrying *Omphalos* (on John Roby Leifchild, b. 1815, see *Wellesley Index* I: 977; Marchand, *Athenaeum*, 226).

95. The only American review I have seen of *Letters from Alabama* appeared in the *American Journal of Science & Arts* (ser.2, XXIX, Jan. 1860, 132, by W[illiam] S[timpson]). It was rarely advertised there (e.g., 'New English Books', *Boston Daily Evening Transcript*, 13 Sept. 1859, 3).

96. *Life*, 290.

97. PHG-[?], 30 Aug. 1859 (Edinburgh).

98. Freeman & Wertheimer-PHG, 68-9.

99. PHG, *Actinologia Britannica*, viii.

100. PHG had originally intended to include the Lucernaria, but excluded them because, as was being recognized at the time, their true affinities were with the Hydrozoa and Medusae (*Actinologia Britannica*, 348, and the anonymous 'Literature of the Sub-kingdom Coelenterata', *Natural History Review* n.s. I, 1861, 427-8).

the group,[101] and he was its 'first adequate monographer.'[102] The result was research 'of the highest order; the descriptions of species attain an unusual level, and the work reveals exceptional insight into the form and life of the animals with which it deals.'[103] In the summary of one newspaper, *Actinologia Britannica* 'may be accounted a national work on the subject.'[104]

Of all his writings, it was this one upon 'wh[ich] his reputation will mainly rest',[105] as Gosse wrote for a solicited biographical entry at the time. In the view of one modern zoologist, some of his other work attained 'equal or greater lasting scientific value,'[106] yet Gosse's scientific colleagues—especially those who cultivated the same field—lauded *Actinologia* for decades.[107] The Irish zoologist E. Percival Wright (1834-1910) called it 'an excellent monograph of our native forms, which will always be a work to refer to.'[108] To the Italian zoologist Angelo Andres (1851-1934), who brought out his landmark study of all known species of sea anemones in 1884, Gosse was 'the revered author' ('*il riverito autore*'), the 'leader of all by merit and character' ('*Il capo di tutti per merito e carattere*').[109] Even seventy-five years after its publication the

101. Freeman & Wertheimer-PHG, 67.

102. H. J. Fleure, 'Alfred Cort Haddon, 1855-1940', *Obituary Notices of Fellows of the Royal Society* III (Jan. 1941), 451.

103. Stephenson, *British Sea Anemones* I: vii.

104. *Belfast News*-Letter, 16 Sept. 1858, 3.

105. See the biographical notice in PHG's holograph, with a postmark for 19 January 1860 (British Library, Add. Mss. 28510, f.115). The notice was published in Griffin's *Dictionary of Contemporary Biography* (1861), 185. The entry in G. H. Townsend (ed.), *Men of the Time* (London: George Routledge and Sons, 7th ed., 1868), 355, gives the same opinion, and thus may also have originated from PHG.

106. Freeman & Wertheimer-PHG, 9, 67.

107. H. B. B[rady]., *Proceedings of the Royal Society of London* 44 (1888), xxvii; *Abstract of Proceedings of the South London Entomological & Natural History Society* (1888), 30; 'Philip Henry Gosse', *Scientific American* 59 (15 Sept. 1888), 160. Similarly I. D. Lawn: 'The great 19th century naturalist P. H. Gosse (1860), in his masterly account of the British sea anemones' (Lawn, 'Behavioural Physiology of Sea Anemones' (University of St. Andrews, PhD dissertation, 1973), 66).

108. E.P. W[right], *Nature* 43 (30 Apr. 1891), 605.

109. Angelo Andres, *Fauna und Flora des Golfes von Neapel.[Vol.] IX. Monographie: Die Actinien [Fauna and Flora of the Gulf of Naples and the adjacent Sea Sections. [Vol.] IX. Monograph: The Actinia]* (Leipzig: Wilhelm Engelmann, 1884), 68. In 1880 Andres had sought PHG's assistance, 'But my increasing years have for some time precluded me from personal investigation among the rocks; and, having published to the world my own researches, I have relinquished the study to my successors' (PHG-Andres, 13 Oct. 1880, CUL Add. 7313,204). PHG owned a copy of Andres' work (*Sandhurst Catalogue,* item #311), and continued corresponding with him (e.g., Corr. Bk., 20 Feb. 1885 *et. seq.*).

English marine biologist T. A. Stephenson (1898-1961) said that "'The Actinologia" has remained, and will continue to remain, a source of inspiration to the discerning'.[110] Gosse's species descriptions were 'so thoroughly and systematically carried out that, although they deal with the externals alone, they remain valid to this day'.[111] Lately an admiring zoologist, calling Gosse a 'superb colorist', noted how his 'incorporation of both ecological awareness and aesthetic sensibility carried through to his scientific monument, *Actinologia Britannica* ... wherein he recounted viewing his light-shy subjects in an aquarium at night, by candlelight, referring to these animals with their floral name as "blossomed beauties."'[112]

These judgments are unsurprising. Notwithstanding the example of a few predecessors, Gosse was on 'virgin soil' in studying sea anemones, wrote Edward Newman in the *Zoologist:* 'Mr. Gosse is the first author on sea anemones who conveys to his reader the idea that he understands what he is writing about; and his plates, printed in colours, most beautifully illustrate his descriptions. Mr. Gosse's style is always delightful; ample without being verbose; perspicuous without repetition.'[113]

Gosse recorded much that was new with precision and succinctness. By including the characters of foreign families and genera, he provided the investigator with an additional aid in identifying hitherto unknown British genera or species.[114] In assigning names to new species and genera, he drew on his familiarity with Greek and Latin to make the name reflect an important characteristic, rejecting the sloppiness which he thought was typical of Linnean specific names.[115] He invented as well a series of vernacular names for the genera which long continued in use.[116]

110. Stephenson, *British Sea Anemones* II: viii.

111. Fleure, 'Alfred Cort Haddon', *Obituary Notices of Fellows of the Royal Society*, 451.

112. J. Malcolm Shick, 'Toward an Aesthetic Marine Biology', *Art Journal* 67 (Winter 2008), 67-8; PHG, *Actinologia Britannica*, 15.

113. [Edward Newman], review of *Actinologia Britannica* in *Zoologist* XIX (1861), 7299.

114. *AMNH* ser. 3, III (Nov. 1858), 368-9. Andres considered this the most important part of the book (Andres, *Fauna und Flora des Golfes von Neapel*, 36).

115. PHG, *Actinologia Britannica*, 211, 339; for a similar opinion of Linnean nomenclature: George Johnston, *British Zoophytes* (2nd ed.), I: 211 fn. In the Introduction to PHG's monograph, he also coined a number of words for the various parts of the teliferous apparatus. Many of these gained general acceptance, and are cited in the *OED*, 1ed. without referencing PHG's priority (cinclides, cnida, craspedum). Others are not mentioned at all (acontia, ecthoreum, strebla, pterygia, peribola).

116. PHG, *Actinologia Britannica*, 137-8fn. Rather than form 'arbitrary aggregations of vowels and consonants,—'Farson', 'Toler", for the genera, he chose words with a meaningful

In his section on the non-adherent forms (*Ilyanthidae*), he included twelve new anemones (one only having been recognized by Johnston, and a number greater than Milne-Edwards gave for the entire world).[117] And throughout the monograph were observations which make it an enduring source of information. One-hundred-and-twenty years passed before another author considered together in a single volume British sea anemones and corals.[118]

Though presented as a research work filled with scientific data, from the day it was released the *Actinologia Britannica* found a highly receptive audience in the general press. 'There are but few books on the Natural History of these Islands,' one scientific reviewer observed, 'that can in any way compare with Mr. Gosse's "*Actinologia Britannica*", whether we regard the evident care and conscientiousness with which it has been got up or the elegance of the illustrations.'[119] Reviewers vied with each other in extolling the excellence of the monograph. They highlighted the descriptions of the form and habits of the anemones,[120] the value of the work for the drawing room and the naturalist,[121] the usefulness of the Introduction in treating structure and physiology,[122] and the economic price for each part.[123]

But it was Gosse's illustrations themselves, reproduced as coloured lithographs from his original watercolours, which drew the most consistent praise (as had been the case earlier with the *Aquarium*). The *Literary Gazette* exclaimed that Gosse

---

etymology. *Actinia mesembryanthemum* (=*equina*) became 'The Beadlet'; *Tealia digitata*, 'The Marigold Wartlet'; *Anthea cereus*, 'The Opelet'; *Phellia picta*, 'The Painted Corklet', &c. See *AMNH* ser. 3, VI (Nov. 1860), 373. For the continued use of these diminutives: N. B. Eales, *The Littoral Fauna of Great Britain. A Handbook for Collectors* (Cambridge: University Press, 4th ed., 1967), 40-6.

117. PHG, *Actinologia Britannica*, 227. This family virtually entirely disappeared in Andres' *Fauna und Flora des Golfes von Neapel* (*Nature*, 1 Jan. 1885, 199).

118. E. A. Robson, review of two works by R. L. Manuel in *Estuarine, Coastal and Shelf Science* (Aug. 1983), 229-30.

119. *AMNH* ser. 3, VI (Nov. 1860), 372; see also *Natural History Review* V (Apr. 1858), 102-3; *Guardian*, 12 Sept. 1860, 816.

120. *Leader*, 7 Aug. 1858, 777; and *AMNH* ser. 3, II (Nov. 1858), 369.

121. *Leader* (7 Aug. 1858), 777; and [G. H. Lewes], *Blackwood's Magazine* LXXXIX (Nov. 1861), 345.

122. [W. S. Dallas, per *Wellesley Index* III: 631], *Westminster Review* XVIII (October 1860), 561; *Literary Gazette* n.s. IV (7 Apr. 1860), 427.

123. *Natural History Review* V (Apr. 1858), 103; *Critic* XVII (31 July 1858), 434; *Atlas*, 8 Aug. 1858, 5; *Globe*, 26 Aug. 1858, [1].

stands alone and unrivalled in the extremely difficult art of drawing objects of zoology so as to satisfy the requirements of science, and reproduce those vivid aesthetic impressions which beautiful combinations of form and colour make upon the minds of those who are familiar with the living creatures whose appearance he depicts. ... he has a facility of entering into the character of the beings he investigates, and depicts them, not as dead specimens, but as imbued with and exhibiting the peculiarities of the life which they enjoy.[124]

In 1863, when Ludwig Reichenbach (1793-1879), Director of the Royal Natural History Museum in Dresden, commissioned Leopold Blaschka (1822-1895), of Dresden, to create glass models of marine invertebrates, they turned to the images of Gosse. Based almost completely on the illustrations in *Actinologia Britannica*, Blaschka (later joined by his son Rudolph) sought with an 'almost ruthless determination to mirror nature in glass.'[125] The result: beautifully fabricated, anatomically-accurate glass sea anemones[126] displayed in artificial aquariums. All but two of the sixty-eight models in the first Blaschka sale catalog of 1870 were based on *Actinologia Britannica*.[127]

Reviewers of Gosse's book, however, had an important reservation. It concerned the author's multiplication of species and genera, and his general classification.[128] Gosse had taken great pains to give diagnoses

124. *Literary Gazette* n.s. IV (7 Apr. 1860), 427. Besides the reviews cited in the previous footnotes, see also: *Spectator*, 31 July 1858, 812; *Guardian*, 18 Aug. 1858), 673; *John Bull*, 4 Sept. 1858, 572; *Gardeners' Chronicle*, 31 Mar. 1860, 291; *Spectator*, 31 Mar. 1860, 311; [J. R. Leifchild], *Athenaeum*, 21 Apr. 1860, 548; and *Zoologist* XIX (1861), 7299.

125. Edward Rothstein, 'What Art Has Made of Nature', *The Wall Street Journal*, 25 Aug. 2016.

126. Drew Harvell, *A Sea of Glass. Searching for the Blaschkas' Fragile Legacy in an Ocean at Risk* (Oakland, CA: University of California Press, 2016), 6-7. The Blaschka glass work has been exhibited in museums: Alicia Rawsthorn, 'Wonders of bygone era; Before digital imaging, craftsmen captured the natural world in glass', *International Herald Tribune*, 21 June 2010.

127. Florian Huber, 'Spiegelbilder vom Meeresgrund. Leopold Blaschkas marine Aquarien' ['Reflections from the Ocean Floor. Leopold Blaschka's Marine Aquaria'], *Berichte zur Wissenschaftsgeschichte* 36 (June 2013), 178, 175; Chris Meechan, 'A Glass Menagerie: The work of Leopold and Rudolph Blaschka', *The Glass Cone* #39 (Spring 1995), 4-5. On Blaschka, see also Foutch, *Arresting Beauty*, chap. 4. Until 1880, Leopold Blaschka relied on PHG's work, but their 1880 catalogue referenced several other zoologists (Huber, 182).

128. *AMNH* ser. 3, II (Nov. 1858), 367-8; *Literary Gazette* n.s. IV (7 Apr. 1860), 428; *Westminster Review* XVIII (October 1860), 561; *NHR* n.s. I (1861), 332; and Thomas Hincks, 'A Catalogue of the Zoophytes of South Devon and South Cornwall', *AMNH* ser. 3, VIII (Aug. 1861), 156fn. In the 'Synopsis of the Families, Genera, and Species of the British Actiniae' (*AMNH* ser. 3, I, June 1858, 414-9), which was followed for the first two parts of *Actinologia*, PHG listed 41 species for 14 genera. When the latter work was completed, there were 44 in 19.

which were carefully crafted and based where possible on more than one character. It was no easy task. For 'The *quaestio vexata*,—What constitutes a species? what a variety?' was, as he knew, 'one which it is much easier to answer theoretically than practically.'[129] Ignoring the recent publication by Darwin, Gosse took the traditional view that 'a species is permanent, a variety transitory,' and thus included seventy 'good' species of anemones and corals[130]—of which only twenty-four had been described in Johnston's *British Zoophytes* (2nd ed., 1847). But how many of these were 'true' species, and how many synonyms?

The difficulty of satisfactorily deciding this species question may be appreciated by glancing at the classification for the genus *Sagartia*, established by Gosse in 1855.[131] At that time, he had divided the old genus Actinia into three new genera—*Sagartia, Bunodes*, and *Actinia*—based mainly on the differences in their thread-capsules (in Gosse's coinage, *acontia*).[132] Besides this character, he was also confronted by a bewildering number of colour varieties, each of which he eventually designated as a species. In 1855 the genus had ten species, and in *Actinologia Britannica*, fifteen. The standard authority on the class subsequently reduced these colour-varieties to one species, and Gosse's fifteen to five.[133]

In all of his descriptions, Gosse was conscious of falling into the trap of establishing species on the basis of a single character (for example, colour or the shape of an organ). Yet he was not always successful in avoiding that danger, and multiplication of species followed as long as external characteristics primarily were considered. A new classificatory approach was needed—comparative anatomy—especially since students of the subject are hindered by the difficulty of clearly defining the evolutionary history of the Anthozoa. Here Gosse fell short in not considering the role which internal comparative anatomy plays as a classificatory tool.[134] It

129. PHG, *Actinologia Britannica*, 50.

130. PHG, *Actinologia Britannica*, v. PHG described Johnston's work as valuable on many points, but 'the almost utter worthlessness of their specific characters has been often confessed' (p. vi.).

131. PHG, 'Description of *Peachia hastata*, a New Genus and Species of the Class Zoophyta; with Observations on the Family Actiniadae', *Trans. Linnean Society* XXI (10 Nov. 1855), 272.

132. This word, which does not have an entry in the *OED* (3ed.), was coined by PHG, *Actinologia Britannica*, xxiv. Contrary to Hertwig, 'Report on the Actiniaria', 17, the acontia were not discovered by PHG. Nonetheless, he appears to have been the first one to have used it as a classificatory tool, the value of which has been generally accepted (T. A. Stephenson, '*On the Nematocysts of Sea Anemones*', *J. Mar. Biol. Assoc.* XVI (May 1929), 190).

133. Stephenson, *British Sea Anemones* II: 305, 308-9.

134. Freeman & Wertheimer-PHG, 67.

was twenty years after the appearance of *Actinologia Britannica* before the systems of all earlier classifiers—Johnston, Milne-Edwards, W. Thompson,[135] Gosse, and others—were improved by the morphological investigations of the Hertwig brothers.[136] It was some fifty-five years later before *Actinologia Britannica* was displaced by T. A. Stephenson's *British Sea Anemones* (1928, 1935).[137]

Unlike some other naturalists,[138] as a systematist Gosse was satisfied to attempt to show affinities rather than reveal perceived patterns of regularity and orderliness in nature. That is not to say that his remarks on the anatomy and physiology of anemones did not reflect ideas he held about form and function in the lower animals. In the Introduction to *Actinologia Britannica*, Gosse stated that the organization of anemones 'is more complex than is usually supposed.'[139] He proceeded to describe the tegumentary and muscular systems, and then the nervous, digestive, circulatory and respiratory, reproductive, and 'teliferous'[140] ones. Little controversy surrounded the two elements in the first group, but the remaining five factors were another matter. In every one of them, Gosse found his views contested by G. H. Lewes.

Recall how Lewes' *Sea-side Studies* (1858) mirrored its author's enthusiasm for science while reflecting his deficient scientific knowledge. Notwithstanding unfavourable notices of the latter aspect of his work, he defended his views. It is true that he never seems to have reiterated his rejection of Spix's discovery of the nervous system of the Actinia,[141] nor

135. W. Thompson, 'Remarks on the British Actiniadae, and Rearrangement of the Genera', *Proc. Zoological Society* ([12 July], 1858), 145-9.

136. Alfred Cort Haddon, *A Revision of the British Actiniae*, Part 1, in *Scientific Transactions of the Royal Dublin Society*, ser. 2, vol. IV (1889), 297, and Hertwig, 'Report on the Actiniaria', 1-2. Haddon's *Revision* was the first one to appear after PHG.

137. C. M. Yonge, 'Thomas Alan Stephenson, 1898-1961', *Biographical Memoirs of Fellows of the Royal Society* VIII (Nov. 1962), 140; 'Obituary. Prof. T.A. Stephenson', London *Times*, 5 Apr. 1961, 15.

138. For the systems of Ehrenberg, Huxley, Agassiz, and others: Mary Pickard Winsor, 'Issues in the Classification of Radiates 1830-1860' (Yale University PhD thesis, 1971).

139. PHG, *Actinologia Britannica*, xi.

140. 'Teliferous' and 'teliferous system' are coinages of PHG from the Latin; he is the only one referenced in *OED* 3ed. to use the term in a zoological application (citing *Actinologia Britannica*).

141. Lewes, *Sea-side Studies*, 118. To be fair to Lewes, many others had doubted Spix's 1809 findings (Winsor, 'Issues in the Classification of Radiates', 38), nor was PHG more successful in verifying them. Nonetheless, he wrote that 'I have little doubt that [ganglia] exist' (*Actinologia Britannica*, xiv), a correct assumption (Stephenson *British Sea Anemones* I: 17-19, and Libbie H. Hyman, *The Invertebrates: Protozoa through Ctenophora* (New York: McGraw-Hill Book Co., Inc., 1940), 596-98).

his belief that they possess no sexual organs.[142] He was more persistent on other issues. All of his researches went to prove that 'the organisation of the Actinia [is] much simpler than other writers seem willing to admit'.[143] He said he deplored the habit of accepting as proven facts which he thought required greater examination.[144]

Such was the case with the prevailing views on digestion and circulation. After a fairly lengthy discussion in *Sea-side Studies* of what is meant by digestion,[145] Lewes concluded that it only occurs when food is chemically altered (not macerated). Since his experiments showed that the fluid in an anemone's stomach is free of acids, and that there is nothing similar to blood or 'chylaqueous' fluid there, Lewes concluded that anemones do not digest food. Rather, they obtain nutrition through sucking sea-water in and out.[146] Lewes' physiological theory was challenged,[147] including by Gosse, who did so both anonymously and under his own name.[148] Lewes declined to accept Gosse's counter-experiments as conclusive, and in reviewing *Actinologia Britannica*, he attempted to defend himself against Gosse's imputation that he had presented a 'foolish hypothesis'.[149]

Another instance in which Lewes thought an 'uncritical laxity' had

142. Lewes, *Sea-side Studies*, 163-8. For PHG's description of the sexual organs: *Actinologia Britannica*, xxi-xxii, 97-8 and Stephenson, *British Sea Anemones* I: 34-6, 91-6. Lewes also incorrectly thought that at least certain anemones are only viviparous (*Sea-side Studies*, 140-2; *Actinologia Britannica*, 117-18; Stephenson, *British Sea Anemones* I: 95-6).

143. Lewes, *Sea-side studies*, 163, 168.

144. Lewes, *Sea-side studies*, 100-1, 153.

145. Lewes, *Sea-side studies*, 207-19.

146. Lewes, *Sea-side studies*, 256-61.

147. *Natural History Review* V (1858), 100. For an earlier description of the simple 'water-and-chyle' circulation in anemones: James D. Dana, *Zoophytes*, (in) *United States Exploring Expedition during 1838, 1839, 1840, 1841, 1842* ... (Philadelphia: Lea and Blanchard, 1848[=1846]), VIII: 35.

148. PHG, 'On the Chylaqueous Fluid in the Actinoida', *AMNH* ser. 3, I (Mar. 1858), 172-5; and [PHG], review of Lewes, *Sea-Side Studies* in *Literary Gazette* (27 Mar. 1858), 297. Freeman & Wertheimer-PHG, 104, tentatively ascribes authorship of the *Sea-Side Studies* review to PHG, based on the fact that he is known to have written for the *Literary Gazette* (PHG-EWG, 26 Apr. 1872, CUL Add. 7041, 53). I have removed the tentative attribution because the writer of the review employs the Latin phrase '*hominum volitare per ora*', which PHG used (PHG-EWG, 10 Feb. 1868, CUL Add. 7041, 11). The review also refers to Lewes twice failing to give priority to PHG's *Naturalist's Rambles* (p. 296).

149. PHG, *Actinologia Britannica*, xvi; Lewes, 'On the Chylaqueous Fluid of the Actiniae', *AMNH* ser. 3, II (Dec. 1858), 417-18; [Lewes], *Blackwood's Edinburgh Magazine* LXXXIX (Mar. 1861), 344-5. Lewes also maintained the view that only mechanical processes of digestion occur in the 'simpler' animals in his *Physiology of Common Life* (Leipzig: Bernhard Tauchnitz, 1860), I: 132-33fn. Both extracellular and intracellular digestion do in fact occur (Stephenson, *British Sea Anemones* I: 90; Hyman, *The Invertebrates*, 595; Juro Ishida, 'Digestive Enzymes of Actinia mesembryanthemum', *Annotationes zoologicae Japonenses* XV, 20 June 1936, 285-305).

encouraged naturalists to accept unproven hypotheses was in the case of the remarkable teliferous (or 'dart bearing') system (another Gosse neologism). When certain anemones are irritated, they shoot out slender white threads 'that you might well mistake for fragments of sewing-cotton dropped from a lady's scissors,' Gosse wrote. But these apparently simple threads are, in fact, 'masterpieces of ingenious contrivance and wonderously elaborate mechanism. Death, nay, myriads of deaths are sealed up in every inch of this thread'. Gosse's description of the system is an example of his masterful descriptive powers:

> Nothing is more wonderful than the structure of this thread, when we examine a minute portion of its length by the aid of the microscope. It is made up of millions of transparent oval or oblong sacs, bags of clear, tough membrane closed at each end, and of such dimensions that five hundred of them, if placed in contact end to end, and three thousand, if laid side by side, would lie within the length of an inch. Within each capsule is seen a wire coiled up loosely, and thus occupying the interior.
>
> Such is the armature as it lies ready for action. But, on the stimulus of the animal will, the oval capsules project from the periphery of the containing thread by thousands, and instantly each shoots its shaft. In other words, the coiled-up wire is evolved with lightning-like rapidity from the smaller end; and that not by direct projection, but by eversion; for, wonderful to tell, the wire is tubular throughout, and in order to be shot it must be completely turned inside-out, just as you invert a stocking.
>
> Well, you see this subtle wire running out, evolving its inner surface as it goes, so quickly that it is only under rare circumstances that the eye can follow the process. But now you discern that even this wire is not a simple tube. For throughout its entire length—a length which often reaches to thirty times that of its capsule—it is ridged with one, two, or three elevated *carinae*, or thickened bands, ... these thickened ridges carry a number of fine stiff bristles, which ... as soon as the progress of the evolution frees them, fly out, and presently assume a retrograde direction as so many reverted barbs.
>
> The force with which this remarkable wire is shot is sufficient, combined with its almost inconceivable tenuity, to enable it to pierce the skin and tissues of the animals with which it comes in contact. ... Moreover, in some way or other, a most subtle poison accompanies

the evolution of the wire, and is injected into every wound made by its intromission. No animal of small size, however vigorous its life, however exalted its rank in the scale of being, can withstand its power.[150]

These thread-capsules had not always been recognized as complex offensive and defensive weapons. When first discovered in 1835 they were thought to be spermatozoa.[151] Their true nature was revealed in 1850 by the Swiss-born, American zoologist Louis Agassiz (1807-1878), who was able to describe the structure of these 'lasso-cells' (as he called them)[152] in spite of the inadequacies of his microscope.[153]

A few years after this, Gosse published his independent researches on the *acontia* in the *Devonshire Coast* (1853), in which he described their structure and method of ejection, and affirmed that they had an offensive rather than generative purpose.[154] These observations were followed by another account of their deadly, poisonous character,[155] and in his 1855 paper on *Peachia hastata* he based his establishment of three new genera on the peculiarities of the thread-capsules.[156]

-V-

In January 1858, Gosse submitted a paper to the Royal Society summarizing his knowledge about the thread-capsules.[157] It benefited from some new observations made by him using an improved microscope, and added a theory which accounted for the emission of the threads from the thread cells as the 'result of vital force'. An abstract of Gosse's

150. [PHG], 'Highwater Mark', *Eclectic Review* ser. 6, I (Jan. 1859), 48-9.

151. C. Th. von Siebold and H. Stannius, *Comparative Anatomy*, 39-40; PHG, *Actinologia Britannica*, xxii. According to Winsor ('Issues in the Classification of Radiates', 45), the discoverer of the thread-capsules, Rudolf Wagner, realised in 1841 that what he had seen were not spermatozoa but nematocysts.

152. 'Lasso-cell' was the term used by Agassiz and others as late as 1885 (*OED* 3ed.).

153. Louis Agassiz, 'On the Structure of Coral Animals', *Proc. American Assoc. Advancement of Science* II (1850), 68-77 (read 14 Aug. 1849).

154. PHG, *Naturalist's Rambles*, 33, 123-6, 405-7, 427-34. Plate 28 is, I believe, the first attempt to picture the different capsules. In this work PHG used the pre-existing terms 'filiferous capsules' or 'thread-capsules'; he had used the word 'threads' in 'Highwater Mark', *Eclectic Review*, 48-9.

155. PHG, *Aquarium* (1854), 115, 143-4, 147-9, and the second edition, p. 148.

156. PHG, 'Description of *Peachia hastata*, a new genus and species of the Class Zoophyta; with observations on the Family Actiniadae', *Trans. Linnean Soc.* XXI, Part 4 (10 Nov 1855), 267-276.

157. The complete original version of the MS (29 foolscap folio leaves with 2 plates illustrating 18 figures) is at the Royal Society (*Archives 1857-58*, AP,40,14), see here folio 1. It is undated.

'Researches on the Poison-apparatus in the *Actiniadae*' appeared in the April *Proceedings* of the Society.[158] So far, so good. Nothing much more to say.

Or is there? Is there significance to the Royal Society's placement of Gosse's 'Researches on the Poison-apparatus' in the *Proceedings*? At first glance, the question itself is odd. The scientist is devoted to reason, the scientist bases decisions on data, the scientist is dispassionate, the scientist aims for truth. Most of us would not see a question here. But exit this imagined construct of a world governed by objective truth for a moment and enter into the human reality, where personalities, opinions, politics, egos, subjectivity, and many other such impulses operate and clash.

Recall: the Royal Society's custom was to place the 'more routine' submissions from its members into its *Proceedings*,[159] preserving the very best research for its *Philosophical Transactions*. Only *la crème de la crème* of human scientific endeavour merited inclusion in its pages. As Thomas Huxley explained, '[I]f all other scientific records in the world were destroyed, the Philosophical Transactions would be an excellent nucleus with which to make a new start.'[160]

What can be the reason to doubt a correct judgment on Gosse's paper? Two anonymous referees argued emphatically that the *Proceedings* is where Gosse belonged. One wrote that 'With one exception and that not a very important one, Mr Gosse's paper does not appear to me to contain much of anything with which [we] were not previously acquainted'. The referee pointed to Louis Agassiz's 1850 memoir and 'to the more detailed and illustrated observations of Mr Agassiz on *Astrangia Danae* ... which were made in 1848 and have been published in one of the volumes of the Smithsonian Contributions to Knowledge.' The referee also disliked the author's 'curious hypothesis' concerning the thread cells ('more novel than probable') and his fondness for neologizing.[161]

---

158. PHG, 'Researches on the Poison-apparatus in the *Actiniadae*', *Proc. Royal Soc.* IX (Apr. 1858), 125-8.

159. Andrew John Harrison, 'Scientific Naturalists and the Government of the Royal Society 1850-1900' (Open University, PhD dissertation, 1989), 6, 82.

160. Huxley's remark, made at a Jan. 1866 lecture in London, is cited in [William M. White (ed.)], *The Journals of Walter White* (London: Chapman and Hall, Ltd., 1898), 196.

161. Referee's report dated 14 Apr. 1858 (Royal Society RR.3.120). While the early discoveries of Agassiz referenced by the referee were published, his memoir was not printed until 40 years later (A. Sonrel [lithographer], *The Anatomy of Astrangia danae [being] Natural History Illustrations Prepared under the Direction of Louis Agassiz [in] 1849*. City of Washington:

A second anonymous referee concurred. The paper did not contain 'a sufficient number of new & important facts'. Besides other detailed objections, the referee also questioned Gosse's 'strange hypothesis' which 'has no support and is in plain contradiction to [the] best known facts of Physics and Physiology'. The conclusion was unavoidable: this work was 'hardly admissible into the Philosophical Transactions.'[162]

And yet the story may not be as straightforward as an initial impression suggests. A credible case for a behind-the-scenes drama outside the imaginary world of objectivity has been suggested by Andrew John Harrison. In his study of the Royal Society in the second half of the nineteenth century,[163] Harrison argues that for well over a dozen years after 1870, Victorian Britain's premier scientific body was controlled by scientific naturalists determined to promote Darwinism. That effort, which was centered around T. H. Huxley, is evident even before that time, he says. It manifested itself in the Society's referee process, which was confined to a relatively small group of men guiding an increasingly elite group of their peers.[164] In their decision-making process, Harrison asserts, this group was neither dispassionate nor disinterested when it came to works by certain of their colleagues.

Enter P. H. Gosse in January 1858. It's worthwhile setting his scientific output in context since his first published work in 1840, the *Canadian Naturalist*. As an independent investigator, he was in the midst of an impressive run. In less than two decades, Gosse had published twenty-six books (some multi-part and all with his own illustrations) and fifty-five articles; he was lecturing throughout Britain, as well as writing on

Smithsonian Institution, 1889, 3)

162. The report is undated (Royal Society RR.3.119). The referee also objected to Gosse's claim that he 'heard a distinct crack or crepitation' when the thread cells burst (PHG's original MS, Royal Society *Archives 1857-58*, AP,40,14, folio 16). 'I cannot but think that this sensation must have been subjective', the referee wrote. 'The [unclear word: cnidae?] are not 1/200th of an inch long. They are inclosed [sic] between two plates of glass and are at least eight or ten inches from the ear. Would it be possible to *hear* a corresponding bulk of gunpowder explode under the conditions of the experiment?' (Emphasis in the original). Nonetheless, PHG repeated the claim (which he had also made in *Naturalist's Rambles* (1853), 123, and *Aquarium* (1854), 149) in *Actinologia Britannica*, xxx.

163. Harrison, 'Scientific Naturalists and the Government of the Royal Society'.

164. The total number of members of the Royal Society had decreased 32% from 1848-78 (1848, 812 members; 1858, 706; 1868, 600; 1878, 549). See Leone Levi, 'The Scientific Societies in relation to the Advancement of Science in the United Kingdom', *Report of the Forty-ninth Meeting of the British Association ... Sheffield in August 1879* (London: John Murray, 1879), 464, paper read 21 Aug. 1879.

religious and ancient history topics.[165] Many of these were popular works drawing on his own meticulous investigations. There were also his non-popular, abstruse studies, displays of skill at the highest levels in the world of science of his day.

During February and March 1855, original research by Gosse was being read in London—one at the Royal Society, one at the Linnean. A third paper followed in March 1856 at the Royal Society, and a fourth that December at the Linnean.[166] All four papers were published in the prestigious *Transactions* of those bodies. They were not trivial. One of the Linnean Society papers included a description and illustration by Gosse of a hydroid animal (a small, inconspicuous aquatic animal) which he named *Lar sabellarum*, Gosse.[167] The modern view is that it is 'one of the most enchanting' of his works.[168] When announced, however, the 'remarkable Hydroid' depicted by 'Mr. Gosse's pencil' was greeted with 'a kind of polite suspicion' and 'an amount of incredulity'. Sceptics assumed that Gosse's illustration of this 'half-mythical' creature was fanciful.[169] That remained the view for the next fifteen years, during which time nothing further was heard about the hydroid. Then the zoologist Thomas Hincks (1818-1899) obtained a hydroid colony. He confirmed that 'extraordinary as [Gosse's illustration] *looks*, it does no more than justice to the original.'[170]

Another of Gosse's papers (this one for the Royal Society) examined the manducatory organs in Rotifera. As previously mentioned, the work helped to earned for him election as a Fellow of that body, and contained results unmodified by other researchers five decades after it appeared.

165. This tabulation is based on Freeman & Wertheimer-PHG.

166. For this output: Freeman & Wertheimer-PHG, 115-17.

167. '... a beautiful drawing accompanied the paper' (notice of the Linnean Society meeting, 2 Dec. in *Gardeners' Chronicle*, 13 Dec. 1856, 822); PHG, 'On a new form of corynoid polypes', *Trans. of the Linnean Society* XXII, part 2 (1857), 113-16. 'The animal is currently known as *Proboscidactyla stellata* (Forbes).

168. Freeman & Wertheimer-PHG, 117.

169. Thomas Hincks, 'On the Hydroid *Lar sabellarum*, Gosse and Its Reproduction', *AMNH* ser. 4, X (Nov. 1872), 313-314.

170. T. Hincks, 'On the Hydroid *Lar sabellarum*, Gosse and Its Reproduction', 313-17 (emphasis in the original); Hincks likely sent PHG an offprint of his article (Corr. Bk., letter from Hincks, Nov. 28, 1872; PHG response 'with 4 Memoirs', Nov. 29). See also Harry K. Harring and Frank J. Myers, 'The Rotifer Fauna of Wisconsin', *Trans. Wisconsin Acad. Of Science, Arts, and Letters* XXV (1930), 353: P. L. Kramp, 'Synopsis of the Medusae of the World', *J. Mar. Bio. Assoc.* XL (Nov. 1961), 300-1; Dale R. Calder, 'The Reverend Thomas Hincks FRS (1818-1899): taxonomist of Bryozoa and Hydrozoa', *Archives of Natural History* 36 (2009), 195, 198. The claim in *Life*, 266, that PHG's paper 'was received with great respect' is incorrect.

T. H. Huxley said it was an 'excellent memoir'; a French authority writing decades afterwards called it a 'masterful study'; a modern assessment is that it was one of his best-ever scientific serial works.

Besides these four papers, during this time Gosse was asked by the Royal Society to provide referee reports on papers being considered for its *Philosophical Transactions*.[171] Meanwhile in December 1857, Gosse had alerted the British public that the first of twelve parts of a study of sea-anemones, *Actinologia Britannica*, with colour illustrations by the author, would soon be issued.[172] After the appearance of only four parts, one reviewer said 'it promises to prove one of the most instructive and interesting monograms [sic] connected with the natural history of our islands which have ever issued from the press.'[173] It was one of Gosse's most important scientific works.[174]

Thus the scene in 1858, when Gosse delivered to the Royal Society his 'Researches on the Poison-apparatus'. No one reasonably doubted that he was a man of science with a name and a reputation. Certainly those who acted as his anonymous referees did not doubt that, though they found no place for his article in the *Philosophical Transactions*. After all, those same referees had recommended him for election as a Fellow of the Royal Society in June 1856. Who were they? The first referee's report, described above, was by George Busk (1807-1886); the other was by Busk's friend, Huxley. Busk and Huxley were two of the top fourteen most frequent referees at the Royal Society from 1859-62, and thus had an inordinate influence on what appeared (and where) in Royal Society publications.[175] The two worked together,[176] and from 1864 were part of

171. PHG provided brief anonymous assessments of two submissions on physiology: John Lubbock on the crustacea *Daphnia*, and J. S. Bowerbank on sponges (PHG-C. R. Weld, 24 Mar. 1857, Royal Society Referees' Reports III, 1855-58, 182; PHG-C.R. Weld, 21 Aug. 1857, Royal Society Referees' Reports III, 1855-58, 29). PHG recommended that both papers be published in the *Philosophical Transactions*, which is what happened.

172. Similar brief announcements of the project appeared in 1857 in the *Birmingham Daily Post*, 7 Dec., 1; *Birmingham Journal*, 12 Dec., 12; and Edinburgh *Caledonian Mercury*, 9 Dec., 1. A detailed description of the project is in the London *Literary Gazette*, 5 Dec. 1857, 1169. The first part is described as published on 1 Mar. 1858.

173. Review, *Belfast News-Letter*, 16 Sept. 1858, 3.

174. Freeman & Wertheimer-PHG, 67-9, and contemporary opinion.

175. Harrison, 'Scientific Naturalists and the Government of the Royal Society', 85.

176. When E. P. Wright solicited Huxley's support in 1860 in expanding the appeal of the *Natural History Review* (which he had founded), Huxley appointed fellow advocates of Darwin's theory to join him in editing the quarterly. Among them was George Busk (DeArce, 'The natural history review (1854-1865)', 253-269; *Natural History Review* VIII (1861), title page).

the X Club, 'a sort of masonic Darwinian lodge, invisible to outsiders: a dining club devoted to science "untrammelled" by any theology.'[177] The group of nine London men of science was active for nearly four decades.[178] Both efforts had the same partisan purpose: to promote Darwinism.[179]

How could it be that Busk and Huxley would allegedly turn against Gosse eighteen months after publicly promoting his career? Harrison has a one-word explanation: *Omphalos*.[180] Busk and Huxley were 'avid scientific naturalists eager to prepare the ground for Darwin's coming revelations,' Harrison correctly observes. Gosse—with his notable record as a field naturalist in five countries, his impressive skill as an observer, his many publications—might have seemed a potential fellow-traveller, a valuable asset. Yes, '*might have seemed*'—but then Gosse delivered *Omphalos* in November 1857, and his challenge to uniformitarian geology laid the matter to rest.

Two months later, Gosse innocently submitted his poison-apparatus research not just to the Royal Society, but unwittingly to two guardians of a naturalistic scientific outlook opposed to his own. Harrison's conclusion: the denial of a place for Gosse's research in the *Philosophical Transactions* 'seems rather more than coincidental ... The rejection of a purely technical paper so shortly [after the publication of *Omphalos*] ... smacks loudly of intent'.[181] And this appears to have been the intent: Honour an opponent of scientific naturalism with the *imprimatur* of recognition in the Royal Society's elite journal? That's not going to happen.

Even though the refereeing process can not be completely free of non-objective factors, one must face the possibility that Gosse's poison-apparatus paper simply did not merit more than an appearance in the *Proceedings*. Except that two subsequent episodes concerning Gosse—of

177. Adrian Desmond and James Moore, *Darwin* (New York: W.W. Norton & Co., 1991, 1994), 526.

178. Ruth Barton, *The X Club: Power and Authority in Victorian Science* (Chicago: University of Chicago Press, 2018), 6; Barton, 'X Club', *ODNB*.

179. G. C. Cook, 'George Busk FRS (1807-1886), Nineteenth-century Polymath: Surgeon, Parasitologist, Zoologist and Palaeontologist', *Journal of Medical Biography* V (1997), 98; DeArce, 'The natural history review (1854-1865)', 262-3; 'Natural History Review', *DNCJ*.

180. Harrison actually cites a second reason why PHG was repudiated: his refusal to provide a sympathetic response to Darwinism when, in the summer of 1857, he was allegedly approached privately after meetings of the Royal Society by J. D. Hooker and Darwin (as described in EWG, *Father and Son*, 1907, 117-119). As explained earlier, this scenario is full of difficulties.

181. Harrison, 'Scientific Naturalists and the Government of the Royal Society', 100 and Chap. IV.

which Andrew John Harrison was unaware, and which are discussed in detail in Chapter 12[182]—strongly suggest that difficult as it is to determine intent, Harrison's suspicion that Gosse's work was boycotted by X Club members—among whom were George Busk and T. H. Huxley[183]— is correct.

Two other examples of how the Royal Society excluded Fellows who deviated from established agnostic naturalism of the X Club during the 1860s and 1870s are instructive. One concerned an evolutionist, another an evolution opponent.

The case which most closely resembles that of Gosse concerns the British neurologist H. C. Bastian (1837-1915).[184] Bastian was initially a favourite of Busk and Huxley. Both had reviewed an 1865 paper by Bastian which they recommended for inclusion in the *Philosophical Transactions*, where it appeared. Both endorsed Bastian for fellowship in the Royal Society in 1867, reflecting their high opinion of him, just as they had both previously recommended Gosse as a Fellow. But then Gosse and Bastian fell from X Club grace: Gosse after 1857 because in *Omphalos* he argued against the uniformitarian/evolutionary mode of scientific thinking, and Bastian after 1870 because—even though he was a prominent evolutionist—he didn't adhere to the scientific naturalist's party line on spontaneous generation and the origin of life.[185]

Both Gosse and Bastian suffered a similar fate at the Royal Society. No research from Gosse completed after *Omphalos* was ever again published in the Royal Society's *Philosophical Transactions*. Meanwhile in 1876, Bastian encountered seemingly inexplicable difficulty in gaining a hearing for a submission he made for the *Philosophical Transactions*. In the end, the paper was rejected and instead published by the Linnean Society. Bastian got the message: the X Club-dominated Royal Society would no

---

182. See pp. 545-561 (esp. p. 555) and 570-581 (esp. pp.580-1).

183. Ruth Barton, 'The X Club: Science, Religion, and Social Change in Victorian England' (University of Pennsylvania, PhD dissertation, 1976), 1.

184. The information on Bastian and the Bastian case is drawn from two works by James E. Strick, 'The British Spontaneous Generation Debates of 1860-1880: Medicine, Evolution, and Laboratory Science in the Victorian Context' (Princeton University, PhD dissertation, 1997); and 'Darwinism and the Origin of Life: The Role of H.C. Bastian in the British Spontaneous Generation Debates, 1868-1873', *Journal of the History of Biology* 32 (Spring 1999), 51-92.

185. Strick: 'The British Spontaneous Generation Debates of 1860-1880', 262; Strick, 'Darwinism and the Origin of Life', 66-7.

longer be a venue for his work.[186] A biographer noted that Bastian 'felt deeply the rejection of his papers to the Royal Society.'[187]

Rough treatment was also meted out by the Royal Society to John William Dawson, Principal of McGill College in Montreal. Dawson had become a Fellow of the Royal Society in 1862, having been put forward by the imperial royalty of geology and paleontology of that time—Charles Lyell, R. I. Murchison, Richard Owen, Andrew Ramsay, Leonard Horner and Hugh Falconer, as well as by Darwin and Huxley.[188] By 1870, Dawson was 'so eminent a geologist', according to *Nature*, that it was unsurprising that the Canadian had been invited to deliver the Bakerian Lecture (the Society's second most senior lecture)[189] on a topic which 'he has made especially his own.'[190] Just prior to the talk, Dawson attended a *conversazione* with 'the *élite* of the scientific world'[191] at the Royal Society's London headquarters at Burlington House in fashionable Mayfair. He afterwards spoke at the Royal Institution.[192] 'Science is lively at the Royal Society,' *Nature* proclaimed, referring in part to Dawson's 'very interesting' Bakerian presentation on May 5.[193]

Notwithstanding this acclaim, Dawson discovered that his high-profile, decade-long opposition to Darwin's theory[194] was problematic. The result of Dawson's stance—he noted his views on evolution in his Bakerian

186. Strick: 'The British Spontaneous Generation Debates of 1860-1880', 287-291.
187. F[rederick]W[alker] M[ott], 'Henry Charlton Bastian (1837-1915)', *Proceedings of the Royal Society of London. Series B*, 89 (1 Aug. 1917), xxiii.
188. 'Certificate of Candidate for Election', Royal Society *Certificates* X, 19. Dawson was elected a Fellow on 5 June 1862.
189. Michael Ruse, *The Darwinian Revolution: Science Red in Tooth and Claw* (Chicago: University of Chicago Press, 1979, 2ed., 1999), 259.
190. 'Notes', *Nature* II (5 May 1870), 12.
191. 'Sir Edward Sabine's Conversazione', *Nature* II (5 May 1870), 8.
192. *Illustrated London News* 56 (21 May 1870), 522 (the talk was on 27 May).
193. 'Notes', *Nature* II (12 May 1870), 32.
194. To cite a few examples of Dawson's anti-Darwinism: In his 20-page review of Darwin's *Origin of Species*, Dawson wrote that 'we fail ... to place confidence in the bridge, thinner than gossamer, which [Darwin] has woven to bear our feet over the gulf that separates the proved ground of specific variability from the mystery of specific difference', and referenced the 'fundamental unsoundness of the argument' (*Canadian Naturalist and Geologist* V, (Feb. 1860), 101, 120). In 1864, Dawson began promoting the discovery of the 'dawn animal of Canada', *Eozoön Canadense*, as proof that Darwin's evolutionary theory was invalid (Rehbock, 'Huxley, Haeckel, and the Oceanographers', 524). A year prior to his Bakerian Lecture, Dawson restated the view that the 'difficulties of Darwinism are many' (Dawson, 'Modern Ideas of Derivation', *Canadian Naturalist and Geologist* n.s. IV (June 1869), 132). On the subjects of 'cosmogony, evolution, the antiquity of man, and creation', there were 'Few works [which] have been better known in the libraries of Christian men of science' than Dawson's 1860 volume, *Archaia* (*The Christian*, 20 Dec. 1877, 847).

lecture[195]—was that a prestigious talk which in the past had virtually been assured of appearing in the Royal Society's *Philosophical Transactions* ended up being rejected.[196] It was instead placed in the *Proceedings*.[197] The lead critic was the X Club's J. D. Hooker.[198] Dawson had also chastised Huxley (albeit privately) for what he took to be sarcastic and inaccurate words about Saint Paul in his address in Liverpool as president of the British Association.[199] Though a somewhat different interpretation has been proposed,[200] I would argue that it was Dawson's anti-Darwinian posture which aroused the ire of those controlling the Royal Society and acting as gatekeepers to it.

Seven years after this 'indignity' Dawson had overcome his ill-feeling towards the Royal Society. He applied for a small grant. He was again

195. Ruse, *Darwinian Revolution*, 259-60; Susan Sheets-Pyenson, *John William Dawson: Faith, Hope, and Science* (Montreal: McGill-Queen's University Press, 1995), 114; 'Fossil Flora of the Devonian Period', *Academy* I (14 May 1870), 208.

196. The referees' reports by geologist Peter Martin Duncan and botanist J.D. Hooker are described in Ruse, *Darwinian Revolution*, 259-60. The harsh critique by Hooker, an X Club member, influenced the report of the third referee, William Carruthers (a paleo-botanist not in the Darwinian camp) in achieving a majority decision not to publish Dawson's lecture in the *Philosophical Transactions*. Hooker wrote Darwin that Dawson's paper was 'perfect trash' (Sheets-Pyenson, *John William Dawson*, 112-17; Susan Sheets-Pyenson, '"Pearls before Swine": Sir William Dawson's Bakerian Lecture of 1870', *Notes and Records of the Royal Society of London* 45 (July 1991), 179, 185).

197. Dawson, 'On the pre-Carboniferous floras of Northeastern America, with especial reference to that of the Erian (Devonian) period', *Proc. Royal Soc.* XVIII, 1870, 333-5. The lecture was summarized in *Nature* II (12 May 1870), 35-6, and the discussion briefly reported in the same issue (p. 32).

198. Sheets-Pyenson, *John William Dawson*, 110-18.

199. Dawson-Huxley, 9 Oct. 1870, cited in John Fenlon Cornell, 'Sir William Dawson and the Theory of Evolution' (McGill University, M.A. thesis, 1977), 29fn.39; 'Professor Huxley's Inaugural Address', Liverpool *Daily Post, Supplement*, 15 Sept. 1870), 1; 'Professor Huxley's Address', *Glasgow Daily Herald*, 15 Sept. 1870, 2.

200. Sheets-Pyenson recognized that being evolutionists, Hooker and Duncan would have 'a strong ideological opposition to whatever Dawson wrote' and that Dawson's 'pronounced opposition to evolution antagonized scientific powerbrokers like Hooker' (Sheets-Pyenson, '"Pearls before Swine"', 185, 187). She notes that Hooker's harsh criticism 'not surprisingly' influenced the judgment of the third referee, Carruthers (p. 187). She believes, however, that the failure to publish Dawson's lecture was not caused by that, nor was it a reflection on the quality of Dawson's lecture. Instead, she points to Dawson's unfamiliarity with 'the tacit assumptions and unspoken conventions that governed the practice of science in metropolitan centres like London' (pp.177, 187). Though Sheets-Pyenson's analysis is impressive, I believe the cases of Bastian, Dawson, and PHG described here, as well as the oft-documented X Club practice of restricting and denying critics of evolution access to prestigious publication in the Royal Society's *Philosophical Transactions*, argue against her interpretation being the sole or primary explanation.

rejected.[201] As a result of the experience, Dawson ceased this type of scientific pursuit in favour of popular writing.[202]

-VI-

It is unknown whether or not at the time Gosse was aware of the background to the criticisms of his 'Researches on the Poison-apparatus'. Yet certainly later, if not then, he knew of the difference in status between an abstract in the *Proceedings* versus full publication in the *Philosophical Transactions*. Regardless, he reprinted his poison-apparatus findings with essentially the same line of argument in *Evenings at the Microscope* (1859) and more fully in *Actinologia Britannica* (1860).[203]

To Gosse's mind, the subject was of more than abstruse interest. It was a wonderful example of Divine ingenuity:

> I do not think that the whole range of organic existence affords a more wonderful example than this of the minute workmanship and elaboration of the parts. ... We must remember that all this complexity is found in an animal which it is customary to consider as of excessively simple structure. But the ways of God are past finding out. These are but part of His ways.[204]

At about the same time that Gosse's memoir was read before the Royal Society, Lewes' investigations on the subject were published in *Sea-side Studies*. He of course granted that the thread-cells exist, but was their function to sting or to poison their enemies? No experiment had been made, he claimed,

> to prove the function so unanimously admitted, not a single test has been applied to strengthen or controvert what was, indeed, but only *plausible*, not *proven*. Accordingly, no sooner did I submit the question to that rigorous verification which Science imperiously requires, than

---

201. Carl Berger, *Science, God, and Nature in Victorian Canada* (Toronto: University of Toronto Press, 1983), 63.

202. Sheets-Pyenson, *John William Dawson*, 118. Sheets-Pyenson writes that Dawson suspected Hooker of involvement in the Bakerian Lecture affair and bore a grudge against him for it. Maybe so, but an 1875 letter in which Dawson thanks Hooker for telling him of the death of Lyell appears cordial (Dawson-J.D. Hooker, 15 Mar. 1875; Kew, *British North American Letters* 195, 194).

203. Freeman & Wertheimer-PHG, 117-18.

204. PHG, *Evenings at the Microscope* (1859), 450. For similar statements, see *Actinologia Britannica*, xl, and *Year at the Shore* (1865), 80-1, 201-3.

it became clear to me that my illustrious predecessors—Wagner, Erdl, Siebold, Quatrefages, Ehrenberg, Agassiz, and Owen—men whom the most presumptuous would be slow to contradict, had admitted the point without proof, because it wore so plausible an air. Let me hope the reader will accuse me of no immodesty in thus controverting men so eminent; he will see that whereas they have only hypothesis on their side, I have accumulated and overwhelming weight of experimental evidence.[205]

Lewes then proceeded to chide Gosse for establishing the new genus *Sagartia* on the basis of 'this purely hypothetical [urticating or stinging] function'.[206] All of Lewes' logical scepticism went for nought, as Gosse did not deem a response worthwhile. It was not long before other investigators brought forward evidence supporting the accepted interpretation.[207]

It is important to note that the disagreement between Gosse and Lewes concerning the description of the physiology and anatomy of anemones was not simply the result of differing scientific investigations. It is true that Lewes' inexperience and meagre knowledge of the materials with which he was dealing put him at a disadvantage. Moreover, Lewes was not adept in the manipulation of specimens under the microscope,[208] inevitably hindering his perception. In the end, however, it was not only what they saw that made the difference. It was what they wanted to see. Lewes came to science with an 'empirical metaphysics' which acknowledged the wonders of the 'complex facts of life' but demanded that they be ordered in a definite progression leading from the lowest to the highest—Man. It was primarily in the shared striving towards a 'Universal Life' that they found a common ground. Gosse, on the other hand, could not help seeing the same scale, but with a differing explanation of it. Man was the Head of Creation not because of his

---

205. Lewes, *Sea-side Studies*, 146, also 152-3. Emphasis in the original.

206. Lewes, *Sea-side Studies*, 150.

207. William Brodrick, 'On the Urticating Powers of the Actiniae Towards Each Other', *AMNH* ser. 3, III (Apr. 1859), 319-20, and Augustus Waller, 'On the Means by Which the Actiniae Kill Their Prey', *Proc. Royal Society* (1859), 722-4. R. McDonnell conjectured in one paper that electricity rather than poison was the power which benumbed the actinians' enemies, but he quickly rejected the hypothesis ('On the Electrical Nature of the Power Exercised by the Actiniae of our Shores', *Proc. Royal Soc.* (1858), 103-7; ibid., (1859), 478-80).

208. Lewes did not learn how to use a microscope until 1856 (Kitchel, *George Lewes and George Eliot*, 171). PHG had bought his first one in June 1849 (*Life*, 222), though he had no doubt used one in Newfoundland, and in Jamaica.

organization, but because he had been given dominion over it by God. Therefore, the 'complex facts of life' represented to him a reflection of the majesty and power of the Creator, and wherever these complexities could be unravelled and appreciated by the investigative man of science they constituted one more tribute to the Creator.

'Did I not truly say that we have here a most elaborate piece of mechanism?' Gosse asked in concluding his description of the teliferous system:

> And surely its wondrousness is greatly enhanced by its minuteness! If we admire the skill of the penman who writes the Decalogue in the area of a threepenny bit, and the Iliad in a nutshell, though with no ulterior end, what shall we say to the skill which forms engines of battle, such as these, and packs them by millions in an inch of thread, not for the useless display of power, but for the defence and sustenation of creatures which Omniscience has devised and Omnipotence had created?[209]

After the publication of *Actinologia Britannica*, Gosse continued to go down to the shore, and write occasionally on new or strange anemones and corals.[210] He found it more difficult to locate specimens. In 1856, he wondered about the cause: perhaps a harsh winter or rapacious amateurs?[211] But in 1861 it was the latter which emerged as the basis for the depletion:

> Ah! gentle reader, I'll whisper a secret in your ear; but don't tell that I said so, for 'tis high treason against the ladies. Since the opening of

209. [PHG], 'Highwater Mark', *Eclectic Review*, 49.

210. PHG, 'On *Aegeon Alfordi*, a New British Sea-anemone', *AMNH* ser. 3, XVI (July 1865), 41-44 (it was not in fact new, but a synonym for *Anthopleura ballii* (Cocks); see Stephenson II: 161); 'A Fresh-water Actinia', *Hardwicke's Science-Gossip* IV (1 Nov. 1868), 247; 'The Depth at Which British Corals are Found, and Mr. J. Gwyn Jeffreys' Views Thereon', *Scientific Opinion* II (22 Dec. 1869), 625; 'New Living Corals', ibid. III (11 May 1870), 421-2 (the corals were not new: William S. Kent, ibid. (25 May 1870), 469, and PHG, ibid. (8 June 1870), 509: 'I can only express my regret that I have unintentionally augmented the vast heap of synonyms, which are the scandal of our natural history'). PHG received a letter from Jeffreys on 25 Dec. 1869, to which he replied that day (Corr. Bk.). Gosse's interesting paper on commensalism in *Adamsia palliata* and *Pagurus* (=*Eupagurus*) *prideauxi* appeared in *Zoologist* (June 1859), 6580-4, on which see *Quarterly Journal of Science* I (Jan. 1864), 172-3, and PHG, *A Year at the Shore* (1865), 246fn.

211. PHG-[?W.A. Lloyd], 19 Sept. 1856 (Edinburgh): 'The caverns here [Tenby] are not what they were in 1854. Some cause or other, either the rapacity of amateurs or the frosts of the winter of 1854-5, has almost quite extirpated the Actiniae that were so abundant then, so that except a few Venusta & mesembryanthemum scarcely any are left. ... I should be very sorry to see Tenby & its caves robbed of their Actiniae.'

sea-science to the million, such has been the invasion of the shore by crinoline and collecting jars, that you may search all the likely and promising rocks within reach of Torquay, which a few years ago were like gardens with full-blossomed anemones and antheas, and come home with an empty jar and an aching heart, all being now swept as clean as the palm of your hand![212]

The amateur and professional collectors thus drove Philip some distance from St. Marychurch, and one of his favourite places became the beach at Goodrington Sands. A successful day's catch would be brought home and examined (often under one of his microscopes) in Gosse's study, the largest sitting-room on the main floor of Sandhurst. Here he worked at his book-covered desk, in his book-lined room, surrounded by aquaria of various sizes. In August 1862 he constructed a new artificial sea-water tank which was soon rich in animal life.[213]

-VII-

On 28 February 1860, Gosse's mother Hannah (whom he had brought up from London almost exactly two years earlier) died at Sandhurst.[214] Leonard Strong officiated at the funeral service, and later in the morning went to see his friends Henry and Mary Curtis at Upton Cottage, 'The Rosery' (presumably members at Strong's Warren Road Room). In mentioning that the 'noted naturalist' Philip Gosse was also the minister at a small Room in St. Marychurch, an immediate curiosity was aroused in the Curtises and their guests, the Brightwen sisters. They all decided

---

212. PHG, 'An Hour Among the Torbay Sponges', *Good Words* II (May 1861), 294. This oft-quoted remark is misdated by scholars, who cite it from an edition of PHG's *Land and Sea*, where it later appeared (first edition, 1865 plus editions into 1879, see Freeman & Wertheimer-PHG, 77-8, 120). Those writers—e.g., Kyriaki Hadjiafxendi and John Plunkett, 'Science at the Seaside: Pleasure Hunts in Victorian Devon', in Nicholas Allen, Nick Groom and Jos Smith (eds.), *Coastal Works: Cultures of the Atlantic Edge* (Oxford: Oxford University Press, 2017), 202-3; Silvia Granata, '"Let us hasten to the beach": Victorian Tourism and Seaside Collecting', *LIT: Literature Interpretation Theory* 27 (2016), 103; Travis, *Rise of the Devon Seaside Resorts*, 169, and many others—in dating PHG's words to 1865 or later rather than to when they originally appeared in 1861, underestimate the speed with which the Devon shore was devastated. The denuding is likewise misdated by EWG to the summer of 1858 in *Father and Son*, 1907, 153-7.

213. The description of the room is from Gosse, 'Reminiscences of My Husband from 1860 to 1888' (*Life*, 355), and the sea-water aquarium from PHG, 'A Sabella Building its Tube', *Intellectual Observer* III (Mar. 1863), 77-8.

214. She was buried at the Torquay Cemetery on Barton Road (CUL Add. 7041, 63); William Gosse, Diary, 31 Mar., 2 Apr. 1858; Sarah Andrews-PHG, 2 Apr. 1858 (CUL Adv. c. 82.5, 57); *Life*, 293.

to visit the Room. Thus did the occasion of one death breed new relationships, for Henry Curtis (b. 1821 or 1822), a landscape gardener, soon became one of Gosse's 'intimate' friends, and one of the Brightwen sisters, Eliza (1813-1900), became Gosse's second wife.[215]

Eliza spent eight months that spring and summer with the Curtises,[216] and continued to attend meetings both at the Room and at Sandhurst, where weekly Bible readings took place. These were conducted by Gosse and the Revd John Eddowes Gladstone (1814-1901),[217] said by Eliza Gosse to be her husband's 'most intimate friend' at the time.[218] Gladstone was a first cousin of the prime minister, but held contrary political views and was a devout Evangelical.[219] As minister of Furrough-Cross Church in St. Marychurch, he was known for his staunch resistance to Tractarianism and Ritualism, and his involvement in the Church Rate controversy in St. Marychurch.[220] While Eliza had apparently been raised as an Anglican, and later became a Quaker, she was already acquainted with prominent Brethren and the movement's tenets, and so found the meetings profitable and congenial.[221] She had attended George Müller's

215. For the incident: *Life*, 353-4. For the Curtises: *Torquay Directory* (15 May 1861), 6; *1871 Census Returns for Torquay*, Enumeration District 9 (RG 10/2085); PHG, 'Reminiscences', II: 438; PHG-Henry Curtis, 2 Jan. 1881 (CUL Add. 7313, 272-3); and PHG, 'A Clever Duck', *Zoologist* XX (Feb. 1862), 7883. According to the Family Collection copy of *Life*, 374, Eliza was born on 10 Apr. 1813.

216. Eliza Gosse, 'Reminiscences of My Husband from 1860 to 1888' (*Life*, 357).

217. 'Death of the Rev. J. E. Gladstone at Braunton', Barnstaple *North Devon Journal* (9 May 1901), 8.

218. Eliza Gosse, 'Reminiscences of My Husband from 1860 to 1888' (*Life*, 355).

219. 'Social and Personal', Bristol *Western Daily* Press, 9 May 1901, 10; Exeter *Western Times*, 12 Feb. 1926, 8.

220. For the church rate issue: *Woolmer's Exeter and Plymouth Gazette*, 27 Oct. 1855, 4 and 'Criticus' [Clayton Walker], *Churches and Chapels of Torquay*, 76-7; *Torquay Directory*, 14 Oct. 1857, 4; on Gladstone, *Crockford's Clerical Directory for 1868*, 257; *Alumni Oxonienses* II (1868), 527; *Life*, 355. According to Walker, Gladstone had been forced into Nonconformity by a ruling of the Court of Arches, which prohibited him from practising within the Church. He left Marychurch in the autumn, 1861.

221. *Father and Son*, 1907, 250, states that Eliza was brought up in the Church of England, but also refers to her as 'that sympathetic Quakerish lady' (ibid., 248). In another place, EWG called her 'a Quaker lady' (Edmund C. Stedman, 'Some London Poets', *Harper's New Monthly Magazine* (1882), 877). Charteris, on the other hand, claimed she was a 'Quakeress by birth and upbringing' (p. 174). If Eliza was indeed a Quaker, she belongs in the long line of Friends whose secession to Brethrenism has been studied in T. C. F. Stunt's excellent 'Early Brethren and the Society of Friends', *CBRF Occasional Paper*, 5-27, and lately in West, *From Friends to Brethren, passim*. It may be significant that one of her brothers, George, belonged to a firm of bankers Gurneys, Tritton, and Overend, who were Quakers (Ford K. Brown, *Fathers of the Victorians*, 342fn.).

church and Orphanage in Bristol, and had stayed with Alexander Thomas Campbell in Exeter.[222]

Shortly after she left town in early September, Gosse sent her a letter 'proposing and urging, in strong terms' marriage, and after 'a week or two of consideration and consultation with friends' she accepted.[223] He was 50 and she was 47 when they were married at the Zion Chapel in Frome by the Revd D. Anthony 'according to the Rites and Ceremonies of the Independents', on 18 December in the presence of six relatives. They returned to Sandhurst that evening, where they were welcomed by gifts from the Brethren, a distraught Sarah Andrews, and a little boy who once again had a mother.[224]

Eliza was not so set in her ways that she was unable to meet the new circumstances into which she now entered. Undoubtedly her economic status was somewhat below what it had been when she had lived under her father's roof (he had been part of a large banking family). And although baptised as a child, she agreed to being baptised as a believer by immersion.[225] Indeed, she adapted so effortlessly to the religious views of her husband that Mary Hannaford, who worshipped with Gosse, assured him that his labours were productive. During 'several months past,' she wrote him, 'I have observed an evident advance in holiness in your dear partner, her prayers are deeper and more experimental'.[226] On Edmund she had a beneficial effect, changing and lightening his mental and physical regimen.[227]

-VIII-

In the early 1860s, Philip looked for new fields of scientific investigation, and he underwent a revival of interest in two of his former studies. He sent his drawings of rotifers to the marine invertebrate collector and

---

222. T. C. F. Stunt, 'Sir Alexander Cockburn-Campbell (1804-1871): A Biographical Note', *BHR* 12 (2016), 22-29; *DEB* I: 235.

223. Gosse, 'Reminiscences of My Husband from 1860 to 1888' (*Life*, 357).

224. Gosse, 'Reminiscences of My Husband from 1860 to 1888' (*Life*, 357). A copy of the marriage certificate is at CUL Adv. c. 82.5, 65; EWG-his parents, 17 Dec. 1885 (Charteris, 179-80; compare *Father and Son*, 1907, 251); *Life*, 357. The marriage was announced in the London *Daily News* (29 Dec. 1860), 7; *Torquay Directory* (2 Jan. 1861), 5; *Essex Standard* (Colchester, Essex) (4 Jan. 1861), 3; and *Gentleman's Magazine* n.s. X (Feb. 1861), 200.

225. *Father and Son*, 1907, 253.

226. Mary Hannaford-PHG, no date (but '?1864' written in pencil by PHG; CUL Add. 7027, 48).

227. *Father and Son*, 1907, 252-4; Edmund C. Stedman, 'Some London Poets' (1882), 878.

zoologist A. M. Norman (1831-1918) in November 1860,[228] and between 1861-6 published a series of descriptive papers on them. But his main occupation at the time was the collection, cultivation, and microscopic examination of tropical orchids.

Ever since his Caribbean days, and subsequent acquaintance with the great orchid nursery of the Loddiges family in Hackney,[229] Gosse had delighted in these lovely flowers. Recall that while in Jamaica, he had not only collected them but projected 'a large illustrated work on the Orchideae' of the country.[230] Years later, the move to Sandhurst provided the facilities to gratify his interest. In 1861, he built an orchid house on the western side of Sandhurst,[231] and began corresponding with collectors and naturalists. He wrote to H. W. Bates (1825-1892) in 1862 and asked for the names of orchid dealers in Brazil. Gosse received orchids from his Jamaican friend, Richard Hill, emphasizing that 'I do not desire species that possess merely a botanical interest, but such as will ornament an Orchid house.' The Sandhurst hothouse soon became well-stocked.[232] Advice was sought from his long-time acquaintances (and now, through marriage to Eliza, distant cousins) the Hookers at Kew. Joseph D. Hooker warned him of the great difficulties involved in imitating the natural environment of orchids, but Sir William J. Hooker (Joseph's father), who sent Gosse a hamper of stove and greenhouse plants, visited Sandhurst in June 1862. A month later Gosse reported that the hothouses were greatly improved, and contained forty species of orchids. To Joseph he had written earlier, 'Though my walk in science has been mainly Invertebrate Zoology, so far as I am known to the world,

228. PHG-A. M. Norman, 19, 21, 26 Nov. 1860 (BMNH, Alder-Norman Letters nos. 526-8); Sidney F. Harmer, 'Canon Alfred Merle Norman, F.R.S.', *Nature* 102 (7 Nov. 1918), 188-9.

229. 'The Loddiges of Hackney', *Athenaeum* (18 Feb. 1899), 214.

230. PHG, 'Jamaica Journal', 31 Jan. 1845; Analysis, 31 Jan. 1845: 'Began to paint Orchids'.

231. Eliza Gosse incorrectly estimates the date of the revival of her husband's interest in orchids as 1866 (*Life*, 359). In 1861 PHG installed a boiler in the cellar (see *Gardeners' Chronicle*, 6 Apr. 1872, p. 471), and letters and surviving MSS confirm that this is when he began his collecting. His letter to Charles Darwin of 30 May 1863 is about his efforts to fertilise orchids (Darwin Correspondence Project, Letter no. 4194, plus others in the Project on this subject). W. R. Hughes noted that in his later years PHG was a grower of orchids 'long before they became popular', and had orchids which flowered for a single day only, and others for a whole year (W.R.H[ughes], 'Philip Henry Gosse, F.R.S.', *Midland Naturalist* XI (1888), 302).

232. PHG-H.W. Bates, 2 Apr. 1862 (LeBL); PHG-R. Hill, 15 Nov. 1862 (Institute of Jamaica, National Library of Jamaica); PHG-J. D. Hooker, 13 Dec. 1861 (Kew, *English Letters* 87/69), and the reply, 15 Dec. (Massachusetts Horticultural Society).

yet gardening is my pet hobbyhorse, my cheval de bataile [*sic*]; & I wd. at any time turn away from a sea anemone to a rare or new flower.'[233]

It was a 'pet hobbyhorse' in the sense that while Gosse knew some things about the geographical distribution of orchids from his time in Jamaica,[234] his knowledge of the embryology, physiology, and cultivation of the order was very limited. Yet an industrious man of science can improve that state of affairs, and Gosse did begin to combine study with collecting, reading up in the literature[235] and keeping careful laboratory notes.[236] When he was unable to identify a specimen, he wrote for assistance to the London *Gardeners' Chronicle*,[237] the influential politically and religiously neutral weekly. He corresponded with other amateur orchid growers,[238] even began to publish a few notes and queries on orchids. It appears that by coincidence, Gosse had become a participant in the latest horticultural fad, the rage for orchids.[239] The onlooker might affirm: What a nice little amusement to pass the time! Yet when it comes to Gosse, such an assumption would be presumptuous.

233. PHG-W. J. Hooker, 28 June, 22 & 31 July 1862 (Kew, *English Letters* 41/349-51); PHG-J. D. Hooker, 19 Dec. 1861 (ibid, 87/70).

234. PHG, *Naturalist's Sojourn in Jamaica*, 481-9 *et passim*.

235. *Sandhurst Catalogue* lists a number of titles related to botany (items #346-376, 427-8) and to orchids specifically (items #358-376).

236. PHG, 'Manuscript Orchid Notes', 'A Synopsis of Cultivated Orchids (manuscript)', 'Notes on Orchids', and 'Botanical Notes' were listed for sale in *Sandhurst Catalogue*, items #449-451. The first three MSS are currently at the Chicago Botanic Garden (Lenhardt Library)..

237. PHG's letters are listed in Corr. Bk., and the replies to queries published in the *Gardeners' Chronicle*. Between 1870-86, PHG made 27 requests for the identification of orchids and other plants. E. Charles Nelson adds PHG contributions overlooked by Freeman & Wertheimer-PHG (many of which relate to orchids) in 'Additions to Philip Henry Gosse's Bibliography: Letters to Newspapers and Horticultural Periodicals 1864-1879', *Archives of Natural History* 41 (Apr. 2014), 172-5.

238. Two of these laboratory journals, Part I (1867-74) and II (1863-75), are at the Massachusetts Horticultural Society. Two others are in the Botany Library, BMNH, one containing clippings from the *Gardeners' Chronicle*, with watercolours of specimens flowered at Sandhurst (1864-75), and the other consisting of a guide to orchid culture and care, arranged by specimen, with notes from the *Gardeners' Chronicle* and *Journal of Horticulture* (c. 1862-3). In 1874 PHG compiled *A Synopsis of Cultivated Orchids* not listed in John Lindley's *Folia Orchidacea* (1852-9) (Mass. Hort. Soc.). During at least the late 1870s and early 1880s PHG also corresponded with H. G. Reichenbach (1823-89), the German orchid expert (Corr. Bk. from at least 14 Dec. 1878 to 20 Dec. 1883). PHG sent him orchids, appearing to bridle at Reichenbach's complaints about their condition upon arrival (rough copy of a letter, PHG-Prof. Reichenbach, 2 Jan. 1878, CUL Adv.c.82.5, 78).

239. 'The modern fashion for any kind of flower is very fickle. At the utmost it lasts a few years and then turns to a new favourite. ... The rage for orchids seems to be on the wane' (review of *The Book of the Royal Horticultural Society, 1862-1863*, in *Athenaeum*, 1 Aug. 1863, 138). Jonathan Smith says that the rage had 'exploded in Europe in recent decades' prior to Darwin's *Orchids* in 1862 (Smith, in Donald and Munro (eds.), *Endless Forms*, 239).

So what was going on? A drama was occurring on two levels. To start from Gosse's vantage point, in 1861 he was probably just enthused about these beautiful plants. Darwin had proposed his theory of evolution two years earlier, but the theory seemed far removed from this hobby. Besides, botanists and many naturalists were not jumping onto the evolution bandwagon. Those most aware of trends in geological science—Charles Lyell, Edward Forbes, Charles Darwin—were the ones most receptive to a generalizing theory which could account for 'historical causes for present day distribution patterns' of flora and fauna.[240]

The highly-regarded botanist J. D. Hooker, on the other hand, felt drawn not to propose wide-ranging theories but to continue to collect and describe.[241] Before 1859, Hooker was famously resistant to the theory—not for religious or philosophical reasons, but because he simply was not persuaded that the scientific record supported evolution. Botanist W. B. Turrill (1890-1961) has insisted that while a scientist examining orchids from around the world in 1858 would have been struck by small-to-extreme variations, they could not be precisely explained. 'Neither special creation nor transmutation appear satisfactorily to account for the diversity,'[242] Turrill has written about those times. The critical factor for Hooker was taxonomic. 'Species fixity' seemed likely, and Hooker was apprehensive that the evolution theory would lead to an out-of-control identification of new species.[243] In other words, if there was no initial reason for Hooker to align with Darwin, there was less reason for Gosse to do so, whether considering his experience or outlook.

In the next year, as mentioned, Gosse published a few notes and queries on orchids. Then came a new book from Darwin, *On the Various Contrivances by Which British and Foreign Orchids are Fertilised by Insects* (1862). It was the first monograph by the scientist after his *Origin*. Darwin thought it would help to support his findings in showing that 'I have worked hard at details.'[244] Yet when it came time to review the book, the *Gardeners' Chronicle* feigned surprise at Darwin's chosen subject.

240. Elizabeth Janet Browne, 'C. R. Darwin and J. D. Hooker: Episodes in the History of Plant Geography, 1840-1860' (Imperial College, PhD dissertation, 1978), 231.
241. Browne, 'C. R. Darwin and J. D. Hooker', 234.
242. Turrill, *Joseph Dalton Hooker*, 91-2.
243. Bellon, 'Joseph Hooker', 23, 212-13, 227.
244. Charles Darwin-John Murray, 24 Sept. 1861, in Francis Darwin (ed.), *The Life and Letters of Charles Darwin* (London: John Murray, 1887), III: 254.

Why was he writing about the 'physiology of fecundation in Orchids'?[245] Why the abstruse topic? Many simply did not get it. The work failed to arouse much debate. Some reviewers did not even connect it with Darwin's theory.[246]

Pretense notwithstanding, the anonymous reviewer in the *Gardeners' Chronicle* did get it. Over the period of a month, *Various Contrivances* was considered so important that it received three detailed notices in the weekly.[247] The final one concluded with a favourable verdict on the book. Then a writer in the *Natural History Review* carefully spelled out what was taking place. *Various Contrivances* was intended to be a footnote to Darwin's theory, demonstrating 'that no hermaphrodite fertilises itself for a perpetuity of generations'[248] Meaning? That if it could be proven that orchids are self-impregnating; that 'the adaptation of all parts of Orchid flowers is [not] for cross impregnation of one flower by the pollen of *another of the same species only*'; or that insects are not almost exclusively the means of this fertilisation—then Darwin's theory would become 'untenable'.[249] But of course Darwin hoped to prove the contrary, and by showing that the complex arrangement of the parts of the orchid was due to natural selection and not design, strike a blow against the notion of teleology in nature.[250]

Gosse read *Various Contrivances*.[251] He was not among those who felt that one could accept Darwin's findings, modify one's religious views, and continue along in life, ignoring the implications of the theory. As we have seen, Gosse rejected the naturalistic, uniformitarian

245. [anon], review of Darwin's *Various Contrivances, Gardeners' Chronicle*, 23 Aug. 1862, 789.

246. Ellegård, *Darwin and the General Reader*, 27, 188.

247. [anon], *Gardeners' Chronicle* 1862: 23 Aug., 789-90; 13 Sept., 863; 27 Sept., 910.

248. Charles Darwin, *On the Various Contrivances by which British and Foreign Orchids are Fertilized by Insects, and on the Good Effects of Intercrossing* (London: John Murray, 1862), 1.

249. [anon], review of Darwin's *Fertilization of Orchids, Natural History Review* n.s. II (1862), 371-3. Emphasis in the original.

250. Michael T. Ghiselin, *The Triumph of the Darwinian Method* (Berkeley and Los Angeles: University of California Press, 1969), 134-7, and Gavin de Beer, *Charles Darwin. A Scientific Biography* (Garden City, N.Y.: Anchor Books, Doubleday & Co., Inc., 1965), 227-37.

251. In November 1972, I saw PHG's copy of *On the Various Contrivances by which British and Foreign Orchids are Fertilised by Insects* (1862), with his bookplate in it, in the collection of Raymond Lister (1919-2001) of Linton, Cambridgeshire. Lister was an author, illustrator, collector, publisher and friend of Dr P. H. G. Gosse. In *Evenings at the Microscope* (1874 ed.), PHG alluded to *Various Contrivances* (p. 123fn.) and cites it as *On the Fertilisation of Orchids*, (p. 156fn.), which was the book's spine title (with the addition of the words 'On the'; Freeman, *Darwin*, 2ed., frontispiece photo).

mode of investigation, and in *Omphalos* proposed a *logical* way to maintain Genesis *and* geology. Now Gosse took a different approach, in *scientifically* testing the joints of the Darwinian armour.

Towards the end of 1862, James Anderson (d. 1899), a nurseryman and award-winning orchid cultivator in Scotland,[252] did experiments which seemed to indicate that some tropical orchids could produce seed-pods *without* the aid of insects. Noting that this was contrary to Darwin's theory, he went straight to the author to get his opinion on the matter. Seeds were sent to both Darwin and Gosse. Under microscopic observation, Gosse at first thought they were all barren. After a more exhaustive search, he found that a very small percentage did contain an embryo. All of this convinced both Anderson and Gosse that the possibilities of self-impregnation had been underrated. Darwin nonetheless responded that he still held that 'I am not shaken in my belief that their structure is mainly related to insect agency.'[253]

Meanwhile, Gosse's discovery of a filament attached to orchid seeds attracted Darwin's attention.[254] Late in May, Gosse corresponded directly with him about insects as impregnating agents. Thinking that he had found orchid structures adapted not for cross- but for self-fertilisation, he innocently wrote Darwin of his hypothesis. The Down House sage was not impressed. While 'prepared to believe anything of these beautiful productions,' went Darwin's understated reply, 'If you could prove the truth of your hypothesis, it would be extremely curious & quite new.'[255] In what is the last known exchange between the two, Darwin urged Gosse to carry on further experiments.[256]

Thus far, the narrative from Gosse's viewpoint. Hidden from his view was theatre taking place behind the curtains.[257]

After the completion of the second edition of *Origin* in January 1862,

252. 'James Anderson', *Gardeners' Chronicle*, 24 June 1899, 414; 'Obituary [of Anderson]', London *Orchid Review* VII (July 1899), 198.

253. All of the correspondence was conducted in the pages of the *Journal of Horticulture* n.s. IV (1863): James Anderson, 'Orchid Cultivation, Crossbreeding, and Hybridising' (17 Mar.), 206-8; PHG, 'Orchid Impregnation' (24 Mar.), 217; Charles Darwin, 'Fertilisation of Orchids' (31 Mar.) 237; James Anderson, 'Fertilisation of Orchids' (21 Apr.), 287.

254. PHG, 'Microscopic Observations on Some Seeds of Orchids', *Journal of Horticulture* n.s. IV (21 Apr. 1863), 287-8; Darwin-J. D. Hooker, 23 Apr. 1863 (CUL DAR 115/191). Darwin referred to this paper in the second edition of *Fertilisation of Orchids* (1877), 147-8.

255. PHG-Charles Darwin, 4 June 1863 and Charles Darwin-PHG, 5 June [1863] (Darwin Correspondence Project, Letters no. 4203, 4205).

256. The letters are all in the Darwin Correspondence Project and quoted in *Life*, 299-304.

257. This paragraph is based on Bellon, 'Joseph Hooker', 292-320.

Darwin had become obsessed with orchids—specifically, their cross-fertilization by insects. Darwin focused on this seemingly arcane topic in systematic botany to provide an actual example of the potent power of his theory to understand nature in a way which eluded proponents of the Design argument. Specifically, his overall goal was two-fold: demonstrate that contrary to the common view, orchids had sexual structures excellently adapted to promoting cross-fertilization by insects. He could attain that goal with a painstaking, technical examination of orchid plant structure, and his theory of evolution by natural selection would be seen to bring order to natural history study. At the same time, Darwin needed to win the support for his theory of key botanists—no one more so than J. D. Hooker. By the fall of 1858, Hooker had become a Darwinian.[258]

On 3 April 1862, at around the very time that Gosse was looking into the subject, Darwin presented his orchid findings to the Linnean Society. Then on 15 May, his *Orchids* book appeared.[259] Among the reviews were the positive ones previously mentioned in the *Gardeners' Chronicle* and *Natural History Review*. We now know what Gosse did not know:[260] both were written by J. D. Hooker.[261] Both had the same intention: 'to commend Darwin's work' and 'to further the interests of Darwinism.'[262] In the former, Hooker argued anonymously that Darwin's 'hypothesis gains in every way by a study of Orchideae'; the latter lavishly praised Darwin's technique and achievement. Gosse's timing had been off. He had coincidentally entered into a deliberation on orchids and species

---

258. Bellon, 'Joseph Hooker', 254-5. Bellon dates the conversion to three months *after* the Darwin-Wallace joint paper at the Linnean Society of July 1858 (end of Sept. 1858).

259. For the date of publication: Freeman, *Darwin*, 2ed., 112.

260. It is possible that in the year before he died, PHG may have become aware of Hooker's views on evolution. Corr. Bk. for 1887 records one letter from 'Fr[ancis] Darwin' (June 1) and another to him (June 2). The exchange may have related to the forthcoming *Life and Letters of Charles Darwin*, edited by his son, Francis. Advance sheets of the work were available in September 1887 (*Athenaeum*, 10 Sept. 1887, 344), with the three-volume work appearing that fall (review in *Spectator*, 26 Nov. 1887, 1619-21). It is also possible (though unlikely) that PHG saw Hooker's anonymous reviews in *Gardeners' Chronicle* and/or *Natural History Review*. He had three volumes each of the former and the latter in his library; the dates for the volumes are not known (*Sandhurst Catalogue*, items #431, 321).

261. For Hooker's reviews of *Fertilisation of Orchids* in *Natural History Review* and *Gardeners' Chronicle*, J. D. Hooker-Charles Darwin, 7 Nov. 1862, in Francis Darwin and A. C. Seward (eds.), *More Letters of Charles Darwin* (London: John Murray, 1903), II: 290-1; for his review in the *Gardeners' Chronicle*, Charles Darwin-J. D. Hooker, 12 Nov. 1862, in F. Darwin (ed.), *Life and Letters of Charles Darwin*, III: 273.

262. Bellon, 'Joseph Hooker', 311.

precisely at the time that Darwin had not only concluded his work on the subject, but successfully converted one of England's premier botanists from an agnostic to a believer in his theory.

Though Darwin rejected as valid Gosse's initial scientific investigations on orchid fertilization, Gosse believed further investigation was warranted. Four years after his exchange with Darwin, he sent some notes on the embryology of orchids to J. D. Hooker. He described numerous instances in which he obtained 'manifestly fertile seeds' from an orchid crossed with a different genus. Wondering if Hooker thought he should send his results to the Linnean Society, Gosse asked: 'Is not this [case] contrary to all the accepted canons of botanic law?' Hooker's answer: Don't publish. Gain a better mastery of the subject.[263]

With that advice, Gosse discontinued his scientific investigations of the order.[264] He had been unable to demonstrate through new scientific evidence the inadmissibility of Darwin's theory. For now.

-IX-

During the first half of the 1860s there is a decline in the quantity of Gosse's published writings. The obvious observation is that Gosse could not forever maintain his punishing publishing schedule—during the 1850s, a remarkable twenty-one titles and 100 articles, almost all universally appealing and successful. Simultaneously, there was a decline in quality, as his 1860s works lacked the enthusiasm and investigative flair which had become hallmarks of Gosse's writings.

Excluding *Actinologia Britannica*, which involved nearly a decade's research, three of the four books Gosse published in the 1860s were compilations from his own writings or not based on new research. In the first series of the *Romance of Natural History* (1860) he attempted to deal with nature not in Dr Dryasdust's way, but in that aesthetic manner which would have pleased Carlyle and long pleased readers.[265] Devoting

---

263. PHG-J. D. Hooker, 7, 10, 13 June 1867 (Kew, *English Letters* 87/72-4), and the replies, 8, 10, 13, [?18] June (Mass. Hort. Soc.). Corr. Bk. registers letters from-and-to 'Dr. Hooker' (e.g., during Apr. 1869).

264. PHG published short notes on this topic during 1862-7. Besides Freeman & Wertheimer-PHG, see Nelson, 'Additions to Philip Henry Gosse's bibliography', 172-5 and E. Charles Nelson, 'Philip Henry Gosse: more additions, mainly horticultural, to his bibliography', *Archives of Natural History* 49 (Apr. 2022), 207-9.

265. 'The popularity of these well-known volumes [*Romance of Natural History*, first and second series] may be looked upon as a standing protest against the common opinion that the

chapters to 'The Vast,' 'The Minute,' 'The Memorable,' 'The Recluse,' 'The Wild,' 'The Terrible,' and 'The Unknown,' he grouped under each of these headings excerpts from diverse sources. In one chapter he expressed his belief in the unicorn, and in another, on 'The Great Unknown,' examined the evidence for and against the existence of a great sea-serpent. He concluded that one exists similar to the fossil Enaliosauria.[266] *Romance of Natural History* went through at least eighteen British printings and ten in the United States, making it one of his most popular works[267]—'one of the most readable and agreeable of all his readable and agreeable books,' as the *Zoologist* said.[268] It was by far the most-reviewed of all of Gosse's books published in America.[269]

Yet as previously discussed, when Gosse tried to duplicate that success in 1861 with a second series, his effort met with mixed reaction. The third of his 1860s books, *Land and Sea* (1865), was mainly a collection of some of his periodical writings from 1853-1863, while *A Year at the Shore* (1865) relied too heavily on his earlier researches and brought together previously serialised articles. The reproduction of the illustrations came out flat and insipid, and are of an untypically poor quality.[270] His only

exact study of natural objects is inimical to a poetic conception and romantic love of nature' (review in *Nature*, 30 Dec. 1869, 236).

266. Some book reviewers considered *Romance* an example of 'book-making' ([J. R. Leifchild], *Athenaeum*, 22 Dec. 1860, 874-6; *British and Foreign Evangelical Review* X (Jan. 1861), 233-4), and in a rare development, one expressed a totally unfavourable appraisal (*Critic* XXI (24 Nov. 1860), 642-3). Nearly all commentators praised it highly (*Zoologist* XXI (1861), 7297-8; London *Daily News* (26 Dec. 1860), 2; *Eclectic Review* n.s. IV (Dec. 1860), 651; *Nonconformist* n.s. XX, 12 Dec. 1860, 995-6; *Gardeners' Chronicle*, 24 Nov. 1860, 1043-4; *Guardian* 10 Apr. 1861, 356; *Ecclesiastic* XXIII (Aug. 1861), 375-7; *British Quarterly Review* XXXIII (1 Jan. 1861), 277; *Gentleman's Magazine* n.s. X (Feb. 1861), 194-5). Most of these referred to the chapter on the sea-serpent in a more serious way than we would do today (see also [G. H. Lewes], *Blackwood's Magazine* LXXXIX (Mar. 1861), 345-8). Only three writers found PHG's presentation unconvincing (*Athenaeum*, *Critic*, *Eclectic*). The issue was still fairly open, as is evident from the large literature on the subject at the time (see W. E. H[oyle], 'Sea-serpent', *Encyclopaedia Britannica* XXI (1886), 9th ed., 608-10). PHG had discussed his disagreement about it with Richard Owen prior to publication (PHG-Owen, 13 Apr. 1860, Amer. Philos. Soc. Lib.).

267. Freeman & Wertheimer-PHG, 70.

268. Review, *Zoologist* XIX (1861), 7298.

269. D. Wertheimer, 'P. H. Gosse's Scientific Reception in America' (unpublished MS).

270. With the exception of the *Athenaeum*, (19 May 1865), 658-9, [J. R. Leifchild]) and the *Christian Remembrancer* XLIX (Apr. 1865), 499—the latter thought there was already a surfeit of books by PHG—all of the reviews of both books praised the letterpress and illustrations. On *Land and Sea*: *Journal of Horticulture* n.s. VIII (7 Mar. 1865), 190-1; *Reader* (27 May 1865), 596; on *Year at the Shore*: *Popular Science Review* IV (1865), 357-9; *Reader*, 11 Feb. 1865, 164; *Eclectic Review* n.s. VIII (Mar. 1865), 289-90; *Evangelical Magazine* XLIII (Apr. 1865), 227; *British Quarterly Review* XLI (Apr. 1865), 547; [W. S. Dallas per *Wellesley Index* III: 637], *Westminster Review* XXVII (Apr. 1865), 601; *London Quarterly Review* XXIV (July 1865), 554-

papers at this time possessing any lasting scientific merit were those on the rotifera.

By the mid-1860s Philip could pretty much do whatever he pleased. He had scientific honours, respect, and (through an inheritance which Eliza received in 1864)[271] the financial means to free himself from the yoke of the printed page.[272] Another reason to turn to other ventures: the audience which had found his seashore writings so acceptable was beginning to fade away during this decade, as the subject became the domain of trained biologists and oceanographers.

After *Omphalos* (1857), Gosse grew increasingly unhappy with what he saw in the scientific world, and felt concern lest he be tainted by 'the rapid apostasy of science to infidelity'.[273] Insofar as infidelity was promoted by the Darwinian theory, he was not wrong in seeing the gradual spread of the idea as a threat. Reviewing the fourth edition of Darwin's *Origin of Species* at this time, the London *Popular Science Review* observed:

> Whatever be the accuracy of the theory which Mr. Darwin has so ably promulgated, it is surprising how many distinguished men of science in all parts of the world have given it their support and countenance. In this country, nearly all the naturalists of repute have admitted the force of Mr. Darwin's opinions; and though few of them are prepared to swear to the truth of the new doctrine, all are ready to admit that the hypothesis of Natural Selection has far more evidence in its favour than any other upon the same subject that has yet been published, and that, furthermore, it is in no way obnoxious to the facts of revelation.[274]

The conclusion about the theory's relation to revelation was that of the reviewer. It was most certainly not Gosse's. Yet his retreat from that

5; and both books together, *Spectator* XXXVIII (29 Apr. 1865), 473. R. N. Gibson has pointed out that the first report of any tidally controlled non-reproductive behavior in a fish occurs in *Year at the Shore* (pp. 215-16), but he did not mention that the observation was not PHG's, but reprinted from a newspaper (Gibson, *J. Mar. Biol. Assoc. U.K.* XLVII (1967), 97). For publishing information on *Land and Sea* and *Year at the Shore*, Freeman & Wertheimer-PHG.

271. Eliza Gosse was to receive the dividends, interest, and income (£400 per annum) from a legacy of £9000 from her uncle John Brightwen during her lifetime (CUL Adv. c. 82.5, 70). See also PHG-Edmund, 22 Feb. 1870 (CUL Add. 7041, 33).

272. In Eliza Gosse's recollections of her husband, she wrote (referring to events some 25 years earlier) that the inheritance freed PHG from the need to earn a living 'in writing or in lecturing' (*Life*, 359). Though PHG occasionally lectured on religious subjects from 1864-70, it is unlikely he was paid to do so. His last scientific lecture was in 1861.

273. The phrase appears in PHG-Henry Dyer, 8 July 1869 (Corr. Bk.).

274. 'The Origin of Species', *Popular Science Review* VI (1866), 66.

world was hesitant and even deceptively stoic, hardly resembling a strategic plan.

Gosse was indifferent when told by J. D. Hooker that under a new bye-law he could no longer remain an Associate of the Linnean Society— although all he had to do was say the word, and he could become a Fellow. 'As I am quite settled now in this remote region,' Gosse replied, '& have probably contributed my little mite to science (all I ever shall contribute) I don't think it worthwhile to become a Fellow.'[275] Similarly, he turned down an invitation from the Plymouth Institution and Devon and Cornwall Natural History Society to join the noted men of science William Pengelly (of Torquay) and C. Spence Bate (of Plymouth) in becoming a member of that group. His explanation to the secretary of the society (who was also a relative) resembled what he had told Hooker:

> Five & twenty years I have been before the world as an author, & for nearly ten years more than that have I been an ardent worker in science; & now I think it time to use the rest that God graciously gives me. To my loving Lord & Saviour who has bought me with his blood, my all is due, & I will try to serve Him as long as I have any power to serve; but science & I may shake hands without my feeling that I owe it any thing.
>
> And so, dear John, the upshot is, that Mr. Pengelly & Mr. Spence Bate must enjoy the honours of the Plymo[uth] Institute, unrivalled by me.[276]

While expressing appreciation to a Canadian naturalist who approached him about bringing out a new edition of the *Canadian Naturalist*, Gosse parenthetically remarked that 'I have now for some time relinquished active literary work.'[277]

275. J. D. Hooker-PHG, 15 Dec. 1861 (Mass. Hort. Soc.), and the reply, 19 Dec. (Kew, *English Letters* 87/70). On 9 Jan. 1862, PHG formally requested that his name be omitted from the list of Associates, which was approved (Linnean Society *Council Minute Book* no.4 (1859-72), p. 82).

276. PHG-John [Shelly], 18 Apr. 1864 (Wertheimer Collection). Shelly was a nephew of PHG's wife, Eliza, and executor of her will. Pengelly was then a Corresponding Member, and Bate a Vice President, of the Plymouth Institution (*Annual Report and Transactions of the Plymouth Institution and Devon and Cornwall Natural History Society. 1864-5* (Plymouth: Isaiah W. N. Keys, 1865), 3-4).

277. PHG-[James Hubbert], 27 Nov. 1867 (Blacker-Wood Library of Zoology and Ornithology, McGill University). The Revd James Hubbert, PhD (d. 1868), was a botanist, active member of the Entomological Society of Ontario and Professor of Natural Science at St. Francis College and Grammar School, Richmond, in the Eastern Townships of Quebec (Montreal *Journal of Education for Lower Canada* X (1866), 93; *Canadian Almanac 1867*. Toronto: W.C. Chewett & Co., n.d., 96). The reason the project was not realised may have had nothing to do with its viability. Hubbert died several months after contacting PHG, having gone shortly before his

Gosse eventually entrusted his orchid collection, which increased to 300 species by 1874, to the sole management of his 'excellent'[278] gardener, James Chudley (b. 1828/9-1908).[279] And in 1865, when invited by natural history publisher Lovell Reeve (1814-1865) to produce a work on orchids, he politely declined. It was not simply that the honorarium was too low, or that he no longer needed the money. For he wrote Reeve that 'as a matter of taste I find the cultivation of Plants more agreeable than the writing of books, even though the subject were one so charming as Orchids; & I confess there is no subject on which I would so willingly write.'[280]

At the same time, however, Gosse began to overcome this self-imposed tranquility with an increasingly urgent need to speak out. Over the course of several years he began expressing his views in public and private, to popular and to religious audiences; he united with like-minded opponents of the Darwinian theory; and he took ever-bolder steps towards ceasing his scientific endeavours.

At least from 1859, he described in his popular lectures the dangers of what he felt were hubristic scientists who claimed that science offered a substitute for religion or religious belief. At the second of two lectures on the 'lower animals' at the Literary and Philosophical Society in Sheffield, for example, a reporter recorded Gosse's sentiments:

> At the conclusion, Mr. Gosse said he had abstained during the entire course from formally speaking on the religious bearings of the subject, because the very object of it was to demonstrate the Divine wisdom and goodness, as seen in the adaptation of the lower animals to their position. But as there was a very prevalent tendency in scientific men to suppose that their peculiar pursuits had the effect of leading them to God, and capacitating them for His presence hereafter, he was desirous of protesting against it. There was no such thing as attaining to religion

death to Florida for health reasons (*Canadian Entomologist* IV (Aug. 1872), 141-2; *Proceedings of the Essex Institute V, 1866-67*. Salem [Massachusetts]: Essex Institute Press, [?1872], 84). PHG's *Canadian Naturalist* was for sale in 1858 (apparently in New York) for $3.60 (*Canadian Naturalist and Geologist* III (1858), 417).

278. PHG, 'Dendrobium Breviflorum, *Lindl.*', *Gardeners' Chronicle* ser. 2, 26 (7 Aug. 1886), 181.

279. PHG-Mrs E---, 23 Apr. 1874 (Corr. Bk.); *Life*, 361; for Chudley's age, EWG-NG, 23 Nov. 1889 (CUL Add.7021,116). For his date of death and other biographical details: Nelson, 'Philip Henry Gosse: more additions, mainly horticultural, to his bibliography', 209fn.1.

280. PHG-Lovell Reeve, Mar. 29, 1865 (Wellcome Hist. Med. Lib.).

by means of scientific pursuits. There was no way of holiness but through the blood of Jesus. And it was only after scriptural knowledge of God that men realized Him in the works of his hand. Mr. Gosse was several times applauded for the felicity of his descriptions, as also at the conclusion.[281]

Several years later he offered fervent advice about developments in science specifically to fellow Christians. As previously mentioned, he was one of the principal speakers at a three-day event marked by prayer and speeches on the 'Sure Word of Prophecy' at Freemasons' Hall in London. Apparently he had not intended on that Tuesday morning, 10 May 1864, to raise the subject,

> but I do feel very strongly the havoc that Satan is making, not only in the world, but even among the children of God, with respect to this very subject. I feel that it is a very solemn thing, that the wolf is sapping the outworks of the fold, and the sheep are looking into one another's frightened faces, not knowing what to do or say. You know what I mean. I mean "the geological argument."[282]

Two opportunities presented themselves to Gosse to join his voice of protest against developments in science to that of others, and he took advantage of them both. Around June 1864,[283] he lent his name to *The Declaration of Students of the Natural and Physical Sciences*.[284]

281. 'Lectures by Mr. Gosse', Supplement to the *Sheffield and Rotherham Independent*, 19 Feb. 1859, 10 (PHG's concluding words also in *Yorkshire Gazette*, 19 Feb. 1859, 7); and *Dundee and Perth Saturday Post*, 5 Feb. 1859, p. [3].

282. *Report of Three Days' Meetings for Prayer and Addresses on the "Sure Word of Prophecy"*, 58. PHG's speech was transcribed in *Report of Three Days' Meetings*, 54-60, with brief summarizing excerpts in *The Revival*, 26 May 1864, 328-9. PHG's words were not always transcribed in precisely the same way in the two accounts.

283. Organizers of the *Declaration* began collecting names of supporters around April 1864 and issued a completed document in mid-May 1865 (W. H. Brock and R. M. Macleod. 'The Scientists' Declaration: Reflexions on Science and Belief in the Wake of *Essays and Reviews*, 1864-5', *British Journal for the History of Science* IX, Mar. 1976, 39-66). I have not seen any indication of PHG's desire to be included in the *Declaration* other than his being listed as the 129th signator ('Original Letters Relating to the Declaration of Students of the Natural and Physical Sciences. 1866', Oxford University, Bodleian MS Add. C.102). Since Thomas Bell, the 138th signator, added his name in a note dated 1 July 1864 (included with the Bodleian MS), that means PHG signed on or before that time. Replies to the *Declaration* are at CUL Add. 5989; see also E.G.W. Bill, 'The Declaration of Students of the Natural and Physical Sciences, 1865', *Bodleian Library Record* V (Apr. 1954), 262-7.

284. The names of 617 of the signators are printed in Samuel Kinns, *The Harmony of the Bible with Science: or, Moses and Geology* (London: Cassell, Petter, Galpin & Co., 2ed., 1882), 475-494, 5-6.

This document, which ultimately included 717 names, asserted that 'researches into scientific truth are perverted by some in our own times into occasion for casting doubt upon the Truth and Authenticity of the Holy Scriptures.'[285] Among the signators were ten people with whom Gosse was associated, including three other Brethren.[286] Then in May 1865, Gosse (as previously discussed) became a founding member and vice-president of the Victoria Institute of London. The aim of this leading evangelical defense organization (in which Gosse remained actively engaged) was to combat the opposition of science 'falsely so-called' to Scriptures. Many vocal anti-Darwinians found it a conducive gathering place, and linked their names to it.

Gosse's definitive dissent, and his most widely circulated one, was preceded by a misstep in 1864. Before appearing as his last popular natural history book, *A Year at the Shore* was serialised in *Good Words*, the Revd Norman Macleod's successful religious monthly. In the concluding words to the final installment in the December issue, Philip vaguely censured those who failed to acknowledge the 'wondrous variety, the incomparable delicacy, elegance, beauty, the transcendent fitness and perfection of every organ and structure' created by the 'all-glorious God'.[287] Such a clichéd, rote recital was not what Gosse intended to convey (though it is possible that he had been prevented by Macleod from expressing his position).

A month later, when the articles were gathered together in book form,[288] he said what he felt. In *A Year at the Shore* (1865), Gosse added two-and-a-half pages to his previously serialised concluding remarks

285. *The Declaration of Students of the Natural and Physical Sciences* (London: Simpkin, Marshall & Co., [1865]), [3].

286. The three Brethren were J. E. Howard, Robert Howard, and James Van Sommer; the others known to PHG were his cousin Thomas Bell, Capel Henry Berger, J. S. Bowerbank, Edward Doubleday, Thomas Rymer Jones, J. Hudson Taylor, and N. B. Ward. C. H. Berger was the son of Capel Berrow Berger (London *Era*, 5 July 1868, 15), who (as mentioned) was associated with Brethren in 1843. C. H. Berger was a devout Christian who attended church and lived with his father at Sion House, Lower Clapton (Liverpool *Daily Post*, 26 June 1868, 7). He worked at Lewis Berger & Sons, London, the family business (London *Journal of the Chemical Society* n.s. VII (1869), iv-v).

287. PHG, 'A Year at the Shore', *Good Words* V (Dec. 1864), 974.

288. *Life*, 305, claims *Year at the Shore* appeared on 24 Jan. 1865. The work was announced by the publisher in October 1864 (*Bookseller*, 31 Oct. 1864, 755), and advertised as 'Immediately will be published' in the *Athenaeum*, 17 Dec. 1864, 834, and '*Next week*' in *The Spectator*, 7 Jan. 1865, 28. The earliest review I've seen is in the London *Reader* V (11 Feb. 1865), 164. Freeman & Wertheimer-PHG, 78-80, 121.

in *Good Words*. Now he made a 'solemn and deliberate protest against the infidelity with which, to a very painful extent, modern physical science is associated.' Not only geological but also popular and learned scientific literature, he wrote, was tending more and more to ignore 'the awful truths of God's revelation,' substituting for it 'a mere sentimental admiration of nature, ... [which] teaches that the love of the beautiful makes man acceptable to God'.

> There is no sentimental or scientific road to heaven. There is absolutely nothing in the study of created things, however single, [*sic*] however intense, which will admit man into the presence of God, or for him to enjoy it. If there were, what need was there that the glorious Son, the everlasting Word, should be made flesh, and give His life a ransom for man?
>
> If I have come to God as a guilty sinner, and have found acceptance, and reconciliation, and sonship, in the blood of His only-begotten Son, then I may come down from that elevation, and study creation with advantage and profit; but to attempt to scale heaven with the ladder of natural history, is nothing else than Cain's religion; it is the presentation of the fruit of the earth, instead of the blood of the Lamb.[289]

And in the book's concluding words, he wrote: 'This will be, in all probability, the last occasion of my coming in literary guise before the public; how can I better take my leave than with the solemn testimony of the Spirit of God, which I affectionately commend to my readers,—THERE IS NO WAY INTO THE HOLIEST BUT BY THE BLOOD OF JESUS.'

More than one reviewer regretted the possibility that they would be deprived of future works from this Christian naturalist,[290] especially because this was (as the *Illustrated London News* put it) 'A delicious book, deliciously illustrated.'[291] But Gosse mainly kept his promise. From

289. PHG, *A Year at the Shore*, 326-7.
290. 'The concluding page of the present volume contains a sentence which has saddened us. ... Men like Mr. Gosse, who believe in God, as well as nature, are only too few among us; we can afford to spare none of them, before the time; and we earnestly hope he may have life and health to put more than one crown yet upon the useful labours of foregoing years' (*London Quarterly Review* XXIV (July 1865), 554). See also *Spectator* XXXVIII (29 Apr. 1865), 473; *Eclectic Review* n.s. VIII (Mar. 1865), 290; *Popular Science Review* IV (1865), 358-9, thought the protest unnecessary and out of place.
291. 'Current Literature', *Illustrated London News*, 25 Feb. 1865, 193.

1865-9, he published only fourteen minor (mainly short) notes in natural history journals.

-X-

Gosse's statement in *A Year at the Shore* was the culmination of his protests. He did, however, have an opportunity in 1869 to reconsider his self-exile from science.

With the annual meeting of the British Association approaching in Exeter, Henry Dyer, of that city (an Open Brethren[292] acquaintance of long standing who was not a naturalist) approached Gosse to speak there during the meeting. The Association, founded in 1831, was frequently called 'the Parliament of Science for Great Britain.'[293] Others characterized it as 'the British Association for the Advancement of Infidelity.'[294] James Reddie, the founder of the Victoria Institute, and many of its members consistently took the latter view. Not surprisingly, the Association's public image made it 'one of the chief arenas of the Darwinian battle'.[295] During the 1860s the increasing public interest in the British Association was likely in part due to discussions at its meetings related to Darwin's theory.

When Dyer invited Gosse to Exeter, Gosse did not likely know that the timing was propitious. At the previous year's Association meeting at Norwich, the important position of president had been occupied by J. D. Hooker. His known support for Darwin's theory was proclaimed in his presidential address. At Exeter, the pendulum swung to the opposition when the physicist G. G. Stokes (1819-1903) became president. Life, Stokes said towards the end of his presidential address at the Exeter meeting in a direct counter to the Darwinians, is a 'profound mystery'. It would be an error to 'forget the First Cause' in trying to understand this 'misty region,' or to 'shut our eyes to the wonderful proofs of design which, in the study of organized beings especially, meet us at every turn.'[296]

292. T. C. F. Stunt, 'New Source Materials for the Open Brethren in the 1850s', 70.

293. Revd Walter Mitchell, Victoria Institute Vice-President, at the 19 Nov. 1866 meeting (*JTVI* I: 222).

294. James Michell Winn, cited in F. O. Morris, *All the Articles of the Darwin Faith* (London: W. Poole, enlarged ed., 1882), iv. Winn was not a member of the Victoria Institute, but did deliver a paper on 'Materialistic Physiology' at the 8 Jan. 1877 meeting (*JTVI* XII,1879, 157). It was separately printed and did not appear in *JTVI* (*JTVI* XIV (1881), 153-4).

295. Ellegård, *Darwin and the General Reader*, 67. Unless otherwise indicated, statements here about the British Association and its meetings are drawn from Ellegård's book, chap. 4.

296. *Report of the Thirty-ninth Meeting of the British Association for the Advancement of*

As it turned out, anti-Darwinian speakers joined Stokes at Exeter. W. D. Michell (d. 1873),[297] who described himself as an archaeologist, in his paper 'Are Flint Instruments of the First Stone Age found in the Drift?'[298] argued against the vast antiquity of man proposed by Darwinians like Sir John Lubbock. Three clergymen opposing evolution also presented papers: the Archdeacon of Exeter, Philip Freeman (1818-1875), who spoke on 'Man and the Animals, being a Counter Theory to Mr. Darwin's as to the Origin of Species';[299] the Revd James McCann (d. 1916), who proposed 'Philosophical Objection [sic] to Darwinism or Evolution';[300] and the Revd F. O. Morris (1810-1893) on 'Difficulties of Darwinism'.[301] With the exception of Morris (who had lectured at the previous Association meeting), all had a connection to the Victoria Institute.[302]

Regardless of whether or not Gosse had known of this protest activity, it seems unlikely he would have joined it. As he responded to Dyer,

Science; held at Exeter in August 1869 [hereafter Report of the Thirty-ninth Meeting] (London: John Murray, 1870), civ.

297. Michell presented a similar paper at the British Association meeting in 1871 ('Is the First Stone Age of Lyell and Lubbock as yet at all Proven?', see *Athenaeum*, 19 Aug. 1871, 243).

298. The title only of the speech is given in *Report of the Thirty-ninth Meeting*, 69 (where the surname is misspelled 'Mitchell'); for a summary, *Exeter and Plymouth Gazette* 27 Aug. 1869, 3. At the Exeter meeting, Part II of John Lubbock's paper 'On the Origin of Civilization and the Primitive Condition of Man' was read (*Report of the Thirty-ninth Meeting*, 137-51).

299. The title only of the speech is given in *Report of the Thirty-ninth Meeting*, 132; for a summary of it, 'Anti-Darwinianism', Exeter *Western Times* 24 Aug. 1869, 3. The speech was read by the entomologist H. T. Stainton, then Secretary of the Biology Section of the British Association.

300. The title only of the speech is given in *Report of the Thirty-ninth Meeting*, 151; for a summary of the 'startling paper' (read by McCann), see 'Anti-Darwinianism', Exeter *Western Times*, 24 Aug. 1869, 3.

301. The title only of the speech is given in *Report of the Thirty-ninth Meeting*, 151; for a summary of it, see 'Anti-Darwinianism', Exeter *Western Times*, 24 Aug. 1869, 3. The reprinted speech included testy correspondence between Morris and T. H. Huxley (Morris, *Difficulties of Darwinism* (London: Longmans, Green, and Co., 1869)). Morris 'found it utterly impossible to deny that if the Darwinian theory, thus carried to its furthest limit, be true, then the Bible is untrue; and when, placed in these two alternatives he decidedly preferred resting his faith on the older Book' (M. C. F. Morris, *Francis Orpen Morris: A Memoir* (London: John C. Nimmo, 1897), 217).

302. G. G. Stokes joined the Victoria Institute in 1877 and was its president from 1886 to his death in 1903; Archdeacon Freeman was an associate member from 1872-5; the Revd James McCann was a member from 1869-93; Michell was never a member, but was a guest at the ordinary meeting of the Institute on 6 June 1870. James Reddie spoke on Sir John Lubbock, and Michell added comments critical of Lubbock and Darwin (*JTVI* VI, 1873, 36-8). At the Ordinary Meeting of the Institute on May 6, 1873, Michell read a paper 'On the so-called Flint Implements of the Drift'. He neglected to give a copy of it to the Institute, died a few weeks later, and the work was never printed (*JTVI* VIII (1875), 3).

For several years I have more & more held myself aloof from companionship with men of science as *such*. I have delivered my own feeble but earnest protest against the increasing tide of scepticism, & in particular, I have determined by God's grace, never to countenance by my presence the British Association. When it was decided that its sitting should be held at Exeter, my first thought was to go away to some distance from home during its meeting. But it seemed to me that this would be a poor & insufficient testimony of my disapproval of it, as my absence might be supposed accidental. It seemed a better protest that I should remain here in my proximity, & take no cognizance whatever of it. If I could influence any Churchman by my counsel, I would say to him, Go not near one of the meetings of the Association; turn from it & pass away:—unless, indeed, you are able to lift up your voice in fearless testimony for the truth of God. I know little of the gentleman you name; but very much doubt whether *he* would be content to stand on God's side against the wise of this world. Indeed, dear brother, I recommend you to be very chary in asking anyone to lecture on such a subject, unless he possess these two qualities: 1. the Knowledge of science, *in its present advanced state*, which would enable him to handle its facts, & 2. That enjoyed oneness with Christ which would enable him to subject every thought to Him, & to be a fool for His dear name's sake. For surely *such* a protest as an instructed Believer ought to give, if he attempt it at all, would cover him with opprobrium & contempt perhaps without parallel in our days. I am too old for it; even if I had the requisite knowledge & the requisite love, which I very decidedly have not.[303]

As it turned out, Gosse was not totally absent from the British Association proceedings. A paper on marine fauna of Devon and Cornwall by C. Spence Bate (1819-1889), then a Vice-President of the Association's Biology section, referenced a letter from Gosse about his sighting of a rare beluga whale in the area in 1832.[304] Some 300 Association members also visited the Torquay Natural History society, near Gosse's home.[305]

---

303. PHG-Henry Dyer, 8 July 1869 (Corr. Bk.). Emphasis in the original. Dyer's initial letter has not been traced, and I have only seen a copy of PHG's original response. In my transcription of this letter and the one of 12 Aug. 1869, abbreviations used in the copy seen have been silently filled out. Emphasis in the original.

304. Williams, 'Another published letter by Philip Henry Gosse', 170-2.

305. *Torquay Directory* (1 Sept. 1869), 3; Hilda H. Walker, *Torquay Natural History Society: The First 125 Years, 1844-1969* (Torquay: Torquay Natural History Society, 1969), 8.

In a follow-up letter, Gosse gave Dyer permission to circulate his previous letter to him in MS, and expanded upon his feelings about the science of the day:

> I have no quarrel with Science, only 'Science falsely so called'. Acquaintance with [the] handiwork of God, searching out his wisdom & P[lan?] & Godhead in [the] things which He made,—this surely is not evil but good; provided you give Him glory, & be subject to His revealed word. My objection is to those bold assertions & deductions of scientific men, which trample under foot his authority, particularly referring to Geology & its kindred sciences, Cosmology, Ethnology, Chronology, some aspects of Philology, &c. The British Association has taken a very prominent place in diffusing *ex cathedra*, this quasi-scientific skepticism; nay, more than skepticism, open, undisguised antagonism to the Word of God. I know there are Christian men in it; but they are mute on these points, & the infidelity is heard unrebuked.[306]

At about this time, Gosse supported other evangelical groups defending the Bible and Christianity against attacks.[307] The Christian Evidence Society, planned in London in 1868 and launched in 1870,[308] was guided by a formidable and influential committee of fifty-five evangelical leaders. It sponsored lectures and a publication,[309] with some forty per cent of the committee members, and fifty-six per cent of the lecturers, also affiliated with the Victoria Institute. Gosse was in contact with the Society from at least 1871, and supported it financially.[310]

306. PHG-Dyer, 12 Aug. 1869 (Corr. Bk.). It is not known if Dyer circulated PHG's 8 July letter. Emphasis in the original.

307. Unless otherwise indicated, the information in this paragraph is from D. Wertheimer, 'Evangelical Alliances Against Science and Secularism in England, 1865-1871' (unpublished paper read at the Annual Meeting of the Canadian Historical Association, June 1975), 23-7.

308. Though the formation of Christian Evidence Society was noted in the *Revival*, 24 June 1869, 277-8, it appears to have begun to attract newspaper notice only from Mar. 1870 (Guernsey *Star*, 5 Mar. 1870, 2; Darlington *Northern Echo*, 9 Mar. 1870, 2). A Scottish CES, modeled after the London one but with branches in Edinburgh and Glasgow, was projected in 1872 ('Christianity & Infidelity', *Quarterly Journal of Prophecy* XXIV (Apr. 1872), 136-7). There was a first-hand report on one of its meetings in 1873 ('Orthodoxy at the "Hall of Science"', in [Charles Maurice Davies], *Orthodox London: or, Phases of Religious Life in the Church of England* (London: Tinsley Brothers, 1873), 227-39. See also Dale A. Johnson, 'Popular Apologetics in Late Victorian England: The Work of the Christian Evidence Society', *Journal of Religious History* XI (Dec. 1981), 558-77.

309. 'The Modern Crusade', *Reynolds's Newspaper*, 26 June 1870, 4-5.

310. Letter from 'Burrows (Ch. Evid', 16 Mar. 1871, listed in Corr. Bk. PHG donated to the Christian Evidence Society from at least 1875 (*Christian Evidence Journal* II (Mar. 1875), 60)

At the same time, Gosse became a member of the Society of Biblical Archaeology,[311] which (among other things) aimed to investigate the antiquities of biblical lands.[312] As a noted Christian naturalist and author of several works on biblical lands and history he was an ideal supporter, making it unsurprising that his letter approving the Society's goals was among those read at the London group's inaugural meeting.[313] Soon, an historic report was made at a Society meeting on the newly-discovered Mesopotamian Epic of Gilgamesh, which contained an ancient account of a great flood. That supported expectations that 'Biblical science,' as one newspaper put it, could 'only corroborate in its main features the simple narrative of the Hebrew Scriptures.'[314]

So Gosse's protest with words led to his standing with others on the ramparts, followed by what was expected to be a final withdrawal from scientific activity. That writer whose name had been a 'household word' among naturalists in the 1850s and early 1860s largely disappeared from the printed page after 1865.[315]

Yet only a few who witnessed this response could have realized that Gosse's statement about his termination of his scientific career masked a double entendre. There was a factor other than the felt apostasy of science which might prevent him from ever again publishing anything.

and corresponded with CES for many years (e.g., Corr. Bk., 1 Dec. 1882).

311. PHG received a letter from the Society of Biblical Archaeology on 22 Feb. 1871 (Corr. Bk.). He was a member of the London organization from its inaugural meeting on 21 Mar. 1871 (*Athenaeum*, 1 Apr. 1871, 404; 'List of Members, December, 1872', *Transactions of the Society of Biblical Archaeology* I (1872), 3) to his death (*Proceedings of the Society of Biblical Archaeology* XII (1890), 129: 'one of our earliest members, he ever gave the assistance and support in his power, which was continued to the last'). On the SBA: Mathieson, *Evangelicals and the Philosophy of Science*, 102-3.

312. *Athenaeum* (7 Jan. 1871), 19-20; *Academy* (1 Feb. 1871), 116.

313. 'Society of Biblical Archaeology', London *Standard* (27 Mar. 1871), 6. The group was founded on 9 Dec. 1870 ('Introduction', *Transactions of the Society of Biblical Archaeology* I (Dec. 1872), ii).

314. London *Graphic*, 7 Dec. 1872, 526; Norman Cohn, *Noah's Flood: The Genesis Story in Western Thought* (New Haven: Yale University Press, 1996), 18-21.

315. The point is made in PHG obituary notices in *Zoologist*, ser. 3, XII (Oct. 1888), 382 and by H. B. B[rady], *Proc. Royal Soc. London* XLIV (1888), xxxviii.

CHAPTER NINE

1866-1875

The 'Sure Word of Prophecy'

We have also a more sure word of prophecy; whereunto ye do well that ye take heed, as unto a light that shineth in a dark place, until the day dawn, and the day star arise in your hearts. (2 Peter 1: 19)[1]

Blessed is he that readeth, and they that hear, the words of this prophecy, and keep those things which are written therein: for the time is at hand. (Revelation 1: 3)

And the Lord said, Who then is that faithful and wise steward, whom the lord shall make ruler over his household, to give them their portion of meat in due season? Blessed is that servant, whom his lord when he cometh shall find so doing. Of a truth I say unto you, that he will make him ruler over all that he hath. (Luke 12: 42-4)

-I-

REVOLUTION AND REACTION WERE WRIT LARGE IN EUROPEAN HISTORY during a six-decade period spanning two centuries. It began in 1789 in France, when the Old Order of monarchy and nobles was uprooted, the peasantry rose up, anti-clericalism held sway, terror and the guillotine were everywhere, wars were declared, and a new government was created by *coup d'état*. Soon empires crumbled or were

1. This passage appears as the epigraph to PHG's first published piece on prophecy: PHG, 'The Signs of the Times', *Christian Lady's Magazine* XX (July 1843), 49.

overthrown, and a period of turmoil seized the Continent again during 1830-1. Even greater upheaval ensued in 1848, when revolution and counter-revolution shook Austria, Denmark, France, Germany, Hungary, Italy, Switzerland and elsewhere. In comparison with Europe, Britain— though shaken by violent political and economic agitation and economic downturn—remained relatively and remarkably stable.

Whether viewed from a social, political, or economic perspective, there was nothing within memory to compare with this churning and change. That this was so was not in dispute; in some quarters, its cause was a matter of debate. By mid-century, Victorians couldn't help wondering: What was the meaning of these rapid, palpable, shocking transformations?

It is sufficient for the present purpose to indicate one of the many ways (in its dual aspect) in which the question was confronted. Some observers and movements, seeing the old anchors cast overboard, the ship helmless, and the crew and passengers paralyzed through fear and uncertainty, grasped the opportunity to steer a new course. These Europeans were gripped with the 'expectation of universal regeneration'. They believed that through their actions, they could bring a millennial period of grace down to earth. The first half of the nineteenth century was, as historian Jacob L. Talmon has argued, an era of 'political messianism'. Utopian schemes flourished as never before.[2]

Others saw the same vessel adrift and were animated by a similar hope of regeneration, yet they took an entirely different course. In fact, the ship—though in turbulent waters—was not adrift. It was heading in precisely the right direction. The Captain—though not visible—was present. The passengers were being guided, amazing to say, towards the appointed destination. According to these observers or 'religious messianists,' no amount of action in this world could be determinative. That is because what was occurring had been predicted some two millennia earlier. The prediction had been shrouded in symbolic language left behind to be decoded. To those who could do so, there was nothing unnerving about the state of the ship—on the contrary, it was reassuring.

2. Jacob L. Talmon, *Political Messianism: The Romantic Phase* (New York: Frederick A. Praeger, 1960, 1968), 15. In his classic study, Norman Cohn argues that Communism and Nazism are heavily indebted to that 'very ancient body of beliefs which constituted the popular apocalyptic lore of Europe'. I have seen no evidence suggesting that the millennialist school of prophecy discussed here could lead to such an outcome (Cohn, *The Pursuit of the Millennium. Revolutionary Messianism in Medieval and Reform Europe and its bearing on Modern Totalitarian Movements* (New York: Harper & Row, 1957, 2ed., 1961), 309).

Events were proving that the repositories of the prediction—the prophetic writings in Scripture—were accurate. History was prophecy realized.

Whatever doubts one may have about the programmes of the political messianists—Saint-Simon, Fourier, Fichte, Marx, Mazzini, and others— their idealistic views may still resonate. Not so with their religious counterparts, whose outlook escapes modern modes of thought. Yet the school of religious messianists—here meant to designate specifically students of the historicist premillennialist school of prophecy, of which P. H. Gosse was a member—were responding to the same set of events as their political and social counterparts. Through books and periodicals, lectures and conferences, sermons and hymns, thousands of Christians in mid-Victorian Britain lived in expectation of the second advent. Their influence during that period, one historian has asserted, has been greatly underestimated.[3]

The year 1848, for example—when revolutions throughout Europe failed—fairly crushed the spirit of the political messianists. The German philosopher Arthur Schopenhauer's pessimistic and philosophic rejection of life found its belated appeal in summing up that mood.[4] The religious messianists, on the other hand, surveying those exact events, looked upwards.

Since the revival of interest in prophecy at the time of the French Revolution, many expositors believed (as previously mentioned) that 1843-7 would witness the second coming of Christ. Many believers were full of 'hopeful excitement,' Gosse recalled: 'With what eager expectation did we devour the accounts of the developments of the earthquake, in every day's newspaper. The watchers were full of confidence, that the great final Day was breaking.'[5] After that did not occur in 1848, some looked to 1855.[6] When that year passed, prophetic heralds (regardless of their chosen earliest possible date for their calculations—or in the Latin jargon of the day, the *terminus a quo*), turned in increasing numbers to 1866-7 as the crucial beginning of the great crisis.[7]

3. Jeanette Sears, 'The Interpretation of Prophecy and Expectations of the End in Britain, 1845-1883' (University of Manchester, PhD dissertation, 1984), 7-51, 337.

4. Frederick Copleston, *A History of Philosophy* (New York: Image Books, 1963, 1965), VII: 2, 28.

5. PHG, 'The Breaking of the Day', *The Christian* I (7 Apr. 1870), 131.

6. PHG wrote in 1856 that according to one calculation, 1855 might represent a signal year, and that '1855 has not yet expired according to scriptural computation' (PHG, '[A note on] Daniel viii.14', *Christian Annotator* III (29 Mar. 1856), 122).

7. Froom, *Prophetic Faith* III: 704. In general, students of prophecy whose writings appeared

Everyone seemingly knew about that dating. The Whig politician and British historian Thomas Babington Macaulay (1800-1859), countering arguments to deny civil rights to Jews in Britain, gave recognition not once but twice to the Christian belief in the second coming.[8] Speaking before a House of Commons committee in 1833, he even cited Christian expectations: 'Many Christians believe that Jesus will visibly reign on earth during a thousand years. Expositors of prophecy have gone so far as to fix the year when the Millennial period is to commence. The prevailing opinion is, I think, in favour of the year 1866; but, according to some commentators, the time is close at hand.'[9] Previously, in an anonymous 1831 piece in the upper-class liberal *Edinburgh Review*, Macaulay argued that 'it passes for an argument' to assert that Jews would not be British patriots because they believe that they would be brought to Palestine 'perhaps a thousand years hence'. Then, indirectly, he referred in laudatory terms to Christians who held related views:

> The Christian believes, as well as the Jew, that at some future period the present order of things will come to an end. Nay, many Christians believe that the Messiah will shortly establish a kingdom on the earth, and reign visibly over all its inhabitants. Whether this doctrine be orthodox or not, we shall not here enquire. The number of people who hold it, is very much greater than the number of Jews residing in England. Many of those who hold it, are distinguished by rank, wealth, and talent. It is preached from pulpits, both of the Scottish and of the English Church. Noblemen, and members of parliament, have written in defence of it.[10]

'All students of prophecy are agreed in believing that the time of our Lord's coming draws very nigh,' proclaimed the London *Bible-Reader's*

from 1800-45 anticipated the second coming around 1847; for those writing between around 1845-66, expectations centred on the 1860s; from the 1870s, predictions extended some 50 years into the future (Sears, 'The Interpretation of Prophecy and Expectations of the End in Britain', Table on p. 291). See also Terlep, 'Inventing the Rapture: The Formation of American Dispensationalism', chap. 4.

8. Macaulay actually spoke on Jewish civil rights a third time, on 5 Apr. 1830. In his maiden speech as a Member of Parliament, he does not appear to have referenced Christian prophecy (the longest summation of his speech I have seen is in the London *Standard*, 6 Apr. 1830, 4).

9. Speech of 17 Apr. 1833, in T. B. Macaulay, *Speeches of the Right Honorable T. B. Macaulay, M.P. Corrected by Himself* (London: Longman, Brown, Green, and Longmans, 1854), 118.

10. [T. B. Macaulay, per *Wellesley Index* I: 473], 'Civil Disabilities of the Jews', *Edinburgh Review* 52 (Jan. 1831), 371-2; Ellegård, *The Readership of the Periodical Press*, 27. This passage (but not Macaulay's 1833 speech) is quoted out of historical context in Froom, *Prophetic Faith* III: 268, and others who cite him.

Journal, R. C. Morgan's evangelical monthly, in 1860.[11] A year later, a poll in America showed that the anticipation of the end days was not restricted to Britain or to millenarian enquirers. Research data revealed that 584 preachers and evangelists—mostly men but a few women, from east to west across the Union in nineteen states, and including Canada and Nova Scotia—held second advent positions. Though not of one mind about the details, they were all on the same page. *Every single one of those surveyed* was convinced that the age was 'near ending'.[12]

Of course with each failure of the predicted dates, the prognosticators of the historicist school lost adherents. The end of the world did not arrive. For many, the movement was discredited.[13] For some, acknowledgement of error was inconceivable.[14] For yet others, 'The End was capable of infinite postponement.'[15] Such individuals were confident that the error was in the calculation. *Humanum est errare*. The hope itself could not be a deception.[16] Expositors like Gosse never stepped back from where they originally stood, no matter how errant their predictions. Gosse explained his reasoning this way:

> Conclusions arrived at have often been propounded with a confidence, and asserted with a claim, which would have been warranted only by inspiration. Repeated failures of chronological calculations, too boldly enforced, have doubtless done great injury, and brought the study of Prophecy into disrepute. We should ever remember, and very distinctly reiterate, that, while the data themselves are divine, and therefore infallibly true, our deductions from them are merely human, and therefore very liable to error.[17]

11. Review of the *Quarterly Journal of Prophecy* publication in *Bible-Reader's Journal* (1 Mar. 1860), 349.

12. 'American Prophetical Literature', *Boston Journal*, 11 Jan. 1861, reprinted in London *Quarterly Journal of Prophecy* 13 (July 1861), 305-7.

13. Sears, 'The Interpretation of Prophecy and Expectations of the End in Britain', 249-50, 269-92; Terlep, 'Inventing the Rapture: The Formation of American Dispensationalism', 193, referring to the American situation.

14. Sarah Kochav notes Cumming exuded confidence in his failed predictions in *The Seventh Vial* (1871): Kochav, 'שיבתם של היהודים לארץ-ישראל והתנועה האוונגלית באנגליה' ('The Evangelical Movement in England and the Restoration of the Jews to Eretz Israel'), *Cathedra: For the History of Eretz Israel and Its Yishuv* (Dec. 1991), 34-5 [Hebrew].

15. Sears, 'The Interpretation of Prophecy and Expectations of the End in Britain', 136.

16. PHG, *The Prophetic Times* (Printed for private circulation, 1871; simultaneously printed in *Quarterly Journal of Prophecy* XXIII (Apr. 1871), 21-2).

17. PHG, 'The Breaking of the Day.- XXIII', *The Christian*, 18 Aug. 1870, 368.

There was another reason why those of the historicist school in this revolutionary era (and for nearly a century afterwards) were so unwavering in their position. They knew what was said about them. They were well aware that their views were often scorned in the secular press[18] and sometimes even by other Christians.[19] Yet they also knew that while many sneered, on occasion outside observers—no matter their background or outlook or the degree to which they might accept the calculators' outlook—affirmed that the religious messianists *might just be correct*.

While a young woman, the verse of the Romantic poet Christina Rossetti (1830-1894), for example, was influenced by the sermons on prophecy of the High Church (and later Roman Catholic) minister, William Dodsworth (1798-1861).[20] The Duke of Wellington (1769-1852), the great British military hero and prime minister, was said to have been convinced after reading Matthew Habershon's works that there were impressive coincidences even after 1848 between political events in Europe and the inferences drawn from prophecy.[21] Henry Fynes

18. The Revd John Cumming (1807-1881), a premillennial historicist, was a frequent target. He is 'an utterly untrustworthy guide as to the affairs of either this world or the next', concluded the London *Saturday Review* ('The Great Tribulation', 15 Oct. 1859, 452).Writing on his lectures in Manchester and Liverpool, one newspaper said they were 'more insufferably silly and egregiously ignorant than any of his former foolish performances. The bitter ridicule to which it has recently subjected him would be sufficient to silence or shame any man whose diseased mind did not exult in being the laughing-stock of his time' ('Dr. Cumming on Prophecy', Liverpool *Daily Post*, 10 Nov. 1860, 3). He was mocked in a cartoon and article in *Vanity Fair*, 13 Apr. 1872, 118-19: 'He has preached before the Queen, and his numerous works—notably "The Great Tribulation", and, more recently, "The Seventh Vial", in which he publishes his interpretation of the prophetic parts of Scripture as revealing the future history of Europe and the End of the World—have acquired a notoriety which cannot be gainsaid. ... we are inclined to hope that the world will last our generation.' On Cumming's career: Sears, 'The Interpretation of Prophecy and Expectations of the End in Britain', 278-84.

19. To cite only two examples of less than sympathetic treatment at this time: 'Modern Prophetic Literature', *Journal of Sacred Literature* X (Oct. 1859), 1-16, and 'The Apocalypse and its Interpreters', *Literary Churchman*, 17 June 1861, 226-9.

20. John O. Waller, 'Christ's Second Coming: Christina Rossetti and the Premillennialist William Dodsworth', *Bulletin of the New York Public Library* 73 (Sept. 1969), 465-482. Dodsworth was a futurist premillennialist (p. 477).

21. According to Matthew Habershon's son, Theodore, the Duke of Wellington commenced 'a correspondence of considerable length' after studying the father's prophetic writings. Theodore does not indicate when this was, the works cited, nor to whom the letters were addressed. See '"The Duke" and Prophecy', *Teignmouth Times and Directory*, 22 Oct. 1858, p. [3]; the claim is derided, with T. Habershon's response, in *Newcastle Journal*, 23 Oct. 1858, 7. In 1843, Capt. Wellesley, a nephew of the Duke of Wellington, 'adopted the tenets [of Brethren] ... and is exceedingly zealous and ardent in aiding in their promulgation and diffusion' (*North Devon Journal*, 21 Dec. 1843, 4; 'William H. G. Wellesley [1806-75]', in Pickering, *Chief Men*, 2ed., 40-1);

Clinton (1781-1852), the English MP, in later life was a Greek and Roman chronologist. Among his publications was *Fasti Hellenici: The Civil and Literary Chronology of Rome and Greece* (1824 and later editions), an oft-quoted study by writers on prophecy which 'proved to demonstration' that the 6,000 years of the world's history would elapse about 1867.[22] His brother stressed this unexpected fact: even though Fynes Clinton reached that conclusion, he was *not* a student of prophecy.[23]

Then there was that Olympian authority of Victorian England known as 'The Thunderer'. *The Times* was the daily newspaper which proposed to speak to all the world on the leading issues of the day.[24] In 1859 it devoted serious attention to prophecy with a 4,100 word, 50-column-inch-long analysis (spanning two-and-a-half out of the six columns on the page) entitled 'The School of the Prophets'.[25] Why so? Because that's what was on people's minds. As the *Christian Observer*, an Established Church monthly with a readership of Evangelical-leaning clergy, explained:

> It is not to be wondered at in the present extraordinary state of the earth, agitated as it is everywhere, and with black clouds portentously overcasting the future, that there should be a turning of Christian men's minds with a general and deep interest to the prophecies in holy scripture, which seem to concern these latter days. The article from the Times ... well illustrates this. Had not a general interest been awakened on the subject, the sagacious editors of that powerful journal would never have admitted such an article into its columns.[26]

To recapture the sentiment of that era, it is worthwhile re-reading *The Times* article, ostensibly a review of three works on prophecy. True

---

Stunt, *Elusive Quest of the Spiritual Malcontent*, 266. Wellesley and PHG were both speakers at the three-day Freemasons' Hall meetings in London on prophecy in 1864.

22. Letter to the Editor by C. J. Fynes Clinton, London *Times*, 5 Nov. 1859, 10. PHG owned a 3-volume edition of *Fasti Hellenici* (*Sandhust Catalogue*, item #497), which could have been the one published in 1834. He also cited this work (PHG, *6000 Years*, 10 fn.b *et. seq.*)

23. Letter to the Editor by C. J. Fynes Clinton, London *Times*, 5 Nov. 1859, 10.

24. *The Times* had earned its reputation for outdistancing its rivals around the 1840s (E. E. Kellett, 'The Press', in G. M. Young (ed.), *Early Victorian England* (London: Oxford University Press, 1934), I: 17).

25. [anon], 'The School of the Prophets', *The Times* (3 Nov. 1859), 5. The article is a review of E.B. Elliott's *Horae Apocalypticae*, Lord Carlisle's *Remarks on the Eighth Chapter of Daniel*, and John Cumming's *Great Tribulation*.

26. 'Prophecy: Its Interpretation, and Our Place in It', London *Christian Observer* 59 (Jan. 1860), 41. The writer assumes the correctness of the historicist viewpoint (p. 50). For the characterization of the *Christian Observer:* Ellegård, *The Readership of the Periodical Press*, 30.

Protestants, claimed the anonymous author[27] in a notably sensitive, intelligent and informed presentation, could not ignore the interpreters of Daniel and Revelation. Those books were, after all, as much a part of the Bible as any other. Moreover, students of the prophetic books did not set themselves up as illuminati. 'They may be mistaken,' the reviewer said, 'but certainly they are not fanatics.' With these premises, *The Times* writer argued their case:

There has arisen during the stirring years which still run their course, a very widespread attention to the study of unfulfilled prophecy. Books on the subject are in great demand, and the supply apparently meets the demand. It is not unnatural to expect this. The last 10 years, dating their beginning at the great European convulsion of 1848, have, without doubt, witnessed so many national complications, social changes, and individual sufferings—event has so rapidly thundered on event, and scene flashed on scene—so altered have the face of Europe and the relations of Cabinets become, and so unsettled is the European sky at this hour, that intelligent and sober-minded men, with no spice of fanaticism in their nature, have begun to conclude that the sublime predictions uttered on the Mount 1800 years ago are being daily translated into modern history. ...

... these writers on prophecy have handled this branch of investigation as others treat geology, chymistry, [sic] or astronomy. It is a legitimate subject of research. The errors of geologists and chymists do not fairly militate against their respective fields, and we do not see why the errors of interpreters of prophecy should be adduced as a reason for ignoring what is difficult, but divinely commended to our study. ... Some of their works are very learned. The *Horae [Apocalypticae]* of Mr. Elliot[t] does credit to the theology of the age. Others are very popular. It is not, therefore, fair in rash and reckless writers to confound the sober, even if mistaken students of a grand text with fanatics and enthusiasts.

27. The *Clerical Journal* claimed 'on good authority' that *The Times* article was written by the Revd John Cumming ('Literary Notes', *Borough of Marylebone Mercury*, 10 Dec. 1859, 2; *Bradford Observer*, 22 Dec. 1859, 3). The allegation is recorded as fact in the Liverpool *Daily Post*, 10 Nov. 1860, 3. Gordon Phillips, the archivist at *The Times*, informed me *in. litt.*, 4 June 1976, that 'By the most rotten luck you have chosen one of the very few days throughout the long run of Editorial Diaries when not even the leader writers are noted, the pages around 3 November 1859 are, for some mysterious reason, blank! This is most rare, I assure you. I am inclined to think that the review in question may well have been the work of either SAMUEL LUCAS or ENEAS SWEETLAND DALLAS who seem to have monopolised book reviewing at that time.'

But, whether these interpretations be right or wrong, there is no doubt that the barometer of Europe singularly—it may be accidentally—corresponds with their deductions from prophecy.

Not surprisingly, this article was immediately seized upon by the prophetic community—and not just by them. 'The remarkable article in the *Times*,' editorialized the *Taunton Courier*, a newspaper serving the West Country, 'is a lucubration of a character so alien from the general productions of the 'Thunderer,' as to have awakened a very wide-spread interest throughout the land.'[28] Reprinted in pamphlet-form, in less than two years *The School of the Prophets* was in its 40th thousand.[29]

The Times reviewer had taken seriously the possibility that human history might be of only 6,000 years duration. It *might* terminate around 1866-7. And as that moment approached, members of the historicist school were increasingly active in spreading the message of watching to fellow Christians. Their school had taught for half a century the importance of the period 1864-72.[30] To the *cognoscenti*, the subject of an article, pamphlet, tract, or chapter in a book headed simply '1866' or '1867', bespoke its contents.[31]

28. [Editorial], *Taunton Courier*, 9 Nov. 1859, 8. For a similar assessment: 'Mission to Sierra Leone', *Dover Express*, 21 Jan. 1860, 3; *The Times* article was excerpted in Horace Welby [pseudonym of John Timbs, 1801-75], *Predictions Realized in Modern Times* (London: Kent and Co., 1862), 247-50. For a critical opinion: *Borough of Marylebone Mercury*, 12 Nov. 1859, 2.

29. For the number of copies printed: *Revival*, 19 Oct. 1861, 128. The British Library holds an early issue of *The School of the Prophets: A Review of Elliott's "Horae Apocalypticae," Lord Carlisle's "Remarks on Daniel VIII.," and Dr. Cumming's "Great Tribulation; or, Things Coming on the Earth"* (London: Morgan & Chase, n.d.). The 16-page pamphlet, published by permission of *The Times* and selling for one penny, appeared by early 1860. The sole review I've seen was in the London *Christian Observer* 59 (Jan. 1860), 40-54, where it was included with eight other publications on prophecy. The pamphlet was advertised as showing 'that politicians are being led, by the course of events, to the conclusion which prophetic students have arrived at from the Word of God. Fynes Clinton's amended chronology, which makes 1867 to be A.M. 6000, is virtually accepted by the reviewer' (*Revival*, 21 Jan. 1860, 24).

30. Terlep, 'Inventing the Rapture: The Formation of American Dispensationalism', 177-9.

31. For example: W. C. Stather, '1866', *The Rainbow. A Magazine of Christian Literature, with Special Reference to the Revealed Future of the Church and the World* III (1 Jan. 1866), 37-40; W. Howell, '1867', *The Voice Upon the Mountains. A Journal of Prophetic Testimony and Evangelistic Effort* I (Feb. 1867), 21-2; John Hampden, '1867', *Voice Upon the Mountains* I (May 1867), 67; Revd John Cumming, '1867', Lecture XXI in *The Great Tribulation* (London: Richard Bentley, 1859), 240-51; and also 'European Convulsions', *Rainbow* III (1 Aug. 1866), 337-8. An article in Michael Baxter's *Signs of our Times. A Monthly Magazine of Second Advent and Prophetic Exposition, and General Intelligence* (1 May 1868), 320-4, lists 120 prophetic works which calculated the end of days with a *terminus ad quem* between 1866-80. Fifty-five based their conclusion on the 1335 years; 53 on the 1260 years; and 10 on the 2300 years or 6000 years of creation.

-II-

Now ever since 1842, Philip Gosse had held to the faith of this historicist school. By 1843 he felt he knew enough about the subject to prepare a Preface to a proposed guide to unfulfilled prophecy, Ἡ Μαρτυρία τῆζ Προφητείαζ (The Testimony of Prophecy).[32] Though the work was never published, an essay by Gosse on the topic did appear that summer.[33] At that time, Gosse was introduced to Brethren, the Christian movement in Britain with the 'densest concentration' of adventist focus.[34] His four books on Bible lands mirrored the historicist interest in history, and his work on the history of Jews, in dwelling upon Catholic persecution of them, followed that school's abhorrence of what they pejoratively called 'Popery'.[35] He had shared the historicist frustrations as 1843-7, 1848, and then 1855-6, had passed without note. He had been disappointed when his wife Emily was not spared death in 1857. He had written to friends, published a few short papers, and given lectures at Tenby and Torquay in 1856 and 1865 and London in 1864, all reflecting his prophetic expectations;[36] he was reading deeply in prophetic books and periodicals.[37] To understand Gosse's devotion to prophecy is to get a glimpse into his 'spiritual workshop'.[38]

The tempo of Gosse's prophetic-fuelled activities quickened as 1866 approached. He felt that he could not be the 'faithful and wise steward'

32. PHG, 'Reminiscences', II: 258-9. The undated Preface is in PHG, 'Testimony of Prophecy'.

33. PHG, 'The Signs of the Times', *Christian Lady's Magazine* XX (July 1843), 49-57.

34. Sears, 'The Interpretation of Prophecy and Expectations of the End in Britain', 336.

35. Sears, 'The Interpretation of Prophecy and Expectations of the End in Britain', 58-71.

36. A copy of a letter to PHG's Jamaica colleague Richard Hill seems to indicate that he had discussed prophecy with him (5 Oct. 1850 in Corr. Bk.). Besides the essay in the *Christian Lady's Magazine*, PHG wrote '"The Saints" of the Revelation' (*London Monthly Review and Record of the London Prophetical Society* II (May 1857), 467-70), and see PHG, *Sacred Streams* (1850), 51-2, 82, 115, 122, 145, 158-9. He delivered four lectures on prophecy while at Tenby, 7-28 Sept. 1856 (*Tenby Observer* IV (5 Sept. 1856)), and one nearly a decade later on 'What is a Christian?' at the YMCA in Torquay on July 24, which dealt with 'Repentance, Worship, Walking with God, and Preparation for Judgment' (*Torquay Directory*, 26 July 1865, 5).

37. The list of works read is long. It includes studies by futurists (J. G. Bellett, Darby, B. W. Newton, Thomas Ryan, S. P. Tregelles, William Trotter), historicists (T. R. Birks, J. W. Bosanquet, E. B. Elliott, G. S. Faber, H. G. Guinness, A. Keith, Isaac Newton, B. W. Savile, C. Wordsworth), and related volumes (J. Blair, Henry Fynes Clinton, W. Lincoln, H. Soltau). PHG also subscribed to the leading prophetic serials of the day: *Quarterly Journal of Prophecy* (*Sandhurst Catalogue*, item #539, 9vols.), *Rainbow* (item #573, 4vols.), *Signs of our Times*, and *London Monthly Review*.

38. The phrase is Albert Einstein's (*geistige Werkstatt*), referring to the value of Newton's theological MSS. (cited in Frank Manuel, *The Religion of Isaac Newton* (Oxford: Clarendon, 1974), 27).

spoken of by Luke the Evangelist if he only watched and waited for the Lord's appearing. Martin Spence has argued that there were historic premillennialists in nineteenth century Britain who were 'optimists, progressives, and materialists'. Many of them had 'a *great* interest in making the world a better place,' he writes, and they 'joined a growing coalition of Christian social activists, which included non-Evangelicals, literary figures, and political radicals' in 'social justice' activities.[39] If so, Gosse—like other historicist premillennialist Brethren such as B. W. Newton and S. P. Tregelles[40]—was not among them. His emphasis in 'preparing the Lord's household' was accomplished through personal testimony and pecuniary support of Christian (frequently missionary) work.[41]

When he had moved to St. Marychurch in 1857, he had placed himself in the midst of so-called 'Romanism and Ritualism' (pejorative polemical terms for perceived Roman Catholic influence in the Church of England and a religious trend towards Anglo-Catholicism),[42] but he had opposed their outlook. The Brethren's Room had been established; converts were won during that 'wave of blessing from the Spirit of God'[43] during the previous decade or so; in 1864 Gosse published in book form *Gosse's Narrative Tracts*,[44] these leaflets being a popular way of 'directing the sinner to the Saviour'.[45] Widely dispersed with astounding sales, seven million of the Gosse tracts (almost all by Emily) were distributed in Britain between 1859-65.[46]

In addition, Gosse spread knowledge about the significance of unfolding

---

39. Spence, *Heaven on Earth*, 51, 204 (emphasis in original), 209. The different social positions of premillennialists in America is discussed by Paul Clifford Wilt, 'Premillennialism in America, 1865-1919, with Special References to Attitudes toward Social Reform.' American University, PhD dissertation, 1970, chap. IV and 134-6.

40. I am grateful to Timothy Stunt for the information on Newton and Tregelles (*in litt.*, 15 Sept. 2022). Sears, 'The Interpretation of Prophecy and Expectations of the End in Britain', 308-13, concludes that there was no consistent position on social reform taken by premillennialists or postmillennialists.

41. PHG–Joseph Anderson, Jr., 7 June 1880 (CUL Add. 7313, 126); *Father and Son*, 1907, 364-5.

42. The area was known as a bastion of these influences from at least 1837: E. B. Elliott, 'Counter-retrospect', *Christian Observer* LXVIII (Dec. 1868), 572; and Freeman & Wertheimer-PHG, 122, no. 338.

43. PHG, 'The Breaking of the Day', *Christian* I (9 June 1870), 250.

44. Freeman & Wertheimer-EG, 30-7, 41-6.

45. 'Distribution of Religious Tracts', London *Wesleyan-Methodist Magazine* ser. 3, XVII (Apr. 1838), 289.

46. Freeman & Wertheimer-EG, 34.

events by participating in major Christian prophetic conferences of the early 1860s. By mid-century, meetings devoted to prophecy were not a new phenomenon in Britain: the Albury Park Conferences and Society for the Investigation of Prophecy had taken place in Surrey in 1826, the Powerscourt Conferences near Dublin in 1831. From the 1850s onward, however, there was renewed activity. The London Prophetical Society was launched in 1855, the Prophetical Alliance in 1859. Then, from 1863 to 1867 (and perhaps beyond), several meetings took place in London 'on the subject of the Lord's Coming.'[47]

The first of these, and the model for the others, was at least partially proposed by the Exclusive Brethren hymn-writer Frances Bevan (1827-1909).[48] It was convened in a schoolroom in Trent Park, East Barnet, London, by the Anglican minister Clarmont Skrine (1820-1886), between 28-30 October 1863.[49] The purpose of the gathering at the Bevan family estate was not to promote a doctrinaire interpretation of the biblical books of Revelation or Daniel but to awaken interest in the subject. As many as 200 people from across the country representing many denominations may have attended at Trent Park. Among them were Evangelicals such as the Revd William Pennefather (1816-1873), founder of the Mildmay Conferences for Christian workers (Gosse had once been invited to attend a conference),[50] and the Revd William Leask (1812-1884), editor

47. On these conferences: Froom, *Prophetic Faith* III: 498, 435; Sandeen, *Roots of Fundamentalism*, 18-22, 34-8, 88-9 and 89fn.19; Rowdon, *Origins*, 86-7ff; Robert Braithwaite (ed.), *Life and Letters of Rev. Wm. Pennefather, B.A.* (London: John F. Shaw & Co., n.d.), 253, 286, 321-3; *London Monthly Review* I: 97.

48. On Bevan: Neil Dickson, 'A Darbyite Mystic: Frances Bevan (1827-1909)', in Neil Dickson and T. J. Marinello (eds.), *Bible and Theology in the Brethren* (Glasgow: BAHN, 2018), 215-47, esp. 231-2.

49. *Revival* IX (5, 12 Nov. 1863), 296-9, 310-3; *Report of Three Days' Meetings for Prayer and Addresses on the "Sure Word of Prophecy"*, 3. Skrine's role appears to have been as an organizer of this, and similar, events (for example: 'Special Prayer Meeting', London *Daily News*, 7 Jan. 1862, 5; special prayer meeting for children, *Pall Mall Gazette*, 12 June 1867, 8). Skrine's first name is sometimes given as 'Clement' (*Crockford's Clerical Directory 1860*); see 'Death of the Rev. Clarmont Skrine', *Isle of Man Times and General Advertiser*, 6 Nov. 1886, 5; obituary, *Evangelical Christendom, Christian Work, and The News of the Churches* XL (1 Nov. 1886), 342; John Foster Kirk, *A Supplement to Allibone's Critical Dictionary of English Literature* (Philadelphia: J.B. Lippincott & Co., 1891), II: 1352, incorrectly gives 1887 as Skrine's date of death.

50. PHG-EWG, 12 Oct. 1868 (CUL Add. 7018,18). PHG said he did not attend Pennefather's conference, and did not indicate when he had been invited. On the Mildmay Conferences: Bebbington, *Evangelicalism in Modern Britain*, 159-161.

of *The Rainbow*. Many Brethren were present—Charles Hargrove, John Hambleton, H. H. Snell, Andrew Jukes, and William Yapp.[51]

The Trent Park Conference was followed by two meetings in London in the next year, both of which Gosse attended and before which he spoke. 'My present business is to wait for Christ, to love Christ, to serve Christ,'[52] Gosse declared at the evening meeting on January 7, during the 1864 'Week of Prayer'. Unlike Trent Park, programmes were held throughout the capital, with Gosse speaking a few minutes walk from the fashionable Lincoln's Inn Fields at Freemasons' Hall in Great Queen Street, Holborn. The *Daily Telegraph* reported that the purpose of this widely-covered international event (corresponding programmes were held simultaneously in France,[53] other European countries, and in Ireland and Scotland) was to discuss 'various matters which are considered to demand especial attention at the present time,' without specifically mentioning prophetic developments.[54] *The Revival*, the widely-circulated and influential interdenominational evangelical weekly,[55] fleshed out the significance of the Week of Prayer. This hugely successful gathering, the newspaper pointed out, was 'unparalleled in the history of the Church of God' and was a 'striking token that the day is at hand'. When the man acknowledged as the 'greatest English-speaking preacher of the century,'[56] the Revd C. H. Spurgeon (1834-92), came to the podium on the first evening, the auditorium had been 'densely packed long before the time appointed for the commencement of the proceedings, [so] that many hundreds of persons were compelled to go away, after having vainly striven to obtain admission.'[57] Declared Gosse's friend, the Brethren

51. For the disapproval of the 'dreamy sentimentalism' that typified the Mildmay Barnet conference in 1863 in the opinion of S. P. Tregelles: T. C. F. Stunt, *The Life and Times of Samuel Prideaux Tregelles: A Forgotten Scholar* (London: Palgrave, 2020), 186-7.

52. *Revival* X (28 Jan 1864), 53. The two 1864 meetings were convened by H. Wilbraham Taylor and John Morley, both Brethren (*Revival*, 19 May 1864, 314).

53. Th. Monod, 'La Semaine de prières a Paris', *Archives du Christianisme au Dix-neuvième Siècle* VI (20 Jan. 1864), 10-11; several London speakers were covered in 'La Semaine de prières a Londres', *Archives* (30 Jan. 1864), 18-20. For 1865, an invitation to the Week of Prayer in London was issued by James Davis and Hermann Schmettau, 'La Semaine de prières du 1er au 8 Janvier 1865', *Archives* (20 Nov. 1864), 277-8, and a 'Semaine de prières' was again held at various locations in Paris (*Archives*, 20 Dec. 1864, 310-311; 30 Dec. 1864, 324).

54. London *Daily Telegraph*, 5 Jan. 1864, 3.

55. P. G. Scott, 'Richard Cope Morgan, Religious Periodicals, and the Pontifex Factor', *Victorian Periodicals Review* V (June 1972), 1-14.

56. Bebbington, *Dominance of Evangelicalism*, 40.

57. 'Mr. Spurgeon on "The State of Churches"', Swansea, Wales *Cambria Daily Leader*, 7 Jan. 1864, 3.

writer Henry Soltau (1805-1875): 'we have been obliged to have a new hymn-book and new tunes, for the rather heavy tunes of old do not suit the new joy bursting from the hearts of the quickened ones of Christ.'[58]

Four months later, Gosse returned to London for a third event (also at Freemasons' Hall), this one specifically devoted to the 'Sure Word of Prophecy'. Once again, both Anglicans and Dissenters lectured during the three-day event, from 9-12 May. Most of the latter were Open Brethren, and the average age was 52. While the printed *Report* played down differences of opinion, apparently they were significant if not overwhelming: one speaker criticised those whom he claimed worshipped Darby instead of God. The remarks of Brethren Leonard Strong ('evidently pressed out by the Holy Ghost'), J. L. Harris, and Gosse (on the 'geological question' and the Epistle to the Ephesians) were noted as significant.[59]

During 1864-7 other prophetic meetings were held within and outside London,[60] and even near Gosse's home at Torquay.[61] It is not known

58. Both *Revival* quotations from *Revival* X (28 Jan 1864), 56, also p. 52; Wertheimer, *Identification*, 10-11.

59. For these meetings: *Revival* X (19, 26 May; 2, 9 June 1864), 314-6, 328-9, 345-7, 354-6, esp. 314-5, 328, 345; *Report of Three Days' Meetings*, and for PHG's speeches, pp. 54-60, 98-100 and Wertheimer, *Identification*, 10-11. The characterization of the speakers is from my analysis. Speakers included C. Skrine and the Revd John Manners (both Anglicans), and the following Open Brethren: Earl of Cavan, J. M. Code, C. Hargrove, J. Hambleton, Robert Howard, Andrew Jukes, W. Lincoln, H. H. Snell, H. W. Soltau, and W. H. G. Wellesley. By the mid-1860s, Jukes' connection with Brethren was tenuous (T. C. F. Stunt-D. Wertheimer, *in litt.*, 9 Sept. 2023).

60. Sears states that the period in Britain from the beginning of the controversy between J. N. Darby and B. W. Newton and Darby's death (i.e., 1845 to 1882) had 'considerable' numbers of prophetical lectures, conferences and societies (Sears, 'The Interpretation of Prophecy and Expectations of the End in Britain', 32).

61. For an 1864 London meeting: Mrs S. A. Blackwood (ed.), *Some Records of the Life of Stevenson Arthur Blackwood K.C.B.* (London: Hodder and Stoughton, 1896), 240-2; for the 1865 London ones: *Evangelist* n.s. III, 1866, advertisement at back; *Revival* XIII (9 Nov. 1865), 276-80; for 1866 (summer): 'London Meetings', Philadelphia *Prophetic Times* V (May 1867), 74-7; and for 1867: *Revival* XV (31 Jan. 1867), 65-6; *Voice Upon the Mountains* I (May 1867), 61, and the special number for June, 97-116; Sandeen, *Roots*, 88-9.

Lectures on prophecy at Torquay were given by the Revd Richard Gwatkin (1791-1870) in 1865, and T. George Bell (1811-1871), editor of *Voice Upon the Mountains*, in 1866 (*Torquay Directory*, 2 Aug. 1865, 5; 28 Mar. 1866, 5; 25 Apr., 5; 16 May, 4; and 9 May, 6, a resume of Bell's lectures; see also Bell's *The Voice of Prophecy: Being Notes of Four Lectures Delivered in the Bath Saloon, Torquay, May, 1866*. London: Partridge, [1866]). On Bell: T. C. F. Stunt, 'An Early Account of the Brethren in 1838 With Some Explanation of its Origins and Context', *BHR* 8 (2012), 3-4. Sears, 'The Interpretation of Prophecy and Expectations of the End in Britain', 167, says Bell was 'connected with Brethren'. The Revd R. Purdon of Torquay edited *The Last Vials* (1848-70), a prophetic journal in which Napoleon III was identified as the Little Horn of the Beast (J. T. White, *The History of Torquay*, 347).

what, if any, involvement he had in them. In any case, 1866 was fast approaching. Gosse's testimony before those Christians 'washed in the Blood' was necessarily extended to a declaration before the Christian community at large.

For many years now, P. H. Gosse, FRS, had been recognized as a naturalist of distinction and popular fame. Everything he wrote about nature reflected without reserve his service to Christ. If, as became clear to him by 1865, most investigators of God's Work did not emphasize the connection and actually opposed it, then he felt it was incumbent upon him to cease his formal scientific work. That is what he did with his protest at the end of *A Year at the Shore,* as previously mentioned. The manifest reason for the protest was the growing 'apostasy of science'; the unstated context was that *all* scientific research would shortly end if—as hoped and expected—the second advent occurred in 1866 or 1867.

When this long-awaited period arrived, Gosse bent all his energies to promulgating his position in pamphlets and articles, doing so with the same skill which had marked all his scientific investigations. There is no gap between Gosse's scientific and religious or prophetic thought. While one may justifiably dissent from the postulates upon which he built his edifices, or point to their heterodoxy, the posture he maintained in scientific and religious pursuits was consistent and followed an internal logic. As B. M. Pietsch has pointed out in regard to American dispensationalists of the latter nineteenth century, Bible study for them (as for Brethren, including Gosse) involved more than 'simple literalism, proof-texting, or conservative retrenchments'. It included 'modernist assumptions', such as that 'knowledge-making required explicit use of method'—what Pietsch calls 'the taxonomic mind':

> ... the Bible must be interpreted to "unlock" its true meaning. ... authoritative biblical knowledge required years of specialized study, study that made use of engineering methods, such as classification, enumeration, cross-referencing, and taxonomic comparison of literary units. The result was a view of the Bible as an internally coherent whole with a progressive unfolding of meaning, meaning that was located in elaborately coded systems of intertextual relationships ...[62]

The harmony between Gosse's religious and scientific thought was

---

62. Pietsch, *Dispensational Modernism,* 3-4, 105.

reflective of what he perceived as the underlying unity of God's creations, nature and the Bible. Both were, by his understanding, formed perfect and complete, and for that very reason animals were incapable of improvement (that is, evolution by natural selection is unthinkable). The Bible, he maintained, 'If it were not flawless ... w[oul]d be worthless.'[63] Both, to be properly understood, had to be assiduously studied: the apparent simplicity of nature (*e.g.*, in the offensive and defensive system in sea anemones) hid an underlying complexity (the teliferous system), while the apparent obscurity of some portions of the Bible (*e.g.*, Daniel and Revelation) were clarified by grasping the correct hermeneutical principle (*i.e.*, the historicist approach). Moreover, while both offered distinctive messages, they supplemented each other. The contemplation of nature made one aware of the 'ever-fresh proofs of [God's] all-pervading care, of his wondrous skill and wisdom, of his glorious majesty and power,' thus providing 'abundant occasion to praise His infinite wisdom and inexhaustible resources.'

This message from nature could not alone tell the born sinner how to act: 'it is to the Book that I [must] turn, and there I learn the mystery of the incarnation; the redemption of a sinner by blood; the payment of my infinite debt; my union with the God-man in resurrection life, on my believing the record; and the sharing of his coming glory.'[64] And although the message was found in many books of Scripture, they are all 'really *one book*, the work of one Mind ... [with] *one subject*, <u>Christ</u>. Embracing a great variety of treatment, & a multitude of *sub*-subjects, every book & every page is ancillary to the one grand design,—*the heading-up of all things in the God-Man, in perpetuity of blessing, secured by Resurrection.*'[65]

This multifaceted coherence of the Bible and nature forced Gosse to take an all-or-nothing approach to them when dealt with separately. Any vacillation, any inconsistency, any allowance for a deviation would be disastrous. In his view, it would not *weaken* the whole integrated structure: it would *destroy* it. That is to say, no problem could be isolated

---

63. Copy of a letter, PHG-F. Max Müller, 25 Oct. 1869 (Corr. Bk.); and see PHG, *Mysteries of God:* 'Nor am I anxious to find any parallelism between the Laws of the Heavenly and the Laws of the Earthly. I am content to rest everything on Authority:—the authority, however, of God, with whom "it is impossible to lie".' (p. vi)

64. These quotations are all from PHG, 'An Hour Among the Torbay Sponges', *Good Words* II (May 1861), 298, 295.

65. PHG-Edmund Gosse, 2 Sept. 1870 (CUL Add. 7041, 40). Emphasis in the original.

as simply a religious or a scientific one. *Omphalos* is a case in point. Whether or not uniformitarian geology provided a correct scientific hypothesis, there was a reason why, over the years, Gosse clung so tenaciously to his omphalotic argument. According to his reasoning, if the world was not created in six days, then the Bible was not all true. If the Bible were not all true, then there was no master plan structured by Death, Resurrection, and the Second Coming. If there was no overarching master plan, all the prophetic writings were meaningless.

The approach to both creations, finally, must be similar. In Gosse's scientific work—even in *Omphalos*—naturalistic explanations of events are always given. In his prophetic studies, too (as we shall see), miraculous occurrences were not to be expected immediately prior to the second advent. Logic must govern all Philip's thought, for 'What then is logic, but the art of finding the truth?'[66] The methods which Gosse used in science—observation and description, classification, experimentation— were also paralleled in his prophetic studies. That was the purpose of historical analysis and a comparative interpretation of texts emphasizing the explication of symbolic language. And just as his refusal to admit the legitimacy of Darwin's theory eventually placed him outside the mainstream of scientific thought, so did his adherence to the historicist mode of prophecy isolate him from the mainstream. After the mid-1860s, the futurist interpretation was dominant in England among evangelicals, including amongst most Brethren.[67]

-III-

The first of Gosse's prophetic writings in 1866, *The 6000 Years of the World's History now Closing*, a 16-page pamphlet published in March, focussed on a Jewish view (not found in Scripture, but adopted by Christians) that the week of creation and the Sabbath rest in Genesis were symbolic of the time allotted to humans on earth. According to one Talmudic opinion,[68] each of God's days of creation would be paralleled

---

66. PHG-Edmund Gosse, fragment of an undated letter (prob. 1868-73) (CUL Add. 7041, 85).

67. Sandeen, *Roots*, 87; PHG, 'On Prophetic Interpretation', *Rainbow* III (1 Apr. 1866), 150-1. Amongst prophetic journals, the *Rainbow* favoured Darbyite futurism (II (1 Apr. 1865), 191-2; III (1 Dec. 1866), 533-42, esp. 534-5). Newtonian futurism was favoured in the *Voice Upon the Mountains* (II (1 Mar. 1868), p. 351; I (1 Dec. 1867), 217-18) and the *Quarterly Journal of Prophecy* (XXII (Oct. 1870), 396; XXIII (Oct. 1871), 387-8).

68. PHG was not a student of the Talmud, where the subject is discussed. A statement in the Babylonian Talmud *Rosh Hashanah* 31a reads: 'The world will last 6000 years, and for 1,000

by six 'days' of 1,000 years of human activity, culminating in a seventh millenary of rest (Sabbath) and renewal (*viz.*, the messianic times). In order to discover how much of the world's history had so far elapsed, Gosse constructed a chronology of Scripture which showed that the 6,000-year period, dated from the creation of Adam, could terminate in 1866. The prediction could not be made with absolute certainty, Gosse acknowledged: 'A writer who should affect minute accuracy from these [chronological] data, must either intend to deceive his readers, or must be himself ignorant of the very principles of chronology.'[69] Nonetheless, said Gosse:

> It is enough to have proved (and this, I am sure, the data do prove) that the end of the sixth millenary must, if the Bible is true, be within a few years of the present time. The probability that 1866 is the *very* year, the *annus mirabilis*, is, however, immensely augmented by the convergence of the great prophetic periods of Scripture; as the Seven Times of Gentile bestial dominion, the 2300 years of oriental devastation, the 1260 years of the Little Horn of the Fourth Beast, and the 1335 years, whose lapse marks the final "Rest".[70]

While reviewers noticed Gosse's pamphlet, only one affirmed that 'Assuredly great and solemn times are at hand—yes, at our very door,' with the consequent need to 'be in a spirit of watchfulness and waiting.'[71]

From an explanation of this hermeneutical principle, Gosse next examined in periodical articles and a pamphlet the underlying foundation which all Christians might be able to accept. His Brethren outlook and his study of prophecy were inspired by that irenical desire. So the great

years it will be destroyed.' Other views on the nature of the 6000-year period are offered in *Sanhedrin* 97a. See also Arnold D. Ehlert, (comp.), *A Bibliographic History of Dispensationalism* (Grand Rapids, MI: Baker Book House, 1965), 8-22, and compare [anon], *The Chronology of the World: Showing the Approaching Termination of the Six Thousand Years of Human History. Computed from the Dates Given in the Scriptures. Intended for the Help of Bible Readers and Students of Prophecy* (London: Morgan and Chase, 1866).

69. PHG, *The 6000 Years of the World's History Now Closing: A Table of Scripture Chronology, with Notes* (London: Morgan & Chase, 1866), 14-15.

70. PHG, *6000 Years*, 15 (emphasis in the original) does not cite the famous 6000-year chronology of Archbishop James Ussher, as did others at the time (e.g., J. W. Bosanquet, *Messiah the Prince, or The Inspiration of the Prophecies of Daniel* (London: Longmans, Green, Reader, and Dyer, 1866), 153, 297).

71. Review in London *Gospel Magazine and Protestant Beacon* n.s. X (1 Aug. 1866), 448. The views in *6000 Years* were noticed, but not endorsed, in *The Rainbow* III (1 Apr. 1866), 190; *Revival* XIV (5 Apr. 1866), 194; and *Quarterly Journal of Prophecy* XVIII (July 1866), 301-2.

diversity of opinions on prophecy, and what he considered the dogmatic assertions of writers, distressed him. 'Beloved brethren,' he remonstrated, 'this is not the way to come at the Truth of God.'[72] It could only result in the 'testimony of Jesus' becoming, 'through our endless contentions, the very laughing stock of the world.'[73]

Nor was the discussion of details before the establishment of canons of interpretation helpful. That order had to be reversed. As an example of how it might be done, he briefly discussed in an April 1866 article in *The Rainbow* a crucial question: According to what principle should Revelation 6-17 (and more particularly the 'great tribulation' spoken of there) be interpreted? Rejecting the futurist claim that the crisis described referred to events *not yet fulfilled*, Gosse argued that the only principle for properly understanding the predictions in the Apocalypse was the historicist one. On that view, the events of the great tribulation had been *continuously unfolding* since the first century AD.[74]

This criticism of futurism in the pages of a monthly whose Congregationalist editor William Leask supported Darby's prophetic views[75] was not about to escape a rejoinder, which came the following month from the Revd Richard Chester (1811-1883), Vicar of Ballyclough (Ballyclogh) and Dromdowney, Ireland.[76] A veteran author, Chester's writings on prophecy appeared in *The Rainbow*, *Voice Upon the Mountains*, and Baxter's *Signs of Our Times*, among other places. In 1870, he countered Gosse's prophetic views in the pages of *The Christian* (discussed later in this chapter). In *The Rainbow* exchange, one finds the central difference between futurism and historicism stated in Chester's article, Gosse's rejoinder in June, and Chester's defense in August.[77]

72. PHG, 'On Prophetic Interpretation', *Rainbow*, 150.

73. PHG, *The Revelation*, 2.

74. PHG, 'On Prophetic Interpretation', *Rainbow*, 150-7; this position is restated in PHG, *The Great Tribulation* (London: Morgan & Chase, [1868]), 9, 14.

75. Sandeen, *Roots of Fundamentalism*, 87-8.

76. On Chester: *Crockford's Clerical Directory for 1860*, 691; George D. Burtchaell & Thomas U. Sadleir, *Alumni Dublinenses* (Dublin: new ed., Alex. Thorn & Co., 1935), 148; J. H. Cole, *Church and Parish Records of the United Diocese of Cork, Cloyne and Ross* (Cork, 1903); and W. M. Brady, *Clerical and Parochial Records of Cork, Cloyne, and Ross* (Dublin, 1863). I am grateful to G. Willis, of the Representative Church Body Library, Braemor Park, Dublin, for information which she supplied from the last two reference books.

77. Richard Chester, 'Principles of Futurist Interpretation', *Rainbow* III (1 May 1866), 222-6; PHG, 'Futurist Principles Examined', *Rainbow* III (1 June 1866), 268-71; Chester, 'Futurist Principles Defended', *Rainbow* III (1 Aug. 1866), 348-52. In Chester's first article he does not explicitly mention PHG and framed his futurist principles in opposition to preterist ones, but it

The disagreement revolved around the question of the literal interpretation and fulfillment of words and predictions in Revelation.[78] Given that symbolic language was used in that book, should it be given priority over literal constructions? Should the literal—or symbolic— fulfillment of symbolic predictions be expected? Chester maintained that the precision of the word of God meant that the plain and literal understanding of statements must be preferred to a figurative one, unless there was express evidence to the contrary. In doing so, 'the fancy of individual commentators' which leads to 'utter despair' is avoided. And even where a prediction is cloaked in symbolic language (as, for instance, the plagues in the seven vials), its precise fulfillment is to be anticipated.[79]

Adopting Chester's line of thought would have pushed Gosse into a corner. It would have meant that terms in the Bible could not have different meanings in different places without explicit warrant from the context. Then a 'day' or a 'year', for example—which Gosse saw as uniformly used in Scripture in their plain sense—could not have a symbolic sense. Then the equation of a day for a year (the 'year-day system')—a key pillar of historicist chronology since the early seventeenth century[80]—would be untenable. Then Gosse would have been forced to admit that 'All unquestionably fulfilled prophecy has had a literal fulfillment.'[81] And by that test, there were serious objections to the historicist assumption that the Papacy was the Antichrist.

Chester's canons of interpretation were a non-starter, and Gosse was unsparing in his attack on that exegesis. 'I cannot think', he noted at one point, 'that my honoured brother really means that there is nothing of symbol in all this; that he really expects these conditions to occur some time or other, in the plain simple common sense of the terms.'[82] This was not to ignore those ideas shared with futurists in particular

seems certain that his action was prompted by PHG's April *Rainbow* article. Chester had once been an historicist, and wished to show why he had abandoned that position (p. 226).

78. Early nineteenth century British millenarians, whether futurist or historicist, were literalists (Sandeen, *Roots*, 103-112, esp. p. 39). However, by around the mid-1840s, literalism in prophetic interpretation was associated solely with futurism and dispensationalism (Froom, *Prophetic Faith* IV, 1220; the discussion below, and *The Christian*, 9 Aug. 1877, 539; 7 Apr. 1870, 129). *Father and Son*, 1907, 75-6, mistakenly attributes a sweeping literalistic exegesis to PHG (on the example cited there: Wertheimer, 'A Son and His Father', 66-8).

79. Chester, 'Futurist Principles Defended', *Rainbow*, 350; Chester, 'Principles of Futurist Interpretation', 225.

80. Stunt, *From Awakening to Secession*, 22.

81. Chester, 'Principles of Futurist Interpretation', *Rainbow*, 223.

82. PHG, 'Futurist Principle Examined', *Rainbow*, 270.

(premillennialism, the expectant attitude), or the belief by millenarians in general in an inerrant and flawless Bible. What Gosse did was only to point to the obvious parting of ways when futurists and historicists approached the prophetic writings. As H. Grattan Guinness, the leading historicist, observed,

> It stands to reason, that if these emblematic visions [in Revelation] are read under the impression that these things are to come to pass *literally*, the conclusion that the book consists entirely of unfulfilled prophecies is inevitable, for most assuredly no such things ever have come to pass.
>
> *Literalists* must therefore be *futurists*, and the abandonment of the first error, is almost certain to lead to the abandonment of the second.[83]

After initial testing of futurist armour, Gosse devoted his fourth prophetic piece in 1866 to a carefully argued defence and elaboration of the foundation of his historicist position. Appearing in July, Gosse regarded highly his 64-page pamphlet *The Revelation: How Is It To Be Interpreted?*[84] He never ceased claiming that its arguments had resisted all attacks,[85] and likely would have set it as a *magnum opus* alongside his *History of the British Sea Anemones.*

In *The Revelation*, Gosse appears to have sought to create a united approach to the prophetic word by convincing Christians to rally around the historicist standard. That's what would appear to have been the case. More likely, the treatise was addressed specifically (though not exclusively) to Brethren. As Christians who were predominantly futurists, they had gone astray (in Gosse's view); as Christians who 'have sought to find a common ground for the union of all saints'[86] there was hope that his appeal would be given a fair hearing. The *Achill Missionary Herald* appreciated Gosse's implicit purpose, commending him for his rejection of futurism notwithstanding the fact that the 'Plymouth Brethren ... the sect of his adoption' largely favoured it.[87]

83. H. Grattan Guinness, *The Approaching End of the Age* (1ed. 1878), 111. Emphasis in original.

84. Freeman & Wertheimer-PHG, 80-1.

85. PHG, 'Breaking of the Day', *Christian* I (17 Mar. 1870), 92; PHG-George Pearse, 12 Dec. 1880 (CUL Add. 7313, 252-3); PHG, *Mysteries of God*, 149 fn.1.

86. PHG, *The Revelation: How Is It To Be Interpreted?*, [iii], also p. 38. Almost all Gosse's citations refer to Darbyites (Darby, William Trotter, J. G. Bellett) or other Brethren (William Lincoln, B. W. Newton).

87. Review of *The Revelation, Achill Missionary Herald* XXIX (11 Dec. 1866), 411. In the second article on PHG's work, the reviewer sensed 'an amount of dissatisfaction with the views

Read this way, *The Revelation* was a critique of the system of futurism known as dispensationalism. This teaching, developed in its modern form by J. N. Darby, had been adopted by Exclusive or 'Darbyite' Brethren and, through him and them, by many millenarians. What was peculiar about dispensationalism, as the late Ernest R. Sandeen pointed out,[88] was not the division of history into precisely circumscribed eras (Latin: *dispensatio*), each of which was governed by an equally distinctive activity of God. That belief was shared by others. Its key features were the so-called 'Jewish interpretation' of the New Testament and the doctrine of the secret rapture.[89]

According to the 'Jewish interpretation', most of Revelation referred not to the Christian Church but to Jews. This was necessarily the case, because (in Gosse's summary of the argument), 'The Church, being heavenly in its origin, calling, and associations, cannot be the subject of predictions whose sphere is the earth. But the main scenes of the Revelation (chaps. vi.-xviii.) are laid on earth; therefore the "saints" mentioned in them cannot be the Church, but are probably Jews after the Church is with the Lord.'[90]

Related to this hermeneutic was Darby's description of the second advent as occurring in not one but two stages. At the end of days, Darby believed, Jesus would first come for the Church. It would be 'raptured' (or removed to Jesus) *secretly*, so as to be unobserved by the world. Then, after a passage of time, Jesus would return again to judge *openly* *with* the Church. In reply to the question whether the Church would suffer through the persecution under the Antichrist's reign during the great tribulation, or be withdrawn beforehand, Darby believed the latter would be case. This was the doctrine of the 'pre-tribulationist rapture'.

Finally, the rapture would be not only secret but sudden—that is, at any moment. In this way, Darby reduced 1,800 years of history to a

---

and spirits of "Brethrenism", which would lead one to hope that Mr Gosse may yet feel it to be his duty to abandon that most erratic, unsettled, and disorderly sect, and to throw the weight of his influence into the scale of *apostolic order*, as well as apostolic truth' (*Achill Missionary* XXX (8 Jan. 1867), 435).

88. Sandeen, *Roots*, 68-70. Much of Sandeen's outstanding work is devoted to an analysis of dispensationalism.

89. The discussion below of Newton and Darby on dispensationalism is based on Rowdon, *Origins*, 230-33; Neatby, *History of Plymouth Brethren*, 104-6; Froom, *Prophetic Faith* IV: 122-5; Sandeen 62-70; Burnham, 'The Controversial Relationship Between Benjamin Wills Newton and John Nelson Darby', Chap. 5.

90. PHG, *The Revelation*, 4.

parenthesis or gap between the two advents. Though nearly expired, the prophetic clock had stopped ticking at the crucifixion. That ended the first advent. Nothing written of in Revelation had been fulfilled since then, nor would it be, until the second advent began—which might occur at any moment—when the clock would run again.

Recall that the heterodoxy of Darby's dispensational understanding of unfulfilled prophecy loomed large over the divisive confrontation between B. W. Newton and Darby in the 1840s. The two men did have a point of agreement: they both adhered to a form of premillennial futurism.[91] Their disputes were many: Newton believed that the Church would not be redeemed until after the great tribulation (thus making him a 'post-tribulationist'); that the second advent was a single event, with no secret rapture or any-moment advent; and that Israel and the Church, far from being discontinuous, were phases of one plan of salvation.

While Gosse never engaged in an open polemical duel with Darby or Newton, eclecticism dominated his appraisal of them. As far as the general approach to prophecy was concerned (their ecclesiastical ideas will be considered later in the chapter), Gosse had nothing in common with the two futurists. Nor did his wife Emily, who as a student of prophecy had annotated her copies of works by Newton and Darby and who (as previously mentioned) had known Newton's first wife, Hannah. Notwithstanding these points of familiarity with Newton, however, Gosse noted that 'she came back with a firmer confidence to the old Protestant [historicist] interpretation.' She was an enthusiast for E. B. Elliott's *Horae Apocalypticae*.[92]

Gosse himself had little good to say about Darby (and Darby, as previously noted, was suspicious of Gosse from his Jamaica days). Darby's views, Gosse said, were 'almost always valuable, though unfortunately hidden beneath a most involved and forbidding phraseology.'[93] But when asked by his son Edmund whether or not he considered himself aligned with 'Plymouth Brethren', Gosse answered: 'I presume by "Plymouth Brethren" you mean the Exclusive,[94] or Darby party, with whom the

91. Burnham, 'The Controversial Relationship Between Benjamin Wills Newton and John Nelson Darby', 232.

92. PHG, *Memorial*, 55-7.

93. PHG, *Memorial*, 56.

94. Early terms used to designate the followers of J. N. Darby included 'Plymouth Brethren' (from at least 1838, see *OED* 3ed.) and 'Darbyite' (from at least 1839, see Sydney, NSW *Australasian Chronicle*, 12 Nov. 1839, 2). The earliest use of the term 'Exclusive Brethren' I've

less you have to do the better. I fear the latter clause of I Thessalonians ii: 15 ['... and they please not God, and are contrary to all men'] too correctly describes them.'[95] And while Gosse opposed Newton in the 'Psalm's heresy,' and referred to his *Thoughts on the Apocalypse* (1844) as containing a 'beautiful and elaborate system' which was 'attractive but most erroneous',[96] he nonetheless shared (though for different reasons) Newton's attitude to dispensationalism.

As an historicist, Gosse's examination of dispensationalism in *The Revelation* concentrated on what futurists ignored: the bond cementing history and the apocalypse. According to Gosse, a knowledge of history was absolutely crucial and not (as all futurists held) utterly useless. Without that historical perspective there was no way to determine when any prophetic prediction had been accomplished. Without that, a short-sightedness developed which led to the naive conclusion that no event which ever occurred could possibly correspond to the grand symbols used by the prophets. Miraculous fulfillments in 'astounding interruptions and violations of natural laws' were anticipated by futurists, an idea which (Gosse said) only appealed to the 'natural proclivity to superstition' in the masses.[97] Without historical perspective, finally, Revelation was viewed as describing the consummation of the end of days in a brief climacteric. That made futurism deficient in its 'practical energy on the people.' Historicists, who could follow the unfolding plan of God in time, knew that that book was really a chronicle of the experiences of the Church in the world from the era after Christ.[98]

So one purpose of *The Revelation* was to show that dispensationalism, being governed by futurist principles, must be fallacious. It also rested on an unstable foundation. Reserving the question of the Church's place

seen is in the title of a book: *The Exclusive Brethren: their Origin and Discipline* (London: William Macintosh, [n.d.], but advertised in the London *Times*, 12 June 1867, 12. The author of this work was apparently 'G.', see 'Conclusion', 52). *OED* (2022) gives the earliest usage as 1879. 'Plymouthism' was used in an obituary of C. J. Davis, an advocate for Exclusive Brethren ('Death of Dr. C. J. Davis at Sedan', *Aberdeen Journal*, 14 Dec. 1870, 6). The best treatment is Dickson, '"Exclusive" and "Open": A Footnote', 82-90.

95. PHG-EWG, 22 Feb. 1868 (CUL Add. 7041, 13). PHG has occasionally been incorrectly assumed to have been aligned with 'Exclusive Brethren' (Burnham, 'The Controversial Relationship Between Benjamin Wills Newton and John Nelson Darby', 247 fn.14).

96. For the description of Newton's *Thoughts*: PHG, *Memorial*, 55, and *The Revelation*, 40fn., 18fn.; on the 'Psalm's Heresy': Rowdon, *Origins*, 258-61; EWG, 'Journal' (CUL Add. 7027, 77), under 12, 16 July 1868, and PHG-EWG, 29 July 1868 (CUL Add. 7018, 9).

97. PHG, *The Revelation*, 53.

98. PHG, *The Revelation*, 61-2; also Guinness, *Approaching End of the Age*, 111-39.

in the great tribulation to another place (and so not touching on the doctrine of the secret or open rapture of the Church and the stage(s) of the advent),[99] Gosse confined his attention to what he felt was the untenable 'any moment' expectation and the 'Jewish' interpretation.[100] Here his position resembled Newton's, as stated above: Revelation concerned the Church,[101] and foretold of its rapture to the Lord at (or after the end of) the great tribulation (and not at any moment).

Yet, after all was said and done, the practical consequence of Gosse's critique of dispensationalism brought him, ironically, to Darby's position concerning the attitude of expectation, not to Newton's. Newton had claimed that an 'any moment' advent was unscriptural; so had Gosse. But whereas Newton therefore rejected Darby's 'blessed hope,' and thought the Lord's coming was far off,[102] Gosse was not obliged to do either. Gosse had traced the ticking of the prophetic clock, and thought it would run out imminently. That is why he could tremblingly conclude his 1866 treatise with this thought:

> If the Presentist interpretation[103] is true, then the whore of Babylon is just on the verge of her doom; the vials are nearly all poured out; the Church's tribulation is almost ended; and the Lord whom we love may at any moment descend to the air, snatch his dead and living ones to meet Him; and resurrection glory, and bridal joy, and denizenship in the Holy City, and session on the Throne of the Lamb, be ours for ever and ever.

99. PHG had already touched on the Great Tribulation in 1866 ('On Prophetic Interpretation', *Rainbow*), and did so at more length two years later. PHG believed, following the historicist scheme, that Christians had already endured most of the tribulation ('On Prophetic Interpretation', *Rainbow*, 150, 154, 157). Nonetheless, he seemed to waver as to whether or not the rapture of the Saints would be secret or public, eclectic or common, antedate or post-date the end of the tribulation. See the undated letter printed in Charteris, 43-4, which—if there was such a letter and it was faithfully transcribed, including as to its context—indicates that PHG was open to accepting 'partial rapture' views (not all believers would be caught-up during the initial stage of Christ's Advent); PHG, 'The Breaking of the Day', *Christian* I (5 May 1870), 184-5; and for his final indecision, *Mysteries of God*, 147-59.

100. PHG, *The Revelation*, 48-50; 6-11, 22-36.

101. PHG had made this point in 1857 in his *London Monthly Review* article on '"The Saints" of the Revelation' (1857), quoting from that article *in extenso* in *The Revelation*, 32-6.

102. Richard Chester, 'Is the Second Advent of Our Lord to be Secret or Manifest?', *The Rainbow* II (1 July 1865), 293-4.

103. 'Presentist' being a synonym for 'Historicist'.

O blessed, cheering, purifying Hope! O joyful consummation! O
rapturous sight of Jesus! What manner of persons ought we to be in all
holy conversation and godliness![104]

-IV-

In the *6000 Years* and *The Revelation*, Gosse had promised his readers
that he would, 'if the Lord will,' provide his reflections on related
prophetic issues. In 1868 he published *The Great Tribulation* (a 16-
page pamphlet on its nature and duration),[105] and in 1871 another on
'The great prophetic periods of Daniel and The Revelation' (entitled *The
Prophetic Times*). When the predictions for 1866 failed to occur, Gosse
issued an updated second edition of *6000 Years* in 1867.[106] He now
pushed off the termination of the six-millennia period to about 1872.[107]
There is no record that his projected studies on 'The Antichrist: Who
or What Is He?' or 'The Year-day Computation of Symbolic Prophecy
Examined'[108] ever appeared. Gosse likely realized that pronouncing on
these subjects would only be to restate the obvious. The identification
of the Papacy with the Antichrist and the assumption that the year-day
system was basic to prophetic interpretation were acknowledged tenets of
historicism.[109] Besides, *The Revelation* gained for Gosse recognition as an
able defender of historicism. H. Grattan Guinness called it 'an admirable
little pamphlet ... which we earnestly commend to the consideration of

104. PHG, *The Revelation*, 63. His attitude to the 'any moment' expectation has been
misunderstood. Because *Father and Son* does not give the grounds for the Lord's imminent
coming (*Father and Son*, 1907, 340-1), Embley assumed that it was not different from Darby's
(Embley, 'Origins and Early Development', 214).

105. A copy of PHG's *Great Tribulation* was not known to Freeman and Wertheimer-PHG,84.
I subsequently located one at the John Rylands Library, University of Manchester. The publishing
information for the work as given in Freeman & Wertheimer-PHG is correct.

106. The second edition of *6000 Years* was advertised in *The Revival* XVI (11 Apr. 1867).

107. Freeman & Wertheimer-PHG, 80, were unable to locate a copy or a review of the second
edition. However Michael Baxter cites the *6000 Years* (not specifying the edition) as among
those works which terminate that period 'about 1872'.(Baxter, *End of This Age about the End of
This Century, and Its Last Week Passover Week, Ending on Thursday, Apr. 11, 1901* (London:
Christian Herald Office, 1887), 26, and 'The End of the 6000 Years from the Creation, in 1890',
New York *Christian Herald and Signs of the Times*, 9 Sept. 1880, 583). In the first edition of
6000 Years, PHG had looked to the year 1866 as inaugurating the End of Days.

108. These works were promoted in advertisements in PHG, *The Revelation*, [64]; Freeman
& Wertheimer-PHG, xiii.

109. PHG, *6000 Years*, 6-7. One did not have to be a devotee of prophetic studies to share
this position. J. W. Dawson (the Canadian geologist and anti-Darwinian) also believed that the
correct translation of the Hebrew *yom* (day) was *eon* (Cornell, 'Sir William Dawson and the
Theory of Evolution', 12).

those who hold futurist views.'[110] Years later, it was said to be a work containing arguments 'which have never been refuted, and which are not capable of refutation.'[111]

During 1866 Gosse also published related materials, including the 16-page pamphlet, *Geology or God; Which? A Supplement to 'Omphalos'* (1866).[112] The 104 entries which he contributed to the Revd Patrick Fairbairn's *Imperial Bible-Dictionary* (2 vols., 1864-66)[113] dealt mainly with animals. They did not touch on prophetic issues, but a number provided an exegetical or hortatory reading, and all supported his belief in an inerrant Bible.[114]

-V-

Notwithstanding all of Gosse's zealous activities during what he believed would be a world-historical moment, no amount of powerful logic can bring the messiah to earth. Having mortgaged his faith to history, what did he do when each passing year yielded 'disconfirmation' of his belief (in the terminology of modern social psychologists)?[115] How did he act towards friends and family, the Church of God at Marychurch over which he ministered, and the world at large?

These are not theoretical questions—Gosse's own son challenged him directly to explain himself. What exactly *was* his father doing? Edmund

---

110. H. Grattan Guinness, *Approaching End of the Age* (1ed. 1878), 132fn.

111. So an editorial by [R. C.] M[organ]., *The Christian*, 23 Aug. 1877, 576 ('His contributions to the paper are generally initialed "M."', according to David Williamson, 'Personal Forces in Religious Journalism. VII.—Messrs. Morgan and Scott of *The Christian*', *The Leisure Hour* (July 1903), 724; see also S. A. Blackwood, 'Prophetic Interpretation', *The Christian*, 9 Aug. 1877, 539). PHG's *Revelation* was favourably reviewed in *The Revival* XV (19 July 1866), 40; *Quarterly Journal of Prophecy* XIX (Jan. 1867), 85; the *Achill Missionary Herald* XXIX (11 Dec. 1866), 411, and XXX (8 Jan. 1867), 434-5, and noted in the Baptist *Freeman* XIII (3 Aug. 1866), 174. It was criticized in the *Voice Upon the Mountains* (II (15 Dec. 1868), p. 171), with a tempered dissent in the *Rainbow* (III (1 Oct. 1866, 476-7); Richard Chester, 'Have the Apocalyptic Seals as yet Been Opened?', IV (1 Feb. 1867), 58-64.

112. Several PHG works were advertised in *The Christian* I (28 Apr. 1870), facing p. 171 (the ad is reproduced in Freeman & Wertheimer-PHG, 81, ix): *The Revelation*; *The 6000 Year* (2ed.); *Geology or God*; and *The Great Tribulation*.

113. Contrary to Freeman & Wertheimer-PHG, 83, the work did not first appear in 2vols. in 1866. Volume I appeared separately in 1864 (publisher's advertisement, *Athenaeum*, 20 August 1864, 229: 'Now ready, Vol. I ... to be completed in 2 vols.').

114. One reviewer found PHG's articles 'well written', but the dictionary as a whole inferior to others and the editing 'so poor, so unscholarly, so narrow' (*Athenaeum*, 29 Dec. 1866, 874).

115. Leon Festinger, Henry W. Riecken and Stanley Schachter, *When Prophecy Fails. A Social and Psychological Study of a Modern Group that Predicted the Destruction of the World* (Mansfield Centre, CT: Martino Publishing, 1956, 2009).

said he seemed like 'a servant sitting at a window ... & letting the house go quite unheeded' and 'not working about the house till the Master come.'[116] To which Philip responded:

> ... perhaps it hardly becomes me to say much; except that it is the very thing I am striving to avoid. For what have I given up the paths of Science, & turned from the praise of men, but that I might labour in my Master's house, & wash the feet of his lowly ones? More than ever, as I see the day approaching, have I of late sought to give up myself to His service,—to stir up, both by tongue & pen, His dear people to practical godliness, & readiness for Him.[117]

That desire to be active among 'His dear people' was a general goal; it applied equally well to Gosse's only child. Though far from the parental home, parental concern was never far off. 'The Coming of the Lord draweth nigh,' went one of Philip's earliest letters to his son. Another concluded: 'Time is short; eternity is at hand.'[118] Edmund was sent copies of the Revd John Cumming's *When Shall These Things Be?* (1868), Bourchier Wrey Savile's *The Apostacy* (1853), and some of Philip's own prophetic writings (which they discussed), and asked if recent archaeological discoveries which seemed confirmatory of the Bible were much talked of among the literati in London.[119] As events in Europe unfolded which looked as though they had been predicted in biblical texts, Philip enquired as to whether his son was constantly watching and taking his own stand for Christ. Philip's correspondence was interspersed with details of his preaching and ministry. Looking over his shoulder, he noted how the Power of Darkness 'under two generals, Popery & Infidelity,' was assaulting the Kingdom of Light.[120] And while Philip gradually realized that his son did not sympathize with historicist

116. EWG's letter to his father containing these words is not extant, but EWG's words are quoted in his father's response to them (PHG-EWG, 11 Mar. 1872, CUL Add. 7041,51). See also *Father and Son*, 1907, 340-1

117. The accusation about idleness was made by EWG, with his father's reply, as quoted, 11 Mar. 1872 (CUL Add. 7041, 51). See also *Father and Son*, 1907, 340-1.

118. PHG-EWG, 18 Feb. 1867 (CUL Add. 7041, 6); PHG-EWG, 12 Oct. 1868 (CUL Add. 7018, 18).

119. PHG-EWG, 8 Feb. 1869 (CUL Add. 7041, 23); PHG-EWG, 23 Mar. 1868 (Add. 7041, 16); EWG's 'Journal', under 17 Nov. 1868 (on the *Great Tribulation*), and PHG-EWG, 30 Mar. 1870 (CUL Add. 7041, 37), on 'The Breaking of the Day'; and PHG-EWG, 9 June 1869 (Add. 7041, 27).

120. PHG-EWG, 5 Oct. 1874 (British Library, Ashley Library, B 3282); PHG-EWG, 6 Jan 1873 (Add. 7041, 56).

views, he still looked, 'with an ever increasing joyful confidence, to have you with me through those bright & blissful ages soon (oh! how soon!) to be begun;—assured that He who hath begun a good work in you will perform it until the Day of Jesus Christ.'[121]

The homefront at St. Marychurch could not be ignored. As those who belonged to the Room were of low social standing with meagre education, nourishment from heaven and earth was needed for them. In 1867 Philip began to plan to build a school room behind the chapel, soon used as a Sunday school;[122] and in the next year, Eliza Gosse joined a newly formed Dorcas Society, which provided clothing for the poor.[123] A few years later a Bible woman was engaged, to go house to house carrying 'the gospel message to the poor people,'[124] as a supplement to Gosse's own pastoral visitations.[125] Lectures were given by Gosse to the young women of the area, and (apparently at an annual meeting of Brethren) on prophecy at Teignmouth.[126] He attended the annual meetings of the Torquay Brethren,[127] spoke twice on the Lord's Day at the Room,[128] and conducted weekday Bible and prayer meetings at home.[129] Some of these meetings (and those at chapel) were devoted to prophetic subjects, touching on topics such as the identification of the Man of Sin with the Papacy, the imminency of the Lord's Coming 'as a thief,' and the restoration of Israel.[130] Concern for the physical and auditory comfort of the worshippers at the Room led Gosse to add backs to the forms in the chapel, and to direct the singing 'in a moderately quick time.' Gosse

121. PHG-EWG, 19 Sept. 1870 (Add. 7041, 45).

122. PHG-EWG, 1 Mar. 1867 (Add. 7018, 3); PHG-EWG, 23 Mar. 1868 (Add. 7041, 16); within a year, 'Mamma's School' [=the Sunday School?] had 55 students (PHG-EWG, 1 Feb. 1868, CUL Add. 7041, 9).

123. PHG-EWG, 12 Oct. 1868 (Add. 7018, 18); PHG-EWG, 8 Dec. 1868 (Add. 7041, 22). On Dorcas Societies: Acts 9: 36; [William Hale White], *The Autobiography of Mark Rutherford and Mark Rutherford's Deliverance*, ed. by Reuben Shapcott (London: Trübner & Co., 2ed., 1888), 29-32; and Kenneth Young, *Chapel* (London: Eyre Methuen, 1972), 105.

124. PHG-EWG, 11 Mar. 1872 (Add. 7041, 51); for Thomas Jury, a later Bible worker: PHG-Thomas Jury, 19 Mar. 1880 (Add. 7313, 60).

125. PHG-EWG, 6 Apr. 1875 (Add. 7018,29); *Life*, 358.

126. To young women: PHG-EWG, 8 Feb. 1869 (Add, 7041, 23); on prophecy: PHG-EWG, 19 Sept. 1870 (Add. 7041, 45), where the event is referred to as an 'annual meeting', without further clarification. PHG's letter is the only source I have seen for this event.

127. PHG-EWG, 11 May 1869 (Add. 7041,25); PHG-EWG, 12 May 1871 (Add. 7041, 47).

128. PHG-EWG, 6 Apr. 1875 (as cited, fn. 66); PHG-EWG, 1 Sept. 1879 (Add. 7018, 32).

129. PHG-EWG, 1 Feb. 1868 (Add. 7041,9); PHG-EWG, 10 Mar. 1868 (Add. 7041, 15); PHG-EWG, 23 Mar. 1868 (Add. 7041, 16); Nellie Gosse-EWG, 1 Sept. 1881 (Family Collection).

130. PHG-EWG, 10 Mar. 1868 (Add. 7041,15); PHG-EWG, 12 July 1875 (Add. 7019, 16); PHG-EWG, 21 Apr. 1868 (Add. 7041, 19).

was considered 'a good singer,'[131] though he disliked the 'Revival Tunes' with their refrains and choruses.[132]

This sowing yielded results. In 1872, a dozen new members joined in fellowship,[133] pleasing Gosse: 'The dear Saints with us are we think growing in grace & love; in practical watchfulness & holiness; in self denial & attendance upon ordinances; in enjoyment of the word of Christ; in waiting for His coming; & in love towards me.'[134] By mid-1875, there were 120 in attendance at the Room, mostly poor.[135]

Gosse's success at Marychurch in creating a harmonious gathering of a sizable number of people, where there had only been an inchoate collection of about a dozen believers when he arrived less than twenty years earlier, was achieved through personal toil and devotion. It had not been a simple task. While his followers accepted his prophetic views,[136] and so differed with him from some Brethren, the relationship was not always smooth sailing. One known episode of discontent threatened to nullify all Gosse's efforts.

As has been noted, the primary source of contention between Darby and Newton, resulting in the schism within Brethren in the 1840s, concerned the interpretation of prophecy. An ecclesiastical and doctrinal issue—what was referred to as 'liberty' of (or 'open') ministry at the Lord's (or Communion) Table—had been another disputed point.[137]

Brethren had, from their earliest days, rejected the need for an ordained ministry and, in accordance with their attempt to revive Apostolic practice, had looked to 1 Corinthians 14 as their model for Church worship. Some interpreted Corinthians as signifying that the

---

131. Thus the judgment of Philip Tocque, who knew PHG in Newfoundland: Tocque, *Kaleidoscope Echoes*, 16.

132. On the forms: PHG-EWG, 20 Apr. 1874 (Add. 7041, 58); the singing: PHG-EWG, 6 Jan. 1873 (Add. 7041, 56).

133. PHG-EWG, 6 Jan. 1873 (Add. 7041, 56).

134. PHG-EWG, 11 Mar. 1872 (Add. 7041, 51); cf. also PHG-EWG, 16 Nov. 1872 (Add. 7041, 55), where he refers to the 'saints' admiration for Eliza as well.

135. PHG-George Pearse, 19 June 1881 (Add. 7313, 380-1); PHG-EWG, 12 July 1875 (Add. 7019, 16).

136. PHG-George Pearse, 19 June 1881 (Add. 7313, 380-1), quoted with differences in *Life*, 367-8; PHG-Rev. James Fanstone, 24 July 1880 (Add. 7313, 163-4).

137. Grass, *Gathering to His Name*, 98-99 and index; Rowdon, *Origins*, 227-30; Neatby, *History of Plymouth Brethren*, 106-9, 207, 213, 337; Embley, 'Origins and Early Development', 156-61, 216-17; Lenz, *"Strengthening the Faith of the Children of God"*, 42fn.26, describes the 'primary difference' between Open and Exclusive Brethren in terms of 'the practice of communion', available to 'all Protestants who profess Christ as Savior' or only on a restricted basis.

service should be conducted openly and freely: any person spontaneously moved by the Holy Spirit should be allowed to address the assemblage. This was, in the end, Darby's own view. Others felt that restrictions needed to be placed on open ministry because in Apostolic times, certain believers had come prepared to speak (I Corinthians xiv:26). Such people, it was argued, ought to be recognized as 'overseers' of the church. An 1844 newspaper report on the Brethren drew attention to its ideal of no paid, official or special ministry and the real-world custom: 'They hold that every male of the church, who feels disposed to address the church, has a right to do so. It happens, however in most of the churches of the Plymouth Brethren, that one individual has greater gifts for edification than any of the rest, and he consequently most frequently addresses the church.'[138] It was Newton's adherence to the belief that there should be a group of recognized 'Elders' which brought the full weight of Darby's condemnation down upon him.

As earlier noted, Gosse had experienced open ministry from his first association with the Brethren in Hackney. His later experiences, likely in Jamaica and certainly in Devon, undoubtedly helped to persuade him that the practice was ineffectual. As Newton, Andrew Jukes, and other Brethren had discovered, open ministry worked well when men of intellect were present (as at Hackney), not so well when the meeting was predominantly constituted of the uneducated poor. In the latter situation, it was a leading personality whose guidance allowed for profitable worship.[139]

Moreover Gosse questioned the New Testament derivation of open ministry. He believed that the Holy Ghost was still operating in the church,[140] though the miraculous gifts of Apostolic times were no longer extant.[141] His conclusion: there was not a perfect congruence between that age and his own time.

This question had also surfaced, tangentially, in Gosse's 1866 writings on prophecy. Was historicism undemocratic, in that it required a knowledge of history, or the erudition necessary to master a *Horae*

---

138. 'Lord Teynham—The Plymouth Brethren', *Dumfries and Galloway Standard*, 27 Nov. 1844, 3.

139. Embley, 'Origins and Early Development', 217; Neatby, *History of Plymouth Brethren*, 92.

140. PHG, 'Praying for the Holy Spirit', *Bible-Reader's Journal* no. 18 (1 June 1860), 404-5; PHG-Mrs Susanna Filby, 20 Mar. 1880 (Add. 7313, 61-2).

141. PHG, 'Reminiscences', II: 255 (cited in *Life*, 377); Embley, 'Origins and Early Development', 217; Neatby, *History of Plymouth Brethren*, 207.

Apocalypticae? Certainly the Revd Chester thought so. He said that it was the futurist (not the historicist) system which allowed every Christian, 'although he be poor and unlearned,' to deal with God's word.[142] So were historicists—in relying on learned men—denying the operation of the Holy Ghost among all believers? That Gosse rejected, and in so doing, hinted at the parallelism between democracy in the interpretation of prophecy and open ministry in worship. In both cases, edification had to come from those overseers or scholars most capable of providing it. 'I have had some experience of peasants and artisans, real converted persons, holy and faithful,' Gosse wrote in 1866,

and I find that a considerable proportion of them are not only dependent on educated persons to translate the mind of God out of Hebrew and Greek into English, but to explain that very English version in a homely conversational way, line upon line, before they can get any correct ideas at all out of it. I should like to see the results, truly set down, of a catechetical examination of the uneducated portion of any gathering of saints in the country parts of England, on the meaning of the detailed symbols of the Apocalypse. I wonder how much of the elaborate system of Mr. Newton's "Thoughts," ... would be educed from those, dear worthy Christian people though they be, who have never learned geography or history, nor even to read with understanding. It may be said this is an extreme case; but if the principle contended for is good for anything, it should apply to such persons, who form so large a portion of our assemblies. Have not such persons received the Holy Ghost? Of course *very much of truth must be taken from others on trust;* or where is the need of human ministry in the Church of God? I daresay I shall be misrepresented by some as denying the presence of the Holy Ghost in the Church. But I appeal to known facts, and plain common sense.[143]

Among Gosse's main differences with Darbyite or 'Exclusive' Brethren were those that revolved around the interpretation of prophecy and open ministry.[144] In the case of the latter, in moving to St. Marychurch in 1857

142. R. Chester, 'Principles of Futurist Interpretation', *Rainbow*, 226.
143. PHG, *The Revelation*, 40fn. Emphasis in original.
144. So PHG himself stated in letters to his son of 3 Mar. 1868 (CUL Add. 7041, 14), and 23 Mar. 1868 (CUL 7041, 16). A third difference concerned the principle of congregational independency or autonomy. Darby and the 'Exclusives' favoured centralization of authority and the strict enforcement of communal discipline through excommunication. PHG and the Open Brethren, on the other hand, preferred local autonomy and the right of each assembly

it was natural that he would assume leadership over 'the little Church meeting in Marychurch'[145] or (as he sometimes referred to it) the 'Church of God'.[146] Gosse did not like being styled 'Reverend'[147] because he said he was appointed by no man. 'Pastor'[148] was an acceptable term because it was the Holy Ghost 'who gave me a pastor's heart, & an overseer's place'[149] over 'a little flock of believers, mostly of low estate in this world, many of whom are my own children in the gospel. We break bread in remembrance of Jesus, & own no sectarian or distinctive name.'[150] Gosse guided his people, for example in being charitable towards others when the need arose.[151]

This 'little flock of believers' seemed to exemplify the true unity and simplicity desired by the Brethren's initial revival. But it was the failure to live up to those ideals—'The Holy War between the two sections of the Plymouth Brethren'[152]—which continued to 'rage' long after the divisiveness of 1848. At St. Marychurch in the fall of 1868, the controversy involved not intra-party but inter-party differences. Gosse's pastor's role

to admit whomever it judged to be fit. PHG's position may be inferred from the way he acted in the baptism of the Bewes children by Leonard Strong. Although he was not pleased with the decision of Strong and Bewes, he accepted it (the episode is discussed later); and on the general subject: Embley, 'Origins and Early Development', 159-60, and Embley, in Wilson (ed.), *Patterns of Sectarianism*, 227.

145. PHG-[Leonard] Strong, 13 Dec. 1872 (Corr. Bk.). Eliza Gosse refers to him as 'the minister of a small congregation' (EG-NG, 5 Feb. 1875, CUL Add. 7019,14).

146. For the usage 'Church of God': e.g., PHG-EWG, 20 Sept. 1882 (CUL Add. 7018, 36). Brethren generally call their churches 'assemblies' (Dickson, 'Hunter Beattie', 147, and for an historic example: Leonard Strong-PHG, 14 Dec. 1872, Corr. Bk.). In the 1890s, the 'Church of God' became a coded way of referring to the Needed Truth faction of Brethren. PHG's use of 'Church of God' did not have a sectarian connotation but reflected the phrase as used in Acts and elsewhere (Neil Dickson-Wertheimer, 1 Feb. 2022).

147. PHG-Messrs [James] Veitch [and Son], 21 Dec. 1880 (Add. 7313, 259). However in newspaper reports mentioning Leonard Strong, he was frequently designated 'Rev. L. Strong, minister of the Brethren's Room, Warren-road' ('Torquay', Exeter *Western Times*, 8 Sept. 1855, 7).

148. PHG-[Leonard] Strong, 13 Dec. 1872 (Corr. Bk.).

149. PHG-Rev. W. E. Jellicoe, 5 Apr. 1881 (Add. 7313, 332); PHG-Albert R. Fenn, 16 June 1880 (Add. 7313, 135-6), and PHG-Rev. Alfred Tilly, 13 Feb. 1880 (Add. 7313, 32).

150. PHG-Miss L. M. Campbell, 25 Nov. 1880 (Add. 7313, 237); PHG-J. H. Gladstone, 3 Oct. 1877 (J. H. Gladstone Papers, seen in the collection of Sir Stephen Holmes, Kent); PHG-George Pearse, 19 June 1881 (CUL Add. 7313,380-1).

151. During a time of economic hardship in Lancashire, the 'Saints at Mary Church, Devon, per P.H. Gosse' donated over £2 to the Lancashire Supplementary Relief Fund (*The Revival*, 18 Dec. 1862, [293]). The Brethren preacher H. Wilbraham Taylor (1847-1899) was involved in the Fund (letter, Colchester *Essex County Standard*, 19 Dec. 1862, 3).

152. The phrase is from 'Devonshire', *Sherborne Mercury* (17 Jan. 1865), 8: 'The difference between the two bodies is very slight in outward aspect'.

came into question. Gosse narrated the development in considerable detail in a letter to his son:

... there was dissatisfaction & murmuring among some of the brethren, & chiefly the active young men, about my taking too prominent a part in ministry; & against the Elders' meeting, the existence of any such body being 'contrary to Brethren's Principles.' Sunday morning, 27th Sept, the brethren remained, & there was some disputing, which induced me to devote the following Sunday evening to a carefully prepared lecture, in which I brought out the very copious New Test. evidence for Church rule by a body of Elders; & showed that the deduction of 'Open Ministry' from 1 Cor. xiv, is utterly worthless. On the following Thursday evening (7th inst.) there was a meeting of the whole church appointed for a solemn discussion. Some (Wm. Oliver in particular) acknowledged that the testimony of Scripture which I had adduced on Sunday evening was quite conclusive, & had changed their judgment. But two or three were contumacious & bitter. So large a portion of the meeting remained silent that I could not determine how the general voice ran; &, as I had been told that the disaffection was wide-spread (though my informant was himself one of the disaffected), Mamma & I, on conferring about it after we came home, felt very discouraged & down-hearted. I cast it much on the Lord, & saw no other chance to restore peace than that I should resign the pastoral charge, & all ministry in the church-meeting; breaking bread with them, but sitting in one of the side seats persistently silent.

Accordingly yesterday morning, after the breaking of bread, I asked the saints to remain, & told them the decision I had come to; though in doing so I was so painfully affected that I could hardly speak intelligibly. The disaffected brethren had absented themselves, & turned out to be only 4 in all, though these are godly & active, being in fact, Lear, Sharem, Towell & Collins. My statement elicited such a profusion of sympathy, & love, & regret, & remonstrance, & encouragement as I could not have looked for. There was but one voice; all protested that it would be unfair to make a whole church suffer for the fault of 3 or 4 malecontents. So many, even of the poorest, protested that they had received much blessing from my ministry; so many begged that I would reconsider my decision, some even vowing that they would never come again if I gave up my Pastorship, that I could not but hear God's voice in it. It was decided that a meeting be held next Thursday, expressly to examine 1 Cor. xiv (brethren's stronghold for 'Open ministry'); & that the disaffected shall be met & remonstrated with, not by me, but by the rest. In the meanwhile, my decision remains in suspensû [*sic*]. Pray for us, that the Lord may bring good out of all this evil; pray that I may still be able to watch over this Church in love; & pray that the dear Brethren in question be not driven away.

    It is all the more painful because these latter are such really earnest sincere, upright men of God; my personal respect & love for such brethren as Lear and Sharem is very great. Yet I am persuaded that they misread the Scripture; that 1 Cor. xiv. has no such bearing as they, led by honoured Brethren's Tracts & teachings, ascribe to it.[153]

This display of what Gosse termed 'the democratic spirit'[154] apparently had an immediate psychosomatic effect. A bodily illness brought on 'a decay of interest in things I had formerly valued, even my plant-house, my orchids, seemed to have lost their charm.'[155] To pass the time, he and Eliza went to Cornwall and on their return home collected sea anemones. By 22 October the rift in 'our little Zion' remained unhealed, which Philip connected to a belief 'especially [among] the uneducated, [in] a superstitious expectation of a quasi-miraculous operation of the Holy Spirit, which is quite unwarranted.' Instead of waiting during worship to be moved by the Spirit, Gosse prepared in advance what he was going to say or teach.

In any event, Gosse's own irenic attitude must have done much to close the breach, although he acknowledged that it was William Oliver and other members who eventually brought peace to the assembly.[156]

-VI-

Exhortations to his son, and ministry over the Church of God, were two of the ways in which Gosse prepared those dear to him for the return of the Great Shepherd. So devoted was he to such service that little time was left for other pursuits (orchid collecting and cultivation being one of the few

153. PHG-EWG, 12 Oct. 1868 (CUL Add. 7018, 18).
154. PHG-George Pearse, 19 June 1881 (CUL Add. 7313,380-1).
155. Information in this paragraph is from PHG-EWG, 22 Oct. 1868 (Add. 7018, 19).
156. PHG-George Pearse, 19 June 1881 (CUL Add. 7313,380-1); and for another instance of dissatisfaction with PHG's leadership position (this time concerning his Bible readings at Sandhurst): PHG-Robert Nelson, 19 Aug. 1881 (CUL Add. 7313, 412-3).

demanding exceptions).[157] In the decade after 1866, his scientific writings were reduced to a trickle in comparison to the ocean which they had been in the ten previous years (in 1874 he brought out a lightly revised, though well-received, new edition of *Evenings at the Microscope*).[158] His interest in politics was mainly confined to its bearing 'on the Kingdom of God.'[159] He declined a request to participate in a mooted plan to provide intellectual amusement in Torquay because

> the very chiefest of all service, I judge to be the making known to poor lost sinners the salv[atio]n wh[ich] God in the Bl[ood] of His Son, has freely prov[ide]d for whosoever will accept it. As He had given me the knowl[ed]ge of this His love, a measure of power of utterance, & heart for the work,—this I strove to do with my might. ... Body, soul, & spirit, I am His ...[160]

More and more, he retreated from this world,[161] awaiting to become part of the next.

In labouring for others he also reached beyond his immediate circle. As previously noted, Gosse supported societies formed to combat the atheism and infidelity of the age. Financial help was given to evangelical workers and missionaries at home and abroad (in China, India, Palestine, and elsewhere),[162] and for tract distribution to missionaries at home and

157. *Life*, 359-60; and the following letters from PHG: to Dr M. Brocas, J. H. Cooke, T. A. Cokayne, C. W. Strickland, 5, 16, 18, 23 Aug. 1871 (all Corr. Bk.); to EWG, 5 Oct. 1874 (British Library, Ashley Library, B3282); CUL Add. 7018, 68 [n.d.]; to EWG, 11 June 1877 (CUL Add. 7019, 22); and other letters.

158. Notes were added and the text was reset but unaltered for the new edition of *Evenings at the Microscope* (Freeman & Wertheimer-PHG, 64, no. 90); PHG-Thomas Burt of the SPCK, 29 May 1873 (Corr. Bk.). Reviewed favourably in *Quarterly Journal of Science* n.s. IV (Apr. 1874), 255-6. F. Jeffrey Bell (1855-1924), a cousin who was Professor of Zoology at King's College London, brought out a revised edition of the book in 1895 (Freeman & Wertheimer-PHG, 62-3, 65).

159. PHG-EWG, 8 Dec. 1868 (CUL Add. 7041, 22); PHG-EWG, 4 May 1869 (Add. 7041, 31).

160. PHG-Henry Jackson, 15 Jan. 1872 (copy of a letter, Corr. Bk.).

161. EWG-PHG, 11 Sept. 1874 (CUL Add. 7018, 60).

162. PHG supported the China Inland Mission (*Life*, 363; PHG-W. T. Berger, 16 Aug. 1860, Corr. Bk.); Zenana Missions to Women in India (PHG-Sir William Muir, 29 Dec. 1880: CUL Add. 7313, 267); Miss Walker-Arnott's school in Jaffa for Arab orphans (PHG-Miss E. Walker-Arnott, 14 June 1880: CUL Add. 7313, 132. The school was begun in 1863: *The Christian*, 26 July 1877, p. 508); the Misses Campbell's harem work in the Orient (PHG-Miss Louise M. Campbell, 18, 25 Nov. 1880: CUL Add. 7313, 231, 237): Papuan missionaries (PHG-Rev. Dr John Ludwig Krapf, 6 Mar. 1870; to Pastor Ansorge, Berlin, 24 May 1870: both in Corr. Bk.); and was a referee for H. Grattan Guinness' East End Training Institute for Home and Foreign Missions, founded in Feb. 1873 (*Illustrated Missionary News*, 1 Apr. 1875, 45). Among others involved in EETI were T. J. Barnardo, W. T. Berger, D. L. Moody, R. C. Morgan, C. H. Spurgeon, and J. Hudson Taylor.

abroad.[163] Letters were exchanged with an impressive number of Brethren and evangelicals.[164] Some years later, when Gosse discovered that he had spare money in his account at the bank, he decided that the best investment was in missions, not stocks.[165]

Even with all this, Gosse did not disregard his own condition and duties. On a mundane level, he handled the household finances.[166] On another, his interest in all facets of biblical history resulted in his supporting the Palestine Exploration Fund from 1869.[167] Engrossed in reading *Chips from a German Workshop* (vol. 1, 1867), a collection of essays by the Orientalist Friedrich Max Müller (1823-1900), Gosse sent a long letter to the author enumerating differences in their assessments of the Rig-Veda, the Hindu sacred text, and its value for comparative religious studies.[168]

EETI was later known as East London Institute for Home and Foreign Missions (*Missionary Echo*, Feb. 1880, insert). PHG was a Referee for that organization (Mrs H. Grattan Guinness, *The Wide World and Our Work In It: or, the Story of the East London Institute for Home and Foreign Missions* (London: Hodder and Stoughton, [1886]), [257]).

163. PHG donated 5,000 tracts to an Open Air Mission (see Corr. Bk. under 20 Aug. 1873); tracts abroad: PHG-Richard Perrens, 18 May 1880 (CUL Add. 7313, 111-12), to Rev. James Fanstone, 24 July, 4 Oct. 1880 (CUL Add. 7313, 163-4, 194-5: offers to send 1,000 tracts).

164. Examples listed in Corr. Bk.: T. J. Barnardo (11 Nov. 1870); E. H. Bennett (22 May 1887); W. H. Bennet (6 Feb. 1885); [J. W.] Bosanquet (16 Feb. 1870); George Brealey (7 Feb. 1872); R. C. Chapman (May 13 1887); Mrs H. G. (Fanny) Guinness (22 May 1874); J. L. Harris (7 June, 6 Dec. 1871); J. E. Howard (1 June 1872); revivalist C. Russell Hurditch (24 Oct. 1875; using the pseudonym 'Septima', his daughter Grace wrote *Peculiar People*, 1935, a reply to *Father and Son* by depicting a happy Brethren upbringing. I am grateful to Timothy Stunt for this information); open-air preacher Gawin Kirkham (11 May 1869; 'The Christian' Portrait Gallery, 185); R. C. Morgan (28 July 1870, etc.; see George E. Morgan, *Veteran in Revival: R. C. Morgan, His Life and Times* (London: Morgan & Scott, 1909), 21, 224-5); G. Müller (10 Nov. 1870); G. Pearse (13 June 1873); B. W. Savile (7 Mar. 1873); H. Soltau (8 Jan. 1873); C. H. Spurgeon (20 July 1872); Leonard Strong (1 May 1872); J. H. Taylor (30 Aug. 1872); W. Yapp (24 July 1872, including noting his death in 1874).

165. PHG-Mrs H. G. (Fanny) Guinness, 26 Mar. 1880 (CUL Add. 7313, 68): he enclosed £60. On Fanny Emma Guinness (1831-1898): Heggoy, *Fifty Years of Evangelical Missionary Movement*, 24; 'Death of Mrs. Guinness, of Cliff College, Curbar', *Derbyshire Times and Chesterfield Herald*, 12 Nov. 1898, 7.

166. See, e.g., the fly-sheet from the Planet Benefit Building & Investment Society, London, dated 29 June 1872 (stuck in Corr. Bk.); for other investments, 'The Account of PHG's Personal Estate at his Death' (CUL Add. 7041, 68).

167. For the Palestine Exploration Fund: Corr. Bk. under 19 Nov. 1869, and PHG-Walter Besant, 3 Jan. 1881 (Add. 7313, 274).

168. PHG-EWG, 4 Aug. 1869 (CUL Add. 7041, 28); PHG-F. Max Müller, 11 Aug. 1869 (Corr. Bk.); Max Müller-PHG, 18 Oct. 1869 (LeBL); reply, 25 Oct. 1869 (Corr. Bk.); PHG- Max Müller, 16 May 1871 (Corr. Bk.). Though not a member of the Victoria Institute, Max Müller's views on philology were cited over the years by a number of Victoria Institute members. Those remarks, and occasional communications from Max Müller, were printed in *JTVI*.

And lest he be found culpable of some transgression against another person by the Lord who is 'coming quickly,' he was constantly concerned to ask forgiveness for any transgression against others: 'I desire to be found of Him in peace without spot & blameless.'[169]

-VII-

Already in the early 1700s Sir Isaac Newton had warned students of prophecy of the danger in becoming too enamored with inferences expositors drew from biblical texts. The great mathematician wrote of the 'folly of Interpreters [who] foretel times and things ... as if God designed to make them Prophets. By this rashness they have not only exposed themselves, but brought the Prophecy also into contempt.'[170]

Gosse, as we have seen, was aware of the danger and in complete agreement with Newton's point. 'The data, the premises, are divine, and therefore infallible,' Gosse said, 'the conclusions are merely human inferences, and therefore liable to error.'[171] He also recognized that if following the Divine plan was like reading a tramway schedule, what role was left for faith? As he put it, 'To be looking for manifest signs at every turn would be now to walk by sight instead of by faith.'[172] Yet that didn't mean to Gosse that Christians could slacken in watching for the Second Advent, or ignore signs marking the arc of history as it bent towards the End Days. 'I attempt not to guess the progress of events yet unfulfilled,' Gosse explained in 1870: 'Events of colossal magnitude seem to be developing day by day; but I will not conjecture these; though I keep my eyes open, and my heart heavenward, to watch what God shall unfold.'[173]

From his first reading of Habershon in 1842, Gosse had studied 'God's infallible almanack of prophetic history ... to see our place there.' During the Franco-Prussian War of 1870-1, some evangelicals avoided the subject. 'We do not meddle with politics,' editorialized the *British Messenger*,

169. PHG-Rev. Robert Govett, 16 Jan. 1872 (Corr. Bk.); PHG-EWG, 1 Mar. 1872 (Add. 7041, 50); PHG-Charles Bathurst Woodman, 7 Oct. 1875 (Corr. Bk.). Woodman was a Baptist minister (d. 1895: *Newcastle Weekly Courant*, 28 Mar. 1896, 3).

170. Quoted in Froom, *Prophetic Faith* II: 665-6. PHG cites Isaac Newton's *Observations on the Prophecies of Daniel* (1733) in his series on prophecy in *The Christian*, 9 June 1870, 6fn.

171. PHG, *Prophetic Times*, 21.

172. PHG, *Sacred Streams*, 38, and the following quotation, p. 51.

173. PHG, 'The Breaking of the Day', *The Christian* I (1 Sept. 1870), 394.

'we are afraid to speculate on unfulfilled prophecy.'[174] Not Gosse. He was avidly reading the *Illustrated London News*[175] and searching the pages of the London *Times*,[176] not in order to discover that one day some Christians had been reported as mysteriously missing but to discern correlations between predictions and accomplished events pointing to the approaching Time. That led him to be standing in expectation 'not only upon the toes, but, so to speak, upon the very tips of the toes.'[177]

Gosse was puzzled when no apocalyptic event occurred in 1866-7. In his unpublished autobiography, he recalled that from Thomas Scott's *Commentary* (1788-92),

> I learned to date the Millennium at 1866, or thereabout. That date is indeed past (I am writing these words Dec. 2. 1868); yet the signs of [the] times lead me to think, that the error of anticipation may not be very great. ... whether I shall be permitted to live to 1876, I know not, nor am anxious to know; since the blessed alternative has, through infinite grace, long ago been accomplished, and I, who was sometime far off, have been brought nigh & reconciled, by the Blood of Christ.[178]

Shortly after this, he began to reach out to other prophetic expositors to learn their thinking on the signs of the times. In 1870 he wrote James Whatman Bosanquet (1804-1877),[179] the treasurer and a financial supporter of the Society of Biblical Archaeology and author of *Messiah the Prince: Prophecies of Daniel* (1866); the Bishop of Lincoln (Christopher Wordsworth, 1807-85), whose *Babylon; or, the Question Examined, Is the Church of Rome the Babylon of the Apocalypse?* (1850; 3rd ed., 1856) was considered 'an unanswerable argument for an affirmative reply' to that query;[180] B. W. Savile (1817-1888), whose ideas on prophecy were

---

174. Editorial, 'The War', *British Messenger*, 1 Oct. 1870, 114.

175. These issues of the *Illustrated London News* are listed in *Sandhurst Catalogue*, item #620.

176. *Life*, 368; E. Charles Nelson, *Archives of Natural History*, 173, cites a letter from PHG published in *The Times* in 1867.

177. PHG, *Sacred Streams*, 51.

178. 'Reminiscences', I: 355, 369.

179. Corr. Bk., under 16 Feb. 1870 (I am assuming PHG's correspondence with 'Bosanquet' refers not to Samuel Richard Bosanquet, a member of the Victoria Institute in 1882, but to James Whatman Bosanquet, see Kirk, *A Supplement to Allibone's Critical Dictionary*, I: 180).

180. Exchange of letters with 'Bp. of Lincoln' is listed in Corr. Bk. under 19 Feb. and 4 Mar. 1870; for the evaluation of the book, H. G. Guinness, *The Approaching End of the Age*, 160.

favored by Gosse;[181] Edward Nangle (1799-1883), founder and editor
of the *Achill Missionary Herald*,[182] an historicist and anti-Catholic
polemicist;[183] and Horatius Bonar (1808-1889), editor of the *Quarterly
Journal of Prophecy*.[184] Gosse was a subscriber to Bonar's journal,[185] and
his correspondence may have related to an article by him which Bonar
published.[186]

Gosse also contacted the venerable Edward Bishop Elliott, then nearly
77, whose *Horae Apocalypticae* on the Book of Revelation had been
recognized as an instant classic when it appeared in 1844.[187] It marked
'the high point of the historicist tradition in British Evangelicalism,'[188]
and Gosse turned to it because he considered it 'beyond all praise as a
guide to prophetic interpretation.'[189] We don't know exactly what Gosse
wrote to other students of prophecy, but we do know what he wrote
Elliott. A rough copy of his 5 March 1870 letter has survived, loosely
inserted in the Correspondence Book in which Gosse listed all letters
sent and received from 1869 to his death in 1888. With this letter, Gosse
included several 'little brochures' on religious subjects.[190] His question
to Elliott was an obvious one:

181. Corr. Bk., May 12, 20, 24, 1870, *et. seq.* cite only 'Savile'. If this does refer to B. W. Savile
(and not Frederick Alexander Savile, a Victoria Institute member from 1871-1907), the exchanges
might have dealt with matters relating to prophecy, or possibly to the Victoria Institute, of which
PHG and BWS (from 1870-6) were members.

182. Corr. Bk. Mar. 2, 9, 10,14, 1870, etc. cite only 'Nangle'.

183. 'For thirty years the *Achill [Missionary] Herald* has been an uncompromising advocate of
the great principles of the Reformation, as embodied in the Articles and Liturgy of the Established
Church, in opposition to Popery, Ritualism, Infidelity, and the manifold errors of Darbyism, in all
its conflicting phases' (*Achill Missionary Herald*, 12 Mar. 1867, 453). Nangle did not sympathize
'with Mr. Gosse in the peculiar views of the body with which he is connected', but did recommend
PHG's *Revelation* (Nangle, letter to the editor dated 12 Dec. 1866, *Christian Observer* 66 (Jan.
1867), 80). *The Revelation* was favourably reviewed in the *Achill Missionary Herald* XXIX (11
Dec. 1866), 411, and XXX (8 Jan. 1867), 434-5.

184. PHG-Horatius Bonar, 19 Jan. 1871 'with [PHG's pamphlets] Rev[elation]n + [Great]
Tribul[atio]n'; HB-PHG, 19 Jan. 1871 ('Bonar'); and 3 Jan. 1885, 'Dr. Bonar' (all Corr. Bk.).

185. PHG had 9 volumes of *Quarterly Journal of Prophecy* in his library (*Sandhurst
Catalogue, item* #539).

186. PHG, 'The Prophetic Times', *Quarterly Journal of Prophecy* XXIII (Apr. 1871), 138-58
(for additional information: Freeman & Wertheimer-PHG, 124).

187. Review, *Christian Lady's Magazine* XXI (Apr. 1844), 372-3.

188. Spence, *Heaven on Earth*, 61.

189. PHG, *6000 Years*, 6fn.

190. PHG included with the letter to Elliott four of his works: *Geology or God; Which?; The
Revelation; 6000 Years of the World's History*; and *The Great Tribulation*.

Permit one, who, though a stranger to you in person, has been for nearly
30 [years] an earnest student of Divine Prophecy, & for the greater part
of that time had had the fullest communion with you in spirit through
your admirable Horae, & Warburton Lecture,—to trouble you with a brief
inquiry, which I am confident ... you will pardon. Often & often, since
the issue of your 5th edition [of the *Horae Apocalypticae* in 1862][191] as
the days have seemed more & more to be closing-in, & especially since
the long expected year 1866 has come, & gone,—& yet our adorable Lord
Jesus delays his appearing,—have I said to myself,—'How I should like
to know Mr. E's thoughts about the times!' & I have eagerly watched
the book-advertisements to see your honoured name once more—but
in vain.[192]

Though Elliott's reply to Gosse has not been traced,[193] it seems likely
he responded with a preview of his *Postscript to the Preface of the Horae
Apocalypticae: on the Expiration of the 1260 Years of Papal Dominion.*
This pamphlet, first published in 1875,[194] apparently reappeared as an
Appendix dated September 1868 and May 1871 in *The Last Prophecy*
(an abridgement of *Horae Apocalypticae* published in 1884 by Elliott's
wife).[195] In the section dated 1868, Elliott confirmed that *yes*, 'the great
New Testament prophetic period of the 1260 years' had been completed
and that *yes*, it had expired, just as he and others had claimed was evident
from a proper reading of the texts.[196] The new discovery was that the

191. PHG owned a copy of Elliott's *Horae Apocalypticae*, 4vols., which likely would have
been the 5ed, published in 1862 (*Sandhurst Catalogue,* item #572).

192. PHG-E. B. Elliott, 5 Mar. 1870 (Corr. Bk.). I have silently filled in the abbreviated words
in this copy of PHG's letter, the ellipsis is in the original. Although this could be a draft of PHG's
letter, I believe it to be a copy.

193. The letter is listed in Corr. Bk.: E. B. Elliott-PHG, 8 Mar. 1870.

194. Advertisement, London *Standard* (29 May 1875), 4 (under the heading: 'New Books and
Recent Editions. This column is restricted to books of the last three months'). I have not seen
this pamphlet except as Appendix I of H.E.E., *The Last Prophecy*, 365-71.

195. H[arriette].E[mily].E[lliott]., *The Last Prophecy: being An Abridgment of the late Rev.
E. B. Elliott's Horae Apocalypticae. To Which is Subjoined His Last Paper on Prophecy Fulfilled
and Fulfilling* (London: James Nisbet & Co., 3ed., 1884), 365-371. 'H.E.E.', the author of *Last
Prophecy*, is identified in an anonymous letter in the *Hampshire Telegraph and Naval Chronicle*
(12 Jan. 1884), 3: '... I have caused a book called the 'Last Prophecy', being an abridgment of
the late E. B. Elliott's 'Hora[e] Apocalypticae', by his widow, to be republished by James Nisbet'.
Harriette Emily (*née* Steele) was Elliott's second wife. They were married in 1835 (London *Times*,
27 Oct. 1835, 4; *Sheffield and Rotherham Independent*, 7 Nov. 1835, 3). 'Harriette' is sometimes
spelled 'Harriett'.

196. H.E.E[lliott]., *The Last Prophecy: Being an Abridgment of the late Rev. E. B. Elliott's
Horae Apocalypticae*, 365-7.

seventy-five years of the Book of Daniel 12 remained unfulfilled.[197] That pushed the second advent to 1941 (1866 + 75 = 1941).

Elliott had become a 'continuationist'. In modern psychological parlance, he had met the challenge of cognitive dissonance.[198] The result: there was no reason to despair. The lesson learned: past terminal dates had intentionally been made to appear real, 'to excite and keep up that lively expectation of his coming as near at hand.'[199] Looking ahead, Elliott's recalculation pushed the crucial year beyond his lifetime and far into the future[200]—as was common among historicists from the 1870s.[201]

Gosse's inquiries coincided with more prophetic outpourings from his pen. All of these new publications affirmed his historicist stance. A letter early in 1870 to the prominent evangelical publication *The Christian*, chiding it for remaining silent on the 'signs of the times', was followed by a series of twenty-four articles appearing over six months on 'The Breaking of the Day', solicited by R. C. Morgan, the weekly's editor and Gosse's friend.[202] Assuming the correctness of historicism (proof of that proposition Gosse believed had already been given in *The Revelation*), he performed the same task *in extenso* which he had undertaken in his 1843 article in the *Christian Lady's Magazine*. Only now he thought that the signs were clearer.

Tracing events from the French Revolution,[203] Gosse interpreted the symbols of the Apocalypse and pointed to the signs heralding the Son of Man. The three 'frog-like demons' (Rev. XVI:13-14)—the Dragon, the

197. H.E.E[lliott]., *The Last Prophecy: Being an Abridgment of the late Rev. E. B. Elliott's Horae Apocalypticae*, 369.

198. Festinger, Riecken and Schachter, *When Prophecy Fails*, 25-30.

199. H.E.E[lliott]., *The Last Prophecy: Being an Abridgment of the late Rev. E. B. Elliott's Horae Apocalypticae*, 371.

200. For Elliott's 'continuationism': E. B. Elliott, 'Counter-retrospect', *Christian Observer* 68 (Dec. 1868), 945-9, esp. 948-9; Froom, *Prophetic Faith* III: 716-22, esp. 721-2. For a critique of the 'Counter-retrospect': Richard Chester, 'Is the Coming of the Lord to be Delayed?', *Voice Upon the Mountains* III (1 Nov., 1 Dec. 1869), 141-2, 166-7.

201. Sears, 'The Interpretation of Prophecy and Expectations of the End in Britain', 291, asserts (without demonstrating) this point.

202. PHG, 'Signs of the Times', *The Christian* I (24 Feb. 1870), 51-2; PHG, 'The Breaking of the Day', *Christian* I (10 Mar.-1 Sept. 1870), 75-394, *passim*. Corr. Bk. records an intensive correspondence between PHG and Morgan from Jan. 1870.

203. PHG characterized the French Revolution as 'inseparably connected with the insane & atheistic effort to change & forget every record of the past history of man; [?as] a piece with the renaming of the years, the months, the days; the abolition of everything sacred & venerable; the reduction of everything to a French-Revolution standard' (PHG-Robert McLachlan, 7 Feb. 1882, CUL Add. 7313,484-5). PHG's words, marked 'Private', were contained with a letter on scientific matters to McLachlan, 'As a Postscript to the preceding, which please tear-off, when read'.

Beast, and the False Prophet—were defined as atheistic lawlessness, Popery, and sacerdotalism or ritualism. One of the great prophetic periods (the 'Seven Times') was analysed at length, with its full termination not later than 1871.[204] Also held up as significant were the great European upheavals of the age, the restoration of the Jews to Palestine,[205] foreign and home gospel missions, the decline and imminent fall of 'the false, foul, idolatrous, cursing, blood-thirsty, sumptuous, greedy, arrogant, blasphemous Papal Church,'[206] the increasing 'number of Perverts made to Popery of late years,' and the sequent threat to Great Britain as 'the chief seat of the true Church of God.'[207] Gosse set 'Negro slavery'—'that dreadful engine of God's providence and man's covetous cruelty'—within his prophetic system. In forcibly extracting an estimated 4.5 million of 'Africa's children' from that continent and bringing them to the Gospel, 'the curse itself ... [had] in a multitude of cases, been turned into a blessing,' Gosse said, thus matching a prophetic prediction about the worldwide preaching of the gospel.[208]

'Nothing seems left to be fulfilled,' Gosse warned, 'but the awful end.'[209] And in a passage which seems to echo (among other things) Elliott's continuationist outlook, he observed:

> ... he who postpones his preparation till he sees Signs which shall force themselves on his unwilling attention, will wait in vain, and be found sleeping. God has been pleased to announce the future, mainly enwrapped in symbol and enigma, so as not to interfere unduly with human freedom, and so as to keep his faithful people in an attitude of expectation throughout the long delay. ...

204. PHG, 'The Breaking of the Day' (18 Aug. 1870), 368-70.

205. PHG did not write extensively on this subject, important as it was to prophetic expositors, perhaps because he felt 'great difficulty in reducing to intelligible order and consistency' the main body of predictions (PHG, 'Breaking of the Day', *The Christian*, 5 May 1870, 184-5). PHG thought his views unorthodox, in that he expected a sudden restoration, coincidental with the rapture of the Church. See PHG, 'Testimony of Prophecy' (under 'The Restoration of Israel', some of which is reprinted verbatim in 'Breaking of the Day'); and the full version (seen in the Family Collection) of his PHG's *History of the Jews*, 471-85. This distinguished PHG from the influential dispensationalist views of J. N. Darby, who believed that the rapture of the Church would ignite cataclysmic events, including the return of Jews to Zion (David S. Yoon, 'The Restored Jewish State And the Revived Roman Empire: The Transmutation of John Nelson Darby's Dispensationalism into Modern Christian Zionism' (UCLA, PhD dissertation, 2010), 143).

206. PHG, 'The Breaking of the Day' (31 Mar. 1870), 115.

207. PHG, 'The Breaking of the Day' (30 June 1870), 285.

208. PHG, 'The Breaking of the Day' (2 June 1870, 238; 1 Sept. 1870, 393).

209. PHG, 'The Breaking of the Day' (17 Mar. 1870), 93.

... I look to the descent of the Lord Jesus into the air ... To this most blessed consummation my eyes are bent; on Himself my hopes are set;— on Himself, not on evolving events. ... I earnestly desire to stir up the hearts of His own ... The least dim indication, the feeblest probability, that He is near, ought to send a joyful thrill through our hearts. It ought; but alas! it does not.[210]

Gosse had gone to considerable effort in preparing the 24-part series in *The Christian*. His composition of some 55,000 words was 'truly a labour of love,'[211] and Morgan himself was pleased with the work.[212] Some readers, however, told Gosse they could see 'nothing but evil in my attempt,'[213] while others complained to Morgan that *The Christian* had only provided room in its pages for an exposition of the historicist schema.[214] That objection was met when Morgan invited a futurist and postmillennialist to argue their positions. Richard Chester (who opposed Gosse in 1866 articles in *The Rainbow*, as discussed) wrote nine essays on 'The Coming Kingdom'.[215] The Revd David Brown (1803-1897), once a premillennialist[216] and later considered 'the champion of post-millennialism'[217] and 'the most capable critic of premillennial teaching in the mid-nineteenth century,'[218] dealt in eight articles with 'The Blessed Hope.'[219] Brown, Principal of the Free Church College, Aberdeen, had been an assistant of Edward Irving's and an attendee at one of the Albury Park Conferences. Unlike the case with Gosse, his series was not original, derived almost verbatim from two existing works.[220]

210. PHG, 'The Breaking of the Day' (1 Sept. 1870), 394.

211. PHG, 'The Breaking of the Day' (1 Sept. 1870), 393.

212. George E. Morgan, *Veteran in Revival: R. C. Morgan*, 259-60.

213. PHG, 'The Breaking of the Day' (1 Sept. 1870), 393.

214. PHG-R. C. Morgan, 30 Mar. 1870; PHG-Bishop S. A. Crowther, 7 May 1870; PHG-Rev. Dr John Ludwig Krapf, 6 Mar. 1870; PHG-Pastor Ansorge, Berlin, 24 May 1870 (all Corr. Bk.); 'To Our Readers', *Christian* I (7 Apr. 1870), 129.

215. *The Christian* I (8 Sept. to 3 Nov. 1870), 403-502, *passim*.

216. William Garden Blaikie, *David Brown D.D., LL.D.: Professor and Principal of the Free Church College, Aberdeen. A Memoir* (London: Hodder and Stoughton, 1898), 89; Bebbington, *Evangelicalism in Modern Britain*, 84-5.

217. William Kelly, *The Second Advent of Christ Premillennial: A Reply to the Rev. D. Brown, D.D.* (Glasgow: R.L. Allan, 1868), [9]; Pietsch, *Dispensational Modernism*, 159.

218. Bebbington, writing in Spence, *Heaven on Earth*, ix.

219. D. Brown, 'The Blessed Hope', *The Christian* (10 Nov. 1870-5 Jan. 1871).

220. The two works were D. Brown, *The Restoration of the Jews* (Edinburgh, 1861), 212-23, and Brown, *Christ's Second Coming: Will it be Premillennial?* (Edinburgh, 1843, 6ed., 1867), 273ff. On Brown: Blaikie, *David Brown*, 32-94, and Kelly, *The Second Advent of Christ Premillennial*, 9. Brown was later attacked by James H. Brookes in America, one of the principle

In 1871 Gosse added a 24-page supplement to his *Christian* papers titled *The Prophetic Times*. It was his last published work on this subject. He occasionally enclosed copies of his pamphlets in letters he wrote from at least 1870 to 1877, and *Prophetic Times* was the one he most frequently sent.[221] That work gave to each prophetic period an 'incipient' and 'mature' (or 'complete') realization, and one of them ('a time no longer') was expected to be fully elapsed by no later than October 1877.[222]

Gosse kept his eye on the signs of the times during the first years of the 1870s, and became increasingly apprehensive as time passed. He was on edge during 1876.[223] He was anxious during 1877.[224] In 1880, he wrote his brother Tom, then 64 years old:

> There is one question in my letter which you do not notice: I repeat it. Are you in accepted fellowship with any part of the Church of God? I have an indistinct recollection that, a good many years ago, you met with believers known simply as Brethren; & I think in communication with them. I never knew why you left them. I have solemn fears, dear Tom, that God may have a controversy with you. ... I am expecting the advent of the Lord for his waiting ones, very immediately;—and Eternity cannot be far from either you or me, even if He do *not* come as I hope. Satisfy my anxieties on this point,—your preparedness for Him.[225]

So Philip was watching, as he believed he must. Yet what was the point if those whom he loved failed to act likewise, through inadvertence or

premillennialist writers there (Pietsch, *Dispensational Modernism*, 103-4; Wilt, 'Premillennialism in America, 1865-1919', 40-1).

221. Based upon my analysis of Corr. Bk. for these years, the pamphlets sent (in order of frequency) were: *Prophetic Times*; *High Numbers of the Pentateuch*; *Revelation*; *Great Tribulation* and *Geology or God*; and the *Christian* series. There is no record in Corr. Bk. of PHG's including one of his religious works with a letter after he sent a copy of *High Numbers* to 'Todd' on 22 Sept. 1877.

222. PHG, *The Prophetic Times*, 15-16, 21. PHG's calculation was based upon the lapsing of 'a time' (360 years) from 31 October 1517, the date on which Luther pinned his theses on the Church door at Wittenberg, regarded as having launched the Reformation. This is explained in PHG-George Pearse, 12 Dec. 1880 (CUL Add. 7313, 252-3).

223. PHG-EWG, 3 Jan. 1876 (CUL Add. 7018, 73).

224. PHG-George Pearse, 12 Dec. 1880 (CUL Add. 7313, 252-3); PHG-EWG, 3 Jan. 1876 (CUL Add. 7018, 73).

225. PHG-Tom Gosse, 2 Aug. 1880 (CUL Add. 7313,165-6). Emphasis in the original. TG was then living in Bath, an active Brethren location since the early 1830s (Grass, *Gathering to His Name*, 50-1), expanding thereafter (letter to the editor, Thomas Hamilton, *Bath Chronicle*, 15 Jan. 1846, 3).

indecision or error? What would become of them? That's why he wrote his brother. That's why he worried: *What will become of my beloved son?*

Father and Son

CHAPTER TEN

1857-1868

Born for Immortality

-I-

'LET EVERY READER THEREFORE PONDER this undoubted truth,' Emily Gosse wrote in the introduction to her book on child-rearing, 'that there is no responsibility committed to man on the earth, so great as that which has been placed in the hands of parents.' For all parents, this involves 'influencing, for good or evil, a being born but yesterday'; for the religiously minded, there is the additional responsibility to guide the child 'born for immortality'.[1] Two years after these words were written, Emily was dead. The formidable duty to which she drew attention now rested with her husband.[2]

For the first few years after 1857, Edmund was under his father's care and that of housekeeper Sarah Andrews. He apparently had few playmates—Benny Jeffries, who lived several doors down from Sandhurst, was an exception[3]—and so his main companion was his father. In fact, he became his father's understudy. When Philip returned one day from visiting Kent's Cavern in Torquay with geologist William Pengelly and others, for instance, Edmund—who Pengelly described as 'a nice

---

1. Emily Gosse, *Abraham and His Children*, x.
2. On the transmission of Godly traits from generation to generation, *Father and Son*, 1907, 226-8. In the following two chapters I have attempted to reconstruct the father and son relations during 1857-75, relying on original printed and manuscript materials from that period. I do not cite all the instances in which this version differs from EWG's accounts. For details: D. Wertheimer, 'A Son and His Father', 45-92.
3. See the entry under 'Benny' in Wertheimer, *Identification*, 4.

boy'[4]—was there. When Philip was preparing his work on sea anemones, Edmund would sometimes go dredging or searching tide-pools with him. In June 1858, the junior naturalist's 'keen and well-practised eye' detected a new species of anemone, the 'walled corklet'.[5] As his father was preparing *Actinologia Britannica*, 'Edmund William Gosse FRS' was writing and illustrating his own *History of the British Sea Anemones and Corals* (only unlike his father's single volume, this was a double-decker). His son drew coloured images of sea anemones and marine creatures and grouped them 'after his own ideas of affinity,' and his father left him in charge of their aquarium when he was away—maintaining it and observing its inhabitants.[6]

Works were not limited to seashore studies. There was *A Manual of British Lepidoptera* (c. November 1858), apparently appearing in the same year as *Zoological Sketches Consisting of Descriptions and Engravings of Animals* (that work was thoughtfully dedicated to his father, 'with the Author's very best love').[7] In 1860 other works issued from this fertile pen, including an *Analysis of the Families of British Butterflies* (3 parts, 100 pages) and *A History of British Ferns* (89 pages).[8] As an author, young Edmund William was hardly less prolific than his mentor.

When left to himself, Willy (his familiar name) never had trouble occupying his time. During these years he read scientific works,[9] and when his father was away from home on a lecture tour, he spent long hours in the greenhouse or out-of-doors. His letters to his father were full of questions about, and illustrations of, what he saw.[10] If he somehow

---

4. Mrs Pengelly-her mother, Mar. 1859, in Pengelly, *A Memoir of William Pengelly*, 81.

5. PHG, *Actinologia Britannica*, 137. *Father and Son*, 1907, 160, incorrectly dates the event to 1859.

6. PHG-C. Kingsley, 5 Jan. 1872 (a copy of the letter in Corr. Bk.).

7. All of these are at LeBL. There is a signed, post-1907 covering note in Edmund's holograph stating that *Zoological Sketches* 'was produced without any help or encouragement from any one.' At least one section of the work on butterflies is endorsed by PHG: 'Begun 6th Nov. 1858, Fin. 12 Nov. 1858'.

8. The first MS, dated 15 June 1860, contains extracts from the *Zoologist* with plates coloured by EWG (seen in the Family Collection). The other work contains plates drawn by the author and dated Oct. 1860, and is modelled on the format of PHG's *Actinologia Britannica* (LeBL).

9. EWG's copy of Samuel P. Woodward's *A Manual of the Mollusca* (London, 1851) is at LeBL. It is inscribed by him: 'I had this book when I was eight years old (1857) and for a long time it was my favourite possession.' Woodward (1821-1865), whose *Mollusca* was a 'class-book on the subject', worked in the Natural History Department of the British Museum (Cowtan, *Memories of the British Museum*, 356-7; Boase III: 1492).

10. EWG-PHG, 3 Apr. 1858 (CUL Add. 7027, 27) and other letters in CUL Add. 7027.

'fell into sin,' Miss Andrews knew the punishment which fit the crime: he was 'not to go into the greenhouse, or to see the animals.'[11]

Perhaps it was on such occasions that he took to writing poetry. Even before he turned 8 and they had moved to Sandhurst he had composed a few 'small scraps in rhyme' and a poem entitled 'The Battle Between a Swan & Two Eagles.' In 1858, Edmund commenced 'The Loss of the Erebus & Terror' (it remained unfinished).[12] Another juvenile piece, 'Lessons for Stray Hours', reflected the environment his father was creating and Miss Andrews was overseeing. One of the questions in this catechism was 'What is a *Man*?', with the faithful response: 'A Mammal, which is civilized, and stands erect, he has a soul.'[13]

It was the last of these characteristics which was now of most direct relevance to Edmund. A soul may be an integral element in defining a person, but what is it that makes a Christian? For Victorian evangelicals, critical factors are the acknowledgement that one is born in a fallen state and that redemption is only possible through the atoning work of Christ. The true realization of these facts is considered a gift and act of God, whereby one gains through a new birth a new life. The mechanism which confirms this response is the sacrament of baptism.

Who is eligible for baptism, and at what stage in one's life is it administered? To Open Brethren, with whom Philip identified, the answer was (and is) that baptism is administered to those who make a personal confession of faith in Christ.[14] Adults could make that conscious personal response—what about a child? Whether adult or child, would the act of baptism have a transcendent meaning? Should it imply an obligation on the one baptised?

Raising these issues only draws attention to the fact that there is no universally accepted understanding of baptism. Unless clarified, misunderstanding is likely to follow.[15] That appears to have been the case with Edmund. In the Christian community in which he was raised,

---

11. Sarah Andrews-PHG, 2 Apr. 1858 (CUL Adv. c. 82.5, 57).

12. EWG, [untitled MS hereafter *Early Writing Career*], LeBL (with a covering initialled note by EWG, 4 July 1909. The MS bears the date 'May 1866', probably added in 1909). The *Erebus* and *Terror* were ships of Sir John Franklin's expedition of 1845 to discover the Northwest Passage. They were abandoned three years later.

13. EWG, 'Lessons for Stray Hours', undated (British Library, Ashley MSS 5721). Emphasis in the original.

14. Bruce, *Who are the Brethren?*, 7.

15. For a discussion on interpreting baptism: Coad, *Brethren Movement*, 275-80.

child baptism was a natural experience,[16] and even though he recalled no precise moment of conversion,[17] the event may have occurred quietly, and been real. Looking back years after the event, the sacrament symbolized to Edmund the culmination of a 'Great Scheme' on the part of his parents who, in dedicating him to the Lord, thereby placed the burden of Christ forever on his shoulders.[18] But his father—in accord with Brethren opinion generally[19]—was consistent throughout his life in placing a different construction on the event. Philip taught that baptism was the mystical symbol of death, burial, and resurrection, the 'rehearsal of the great work for which He came into the world.' The symbol itself, in his understanding, had no transformative spiritual value. It placed no burden upon the one baptised.[20] As Philip would explain to his son:

> I cannot concur with you in your thoughts about baptizing children, nor in your regret that yourself [*sic*] was enabled to confess your union with Christ so young. Of course all depends on the *reality*, the *truth*, of such confession. If you had *really* accepted Christ as your Saviour then, you were *really* united to Him in His penal death, & in His resurrection; & was it not right to avow this? You speak as if some heavy burden had been laid upon you, to which your youth was unequal; but, assuming that your faith, (although a *child's* faith), was real, your *new life* was real, & the indwelling Holy Ghost in you was real. The public avowal of this,—whatever your after experience,—was, I am sure, a source of strength; not of weakness. You do not, I hope, look on baptism as a

16. In the 19th Century Brethren assembly at Bearwood in Birmingham, England, Jean M. Johnson found that no baptisms of children under 15 are known to have taken place. She thus concludes that EWG's baptism at the age of 10 'was unusually early' (Johnson, 'Brethren in Bearwood: The Earliest Days', in Dickson and Grass, eds., *Growth of the Brethren Movement*, 100). That may well have been the case for that assembly, but it is not hard to cite counter examples (notwithstanding EWG's claims concerning his child baptism in *Father and Son*, 1907, 209-217). The 1872 baptism of the four Bewes children—aged 9-14—is discussed here later. Three daughters of Henry W. Soltau, a friend of PHG's, were baptised at the ages of 10, 11, and 12 (Mildred Cable and Francesca French, *A Woman who Laughed*, 38). In modern times, Patricia Beer (d. 1999), brought up in a Brethren household, was baptised when she was 12 (Beer, *Mrs Beer's House* (London: Macmillan, 1968), 141-5).

17. *Father and Son*, 1907, 229, 205.

18. Wertheimer, 'A Son and His Father', 60-66, argues that surviving documents do not support EWG's claim about a dramatic 'Great Scheme'.

19. Bebbington, *Dominance of Evangelicalism*, 158.

20. 'To ascribe to the mere performance of the [baptism] rite upon the body, a spiritual change of the most stupendous character, in the person so treated, is not only without any real support from Scripture, but quite contrary to all its teaching' (PHG, *Mysteries of God*, 72).

vowing or promising to do any thing,—an aspect wholly unwarranted by Holy Scripture:—it is, "an answer," an avowal, "of a conscience, good toward God, through the resurrection of Jesus Christ."—as [1] Peter iii.21, describes it. The baptized one, dramatically, in a sort of *tableau vivant*, makes this declaration. "Christ was buried under the floods of God's wrath as the punishment of sin. But He stood as *substitute for me*, therefore it was *I* that was so slain & buried. He was raised again, by God Himself, in token that the sin was wholly removed from God's judicial sight. But He stood as *substitute for me*; therefore it was *I* that was justified, on the ground of that axiom in Rom. vi. 7, "He that has died is justified from sin"; [See Greek] [*sic*]—viz. by having exhausted the penalty. And this I openly confess.[21]

It was apparently just after Edmund turned 10-years-old that he was guided by his father into a public confession of Christ as his personal Saviour. After an examination by members of the Marychurch Brethren, the transformation was judged heartfelt and genuine. At the time, public baptisms for an individual adult or a group of adults were commonly attended by others.[22] Whether child baptisms were similarly witnessed is unknown, but Edmund later claimed that because of his youth, his baptism attracted unusual, widespread attention.[23]

As we have seen, Thomas Gosse had undergone an evangelical conversion on 22 July 1790; Philip had 'closed with Him' in 1832; on 12 October 1859, under the supervision of Philip's friend and colleague Leonard Strong, a third generation of Gosses entered into new life. The

21. PHG-EWG, 6 Jan 1873 (CUL Add. 7041, 56). Emphasis in the original. PHG's understanding of the meaning of baptism remained constant from at least 1850: PHG, *Sacred Streams* (1850), 221-4; PHG's note in *Bible-Readers Journal*, no. 19 (1 July 1860), 430; and PHG, *Mysteries of God*, 1884, chap. VI and 70, 72.

22. I have found Brethren baptisms occasionally documented in newspaper reports between 1841-69. Scarborough, North Yorkshire: Rebecca Tindall baptized by John Howard of Tottenham (*Leeds Mercury*, 9 Oct. 1841, 7); Dartmouth: unstated number of people baptised (*Trewman's Exeter Flying Post*, 8 July 1858, 5); Exmouth: 11 men and women baptised (*Trewman's Exeter Flying Post*, 22 Aug. 1860, 7); Crediton: unstated number (Barnstaple *North Devon Journal*, 27 June 1867, 8); Poole: 6 people (Yeovil *Western Gazette*, 19 Mar. 1869, 8).

23. *Father and Son*, 1907, 209-16. 'Those were days when newspaper enterprise was scarcely in its infancy, and the [baptism] event owed nothing to journalistic effort. In spite of that, the news of this remarkable ceremony, the immersion of a little boy of ten years old "as an adult", had spread far and wide through the county' (p. 211). I searched unsuccessfully for a mention of EWG's baptism in the *Torquay Directory* for 1859 and 1860.

event took place at the Brethren's Warren Road Room in nearby Torquay, where Strong was the leader.[24]

-II-

Around July 1860 Edmund contracted whooping cough and, a change of air being recommended, Philip took him in the middle of the month on a trip to Dartmoor and the primeval oakwood of Wistman's Wood.[25] Shortly after their return, Edmund was enrolled in the 'Classical, Mathematical, & Commercial' day school of Nicholas T. Menneer (1833-1903)[26] at Trafalgar Villa in St. Marychurch.[27] This young Penzance-born principal had been preparing students for the Oxford and Cambridge exams first at Sydney House in Torquay as early as 1857, and later that year in St. Marychurch.[28] In the early 1860s there was more than one preparatory school in St. Marychurch and environs,[29] and it seems plausible that Gosse was influenced to send his son to Menneer's school by his friend the Revd J. E. Gladstone, who had a son at Menneer's.[30] Edmund would spend two-and-a-half years at Montvidere House (to which Menneer

24. According to EWG's account, he was baptised on the date given above, shortly after his tenth birthday (*Father and Son*, 1907, 210). For the place of the event: Wertheimer, *Identification*, 9. In PHG-EWG, 6 Jan. 1873 (CUL Add. 7041,56) it is stated that EWG was 'eleven years old' at that time, which would put the event to 1860. I have been unable to uncover any conclusive evidence in favour of one or the other of these possibly contradictory statements. Other references to the event provide no clarification (CUL Add, 7041, 30, and Stedman, 'Some London Poets' (1882), 877). It could be that PHG meant that EWG was in his eleventh *year*, i.e., 1859. This date seems more probable for the reason stated in *Father and Son*, 1907, 210, that the baptism took place in Torquay because the St. Marychurch Brethren lacked the proper facilities. They did not move to the more commodious Room on Fore Street until 9 July 1860 (*Life*, 356).

25. PHG, 'Dartmoor and the Dart', *Intellectual Observer* III (June 1863), 318, and for the year of the excursion: PHG-Rev. J. B. Paton (editor of the *Eclectic Review*), 8 Aug. 1860 (Wellcome Historical Medical Library).

26. For Menneer and his school: Wertheimer, *Identification*, 7-8. The surname is frequently misspelled 'Meneer' (including in Wertheimer, *Identification*); for the correct spelling: letter to the editor from F. B. Menneer, 'Mr. G. C. Menneer', *Torquay Herald and Express*, 21 Mar. 1929, 8. For biographical details: 'Death of Mr. N. T. Menneer', Penzance *Cornishman*, 26 Mar. 1903, 2; and *1871 Census Returns for Torquay [St. Marychurch]* (Enumeration District 10, RG 10/2087). Statements about Menneer and his school in *Father and Son*, 1907, 240-6 (where he is referred to as 'Mr. M.') are mostly inaccurate.

27. Wertheimer, *Identification*, 7.

28. Advertisements, Exeter *Western Times*, 4 July 1857, 8; and 24 Sept. 1862, 4.

29. For H. N. Madden's school at St. Marychurch: *Trewman's Exeter Flying Post*, 3 July 1861, 8.

30. F. E. Gladstone, a son of J. E. Gladstone, was at Menneer's school (Truro *West Briton and Cornwall Advertiser*, 20 Aug. 1858, 3); on the PHG-Gladstone friendship: *Life*, 355. *Father and Son*, 1907, 240, does not mention Gladstone, but says Menneer had 'begged [PHG] for the favour of a visit' concerning his school. Both scenarios could be correct.

had moved in 1861)[31] with seventeen pupils, ranging in age from 9 to 16 years old (but mainly around age 13).[32] Here Edmund studied English composition, Greek and classics, history, geography, drawing,[33] and probably also natural philosophy and Scriptures.

Before the spring holidays in June and in December 1862 he took the public examinations. Edmund's own progress was certainly creditable if not outstanding. In the former exam he placed first in the school in history and geography, third in classics, and also received a prize in mathematics.[34] In the Cambridge University Local Examination in December, when Edmund was 13, he obtained third class honours for students under 16.[35]

During his holidays and free periods, Edmund continued to expand his intellectual horizons. He began to read general literature (even past bound volumes of the London literary weekly, *The Athenaeum*),[36] and taught at the Marychurch Sunday school;[37] on one of his walks between Montvidere and Sandhurst he apparently met the retired and newly converted dramatist James Sheridan Knowles (1784-1862), whose arrival in Torquay had caused a public stir.[38] During the summer break from school in 1861-2 his stepmother, Eliza, took him on one trip to see her relatives in Norfolk and another to visit once again Dartmoor and the surrounding area.[39]

It was just after Edmund returned from the December Cambridge examination that his father decided to withdraw him from Montvidere. This action might seem strange considering that Philip had the highest regard not only for Menneer's teaching abilities but also for the way in

31. Advertisement, Exeter *Western Times*, 4 July 1857, 8. Charteris, 12, mistranscribed the name from a letter as 'Mt. Veden' (Wertheimer, *Identification*, 7).

32. *1871 Census Returns for Torquay* (as cited).

33. The drawing master was Mr. Dames (PHG-EWG, 12 July 1875; CUL Add. 7019,16), the father of Mansell Dames.

34. *Torquay Directory*, 18 June 1862, 5; for his study of Greek in 1862: PHG-W. J. Hooker, 22 July 1862 (Kew, *English Letters*, XLI: 350), and for his fondness for geography: *Father and Son*, 1907, 231.

35. *Torquay Directory*, 18 Feb. 1863, 5; Exeter *Western Times*, 19 Feb. 1863, 1.

36. Edmund Gosse, 'Readers and Reviewers', *Athenaeum*, Jan. 1916, 9 (referring to 3 bound volumes of the *Athenaeum*; *Sandhurst Catalogue*, item #610, lists 2 volumes).

37. *Father and Son*, 1907, 265-6.

38. Wertheimer, *Identification*, 7. Knowles was a friend of William Pengelly, whom he visited in Nov. 1861 (Pengelly, *Memoir of William Pengelly*, 115).

39. For the visit to Norfolk in 1861: EWG, 'Earlham', in *More Books on the Table* (London: William Heinemann Ltd., 1923), 189-91; and to Dartmoor in 1862: PHG-W. J. Hooker, 16 Aug. 1862 (Kew, *English Letters* XLI: 347).

which he was able to win 'the love & confidence of his pupils.' 'Yet there is one thing which I greatly desire for Willy, who is wanting at Mt. Videre,' Philip wrote Menneer at the end of 1862:

> A converted child himself, he needs spiritual companionship, & this he does not meet with. He does not find one boy who is of the slightest help to him spiritually. You may say, he ought to stand out for Christ + give the tone to the school. Perhaps he ought; but he does not. He lacks the courage; his spirits are high; he loves play as much as any; + he is carried away by the general tone, which, without being morally evil, is *earthly*. With his youth, + his subordinate position in the school, I do not see well how it c[ou]ld be otherwise. But we think we discern the result in the deteriorations—or at least the dulling—of his spiritual life.
>
> Now I had rather see him a warm devoted man of God than the brightest scholar or the most successful businessman in the world. And this I seek for him, whatever sacrifice it may involve. ...
>
> I know a school in wh[ich] a good number of the older boys are converted to God, + among whom there is a recognized Xtian circle whose influence is manifest for blessing. I think if Willy were among them, he would be in a nursery for his soul. ... I am anxious ... to assure you that what I have told you is not only the *true* reason, *but the only reason* for my withdrawing him. ... I shall tell all who may be interested in knowing, + you may safely do so too, that my purpose does not in any way diminish my estimate—my very high appretiation [*sic*] of you as an able, faithful, successful + most kind preceptor.
>
> I may say, moreover, that it is sorely against Willy's desire, to be removed; he w[ou]ld desire no other master than you.[40]

The new school which Philip had found was the 'boarding and day school for gentlemen' run by Thomas Edgelow (1802/3-1875)[41] and his wife, located at Thorn Park, Coombe Vale, in the neighbouring seaport town of Teignmouth.[42] Like Menneer, the Edgelows were experienced school proprietors—Edgelow's school had been in existence at least since

40. Copy of a letter not in PHG's holograph, PHG-N. Menneer, 23 Dec. 1862 (CUL Add. 7024, 41). Emphasis in the original.

41. Edgelow: 'Deaths', London *Morning Post*, 1 July 1875, 8; Exeter *Western Times*, 2 July 1875, 8.

42. Wertheimer, *Identification*, 5-6.

1858. Unlike Menneer, the Edgelows were Brethren.[43] When Edmund enrolled there (probably in January 1863), two of Leonard Strong's sons—Robert Dundas (three years older than Edmund) and James (one year older)—were already in attendance (years later, Robert, then a lawyer, married Edgelow's daughter, Caroline).[44] In a letter to Thomas Edgelow, Philip agreed to the annual tuition (including board) of £50, and emphasized:

> I want W[illy]'s *soul* to prosper, above all things else; ... I beseech you, & yr dear wife, occasionally to say a word to his heart & conscience *in private*. It is my desire that his talents may be hereafter used in the Lord's service; & I w[ou]ld have his studies & his fellowships, all to be ancillary to this object.[45]

Edmund spent the next three years at Thorn Park, studying (among other things) French, Latin,[46] and continuing with Greek. But whether he enjoyed himself, or whether his soul prospered, is difficult to tell.[47] His father, who now only saw him on weekends, could bring him to religious conventions—such as the one at Freemasons Hall on prophecy in May 1864[48]—but otherwise he had to hope that the changed atmosphere was having its effect. As far as his studies were concerned, Edgelow thought that his 'extreme forgetfulness' was a pronounced and uncorrected fault.[49]

43. EWG's claim that the Edgelows were Brethren (*Father and Son*, 1907, 302) would seem to be confirmed by the salutation PHG used in a letter, 'Mr d[ea]r Brother' (PHG-T. Edgelow, 20 Jan. 1863. CUL Add. 7018,39. In another letter, however, PHG addressed him 'Dear Sir', PHG-T. Edgelow, 31 Jan. 1866, CUL Add. 7027,56. Both letters are copies, not in PHG's holograph). It would also seem to be supported by the fact that Leonard Strong's son Robert married Edgelow's daughter, Caroline (see next footnote below). Brethren had a meeting room in Teignmouth from at least 1837-8 (Grass, *Gathering to His Name*, xix, 42). In 1858, it was on Bitton Street (*Teignmouth Gazette*, 3 Jan. 1858, 7). For a negative account of Edgelow's exploitation of one of his teachers: T. C. F. Stunt, 'The *Via Media* of Guicciardini's Closest Collaborator, Teodorico Pietrocola Rossetti', in L. Giorgi and M. Rubboli (eds.), *Piero Guicciardini 1808-1886: un Riformatore religioso nell'Europa dell'ottocento* (Florence: Olschki, 1988), 142-3, 151-2.

44. 'Marriages', *Exeter and Plymouth Gazette* (31 Dec. 1869), 5.

45. Copy of a letter, PHG-T. Edgelow, 20 Jan. 1863 (CUL Add. 7018,39). Emphasis in the original.

46. EWG's copy of *Q. Horatii Flacci. Opera Omnia* (1865), seen in the Family Collection, bears the inscription: 'Out of this little book ... I read Horace at school nearly 40 years ago. E. G. Oct. 1904'.

47. In *Father and Son*, 1907, 312-317, EWG wrote that his years at Edgelow's were lonely and unhappy. In an earlier recollection, he claimed that he found 'congenial sports and comrades.' (Edmund C. Stedman, 'Some London Poets' (1882), 878).

48. Wertheimer, *Identification*, 10-11.

49. T. Edgelow-PHG, 14 June 1864 (CUL Add. 7027, 44).

Otherwise he showed annual improvement. Edmund stood eighth in the second examination of the 1864 school year (having moved up one position from the previous exam), took Junior First Class honours in the Cambridge Local exam of December 1864,[50] Senior First Class honours in 1865[51] (third for all of England in English, fifth for German),[52] and in 1866 received a Senior Candidate prize for passing exams in Scripture, English history, Latin, Greek, French, German, and Zoology. He was also awarded a certificate for 'Pope's Works' and Homer's *Illiad* and *Odyssey*.[53]

It was a month after Edmund's sixteenth birthday that Philip began thinking about an occupation for him. From what we know, Philip did not believe that his son must become a missionary or minister in order to be 'used in the Lord's service', as his son later thought.[54] To Philip, there were many ways to serve.[55]

Late in October 1865, Philip enlisted the assistance of his friend, the Revd Charles Kingsley, in finding a job for Edmund.[56] Kingsley contacted his relative, Theodore Walrond, an Examiner to the Civil Service Commission, who suggested to Kingsley that young Gosse try for the position of 'Junior Assistant' at the British Museum. The examination was non-competitive and modest (writing, spelling, elementary mathematics, and a knowledge of an ancient or modern language), and it 'is one of the few places in the Civil Service at all worth having, which are open to a youth of 17.' The pay, to be sure, was poor, and promotion slow, but an individual with literary and scientific tastes might at least keep

50. 'University Intelligence', London *Standard*, 3 Feb. 1865, 3.

51. *Exeter and Plymouth Gazette*, 9 Feb. 1866, 5.

52. Copy of a letter, PHG–J. Winter Jones (Principal Librarian, British Museum), 10 Sept. 1866 (CUL Add. 7027, 66).

53. 'Oxford and Cambridge Local Examinations', Exeter *Western Times*, 21 Sept. 1866, 8; 'Cambridge', *Exeter and Plymouth Gazette*, 21 Sept. 1866, 6.

54. Compare EWG's claim that 'I cannot recollect the time when I did not understand that I was going to be a minister of the Gospel' (*Father and Son*, 1907, 31) with his 1875 statement that 'I was brought up to be a naturalist' (Wertheimer, 'A Son and His Father', 75fn.75).

55. 'If it is service you really want, the Master will do it. But remember, service must be of His choosing, not yours. I think you a little misunderstood Mamma's observations. ... she was not spurring you to go out as a missionary to the heathen; she alluded to Missions as a sphere of legitimate interest. But there are other ways of serving Christ besides missions & hymn-writing: though I doubt if He would own modern fashionable poetry as one' (PHG–EWG, 1 Feb. 1868, CUL Add. 7041,9).

56. C. Kingsley–PHG, 31 Oct. 1865. There are 17 more letters from Kingsley–PHG on this subject in Add. MSS. 7027.

those interests alive there.[57] Kingsley told Philip he thought it a perfect fit.[58] Moreover, it was an attainable position because Kingsley knew the Museum Trustees responsible for the nomination—the Lord Chancellor (Lord Cranworth, Robert Monsey Rolfe); the Speaker of the House of Commons (John Evelyn Denison); and the Archbishop of Canterbury (Revd Charles Thomas Longley).[59]

Another avenue of exploration led Philip to the Royal Gardens at Kew. This was a jarring misjudgment. By 1865, after all, Gosse had turned away from scientific work because of what he felt were the atheistic tendencies of its practitioners—and now he was turning to Joseph Hooker, Assistant Director at Kew,[60] to find suitable employment for his son? Surely he knew—or at the very least, suspected—that Hooker was in the Darwinian camp.[61] Yet he wrote his relative anyhow to ask if there was a position available, claiming that his son's 'predilections are scientific, & he is a boy of moral, honourable & gentlemanly principle, industrious, & trained to habitual obedience.' The latter characteristics may have been accurate, but *scientific predilections*? As it turned out, Hooker was not encouraging, so Philip dropped the subject. He acknowledged that in fact his son could not be called a botanist. Besides, the scale of remuneration was too low.[62] The request suggests panic on Philip's part, and is hard to fathom.

Philip thus had to return to Plan A, without doubt a fraught option. In the Great Metropolis, Edmund would be far away and out of sight. The 'sleazy nightside' of the city was only one of the undeniable enticements which could lure a 17-year-old in a dangerous direction. On the other hand, did not Philip himself have pleasant memories of his time spent at the British Museum some thirty years earlier? Would not the move do his

57. Copy of a letter, T. Walrond-C. Kingsley, 1 Nov. 1865 (CUL Add. 7027, 51); 'Theodore Walrond [1824-87]', London *Spectator* 60 (25 June 1887), 858-9; Boase III:1175; Walrond was married to Kingsley's niece Charlotte ([Frances E. Grenfell Kingsley] (ed.), *Charles Kingsley: His Letters and Memories of His Life* I: 487).

58. C. Kingsley-[PHG], 2 Nov. 1865 (CUL Add. 7027, 52).

59. PHG-T. Edgelow, 31 Jan. 1866 (CUL Add. 7027,56).

60. J. D. Hooker was Assistant Director at Kew during his father's directorship (*Gardeners' Chronicle*, 2 Sept. 1865, 819), and succeeded him following his death (*Gardeners' Chronicle*, 23 Sept. 1865, 890).

61. J. D. Hooker was initially resistant to Darwinian evolution but became a convert in 1858: Bellon, 'Joseph Hooker', 216, 254-8. The introduction to Hooker's *Flora Tasmaniae* (1860) 'essentially proclaims his acceptance of evolutionary ideas and the theory of natural selection' (Turrill, *Joseph Dalton Hooker*, 93).

62. PHG-J. D. Hooker, November 1 and 8, 1865 (Kew, *English Letters* LXXXVII: 71, 75).

son good and expand his horizons, as had Philip's overseas trips while a young man? Could the Museum environment be so spiritually harmful? Moreover, if he associated Edmund with his Brethren acquaintances in the city, would that not counter any negative impact? Considered logically, the situation did seem to have its virtues.

On 28 November 1865, therefore, Edmund took the train to London to meet the Museum's Principal Librarian, Antonio Panizzi.[63] Kingsley introduced him. Panizzi told Edmund that a knowledge of modern European languages would be of great advantage in securing a position.

Soon after he returned to St. Marychurch, Philip wrote Edgelow of the new prospects. Henceforth, he wanted his son to concentrate on literature, languages, and developing a neat hand. Should Edmund get the appointment, Philip wrote Edgelow, he would be withdrawn from the school after his 17th birthday.[64]

During the ensuing nine months Edmund was thus put through a rigorous programme, acquiring an elementary knowledge of Italian, Hebrew, Danish, and Swedish, and progressing in Latin, Greek, German, and French.[65] His father's wish that he should also study literature had a marked effect upon his intellectual growth. Edmund became a voracious reader,[66] and for the first time since his poem 'Farewell' was written in 1860 he returned with sudden passion to the writing of poetry. At first Edmund composed under the inspiration of the poet Gray, until in the middle of March he began the poem 'Summer' (his first original effort). Other poems followed in a flood of inspiration, and included a morbid ballad, hexameter verse modelled after Kingsley's *Andromeda* (1858), a blank-verse comedy, a hymn, and a translation from Goethe (the last mentioned being made after a tooth had been extracted).[67]

63. PHG-J. Winter Jones, 10 Sept. 1866 (CUL Add. 7027, 66).

64. Copy of a letter, PHG-T. Edgelow, 31 Jan. 1866 (CUL Add. 7027, 56).

65. PHG-C. Kingsley, 18 June 1866, and PHG-J. Winter Jones, 10 Sept. 1866 (CUL Add. 7027, 58, 66). In his valuable work, Elias Bredsdorff incorrectly concludes that EWG could not have studied Swedish at this time because in 1871 he did not know or understand a word of Norwegian (*Sir Edmund Gosse's Correspondence with Scandinavian Writers* (Copenhagen: Scandinavian University Books, 1960), 1).

66. *Father and Son*, 1907, 335. One of the novels EWG recalled reading, perhaps at this time, was Hannah More's most popular work, *Coelebs in Search of a Wife* (1809): EWG, *Leaves and Fruit* (London: William Heinemann Ltd, 1927), 145.

67. EWG, *Early Writing Career*, pp. 1-[7]. *Father and Son* contains no mention of Gray, but claims that the muse came to him as a result of hearing his father read Virgil (1907, 185-7). At another time, EWG told PHG that his poetic power came in direct answer to prayer (PHG-EWG, 25 Oct. 1867, CUL Add. 7041, 8).

By the end of September 1866, following some further correspondence,[68] the position at the Museum must have seemed secured. Philip wrote to Miss Anne Buckham (b. 1810/11) in London to ask if Edmund might come to live with her. Perhaps Philip knew of her through her activities with Brethren; at any rate, she was pleased to have the young man as a boarder, and would charge one guinea per week, all inclusive.[69]

Edmund was finally nominated for the position of 'Junior Assistant or Transcriber' in the Department of Printed Books on 12 December. Later that month, on a 'dreary winter evening, my heart full of sorrowing love', Philip left him in London in his new home.[70]

-III-

Through an uncanny set of events, Edmund now found himself in circumstances paralleling those of his father in 1843. Both carried on work at the British Museum; both lived in north London. The distance which separated these two places also represented the two worlds in which they dwelled.

At 6 Tottenham Terrace, White Hart Lane, in Tottenham, Edmund lived with three unmarried women. Miss Buckham (the same age as his father) was the head of the household. She had been a member of the Committee of the Ladies' Chinese Association, a missionizing society.[71] An annuitant, Mary Ann Baker (1795/98-1884), who had commenced in 1844 a lifelong friendship with Anne Buckham, was also there. Baker had been converted in early life and knew many New Testament books by heart. Mary Daniels, the 50-year-old servant, completed the household.[72]

68. PHG-J. Winter Jones, 10 Sept. 1866 (CUL Add. 7027, 66); PHG-C. Kingsley, 18 June 1866 (CUL Add. 7027, 58); C. Kingsley-PHG, 18 Sept. 1866 (Princeton University, Morris L. Parrish Collection).

69. A. Buckham-PHG, 1 Oct. 1866 (CUL Add. 7024, 46).

70. PHG-EWG, 21 Jan. 1870 (CUL Add. 7042, 30); for the nomination: CUL Add. 7027, 73. *Life*, 360, and Edmund C. Stedman, 'Some London Poets' (1882), 878, confirm that PHG accompanied EWG to London in 1866. EWG inaccurately described the event in 1875, managing 4 errors in 27 words: 'In January 1867 [*sic*] I came to London alone to win my livelihood. I obtained a position to a junior post in the Library of the British Museum' (Bredsdorff, *Sir Edmund Gosse's Correspondence*, 82).

71. *Occasional Paper*, stuck in the British Library copy of the *Chinese Missionary Gleaner* II (Apr. 1857), between pp. 52-3.

72. *1871 Census Returns for Edmonton (Tottenham)*, Enumeration District 9, p. 29; [?PHG], 'In Memoriam [Miss Baker]', single sheet, [1884] (CUL Add. 7027, 49). This notice states that she died in her 89th year, but according to the *Census Returns*, she was 86. Freeman & Wertheimer-PHG, 86-7, doubt the notice about Miss Baker was by PHG.

One-and-a-half miles from Tottenham Terrace was Brook Street, and it was the Brethren Chapel there which they attended. Founded by John Eliot Howard (1807-1883), the quinologist and former Quaker, the Chapel was in existence when Philip Gosse had lived in London, dating to 1838. In 1849, the Tottenham Brethren got caught up in the controversy between Darby and leaders of Bethesda Chapel in Bristol, and broke with the former over the question of exclusion of believers from the Lord's Table.[73] They thus came to hold Open Brethren views.

Now Philip Gosse knew many of the members of this circle with whom Edmund came in contact. It was at the home of Robert Howard (1801-1871), John Eliot's older brother and partner in the pharmaceutical firm of Howard and Sons,[74] that Philip and Emily had married in 1848.[75] Mary Stacey (one of the oldest, if not the oldest, of this circle) knew Philip and Emily from 1856. In 1857, when she and Miss Buckham were members of the Committee of the Ladies' Chinese Association, Rachel Lloyd (Mrs Robert) Howard[76] of Bruce Grove was the treasurer, and Maria (Mrs John E.) Howard[77] of Lordship Lane, the secretary.[78] William Thomas Berger[79] played an outsize role in Philip Gosse's life, as earlier described, in introducing him to Brethren and corresponding with him while he was in Jamaica.[80] Other friends of his father who Edmund may not have

73. West, *From Friends to Brethren*, 13-14, 241.

74. The Howard and Sons partnership began in 1858 (West, *From Friends to Brethren*, 3, 31-2).

75. H. C. H[itchcock]., 'A Little of our History', *Brook St. Chapel, Tottenham Magazine* no. 4 (Nov.-Dec. 1962), 7-10 (I am grateful to F. Roy Coad for lending me this number); Coad, *Brethren Movement*, 159, 301; John M. Thomson, 'David Howard [obituary notice]', *Journal of the Chemical Society, Transactions* CXI (1917), 342-4; obituary notice of Robert Howard FCS, *J. Chem Soc.* 25 (1872), 349-50; Stunt, 'Early Brethren and the Society of Friends', 20-3. Mr. H. C. Hitchcock has informed me (*in litt.*, 27 Jan. 1974) that the records of Brook St. Chapel indicate that EWG was 'Received 19.1^{18}.68' at Brook Street. This evidently refers to his formal membership application, for he was certainly in contact with the circle from his arrival in London.

76. West, *From Friends to Brethren*, 257.

77. West, *From Friends to Brethren*, 13, 257.

78. *Occasional Paper* inserted in the *Chinese Missionary Gleaner* (as cited); in 1853, the Howard women held the same positions (*Chinese & General Missionary Gleaner* II, Mar. 1853, 80); Braithwaite, *Life & Letters of Pennefather*, 306; Stunt, *Early Brethren and the Society of Friends*, 21-2; *Life*, 262.

79. 'How charming the old town of East Grinstead is. I have found the house where I stayed in 1867, it is called Saint Hill. I remembered the name because the host was a Plymouth Brother friend of father's, and all the guests were 'saints'. My first 'weekend Party',—I remember how dismal it was. I have never been at E. Grinstead since' (Postcard of EWG-Nellie Gosse, 5 August 1917, CUL Add. 7025, 67). 'Saint Hill' was the name of W. T. Berger's home.

80. For Berger's address at Saint Hill at this time, see *The Christian*, 14 July 1870, 315; and *1871 Census Returns for East Grinstead (Sussex)*, Enumeration District 4, p. 5; an image

known in Tottenham were Charles Frearson Hargrove (who was not connected with the Tottenham band until a year before his death in 1869).[81]

At the British Museum, some three-and-a-half miles from Tottenham, the situation was quite unlike what Philip had remembered. The old guard had passed, or was passing: Adam White was gone, James Cates, the Superintendent of the Reading Room in 1839, had died in 1855, and by 1871 Marshall was superannuated and Robert Cowtan was publishing his *Memories of the British Museum*.[82]

On Thursday, 24 January 1867, Philip received the notice of Edmund's appointment to the Museum, and on the following day, or probably the next Monday, Edmund presented himself to Thomas Watts (1811-1869), the Keeper of Printed Books.[83] Edmund's duties were certainly monotonous, the conditions deplorable, and the salary of £90 hardly princely, but at first he did not seem to mind overmuch. At nine each morning he and fourteen of the other staff of the Transcribers began their work,[84] which continued until 4 o'clock. Ever since 1830 the Museum had employed people to copy the titles of all accessions to the Library in quadruplicate. As the Transcribers were not instructed to economize on space, the manuscript catalogue exploded from 250 volumes in 1850 to 2,250 in 1875.[85]

In these first years, even if Edmund's supervisors were tyrants, his companions were pleasant.[86] Working 'so infinitely underground that they were almost buried—in ill-lighted rooms with a smell of dry-rot,' they broke the tedium whenever possible. Playing cricket against the

of Saint Hill is in M. G. Guinness, *The Story of the China Inland Mission* (London: Morgan & Scott, 2vols., 1900), I: 228-9.

81. Hargrove died at Robert Howard's home (Robert Braithwaite, *Life & Letters of Rev. William Pennefather, B.A.* (London: John F. Shaw & Co., cheap edition, n.d.), 445-6).

82. PHG-EWG, 16 Nov. 1872 (CUL Add. 7041, 55). PHG and Cowtan exchanged letters, and PHG sent him an offprint of his Victoria Institute paper on 'The High numbers of the Pentateuch' (Corr. Bk., Dec. 8 and 10, 1872).

83. PHG-EWG, 24 Jan. 1867 (CUL Add. 7041, 3); J. Winter Jones-T. Watts, 25 Jan. 1867 (Dept. of Printed Books, British Library, Miscellaneous Departmental Reports, 1867, item 347, ff. 132-3); Edward Miller, *That Noble Cabinet. A History of the British Museum* (London: Andre Deutsch, 1973), 155 and fn., 284-6.

84. Charteris, 18-19.

85. Arundell Esdaile, *The British Museum Library* (London: George Allen & Unwin, Ltd., 1946), 133-5. The catalogue was not printed until 1880.

86. PHG-EWG, 18 Feb. 1867 (CUL Add. 7041, 6); Charteris, 19; Miller, *That Noble Cabinet*, 286.

door of the Principal Librarian was one of their occupations.[87] Edmund's fellow-clerks, as he later recalled, 'were a merry set of grown-up children, who looked upon life as a "lark", and the office as a benevolent institution for the encouragement of their giggling. With them he did a fair amount of work and perhaps an unfair amount of talking and laughing.'[88]

-IV-

With Edmund now some 200 miles from Sandhurst, father and son no longer had the opportunity for the occasional face-to-face weekend contact. Their sole form of communication was the written word. Relatively little of that correspondence survives, but what is available is a gripping record of how two loving people looked ahead from different images of their shared past toward a different anticipated future. These were writers gifted in expressing their emotions and sharing their ideas, and in reading their letters today one feels like an eavesdropper witnessing an unfolding drama.

During these first two years away from home, Philip's letters were full of counsel, admonition, and love. He wished his son to view him as his 'Guide, philosopher, & friend'.[89] He wanted to be known as 'The worthy father of a worthier son,' and thought of the dictum of Solomon, 'He that begetteth a wise child shall have joy of him.'[90] Edmund welcomed the guidance, responded to the advice, and matched love-for-love.

Philip was methodical. In replying to a letter, he had a plan. He wrote out his thoughts and then reviewed what his correspondent had written, 'ab initio, in order to see if I have omitted to notice anything. If so, I add my reply ... *unless I purposely pass it* over.'[91] This irritated Edmund. It made his father's communications disappointing, he later said, not from lack 'but from excess of care': 'his letters, even to the members of his own family, were often so stiff and sesquipedalian as to produce a repellent effect, which was the very last thing that he intended. Letters,

87. 'The British Museum Forty Years Ago. Mr. Gosse's Reminiscences', London *Daily Graphic*, 11 Oct. 1906, 10.

88. EWG, 'Tristram Jones. Fragment of an Autobiographical Romance' (CUL Add. 2768/15), 25.

89. PHG-EWG, 8 Feb. 1868 (CUL Add. 7041, 10); and 20 Aug. 1868 (Add. 7018, 11).

90. PHG-EWG, 18 Feb. 1867 (CUL Add. 7041, 6); 20 Nov. 1868 (Add. 7018, 21); Proverbs 23: 24 (KJV).

91. PHG-EWG, 25 Feb. 1867 (CUL Add. 7018, 2). Emphasis in the original.

to be delightful, must be chatty, artless, irregular; anything of obvious design in their composition is fatal to their charm.'[92]

Philip sent his son violets,[93] headed one letter 'Fili mi dilectissime' ('My dearest son'), and ended another: 'I throw the arms of my love around you.' Edmund was 'my own sweet darling,' 'My beloved Son,' 'My darling Child,' 'My dearly beloved Boy.' He himself was 'Your tender loving Father,' and Philip and Eliza had an 'ever bubbling-over ... fountain of love in our hearts towards you.' Wrote Philip: 'I do delight to discern the simplicity of your child-like love to us; your Mamma & I often say to each other with congratulations, that our dear boy is not at all changed by his manhood, except that his love is tenderer and deeper.'[94]

When Philip heard 'terrible accounts' of a relative who was Edmund's contemporary, he was 'heartily thankful ... for the love & grace & goodness of my own beloved boy.'[95] And, writing just ten years after 'your own beloved sainted mother commended you with her dying breath to the care of her faithful covenant God,' Philip mused: 'If she can look down & see you now, I think she adoringly owns that her prayers have been answered.'[96]

Edmund responded in kind. No sooner did his father write him of a severe sore throat, than his son began intercessory prayers for him.[97] Edmund reminded his father that 'your letters are like angel visits to me, and ... if you should out of the overflowing of your heart give me a long epistle, it will be the better taste of the 'all-too-precious you' that I cannot personally chatter to.'[98]

There were problems and misconstructions—that was inevitable and unavoidable. Philip was aware that he was a 'somewhat critical' father. He knew that he was 'anxious, perhaps nervous & fidgetty,' about Edmund's welfare. 'Forgive the nuisance, for the sake of the love,'[99] he said. Philip hoped that given his intent, Edmund did not 'feel ashamed, as if I had imputed fault.'[100]

92. *Life*, 343.
93. EWG, *Journal*, 28 Nov. 1868.
94. PHG-EWG, 25 Oct. 1867 (CUL Add. 7041, 8).
95. PHG-EWG, 1 Mar. 1867 (CUL Add. 7018, 3).
96. PHG-EWG, 1 Mar. 1867 (CUL Add. 7018, 3).
97. PHG-EWG, 4 and 20 Aug. 1868 (CUL Add. 7027, 75; Add. 7018, 11).
98. EWG, *Journal*, 12 Aug. 1868.
99. PHG-EWG, 20 Nov. 1868 (CUL Add. 7018,21).
100. PHG-EWG, 11 Feb. 1867 (CUL Add. 7018, 1).

Have my letters made your heart ache, my precious boy, with the
impression that I expected you to try to crush or slight me? How strange
that my style should be so obscure as to convey an impression, towards
which I have never felt the most distant approach! My solicitude has
never been that you should not love *me* (of that I have had no doubt),
but that you should not love *God*. The times are *very* dark; I cannot help
seeing the abounding evil, the rapidly increasing insolence of infidelity;
& my love makes me warn you. Do not accuse me of being sepulchral in
my tones, because I am hortatory. Who should give a child holy counsel,
but a father?[101]

Years later, Edmund called their correspondence from those days
a 'postal inquisition'. Our memory can play tricks on us. Edmund
remembered that no sooner had he settled in London than letters reached
him from Sandhurst 'almost daily,' with answers required by return
post.[102] To be sure, Edmund was not the only one to chaff under what
could be Philip's pestering—his brother William said the same thing.[103]
Nonetheless E. P. Wright, admittedly not a family member but a colleague
of Philip's, specifically objected to Edmund's claim that his father's letters
were disappointing.[104]

As to a constant flood of inquisitions emanating from Philip, from
the perspective of decades perhaps that is how it seemed. As it turns
out, data exists on the subject. We know that the state of affairs was
not as Edmund recalled. While no authoritative inventory exists of the
number of father-son letters during 1867-8, from April 1869 until shortly
before his death Philip kept a Correspondence Book in which he listed
almost every letter he wrote or received—some 15,000 in all. For every
year between 1869-75, Edmund wrote his father more letters than he
himself received (averaging for this period thirty-three letters per year
from Philip, and forty-six from Edmund).[105]

101. PHG-EWG, 25 Oct. 1867 (CUL Add. 7041,8). Emphasis in the original.
102. *Father and Son*, 1907, Epilogue, 346.
103. '... a British Messenger came this even[in]g. I can't move or turn without being haunted
& dunn'd with Henry's papers to the annoyance & trouble of various other persons—this meddling
officiousness is quite disagreeable—I don't want his papers nor this authoritative thrusting them
upon me—unasked, & quite unasked for—let him mind his own affairs' (William Gosse, Diary
under 8 Mar. 1857).
104. E. P. W[right], review of *Life*, *Nature* XLIII (30 Apr. 1891), 606. PHG and Wright
corresponded at least in 1877; see Corr. Bk. under Jan. 22, 27, 1877.
105. The following is the number of letters listed in the Correspondence Book (with the

Today, an onlooker reading the father-son exchanges winces at the sharpness and insistence of Philip's queries. No matter how well intentioned, one wishes that the father would have acknowledged in his heart that 'we have to allow our children the space to be themselves if we are to be good parents.'[106] Perhaps his inflexibility forced Edmund into evasive, opaque, even dishonest responses. One feels sympathy with both men as they confronted profound personal matters.

-V-

During Edmund's first two years in London his relations with his father were more than satisfactory. Philip's thoughts of arriving in Newfoundland as a 17-year-old prompted him to share some of the things he had learned there.[107] Edmund should get a code of etiquette (his brother William had given him one on setting foot in the colony).[108] Edmund should keep a record of his correspondence. He should be frugal. He should set aside savings (his father committed to doubling whatever amount he saved).[109] From time to time, Philip pointed out orthographic or stylistic errors in his letters.[110]

After touching on practical matters, Philip invariably turned to asking about his son's spiritual state. Here are some ways in which he did that in early 1867:

[January 30]

Remember my counsel of being chary of yielding your intimacy, until you know that the persons seeking it are safe & worthy. And don't be afraid of letting it be known that you are Christ's. Show your colours.[111]

number of those surviving given in parenthesis): 1869: from PHG, 23 (7); from EWG, 42 (nil); 1870: PHG, 61 (17); EWG, 86 (2); 1871: PHG, 28 (2); EWG, 43 (2); 1872: PHG, 32 (7); EWG, 40 (3); 1873: PHG, 32 (2); EWG, 36 (5); 1874: PHG, 34 (3); EWG, 44 (11); 1875: PHG, 22 (2); EWG, 28 (4). Seven year total: from PHG, 232 (40); from EWG, 319 (27) For the year 1867, 9 letters survive from PHG, 2 from EWG; for 1868, 37 from PHG, 2 from EWG. I have found very few letters to or from PHG which are not listed in Corr. Bk.

106. Jonathan Sacks, *Studies in Spirituality. A Weekly Reading of the Jewish Bible* (New Milford, CT: Maggid Books, 2021), 19.

107. PHG-EWG, 5 Feb. 1868 (CUL Add. 7041, 5).

108. PHG-EWG, 11 Feb. 1867 (CUL Add. 7018, 1).

109. PHG-EWG, 18 Feb. 1867 (CUL Add. 7041, 6); PHG-EWG, 24 Jan. 1867 (CUL Add. 7041, 3), and 11 Feb. 1867 (CUL Add. 7018, 1).

110. E.g., PHG-EWG, 18 Feb., 1 Mar. 1867 (CUL Add. 7018, 3); PHG continued the habit throughout his life.

111. PHG-EWG, 30 Jan. 1867 (CUL Add. 7041, 4); for the same advice, PHG-EWG, 25 Feb.

[February 5]

I am glad you enjoy the Lords days. From what I remember I used
rather to prefer Mr. J.E. H[oward] to his brother, Robert; but both
are instructive. Glad, too, you have a S[unday] S[chool] class to your
mind. ... My fatherly love has never been anything like so strong since
you have been in London. You are very constantly on my heart in prayer,
& this no doubt augments love. And your manifest love to us, & your
filial demeanour all commend you to my heart. Let me know that you are
walking in the truth, & that your heart is right with God; & all is well.[112]

[February 18]

I am glad you like your companions: tell me plainly, is the conversation
such as you can listen to without defilement? I do not mean, Is it
other than secular? This I could not expect; political, metaphysical,
argumentative, jocose, bantering,—all this it might be, of course; but
tell me whether it is lascivious. If you would rather, you may write
your answer on a separate scrap of paper, & it shall meet no eye but
mine, nor shall the subject be mentioned to anyone else. I can do this
now, as Mamma is from home. I know what office talk was when I was
young; & I am jealous, as a father for my son. ... Do you get any spiritual
companionship with any of the young men there? ... Do you find the
ministry of the Word pleasant; &, above all, profitable? ... The Coming
of the Lord draweth night.[113]

During these early years, Edmund was trying to live up to the high
Christian ideals he had embraced at his conversion. His declaration
in one letter that he fully intended to be on the Lord's side was 'just
what I have been wanting,' his father responded.[114] 'Oh! I thank God I
have a praying son.'[115] Although Edmund was at first hesitant to speak
at prayer meetings, it appears that others could tell that he was among
the converted.[116] In the summer of 1868 Edmund met another junior

1867 (CUL Add. 7018, 2).
   112. PHG-EWG, 5 Feb. 1867 (CUL Add. 7041, 5).
   113. PHG-EWG, 18 Feb. 1867 (CUL Add. 7041, 6).
   114. PHG-EWG, 25 Oct. 1867 (CUL Add. 7041, 8).
   115. PHG-EWG, 20 Aug. 1868 (CUL Add. 7018, 11).
   116. PHG-EWG, 1 Mar. 1867 (CUL Add. 7018, 3); PHG-EWG, 3 Mar. 1868 (CUL Add. 7041, 4).
EWG used to take part orally in prayer while a student. For EWG's religious fervour at this time:

assistant at work, a Nonconformist (not a member of the Brethren) some eight years older than himself, Charles Albert Legh Walker.[117] He wrote his father that he found 'Charlie's' companionship spiritually profitable.[118] They went together to hear the Presbyterian minister Adolph Saphir (1831-1891), a converted Jew, speak at Great Marlborough Street on 'Romanism & Rationalism' later that winter. It was only 'profound and Elegant', not interesting.[119]

A few months after he had arrived in London Edmund began thinking of conducting one of the Brook Street Sunday School classes, as he had done at St. Marychurch. Within a year he was leading one, and enjoying the experience. Attendance was good. 'I have the interest of these unfledged souls very earnestly upon me,' he wrote on 13 December 1868 in his *Journal*, which he sent to his father. 'Lately I have been much led to pray for grace to lay the heart-truth rather than the head-truth before them. Pray for me in this.'[120] At the Sunday School he would address his pupils for as much as half-an-hour; at his second address of 1868 he spoke on the biblical Joseph.

> The children were very attentive, and answered the incidental questions I put to them, with very pleasing alacrity. I drew as well as I could the typical portrait of Christ as shadowed in Joseph and wound up with a short declaration of the gospel. We then sang a hymn, and I concluded with a few words of prayer.[121]

While he was teaching, he was also learning. He attended Bible-reading meetings along with Messrs Robert Howard, Heath, Hargrove, 'Brother Mary Stacey', and others.[122] On his own initiative he studied the Book of Ezekiel, and found 'a wonderful sweep of withering satire in the

George C. Williamson, 'Edmund Gosse as a Boy: A Reminiscence', *London Mercury* XVIII (1928), 633-5. If Williamson's memory can be trusted, statements on p. 634 date the incidents to 1866-7.

117. Walker remained for a number of year at the British Museum, eventually being promoted from junior to senior assistant (London *Morning Post*, 5 Apr. 1876, 6).

118. PHG-EWG, 12 Oct. 1868 (CUL Add. 7018, 18). Walker was 27 on 6 Aug. 1868 (EWG's *Journal*, 6 Aug.1868). Walker later visited Sandhurst (PHG-EWG, 11 May 1869, CUL Add. 7041,25). Letters between PHG-Walker for 1869-70 are listed in Corr. Bk.

119. EWG, *Journal*, 26 Nov. 1868. There are entries in Corr. Bk. for 'Saphir' (e.g., 8, 13 Dec. 1887). On Saphir: '*The Christian' Portrait Gallery*, 327-9.

120. PHG-EWG, 5 Feb. 1867 (as cited); PHG-EWG, 22 Feb. 1868 (CUL Add. 7041, 13); EWG, *Journal*, 26 July, 20 Sept., 22 Nov., 13 Dec. 1868; and PHG-EWG, 8 Aug. 1868 (CUL Add. 7018, 10).

121. EWG, *Journal*, 29 November 1868.

122. EWG, *Journal*, 18 November, 1 Dec. 1868.

early chapters wh[ich] I think we often miss, as we do so much else in
the Scriptures, by reading it in fragments.'[123] On another occasion, after
everyone at Tottenham Terrace had gone to bed, he stayed up to study
the First Epistle to the Thessalonians, while 'praying with my heart full
of yearning love for those dear people under whose roof I was sleeping,
and for you [his father], as I hoped, just got to rest after your arduous
day of service.'[124]

But it was above all the Young Men's Prayer Meetings at Brook Street
which Edmund found most impressive. When his father warned him
that perhaps all of his activities at Brook Street after Museum hours
were exhausting him, Edmund agreed he should reduce them. Not these
Prayer Meetings: 'to me [they are] the most vital of all ... 'the spirit,
truly, is willing, but the flesh is weak.'"[125] Earlier, he had brought two
teenage boys with him to a Meeting: 'On the way I took the opportunity
of speaking a little to them for their eternal welfare. It was quite a small
meeting, only 12 present, and of these the only unconverted were my
two friends. I prayed all the more earnestly as having in them a personal
interest, and we sang at my request "Nearer, my God, to thee." I hope
these meetings will be sustained; they are very healthful to my soul.'[126]
The two boys (aged 18 and 14) ceased to attend within a month, and
Edmund was disheartened at the small turnout (apparently never more
than about a dozen people). Indeed, he could hardly blame the boys for
not returning. The meetings were 'dull as dull can be for those who have
no vital interest in its exercises' yet 'I do thank God for putting the idea
of them into somebody's brain.'[127]

During 1867-8 Edmund's religious activities were not limited to
being present at lectures and prayer meetings, teaching at Sunday
school, participating in Bible readings and the like. He also visited the
Howards and knew well Robert's son, Theodore (1837-1914),[128] who
was active at Brook Street. Theodore was later to gain a reputation as

123. EWG, *Journal*, 14 November 1868.
124. EWG, *Journal*, 12 August 1868.
125. EWG, *Journal*, 21 Nov. 1868, and PHG-EWG, 20 Nov. 1868 (CUL Add. 7018, 21).
126. EWG, *Journal*, 12 November 1868.
127. EWG, *Journal*, 10 Dec. 1868, and 3 Dec. 1868: 'I wish more persons would be induced
to attend: you would smile to hear us sing. We have neither ear nor voice, but like Mr. Curtis,
we sing out with a will'.
128. M[arshall]. B[roomhall]., 'In Loving Memory of Mr. Theodore Howard', *China's Millions*,
51-2; West, *From Friends to Brethren*, 257.

the Home Director of the China Inland Mission,[129] following his uncle, John Eliot Howard, 'one of the oldest friends' of the Mission.[130] Edmund dined on occasion at Mary Stacey's,[131] who had known his mother. In February 1867 he went to hear the wildly in-demand Congregationalist preacher, Newman Hall (1816-1902). Edmund may have been present as ministers (including Hall) preached simultaneously in London on how to encourage the working class to attend church.[132] Edmund also apparently attended one of the Revd William Pennefather's Mildmay Conferences in November 1868.[133]

Edmund's involvement with the man who gained fame as the founder of Barnardo's Homes was around 1868. Thomas J. Barnardo (1845-1905), inspired by J. Hudson Taylor (1832-1905) to become a missionary to China, had moved from Dublin to London in April 1866. But he changed his mind about his career path, and turned instead towards the unconverted in London with 'Important Ragged School Work in the East End'.[134] With that goal in mind, he enlisted the voluntary help of forty or fifty 'earnest Evangelical Brethren and sisters'. Edmund was a natural for the task. He had tagged along as a child with his mother when she went among the poor; he had participated in prayer meetings, taught Sunday School and young men; he had effectively led others towards belief (as exemplified by a Mr Anderson, who, in his dying moments, mentioned Edmund by name).[135] An added bonus: Barnardo had aligned with Open Brethren in both Dublin and at Sidney Street, Stepney,[136] and maintained

129. EWG, *Journal*, 19 July, 22 Nov., 3 Dec. 1868; Guinness, *Story of the China Inland Mission*, I: 454-5. In 1884 Theodore Howard was Chairman of the Council of the CIM (*China's Million's* IX (Aug. 1884), 108). He was known as a 'life-long friend of the Mission' (Dr & Mrs H. Taylor, *Hudson Taylor and the China Inland Mission* (1918), 318).

130. The characterization is by J. Hudson Taylor, in M[arshall]. B[roomhall]., 'In Loving Memory of Mr. Theodore Howard', *China's Millions*, 51.

131. EWG, *Journal*, 13 December 1868.

132. PHG-EWG, 1 Mar. 1867 (CUL Add. 7018, 3) notes that EWG heard the Revd Hall speak, without further details. On Christopher Newman Hall's speech of Sunday, Feb. 24: *Pall Mall Gazette*, 25 Feb. 1867, 7; on the 21 Jan. 'Conference of the Clergy and the Working Classes in London' to 'ascertain, if possible, the reasons why so many of the latter do not attend either church or chapel': *Glasgow Daily Herald*, 22 Jan. 1867, 3; and London *Daily News*, 22 Jan. 1867, 3.

133. PHG-EWG, 12 Oct. 1868 (Add. 7018, 18).

134. *The Revival*, 25 July 1867, 411-12.

135. EWG, *Journal*, 15 June 1868, and PHG-EWG, 29 July 1868 (CUL Add. 7018, 9).

136. On Barnardo: J. Wesley Bready, *Doctor Barnardo. Physician, Pioneer, Prophet* (London: George Allen & Unwin Ltd, 1930, 3rd impression, 1932), 55-67, 92-7; Grass, *Gathering to His Name*, 245; Coad, *Brethren Movement*, 171, 179-80, 305; T. C. F. Stunt, 'Thomas Barnardo: The Man and the Myth', *The Harvester* (Oct. 1979), 279-82; and Barnardo's early articles in *The Revival*, 'The Gospel in the East End', 29 Oct. 1868, 599-600; 'East-End Juvenile Mission',

462 Philip Henry Gosse

millenarian views in the metropolis.[137] Notwithstanding this profile, Edmund felt unsuited for Barnardo's East-End Juvenile Mission and remained there only briefly. 'I did not make a success of it,' he recalled, 'the people intimidated me, which was fatal.'[138] Missionary service in China was not more appealing, even after Edmund heard Hudson Taylor speak on the subject in October 1871.[139]

Philip was naturally encouraging as his son strived for holiness. 'Your word,—"it is very hard indeed to walk with Christ,"' Philip said at the end of 1868,

> fills me with thankfulness; for I think it shews you are making a step in the ways of God. The secret of service is experience: you have begun to *serve* the Lord; well, his response to this effort is, his revealing to you somewhat more of your own heart, ... But do not be discouraged; if you were not *earnestly trying* to walk with Christ, you wd. not be conscious of any great difficulty in the matter. I solemnly assure you *I* find it as hard, *now*, after nearly 37 years' experience, to walk with God, as ever I did.[140]

The issues which proved most contentious at this time revolved around money, religion, and literature. Of these, the first was of least importance,

31 Dec. 1868, 727-8, and other reports. Barnardo sought the advice of the *Revival's* editor, R. C. Morgan (PHG's friend), when he began his work in London (H. Simonis, *The Street of Ink: An Intimate History of Journalism*. London: Cassell and Co., 1917, 305); PHG's Corr. Bk. lists letters to 'Bernardo' on 1 Mar. 1870, and to 'T. J. Barnardo', 10 Nov. 1870, and many other instances. EWG's recollection of his work with Barnardo in 1868 more likely took place between 1868-70. W. J. Nowell, Librarian of Dr Barnardo's, informed me (*in. litt.*) that very little material survives there for the period 1867-70. Additionally, it was customary for Barnardo to mention his many helpers without citing them by name. H. C. H[itchcock]., in 'A Little of our History', 8, states that Barnardo was baptised at Brook Street, while Brealey states this was done in Oct. 1862 in Dublin (Brealey, 47). There may be no contradiction.

137. Gillian Wagner, 'Dr. Barnardo and the Charity Organisation Society: A re-assessment of the Arbitration Case of 1877' (London School of Economics, PhD dissertation, 1977), 13.

138. The sole source for EWG's activity with Barnardo is the letter, EWG-Evan Charteris, 29 Sept. 1905, printed in Charteris, 293-5.

139. EWG-PHG, 24 Oct. 1871 (CUL Add. 7018, 47; printed in Charteris, 36-7). Corr. Bk. lists PHG-Hudson Taylor correspondence at least as early as 1872. Hudson Taylor, who founded the China Inland Mission (Griffith John, 'In Memoriam: The Rev. J. Hudson Taylor, M.R.C.S., F.R.G.S.', *China's Missions* n.s. XIII, Oct. 1905, 131) knew W. T. Berger, who was involved with the CIM for many years. He had met Theodore Howard in 1851 (M[arshall]. B[roomhall]., 'In Loving Memory of Mr. Theodore Howard', *China's Millions*, 51) or around 1853 (Taylor, *Hudson Taylor in Early Years*, 171fn). Hudson Taylor was also associated with Brook Street for a short time (Coad, *Brethren Movement*, 76), and ran one of the notable 'Brethren-influenced 'faith mission[s]' at around this time (Grass, *Gathering to His Name*, 245).

140. PHG-EWG, 14 Dec. 1868 (CUL Add. 7018, 23). Emphasis in the original.

although Edmund's low income at the Museum gave it a certain irregular prominence. Philip had advised Edmund to keep an account of his spending, but even though at first he regularly helped him with expenses (such as travelling to and from London and St. Marychurch), Edmund was hopelessly inept at balancing his books. 'I wish I could understand the money-matters,' went one letter at the end of 1868, after calculations had shown a high tailor's bill, 'but I get so puzzled and stupid when I hammer over my accounts. ... Do not be very angry. I am very humble and sorry. ... O dear Papa, I am so miserable. I did not expect ever to have to write you like this.'[141] Philip was comforting and told Edmund he need not be distressed.

The issue, however, persisted. Which got Edmund to thinking: Why did he have to pinch pennies when the family had plenty of money? Because, as his father remonstrated, he himself had known what it was like to have to live modestly. He had only the precarious income of £160 when Edmund was born in 1849, and his reputed wealth at Sandhurst was possible only because Eliza had an inheritance which he was allowed to use during her lifetime. Philip was echoing the words of Samuel Smiles's *Self-Help*, a spirit-of-the-age guide: 'Prudence, frugality, and good management are excellent artists for mending bad times.'[142] Though Edmund felt his father's decision to cease paying for his railway tickets was the result of pique, Philip saw it otherwise. By the beginning of 1870, Edmund's salary had increased by £30 to £120, with no additional expenses. 'When I reflect how many years of my life I passed with an income hardly reaching the half of yours [£120], & yet lived happily, & I humbly trust usefully,—I cannot think you have much to complain of in pecuniary matters.'[143]

141. EWG-PHG, 14 Dec. 1868 (CUL Add. 7018, 43), and PHG's reply, 18 Dec. 1868 (Add. 7018, 24); also EWG's letter, 13 Jan. 1868 (Add. 7018, 42).

142. Samuel Smiles, *Self-Help; with illustrations of Character and Conduct* (London: John Murray, 1859, 12th thousand 1860), 217, quoting 'Samuel Drew, the philosophical shoemaker'.

143. PHG-EWG, 21 Jan. 1870 (CUL Add. 7041, 30), and PHG-EWG, 1 Sept. 1879 (Add. 7018, 32). For some context: while a medical student around 1836, Edward Forbes lived on an annual 'liberal allowance from his father' of £120. In 1842 he was paid £100 a year as Professor of Botany at King's College, London, while at the same time earning £150 as curator of the Geological Society of London (George Wilson and Archibald Geikie, *Memoir of Edward Forbes, F.R.S.* (Cambridge and London: Macmillan and Co., 1861), 150 and 150fn., 324). In around 1859, Albert Günther made £200 cataloguing the fish collection at the British Museum (*ODNB*). By late 1854, T. H. Huxley was earning £700 a year (*ODNB*), and before he got married in 1855, he recalled that 'we agreed we would marry whenever we had £200 a year. Well, we have had more than twice that to begin upon.' In 1859, while earning £600 and expecting a gradual raise to £800, Huxley

In the religious sphere, it is hard not to feel that Edmund's upbringing left him ill-equipped to meet the challenges of life in London, even in his supportive environment there. He felt his father's 'almost exclusively doctrinal' training of him went over his head.[144] He was confused by some concepts. Take 'separation from the world', for example. Philip would remind him of the dictum, 'Love not the world, neither the things that are in the world. If any man love the world, the love of the Father is not in him' (1 John 2: 15). Well and good—but what did this look like in practice? Or another example: Edmund had grown up among Brethren who sought a return to essential Christian values. What of communion with other Christian believers? If it was not appropriate, why not? And if one could aspire to it, why remain among Brethren?

To point out these issues is not to impute faulty child-rearing practices to Philip. His challenge was to transmit to the next generation the belief system he had discovered for himself and later developed as a mature adult. He had to prepare his child to receive those values while teaching him why they are important, suitable to the child and worth preserving. This is an awesomely difficult task. There are no guarantees one will succeed. Parenting is never easy.

Initially, Edmund looked to his father for clarity. He asked him about 'Plymouth Brethren'—by which Philip understood that he meant the Darbyite or Exclusive section—and (as previously noted) Edmund was told that 'they please not God, and are contrary to all men' (1 Thessalonians 2: 15).[145] Nor did Philip consider himself identified with '"brethren"… as a distinctive body of Christians.'[146] What he meant by that was that he

---

commented: '... it is the greatest possible blessing to be paid at last, and to be free from all the abominable anxieties which attend a fluctuating income. I can tell you I have had a sufficiently hard fight of it' (Huxley (ed.), *Life and Letters of Thomas Henry Huxley* I: 233). In 1871, Huxley's income was £1,000 ([William M. White (ed.)], *Journals of Walter White*, 237).

Economic historians are circumspect about relating wages to class, but an income of £160 in mid-century London (especially with a family) would place one higher than a skilled worker (up to £73 per annum) and perhaps in the lower middle class (on the first, S. G. Checkland, *The Rise of Industrial Society in England 1815-1885* (London: Longman, 1964, 1971), 36, 232; on the second, Geoffrey Best, *Mid-Victorian Britain 1851-75* (London: Weidenfeld and Nicolson, 1971), 90). Judith Flanders says 'the prosperous middle class' could expect an annual income of £200-300 at about this time (Flanders, *Inside the Victorian Home*, 347).

144. *Father and Son*, 1907, 100.

145. PHG-EWG, 22 Feb. 1868 (CUL Add. 7041, 13).

146. PHG-EWG, 3 Mar. 1868 (CUL Add. 7041, 14). As previously noted, '... the denial that one is, or can be, 'Brethren' is still considered by some a mark of genuine Brethrenism' (West, *From Friends to Brethren*, 241).

preferred a non-sectarian vision (the 'Open Brethren,' a term only just then coming into use)[147] to that of 'Plymouth Brethren' (*i.e.*, Darbyite or 'Exclusive Brethren'). That's why Philip added that he was 'quite content' that Edmund 'should be under the teaching of the dear Messrs. Howard, & that you should call yourself a Baptist.'[148] So when Edmund told him that he attended other religious services, his father was unfazed. 'I am glad too that your evening food, at the Presbyterian Church, compensated for your unsatisfied hunger in the morning,' Philip wrote. 'Bear a word of counsel. Seek to make personal prejudices & dislikes (even though not unreasonable) quite subordinate, when anyone says, "I have a message from God unto thee!"'[149] The pronouncement carried a caveat:

> I see you are captivated with the Liturgy of the Ch. of England. "Our beautiful liturgy", is the common phrase; beautiful it confessedly is, as a composition; its sentences are faultless in structure, its cadences most musical; & if the object of the assembling of the Church of God were the gratification of a refined taste, surely this "beautiful Liturgy" would be a complete success. But is this worship? Is this the worship of the Redeemed & accepted Family, within the Holiest? ... You confess to love *truth*, & I believe you do. What is beauty of phrase, devoid of truth? "Is the Liturgy true?" is the question. ... If not, could you go to God with it?[150]

147. *OED* (3ed.) gives the first use of 'Open Brethren' as 1879, but it dates from at least 1874 ('Another section has just come into existence in the secession of a third party from the Baptist Church. ... they are understood to belong to the 'open' brethren' ('Formation of New Religious Bodies', Selkirk, Scotland *Southern Reporter*, 5 Mar. 1874, 2). Neil Dickson's invaluable '"Exclusive" and "Open": A Footnote', *BHR* 19 (2023), 82-90, is the first study of the historical usage of those terms.

148. On the Howards at Tottenham: West, *From Friends to Brethren*, 241. The theological gap between Brethren and Baptists was not insurmountable and frequently overcome. Brethren in Kingsbridge, Devon, for example, drew seceders from the Baptist chapel there in forming a community at least in 1841 (Exeter *Western Times*, 16 Jan. 1841, 2; 'Kingsbridge.—The Plymouth Brethren', Exeter *Western Times*, 4 Dec. 1863, 5). Brethren leader R. C. Chapman famously moved from Baptists to Brethren at Barnstaple around 1848 (William F. Gardiner, *Barnstaple: 1837-1897* (Barnstaple: Ralph Allan, 1897), 101, 103, 154; Grass, *Gathering to His Name*, 39). In Scotland in the early 1870s, some members of a Baptist Church in Galashiels joined an existing 'Close' Brethren meeting. Other members established a new Baptist meeting; and yet a third group from the Baptist Church formed a new Open Brethren assembly ('Formation of New Religious Body', Selkirk, Scotland *Southern Reporter*, 5 Mar. 1874, 2). Neil Dickson provides an introduction to statistical sampling of Brethren and Baptists in 'Brethren and Baptists in Scotland', *Baptist Quarterly* 33 (Oct. 1990), 372-87.

149. PHG-EWG, 8 Aug. 1868 (CUL Add. 7018, 10); in the next month EWG attended a meeting for all Dissenters at the Independent Church in Edmonton and found it 'useful to my own soul.' (*Journal*, 23 Sept. 1868).

150. PHG-EWG, 2 May 1868 (CUL Add. 7041, 20). Emphasis in the original.

There were also inquiries about other theological topics. One evening in July 1868, while playing croquet at the home of the Beddows's, a Brethren family, Edmund participated in a three-hour discussion about workers in the East End of London who believed that they had obtained a state of 'sinless sanctification' (presumably a reference to the notion of 'Christian perfection' or 'perfect love' or 'perfect sanctification' which, as we have seen, Philip had encountered under different circumstances in Alabama). 'How startling this is! But surely it is unscriptural,' Edmund wrote in his *Journal*. He was 'tired and nervous' and wanted to tell his father about 'their extraordinary and fascinating dogmas':

> They believe that Xtians once saved (or justified) may fall away and be for ever lost! I cannot find that they can bring sufficient proof of this terrible and distressing doctrine. Their minor tenets are, womens' & childrens' preaching, ecstatic praise to God, immense zeal for the salvation of souls, earnest home missionary labour, and practical sanctity. They say that no one can convict them of sin, and that their inner life is as holy as their outer. They consider this sinless sanctity not only attainable, but frequently attained; and they think that none who do not attain it will be ultimately saved. As few attain it in life, they think most saints reach it in the near approach of death.[151]

The subject troubled Edmund, and in that connection he read a tract by Benjamin Newton 'which strikes me as powerfuly logical and commendable. This strongly opposes the 'sinless sanctity' but they say that Newton is fearfully heretical; so I do not know what to think.'[152] Philip addressed a lengthy letter to him on the subject, only to inadvertently make matters worse. Miss Buckham said she thought Philip unfairly prejudiced against Newton. 'Between you be it!' wrote Edmund, ending the discussion.[153]

Inevitably the question of separation from the world arose. It lead to

151. EWG, *Journal*, 11 July 1868. According to EWG, both R. C. Morgan and William Booth embraced 'sinless sanctification' (Booth was a frequent visitor to Morgan's *Revival* office: George E. Morgan, *Veteran in Revival: R. C. Morgan*, 155-6). On Booth's understanding of the doctrine of sanctification: John Rosario Rhemick, 'The Theology of a Movement: The Salvation Army in its Formative Years' (Northwestern University, PhD dissertation, 1984), 77-97.

152. EWG, *Journal*, 12 July 1868. J. N. Darby had early opposed Wesleyan Christian perfectionism (Larry Edward Dixon, 'The Pneumatology of John Nelson Darby (1800-1882)' (Drew University, PhD dissertation 1985), 302-5; Burnham, 'The Controversial Relationship Between Benjamin Wills Newton and John Nelson Darby', 159).

153. PHG-EWG, 29 July, 8 Aug. 1868 (CUL Add. 7018, 9-10); EWG, *Journal*, 16 July 1868.

some heated exchanges.[154] Philip believed that Edmund should enjoy interaction with others—*provided* it was in a godly group. But when he wrote his father that he had spent a day—the Lord's Day—at the home of his British Museum colleague Dorset Eccles, a 'professed infidel,'

> ... we could only grieve. Your heart responded to the sweetness of the name of Jesus, in the Hymn at Church; but did it appear to you that you were glorifying that Name, in spending all the rest of that day as the guest of one who tramples it under foot? You tell us how congenial you found the talk around the dinner table. I do not know how to reconcile these two things:—the sweetness of the name of Jesus in your ear and yet the congeniality of the talk at the table of an infidel.

Philip then told him how he had once refused an invitation to dine at the home of a Unitarian because 'the Divinity of my Lord was denied' there. He added:

> Many passages of my life will not bear retrospect without a measure of sorrow & shame; but O my dear Willy, I have never been ashamed of the line I took then; ... I want to see you a noble unflinching Christian: I want to see you cherishing the same feelings of sensitive honour, gratitude, & love towards the Lord Jesus, that you do towards me. Would you go willingly, pleasedly, gaily into the society of persons, however witty & well-behaved, who were my professional enemies, & who hated my very name? I am sure you would not. O draw the parallel yourself.[155]

Edmund didn't see things that way. 'Our duty in this world, is, it seems to me, to soften men's hearts, not to harden them,' he wrote. And even though his father added that he would visit an unconverted man though not a sceptic or Socinian,[156] to Edmund the clarification meant little.

---

154. More than one member of the Brethren has foundered on this issue and been surprised by how appealing 'the world' might actually be. Thus Arnott, *The Brethren*, 21-2, 172, 193, and Beer, *Mrs Beer's House*, 146.

155. PHG-EWG, 20 Aug. 1868 (CUL Add. 7018, 11), quoted in part (with errors of transcription) in Charteris, 23-4. I have been unable to trace the Birmingham newspaper referred to by PHG.

156. PHG-EWG, 24 Aug. 1868 (CUL Add. 7018, 13), excerpts in Charteris, 24. The term 'Socinian' could be used as a synonym for Unitarian, which is probably what PHG intended. '... every Socinian is an Unitarian, but every Unitarian is not a Socinian. An Unitarian is a believer in the personal unity of God; a Socinian is a believer in the personal unity of God, who also holds Jesus Christ to be both a man and an object of religious worship' (J. Burns (ed.), *Evans' Sketch of the Denominations of the Christian World* (1851), 74-75fn.). H. J. Slack, whose work PHG praised, was a Unitarian (G. J. Holyoake, 'Obituary. Mr. Henry James Slack, F.G.S., F.R.M.S.',

He daringly called his father's theology 'narrow'. '[B]ut is it narrower than God's?', came the retort. 'Does it not seem narrow to you, because you have imbibed the lax, broad, notions of such fascinating writers as [Charles] Kingsley, instead of making the written Word your only standard of truth?'[157]

Separation from the world meant more than just keeping a safe distance from infidels. 'Thy Word is a lamp unto my feet, and a light unto my path,' as the Psalmist wrote (CXIX:105), but for Brethren, who eschewed religious traditions and authority in general, it was *the* lamp. They were 'extremists' in seeing the Bible alone as their guide,[158] and one of the highest compliments which could be paid to one who had 'gone before' was that he was a man of 'one Book'. The usefulness or value of other literature was not entirely clear.

-VI-

The poetic muse which had attracted Edmund during his last year at St. Marychurch continued to exercise its influence in London during 1867-8. He wrote more poems, one of which his father submitted for publication, and a few of which Philip read to friends. These all praised.[159]

Moreover, Philip assured his son that he did not think 'the buying of books of sound literature "wicked waste,"' and sent him a copy of Robert Southey's poems as an example. He himself had just been re-reading the chief epic of that poet, *The Curse of Kehama* (1810), and

London *Daily News*, 27 June 1896, 4). I do not know if PHG was aware of that fact.

157. PHG-EWG, 18 Sept. 1868 (CUL Add. 7018, 15). PHG had been reading Kingsley's *Alexandria and Her Schools* (1854) and said he admired his 'vigour of thought & expression; his wide benevolence, his scorn of all that is mean & selfish; but I cannot help feeling that in very many cases his theology is not the theology of the Holy Scriptures. He frequently quotes sayings of our Blessed Lord, of Paul, &c., but appropriated to very different senses from theirs; & he makes broad assertions, which can be directly, flatly contradicted by the inspired Word. ... Kingsley speaks sneeringly of the doctrine that sinners shall be punished with eternal torments: but do *you* turn to Matt. xxv.41; xii.42; Mark ix.43-49; Rev. xiv.10,11; xx.15 (compared with ver.10). Read these in the Greek, & say whether an eternal hell is not an awful truth, unless the Lord Jesus was a liar' (emphasis in the original).

158. Bebbington, 'The Place of the Brethren Movement in International Evangelicalism', in Dickson and Grass, eds., *The Growth of the Brethren Movement*, 252; Bebbington, *Evangelicalism in Modern Britain*, 12-14.

159. EWG's poem on 'Hope' was submitted to *Good Words* but not published (PHG-EWG, 5 Feb. 1867, CUL Add. 7041, 5; Charteris, 16). For the other poems: PHG-EWG, 18 Sept. 1867 (CUL Add. 7041, 7). The next day EWG wrote that he intended to commence a poem on 'Devon Legends and Idylls' (EWG-PHG, 19 Sept., Add. 7018, 40). There is a MS collection of EWG's poems at Cambridge from c. 1867-8 (Add. 7035/VI).

thought it characterized by 'wonderfully grand imagination & power.'[160] On Edmund's recommendation, Philip and Eliza read and admired *A Story of Doom, and Other Poems* (1867), by Jean Ingelow (1820-1897).[161] Poetry was not *ipso facto* ungodly, Philip said:

> I joyfully admit the blamelessness & freedom from danger of poetic literature in comparison with science,—the science of *this* age. I have repeatedly thanked God, long before your present letter, that He had not allowed you to follow your father's line of natural science, but had led your tastes in another direction,—on this very account. I can add many admirable Christian Poets to your list; and fully admit that the prevalent tendency of poetry is certainly not towards scepticism.

But in a prophetic warning, Philip added: 'Where it *is* evil, it is rather to sensuousness & lasciviousness. These are the rocks for a young Christian Poet to avoid. Another, yet more dangerous, is the mawkish sentimentalism which idolizes man & nature.'[162]

Meanwhile Edmund sent some of his writings to Algernon Charles Swinburne (1837-1909) in September 1867, which startled his father when he learned of it three months later.[163] That's because the aestheticism promoted in Swinburne's controversial *Poems and Ballads* (1866) represented (in the words of one reviewer) a 'revolt against the current notions of decency and dignity and social duty.'[164]

Edmund nonetheless defended his action. He claimed he had intended nothing more than to get an opinion of his talents, 'as one gentleman to another'. While Swinburne declined to share his assessment, a friend at the Museum was 'severely critical'.[165] He now felt that his father, too, had been hiding his true feelings:

160. PHG-EWG, 18 Sept. 1867 (CUL Add. 7041, 7), and *Father and Son*, 1907, 336, which gives an earlier date for the gift of Southey's poems.

161. Ingelow's poem imitated Robert Pollok's *Course of Time* (which, as previously mentioned, PHG had read many years earlier): Gribben, 'Scottish Romanticism, Evangelicalism and Robert Pollok's *The Course of Time* (1827)', 30.

162. PHG-EWG, 25 Oct. 1867 (Add. 7041, 8). Emphasis in the original.

163. EWG-PHG, 31 Dec. 1867, with a postscript of 2 Jan. (CUL Add. 7018, 41); Ifor Evans, *English Poetry in the Later Nineteenth Century* (London: Methuen & Co Ltd, 1933, 2ed., revised, 1966), 71-6. Swinburne's letter, dated 14 Sept. 1867, was printed in E. Gosse and T. J. Wise (eds.), *The Complete Works of Algernon Charles Swinburne*, vol. XVIII (London: William Heinemann Ltd, 1927), 54-5.

164. 'Mr. Swinburne's New Poems', London *Saturday Review* XXII (4 Aug. 1866), 145; 'Swinburne (Algernon Charles)', in Wheeler, *Biographical Dictionary of Freethinkers*, 310.

165. EWG-PHG, 31 Dec. 1867 (CUL Add. 7018, 41).

... you seem rather to take for granted that I have not the least chance
of success simply from the authority of a young critic [at the British
Museum] of whom you know nothing. This inclines me to believe that
you have long thought the same and have only concealed your feeling
from a fear to wound, more especially as you tell me you are praying [to]
God to give me a new object of attention, so that it evidently appeared
to you lost labour to pray for more skill in the present object. ... I am
very sorry that you should have jumped so readily to the dreadful
conclusion. ... But I constantly ask you for real analytical criticism and
you *never* give it, have never thought of doing so since I have been
up here.

I feel sick and stupid. Are you never coming up to London? I should
feel better if I could talk to you.[166]

Two weeks later, Edmund had somehow sufficiently overcome feelings
of low self-esteem to allow him to ask his father to pay to publish a volume
of his poems. In a 16-page response, Philip estimated the cost to do so
would be about £50. That in itself was not an issue; two obstacles were,
however.

Firstly, Philip did not believe Edmund was ready to appear before the
world in cloth and gilt. He was in an 'immature condition' as a poet. 'Go
on writing, if you will,' he said, 'be gaining wisdom, judgment, maturity
of taste; but repress the eagerness with which you now crave fame.'[167]
The point was a recurring issue:

You say you *trust* you do not crave fame & ask me why I say you do.
When have I said so? Yet this I will say; the desire of fame is a most
treacherous insinuating temptation, & sure to grow. And if you have
it not, then why do you want to publish? If you have *really* no desire
"hominum volitare per ora",[168] does not the writing of the poems answer
every end?[169]

166. EWG-PHG, 13 Jan. 1868 (CUL Add. 7018, 42). Emphasis in the original.
167. PHG-EWG, 1 Feb. 1868 (CUL Add. 7041, 9), printed in part in Charteris, 14-16.
168. Virgil, *Georgics* III:9: '*virûm volitare per ora*' (translated as 'to get into people's mouths,
become the common talk', in Charlton T. Lewis and Charles Short, *A Latin Dictionary* (Oxford:
1879, 1962), 1281). PHG also used this Latin phrase in PHG-EWG, 18 Feb. 1867 (CUL Add.
7041, 6).
169. PHG-EWG, 10 Feb. 1868 (CUL Add. 7041, 11). Emphasis in the original. In a letter
PHG-EWG, 1 Feb. 1868 (CUL Add. 7041, 9), he had advised EWG to 'repress the eagerness with
which you crave fame.' The warning was not unwarranted, as is evidenced by more than one
statement of EWG's that his father should do more to promote his own reputation (18 Feb. 1867;

Secondly, Edmund had not shown his father the poems he intended to publish. Philip suspected that he would not be pleased with his son's poetic taste. Edmund, for example, admired F. W. H. Myers' *St. Paul* (1867), likely captivated by the linkage in lush poetic diction of Greece and the Gospels (many years later, Edmund said that Myers's stanzas were 'extraordinary' but also filled with 'doctrinal extravagances').[170] After reading *St. Paul*, Philip and Eliza agreed in their appraisal. Philip did not mince words:

> ... I will ask you, How can you be captivated by this turgid rant? When the brass-band in front of a puppet show in a village-fair plays up, the open-mouthed bumpkins have all their attention given to the negro fellow that clangs together two cymbals, or brass plates: the more noise, the more music. Myers's clangour reminds me of this. Where are the *thoughts* amidst all this clash of words? ... As I read, I caught myself continually saying, "What trash! What stuff is this!" & this, I am sorry to say, not seldomly, in stanzas that *you* have pencil-marked as if with admiration. ...
>
> ... the noblest in Poetry is ever the simplest: ... our best poets know nothing of this craving after the uncouth, the intense, the obscure, the mystical. You will perhaps impatiently say that you know all this. I reply, I thought you *did* know it, but that you know it *now* I doubt. How else could you admire such a style as Myers'? ...
>
> You speak of a "longing aspiration for what is beautiful & true." Can you ever find anything more beautiful, anything more true, than the Just suffering for *you* the unjust, to bring *you* to God? The verses that such as Myers write, are not beautiful, if I know anything of literary worth, & I am quite sure they are not true. ... You speak of a desire to serve your generation; to serve Christ; a noble ambition indeed; for which in you even if feeble, I am most thankful. The good Lord deepen it, & guide

3 Mar. 1868, both as cited).

170.   For EWG's later view of 'Frederic Myers' Poems': EWG, *More Books on the Table*, 39-44. EWG further characterised *St. Paul* as 'a series of disjointed ejaculations by a converted Greek, who was far from indifferent to the charms of honeyed diction. ... It is an even more serious fault that the poem has no definite object or end, no coherence.' (p. 43) In this essay, EWG related how 'a spinster Plymouth sister' gave away many copies of the book, first changing the 'Puseyite cross' on its cover into a star (p. 41). In an earlier letter to Myers himself, EWG claimed that an old evangelical aunt had snatched the book from him and returned it *sans* cover, which had been burned because of the 'Popish cross' (EWG-F. W. H. Myers, 10 Oct. 1882; Myers Papers, Trinity College Cambridge, Add. 2, f. 75).

it! But, my own darling boy, there is no such thing as serving Christ without taking up the cross. ... You alluded to Cowper; his poetic talent was always on the side of holiness & right. When not directly religious, it was always manly, sterling, simple, good; his humour is always pure, his laughter is like the merry guffaw of a guileless child. And how often he speaks out, clearly & strongly, with no uncertain sound, for scriptural truth, for God & Christ! I shall rejoice to see your name in the literary world, if you take a stand, decidedly, indubitably, on the side of Christ. ... But I should feel stricken down by a terrible calamity in my hoar hairs, if my only son took his place in the ranks of the frothy, sentimental spouters of the day, avoiding the blessed Name which is above every name, or touching it only to pollute it. Spare me this agony, my darling child.[171]

In writing this letter, Philip 'earnestly cried again & again to God, that I might answer you wisely & lovingly.' He was pained at the thought that he might not have done so. Within a week, he had his reply to the 'bitter draught' of medicine, when Edmund told him that he agreed with his father's canons of poesy. 'Perhaps, however, I in my unskill, made it bitterer than was needed,' Philip admitted. 'If I did, I ask your forgiveness.'[172]

Even with such assurances Edmund was still hesitant to send samples of his poetry, and he only did so after coaxing. When Philip received the first batch of poems he devoted all day to analysing one of them, 'Parnassus in a Mist'.[173] Some of the poems he praised, such as 'Noadiah' and 'Jonathan'.[174] In others, however, 'there seems to me an unnaturalness, & unhealthiness, ... which you would do well to avoid. The incidents are too often impossible, at least, utterly improbable.'[175]

The poets who influenced Edmund at this time seem to have fallen into

---

171. PHG-EWG, 1 Feb. 1868 (CUL Add. 7041, 9; printed in part in Charteris, 14-16). Emphasis in the original. For a view of Myers which is similar to, though not as harsh as, PHG's: J. A. Symonds, in Alfred H. Miles (ed.), *The Poets and Poetry of the Century* (London: Hutchinson & Co., n.d.), VIII:63.

172. PHG-EWG, 8 Feb. 1868 (with a note the following day) (CUL Add. 7041, 10); PHG-EWG, 15 Feb. 1868 (Add. 7041, 12).

173. PHG-EWG, 3 Mar. 1868 (CUL Add. 7041, 14).

174. PHG-EWG, 10, 23 Mar. 1868 (CUL Add. 7041, 15-16). Charteris, 11, interpreted a remark in *Father and Son*, 1907, 342, as referring to 'Jonathan', 'a tragedy in pale imitation of Shakespeare'. If this is correct, the date of writing has been placed too early in *Father and Son*.

175. PHG-EWG, 15 May 1868 (CUL Add. 7018, 4).

two camps. He admired Milton and Robert Browning;[176] Jean Ingelow as well as the *Belshazzar* (1822) of H. H. Milman;[177] he thought Longfellow a 'drivelling poetaster'. Simultaneously he was also reading the verses of the 'new age', not only those of Myers and George Macdonald (1824-1905),[178] but also William Morris's *Defence of Guenevere* (1868),[179] and undoubtedly Swinburne, too. Nonetheless, it was not until he began to converse with John Arthur Blaikie (1848-1917) that he had much encouragement from his friends in either of these directions. Charlie Walker's temperament was opposed to poetry; Dorset Eccles (b. 1843),[180] a co-worker at the Museum since 1860 and an assistant there,[181] 'knows nothing and cares less for poetry'; and Mansell Longworth Dames (b. 1850/1), a bright fellow-student at Menneer's Montvidere school[182] and

176. EWG, *Journal*, 25 July, 2 Dec. 1868.

177. EWG, *More Books on the Table*, 39.

178. One of the themes of Macdonald's popular verse was the rejection of his former religious beliefs in favour of 'an amalgam of Browning, Carlyle, and such German philosophy as is within reach, and the cheerful but unsupported assumption that God approves of the change' (Evans, *English Poetry in the Later Nineteenth Century*, 308-9). In PHG-EWG, 1 Feb. 1868 (CUL Add. 7041, 9) is the passage: 'A lost sinner saved from deserved Hell by the atoning blood of Jesus,—this is the very sum and substance, the foundation and topstone of Paul, as of every true believer. ... but where do you find it in Myers, in Macdonald, in any of the fashionable writers? No; the atoning Blood of Jesus must ever be an unfashionable theme.' Nonetheless, EWG continued to be attracted to Macdonald. A copy of *Madrigals, Songs and Sonnets* (1870) at the Colbeck Collection at the University of British Columbia Library is inscribed by EWG to Macdonald. The pages are uncut.

179. ' ... I do not remember being often more severely snubbed than I was by my dear father when, in the year 1867, I spent six shillings—I think that was the sum—on a volume of what he called 'rubbishy minor verse' to which I felt irresistibly attracted. It was certainly a very obscure book then; it was *The Defence of Guenevere* by Mr. William Morris. ... it was the beginning of my bibliomania' (EWG, preface to *A Catalogue of a Portion of the Library of Edmund Gosse*, complied by R. J. Lister. London: The Ballantyne Press, privately printed & limited to 65 copies, 1893). Morris' book appeared in 1868, not 1867. According to J. K. Robinson, 'A Neglected Phase of the Aesthetic Movement: English Parnassianism', *PMLA* LXVIII (Sept. 1953), 753, this book was important in introducing French materials to English readers without arousing Francophobia. It thus had an influence on the English Parnassian movement, of which EWG was later a member.

180. [John] Bernard Burke and Ashworth P. Burke, *A Genealogical and Heraldic History of the Peerage and Baronetage, the Privy Council, Knightage and Companionage* (London: Harrison & Sons, 74ed., 1912), 2181. Eccles retired in 1908; see also 'Home Office List. Imperial Service Order', *Aberdeen Daily Journal*, 9 Nov. 1903, 5.

181. Burke and Burke, *A Genealogical and Heraldic History*, 2181; Eccles is described as an 'assistant in the British Museum' in the case of an ex-servant who was stalking him: 'Singular Charges against a Young Woman', *Liverpool Mercury*, 14 Mar. 1873, 7.

182. 'The Cambridge Local Examinations', *Woolmer's Exeter and Plymouth Gazette*, 13 Feb. 1863, 7; 'Torquay. Cambridge Middle Class Local Examination', Exeter *Western Times*, 3 June 1864, 8. In 1866, Dames placed third in 'aggregate merit' for all of England in the Senior Division, Oxford exams. EWG, who at that time won a certificate for Seniors (Cambridge), was then at Edgelow's school (both are cited in *Exeter and Plymouth Gazette*, 21 Sept. 1866, 6).

the son of Edmund's old drawing master there, had different interests.[183] Besides, Dames had already passed the exam to enter the India Civil Service,[184] and he appeared 'unsaved' to Philip.

While the London-born Blaikie, the son of a wine merchant, had no formal education, he was a voracious reader.[185] He apparently met Edmund in Torquay in 1867 when he was home on holidays. Their friendship was slow to develop. At first, Edmund described Blaikie to his father as 'queer and rather uncouth in appearance. I like his letters better than his talk. We hardly agree at all. He is a very rank Tory ... and thinks meanly of Dissenters from Milton downwards. Need I say, we fight?'[186]

After visiting him in July 1868, however, they found a shared area of interest. Blaikie became a 'great treasure to me as being the only one of my intimate ... friends who is poetico-literary.'[187]

-VII-

It was only natural that during Edmund's first two years in London he was attached heart and mind to Sandhurst. Slowly he was trying to figure out his own world-view. That was natural, too. A loving father observed the transition: 'I see more & more, & wonder as I see, in how many things your idiosyncrasy is moulded after mine; while in others you have quite a groove of your own.'[188]

One way in which Edmund could attain equality of standing with his father, as one adult to another, was through writing. If Edmund could become a published and lauded poet, might father and son not meet as equals in the world of letters? That could help, but he needed to do more. To 'fashion his inner life for himself,'[189] he needed a replacement for his father and Sandhurst—a new source of meaning in life, a new support system, a new path.

Edmund had to figure out: If not born for immortality, then what?

183. EWG, *Journal*, 4 Aug. 1868.

184. 'India Civil Service', London *Daily News*, 18 May 1868, 3; 'Torquay', *Exeter and Plymouth Gazette*, 29 May 1868, 7; PHG-EWG, 9 Apr. 1868 (CUL Add. 7041, 18).

185. Biographical details from his obituary in the *Westminster Gazette*, 29 Dec. 1917; clipping at CUL Add. 7027, 88.

186. EWG, *Journal*, 25 July 1868.

187. EWG, *Journal*, 4 August 1868.

188. PHG-EWG, 29 May 1869 (CUL Add. 7041, 26).

189. *Father and Son*, 1907, 374.

CHAPTER ELEVEN

1868-1875

'You are My Joy & Crown'

-I-

THAT EDMUND VIEWED HIMSELF AROUND 1868-69 as pretty much his father's child is attested to by his unpublished autobiographical novel, 'Tristram Jones'. In a reflective moment, he describes the moustache of Tristram Jones—Tristram being a pseudonym for himself, and the moustache surely a symbol of his embryonic ego—as 'so small that it constantly eludes his [Tristram's] grasp.' Tristram, he wrote,

> has plenty of characteristics, [though] he has as yet, properly speaking, developed no character at all. The best thing we can find in him is a happy negation of all strong vicious impulses. He is good-natured, affectionate, impressible, but the impressions fade away like morning dew beneath the rays of a new book or a new friend. We might even say that each night leaves his soul a smooth palimpsest on which, next day, the household gods may scribble what they will. His ideas of men and human affairs are mostly taken from books, and tinged with the shifting colours of his own fancy. His intellectual is more satisfactory that [sic] his moral side; he had read much and variously, considers self-culture the first aim in life. In fact he is at present just a clever young Philistine and nothing more, of whose future it is impossible to prophecy, [sic] since it depends on psychic forces from without, which are as much beyond human providence as the knowledge that there will be a storm tomorrow or a star-lit sky tonight.[1]

1. EWG, 'Tristram Jones', 6-7. Only part of this untitled novel survives. A holograph note

The forces which could shape Edmund into an independent man were not quite as indeterminable as he thought. Chance certainly played its part. Like Tristram, he was striving to endow himself with 'firmness, manliness, self-reliance, a strong will directed to the attainment of high aims.'[2] The influence of three separate factors helped to point him towards that goal.

One of the households active in the Tottenham Brethren circle was the Beddows family, whom Edmund would frequently visit in 1868 to play cricket, to discuss theological issues, or to attend one of a series of Bible-reading meetings.[3] Edmund was enamoured with their daughter Emma, who was older than he was. Mesdames Buckham and Baker frowned on the Beddows's, thinking them parvenus lacking breeding.[4] Edmund himself soon realised that he did not in fact love Emma. She was not the type who would encourage the ideals he wished to advance.

It appears that no sooner did one budding romance end than a more serious one ensued. Edmund first met Mary Johnson, who was slightly older than he was, about a month after he broke off with Emma Beddows, in July or perhaps August 1868.[5] A year-and-a-half later he informed his father that he intended to become engaged. 'Let me at once say, that you have my fullest sympathy, & dear Mamma's also,' Philip said.

> I have long held that a pure & honourable affection, set upon a worthy
> object, is of very great value to a young man, as tending to sober his
> thoughts; to give a purpose to his life; to supply a lode-star to his wayward

added by EWG on Sept. 9, 1902, describes it as here noted, and gives it a tentative date of 1872. Though internal evidence is inconclusive, this date would seem to me correct, or one for 1872-3. The MS was unknown to Charteris when he worked on his EWG biography, which appeared by Mar. 1931 (J. C. Squire, 'Sir Edmund Gosse [review of Charteris]', London *Observer*, 29 Mar. 1931, 4). EWG had given the MS to Norman Gullick 'Many years ago', and in 1931 he returned it to Dr Philip Gosse (Gullick-P. H.G. Gosse, 5 Apr. 1931, CUL Add. 7032, 96).

2. EWG, 'Tristram Jones', 13.

3. EWG, *Journal*, 11, 19 July and 1 Dec. 1868.

4. EWG, 'Tristram Jones', 7. The distinctive social and religious aspects of Dissent and the Church of England are themes dealt with in EWG's anonymous novellette, 'The Unequal Yoke'. That work appeared in three parts in the *English Illustrated Magazine* III (Apr., May, June 1886), 500-12, 562-76, 604-15. A facsimile edition was published in 1975 (*The Unequal Yoke (1886). A Novel By Sir Edmund Gosse*. Introduction by James D. Woolf. Delmar, NY: Scholars' Facsimiles & Reprints, 1975). The reviews were generally favourable, with the most complete notice of the first part in the New Orleans, Louisiana *Times-Democrat*, 11 Apr. 1886, 5. Too little is known about Emma Beddows and Mary Johnson to be able to tell to what extent the novellette may have been autobiographical.

5. EWG, *Journal*, 9 July 1868.

inclinations; to give him an increased sense of duty & responsibility, as a *prospective* husband & father; to supply additional motives for controlling his passions; & so, specially assuming that both he & his love be earnest believers, helping him to maintain his holy walk with God.[6]

As had been the case earlier when Edmund mooted publishing a volume of poems, his father once again counselled 'Do nothing rashly.' Wait a year or two. Think about this: Had Edmund asked for God's guidance? What type of Christian was she? Was Mary 'truly converted to God?' Would he discuss Mary with Miss Buckham? What did Mary do, what was the position of her father, what was her lifestyle? 'What are her tastes & habits? Is she musical? Does she care for art? Is she given to reading? Is she well-informed? Quiet or dressy? Retiring or forward? Self-possessed in company, or shy & timid? Plain or comely? Tall or short?' Philip concluded this whir of queries by praying that if 'you and your love be spared to be one, your own home may be as full of love & brightness as the one in which you were brought up.'

But misfortune was on the doorstep. In a letter which Philip received on 18 May 1870, Edmund informed him that Mary had suddenly become seriously ill.[7] Replying that same day, Philip added thoughts which had comforted him when, in anguish, he had watched his wife die.

> Should your Mary be removed to the presence of the Lord, it is you who will be left to mourn alone, with a heart broken, & tenderest affections blighted. For you I feel; for you I pray. You say you lay your burden fully on the Lord. O what a mercy is this! ... May he give you *all comfort*, & prove to you now, <u>all</u> that you need! I do not at all doubt that His gracious end in this most heavy affliction is to bring you nearer to Himself; to empty your earthy pitcher, your "broken cistern," that He may fill you from His own fulness.[8]

Edmund found his father's conventional evangelical message hard to accept, and it is obvious that they argued about it. Tristram Jones had said that 'When we are angry we often attack with virulence something

---

6. PHG-EWG, 22 Feb. 1870 (CUL Add. 7041, 33). Emphasis in the original. EWG's intention to become engaged is known from PHG's reply.

7. For the receipt of the letter, see Corr. Bk. The letter itself has not been traced.

8. PHG-EWG, 18 May 1870 (CUL Add. 7041, 35). Emphasis in the original.

that is peculiarly dear to us,'[9] and in such an understandably fraught state the antagonism was heightened. Philip could only plead that Edmund should continue to 'tell Jesus' of his sorrow, and draw the implied lesson in doing so:

> I earnestly implore you, my darling, my only Child, whom from earliest infancy I have ever presented to God in faithful importunate prayer,— whom I long for in the bowels of Jesus Christ,—I intreat you, do not become angry, & say I have no sympathy for your sorrow. Do not say I rudely sear your wounded heart by a long tirade of Theology. I deeply feel your sorrow; but I desire to turn it to account: I earnestly desire that it may not be "the sorrow of the world that worketh death," but a "godly sorrow," laying you low at His feet, who wounds to heal. I want to see you happy. I want to do you good. I desire for you the *very best* good: the *very happiest* happiness. ... O my beloved Child! give me this desire of my heart! let me have this joy of you! Choose the better part! ... It is not for His pleasure that He inflicts this sharp & deep wound on your heart, but for your profit, that you may be partaker of His holiness. ... *This is your first great sorrow*. May it have a mighty influence in shaping your manhood for eternity.[10]

Two weeks later Mary Johnson was dead.[11] Was Edmund reconciled to his loss in the same manner as Philip had been to Emily's 'home call'? One letter suggests that he found comfort in his father's words.[12]

-II-

During the time that Edmund's love for Mary was flourishing, he came into contact with a group of young poets at the British Museum who were to have an inordinate influence on him. They encouraged Edmund in his search for a world-view unlike that of Sandhurst, and helped him to gain both status and independence. In the process, a profound chasm was opened between father and son which remained unbridgeable.

It is obvious that Edmund's early London poetry was not the poetry

---

9. EWG, 'Tristram Jones', 12.

10. PHG-EWG, 18 May 1870 (CUL Add. 7041, 35). Emphasis in the original.

11. Death notice, 'Johnson, Mary J., daughter of Mr. G. R., of Sturry, Kent, at Bayswater, aged 21, May 31' (*Pall Mall Gazette*, 2 June 1870, 5).

12. PHG-EWG, 20 June 1870 (CUL Add. 7041, 38).

of Philip Gosse.[13] As a youth in Newfoundland, Philip had known what it was like to be inspired by the muse, but he also thought that poetry must display a specific contour. The subject need not be religious—though his own major composition, 'The Restoration of Israel', contained ideas of unfulfilled prophecy—but Philip judged the inspirational as perhaps the highest form of verse.[14] Had not Emily Gosse's own compositions been largely of this sort?

Having few friends at Tottenham,[15] and with London acquaintances who (with the exception of Blaikie) were not interested in poetry, Edmund at first was left to make his own literary discoveries. He was balanced between the old and new, and sought advice from both. Swinburne we know was noncommittal, but he did receive encouragement from the poet and novelist, Jean Ingelow. The style of her verse had been influenced by Coleridge, Wordsworth, and Tennyson (among others), and was both clear and simple. It was this (together with an introspective, didactic, or religious tone) which made her lyrics and ballads so widely read,[16] even (as previously mentioned) by an admiring Philip Gosse.[17]

Towards the end of May 1869 Edmund attended one of Miss Ingelow's London garden parties. Since she was acquainted with most of the poets, painters, and writers of her time, it is fair to speculate that Edmund may have made some useful connections through her. But Miss Ingelow's admiration of Edmund's poetry was enough of a justification for him to go to the party. Moreover, his father did not object. Philip was not surprised that Miss Ingelow was 'gratified with your Poems: I am sure she was; for they possess very much of beauty and genuine feeling, with great facility & melody of expression.'[18] A word of warning was necessary, however. 'Wine will probably be abundant;' Philip wrote, 'drink very cautiously. Go with prayer beforehand; be on your guard; & walk circumspectly. Mamma and I will pray that God may be to you 'a Sun & a Shield!'"[19] As it

13. PHG-EWG, 15 May 1868 (CUL Add. 7018, 4).

14. On PHG's *Gems*, see 'Reminiscences', II: 139, 183. In 1868, EWG had borrowed *Gems*, vol. II (dated Jan. 1835) and perhaps also vol. I (EWG-PHG, 13 Jan. 1868; CUL Add. 7018, 42).

15. EWG, 'Tristram Jones', 25 (referring to c. 1868-69).

16. *Athenaeum*, 24 July and 7 Aug. 1897, 129, 193-4; Saunders, *Celebrities of the Century*, 596; 'Ingelow, Jean', *DNB* XXII: 903; EWG, *More Books on the Table*, 140.

17. Besides the letter already cited: PHG-EWG, 22 Oct. 1868 (CUL Add. 7018,19).

18. PHG-EWG, 29 May 1869 (CUL Add. 7041, 26).

19. PHG-EWG, 4 May 1869 (CUL Add. 7041, 31). This portion of the letter has inadvertently been bound apart from the rest (Add. 7041, 24).

turned out, the warning was unnecessary. The dinner was quiet. Edmund reported that he did not enjoy 'drawing-room small talk'.[20]

The young poetic traveller was to make only a brief stop at Miss Ingelow's before continuing to fairer pastures. Although he was to glance back at the ground which he had covered, he never returned to it. During 1869-70 he met new friends at the British Museum who led him to British practitioners of two contemporary artistic trends, Parnassianism and Pre-Raphaelitism. The former had emerged in France from *l'art pour l'art* movement of the 1840s and 1850s. It was an aesthetic in which art is autonomous, unaffected by externalities, emphasizing features such as formalism, objectivity, the historic, and the exotic.[21] Pre-Raphaelitism, in reacting against an industrializing society, sought to depict—in painting and poetry—nature and truth 'as they are'. Freed from tradition, they were critics of their society and the state of art, and looked instead for their inspiration to the supposed simplicity of the medieval world.[22]

20. PHG-EWG, 29 May 1869 (CUL Add. 7041, 26). Part of this letter (which also appears in *Father and Son*, 1907, Epilogue, 357) is worth quoting:

'By the way we are reading [James Ewing] Ritchie's Nightside of London [1857]; a remarkable, nay a frightful, exhibition of the pitfalls & snares which surround on every hand the thoughtless giddy youth of London. Women & wine: whoredom & drunkenness; seem to be the Devil's most successful baits. I would not ask you to read it; for to a young man the very description of such scenes is inflammatory & defiling: but it is a ghastly comment on the first nine chapters of Proverbs. Both Mamma & I have heartily thanked God that your home lies so far away from dissipated London, that you are thrown out of the range of the fowler's net; that you escape the temptation of walking the treacherously-baited streets at night, unless you wilfully choose it. (Prov. ii.10-16) You charge me in one place with being suspicious; & I fear I cannot deny the charge. But I can appeal to your own sensible & thoughtful mind for a considerate allowance. My deep & tender love for you; your youth & inexperience; the temptations that beset you; the examples of other young men: your distance from parental counsel; our absolute & painful ignorance of all the details of your daily life, except what you yourself tell us:—try to throw yourself into the standing of a parent, & say if my suspiciousness is unreasonable. I rejoicingly acknowledge that, from all I see, you are pursuing a noble, virtuous, steady, worthy course. You allude to your frequent adoption of my advice: I am exceedingly gratified: not mainly, I trust, because it touches my self-love; but because it shews grace & subjection in you, which is lovely & of good report. One good thing the expression of my suspiciousness does:—ever & anon it brings out from you unexpected assurances, which greatly refresh & comfort me. And again, it carries me ever to God's Throne of Grace on your behalf in earnest, pleading, importunate prayer; & then God gives me answers of peace.'

EWG thought the serious attention to Ritchie's book 'just a little funny'. PHG recognized that it did not give a fair picture of London, but he reiterated the possible dangers (PHG-EWG, 9 June 1869, CUL Add. 7041, 27).

21. Bridget Behrmann, 'The Parnassian Moment and the Experimental Poem, 1866-1876' (Princeton University, PhD dissertation, 2017), 8-27.

22. 'Pre-Raphaelite' and 'Pre-Raphaelitism' are notoriously elusive terms. A tortuous example

Arthur William Edgar O'Shaughnessy (1844-1881) and Théophile-Jules-Henri Marzials (1850-1920) were two of Edmund's guides. The former was nominated to the Museum in 1861 as a Transcriber. In the next year he moved to the Zoology Department, having been outrageously chosen over the well-known entomologist Henry Walter Bates as the result of Sir Edward Bulwer Lytton's patronage. O'Shaughnessy never became anything more than a competent herpetologist,[23] as he disliked both his work and natural history. But such deficiencies and problems were only superficial irritants affecting one whose true vocation was, after all, poetry. He was an intimate of the later Pre-Raphaelites, and knew Ford Madox Brown, William Morris, W. Bell Scott, and Swinburne. Moreover, O'Shaughnessy's Francophilia led him to visit that country during his holidays, and he was the first to bring back to his Museum friends news of the Parnassians. His first volume of verse, *An Epic of Women and Other Poems* (1870), seemed to follow the predominant tendency of art for morality's sake, and was well received; but he soon espoused the Parnassian ideal. Edmund apparently met O'Shaughnessy in 1870,[24] and was never particularly close to him.[25] He spoke highly of his poetry, even if he felt it was of 'exceedingly unequal' quality.[26]

Theo. Marzials, as he was known, was a more intimate friend of

at definition is EWG, 'Dante Gabriel Rossetti', New York *Century Magazine* XXIV (Sept. 1882), 718-25, esp. 721, 719. For attempts at a definition over the past 65 years: William Evan Fredeman, 'The Pre-Raphaelites and Their Critics: A Tentative Approach Toward the Aesthetic of Pre-Raphaelitism' (University of Oklahoma, PhD dissertation, 1956), 182-6, and Aurélie Petiot, *The Pre-Raphaelites*. Translated from the French by Jane Marie Todd (New York: Abbeville Press, 2019), 12, 64.

23. This is a fair judgment of O'Shaughnessy's scientific achievement, notwithstanding that the naturalist Richard Owen spoke of him with 'deep ... respect' (*Nature* 23, 24 Feb. 1881, 402), and said that he had an 'honourable degree of reputation' for his work at the Natural History Department of the British Museum ('The Late Mr. Arthur O'Shaughnessy', London *Daily News*, 1 Feb. 1881, 5).

24. In a signed obituary notice, EWG says he had known O'Shaughnessy for 11 years (EWG, 'Arthur O'Shaughnessy', *Academy*, 5 Feb. 1881, 98. EWG incorrectly gives his year of birth as 1846).

25. A valuable biographical account of O'Shaughnessy's Museum career is W. D. Paden's 'Arthur O'Shaughnessy in the British Museum; or, the Case of the Misplaced Fusees and the Reluctant Zoologist', *Victorian Studies* VIII (Sept. 1964), 7-30. See also: EWG, 'Arthur O'Shaughnessy', *Silhouettes* (London: William Heinemann Ltd, 1925), 173-9; Evans, *English Poetry in the Later Nineteenth Century*, 138-9; Richard Garnett, in Miles, *Poets and Poetry of the Century* VIII: 171-2; EWG-E. C. Stedman, 18 June 1881, in Mattheisen and Millgate, *Transatlantic Dialogue*, 83; Robinson, 'A Neglected Phase of the Aesthetic Movement: English Parnassianism', 744. The discussion in Charteris, 13-14, of EWG's early friendships with poets at the Museum, is inadequate and misleading.

26. EWG, 'Arthur O'Shaughnessy', *Academy*, 5 Feb. 1881, 99.

Edmund's—intimate enough to have encouraged one scholar to describe their relationship as 'probably homosexual.'[27] Marzials was born in France to a Protestant family whose father was a pastor. The family moved to London, and in September 1870 Theo joined the staff of the Museum as a junior assistant. A few months later he was a Transcriber in the Department of Printed Books, and that is where he met Edmund. Their friendship was cemented when the handsome Marzials[28] read in 1870 to his new acquaintance the first draft of his *Passionate Dowsabella (A Pastoral)*, published in book form in 1873. ' … I then thought and said [it] was a poetical revelation,' Edmund later recalled. An ecstatic Theo 'suddenly kissed me, in our workroom at the British Museum, in a paroxysm of innocent gratification.'[29] Marzials' attachment to Parnassianism secured him a place in Edmund's new circle of friends.

The last member of the Parnassian quartet, whom Edmund possibly met at this time, was John Payne (1842-1916). Though Payne was a practising solicitor and not at the Museum,[30] and was apparently not particularly close to Edmund,[31] he was a friend of O'Shaughnessy.[32]

Before the late 1860s there had been little literary communication

27. John M. Munro, *Selected Poems of Theo. Marzials* (Beirut, Lebanon: American University of Beirut, 1974), 7-8. Michael Hatt refers to EWG as among the 'homosexual men' who were acquaintances of English sculptor Hamo Thornycroft (Hatt, 'Near and Far: Homoeroticism, Labour and Hamo Thornycroft's *Mower*', *Art History* 26, Feb. 2003, 26). Jason Edwards, 'Edmund Gosse and the Victorian Nude', *History Today* (Nov. 2001), 34, discusses sexual issues and cites EWG's relationship with Thornycroft. General details about Marzials are in *ODNB*. 'The Late Mr. Marzials', London *Times* (18 Feb. 1920), 18, states that Marzials was 'of Venetian extraction'. Biographical details which follow here are mainly from Munro, *Selected Poems of Theo. Marzials*, 1-23.

28. W. D. Paden, 'A Neglected Victorian Poet: Theo. Marzials', *Notes and Queries* 210 (Feb. 1965), 62.

29. EWG's specific denial of 'a filthy interpretation' to being kissed by Marzials is in Paul F. Mattheisen, 'Gosse's Candid "Snapshots"', *Victorian Studies* VIII (June 1965), 340.

30. Charteris, 14, implies Payne was employed at the British Museum: this is corrected by *The Autobiography of John Payne*, with preface and annotations by Thomas Wright (Olney, near Bedford: Thomas Wright, 1926), 47-8 and fn. 131; 'Payne, John', in Joseph McCabe (comp.), *A Biographical Dictionary of Modern Rationalists* (London: Watts & Co., 1920), 590-1.

31. See *Autobiography of John Payne*, 18, where Payne claims to have been condemned in 1902 by a clique composed of '*****, Lang', and others. '*****' is identified by Wright as 'a well-known man of letters alive to-day.' According to Robinson ('A Neglected Phase of the Aesthetic Movement: English Parnassianism', 751fn.50), this 'is obviously Gosse'. It is possible that EWG did not actually meet Payne in 1869-70. Richard Garnett (1835-1906), another Museum worker friendly with EWG, wrote that Payne's 'life, so far as known to the public or ourselves, is marked solely by his appearances as an author' (Miles, *Poets and Poetry of the Century* VIII:37).

32. Payne's *Masque of Shadows* was dedicated to O'Shaughnessy, and O'Shaughnessy returned the compliment in *An Epic of Women* (both published in 1870).

between London and Paris, and it may seem odd that a herpetologist, a solicitor, and two clerks who scribbled all day on chits of paper should have become pronounced Gallicans. They did have their reasons. Marzials and O'Shaughnessy had lived or visited France; Gosse would later trace a real (or imagined) ancestry to a Huguenot family of Bordeaux.[33] They were young and ambitious, eager to pursue unexplored paths, and widely read. And the path to France had already been opened in the late 1850s by William Morris, Swinburne, and Dante Gabriel Rossetti (these three later opposed what they themselves had introduced).[34]

What was being brought to England was a 'poisonous honey stol'n from France,' as the English Poet Laureate Tennyson advised in 1873 in attempting to arouse opposition to the trend. It was the importation of the aesthetic theory of Gautier and the practice of Banville and others, including François Villon. The English Parnassians were inspired by these writers to place form above function, or to make function a factor of form. The only creation of man which lasted, they felt, was Art, and the highest achievement was a perfect sculpting of that Art. The ideas embodied in that Art were secondary, and considered escapist.

Each of the above-mentioned individuals of the British Museum quartet showed the influence of Parnassianism in his verse. Some of the old French forms were to be found in Marzials' *Gallery of Pigeons* (1873) and Gosse's *On Viol and Flute* (1873); O'Shaughnessy translated the *Lays of Marie de France* (1872) and Payne dedicated his *Intaglios* (1871) to Banville and translated Villon. Their verse was melodious and could be 'in some ways very brilliant indeed,' but *au fond* (in the view of one critic) it was 'incoherent ineffectual ecstasy.'[35] To this group, as the poet and pre-Raphaelite painter William Bell Scott (1811-1890) explained,

---

33. *Banquet à M. Edmund Gosse, Restaurant Durant, Paris, Mardi le 9 Février, 1904* (cited in Charteris, 510).

34. These paragraphs on Parnassianism are (unless otherwise stated) based on Robinson, 'A Neglected Phase of the Aesthetic Movement: English Parnassianism', 733-54; Munro, *Selected Poems of Theo. Marzials*, 18-23.

35. G. A. Simcox in *The Academy* IV (15 May 1873), 181-2 (reviewing Marzials' *Pigeons*); on the lack of substance in these poems: the review of O'Shaughnessy's *Lays of France, Athenaeum* (6 Jan. 1872), 8-9, and Richard Garnett, in Miles, *Poets and Poetry of the Century* VIII: 171-2 ('He would have been a great as well as a genuine poet if this gift of music had been associated with the gifts of the thinker'); on Payne's *Intaglios*: F. Leary in *The Dark Blue* I (May 1871), 397-9, and *Athenaeum* (18 May 1872), 618-19. EWG's volume was subject to the same criticism, and is discussed later in this chapter.

new *forms* were everything; French verses, rondels, and rondeaux being the perfect thing with them; imagination, knowledge of life, insight, and power of thought, the motive or sentiment, were very well, but not to be had, so not to be required. English heroic verse was presumed by them to be dead and buried; ballad quatrains, blank verse, and so forth, were all spoken of with contempt. ... what matters the sense, motive, or morals of a poem, if it is beautiful? Art above everything! One of them [EWG] called the year of the Franco-German war (that war that changed the face of Europe, reversed the position of the two countries, ensured the independence and unity of Italy, and broke the power of the Papacy) "the year when Regnault died."[36]

Regardless of his father's known opposition to the English Parnassian outlook, Edmund next wedged himself into the English Pre-Raphaelite circle. In March 1870, he sent a note to W. B. Scott discussing some points in that author's *Life and Works of Albert Dürer* (1869). Scott, who said he confused Edmund with a man who had bought a painting from him, invited him to visit. Instead of finding 'the portly gentleman of middle life' at his doorsteps, Scott was startled to find someone in his twenties. 'We took to him, however,'[37] and Scott became the source of valuable introductions. Scott was said to know 'nearly everybody, young or old, of any importance in literature and art,' particularly those in the pre-Raphaelite movement.[38]

Perhaps it was on Scott's recommendation that Edmund met Christina Rossetti in the winter of 1870-71.[39] In December 1870, he was 'presented'

36. W. Minto (ed.), *Autobiographical Notes of the Life of William Bell Scott* (London: James R. Osgood, 1892), II: 192, 197-8. 'The Year Regnault Died' is a reference to EWG's '1870-71', in EWG, *On Viol and Flute* (London: Henry S. King & Co., 1873), 207-11. The French painter Henri Regnault (1843-1871) died in action during the war. On Scott: Rodney K. Engen, *Dictionary of Victorian Engravers, Print Publishers and Their Works* (Cambridge: Chadwyck-Healey, 1979), 175.

37. Minto, *Autobiographical Notes* II: 193-4; Charteris, 24, cites the letter but omits the fact that the meeting was based on a misunderstanding.

38. Cosmo Monkhouse, 'Obituary. William Bell Scott, LL.D., H.R.S.A.', *Academy* (6 Dec. 1890), 529.

39. EWG, 'Christina Rossetti', New York *Century Magazine* 46 (June 1893), 216; EWG, *Critical Kit-Kats* (London: William Heinemann, 1896), 157. Original etchings by Alma-Tadema appeared in W. B. Scott's *Poems, Ballads, Studies from Nature, Sonnets* (1875), and the frontispiece to EWG's 1879 *Studies in the Literature of Northern Europe* was by him (Engen, *Dictionary of Victorian Engravers, Print Publishers and Their Works*, 16). Scott was an 'intimate friend' of Dante Gabriel Rossetti (Monkhouse, 'Obituary. William Bell Scott, LL.D., H.R.S.A.', 529-530). McCabe, *Biographical Dictionary of Modern Rationalists*, 283-4.

to A. C. Swinburne. The note from the hostess who brought them together
read: 'Algernon took to you at once, as is seldom the case with him.'[40]

-III-

Surviving letters show that during this time father and son nattered about
the aquarium which Philip had sent him, the health of its sea anemones,
and the 'Tottenham Actinological Society'.[41] There is nary a word about
Edmund's new literary associations. Then the two met face-to-face on
two (or maybe three) occasions in 1868, and at least twice in 1869.[42] We
know that by early 1870, in his twenty-first year, a crisis erupted between
the two. Reflecting on it nearly four decades later, Edmund located that
as the cause of his determination to separate from his father and take 'a
human being's privilege to fashion his inner life for himself.'[43]

Did Edmund actually feel that way at the time? And what did he mean
by what he said later in life? Was he referring to an inner thought? An
actual event? An imagined reality? Only Edmund knew whether it was
the first scenario, and only he knew whether he *imagined* this is what
had happened *at that time*.

What we do know is that surviving documents provide no support for
a narrative in which Edmund affirmatively separated from his father's

40. EWG, *Portraits and Sketches* (London: William Heinemann Ltd, 1912, new impression,
1924), 7. EWG had first seen Swinburne on 10 July 1868 (Journal, 11 July 1868; Charteris, 19).
The note cited here rings true: Swinburne publicly defended EWG when attacked by Churton
Collins (Swinburne, 'The Literary Record of the 'Quarterly Review'', *Athenaeum*, 6 Nov. 1886,
600-1), while 'The celebrated German critic, Herr Edmund W. Gosse, regards Algernon Charles
Swinburne as the greatest of the three living poets, Tennyson and Browning being the other two'
(*Oakland [California] Tribune*, 10 Nov. 1877, 2).

41. In October 1868, PHG offered to send EWG 'the large quadrangular tank (it is a historic
relic, for it is the first private Aquarium that was ever made, & ought to be an heir-loom in my
family)'. On December 11, it was sent-off, the Tottenham household already having commenced
a study of PHG's *Handbook* a few weeks earlier. Shortly thereafter, PHG began to send them
stock to fill it, and EWG kept him acquainted with the tank's progress in the 'Journal of the
Tottenham Actinological Society. 1869'. The specimens did not fare well, and PHG had to send
further instructions on keeping the aquarium clean (*Journal*, 17 Nov. 1868; 16 Apr.-6 May 1869;
PHG-EWG, 22 Oct., 27 Nov., 14 Dec. 1868; 4 May 1869; CUL Add. 7018, 19, 22-3, and Add. 7041,
24). The aquarium was kept until 1893, 'when it fell to pieces' (Charteris, 456-7).

42. For the visits to Sandhurst in September and December 1868: PHG-EWG, 3 Sept. 1868,
8 Feb. 1869 (CUL Add. 7018, 14; Add. 7041, 23). EWG probably also visited his parents while at
Poole in May 1868 (PHG-EWG, 8 May 1868; CUL Add. 7041, 21). PHG had apparently come up
to London in December 1868, when EWG severely cut his hand (PHG-EWG, 21, 26 Dec. 1868; 4,
11 May 1869; CUL Add. 7018,25-6; Add. 7041, 25, 31). In 1869, he visited Marychurch in January
and August (PHG-EWG, 21 Jan. 1870, 9 June 1869; CUL Add. 7041, 27, 30).

43. *Father and Son*, 1907, Epilogue, 374.

orbit in 1870. The final divide between son and father occurred a few years later, and was influenced by other developments.

Here was the background to the 1870 crisis. From a narrow perspective, the immediate cause was two-fold. There were problems with money, and there were problems over Philip's continued exhortations about his son's spiritual welfare. Edmund was tiring of having to deal with both of them. It is true that at first, Edmund accepted that a certain supervision was necessary and prudent, given his general unworldliness. That was then. Gradually he had learned the required lessons, and he concluded that the wealthy occupant at Sandhurst was losing touch with his situation.[44] Advice about frugality had become an end in itself.

As he began his fourth year in London on his own, Edmund bridled at the never-ending recommendations. 'I can quite understand how my anxiety for you may be irksome,' Philip admitted,

> especially as I see how defective I am in tact, & in the art of making things pleasant. The baby in Wordsworth is "*Fretted* with sallies of his Mother's kisses", they tease him; & interrupt his play; & he does not like them: yet they are the inevitable expressions of an unutterable unfathomable love. If I saw symptoms of typhus or of consumption in your body, shd. not I be anxious? How much more when I discern what I cannot but regard as alarming symptoms of spiritual disease? It is not that I have "hard thoughts" of you: it is not a matter of blame, but of deep anxiety & sorrow. I know you love *me*; but do you love *God*? I think of your dying Mother's prayers; of your early promise; of my joy & thankfulness when you avouched the Lord to be your Saviour; & I want to know what of this remains. You take your place still with the people of God; but is your faith "the faith of God's elect?" This is what I am most anxious to know, & oh! how willing to believe.[45]

The son had looked to the past, and found two sources of tension with his father; he now looked to the present and future, and found two others. In November 1868, Edmund bought a second-hand English-Greek New Testament, and began to read it carefully.[46] Early in the next year he spoke of religious doubts. Were the Scriptures really a divinely inspired work? Philip responded by sending him William Page Wood's

44. EWG-PHG, 19 Jan. 1870 (CUL Add. 7018, 44). The letter exists only as a fragment.
45. PHG-EWG, 4 Aug. 1869 (CUL Add. 7041, 28). Emphasis in the original.
46. EWG, *Journal*, 19, 30 Nov. 1868.

The Continuity of Scripture (1867). 'Read his preface with Care,' Philip advised, 'the reasonings of an English Judge must be worth weighing. Tell me how you like it.'[47]

When Edmund visited Sandhurst in August 1869 he made no attempt to hide his emerging persona. Gone was Tristram Jones, the one who 'as yet, properly speaking, [had] developed no character at all.' Gone was the young man who had drawn spiritual sustenance from the Young Men's Prayer Meetings or Sunday school teaching. Several months after that summer visit the transition was captured in moving, blazingly honest, carefully argued and blunt exchanges. We can read them today because, remarkably, Edmund chose to preserve many of them.

Philip began his 15-page letter of 21 January 1870, by acknowledging that he knew that 'my only child was fast tending to a condition of alienation from me. I am most thankful that you feel, *with me*, that such a condition is most earnestly to be deprecated.' He summarized all of the attempts which had been made to lead his son in a godly path: his mother's solemn charge and his father's choice of an appropriate housekeeper, the right schools, a second wife, a good occupation for Edmund and a wholesome residence for him. Philip had tried to make his son's Sundays beneficial, '& in multitudes of lesser things, I have sought to act for you, not in the light of this present world, but with a view to Eternity.'

During Edmund's first two years in London, Philip said, things seemed good. The life he led seemed to reflect the fact of a re-birth.

> But of late, & specially during the past year, there has become manifest a rapid progress towards evil. [I must beg you here to pause, & again look up to God for grace to weigh what I am about to say; or else wrath will rise, and I shall have done you evil, & not good.]
>
> When you came to us in the summer, the heavy blow fell full upon me; & I discovered how very far you had departed from God. It was not that you had yielded to the strong tide of youthful blood, & had fallen a victim to fleshly lusts ... It was not this; it was worse. It was that horrid, insidious infidelity, which had already worked in your mind and heart with terrible energy. Far worse, I say, because this was sapping the very foundation of faith, on which all true godliness, all real religion, must rest. Nothing seemed left, to which I could appeal. We had, I found, no

47. PHG-EWG, 8 Feb. 1869 (CUL Add. 7041, 23); *Father and Son*, 1907, Epilogue, 353.

common ground. The Holy Scriptures had no longer an authority: you had learned to deny their inspiration ....

Do not think I am speaking in passion, & using unwarrantable strength of words. Do, as a man of thought & reason, weigh this matter deeply. If the written Word, to which our Lord Christ ever came as a final appeal, is not absolutely authoritative, what do we *know* of God? What more than we can *infer*, that is, *guess*,—as the thoughtful heathens did,— Plato, Socrates, Cicero—from dim & mute surrounding phenomena? What do we know of eternity? of our relations to God? especially of the relations of a *sinner* to God? what of reconciliation? what of the capital question,—How can a God of perfect spotless rectitude deal with me a corrupt sinner, who have trampled on those of His laws which were even written on my conscience?

You may say, "I *think* He will be lenient towards me." Yes, it is at present convenient to think so: but what if He have reasons for thinking otherwise? And of this you know absolutely nothing, except what you learn from his written Word, which unhappily you have persuaded yourself to treat as of no *authority* (since, if the authority be not absolute, it is no *authority*); & thus the awful Future, into which you are plunging, is midnight darkness.

Oh! Willy! my loved & cherished child! is it come indeed to this? is it thus that I must think of you? having cast down the ancient landmarks have you nothing better than this spider's web to set in place of the Faith once delivered to the Saints? The blinding tears fill my eyes as I write, to think of the contrast between my child of today & my child of a few short years ago.

And you can make a jest & a scoff of my "sorrowing Heart"! you can be indignant that I should think more of this dreadful disease of your soul than of any disease of your body! When God laid His hand upon you, I hoped that you might listen in humility to His voice; & wrote you that long & earnest appeal, which you contemptuously describe as "full of argumentative theology," but of which you took no further notice.

O Willy! How could you write that bitter scornful letter, denouncing in course terms my "Calvinistic religion?["] Was this a reply to my "argumentative theology?["] How could you say "that if you would leave the Church & once more sign yourself P[lymouth] B[rother], there wd be no bounds to the love & praise & all tender attention you wd have from me"? This is not true. If your sincere convictions led you to the

communion of the Ch. of England, I would not say a word against it. ...
It is not your having left "Brethren" (so called), if indeed you have left
them, which you had never told us of,—that grieves me, but your having
forsaken the sure word of Truth for the dark mazes of infidelity. And all
your reiterated protestations that you cannot charge yourself with any
thing to account for my displeasures, would utterly amaze me, only that
I remember what is written of another form indeed of evil,—"She eateth
& wipeth her mouth, & saith, *I* have done no wickedness!"[48]

That dreadful letter of yours[49] I had intended, after much prayer, to
pass by in entire silence; but your apparently sincere inquiries after the
cause of my sorrow have led me to go to the root of the matter, & I could
not stop short of the development contained in that communication. It
is with pain, not in anger, that I now refer to it; hoping that you may be
induced to review the whole course of which this is only a stage, before
God. If this grace were granted, oh! how joyfully should I bury all the past,
& again have sweet & tender fellowship with my beloved Son, as of old!

You will say that you have a right to think for yourself in these
matters,—for so I understand your demand of "the privileges of a
belligerent power." I know that you *must* think for yourself; you *must*
answer for yourself at the bar of God; I *cannot* take this solemn & most
weighty responsibility from you, if I would. But have *I* not rights too?
You are yet a youth. I am your parent. Have not I the right to counsel,
to suggest, to entreat; & if I see you choosing fatal error, have I not the
right to remonstrate? Have I not the right to *grieve*?

Well, I have, at least, the right to pray. And this I do, and will do,
fervently and instantly; that He, in whose hand are all hearts, may turn
your heart back again.[50]

---

48. Proverbs 30: 20.

49. This letter has not been traced. Writing in *Father and Son*, 1907, 372, EWG described
the conflict with his father as having reached an inflection point when he told him *face-to-face*
about his need to be left alone. That does not accord with what PHG wrote at the time. The
sentence which reads in the MS 'That dreadful *letter* of yours I had intended ... to pass by in
entire silence; ... I could not stop short of the development contained in that *communication*' was
changed in *Father and Son* to read: 'This dreadful *conduct* of yours ... the development contained
in *this letter*' (emphasis added in both sentences). See Wertheimer, 'Son and Father', 65. Harold
Nicolson (1886-1968) recalled a visit to his friend EWG in 1927, seven months before EWG died,
when EWG's memory 'was as fresh as that of a young man's.' Nicolson said EWG told him that
'the end' of *Father and Son* 'had been slightly "arranged". There was no dramatic breach' with
PHG, 'but they continued on terms of mutual politeness till his father's death' (James Lees-Milne,
Harold Nicolson: A Biography. Volume 1, 1886-1929. Hamden, Conn.: Archon Books, 1981, 317).

50. PHG-EWG, 21 Jan. 1870 (CUL Add. 7041,30). Emphasis and square brackets in the

In the remainder of the letter, Philip took up the other points which had troubled his son. 'You accuse me of constant suspicion of you,' he wrote. 'I do not like recrimination, but I must say this, that what you call suspicion is the puzzlement arising from your reluctance to give me full & clear information.' Edmund's finances supplied the case in point. His accounts were garbled and unbalanced, his father asserted, and as long as he gave him money he felt it acceptable to inquire about how it was being spent. 'You speak of these things as if you thought attention to money matters were meanness; but this [is] a puerile, foolish notion, which you will be ashamed of by and by.'

In conclusion, he asked his son to give the same care to reading the letter as had gone into writing it: 'for the subject is, in my esteem, one of the most momentous weight ... strive to consider the whole from my point of view; & that with much earnest prayer for self-abnegation, & for Divine illumination.'

Philip had begun to write his reply on a Friday, and on that day, the next two days and the following Wednesday, he received letters from his son.[51] It was the last of these, arriving on the morning of one of the Bible-Reading Meetings, which confirmed that the father's communications had achieved their goal.

> With tears, no longer of sorrow, but of joy & thankfulness, I have read your dear letter. ... Dear Mamma & I have been most anxiously crying to God, ever since my letter was written, that it might not wound & irritate, but truly help you; but, indeed, our faith did not reach such an answer as this. And one very blessed result is, that it brings God *very nigh*, as a *Living* God, & an Answerer of prayer.
>
> Very thankfully do I accept your loving confidence as to the exercises of your own mind. If you will continue to grant it, laying before me from time to time your difficulties, do not fear that I shall be intolerant of them; I will joyfully, as God shall enable me, try to meet them; & possibly *two* minds, both subject to God, may overcome difficulties which seemed insurmountable to one alone. The great joy, the bright light, is that "now you are *most desirous* to believe." *This* will remove mountains.

original. This letter, which is now at Cambridge (Add. 7041, 30), was printed in part in the epilogue to *Father and Son*. Some words and entire sections have been silently omitted, and the purport of the letter altered by EWG (see previous footnote).

51. Letters from EWG are recorded in Corr. Bk. for January 20, 21, 22, 26, 1870.

Perhaps the sweetest word in your sweet letter is that in which you avouch your confidence that Christ died for *you*, & your love to Him on this account. This I yearned for, more than anything; I knew the confession could not be forced; & I did not know how far the disease might have gone, & feared the worst. Blessed be God! this fear proves groundless; & I can still with undoubting confidence look on my beloved boy as indeed partaker of like precious faith with us. This alone removes a mountain from my heart ... & I will ask grace that I may not drive you faster than you are able to go. We are at one again; one in spirit; one in heart; one in the deepest foundations, one in highest interests; one in hope; one in eternal destiny. Thank God! Thank God!

The letter you mention I inclose;—without again reading it, for I do not wish it to live in memory; though the present joy obliterates that past pain. ...[52]

During the next six months, while one subject was uppermost in Philip's mind, Edmund's thoughts were directed elsewhere. His attachment to Mary Johnson was one issue, his renewed desire to become a published poet another. Having waited nearly two years since he originally raised the latter subject, in November 1869 he once again spoke of it to his father.[53] This time, Edmund got the go-ahead for a volume of poems by him and his friend John Blaikie. By March 1870, Philip had received estimates for the cost of a privately printed edition (500 copies would run approximately £40, including binding). If 270 of these were sold, all expenses would be met (that assumed about a 3s. profit per copy sold). Philip offered to manage the commercial and artistic part of the work, and correct the proofs. But before doing anything, he wanted to see his son's poems. Those of his collaborator Blaikie he would read, too (Blaikie's share in the arrangement was £20, paid in advance).[54]

When the referee examined Blaikie's work, he focussed upon the style and ignored the content. Philip found some of his phrases 'unintelligible,' and the whole displayed an obscurity and 'Uncouthness of language

52. PHG-EWG, 26 Jan. 1870 (CUL Add. 7041, 32). Emphasis in the original. EWG's letters referred to here have not been traced.

53. PHG-EWG, 4 Nov. 1869, and PHG-George E. Bulger, 9 Nov. 1869 (both in Corr. Bk.).

54. PHG-EWG, 25 Mar. 1870 (CUL Add. 7041, 34). According to PHG's calculations, the boarding (*viz.*, binding) of the book would cost 38s. or 40s. per 100, and for printing 500 copies, £24; 750, £28; 1000, £31. If the book sold for 5s., about one-third would be taken as the publisher's share.

or riggedness [*sic*] of expression.' Philip's approach annoyed Blaikie, though the focus may have worked to his advantage. It kept Philip away from religious matters where, as Blaikie acknowledged, 'I am only half a churchman.'[55]

The scrutiny of Edmund's verse was intense. At first, Philip did not like what he saw. The poems became a focal point in Philip's struggle to insure that his son had completely expunged traces of infidelity from his thought. There was an urgency to Philip's words because 1870-1 signalled more than warfare between France and Prussia. The second advent was at hand. In the middle of May, he explained why the stakes were so high:

> Every day, & every hour in the day, I am contemplating the imminent approach of my beloved Lord. He has said,—"One shall be taken, & another left." The terrible thought constantly obtrudes,—"What if I be taken, & my child left!" Do not be too rashly sure that this cannot be, because you are a true believer. Many earnest students of prophecy maintain, from many very startling Scriptures (& I dare not affirm that they are in error) that when the Lord will descend into the air, He will snatch up only those (of the living) who are really watching for Him, leaving a mass of careless, worldly (though *real*) Christians, to pass through all the horrors that then will be poured on the earth. Read Luke xxi.36; what do you infer from the middle clause?[56]
>
> I will not intrude on your grief [at Mary Johnson's illness] with criticism on your Poetry. But the whole tone of it exercises me much before God, for I cannot help seeing that your thoughts run altogether in the same channels as those of unconverted men. They are not immoral; but they are *earthly*; even the allusions to higher things are not such as the Holy Ghost begets in the heart of a believer, derived from His own revealed Word, but mere sentiment, the fruit of the natural heart. Can God smile on this?[57]

The religious deficiencies which Philip spotted were coincidentally heightened at this time by some correspondence which he had with James

55. J. A. Blaikie-PHG, 14 May 1870 (LeBL). Blaikie was grateful for the suggested corrections, one of which was '"Leaves" do not "moan"—that is true' (instead he wrote: 'There is a murmur in the leaves on high', cited in review of J.A. Blaikie, *Love's Victory. Lyrical Poems*, in *Athenaeum*, 16 July 1892, 49).

56. Luke 21: 36: 'Watch ye therefore, and pray always, that ye may be accounted worthy to escape all these things that shall come to pass, and to stand before the Son of man.'

57. PHG-EWG, 18 May 1870 (CUL Add. 7041, 35). Emphasis in the original.

Green, his long-ago school-mate and his deceased sister Elizabeth's husband. In acknowledging a copy of Green's *Shadow & Sunshine; or, Claverton Churchyard*, Philip ended his letter: 'The night is far spent, & the day is at hand. ... Soon our Lord Jesus will come; O to be found of Him in peace, without spot and blameless!'[58] And about a year and a half later, after Green had sent him a second edition of the poems, dedicated to him, Philip added: 'It is a joy for me to hail you as a fellow-heir of the grace of life, & to see that your aims are towards the glory of His holy name.'[59]

In the meantime, Edmund was showing himself unwilling to yield to his father's voice. They continued to argue about the proper interpretation of Scriptures, focussing on separation from the world and prophecy, as well as Philip's continuing spiritual exhortations. At one point, Edmund shocked his father by asking if he had ever read the Gospels (Edmund seemed to place a higher value on them than on the Apostolic Epistles). 'I assure you I have read the Gospels;' Philip declared. ' ... I think just as highly of them as of the Epistles; not a whit more highly, nor less.' And he continued: 'I want only to know what God speaks; this has long been my earnest study; not, as you erroneously suggest, "to make the Scriptures prove my preconceived view of the Will of God", but by searching the Word *in all its parts*, & weighing the whole.'[60] But the question was not only what God *said*, but what He *meant*, that was disputed:

> ... You [Edmund] cite his saying, "Ye are the light of the world!" as if you understand by it, companionship with the world. But is this a fair exegesis? Read it with His own practical comment. He said emphatically,—"I am *the* light of the world." Did this involve any companionship in Him with it? "The world cannot hate *you*," He said to his unbelieving relatives (John vii. 5, 7);—"but Me it hateth, because *I testify* of it, that the works thereof are evil."
>
> O my beloved child! this is what I understand by being "the light of the world". It is, walking with Christ in a path of separation from it, & thence testifying against its evil; yes, & *getting its hatred* for so doing.

58. PHG-J. Green, 7 Feb. 1870 (CUL Adv. c. 82.5, 68).

59. PHG-J. Green, 29 Aug. 1871 (CUL Add. 7035/X/1); PHG-J. Green, 30 June 1871 (Adv. c. 82.5, 80). J. Green, *Shadow & Sunshine; or, Claverton Churchyard* (Bath: Printed for the Author, second ed., [1871]). Green was the author of *Popery, the Antagonist of Liberty*, and poetical works.

60. PHG-EWG, 20 May 1870 (CUL Add. 7041, 36). Emphasis in the original. What EWG wrote is only known from the references in PHG's reply.

Is that what *you* understand by being lights in the world? If not, who studies the Gospel best, you or I?

My dear Boy, gladly do I assure you that you have not "forfeited my love" by speaking out. The more fully you will discuss these themes the better I shall be pleased; always assuming, as I said before, that the Word is paramount. It is because you have studied them slightly, (forgive my plainness), & in other's twilight, that you have not discerned their heavenly meaning.[61]

Philip had also sent Edmund the first two numbers of his prophetic study of 'The Breaking of the Day', serialised in *The Christian*. There Philip had detailed the evidence which he was convinced pointed to the second advent. Edmund found the facts weak and the proofs flimsy. His father countered that he had not read carefully.

In the end, Edmund still thought that his father was trying to compel belief, not to offer beneficial advice. What the one saw as attempts to warn, the other viewed as efforts to be forced into a Procrustean bed. 'Why will you persist in saying I '*reproach*' you?', Philip asked in his letter of May 20:

Why will you consider my warnings & intreaties unkind? I see my child merrily pulling flowers in a wood, & an assassin aiming at his life from behind a tree. I interrupt his sport with a loud cry of warning; & I am harsh & selfish for doing so! He is walking across a path whose greened surface conceals a treacherous pit. I have traversed the same path before him, & have, not without cost, learned the danger; & I intreat him to choose a safer, though less inviting, path. And this is unkind! My experienced eye discerns in him germs of a fatal disease; & I am importunate with him to have recourse to preventive & remedial measures. And this is my narrow, frozen prejudice, which grudges him his enjoyments![62]

And ten days later, Philip expanded the arguments:

You ask me not to be displeased if you remind me that I am "thoroughly determined that I am perfectly right"; & you are afraid that "argument & evidence are not much valued by me now". Is this true? I am content, nay

61. PHG-EWG, 20 May 1870 (CUL Add. 7041, 36). Emphasis in the original.
62. PHG-EWG, 20 May 1870 (CUL Add. 7041, 36). Emphasis in the original.

eager, that *everything* wh. I hold should be tested by the Word of God; & my letter was *all* argument: whereas you give me absolutely none. ...

You say I bring a charge against you, which you pronounced unjust & untrue, that your expressions of spiritual emotion & experience to me have been "mere sentiment"; and "what the smile of God could not rest on." And you put quotation-marks, just as above; so as to imply that you are quoting my *ipsissima verba*; & you appeal to my calmer judgment whether such an accusation is not ungenerous.

Will you kindly send me the letter, or the sheet, in which I make such a charge. I am absolutely unconscious of ever having had such a thought. Look again, & see if any words of mine will really bear such a construction. ... Whenever you have given me your confidence on the inward workings of your own heart, your trials, your temptations, your faith, your feelings,—I have ever felt the fullest sympathy for them, & have treated them with the tenderest delicacy & reverence.

You effect to be much puzzled to come at my meaning. I do not think that my language is so obscure that I cannot manage to express what I mean. I do not believe you are so dull as not readily to catch that meaning. I had pressed on you that God says, "Give me thy heart." You ask if I meant that you "should study for the church." This is unworthy of my dear Boy. You know perfectly what I mean; you had not a suspicion that I meant what you suggest. You know well, in your inmost soul, that you have <u>not</u> given God *your* heart; & I am sure you know quite well, what *giving him your heart* implies. You do not like it; but do not say you do not know what it means. You call it monasticism; but, I fear, only on the old principle, Give a dog a bad name, & hang him. ...

It is not a question of doubtful interpretation. If Jesus was in any sense the exponent of the mind of God, *there stand his words*, clear & full & unambiguous; plenty of them; on multitudes of occasions; in various combinations & connexions;—there, I say, are *his words*. When I was very little older than you, I felt their power. I acknowledged their claim; & though I, with sorrow, confess very many trespasses, very many treasons, against his authority, yet I can boldly say, I have, throughout these eight & forty years,[63] owned his claim as the supreme law of my life. That life has not been an unhappy one: I am sure you

---

63. PHG experienced his evangelical conversion in 1832, when he was 22. In 1870, he was 60. PHG should have written, 'eight & thirty years'.

know, whatever you may say, it has not been a "monastic" or gloomy one. I have selected my friends from the friends of Christ; I have sought to "serve my generations by the will of God"; I have not been ashamed to confess the Blessed Name of Jesus; I look forward, with an humble hope, that He will not be ashamed of me. Is it strange that I ardently wish *you* to serve & confess & follow the same loving Master?

You appeal to my "calmer judgment." All my verdict on this matter is calm. I write nothing in passion:—why should I? It is not my own interest, that is concerned. What gain wd. it be to *me* that you should accept my counsels, save the indirect gain that would flow to me from your benefit? Because you are my own flesh & blood; "my own bowels"! Would it not be simpler, easier, for me just to let you alone, & leave you to take your own course? And this I should certainly do, only that I love you dearly.[64]

This kind of emotionally draining correspondence could not long continue, and the returns were bound to be diminishing. If the two could have calmly discussed their differences in person, some mutual understanding might have ensued—that's what Philip thought.

-IV-

Towards the end of June, there were startling developments. Mary Johnson died (as previously mentioned), and as a result of this strain on Edmund, Miss Buckham suggested that it might be a good idea if he would accompany her nephew and niece on a trip to Switzerland. It would also 'greatly enlarge his mind, his knowledge of books is much more extensive than of persons,' she wrote Philip.[65] Before a decision was made, Philip received a new poem from his son dealing with the death of Christ. He saw it as a stunning reversal: 'We had no notion of what our darling was capable of. The subject is noble & the treatment is noble,' Philip wrote. To be sure, a letter followed full of details for suggested corrections—without alluding to the atoning character of Christ, the poem 'is like "Hamlet" without the Prince of Denmark's part'—but these could be worked out later.[66] The poem may have smoothed the way to

64. PHG-EWG, 30 May 1870 (CUL Add. 7041, 37). Emphasis in the original.
65. Anne Buckham-PHG, 24 June 1870 (CUL Add. 7027, 47; see also Add. 7027, 45).
66. PHG-EWG, 20 June 1870 (CUL Add. 7041, 38); also PHG-EWG, 25 June 1870 (Corr. Bk.).

acceptance of Buckham's proposed trip. Philip now offered to pay for it, as long as Edmund kept a copious journal for his parents.[67]

Good news followed good news. On 25 June, Philip returned to Edmund's poetry book project. He composed a proposal to be sent, and then personally delivered by Edmund, to Macmillan, the London publisher. When nothing came of this, they tried Longmans two weeks later. Success![68]

On 15 July, tensions which had been mounting in Europe came to a head. Though fighting between France and Prussia had not been expected, on the next day France declared war.[69] That meant one thing: a trip to Switzerland was out of the question, so Denmark was considered.[70] It also meant another: Maybe Philip was correct about his second advent expectations. As he wrote his son:

> Though you don't, & perhaps won't, accept my thoughts on Prophecy, yet, I pray you, keep your eyes open, & maintain a very close walk with God; & betake yourself frequently & diligently to the blood & sprinkling (1 John i.9), that your daily trespasses may be cleansed away: lest That Day take you unawares.
>
> The sudden breaking out of what promises to be a general European war of colossal proportions, at the very moment that the Papacy crowns its arrogant blasphemy,—is surely a loud cry, "Watch!"[71]

Edmund responded by admitting that he did see grounds for watching. Also, prudence dictated not a holiday to the Continent but one closer to home. Scotland was selected, and on or about 30 July he set off, accompanied by Mansell Dames.[72]

The three-week journey to Scotland took the two to the Central

67. PHG-EWG, 25 June 1870 (Corr. Bk.); PHG-EWG, 22 July 1870 (CUL Add. 7041, 41), which indicates the amount paid was £20.

68. PHG-EWG, 25 June 1870; PHG-Macmillan, publisher, same date (both letters in Corr. Bk.); according to the latter, EWG had once been introduced to Macmillan by Kingsley. PHG made the proposal (later accepted) that the volume be published at the author's expense, and printed by R. Clay, Sons, and Taylor, who had printed several of his books. He would see it through the press, and it was to appear in the style of Tennyson's *Holy Grail* (1870); see also Corr. Bk. under 4 July 1870 (letter to Longmans & Co.).

69. 'The War', *Illustrated London News* 57 (23 July 1870), 78.

70. EWG-PHG, 18 July 1870 (CUL Add. 7018, 45).

71. PHG-EWG, 20 July 1870 (CUL Add. 7041, 39).

72. PHG-EWG, 22 July 1870 (CUL Add. 7041, 41), and PHG-EWG, 13 Sept. 1870 (Add. 7041, 42, 44). It is difficult to tell exactly when EWG began his trip, but evidence suggests July 30 (Corr. Bk.).

Highlands and the Hebrides. Edmund recorded many strange and 'never to be forgotten' things. He commented briefly upon the natural history of the area, objected to the smoking of tobacco and drinking of spirits on the ship from London, and said that a church which he saw was 'in modern parlance absurdly called a Cathedral.'[73] But it was obvious that, in many small details, Edmund was not pursuing his father's path. He made no attempt to draw Mansell towards religious belief;[74] he admired the natural beauty of some of the sites—'I found my cheeks flushed, and my heart beating fast'[75]—yet there was no connection made to God's wisdom in creation. His Sundays were notable for the sparse way in which he wrote about them. Though Edmund pronounced that 'I hate the Scotch,' he was interested in seeing the National Gallery in Edinburgh and some books of the Elizabethan poet Thomas Lodge.[76] He concluded his Journal with a word of thanks for 'this glorious outing ... to the best of Fathers that ever lived.'[77]

With Edmund's return to London on 22 August, 1870, his correspondence with his father began where it had left off. But there was a difference—so Philip thought, with a certain justification. He felt Edmund's questions about the Bible were being resolved. He rejoiced that his son was recognizing the '*wondrous coherency & divinity*' in the Holy Scriptures,[78] and for his twenty-first birthday his parents sent him Henry Alford's four-volume edition of the Greek New Testament (1849-1861).[79] He was gratified that Edmund was seeking his help in 'watching'; he learned his son was undertaking 'lowly work for Him,' and that he had become the Superintendent of the Brook Street Sunday school. Moreover, Edmund had decided to remain in communion with the Brethren at Tottenham.[80] All was positive:

73. EWG, 'Journal in Scotland', August 1870 (National Library of Scotland, MS 2562), f. 11. There is a summary of the Journal in W. M. Parker, 'A Modern Tour to the Hebrides. The Criticisms of Edmund Gosse', *Scots Magazine* XXXIV (Jan.-Feb. 1941), 263-72, 341-50, and Charteris, 26-9.

74. PHG-EWG, 9 Apr. 1868 (CUL Add. 7041, 18); PHG-EWG, 22 July 1870 (CUL Add. 7041, 41).

75. EWG, 'Journal in Scotland', f. 13.

76. EWG, 'Journal in Scotland', ff. 3 (verso), and 35; EWG, 'Thomas Lodge', in EWG, *Seventeenth-Century Studies. A Contribution to the History of English Poetry* (London: Kegan Paul, Trench & Co., 1883), 3-40.

77. EWG, 'Journal in Scotland', ff. 35, 36.

78. PHG-EWG, 2 Sept. 1870 (CUL Add. 7041, 40). Emphasis in the original.

79. PHG-EWG, 19 Sept. 1870 (CUL Add. 7041, 45); *Father and Son*, 1907, Epilogue, 353.

80. PHG-EWG, 13 Sept. 1870 (CUL Add. 7041, 42, 44).

I do not prescribe to you any particular mode of exhibition of your
obedience & love to your Lord. All I was most anxious about, (& this
I now with joy learn of you,) was that your heart was really habitually
dealing with Himself. *How* He shall lead you I am quite content to
leave to Him,—now that I know you do truly yield yourself to Him.
Whether you break bread with "Brethren", or worship with the Church
of England, or with godly Dissenters;—whether you spend your time &
talents in active service for souls for Jesus' sake;—whether you regulate
your friendships & your daily conversation by the principle of confessing
Christ & taking up the Cross;—and in what degree, & in what mode, these
are settled;—while I by no means think unimportant, yet all these I am
content to leave to your own selection & decision, if only I know that you
are habitually walking with God, as *Father, in the light*.[81]

And yet. The son's actions indicate either that he was withholding
information from his father, or that his father was listening only for
that which he wanted to hear.

Edmund and Blaikie's *Madrigals, Songs and Sonnets* appeared in
December 1870,[82] bearing a dedication (without explanation) to Mrs
Henry Curtis, of Torquay.[83] Philip's judgment was that the whole
would do both authors credit, and he was especially pleased with the
simplicity of Edmund's verse. He even found nothing to complain of in
its religious content,

except what I may call nature-worship; while here & there occur
recognitions of God. In "The Tomb [in the Garden]", however, which
I think, *in every respect*, the very centre & gem of the book, you have
sought to make the blessed <u>Son of God</u> the object of your readers'
admiration & adoration,—as well as of your own. And for this effort to
exalt the Beloved Saviour with your Poetic talent, I doubt not that He
will bless & exalt *you*.[84]

81. PHG-EWG, 2 Sept. 1870 (CUL Add. 7041, 40). Emphasis in the original.

82. EWG and J. A. Blaikie, *Madrigals, Songs, and Sonnets* (London: Longmans, Green,
and Co., 1870). Though the book was announced for 5 December, it may have been delayed. The
earliest review I have seen is in the *Manchester Guardian*, 28 Dec. 1870, 3.

83. Mary Curtis lived with her husband, Henry Curtis, at Upton Cottage, or The Rosary.
She was 57 in 1871, he was 50 (*1871 Census Returns for Torquay*, Enumeration District 9, RG
10/2085). As previously mentioned, when EWG's stepmother Eliza first met PHG, she was
staying with them.

84. PHG-EWG, 8 Dec. 1870 (CUL Add. 7018, 27). Emphasis in the original. Charteris, 31-2.
In EWG's 'The Poet to Nature', he refers to himself as 'thy child and worshipper, thine own!'

The major literary publications did not notice the work, and it received mixed comment in the press.[85] Only a dozen copies were sold.[86] The burning desire to become '*hominum volitare per ora*' remained, no thirst had been quenched, and Philip's warnings about the danger which striving for ego gratification might pose to him in drawing his affections away from Jesus and to the world, went for nought.[87]

Madrigals, Songs and Sonnets did have its positive side. Both Swinburne and Dante Gabriel Rossetti (1828-1882) were said to have 'praised very highly' the sonnet on 'Webster'.[88] That was one door opened. Edmund also gained entrance into *The Athenaeum*, the 'indispensable' literary and scientific weekly, where he was by May 1871 a member of the regular staff.[89]

Perhaps at this time he was introduced to Tennyson by W. R. S. Ralston (1828-1889), an Assistant in the Department of Printed Books who pioneered in the introduction into England of popular Russian

(EWG and Blaikie, *Madrigals, Songs, and Sonnets*, 6).

85. No review of *Madrigals* is recorded in 'An Edmund Gosse Bibliography', Boston *Literary World* XVI (16 May 1885), 172-3, or Paul F. Mattheisen, 'Edmund Gosse: A Literary Record' (Rutgers University, PhD dissertation, 1958), but the book did receive a good deal of press coverage. For positive reviews: *Torquay Directory*, 4 Jan. 1871, 3; *Illustrated London News* 58 (14 Jan. 1871), 35 ('contains many things of considerable merit'); *Athenaeum*, 21 Jan. 1871), 78: 'the poems have a power of melodious versification that promises well'; Exeter *Western Times*, 24 Jan. 1871), 8: '... a [happy] contrast to the showy and blatant efforts sometimes designated as poetry'; and *Bristol Mercury and Western Counties Advertiser* (26 Aug. 1871, 6: 'a dramatic sketch, 'The Tomb in the Garden', ... is of superior merit both as regards conception and execution'). Less favourable reviews: *Manchester Guardian*, 28 Dec. 1870, 3: 'Messrs. Blaikie and Gosse are verse-makers. To say that they are poets would be untrue'; London *Examiner*, 7 Jan. 1871, 19-20: 'The poems never rise above that fatal mediocrity which neither gods nor men can endure'; London *Graphic*, 8 Apr. 1871, 7: '... the work of men of culture, but we cannot conscientiously say it is poetical'.

86. According to *The Candid Friend* (22 June 1901), 297, only 12 copies of *Madrigals* were sold. In July 1899, one of 40 copies of the book then known to exist was auctioned at Sotheby's (the others had been destroyed by the authors: 'Book and Curio Sales', *Glasgow Herald*, 22 July 1899, 7). EWG later thought that only a few of his sonnets showed promise (EWG-L. N. Chase, 16 May [1917], in Mattheisen and Millgate, *Transatlantic Dialogue*, 297).

87. PHG-EWG, 21 Oct. 1870 (CUL Add. 7041, 46), and PHG-EWG, 8 Dec. 1870 (CUL Add. 7018, 27).

88. EWG, in Mattheisen and Millgate, *Transatlantic Dialogue*, 297; Bredsdorff, *Sir Edmund Gosse's Correspondence*, 82.

89. PHG-EWG, 12 May 1871 (CUL Add. 7041, 47). Likely the more correct description is that EWG was a regular 'contributor'. For the characterization of the *Athenaeum*: Ellegård, *The Readership of the Periodical Press*, 22. EWG could have come to the *Athenaeum* via D. G. Rossetti, a contributor (sometime between 1846-69), or Richard Garnett, another reviewer (Marchand, *Athenaeum*, 90, 225).

literature[90] and was supportive of Edmund's work.[91] Edmund later remembered having been gratified that the Poet Laureate had read some of his verse, 'and was vaguely gracious about them. He seemed to accept me as a sheep in the fold of which he was, so magnificently, the shepherd.'[92] Edmund moved quickly to exploit these new connections. He attended the fortnightly meetings at the homes of members of the Pre-Raphaelites in mid-1871, and was said to have been called 'Our youngest Poet' by D. G. Rossetti.

His extended family was watching. In a letter concluding with the words 'to be *burnt* as soon as read,' Mary Ann Baker reported to Philip on the developments. The frequent 'meetings at the houses of these Celebrities' were concerning. They were exhausting Edmund, and they were lowering 'the spiritual tone'. Edmund acknowledged the latter point, but said that they are '*needful*' as a learning experience. Yet there was also reassurance. Edmund told Mary Ann Baker that he declined to visit the literati on Sundays, telling his hosts: never on '*that day.*' Using his Greek New Testament, he studied Scriptures in the evenings with Baker, when possible. And prior to setting off for Norway in June,[93] he made sure that Baker and Anne Buckham 'commend me to God.'[94]

On balance, a hopeful attitude seemed justified. Philip's mind was at ease. This is how he summed up the situation in an August 1871 letter to James Green:

> Very lately I had the great joy of finding satisfactory evidence ... that my brother William has closed with God's offer of mercy, & accepted Jesus as his own Saviour. And now, there is not one very near & dear to me by natural ties, of whom I have not a confident recognition, as in that happy band, who are redeemed with the Blood of the Lamb. To God Jehovah be all praise![95]

90. J. S. C., 'W. R. S. Ralston', *Academy* 36 (10 Aug. 1889), 87. Ralston first met EWG in 1867 (Ralston, 'A Testimonial to Mr. [Edmund] Gosse', *Pall Mall Gazette*, 28 Oct. 1886, 2).

91. Ralston defended EWG against Churton Collins: Ralston: 'The 'Quarterly Review' and Mr. Gosse', *Athenaeum* (6 Nov. 1886), 601-2.

92. EWG, *Portraits and Sketches*, 130-3.

93. Bredsdorff, *Sir Edmund Gosse's Correspondence*, 83.

94. M. A. Baker-PHG, 13 July 1871 (CUL Add. 7018, 28). Emphasis in the original.

95. PHG-J. Green, 29 Aug. 1871 (CUL Add. 7035/X/1).

-V-

In the fall of 1870 Edmund had turned 21. He was making his way in life: twice he nearly married, at his work he found friends with like-minded literary inclinations and aspirations, he became a published poet, and he had wedged himself into the company of the trending versifiers of the day. Throughout, he had managed to include his spiritual life in these changes and to manage his father's expectations of him. In 1871 he began another chapter of growth when his life was transformed by his engagement with the literary landscape of Norway and later Scandinavia.

Even a few years later he said he was unable to recall what it was that attracted him to the North.[96] The disclaimer is hardly credible. If there was little literary intercommunication between London and Paris at this time,[97] there was none between England and Scandinavia. It was *terra incognita*, and the first explorer could achieve fame. Such a pioneer was waiting at the docks, one who (as previously mentioned) already had the rudiments of the 'Dano-Norwegian' language, and who would have visited the area earlier had not the Franco-Prussia War intervened.

Edmund was to visit Scandinavia three times between 1871-4, but his first tour provided almost no hint as to the importance the area would have for him. From around mid-June to the first days of August he visited Norway by himself.[98] He could not speak the language and was unfamiliar with the literature, so he concentrated on the scenery of coastal districts. The result was that, when he returned home he wrote—what even then was not uncommon[99]—a travelogue, this one on the Lofoden Islands, northwest of Norway.[100] This *Fraser's Magazine* piece was his first periodical publication.[101]

Then there was that 1871 episode in Trondheim. Wandering into a bookstore, he asked 'if there were any Norwegian poets!!' He was shown Henrik Ibsen's *Digte* (*Poems*), which had only just appeared. Though he admittedly couldn't understand a word in it,[102] back in London he consulted with W. R. S. Ralston at the British Museum and R. H. Hutton,

96. Bredsdorff, *Sir Edmund Gosse's Correspondence*, 82-3.

97. Bredsdorff, *Sir Edmund Gosse's Correspondence*, 22.

98. Bredsdorff, *Sir Edmund Gosse's Correspondence*, 83. *Corr.Bk.* registers PHG-EWG letters, but without stating EWG's location.

99. Bredsdorff, *Sir Edmund Gosse's Correspondence*, 2.

100. EWG, 'The Lofoden Islands', *Fraser's Magazine* n.s. IV (Nov. 1871), 563-74.

101. Charteris, 35; Bredsdorff, *Sir Edmund Gosse's Correspondence*, 2, 316.

102. Bredsdorff, *Sir Edmund Gosse's Correspondence*, 83.

editor of *The Spectator*, a broad-minded, political weekly with a literary emphasis. The former knew Norwegian, and the latter advised Edmund if he wanted to get more articles published, a good tactic would be to write on 'something out of the way, Scandinavian literature for instance.' During 1871-2 Edmund thus studied anew the Dano-Norwegian languages,[103] achieving a satisfactory reading level within three months. In March 1872 his review of *Digte* was published by Hutton. It was the first time that Ibsen's name appeared in Britain (his forename was twice misspelled 'Henrick').[104]

Edmund soon discovered that while he was able to publish another article in 1871,[105] getting Ibsen into print a second time was not so easy. During 1872 he talked and wrote a great deal about the poet, but Mesdames Baker and Buckham advised him that he would weary people with the constant chatter about 'Mr. Gibson'. The two women were right: several articles on Ibsen by Edmund were submitted and rejected. Philip Harwood (1809-1887),[106] editor of the leading political-literary *Saturday Review*, said that Edmund's review of Ibsen's *Peer Gynt* was so fulsome in its praise of an unknown writer that he needed a second appraiser to confirm the assessment. None was forthcoming, so he did not publish it. Finally James Anthony Froude (1818-1894)[107] of *Fraser's Magazine*, and in 1873 John Morley (1838-1923)[108] of the *Fortnightly Review*, the liberal-radical monthly, accepted Edmund's essays, and from then on no further hindrance lay in his way.[109]

103. Bredsdorff, *Sir Edmund Gosse's Correspondence*, 2, 83; Charteris, 39.

104. Bredsdorff, *Sir Edmund Gosse's Correspondence*, 24; [EWG], 'Ibsen's New Poems', *Spectator* 45 (3 Mar. 1872), 344-5. Ibsen's forename was correctly spelled in the index to the volume and once in the text; *DNCJ*, 589; Ellegård, *The Readership of the Periodical Press*, 24-5.

105. [EWG], 'George Cruikshank', *Spectator* 44 (2 Dec. 1871), 1465-6. EWG's anonymous review of *A Descriptive Catalogue of the Works of George Cruikshank* is identified in PHG-Charles Kingsley, 5 Jan. 1872 (Corr. Bk.). This article has not been previously ascribed to EWG.

106. McCabe, *Biographical Dictionary of Modern Rationalists*, 328. Harwood's rejection seems odd, given that he was the first to introduce the biblical critic David F. Strauss's work to England (Thrane, 'The Rise of Higher Criticism in England, 1800-1870', 285).

107. McCabe, *Biographical Dictionary of Modern Rationalists*, 272-3; Wheeler, *Biographical Dictionary of Freethinkers*, 139-40.

108. McCabe, *Biographical Dictionary of Modern Rationalists*, 533-4; Wheeler, *Biographical Dictionary of Freethinkers*, 234.

109. Bredsdorff, *Sir Edmund Gosse's Correspondence*, 183-4 fn. 118; [EWG], 'A Norwegian Drama [*Peer Gynt*]', *Spectator* 45 (7 July 1872), 922-3; EWG, 'Norwegian Poetry Since 1814', *Fraser's Magazine* n.s. VI (1 Oct. 1872), 435-49; EWG, 'Ibsen, the Norwegian Satirist', *Fortnightly Review* XIII (1 Jan. 1873), 74-88; Ellegård, *The Readership of the Periodical Press*, 24; *DNCJ*, 227-8; for EWG's other writings on Scandinavia: bibliography in Bredsdorff.

The interest in Scandinavian literature was influencing Edmund's relationship with his father in three ways: he was becoming an established critic, was earning money in the process,[110] and was widening his knowledge of the world. Undoubtedly the last of these factors was the most important, and two men whom he met in London in the spring of 1872 greatly helped him expand his horizons. He was introduced to the 'most popular Danish divine of his day',[111] the Lutheran Dean of Holmen's Church in Copenhagen, Bruun Juul Fog (1819-1896), as someone with an interest in Danish literature, and showed Fog around London.[112] At the same time, Ibsen put Edmund in touch with the Norwegian linguist Jakob Løkke (1829-1881). He acted as a guide during Løkke's frequent trips to England, while Løkke was an almanac of information about Norwegian affairs for Edmund.[113] Certainly Fog, and probably Løkke as well, invited Edmund to visit the North again.

The result was that two weeks during the summer of 1872 were spent at the home of Dean Fog in Copenhagen, and an equal amount of time with Løkke in Christiania. While he was in Denmark (13-27 July) he was introduced to Fog's circle of friends, including the Danish poets Hans Christian Andersen[114] and Frederick Paludan-Müller (1809-1876), the Danish bishops Grundtvig[115] and Martensen,[116] and many others.[117] And between 29 July and 13 August he met a number of Løkke's ultra-conservative friends,[118] as well as the Norwegian political writer Ludvig Kristensen Daa[119] (to whom he showed an introduction from Tennyson)

110. By October 1872, EWG had earned £20 for that year (EWG-PHG, 5 Oct. 1872; CUL Add. 7018, 50). In 1874, this increased to more than £112, and more than £187 in 1875 (Charteris, 94).

111. E[dmund] G[osse], 'Bishop Fog', *Athenaeum*, 7 Mar. 1896, 314-15.

112. EWG, 'Two Northern Prelates', *Cornhill Magazine* n.s.XXXI (Aug. 1911), 191; EWG, *Two Visits to Denmark: 1872, 1874* (London: Smith, Elder, & Co., 1911), 21.

113. Bredsdorff, *Sir Edmund Gosse's Correspondence*, 3-4. Løkke visited Edmund at both the Museum and Tottenham (Bredsdorff, 195fn.303).

114. Edmund W. Gosse, 'Hans Christian Andersen', *Academy* VIII (14 Aug. 1875), 168-9.

115. Unsigned obituary, 'Bishop Grundtvig', *Spectator* 45 (21 Sept. 1872), 1199-1200, attributed to EWG by Bredsdorff, *Sir Edmund Gosse's Correspondence*, 316.

116. E[dmund]. W[illiam]. G[osse]., 'Hans Lassen Martensen', *Athenaeum* 16 Feb. 1884), 214-5; 'Bishop Martensen', *The Expositor* ser. 3, vol. I (Jan. 1885), 59-68.

117. EWG, *Two Visits to Denmark*, 70-130; EWG, Bredsdorff, *Sir Edmund Gosse's Correspondence*, 4-5.

118. In politics, Løkke 'became a high-and-dry conservative, of a kind very rare to meet with in Norway—a Tory of the most grimly despairing species' (Edmund W. Gosse, 'Obituary. Jakob Løkke', *Academy*, 15 Oct. 1881, 293).

119. Unsigned obituary note, *Academy* XI (23 June 1877), 555, attributed to EWG by Bredsdorff, *Sir Edmund Gosse's Correspondence*, 326.

and the Norwegian poet Bjørnstjerne Bjørnson (1832-1910), a radical outside of this group.[120]

Although all of these connections aided Edmund in furthering his career, it was his friendship with Dean Fog which had a striking influence. Here was a young Englishman, emerging from the influence of a father whose overwhelming confidence in his understanding of the true in religion was so pronounced, staying at a future bishop's home. And yet how differently they observed the Lord's Day. In Copenhagen, the observance actually began on the previous afternoon and ended twenty-four hours later. And when the Sunday mid-day meal was over, Edmund was shocked to find how quickly the atmosphere and tone of conversation changed. On one occasion, his hosts immediately began to entertain him on the piano.[121]

The attitudes were also different. For Philip, anything which in its alpha and omega was worldly, was evil. Fog saw no objection to secular music, nudity in painting and sculpture, philosophical debate, or dancing and the drama.[122] Gradually it must have dawned upon Edmund that the guardian of truth was protecting something which was relative and not absolute.

-VI-

As the ego of Tristram Jones went from strength to strength during 1871-2, finding new friends and coming into contact with new ideas, writing for publications such as *Fraser's*, the *Spectator*, the *Academy*, and the *Athenaeum*, Edmund found himself in a state of almost unrelieved tension with his father. There might be smiles, but these seemed to be intermissions between frowns. Edmund knew what he wanted, and it is evident that with a new-found will he was determined to get it.

About three months after he had returned from the Lofoden Islands, he was back again dining with the Pre-Raphaelites. On 19 October 1871, he was at W. Bell Scott's, where he met William Allingham (1824-1889),[123]

120. Unsigned obituary, 'Death of Bjørnson. (From Our Own Correspondent.)', London *Times*, 27 Apr. 1910, 5, attributed to EWG by Bredsdorff, *Sir Edmund Gosse's Correspondence*, 335; EWG, 'A Visit to the Friends of Ibsen', *Aspects and Impressions* (London: Cassell and Co., 1922), 247-59; Bredsdorff, *Sir Edmund Gosse's Correspondence*, 5; 'Bjornson (Björnstjerne)', in Wheeler, *Biographical Dictionary of Freethinkers*, 44-5.

121. EWG, *Two Visits to Denmark*, 30.

122. EWG, *Two Visits to Denmark*, 247.

123. McCabe, *Biographical Dictionary of Modern Rationalists*, 17-18.

a minor poet and sub-editor of *Fraser's*; Charles Edward Appleton (1841-1879), the founder and editor of the *Academy* and his assistant editor, Francis Hueffer (1845-1889);[124] and Christina and Dante Rossetti. 'It was very kind of Mr. Scott, I think, to ask me to a little party of people who were all sure to be useful to me,' he wrote his father. Edmund then proceeded to tell him of another such gathering he attended five days later. This one was notable because the host, the painter Ford Madox Brown (1821-1893),[125] thought that William Morris (1834-1896)[126] would like to meet Edmund. A date was set. 'I tell you these little particulars because you told me you liked to know them,' Edmund added, '& because they are all significant as steps gained in my profession.'[127] Apparently at this time Edmund was also introduced to the minor Pre-Raphaelite poet Philip Bourke Marston (1850-1887),[128] whose sister Eleanor later married O'Shaughnessy. On 13 January 1872, 'The great poet, who is the biggest lion I have been introduced to yet,'—as William Morris was described—'was very benign, and was good enough to say "he had heard all about me."'[129]

Philip congratulated his son on his published writing,[130] yet behind the scenes he was maneuvering to separate Edmund from his British Museum associations. On the face of it, Philip's actions are mystifying. He claimed (in a letter to the Revd Charles Kingsley early in 1872, again seeking his assistance) that Edmund needed to look for a new position because he would soon be paid the maximum salary allowed and had no prospects for advancement. He even suggested that Edmund could replace his father's seriously ill friend, William Baird (1803-1872), an assistant in the Zoology Department at the Museum. 'To fill such a post as the one B[aird] had held, wd. be a g[rea]t del[igh]t to my son,' Philip told Kingsley, for his only child had long been interested in the invertebrates, Baird's specialty.[131]

124. McCabe, *Biographical Dictionary of Modern Rationalists*, 365.
125. McCabe, *Biographical Dictionary of Modern Rationalists*, 116-17.
126. McCabe, *Biographical Dictionary of Modern Rationalists*, 535.
127. EWG-PHG, 24 Oct. 1871 (CUL Add. 7018, 47); Charteris, 36-7; Walker, 'The Life and Work of William Bell Scott', 195. '... for some years [Scott was] one of the most valued of the staff of the *Academy*' (Monkhouse, 'Obituary. William Bell Scott, LL.D., H.R.S.A.', 529).
128. EWG, 'A Blind Poet', *Leaves and Fruit*, 308; London *Morning Post* (1 Feb. 1881), 5; 'Marston (Philip Bourke)', in Wheeler, *Biographical Dictionary of Freethinkers*, 219.
129. EWG-PHG, 15 Jan. 1872 (CUL Add. 7018, 48); Charteris, 38-9.
130. PHG-EWG, 27 Oct. 1871 (CUL Add. 7041, 48), referring to the Lofoden Islands article.
131. PHG-C. Kingsley, 5 Jan. 1872 (copy of a letter in Corr. Bk.).

The first claim is unpersuasive, and Philip knew the second was preposterous. Edmund told him as much when, a week later, Philip described the plan he had set before Kingsley. Edmund admitted that he could eventually become 'a really valuable, though never brilliant, servant of the Trustees' as a zoologist. It's just that he had no desire to do so:

> To make Zoology my life-study, ... I do not see my way to yet; that is, if you mean to the disregard of those branches of literature in which I am just now beginning to ascend towards some position. Belles-lettres would always be my delight in moments of relaxation, and I suppose the objects of my serious home-study. Having begun under such good auspices, & having just pushed myself with so much difficulty into a powerful clique, it seems to me it would be stupid to throw literature over for so small a chance as this is. I can cultivate both well, I believe, but I shall never, I suppose, be a scientific discoverer.[132]

Edmund was so eager to allow his new light to shine, and Philip so concerned to direct it to another source, that neither of them commented on how only a short while earlier Philip had been thankful that his son had not followed in his footsteps as a naturalist.

In truth, what seems to have troubled Philip was not his son, it was his son's circle of friends. From his Newfoundland days, Philip could recall the profound strength which he drew from his fellow clerks—Apsey, St. John, Jaques, Sprague, Newell, Lush. After his time in Hackney, he never lost touch with the Bergers, Pearse, or Emily Bowes. During his visits to the British Museum he met White, Westwood, Doubleday, Gray, and Baird. Wherever Gosse journeyed he gravitated towards other Christians—sincere, devoted, and thoughtful ones, like himself. They provided psychological support, comradeship, a shared vision of life. And Edmund? True, his father had arranged introductions to Baker, Buckham, the Howards, even Berger, and he had met the Beddowses and Johnsons. But the ones Edmund sought out on his own were freethinkers and rationalists—Dames, Payne, Marzials, Scott, Rossetti, Swinburne, Morris, Brown, and Marston, and from Scandinavia, Ibsen and those around him.

An extant letter suggests that this issue may well have been the one

---

132. EWG-PHG, 15 Jan. 1872 (CUL Add. 7018,48). '1871' has been changed to '1872', with '2' written in red, likely by PHG.

which impelled Philip to try to extricate his son from what he thought
was a poisonous environment. From the middle of January until at least
early March father and son were again at odds. 'The D[uke] of Somerset[133]
has just told us—though indeed we knew it well enough without his
testimony, that "society" quite rejects the Bible,' Philip wrote anxiously:

> And you know it as well as he. The literary, the scientific, the artistic,
> the polite, the fashionable, circles of London, are utterly alien from
> Christ. I am certain you know this; however you may know of individuals
> who secretly reverence Him. Now it is into this "society," that you are
> obtaining access; and it greatly excites my fears. O my Willy! you are
> walking in slippery places! Do you not feel that there is the sorest
> temptation to be ashamed of Christ in those circles? You confess Him
> at Tottenham. Yes, but there is no cross in the confession *there*. Do you
> confess Him in London? Do the people at the Museum,—do those at Mr.
> Madox Brown's,—know you are a Christian? Do you desire that it should
> be known; and *seek for* suitable occasions to let it be (unostentatiously,
> but decisively) known? I am not saying *no* to these questions; I do not
> certainly know; I earnestly wish to know; but you always evade a direct
> answer. ... Ask yourself whether the Name of Jesus is dearer to you
> than anything else. If you cannot uprightly say yes; *be sure there is
> something wrong*; & be warned to set it right without delay. ... But it is
> your own matter: as you make your bed, so you must lie. Do not think
> of "making the best of both worlds": there is no such thing: it is Satan's
> lie (Luke XVI.13). ...[134]

Edmund did reply soon, but the answer gave no satisfaction. In fact,
Philip responded with a letter he promptly regretted writing because
it 'failed in regard to the spirit of meekness.' He had asked God's
forgiveness, and Edmund's understanding:

> ... I lovingly <u>beseech</u> you, by the Grace of Christ; by the powers of the
> World to come; by the awful Tribunal before which you must shortly

133. On Edward Adolphus Seymour (1804-1885), Duke of Somerset: Wheeler, *Biographical
Dictionary of Freethinkers*, 302; McCabe, *Biographical Dictionary of Modern Rationalists*, 731.
PHG here refers to Somerset's *Christian Theology and Modern Scepticism* (1872), 'a trenchent
attack on orthodoxy' (Wheeler) in which the author 'rejects all miracles, denies the authority
of the Gospels, and opposes dogma and priesthood', though accepting a 'Supreme Intelligence'
(McCabe).

134. PHG-EWG, 6 Feb. 1872 (CUL Add. 7041, 49). Emphasis in the original.

stand; by the eternal results which thereon depend;—deeply & frequently ponder my late letter to you. For *these*, you must distinctly give account. God Himself has been, & is still, speaking to you, through me; and you cannot lay them lightly aside, & turn to merriment & forget them,—you cannot do this, without grieving (not me alone, but) the Holy Spirit of God, by whom you are sealed; without putting a grave affront upon (not me alone, but) that Loving Son of God, who once gave His blood freely for you. ...

I now close; asking you, in filial love, to pass by all that has given you pain in my correspondence, except as you may "suck honey out of the flinty rock"; and to believe me to remain, with unchanging affection, & with earnest hope that my labour shall not be in vain in the Lord,—and with tenderest love of dear Mamma. ...[135]

On 11 March, Philip found the tables turned, as his son put him on the defensive. It was all well and good that criticisms of Edmund's activities should come from Sandhurst, but what of the critic's own attitude? Was Philip not like 'a servant sitting at a window ... letting the house go quite unheeded ... not working about the house till the Master come'? The charge was denied: 'it is the very thing I am striving to avoid.' Countered the father:

For what have I given up the paths of Science, & turned from the praise of men, but that I might labour in my Master's house, & wash the feet of his lowly ones? *More than ever*, as I see *the day* approaching, have I of late sought to give up myself to His service,—to stir up, both by tongue & pen, His dear people to practical godliness, & readiness for Him. Nay, what were my late long letters to you, but the earnest devotion of time & thought & labour to *your* best interest, for Jesus' sake, because I believed I had caught sight of His near approach? ... Luke xii.42-44[136] is the secret of what, in my spirit & conduct, seems to you so peculiar. Oh! it is what *He prescribes* that I want to be doing. Other, even "earnest, Christians," are no rule for me.

---

135. PHG-EWG, 1 Mar. 1872 (CUL Add. 7041, 50). Emphasis in the original.
136. Luke 12: 42-4: 'And the Lord said, Who then is that faithful and wise steward, whom *his* lord shall make ruler over his household, to give *them their* portion of meat in due season? Blessed *is* that servant, whom his lord when he cometh shall find so doing. Of a truth I say unto you, that he will make him ruler over all that he hath' (KJV).

> I do not prescribe my own mode of life as a rule for you. You have
> a path of activity to pursue ... a path of honourable usefulness to your
> generation. I wish merely to see in you *the principle* of pleasing Christ,
> *so paramount* as to guide & govern all your doings. If I could be sure
> that you had decisively placed yourself under this rule –"Lord, what
> wilt *Thou* have me to do?"—I could cheerfully leave all the details to
> your own wisdom.[137]

During the remainder of 1872—both before and after Edmund's
second visit to Scandinavia—father and son seem to have set aside
their differences and found more pleasant topics to discuss. Philip
complimented Edmund for having moved onto a new literary path. It
seemed to Philip that Scandinavians were serious, God-fearing people,
and that this field 'had been opened for you by our gracious Lord, in
answer to prayer; & I trust his smile may consciously attend you in the
pursuit of it.'[138] He was also impressed with the extensive knowledge
which Edmund had gained in Northern languages, and he praised his
literary reviews (though hoping that Edmund did not intend to devote his
life to being a critic).[139] In the fall of this year, Edmund fulfilled requests
from his parents to provide them with sketches of how he spent a weekday
and Lord's Day. On his twenty-third birthday he wrote about the former,
prefacing it with a reflection on the previous year:

> ... I am conscious of many things to call forth great gratitude to God from
> me. He has preserved you both in health & strength, he has granted me
> much success, and given me much pleasure, and introduced me to kind
> friends and a wider sphere of interest. Beside this He has granted me
> more settled health than I have ever enjoyed in twelve months before.
> In all temporal blessings I am fortunate above my fellows, or I will not
> say fortunate, for that implies chance, and it is not chance, but this good
> hand of God that gives me these.[140]

A few weeks later he described a typical Sunday. He answered his
father's queries about whether he still participated in the Sunday school,

---

137. PHG-EWG, 11 Mar. 1872 (CUL Add. 7041, 51). Emphasis in the original.
138. PHG-EWG, 23 Apr. 1872 (CUL Add. 7041,52).
139. PHG-EWG, 26 Aug. 1872 (CUL Add. 7041,53).
140. EWG-PHG, 21 Sept. 1872 (CUL Add. 7018, 49).

and which church he went to,[141] in writing that he now affiliated with the Church of England (at Tottenham he worshipped at Brook Street). Theodore Howard was the Superintendent of the Sunday school, but Edmund still handled a class of about twelve boys (aged 13 to 15). On Sunday evenings, Edmund translated from Danish one of Dean Fog's sermons for Mesdames Baker and Buckham, 'and greatly are we all impressed and delighted by them.' A hymn and perhaps Scripture reading concluded the day.[142]

Towards the close of 1872, the irrepressible doubts reappeared in Philip's mind. Although there had been an evident revival of religious feeling on Edmund's part, his secular life continued to be suspect.[143] He told his father that he was writing some new poems (no comment on that has survived). Then, one day in November, Philip encountered his physician, Dr Thomas Finch (1824/5-1895). Gosse mentioned with pride his son's literary work, noting that he was writing for *The Academy*. Sometimes a parent boasts of a child's achievement and knowingly gilds the lily. Philip had already told Edmund that he was less than enamoured with that journal's theology section (unsurprisingly, given that *Academy* writers supported the Higher Criticism of the Bible).[144] Now he wrote Edmund of Finch's unexpected words, which exploded the father's prideful pretense: 'The Academy! that's a rather heretical paper, isn't it? Eckel writes in it, & Huxley!'[145] Finch's comment 'hurt me much,'[146] Philip wrote. Not less revealing: Philip did not recognise the name of the biologist Ernst Haeckel (1834-1919), the leading German propagandist for Darwin (the German equivalent as Darwin's 'bulldog'[147] to Huxley). It was confirmation of how out of touch Philip had become with attackers of the faith.

---

141. PHG-EWG, 24 Sept. 1872 (CUL Add. 7041, 54).

142. EWG-PHG, 5 Oct. 1872 (CUL Add. 7018, 50). In the next month, EWG solicited and gained the Superintendency of the Sunday school (PHG-EWG, 16 Nov. 1872. CUL Add. 7041, 55).

143. EWG-PHG, 5 Oct. 1872 (CUL Add. 7018, 50).

144. EWG-PHG, 15 Jan. 1872 (CUL Add. 7018, 48); John Curtis Johnson, 'The *Academy*, 1869-1896: Center of Informed Critical Opinion' (Northwestern University, PhD dissertation, 1958), 235-6.

145. Huxley did write for the *Academy* and did review works of Haeckel there, but Haeckel was not an *Academy* contributor (Johnson, 'The *Academy*, 1869-1896', 59, 283, 285).

146. PHG-EWG, 16 Nov. 1872 (CUL Add. 7041, 55).

147. Rupke, *Richard Owen*, 206; 'Haeckel (Ernst Heinrich Philippo August)', in Wheeler, *Biographical Dictionary of Freethinkers*, 160.

-VII-

After four years of corresponding, father and son had explored their conflicting attitudes in a fraught relationship. The points had been made and the positions had been staked out. In painful detail over a three month period, each side now summed up its interpretation of the past, present, and future. Armageddon was at hand.

In part, this final battle was triggered by what in different circumstances would have been an instructive dispute about believer's baptism for children. Around the beginning of December 1872,[148] Wyndham Edmund Bewes (1821/2-1884)[149] of Torquay desired that four of his children[150]—the sisters Jessie C., Edith L., and Alice Goddard[151] were 9, 11, and 12 years old respectively,[152] and their brother Edward had just

148. In Corr. Bk., the earliest letter from PHG-Bewes is dated 16 Dec. 1872, from Bewes-PHG is Dec. 19. Letters of unknown content were exchanged between PHG-Leonard Strong in the previous month.

149. In the extant correspondence of PHG, Leonard Strong, and Bewes, Bewes is only referred to as 'Col. W. Bewes' or 'Col. Bewes', without further identifying data for him or the children in question. That data has been reconstructed here for the first time using contemporary newspaper articles and other sources. On W. Bewes: 'Deaths', London *Reynolds's Newspaper*, 20 July 1884, 6; his age is given in *Whitstable Times*, 26 July 1884, 4; J. T. White, *The History of Torquay*, 348. He was the son of Thomas Bewes, MP for Plymouth (d. 1857, Boase I: 267); 'Married', London *Morning Chronicle*, 14 June 1855, 7; 'Marriages', *Annual Register 1855* (London: F. & J. Rivington, 1856), 228.

150. W. E. Bewes and his wife Mary had many children. Their eldest son was Wyndham Anstis Bewes (b. 16 Aug. 1857: London *Morning Post*, 21 Aug. 1857, 8; Joseph Foster, *Men-at-the-Bar: A Biographical Hand-list of the Members of the Various Inns of Court* (London: Hazell, Watson, and Viney, 2ed., 1885), 36), and another daughter, Helen ('Death of Mrs. Wyndham E. Bewes', Plymouth *Western Morning News*, 11 Mar. 1899, 8).

151. For the full name 'Alice Goddard', where she is referred to as the second Bewes daughter, see 'Marriages', London *Standard* (23 Nov. 1888), 1.

152. Determining the ages of the three Bewes girls (whose names we know from the PHG correspondence) with total confidence is difficult but possible. Newspaper birth notices at the time list the precise date and location for the birth of a son or 'a daughter' and the name of the father. They do not reveal the mother's name, and only the name of a newborn *son* is printed. It is thus not possible from newspaper reports to associate all the Bewes daughters with a particular date of birth. The 1871 Census Return for Greenwich (where the Bewes family was then living), taken on 2 Apr. 1871, is helpful (I am grateful to Timothy Stunt for bringing this information to my attention).

JESSIE: According to the 1871 Census, at the time Jessie was 7, which coordinates with the birthdate of a 'daughter' on 25 Oct. 1863 (London *Morning Post*, 28 Oct. 1863, 8; *Dover Express and East Kent Intelligencer*, 31 Oct. 1863, 3; London *Lloyd's Weekly Newspaper*, 1 Nov. 1863, 11). In December 1872, Jessie was 9 (in the 1871 Census the name is 'Jessie C.', in correspondence it is also spelled 'Jessy' and 'Jesse').

EDITH: According to the 1871 Census, at the time Edith was 9, which coordinates with the birthdate of a 'daughter' on July 19, 1861 (*Morning Post*, 26 July 1861, 8). In December 1872, Edith was 11.

ALICE: According to the 1871 Census, Alice Goddard was 11-years-old at the time, which

turned 14[153]—should be simultaneously baptized. Bewes, a member of Gosse's Assembly at St. Marychurch, was a well-to-do,[154] retired military man of the British Army's 73rd Regiment who had served in India[155] and attained the rank of colonel. In 1855, he married Mary Soltau (1827/8-1899), a daughter of George William Soltau (1801-1884) of Little Efford.[156] In so doing, Bewes became related to Soltau's older brother, Henry William Soltau (who, as previously mentioned, was a friend of Philip's). In family mythology, H. W. Soltau's people had disowned him when he seceded from the Church of England to align, in its early days, with Brethren.[157] He was eventually with Open Brethren[158] and his daughter Henrietta E. Soltau (1843-1934) was prominent among them.[159] Several years after marrying, Col. Bewes was involved with evangelical groups such as the British Army Scripture Readers' Society[160] and the East London Mission and Relief Society (of which he was for a time an Hon. Secretary).[161]

The initial approach to Gosse was about Jessie and Alice's 'admission into the Church of God' at St. Marychurch.[162] Gosse interviewed them and approved the plan. Then the Bewes parents added Edith and Edward, convinced that they have 'believed on the Lord, for the increase of our

coordinates with the birthdate of a 'daughter' on Feb. 15, 1860 (London *Morning Post*, 22 Feb. 1860, 8; *Royal Cornwall Gazette*, 24 Feb. 1860, 5). From 'Marriages' (London *Standard*, 23 Nov. 1888, 1), we know her full name, and that she was the second Bewes daughter. In December 1872, Alice was 12.

153. Edward was born on 1 Dec. 1858 (*Lloyd's Weekly London Newspaper*, 12 Dec. 1858, 11).

154. Bewes left an estate of £32,000 ('Recently Proved Wills', London *Pall Mall Gazette*, 19 Sept. 1884, 10; *Manchester Courier*, 19 Sept. 1884, 3).

155. Bewes' reference to his military service in India is noted in the Plymouth *Western Morning News* (23 Nov. 1861), 3. After his death, his wife donated a wasp specimen from India to the London Zoological Society (*Nature*, 13 Oct. 1892, 575).

156. W. E. Bewes and Mary Soltau married on 11 June 1855 (London *Standard*, 13 June 1855, 4; 'Marriages', *Annual Register 1855* (London: F. & J. Rivington, 1856), 228). On G. W. Soltau: [John] Bernard Burke, *A Genealogical and Heraldic Dictionary of the Landed Gentry of Great Britain and Ireland* (London: Harris, 1858), 1119; 'Funeral of Mr. Geo. W. Soltau', Plymouth *Western Morning News*, 31 May 1884, 5.

157. The claim of a family rupture was made by W[illiam]. S[oltau]., 'Henry William Soltau', in Henry Pickering, *Chief Men Among the Brethren* (2ed. 1931), 86. Timothy Stunt (*in. litt.* and Stunt, *Elusive Quest of the Spiritual Malcontent*, 286fn.20), doubts that there was family hostility to Soltau's alignment with Brethren.

158. F. Roy Coad, 'Soltau, Henry (William)', *DEB* II: 1033; Pickering, *Chief Men* (2ed. 1931), 84-88.

159. Harold Rowdon, 'Soltau, Henrietta Eliza', *ODNB* (2004).

160. On BASRS, see Plymouth *Western Morning News*, 23 Nov. 1861, 3.

161. Advertisement, London *Morning Post* (10 Feb. 1871), 1.

162. PHG-Leonard Strong, 13 Dec. 1872 (Corr. Bk.).

joy & thankfulness.' Apparently they next approached Leonard Strong, of the Warren Road Room in Torquay, about the simultaneous baptism of all their children. Strong approved. Gosse balked. Strong consulted with Gosse, who said he had yet to speak with Edith and Edward about their new religious state, and thus was unable to 'propose them for fellowship as yet'. Moreover, the custom at Gosse's Assembly was that candidates for fellowship have their name announced prior to baptism to allow for possible objections.[163] Gosse urged delay. Neither the children nor their parents saw any reason to do so. Although the subject was not raised in the surviving correspondence, the Bewes parents may have felt a private urgency to have their children baptized as a public affirmation of the children's faith due to the fact that another child had died several years earlier, aged 14 months.[164]

Following a brief correspondence between Bewes, Gosse, and Strong,[165] all four children were baptised at the Warren Road Room on 25 December at 2:30 p.m.[166] Gosse did not attend. Clearly miffed at the Bewes parents (who were considerably younger than Gosse) for going from one religious leader to another in order to obtain the desired result, he suggested Bewes ponder the command in Hebrews 13: 17: 'Obey them that have the rule over you.'[167] And he told Leonard Strong that, though the process by which the baptisms took place was 'very irregular', the 'slight upon myself as a pastor, & upon the Church over wh[ich] the H[oly] G[host] has made me overseer, I will for Jesus' sake, willingly pass over.'[168] Ultimately that is what he did: he told Col. Bewes that his children would be welcomed at St. Marychurch, and he maintained contact with the Bewes girls for years to come.

163. PHG-Col. Bewes, 16 Dec. 1872 (Corr. Bk.).

164. Cecil R. Bewes, born in 1865, died on 6 May 1866, aged 14 months (*Dover Express and East Kent Intelligencer*, 11 May 1866, 3).

165. PHG-Leonard Strong, 13 Dec.; Strong-PHG, 14 Dec.; PHG-Col. W. Bewes, 16 Dec.; Strong-PHG, 19 Dec.; Bewes-PHG, 19 Dec.; PHG-Bewes, 20 Dec.; PHG-Strong, 20 Dec. 1872 (all original letters, or copies of PHG's, in Corr. Bk).

166. EWG wrote that his baptism, about a dozen years earlier, was at night (*Father and Son*, 1907, 212). Newspaper reports of baptisms in the west of England which I have seen do not state when the baptisms took place, though the fact that several were in running water and were observed outdoors by locals suggests they were not at night. See *Trewman's Exeter Flying Post*, 8 July 1858, 5, in the Dart River; *Trewman's Exeter Flying Post*, 22 Aug. 1860, 7, at the beach at Exmouth; Barnstaple *North Devon Journal*, 27 June 1867, 8, at Coleford, Crediton; Yeovil *Western Gazette*, 19 Mar. 1869, 8, outdoors near Poole; *Aberdeen Journal*, 27 June 1879, 6, in the Teviot River.

167. PHG-W. Bewes, 20 Dec. 1872 (Corr. Bk.).

168. PHG-Leonard Strong, 20 Dec. 1872 (copy of a letter, Corr. Bk.).

Even before the Bewes matter was resolved, Gosse wrote about it to his son in London.[169] To Philip, the issue was not the *idea* of child baptism—neither he nor Strong questioned that.[170] In fact to Gosse, terms like adult or infant baptism were meaningless: 'The point is not between adults and children, but between believers and unbelievers. If little children are believers, youth is no objection. That the Spirit can work a living faith in very little children, there is abundant precious evidence.'[171] What was at issue with the Bewes children was the *process* by which it had taken place.

Edmund, however, was not interested in details. When he heard of the episode, he told his father that he regretted having been baptised as a child. Philip did not agree. He was sure that it had been a lasting influence for good. 'Your recent revival confirms my confidence (long indeed wavering) that your confession was no mistake, but a blessed reality;' he said, '& this being so, I am sure it has never harmed you.'[172]

It was not long before Philip had cause to change his mind.

-VIII-

At the end of December 1872, Edmund's paper on 'Ibsen, the Norwegian Satirist' was published in the *Fortnightly Review*, followed in February by his anonymous review in the *Spectator* of the Danish poet Paludan-Müller's *Sex Digte* (*Six Poems*).[173] Edmund did not send the articles to his father, but he apparently did tell him about them. Philip took them out of the library.[174] During the next four weeks, a gripping and exhausting exchange ensued.

169. EWG-PHG, 18 Dec. 1872, referenced but not quoted in PHG-EWG, 6 Jan. 1873 (CUL Add. 7041,56). Corr. Bk. records a letter from EWG dated Dec. 19; PHG wrote him on 1 Jan. 1873, but did not specifically respond to that letter. The disposition of the letter is unknown.

170. 'In the matter of children I feel I must be as ready to receive them when God has given them to Christ as grown persons' (Strong-PHG, 14 Dec. 1872, Corr. Bk.); '... I have a special delight in suffering little children to come to Jesus' (PHG-Col. Bewes, 16 Dec. 1872, Corr.Bk.)

171. PHG, *Mysteries of God*, 65-6.

172. PHG-EWG, 6 Jan. 1873 (CUL Add. 7041, 56).

173. Edmund W. Gosse [signed], 'Ibsen, the Norwegian satirist', *Fortnightly Review* n.s. XIII (Jan. 1873), 74-88 (this issue was advertised in the *Athenaeum*, 28 Dec. 1872, 836); [EWG], 'Frederik Paludan-Müller [review of *Sex Digte*, 1872]', London *Spectator* 46 (1 Feb. 1873), 142-3 (this is not listed in the excellent bibliography in Bredsdorff, *Sir Edmund Gosse's Correspondence*, 317). EWG called Paludan-Müller 'one of the greatest and most original poets of our time' (EWG, 'Frederik Paludan-Müller', *Athenaeum* 6 Jan. 1877, 18) and *Kalanus* 'a work of extraordinary genius' ('Frederik Paludan-Müller', *Academy* 6 Jan. 1877, 9). EWG's *Studies in the Literature of Northern Europe* (1879) contains an analysis of *Kalanus* (pp. 188-194), which he incorrectly dates there (as in the *Spectator*) to 1857 (p. 185).

174. PHG-EWG, 14 Feb. 1873 (CUL Add. 7041, 57). PHG wrote that he got the *Fortnightly*

It started with Philip's letter of 10 February, in which he wondered 'if there are not several things,—lines of thought, expressions and allusions,—in both your last papers, which you would hardly like to be examined at the Judgment Seat of Christ.' The books Edmund was reviewing were 'frivolous and profane'. They did not reflect that he was 'walking and working under your Master's eye.'[175] It was hard to dismiss Philip's point: Ibsen was known in Britain as 'an open unbeliever in Christianity.'[176]

Three days later came Edmund's first rebuttal. 'Your remarks on my printed papers have, down to the immediate past, been so encouraging, so warmly laudatory, that I confess at first your letter took my breath away,' he said. Were there 'lines of thought, expressions and allusions' in his two articles of which he might not be proud? 'To this question,' Edmund said,

> implying as it does, a reproof of the most serious kind, I answer, most solemnly, No, or if there are, I am not cognizant of them. It is not affectation when I say that I have, in the light of this question, gone through both the papers referred to, and I am absolutely without a guess as to the position of the lines of thought, expressions & allusions you speak of, and I cannot even form an idea of their nature. Both of these papers were read aloud to the ladies here [Mary Ann Baker and Anne Buckham] while they were in MS. & they perceived nothing amiss. I have prided myself in writing nothing that should ever hinder anyone a handbreath on his journey heavenward.

Nor did Edmund feel the books he reviewed were 'frivolous and profane':

> You call me to "go before God in self-abasement and self-repudiation." Indeed in no other attitude dare I as a pardoned creature conscious of constant sin and defilement, go before Him. But in this matter of my public life as a man of letters, in which your conscience so strongly condemns me, my own conscience condemns me not. I have striven to

from the library, and presumably also borrowed the *Spectator* from there.

175. The letter has not been traced, but is recorded in Corr. Bk. and quoted in EWG's letter of 13 Feb. 1873.

176. 'Ibsen (Henrik)', in Wheeler, *Biographical Dictionary of Freethinkers*, 183.

do honest work in the world, such as was given me to do, & to carry it out in an upright, honest and manly way.[177]

Philip sat down the same day he received this letter and shot off a reply. He wrote at the top 'No. 2.' Though he addressed it 'My dearly beloved Son,' the gloves had come off. If Edmund could not come to his meaning, he would have to state it directly, even painfully.

The very fact that my past notices have been laudatory, which seems to you so inconsistent with my present tone, is but proof of my reluctance to reprove. My judgment of the *matter* on which you wrote has never varied; but I cherished hope that you would soon select something better; and meanwhile I could honestly praise the *manner;*—the skill, & taste, & learning, that you displayed. Have I ever lauded the *texts* of your comments? O believe, how far rather I would praise than blame. ...

... The written Word of God is the infallible rule, by which conscience must be guided; to which it must be subject. ... Now here is the point at which, I think, you begin to go wrong: here you diverge from the straight line. I fear you have not bowed every thought to the written word. "What hath the Lord spoken?" must be the ultimate appeal for a Christian. ... Do you accept, *animo pleno* [wholeheartedly],[178] this canon? *O tell me this*, my dearest child ...

Will you honestly tell me what you understand by *"the world"*, of which the Lord Jesus says, "Me it hateth, because I testify of it, that the works thereof are evil"? (John vii. 7); that "it seeth not, neither knoweth" the Spirit (xiv.17); that it "hateth" His disciples, & Him (xv.18,19; xvii.14; 1 John iii.13); & which we are so solemnly warned not to love (1 John ii.15,16)? I ask you very specially & urgently to tell me this. ... Can you take these sayings, just as they stand, all of them, before God, & say, in His sight, you have a conscience void of offence <u>before Him</u>? Do, I pray you, answer this openly & fully; for here, I firmly believe, lies the issue between us.

The writings which you criticise, & translate, & commend, & so help to publish, are essentially "of the World";—in that sense of "the World" that it hateth the Lord Jesus, & His little flock; that it seeth not nor knoweth the Spirit. Is it not so, darling Willy? Can you think that Ibsen,

177. EWG-PHG, 13 Feb. 1873 (CUL Add. 7018, 51).
178. I am indebted to Timothy Stunt, *in litt.*, for clarifying the Latin term.

that Pal. Müller, estimable though they may be in many respects, love Jesus the Lord? Do they love *you*, because you are His? Would they love you *better*, if you told them you are washed in His blood; if you spoke to them of His preciousness?...

Nor can you evade these questions, or escape answering them, now that they are thus pointedly presented to you, without receding from your ground of a good conscience before God. Here are God's own awful words: how will you answer them at the Judgment-seat of Christ? ...

You solemnly declare in answer to a question of mine, about certain lines of thought, expressions & allusions in your last two Papers,—that you are not cognizant of such; that you are absolutely without a guess what I mean. I have no desire to search out fault with a microscope; but I should have supposed you wd. readily discern what I refer to. But since you cannot, I must be more definite. Yet please believe that I did not wish to enter into these details.

The Memoir on Ibsen is not in my hands, as I got The Fortnightly from the Library, therefore I must trust chiefly to memory. Yet I observed the following. The reference to Ezekiel was objectionable. Jehovah, by his Prophet, denounces, under the figure of adultery, the faithlessness & idolatry of both the Kingdoms of Israel. To speak of this as *satire* was a mistake;[179] & to bring the words of the Holy Ghost into mere literary comparison with those of modern satirists, or those of such as Juvenal, was profane & shocking to a reverent spirit.

Later on, in "Love's Comedy", your Author takes the great Name of God profanely; & you follow him without scruple, & without remonstrance; although you know "Jehovah will not hold him guiltless that taketh His name in vain."

"Brand" appears, from the description, to be a coarse caricature of godliness, as if hypocrisy, like "Mawworm" in The Beggar's Opera (I think), or like "the Shepherd" in Nich[ola]s Nickleby. Such are portraits, drawn by enemies, of persons who take the Lord Christ for Master, & confess His Name; such as, in a small way, have been drawn of me; such as will be drawn of you, if you will be faithful to Him. ...

---

179. In 'Ibsen, the Norwegian Satirist', 75, EWG wrote: 'Modern life is a thing too complex and too delicate to bear such satire as thrilled through the fierce old world. In Ezekiel we see the thunders and lightnings of the Lord blasting the beautiful evil body of Aholah; in Juvenal, the iron clank of horse-hoofs is ringing on the marble pavement, till in crushing some wretched debauchee, they mingle his blood with the spilt wine and the vine-wreaths'.

I come to [Paludan-Müller's] "Kalanus." Here the poet aggrandizes &
glorifies a subtle system of false religion; & you present it all to English
readers, without reproof, without a caveat. This Buddhist idolatry, which
carries captive hundreds of millions of the human race, is one of the
subtlest, & most successful devices of the Arch Adversary of God & man.
Yet this is dressed up attractively; the expression "incarnate Godhead"[180]
is blasphemously applied to it. ...

By & by the hero of all this glorification, in *suicide* is described as "his
soul rising to the skies"; as being-absorbed "into the Universal Oneness
that is spirit and light."[181] ... I will not more than allude to the foul scene
of the harlots.[182]

This eight-page letter of Philip's was followed by another of the same
length on 21 February; Edmund replied the next day; Philip followed
with eight more pages on the 23rd, and twenty more on the 25th; on the
28th Edmund wrote again.[183]

Edmund had now been confronted with two questions which had
receded (and later surged) in prominence during a good part of his life.
Were the Scriptures—in spirit and word—of Divine origin? Did they
enjoin upon all believers—with incontrovertible authority—the necessity
to remain separate and aloof from the World? Summoning up an answer
to them was a significant step in Edmund's determination to separate
himself from his father in order to establish an independent identity.

He set out to do just that on 4 March 1873, in a 3,300-word letter in
which he was not less blunt than had been his father. Unsurprisingly, it
shows signs of stress (the letter was thirty-eight pages misnumbered as
thirty-six, and there were ten sections, not the eight numbered ones),

180. In 'Frederik Paludan-Müller', *Spectator*, 142, EWG wrote that Kalanus is described by
Paludan-Müller as 'an Indian, born by the Ganges, and brought up in a temple of Brama' who
worships 'the Invisible Unity whom men call Brama. Day after day, kneeling by the river-side
among the palms, he has prayed and longed for a manifestation of the incarnate Godhead'.

181. In 'Frederik Paludan-Müller', *Spectator*, 143, EWG wrote: '... Alexander [the Great]
sanctions the burning of Kalanus. The philosopher approaches his own fiery tomb with a solemn
elation, a sublime joy. Dismissing the troops, casting aside the adornments that Alexander has
sent to do him honour, he gathers his own countrymen about him, mounts the pyre, and in the
midst of a choral invocation to the spirit of Brama, expires, his soul rising to the skies like wine
poured out into the fire. The chorus around proclaim his absorption into the Universal Oneness
that is spirit and light'.

182. PHG-EWG, 14 Feb. 1873 (CUL Add. 7041, 57). Emphasis in the original.

183. The length of these letters (none of which has been traced) is given in Corr. Bk.

yet it is remarkably mature, thoughtful and articulate. Edmund began
with this declaration:

> ... let me say that I will plainly and without concealment state my views
> and convictions; the attitude in which I receive your exhortations, and
> my judgments concerning them, laying down, for once, unflinchingly,
> the differences that I perceive to exist between your view of the Will of
> God towards us, and mine, not forgetting ... that which we indubitably
> hold in common. ...
>
> You promise me sympathy, yet you warn me not to render sympathy
> impossible. You urge and insist on plain dealing, yet you imply that plain
> dealing will be insupportable to you. I am obliged to say that you are
> very little acquainted with the conditions and growth of my spirit. You
> speak of yourself as a surgeon, probing into a wound. Throughout, you
> speak of a great crisis in my life. I must plainly tell you that I perceive
> no crisis. You take for granted that you have to deal with a blunt and
> sleepy conscience, an ignorant mind in spiritual things, a dull soul that
> needs stabbing into painful and sudden wakefulness. ... I have spoken
> of increased pleasure in spiritual matters, and hence, apparently, you
> judge that my soul is unconsciously drifting towards a crisis. But it
> is not so. It is true that I have of late enjoyed a fuller sense of divine
> pleasures, of the value of prayer, and the assurance of God's gracious
> favour, but my intellectual perception has been ahead of my emotional
> appreciation, and I have not been drifting helmless and pilotless. I have
> read no religious books ... they do not appeal to me. I have read and
> reread the word of God alone. No book has been so much in my hands
> during the last year as the Bible. ... I have striven to put away from me
> all that I have merely gained by tradition, and sought to arrive at the
> real drift myself. And minute criticisms and obscure passages have had
> no importance for me. My desire has been to grasp in some measure the
> meaning of the great scheme of Salvation, to perceive its devolpment
> [*sic*] in the past and its character in the future.

Edmund first took hold of one problem—the verbal inspiration of
the Scriptures—and cast it aside. More than a year earlier he had gone
through the New Testament to investigate the point. He concluded from
discrepancies in apparently verbatim reports of what Jesus had said, that
'It is obvious to me that the inspiration of the Scriptures is one of tenour

and matter, not of word.' Edmund's exercise occurred not long after the appearance of his father's paper at the Victoria Institute, in which Philip had made precisely the opposite argument in upholding the probable accuracy of high numbers in the Pentateuch.

Then, after a slight digression (and lapse of time), Edmund confronted the other problem. He put it this way: 'What is the proper mutual attitude of the Church and the World in our own times?' and added: 'it is increasingly plain to me that in these few words lies the core of all our argument.' After summarising his father's view on the matter, he set down his analysis, which entailed an important historical critique:

> Well, this belief [in separation], (which for a long time in obedience to the authority of those whose age and study entitled them to my deep respect, I held, even to the continual vexing of my conscience, self-wounded with divers imaginary offences), I do not [*sic*] longer hold. And since you give me a caveat against the supposition, that a thing must be wrong because it is agre[e]able, I will give you another against thinking all things undesirable necessarily right. ... Of course, especially to a person of my temperament, the idea of separation from the pursuits and desires of my fellows is very distasteful; and ... the very consciousness that my heart naturally went out in genial sympathy to all sorts of people, merely for themselves, without any impulse to teach them, for a long time staggered me; still I determined that I would not be biassed by preconceived impressions in my study of the Word, and it gradually grew into a conviction with me that this separation was a wholly uncalled-for, scarcely even desirable state, in a protestant [*sic*] land like ours. When we think of what Greece, Italy, Asia were in the beginning of the Christian era and contrast the life then and there with life now and here, the difference is not one of degree but character. ... Are we not apt sometimes to think that what was said to Corinth 1850 years ago is said exactly to England today?
>
> ... As to your saying that I live one life in Tottenham and one in town, it is a mistake. Everybody who cares to know, in London, knows I am Superintendent of a little Dissenting Sunday-School; and everybody who cares to know at Brook Street knows I am a poet-critic and litterateur. You only have found these things inconsistent.

As a collateral point, Edmund added later in the letter that he not only felt no compulsion to interpolate commands from biblical times into the Victorian era, but that he saw no reason to assume that a tiny band of people represented the sum total of those who were the 'elect'. If there is no belief that those who faintly perceive the truth will also be saved, then

> how can we find in the great mission of Christ anything but a failure? ... Hence, when I walk among my fellow mortals, I do not feel myself alone among the damned, but as one who owes it to unusual grace that he perceives what is hidden from the bulk of his brothers and sisters, who shall all one day arise into the perfect light of day.

Before concluding the letter, Edmund acknowledged his father's efforts as a parent. He could not praise all aspects of his upbringing,

> but I do think that the general tenour of your example, especially the deep consciousness I had that you sought with all your heart to bring me up for God, had an immensely beneficial effect on my character. I believe you even suffer now from the effects of your training, for if you had been less unflinching, less logical and firm in your education of me, it would be easier than it now is to lean on other people's opinion and hold two views at once. You did your best to give me a stiff backbone. I am desirous of saying how much I feel I owe to your pious training. ...[184]

And so—what was left? 'I believe in Christ, the God-Man, who gave his blood to take away the sins of the world,' Edmund avouched. 'Beyond this I do not know that I have any creed.'

Edmund was understandably stressed—he fled to the sea-side that April with a fever.[185] He had written, 'There are some things in which we really must bear with one another' and that 'I think you are the most difficult Father to satisfy in all the wide world.' What words did Philip now set to paper? We don't know. His letter may have brought about an urgent

184. EWG-PHG, 4 Mar. 1873 (CUL Add. 7018, 52). The letter is printed in full, with a few minor errors and omissions, in Charteris, 45-56.

185. Another interpretation of the entries in Corr. Bk. is that EWG sent only the first 10 pages to his father on 5 Mar., and the remainder on 13 Mar. (or in parts, on 13, 17, and 21 Mar.). While he was writing, EWG received the note of encouragement from his father which he mentions at the end of his letter (Charteris, 56), and which, according to Corr. Bk., was sent 6 Mar. There is no further letter recorded to EWG until 18 Mar. Then sometime in April, as he wrote P. C. Asbjornsen on 15 June 1873, EWG became ill, and went down to the sea-side, and presumably to Sandhurst (the letter is quoted in Bredsdorff, *Sir Edmund Gosse's Correspondence*, 61-2). On at least one other occasion, EWG suffered a headache in replying to his father's strictures (PHG-EWG, 8 Feb. 1868. CUL Add. 7041, 10).

meeting between father and son, either in London or at Sandhurst the next month.[186] Or perhaps there was no personal encounter as Edmund weighed anchor and prepared to sail for his new world.[187]

-IX-

Whatever Philip's response was, Edmund's attitude had been revealed. His course of action was now predictable. Slowly and inexorably during the next two and a half years, the old was supplanted by the new.

He continued to write about Ibsen and other literary figures of the North, to correspond with them, and to welcome them to London. The minor Danish poet Carl Andersen (1826-1883) and his wife visited Edmund at Tottenham in the summer of 1873, but 'a variety of circumstances' prevented Edmund from returning to Scandinavia that year.[188] Edmund also hosted Dean Fog as the two toured Wales and the Midlands during July and August. It was probably at the start of their travels that they visited St. Marychurch, at Philip's request. There, according to Edmund, his father argued with Fog about the atonement, and the Dane left astonished 'at the rigidity of the local religious institutions.'[189] Nonetheless, they reportedly respected their differences. 'Your son is truly dear to my heart,' the Dean wrote Philip, 'and I pray

186. It is known that PHG visited London some time in 1873 (*Life*, 360). The evidence suggesting that the visit may have coincided with EWG's letter (though admittedly conjectural) is based upon the following interpretation of entries in Corr. Bk. While there are gaps in Corr. Bk. of up to four days in 1873 during which neither letters to nor from PHG have been listed, there is only one occasion during which five days passed, viz. between 8-12 Mar. The scenario would thus have been that EWG began writing his letter on 4 Mar. after work, and stopped late at night. On the blank side opposite page 10 of the original letter, EWG wrote: 'I have written far into the night, and my head forces me to stop. As soon as possible I will continue. Your loving son Edmund W. Gosse' (this sentence is not quoted in Charteris). On the next day, EWG continued and completed the letter, sending it to his father, along with an invitation for him to come to London. PHG received the letter the same day (Corr. Bk. records a letter received from EWG on 5 Mar.), responded on 6 Mar., and left for London on Friday, 7 Mar., returning on the 13 Mar. to Sandhurst, and getting another letter from EWG that day (as listed in Corr. Bk.).

187. In the 4 Mar. 1873 letter, EWG intentionally digressed on occasion, offering notable critiques of his father's work. Firstly, he compared him negatively with the Darwins and Huxleys of the scientific world (he repeated the critique in *Life* and *Father and Son*). EWG wrote: 'One observer notes down microscopic details and laboriously stores up what seems chaotic material; another, incapable of microscopic work, seems called to compare one large body of facts with another, and form wide theories.' EWG also wrote: 'The study of poetry seems to me a loftier one than that of microscopic zoology; it does not seem so to you.'

188. EWG, *Two Visits to Denmark*, 181, 135; Bredsdorff, *Sir Edmund Gosse's Correspondence*, 6, 249fn.31. During the winter of 1872, Edmund had translated Ibsen's 'Love's Comedy' into blank verse, but 'no one would publish, or so much as read it' (Bredsdorff, 184fn.118).

189. EWG, *Two Visits to Denmark*, 35-6.

God that I may be useful to him also in respect of that which is in reality the only useful thing.'[190]

In 1874, Edmund published more articles on Scandinavia than in any previous year. In one on Norway he got so many of the facts wrong that he felt embarrassed to return there.[191] So instead he visited Dean Fog again in Copenhagen between 10-29 May, where he met an impressive new group of literary and musical celebrities, including the Danish literary critic Georg Brandes (1842-1927), with whom he formed a close friendship.[192]

Another essay that Edmund wrote at this time on Scandinavia is illuminating. Presumably to please his father, he became a member of the Victoria Institute in London on 31 October 1873, the heavily evangelical defence group against evolution and Bible criticism. On 20 April in the following year he read before it an essay on 'The Ethical Condition of the Early Scandinavian Peoples'. The meeting was advertised, open to the public,[193] well-attended,[194] with a vigorous discussion afterwards. But to Edmund the Institute seemed 'little more than a Debating Society, where young men and old parsons get up to hear themselves speak, not because they have anything to say.'[195] A revealing point was raised by a few of the speakers,[196] who questioned Edmund's claim that the spread of Christianity in many places had hindered the flourishing of the arts. Edmund's apparent acceptance of this view was seemingly a reflection of his spiritual travels.[197]

It has already been mentioned that less than two years after the appearance of *Madrigals, Songs, and Sonnets* Edmund had written his

190. B.Fog-PHG, 14 Aug. 1873 (CUL Adv. c. 82.5, 76); EWG-Eliza Gosse, 15 Aug. 1873 (CUL Add. 7018, 55).

191. Bredsdorff, *Sir Edmund Gosse's Correspondence*, 8; EWG, 'The Present Condition of Norway', *Fraser's Magazine* n.s. IX (Feb. 1874), 174-85.

192. Bredsdorff, *Sir Edmund Gosse's Correspondence*, 8-9; EWG, *Two Visits to Denmark*, 148-364 (EWG also made a brief visit to Sweden); 'Brandes (Georg Morris Cohen)', in Wheeler, *Biographical Dictionary of Freethinkers*, 53. EWG-PHG, 18, 25 May 1874 (CUL Add. 7018, 57-8). PHG had given EWG £25 to enable him to visit Copenhagen (Corr. Bk., under 20 Apr. 1874, and PHG-EWG, same date, CUL Add. 7041, 58).

193. Advertisement, *Academy* (18 Apr. 1874), [417].

194. The *Illustrated London News* referred to it as 'a full meeting' (25 Apr. 1874, 391).

195. EWG-PHG, 22 Apr. 1874 (CUL Add. 7018, 56).

196. The point was not mentioned in coverage of EWG's talk in the London *Morning Post*, 21 Apr. 1874, 6; *Illustrated London News*, 25 Apr. 1874, 391; or *Academy*, 25 Apr. 1874, 468.

197. EWG, 'The Ethical Condition of the Early Scandinavian Peoples', *JTVI* IX (1875), 84-100, and the discussion, pp. 100-8, esp. pp. 94, 101-5, 107. In mentioning that he had received a dozen offprints of the article, PHG did not comment on it (PHG-EWG, 12 July 1875, CUL Add. 7019,16).

father that he was once again composing new poems. During 1873 he wrote constantly: 'It seems absolutely necessary now to me to publish,' as he told W. Bell Scott.[198] Inspired by the Parnassians, Rossetti, Swinburne (with whom he was now on intimate terms) and the ethical influence of Whitman,[199] he did not, as before, look to Sandhurst for advice or consent.

On Viol and Flute, which appeared at the beginning of December 1873, was primarily planned and executed by the author alone.[200] The volume was dedicated to Bell Scott (who drew the unsigned woodcut on the title-page) and Edmund's Norwegian friends (some of the poems were written while on the Continent, and one was entitled 'To Henrik Ibsen in Dresden'). Notwithstanding Edmund's misleading claims, reviews were mixed.[201] As far as the style was concerned, it garnered some positive pronouncements.[202] D. G. Rossetti and Robert Browning

198. EWG-W. B. Scott, 26 Feb. 1873 (LeBL). There is an unusually intense series of letters registered between EWG-PHG at this time in Corr. Bk., which may be related to this writing (EWG-PHG, 11,14,22,28 Feb.; PHG-EWG, Feb. 10, 14, 21 ['8 pp.'], 23 ['8 pp.'], 25 ['20 pp.']).

199. EWG, *Portraits and Sketches*, 7; EWG-L. N. Chase, 16 May [1917], in Mattheisen and Millgate, *Transatlantic Dialogue*, 297.

200. The launch of *On Viol and Flute* did not go smoothly. It was being promoted as early as October 1873 (*Academy*, 15 Oct. 1873, 384: 'We learn that Mr. E. W. Gosse of the British Museum, has in the press a volume of Lyrical Poems. It will be entitled *On Viol and Flute*, and will have a frontispiece by Mr. W. B. Scott'). A month later, the *Athenaeum* (22 Nov. 1873, 663) noted that a 'young writer, Mr. Gosse, of the British Museum, is about to publish a volume of short poems, to which unity is given by a musical theme'. There is a copy of *On Viol and Flute* in the Colbeck Collection, University of British Columbia, which includes advertisements at the back dated Nov. 1873 listing the book as already published (no price is given). But the earliest 'Just ready' advertisement seen was in the London *Daily News* (8 Dec. 1873, 4), and it was also advertised (without those words) in the *Athenaeum* (6 Dec. 1873, 717) and *Academy* (15 Dec. 1873, 470). I have not seen the review in the *Sunday Times* (21 Dec. 1873) or *Morgenbladet* (Norway, 19 Dec.1873). The earliest reviews I have found were in the *Westminster Review* n.s. XLV (1 Jan. 1874), 298 [by J.R. de Capel Wise, per *Wellesley Index* III:650], *The Spectator* XLVII (3 Jan. 1874, 18-20), and *Athenaeum* (3 Jan. 1874) 18-20.

The book was paid for by EWG himself, 500 copies costing £35.5s. (CUL Add. 7027, 104). PHG had it in his library (*Sandhurst Catalogue*, item #493). I am not aware that he commented on it.

201. In January 1875, EWG claimed the poems 'met with almost unanimous praise from the press' (Bredsdorff, *Sir Edmund Gosse's Correspondence*, 84) and later that they were 'received by English readers with much favour' (EWG, *Two Visits to Denmark*, 140). 'An Edmund Gosse Bibliography', Boston *Literary World*, 172, cites no reviews of *Madrigals, Songs, and Sonnets* and four for *On Viol and Flute*. The excerpts appearing in the bibliography give the impression that they were favourable. Some did point to positive aspects of EWG's poems, but no review is totally favourable and two were mainly negative.

202. *Examiner* (24 Jan. 1874), 89-90; A. Lang in *Academy* (31 Jan. 1874), 108; [Richard Garnett], *Illustrated London News* (21 Feb. 1874), 175; [J. R. de Capel Wise], *Westminster Review* n.s. XLV (1 Jan. 1874), 298. I have not seen the reviews of the book in the *Graphic* or *Public Opinion*. A second edition appeared on 1 Nov. 1875 (not 'within a few months', as Charteris claims, p. 42; see Diary for 1875 of Nellie Gosse, LeBL, under that date). There were seven imperfect rondeaus in the book (J. K. Robinson, 'Austin Dobson and the Rondeliers', *Modern Language*

were said to have been struck 'very forcibly' by the 'The Mandrakes' poem.[203]

And well they ought to have been, given that critics of the Pre-Raphaelite movement like the *Spectator* noted that, in accordance with poets of the 'fleshly school,'[204] physical sensations were placed above spiritual matters in the volume. With some of his verse Edmund had perpetrated a *bêtise* (act of foolishness or stupidity), the *Contemporary Review* said.[205] Richard Garnett (a friend of Edmund's) found it difficult to discern 'moral purpose, intellectual enlightenment, spiritual interpretation, or poetic story' in *Viol and Flute*. The critiques were on point: there was no attempt to hide a philosophy of life which mixed Art with sensualism:

> *And these make up my sum of life's desire,—*
> *To live for ever in the sun's broad fire,*
>   *To know and love strong men and shapely girls,*
> *And nobly working till the end aspire.*
>
> *With colour, verse, and harmony to frame*
> *A house of beautiful delights, whose name*
>   *May stir the world with pleasure like fine pearls,*
> *Strung on a gold thread gleaming as a flame.*
>
> *There have been sage philosophers who found*
> *That pleasure was a dream, and song mere sound;*
>   *They passed, and left us poorer; now, ah me!*
> *I wonder what they dream of underground!*
>
> *For lying in the narrow earth they miss*
> *All consolations of remembered bliss,*
>   *The scent of wine, blown air and glowing sea,*
> *The songs we sing, the kisses that we kiss.*
>
> *For us no learning is worth half the lore*
> *Of knowing what the breakers tell the shore;*

Quarterly XIV, 1953, p. 34).

203. Anonymous review of *The Poets and the Poetry of the Century*, ed. by Alfred Miles, in *Athenaeum* (23 Sept. 1893), 412; EWG, 'The Mandrakes. A Study in Grotesque', *On Viol and Flute*, 156-177.

204. *Spectator* 47 (3 Jan. 1874), 18-20; [Garnett], *Illustrated London News* (21 Feb. 1874), 175; the *Athenaeum* reviewer (10 Jan. 1874, 51-2) had nothing good to say; see also P. F. Mattheisen, 'Edmund Gosse: A Literary Record', 16-19. Garnett is identified as the author of the *ILN* critique in EWG-W. B. Scott, 13 Dec. 1873 (LeBL).

205. Henry G. Hewlett, 'Modern Ballads', *Contemporary Review* 26 (Nov. 1875), 978.

> No science half so wise as what the bee
> Is murmuring while he feels the lily's core.
>
> So listen while I tell you my delights
> On sunny afternoons and starry nights,
>   What secrets Love has whispered low to
> And what I know of Nature's mystic rites.[206]

As far as its religious content, the work was as Christian as one would expect from a student of Swinburne's 'amatory paganism'.[207] Thoughts such as

> I do not hunger for a well-stored mind,
> I only wish to live my life, and find
> My heart in unison with all mankind[208]

spoke clearly of the author's antagonism towards the idea of separation from the World.

Edmund's drive to succeed in the literary world continued to gain him introductions into new circles. In April 1874 he attended one of the meetings of the Pen and Pencil Club, at the home of Peter Taylor, MP (1819-1891), where he met Austin Dobson (1840-1921).[209] Edmund and Dobson coincidentally and independently began using French forms of verse in 1875,[210] and the two together did more to encourage 'the naturalization into English verse of certain medieval French poetic forms' than anyone else.[211] At the same time, the acquaintance with Taylor led Edmund to become a contributor, in the autumn of that year, to the London *Examiner*, for which Taylor was the proprietor.[212] Politically on the left, 'atheist and republican,' its circulation was in decline though

206. EWG, *On Viol and Flute*, 4-5. Italics in original.
207. EWG, 'Mr. Swinburne', New York *Century Magazine* 64 (May 1902), 103.
208. EWG, *On Viol and Flute*, 47. Italics in original.
209. EWG, *Firdausi in Exile and Other Poems* (London: Kegan Paul, Trench & Co., 1885), is dedicated to Dobson; see also EWG, 'Austin Dobson', *Silhouettes* (London: William Heinemann, 1925), 183-90.
210. R[obert] C[olville], 'Mr. Henry Austin Dobson, LL.D. A Chat with the Famous Poet and Writer on the Eighteenth Century', London *Great Thoughts from Master Minds*, ser. 6, IV (1908), 376. In 1908, Dobson kept a portrait of EWG in his study (p. 378).
211. J. K. Robinson, 'Austin Dobson and the Rondeliers', 31; Charteris, 81.
212. Bredsdorff, *Sir Edmund Gosse's Correspondence*, 84. 'The *Examiner* I write for constantly', EWG told Georg Brandes on 26 Oct. 1874, '... we are atheist and republican, and I write on poetry every week, do dramatic criticism, etc.' (Paul Krüger (ed.), *Correspondance de Georg Brandes. Lettres choisies et annotées*. Copenhagen: Rosenkilde og Bagger, 1956, II:36).

the weekly managed to attract top writers.[213] Among them was Edmund, whose articles (in the words of a colleague) 'shone with a radiance of their own'.[214]

It was at the on-going meetings of the Pre-Raphaelites that Edmund met his future wife, Ellen ('Nellie') Epps (1850-1929). She was a minor artist in her own right, and a daughter of the surgeon George Napoleon Epps (1815-1874), whose step-brother, John Epps had (as previously mentioned) treated Emily Gosse during her last days.[215] But Edmund, who was presumably unaware at this time of the connection with his mother,[216] was nonetheless bound to make the acquaintance of this 'beautiful' woman,[217] for the Bell Scott and Epps families were old friends.

In October 1874, Edmund wrote his father of his affection for Nellie. He said he had known her for slightly more than four years (according to another version, he knew her for less than a year).[218] A month and a half later came a brief note stating that 'Nellie has suddenly capitulated and without terms!', and a wedding was planned.[219] Although Nellie came from a modestly religious family—she and her mother on occasion attended a Wesleyan Chapel—this was not the force which attracted the two. It was their agreement about so many points, and Nellie's impressively 'massive head' which Edmund wrote of, not her religious beliefs. So that when Eliza Gosse wrote to Nellie describing the Sandhurst life-style, her statements were probably intimidating:

213. Ellegård, *The Readership of the Periodical Press*, 23; *DNCJ*, 211.

214. William Robertson Nicoll recalled 'the days when I was a humble fellow contributor with [EWG] to the *Examiner* how the articles of E.G. shone with a radiance of their own' ('The Correspondence of Claudius Clear [W. R. Nicoll]: "*Father and Son*"', *British Weekly*, 31 Oct. 1907, 93). For PHG's critique of EWG's anonymous review of 'Queen Mary' ('Mr. Tennyson's Drama', *Examiner*, 26 June 1875, 717-719): PHG-EWG, 12 July 1875 (CUL Add. 7019,16).

215. *Life*, 270; Charteris, 66; for her birth certificate, CUL Add, 7027,107; Ellen C. C. Needham, *English Female Artists* (London: Tinsley Brothers, 2vols., 1876), II: 94-5.

216. EWG was familiar with his father's *Memorial of the Last Days* of Emily Gosse, where Epps is mentioned (though not by name) as 'another homoeopathic physician' (p. 50). EWG may not have known his identity until he wrote *Life* in 1890, where Epps is identified as having provided medical attention to his mother (p. 270).

217. NG was thus described during the lecture tour with EWG to America (Topeka, Kansas *Weekly Commonwealth*, 5 Feb. 1885, 7).

218. In 1882, EWG said he knew Nellie for less than a year when he proposed. Lawrence Alma-Tadema (1836-1912), Nellie's uncle, having 'read and admired' *On Viol and Flute*, 'sought out the author, and introduced him to his own home. Here Gosse met Miss Nellie Epps' (E. C. Stedman, 'Some London Poets', 878).

219. EWG-PHG, 24 Oct. 1874 (CUL Add. 7018, 47); EWG-PHG, 2 Dec. 1874 (CUL Add. 7018, 64); EWG-PHG, 12 Dec. 1874 (CUL Add. 7018, 61, 64-5; Charteris, 67, 71-2).

We are such tarry-at-homes that I fear we must not look forward to meeting except you come to see us here. We are very quiet people & mingle but with few. My husband always has been of home & quiet propensities. Willie will tell you he is the minister of a small congregation here chiefly among the poor; & I spend a good deal of time in visiting among them, & seeking to arouse them to give greater heed to the matters of eternal interest & to induce them to "seek first the kingdom of heaven". This, dear Nellie, we, you & I, must make our first thought; God who had been so good & gracious to us, especially in the gift of His Son, is worthy of our whole hearts; which He asks of us, ... Tell me a little of your thoughts on these great and momentous subjects. It is our first & greatest anxiety that you should lead one another in the ways of God. I do not mean that you will have to give up in a morose & melancholy way. *You* will be the receiver; God is the Giver.[220]

With the imminent prospect of marriage, Edmund began saving money.[221] Having expressed discontent with the drudgery as a Transcriber at the Museum, he sought more remunerative work.[222] One position came up in the Museum, and Edmund himself enlisted Kingsley's help again, and that of the Trustees and others, but the job seemed certain to go to Edmund's friend, Dorset Eccles. Another position then opened at the Board of Trade, where Edmund's knowledge of Scandinavian languages helped him to secure the post of Translator. The salary was £400 per year.[223]

-X-

Ties with the past were now broken in quick succession. Edmund had severed his association with Brook Street in 1874;[224] sometime before

220. Eliza Gosse-Nellie Epps, 5 Feb. 1875 (CUL Add. 7019, 14 Emphasis in the original); for the visit to a Wesleyan Chapel: Diary for 1875 of Nellie Gosse (24 Jan.; also 13 June: 'To Morington Church with Mamma').

221. EWG-PHG, 5 Nov. 1874 (CUL Add. 7018, 62: Charteris, 70).

222. As late as 21 Sept. 1872, EWG had told his father that he found the variety of work at the Museum agreeable (CUL Add. 7018, 49); in May of the next year it had become 'dull and labourious' (EWG-Alice Boyd, 6 May 1873, cited in Vera Walker, 'The Life and Work of William Bell Scott, 1811-1890' (University of Durham, PhD dissertation, 1951), 193-4). Later in that year, the subject of low wages for civil servants received public attention, though no action was taken (*Athenaeum*, 16 Aug. 1873, 211-12).

223. EWG-PHG, 12 Dec. 1874 (CUL Add. 7018, 65); EWG-PHG, 4 Aug. 1875 (CUL Add. 7018, 69: Charteris, 75-6).

224. Records of Brook St. Chapel state for EWG: 'Removed to Place not named 1874' (as per

August 1875 he left Tottenham and moved to 26 Alfred Place, St. Giles; he quit the Museum, and officially entered the Board of Trade on 24 August (where Austin Dobson headed another department); he ended his membership in the Victoria Institute before the end of the year.[225]

Edmund's relationship with his father became less intense. In 1867, Philip had realised that his son came home from work exhausted, and so asked if he could manage to write home once a week.[226] There had been an initial burst of enthusiasm, but by 1874, letters were arriving about every three weeks. Moreover, while they were full of pleasant chatter, the surviving correspondence suggests that father and son were on tenterhooks. When an issue arose, Edmund had frankly to admit that he was reluctant to share details of his life. 'Why do you do your better nature such a wrong?' Edmund asked his father.

> Why do you insist on stretching everyone on your own self-measured bed and cutting off feet and ancles [sic] because they push out further than yours do? You insist, more than any professional theologian I have ever met, on your own insight into theology. ... If you will but [re]strain your natural instinct to mould and fashion the character of your own child ... we may always continue to strengthen and help one another, and we may then lay down one another's letters with a sense of full enjoyment, and not with a disappointed sense of yearning.[227]

It is also apparent that Edmund avoided personal contact with his father. Philip might offer to discuss with him the descent of the Israelite tribes from the Teutons, but (using words which many a loving parent has uttered) only 'If ever you come to see us again.'[228] During 1873-4, Edmund's sole known visit to Sandhurst was when he was accompanied by Dean Fog. Yet in 1873, he twice was at The Grove, near Stanmore, the home of Eliza's brother and wife, George and Eliza Brightwen, 'where I have spent my days in rowing over the lake, basking in the sun half-naked, and reading 'Consuelo' among the bulrushes.'[229] In 1874, he took

H. C. Hitchcock-D. Wertheimer, 27 Jan. 1974).

225. EWG's name last appears in a Victoria Institute membership list in *JTVI* IX, 1876, 380 (preface dated 31 Dec. 1875).

226. PHG-EWG, 1 Mar. 1867 (CUL Add. 7018, 3).

227. EWG-PHG, 18 May 1874 (CUL Add. 7018, 57; Charteris, 60-1).

228. PHG-EWG, 20 Apr. 1874 (CUL Add. 7041, 58).

229. EWG-W. B. Scott, 30 Sept. 1873 (LeBL), and EWG-Eliza Gosse, 28 June 1873 (CUL Add. 7018, 54). George Sand's novel *Consuelo* appeared in English in Britain in 1847.

a whirlwind tour to Cornwall with Elise C. Otté (1818-1903), a writer
and translator on Scandinavia and on natural history whom Edmund
considered 'one of the most learned women of her time'.[230] On the way
there they stopped at Newton Abbott, at the very doorsteps of Sandhurst.
He said he 'felt stung with compunction at being so near and yet not
coming to Marychurch. But the time we had was so short that a visit
would have made the Lizard impossible.'[231] In May 1875, the year of his
marriage, Edmund did visit his parents.[232]

For Edmund, it was too late in the day to be discussing religion with his
father. His mind was elsewhere while he conversed with the literary elite
at the Savile Club in London, or helped to found the British Scandinavian
Society.[233] He might, on occasion, indulge a whim of his father and
accompany Nellie to hear the revivalists Moody and Sankey,[234] but no
soul-stirring resulted. When an aspiring poet sent Edmund some of her
poems, he warned against writing too much in a religious vein: 'There is
little new to be said on this august subject, & poetry, to be good, should be
also new. The development of the human soul, the beauty of the physical
world, passion & delight & pain, these are the great & inexhaustible
subjects of poetry, & religion must not do more than illuminate these.'[235]

At Sandhurst, recognition of Edmund's chosen life companion came
in typical Gossean fashion: Philip sent Nellie a large selection of rare
and beautiful orchids.[236] The father urged his son to go earnestly before

230. Edmund Gosse, 'Miss Otté', *Athenaeum*, 2 Jan. 1904, 15.

231. EWG-PHG, 3 Aug. 1874 (CUL Add. 7018, 59); on Otté: entry by EWG in *DNB*, and
almost the identical signed notice in the *Athenaeum*, 2 Jan. 1904, 15.

232. Diary for 1875 of Nellie Gosse (7 May).

233. For the Savile Club, which EWG first attended in the winter of 1874 when Andrew
Lang and George Saintsbury entertained Thomas Hardy: EWG, *Silhouettes*, 378; for the British
Scandinavian Society, founded in late January or early February 1875: Bredsdorff, *Sir Edmund
Gosse's Correspondence*, 189fn.200.

234. Diary for 1875 of Nellie Gosse (1 Apr.); and PHG-EWG, 6 Apr. 1875 (CUL Add. 7018,
29). EWG and NG heard Moody and Sankey speak at an unknown London location on April
1. That day the Americans held meetings at Exeter Hall at noon and the Agricultural Hall at
8 p.m. (advertisement, London *Standard,* 2 April 1875, 1; 'The Moody and Sankey Services',
London *Daily News,* 2 April 1875, 3). 'They attract overwhelming crowds, they are reported
in the newspapers, their portraits are in the shop-windows, and their names in everybody's
mouth. ... Everything they attempt is on a colossal scale. ... At their huge meetings are people of
every class—nobility of both sexes, Churchmen and Dissenters, deans and canons, Ritualists and
Irvingites, Plymouth Brethren and Primitive Christians, members of Parliament, professional
men, merchants, traders, down to stall-keepers and costermongers' (London *Morning Post,* 2
April 1875, 4).

235. EWG-Miss K. Hansen, 25 Mar. 1875 (CUL Add. 7019, 15).

236. Diary for 1875 of Nellie Gosse (14 May); Nellie Epps-PHG, 14 May 1875 (CUL Adv. c.

God and plead for His blessing of their union,[237] with unknown results. Edmund was a month shy of turning 26 and Nellie was 25 when they were married in London on 13 August 1875. They received a telegram from Scandinavian friends, and George Brightwen (Eliza Gosse's brother) and Miss Buckham were there.[238] Some letters were exchanged,[239] but neither Philip, who was then 65, nor Eliza, 62, found it possible to leave Sandhurst for the happy event.

-XI-

The transmission of a religious worldview with specific traits was a goal above all others for Edmund Gosse's parents, as we know. Describing the external factors impacting that upbringing between 1857 and 1875—for Edmund, roughly between the ages of 8 and 26, and for Philip between the ages of 47 and 65—tell part of the story. Glimpsing the intimate thoughts of father and son as set down in a remarkable correspondence provides another part. Together, the two constitute an insight into the challenges of child-rearing. No matter how well-intentioned or devoted or loving, parenting is a humbling experience.[240] Sometimes there is success; this one, judged by its goal, failed. Making one's way in the world from childhood to adulthood is not without its trials. No matter how respectful or sensitive or sharing, during those formative years the pull between individuation and continuity is intense. Errors, misjudgment, and bruised egos are inevitable for parent as they are for a child.

Edmund famously told the story of his upbringing in his masterpiece, *Father and Son*.[241] This was the product of a writer who possessed 'a

---

82.5, 75): 'In thinking of you now, I shall imagine you as always surrounded by this strange and beautiful vegetation.'

237. PHG-EWG, 12 July 1875 (CUL Add. 7019, 16).

238. Bredsdorff, *Sir Edmund Gosse's Correspondence*, 10, 73; EWG-PHG, 12 Aug. 1875 (CUL Add. 7018, 70: Charteris, 78); marriage certificate (CUL Add.7028, 2).

239. Corr. Bk. lists the following letters received or sent: 13 Aug. (from N. Epps, EWG); 19, 27, Aug.; 5, 18, 26, 28, 29 Sept. (from EWG); 10, 19, 27, Aug.; 27, 28 Sept. (PHG-EWG).

240. This is a saying of Gila Wertheimer.

241. During an eleven year period, a 'Five Best' column by different writers in *The Wall Street Journal* has several times singled out *Father and Son*. In 'Masterpiece: His Father, the Believer', Dan Hofstadter called it 'the finest Edwardian literary response to those puzzling Victorians [...] a model of how one generation may compassionately reconsider its immediate forebears' (27 October 2012, C13). Other columns have noted its portrayal of father-son relationships ('Five Best: Alexander Waugh on books that capture the complexities of father-son relationships', 12 June 2008, W8; 'Five Best: Erica Wagner on memoirs of fathers by their sons', 22 July 2017, C10); family trouble ('Five Best Books on Family Trouble: Claire Tomalin', 24 November 2018, C12); and as a childhood memoir ('Five Best Memoirs of Childhood: Laura Marcus', 16 February 2019, C8).

gifted and skillful literary hand with an acute sense of audience and of dramatic effect'.[242] Edmund was 58 when his interpretation of his early years was published—at almost exactly the same age as his father when he had sent his only child to London to earn a living. Looking back from that mature position, Edmund came to this conclusion: What he had experienced transcended the familial. It was archetypal, it was 'a struggle between two temperaments, two consciences and almost two epochs. ... Of the two human beings ... one was born to fly backward, the other could not help being carried forward.' Set in that context, Edmund wrote, it was 'inevitable' that the relationship would end in 'disruption'. Nor was the resulting portrayal, astonishing as it was, imagined: that was Edmund's commitment. *Father and Son* was 'a *document*', it was 'a record' which was 'scrupulously true.'[243]

One would not wish to deny that Edmund may well have given expression in this work to what he felt was the truth of a lived experience. And indeed *Father and Son* resonated with many readers, who sent the author letters because they wanted him to know that his recollection of 'breaking away from the bondage of the old religious order' was also their story.[244] What also cannot be denied—and this I have documented elsewhere—is that *Father and Son* may ring true on one level but is not true on another. It was not as promised. It is replete with factual errors, misinterpretation, misrepresentation, dissimulation, conflicting accounts, and faulty transcriptions.[245]

How did Philip assess this relationship? We have no *Son and Father* to tell us. As it turns out, however, we have something almost as good. Hidden away in their correspondence we have four words. I believe they tell the father's story.

In 1869, when Edmund was a 19-year-old teenager living in London yet still within his father's sphere of influence, Philip expressed his parental feelings towards him. Alluding to the Apostle Paul's words to believers,[246] he called Edmund

242. Michael Millgate-D. Wertheimer, 9 Sept. 1973.

243. For these quotations: Wertheimer, 'A Son and his Father'. Emphasis in the original.

244. R[obert] C[olville], '"*Father and Son*." An Interview with Mr. Edmund Gosse, LL.D.', London *Great Thoughts from Master Minds*, ser. 6, IV (4 Apr. 1908), 9 (excerpts in the New York *Literary Digest*, 16 May 1908, 794-5, and Hobart, Tasmania, *Mercury*, 4 Sept. 1908, 3).

245. Wertheimer, 'A Son and his Father', 57-69.

246. Philippians 4: 1; 1 Thessalonians 2: 19.

my darling Son, my pride, my joy & crown.[247]

In the next year, Philip explained what he meant:

> You are my joy & crown: & [so] you will be, I am sure, in that great hastening day, that day wh. never shall be followed by night, when together we stand before the Son of Man, & look up into His face of love, & hear His happy "Well done!"[248]

Twelve years passed. It was 1882. Philip was reminiscing to his son about shared events of the past. It was on the very day before Edmund turned 33,

> which was the age of our adorable Lord Jesus, when He suffered for sin. What a joy it would be to me, if I could associate with this your birth-day the knowledge that you had come back to his feet, with mourning and confession, & a true change of heart!

By then, his original hope for his son had all but vanished. If not that, then *this:* Whatever good, whatever good deeds, Philip did in his life— *that* would be his reward. The four key words now pointed in a new direction. Perhaps conscious—perhaps not—of what he had previously written, he shared this revealing thought with his son:

> Twenty-five years ago, next Wednesday, I, and you, and Miss Andrews walked down to the Public Room [in St. Marychurch]:—and I began that pastoral intercourse with the little simple Church of God in this village, which has been such an uninterrupted delight to me here, and will be my joy & crown, by and by.[249]

247. PHG-EWG, 29 May 1869 (CUL Add. 7041, 26).
248. PHG-EWG, 2 Sept. 1870 (CUL Add.7041, 40).
249. PHG-EWG, 20 Sept. 1882 (CUL Add. 7018, 36).

PART IV

1875-1888

Last Years

CHAPTER TWELVE

1875-1888

As Age Lengthens Its Shadow

-I-

'WHAT DO YOU DO WHEN you have achieved it all, when you have risen to whatever career heights fate or providence has in store for you?' asks Jonathan Sacks. 'What do you do as age lengthens its shadow, the sun sinks, and the body is no longer as resilient, or the mind as sharp, as it once was?'[1] Few who reach this stage in life can elude confronting this human dilemma, famously formulated in Ecclesiastes. The answer is rarely straightforward or simple.

In Philip Gosse's case, from an outsider's vantage point his last years were marked by intellectual and personal seclusion. This was not traceable to any one factor, but to several. For one thing, his travels abroad during twenty years of his life had insured that early acquaintances would forever be distant from him. He did maintain contact with many of his friends, as he was an avid letter writer (during the last nineteen years of his life, on average he wrote or received over two letters every day of the year).[2] Yet even the liveliest of correspondences is no match for that day-to-day interaction which deepens and refreshes relationships, and inevitably it became difficult to sustain or rekindle past fervour. Always pleased to hear from one of the Jaqueses, W. C. St. John, George Pearse, W. T. Berger, or R. C. Morgan, Gosse eventually knew nothing of Richard

---

1. Jonathan Sacks, *Judaism's Life-Changing Ideas* (New Milford, CT: Maggid Books, 2000), 293; *Ecclesiastes/Kohelet* XII: 1-8.
2. PHG's Corr. Bk. lists 15,000 letters to and from him between April 1869-May 1888.

Hill, and after the passage of years Charles Kingsley wondered what had become of him.[3]

More profoundly, this increasing seclusion is traceable to deeply embedded, life-long character traits, and the results which flowed from them. From boyhood, as previously noted, Gosse was much like his father, 'bookish, inward, craving after affection.' As an introvert, he often preferred his own company, or solitude in nature, to associations with others. 'My darling,' he said to Eliza in quoting the poet Edward Dyer, '"My Mind to Me a Kingdom Is"'.[4] A seemingly photographic memory encouraged his confidence in his own perceptions and supported an attitude of confidence in his conclusions. Gosse felt that once he had discovered by careful thought and investigation that which was correct or true, he clung to it, and argued for it, tenaciously, with that 'impulsive eager spirit' and 'warmth of imagination' which characterised him.[5] His unbending personality is reflected in his distinctive handwriting: sharp, precise, artful and virtually unchanged from manhood to his very last days.

By the time Gosse was in his mid-thirties, the religious search for a solid and immutable resting place was over. By then, he was adhering to Brethren views and lifestyle. He was firmly convinced that Jesus' Second Advent could be predicted and would occur during his lifetime. And he was publicly affirming the validity of the biblical account of the formation of the world, 'not by evolution, as the lying science of the day teaches, but by his creating word.'[6] From these positions Gosse never deviated, even when, in the 1860s, they were given up by the majority of his scientific and religious colleagues. They gave Gosse's life meaning. 'Yes, I am a happy man,' he once told a correspondent,

3. On Hill: PHG-[C. J. G. Rampini, author of *Letters from Jamaica*], 17 Sept. 1874 (Corr. Bk.), and PHG's letter listed in Corr.Bk. to Hill, under 14 Oct. 1874. Hill died in 1872. In 1856, Charles Darwin had asked PHG for a contact in the West Indies to assist him in his study of pigeons, and PHG referred him to Hill (Darwin-PHG, 22 Sept. [1856], PHG-Darwin, 28 Sept. [1856], in Darwin Correspondence Project LETT-1958 & 1962); on Darwin's friendship with Hill: Desmond and Moore, *Darwin's Sacred Cause*, 313-15. On Kingsley: CK-William Pengelly, 26 Aug. 1870, in Mrs Hester F. Julian, 'The Scientific Correspondence of Charles Kingsley and William Pengelly', *J. Torq. Nat. Hist. Soc.* II (1920), 370.

4. *Life*, 359, 331.

5. Obituary notice, *The Christian* (21 Sept. 1888), 886.

6. PHG, *The Mysteries of God*, 2.

For I am assured that *God loves me!* Observe, my dear friend, it is not "religion," I mean; it is not that I am a good man, decent, moral, decorous: it is something quite independent of this; quite antecedent to it. It is that the Almighty, the Holy, *God has loved me*; and I believe it, upon His own word.[7] Is not this enough to make me happy? And he has secured my full, perfect, uninterrupted, unimaginable, happiness, for all eternity; and *assures me* that He has. And all this is as fully open for you, as for me, if only you will accept it.[8]

-II-

An unexpected image of Gosse's last years comes into view when we turn from his character traits and religious outlook to the life of the naturalist as 'age lengthens its shadow.' Recall that Gosse had intended to give up active scientific pursuits by 1865. In *Actinologia Britannica*, he thought he had produced the work by which he would be known in the scientific world. And at age 55, according to one calculation, he was likely past the age at which he would do his best work.[9]

His interest in nature, however, was irrepressible. In a modest fashion, in the next decade he continued to write about, and cultivate, orchids. At least one of his orchids was awarded a prize by the Royal Horticultural Society;[10] at his death, he is reputed to have had one of the finest private orchid collections in the area.[11] Apparently a long time—fifteen years— had elapsed since Gosse last kept sea animals in an aquarium.[12] Then, during 1875-7 he once again collected specimens, dredged for them in Torbay with A. R. Hunt (1843-1914), and—because he was not *au courant* with the latest scientific discoveries—hesitatingly published descriptions

7. 1 John 4: 16.

8. PHG–George E. Bulger, 27 Mar. 1880 (CUL Add. 7313, 69). Emphasis in the original. PHG expressed the same thought in his tract 'A Dollar's Worth' [1859], PHG and EG, *Narrative Tracts* (Freeman & Wertheimer-PHG, 99).

9. With explicit reservations about the general applicability of his findings, C.W. Adams calculated that for 4,204 scientists living after 1600, 'The Age at Which Scientists Do Their Best Work' is 43 (Adams, *Isis* 36, Oct. 1946, 166-169).

10. The first-class certificate 'so well deserved' was for C. Sandhurstiana, exhibited in South Kensington in Dec. 1884 ('Calanthes', *Gardeners' Chronicle*, 26 Dec. 1885, 808).

11. Obituary notice of PHG, *The Academy* XXXIV (1 Sept. 1888), 140. Some of the orchids, as *Calanthe Chudleyana* (after PHG's gardener) and *C. Sandhurstiana* (after his house) were hybrids (*Gardeners' Chronicle*, 14 Dec. 1872, 1651); others were extremely rare (*Gardeners' Chronicle*, 5 May 1877, 573; *Life*, 360).

12. *Life*, 308; in Mar. 1876 PHG had two tanks (one of 11, the other 7.5, gallons) repainted and reglazed (PHG, *The Aquarium*, MS notes, LeBL).

of new genera and species.[13] In June 1876, with the assistance of his old friend, W. A. Lloyd, he constructed at Sandhurst a large forty-nine-gallon aquarium according to the plan of the one at the Crystal Palace, with a reservoir and cistern of more than 330 gallons.[14]

A great deal of physical exertion was necessary to carry out this sort of activity, and though Gosse was in basically sound health, his 68 years were beginning to make the hobby difficult to enjoy. An attack of aphasia in 1874, an aching back, perhaps even his ten new false teeth,[15] directed him into a quieter avocation. So Gosse, citing Horace's dictum that 'If you drive nature out with a pitchfork, she will soon find a way back,'[16] found himself with a new burst of scientific energy. 'Fifty years ago I began my scientific career, with Lepidoptera,' Gosse wrote to the American entomologist W. H. Edwards (1822-1909), 'in my old age, after some inconstancies, I return to my first love!'[17]

What began as an innocent recreation soon took on the proportions of a serious enterprise. It reflected 'a marvellous rejuvenescence near the age of seventy,' in the words of one who knew him.[18] The purchase of some cocoons led to the rearing of larvae, and then to the study of their transformations; this, in turn, was followed by further acquisitions of tropical Lepidoptera from Alfred Wailly and William Watkins, London-based dealers. In February and March 1879 Gosse's biography of the

13. While dredging with Hunt on 10 Aug. 1877, Hunt hauled in a shrimp and a mollusk, both of which PHG considered new additions to British fauna: PHG, 'On *Bellidia huntii*, a Genus and Species of Crustacea Supposed to be New', *AMNH* ser. 4, XX (Oct. 1877), 315, and a second PHG paper, 'On *Hancockia eudactylota*, a Genus and Species of Mollusca, Supposed to be New', also *AMNH*, ser. 4, XX (Oct 1877), 316-19. *Bellidia Huntii*, a shrimp, was in fact new, though the genus (=*Hippolyte huntii*) was incorrect: R. A. Alvarez, 'Crustáceos Decápodos Ibéricos', *Investigacion Pesquera* XXXII (Aug. 1968), 121-2. Other dredging excursions are described in PHG-EWG, 11 June 1877 (CUL Add. 7019, 22) and *Life*, 306-12. On Arthur Roope Hunt: obituary in London *Times* (23 Dec. 1914), 5, funeral notice in Exeter *Western Times* (29 Dec. 1914), 6, and J. Charteris Johnston, '"Literary" Torquay', *Report and Trans. of the Devonshire Association* L (1918), 300. For Hunt's comments on *Father and Son*: Hunt, 'Mr. P. H. Gosse and Mr. Edmund Gosse', *Torquay Directory* (15 July 1908), 6.

14. PHG-William R. Hughes, 20 Nov. 1878, printed in PHG, 'A Marine Aquarium', *Midland Naturalist* II (Jan. 1879), 1-6; Lloyd and the entomologist J. T. Carrington (1846-1908) both came to Sandhurst to help plan the aquarium (*Life*, 308-9). Corr. Bk. lists a number of letters from 'Lloyd' and some from 'Carrington' during 1876 (esp. June-July).

15. *Life*, 363; PHG-EWG, 15 Mar. 1878 (CUL Add. 7018, 30).

16. 'Naturam expellas furca, tamen usque recurret' (Horace, *Epistles* I: x,24), cited in 'PHG-A. B. Farn, 7 Sept. 1880 (CUL Add. 7313, 186-7); PHG-EWG, 15 Mar. 1878 (CUL Add. 7018, 30).

17. PHG-W. H. Edwards, 17 Feb. 1882 (State of West Virginia, Department of Archives and History; a copy is at CUL Add. 7313,489); *Life*, 313-4.

18. [F. Jeffrey Bell], *Athenaeum* (18 Apr. 1891), 508.

Great Atlas moth of Asia, whose wing-span could reach nine inches, appeared in the *Entomologist*;[19] on October 1, Gosse was elected an Ordinary Member of the Entomological Society of London.[20] Two months later, he communicated a paper to the Society,[21] and in the next few years published modest articles based on his collecting.[22]

That entomological greed which had afflicted Gosse some forty-five years earlier in Newfoundland now returned. He needed to have a new cabinet made to house his specimens, which by September 1879 numbered more than a thousand.[23] His zeal bordered on the ecstatic, pushing everything else to the side. 'Father is extremely hearty and in high spirits,' Edmund recorded during a visit to Sandhurst, 'talking away most volubly, but his whole heart and time are given up to the butterflies. It is quite curious: I think I never saw him so absorbed in anything. He can only spare us an hour this morning, and another hour this afternoon.'[24]

Not satisfied with the variety of insects supplied him by English dealers, Gosse appealed directly to collectors in foreign countries, reminiscent of his call for help in researching his sea anemones book. By the end of 1880 missionaries and Englishmen in all parts of the world were addressing cigar, wooden, or tin boxes full of butterflies and moths, tucked in three-cornered envelopes, to Sandhurst.[25] The Anglican minister J. Leslie

19. PHG, '*Attacus Atlas:* A Life-history', *Entomologist* XII (Feb.-Mar. 1879), 24-41, 67-75 (published in pamphlet form in the same year). On his return to London from Alabama in 1839, PHG had purchased a preserved specimen of this magnificent moth, which he still had 40 years later.

20. *Proceedings of the Entomological Society ... for 1879*, p. xliii; 'Entomological Society', *Nature* (23 Oct. 1879), 620.

21. PHG, 'On *Papilio homerus*, Its Ovum and Larva', *Proceedings of the Entomological Society ... for 1879*, Part 5 [5 May 1880], lv-lviii (the abstract was read at the Dec. 3 meeting); 'Entomological Society', *Nature* (1 Jan. 1880), 219. This is the first printed record of the larva of this Jamaican swallow-tail butterfly (Brown and Heineman, *Jamaica and its Butterflies*, 335).

22. PHG, '*Urania sloanus* at Home', *Entomologist* XIII-XIV (June 1880; Nov. 1881), 133-5, 241-5; 'The Butterflies of Paraguay, and La Plata', *Entomologist* XIII (Sept. 1880), 193-205; '*Ornithoptera Brookeana*, Wall[ace]. (Description of female)', *Entomologist* XIV (July 1881), 156-7; [a letter on Trioza crithmi] in J. Scott, 'Description of a Species of Psyllidae Recently New to Great Britain', *Entomologist's Monthly Magazine* XIX (Aug. 1882), 64-6; '*Charis zabua*, Gosse, = *Lemonias tenellus*, Burm[eister]', *Entomologist* XVI (Feb. 1883), 42.

23. For the cabinet: PHG-George Gascoyne, 30 July 1878 (Corr. Bk.), and the entry there under 3 July 1878; on the number of insects: PHG-EWG, 21 Sept. 1879 (CUL Add. 7018, 33).

24. EWG-Nellie Gosse, 6 Oct. 1879 (CUL Add. 7019, 58).

25. A record of these transactions was kept by PHG in a copying book, now at Cambridge (Add. 7313); *Life*, 361-2.

Mais, BA[26] and his two sons sent specimens from Jamaica; Richard and Thomas Perrens, and their uncle, William King Perrens, from Paraguay and Argentina; the Revd James Fanstone, from Pernambuco, Brazil; W. L. Mesman of Celebes (at whose farm Alfred Russel Wallace had once stayed);[27] the Revd Louis C. Biggs, M.A., Colonial Chaplain of Penang, from Malacca (Malaysia);[28] the Revd John Jackson from Honduras; James H. Man from British Guiana; the Revd James Pascoe (1841-1888), founder of the Mexican Evangelical Mission, from that country;[29] and others from the United States and China. Yet even this did not suffice: an agent bought West African Lepidoptera at an auction,[30] Otto Staudinger (1830-1900) and Andreas Bang-Haas (1846-1925), dealers in Dresden, were contacted; when he encountered difficulty identifying new acquisitions, he sought help from experts.[31] As Gosse's collection grew to between 2,000 and 3,000 diurnal Lepidoptera in three cabinets, he sold or exchanged the surplus with Herbert W. Marsden, of Gloucester, a dealer in books and specimens for entomologists and others.[32]

26. Mais had been in Jamaica since 1860, where he was a Stipendiary Curate (*Blue Book. Island of Jamaica. 1870*. Kingston: George Henderson & Co., 1871, pp. L70; L(n); S48); *The Handbook of Jamaica for 1881* (Kingston: Government Printing Establishment, 1881), 339. Mais apparently knew Mrs Sturridge, a Wesleyan acquaintance of PHG's from his Jamaica years (PHG-J. L. Mais, 16 Oct. 1880, CUL Add. 7313,210).

27. PHG-W.L. Mesman, 12 Mar. 1880 (CUL Add. 7313,46-7); A. R. Wallace, *The Malay Archipelago* (London: Macmillan, 1872), 226-231 (PHG owned a copy of this book, *Sandhurst Catalogue*, item #336).

28. Biggs: 'Ecclesiastical News', *Yorkshire Herald*, 5 Oct. 1899, 2; *Madras Mail* (India), 24 Nov. 1881, 2; Biggs was the Colonial Chaplain of Penang from 1885-97, and editor of *Hymns Ancient and Modern, Annotated*, 1867 (*Crockford's Clerical Directory for 1901*, 118).

29. Pascoe: 'Founder of the Mexican Evangelical Mission', '*The Christian' Portrait Gallery*, 279-81. Pascoe's missionary work in Mexico was known in England through printed accounts and personal reports at Mildmay Conferences (e.g., *Christian*, 7 Dec. 1877), and PHG had donated £66 to it over three years (PHG-J. Mercer, 18 Aug. 1880, CUL Add. 7313, 176). They had similar prophetic positions (letter of 5 Mar. 1881).

30. PHG-George C. Harvey, 3 Feb. 1880 (CUL Add. 7313, 26).

31. They included A. G. Butler; A. Doncaster; W. H. and H. Edwards (both from America); J. D. Hooker; and the lepidopterist and future President of the Entomological Society of London, Lord Walsingham (Thomas de Grey, 6th Baron Walsingham, 1843-1919; Walsingham is listed in Corr. Bk., 18, 21 June 1878).

32. On the number of insects: PHG-Arthur Doncaster, 7 Feb. 1881 (CUL Add. 7313, 294) and PHG-Alfred Wailly, 18 Mar. 1881 (CUL Add. 7313, 322-3); on the sales: PHG-John C. Stevens, 28 Feb. 1881; PHG-H. W. Marsden, 7 Mar. 1881; PHG-W. L. Mesman, 10 Jan. 1882 (all CUL Add. 7313, 314; 320; 474-5), et. seq.; on H. W. Marsden: *Year-Book of the Scientific and Learned Societies of Great Britain and Ireland* (London: Charles Griffin and Co., 1885), advertisement on p. [235]. Marsden supplied PHG with a copybook (now at CUL Add. 7313,1)—this type of copybook remained in use in England into the 1960s—which PHG used for his correspondence (PHG-Marsden, 28 Nov. 1879).

Gosse's memory of his own unhappy experiences with Hugh Cuming in Jamaica made him a model correspondent and agent. Transactions were conducted 'as between gentlemen & friends, not as between a customer & a dealer.'[33] In introducing himself, Gosse would relate something of his own background as a Christian and a naturalist, give specific instructions as to what he wanted,[34] how it was to be identified, captured and packaged,[35] and what price he would pay.[36] He even obtained a ruling from the Post Office in London on the proper charges for transmitting dried butterflies and moths.[37]

Usually the first step—convincing non-scientists to mail him insects—was the most challenging. Here Gosse's powers of persuasion, and his winning and open manner, served him well. Missionaries especially found it difficult to decline a request. Gosse could, after all, suggest beneficial incentives other than that of being paid for getting exercise out-of-doors. 'The reverent study of these beauteous handiworks of our God's wisdom, love & skill is not unworthy of one who knows His higher & greater work of Redemption,' as he wrote the Revd James Pascoe. But perhaps the pressure of the Lord's work was too demanding? Then, Gosse suggested, try training a young person:

> ... in a few days, if he is naturally clever & thoughtful, he will have become
> an expert. He will soon want to know something of the *nature* of the
> creatures he is catching: he will begin to *observe*; thus he will, as it were,
> have been endowed with a new sense, a source of immense enjoyment,

33. PHG-Alfred Denny, 7 Jan. 1881 (CUL Add. 7313, 280-1).

34. PHG desired species, not just specimens (PHG-J. Fanstone, 4 June 1880; CUL Add. 7313, 123-4) from the following families: Papilionidae, Heliconiidae, Nymphalidae, Morphidae, and Erycinidae. He declined those from Danaidae, Satyridae, Lycaenidae, Pieridae, and Hesperiidae (PHG-A. B. Farn, 7 Sept. 1880; CUL Add. 7313, 186-7).

35. By early 1880, PHG was enclosing printed *Instructions* in letters to his collectors (Freeman & Wertheimer-PHG, 86). Sometimes he went beyond this, as when he compiled a special handbook which was 'a sort of coup d'oeil of the arrangement of Butterflies (of which about 9500 species are registered) into their Families' (PHG-L. C. Biggs, 14 Apr. 1880; CUL Add. 7313, 80-1). For another correspondent, he prepared an identification book into which the wings of different species could be pasted (PHG-R. Perrens, 18 May 1880; CUL Add. 7313, 111-12).

36. PHG offered from 4d. to 1s. per specimen, delivered to him post free (PHG-G. C. Harvey, 16 Jan. 1880; PHG-J. Pascoe, 18 Aug. 1880; both CUL Add. 7313, 14-15; 174-5). He himself had been paid 1s.6d. by the British Museum for his Jamaican butterflies, and they chose only the ones they wanted (PHG-A. Hodgson, 25 Feb. 1880; CUL Add. 7313, 38).

37. PHG-Secretary of the Post Office, London, 15 Nov., 6 Dec. 1880 (both CUL Add. 7313, 228, 245-6).

a lever for elevation of mind & character; possibly, a preparation for the entrance of the Grace of God into his heart. Is it not worth the trial?[38]

Once the door was opened, Gosse showed he cared about his correspondents. He would send them copies of his own works (including the *Memorial* of Emily Gosse), those of the novelists Walter Scott and Bulwer-Lytton, or the English astronomer and freethinker Richard Proctor;[39] occasionally Gosse's *Narrative Tracts* were included. And, always mindful that 'to have had Jesus divinely revealed to us … is incomparably better than all knowledge besides!',[40] he diplomatically inquired about his collectors' religious views.[41]

Simultaneously, Gosse was also busy building up his entomological library.[42] Here he encountered a problem. All his life he was an avid reader and book lover, but matters had got out of hand. Because the closest library was fifty miles away,[43] when possible Gosse would try to borrow scientific works from the Royal or Entomological societies, or from fellow naturalists.[44] Yet as he continued to accumulate books, he had 'ever less & less book-*room*'.[45]

At his Sandhurst home, books were everywhere: in the morning, dining, and sitting rooms, in his library and his laboratory, in hanging or open shelves made of walnut, mahogany, or stained wood.[46] As Eliza Gosse described Sandhurst, 'Shelves surrounded the walls, filled with books ready for reference on each branch of his many literary studies; a large glass-fronted bookcase stood against the wall, opposite to the chair

38. PHG-J. Pascoe, 18 Aug. 1880 (CUL Add. 7313, 174-5). Emphasis in the original.

39. PHG enjoyed the works of Proctor, including *Other Worlds Than Ours* (1870) and *Orbs Around Us* (1872) (PHG-J. Pascoe, 29 Nov. 1880, CUL Add. 7313, 239-40; PHG-J. Pascoe, 11 Dec. 1880, CUL Add. 7313, 250-1; 'Proctor (Richard Anthony)', in Wheeler, *Biographical Dictionary of Freethinkers*, 265; McCabe, *Biographical Dictionary of Modern Rationalists*, col. 623-4.

40. PHG-Mrs [Fanny] Perrens, 12 Feb. 1881 (CUL Add. 7313, 300-1).

41. See, *e.g.*, PHG letters to Richard Perrens (18 May 1880; CUL Add. 7313, 111-12), W. L. Mesman (18 Apr. 1881; CUL Add. 7313, 342), and James Pascoe (29 Nov. 1880, CUL Add. 7313, 239-40; 5 Mar. 1881, CUL Add. 7313, 318-19).

42. The works of Butler, Distant, Felder, and Hewitson, listed in the *Sandhurst Catalogue*, items #275-6, 279, 266, 268-9, were all acquired between 1880-2. By January 1881, PHG already possessed works of insect collectors Pieter Cramer, Edward Donovan, Edward Doubleday, Dru Drury, E. J. C. Esper, J. O. Westwood, and others (CUL Add. 7313, 284).

43. PHG-L. C. Biggs, 9 Nov. 1880 (CUL Add. 7313,224).

44. Royal Society: PHG-Walter White (1811-1893), 13 June 1881 (CUL Add. 7313, 374) and 22 June 1881 (CUL Add. 7313, 384); Entomological Society: PHG-Ferdinand Grut, 12 June 1880 (CUL Add. 7313, 131); correspondents: P. C. T. Snellen, 16 June 1881 (CUL Add. 7313, 378).

45. PHG-[Mary] Hamer, 28 Nov. 1881 (CUL Add. 7313, 445). Emphasis in the original.

46. The characterization of PHG's library is based on my analysis of *Sandhurst Catalogue*.

in which he sat always, during the winter, with his back to the fire, at a large table covered with books, papers, and implements.'[47] In all, he had at least nine bookshelves totaling well over 165 linear feet of shelving to hold some 2,000 volumes.[48] Most of the volumes (as opposed to titles) dealt with religious topics (37.3%), followed by scientific subjects (28.5%), and reference, literary, and historical works (20.6%). He also had at least 262 volumes from thirty-two different serials, heavily weighted to science (13.6%).

-III-

Notwithstanding intentions, it was not until Gosse was 70 that he could finally declare himself 'out of the scientific world'[49] (as he described his situation in 1880 to Ferdinand Grut, 1820-91, the Librarian at the Entomological Society).[50] It had taken him fifteen years to get to that point. Separation was difficult. To be accurate, for Gosse it was impossible. He was addicted to nature study.

We have seen how, some twenty years earlier, Gosse had casually revived his interest in orchids: growing and collecting, followed by study. Now for insects, it was step-and-repeat: collecting, followed by study. His son Edmund, who was busy with his own life although familiar with his father's latest obsession, did not understand what was happening. He described it as 'a new hobby' for his aged parent, or, 'more strictly speaking, his earliest hobby resuscitated.'[51] As was typical of his portraits of his father, there could be elements of truth in what Edmund Gosse wrote about him, but they were frequently mostly untrue[52]—or, as in this case, missed the point.

47. Gosse, 'Reminiscences of My Husband from 1860 to 1888' (*Life*, 355).

48. *Sandhurst Catalogue* gives the dimensions of many, but not all, of the book shelves. They ranged from a narrow, two-foot six-inch wide, 7-tier shelf (#218) to an 11-foot nine-inch wide, 7-tier one (#216). The *Catalogue* likewise lists many book titles or subjects, but not all. I calculated that PHG had not fewer than 1,933 volumes.

49. PHG-Ferdinand Grut, 19 July 1880 (CUL Add. 7313, 158). In the summer of 1880, A. C. Haddon with A. R. Hunt's help, took a Cambridge University group to Torbay to set-up a marine biological station (*Nature* XXII, 30 Sept. 1880, p. 517). PHG is not known to have been aware of it.

50. 'Ferdinand Grut, F.L.S.', *Entomologist's Monthly Magazine* ser. 2, II (1891), 251-2.

51. EWG, *Life*, 313-18. This account is but one example confirming E. P. Wright's 1891 observation that to write his father's biography required 'over and above literary skill, not only a most tolerant sympathy with the religious views and feelings of the man, but also a large acquaintance with the studies of his life, and neither of these qualifications does Mr. Edmund Gosse lay claim to' (review of *Life* in *Nature*, 30 Apr. 1891, 606).

52. On this general point: Wertheimer, 'A Son and His Father.' The details of PHG's research

Philip Gosse was not the type to engage in hobbies. Yes, he thrilled
at the beauty of flowering plants and loved studying insects. Yes, he
feared (like other premillennialists) that 'science' undermined trust in the
certainty of second advent expectations.[53] Unlike students of prophecy,
however, Gosse was not doomed to complaining from the sidelines. He
was an accomplished student of nature. He had weapons to test the
conclusions of science. Thus the implicit purpose, and the significance,
of Gosse's study of plants and insects at the age of 70: the scientific
questioning, if not the overthrow, of the Darwinian theory.

Up until 1880 there is no hint of this aim in Gosse's entomological
researches. What happened at this time was that while Philip Gosse
was collecting tropical insects he was also examining them under the
microscope. And eventually his attention was drawn to the form and
structure (or morphology) of those organs, peculiar to male butterflies,
which hold the female during coition. In comparing this genital armature
in the genus *Euryades* with that in *Papilio* and *Ornithoptera*, Gosse soon
realised that he had struck upon an abstruse, yet novel and important,
field of work. Species even in the same genus, hitherto classed together
because of similar form, colouring, and markings, were found to have
clasping organs which, in shape and structure, were distinct.[54] What
could that signify?

There were two implications from this observation. On the one hand,
a diagnosis of these organs could provide systematists with a sure tool
for grouping truly related species, replacing the former reliance on
external characters. That was important for the systematist. But of critical
interest to Gosse was the possibility that his researches might shed light
on that vexatious question, What is a species? Could it be that the best
way to account for the diversity of detail in the armature was to reject
the evolutionary understanding of species, and return to the old 'fixity'
definition? Gosse decided to find out.

Gosse knew that his long-time entomologist friend J. O. Westwood
would appreciate this line of inquiry. Westwood was the 'pre-eminent'
entomological systematist of his day,[55] and a well-known Darwin critic

on butterflies were first described in D. L. Wertheimer, 'Philip Henry Gosse', 491-7.

53. Sears, 'The Interpretation of Prophecy and Expectations of the End in Britain', 129-130.
54. PHG, 'On the Clasping-organs Ancillary to Generation in Certain Groups of the
Lepidoptera', *Transactions of the Linnean Society*, ser. 2, II (Zoology) (Apr. 1883), 267-8.
55. J. F. M. Clark, *Bugs and the Victorians* (New Haven: Yale University Press, 2009), 121.
Westwood was called the 'Nestor' of entomology of his time whose literature he 'enriched with

(Darwin had incorrectly attributed to him a negative review of his *Origin of Species* in the *Athenaeum*).[56] Gosse wrote him:

> The subject grows in interest & in importance, as I pursue it; &, I suspect, will afford some arguments adverse to the development hypothesis of MM. Darwin & Wallace. I yesterday and to-day examined the intravalvular apparatus of *Pap. Mireus, Pap. Bromius*, and *P. Phorcas*; insects so closely allied (espec[iall]y the former two) that they might well be considered mere varieties of one species, slightly modified by local or climatal conditions. But the prehensile armature differs widely, essentially, in each of these, from that in either of its allies. May we not reasonably argue that each is an original creation?[57]

It was this possible implication which Gosse wished to develop. By April 1881, he had some notes and drawings which he was thinking of publishing.[58] During the spring and summer he was feverishly absorbed in examining specimens of *Papilio* and *Ornithoptera*: 'I care about nothing else at present,' he wrote to his son.[59] Gosse ordered materials from dealers, borrowed books from the Royal and Entomological societies, and purchased new equipment for his microscope.[60] He also corresponded

a number of beautiful volumes' ('Prof. Westwood', *Athenaeum*, 7 Jan. 1893, 27). He had also achieved prominence for his paleographic illustrations of medieval MSS (Lovell Reeve (ed.), *Portraits of Men of Eminence in Literature Science, and Art*, II: 100-2).

56. Gene Kritsky, 'Entomological Reactions to Darwin's Theory in the Nineteenth Century', *Annual Review of Entomology* 53 (2008), 352; Muriel Blaisdell, 'Natural Theology and Nature's Disguises', *Journal of the History of Biology* XV (Summer 1982), 175: 'Westwood retained his confidence in the reality of distinct created species until his death in 1893 and argued forcefully with both Wallace and Bates at the Entomological Society throughout the 1860s and 1870s.' The *Athenaeum* review was by J. R. Leifchild (Marchand, *Athenaeum*, 226).

57. PHG-Westwood, 22 June 1881 (CUL Add. 7313, 385); for the statement of Westwood's views on evolution: Westwood's letter, *Gardeners' Chronicle*, 11 Feb. 1860, 122, and F. Burkhardt in T. F. Glick, ed., *The Comparative Reception of Darwinism* (Austin: University of Texas Press, 1974), 62.

58. 'I have been making some notes, & drawings of these parts [prehensores], which I may possibility publish' (PHG-F. Du Cane Godman, 13 Apr. 1881, CUL Add. 7313, 335). *Life*, 316, states that Ray Lankester visited PHG in April 1881, and cites a PHG diary entry: 'encouraged by E.R.L., I have begun my monograph on the *Prehensores.*' The diary has not been traced and the assertion cannot be verified, although it may be correct. There is no known correspondence between PHG-Lankester, and Lankester did not confirm the claim in his reader's report on PHG's *Prehensores* paper (see below, 553).

59. PHG-EWG, 5 July 1881 (CUL Add. 7313, 395).

60. For these, see the following letters from PHG, all in 1881 (unless otherwise indicated): to P. C. T. Snellen, 16 June, 29 July (CUL Add. 7313, 378, 405), to J. C. Stevens, 23 Apr. (Add. 7313, 345), to H. W. Marsden, 3 May (Add. 7313, 354), and to R. Perrens, 11 May (Add. 7313, 360-1); to Walter White, 13, 22 June, 31 Aug. (Add. 7313, 374, 384, 415), to F. Grut, 14 Jan. 1882 (Add.

with experts, including the naturalist and entomologist Frederick DuCane Godman (1834-1919), the first part of whose gigantic *Biologia Centrali-Americana* (1879-1915, 63 vols.), co-authored with Osbert Salvin, had just appeared in September 1879.[61] Westwood referred Gosse to the investigations of the Scotsman, Francis Buchanan White, and the Dutchman, Willem de Haan[62] (Edmund Gosse was soon translating the latter for his father); J. H. Gladstone (1827-1902), a past President of the Chemical Society, was consulted about a related matter.[63]

Gosse was convinced of the 'almost absolute novelty' of his observations.[64] He said that, showing that he was apparently unfamiliar with the trend of scientific thinking among entomologists during his own time (or, not less likely, knew of it and refused to accept it). It was one thing for Gosse in his entomological studies before Darwin to adhere to a belief in the immutability of species. When the *Origin of Species* appeared in 1859, Darwin himself was erroneously convinced that entomologists were his leading critics.[65] Some were—such as W. C. Hewitson,[66] Andrew Murray,[67] Edward Newman,[68] J. O. Westwood, and T. V. Wollaston in Britain; Léon Provancher (the 'father of French-Canadian Entomology')[69]

7313, 477); and to Messrs Hunter & Sands, 13 June (Add. 7313, 375), and the optical instrument makers Messrs Negretti & Zambra, 21 June (Add. 7313, 382). PHG corresponded with Negretti & Zambra from at least April 1869 (Corr. Bk.).

61. PHG and Godman corresponded from 1880 (16 Oct. 1880, CUL Add. 7313,212-3).

62. PHG-Westwood, 13 June 1881 (CUL Add. 7313, 373). White, de Haan, and the Americans S. H. Scudder and E. Burgess (1870), had given previous attention to the subject in butterflies. No one informed Gosse of a fourth author, Jules Pierre Rambur, who had published on it in 1839: S. H. S[cudder]., 'The Male Genital Armature of Lepidoptera', *Science* II (6 July 1883), 22.

63. PHG-EWG, 2, 5 July 1881 (CUL Add. 7313, 393-5); PHG-Gladstone, 15 Aug., 14 Sept., 14 Nov. 1881 (CUL Add. 7313, 408, 417; the last letter was seen in the Gladstone Papers in the possession of Sir Stephen Holmes, of Kent). PHG may have first encountered, but certainly knew of, Gladstone as a fellow member of the Victoria Institute.

64. PHG, 'Clasping-organs', 265; 'Clasping Organs, accessory to generation, in Lepidoptera', *Journal of the Royal Microscopical Society* ser.2, III (Oct. 1883), 650.

65. Kritsky, 'Entomological Reactions to Darwin's Theory', 351-60, argues that the concern was based on misinformation. Darwin's misstatement is repeated by Sorensen, *Brethren of the Net*, 210.

66. Kimler, 'One Hundred Years of Mimicry', 246fn.3.

67. Clark, *Bugs and the Victorians*, 113.

68. Clark, *Bugs and the Victorians*, 114; Edward Newman, 'The Death of Species', *Zoologist* ser.2, IV (Feb. 1869), 1529-1542; 'Newman, Edward', *ODNB, DNCJ*.

69. Mélanie Desmeules, 'La contribution entomologique et taxinomique de l'abbé Léon Provancher' (Université du Québec in Chicoutimi, MA thesis, 2003), 90-1; for the condemnation of uniformitarian geology and *le darwinisme* by Provancher (1820-1892), an ordained Catholic priest in Québec: Greig Houlden, 'Materialism, Man, and the Moral Order: Canadian Responses to Darwinian Evolutionary Naturalism' (University of British Columbia, BA essay, 1975), 61-83. For the characterization of Provancher: Fyles, 'The Rise in Public Estimation of the Science of

in Canada; or S. H. Scudder, in America. 'Mr. Darwin's theory seems to have few friends among entomologists,' the Lepidopterist Edwin Birchall (1819-1884) observed in the *Zoologist* in 1861, 'and perhaps his happiest illustrations are not from our branch of Science'. He added: 'but how few of us have really studied the question, and can say what Entomology does teach on the subject of specific variation!'[70]

But times change, and entomologists' views changed. By the 1880s, entomologists—in effect responding to Birchall's question—were making a 'significant and enduring contribution' to buttressing Darwin's theory.[71] With studies drawn from North and South America, Asia, and Africa, entomologists had emerged as 'among those best qualified' to assess issues raised by the evolutionary theory. Having done so, they now stood behind it.[72] Included among the entomologists who turned to the evolutionary theory to give direction to their investigations were (in England) H.W. Bates, F. DuCane Godman, R. McLachlan, Raphael Meldola (Darwin's 'entomological bulldog'),[73] Edward B. Poulton,[74] O. Salvin, and A. R. Wallace; in America, S.H. Scudder[75] and W.H. Edwards (the two most notable Lepidopterists there),[76] and A. S. Packard;[77] and in South Africa, Roland Trimen.[78] Until Darwin's *Origin*, entomologists in England had been focused on cataloguing and classifying the vast number of insects they found, trying to figure out their relations without

Entomology', 44.

70. Edwin Birchall, 'Notes on a Trip to Loch Rannoch', *Zoologist* XIX (1861), 7521.

71. Kritsky, 'Entomological Reactions to Darwin's Theory', 345, 357; Clark, *Bugs and the Victorians*, 119.

72. Sorensen, *Brethren of the Net*, 198.

73. Clark, *Bugs and the Victorians*, 119. Meldola, a naturalist, chemist and physicist, was 'famous as an ardent champion of evolution' whose 'chief biological interest lay in the study of evolution in relationship to insects' (James Marchant, *Raphael Meldola*. London: Williams and Norgate, 1916, 127-8, 94).

74. Clark, *Bugs and the Victorians*, 106; Kimler, 'One Hundred Years of Mimicry', 175-8, Chap. 4.

75. Scudder opposed Darwinism until about 1870, when he accepted the evolutionary theory (Sorensen, *Brethren of the Net*, 199). Ronald L. Numbers offers a more nuanced assessment of the change, placing Scudder among 'theistic evolutionists' (Numbers, *Darwinism Comes to America* (Cambridge: Harvard University Press, 1998), 40). Possibly Scudder was influenced by his study of insect fossils, being the 'first great paleoentomologist' (E.O. Essig, 'A sketch history of entomology', *Osiris* II (1936), 108).

76. C. J. S. Bethune, 'William Henry Edwards', *Canadian Entomologist* XLI (Aug. 1909), 245.

77. T. D. A. Cockerell, 'Biographical Memoir of Alpheus Spring Packard, 1839-1905', *Biographical Memoirs of the National Academy of Sciences* IX (1920), 197.

78. Alan Cohen, 'Roland Trimen and the 'Merope' Harem', *Notes and Records of the Royal Society of London* 56 (May 2002), 205-18; Kimler, 'One Hundred Years of Mimicry', 159-60.

the benefit of any over-arching organizational principle. True, there was God's plan of creation. Understanding that demanded description. But Darwin's theory offered another approach, one which focused not on unchanging species but their dynamic origin.[79]

Nonetheless confident in the importance of his investigation, Gosse had a completed manuscript by October. It contained descriptions of structures associated with coition in sixty-nine butterfly species belonging to two genera, illustrated by 196 magnified figures.[80] During the past six months Gosse had usually been at his microscope from 5 o'clock every morning.[81] Unsurprisingly, he was no longer satisfied to have the fruits of his labouring appear in an entomological journal, as originally intended.[82] That month, Gosse mailed the text of some 45,000 words (written on note paper)[83] and his illustrations to T. H. Huxley, the biological secretary of the Royal Society. He asked Huxley 'the kind favour that you will bestow a brief glance on them [text and illustrations] … and if they appear to you to be worthy, that you will back them' for publication in the *Philosophical Transactions*.[84] Four days later, Huxley acknowledged receipt of the material 'with a kind word.'[85] Gosse likewise heard from Herbert Rix, a clerk at the Royal Society.[86]

With this action Gosse launched an episode—hitherto unexplored—which sheds light on the promotion of Darwinism in Victorian England; the development of entomological studies vis-à-vis the evolution theory; the conduct of the Royal Society; and (not least) the nature of Gosse's opposition to evolution.

79. Kimler, 'One Hundred Years of Mimicry', 11-19.

80. PHG-W.B. Pryer, 8 Dec. 1881 (CUL Add. 7313,455-6). This may represent a reduction of illustrations for the final version. PHG wrote that there were 'about 300 figures' (PHG-P.C.T. Snellen, 7 Dec. 1881, CUL Add. 7313, 454). *Life*, 316, wrote of 'nearly two hundred figures'.

81. PHG-Rev. J. Fanstone, 14 Oct. 1881 (CUL Add. 7313, 420-1).

82. PHG-P. C. T. Snellen, 21 Apr. 1881 (CUL Add. 7313, 344).

83. 'P.S. Might I suggest that *long* papers such as this written on *note* paper are in an extremely inconvenient form for analysis?' (Robert McLachlan referee's report, n.d., Royal Society RR.9.41. Emphasis in the original).

84. PHG-Huxley, 10 Oct. 1881 (Royal Society, Misc. Corr. XII, 1880-83, f. 276; and a copy of the letter, CUL Add. 7313, 423).

85. PHG-EWG, 1 Nov. 1881 (CUL Add. 7313, 427). Corr. Bk. records the 10 Oct. letter to Huxley and the 14 Oct. reply.

86. Corr. Bk. records an 17 Oct. letter from 'Rix (Roy. S.)'; see 'The Rev. Herbert Rix, Royal Society, 1879-95', *Notes and Queries* ser. 11, VI (26 Oct. 1912), 327.

-IV-

Initially, the review process for Gosse's paper appeared to be going as hoped. Then on 22 October another letter came from the Royal Society, this time from Walter White (1811-1893), the Assistant Secretary. Gosse was invited to prepare an abstract of his article, which would be read at an upcoming meeting. Without being assessed by outside readers the abstract would be printed in the Society's *Proceedings*.[87] What did this mean?

On the face of it, the referral to the *Proceedings* was a pro forma matter. It may have reflected Huxley's support for quickly publishing the research of Royal Society fellows.[88] Alternatively, it was possible that it signalled good news. A paper from Gosse, a naturalist with an established reputation, was being given preferential treatment—an official stamp of approval, so-to-say—without discussion by his colleagues or the commencement of the referee process.[89] More likely—and this third possibility is what Gosse feared—it signaled not acceptance and not recognition, but peremptory dismissal. That would be a development well below his expectations. Even before the paper was one of twelve read on 17 November and then printed in the *Proceedings*,[90] Gosse was concerned that his text would never be printed in the prestigious *Philosophical Transactions*. Additionally, he could not help thinking that 'my drawings would be relegated to the Society's Closets, & never see the light.'[91]

87. Corr. Bk., White-PHG, 22 Oct. 1881, with a response from PHG on Oct. 24. White's letter has not been traced but is summarized in PHG-EWG, 1 Nov 1881 (CUL Add. 7313,427).

88. [William M. White (ed.)], *Journals of Walter White*, 271.

89. Andrew John Harrison has documented how Herbert Rix at the Royal Society frequently sought the advice of the physiologist Michael Foster (1836-1907) in the late-1880s and early-1890s to mark those submitted papers favoured as 'safe' for publication even prior to discussion or formal assessment (Harrison, 'Scientific Naturalists and the Government of the Royal Society', 93).

90. PHG, 'The Prehensores of Male Butterflies of the Genera *Ornithoptera* and *Papilio*', *Proc. Royal Society* XXXIII (1881), 23-7. All 12 papers read at the Nov. 17 meeting are listed in the *Athenaeum* (12 Nov. 1881, 635, and 26 Nov. 1881, 706, only two of them are given in *Nature*, 8 Dec. 1881, 142-3). *Life*, 316, claims that Huxley read the PHG abstract; the report on the meeting in the *Proceedings* is mum on the point.

91. PHG-EWG, 1 Nov 1881 (CUL Add. 7313,427). A year earlier, as previously mentioned, PHG had submitted a paper 'On *Papilio homerus*, its ovum and larva' to the Entomological Society of London. It appeared in its *Proceedings* and was not published in its *Transactions* (the article is incorrectly given as from the *Transactions* in the Royal Society *Catalogue of Scientific Papers* and in Stageman, *Bibliography of the First Editions of Philip Henry Gosse*, 82; see Freeman & Wertheimer-PHG,126). Only an abstract of PHG's paper appeared, which disappointed him (PHG-R. Meldola, Entomological Society Secretary, 23 Jan. 1880; PHG-Rev. J. L. Mais, 13 Feb. 1880, both CUL Add. 7313, 20-1; 34). The paper, however, was not original research by PHG;

Gosse asked his son, who was living in London, to attend the 17 November Royal Society evening meeting, the first of the season, and let him know if there was any reaction to his paper. Then Philip learned that the paper was to be anonymously peer-reviewed, something of which he had been apparently unaware. He wrote Edmund that he hoped Ray Lankester (1847-1929), Professor of Zoology at University College London, would be one of the paper's referees, since he was 'one of our ablest zoologists & zootomists.'[92] Edmund dutifully reached out to Lankester[93] (the two may have become acquainted during the overlapping years they were contributors to the *Academy*).[94] Looking at the matter from our vantage, Ray Lankester's involvement is not without its irony. He was 'the greatest morphologist' of his time,[95] and was also the best-known proponent of Darwinian evolution in the post-Huxley era.[96] He also had a reputation as being 'even more disliked' by the 'faithful' than 'the combative agnostic Huxley.'[97] On the other hand, Lankester recalled having met Philip in his father's house as a child,[98] and was unusual among Darwinians in that he retained an outspoken public admiration for him.[99]

he communicated observations by the Revd J. Leslie Mais and his sons, who collected insects for him in Jamaica.

92. PHG-EWG, 1 Nov 1881 (CUL Add. 7313, 427). A 'zootomist' is a comparative anatomist. *OED*, 3ed., cites only two usages during the Victorian era.

93. PHG-EWG, 1 Nov 1881 (CUL Add. 7313, 427) clearly states this sequence of events. *Life*, 316-18, however, gives a different account of the chief persons involved in the stages leading to the publication of the manuscript. EWG asserts that it was Lankester who first encouraged PHG to initiate his study, and that Michael Foster (secretary of the Royal Society from 1881-1903) played a role towards that end. Certainly Robert McLachlan's aid was more notable, as is evident from numerous letters between him and PHG. EWG dedicated the *Life* of his father to Lankester, who remained an important enough friend of EWG's to be counted among the mourners at his funeral ('Funeral. Sir Edmund Gosse', London *Times*, 22 May 1928, 19).

94. During 1871-73, EWG and Lankester wrote for the London *Academy*, then a fortnightly (Johnson, 'The *Academy*, 1869-1896', 78-9).

95. 'News and Views: Sir Edwin Ray Lankester (1847-1929)', *Nature* 159 (31 May 1947), 734.

96. John Bellamy Foster, 'E. Ray Lankester, Ecological Materialist', *Organization & Environment* 13 (June 2000), 233;); 'Lankester (Edwin Ray)', in Wheeler, *Biographical Dictionary of Freethinkers*, 199-200; McCabe, *Biographical Dictionary of Modern Rationalists*, col. 423.

97. 'Obituary. A Great Scientist. Sir E. Ray Lankester', London *Guardian* (16 Aug. 1929), 6.

98. Joseph Lester, *E. Ray Lankester and the Making of Modern British Biology*. Edited by Peter J. Bowler (BSHS Monographs, Number 10. Oxford: British Society for the History of Science, 1995), 10.

99. Ray Lankester referred to PHG as 'a great naturalist, who loved the sea-shore and its rock-pools enthusiastically ... and gave beautiful coloured pictures of them', and whose books were 'of high scientific value' (Lankester, *Diversions of a Naturalist*, 83). As has been noted, in reviews of PHG's scientific works, Lankester's father, Edwin Lankester, also spoke highly of

While awaiting the reports, Gosse continued his investigations, making additional drawings and corresponding with Robert McLachlan (1837-1904) about his authoritative *Catalogue of British Neuroptera* (1870). In 1877, McLachlan had been elected a Fellow of the Royal Society, one of the few entomologists to achieve that distinction.[100] His *Monographic Revision & Synopsis of the Trichoptera of the European Fauna* (1874-80; Supp., 1884), had anticipated Gosse's researches for other orders.[101]

On 1 December, Gosse asked Walter White at the Royal Society to return his original manuscript, which (Gosse added) he expected would be printed 'in extenso' by the Society.[102] White responded that it was not certain that it would appear in the *Philosophical Transactions*.[103] Gosse was not waiting. He sent copies of his abstract to noted entomologists: the American W. H. Edwards and the Dutch Lepidopterist P. C. T. Snellen (1832-1911), the latter giving a 'flattering estimation' of the paper.[104]

As it turned out, Lankester and McLachlan were selected as referees. Early in 1882 both submitted favourable assessments, recommending full publication in the *Philosophical Transactions*.[105] Lankester was insistent that the Society accept the paper with all of its drawings by Gosse, who was a 'venerable [Royal Society] Fellow' whose 'work in past years has been of very great value and interest.'[106] The analysis

PHG. Lankester is said to have 'strongly believed that arguments were a necessary part of the way the human intellect worked things out' so he 'did admire some of those who were attacking him simply because they were speaking their mind' (Boulter, *Bloomsbury Scientists*, 32).

100. Wale, '"The Sympathy of a Crowd": Periodicals and the Practices of Natural History in Nineteenth-Century Britain', 137.

101. For example, PHG-McLachlan, 21 Nov. 1881 (CUL Add.7313, 439-40). Copies of some PHG letters are at CUL, McLachlan's letters are listed in Corr. Bk. McLachlan's researches on the *Trichoptera* contained 59 plates with 2,000 figures. His eyesight never recovered from the strain of producing them (obit. notice, *Proc. Royal Society* LXXV (June 1905), 368).

102. PHG-Walter White, 1 Dec. 1881 (a copy is at CUL Add. 7313, 448, the original is at the Royal Society, *Miscellaneous Correspondence* XII (1880-3), 224).

103. W. White's warning is derived from PHG's description of it in his same-day response to White's letter (PHG-W. White, 3 Dec. 1881, Add. 7313, 451).

104. PHG-W. H. Edward, 17 Feb. 1882 (State of West Virginia, Department of Archives and History; a copy is at CUL Add. 7313, 489); PHG-P. C. T. Snellen, 14 Dec. 1881 (CUL Add. 7313, 458). PHG enclosed with this letter a copy of the abstract of his paper, and it is not clear if Snellen's words related to PHG's description of his paper or to something more substantive, or what PHG sent. Harrison notes ('Scientific naturalists and the government of the Royal Society', 10) that authors whose research appeared in *Philosophical Transactions* received 100 free offprints, those with abstracts in the *Proceedings* received none.

105. For the reports of McLachlan and Lankester: Royal Society, RR.9.41-2; the former is undated, the latter dated 16 Jan. [1882].

106. Ray Lankester-G.G. Stokes, 16 Jan. [1882] (Royal Society, Referees' Reports vol. IX,42, RR.9.42). Stokes was secretary of the Royal Society from 1854-85.

by McLachlan, who was regarded as 'among the most prominent' of those in the London entomological world during the last half of the nineteenth century,[107] was more cogent. He knew from his own parallel and painstaking studies how valuable the genital organs were as guides for the systematist. Confident that Gosse's observations were correct ('so far as correctness can be obtained in dry insects, and limited materials in some cases'), he therefore asserted that, with a few possible changes, the paper merited publication. It was likely 'to do real scientific service, and to excite attention to a subject that has received only the slightest consideration in Lepidopt[e]ra,' McLachlan said. 'The drawings should also be reproduced; they are very beautiful, in some cases possibly too highly finished.'[108] McLachlan added that since he was unfamiliar with the butterfly groups with which Gosse dealt, the Society might wish to elicit the opinion of someone who had worked in that specific area. He suggested Osbert Salvin (1835-1898), a favourite among naturalists for his 'generally sound' scientific advice.[109]

Although Lankester and McLachlan were in agreement in recommending Gosse's findings for the *Philosophical Transactions*, a third opinion was sought from Salvin. This was highly irregular. Just five years earlier, the physicist John Tyndall, who had been a Fellow of the Royal Society since 1852, described the Royal Society's procedure in assessing papers for publication, as follows:

> You know the habit of the Royal Society is to place every paper presented for the Philosophical Transactions in the hands of two referees, who are chosen for their acquaintance with the subject. They report to the Council favorably or unfavorably as the case may be. This caution is not at all observed with regard to the Proceedings where many things of doubtful value are permitted to appear.[110]

Gosse's research had been examined by two referees. Both were notable men of science. Both were familiar with Gosse's subject. Both recommended publication in the *Philosophical Transactions*. And yet the review process for Gosse's submission continued with Salvin. The logical

---

107. W. F. K., 'Robert McLachlan, F.R.S.', *Nature* (2 June 1904), 106.
108. McLachlan, referee's report, n.d. (Royal Society RR.9.41).
109. Obituary notice, 'Osbert Salvin', *The Entomologist* XXXI (July 1898), 176.
110. Tyndall-Louis Pasteur, 17 Jan. 1877, quoted in Strick, 'The British Spontaneous Generation Debates of 1860-1880', 290.

explanation for this unconventional treatment is that two referees had not delivered the rejection desired by those who ran the Royal Society.

One needs to parse the peer-review report which was received from Salvin. A convert to the theory of evolution after reading Darwin's *Origin* and doing natural history field work in Guatemala,[111] Salvin wrote (seemingly intending marvellous understatement) that Gosse's paper 'bears evidence of having been prepared with great care.' The author's focus on only part of the genital apparatus, however, he thought misguided. Nor were the results of 'sufficient precision, novelty, or importance' to justify publication in the *Philosophical Transactions.* Nonetheless, because the subject had not received the attention it deserved, Salvin concluded that 'I should be sorry if the Memoir were not published somewhere.' Translation: 'somewhere' where *la crème* is good enough, but not here in the *Philosophical Transactions*, where only *la crème de la crème* will do. A noteworthy fact is that Salvin was then vice-president of the Zoological Society.[112] He was in a position to promote publication in their journal. Instead, he proposed the Linnean Society as a suitable venue.[113]

Gosse was again experiencing the boycott of his work at the Royal Society which had first surfaced in 1858, as mooted by Andrew John Harrison and previously discussed.[114] After 1870, the Huxleyite scientific naturalists were in firm control of the Royal Society; in 1883 they were at the height of their influence.[115] The agenda of these agnostic naturalists was to rally around the pro-Darwinian camp while preventing opponents from gaining a hearing.

In focussing on comparative entomology and morphology, Gosse had presented a piece of research which was more sophisticated than his earlier great work on sea anemones. Since its publication entomologists have called the memoir a 'classical' contribution[116] and an 'elaborate and beautifully illustrated paper';[117] some have disapproved of Gosse's

111. F. DuCane Godman, speaking at the 6 June 1916 meeting of the Zoological Society, quoted in *Proceedings of the General Meetings for Scientific Business of the Zoological Society of London, 1916* (London: Longmans, Green, n.d.), Pt. II: 542.

112. 'Zoological [Society]', *Athenaeum* (27 May 1882), 671.

113. Salvin, referee's report, 30 June 1882 (Royal Society RR.9.43).

114. See above, pp. 356-365 (esp p.361).

115. Harrison, 'Scientific Naturalists and the Government of the Royal Society', iv, 411.

116. 'Current Notes and Short Notices', *Entomologist's Record* XXVII (15 Apr. 1915), 90.

117. G. T. Bethune-Baker, 'What are the Tegumen and Valvae in the armature of the Lepidoptera?', *Entomologist's Record* XXVII (15 Feb. 1915), 32. Besides the laudatory remarks

techniques.[118] Yet recall that Gosse was intending to do more than contribute another abstruse study to the world of science. He believed that the details he had uncovered were 'certainly novel' and important, 'opening unexpected lines of agreement & divergence between species.'[119] He hoped to call into question, if not to disprove, the validity of Darwin's theory, and to do so not from a religious, but from a purely scientific, perspective. To Gosse it was a matter of urgent importance. To insure that this point was not missed by readers, he included some three pages discussing his conclusions.

In their referees' reports, Lankester and McLachlan urged the excision of those remarks. 'The only suggestion I have to offer in regard to emendation or curtailment –,' Lankester wrote, 'is that the author should be requested to remove from the MS, before printing, all references to theological topics which have not, I think he will see, a necessary place in a treatise on the structure of the genital organs of Butterflies, & may give offence to some sensitive minds ...'[120] There is a dismissive aspect to McLachlan's concurrence: 'I think the remarks on pp. 62-65 might be omitted with advantage: no doubt they are strictly in keeping with the

of Scudder ('The Male Genital Armature of Lepidoptera', 22), McLachlan, and Lankester, see also the obituary notice of PHG in *Entomologist's Monthly Magazine* XXV (Oct. 1888), 113-14: 'All Entomologists must be glad to see the tendency among Lepidopterists of late years to place special value on structural characters, and to recognize this work of Mr. Gosse ['On the clasping organs'] as a valuable contribution to that view of the subject'.

118. British entomologist Frank Nelson Pierce (1861-1943) later referred to PHG's 'beautifully illustrated' study, but echoed comments of Salvin. Pierce asserted that the majority of the drawings were misleading and often incorrect because he only used dried specimens, and that the entire armature should have been examined (Pierce, *The Genitalia of the Group Noctuidae of the Lepidoptera of the British Isles. An Account of the Morphology of the Male Clasping Organs* (Liverpool: A. W. Duncan, 1909), 2-3). A later researcher, citing Pierce's work, agreed with his assessment: PHG's work was 'beautifully illustrated', but 'The majority of the drawings were incorrect or misleading because of the manner in which they were represented' (George Henry Hammond, 'The Genitalia of Graptolitha Hbn. (*Cucullinae, Noctuidae*)' (McGill University, MSc thesis, 1924), 2).

More recently, PHG's 1881 (*Proc. Roy. Soc.*) and 1883 (*Trans. Linn. Soc.*) studies have been severely criticized as contributing to the 'chaotic' terminology used to describe the genitalia in Lepidoptera. 'However elegantly styled and handsomely illustrated (the second paper) [by PHG] ... they contain serious errors, due to the crude working method of the author (maceration of chitin and sclerotin with KOH not being known at the time, the genitalia were inspected in dry and shriveled condition, after one *valva* having been removed 'with a sharp pen-knife')' (A. Diakonoff, 'Considerations on the Terminology of the Genitalia in Lepidoptera', *Lepidopterists' News*, (1954), 69).

119. PHG-R. McLachlan, 6 Mar. 1882 (CUL Add. 7313,492-3).

120. Ray Lankester-G.G. Stokes, 16 Jan. [1882] (RR.9.42).

ideas of the author of "Omphalos", but somewhat out of place—as they now stand—in the Philosophical Transactions.'[121]

More importantly, McLachlan's own studies on the purpose of the structural variations of these organs—which Gosse was unable to clarify[122]—far from raising doubts about the validity of Darwin's theory, actually reinforced McLachlan's support for it. 'Having long since given in my adherence to the doctrine of evolution,' McLachlan had argued a few years earlier, 'I can only remark that my faith in the ground-work of that doctrine has been materially strengthened.' In this case, variations in the armature had to be correlated with the physical environment, and seen as another example of advantageous adaptations in the struggle for survival in nature.[123] Salvin did not comment on Gosse's three pages.

Notwithstanding Gosse's wishes, behind-the-scenes negotiations reveal that praiseworthy as the paper might be, it was sailing the scientific seas without prospects of finding a safe port at which to dock. In February 1882, the Council of the Royal Society had purportedly determined that the memoir was 'of too limited and special a nature' for the *Philosophical Transactions*, G. G. Stokes,[124] the secretary of the Society, told G. J. Romanes, the secretary of the Zoological Section of the Linnean Society.[125] This odd conclusion for an organization which regularly published papers on abstruse subjects was delivered straight-faced. Stokes wondered if there was any chance that the Linnean might print it? Then the day before Stokes wrote Romanes, he heard from P. L. Sclater, Secretary of the Zoological Society of London, that it wouldn't be 'expedient' for them to take it, either. The reasons appear to have been

121. McLachlan, referee's report, n.d. (Royal Society RR.9.41).

122. PHG, 'Clasping-organs', 279-80.

123. R. McLachlan, *A Monographic Revision & Synopsis of the Trichoptera of the European Fauna* (London: John Van Voorst, 1874), Part I: iii.

124. It is worthwhile comparing PHG's experience with the Royal Society in 1882 with that of J. W. Dawson in 1870 (as previously discussed). Both men corresponded with Walter White and G. G. Stokes at the Royal Society; both had their submissions read in the first instance by two referees who were advocates for the evolution theory; both ended up having three referees (in the case of PHG, the first two recommended publication, the third opposed it; for Dawson, of the first two referees one favoured, the other opposed, publication, and the third opposed it as well); both waited a considerable time before learning the fate of their paper (PHG, some 18 months; Dawson, 12 months); both had their submissions rejected for publication in the Society's *Philosophical Transactions* after their work had been excerpted in the *Proceedings*.

125. G. G. Stokes-G. J. Romanes, 24 Feb. 1882 (Royal Society RR.9.45). When I saw this letter at the Royal Society, its poor condition made it almost undecipherable.

a backlog of papers and a shortage of funds,[126] especially common in instances in which a scientific paper required illustrations.[127]

A week later, Romanes seemed to close out the Linnean Society as an option. 'There is no question that the paper is one which ought to be published,' he said, but it had been determined that the cost of printing the plates 'would be greater than the finances of the Society could at present sustain.' Regretting that the paper might not appear 'through a mere lack of funds,' Romanes asked whether Gosse, or the Royal Society, 'could assist.'[128]

Gosse had been kept in the dark about the negotiations, and was puzzled when McLachlan broke the news in March. After thanking McLachlan 'for the very kind interest you have taken in my Paper, & your appreciation of the researches,' he added:

> Since you expressly say the rejection of the paper [from the *Philosophical Transactions*] is not on its merits, am I to understand that the expense is *their* [the Royal Society's] difficulty? You indeed say they consider it *unsuited*; but Animal Physiology is not infrequently treated in the Phil. Trans., as witness Mr. Parker's vol. on the Batrachian skull,[129] and even my own two papers on Rotifera which appeared in the Ph. Trans. six and twenty years ago.[130]
>
> If the cost of plates,—which I know will be great,—is the chief impediment to the Roy. Soc. publishing my Memoir,—that would be easily overcome. I would think little of guaranteeing a sum of £50 towards the expenses and that, whether I were reimbursed by the Gov[ernmen]t Grant or not. ... At all events, the observations having

126. P. L. Sclater-G. G. Stokes, 23 Feb. 1882 (Royal Society RR.9.44). Upon becoming secretary of the Zoological Society in 1859, Sclater had tackled these two organizational issues (A. H. Evans, 'Obituary. Philip Lutley Sclater', *The Ibis* ser. 10, I, Oct. 1913, 645).

127. Harrison, 'Scientific Naturalists and the Government of the Royal Society', 19-20.

128. G. J. Romanes-G. G. Stokes, 4 Mar. 1882 (Royal Society, RR.9.46). Romanes was one of Darwin's 'strongest supporters' (Joel S. Schwartz, 'Out From Darwin's Shadow: George John Romanes's Efforts to Popularize Science in *Nineteenth Century* and other Victorian Periodicals', *Victorian Periodicals Review* 35 (Summer 2002), 133).

129. William Kitchen Parker, 'On the Structure and Development of the Skull in the Urodelous Amphibia', *Philosophical Transactions of the Royal Society of London*, vol. 167, Part 2 (London: Taylor and Francis, 1878), 529-598.

130. PHG refers to his *Philosophical Transactions* papers 'On the structure, functions, and homologies of the Manducatory organs in the Class Rotifera' and 'On the dioecious character of the Rotifera', published respectively in 1857 and 1858 (Freeman & Wertheimer-PHG, items #268, 273).

been made, ought not to be hidden in the Archives: indeed, I think it would be shameful, of such a Society as the Royal, to hide them there.[131]

In the end, a financial arrangement was worked out with the Linnean Society in March 1882. During the second half of the nineteenth century, scientific papers were increasingly accompanied by illustrations whose reproduction was growing more and more expensive.[132] The estimated cost for the 80-page text (£40) and the eight illustrative plates with 203 figures (£50) was largely met by a £50 grant from the Royal Society, and £25 from Gosse himself.[133] On 6 April the Linnean Society formally agreed to place Gosse's research in its *Transactions*.[134] The memoir was the last to be read at the meeting of the Linnean Society on 4 May 1882.[135]

Three matters remained to be discharged before publication. Firstly, there was the final form in which the study would appear. Gosse wanted an index to the text and plates (an index was a feature of all of his scientific works); James Murie, the Linnean's librarian, agreed to compile one.[136] Then there were the drawings. Gosse was concerned that the illustrations should be done in a consistent tone. To insure that, he insisted that the proofs for each plate be approved by him. 'The mode & vehicle of illustration,' he wrote to Murie,

> I confidently leave to you. Lithography is *soft*; but is apt to be *indefinite*, is it not? And these microscopic details of mine demand great precision of definition. The illustrations of my Memoirs on Rotifers, in Phil. Trans., 1856 and 1857, were beautifully rendered: these were, if my memory does not fail me, on steel, by Mr. [James] Basire.[137] The plates

131. PHG-R. McLachlan, 6 Mar. 1882 (CUL Add. 7313, 492-3). The annual Government Grant for scientific research to the Royal Society began in 1849 at £1,000 (Harrison, 'Scientific Naturalists and the Government of the Royal Society', 26-31).

132. Harrison, 'Scientific Naturalists and the Government of the Royal Society', 19-20.

133. For the estimated cost, see G. J. Romanes-G. G. Stokes, 4 Mar. 1882 (Royal Society, RR.9.46); for the grant, Linnean Society *Council Minute Book* No. 6 (1881-91), 37 (under 16 Mar. 1882); for PHG's share, ibid., p. 100 (under 7 June 1883). For his payment, PHG received 50 extra copies, of which he still had 20 at his death (*Sandhurst Catalogue*, item #486).

134. As previously indicated, Osbert Salvin had suggested the Linnean Society for PHG's paper in his Referee's Report. But his report is dated 30 June 1882, and by that time the paper had already been accepted by the Linnean.

135. 'Linnean [Society]', *Athenaeum* (27 May 1882), 671; 'Linnean Society, May 4', *Nature*, 1 June 1882, 119. It appears that PHG was present at the meeting, having perhaps gone up to London for the day (there is no listing in Corr. Bk. for any letters received on May 4).

136. PHG-J. Murie, 23 May 1882 (Linnean Society).

137. James Basire (1796-1869) was the last of the English printmakers and engravers with that name (*ODNB s.v.* 'Basire, Isaac'). PHG correctly recalled Basire's work for him.

of my Paper on Lar Sabellarum,—In Linn. Tran., 1857, was by Mr. [G.] Jarman;[138] very nice, but the subject was less a test than the former, *and than the present*. But you will, I am sure, commit the work to artists who will not dishonour the Linnean Society,—nor me. And I doubt not that I shall be satisfied with your selection.

With your proposal to intrust the Plates to different artists, I quite concur; for I greatly desire that publication be not needlessly delayed. Provided only such artists be chosen, as possess the same style. ...[139]

Finally, there was the matter of Gosse's comments on the implications of his findings. In June, he promptly returned the proof of his paper to Murie at the Linnean; meanwhile by September he had heard nothing further. The Society, he told McLachlan, had shown him 'scant courtesy'.[140] Once again, Gosse was out of the loop. It was his reflections spanning three pages which were causing heartburn for the Linnean, as likely had been the situation for the Royal and Zoological societies. Gosse was reputedly convinced by the argument of Ray Lankester that if the Royal Society permitted a defence of Christianity in one of its scientific papers it could hardly prohibit a defence of atheism under similar conditions.[141] Whether or not this was how the case was resolved is unknown. What is known is that differences of opinion at the Royal Society could be tolerated, as long as they involved disputes between evolutionists.[142]

Ultimately most of Gosse's offending words were deleted or reduced by

138. Jarman later engraved seven plates for R. McLachlan's *Monographic Revision ... of Trichoptera* (1884).

139. PHG-J. Murie, 23 May 1882 (Linnean Society). Emphasis in the original. All of the figures were drawn by PHG, and the lithographic work was done by Frederick Huth (fl. 1881-1905) of Edinburgh (for whom see Engen, *Dictionary of Victorian Engravers, Print Publishers and Their Works*,109).

140. Dating for this letter is based on my interpretation of PHG-R. McLachlan, [summer or autumn] 1882 (Linnean Society, Gosse MSS). According to the letter, PHG received the proof for his paper on 13 June and returned it promptly. Corr. Bk. lists a letter to 'Murie L.S.' on 16 June. The only letter listed in Corr. Bk. to McLachlan after 13 June is dated 22 Sept., with a 25 Sept. reply from McLachlan.

141. *Life*, 318.

142. An 1866 paper by C. H. Bastian printed in the Royal Society's *Philosophical Transactions* received glowing anonymous referees' reports from George Busk and T. H. Huxley, with a significant difference. Huxley recommended changes to Bastian's concluding remarks 'as they contain one or two inaccuracies in matters of fact.' Busk, however, stated that 'I see no reason ... why [Bastian] should not be allowed to express his own views in the way he has done' (both reports quoted in James Edgar Strick, 'The British Spontaneous Generation Debates of 1860-1880, 89-90). As previously noted, Bastian, Busk, and Huxley were all supporters of Darwin's theory.

mutual agreement, until on 16 November 1882, there remained only the '[final] paragraph of the MS. in question.' On 7 December it was reported that Gosse had agreed to its omission.[143] No record has been traced of what Gosse stated in that paragraph, yet the careful reader would not miss Gosse's rejection of Darwin's theory. This paragraph, coming at the end of his description of the one butterfly species, stated:

> Can these [species] be descended from a common parentage? and are the diversities merely the result of changes in the climate, soil, and food produced on a party of emigrants, in the course of many generations? Or are they not, rather, powerful, if unexpected, witnesses to the primal diversity of *Papilio Nireus* and *Papilio Bromius*, as distinct creations of the Almighty God?[144]

While these maneuverings were taking place, Gosse undertook new microscopical researches. Probably realising that his attempt to challenge Darwin's theory scientifically had not succeeded, some of these were left in manuscript.[145] Some five years after beginning his new investigations into butterflies, Gosse's researches were finally issued in the *Transactions* of the Linnean Society, one of England's most prestigious scientific organizations. He promptly began to send out offprints of his article.[146]

-V-

During the next two years (1883-5), the only other known scientific matter occupying Gosse's attention was bringing out a new edition of *Evenings at the Microscope*, which in 1884 was still called 'by far the best book of its

143. Linnean Society, Council Minute Book, no.6, pp. 42, 67, 70. According to *Life*, 317-18, PHG balked at the Council's suggestion that he remove the offending reflections even after he had received proofs of the text. Lankester finally convinced him that it was the right thing to do.

144. PHG, 'Clasping-organs', 320.

145. See PHG, 'Clasping-organs', 332-4, esp. 334 fn. One of the notebooks containing new 'Descriptions of the Genital Prehensors in the Papilionidae' is now in the Entomology Library, British Museum (Natural History). Another notebook, and one of illustrations, together with that one, are listed in *Sandhurst Catalogue*, item #446 (which may be the same as the MS currently at the Stony Brook University Libraries, New York).

146. For example, to the Keeper of Zoology at the British Museum Natural History: PHG-Dr [Albert] Günther, 22 May 1883 (A. Günther Collection, British Museum (Natural History), Box 16). Letters to Günther are listed in Corr. Bk. (e.g., 22 Mar. 1882). Though Günther 'never really expressed his views on Darwin's theory, he contributed much in favour of it and had several friends who were avowed evolutionary biologists' (Savithri Preetha Nair, 'Edgar Thurston at the Madras Museum (1885-1909): The Multiple Careers of a Colonial Museum Curator', in Sarah Longair and John McAleer (eds.), *Curating Empire: Museums and the British Imperial Experience* (Manchester: Manchester University Press, 2012), 170).

kind.'[147] The task was hardly onerous, as almost nothing new was added. Take the chapter on the 'Wheel-bearers', or rotifers. It followed the first edition of 1859 (Gosse had not done work on that class of microscopic animals since 1866),[148] even though professional and amateur naturalists had published numerous faunal and anatomical research in which new species were described.[149] This material remained unculled in various learned and popular serials, awaiting a comprehensive review to replace that of W. C. Williamson in the final edition of Pritchard's *History of the Infusoria* (4th ed., 1861). W. Saville Kent's valuable[150] *Manual of Infusoria* (3 vols., 1880-82) might have done this, had it considered the Rotifera.

Gosse might also have filled the void. At this time, however, he did not have the desire, ability, or energy to do so. That was the case notwithstanding his references to Rotifera being his 'own special delight' in all of the animate world,[151] dating to his first research in the 1850s, as previously mentioned.[152] In the early 1860s, he returned to the subject with a series in the *Popular Science Review* (1861-63) intended for advanced students.[153] The illustrations were by the author, engraved by Tuffen West (1823-1891),[154] an accomplished naturalist whose work was in demand among colleagues.[155] Apparently Gosse had been thinking of popularizing Rotifera with a work titled *The Pond Raker*.[156] If so, it never appeared, possibly because Gosse had been pre-empted by his friend H. J. Slack (1818-1896), 'an excellent and careful observer',[157] in

147. H. J. Slack, 'Pleasant Hours with the Microscope', *Knowledge* IV (23 Nov. 1883), 317. Slack's competitive work, *Marvels of Pond-Life*, had appeared in its 4ed. by 1880 (Freeman, *British Natural History Books*, 316).

148. PHG, 'Dinocharis Collinsii; a Rotiferon New to Science', *Intellectual Observer* X (Nov. 1866), 269-72.

149. De Beauchamp, 'Recherches sur les Rotifères', 12.

150. Ray Lankester, review of *A Manual of the Infusoria*, *Nature* XXII (26 Apr. 1883), 601-3.

151. The same words appear in the 1859 (p. 272) and 1884 (p. 223) editions of PHG, *Evenings at the Microscope*.

152. See above, 176-186.

153. Freeman & Wertheimer-PHG, 120.

154. Britten and Boulger, *Biographical Index of Deceased British and Irish Botanists*, 321.

155. Tuffen West also illustrated Lionel Beale's *Microscope* (1854); Rymer Jones' *Aquarian Naturalist*, 1858; J. G. Wood's *Common Objects of the Microscope* (1861); and Edwin Lankester's *Half Hours with the Microscope* (1874 ed.). Nancy Anderson, 'Observing Techniques: Images from the Microscopical Life Sciences, 1850-1895' (University of Michigan, PhD dissertation, 2002), 162-3.

156. *Life*, 256, is the sole source for this information.

157. PHG, 'Contributions to the History of the Rotifera, or Wheel Animalcules. II. The Floscules (Floscularia)', *Popular Science Review* I (Jan. 1862), 161fn.

Marvels of Pond-life (1861).[158] As it happened, however, all of Gosse's published material, together with his unpublished portfolios and journals on Rotifera, were now to be brought together and put to use by someone else—the microscopist Charles Thomas Hudson (1828-1903)—in an entirely new monograph.

Hudson had received his BA (1852), MA (1855), and LLD (1866) at Cambridge and spent a 27-year-long career as a beloved headmaster[159] (for a time second master, and then Headmaster, at Bristol Grammar School, before founding, in 1861, Manilla Hall, a private school in Clifton, where he remained until 1881).[160] While his earliest investigations on Rotifera date to around 1854,[161] thirteen years elapsed before he published on them, in the *Proceedings of the Bristol Naturalists' Society*. This, and other articles which followed, attracted no particular notice. Then one day he unexpectedly earned a reputation as an able researcher in the Darwinian era.

In July 1871, Hudson brought home a collecting bottle for Rotifera which he had dipped into a previously visited pond near his home in Clifton, in the port city of Bristol.[162] Thus began a hitherto undescribed story which was to form a notable part of Hudson's scientific career and, inadvertently, a minor one in Gosse's as well.

Surveying his catch later that day under the microscope, Hudson took note of several rotifers, all previously known to him. One creature, however, was 'very extraordinary'. Hudson was certain it was quite

158. Hudson & Gosse I: 21.

159. Hudson's students were known as 'Hudsonians' (advertisement, Bristol *Western Daily Press*, 30 May 1881, 8). Hudson was given an engraved silver tray and a cheque for 100 guineas by former students after the conclusion of his time at Manilla Hall (the place was then demolished: 'The March of Bricks and Mortar', *Bristol Mercury*, 5 Nov. 1881, 12; 'Presentation to Dr. C. T. Hudson', *Bristol Mercury*, 28 Nov. 1881, 3).

160. Obit. notices, *J. Royal Micro. Soc.* (Feb. 1904), 48-9 and London *Times* (27 Oct. 1903), 6; *DNB, ODNB, Dictionary of Nineteenth-Century British Scientists* II:1020-1. Hudson founded Manilla Hall after failing to be named head of the newly-established Clifton College (*Alumni Cantabrigienses* Part 2, III:472).

161. Hudson & Gosse II: vi.

162. This paragraph is based on C. T. Hudson, 'On a New Rotifer', *Monthly Microscopical Journal* VI (1 Sept. 1871), 121-4, also p. 215; Hudson, 'On Pedalion Mira', *Quarterly Journal of Microscopical Sciences*, n.s. XII (Oct. 1872), 333-8; Hudson & Gosse II: 132. Pedalion's current name is *Hexarthra mira* (Hudson, 1871) (G. M. Neal, 'Application for the stabilisation of the name for the Genus of the Class Rotifera formerly known as 'Pedalion' Hudson, 1871, or 'Pedalia' Barrois, 1878, including a request for the use of the plenary powers to vary the type species of the genus 'Hexarthra' Schmarda, 1854, and to suppress the trivial name 'Polyptera' Schmarda, 1854, published in combination with that generic name, and matters incidental thereto', *Bulletin of Zoological Nomenclature* VI, Sept. 1951, 73-8; World Register of Marine Species - WoRMS).

unlike anything he—or anyone else—had ever seen, and he didn't know what to make of it. It measured only about 1/120th of an inch long and was complex in its organization. Hudson knew that, viewed internally, it looked like a rotifer. Viewed externally, however, its body cavity, plumes and six hollow 'good-sized limbs' worked by muscles suggested not a rotifer but (with its paired appendages and segmented features) an arthropod (examples of this phylum are insects or lobsters). In recognition of its oar-shaped limb or rudder (Greek, *pedalion*) which guided it in the water—Hudson calculated it could dart and skip at 200 miles per hour—he called it *Pedalion mirum*.

Hudson's initial report of his findings appeared in the *Monthly Microscopical Journal* of the Royal Microscopical Society in London that September. Much as he had done with previous discoveries, he described this one in an understated way as simply a new rotifer.[163] Focusing on *Pedalion*'s external form, he withheld judgment on its affinity to other creatures. Meanwhile he continued searching for living samples to help him solve this puzzle. Inquirers asked him to provide them with one, but the pond which had yielded the first creature had been drained by its owner. 'I could only reply that the rotifers had vanished,' he said glumly.[164] It turned out that *Pedalion* was, and continued to be, 'a great rarity'.[165] Though it was found at some sites on the Continent during the ensuing decades, one researcher writing a half-century after Hudson's pond dip said that during that time it had only been retrieved from three places in Britain.[166]

Another year passed before Hudson read another paper on *Pedalion*, illustrated by slides, at a meeting of the Royal Microscopical Society.[167] His presentation was printed in the October 1872 issue of the *Quarterly Journal of Microscopical Science* (one of the leading zoological

---

163. C. T. Hudson, 'On a New Rotifer', *Monthly Microscopical Journal* VI (Sept. 1871), 121-4.
164. C. T. Hudson, 'On Pedalion Mira', 333.
165. Hudson & Gosse I: 37; W.T. Calman, 'A New Pedalion', *AMNH* ser. 6, XI (1893), 332.
166. Alfred E. Harris, 'Ceratium and Pedalion', *Nature* 108 (10 Nov. 1921), 340; 'When 'finds' were made these were placed under the microscope immediately, with the result that Mr. Gardner-Williams located a speciman [*sic*] of the rather rare Rotifer Pedalion Mirum' ('[Chester Society of Natural] Science Society's Visit to Eaton Park', Chester *Cheshire Observer*, 2 Aug. 1941, 8).
167. *Nature* VI (10 Oct. 1872), 487. The meeting took place Oct. 2.

publications),[168] together with an analysis by Ray Lankester,[169] co-editor of the *Journal* who had recently been appointed to a Natural Science Fellowship at Exeter College, Oxford, where he taught.[170] Before his supply ran dry, Hudson had managed to send living specimens to Lankester who, though only twenty-five years old, was establishing a scientific reputation. He had already published extensively and had connections with Darwin, Huxley, Haeckel, Dohrn, and other evolutionists. Lankester later recalled his reaction when looking at *Pedalion* under the microscope for the first time: it was 'so astonishing and wonderful a little beast,' he said, that 'I could not believe my eyes, and thought I must be dreaming.'[171] With Lankester's three-and-a-half-page commentary now confirming the accuracy of Hudson's work, it was time to move beyond the descriptive to the classificatory. With limbs like an insect and other features unlike any insect, Hudson wondered if his first assumption had been incorrect: Was *Pedalion* really a rotifer?[172]

Regardless of its rarity or elusive definition, *Pedalion* had become—and long remained— a sensation. The *Athenaeum* immediately pronounced Hudson's find 'the most remarkable zoological discovery' of 1872,[173] the word 'remarkable' appearing again and again, and not only in 1886 in reference to *Pedalion* in the Ninth Edition of the *Encyclopaedia Britannica*.[174] A few years later, when Hudson was nominated to become a Fellow of the Royal Society, his highlighted accomplishments—published papers in various scientific journals, his status as President of the Royal

168. From 1869, Ray Lankester was co-editor with his father Edwin Lankester of the *Quarterly Journal*; while edited solely by Ray Lankester, the *Quarterly Journal* was said to be 'the leading British journal of scientific zoology and acquired a world-wide reputation' (E[dwin]. S. G[oodrich]., 'Edwin Ray Lankester—1847-1929', *Proceedings of the Royal Society of London. Series B* 106 (5 Aug. 1930), xiv); see also Lester, *E. Ray Lankester*, 8, 79.

169. E. Ray Lankester, 'Remarks on Pedalion', *Quarterly Journal of Microscopical Science* n.s. XII (1872), 338-342.

170. 'Notes', *Nature* VI (27 June 1872), 169 (correcting a misstatement in the issue of 20 June 1872, 149).

171. Ray Lankester, *Secrets of Earth and Sea* (London: Methuen & Co. Ltd, 1920), 161-2.

172. C. T. Hudson, 'Is Pedalion a Rotifer?' *Monthly Microscopical Journal* VIII (1 Nov. 1872), 209-16.

173. *Athenaeum* (5 Oct. 1872), 435; same in Liverpool *Daily Post*, 7 Oct. 1872, 7; London *Guardian*, 9 Oct. 1872, 3; 'A Singular Rotifer', *Hardwicke's Science-Gossip* VII (1872), 256.

174. A. G. B[ourne], 'Rotifera', *Encyclopaedia Britannica* (Edinburgh: Adam and Charles Black, Ninth Edition, 1886), XXI: 5. Bourne had been an assistant and junior colleague to Ray Lankester (J. Stanley Gardiner, 'Alfred Gibbs Bourne, 1859-1940', *Obituary Notices of Fellows of the Royal Society* III (1941), 545). Another one-time Lankester assistant, George Herbert Fowler, anonymously stated the need for 'additional evidence' before being convinced about the affinity claims concerning *Pedalion* (*Athenaeum*, 26 Apr. 1890, 534).

Microscopical Society, and even the fact that he was the 'chief living authority' on Rotifera—were skimmed over in light of his discovery of the 'genus *Pedalion* ... one of the most remarkable & important contributions to animal morphology of the passed [*sic*] twenty years.'[175] The leading scientific weekly *Nature* concurred. In reviewing its first twenty years of publication, it called *Pedalion* among 'the more striking zoological discoveries' during those decades.[176] When Hudson died in 1903, his obituary in scientific publications, *The Times*, and elsewhere, connected his life-work to *Pedalion mirum*.[177] Early into the twentieth century *Pedalion* was (to a noted Scottish-American scientist) that 'remarkable genus of rotifers'.[178]

What was it about the mysterious *Pedalion* that made it such a phenomenon? A plain interpretation of the finding might suggest it was its scarcity or oddity. A more fruitful answer lies in recalling an aspect of Charles Darwin's theory of evolution by natural selection. According to Darwin, life forms had emerged over time from a common ancestry. If the theory were correct, countless transitional stages (or links) pointing to a remote common ancestry existed between one form and another. In the *Origin of Species*, Darwin confronted the fact that while *in theory* he believed this must be the case, *in fact* there was then no evidence of it. As Darwin put it: '...why, if species have descended from other species by insensibly fine gradations, do we not everywhere see innumerable transitional forms?'[179] It is not relevant here to provide Darwin's response: what is relevant is that, notwithstanding a lack of hard evidence, Darwin insisted on this assumption.[180] His position set off a search by his supporters for what popularly became known as 'missing links'. Opponents emphasized that the obvious absence of links was a weakness in the theory, perhaps even a devastating blow to it.[181]

175. Royal Society *Certificates* XI (1881-95), 166 (biographical notices of the 15 candidates proposed at the same time as Hudson were printed in *Nature* XXXIX (18 Apr. 1889), 586-8).

176. Editorial, 'Twenty Years', *Nature* 41 (7 Nov. 1889), 3.

177. Obituaries in London *Times*, 27 Oct. 1903), 6; *Nature* 68 (29 Oct. 1903), 627; *Journal of the Royal Microscopical Society* (1904), 48-9; *DNB* (1912), Supplement II.

178. John Muirhead Macfarlane, *The Causes and Course of Organic Evolution: A Study in Bioenergics* (New York and London: Macmillan Co., 1918), 529-30.

179. Darwin, *Origin of Species*, 1859, 171-2; Chap. VI: 'Difficulties on Theory' deals with 'Difficulties on the theory of descent with modification—Transitions—Absence or rarity of transitional varieties'.

180. Charles Darwin, 'Origin of Species', *Athenaeum*, 9 May 1863, 617.

181. Ellegård, *Darwin and the General Reader*, 216, 333-4.

After the publication of Darwin's *Origin of Species* in 1859 and *Descent of Man* in 1871, and works by like-minded investigators, the most popularly sought link was between humans and apes.[182] Ernst Haeckel, for example, the evangelist in Germany for Darwin, was determined to identify that gap. In 1866, he thought he had found the intermediate link between primates and humans.[183] Others sought less startling linkages. In 1863, Henry Walter Bates, the Englishman who spent eleven years observing and collecting various species in the jungles of Brazil, delighted Darwinians and provided impressive evidence for the theory in describing 'transition forms' of tropical butterflies.[184] In 1868, Huxley spoke of transitional forms showing an affinity between birds and reptiles.[185]

Identifying missing links aided in the resolution of a fundamental issue for scientific naturalists. Darwin's words led men of science everywhere to attempt to reach back deep in time in hopes of identifying the very beginnings of life.[186] The belief was that it was possible to identify the primordial organic forms from which animals and plants had descended—no Supreme Being necessary.

The discovery of *Eozoön Canadense* in 1858 in Canada was thought to be one such revelation. *Eozoön* was said to be 'the greatest discovery in geology for half a century at least,'[187] but whether it confirmed Darwin or refuted him (as the Canadian geologist John William Dawson claimed) was a dispute which lasted for nearly fifty years.[188] From 1860-1880, the attempt to demonstrate that life had emerged from non-life via

182. Peter C. Kjærgaard, 'The Missing Link and Human Origins: Understanding an Evolutionary Icon', in Kris Rutten, Stefaan Blancke, and Ronald Soetaert, *Perspectives on Science and Culture* (West Lafayette, Indiana: Purdue University Press, 2018), 93-7; Ellegård, *Darwin and the General Reader*, 216.

183. Nolan Heie, 'Ernst Haeckel and the Redemption of Nature' (Queen's University, Kingston, Ontario, PhD dissertation, 2008), 306-7, 334-5, 350.

184. Henry Walter Bates, *The Naturalist on the River Amazons* (London: John Murray, 1863), I: 255-61: '... transition forms [linking] between the two species [of butterflies]', p. 258; the value of Bates' evidence was challenged in *London Quarterly Review* XXII (Apr. 1864), 60; Ellegård, *Darwin and the General Reader*, 216.

185. 'Professor Huxley on the Missing Link', *British Medical Journal* I (15 Feb. 1868), 148.

186. H. Charlton Bastian, *The Beginnings of Life: Being Some Account of the Nature, Modes of Origin and Transformations of Lower Organism* (London: Macmillan and Co., 2vols., 1872).

187. Charles F. O'Brien, '*Eozoön Canadense*, 'The Dawn Animal of Canada'', *Isis* 61 (Summer 1970), 208; O'Brien, citing the opinion of mineralogist T. Sterry Hunt, and p. 206; O'Brien, 'The Word and the Work: A Study of Sir William Dawson and Nineteenth Century Controversies Between Religion and Science' (Brown University, PhD dissertation, 1968), 171-208.

188. Robert John Taylor, 'The Darwinian Revolution: The Responses of Four Canadian Scholars' (McMaster University, PhD dissertation, 1976), 54-5; Juliana Adelman, 'Eozoön: Debunking the Dawn Animal', *Endeavour* 31 (Sept. 2007), 94-8.

'spontaneous generation' received widespread attention. In Britain, T. H. Huxley found it in sediment retrieved from the bottom of the Atlantic Ocean and in 1868 called it *Bathybius haeckelii;*[189] during this time, the English physician Henry Charlton Bastian likewise argued for the emergence of the living from the non-living.[190] In 1872, another Haeckel supposition—the Gastraea theory—posited that all life could be traced to amoeboid blobs of jelly, from which it had emerged.[191]

It is within this historical context of the search for affinities and origins that the meaning attached to the 'remarkable' *Pedalion* can best be understood. Due to an absence of paleontological evidence (as previously mentioned), a consensus view on the classification of Rotifera was elusive. At various times Rotifera had been ranked with crustaceans (primarily aquatic animals in the Phylum Arthropoda), or by the majority with the Phylum Annelida (segmented worms). Interjecting the *Pedalion* discovery into the mix seemed to justify the minority view that a link between Rotifers and arthropods was possibly the correct one (this was Gosse's view).[192] Even Huxley, who had initially belittled the comparison, was now open to that conclusion.[193]

In the zoological arena, no one was a more prominent enthusiast for *Pedalion* than Ray Lankester,[194] who (as previously noted) was a devoted Darwinian 'for long the dominating figure among British zoologists.'[195] In a notable 1870 paper, he developed ideas about evolutionary morphology,[196] spending a lifetime in science applying evolutionary

189. Rehbock, 'Huxley, Haeckel, and the Oceanographers', 504-33; Strick, 'The British Spontaneous Generation Debates of 1860-1880', 19-20; '... in 1875 the eminent biologist [Huxley]' acknowledged *Bathybius* was not as he claimed 'a living expanse of protoplasmic substance, a new and exceedingly primitive organism ... which he supposed to line the bottom of the Atlantic Ocean' but 'little more than sulphate of lime' (review of M. C. Cooke, *Toilers in the Sea*, in *Saturday Review*, 4 Jan. 1890, 24).

190. Strick, 'The British Spontaneous Generation Debates of 1860-1880', 22-6 and *passim*; Bastian, *Beginnings of Life* II: 1-167.

191. Heie, 'Ernst Haeckel and the Redemption of Nature', 168; Cole, *History of Protozoology*, 34.

192. Hudson & Gosse II: pp. [v], [131]-134.

193. T. H. Huxley, *A Manual of the Anatomy of Invertebrated Animals* (London: J. & A. Churchill, 1877), 193.

194. Although the secondary literature on Lankester is not as extensive as for many other notable Victorian naturalists, none of the works which I have seen on him mention his nearly five-decade effort to promote *Pedalion*.

195. E[dwin]. S. G[oodrich]., 'Edwin Ray Lankester', x.

196. Devin Susanne Yagel Gouvêa, 'Essentially Dynamic Concepts and the Case of "Homology"' (University of Chicago PhD dissertation, 2021), 33-4, 51-2.

theory to comparative anatomy, embryology, and classification in order to create a 'tree of evolutionary relationships.'[197] In 1872, he was the first to add his findings about *Pedalion* to those of Hudson for the benefit of those 'interested in speculations upon the genealogy of the animal kingdom.'[198] When Hudson's application for fellowship in the Royal Society came up, Lankester was the one who appended the note about *Pedalion's* historic contribution to animal morphology.[199] On the basis of *Pedalion's* peculiar characteristics, Lankester created a phylum (which he named 'Appendiculata') with three branches: the Arthropods, Annelids, and Rotifers. All three branches started from a common ancestry with characteristics resembling *Pedalion* and other forms, in Lankester's schema.[200] A half-century after Hudson's original discovery,[201] the eminence who had become 'Sir Ray Lankester' devoted the better part of a chapter in his *Secrets of Earth and Sea* to rhapsodizing about *Pedalion*, with its 'astounding "blend" of characters'."[202] He wrote:

> There is little doubt that the wheel animalcules [Rotifera] are related in pedigree to the primitive ancestors of the marine segmented or annulate worms, which also gave rise to the ringed leg-bearing jaw-footed creatures with hard skin, called Crustacea, Arachnids and Insects (the Arthropods). ... The Rotifers are probably a dwindled pygmy race descended from ancestors of ten or a hundred times their linear measurement. ... the wheel animalcules give evidence of relationship to the Crustacea—that is to say, it appears to be probable that they were derived from the common ancestor of marine worms and Crustacea before those two lines of descent had diverged.[203]

197. Lester, *E. Ray Lankester*, 80; Goodrich, 'The Scientific Work of Edwin Ray Lankester', 378.

198. Lankester, 'Remarks on Pedalion', 338.

199. The statement appears under 'Qualifications' in Hudson's 'Certificate of a Candidate for Election' to the Royal Society (Royal Society, *Certificates* XI, (1881-95), 166, dated 7 June 1888).

200. E. Ray Lankester, 'Limulus an Arachnid', *Quarterly Journal of Microscopical Science* n.s. XXI (Oct 1881), 640; B[ourne], 'Rotifera', XXI: 7.

201. According to later researchers, the morphological significance of *Pedalion* was greatly exaggerated (de Beauchamp, 'Recherches sur les Rotifères', 13, 43; Harring and Myers, 'The Rotifer Fauna of Wisconsin', 396-7fn.3). The genus has been considered a synonym of *Hexarthra* Schmarda (H. B. Ward & G. C. Whipple, *Fresh-water Biology* ed. by W. T. Edmondson (New York: John Wiley & Sons, 2ed., 1959), 441). Currently, even with DNA-based research techniques, the place of rotifers in the 'animal tree of life' is an open question (Gregor F. Fussmann, 'Rotifers: Excellent Subjects for the Study of Macro- and Microevolutionary Change', *Hydrobiologia* (2011), 662: 12,16).

202. Lankester, *Secrets of Earth and Sea*, the immediate quotation is from p.162.

203. Lankester, *Secrets of Earth and Sea*, 171. The discussion of *Pedalion* (chap. XIII) is

Ever watchful for evidence supporting Darwin's theory, Lankester was convinced that a fragment of a skull and a lower jawbone of a creature found between 1908 and 1915 in a gravel deposit at Piltdown, some sixty miles south of London, was 'of immense importance ... the most startling and significant fossil bone that has ever been brought to light.'[204] He said it represented 'a real "missing link," an animal intermediate in great and obvious features' between apes and humans.[205]

In 1953, Piltdown man was confirmed to have been a hoax.[206]

-VI-

The famed discoverer of *Pedalion* had accumulated enough new information by 1881 to begin the preparation of a monograph on British Rotifera, to be issued by the Ray Society. This was to utilise Gosse's buried MS journals and drawings, which Hudson had borrowed, perhaps in 1879.[207]

The two naturalists had, in fact, been corresponding at least from 1870,[208] yet it was not until Gosse had finished with his devotion to insects that their association became a collaboration. They were apparently encouraged by Ray Lankester to do so,[209] and they were a good match. Like Gosse, Hudson was attuned to the need to classify, measure and

followed by another on Rotifera.

204. Lankester, *Diversions of a Naturalist*, 284 (Chap. XXX is entitled 'The Missing Link').

205. Lankester, *Diversions of a Naturalist*, 288.

206. Wilfrid Le Gros Clark, *History of the Primates: An Introduction to the Study of Fossil Man* (London: British Museum (Natural History), 1949, 10ed. 1970), 103-4; Lester, *E. Ray Lankester*, 181-2.

207. *Quarterly Journal of Microscopical Science*, n.s. XXI (Apr. 1881), 378; Richard Curle, *The Ray Society. A Bibliographical History* (London: Printed for the Society, 1954), 26; PHG-Hudson, 2 Mar. 1881 (CUL Add. 7313, 327); *Life*, 318-9; *Nature* (14 Apr. 1881), 565.

208. See Corr. Bk., under 15 November 1870. In September 1875, Corr. Bk. lists letters from both Ray Lankester (e.g., Sept. 15) and 'Dr. Hudson' (e.g., Aug. 20). The letters have not been traced.

209. Ray Lankester states that 'It was my good fortune to bring these two devotees of the Rotifera ... together ... to induce them to write a conjoint work' on Rotifera (Lankester, *Secrets of Earth and Sea*, 158). Lankester did not actually bring them together because they already knew each other and their work through correspondence. Lankester apparently meant that he had recommended that they collaborate on a work on the subject (*Life*, 318-9, dates Lankester's recommendation to 1879, when Lankester 'advised' Hudson 'to place himself in relation' to PHG for a work on Rotifera). Seemingly contradicting that interpretation of Lankester's claim is an advertisement on the paper covers of Hudson & Gosse II (seen at the British Museum, Natural History) where it states: 'The two authors, independently of each other, had for many years been accumulating materials for a monograph on the Rotifera ... and had almost abandoned the intention, when they chanced to become acquainted with each other's design'.

weigh a creature, and had imposing artistic and observational skills. But what most appealed to Hudson was to learn 'of the way [the creature] lives, of the craft with which it secures its prey or outwits its enemies, of the home that it constructs, of its charming confidence or its diabolical temper, of its curious courtship, its droll tricks, its games of play, its fun and spite, of its perplexing stupidity coupled with actions of almost human sagacity.' To gain information about such life habits, he was prepared (as Gosse had done) to invest 'patient and accurate observation,' which he recognised (using veiled language) 'may help—does help many—to worthier conceptions of the unseen, to loftier hopes, to higher praise.'[210]

So at the beginning of 1885, or end of 1884,[211] the veteran analyst of the rotiferon manducatory organs resumed new researches: hunting for rotifers in ponds, ditches, gutters, and other likely haunts, daily examining his catches under the microscope, extracting and revising old observations, and issuing a public appeal for help.[212] Gosse was in good health (no longer being troubled by diabetes, of which he had shown symptoms in 1884), and typically energetic.[213] Vials of living organisms were sent to him by Thomas Bolton (1831-1887) of Birmingham,[214]

210. C. T. Hudson, 'On Some Needless Difficulties in the Study of Natural History', *Nature* 40 (20 Feb. 1890), 375-6.

211. See Hudson & Gosse II: 19, and Corr. Bk., which lists PHG-Hudson letters from 3 Nov. 1885. In one place in *Life*, 319, EWG claims the researches were begun in 1879; in another (p. 371), Eliza gives 1885 as the year. Both appear approximately correct.

212. PHG, 'Marine Rotifera', *Field* LXVI (29 August 1885), 322; EWG-'My beloved Parents', 17 Dec. 1885 (Charteris, 179-80). A series of PHG's scientific journals, variously titled *The Infusoria of Britain*, vols. II-III (BMNH, Zoology Library), *Infusoria.4* [vol. IV] (seen in R. B. Freeman Collection), and *Rotifera* vol. V (BMNH, Zoology Library), preserve a register of his activities. Excerpts were made from vols. II-III (covering 1849-54, with additions in 1885); vols. IV (1 Sept. 1886-Oct. 1887) and V (18 Feb.-6 Oct. 1887) contain new material.

213. *Life*, 370.

214. 'The Late Mr. Thomas Bolton', *Birmingham Daily Post* (11 Nov. 1887) 4; 'Death of Mr. T. Bolton', *Journal of the Royal Microscopical Society* ser. 2, VII (Dec. 1887), 1040. Several Rotifera were named after Bolton in recognition of his contribution (W. Hillhouse, 'Thomas Bolton, F.R.M.S.', *Midland Naturalist* X (1887), 299). Bolton was a Fellow of the Royal Microscopical Society. See Freeman, *British Natural History Books*, 54 and Bolton's portfolio of his drawings at BMNH. W. S. Kent's *Manual of Infusoria*, vol. III (also BMNH) contains a flyer from Bolton tipped in at the back of the volume headed: 'Living Specimens for the Microscope. ... Thomas Bolton has for some time been supplying a series of interesting living organisms both Zoological and Botanical to Microscopists and other students of Biology' (dated 5 Nov. 1880). R. B. Freeman noted (*in litt.*, 21 June 1972) that Bolton would send about 27 tubes of living (or sometimes dead) microscopical material, with descriptions, to subscribers who paid one guinea per six months. Some of the descriptions include excerpts from PHG writings. See T. Bolton, *Portfolios of drawings, and descriptions of living organisms, (animal and vegetable), illustrative of freshwater and marine Life, which have been sent out with the living specimens* (London: David Bogue, 1879-83).

Joseph Sinel of Jersey,[215] and the 'successful' researcher John Hood (1831-1914) of Dundee (who identified many of the species found in his area);[216] letters were exchanged with J. E. Lord,[217] Mesdames Davies and Beachey,[218] and other amateurs.[219] At the beginning of 1885 word got out about the projected treatise.[220] Gosse's efforts attracted attention: 'The veteran scientist, Gosse, is 76, but is hard at work on the texts and plates of his new volume of the *Rotifera,*' a Cornwall newspaper noted,[221] and the progress of the work was duly followed.[222] Gosse was 'absolutely free from the slightest spice of scientific jealousy,' Hudson recalled after his colleague's death. The elder scientist had lent him 'the whole of his beautiful drawings,' to make use of as he saw fit.[223] Meanwhile Hudson found time to deliver an 'entertaining and instructive' lecture in Bristol on Rotifera.[224] He said he believed these microscopic creatures 'had wills and minds of their own ... brains and a well-developed nervous system.'[225]

The new monograph, transformed into an examination of the Rotifera

215. Sinel flyers (1889-90) are in a portfolio of drawings by T. Bolton at BMNH. Earlier, he was providing embryological specimens for the microscope (*Journal of the Royal Microscopical Society* ser. 2, III (Aug. 1883), 614). Before he became an author, Sinel occasionally lectured at the Guernsey Society of Natural History (Guernsey *Star*, 17 Oct. 1889, 2) and elsewhere ('"The Wonders of the Shore"', Guernsey *Star*, 6 Feb. 1890, 2).

216. 'John Hood ... to whose successful researches this work bears grateful witness' (Hudson & Gosse I: 83; a number of species cited in this work were named after him with the specific name *Hoodii*). Hood's copy of Hudson & Gosse (3vols.), seen at the University of St. Andrews at its Dundee campus, is described in A. D. Peacock, 'John Hood of Dundee. Working-man Naturalist', *Scots Magazine* (1939), 410-1; 'Death of Famous Naturalist. Dundee Man Who Gained World-Wide Reputation for Microscopic Research', Dundee *Courier* (13 July 1914), 6; Dundee *Evening Telegraph* (13 July 1914), 1; *Nature* 93 (6 Aug. 1914), 589.

217. J. E. Lord belonged to a younger generation of researchers stimulated by the work of Hudson & Gosse (Walter Koste and Eric D. Holloway, 'A Short History of Western European Rotifer Research', *Hydrobiologia* vol. 255/256 (Apr. 1993), 566). Articles by Lord and Hood on Rotifera appeared in *Hardwicke's Science-Gossip*. 'I yield to none in admiration of [PHG's] many great gifts; and indeed for years I enjoyed the privilege of his friendship, and frequent correspondence' (Lord, 'Notes on Rotifers', *Hardwicke's Science-Gossip* (Sept. 1890), 201).

218. Theodora Beachey, her sisters and father, attended the Fore Street Room (PHG-W. K. Perrens, 9 May 1881; CUL Add. 7313, 358).

219. For all these: Corr. Bk., 1885-88; PHG-J. D. Hooker, 14, 28 July 1885 (Kew, *English Letters* LXXXVII: 79-80).

220. *Edinburgh Evening News*, 23 Jan. 1885, 4.

221. Penzance, Cornwall *Cornishman*, 22 Oct. 1885, 4.

222. Hudson & Gosse 'have passed for press the first part of their book on "The Rotifera, or Wheel Animalcules"' (Kent *Sevenoaks Chronicle*, 25 Dec. 1885, 3; *Leeds Mercury Weekly Supplement*, 26 Dec. 1885, 8).

223. Hudson, *Journal of the Royal Microscopical Society* ser. 2, vol. 8 (1888), 1061.

224. *Bristol Mercury*, 9 Dec. 1885, 3.

225. Bristol *Western Daily Press*, 9 Dec. 1885, 5.

of the entire world, appeared in six parts between January and October 1886.[226] Proofs were revised by Gosse,[227] and his contributions carefully designated with his initials. As the initiation, classification, and all the preparatory labour were Hudson's, Gosse insisted that his own name appear on the title-page as an assistant, recalling Richard Hill's status in the *Naturalist's Sojourn in Jamaica*. Though it was against Hudson's wish, this was the way in which the work was presented.[228] Nonetheless, posterity has its own compromise: *The Rotifera* has always been known as 'Hudson & Gosse'.

The work, which appeared in two volumes in October 1886, ushered in the third period of rotiferan studies (following the initial discoveries of Leeuwenhoek in 1676 and the landmark research of Ehrenberg). It was illustrated by thirty plates drawn in almost equal number by each author, with analyses of 250 Rotifera species, of which nearly half (120) were new to science (80 were discovered by Gosse).[229] A *Supplement*, adding another 150 new species, followed in September 1889. There were 750 copies published of each of the three volumes.[230]

The Rotifera may have appeared to outsiders as the successful culmination of years of research undertaken at an earlier period, but its authors knew otherwise. Hudson, who was elected President of the Royal Microscopical Society in 1888 and an FRS in June 1889, busily added new data during the next three years.[231] Nor was Gosse languid. He was nearly 78 when the first of three illustrated studies was read before the Royal Microscopical Society. Said Society President, W. H. Dallinger: 'they were proud—he used the word advisedly—to have the paper.'[232] Up until October 1887, when Gosse was designated one of their few Honorary Fellows,[233] he was still at his microscope. Some five dozen large coloured illustrations of newly identified Rotifera drawn by Gosse at around this

226. For the history of the publication: Freeman & Wertheimer-PHG, 88-91.
227. Hudson & Gosse I: v.
228. *Life*, 319-20.
229. Hudson & Gosse I: v.
230. Freeman & Wertheimer-PHG, 89; Hudson & Gosse *Supplement*, v.
231. See *Certificate of a Candidate for Election, op. cit.*; 'The Royal Society Selected Candidates', *Nature* 39 (18 Apr. 1889), 587; Hudson, *The Original Drawings of the Rotifera* (Clifton, 1886; Royal Society, MS. 132).
232. Dallinger, in *JRMS Proceedings*, ser. 2, VII (Feb. 1887), 181; PHG, 'Twenty-four New Species of Rotifera'; 'Twelve New Species of Rotifera'; 'Twenty-four More New Species of Rotifera', *JRMS*, ser. 2, VII (1887), 1-7, 361-7, 861-71. A PHG letter to 'Dallinger' is recorded in Corr. Bk. for 12 May 1886.
233. *JRMS* ser. 2, vol. 8 (Dec. 1887), 1070 (for 12 Oct. 1887).

time indicated to Hudson that 'his hand and eye were as perfect [then]' as they had been when first they met.[234]

Gosse did not live to see the publication of the *Supplement* to *The Rotifera* in 1889, but 'his work did not slacken towards the close of his life.'[235] Sixty of the 150 new species described there had been discovered by him.[236] In a wonderfully generous tribute, in their last published work Hudson lauded his colleague, referring to his 'great knowledge and experience, his keen powers of observation, his artistic skill, and his rare gift of description [which] are known to all, and have made him *facile princeps* among the writers on the Rotifera'.[237]

'The one thing wanting in a microscopist's library has hitherto been a fairly complete book on Rotifers with a sufficiency of illustrations,' the *Journal of the Royal Microscopical Society* commented following its commendatory notice of the first part of the work.[238] Subsequent reviewers searched their thesaurus to find ways to praise in different words the text and figures. Their synonyms: 'magnificent', 'excellent' and 'very excellent', 'first-class', 'splendid', 'superb', 'capital and thorough', 'great' and 'fine', 'remarkable'.[239] Observed the London *Pall Mall Gazette*:

> The extreme minuteness, accuracy, and beauty of the drawings have never been equalled in this particular department, and never exceeded in any line of investigation. It would be impossible to convey in greater perfection a just idea of the appearance, the detailed anatomy, or the structure and habits of these beautiful little denizens of our pools and

234. Hudson, *JRMS* ser. 2, vol. 8 (1888), 1061. The drawings—described as having been made 'within six months of his death'—were provided to Hudson by EWG, apparently after his father's death.

235. Review of Hudson & Gosse *Supplement* in *Knowledge* XIII (1 Nov. 1889), 15. Immediately after recovering from an illness when he was 78, he 'returned to his investigation of the Rotifera' (*Athenaeum*, 5 May 1888, 571).

236. Hudson & Gosse *Supplement*, [v]; Hudson, *JRMS* ser. 2, vol. 8 (Dec. 1887), 1070. Today about 1,000 good rotifer species are known for the entire world.

237. Hudson & Gosse *Supplement*, vi.

238. 'Hudson's "Rotifera"', *JRMS* ser.2, VI (Feb. 1886), 79. The same sentiment was expressed in 'New Work on the Rotifera', *Hardwicke's Science-Gossip* XXII (Apr. 1886), 90.

239. *QJMS*, n.s. XXVI (Apr. 1886), 508; *Journal of the Quekett Microscopical Club*, ser. 2, II (1886), 279; ser. 2, IV (1889), 86; IV (1890), 86; *Knowledge* IX (1 Mar. 1886), 144-5; IX (1 June 1886), 257-8; X (1 Dec. 1886), 46 (notice only); XIII (1 Nov. 1889), 14-15; *Hardwicke's Science-Gossip* XXII (Apr., June-July, Oct., 1886), 90, 140, 165, 234; XXIII (Jan. 1887), 16-17; *Saturday Review* LXII (18 Sept. 1886), 399-400; LXIII (19 Mar. 1887), 419; LXIX (4 Jan. 1890), 17; *Pall Mall Gazette*, 30 Nov. 1886, 5; *Hardwicke's Science-Gossip* XXV (Nov. 1889), 254; [George Herbert Fowler], *Athenaeum*, 26 Apr. 1890, 534; C. S. Minot, *Science* VII (30 Apr. 1886), 402-3; IX (17 June 1887), 598-9.

streams than Dr. Hudson and Mr. Gosse have now conveyed to us in their present volumes.[240]

'In fact,' one reviewer advised, 'a microscopical library is as incomplete without [Hudson & Gosse] as would an ordinary one on whose shelves neither the Bible nor Shakespeare found a place.'[241] At least one provincial library is known to have heeded the advice.[242] Rotifers as an example of 'another curious little creature found in water', even attracted newspaper attention.[243] Hudson & Gosse was called the 'standard monograph on the subject',[244] 'the most complete and exhaustive history of the Rotifera in any language',[245] a work long known as 'the rotiferist's "Bible".'[246]

As is the case with all scientific works of this kind, subsequent investigations have noted shortcomings in the volumes. Even in 1886, the concentration on description and observation, at the expense of a treatment of morphological problems, was considered a serious fault;[247] by the end of the century, though the work was 'for general inquirers the last word on the subject', an 'improved edition' was called for,[248] and Hudson's classification (a modification of that of Ehrenberg, Dujardin, and Leydig) was acknowledged to be 'unnatural.'[249] In 1912, the number of known Rotifera worldwide had doubled from Hudson & Gosse;[250] the confusion in nomenclature, introduced and perpetuated here, was not corrected until 1913;[251] and even though Gosse was considered 'so

240. 'Living Specks', *Pall Mall Gazette*, 30 Nov. 1886, 5.

241. *Knowledge* IX (1 June 1886), 258.

242. The Southampton library purchased the two-volume *Rotifera* (*Hampshire Advertiser County Newspaper*, 16 July 1887, 3).

243. 'The Children's Hour', *Nottinghamshire Guardian*, 20 Aug. 1886, 3.

244. The words used in the entry for Hudson & Gosse in *DNB* (1912), Supplement II: 315.

245. *Journal of the Quekett Microscopical Club*, ser. 2, IV (1890), 86.

246. H. G. S. Wright, 'Philip Henry Gosse's Microscope', *The Microscope* IX (Jan.-Feb. 1953), 113.

247. See the two reviews in *Science*, cited above.

248. Walter Wesché, 'Notes on Rotifera', *Science-Gossip* n.s. VIII (Oct. 1901), 133, 135.

249. Hudson, 'An Attempt to Re-classify the Rotifers', *QJMS* n.s. XXIV (July 1884), 335-56; Hudson & Gosse I: 25-32; Marcus Hartog, 'Rotifera, Gastrotricha, and Kinorhyncha', in *Cambridge Natural History*, ed. S. F. Harmer and A. E. Shipley (London: Macmillan & Co., 1896), II: 220; E.-F. Weber, 'Faune rotatorienne du bassin de Léman', *Revue Suisse de Zoologie* V (1898), 265; de Beauchamp, 'Recherches sur les Rotifères', 13-14; Wesenberg-Lund, 'Contributions to the Biology of the Rotifera', 210, 213.

250. In 1912, C. F. Rousselet (1854-1921), an authority on Rotifera, stated that he had by then listed 607 new Rotifera species discovered since the completion of Hudson & Gosse (which had recorded 400 species): *Nature* 89 (21 Mar. 1912), 77. PHG and Rousselet had corresponded (e.g. Corr. Bk., 8 June 1887).

251. Harry K. Harring, 'Synopsis of the Rotatoria', *Bulletin of the United States National*

eminent an authority, and so careful an observer,' that a microscopist warned 'we ought to be very careful ere we say that he was in error,'[252] advances in electron and laser-scanning microscopy, together with other innovative techniques, have yielded new insights. One can only picture what can be seen; and Gosse's microscope, with three object-glasses, made around 1840 by Hugh Powell, though better than Andrew Ross's of 1855 and considered state-of-the-art during his lifetime,[253] lacked aperture for the higher powers. This made it impossible for Gosse to elucidate minute details. Moreover, he was unable to use his binocular attachment (probably added in the 1860s) because he was short-sighted in one eye.[254]

Yet notwithstanding these deficiencies, after nearly a century no single work replaced it. Immediately upon publication it generated a burst of attention by naturalists to this class,[255] even an American guide to facilitate the use of the work.[256] One naturalist born nearly three decades after Gosse died recalled how, as a young boy, he intently studied Hudson & Gosse and even memorized a long, lyric passage in the book by Hudson which describes 'what a world of wonders' would be seen if 'we could shrink into living atoms and plunge under the water.' He went on to devote his career to studying Rotifera.[257]

The French zoologist Paul Marais de Beauchamp (1883-1977),

Museum LXXXI (1913), 1-226; cf. also E. Hollowday, 'Introduction to the Study of Rotifera', *Microscope* VI (Sept.-Oct. 1949), 225.

252. George Western speaking at the meeting of 21 Nov. 1890, in *Journal of the Quekett Microscopical Club* ser. 2, IV (1890), 295.

253. Lankester, *Secrets of Earth and Sea*, 157.

254. In 1903, PHG's microscope was displayed before a meeting of the Royal Microscopical Society in London, from which the above information is taken (*JRMS Proceedings* (1903), 117-18; also 1901, pp. 728-9, and H. M. Malies, 'The Microscope During the Last Hundred Years', *Microscope* X (Jan.-Feb. 1955), 116). PHG's microscope was sold at the Sandhurst auction in 1900 (*Sandhurst Catalogue*, item #233), and repurchased by EWG, who gave it to his son in 1913 (EWG-Philip H. G. Gosse, 4 Aug. 1913; CUL Adv. c. 82.5, 63). Its disposition is unknown.

255. Hussey, 'An Historical Survey of the Collection and Study of Rotifers in Britain', 238 (chart and text).

256. The American work was by T. S. Stevens in the *Journal of the Trenton (N.J.) Natural History Society* (1887). The *Journal of the Royal Microscopical Society's* view was that 'the intention [of Stevens' work] is no doubt good, but the result is not satisfactory' (ser. 2, VII, 1887, 405).

257. W. T. Edmondson, 'Rotifer Study as a Way of Life', *Hydrobiologia* 186/187 (1989), 2. The memorized passage by Hudson concludes: 'Time and space ... would fail me to tell of all the marvels of the world beneath the waters. They would sound like the wild fancies of a child's fairy tale, and yet they are all literally true; and, moreover, nearly all of them are true of that Rotiferous world which it is my purpose to describe.' (Hudson & Gosse I:3-4).

considered among the 'greatest rotiferologists' of the last century who had set a new standard for such studies in 1909 which ushered in the fourth period of rotiferan studies, summarized the assessment of field workers. He wrote that,

> ... in spite of everything, what makes the work both valuable and indispensable, and has made it the basis for all subsequent studies, is the profound knowledge of the group, more empirical than reasoned, acquired by the authors by dint of seeing Rotifers, and the enormous mass of scattered facts, sketches from nature and personal observations that have been juxtaposed to make this book.[258]

'I only wish to add,' the Danish zoologist Carl Wesenberg-Lund (1867-1955) remarked in 1923 about Hudson & Gosse,

> that even if I have been forced to attack the system of the learned English authors, my admiration for what these two Scientists have done to promote science in this difficult domain of natural history, has in no way been abated. It will always be the work to which all students of this group of animals will return; in my opinion this is mainly due to the excellent and exact contour drawings of the animals, which only rarely give room for doubts with regard to the conception of the animals which the authors have described.[259]

Hudson & Gosse is invariably referred to as a 'great work,'[260] although a twentieth-century German rotifer researcher called it 'monumental'[261] and two British specialists termed it a 'magnificent work ... containing some of the finest illustrations yet produced.'[262] Today it is singled out

258. '... ce qui rend malgré tout l'ouvrage précieux et indispensable, et lui a valu de servir de base à toutes les études postérieures, c'est la connaissance du groupe profonde, d'ailleurs plus empirique que raisonnée, acquise par les auteurs à force de voir des Rotifères, et la masse énorme de faits épars, de croquis d'après nature et d'observations personnelles qui ont été juxtaposés pour en faire ce livre': de Beauchamp, 'Recherches sur les Rotifères', 13 (and for the assessment of his status, Koste and Hollowday, 'A Short History of Western European Rotifer Research', 567).

259. C. Wesenberg-Lund, 'Contributions to the Biology of the Rotifera', 216.

260. Francis Adams Pray, 'Ecological Observations on the Spring and Winter Rotifer Populations of a Pond in West Central Indiana' (Purdue University, MA thesis, 1949), 6.

261. Josef Donner (1909-89), *Rotifers*. Translated and adapted by H. G. S. Wright (London: Frederick Warne & Co., 1966), ix.

262. Koste and Hollowday, 'A Short History of Western European Rotifer Research', 566.

as one of the 'beautifully illustrated works published [in the 1800s] that still offer an excellent depiction of these animals.'[263]

The collection here of accolades for Hudson & Gosse spanning a century might seem excessive in number and unnecessarily repetitious, given that the quality of Hudson & Gosse has never been a topic of discussion. Yet it usefully draws attention to something which might easily be overlooked and *is* worth discussing—namely, the *absence of any comment* on Hudson & Gosse in the pages of *Nature*, Britain's premier scientific publication at the time.[264] Why would that be? What is the argument that the absence of attention should draw our attention to its absence?

The Rotifera was 'a credit alike to private research and private enterprise' in Britain.[265] It demonstrated 'the greater energy, industry, and skill' of Rotifera studies there, where naturalists added 'two-and-a-half times as many species, as the naturalists of all other countries put together.' This was achieved especially through the efforts of Gosse.[266] It's not that *Nature* was unaware of the work: it was sent the individual parts of *The Rotifera*, and listed them as they appeared.[267] It's not that *Nature* editors would have overlooked the fact that the three volumes of Hudson & Gosse were hailed by contemporaries worldwide: in Britain, by the *Athenaeum*, *Pall Mall Gazette*, and *Quarterly Journal of Microscopical Science* (each carrying one review), *Saturday Review* and *Journal of the Quekett Microscopical Club* (each three reviews), *Nature's* rival *Knowledge* (four notices),[268] or *Hardwicke's Science-*

263. Wallace, Snell, and Smith, 'Phylum Rotifera', in *Thorp and Covich's Freshwater Invertebrates*, 2015, 227.

264. Baldwin, '*Nature* and the Making of a Scientific Community, 1869-1939', 69.

265. *Hardwicke's Science-Gossip* XXV (Nov. 1889), 254.

266. C. T. Hudson, 'The President's Address' at the Annual General Meeting, 13 Feb. 1889, *Journal of the Royal Microscopical Society* Pt. 1 (Apr. 1889), 170 (also reported in *Athenaeum*, 2 Mar. 1889, 284).

267. *Nature* acknowledged in its pages receiving copies of *The Rotifera* as they appeared under 'Books and Pamphlets Received', as follows: Part I, *Nature* (21 Jan. 1886), 279; Part II (11 Mar. 1886), 456; Part III (15 Apr. 1886), 576; Part IV (20 May 1886), 72; Part VI (11 Nov. 1886, 48) and *Supplement* (26 Sept. 1889), 540. I did not see that Part V was received. *Hardwicke's Science-Gossip* also received the parts as issued (beginning with *Science-Gossip* XXII (Apr. 1886), 90), as well as Part V (*Science-Gossip* XXII (Oct. 1886), 234). *The Spectator*, 28 Aug. 1886, 1159, acknowledged receipt of Parts IV and V at the same time. This may have been the case with *Nature*, and the listing of Part V may have been accidentally omitted.

268. On *Knowledge*: Bernard Lightman, '*Knowledge* Confronts *Nature*: Richard Proctor and Popular Science Periodicals', in Louise Henson, et. al., *Culture and Science in the Nineteenth-Century Century Media* (London: Routledge, 2004), 199-210. PHG sent copies of *Knowledge* to

Gossip (five notices); in France, where it was called 'the beautiful work' ('le bel ouvrage') with its '30 magnifiques' plates;[269] in Germany, where the reviewer spoke of the authors' latest 'great works' ('in dem neuesten großen werke');[270] in Denmark, where it was 'their great Monograph' ('i deres store Monografi'),[271] or in America, where it was reviewed twice in *Science*, a publication which aimed to be the American equivalent of *Nature*[272] (C. S. Minot, the Harvard embryologist and evolution supporter,[273] called the first two parts 'a very excellent work'[274] and the last four 'welcome alike to the professional and to the amateur naturalist. ... a capital and thorough treatise'[275]).

It also can't be that the authors did not meet *Nature's* definition of what constituted a 'man of science'. Neither was a man of letters or a clergyman-naturalist who dabbled in science; both were unquestionably individuals who sought 'scientific truth' and spent time on 'original research.'[276] It cannot even be that *The Rotifera* was too abstruse a work or was in a subject area outside *Nature's* core interests. In 1877, *Nature* found space to mention a monograph on Rotifera, apologizing that it could do no more than refer to the work's existence because it was written entirely in Hungarian.[277] In 1883, Ray Lankester wrote a lengthy review of W. Saville Kent's *Manual of Infusoria*;[278] in 1887, there was a report on the contributions to theoretic biology of the German evolutionary biologist August Weismann (1834-1914) which included that writer's view on parthenogenesis (asexual reproduction) in Rotifera.[279] The author of

a correspondent so that he could follow 'the progress of science. It is, unhappily, tainted with the godlessness of all science, nowadays' (PHG-Richard Perrens, 5 Dec. 1881, CUL Add. 7313, 452).

269. Review of Hudson & Gosse *Supplement*, by J. Pelletan, editor of the Paris *Journal de Micrographie* (Oct. 1889), 497-8.

270. Leipzig *Zoologischer Anzeiger* XIII (1890), 609.

271. C. Wesenberg-Lund, *Danmarks Rotifera. Grundtrækkene i Rotiferernes Økologi, Morfologi og Systematik* [*Denmark's Rotifera. The Basic Features of Rotiferan Ecology, Morphology and Systematics*] (Copenhagen: Bianco Lunos Kgl. Hof-Bogtrykkeri (F. Dreyer), 1899), 5.

272. Baldwin, '*Nature* and the Making of a Scientific Community, 1869-1939', 106-7.

273. Frederic T. Lewis, 'Charles Sedgwick Minot', Philadelphia *Anatomical Record* X (Jan. 1916), 139-40.

274. C.S. Minot, '*The Rotifera*', *Science* VII (30 Apr. 1886), 402.

275. C.S. Minot, '*The Rotifera*', *Science* IX (30 Apr. 1886), 598-9.

276. Baldwin, '*Nature* and the Making of a Scientific Community, 1869-1939', 134.

277. 'Hungarian Rotifers or Wheel-Animalcules', *Nature* 17 (13 Dec. 1877), 128.

278. *Nature* 27 (26 Apr. 1883), 601-3.

279. G. Herbert Fowler, 'Professor A. Weismann's Theory of Polar Bodies', *Nature* 37 (8 Dec. 1887), 134-6.

that signed article was G. Herbert Fowler (1861-1940), a zoologist and assistant to Lankester. Two years later, Fowler anonymously sang the praises of the completed three-volume Hudson & Gosse—not in *Nature* but in the *Athenaeum*.[280]

While it is always unwise to discount negligence or incompetence as factors, I would argue that if we follow the evidence presented here, the most probable explanation of *Nature's* conduct is inarguable. In 1881, when word got out that Hudson was preparing a volume on British rotifers to be published by the Ray Society, *Nature* alerted its readers to that newsworthy development. Their notice added that Hudson would use 'Mr. P. H. Gorse's [*sic*] beautiful drawings of Rotifers'[281] (was 'Gorse' a simple typographical error or the result of Gosse's name no longer resonating with readers of *Nature*?). Nearly five years later, when the first installment of Hudson's work appeared under the highly reputable Longmans, Green, and Co. imprint, *Nature* ignored it. The difference? The work was no longer simply *using* Gosse's illustrations. The senior naturalist had been more engaged in the work than initially anticipated. *The Rotifera* was now 'By C.T. Hudson, LL.D. Cantab., Assisted by P. H. Gosse, F.R.S.'

Thus did Hudson's work fall victim to a three-decades-old boycott of Gosse by Britain's 'young guard of science.' Those men—Huxley and some other members of the X Club, as well as *Nature's* founder and editor, Norman Lockyer (1836-1920)—acted as the self-appointed 'elite of the Victorian scientific world,'[282] with *Nature* being their 'important mouthpiece'.[283] In the words of one newspaper, *Nature* was the venue for the 'detective police of science,'[284] the ones who searched for offenders against the accepted scientific orthodoxy in order to cancel their work by denying it the attention which it deserved. Their goal was to establish

280. [George Herbert Fowler], *Athenaeum* (26 Apr. 1890), 534.

281. *Nature* 23 (14 Apr. 1881), 565. The notice was based upon the *Quarterly Journal of Microscopical Science* (n.s. XXI, Apr. 1881, 378), where PHG's surname is correctly spelled.

282. Frank M. Turner, 'The Victorian Conflict between Science and Religion: A Professional Dimension', *Isis* 69 (Sept. 1978), 362; Baldwin, '*Nature* and the Making of a Scientific Community, 1869-1939', 68.

283. Peter C. Kjærgaard, "Within the bounds of Science': Redirecting Controversies to *Nature*', in Louise Henson, et. al., *Culture and Science in the Nineteenth-Century Century Media* (London: Routledge, 2004), 212.

284. 'New Publications', *Boston Globe*, 1 Nov. 1872, 1. Although the catchy phrase is not defined, it is unlikely that it was meant in the way in which I have here used it.

'agnostic naturalism as the proper basis for scientific inquiry' and to 'exclude their opponents from scientific discourse.'[285]

The result: even an undeniably landmark scientific work by two Englishmen—Hudson with Gosse—was to be intentionally snubbed.

Neither Hudson nor Gosse was part of the scientific elite. The future president of the Microscopical Society and soon-to-be FRS, as well as his 'assistant,'[286] remained outsiders. And not just outsiders, but suspect ones. It's true, as an anonymous reviewer of Hudson & Gosse mused, that the discoverer of *Pedalion mirum* had seemingly allowed for a major step forward in understanding how the Rotifera, as 'highly advanced products of evolution,' illustrated Darwin's theory. The reviewer added to this commendation these mocking words: 'Not that Mr. Gosse at least would allow the inference; for the veteran naturalist still stands out almost alone against the new-fangled theories of evolution and natural selection.'[287] When these words were written, Gosse had long been absent from the world of science. When he resumed important scientific researches after a lapse of years, 'there were many who failed at first to connect the eminent zoologist of 1850-60 with the worker of 1880.'[288] Obviously not everyone. A badge of imputed shame was forever to haunt the author of *Omphalos* among the elite of Victorian science.

By his association with Gosse, Hudson bore that mark. Moreover, Hudson's own words may well have condemned him. 'The study of these animals specks, (in which teeth, stomach, muscles, and even a brain lie hidden in the compass of an invisible mote),' Hudson wrote at the conclusion of the preface to Volume 1 of *The Rotifera*, 'irresistibly leads the mind to the contemplation of Him, whose almighty hand is as visible in an atom of this animated dust, as it is in the myriad sparkles of the starlit heaven.'[289] Expressing such a heretical thought would hardly endear Hudson to the guardians of *Nature's* agnostic or scientific naturalism.

285. Baldwin, '*Nature* and the Making of a Scientific Community, 1869-1939', 68.

286. Though having long before mainly dropped from public attention, three PHG works published by James Nisbet—*Romance of Natural History*; *Life*; and *Land and Sea*—were advertised in the first issue of *Nature* (4 Nov. 1869, 36).

287. 'Living Specks [review of Hudson & Gosse, *Rotifera*]', *Pall Mall Gazette*, 30 Nov. 1886, 5. References in the review to *Pedalion* and to rotifers being 'degenerate types of early articulate animals' suggest that Lankester was possibly the reviewer, though I have not seen references to his writing for this London daily newspaper. See Lankester, *Degeneration: A Chapter in Darwinism* (London: Macmillan and Co., 1880), 52, 56-7.

288. [F. Jeffrey Bell], *The Athenaeum* (18 Apr. 1891), 508.

289. Preface (signed 'C.T.H.'), Hudson & Gosse I:vi.

-VII-

In the last thirteen years of his life, Gosse the naturalist was absorbed with his rotifers, butterflies and other insects, and orchids. Orchids galore! During the month of July 1877 he had in flower at Sandhurst seventy-nine orchids (some in multiple varieties).[290] Meanwhile he maintained, with a sure hand, his remarkable talent as a scientific illustrator. His son unwittingly bore testimony to that skill. In 1878, Edmund visited their cousin Thomas Bell, the retired zoologist and former president of the Linnean Society, in Selborne, Hampshire. Previously ill and then nearly 86, he 'talked with the utmost vivacity and clearness,' Edmund wrote his father,

> ... and spoke of you with the greatest admiration and affection. He was delighted with a joke at my expense: he told Mrs. Salter to bring him the collection of tropical insects you had given him, & accordingly she brought a box of large lepidoptera, with pins through their bodies, at which I looked with great respect, until Mr. Bell could not refrain from laughing, & then I saw they were admirable mimics in cardboard. He said many naturalists had been taken in by them, & that no one had ever lived, to his knowledge, not even [J.O.] Westwood, who was so consummate an artist in insects as you were.[291]

Philip Gosse loved all of these pursuits, as his unflagging and industrious devotion to them attests. Yet, as we know, he loved something far more.

When describing himself, Gosse spoke (in the phrase favoured by the famed religious leader John Wesley) of '*homo unius libri*' ('a man of one book').[292] 'God,' Gosse wrote in the same place, 'never asks faith without evidence.' To this man of one book, the basis of all other facts could be epitomised in one simple word: resurrection. Everything led up to it, away from it, and would return to it. He looked for the promise

---

290. PHG, 'Orchids in July', *Gardeners' Chronicle* (18 Aug. 1877), 214 (this item is not cited in Freeman & Wertheimer-PHG). For an earlier list, 'Dendrobiums in Flower [at Sandhurst]', *Gardeners' Chronicle*, 22 Apr. 1876), 536.

291. EWG-PHG, Derby Day [=5 June], 1878 (CUL Add. 7018, 76). EWG mistakenly wrote that Bell was 86 at the time. In an earlier letter, EWG told his father he had reviewed Bell's important edition of Gilbert White's *Natural History of Selborne* (PHG-EWG, 15 Mar. 1878, CUL Add. 7018,30).

292. PHG, *Mysteries of God*, vi; the phrase is cited in Coad, *Brethren Movement*, 248, as reflecting the Bible's place among early Brethren.

inherent in it; his life was a testament on its behalf, the Church of God at St. Marychurch his own 'joy & crown'.

During this time, Gosse's ministrations at the Room continued in that pattern already outlined. Pastoral visits by him or appointed workers were combined with Bible and prayer meetings at home and at the chapel;[293] his discourses, always carefully expressed,[294] were sometimes based on his *Sacred Streams*,[295] and reflected the common evangelical habit of believing that the Old Testament offered the key to interpreting the New.[296] When Gosse was sick, he was not averse to having someone else preach in his place.[297] Around 1880, William King Perrens, formerly one of his entomological collectors in Argentina, later a town missionary in Torquay[298] and a friend,[299] began to share in his labours.[300]

Regardless of the advance in the acceptance of Darwinism as the century progressed, a new edition of *Sacred Streams* showed that there was yet an appreciative audience for other views.[301] It contained what is 'so greatly needed in works of this nature,' declared the Anglican *Christian Observer*, 'a spiritual tone' which pervaded the book.[302] 'Few living lovers of science wield a more attractive pen than Mr Gosse,' said the *Glasgow Herald*, 'none surpass him in gentle reverence and

293. E.g., Nellie Gosse-EWG, 1 Sept. 1881 (Family Collection).

294. PHG, 'On Emphasis in Reading Scripture', *Bible-Reader's Journal* No. 5 (1 May 1859), 82 (partly reprinted in PHG, 'Emphasis in Reading Scripture', *The Christian*, 7 Mar. 1872, 12, which is not listed in Freeman & Wertheimer-PHG).

295. PHG-Theodora Beachey, 12 Sept. 1880 (CUL Add. 7313, 188).

296. PHG, *Mysteries of God*, 2; Gosse, 'Reminiscences of My Husband from 1860 to 1888' (*Life*, 354).

297. PHG-EWG, 5 Oct. 1874 (British Library, Ashley Library B 3282), referring to Revd James T. Gwyther (d. ?1885), a Congregationalist (and member of the Victoria Institute, 1880-5); in 1880, while PHG was suffering from sciatica, William King Perrens 'supplied my lack of service in ministry of the Word' (PHG-Miss Fanny Perrens, 15 Mar. 1880, CUL Add. 7313, 53).

298. 'Town Missions', *Exeter and Plymouth Gazette* (18 Dec. 1885), 7.

299. After Perrens' second marriage (Truro *Royal Cornwall Gazette*, 15 Oct. 1880, 5), PHG welcomed the couple to 'the Table of the Lord' in St. Marychurch (PHG-WKP, 29 [Oct.] 1880, CUL Add.7313,221). PHG named a butterfly from Argentina after WKP, who had collected it for him (PHG-WKP, 10 Sept. 1880, CUL Add. 7313, 189-90; PHG, 'The Butterflies of Paraguay, and La Plata', *The Entomologist* XIII (Sept. 1880), 195). WKP spent time in Florence (PHG-WKP, 9 May 1881, CUL Add. 7313, 358-9). On 12 Apr. 1883, WKP, 'gentleman', was a witness to PHG's will (Public Record Office, Somerset House, London).

300. For PHG's first letter to WKP, 7 Jan. 1880 (CUL Add. 7313, 10-12); cf. also PHG-George Pearse, 19 June 1881 (CUL Add. 7313, 380-1; apparently reprinted, with changes, in *Life*, 364, 367-8).

301. PHG, *Sacred Streams: The Ancient and Modern History of the Rivers of the Bible* (London: Hodder & Stoughton, new ed., 1877); Freeman & Wertheimer-PHG, 36-8.

302. *Christian Observer* (Dec. 1877), 965.

unaffected piety.'[303] The eminent preacher C.H. Spurgeon added this praise: 'Here is a great treat for the Christian reader. ... Mr. Gosse blends the naturalist and the earnest believer ... and makes the Rivers of the Bible stream with instruction.'[304]

Gosse also continued with the Scripture Reading meetings which had provided his introduction to Brethren four decades earlier. They were held on Thursdays at his home, from eleven to noon, when a few men from the area 'read & discuss the Sacred Word.'[305] He was ever on the hunt for recruits, sometimes trying to entice locals who shared his interests in natural history. Among them was the barrister A. R. Hunt, of Torquay, a former president of the Torquay Natural History Society.[306] Hunt was a 'gentleman of fortune'[307] who, during some thirty years of acquaintance with Gosse[308] had acquired a reputation as a Devon naturalist,[309] sometime assisting Gosse in dredging excursions. Since Hunt was a 'man of leisure', time was not an issue; moreover, Gosse believed that they were 'one in faith; one in hope.' He told Hunt about the meetings: 'Will you come once, & see?'[310] Hunt declined with 'some severe criticism on our Scripture conferences.' Undeterred, Gosse wrote: 'Suppose you were to *try* my meeting, just for once!'[311] Several years later, he mentioned his regret that he was unable to personally thank William Lavers (d. 1894), a wealthy solicitor and president of the Torquay District Gardeners' Association[312] and one-time president of the Torquay Natural History Society[313] for the exotic tropical plant (*Nepenthes*) which he

303. *Glasgow Herald* (6 Dec. 1877), 2.

304. C. H. Spurgeon in *Sword and the Trowel*, cited in Charles Stanford, *Homilies on Christian Work* (London: Hodder and Stoughton, 1879), publisher's advertisements p. [200], and other places. There is a favourable review of the 1883 issue of *Sacred Streams* in *Sword and the Trowel* XX (Mar. 1884), 144.

305. PHG-A.R. Hunt, 3 Feb. 1882 (CUL Add. 7313, 480).

306. Walker, *Torquay Natural History Society*, 45,6. Hunt was president from 1879-81.

307. PHG-EWG, 11 June 1877 (CUL Add. 7019, 22).

308. A. R. Hunt, 'Mr. P. H. Gosse and Mr. Edmund Gosse', *Torquay Directory* (15 July 1908), 6.

309. [Obituary], 'Mr. A. Roope Hunt', London *Times*, 2 Jan. 1915, 5.

310. PHG-A.R. Hunt, 3 Feb. 1882 (CUL Add. 7313, 480).

311. PHG-A.R. Hunt, 8 Feb. 1882 (CUL Add. 7313, 486). Emphasis in the original. After PHG's death, Hunt was an Associate member of the Victoria Institute (1897-1900).

312. *Exeter Flying Post* (13 Aug. 1892), 5; 'Personal', Penzance *Cornishman*, 20 Sept. 1894), 6; *Devon and Exeter Daily Gazette*, 22 Nov. 1894, 2.

313. Walker, *Torquay Natural History Society*, 45.

dropped off at his house. Gosse had been engaged in a Scripture reading which he chose not to interrupt.[314]

Meanwhile, Gosse indulged in his life-long habit of inquiring into the religious status of other naturalists, hoping to identify those who shared his outlook. His *Actinologia Britannica*, for example, had barely appeared in February 1860[315] when he sent a copy to the naturalist H.W. Bates 'as a token of regard':

> I have read your numerous letters from Brazil published in the "Zoologist" with great interest, partly, doubtless, because I know a little of tropical collecting;[316] ... From one or two expressions dropped here & there in your letters, I have formed a suspicion, moreover, that you are one of those who love the Lord Jesus, & if so this would be an additional & a far stronger bond of sympathy between us. For there is no union so strong as that between the "holy brotherhood, partakers of the heavenly calling,"—who have by grace been drawn to believe in Jesus. Whether I am mistaken in this conclusion, I do not know ...[317]

Replied the agnostic Bates:[318]

> There will be differences of opinion between us I have no doubt, on mere matters of undemonstrable Dogmatic theology; but in the more essential points of true religious feeling & spirit, I hope in anything I may hereafter write & publish to continue & increase the good opinion you appear to have of me.[319]

Two years later, Gosse wrote to Bates of his pleasure at learning that he would be publishing 'a continuous account of his travels.' He was certain

---

314. PHG-W. Lavers, 8 Sept. 1887, cited in Peattie, *Gathering of Birds*, 208.

315. Freeman & Wertheimer-PHG do not give a date for the appearance of *Actinologia* in book form. The earliest review I have seen in that state was in the London *Critic* XX (24 Mar. 1860), 364-5.

316. PHG and Bates also shared an interest in diurnal Lepidoptera and Coleoptera, especially Carabidae (on Bates's systematic work on these butterflies: 'Henry Walter Bates', *Psyche* VI (Apr. 1892), 249).

317. PHG-H.W. Bates, 13 Feb. 1860 (LeBL). This letter is reprinted, with Bates' reply, by Clodd, 'Memoir', in H. W. Bates, *The Naturalist on the River Amazons*, lxxxvi-lxxxvii.

318. Bates was an agnostic, according to Clodd's 'Memoir', in H. W. Bates, *The Naturalist on the River Amazons*, lxxxvi. H. Lewis McKinney writes that 'Bates's Unitarian religious views did not hinder his acceptance of natural selection' (*DSB* I (2008), 501).

319. Bates-PHG, undated, but a reply to PHG's 13 Feb. letter (LeBL; reprinted in Clodd, 'Memoir', in H.W. Bates, *The Naturalist on the River Amazons*, lxxxvi-lxxxvii).

it would be 'absorbingly interesting' and looked forward to purchasing it.[320]

Had Gosse been abreast of the latest natural history developments, he could have been aware that Bates had already presented his ideas on butterfly mimicry at the Linnean Society.[321] Bates's research provided one of the earliest confirmations of Darwin's theory.[322] When Gosse subsequently read *The Naturalist on the River Amazons*, published in 1863, he would have realized that Bates's support for Darwin's natural selection mechanism was rooted in his field research in the Amazon region.[323]

Two examples of this type of outreach by Gosse occurred in 1881. In one instance, he noticed that in mailing out butterfly specimens, Arthur Doncaster (of Watkins and Doncaster, natural history and entomological suppliers on the Strand in London) habitually used printed papers of Baptist missionaries of the Congo, even some 'advocating Believers' Baptism': 'I venture to infer that you are one of those favoured few, who "has washed their robes … in the Blood of the Lamb." If this is so,—and I hope I am not mistaken,—there is a sympathy between us far deeper, & far more lasting, than any that grows out of kindred scientific proclivities.'[324] As it turned out, Gosse *was* mistaken:

> I am sorry I had misinterpreted the meaning of the printed papers …
> sorry, for your sake. For oh! it is a happy thing to be a believer in Christ.
> I do not emphasize "particular views." These are *comparatively* of little
> importance. The "great gulf" is not between Baptist & Friend;—but
> between dead in sins & alive to God; between saved in Christ & exposed

320. PHG-Bates, 2, 7, and 24 Apr. 1862 (LeBL). PHG's copy of Bates' *Naturalist on the River Amazons*, a 2 vol. set which appeared in 1863, is listed in *Sandhurst Catalogue*, item #335.

321. Bates's 'Contributions to an Insect Fauna of the Amazon Valley,—Lepidoptera, Heliconidae', was read at the Linnean Society on 12 Nov. 1861, following a paper by Darwin (*Athenaeum*, 30 Nov. 1861, 731).

322. Kimler, 'One Hundred Years of Mimicry', 5.

323. Clodd, 'Memoir', in H. W. Bates, *The Naturalist on the River Amazons*, liii, lxxxiii; Kimler, 'One Hundred Years of Mimicry', 77-8. It is not unlikely that the 'Bates' from whom PHG received a letter on Oct. 17, 1871, and to whom on the next day he apparently sent a copy of his *Naturalist's Sojourn in Jamaica*, was Henry Walter Bates (Corr. Bk., 18 Oct. 1871; there is no trace of either letter).

324. PHG-[unnamed correspondent], 25 Nov. 1881 (CUL Add. 7313,443). For the identification of the unnamed correspondent as Doncaster: PHG-A. Doncaster, 1 Dec. 1881 (CUL Add. 7313, 449).

to the wrath of God. O my dear friend, never mind particular views, till this vital question is settled.[325]

Another instance took place on the last day of 1881. In thanking the publisher John Van Voorst for lending him a biographical sketch of the naturalist W. C. Hewitson, Gosse asked whether he knew if Hewitson was 'a real (not a merely professed) *Christian.*' Gosse added:

> But perhaps you yourself, my valued friend, may know the happiness of reconciliation to God by the Blood of Christ. How it would increase my thanksgivings of the new year, if you told me this. If you do not yet know this happiness, I can wish you no kindlier wish than that it may become yours, with the opening year![326]

-VIII-

In the nearly three decades that Gosse lived in St. Marychurch, the town of a few thousand when he first arrived in 1857 nearly doubled in population to 5,800 (the rate of increase for nearby Torquay was similar).[327] He found about a dozen believers there who were cared for by pastoral visits from Torquay (and likely Newton Abbot).[328] Initially, it appeared that Gosse's Church of God experienced little increase. During a Sunday evening in 1860, there were 30-40 present;[329] on New Year's day in 1876, thirty people attended an assembly at 'our little Chapel' at 7 a.m. on a Saturday.[330] Later, thanks to Gosse's ongoing leadership, the rate of growth appears to have far outstripped the demographic increase in Marychurch. In the summer of 1880, the church consisted of 'about

325. PHG-A. Doncaster, 1 Dec. 1881 (CUL Add. 7313, 449). Emphasis in the original.

326. PHG-John Van Voorst, 31 Dec. 1881 (emphasis in the original; the copy seen was a typescript from the original MS, made available to me by R. B. Freeman; the holograph letter was auctioned in 1972 by Charles Kirke Swann of London; see CUL Add. 7313, 468). Van Voorst apparently provided PHG with a copy of either Dennis Embleton's *Memoir of the Life of Mr. W. C. Hewitson, F.L.S.* (1879), or an excerpt or review of that work appearing in the *Natural History Transactions of Northumberland, Durham, and Newcastle-on-Tyne* Vol VII (?1878), 223-35. The *Memoir* and the article in the *Natural History Transactions* may be the same: I have not see the former work. According to Corr. Bk., Van Voorst's letter to PHG was dated 29 December 1881. PHG did not record any letter from Van Voorst between that date and 5 April 1882.

327. *Black's Guide to Devonshire* (Edinburgh: Adam and Charles Black, 13th ed., 1889), 82 (Torquay's population was 24,767, p. 76).

328. PHG-G. Pearse, 19 June 1881 (CUL Add. 7313, 380-1).

329. Gosse, 'Reminiscences of My Husband from 1860 to 1888' (*Life*, 354).

330. PHG-EWG, 3 Jan. 1876 (CUL Add. 7018, 73).

100 souls,'[331] which increased by twenty percent in 1881.[332] At that time, it was nearly standing-room only and it seemed possible that the Room would no longer be large enough.[333]

Of course there was no diminution, either, in that near conviction that the 'Sure Word of Prophecy' would be fulfilled while Gosse was amongst the living. With October 1877 approaching, he once again thought he 'heard that prophetic hour struck on the Clock of God's providence,' being 'deeply persuaded that the Lord Jesus is near, even at the doors; & that I shall not be ashamed of my hope.'[334] But 'when 1877 passed, after the first feeling of disappointment, I set myself to discover where the failure was—And I soon found my mistake.'[335]

In 1878, he read the proofs of *The Approaching End of the Age Viewed in the Light of History, Prophecy, and Science* (1878), by his friend the Revd Henry Grattan Guinness (1835-1910), the last major premillennial historicist. It did not help. He was unconvinced by Guinness's chronological data, which (in common with 'continuationists' of the 1870s like E. B. Elliott) focussed on a *terminus ad quem* far off in 1923[336] or 1934.[337] The miscalculation was not that egregious, Gosse thought, which is why in 1880 he was still 'looking for that blessed Hope, his glorious appearing, which I judge to be very near at hand.'[338]

331. PHG-James Fanstone, 24 July 1880 (CUL Add. 7313,163-4).

332. 'There are about 120 in the fellowship, mostly poor people' (PHG-G. Pearse, 19 June 1881, CUL Add. 7313, 380-1).

333. PHG-W. K. Perrens, 9 May 1881 (CUL Add. 7313, 358-9). I do not know what involvement, if any, PHG had in the creation of the Babbacombe Gospel Hall in 1887, an offshoot of the Marychurch assembly (Beattie, *Brethren*, 67).

334. PHG-EWG, 3 Jan. 1876 (CUL Add. 7018, 73).

335. PHG-James Pascoe, 5 Mar. 1881 (CUL Add. 7313, 318-19).

336. PHG-H. G. Guinness, 3 Oct. 1878 (Corr. Bk.); PHG-Mrs H. G. [Fanny] Guinness, 24 Mar. 1880 (CUL Add. 7313, 65-6); a number of letters exchanged between PHG and 'Guinness' are recorded in Corr. Bk. for Jan. 1878. PHG 'saw portions of the prophetic parts of this work [*Approaching End of the Age*] while it was passing through the press' (HGG, *Approaching End of the Age*, 1878, viii), and HGG commended PHG's *Revelation* (*Approaching End*, 132fn.). The tenth edition of *Approaching End* (1886) was the last to appear during PHG's lifetime, but as far as is known PHG was only involved with the first edition of 1878. By the tenth edition, 17,000 copies had been sold. See also Froom, *Prophetic Faith* IV, 1194-1203, and for HGG's debate in 1887 with Canon A. R. Fausset on the advent: Sandeen, *Roots of Fundamentalism*, 147. Guinness was said to have joined the Brethren (*Cheltenham Chronicle*, 9 Oct. 1860, 8), an assertion he long denied (*Torquay Directory*, 30 Jan. 1861, 5; advertisement, 'To the Presbyterian Ministers of Ulster', *Belfast News-Letter*, 18 July 1863, 4).

337. H. Grattan Guinness and Fanny Guinness, *Light for the Last Days: A Study Historic and Prophetic* (London: Hodder and Stoughton, 1886, 2ed., (1888)), 163, 211.

338. PHG-James Fanstone, 24 July 1880 (CUL Add. 7313,163-4).

At the end of that year, Gosse concluded that in starting his calculations from 1517—when Martin Luther was regarded as having launched the Reformation by pinning his theses on the Church door at Wittenberg—and adding a 'Time' of 360 years, he had committed an elementary textual oversight. 'The special point for the Vision' in Revelation 10, he noted,

> is the [not open, but] open*ed* book, i.e., I judge, the Bible. This looks at Luther's publication of the Scripture in the German vernacular, which was not till the autumn of 1521. Now the Divine ANGEL has the book opened in his hand (See ver. 2) when He swears that august oath ... that 'there shall not be yet a TIME[339] till the Mystery of God be finished.' Which mystery is, I suppose, the presence of the Church, the Body of Christ, upon the earth. ... If my interpretation is right, the Appearing of the Lord cannot overpass the year 1881.[340]

In 1881, when deadly earthquake activity was reported in Europe and in Italy some 110 miles from Rome, Gosse was not the only one to take note of the 'portentous frequency' with which this was occurring.[341] He reminded a friend that he had 'long inferred from Holy Scripture' that 'Rome,—probably the whole of Papal Europe,—will be swallowed by an earthquake, wh[ich] will change the Mediterranean into a Volcanic Crater'.[342] He continued to expect the 'Great Shepherd' to appear[343] late into that year, and to commend Guinness for his prophetic studies.[344] Whether he subsequently discovered reasons for fastening upon dates beyond 1881 is not known.

One thing Gosse was not prepared to do was to set aside his intricate hermeneutics and grasp at what he deemed sensationalist prophetic claims 'propounded with a confidence ... warranted only by [Divine]

339. Meaning: 360 years.

340. PHG-George Pearse, 12 Dec. 1880 (CUL Add. 7313, 252-3). Emphasis and square brackets in the original.

341. 'Earthquakes are Occurring in Various Parts of Europe with portentous frequency', New York and London *Christian Herald and Signs of Our Times*, 3 Mar. 1881, 144; Michael Baxter, 'The Coming Great Earthquake. A Great Earthquake Predicted in Scripture', *Christian Herald and Signs of Our Times*, 12 May 1881, 295.

342. PHG-W.K. Perrens, 9 May 1881 (CUL Add. 7313, 358); 'The Earthquake at Casamicciola', London *Times*, 12 Mar. 1881, 7; 'A Season of Earthquakes', Glasgow *North British Daily Mail*, 9 Apr. 1881, 4.

343. PHG-James Fanstone, 14 Oct. 1881 (CUL Add. 7313,420-1).

344. PHG in *The Christian*, cited in 'Press Notices of the First Edition [1886]' in H. Grattan Guinness and Fanny Guinness, *Light for the Last Days*, [435]. I have not seen the first edition of this work or the issue of the *Christian* in which PHG's words appear.

inspiration.'[345] That's what was asked of him in 1881, when Frederick Boyce, a one-time missionary with the London City Mission,[346] sent him his pamphlet 'on the near coming of our Blessed Lord.'[347] Writing in the *Prophetic News* edited by 'Prophet Baxter' (who from 1861 became notable for predicting the end of the world),[348] Boyce claimed that in October 1878 'very important revelations were made to him.' Among them was that it was 'revealed that the Almighty God was near, while a voice solemnly declared that the Second Advent of Jesus Christ would be accomplished within ten years.'[349] Leading up to 1888, 'the religion of the present day will undergo a terrible shock,' Boyce warned.[350]

Gosse would have nothing to do with this. 'You claim to have a prophetic message from God,' he wrote Boyce as he proceeded to cite the biblical sources by which a true prophet could be discerned from a false one. 'You are a prophet,' Gosse concluded: 'very well, show your miraculous credentials.'[351]

In the meantime, Gosse continued to preach and write, bringing together some of the expositions he had delivered on Sundays in *The Mysteries of God* (1884).[352] The appearance of the book towards the

345. PHG, 'The Breaking of the Day.—XXIII', *The Christian*, 18 Aug. 1870, 368

346. On this group: 'London City Mission', *The Christian*, 11 May 1882, 375.

347. PHG-Frederick Boyce, 3 Sept. 1881 (CUL Add. 7313, 416). Judging from the contents of PHG's letter, he was almost certainly referring to Boyce's 'The Next Eight Years in Relation to Christ's Advent', *Prophetic News and Israel's Watchman* n.s. (Jan. 1881), 23-6. The article has not been traced in pamphlet form.

348. *Prophetic News* was published by Michael Paget Baxter (1834-1910), known as 'Prophet Baxter'. He 'Periodically prophesied the end of the world, the non-fulfilment of which didn't in the least discourage him from further efforts and new dates' ('A Remarkable Man. Prophet Baxter is Dead in London—What He Foretold', Kingston, Ontario *Daily British Whig*, 1 Feb. 1910, 1; 'The Rev. Michael P. Baxter Dead', New York *Christian Herald*, 2 Feb. 1910, 98; Sandeen, *Roots of Fundamentalism*, 98; T. C. F. Stunt, 'Baxter, Robert Dudley', *DEB* I: 69). Baxter was an historicist, 'mid-tribulational' rapturist (Sears, 'The Interpretation of Prophecy and Expectations of the End in Britain', 284-90). PHG found Baxter's *Christian Herald and Signs of Our Times* 'odd' (PHG-G. Pearse, 12 Dec. 1880, CUL Add. 7313,252).

349. Boyce, *Prophetic News*, 23.

350. Boyce, *Prophetic News*, 25.

351. Apparently Boyce sent PHG his pamphlet 'with compliments' and without a covering letter, since the first letter by Boyce listed in Corr. Bk. is from Sept. 9. Boyce again wrote PHG on Nov. 9, 1881. No copies of letters from Boyce have been traced. Sears, 'The Interpretation of Prophecy and Expectations of the End in Britain', 318-26, recounts the story of William Thomas of Yorkshire, a 'bizarre' prophetic student of the 1838-60 period perhaps not unlike Boyce.

352. *Life*, 368-9, states the sermons were delivered on Sunday *mornings*. At least some material came from Sunday *evenings*. 'Last night [Sunday, Apr. 24] I preached on the solemn subject of 'The Great White Throne' of Rev. xx., connected with the two-fold resurrection announced by the Lord Jesus in John v.29' (PHG-James Fanstone, Brazil, 25 Apr. 1881, CUL Add. 7313,346). PHG's *Mysteries of God* contains references to that subject.

end of his life capped the public expression of a lifetime of consistent, simultaneous devotion to religious and scientific studies. In the very same annual volume of *The Bookseller* in which the appearance of *Mysteries of God* was included was an announcement of the impending six-part work on *Rotifera* by C. T. Hudson & Gosse. That *Bookseller* also provided a nod to the future. It cited volumes on Thomas Gray and the history of English literature; introductions and edited versions of various works; and a book of poetry—all by the Clark Lecturer of English Literature at Cambridge University, Edmund Gosse.[353]

Mysteries of God was a disappointing and unexpectedly controversial volume, deliberately narrow in its focus and appeal, and (despite Gosse's denial) painfully speculative.[354] As an expositor, he was harnessed with blinders, looking neither to the right nor left, scrutinizing Scripture 'as with a microscope,'[355] ignoring all modern critical apparatus and research. He spoke only to Believers, 'by which term I mean, not merely such persons as assent, philosophically, to the truth of God's existence, and of the Bible as being his Word, but such as, on the authority of that Word, have come to Christ as lost sinners, and rested on Him for personal salvation.'[356]

Some of the essays dealt with 'Things Coming on the Earth,' 'The New Jerusalem,' and 'The New Earth' (chaps. 22-4), others reiterated the arguments of *Omphalos* (20-1), and yet another contained extravagant conjectures about 'The Colonization of Worlds' (25). His three chapters on 'Christ in the Psalms' (14-16), moreover, met with particularly strong objections, even condemnation. Viewing the whole Book of Psalms as in fact a life of Jesus (a characteristically Brethren approach), Gosse seemed to reduce the mystery of Jesus' earthly God-Man status to an assertion that he was human in abilities and faculties; that he had consequently

The British Library copy of *Mysteries of God* bears an accession stamp for 31 Dec. 1884 (Freeman & Wertheimer-PHG, 87), but there is an advertisement for the book in the *Glasgow Herald*, 27 Nov. 1884, 2.

353. *The Bookseller* (London: Bookseller, 1885), *passim*.

354. Though I find his interpretation unconvincing, a creative reading of PHG's 'futurist speculations' in *Mysteries of God* as 'an evangelical analog to the imaginings of Verne, Wells, and others', is provided by Brett Malcolm Grainger, 'Close Encounters of the Victorian Kind: the Sci-Fi Fundamentalism of Philip Henry Gosse', *Religion & Literature* 53 (Autumn 2021), 83-98.

355. PHG, *Mysteries of God*, iii. PHG used this expression in his *Prophetic Times*, 22, and in other places.

356. PHG, *Mysteries of God*, iii.

suffered physical disease (perhaps leprosy);[357] and that he had become vicarious not on the cross but at the beginning of his ministry.[358] Gosse knew that such speculative thoughts on unclearly defined subjects in Scripture, even though they were tentatively stated and came from a deeply devout Christian, would very likely provoke objections. After all, nearly forty years earlier similar deductions by B. W. Newton roiled Brethren.[359]

In *Sword and the Trowel*, editor C. H. Spurgeon took the high road.[360] After complimenting Gosse for 'his large acquaintance with nature, and his profound reverence for the Word of the Lord,' he added: 'We are always instructed by what Mr. Gosse has to say, whether we accept his opinions or not.'[361] But William Henry Bennet (1843-1920), a leading Open Brother[362] who edited the *Golden Lamp* (the first serial specifically aimed at Open Brethren),[363] would have nothing of that. He was stinging in his rebuke, and insistent. Without once citing by name *Mysteries of God* or its author, he warned of the danger of adding 'our inferences' to 'inspired statements ... lest we unintentionally dishonour Him'.[364] He pursued his critique against Gosse in private conversation, letters,[365] and in two obliquely worded articles.[366] *Mysteries of God* received little attention in the press, and then mainly unfavourably.[367] Even Methodist

357. PHG, *Mysteries of God*, 182-4.

358. PHG, *Mysteries of God*, 188-92.

359. Neatby, *History of the Plymouth Brethren*, 132-45; Coad, *Brethren Movement*, 147-52.

360. I am assuming, as seems to be assumed by others, that Spurgeon authored the book review section of *Sword and the Trowel* (see, e.g., Albert R. Meredith, 'The Social and Political Views of Charles Haddon Spurgeon, 1834-1892' (Michigan State University, PhD dissertation, 1973), 102, 245).

361. *Sword and the Trowel* XXI (May 1885), 236.

362. Coad, *Brethren Movement*, 70fn.; obituary, Yeovil *Western Gazette*, 17 Dec. 1920, 4; 'The Falling Asleep of Mr. W. H. Bennet', *Echoes of Service*, Jan. 1921, 3-5.

363. Grass, *Gathering to His Name*, 152.

364. W. H. B[ennet]., 'The Holy One of God', *Golden Lamp* n.s. VIII (Aug. 1885), 174.

365. PHG, *Humanity of the Son of God*, 4. Corr. Bk. records PHG-Bennet letters between Feb.6-Apr. 12,1885: 7 letters from WHB, 5 from PHG.

366. Bennet's other article was 'When Did Christ Become the Sin-bearer?', *Golden Lamp* n.s. VIII (Sept. 1885), 193-7.

367. The claim of Eliza Gosse (*Life*, 371) that the book was favourably received is unwarranted. It is true that the book was reprinted from the same sheets in Toronto (Freeman & Wertheimer-PHG, 88); excerpts were published in *The Christian* (19 Mar. 1885), 215-6, and (though not credited to *Mysteries of God*) posthumously in Michael Baxter's *Christian Herald and Signs of Our Times* (PHG, 'The New Jerusalem', 11 Oct. 1888, 647) and *Prophetic News and Israel's Watchman* (PHG, 'Things Coming on the Earth', Nov. 1888). The book was graciously reviewed in *Sword and the Trowel* XXI, May 1885, 236, and was also praised in an obituary notice in *The Quiver* n.s. 3, XXIV (Nov. 1888), 78.

publications, which three decades earlier had been sympathetic to *Omphalos* (as previously noted), were among the severe reviewers.[368] In response, in 1886 Gosse specifically addressed the points raised by Bennet and those Brethren whom he had offended in the privately circulated, 32-page pamphlet *Humanity of the Son of God: According to Scripture.*

To an extent, the whole affair tarnished Gosse's reputation as a man of God, among some and at least temporarily. In response, R. C. Morgan spoke up for his friend:

> ... whatever error may have been fallen into by Mr. Gosse, it was an error of judgment merely, and not of heart. The heart of no man on earth beat truer to the Son of God than his. Some have accused him of deliberately dishonouring the name of Jesus. Is it not preposterous to suppose that a man who has spent sixty long years in honouring the Son, even as he honoured the Father, should suddenly at the last turn round and wilfully dishonour Him? It is the *intent* which gives a character to the word or deed. It is possible to utter the words "Lord Jesus" with deepest

The entry in Corr. Bk. under 5 Feb. 1885 PHG points to a reality different than that claimed by Eliza Gosse. That entry is annotated: 'Hodder & St[oughto]n [crit. [*sic*]', possibly referring to critical reviews sent to him by the publisher of *Mysteries of God*. In the *British Quarterly Review* LXXXII (1 July 1885), 254, a once-distinguished publication now in decline (*DNCJ*, 79), the reviewer said 'We have been disappointed in Mr. Gosse's book ... we have a series of addresses of an unctuous character, which our readers will understand when we say, like the addresses characteristic of Plymouth Brethren'. Two unfavourable reviews appeared in the *United Presbyterian Magazine* (Edinburgh) n.s. II (Apr. 1885), 178-9, and n.s. II (Nov. 1885), 512 (by 'J. L.'). 'We admire Mr. Gosse's intellectual courage and independence, but think him sometimes crotchety and quixotic', the first *UPM* review stated, while 'J. L.' complained of PHG's 'literal mode of interpretation which he carries out with considerable thoroughness and much ingenuity', and concluded: 'We cannot but speak respectfully of a writer whose spirit is so devout and earnestly evangelical ... but we are his true friends when we advise him not to meddle with Greek or Hebrew.'

For the Toronto edition of *Mysteries of God*, which was published by S. R. Briggs (a relative of Ann Jaques: 'Reminiscences Awakened', St. John's, Newfoundland *Evening Telegram*, 10 Dec. 1895, 4): Freeman & Wertheimer-PHG, 87-8.

368. A writer in the *Wesleyan-Methodist Magazine* (ser. 2, X, Jan 1886, 75) acknowledged PHG's 'persevering, reverent, loving, and scholarly searching of the Scriptures', adding: 'On the other hand, there is scarcely an essay from which we we are not compelled to dissent more or less seriously.' A similar appraisal was offered by the *Canadian Methodist Magazine* (XXIV, Nov. 1886, 486) concerning the Canadian printing of the book: 'We think that [PHG] is a much better authority on scientific than in Biblical exposition, and even in science he has some extraordinary views. There can be no question as to the devoutness of his spirit, and many important religious lessons can be learned from the present volume. But, with all his scholarship, we think his interpretation often visionary and misleading. ... Serious criticism is wasted on such vagaries as these'.

reverence, or so to utter them in mockery that it becomes blasphemy. Could such a man as Philip Henry Gosse proved himself to have been, by a life spent in the loving service of God and man, have possibly intended to dishonour the Saviour, whom he so loved, by what he has written?[369]

-IX-

Though Philip could be 'grave and somewhat stern' to friends, 'bore rule' at home, and considered himself 'a shy man', he not unexpectedly showed a different side to his own family. He had 'a good deal of humour and fun,'[370] said his wife Eliza, and was diligent in following the state of his relations' welfare. Towards the end of his life, Philip corresponded with his brothers William and Thomas and helped to support them, notwithstanding what we have seen as Thomas's unfamilial conduct after the disastrous financial investment of 1854.[371]

All evidence points to Gosse's relationship with his son becoming less ardent after 1875. From the father's perspective, Edmund's rejection of his childhood affirmation of a new birth was, at the very least, errant conduct. That does not mean that he was not a loving and dutiful child. He visited Sandhurst each year and presented most of his new books to his father. One does not have to search for evidence of filial piety, though neither was comfortable with the lifestyle of the other. The relationship had fractured, never to be repaired.

For his part, though letters to Edmund decreased in number,[372] Philip kept trying and hoping—trying to prod his son to return to his earlier belief, hoping to see signs that this might yet happen. After Edmund and Nellie had visited Sandhurst on their honeymoon, Philip reiterated his adherence to the importance of prophecy and the nearness of the Dawn. He wrote: 'O my dear children; I have the gravest fears that neither of you is resting on the only sure foundation,—the Blood of the Lamb.'[373] When their first child, Emily Teresa, was born (though known as 'Tessa'

369. [R. C. Morgan], obituary of PHG in *The Christian* (21 Sept. 1888), 886 (reprinted in *'The Christian' Portrait Gallery*, 110-13). Emphasis in the original.

370. Gosse, 'Reminiscences of My Husband from 1860 to 1888' (*Life*, 357-8).

371. For William Gosse: PHG-EWG, 27 Aug. 1886 (CUL Add. 7018, 37); EWG-Nellie (undated, prob. 1887) (CUL Add. 7020, 135); for Thomas Gosse: PHG-Thomas Gosse, 23 July, 2 Aug., 5, 8, 13 Oct. 1880; 3 Dec. 1881 (CUL Add. 7313, 162, 165-6, 196, 200, 207-8, 450).

372. PHG-EWG, 15 Mar. 1878 (CUL Add. 7018, 30).

373. PHG-EWG, 3 Jan. 1876 (CUL Add. 7018, 73); diary of Nellie Gosse for 1875, under 6-11, 13-16 Sept. (LeBL).

she was presumably named after Emily Gosse), Edmund turned to his poetic muse to address a thought to the 'Dear child of mine'.[374] To the grandfather it was also a moment to rejoice, but in religious, not poetic, tones: 'Well; accept your precious gift from the hand of God, who thus once more says to you, "My son, give me thy heart!" Oh! could I receive a letter from you, that you have returned in the simplicity of your early faith, to Jesus as a Saviour!'[375] Similar words followed the birth of their second child.[376]

Philip continued to congratulate his son on his success as a littérateur, complimenting him on each new book. An acknowledgment in 1879 went like this:

> O that God would lead you to lay all your talents, & all your honours, at the foot of the Cross of Christ! Then I should be glad, indeed! Will you never give me one peep into your heart's feelings towards Him? I have long abstained from obtruding "religion" upon you; will you not confess that I have? though "my heart was hot within me, & the fire burned." & have waited in hope that you would at length give me your confidence, & not keep this wide dark chasm between your heart & mine, while we talk lightly of trifles.[377]

Edmund's *New Poems* (1879) he read 'with inexpressible sadness' because the verses 'will not look beyond the grave'.[378] On Edmund's thirty-third birthday, having attained that age when Jesus died on the cross, Philip yearned for his son 'a true change of heart!'[379]

It may be that Edmund and Nellie evinced, in relation to their high social position, a moderately religious life during this period, and for some years after it. Occasionally they went to church, though Edmund was bored with sermons.[380] He preferred to stay nearby at The Grove,

---

374. Edmund W. Gosse, 'To Teresa', *Athenaeum* (26 Nov. 1881), 702. Emily Teresa was born 14 Sept. 1877 (d. 1951).

375. PHG-EWG, 17 Sept. 1877 (CUL Add. 7018, 75).

376. PHG-EWG, 1 Sept. 1879 (CUL Add. 7018, 32): Philip Henry George Gosse was born 13 Aug. 1879 (d. 1959).

377. PHG-EWG, 14 Mar. 1879 (CUL Add. 7018, 31), acknowledging receipt of EWG's *Studies in the Literature of Northern Europe* (1879). The quotation references Psalm 39: 3 (KJV).

378. PHG-EWG, 14 Nov. 1879 (CUL Add. 7018, 34).

379. PHG-EWG, 20 Sept. 1882 (CUL Add. 7018, 36).

380. Tessa Gosse's Diary for 1891 (seen in the Family Collection) lists six occasions when some or all of the family went to church; for the instance of EWG sleeping through a sermon, EWG-NG, undated (from internal evidence = 1883), CUL Add. 7020, 30; see also CUL Add.

near Stanmore, the home of the George Brightwen relations, rather than at Sandhurst, for he heard 'no religious conversation' there.[381] At Marychurch, on the contrary, he was 'vigorously tussled with on the religious question ... but I drove the war smartly back into the enemy's camp, & we came out of it quite happy and smiling.'[382] Nor did they prevent their children from experiencing the old-time practices. Once, Edmund even asked his father to compose for, and teach to, Tessa a prayer to say each night.[383]

These little signs that belief was not totally absent from the younger Gosses' lifestyle may have been the reflection of nothing more than habit, social custom, or parental respect. Or perhaps they were a recognition that, as the Psalmist proclaimed, 'Our days may come to seventy years, or, given the strength, eighty years ... They quickly pass, and we fly away' (Ps. 90: 10). Philip was just half-a-year short of the three score and ten-year milestone when Edmund contemplated the inevitable. He recollected that his father was

> rather severe and unbending to me when I was a child, and I went about the empty house in some dread of him. But now he is clingingly affectionate and apologetic for trouble that he gives. I parted from him yesterday with tears in my eyes; there is something overwhelmingly painful in seeing the peculiar expression of weakness asking for forbearance, in the eyes of a man that has been very highhanded and stubborn. I hope my fears about his health may be unfounded: but I realized yesterday, with terror and for the first time, that his vehement eager life would not last for ever.[384]

Several years later, with the son seeing the infirmities of his 77-year-old father, he again gave free rein to new emotions. His father was 'very sweet and gentle, wonderfully mellowed at last by the softening hand of age,' Edmund wrote to a friend, 'and I have felt an affection for him and pleasure in his company, this visit, that I am afraid I never really felt before. And so, in the evening there is light.'[385]

7021, 13.
    381. EWG-NG, undated (but in pencil: 13.5.83), CUL Add. 7020, 8.
    382. EWG-NG, 7 Apr. 1883 (CUL Add. 7020, 7).
    383. PHG-EWG, 11 Nov. 1880 (CUL Add. 7313, 225).
    384. EWG-Hamo [Thornycroft], 7 Oct. 1879 (Charteris, 117).
    385. EWG-Hamo [Thornycroft], 22 Sept. 1887 (Charteris, 210, 214).

During most of 1887, Philip was—though now hard-of-hearing—in good health,[386] carrying out and publishing his investigations on the Rotifera,[387] naming a new one after Tessa,[388] complimenting his grandson on his scientific drawings,[389] lending his drawings, sketches and related material on sea anemones to A. C. Haddon (1855-1940),[390] who was then preparing a revision of the British Actiniae.[391] Haddon was a zoologist (subsequently the 'doyen of British anthropologists')[392] who had early come under the influence at Cambridge of evolutionary thinking.[393] In September, all of the Gosses—grandfather and grandmother, son and daughter-in-law, and three grandchildren[394]—spent a memorable day hunting for sea creatures at Goodrington Sands, Devon.

Gosse had purchased a £5 telescope from London opticians decades earlier which 'exceeded' expectations and allowed him to distinctly view double-stars.[395] During October, many an evening was devoted by Philip and Eliza to gazing through their telescope in search of these heavenly bodies, no doubt dreaming and musing over the expected colonization of the planets in the millennium.[396] Towards the end of the year, while engaged in this pleasurable activity, he suffered an attack of bronchitis.[397]

386. EWG-NG, 7 Apr. 1883 (CUL Add. 7020,7); *Life*, 335.

387. Freeman & Wertheimer-PHG, entries 399-401.

388. *Mytilia Teresa*: PHG, 'Twenty-four New Species of Rotifera', *JRMS*, ser. 2, VII (Feb. 1887), 3.

389. PHG-Philip Henry George Gosse, 19 Apr. 1887 (Family Collection); cf. also PHG-'Master Philip Henry Gosse', 1 Sept. 1885 (CUL Adv. c. 82.5, 79).

390. Haddon, *Revision of the British Actiniae*, 451.

391. PHG-[A. C. Haddon], 28 Nov., 10 Dec. 1887 (Horniman Museum, London, Haddon MSS).

392. C. G. Seligman, 'Dr. A. C. Haddon, F.R.S.', *Nature* 145 (1 June 1940), 848.

393. Fleure, 'Alfred Cort Haddon, 1855-1940', 450.

394. PHG-Teresa Gosse, 12 Sept. 1887 (Family Collection); *Life*, 321-2; Sylvia Laura Gosse was born on 14 Feb. 1881 (d. 1968).

395. Advertisement, 'The £5 Telescope. Testimonial from P. H. Gosse, Esq., F.R.S.', London *Times* (3 Apr. 1867), 1. The first to note this advertisement was E. Charles Nelson, *Archives of Natural History*, 173-4, who cites a later edition of *The Times* in which the same advertisement appeared (it also ran in the London *Illustrated London News*, 7 Mar. 1868, 244). EWG, *Early Writing Career* [?May 1866] (LeBL), refers to having used this telescope as a teenager.

396. PHG, *Mysteries of God*, 302ff. PHG owned several works related to celestial objects (*Sandhurst Catalogue*, items #391-2, 400).

397. *Life*, 322-3. Untypically, between 22-30 Aug. no letter from PHG is listed in Corr. Bk. PHG was apparently also ill at the end of September (EWG-NG, 27 Sept. 1887; CUL Add. 7021, 19), though he managed to keep up his letter writing, with some gaps.

-X-

Sunday, 8 January 1888, was the last occasion on which Gosse spoke at the Room. He was present twice more, sitting quietly in his accustomed place in the corner of the room near the window.[398] Likely in February, he had a heart attack.[399] Edmund met with his father's physician, Alfred Midgley Cash of Torquay, who 'gives F. an extreme limit of a year.' The end, Dr Cash predicted, 'will be quite sudden.'

Edmund also told Nellie towards the end of March that, as his father recovered, he was 'remarkably cheerful ... most affectionate & gentle, and liked me to hold his hand.'[400] Edmund found him a 'fearful fidget':

Rap, rap! [I fly up]
F   I want to see your Mother.
I   Can't I do anything for you?
F   No! thank you, I won't trouble you, I'm chilly.
      [I fly down]
I   Mother, what does he have on when he is chilly?
M   Oh, the rug in the drawing-room.
      [I fly up with the rug.]
F   Hasn't your mother come?
I   She's so tired. May I wrap your shoulders in this?
F   No! I want to see your Mother.
      [I go down very slowly. Mother ascends.]
This goes on four times an hour.[401]

It wasn't until later in April that Philip regained his physical and mental health sufficiently to allow him to return to his microscope.[402] His final article was submitted for publication later that month and published that July, precisely sixty-two years after his name first appeared in print as an author.[403] An endorsement 'From Personal Knowledge' of the successful

398. Gosse, 'Reminiscences of My Husband from 1860 to 1888' (*Life*, 354, 371); obituary in *The Christian* (21 Sept. 1888), 886.

399. There are no letters to or from PHG listed in Corr. Bk. for the month of February.

400. EWG-NG, 28 Mar. 1888 (CUL Add. 7021, 32).

401. EWG-NG, 29 Mar. 1888 (CUL Add. 7021, 33) (square brackets in the original); EWG-George A. Armour, 5 Apr. 1888 (Princeton); EWG-NG, 28 Mar. 1888 (CUL Add. 7021, 32); Charteris, 222.

402. 'The friends of Mr. P.H. Gosse will be glad to learn that he has entirely recovered from the alarming illness under which he was suffering at Easter. Mr. Gosse, who, in his seventy-ninth year, preserves his microscope-eye, has returned to his investigation of the Rotifera' ('Science Gossip', *Athenaeum*, 5 May 1888, 571, reprinted in *Leeds Mercury*, 9 May 1888, 8); EWG-G. A. Armour, 2 May 1888 (Princeton). In 1888, Easter Sunday was 1 Apr.

403. PHG's last published work during his lifetime was dated 20 Apr.: 'The Boar-fish (*Capros aper*. Cuv.; *Lens aper*, Linn.)', *Hardwicke's Science-Gossip* XXIV (July 1888), 163.

candidacy of C. T. Hudson to become a Fellow of the Royal Society was signed, in an uncharacteristically shaky signature, by 7 June 1888.[404] A request from him to the *Gardeners' Chronicle* to identify a milkwort plant (*Polygaloides chamaebuxus*) was published posthumously.[405]

Into May, as the last entries in his Correspondence Book indicate, he was occupied with Rotiferan studies.[406] A few weeks later, his health failed again, and Nellie went down to Sandhurst to assist Eliza in caring for him. Nellie was there for the next four months with their three children.[407] In the meantime Edmund could only manage a few visits to Torquay. He had to remain some 200 miles away in London or attend to his duties as Clark Lecturer at Cambridge while trying to complete a study on William Congreve. Timely telegrams apprised him of his father's health. 'You ask whether I should come at once in case of his death,' he wrote Nellie. 'I should come instantly; but I hope you will be able to send for me before that.'[408] When the Congreve work was completed on 29 May, Edmund began to read 'a very curious & interesting little book on Dying—Dr. Monk's "Euthanasia".'[409]

From May until August, Philip was forced to spend nearly all of his time in his armchair, restrained from involvement in his normal activities. It was 'irksome and depressing to a man of his active mind,'[410] and stressful for those who cared for him. Towards the end of the summer, Edmund

404. C. T. Hudson's 'Certificate of a Candidate for Election' to the Royal Society (Royal Society, *Certificates* XI, 1881-95, 166), recommended 7 June 1888. Hudson was elected on 6 June 1889 (*Nature*, 13 June 1889, 162).

405. 'Notices to Correspondents', *Gardeners' Chronicle* ser. 3, IV (17 Nov. 1888), 583. The last entry in Corr. Bk. is for 8 May 1888.

406. Letters in Corr. Bk. to and from S. G. Osborne, Beachey, Sinel, Hood, Lord are registered from the end of 1887 to the end of the book. For the identification of Osborne as a collector: Hudson & Gosse I: 10, 186, 194, 207.

407. EWG-NG, 4 Apr. 1888 (CUL Add. 7021, 35); EWG-George A. Armour, 13 Apr., 9 Aug. 1888 (Princeton).

408. EWG-NG, [22 May 1888] (CUL Add. 7021, 44).

409. EWG finished *Life of William Congreve* on May 29 (EWG-NG, 29 May 1888, CUL Add. 7021, 49) and the proofs reached him two weeks later (EWG-NG, 13 June 1888, CUL Add.7021,57). The chapter on the 'General and Medical Treatment of the Dying' in William Munk's *Euthanasia; or, Medical Treatment in Aid of an Easy Death* (London: Longmans & Co., 1888) was called 'a most carefully written and valuable one, and we should suggest its publication in the form of a pamphlet for distribution among nurses and others who are in attendance upon the moribund' (*Saturday Review*, 18 Feb. 1888, 213). The word 'euthanasia' in the title did not have the modern signification of 'mercy killing' but indicated managing pain and dealing with anxiety about dying (Judith Flanders, *Inside the Victorian Home*, 367fn.).

410. Obituary in *The Christian* (21 Sept. 1888), 886. The last entries in Corr. Bk. are for two letters received, and one letter written, on 8 May.

was urging his wife—in a letter marked PRIVATE with three underscorings—
to get some rest.[411]

Then it was 23 August, 1888. Two-and-a-half decades earlier Philip
had told a friend he was not afraid to die.[412] Thinking of the second
coming, he now left his Greek New Testament open to John 17, containing
Jesus' words to his disciples: 'Father, the hour is come' (v. 1).

Philip prayed for the members of his Fore Street chapel. Likely he
also had in mind another prayer, one which had occupied him since his
first momentous encounter with sacred prophecy in June 1842. At that
time, 'I immediately began a practice,' he said, 'which I have pursued
uninterruptedly for forty-six years, of constantly praying that I may be
one of the favoured saints who shall never taste of death, but be alive
and remain until the coming of the Lord, to be "clothed-upon with my
house which is from heaven."'[413]

It was not to be. It was one o'clock in the morning—the very hour that
Emily Gosse had died, thirty-one years earlier.[414] The nurse who was then
with him heard him say: 'It is all over. The Lord is near! I am going to my
reward!' After painful delirium and aphasia (which can make it difficult
to speak or write), 'Without sigh or struggle he "fell on sleep"'[415]—'never
to be broken until the sound of the last trumpet.'[416] His final utterance:
'The Lord *is* here! The Lord *is* present!'[417] Philip Henry Gosse was 78.

411. EWG-NG, [14 Aug. 1888] (CUL Add. 7021, 81).

412. So he told W. R. Hughes, in conversation, about 25 years earlier (obituary notice of PHG, *Midland Naturalist* XI (1888), 297). PHG knew Hughes from at least July 1863 (W. R. Hughes, 'Lepidogaster bimaculatus in an Aquarium', *Zoologist* XXII (1864), 9132). Hughes dedicated the booklet-edition of his *Principles and Management of the Marine Aquarium* (1875) to Gosse, 'with feelings of sincere gratitude and respect'.

413. 'Reminiscences', II: 253. The references is to 2 Corinthians 5: 2. In 1881, PHG similarly wrote: 'For 40 years I have used Luke xxi.36 & acted upon it, in pleading with God, for myself personally' (PHG-James Pascoe, 5 Mar. 1881, CUL Add. 7313, 318-19. The verse from Luke reads: 'Watch ye therefore, and pray always, that ye may be accounted worthy to escape all these things that shall come to pass, and to stand before the Son of man').

414. PHG, *Memorial*, 79; *Life*, 270, 323, 372.

415. EWG-Horace H. Furness, 7 Oct. 1888 (Princeton); PHG obituary in *The Christian* (21 Sept. 1888), 886; *Life*, 372.

416. The phrase is used in 'Sudden Death', *North Devon Journal* (22 Dec. 1853), 8.

417. For his last words, *The Christian* (21 Sept. 1888), 886. Emphasis in the original. There are six accounts of aspects of PHG's death published between 1888-1890, including one from 1927. The earliest, from the *Torquay Times* (13 Sept. 1888, 6), mentions that EWG 'was with his father at the time of his death.' *The Christian, q.v.,* attributes a number of remarks to PHG in his last days, including his final one: 'The Lord *is* here!' 'The Lord *is* present!' In a letter from EWG to the American Shakespearean scholar H. H. Furness (1833-1912), he wrote: 'The end too was very painful, with long-drawn delirium and loquacious aphasia. At last he fell asleep, and passed

At his death he had accumulated a sizable estate of some £16,196, which he bequeathed (with the exception of £1,000 for Edmund) to Eliza.[418] He had spent his last 31 years in St. Marychurch, yet he was hardly known there outside his own immediate (if ample) circle.[419] On his headstone is this verse from the Book of Revelation (22: 20):

> He which testifieth these things saith, Surely I come quickly. Amen.
> Even so come Lord Jesus.

In his correspondence and writings, Gosse had cited verses which highlighted the attitude of watchfulness and its impact on proper conduct.[420] These words from Revelation, which served in 1870 as the epigraph to the final installment in his series on 'The Breaking of the Day,'[421] form an appropriate complement to that concern, and mark the place near his mother at Torquay cemetery where he was set down on 27 August 1888, the burial being witnessed by a 'large congregation.'[422]

away in peace' (EWG-HHF, 7 Oct. 1888; Princeton). *Life* (1890), 323, states PHG died just before one o'clock in the morning; Eliza Gosse's "Reminiscences of My Husband from 1860 to 1888" (*Life*, 372) affirms that, and adds that he told a nurse who was with him: 'It is all over. The Lord is near! I am going to my reward!' Eliza Gosse does not note that anyone else was in the room with PHG at his death. She wrote that her husband was 'buoyed up almost to the last' with the hope that Jesus would come before he died. Earlier, she seems to have contradicted herself: '... its nonfulfillment was an acute disappointment to him. It undoubtedly was connected with the deep dejection of his latest hours on earth' (p. 367). The sixth account is a record of a visit of the biographer and politician Harold Nicolson to EWG seven months before EWG died. According to that record, PHG 'as he grew older, became crazy,' ultimately believing God had 'betrayed' him. 'He turned against God, reviling him for treachery. He shouted blasphemies while Gosse and Lady Gosse essayed to hold him down.' EWG told Nicolson his father died at 3 a.m. (Lees-Milne, *Harold Nicolson*, 317). I have followed here what I believe to be the most likely scenario.

418. Probate of Will of PHG, granted 12 Oct. 1888 (Public Record Office, Somerset House, London). A detailed account of his personal estate is at CUL Add. 7041, 68.

419. Thus PHG's obituary notice, *Torquay Times*, 13 Sept. 1888, 6.

420. The epigraph to PHG, *6000 Years of the World's History Now Closing*, cites Rev. 16: 15 and Mark 13: 35, 37, and the one to *The Revelation: How Is It to be Interpreted?* cites Rev. 1: 3, and see there p. 63.

421. PHG, 'The Breaking of the Day.—XXIV', *Christian* I (1 Sept. 1870), 393, where the phrasing is somewhat different from the tombstone: 'He which testifieth these things saith, Surely I come quickly, Amen. Even so come, Lord Jesus.' The verse also appears as the final sentence in H[arriette]. E[mily]. E[lliott]., *The Last Prophecy: Being an Abridgment of the late Rev. E. B. Elliott's Horae Apocalypticae*, 364 (again, with different phrasing), and was also used as the epigraph to John Coleman's *"The Time of the End"*, title page, the Brethren pioneer in Jamaica whom PHG had known while he sojourned there.

422. 'Death of Mr. P. H. Gosse, F.R.S., of St. Marychurch', *Torquay Directory*, 29 Aug. 1888, 5; *Torquay Times*, 13 Sept. 1888, 6; *Life*, 323.

CHAPTER THIRTEEN

Afterwards

-I-

EDMUND AND NELLIE WERE PRESENT at Philip's death, and retreated to Cornwall for a fortnight after the funeral 'to get a thorough nervous rest.'[1] Nellie had spent the previous four months helping out at Sandhurst. Before September, Edmund had returned to London. Nellie remained behind to care for Eliza, for which Edmund was duly grateful.[2]

On the exact same day that Philip died—only in 1893, five years later— his elder brother William passed away in London, aged 85. When he was 14 he had left England for a clerkship in the mercantile trade in Newfoundland, and after some 14 years he had set off there on his own as a painter (including of miniature portraits), mainly in St. John's, from 1836-42.[3] Even though William (like Philip) never studied art,[4] William has been called the 'most successful' of the painters living in Newfoundland during the first half of the nineteenth century.[5] He returned in 1842 to England, later working full time at the London photographic studio of Maull & Co. on Cheapside,[6] and then as a miniature painter of

---

1. EWG-'My very dear Friends [George and Barbara Armour]', 7 Oct. 1888 (Princeton); EWG-H. H. Furness, 7 Oct. 1888 (Princeton). I am grateful to Prof. Paul F. Mattheisen for bringing these letters to my attention.

2. EWG-NG, 29 Aug. 1888 (CUL Add. 7021,82).

3. 'Reminiscences', I: 96; 'Gosse, William', *Encyclopedia of Newfoundland and Labrador* II:576.

4. 'Reminiscences', I: 89.

5. Bert Riggs, 'William Charles St. John portrait [by William Gosse]', Finding Aid, Archives and Special Collections, Memorial University, Newfoundland (1997).

6. PHG-EWG, 10 Mar. 1868 (CUL Add. 7041,15). PHG had his portrait taken at Maull and Polyblank in 1855 (*ODNB*) and, as mentioned, had failed in his attempt to have one also done there for Emily.

photographs in London.[7] A life-long bachelor, William struggled to meet expenses, managing an adequate subsistence in later years thanks to annual financial support from Philip and Edmund[8] (he was an irregular visitor at Edmund and Nellie's home).[9]

His admiration for his brother was enormous, the occasional irritation notwithstanding. Philip's life, he said, was 'a remarkable instance of a struggling genius under most trying difficulties.'[10] The two brothers maintained regular contact throughout their lives. When Edmund learned from a cousin of William's failing health, he rushed to see him. Once there, 'I felt sure that he was sinking,' Edmund told Nellie, 'and stayed with him. He died very peacefully on the stroke of noon.' He was buried at Highgate Cemetery.[11]

Philip's younger brother, Thomas, whose visit to his brother's Canadian farm in 1837 ended in failure, had remained a wayward member of the family.[12] After the death of Emma Budden, his first wife,[13] he had married Fanny, fathering at least seventeen children.[14] Operating from Bath, he worked for years as a share broker, gaining a commission based on the number of shares in a trade.[15] Mines in Cornwall were his specialty: at one time lead and silver,[16] at another, gold. William believed Thomas was the 'Bath shareholder' who attempted to conceal the fact that a claimed

7. PHG-John Bemister, 21 Dec. 1871 (Corr. Bk.). Like PHG, WG produced miniature drawings of natural objects. WG's *Wild Flowers and Fruits of Newfoundland from Nature* (c. 1830) were of 'outstanding quality' and 'more lyrical' than illustrations by PHG or Thomas Gosse, their father (Raymond Lister, 'William Gosse's Botanical Miniatures', *Gardeners' Chronicle*, 26 Apr. 1952, 140). William Gosse's Diary, *passim*, contains detailed references about portraits he did, including his earnings.

8. WG was to receive £20 p.a. from EWG and £40 p.a. from PHG, which made WG 'rapturously happy and grateful' (EWG-NG, undated [prob. 1887], CUL Add. 7020, 135).

9. For example, WG-NG, 12 Dec. 1891 (CUL Add. 7028, 76).

10. WG-EWG, 8 Jan. 1891(CUL Adv.c.82.5,1).

11. EWG-NG, Wednesday [=23 Aug. 1893] and 24 Aug. 1893 (CUL Add. 7022, 79-80).

12. 'Notes on Pedigrees [Gosse family]', Freeman & Wertheimer-PHG, 130 and 131fn.11.

13. TG married Emma on 7 July 1840 in Wimborne, and the couple had three children (CUL Add. 7041, 63-4): Philip Henry Gosse [Jr.] (1842-5); Thomas Gosse (1843-4); and Elizabeth Emma Gosse (b. 1845).

14. TG married Fanny on 14 Dec. 1869 (Bath Chronicle, 16 Dec. 1869, 5). TG had more than 17 children, in total. Besides those he had with Emma Budden, William Gosse noted in his Diary (under 13 Aug. 1857): '... "Tom Gosse" was reported to be the father of Mrs. T. Jelly's child some time ago'.

15. Gosse, *The Gosses: An Anglo-Australian Family*, 'The Gosse Family' genealogy is at the back of the book, and p. 63.

16. 'Treburget United Silver and Lead Mines', *Bath Chronicle* (27 May 1852), 2 (TG was the secretary for the mines' company).

discovery of gold was a fraud which had 'no other object in view than that of filling' the pockets of the promoters.[17] Many lost their investments, including (as we have seen) Philip and Emily. William also interpreted a *Bath Chronicle* death announcement which connected Emily Gosse to Thomas as an effort 'to associate his own name which has been a public stench for years, with a spotless and distinguish'd name like Henry's.'[18]

Nonetheless, William did communicate with Thomas—though only 'by [their] Mother's request.'[19] William's dislike for his brother was long-lasting;[20] Philip proved long-suffering.[21] When Thomas, then father to eleven children, fell into uncontrollable debt in 1880, he appealed to Philip for financial assistance. 'God is trying you heavily,' Philip responded.[22] He agreed to give him £10 quarterly.[23] The funds were preceded by Philip's 'plain stern words' which 'I am grieved to find ... have failed.'[24]

In 1890, two years after the death of his wife Fanny,[25] eight of their children moved to New Zealand.[26] Thomas (who remained behind) died at the age of 81 in 1898 in Bath.[27] In 1927, a Scots Presbyterian minister in Wellington, New Zealand, contacted Edmund to request that he provide financial aid to his struggling cousins. Edmund made no attempt to hide his singular lack of interest in doing so.[28]

17. For the accusation, William Gosse, Diary (under 14 February 1857); the activities of the 'Bath shareholder' were reported in *The Mining Journal* xxiv (2 Sept. 1854), 587.

18. William Gosse, Diary (under 14 February 1857). The announcement appeared in the *Bath Chronicle* (12 Feb. 1857, 4): 'DEATHS. ... Feb. 10, Emily, the wife of P. H. Gosse, Esq., F.R.S., of London, the brother of Mr. Thos. Gosse, of this city.'

19. William Gosse, Diary (under 30 Sept. 1857).

20. 'Why has he [William] such an antagonism to my uncle Tom, if the question be a discreet one?' (EWG-PHG, 15 Jan. 1872, CUL Add. 7018,48).

21. PHG dedicated his *Introduction to Zoology* (1844, I: iii) 'To my brother, Thomas Gosse ... my early companion in zoological pursuits ... in testimony of an affection, which the lapse of years serves but to strengthen and increase'. PHG's Corr. Bk. lists many letters between him and his brothers between 1869-88. The last page of the book, covering 4 Mar. -8 May 1888, registers communications to and from William (including a letter to William on 23 Apr., a day before William's eightieth birthday); one on 1 Mar. to 'Fanny Gosse' (Thomas' second wife) and a response, 17 Mar.; and one from 'Gosse (Bath', on 2 Apr., which was never answered.

22. PHG-TG, 23 July 1880 (CUL Add. 7313,162).

23. PHG-TG, 3 Dec. 1881 (CUL Add. 7313,450).

24. PHG-TG, 8 Oct. 1880 (CUL Add. 7313,200).

25. Fanny Gosse died on 10 July 1888 in Bath (*Bath Chronicle*, 12 July 1888, 5).

26. Gosse, *The Gosses: An Anglo-Australian Family*, 'The Gosse Family' genealogy.

27. Thomas Gosse died on 8 Feb. 1898 ('Births, Marriages, and Deaths', *Bristol Mercury*, 11 Feb. 1898, 8); 'Death of Mr. Thomas Gosse', *Bath Chronicle*, 17 Feb. 1898, 5; 'Bath Chess Club', *Bath Chronicle*, 7 Apr. 1898, 2; 'The Bath Chronicle Index', *Bath Chronicle*, 29 Dec. 1898, 6.

28. Revd J. Gilson Smith-EWG, 12 Dec. 1927 (CUL Add.7032,17), and the reply, EWG-J. Gilson Smith, 22 Jan. 1928 (CUL Add. 7032,21a-b).

Eliza lived to 87 and never remarried. Many years earlier, Philip had called her 'a true yoke-fellow,—in love, in spirit, and in service'[29] who was 'in no sense unfit to pair with my sainted Emily.'[30] After Philip's passing, Eliza believed that Thomas Finch, a doctor and neighbour who had also cared for her husband, had his eye on her. 'But I really could not think of such a thing,' she told Edmund. 'After your Father, any one would seem such a descent!'[31] During an 1890 trip to Sandhurst as Edmund was working on a full-length biography of his father, he consulted with Eliza about its contents. That was a mistake: 'But oh! what a time I have been having of it,—not unfriendly at all, you understand, but dense, suspicious, blunt, confusing & confused. Each sentence misunderstood, a thousand irrelevant questions asked about each turn of the Biography,—!! Well, well! I am alive,—just alive.'[32]

Five years after Philip's death, Edmund remarked that she was 'in marvellous health & spirits, I think I never saw her better ... Wonderful woman, Mother! Up & at breakfast at 8, trotting about all the morning.'[33] A few years later, he gossiped to his son: 'Have you heard that Grandmamma Gosse took in a missionary at Sandhurst last week, & he had a fit and died there? Very upsetting to Grandmama [sic].'[34]

Edmund was in Paris before, and perhaps at, the time of her death in 1900, after a few hours' illness.[35] Nellie was with her during her final days. From an estate of over £21,000, Eliza bequeathed £50 to be distributed 'among the poor or for the benefit of the Brethren's meeting at St. Mary Church or persons attending the same.'[36]

---

29. PHG-W. E. Jellicoe, 5 Apr. 1881 (CUL Add. 7313,332).

30. PHG-George Pearse, 19 June 1881 (CUL Add. 7313, 381).

31. For Eliza's conjecture: EWG-NG, [13 Dec. 1893] (CUL Add.7022, 37); for Finch's death: EWG-NG, 30 Apr. 1895 (CUL Add. 7023,6), and for his photo: CUL Adv.c.82.5,69.

32. EWG-NG, [16 July 1890] (CUL Add. 7021, 129). *Life* was completed the next month ('Mr. Edmund Gosse has completed his life of his father ... and it will be published early in the autumn', in 'Literary and Other Notes', London *Times*, 22 Aug. 1890, 3).

33. Letters EWG-NG, 14 Mar. 1895 (CUL Add.7022,106-7).

34. EWG-Philip Henry George Gosse, 5 Aug. 1896 (CUL Add. 7029, 21). EWG does not cite the individual's name, but it was Albert R. Fenn (1832-1896), a Madrid missionary who died at Marychurch on 3 Aug. ('Falling Asleep of Mr. Fenn', *Echoes of Service* no. 364 (Aug. 1896), 244). PHG had corresponded with him at least in the 1870s-80s.

35. Eliza Gosse died 14 Oct. 1900: London *Times* (16 Oct. 1900), 1; 'Wills and Bequests', London *Morning Post*, 16 Nov. 1900, 2 and London *Daily News*, 17 Nov. 1900, 9. Nellie was with her the month before she died (EWG-NG, 5 Sept. 1900, CUL Add. 7029,60); EWG was in Paris a week before her death (EWG-NG, 8 Oct. 1900, CUL Add.7023,118).

36. Probate of Will of Eliza Gosse, granted 13 Nov. 1900 (Public Record Office, Somerset House, London). The language in 'Wills and Bequests', London *Morning Post*, 16 Nov. 1900,

Nellie, who early in life had studied art, was married to Edmund for over fifty-three years. She died in London following a long period of ill-health in 1929, aged 80.[37]

In spite of the spiritual estrangement with his father, which left a scar of guilt feelings on the son, Edmund had emerged as his own man by the time of his father's death. He had changed his (literary) name by dropping his 'W.' middle initial;[38] he was the author of over sixteen books and pamphlets, thirty contributions to serials (some of which appeared in American editions), introductions to over thirty scholarly studies and over a dozen biographical entries in reference works[39]—he had, in other words, learned the secret of 'Making a Name in Literature.'[40] He lectured in America to a triumphant reception;[41] though never having attended a university, he manoeuvred to succeed Leslie Stephen as the second Clark Lecturer in English literature at Trinity College, Cambridge.[42] He had weathered a withering attack on his scholarship by Churton Collins.[43] With hard work and determination, Edmund gradually interpreted his past to his satisfaction.

In interviews he gave during much of his life and in articles and books which he wrote, he frequently recalled his upbringing while promoting his father's scientific record of achievement.[44] The father who glowed in the son's memory was *The Naturalist of the Sea-shore*.[45] The one who spoiled it all was the minister of the Word who, in unwisely trying to compel belief, had only produced unbelief.[46] Edmund, when 58, summed

---

2, is slightly different.

37. Nellie Gosse died on 29 August 1929: 'Lady Gosse', *Manchester Guardian*, 31 Aug. 1929, 7; Ellen C. Clayton, *English Female Artists* (London: Tinsley Brothers, 1876), II: 94-5.

38. New York *Critic* n.s. II (20 Sept. 1884), 138.

39. 'An Edmund Gosse Bibliography', Boston *Literary World*, 172-3.

40. Edmund Gosse, 'Making a Name in Literature', New York *Forum* VIII (Oct. 1889), 189-198 (repr. in EWG, *Questions at Issue* (London: William Heinemann, 1893), 115-133).

41. Peters and Halliburton (eds.), *Edmund Gosse, America. The Diary of a Visit, Winter 1884-1885, op. cit.*

42. Clark Lectureship announced: *The Athenaeum*, 10 Mar. 1883, 315; competition for the Clark Lectureship, 7 Apr. 1883, 444; EWG appointed to succeed L. Stephen, 17 May 1884, 633; EWG begins lectures, 18 Oct. 1884, 497.

43. Phyllis Grosskurth, 'Churton Collins: Scourge of the Late Victorians', *University of Toronto Quarterly* 34 (Apr. 1965), 254-68; D. Wertheimer, 'A Son and His Father', 2-3.

44. This is analysed in D. Wertheimer, 'A Son and His Father', 5-6.

45. The title of EWG's 1890 biography of his father was *The Life of Philip Henry Gosse F.R.S.*, changed in 1896 when the work was re-issued to *The Naturalist of the Sea-shore: The Life of Philip Henry Gosse*.

46. This is the meaning of the epigraph to *Father and Son*, and at least formally to the entire work. The epigraph (which appeared in all printings of *Father and Son* during EWG's lifetime) is

up his view of the relationship this way: '[W]hat a charming companion, what a delightful friend, my Father would have been, and would pre-eminently have been to me, if it had not been for this stringent piety which ruined it all.'[47]

No minute memorial of Philip's last days, in the style of his heart-wrenching tribute to Emily, was ever compiled. Yet Edmund was not negligent in shaping his father's reputation for posterity. Within a week of Philip's passing he had written and placed a 1,300-word obituary in *The Athenaeum*.[48] Others appeared in the equally prestigious literary weeklies *The Academy* and *Saturday Review*, written by acquaintances of Edmund's. He was interviewed by at least one publication, and watched the newspapers for other obituaries.[49] Then a big break: the 'Dictionary of National Biography ... has now just reached G,' he wrote Eliza. The editor, Leslie Stephen, whom he had known for some fifteen years, had

---

an untranslated aphorism in German by the philosopher Arthur Schopenhauer (1788-1860): 'Der Glaube ist wie die Liebe: er lässt sich nicht erzwingen'. The phrase is from Schopenhauer's last work, *Parerga und Paralipomena: Kleine Philosophische Schriften von Arthur Schopenhauer* (Leipzig: Haffman's Verlag, [1851], 1988), II: 345). In R. J. Hollingdale's translation, the entire sentence reads: 'Belief is like love: it cannot be compelled; and as any attempt to compel love produces hate, so it is the attempt to compel belief which first produces real unbelief' (Hollingdale (trans. and ed.), *A. Schopenhauer. Essays and Aphorisms* (Middlesex, England: Penguin Books, 1970), 197).

With one exception, when the work appeared no reviewer of *Father and Son* explicitly took note of the aphorism, even though it is indirectly alluded to in *Father and Son*. The reviewer in the London *Christian World* (14 Nov. 1907), Supplement, 22, noted that *Father and Son* 'is above all things a warning of how not to teach religion to children. Its lesson cannot be better put than in the words of Schopenhauer, which the author has chosen as its motto' (where the aphorism is translated: 'Faith is like love; it cannot be forced'). In Cecil Ballantine's edition of *Father and Son*, it is translated as 'Belief is like love; it cannot be commanded' (Ballantine (ed.), *Father and Son*. London: Heinemann, 1970, xvii).

47. *Father and Son*, 1907, Epilogue, 366.

48. EWG-NG, 31 Aug. 1888 (CUL Add. 7021,83); [EWG], 'Mr. Philip Henry Gosse, F.R.S.', *Athenaeum* (1 Sept. 1888), 294-5 (I am grateful to Marion Fleischer, of the London *New Statesman*, for confirmation of EWG's authorship). In 1871, EWG was on the regular staff of *The Athenaeum* (CUL Add. 7041,47).

49. Though EWG stated the fact, it is not known which publication(s) interviewed him. Many of the early obituary notices contained similar information: 'Death of Mr. Philip Henry Gosse, F.R.S., of St. Marychurch', *Torquay Directory*, 29 Aug. 1888, 5; *The Academy* 34 (1 Sept. 1888), 140-1 (EWG thought the author was James Sutherland Cotton, CUL Add. 7021, 83); [Middleton-Wake], *Saturday Review* 66 (1 Sept. 1888), 263-4; 'The Late Mr. P. H. Gosse, F.R.S.', *Illustrated London News* 93 (1 Sept. 1888), 279; 'Death of Mr. P. H. Gosse, F.R.S., of St. Marychurch', *Torquay Times*, 13 Sept. 1888, 6; [R. C. Morgan], 'Mr. Philip Henry Gosse, F.R.S.', *The Christian*, 21 Sept. 1888), 1.

asked him to write the entries for both his father and mother in that monumental work.[50]

In 1890, Edmund published a nearly 400-page biography of his father, followed by a work of equal length in 1907 about his own first two decades growing up. In writing of his early years, Edmund may have given expression to what he felt was the truth of a lived experience. The death of his mother when he was 7-years old may have been traumatizing, he may have felt trapped by the way in which he was raised and the expectations placed on him, and he may have been crushed by a father who loved him too much, worried about him too much (in a phrase popular in the United States today, he was a 'helicopter parent'), and was afraid to allow him the space he needed to grow.[51]

Edmund Gosse's response was to handle these issues as he did others during his career as a man of letters. One characterization was that he was 'charmingly inaccurate' in his writings, 'but, if he slips, they are not serious ones.'[52] Not true and not true. The stories he told about his father, and growing up in his parents' home, were neither the former nor the latter. Recognizing that we 'cannot change the past,' Edmund exercised 'the power of reframing' to change the way he *thought about* the past, thus freeing himself to create a future of his own design.[53] He claimed in *Father and Son* that the way he did it was scrupulously accurate. He said that his 'record' could have 'no value that is not based on its rigorous adhesion to truth', and that 'none ... have challenged the general accuracy of the record'. With certitude we now know that many events did not occur as described.[54]

Months after the appearance of *Father and Son*, Edmund emphasized in an interview his conviction that faith, 'in its old and strict sense, has almost died out.' Yet he saw a role for religion and God. In the future, the former 'will deal more with man than with God.' And as for the latter, 'no sane man denies the existence of God. ... Man can form no conception of

---

50. EWG-NG, 31 Aug. 1888 (CUL Add. 7021, 83).

51. A reviewer of *Father and Son* expressed this thought as PHG's 'congenital incapacity to see things from another's point of view' (London *Daily Telegraph*, 25 Dec. 1907, 12).

52. 'Edmund Gosse', *Washington Post* (18 May 1928), 6.

53. The kernel of this thought is contained in a different context in Jonathan Sacks, *Studies in Spirituality*, 53.

54. Wertheimer, 'Son and Father', 47, 70.

the solemnity of life, of its complexity and mystery, without admitting that there must be a central guiding and moral intelligence.'[55]

In a hitherto overlooked way, Edmund added an exclamation point to his escape from his father and his upbringing. In 1916, when Edmund was 66, he jotted down this note to his heirs: he wanted his body to be cremated at Golders Green, Hampstead, in London, 'if it should be perfectly convenient.'[56] His biographers do not mention the request. It lacks an explanation, and none is known with certainty. But it is of no small interest, because it represents the ultimate act affirming Edmund's rejection of the faith in which he had been raised.

At the time Edmund wrote of cremation, the movement in England to incinerate the human corpse rather than bury it was just over four decades old.[57] Up until then, even the most convinced atheist—someone like Austin Holyoake, for example, who died in 1874—was still buried.[58] The number of cremations had been steadily increasing in the United Kingdom, with forty per cent of those in 1906 taking place at the twelve-acre Golders Green site.[59]

For a number of Edmund's friends, cremation was a viable option. Literary figures Henry James (1843-1916) and Thomas Hardy (1840-

55. R[obert]. C[olville]., '"*Father and Son.*" An Interview with Mr. Edmund Gosse, LL.D.', 9-10.

56. EWG's note is dated 30 Apr. 1916 (CUL Add.7032, 48). The writer Henry James, whose funeral EWG attended on 3 March 1916, was also cremated at Golders Green ('Funeral of Mr. Henry James', London *Times*, 4 March 1916, 9). The Golders Green crematorium was opened in 1902 (Lisa Kazmier, 'Leading the World: The Role of Britain and the First World War in Promoting the 'Modern Cremation' Movement,' *Journal of Social History* 42, Spring 2009, 563).

57. Lisa Ann Kazmier, 'A Modern Landscape: The British Way of Death in the Age of Cremation' (Rutgers University, PhD dissertation, 2005), 71.

58. 'An Atheist's Funeral [Austin Holyoake]', in Davies, *Heterodox London* II: 397-408 and Austin Holyoake, 'A Burial Service', 180-185. Holyoake, the brother of G. J. Holyoake and the life-long friend of Charles Bradlaugh (McCabe, *Biographical Dictionary of Modern Rationalists*, col. 357), was buried in Highgate Cemetery.

59. J. C. S[winburne].-H[anham]., 'Cremation', *Encyclopaedia Britannica* VII (New York: Encyclopaedia Britannica Co., 11th ed., 1910), 406-7.

1928) pursued that path,[60] as did zoologist Ray Lankester (1847-1929).[61] Others, inaugurating a 'New Dispensation,' affirmed that cremation would 'make the world understand that the body will not rise again in the flesh, but in the spirit.'[62] Traditional Christian believers were aghast.[63] The first three of the five time-honoured words of consolation pointing to immortality—'Not lost, but gone before'—had been struck out, leaving only the pathetic 'Gone before.'[64] To the 'unregenerate world,' said P. H. Gosse, the grave is 'dark indeed; through which not a gleam of light penetrates.'[65] Those who inhabit that world face an 'awful Future' as they plunge towards 'midnight darkness.'[66] But to those who (like Edmund's mother Emily) looked to a bodily resurrection, the future is bright when one's 'dust ... awaits ... the morning of the FIRST RESURRECTION.'[67]

Edmund William Gosse died on 16 May 1928, aged 78,[68] not long after an operation in a West End nursing home in London.[69] A two-page leaflet, with hymns,[70] was prepared for the funeral service, which took

60. For James: EWG, 'Henry James', in EWG, *Aspects and Impressions*, 53; for Hardy: Michael Millgate, *Thomas Hardy: A Biography* (New York: Random House, 1982), 575. In a high-profile instance, the remains of the poet Percy Bysshe Shelley were cremated in 1822 (Kazmier, 'A Modern Landscape', 54, 83, 88); G. H. Reade, 'The Protestant Burial Ground at Rome', *Great Thoughts from Master Minds* ser. 6, III (5 Oct. 1907), 21. Before the cremation movement gained momentum, a bold objector to religious rites like the Pre-Raphaelite poet Philip Bourke Marston (1850-1887) chose to be buried 'in unconsecrated ground at Highgate, and without religious service': 'Marston (Philip Bourke)', in Wheeler, *Biographical Dictionary of Freethinkers*, 219.

61. Lester, *E. Ray Lankester*, 215.

62. This was one of the objects of the British National Association of Spiritualists (cited in Davies, *Heterodox London* II: 34).

63. Lisa Kazmier, 'Leading the World', 558.

64. 'Probably no such speaking symbol of the difference between the two systems could be instanced as the negative one of the quiet elimination from thought and speech of the words 'Not lost" (Davies, *Heterodox London* II: 398-9).

65. PHG, *The Mysteries of God*, 73.

66. PHG-EWG, 21 Jan. 1870 (CUL Add. 7041,30).

67. A photograph of EG's tombstone, on which these words were incised, is in Boyd, *Emily Gosse*, 62.

68. At one time, EWG had made these calculations on a slip of paper:
 'April 1 1810 - August 23 1888 = 78 + 3 months.
 I shall be the same age if I live until Feb. 23.1928.'
And on the line below, in the holograph of P.H.G. Gosse (EWG's son), was added:
 'My father: who wrote this: died on May.16.1928 at the age of 78 + 5 months + 25 days.'
 (undated note, in EWG's holograph, CUL Adv. c. 82.5, 81).
EWG erred in giving his father's birth date, which should have been 6 April, and he miscalculated the time lived, which should have been 78 years, 4 months, 17 days (*Life*, 323).

69. 'Our London Letter', *Devon and Exeter Gazette*, 18 May 1928, 16; London *Times*, 17 May 1928, 20.

70. The funeral service leaflet is at LeBL (D-2 FUN, Box 3).

place at noon on Monday, 21 May at St. Marylebone Parish Church. It marked the end of a family journey which had commenced in 1798 when his maternal grandparents were married at that church, and continued in 1807 with his mother's baptism there.[71]

Now 209 people gathered for Sir Edmund: men and women of literary attainment and from the world of print, members of the order of chivalry, politicians, officials from Scandinavian countries and France, and university representatives—a slice of the elite of British society.[72] So 'large and distinguished' was the 'congregation' that *The Times* listed every single person by name and distinction.[73] Gosse's body was then taken to Golders Green, where it was cremated.[74]

The memorial headstone at the East Finchley Cemetery and Crematorium in London is inscribed: 'Edmund Gosse, C.B., Kt., Poet— Critic ... Son of Philip Henry Gosse, F.R.S. & Emily Bowes'. He left an estate of nearly £50,000.[75]

-II-

Obituaries and appreciations of P. H. Gosse published in England, the United States, Canada, Germany, and Australia recorded his devotion to the study of natural history stretching over half-a-century, from the earliest days of Queen Victoria's reign to near its closing years. Some notices added: he was a *Christian* naturalist.

Gosse was fortunate in this way: he was perfectly suited for the career which developed unexpectedly in Newfoundland when he was 22. It was there, in the outdoors, where he determined on his own to become a man of science; it was in London, a decade later, among museum staff who became friends that he gained encouragement for this work. It was a courageous, boldly independent move on the part of one who, though lacking in formal educational background and social status, or organizational, university or governmental support, hewed a remarkably

71. Boyd, *Emily Gosse*, 25fn.5.

72. 'Sir Edmund Gosse', *Manchester Guardian*, 22 May 1928, 12.

73. London *Times,* 22 May 1928, 19. Newspaper listings of distinguished funeral attendees were not then uncommon.

74. On the funeral and cremation: 'Sir Edmund Gosse's Funeral', Dundee, Scotland *Evening Telegraph,* 22 May 1928, 2; 'The Late Sir Edmund Gosse', *Manchester Guardian,* 19 May 1928, 10.

75. Probate of Will of EWG, granted 24 July 1928 (Public Record Office, Somerset House, London). *The Times* obituary, 17 May 1928, 20, was likewise headed: 'Sir Edmund Gosse. Poet and Critic'.

innovative path. Seven decades after his death, one writer summed up the result: 'generations of naturalists have followed in this great pioneer's footsteps and even to-day find inspiration in his writings.'[76]

And he was privileged in this way: he remained firm in the faith discovered by him as a 'convert of the revival'[77] at Carbonear, Newfoundland in 1832 in the company of clerks who shared his rebirth. That faith infused his life with meaning and was later reformulated and energized in London amongst Brethren. Some of those Brethren tracked him across the world; a number of them, and those from 1832, never left him.

With his journey completed, we are drawn back to the 13-year-old boy at a boarding-school in Blandford, near Poole in Dorset, listening to him as he was setting off on his travels. Philip Henry Gosse's wish in 1823:

> ... that when Death approaches, I may leave this world with faith, and a full hope of a glorious immortality![78]

There is no reason to doubt that this is what he did.

76. [W. J. Rees], *Times Literary Supplement*, 30 Sept. 1955, 580 (the author was identified for me *in. litt.*, 18 Feb. 1972, by Arthur Crook, then Editor of the *TLS*).

77. Smith, *History of the Methodist Church* II: 173.

78. PHG, 'On Virtue', in 'Themes or Pieces of Juvenile Composition, by P. H. Gosse, at Blandford. From Jan.y 1823, to Xmas, 1823' (LeBL).

APPENDIX

[1877]

'Fairy: A Recollection'

An Unpublished Manuscript[1]

P. H. GOSSE WAS A GIFTED LITERARY STYLIST. He knew what he wanted to say and had the vocabulary at hand to say it, expressing himself in a clear and precise manner. He wrote effortlessly, judging from his manuscripts and correspondence, so that revisions or corrections virtually never appear in his handwritten pages.[2] Gosse's writings convey a warm, caring, and emotional side to his personality, even when he mixed observations in minute and excruciating detail with loving reflections. It is for these reasons that Gosse was able to publish so much good material over the decades, for which he received from readers and reviewers an exceptionally consistent amount of positive feedback.

One finds these literary features in this memoir, which Gosse wrote upon the death of his nearly 6-year-old pet cat, Fairy (1871-1877). Notwithstanding obvious differences, this work recalls the author's *Memorial of the Last Days on Earth of Emily Gosse*, written two decades earlier, about the life and traumatic, painful death of his first wife. The

1. This formally undated MS consists of 46 pages, each page being composed of a 9" x 7" sheet of paper, folded in half, and written on one side (so that each page is 7" x 4-1/2", written lengthwise). The pages are folded into four 'signatures', each having 6 single folded sheets. It was donated to the Cambridge University Library by Dr Philip H. G. Gosse, the author's grandson, on 8 Nov. 1951 (Add. 7325). Jennifer S. Gosse, Dr Gosse's daughter, has kindly granted permission to publish this manuscript here. It was previously transcribed in D.L. Wertheimer, 'Philip Henry Gosse', 527-47, and is annotated here for the first time.

2. EWG wrote similarly of his father's diaries (*Life*, 168-9).

former, though published, was not intended as a conventional biography but 'for the stirring up of the faith and love of those who knew her not, and thus to the extension of his own glory.'[3] The latter, which remained unpublished and is here annotated for the first time, had a more cathartic purpose in mourning the loss of a domestic animal. Gosse here recalls Fairy's habits, the ways in which she brightened his life, and some musings about animals.

All of his life Gosse enjoyed studying vertebrates and invertebrates and observing their habits.[4] He had a fondness for cats, in contrast to some naturalists—the Frenchmen Buffon and Toussenel are examples— who disapproved of their character, appeared obsessed with their sexual habits, and despised them.[5] Gosse had cats in his household since at least his mid-30s, when he lived in Jamaica.[6]

Gosse occasionally mentioned his cats in correspondence with his son between 1872-7, including telling Edmund of Fairy's death. 'My sweet little confiding Cat Fairy died in child-birth six weeks ago,' Philip said:

> I had procured, since, two kittens, of which one, the prettiest + meekest, has now died, leaving a most rampageous impudent romping little hoyden; which we call Bruin, for she has 6 toes + perfect talons on each of her two fore + one hind foot; her feet thus furnished are wondrously splay + bear-like. I was inclined to call her Ishbi-benob, or Ben-rapha;[7] only that these names would have been rather harsh to call a pussy by.[8]

Philip and Eliza Gosse continued to have cats at Sandhurst after Fairy, but none is known to have matched her personality. 'The cursing cat and her idiot son are grown to an enormous size,' Edmund said about different cats during a visit there, 'and still, after all these years, they swear at one another, as strangers, when they first meet in the morning.'[9]

A fondness for cats was a feature of other Gosse households. Edmund

3. PHG, *Memorial*, [iii].
4. PHG described general characteristics of cats in his *Life in its Lower, Intermediate, and Higher Forms*, 1857, 341-5.
5. Kete, *The Beast in the Boudoir*, 117-21.
6. A cat and its offspring lived with PHG at Bluefields, Jamaica ('Jamaica Journal' 16 Apr. 1845).
7. Ishbi-benob was a descendant (Hebrew, *ben*) of the giant Rapha (Deut. 2: 11) who wanted to kill King David (2 Sam. 21: 15).
8. PHG-EWG, 11 June 1877 (CUL Add. 7018,22; excerpts from this letter appear in *Life*, 312).
9. EWG-NG, 7 Apr. 1883 (CUL 7020, 7).

loved cats.[10] Before he was married, he kept a 'great white cat' which greeted him when he awoke at 7 a.m. 'He jumps on the bed to caress me, and that wakes me,' he told his father. 'I play with him for a few seconds, & then I get up and go down into the back-kitchen to have my tub. ... breakfast is ready at 7.30. We, the cat & I, go into my sitting-room, & the cat being settled in the corner on his rug, I eat my breakfast.'[11] Gosse grandchildren Philip Henry George (1879-1959) and Sylvia (1881-1968) shared those sympathies.[12]

If there is truth in the assertion that for Victorians animals were 'mass commodities and living souvenirs at a particularly significant moment in the development of consumer society,' Gosse does not exemplify it. Nor does 'Fairy' confirm the claim that for Victorians, even when pets 'were objects of emotional attention, animals could be objects of affection and cruelty in equal measure.'[13] 'Fairy' recalls the life of a beloved family pet.

The following text has been transcribed by me and all notations are mine, unless otherwise indicated.

10. Lawrence Alma Tadema, 'An Early Portrait of Edmund Gosse', *Cornhill Magazine* n.s. 67 (Dec. 1929), 755. EWG's essay on 'Cats', *Selected Essays (Second Series)* (London: William Heinemann Ltd., 1928), 177-183, is a review of a book on cats.

11. EWG-PHG, 21 Sept. 1872 (CUL Add. 7018,49).

12. Kathleen Fisher, *Conversations with Sylvia. [Laura] Sylvia Gosse, Painter, 1881-1968*, edited by Eileen V. Smith (London: Charles Skilton, 1975), 44, 96.

13. Both quotations are from Sarah Amato, 'Curiosity Killed the Cat: Animals in Nineteenth-Century British Culture' (University of Toronto, PhD dissertation, 2008), 7-8.

Fairy.

———————

APRIL 18TH 1877. This has been a day full of sorrow: my little pet Cat Fairy is dead.

She has been pregnant for about two months, & has been of late very heavy & drowsy, sleeping most of the day on the sofa. Yesterday morning she seemed so uneasy during her usual visit to us in bed, that I had carried her down in my arms even before I was quite dressed, & put her into her kennel. Here she soon gave birth to a kitten, & during breakfast we saw her licking the new-born. I thought I could glimpse another, at least; but the entrance was narrow, so that I could not be sure, and I did not choose to disturb her.

She would not notice food all day; nor did she leave the kennel so far as we saw; and being on the verandah, just outside the din[in]g room window,—our sitting-room, she was under our eyes.

On my coming down this morning (18th) I found she was not in her kennel, where one kitten only was sprawling,—white with a few black spots,—and presently I discovered her, in the midst of the N.E. border, crouched belly to earth, which she had slightly scooped away to receive her body. She was inert, made no response when I spoke to her, and scarcely moved as I tenderly stroked her. Something was wrong, evidently: she had more young, & could not bring them forth. Her vulva was dropping dark blood. I gently lifted her, & carried her to her kennel, the roof of which was hinged, so that I could lay her into it. The kitten began to root at her teats, but she took no notice, save that she pushed it away with her hind foot, once, when it hurt her.

By and by I saw her similarly crouched on the earth of another border; & now, thinking that possibly instinct might teach her that the fresh earth had some medicinal influence, I let her alone. But my heart was full of sorrowing pity, & of sad regret that I could afford her no help.

Before noon, she had moved again, & was on the farther side of the Cypress tree. Here, as I approached her, she just lifted her head, & made, or rather attempted to make, her usual little note of recognition, but it was a horrid, unearthly croak. Presently, as she slightly moved, I saw that there was something protruding, which seemed a kitten, but motionless and bloody. I at once thought that here might be a possibility of aid:

calling Chudley[14] to me, I laid her on her side, quite unresisting and passive; and, while he gently held her head, I managed to take hold of the protruding muzzle of the kitten with my thumb & fingernails; then, steadily pulling, I gradually got the head through, after which the body came with no difficulty. It was quite dead, & the hind parts were already putrescent.

The dear little Fairy once uttered a slight moan, as I was pulling, but did not appear to suffer much from the operation. Indeed all day she was evidently in a torpid comatose state; and this was a comfort, that she seemed to have no agony; only we could not tell what she had suffered during the night. And we knew she could have no anticipations, no mental anxieties.

When the second kitten was thus ejected, I left her under the Cypress, hoping that she now might rally,—if indeed there were no more within; but if there were, we knew that death was inevitable, for she had manifestly no strength for parturition. Her head gradually sank forward, till her little face rested on the earth, & thus she remained without moving for an hour or two more. I look on her occasionally; and, at length, as it seemed that the damp ground, & the very chill air must be inimical to her, I bade Chudley drown the poor starving kitten, for whom there was no hope; and, having laid a softer bed of dry moss in the kennel, I carried it down to Fairy. Then I very gently & carefully laid her in it, & replaced it in the verandah, she quite passive as before. Henceforth she scarcely stirred her position, and I no more disturbed her, till about 6 p.m., when by the coldness of her body, the incipient stiffening of her limbs, & the glazing of her eyes, I saw, with an intense sorrow, that my dear little pet was past hers.

We did not move her that night; but the next morning (19th) I opened the abdomen, & found a third kitten in the uterus, dead of course, but not putrid, & not yet approaching the vulva. Then I saw, not without satisfaction, that no help, no care, on our part, could possibly have averted the end. Chudley immediately dug a hole at the bottom of the garden, in which I laid her, & covered her; &, having restrained my emotions before my servant, I came into the parlour & wept.

Her little grave may be thus identified. A line from the S.W. wall (a), 3 ft. 6 in. long, and a line from the S.E. wall (b) 12 inches long, at right

14. James Chudley was PHG's gardener.

angles, would meet in a point just over the centre of the grave. She lies just under the spot where she had so often sat, on the top of the wall, to watch for my return from my walks.[15]

The sorrow which the death,—so sudden & unexpected, of this little animal has produced in me is something that I could not have anticipated: it surprises me as I feel it; it is rather that which one feels on the loss of a loved human relative than for a mere brute creature. At every thought of her sweet little face, her pretty confiding ways, her eloquent affection for us, my tears burst out afresh, and I cannot control my grief, unseemly as it appears. It is however a comfort that no human eye beholds it, except my Eliza's, and she sympathizes with it, &, in a measure, partakes it.[16]

The dear little thing, though already petted & loved, entwined herself strongly around my heart by her behaviour when we returned from our visit to Cornwall last summer, as I have recorded in my Diary under date of 23rd Aug. 1876. Chudley told me that during our week's absence she had moped about the garden, dull & silent, not associating with the other Cats, of which we then had two, Chinchy and Beauty. But as soon as she saw me, she could scarcely contain her joy: her rubbings, & rollings, and mewings in a very peculiar tone, now & then mingled with those little inward crooning sounds which Cats make to their kittens, continued all the afternoon & evening; & were remarked by the servants; & these, not only when we were in sight. Immediately after that,—I think the very next day,—she began a habit which she maintained almost without a single exception to the morning before she died. She found out, quite spontaneously, the chamber where we slept; and managed to reach us. At first, she used to climb up the Wistaria to my study-window, thence making her way across the porch & orchid-house roof to the margin of the verandah, up which she would spring, at a strong & calculated leap, to our chamber-window sill. But latterly she climbed directly up the verandah-pillar, aided by the stem of the Periploca. In general, she announced her arrival on the sill, by a little mew, & then awaited the opening of the window. For a month or two past she had come earlier,

15. There is an illustration of this plan by PHG.

16. 'The chief utility of the Cat to man, is its habit of preying upon the rats and mice which infest our dwellings. A good mouser will follow up the pursuit of these pests, with a sort of *professional gusto*, quite independent of the promptings of hunger ... It is, however, very frequently kept as a pet, and loved for its own sake, though there may be no mice to be destroyed. The Cat's susceptibility of kindly affections has been much underrated' (PHG, *Natural History. Mammalia* (London: SPCK, 1848), 73-4). Emphasis in the original.

even before we were stirring; but if I was asleep her little mew was sure to awaken me, & I would jump out to let her in. She would give a few rubs of thanks, & then leap up on the bed, often before I could get in myself. When the weather was rainy, & she would come with wet paws & fur, it was necessary to wipe her with a towel; she did not like this operation; and would try to evade it if she could;—but she never resented it; & by & by seemed to know when it was necessary, & submitted with a good grace.

Of late, Eliza & I had taken her into bed, when she would cuddle on our arms,—on E's first, & then, after she considered she had been there long enough, on mine; her meek little face just visible under the bed-clothes. Here she would purr in great enjoyment, for perhaps, half-an-hour, & then push out, & lie the rest of the time on the counterpane, in some hollow among our feet or between our bodies:—quite still, but her bright eyes active, her paws tucked in, her chin resting as was her habit. While we were dressing she would remain in the room, very quiet,—always watching for a little play with my watch-chain, when I put my watch into my pocket,—till we were ready to go down to breakfast. Then she would rattle down the lower flight of stairs before our feet,[17] & impatiently expect her breakfast, taking the bits and scraps which we offered her from our fingers, & mine from the proximate elbow of my great fireside chair.

Fairy was littered May 6. 1871. In the previous summer the cat of our next neighbour, Mrs. Williams had a litter of kittens, under a bush on our side of the dividing wall of the garden: just before our first visit to Bowden-derra. Of the kittens thus thrust upon us, without our will, we agreed to adopt one; & my Eliza selected one to which from the resemblance of the grey fur marked with soft darker bars, to the fur of a Chinchilla, we gave the name of Chinchy. In the spring following she brought forth 3 kittens, of which we preserved one, which I named Fairy. She was very much like her mother in colour and markings, only that the latter were more decidedly black. A patch of black on one cheek reaching to the nose, rather marred the beauty of her face, which in Chinchy was spotless white. Yet the expression of Fairy's face was very much superior in sweetness & gentleness to her mother's; for Chinchy always wore a

17. 'It struck me as very curious & funny that your favourite white pussy comes up to greet you; for our gentle Chinchy comes up often (she did this morning) mewing at our bedroom door, to be let in to us while we are dressing, & always accompanies me, step by step, down stairs' (PHG-EWG, 24 Sept. 1872; CUL Add.7041,54).

cross, ill-tempered aspect, a correct index to her temper, which was surly & uncertain;—but Fairy, to me at least, & latterly, since her affection for me had become so decided, had a very meek & gentle face. And this also was a true indication of her disposition.

At first, when her kittenhood was past, she was not an amiable cat: she avoided her mother, & seemed to dislike companionship; & when, in the course of years other cats were born & grew up (for, we kept for several years three cats altogether on the premises), Fairy always shunned them in her prowlings about the garden; or, at least, never affected their company. She was a querulous crying cat for the first two or three years, perpetually mewing in a complaining tone. Thus she was not a general favourite: I do not know how it was that I took to her, but she gradually became my special pet; & much of her unpleasingness of manner wore away.

She was very gentle; I do not recollect her ever scratching or biting in anger; when hurt in being handled, or when teased by being held against her will, she would struggle, or mew, but never retaliate. Her claws were very sharp; & when being fed, she would rear up & grasp our hands as she took the morsel, with protruded claws: it was a pretty trait in Chinchy, that she always retracted her talons, when fed in this way, & so seized our fingers with velvet paws;[18] but Fairy never learned this courtesy. She had, too, the habit, when lying, in playful mood, on chair or sofa, if we approached her with caresses, of receiving them with manifest enjoyment, quietly; but if the hand were withdrawn, one paw with extended talons was darted like lightning after it, not spitefully, but very evidently with the desire of retaining its pleasant company. From these two causes, our hands very usually bore sundry marks of Fairy's blood-shedding; but never of her malice.

Our Cook dislikes Cats in general, & Fairy in particular; hence the latter had no tolerance in the kitchen, & very little at the back door. Thus she was dependent for a living on the bits she received from our fingers

18. 'Every child knows, who has handled the velvet paw of a Cat, in its ordinary condition, the talons are quite concealed, but that in excitement they are are forcibly thrown forward. The last joint of each toe, the tip of which is encased by the claw, is, in rest, drawn back, either upon, or at the side of, the preceding joint, by the force of two elastic ligaments. From this position it is in an instant extended, by the contraction of a muscle beneath the toe, the tendon of which passes under the head of the last joint, as under a pulley, and is attached to the base of the claws. When the contraction ceases, the claw again springs back to its place, and lies concealed in a deep fold of the skin' (PHG, *Life in its Lower, Intermediate and Higher Forms*, 1857, 341-2).

at meals,—supplemented by her own foraging at our neighbours' waste-heaps, & by her success in catching prey. She evidently took a pride in her own successful skill. She would sometimes come to the parlour-window with a peculiar mew to ask notice, & when we opened the window she would drop at our feet a mouse, or a bird, or sometimes a filthy fowl's head, or mass of garbage, which she had found on some dust-heap. Then she would rub herself on the ground, or on our shoes, meaning, very clearly, 'A'nt I a good Cat?' Nor would she begin to eat her prize till she had secured our notice & approval.

She showed no propensity to thieve in the house; we might leave her alone in the parlour with all the breakfast spread; but though hungry, she would not attempt to help herself. The only apparent exception to this honesty was, that on one or two occasions, in very cold weather, when the butter has been too hard to spread, we have put it down on a hassock before the fire, and presently we have found Fairy busy licking it. But we could not scold her, for she had manifestly thought it was put down for her special use.

Scrupulously clean, too, she was in her habits. Latterly she became so thoroughly a parlour-cat, that we would leave her lying on the sofa, alone, while we went to meeting; & never found that she had abused our confidence. Her sense of propriety was equal to our own.

For two or three summers back, she showed her love to me, thus. On my return from the usual afternoon-walk to the back gate, as I approached it from the road, I would hear her peculiar little cry; &, looking about, would presently discover my Fairy, crouched on the garden wall close by the gate, concealed among the bushes. She had certainly watched my going-out, perhaps a couple of hours before; and whether she had taken her watch-place immediately, & waited patiently till I returned, or had learned to estimate the probable time of my absence, or had distinguished, as she roamed the garden, by her acute ear, my footstep from that of the scores of other passengers, & had then jumped up to welcome me,—I cannot tell. Her pleasure at meeting me was unmistakable: she would not, in general, allow me to take her down from her post; but, as soon as I had opened the garden door, she would jump down, and running a few steps in front of my feet, would rub her face on the grass, & lie down on her side, & wallow just before my feet, & then allow me to take her up, & bring her into the house in my arms. If, however, she happened to be sitting on the verandah when I came in at the lower gate, she would gallop down the lawn with a cry of pleasure to meet me, & roll on the grass when she got to me.

Sometimes, but rarely, she was playful & roguish; would tempt me to approach her, but refuse to be caught, darting away the moment I came close, & spring-up the trunk of one of the Elms, while they existed, or, latterly, up the Cypress. At the foot of this latter tree, under its sweeping boughs, was one of her favourite places, but thence, or from any other part of the garden, she would come galloping up the lawn, when called from the parlour window.

As I have already said, it was from the end of last August & onward that our tenderest recollections of Fairy date. The other two cats, Chinchy & a male which we had called Beauty, I had reluctantly ordered to be destroyed, as they were always subjects of complaint & dislike to the gardener, and thus Fairy became our only one. Thenceforth she was a great deal more our habitual pet, inhabiting the sitting-rooms with us, particularly at meals, & through the lengthening winter-evenings. Her ordinary place was either on the hearthrug, or on the foot of the sofa.

About this time I found, accidentally, that my whistling had power of constraining her approach to me. If she was indolent, or sleepy, lying on the hearthrug, & I was reclining on the sofa, I might call 'Puss! Puss!' or 'Fairy! Fairy!' in vain; but if I whistled, not necessarily in a tune, at the first note she would spring up, & come to me. Almost immediately after I discovered this, there appeared several contributions from correspondents in 'Science Gossip,' which described*[19] the habit of sundry specified Cats, of coming to a person whistling. Most of these also mentioned that the cat would put her mouth close to the lips of the person whistling, which, too, was the custom of Fairy. After a while I noticed that she felt a sort of necessity laid upon her;— that sometimes it w[oul]d have been more agreeable to her to remain where she was, but that she was bound to come. Sometimes if asleep, at the first whistled note, she would just open her eyelids, & then close them again without stirring, as if she had not heard: but if I persevered in whistling, she

19. [PHG note:] *By reference, I find that these notes in '[*Hardwicke's*] Sci. Gossip' were all in the year 1875. As I read the magazine regularly, & as I am quite certain that I noticed the habit in Fairy, before the first of these appeared, it follows that what I have recorded above must have first occurred at least a year & a half earlier than I have above stated. [Editor's note: for the information from *Hardwicke's Science-Gossip*, see issues of 1 June, 1 Oct., 1875, pp. 142, 166, 191, 211, 213, 237].

w[oul]d presently jump suddenly up, trot across the room, put her face to mine, and instantly return to her place & position, as if an unpleasant but unavoidable duty were performed. This apparent sense of duty I frequently observed, & pointed it out to Eliza. Whenever Fairy, after mewing at the window, was admitted, she almost always made some little manifest expression of thanks, usually by coming up to one of us, & giving a little rub of her face. But occasionally she would omit this, & walk straight away to the hearth-rug. In this case I had but to say 'Fairy!' in a reproving tone, & she would, as quite recognizing her omission, come & perform the expected act of gratitude. Such things as these often caused in me deep musings. I have somewhere read the remark, 'Man is the God of the dog,'[20] and certainly, in many particulars, the interrelations of this little creature to me & of me to her, seemed to dimly shadow out those between the Almighty God & his creature Man. The vast superiority in the scale of existence, yet the kindly loving care, the watchfulness for her comfort, the provision for her supply, the response to her mute appeals, the tender affection that I felt for her, most of which she doubtless, had no comprehension of, often presented themselves to me as somewhat, however distantly, like what the Blessed God is, and exercises, towards us. While there was much in her,—of subjection, of duty, of confidence & trust, of taste for our society, or real responsive love,—much that eloquently said to me,—'thus oughtest thou to be to God!' And Isaiah i. 2, 3, seems to show that such a comparison is not irreverent.[21] And now that the dear little thing is gone, the question recurs again and again, with painful pertinacity,—'Is there any hereafter, any resurrection, any life to come, for the inferior creatures?' a question on which the written Word is intensely mute, uttering not a syllable, Yea or Nay![22] For, certainly, Eccles. iii. 21 determines nothing on this point.[23]

20. The saying is often attributed to Robert Burns (W. Lauder Lindsay, *Mind in the Lower Animals in Health and Disease* (New York: D. Appleton and Co., 1880), I: 221).

21. Isaiah 1: 2-3 (KJV): 'Hear, O heavens, and give ear, O earth: for the LORD hath spoken, I have nourished and brought up children, and they have rebelled against me.

'The ox knoweth his owner, and the ass his master's crib: but Israel doth not know, my people doth not consider.'

22. 'The beasts of the field, which, as far as we know, have no life after this, have no power to think of the future; if we [humans] were made only for the world, it is but reasonable to conclude that we also should have our thoughts and desires bounded by the present ... [but] God made man to live for ever; He has revealed this in his word' (Emily Gosse, 'The Sceptical Traveller', in PHG and EG, *Narrative Tracts*, 'Gospel Narrative Tract' no. 59. The tract was first published in 1861: Freeman & Wertheimer-EG, 57).

23. Ecclesiastes 3: 21 (KJV): 'Who knoweth the spirit of man that goeth upward, and the

She asked for drink in this way. A terra-cotta jar of water set in a shallow saucer, constantly stood on the dining-table between meals. When she was thirsty, she would leap on the table, & stand or sit looking at the jar, till I poured out a little water into the saucer for her, when she would lap it up. After waiting a few moments, if no notice were taken, she would rub her nose against the neck of the jar, but utter no sound. Whether this expectant habit had been taught her by my having at some time given her drink in this way, or whether it originated in her own shrewd observation that water was there, I cannot certainly say; I have no recollection of the former.

In the long winter evenings as we sat in our arm-chairs on either side of the fire, Fairy would occasionally sit in our laps,—preferring E.'s, as more comfortable. But she much more affected the dark & cosy hollow in the seat of the chair behind our body. Here she would luxuriate, rolling herself over on her side or back, and stretching out her limbs in great enjoyment; an enjoyment wh[ich] she proved & acknowledged by profusely licking the hand when it was put back to touch her.

This operation of licking was a favourite mode of showing her special affection. As I reclined on the sofa, she would sometimes jump on my body, spontaneously, & begin licking my fingers;—or sometimes my nose, eyes, & cheeks; or she would make her way to the head of the sofa, &, crouching there, would begin an earnest licking of the hair of my head, as if I had been her kitten, the evident affection making the operation not unpleasant to me.

I have described how she used to make her way to our chamber by climbing the Wistaria stem beneath my study-window. But she would also occasionally make the study-window her terminus, climbing up in the forenoon, on purpose to visit me, and announcing her approach not only by the rustling of the leaves, but by her gentle cry. And often I would hear the same little call, &, on getting up & looking out of the window, would see Fairy sitting on the gravel just below, looking up. Then, as soon as I had showed my face at the window, she would be satisfied, & go on her own avocations.

I feel sure that her ear, made acute by affection, could distinguish my footstep, when she could not see me, & when I had not spoken. Often, when I have been in the chief Orchid House alone, she has called to me

spirit of the beast that goeth downward to the earth?'

from the Verandah, when I feel confident she had not seen me. In all such cases she wanted nothing but recognition; a word of salutation always satisfied her.

At the beginning of October last, as she had become so wholly a parlour pet, I provided a little house for her.[24] She had hitherto slept, as we supposed, in the corners or boxes or hampers crowded in the Shed of the Stoke-hole behind the Fernery. This was warm enough, but dirty. Winter was coming-on: and I did not like the thought of her being turned out late at night, in rain or snow, to seek her distant lodging. She had, in former winters, been liable to take cold, with troublesome cough. I wished her to be more comfortably housed. So I procured a small old packing-box, and making one half of the lid to open with hinges, & shut with a hook, & cutting a square hold in one side, for a door, I gave it a coat or two of black paint to give it a decent appearance: then I tacked a bit of old carpet over the floor and walls, quilting this for softness & warmth. Thus a nice little Kennel was made, about 15 inches square, which I set beneath the verandah close to the side of the dining-room window.

A little art was necessary to induce Pussy to adopt the residence. I first put her in from above, thro' the lifted lid, but she instantly crept out through the little square door. I repeated this a few times, by which she learned the use of the door for exit, at least. Then I put a bit of meat, which she was eagerly expecting from my fingers, into the Kennel, which she immediately drew out to eat, inserting, however, only her head, & stretching out her neck to the utmost, not venturing as yet, to trust her feet within.

I began to fear I had lost my labour, & that she would not understand the suitability of my gift: but, in a few days, I was pleased to see that she crept in of her own accord, & settled herself comfortably. Henceforward all was well: the kennel was her sanctum; not only by night, but even by day, when the parlour window was shut, & was not presently opened to her. During the winter storms, when furious rains from East & south would beat-in under the verandah-roof, the wet would occasionally soak into her bed; & I w[oul]d shift its position, having first dried it. In general, she was quite ready to leave her berth, on the opening of the parlour-window; but sometimes, she was manifestly so cosy, that even

24. The kennel, as here described, was sold with other household furnishings from PHG's home after the death of Eliza Gosse in 1900 (*Sandhurst Catalogue*, item #161: 'Grate ornament, hassock, "Cat" door porter, two bordered linoleum mats, and one wool mat').

the temptation of the lifted sash, & our inviting voices, were lost upon her: she would not move, but only looked up with her soft black eyes, & lay still.

When turned out at night to go to her bed, she would never creep directly into her kennel;—but invariably, even if the night were dark and stormy, she would walk-on to the edge of the verandah, & there sit down, looking out upon the weather for five or ten minutes, before she turned back to her house.

She became pregnant in February of this year (1877). She had often had litters of kittens,[25] which were always drowned as soon as they were born, except, I think on one sole occasion, when we allowed her to rear one which we named Darky, & which we gave away subsequently. She generally selected for her nest a hollow in the centre of the great mass of Pampas-grass, very well concealed by the arching leaves. This cavity, by the repeated adoption of it for this use, by both Chinchy & Fairy, had been worn into an ample smooth commodious cavern, quite dry in all weathers. The abstraction of her new-born kittens never appeared to give her much sorrow; after an hour or two's anxiety, & a few signs of distress, she seemed to forget all, & the only apparent result was that she became more fondling and loving to us, & more exigeant of our caresses.

One of her confinements was marked by circumstances wh[ich] are well worthy of being recorded; though the occurrence illustrates rather the moral excellencies of Chinchy than of Fairy. In May, 1873, both the Cats were pregnant together:—Chinchy was brought to bed first, & we had assigned her a shallow basket on the Verandah, where she was lovingly performing the office of a mother, to two kittens, which had been spared her.[26] Just a week after, Fairy's time came. We had observed her early, restless & uneasy, evidently looking about for a suitable retreat. She had not then become so dear to us, & we had left her to provide her own accommodation.

In the forenoon Eliza & I were in the Orchid house recess, whence

25. 'Chinchy had on Saturday [18 Apr.] 4 kittens, of which one survives; *something* having happened to 3 of them' (PHG-EWG, 20 Apr. 1874, CUL Add.7041,58). Emphasis in the original.

26. In June 1873, PHG wrote EWG about Fairy and Chinchy, and may well have referenced the episode which was later related in this paragraph. In reply, Edmund commented: 'I was perfectly charmed with your little idyllic narrative of Chinchy and Fairy. How sweet it was of Chinchy to give way, & how very strange and interesting that they should converse together so distinctly. It is extremely interesting & valuable as a contribution to the evidence of the exi[s]tence of moral & rational characteristics in animals' (EWG-PHG, 9 June 1873; CUL Add. 7018,53).

we could see the whole Verandah-area. We saw Fairy wandering about; presently she approached Chinchy's basket, and anxiously peeped over the edge. To our amazement, Chinchy made some slight movement of her body, manifestly inviting Fairy to share her accomodation, which already seemed barely sufficient for herself. Fairy instantly jumped in, & Chinchy welcomed her most lovingly. The invitation & the welcome were absolutely indubitable, by both of us. [*sic*] We hastened into the house, & from the parlour-window, peering cautiously into the now crowded basket, saw Chinchy not attending to her own kittens, but performing all the duties of a midwife, in the tenderest manner, to Fairy. Thenceforth they occupied the basket in common, quite amicably; which was the more observable, because, as I have already intimated, they had not been on very good terms. All that I have stated is literally true, without the least exaggeration or colouring: it was witnessed by us both, with the utmost wonder and admiration.

In her pregnancies she had always seemed much burdened & uncomfortable as parturition drew on. But on the last occasion, perhaps because she was more under our habitual observation, her gravid condition was particularly patent. She was very unwieldy, lying at full length on her side, often; spending much of her time by day, sleeping on the sofa. Now & then Eliza used a little comb, reserved in a drawer for the purpose, to remove loose hairs of her coat; & this operation, Fairy came to enjoy greatly; stretching herself out, and closing her eyes, while it was going on.

Her agility was diminished by her gravid state; yet, as I have said, she continued to the last morning, to spring up to the verandah-roof to greet us. It is possible that these efforts themselves occasioned her death. Perhaps the muscular strain was hurtful: perhaps she loosed her hold & fell; causing the death of her unborn progeny.

Daisy and Brue.

On the death of Fairy, I began at once to look out for a kitten, to fill up the blank left by her loss. On the 17th May I obtained, for a shilling, of Charles Darcy's little son a pretty little thing about six weeks old, of the soft chinchilla pattern.

She was very meek & confiding; sought our company; could not bear being put outside the window, but w[oul]d cry, her voice now & then rising to a passionate earnestness, rearing up against the window-pane, till we let her in. She took to Fairy's vacant kennel immediately. I gave her the name of Daisy.

The first night, fearing she might roam away, I took her in the kennel into Mary's pantry, where she did well; & the next night too. But on the third night (of Sat., 19th Apr.) I left her in the kennel on the verandah. On Mary's opening the window next morning, she found a great black cat in the kennel, with Daisy, who was crying; on being disturbed, he came out, &, seizing Daisy in his mouth, rushed across the lawn, and dropped her only at the bottom of the garden, when Mary came up with him. The kitten turned up its eyes, & seemed dying; blood oozed from above & below her neck; she could walk with difficulty, trembled and staggered. She must have been fatally injured by this brute's assault, [from] which she never fully recovered.

But I had had the offer of a second kitten, from Mrs. Raven, which also I had accepted. And on the 21st of May, the second day after poor Daisy's rencontre, this one was sent to us. It was born on the 7th April/77[,] is of the same pattern, but more vividly marked, & on a browner ground, with no part white, which is a defect. Her face is eager, sharp, & fierce, highly contrasted with the gentle expression of Daisy. And her manners do not belie her countenance. Savage and tyrannic from the very first, though a very tiny mite, she began at once to assert her mastery, growling & spitting, & swearing, & striking at her gentle companion. Her feet we saw at once to be of unusual size; her legs seemed to be elevated on stout broad pedestals: they were like bears' feet; & so (and partly with allusion to her brown hue) I gave her the name, Bruin. This great development of feet I presently saw was a monstrosity. Each of the fore, & one of the hind paws, has six perfectly taloned toes,—the thumb in each being doubled. And this peculiarity, I am told, marks a breed, which is not very uncommon.

On the day of Brue's arrival, I introduced her to her companion; but the spitting and striking of the termagant so astonished & terrified the gentle Daisy that she meekly sought refuge in her kennel, keeping close most of the day, Bruin peeping & growling at her from outside; but refusing to enter, & remaining all day, utterly implacable. At night I gave a basket to each, & put them under the kitchen-stairs. But Mary found it necessary presently to separate them, taking Daisy into her Pantry.

The next morning early I turned them both on the Verandah. Brue a little more tolerant, cautiously approached, and sniffed the nose of Daisy, but growling & snarling all the time. Each in turn got possession of the kennel, to the exclusion of the other: but having left them a few minutes I found them both ensconced, lying together in peace.

D. ate meat freely from the first, but cared little for milk. B. lapped milk only, scarcely touching meat for several days.

By the 23rd both appeared to recognise the kennel as the common home, in which they coiled together. And by this evening they played together, each using her paw in mock fight;—they both pursued me on the lawn; & both pursued a cork at the end of a string. From this night they slept in the kennel on the verandah, and were no more visited by the black Tom, so far as I know.

Brue became very full of life & play; Daisy more & more inert & dull. She slept in the kennel most of the time, never responding to Brue's play, except by a languid raising of her paw, when it became annoying, but never playing herself. In the evenings, I generally took them down on the lawn, when Brue would scamper every where, refusing to be caught, leaping up the Cypress & then crawling along a horizontal bough, or jumping up the willow in the corner. Daisy would come to me, & follow me slowly, rarely breaking into a run. Gradually she became more & more feeble, & her flanks perceptibly fell-in, though she still ate her food: till the morning of June 9th, when she refused it. She could with difficulty come out of her kennel. And about 8 in the evening, I found her just dead; warm & limp, but the heart had ceased to beat. I took the tiny body into my hands, & carried it away not wishing Brue to see it. The sweet gentle face, had the same meek expression to the last.

We remarked that Bruin would not as she usually did, go into the Kennel, so long as we were up & could see; but sat about on the verandah. And I do not think that she ever went into it of her own accord afterward; during a month that I allowed it to remain there. About that time, I put her towards it, but she strenuously resisted: I lifted the lid, & put her in, but she instantly shot out through the hole, & seemed to have a horror of the place. So about the middle of July I put a large flower-pot on its side in the same spot, with a little straw in it, having removed the Kennel, at least for awhile. Into this pot Brue immediately went of her own accord, & made it her constant sleeping-place.

She had now become quite plump: she had learned her name; or, at least, came bounding to my call from any part of the garden within hearing.

She is now very fully of play, & of a mock fierceness, arching her back, erecting her hair, holding her head obliquely, & going sidewise, & then springing on an object or leaping into the air. She likes to lie crouching, with quivering spine, & leap upon my hand, biting & using all her four paws; then, in a moment, shooting away, to return, ventre à terre, as before. All this particularly in the evening twilight.

On the 26th of July, as I was getting up, before 6 in the morning, the house not being yet open, I looked out of the bedroom window, & peered down on that small portion of the end of the Verandah which is visible, thinking that possibly she might be there. Not seeing her, I called 'Brue! Brue!' Presently I fancied I heard a faint response from beneath, which was presently repeated, but seemed to come from different quarters below, & even from round the house, as if she were seeking the source of the call. I ceased to call, & had no thought of seeing her, but in a few moments her mewing became plainer & nearer; &, looking again out, I saw her little face appear above the Verandah shoot, just before the window. She looked anxious, but scrambled up, & then, having rested a moment, she carefully walked, (not sprang, as Fairy used to do) up the Verandah roof, & with ease jumped up to the window-sill, when I rewarded her with caresses, & she expressed her satisfaction with a loud purr.

Sept. 21. 1877.

FROM THE LAST DATE BRUEY HAS, with scarcely an exception, come up to our bedroom window in the same way, every morning. She soon became somewhat tiresome, coming up long before daybreak, & even several times early in the night; but we refused to notice her till morning; & she would coil herself up in the left-corner between the two sashes of the double-window, & sleep the hours away there. Unfortunately having scrambled up, by the stem of the Periploca, she could not get down; nor has she even yet, I believe, learned to find her own way down, reaching only to the corner of the hot-house roof, whence I have to hold out my arm steady, that she may cautiously venture on it, & descend by my shoulder & body. Thus she is dependent on our window being opened to receive her; & what she will do, when in winter, we close the outer sash, so that she cannot get to the window-sill, is a matter of some anxiety.

After a while I again tried the old Kennel, having well aired it, & removed the straw; but she at once manifested the same revulsion to it as before. And though, by placing within her saucer of food, she was enticed to enter & eat, yet she would suddenly retreat & dart away as if frightened; & I do not think she ever slept in it, or even entered it, of her own accord. Yet she would play about it, & sit on the top. She had chosen a sleeping-place for herself under the shadow of the spreading Cypress on the lawn; I think on the base of one of the lower horizontal boughs.

But about 10 days ago I found another box, in which I put a bed, of hay, & tilted it on its side, with its open top facing the parlour-window, a few inches distant, so as just to admit access. This she took-to quite kindly; & here she sleeps every night now, coming up to the bedroom window after day-light. Then I take her in, & she purrs in my arms loudly, & has learned to cuddle in my arms, & in Eliza's, (for she is not satisfied unless she divides her attentions between us) until we get up: her manners now having become very closely similar to Fairy's.

She is extremely fond of having a piece of paper crumpled-up tightly in a globular form, & thrown to her on the carpet: this she dashes at, strikes with her paws, & very skilfully makes to fly from side to side, she pursuing; & constantly takes up with her mouth, & carries from place to place, much more in the manner of a dog than of a cat. I call the plaything her 'mouse'; & she has certainly learned to know the name; for I have only to say 'Mouse!' when, if she is ever so inert, she becomes on the qui vive in a moment, she looks into my face with sparkling eyes, & is all ardour & expectation.

She is quite a parlour cat; never straying by any chance into the kitchen; rarely going to the back of the house; rarely seen on the lawn, except to run down to the shadowing Cypress, or to gallop back at our call; but making her world almost limited to the rooms that we inhabit, & to the stairs, & the verandah. She seems to have not the power of mewing: when she is in distress her attempt is a most weak undertoned inward sort of cry, scarcely audible. Yet it awakes me when uttered outside the bedroom window.

Select Bibliography

The following Bibliography is an extensive, though not all-inclusive, inventory of works examined.

I. Unprinted Sources
A. MANUSCRIPTS

Libraries:

American Philosophical Society, Library (Philadelphia)
> Letters from PHG to P. W. Maclagan and Richard Owen.

British Library
> Letters from PHG to EWG, and from C. Kingsley to PHG, Ashley Papers, B 3282, Additional Manuscripts 41299, ff. 149-50;
> Curriculum vitae by PHG, [1860], Additional Manuscripts 28510, f. 115;
> EWG, 'Lessons for Stray Hours', n.d., Additional Manuscripts 5721.

British Museum (Natural History)
> Letters from PHG in Owen Correspondence, vol. XIII, f. 209; A. Günther Collection, Box XVI; Zoology Library, Foreign Letters, vol. II, no. 73; and Alder-Norman Letters, nos. 526-8;
> Gosse, P.H. 'Nereis prolifera' [n.d.];
> ———. 'The Infusoria of Britain', vols. II-III (1849, with later additions);
> ———. 'Exuviation of [a] Prawn', 1854;
> ———. 'Anemones [Actinologia]', n.d. [1858-60];
> ———. 'Culture [of orchids]', n.d. (c. 1862-3);
> ———. 'Orchids and their Culture', n.d. (c. 1864-75);
> ———. 'Description of the Genital Prehensores in the Papilionidae', 1882;
> ———. 'Rotifera. [Vol.] V', n.d. (1887).

Cambridge University Library, Gosse Papers
> Gosse, Edmund. 'Poems', n.d. (c. 1867-8), Additional Manuscripts 7035/II;
> ———. 'Tristram Jones: Fragment of an Autobiographical Romance', n.d. (?1872), Additional Manuscripts 2768/15;
> ———. 'Book of Gosse', 2 vols., 1875-1928, Additional Manuscripts 7034-7035/1;
> Gosse, Emily. 'Recollections of the Earlier Life of Emily Bowes, to the year 1835', n.d., Additional Manuscripts 7035/II;
> Gosse, P.H. 'Zoology of Jamaica. 1846' (actually, the manuscript for Gosse's *Birds of Jamaica*, 1847), Additional Manuscripts 7040;
> ———. 'Anecdotes and Reminiscences of My Life', 2 vols., Additional Manuscripts 7016-7. Vol. 1 (composed 1868-69), covers 1810-26; Vol. 2 (composed 1869-88), covers 1827-1844;
> ———. 'Fairy: A Recollection. 1877', Additional Manuscripts 7325 [see *infra*, Appendix];

> Correspondence:
> Gosse, Edmund. Additional Manuscripts 7019-26, 8 vols.; 7027-32, 6 vols. (an extra-illustrated copy of Evan Charteris' *Life & Letters of Sir Edmund Gosse*, interleaved with letters and other material);
> ———. *The Life of Philip Henry Gosse, F.R.S.* An extra-illustrated copy of the book interleaved with letters and other material, including letters from Emily Gosse, Adv. c. 82.5;
> Gosse, P. H. [Letters to EWG], Additional Manuscripts 7033;
> ———. [Letters to EWG], Additional Manuscripts 7018, 7041;
> ———. Copy Book, Additional Manuscripts 7313.

Chicago Botanic Garden (Glencoe, Illinois)
> *See* Massachusetts Horticultural Society (Boston)

Darwin Correspondence Project (https://www.darwinproject.ac.uk/)
> Letters, 1856-64 (from PHG-CD, 4 letters; from Charles Darwin-PHG, 6).

Duke University, William R. Perkins Library (North Carolina)
> Letter from PHG to W. E. Shipton.

Edinburgh University Library
> Letters (6) from PHG to W. A. Lloyd, and 39 to an unnamed correspondent (also Lloyd), La. 425/22.

Horniman Museum and Library (London)
> Collection of original sketches and drawings of British sea anemones and corals, by PHG and his correspondents, 1839-61;
> A. C. Haddon Papers.

Institute of Geological Sciences (London)
> Letters (3) from PHG to C. W. Peach, 1/527;
> Letter, Edward Forbes to PHG.
Institute of Jamaica (Kingston)
> *See* National Library of Jamaica
Leeds University, Brotherton Library, Brotherton Collection
> Gosse, Edmund. 'History of the British Sea Anemones and Corals', 2 vols., n.d.;
> ———. Diary, 1857;
> ———. 'A Manual of the British Lepidoptera', 1858;
> ———. 'Zoological Sketches Consisting of Descriptions and Engravings of Animals', 1858;
> ———. 'A History of British Ferns' [1860];
> ———. 'Album', 1865;
> ———. [Early Writing Career memoir], n.d. (?May 1866).
> Gosse, Ellen. Diary, 1875;
> Gosse, Emily. Diary, 1849[-1855];
> ———. Diary, 1854;
> Gosse, P. H. 'Themes or Pieces of Juvenile Composition, by P. H. Gosse, at Blandford, from Jany. 1823, to Xmas, 1823.'
> ———. 'Letters from Jamaica, 1844-5;
> ———. 'The Aquarium', n.d. (1854-76).
Linnean Society (London)
> Letters (4) from PHG to E. R. Alston, J. J. Bennett. R. McLachlan, and J. Murie;
> General Minute Book No.6 (1844-50);
> 'Certificates of Fellows, Foreign Members & Associates, 1846-56';
> Council Minute Book No. 6 (1881-91);
> MS. of PHG's paper on *Peachia hastata*, printed in the Society's *Transactions* (1855).
Massachusetts Horticultural Society (Boston)
> *The items listed here are now in the Chicago Botanic Garden (Glencoe, Illinois)*
> PHG, [Manuscripts on orchid culture], Part I (1867-74), Part II (1863-75);
> ———. 'A Synopsis of Cultivated Orchids (Supplementary to John Lindley's *Folia Orchidae*, by P. H. Gosse)', 1874;
> Letters (4) from J. D. Hooker to PHG, and four others to PHG from Charles Leach.
Mayfield Library (Bethesda, Maryland)
> PHG, MS. draft of 'Sanguinaria', n.d. [printed in *Hardwicke's Science-Gossip* II, 1 Nov. 1866, 263].
McGill University, Blacker-Wood Library of Zoology and Ornithology (Montreal)
> Letter from PHG to [James Hubbert].
National Library of Jamaica (Kingston)
> PHG, 'A Voyage to and Residence in Jamaica, from 1844 to 1846', MS. 39;
> Letter from PHG to R. Hill.
National Library of Scotland (Edinburgh)
> Gosse, Edmund. 'Journal in Scotland, August, 1870', MS. 2562.
National Museums of Canada (Ottawa)
> Gosse, P.H. 'Entomologia Terrae Novae', 64(+)pp., 232 illustrations, n.d. [?1836], *OGJ.G67.
Natural History Museum (London)
> *Previously known as* British Museum (Natural History), q.v.
Newfoundland Provincial Archives, T. B. Browning Collection (St. John's)
> Sketch book of Conception Bay, Newfoundland, in the 1830s and 1840s [?by William Gosse] (P6[A]1).
Princeton University (New Jersey)
> Letter, C. Kingsley-PHG;
> Letters (4), EWG to George A. Armour;
> Letter, EWG to Horace H. Furness.
Public Archives of Canada (Ottawa)
> Gosse, P.H. 'The Farm Journal of P. H. Gosse from the Season of 1837', M.G. 24 I 63.
Royal Botanic Gardens, Kew (Richmond, Surrey)
> Letters (24) from PHG to J. D. Hooker, English Letters XXI, LXXXVII, *Jamaica Letters* CCX;
> Letters (7) from PHG to W. J. Hooker, *English Letters* XXXI, XLI.
Royal Society of London
> 'Certificates of Candidates for Election', vols. IX (1840-60), f. 373; XI (1881-95), f. 166;
> Referees' Reports by George Busk, T. H. Huxley, W. B. Carpenter, Arthur Farre, R. McLachlan, E. Lankester, and O. Salvin, on papers by PHG printed in the Society's *Transactions* or *Proceedings*, R.R. 3, ff. 114-20; R.R. 9, ff. 41-3;
> Referee's Reports by PHG, R.R. 3, ff. 29, 182;
> Letters (2) to T. H. Huxley and W. White, *Misc. Corr.* XII (1880-3), ff. 224, 276;
> MSS. of 3 papers by PHG, printed in the Society's *Philosophical Transactions* or *Proceedings*;
> Hudson, Charles T., 'The Original Drawings of the Rotifera', Clifton, 1886, MS. 132.
Shoreditch District Library, Department of Archives (London)
> Letter from Edmund Gosse, Bagust Collection vol. XI, f. 100.

Society for Promoting Christian Knowledge (London)
    Minutes of the General Literature & Education Committee [GLC], 1843-95.
Victoria and Albert Museum, Print Room (London)
    Thirty-three wood engravings (mostly proofs), executed by the Dalziel Brothers and Joseph Swain, for
        PHG's *A Year at the Shore* (1865).
Wellcome Historical Medical Library (London)
    Letters (6) from PHG to various individuals.
West Virginia, State Archives (Charleston)
    Letters (3) from PHG to W. H. Edwards.
West Yorkshire Archives (Leeds)
    Symington Collection, Box 7, *c.* 1860-70 (notes on members of the Brethren assembly in St. Marychurch).

Private Collections:
Geoffrey Barrow (Kent)
    PHG, 'Η Μαρτυρία τῆζ Προφητείαζ ['The Testimony of Prophecy', *c.* 13 May 1843- 5 Oct. 1850], containing
        copies of letters, memoranda, and various cuttings and studies on prophetic subjects.
Peter A. Brannon, Family Collection (Alabama)
    Copy of PHG, *Letters from Alabama*, with 600 extra-illustrations (some photocopies of this supplied by
        courtesy of Mr Brannon's widow and Milo B. Howard, Jr., Director, Department of Archives and
        History, State of Alabama).
F. Roy Coad (Carshalton, Surrey)
    H. C. H[itchcock]., 'A Little of our History', *Brook St. Chapel, Tottenham Magazine* (1962).
R. B. Freeman (London)
    PHG, *Infusoria. 4* [Vol. 4] and rotating the MS it opens to *Journal* [miscellaneous natural history notes,
        1846-87], plus loose letters.
    Printed natural history leaflets.
Jennifer Gosse (Berkshire). Gosse Family Collection
    [Bowes, Emily]. Notebook, n.d. [*c.* 1835];
    Gosse, Edmund. 'Analysis of the Families of British Butterflies', 3 parts, [1860];
    Gosse, Eliza. Portfolio of Sketches, n.d.;
    Gosse, P. H. Drawings of exotic butterflies (c. 1846-77);
    ———. 'Entomologia Alabamensis', 1838;
    ———. 'Gems, Collected by P. H. Gosse. "Orient pearls at random strung. —" Newfoundland. Octr. 1830',
        Vol. I [a selection of favoured poems];
    ———. 'Jamaica Studies', 1844-46, contains natural history illustrations made in Jamaica, plus various
        other drawings, including the original plates for PHG's *Aquarium* (1854);
    Gosse, Teresa ('Tessa'). Diary, 1891;
    Gosse, Thomas. 'Memoirs', n.d. (c. 1822-34);
    ———. 'Hebrew Memoirs; Meant to Elucidate, in Sacred Writ, the Story of the Early Descendants of the
        Holy Patriarchs, in Canaan', n.d. [?1837];
    ———. 'Lectures, on the Earliest Times: with the View to an Illustration of the Poem, on the Baleful
        Attempt to Repossess Paradise', n.d. [?1839];
    Gosse, William. 'Wild Flowers & Fruits of Newfoundland, from Nature', n.d. [*c.* 1830];
    ———. Diary, 1857-8;
    Family albums of photos and *cartes-de-visite*.
H. C. Hitchcock (London)
    Brook St. Chapel records.
Sir Stephen Holmes (Kent)
    Letters (2) from PHG to J. H. Gladstone, and one from F. Petrie.
G. C. D. Howley (Purley, Surrey)
    H. Pickering, *Chief Men Among Brethren* ([1918]).
    Report of Three Days' Meetings for Prayer, and Addresses on the 'Sure Word of Prophecy' ([1864]).
H. F. V. Johnstone (Poole, Dorset)
    Gosse, P.H. 'Correspondence Book' (copies of several letters written by PHG, and a nearly complete index
        to all letters to and from him from 1869 to 1888);
    Gosse, Thomas [the father]. 'Why am I a Christian?' (1843);
    Hardy, Evelyn. 'The Limner: Being the Life of Thomas Gosse, 1765-1844.' Typescript, 2 vols., n.d. [?1938].
Charles Kirke Swann (London)
    Letter, PHG-John Van Voorst, 31 Dec. 1881 (on 2 Oct. 1974, R. B. Freeman provided me with a typescript
        copy of the letter, based upon the original MS loaned to him by Charles Kirke Swann of London, who
        was to auction it off; see CUL Add. 7313, 468).
Douglas Wertheimer (Skokie, Illinois)
    Letter from PHG to John [Shelly], 18 April 1864;
    Letter from EWG to Lady Tennant [Viscountess Pamela Grey], 30 May [*s.a.*];
    Smith, K.G.V. (compiler). 'An Annotated Index to Insects Mentioned in *Letters from Alabama* (1859) by
        P. H. Gosse.' Typescript, [1974].

B. DISSERTATIONS, CENSUS RETURNS, UNPUBLISHED MATERIAL, MISCELLANEOUS

The Athenaeum. The file copies of this periodical, identifying the anonymous authors of articles and reviews, were examined at the office of the *New Statesman*, London, for 1840-90, *passim.*

Baldwin, Melinda Clare. '*Nature* and the Making of a Scientific Community, 1869-1939.' Princeton University, PhD dissertation, 2010.

Bell, Jr., Whitfield J. 'Science and Humanity in Philadelphia 1775-1790.' University of Pennsylvania, PhD dissertation, 1947.

Bellon, Richard Donald. 'Joseph Hooker and the Progress of Botany, 1845-65.' University of Washington, PhD dissertation, 2000.

Booth, John Derek. 'Changing Forest Utilization Patterns in the Eastern Townships of Quebec, 1800 to 1930.' McGill University, PhD dissertation, 1971.

Brookes, Alan Alexander. 'The Exodus: Migration from the Maritime Provinces to Boston during the Second Half of the Nineteenth Century.' University of New Brunswick, PhD dissertation, 1978.

Byrne, John Francis. 'The *Reader:* A Review of Literature, Science and the Arts, 1863-1867.' Northwestern University, PhD dissertation, 1964.

Byrne, Pat. 'Folk Tradition, Literature, and a Society in Transition: Newfoundland.' Memorial University of Newfoundland, PhD dissertation, 1994.

Cain, A. J. 'The Omphalotic Argument in the Early Nineteenth Century: Penn and Gosse.' Typescript, 1972 (loaned by the author).

Census Returns. Public Record Office (London).
    1841 Census Returns (Hackney), Enumeration District 4.
    1851 Census Returns (Hackney), Enumeration Districts 3, 6.
    1861 Census Returns (Kensington, London), Enumeration District 23.
    1861 Census Returns (St. Marychurch, Devon), Enumeration District 8.
    1871 Census Returns (St. Marychurch, Devon), Enumeration Districts 19-22.
    1871 Census Returns (Torquay, Devon), Enumeration Districts 3-4, 9.
    1871 Census Returns (East Grinstead, Sussex), Enumeration District 4.
    1871 Census Returns (Edmonton, Tottenham), Enumeration District 9.

Chafe, Edward-Vincent. 'A New Life on "Uncle Sam's Farm:" Newfoundlanders in Massachusetts, 1846-1859.' Memorial University of Newfoundland, MA thesis, 1982.

Desmeules, Mélanie. 'La contribution entomologique et taxinomique de l'abbé Léon Provancher.' Université du Québec in Chicoutimi, MA thesis, 2003.

Dickson, Neil T. R. 'The History of the Open Brethren in Scotland 1838-1999.' University of Stirling, PhD dissertation, 2000.

Downs, Randall L. 'The Influence of the Moravian Missions Movement on Baptist Global Missions.' Mid-America Baptist Theological Seminary, PhD dissertation, 2018.

Doyle, Marjorie M. 'A Biography of Philip Tocque (1814-1899).' Memorial University of Newfoundland, MA thesis, 1986.

Duffy, Rebecca. 'The Age of Aquaria: The Aquarium Pursuit and Personal Fish-Keeping, 1850-1920.' University of Delaware, MA thesis, 2018.

Embley, Peter L. 'The Origins and Early Development of the Plymouth Brethren.' Cambridge University, PhD dissertation, 1966.

Everitt, Judith. 'Philip Henry Gosse. A Victorian Case-history.' University of Sussex, D.Phil. dissertation, 1969.

Cornell, John Fenlon. 'Sir William Dawson and the Theory of Evolution.' McGill University, MA thesis, 1977.

Goodrum, Matthew. 'Marine Zoology in Britain 1820-1860: The Emergence of the Aquarian Naturalists.' University of Oklahoma, MA thesis, 1990.

———. 'The British Sea-Side Studies, 1820-1860: Marine Invertebrates, the Practice of Natural History, and the Depiction of Life in the Sea.' Indiana University, PhD dissertation, 1997.

Gracie, William J. 'Father-Son Conflict in Selected Victorian Autobiographies and Autobiographical Novels.' Northwestern University, PhD dissertation, 1969.

Hanawalt, Mary Wheat. 'The Attitude of Charles Kingsley Toward Science.' University of Iowa, PhD dissertation, 1935.

Harper, George G. 'A Study of the Prose Works of Sir Edmund Gosse, 1872-1907.' Northwestern University, PhD dissertation, 1959.

Harrison, Andrew John. 'Scientific naturalists and the government of the Royal Society 1850-1900.' Open University, PhD dissertation, 1989.

Heggoy, Willy Normann. 'Fifty Years of Evangelical Missionary Movement in North Africa, 1881-1931.'Hartford Seminary Foundation, PhD dissertation, 1960.

Helmstadter, Richard J. 'Evangelical Conversion.' Paper read at the Annual Meeting of the Canadian Historical Association, Edmonton, Alberta, 7 June 1975.

Hinton, D. A. 'Popular Science in England, 1830-1870.' University of Bath, PhD dissertation, 1979.

Hollett, Calvin. 'A People Reaching for Ecstasy: The Growth of Methodism in Newfoundland, 1774-1874.' Memorial University, PhD dissertation, 2008.

Houlden, Greig. 'Materialism, Man, and the Moral Order: Canadian Responses to Darwinian Evolutionary Naturalism.' University of British Columbia, BA essay, 1975.

Kimler, William Charles. 'One Hundred Years of Mimicry: History of an Evolutionary Exemplar.' Cornell University, PhD dissertation, 1983.

Levin, Martin. 'Aspects of the Confessional Form in Edmund Gosse's *Father and Son*.' Master's essay, University of Toronto, 1972.

Manderson-Jones, Marlene. 'Two Chapters from the Life of Richard Hill.' Typescript, 53pp. Department of History, University of West Indies, n.d. [?1975].

Martin, Janette Lisa. 'Popular political oratory and itinerant lecturing in Yorkshire and the North East in the age of Chartism, 1837-60.' University of York, PhD dissertation, 2010.

Mathieson, Stuart. 'The Victoria Institute 1865-1932: A Case Study in the Relationship between Science and Religion.' Queen's University Belfast, PhD dissertation, 2018.

Mattheisen, Paul F. 'Edmund Gosse: A Literary Record.' Rutgers University, PhD dissertation, 1959.

McIver, Thomas Allen. 'Creationism: Intellectual Origins, Cultural Context, and Theoretical Diversity.' University of California Los Angeles, PhD dissertation, 1989.

Moore, James R. 'The Post-Darwinian Controversies. A Study of the Protestant Struggle to Come to Terms with Darwin in Great Britain and America, 1870-1900.' University of Manchester, PhD dissertation, 1975.

Morison, William J. 'George Frederick Wright: In Defense of Darwinism and Fundamentalism, 1838-1921.' Vanderbilt University, PhD dissertation, 1971.

Newton, Kenneth John. 'A History of the Brethren in Australia, with Particular Reference to the Open Brethren.' Fuller Theological Seminary, PhD dissertation, 1990.

Nicol, Adam L. 'The Romance of Natural History: The Imaginative Project of Philip Henry Gosse.' University of Western Australia, PhD dissertation, 2010.

O'Brien, Charles Francis. 'The Word and the Work: A Study of Sir William Dawson and Nineteenth Century Controversies Between Religion and Science'. Brown University, PhD dissertation, 1968.

Parsons, Jacob. 'The Origin and Growth of Newfoundland Methodism 1765-1855.' Memorial University of Newfoundland, MA thesis, 1964.

Patrick, April Nicole. 'A Sentence of Death Had Been Passed on Her: Representing the Experience of Breast Cancer in Britain through the Long Nineteenth Century.' Texas Christian University, PhD dissertation, 2007.

Penner, Louise. 'Narrative under the Microscope: Evidentiary Discourses in Victorian Literature and Culture, 1829-1876'. Rice University, PhD dissertation, 2000.

Pietsch, Brendan. 'Dispensational Modernism.' Duke University, PhD dissertation, 2011.

Porter, Roger J. 'The Double Self: Autobiography and Literary Form in Gibbon, De Quincy, Gosse, and Edwin Muir.' Yale University, PhD dissertation, 1967.

Roberts, Windsor Hall. 'The Reaction of the American Protestant Churches to the Darwinian Philosophy 1860-1900.' University of Chicago, PhD dissertation, 1936.

Rozwadowski Helen Margaret. 'Fathoming the Ocean: Discovery and Exploration of the Deep Sea, 1840-1880.' University of Pennsylvania, PhD dissertation, 1996.

Sears, Jeanette. 'The Interpretation of Prophecy and Expectations of the End in Britain, 1845-1883.' University of Manchester, PhD dissertation, 1984.

Shingleton, Royce Gordon. 'Rural Life in the Old South: the British Travelers' Image, 1820-1860.' Florida State University, PhD dissertation, 1971.

Smith, Françoise Noël. 'The Establishment of Religious Communities in the Eastern Townships of Lower Canada, 1799 to 1851.' McGill University, MA thesis, 1976.

Strick, James Edgar. 'The British Spontaneous Generation Debates of 1860-1880: Medicine, Evolution, and Laboratory Science in the Victorian Context.' Princeton University, PhD dissertation, 1997.

Terlep, Alan Thomas. 'Inventing the Rapture: The Formation of American Dispensationalism, 1850-1875.' University of Chicago, PhD dissertation, 2010.

Turner, Michael Kenneth. '"Redeeming the Time": The Making of Early American Methodism.' Vanderbilt University, PhD dissertation, 2009.

Walker, Vera. 'The Life and Work of William Bell Scott, 1811-1890.' University of Durham, PhD dissertation, 1951.

Wertheimer, Douglas. 'The Victoria Institute, 1865-1919: A Study in Collective Biography Meant as an Introduction to the Conflict of Science and Religion after Darwin.' Master's Essay, University of Toronto, 1971.

———. 'Evangelical Alliances Against Science and Secularism in England, 1865-1871.' Paper read at the Annual Meeting of the Canadian Historical Association, Edmonton, Alberta, June 1975.

———. 'Philip Henry Gosse: Science and Revelation in the Crucible.' University of Toronto, PhD dissertation, 1977.

———. 'On the Battlefield of Science and Revelation: P. H. Gosse as a Lecturer, 1855-1870.' Unpublished MS, 2022.

————. 'P. H. Gosse's Scientific Reception in America.' Unpublished MS, 2023.

Whalen, Robert Kieran. 'Millenarianism and Millennialism in America, 1790-1880.' State University of New York at Stony Brook, PhD dissertation, 1971.

Whelan, Maudie. 'Journalism in Newfoundland: A Beginning History.' Carleton University, Master of Journalism, 1993.

Whitman, Birgit. 'Breast Cancer: Patient Narratives and Treatment Methods.' University of Glasgow, PhD dissertation, 2004.

Wilkinson, Paul Richard. 'John Nelson Darby and the Origins of Christian Zionism.' University of Manchester, PhD dissertation, 2006.

Wills. Public Record Office (London)
    Baxter, Nadir: Proved 11 May 1848.
    Habershon, Matthew: Proved 23 Nov. 1852.

Wills or Letters of Administration. Somerset House (London)
    Berger, William Thomas: Probate of Will granted 31 Jan. 1899.
    Gosse, Edmund: Probate of Will granted 24 July 1928.
    Gosse, Eliza: Probate of Will granted 13 Nov. 1900.
    Gosse, Philip Henry: Probate of Will granted 12 Oct. 1888.
    Gosse, Philip Henry George: Probate of Will granted 11 Feb. 1960.
    Morgan, Richard Cope: Probate of Will granted 1 Dec. 1908.
    Strong, Leonard: Probate of Will granted 6 Sept. 1875.

Winsor, Mary Pickard. 'Issues in the Classification of Radiates, 1830-1860.' Yale University, PhD dissertation, 1971.

Witter, Steven R. 'An Analysis of the Leadership Practices of the Churches of the Plymouth Brethren Movement in the United States.' Capella University, PhD dissertation, 2007.

Woolf, James D. 'Sir Edmund Gosse: A Biographical and Interpretive Study.' Vanderbilt University, PhD dissertation, 1953.

II. Printed Sources

A. BOOKS AND PAMPHLETS

Adams, George. *Essay on the Microscope; Containing a Practical Description of the Most Improved Microscopes; a General History of Insects, their Transformation, Peculiar Habits, and Oeconomy: an Account of the Various Species, and Singular Properties, of the Hydrae and Vorticellae; a Description of Three Hundred and Eighty-three Animalcula: With a Concise Catalogue of Interesting Objects: A View of the Organization of Timber, and the Configuration of Salts, when Under the Microscope.* 2nd ed., ed. by Frederick Kanmacher. London: Dillon and Keating, 1798.

Adams, H. G. *The Sea-side Lesson Book: Designed to Convey to the Youthful Mind a Knowledge of the Nature and Uses of the Common Things of the Sea Coast. In a Series of Familiar Descriptive Chapters; with Questions for Examination, and Explanations of the Meanings of the Scientific Terms.* London: Groombridge & Sons, 1856.

Akenson, Donald Harman. *Exporting the Rapture: John Nelson Darby and the Victorian Conquest of North-American Evangelicalism.* New York: Oxford University Press, 2018.

Allen, David Elliston. *The Naturalist in Britain. A Social History.* London: Allen Lane, 1976.

Allom, Elizabeth Anne. *Sea-side Pleasures: or a Peep at Miss Eldon's Happy Pupils.* London: Aylott and Jones, 1845.

Anker, Jean. *Bird Books and Bird Art.* Copenhagen: Leven & Munksgaard, 1938.

Anon. *A Brief Record of the Last Days of Robert Howard.* Printed for Private Circulation, 1871.

————. *Affection's Tribute to the Memory of Samuel Berger, Esq., Jun., of Homerton, Middlesex; with a Short Account of His Brother, Mr. Thomas Berger.* London: Printed for the Author, 1853.

————. *Canada, Nova Scotia, New Brunswick, Newfoundland, etc. With the History, Present State, and Prospects of These Colonies, in Regard to Emigration.* London: Cradock and Co., 1843.

————. *Catalogue of Furniture and Effects, Valuable Books, and Orchids [belonging to PHG and Eliza Gosse]. Sandhurst, Torquay Road, St. Marychurch.* Torquay: Directory Office, [1900].

————. *The Declaration of Students of the Natural and Physical Sciences.* London: Simpkin, Marshall & Co., [1865].

————. *Hints for the Formation of a Fresh-water Aquarium.* London: SPCK, [1857].

————. *Periodical Accounts Relating to the Missions of the Church of the United Brethren, Established among the Heathen.* London: For the Brethren's Society, Vol. XVIII, 1846[-48].

————. *Principles of Collegiate Education Discussed and Elucidated, in a Description of Gnoll College, Vale of Neath, South Wales; A National Institution Adapted to the Wants of the Age.* London: Edward Stanford, 1857.

————. *Report of Three Days' Meetings of Prayer, and Addresses on the "Sure Word of Prophecy", held in Freemasons' Hall, May, 9th, 10th, & 12th, 1864.* London: William Yapp, [1864].

————. *The School of the Prophets: A Review of Elliott's "Horae Apocalypticae", Lord Carlisle's "Remarks on Daniel VIII", and Dr. Cumming's "Great Tribulation; or, Things Coming on the Earth"*. London: Morgan & Chase, [1860].

————. *Synopsis of the Contents of the British Museum*. 44th ed. London: G. Woodfall & Son, 1842.

————. *Testimonials in Favour of Mr Adam White, during Twenty-five Years Assistant in the Zoological Department, British Museum*. Edinburgh: Thomas Constable, 1865.

'Arachnophilus' [Adam White]. *A Contribution Towards an Argument for the Plenary Inspiration of Scripture, Derived from the Minute Historical Accuracy of the Scriptures of the Old Testament, as Proved by Certain Ancient Egyptian and Assyrian Remains Preserved in the British Museum*. London: Samuel Bagster & Sons, 1851.

Arlidge, J. T., and W. Archer, A. Pritchard, J. Ralfs, and W. C. Williamson (eds.). *A History of Infusoria*. 3ed. London: Whittaker and Co., 1852.

Arnott, Anne. *The Brethren. An Autobiography of a Plymouth Brethren Childhood*. London: A. R. Mowbray & Co., Ltd., 1969.

Barber, Lynn. *The Heyday of Natural History 1820-1870*. London: Jonathan Cape, 1980.

Barlow, Nora (ed.). *Darwin and Henslow. The Growth of an Idea. Letters 1831-1860*. London: John Murray, 1967.

————. *The Autobiography of Charles Darwin*. New York: W. W. Norton & Co., 1969.

Beattie, David J. *Brethren: The Story of a Great Recovery*. Kilmarnock: John Ritchie Ltd., [1939].

Bebbington, David W. *Evangelicalism in Modern Britain: A History from the 1730s to the 1980s*. London: Routledge, 1989, 2005.

————. *The Dominance of Evangelicalism: The Age of Spurgeon and Moody*. Downers Grove, Illinois: InterVarsity Press, 2005.

Becker, Bernard H. *Official Handbook to the Royal Aquarium ... With a Description of the Aquarium by W. A. Lloyd*. London: Charles Dickens & Evans, 1876.

Beer, Patricia. *Mrs Beer's House*. London: Macmillan, 1968.

Bellows, William. *Edmund Gosse. Some Memories*. London: R. Cobden Sanderson, Ltd., 1929.

Berger, Carl. *Science, God, and Nature in Victorian Canada*. Toronto: University of Toronto Press, 1983.

Berger, Thomas B. *A Century & a Half of the House of Berger*. London: Waterlow & Sons, Ltd., 1910.

Berger, William Thomas. *Wages of Sin & Everlasting Punishment*. London: Elliott Stock, 1886.

Bigelow, John. *Jamaica in 1850*. New York: George P. Putnam, 1851.

Bishop, James (ed.). *Handbook of Plain Instructions for the Construction and Management of Fresh-Water Aquaria for Goldfish, etc., and Proper Treatment of the Plants, Fish, Molluscs, Beetles, etc., Kept Therein, or in Glass Globes*. London: Dean and Son, [1856].

Blackwood, Mrs S. A. (ed.). *Some Records of the Life of Steven Arthur Blackwood K.C.B.* London: Hodder and Stoughton, 1896.

Blaikie, William Garden. *David Brown D.D., LL.D.* London: Hodder & Stoughton, 1898.

Boulter, Michael. *Bloomsbury Scientists. Science and Art in the Wake of Darwin*. London: UCL Press, 2017.

B[owes]., E[mily]. *Hymns and Sacred Poems*. 2nd ed. Bath: A. E. Binns, 1832.

————. *Hymns and Sacred Poems*. Second Series. Bath: A. E. Binns, 1834.

Boyd, Robert. *Emily Gosse: A Life of Faith and Works*. Inverness: Olivet Books, 2004.

Braithewaite, Robert (ed.). *Life and Letters of Rev. Wm. Pennefather, B.A.* London: John F. Shaw & Co., n.d.

Braybrooke, Patrick. *Considerations on Edmund Gosse*. London: Drake's Ltd., [1925].

Bready, J. Wesley. *Doctor Barnardo. Physician, Pioneer, Prophet*. London: George Allen & Unwin Ltd., 1930, 3rd impression, 1932.

Bredsdorff, Elias (ed.). *Sir Edmund Gosse's Correspondence with Scandinavian Writers*. Copenhagen: Scandinavian University Books, 1960.

[Brightwell, Cecilia Lucy]. *Memorials of the Life of Mr. Brightwell, of Norwich*. Norwich: Printed for Private Circulation, 1869.

Brown, A. W. *The Metaphysical Society, 1869-1880*. New York: Columbia University Press, 1947.

Brown, Candy Gunther. *Word in the World. Evangelical Writing, Publishing, and Reading in America, 1789-1880*. Chapel Hill: University of North Carolina Press, 2004.

Brown, F. Martin and Bernard Heineman. *Jamaica and its Butterflies*. London: E. W. Classey, 1972.

Brown, Ford K. *Fathers of the Victorians*. Cambridge: Cambridge University Press, 1961.

Bruce, F. F. *Who are the Brethren?* London & Glasgow: Pickering & Inglis Ltd., Witness Booklet No.1, 1962.

————. *Answers to Questions*. Exeter: Paternoster Press, 1972.

Brugmans, Linette F. (ed. and trans.). *The Correspondence of Andre Gide and Edmund Gosse 1904-1928*. London: Peter Owen Ltd., 1960.

Buchner, John Henry. *The Moravians in Jamaica*. London: Longman, Brown, & Co., 1854.

Bunbury, Frances J. (ed.). *Life, Letters and Journals of Sir Charles J. F. Bunbury, Bart.* 3 vols. London: Printed for Private Circulation, 1894.

Burkhardt, Frederick and Sydney Smith (eds.). *The Correspondence of Charles Darwin. Volume 5: 1851-1855.* Cambridge: Cambridge University Press, 1989.

Butler, Henry D. *The Family Aquarium; or, Aqua Vivarium.* New York: Dick & Fitzgerald, [1858].

Cable, Mildred and Francesca French. *A Woman who Laughed. Henrietta Soltau Who Laughed at Impossibilities and Cried: 'It Shall Be Done'.* London: China Inland Mission, 1934.

Cardwell, D. S. L. *The Organisation of Science in England.* London: Heinemann Educational Books, 1957, 1972.

Case, Henry W. *On Sea and Land, On Creek and River. Being an account of experiences in the visitation of assemblies of Christians in the West Indies and British Guiana; with Reminiscences of Pioneer Missionaries and of the Slave Trade formerly carried on from Bristol.* London: Morgan and Scott, 1910.

Catwell, Sylvan R. *The Brethren in Barbados: Gospel Hall Assemblies 1889-1994.* Barbados: Sylvan R. Catwell, 1995.

Chadwick, Owen. *The Victorian Church.* London: Adam and Charles Black, 2 parts, 1966, 1970.

Channell, Leonard Stewart. *History of Compton County and Sketches of the Eastern Townships, District of St. Francis and Sherbrooke County.* Cookshire, Quebec: Published by L. S. Channell, 1896.

Charteris, Evan. *The Life and Letters of Sir Edmund Gosse.* London: William Heinemann Ltd., 1931.

Chesson, W. H. (ed.). *Eliza Brightwen: The Life and Thoughts of a Naturalist.* London: T. Fisher Unwin, 1909.

Chester, Richard. *The Coming of the Lord. How Should we Regard It? as Distant? or Near at Hand?* London & Dublin: Dublin Tract Repository, [?1864].

Clarke, John. *Memorials of Baptist Missionaries in Jamaica, including A Sketch of the Labours of Early Religious Instructors.* London: Yates & Alexander, 1869.

Clarke, John, W. Dendy and J. M. Phillippo. *The Voice of Jubilee: A Narrative of the Baptist Mission, Jamaica, from its Commencement; with Biographical Notices of its Fathers and Founders.* London: John Snow, 1865.

Coad, F. Roy. *A History of the Brethren Movement. Its Origins, its Worldwide Development and its Significance for the Present Day.* London: Paternoster Press, 1968.

Cole, Francis J. *The History of Protozoology. Two Lectures Delivered before the University of London at King's College in May 1925.* London: University of London Press, 1926.

[Coleman, John]. *Hymns Arranged for the Use of Christians.* Bradford: W. H. Blackburn, 1846.

Coleman, John. *Prophecy Unfolded; or, Eternal Redemption: with Providential Agencies, the Second Advent of the Lord Jesus Christ, the Restoration of Israel, &c..* London: J. B. Bateman, 1861.

———. *"The Time of the End", or, Prophecy Unfolded: being Thoughts upon God's Dispensational Dealings with Man, as Consummated in the Second Advent of the Lord Jesus Christ.* London: Wertheim, MacIntosh, & Hunt, 2nd edition [of *Prophecy Unfolded*], 1862.

Coleman, William. *Georges Cuvier, Zoologist. A Study in the History of Evolution Theory.* Cambridge, Mass.: Harvard University Press, 1964.

'Criticus' [=Clayton Walker], *The Churches and Chapels of Torquay.* Torquay: MacKenzie & MacDonald, [1905].

Croft, L[aurence]. R. *The Life of Philip Henry Gosse.* Preston: Elmwood, 2000.

Cumming, John. *The Great Tribulation; or, Things Coming on the Earth.* London: Richard Bentley, 3rd thousand, 1859.

Cundall, Frank. *Biographical Annals of Jamaica. A Brief History of the Colony Arranged as a Guide to the Jamaica Portrait Gallery: with Chronological Outlines of Jamaica History.* Kingston: Institute of Jamaica, 1904.

———. *Historic Jamaica.* London: West India Committee, 1915.

[Dallas, Mrs A. R. C.]. *Incidents in the Life and Ministry of the Rev. Alex. R. C. Dallas, A.M.* London: James Nisbet & Co., 1871.

Dance, S. Peter. *Shell Collecting. An Illustrated History.* Berkeley and Los Angeles: University of California Press, 1966.

———. *The Art of Natural History: Animal Illustrators and their Work.* Woodstock, NY: Overlook Press, 1978.

[Darby, John Nelson]. *Letters of J. N. Darby: Supplement. Correspondence with G. V. Wigram. Volume 1: 1838-1855.* Chessington [England]: Bible and Gospel Trust, 2019, reprinted 2021.

[———]. *Letters of J. N. Darby: Supplement. Correspondence with G. V. Wigram. Volume 2: 1856-1878.* Chessington [England]: Bible and Gospel Trust, 2019, reprinted 2021.

[———]. *Dialogues on the Essays and Reviews, by One Who Values Christianity for its Own Sake, and Believes in it as a Revelation From God.* Part I. London: W. H. Broom, 1862.

Darwin, Charles. *On the Origin of Species by Means of Natural Selection.* London: John Murray, 1859.

———. *On the Various Contrivances by Which British and Foreign Orchids are Fertilized by Insects.* London: John Murray, 1862; 2nd ed., 1877.

Darwin, Francis (ed.). *The Life and Letters of Charles Darwin.* London: John Murray, 3 vols., 1887.

Darwin, Francis and A. C. Seward (eds.). *More Letters of Charles Darwin*. London: John Murray, 2 vols., 1903.

Davies, Arthur Morley. *Evolution and its Modern Critics*. London: Thomas Murby & Co., 1937.

Dawson, John William. *Archaia; or, Studies of the Cosmogony and Natural History of the Hebrew Scriptures*. Montreal: B. Dawson & Son, 1860.

Day, Mrs C. M. *History of the Eastern Townships, Province of Quebec, Dominion of Canada, Civil and Descriptive*. Montreal: John Lovell, 1869.

Desmond, Adrian and James Moore. *Darwin's Sacred Cause: How a Hatred of Slavery Shaped Darwin's Views on Human Evolution*. Boston: Houghton Mifflin Harcourt, 2009.

Dickson, Neil T. R. and Tim Grass (eds.). *The Growth of the Brethren Movement: National and International Experiences. Essays in Honour of Harold H. Rowdon*. Bletchley, Milton Keynes: Paternoster, 2006.

Donald, Diana and Jane Munro (eds.). *Endless forms: Charles Darwin, Natural Science and the Visual Arts*. New Haven: Yale University Press, 2009.

Doncaster, Islay. *In the Footsteps of the Naturalists*. London: Phoenix House, 1961 (Chap. VI is devoted to Gosse, 'Explorer of the Sea-shore' for a young audience).

Donner, Josef. *Rotifers*. Trans. and adapted by H. G. S. Wright. London: Frederick Warne & Co., 1966.

Dupree, A. Hunter. *Asa Gray, 1810-1888*. New York: Athenaeum, 1959, 1968.

Durant, T. *Memoirs and Select Remains of an Only Son Who Died November 27th, 1821, in his Nineteenth Year; While a Student in the University of Glasgow*. Poole: J. Lankester, 2 vols., 1822.

Eales, N. B. *The Littoral Fauna of Great Britain. A Handbook for Collectors*. Cambridge: At the University Press, 4th ed., 1967.

Edmonds, F. S. *Chronicles of St. Mary Church*. Torquay: Charles G. Jowitt, 1925.

Eiseley, Loren. *Darwin's Century*. Garden City, N.Y.: Doubleday & Co., Inc., 1958; Anchor Books, 1961.

Ellegård, Alvar. *The Readership of the Periodical Press in Mid-Victorian Britain*. Göteborg: Göteborgs Universitets Arsskrift, Vol. LXIII, 1957.

———. *Darwin and the General Reader. The Reception of Darwin's Theory of Evolution in the British Periodical Press, 1859-1872*. Vol. LXIV. Göteborg: Göteborgs Universitets Arsskrift, 1958.

Elliott, Edward Bishop. *Horae Apocalypticae; or, A Commentary on the Apocalypse, Critical and Historical; Including Also an Examination of the Chief Prophecies of Daniel*. London: Seeley, Jackson, and Halliday, 1844; 5ed., 4 vols., 1862.

———. *Warburtonian Lectures, Preached in Lincoln's Inn Chapel, in the Winters from 1849 to 1853. On the Christian Church's Institution, and Declension into Apostacy; the Apostate Church's Heading by the Romish Antichrist; and the Counter-witness-church's Prophesying in Sackcloth, All as Predicted in Scripture, and as Fulfilled*. London: Seeley, Jackson, and Halliday, 1856.

E[lliott]., H[arriette]. E[mily]. *The Last Prophecy: being An Abridgment of the late Rev. E. B. Elliott's Horae Apocalypticae. To Which is Subjoined His Last Paper on Prophecy Fulfilled and Fulfilling*. London: James Nisbet & Co., 3ed., 1884.

English, Mary P. *Victorian Values: The Life and Times of Dr. Edwin Lankester M.D., F.R.S.* Bristol: Biopress Ltd., 1990.

Esdaile, Arundell. *The British Museum Library*. London: George Allen & Unwin, Ltd., 1946.

Essig, E. O. *A History of Entomology*. New York: Macmillan, 1931.

Evans, Ifor. *English Poetry in the Later Nineteenth Century*. London: Methuen & Co. Ltd., 1933, 2nd ed., revised, 1966.

Findlay, G.G. and W.W. Holdsworth. *The History of the Wesleyan Methodist Missionary Society*. London: Epworth Press, 5 vols., 1921.

Flanders, Judith. *Inside the Victorian Home: A Portrait of Domestic Life in Victorian England*. New York: W.W. Norton & Co., 2004.

Forsberg, Laura. *Worlds Beyond: Miniatures and Victorian Fiction*. New Haven: Yale University Press, 2021.

Fox, Sarah E. (ed.). *Edwin Octavius Tregelles: Civil Engineer and Minister of the Gospel*. London: Hodder and Stoughton, 1892.

Fraser, Robert W. (ed.). *Ebb and Flow. The Curiosities and Marvels of the Sea-shore. A Book for Young People*. Edinburgh: John Menzies, 1860.

———. *Seaside Divinity*. London: James Hogg and Sons, 1861.

Freeman, R. B. *The Works of Charles Darwin: An Annotated Bibliographical Handlist*. London: Dawsons of Pall Mall, 1965. Second edition: Chatham: Wm Dawson & Sons Ltd., 1977.

———. *Classification of the Animal Kingdom: an illustrated guide*. London: English Universities Press Ltd., 1972.

———. *British Natural History Books, 1495-1900. A Handlist*. Folkestone, Kent: Dawson Publishing, 1980.

Freeman, R. B. and Douglas Wertheimer. *P. H. Gosse: A Bibliography*. Folkestone, Kent: Dawson Publishing, 1980.

Frey, Hans. *Das Aquarium von A bis Z*. Leipzig: Neumann Verlag, 1959.

Froom, Le Roy Edwin. *The Prophetic Faith of Our Fathers. The Historical Development of Prophetic Interpretation.* 4 vols. Washington, D.C.: Review and Herald Publishing Assoc., 1946-54.

Fyfe, Aileen. *Science and Salvation: Evangelical Popular Science Publishing in Victorian Britain.* Chicago: University of Chicago Press, 2004.

Ghiselin, Michael T. *The Triumph of the Darwinian Method.* Berkeley and Los Angeles: University of California Press, 1969.

Gillispie, Charles Coulston. *Genesis and Geology.* New York: Harper Torchbooks, 1951, 1959.

——. *The Edge of Objectivity.* Princeton: Princeton University Press, 1960.

Glick, T. F. (ed.). *The Comparative Reception of Darwinism.* Austin: University of Texas Press, 1974.

Gosse, Edmund. *Aspects and Impressions.* London: Cassell and Co., 1922.

——. *Critical Kit-Kats.* London: William Heinemann Ltd., 1912.

[——]. *Father and Son: A Study of Two Temperaments.* London: William Heinemann, 1907.

——. *Firdausi in Exile.* London: Kegan Paul, Trench & Co., 1885.

——. *Leaves and Fruit.* London: William Heinemann Ltd., 1927.

——. *The Life of Philip Henry Gosse, F.R.S.* London: Kegan Paul, Trench, Trübner & Co., Ltd., 1890.

——. *More Books on the Table.* London: William Heinemann Ltd., 1923.

——. *On Viol and Flute.* London: Henry S. King & Co., 1873.

——. *Portraits and Sketches.* London: William Heinemann Ltd., 1912; new impression, 1924.

——. *Silhouettes.* London: William Heinemann Ltd., 1925.

——. *Two Visits to Denmark: 1872, 1874.* London: Smith, Elder, & Co., 1911.

Gosse, Edmund and John Arthur Blaikie. *Madrigals, Songs and Sonnets.* London: Longmans, Green, and Co., 1870.

Gosse, Edmund and T. J. Wise (eds.). *The Complete Works of Algernon Charles Swinburne.* Vol. XVIII. London: William Heinemann Ltd., 1927.

Gosse, Emily. *Abraham and his Children; or, Parental Duties Illustrated by Scriptural Examples.* London: Nisbet and Co., 1855.

[——] & [Gosse, P. H.] *Sea-side Pleasures.* London: SPCK, 1853. Chapter 4 only attributed to her. *See also* B[owes]., E[mily]., and GOSSE, PHILIP HENRY AND EMILY GOSSE, joint authors.

Gosse, Fayette. *The Gosses: An Anglo-Australian Family.* Canberra, Australia: Brian Clouston, 1981.

Gosse, Philip Henry. *Actinologia Britannica. A History of the British Sea-anemones and Corals.* London: John Van Voorst, 1860.

——. *The Aquarium: An Unveiling of the Wonders of the Deep.* London: John Van Voorst, 1854; 2nd ed., 1856.

——. *Assyria: Her Manners and Customs, Arts and Arms: Restored from Her Monuments.* London: SPCK, 1852.

——. *The Birds of Jamaica.* Assisted by Richard Hill. London: John Van Voorst, 1847.

——. *The Canadian Naturalist. A Series of Conversations on the Natural History of Lower Canada.* London: John Van Voorst, 1840.

——. *Evenings at the Microscope; or, Researches Among the Minuter Organs and Forms of Animal Life.* London: SPCK, 1859.

——. *Geology or God: Which? A Supplement to "Omphalos".* London: Morgan & Chase, 1866.

[——]. *Glimpses of the Wonderful.* London: Harvey and Darton, 1845.

——. *The Great Tribulation.* London: Morgan & Chase, [1868].

——. *A Handbook to the Marine Aquarium: Containing Practical Instructions for Constructing, Stocking, and Maintaining a Tank, and for Collecting Plants and Animals.* London: John Van Voorst, 1855; 2nd ed., 1856.

——. *The History of the Jews, from the Christian Era to the Dawn of the Reformation.* London: SPCK, 1851.

——. *The Humanity of the Son of God: According to Scriptures.* Printed for Private Circulation, 1886.

——. *Illustrations of the Birds of Jamaica.* London: John Van Voorst, 1849.

——. *An Introduction to Zoology.* 2 vols. London: SPCK, [1844].

——. *Land and Sea.* London: James Nisbet and Co., 1865.

——. *Letters from Alabama, (U.S.) Chiefly Relating to Natural History.* London: Morgan and Chase, 1859.

——. *Life in its Lower, Intermediate, and Higher Forms: or, Manifestations of the Divine Wisdom in the Natural History of Animals.* London: James Nisbet and Co., 1857.

——. *A Manual of Marine Zoology for the British Isles.* 2 Parts. London: John Van Voorst, 1855-56.

——. *A Memorial of the Last Days on Earth of Emily Gosse.* London: James Nisbet & Co., 1857.

——. *The Monuments of Ancient Egypt, and Their Relation to the Word of God.* London: SPCK, 1847.

——. *The Mysteries of God: A Series of Expositions of Holy Scripture.* London: Hodder and Stoughton, 1884.

——. *Natural History. Birds.* London: SPCK, 1849.

——. *Natural History. Fishes.* London: SPCK, 1851.

————. *Natural History. Mammalia.* London: SPCK, 1848.

————. *Natural History. Mollusca.* London: SPCK, 1854.

————. *Natural History. Reptiles.* London: SPCK, 1850.

————. *A Naturalist's Rambles on the Devonshire Coast.* London: John Van Voorst, 1853.

————. *A Naturalist's Sojourn in Jamaica.* Assisted by Richard Hill. London: Longman, Brown, Green, and Longmans, 1851.

————. *The Ocean.* London: SPCK, 1845.

————. *Omphalos: An Attempt to Untie the Geological Knot.* London: John Van Voorst, 1857.

————. *Popular British Ornithology; Containing a Familiar and Technical Description of the Birds of the British Isles.* London: Reeve, Benham, and Reeve, 1849.

————. *The Prophetic Times.* Printed for Private Circulation, 1871.

————. *The Revelation: How is it to be Interpreted?* London: Morgan and Chase, 1866.

————. *The Romance of Natural History.* London: James Nisbet and Co., 1860.

————. *The Romance of Natural History. Second Series.* London: James Nisbet & Co., 1861.

————. *Sacred Streams: The Ancient and Modern History of the Rivers of the Bible.* London: C. Cox, 1850.

————. *The 6000 Years of the World's History Now Closing: A Table of Scripture Chronology, with Notes.* London: Morgan and Chase, 1866. 2ed., 1867 [no known copy].

[————]. *Tabular View of the Orders & Families of Fishes.* London: Edward Stanford, 1856.

————. *Tenby: A Sea-side Holiday.* London: John Van Voorst, 1856.

————. *Text-book of Zoology, for Schools.* London: SPCK, 1851.

[————]. *Wanderings Through the Conservatories at Kew.* London: SPCK, 1856.

————. *A Year at the Shore.* London: Alexander Strahan, 1865.

Gosse, Philip Henry, and Emily Gosse. *Narrative Tracts.* London: Morgan and Chase, [1864].

[————] & [————]. *Sea-side Pleasures.* London: SPCK, 1853.

See also HUDSON, CHARLES THOMAS.

Gosse, Thomas (ed.). *The Bee and Blossom Magazine,* no.1 ([1835], ?no more published).

Granata, Silvia. *The Victorian Aquarium. Literary Discussions on Nature, Culture, and Science.* Manchester: Manchester University Press, 2021.

Grass, Tim. *Gathering to His Name. The Story of Open Brethren in Britain and Ireland.* Milton Keynes, England: Paternoster, 2006.

Green, James. *Shadow & Sunshine; or, Claverton Churchyard.* Bath: Printed for the Author, 2nd ed., [1871].

Greene, John C. *American Science in the Age of Jefferson.* Ames, Iowa: Iowa State University Press, 1984.

Guinness, H. Grattan. *The Approaching End of the Age Viewed in the Light of History, Prophecy, and Science.* London: Hodder and Stoughton, 1878.

Guinness, M. G. *The Story of the China Inland Mission.* 2 vol. London: Morgan & Scott, 1900.

Gunn, Gertrude E. *The Political History of Newfoundland 1832-1864.* Toronto: University of Toronto Press, 1966.

Gunther, Albert E. *A Century of Zoology at the British Museum through the Lives of Two Keepers 1815-1914.* London: Dawsons, 1975.

Haber, Francis C. *The Age of the World. Moses to Darwin.* Baltimore: Johns Hopkins Press, 1959.

Habershon, Matthew. *An Historical Dissertation on the Prophetic Scriptures of the Old Testament, Chiefly Those of a Chronological Character; Shewing their Aspect on the Present Times, and on the Destinies of the Jewish Nation.* London: James Nisbet and Co., 2nd ed., 1840.

Haight, Gordon S. (ed.). *The George Eliot Letters.* 7 vols. New Haven: Yale University Press, 1954-6.

————. *George Eliot. A Biography.* Oxford: Clarendon Press, 1968, 1969.

Halévy, Élie. *A History of the English People in the Nineteenth Century.* Translated from the French by E. I. Watkin. London: Ernest Benn Ltd., 6 vols., English 1932-52, reprint 1964.

Hamera, Judith. *Parlor Ponds: The Cultural Work of the American Home Aquarium 1850-1970.* Ann Arbor: University of Michigan, 2012.

[Hark, Walter and Augustus Westphal]. *The Breaking of the Dawn: Or, Moravian Work in Jamaica 1754-1904.* Belfast: Wm. Strain & Sons, [1904].

Harmer, S. F. and Shipley, A. E. (eds.). *Cambridge Natural History.* Vol. II. London: Macmillan & Co., 1896.

Harper, John. *The Sea-side and Aquarium; or, Anecdote and Gossip on Marine Zoology.* Edinburgh: William P. Nimmo, 1858.

Harvell, Drew. *A Sea of Glass. Searching for the Blaschkas' Fragile Legacy in an Ocean at Risk.* Oakland, CA: University of California Press, 2016.

Harvey, W. H. *The Sea-side Book; Being an Introduction to the Natural History of the British Coasts.* London: John Van Voorst, 1849; 3rd ed., 1854; 4th ed., 1857.

Hibberd, Shirley. *The Book of the Fresh-water aquarium; or Practical Instructions, on the Formation, Stocking, and Management in all Seasons, of Collections of River Animals and Plants.* London: Groombridge & Sons, 1856.

————. *Rustic Adornments for Homes of Taste.* London: Groombridge & Sons, 1856.

————. *The Book of the Marine Aquarium; or Practical Instructions on the Formation, Stocking, and Management in all Seasons, of Collections of Marine Animals and Plants.* London: Groombridge & Sons, new ed., 1869.

Hill, Richard. *Lights and Shadows of Jamaica History; Being Three Lectures, Delivered in Aid of the Mission Schools of the Colony.* Kingston: Ford & Gall, 1859.

Houghton, W. *Sea-side Walks of a Naturalist with His Children.* London: Groombridge & Sons, 1870.

[Howard, Mary Matilda]. *Ocean Flowers and Their Teachings.* Bath: Binns and Goodwin, 1846.

Hudson, Charles Thomas. *The Rotifera; or Wheel-Animalcules.* Assisted by P. H. Gosse. 2 vols. London: Longmans, Green, and Co., 1886.

————. *The Rotifera; or Wheel-Animalcules, both British and Foreign. Supplement with illustrations.* Assisted by P. H. Gosse. London: Longmans, Green, and Co., 1889.

Hughes, W. R. *On the Principles and Management of the Marine Aquarium.* London: John Van Voorst, 1875.

Humphreys, H. Noel. *Ocean and River Gardens: A History of the Marine and Fresh-water Aquaria, with the Best Methods for their Establishment and Preservation.* London: Sampson Low, Son, & Co., 1857.

Huxley, Leonard (ed.). *Life and Letters of Thomas Henry Huxley.* London: Macmillan and Co., 3 vols., 1903.

————. (ed.). *Life and Letters of Sir Joseph Dalton Hooker.* London: John Murray, 2 vols., 1918.

Huxley, T. H. *A Manual of the Anatomy of Invertebrated Animals.* London: J. & A. Churchill, 1877.

Hyman, Libbie H. *The Invertebrates: Protozoa through Ctenophora.* New York: McGraw-Hill Book Co., Inc., 1940.

Introvigne, Massimo. *The Plymouth Brethren.* Oxford: Oxford University Press, 2018.

Ironside, H. A. *A Historical Sketch of the Brethren Movement. An Account of Its Inception, Progress, Principles and Failures, and its Lessons for Present Day Believers.* Grand Rapids, Michigan: Zondervan Publishing, 1942.

Jacks, L. P. (ed.). *From Authority to Freedom: the Spiritual Pilgrimage of Charles Hargrove.* London: Williams & Norgate, 1920.

James, Louis. *Fiction for the Working Man 1830–1850.* London: Oxford University Press, 1963.

Johnson, E. D. H. (ed.). *The Poetry of Earth. A Collection of English Nature Writings from Gilbert White of Selborne to Richard Jefferies.* New York: Atheneum, 1966, 1974.

Jones, Thomas Rymer. *The Aquarian Naturalist. A Manual for the Sea-side.* London: John Van Voorst, 1858.

Kelly, William. *The Second Advent of Christ Premillennial: A Reply to the Rev. D. Brown, D.D.* Glasgow: R. L. Allan, 1868.

Kemp, George Edward. *Kemps of Ollantigh and Kemps of Poole. Being a brief outline of the Ancient Kemp family of Ollantigh Manor, Wye, Kent County, and a brief history of the Kemp Family of Poole, Dorset county, England, and some of the descendants in the United States.* Seattle, Washington: McKay Printing Co., 1939.

King, Amy M. *The Divine in the Commonplace: Reverent Natural History and the Novel in Britain.* Cambridge: Cambridge University Press, 2019.

Kitchel, Anna Theresa. *George Lewes and George Eliot. A Review of Records.* New York: John Day Co., 1933.

Klaver, J. M. I. *Geology and Religious Sentiment. The Effect of Geological Discoveries on English Society and Literature between 1829 and 1859.* Leiden: Brill, 1997.

Lankester, Edwin. *The Aquavivarium, Fresh and Marine.* London: Robert Hardwicke, 1856.

Lankester, Edwin Ray. *Degeneration. A Chapter in Darwinism.* London: Macmillan and Co., 1880.

————. *Diversions of a Naturalist.* London: Methuen & Co., 1915.

————. *Secrets of Earth and Sea.* London: Methuen & Co. Ltd, 1920.

Lazenby, Marion Elias. *History of Methodism in Alabama and West Florida. Being an account of the Amazing March of Methodism through Alabama and West Florida.* [?Nashville]: North Alabama Conference and Alabama-West Florida Conference of the Methodist Church, 1960.

Lench, Charles. *The History of the Rise and Progress of Methodism on the Western Bay Circuit, first as part of Carbonear, then Blackhead, and afterwards for 35 Years as a Separate Circuit with a Bird's-eye View of Carbonear, Freshwater, Blackhead, Lower Island Cove and Old Perlican Circuits.* [?St. John's, Newfoundland]: Barnes & Co., [?1912].

————. *The Story of Methodism in Bonavista And the Settlements visited by the Early Preachers.* S.n.: 1913.

Lester, Joseph. *E. Ray Lankester and the Making of Modern British Biology.* Edited by Peter J. Bowler. BSHS Monographs, Number 10. Oxford: British Society for the History of Science, 1995.

Levere, Trevor H. and Jarrell, Richard A. (eds.) *A Curious Field-book: Science & Society in Canadian History.* Toronto: Oxford University Press, 1974.

Lewes, George Henry. *Sea-side Studies at Ilfracombe, Tenby, the Scilly Isles, & Jersey.* Edinburgh & London: William Blackwood and Sons, 1858; 2nd ed.,1860.
———. *The Physiology of Common Life.* Leipzig: Bernhard Tauchnitz, 1860.
Lightman, Bernard. *Victorian Popularizers of Science: Designing Nature for New Audiences.* Chicago: University of Chicago Press, 2007.
Lindroth, Carl H. *The Carabid Beetles of Newfoundland.* Entomologiska Sällskapet i Lund [Entomological Society of Lund, Sweden], Opuscula Entomologica Supplementum XII, 1955.
Lineham, Peter J. *There We Found Brethren: A History of Assemblies of Brethren in New Zealand.* Palmerston North: G.P.H. Society, 1977.
Lister, Raymond. *Thomas Gosse: A Biographical Sketch of an Itinerant Miniature Painter of the Early Nineteenth Century.* Linton, Cambridge: Golden Head Press, 1953.
———. *British Romantic Art.* London: G. Bell & Sons, 1973.
Livingstone, David N. *Dealing with Darwin. Place, Politics, and Rhetoric in Religious Engagements with Evolution.* Baltimore: Johns Hopkins University Press, 2014.
Livingstone, David N., Hart, D. G. and Mark A. Noll (eds.). *Evangelicals and Science in Historical Perspective.* New York: Oxford University Press, 1999.
[Lloyd, William Alford]. *The Marine Aquarium. (SALE LIST.).* London: Hayman Brothers, [1856].
Lloyd, William Alford. *A List, with Descriptions, Illustrations, and Prices, of Whatever Relates to Aquaria.* London: Hayman Brothers, 1858.
———. *A Supplement to "A List, with Descriptions, Illustrations, and Prices, of Whatever Relates to Aquaria"; Containing Practical Instructions for their Management, and a Description of a Series of Tanks in Which Cheapness of Cost and Efficiency of Action are Combined to an Extent Hitherto Unattained.* London: Hayman Brothers, 1860.
———. *A Guide Book to the Marine Aquarium of the Crystal Palaces Company (Limited).* London: R. K. Burt & Co., 1872.
Lysaght, Averil M. *Joseph Banks in Newfoundland and Labrador, 1766. His Diary, Manuscripts and Collections.* Berkeley: University of California Press, 1971.
McLachlan, Robert. *A Monographic Revision & Synopsis of the Trichoptera of European Fauna.* London: John Van Voorst, Part I, 1874.
Magee, Judith. *The Art and Science of William Bartram.* University Park, PA: Pennsylvania State University Press, 2007.
Malcomson, Robert W. *Popular Recreations in English Society 1700-1850.* Cambridge: University Press, 1973.
Manuel, Frank E. *The Religion of Isaac Newton.* Oxford: Clarendon, 1974.
[Mark, Walter]. *Retrospect of the History of the Mission of the Brethren's Church in Jamaica, for the Past Hundred Years.* London: William Tyler, [?1854].
Mathieson, Stuart. *Evangelicals and the Philosophy of Science: The Victoria Institute, 1865-1939.* London: Routledge, 2020.
Mattheisen, Paul F. and Michael Millgate (eds.). *Transatlantic Dialogue: Selected American Correspondence of Edmund Gosse.* Austin: University of Texas Press, 1965.
Members of the Natural History Society of Jamaica. *Glimpses of Jamaican Natural History.* Kingston, Jamaica: Institute of Jamaica, 2ed., Vol. 2, 1949.
Merrill, Lynn L. *The Romance of Victorian Natural History.* New York: Oxford University Press, 1989.
Merton, Francis S. *Handbook to the Aquarium; Being a Popular Description of the Best and Cheapest Method of Making and Managing an Aquarium; with Some Observations on the Habits and Localities of the British Fresh-water Shells.* London: Whitely & Co., 1856.
Miles, Alfred H. (ed.). *The Poets and Poetry of the Century.* London: Hutchinson & Co., Vol. VIII, n.d.
Miller, Edward. *That Noble Cabinet. A History of the British Museum.* London: Andre Deutsch, 1973.
Milne-Edwards, Henri. *Histoire Naturelle des Coralliaires, ou Polypes Proprement Dits.* Paris: A la Librairie Encyclopédique de Roret, Tome I, 1857.
Minto, W. (ed.). *Autobiographical Notes of the Life of William Bell Scott.* London: James R. Osgood, 2 vols., 1892.
Mitchell, D. W. *Guide to the Gardens of the Zoological Society of London.* 3rd ed., revised by P. L. Sclater. London: Bradbury and Evans, 1859.
Mitchell, P. Chalmers. *Centenary History of the Zoological Society of London.* London: Printed for the Society, 1929.
Moore, James R. *The Post-Darwinian Controversies. A Study of the Protestant Struggle to Come to Terms with Darwin in Great Britain and America, 1870-1900.* Cambridge: Cambridge University Press, 1979, 1981.
See also DESMOND, ADRIAN and JAMES MOORE
Morgan, George E. *Veteran in Revival: R. C. Morgan, his Life and Times.* London: Morgan & Scott, 1909.

Morris, F. O. *Difficulties of Darwinism. Read before the British Association at Norwich and Exeter in 1868 and 1869. With a Preface and a Correspondence with Professor Huxley*. London: Longmans, Green, and Co., 1869.

Moyles, R. Gordon. *"Complaints is Many and Various, but the Odd Divil Likes It": Nineteenth Century Views of Newfoundland*. Toronto: Peter Martin Associates, 1975.

Mullen, Gary R. and Taylor D. Littleton. *Philip Henry Gosse: Science and Art* in Letters From Alabama *and* Entomologia Alabamensis. Tuscaloosa: University of Alabama Press, 2010.

Munro, John M. *Selected Poems of Theo. Marzials*. Beirut, Lebanon: American University of Beirut, 1974.

Neatby, William Blair. *A History of the Plymouth Brethren*. London: Hodder and Stoughton, 1901.

Nicoll, W. Robertson. *My Father. An Aberdeenshire Minister 1812-1891*. London: Hodder and Stoughton, 1908.

Nicolson, Marjorie H. *The Microscope and English Imagination*. Northampton, Mass.: Smith College Studies in Modern Languages XVI, 1935.

Numbers, Ronald L. *The Creationists: The Evolution of Scientific Creationism*. Berkeley: University of California Press, 1992, 1993 pb.

Orr, J. Edwin. *The Fervent Prayer*. Chicago: Moody Press, 1974.

Osborn, Herbert. *Fragments of Entomological History, Including Some Personal Recollections of Men and Events*. Columbus, Ohio: Published by the Author: vol. I, 1937; vol. II, 1946.

———. *A Brief History of Entomology, Including [the] Time of Demosthenes and Aristotle to Modern Times with over Five Hundred Portraits*. Columbus, Ohio: Spahr & Glenn Co., 1952.

Payne, Christiana. *Where the Sea Meets the Land: Artists on the Coast in Nineteenth-Century Britain*. Bristol: Sansom & Co., 2007.

Pengelly, Hester (ed.). *A Memoir of William Pengelly, Torquay, F.R.S., Geologist, with a Selection of His Correspondence*. London: John Murray, 1897.

Petley, Christer. *Slaveholders in Jamaica: Colonial Society and Culture During the Era of Abolition*. London: Pickering & Chatto, 2009.

Pierce, F. N. *The Genitalia of the Group Noctuidae of the Lepidoptera of the British Isles. An Account of the Morphology of the Male Clasping Organs*. Liverpool: A. W. Duncan, 1909.

Pierson, Arthur T. *James Wright of Bristol*. London: James Nisbet & Co., Ltd., 1906.

Pietsch, Brendan M. *Dispensational Modernism*. Oxford: Oxford University Press, 2015.

Pratt, Anne. *Chapters on the Common Things of the Sea-side*. London: SPCK, 1850.

Prowse, D. W. *A History of Newfoundland from the English, Colonial, and Foreign Records*. London: Macmillan and Co., 1895.

Roberts, Mary. *The Sea-side Companion; or, Marine Natural History*. London: Printed for Whittaker & Co., 1835.

Rowdon, Harold H. *The Origins of the Brethren, 1825-1850*. London: Pickering & Inglis Ltd., 1967.

Rupke, Nicolaas A. *Richard Owen: Biology without Darwin*. Chicago: University of Chicago Press, 1994, revised ed., 2009.

Sacks, Jonathan. *The Great Partnership: Science, Religion, and the Search for Meaning*. New York: Schocken Books, 2011.

St. John, William Charles. *A Catechism of the History of Newfoundland, from the Earliest Accounts to the Close of the Year 1834, for the Use of Schools*. St. John's: J. M'Coubrey, 1835; revised edition with a modified title, Boston: George C. Rand, 1855.

Sandeen, Ernest R. *The Roots of Fundamentalism. British and American Millenarianism 1800-1930*. Chicago: University of Chicago Press, 1970.

Saville-Kent, W. *Official Guide Book to the Manchester Aquarium*. 3rd ed. Manchester: The Main Printing, Stationery & Paper Co., Ltd., 1875.

Scherren, Henry. *The Zoological Society of London: A Sketch of its Foundation and Development and the Story of its Farm, Museum, Gardens, Menagerie and Library*. London: Cassell and Co., 1905.

Sclater, P. L. *A Record of the Progress of the Zoological Society of London during the Nineteenth Century*. London: William Clowes & Sons, 1901.

Secord, James A. *Victorian Sensation: The Extraordinary Publication, Reception, and Secret Authorship of* Vestiges of the Natural History of Creation. Chicago: University of Chicago Press, 2000.

Sheets-Pyenson, Susan. *John William Dawson: Faith, Hope, and Science*. Montreal: McGill-Queen's University Press, 1995.

Shipton, Anna. *"Tell Jesus." Recollections of Emily Gosse*. London: Morgan and Chase, [1863].

———. *The Upper Springs and the Nether Springs; or, Life Hid with Christ in God*. London: James Nisbet & Co., 1882.

Siebold, C. Th. von, and H. Stannius. *Comparative Anatomy*. Translated from the German, with Notes and Additions by Waldo I. Burnett. London: Trübner & Co., vol. I, 1854.

Simonetta, Alberto Mario. *Short History of Biology from the Origins to the 20th Century*. Firenze: Firenza University Press, 2003.

Slack, H. J. *Marvels of Pond-life; or, a Year's Microscopic Recreations among the Polyps, Infusoria, Rotifers, Water-bears, and Polyzoa.* London: Groombridge and Sons, 1861.

Smith, J. E., and J. D. Carthy, G. Chapman, R. B. Clark, and D. Nichols (eds.). *The Invertebrate Panorama.* London: Weidenfeld and Nicolson, 1971.

Smith, Jonathan. *Charles Darwin and Victorian Visual Culture.* Cambridge: Cambridge University Press, 2006.

Smith, T. Watson. *History of the Methodist Church within the territories embraced in the late conference of Eastern British America, including Nova Scotia, New Brunswick, Newfoundland, Prince Edward Island and Bermuda.* 2 vols. Halifax: Methodist Book Room, Vol. I, 1877; Halifax: S.F. Huestis, Vol. II [1890].

Sonrel, A. (lithographer). *The Anatomy of Astrangia danae [being] Natural History Illustrations Prepared Under the Direction of Louis Agassiz [in] 1849.* City of Washington: Smithsonian Institution, 1889.

Sorensen, W. Conner. *Brethren of the Net: American Entomology, 1840–1880.* Tuscaloosa: University of Alabama Press, 1995.

Sowerby, George Brettingham. *Popular History of the Aquarium of Marine and Fresh-water Animals and Plants.* London: Lovell Reeve, 1857.

Spence, Martin. *Heaven on Earth. Reimagining Time and Eternity in Nineteenth-Century British Evangelicalism.* Eugene, Oregon: Pickwick Publications, 2015.

Stageman, Peter. *A Bibliography of the First Editions of Philip Henry Gosse, F.R.S.* Cambridge: Golden Head Press, Ltd., 1955.

Stark, R. M. *The Marine Aquarium. Directions for its Preparation and Management.* Edinburgh: Edmonston and Douglas, 1857.

Step, Edward. *By the Deep Sea. A Popular Introduction to the Wild Life of the British Shores. With 122 Illustrations by P. H. Gosse, W. A. Pearce, and Mabel Step.* London: Jarrold & Sons, 1896.

Stephenson, Thomas Alan. *The British Sea Anemones.* London: Printed for the Ray Society, vol. I, 1928; II, 1935.

Stewart, D. B. (ed.), *Gosse's Jamaica 1844-45.* Kingston, Jamaica: Institute of Jamaica Publications, 1984.

Stott, Rebecca. *Theatres of Glass: The Woman Who Brought the Sea to the City.* London: Short Books, 2003.

Stunt, Timothy C. F. *From Awakening to Secession: Radical Evangelicals in Switzerland and Britain 1815-35.* Edinburgh: T&T Clark, 2000.

Summerton, Neil. *'I thanked the Lord, and asked for more': George Müller's Life and Work.* Glasgow: Brethren Archivists and Historians Network, 2022.

Tatford, Frederick A. *That the World May Know. Vol. 10: The Islands of the Sea (also including Aborigines, Maoris and Amerindians).* Bath: Echoes of Service, 1986.

Taylor, Dr and Mrs Howard. *Hudson Taylor and the China Inland Mission.* London: Morgan & Scott, 1918.

Taylor, J. E. *Half Hours at the Sea Side; or, Recreations with Marine Objects.* London: David Bogue, 1872, 4th ed., 1880.

———. *The Aquarium. Its Inhabitants, Structure, and Management.* Edinburgh: John Grant, 1876, new ed., 1901.

Thompson, Augustus C. *Moravian Missions.* London: Hodder and Stoughton, 1883.

Thomson, Keith. *Before Darwin: Reconciling God and Nature.* New Haven: Yale University Press, 2005.

Thwaite, Ann. *Edmund Gosse: a literary landscape 1849-1928.* London: Secker & Warburg, 1984.

———. *Glimpses of the Wonderful: The Life of Philip Henry Gosse 1810-1888.* London: Faber and Faber, 2002.

Tocque, Annie S.W. (ed.). *Kaleidoscope Echoes, being Historical, Philosophical, Scientific, and Theological Sketches, from the Miscellaneous Writings of the Rev. Philip Tocque, A.M.* Toronto: Hunter, Rose Co., Ltd., 1895.

Tocque, Philip. *Wandering Thoughts, or Solitary Hours.* London: Thomas Richardson and Son, 1846.

———. *A Peep at Uncle Sam's Farm, Workshop, Fisheries, &c.* Boston: Charles H. Peirce and Co., 1851.

———. *Newfoundland: As It Was, and As It Is In 1877.* Toronto: John B. Magurn, 1878.

Turrill, W. B. *Joseph Dalton Hooker.* London: Thomas Nelson and Sons Ltd., 1963.

Twyman, Michael. *A History of Chromolithography: Printed Colour for All.* London: The British Library, 2013.

Van Sommer, James. *Lay Service: Its Nurseries and its Spheres.* London: John F. Shaw & Co., [?1881].

Van Sommer, Jr., James. *Records of the Van Sommer Family.* Bath: The Ralph Allen Press, 1945.

Vickery, V.R. and D. K. McE. Kevan. *A Monograph of the Orthopteroid Insects of Canada and Adjacent Regions.* Ste. Anne de Bellevue, Quebec: Lyman Entomological Museum and Research Laboratory, Memoir no. 13, vol. I, 1983.

Walker, Hilda H. *Torquay Natural History Society: The First 125 Years, 1844-1969.* Torquay: Torquay Natural History Society, 1969.

Ward, H. B. and G. C. Whipple. *Fresh-water Biology.* 2nd ed., ed. by W. T. Edmondson. New York: John Wiley & Sons, 1959.

Ward, Nathaniel Bagshaw. *On the Growth of Plants in Closely Glazed Cases*. London: John Van Voorst, 1842.

Ward, Stephen H. *On Wardian Cases for Plants, and their Applications*. London: John Van Voorst, 1854.

Wells, T. Spencer. *Cancer Cures and Cancer Curers*. London: John Churchill, 1860.

West, Anson. *A History of Methodism in Alabama*. Nashville, TN: Printed for the Author, 1893.

West, Gerald T. *From Friends to Brethren: The Howards of Tottenham—Quakers, Brethren, and Evangelicals*. Troon, Ayrshire: Brethren Archivists and Historians Network, 2016.

White, Adam. *Heads and Tales*. London: James Nisbet & Co., 1870.
    See also ARACHNOPHILUS.

White, Andrew Dickson. *A History of the Warfare of Science with Theology in Christendom*. New York: Dover Publications, Inc., 1896, 2 vols., 1960.

White, J. T. *The History of Torquay*. Torquay: Torquay Directory Office, 1878.

[White, William M., editor]. *The Journals of Walter White*. London: Chapman and Hall, Ltd., 1898.

Williams, Charles. *Pickings on the Sea-shore; or, Cliffs, Sands, Plants, and Animals: A Hand-book for Brighton, Ramsgate, Folkestone, Dover, Hastings, the Isle of Wight, Scarborough, and Other Parts of the Coast; and for the Vivarium at Home*. London: Judd and Glass, 1857.

Wilson, Bryan R. *Patterns of Sectarianism: Organisation and Ideology in Social and Religious Movements*. London: Heinemann, 1967.

———. (ed.). *Religious Sects. A Sociological Study*. London: Weidenfeld and Nicolson, 1970.

Wilson, Robert. *Methodism in The Maritime Provinces*. Halifax: S.F. Huestis, 1893.

Wilson, William. *Newfoundland and Its Missionaries*. Cambridge, Mass.: Dakin & Metcalf, 1866.

Winslow, Octavius. *The Standard and the Standard-bearer. A Tribute to the Memory of the Rev Edward B. Elliott, M.A.* London: James Nisbet & Co., 1875.

Wood, J. G. *The Common Objects of the Sea Shore; Including Hints for an Aquarium*. London: G. Routledge & Co., 1857.

Wood, Theodore. *The Rev J. G. Wood: His Life and Work*. London: Cassell & Co., Ltd., 1890.

Woolf, James D. *Sir Edmund Gosse*. New York: Twayne Publishers, Inc., 1972.

———. (introduction). *The Unequal Yoke (1886). A Novel By Sir Edmund Gosse*. Delmar, NY: Scholars' Facsimiles & Reprints, 1975.

Yonge, C. M. *The Sea Shore*. London: Collins, 1949, 1972.

Young, Kenneth. *Chapel*. London: Eyre Methuen, 1972.

B. ARTICLES

Abate, Dante, Sorin Hermon, Stefania Lotti, and Gianna Innocenti. '3D Scientific Visualisation of 19th Century Glass Replicas of Invertebrates', *2017 IEEE 13th International Conference on e-Science* (Oct. 2017), 533-41.

Adelman, Juliana. 'Eozoön: Debunking the Dawn Animal', *Endeavour* 31 (Sept. 2007), 94-8.

Agassiz, Louis. 'On the Structure of Coral Animals', *Proc. of American Association for the Advancement of Science* II (1850), 68-77.

Ainley, Marianne Gosztonyi. 'Science in Canada's Backwoods. Catharine Parr Traill', in Barbara T. Gates and Ann B. Shteir. *Natural Eloquence: Women Reinscribe Science*. Madison: University of Wisconsin Press, 1997, 79-97.

Alder, Joshua. 'A Catalogue of the Zoophytes of Northumberland and Durham', *Trans. Tyneside Naturalists' Field Club* III (1856), 93-162.

Alexander, Bob. 'William Alford Lloyd, 1824-1880', http://parlouraquariums.org.uk/ [website only, 34 unnumbered pages, n.d. but 2012].

Allen, D. E. 'Natural History and Social History', *Journal of the Society for the Bibliography of Natural History* VII (June 1976), 509-16.

———. 'Tastes and crazes', in Nicholas Jardine, J. A. Secord and E. C. Spary (eds.). *Cultures of Natural History* (Cambridge: University Press, 1996), 394-407.

Anderson, James. 'Fertilisation of Orchids', *Journal of Horticulture* n.s. IV (21 April 1863), 287.

———. 'Orchid Cultivation, Cross-breeding, and Hybridising', *Journal of Horticulture* n.s. IV (17 March 1863), 206-8.

Andrews, John S. 'Philip Henry Gosse, F.R.S.', *Library Association Record* XXVIII (June 1961), 197-201.

Anon. 'The Apocalypse and Its Interpreters', *Literary Churchman* (17 June 1861), 226-9.

———. 'The British Museum Forty Years Ago. Mr. Gosse's Reminiscences', *Daily Graphic* (11 October 1906), 10.

———. 'Clasping Organs, accessory to generation, in Lepidoptera', *Journal of the Royal Microscopical Society* ser.2, III (Oct. 1883), 648-50.

———. 'A Day's Excursion in Newfoundland', *Fraser's Magazine* XXXII (Dec. 1845), 740-2 [author unidentified in *Wellesley Index*].

———. 'Death of a Man Converted by Emily Gosse's 'Stray Sheep'', *Revival* X (18 Feb. 1864), 101.

———. 'European Convulsions', *Rainbow* III (1 Aug. 1866), 337-8.

————. 'Modern Prophetic Literature', *Journal of Sacred Literature* X (Oct. 1859), 1-16.

————. 'Noch ein Besuch im zoologischen garten des Regentsparks zu London', *Die Gartenlaube* IV (1856), 385-6.

————. 'On Tract Distributing', *The Revival* XIII (5 Oct. 1865), 207.

————. 'Our Religious Societies', *Christian Work* (1 Nov. 1865), 495-501; (1 Feb. 1866), 55-63.

————. 'Paragon Hall, Hackney, London, 1850-1954', *The Witness* LXXXIV (Dec. 1954), 238.

————. 'Retrospect of the History of the Mission of the Brethren's Church in Jamaica for the past Hundred Years', in *Periodical Accounts Relating to the Missions of the Church of the United Brethren, Established Among the Heath* (London: For the Brethren's Society, 1853), XXI, 283-98, 337-60.

————. 'The School of the Prophets', London *Times*, 3 Nov. 1859, 5.

————. 'The Value of Tracts', *The Evangelist* n.s. III (1868), 91-2.

————. 'Wie er= und behält man den Ocean auf dem Tische, oder das Marine=Aquarium', *Die Gartenlaube: illustriertes familienblatt* III (1855), 503-6.

Armstrong, Isobel. 'The Microscope: Meditations of the Sub-Visible World', in Roger Luckhurst and Josephine McDonagh (eds.). *Transactions and Encounters: Science and Culture in the Nineteenth Century*. Manchester: Manchester University Press, 2002, 30-54.

Arnold-Foster, Agnes. 'Gender and Pain in Nineteenth-Century Cancer Care', *Gender & History* 32 (March 2020), 13-29.

Atz, James W. 'The Myth of the Balanced Aquarium', *Natural History* (American Museum of Natural History) 58 (Feb. 1949), 72-77, 96.

B[adham]., C. D. 'Periwinkles in Pound', *Fraser's Magazine* LI (May 1855), 531-48.

Baker, D. B. 'Alfred Russel Wallace's record of his consignments to Samuel Stevens, 1854-1861', *Zoologische Mededelingen* 75 (2001), 251-341.

Barber, Bernard. 'Resistance by Scientists to Scientific Discovery', *Science* n.s. CXXXIV (1 Sept. 1961), 596-602.

Barnardo, T. J. 'The Gospel in the East End', *The Revival* (29 Oct. 1868), 599-600.

————. 'East-End Juvenile Mission', *The Revival* (31 Dec. 1868), 727-8.

Barton, Ruth. '"An Influential Set of Chaps": The X-Club and Royal Society Politics 1864-85', *British Journal for the History of Science* 23 (March 1990), 53-81.

————. 'Just before *Nature:* The Purposes of Science and the Purposes of Popularization in some English Popular Science Journals of the 1860s', *Annals of Science* 55 (1998), 1-33.

————. '"Huxley, Lubbock, and Half a Dozen Others": Professionals and Gentlemen in the Formation of the X Club, 1851-1864', *Isis* 89 (Sept. 1998), 410-44.

————. 'Scientific Authority and Scientific Controversy in *Nature:* North Britain against the X Club', in Louise Henson, et. al. (eds.). *Culture and Science in the Nineteenth-Century Century Media* (London: Routledge, 2004), 223-35.

Beauchamp, Paul Marais de. 'Recherches sur les Rotifères. Les formations tégumentaires et l'appareil digestif', *Archives de Zoologie Expérimentale et Générale*, 4e ser., X (25 Jan. 1909), 1-410.

Beer, Patricia. 'Happy Few', review of Max Wright, *Told in Gath*, in *London Review of Books* 13 (23 May 1991), 12.

Beiermann, Lea. 'Reproducing Rotifers: 'Working Images' and the Making of a Microscopy Community in the Nineteenth Century', *Transactions of the American Philosophical Society* n.s. 111 (2022), 20-44.

B[ennet]., W. H. 'The Holy One of God', *Golden Lamp* n.s. VIII (Aug. 1885), 169-74.

————. 'When Did Christ Become the Sin-bearer?' *Golden Lamp* n.s. VIII (Sept. 1885), 193-7.

Bethune, C. J. S. 'The Rise and Progress of Entomology in Canada', *Trans. Royal Society of Canada*, sec. IV (1898), 155-65.

Betts, John Rickards. 'P. T. Barnum and the Popularization of Natural History', *Journal of the History of Ideas* XX (1959), 353-68.

Bill, E.G.W. 'The Declaration of Students of the Natural and Physical Sciences, 1865', *Bodleian Library Record* V (April 1954), 262-7.

Blackwood, S. A. 'Prophetic Interpretation', *The Christian* (9 Aug. 1877), 539.

Blaisdell, Muriel. 'Natural Theology and Nature's Disguises', *Journal of the History of Biology* XV (Summer 1982),163-89.

Blake-Hill, P.V. 'The Macmillan Archive', *British Museum Quarterly* XXXVI (Autumn 1972), 74-9.

Borges, Jorge Luis. 'The Creation and P. H. Gosse' [1941], *Other Inquisitions 1937-1952*, trans. by Ruth L. C. Simms (New York: Washington Square Press, 1965, 1966), 22-5.

Borsay, Peter. 'A Room with a View: Visualising the Seaside, *c.* 1750-1914', *Transactions of the Royal Historical Society*, 6th ser., 23 (2013), 175-201.

Bout de Charlemont, Hippolyte. 'Notes pour server a l'histoire des aquariums', *Bulletin Mensuel de la Société Nationale d'Acclimatation de France* ser. 4, vol. 3 (Jan. 1886), 30-44.

Bowler, Peter J. 'Scientific Attitudes to Darwinism in Britain and America', in David Kohn (ed.), *The Darwinian Heritage*. Princeton: University Press, 1985, 641-681.

————. 'Are the Arthropoda a Natural Group? An Episode in the History of Evolutionary Biology', *Journal of the History of Biology* 27 (Summer 1994), 177–213.

————. 'In Retrospect. Charles Darwin and his Dublin critics: Samuel Haughton and William Henry Harvey', *Proceedings of the Royal Irish Academy: Archaeology, Culture, History, Literature* 109C (2009), 409-20.

Boyd, Robert. 'Mother and Son', *Harvester* (Nov. 1962), 52, 169.

————. 'Bibliographical: Philip Henry Gosse, 1810–1888', *CBRF Broadsheet* no. 2 (March-April 1969),4–5.

————. '"Father and Son"—A New Look', *The Witness* (July 1975), 264-66.

————. 'Gosse, Emily', *Dictionary of Evangelical Biography* I (1995), 460.

————. 'Gosse, Philip Henry', *Dictionary of Evangelical Biography* I (1995), 460.

Boyd, Robert and Harold H. Rowdon. 'Gosse [*née* Bowes], Emily', *Oxford Dictionary of National Biography* (online, 2004).

Brock, W. H. 'The Warington-Gosse Aquarium Controversy: Two Unrecorded Letters', *Archives of Natural History* 18 (1991), 179-183.

————. '*Glaucus:* Kingsley and the Seaside Naturalists', repr. in William H. Brock, *Science for All: Studies in the History of Victorian Science*. Brookfield, VT: Variorum, 1996, 25-36.

Brock, W. H. and R. M. Macleod. 'The Scientists' Declaration: Reflexions on Science and Belief in the Wake of *Essays and Reviews*, 1864-5', *British Journal for the History of Science* IX (March 1976), 39-66.

Broderip, W. J. 'On the Utility of Preserving Facts Relative to the Habits of Animals, with Additions to Two Memoirs in "White's Natural History of Selborne"', *Zoological Journal* II (April 1825), 14-17.

Brodrick, William. 'On the Urticating Powers of the Actiniae Towards Each Other', *AMNH* ser. 3, III (April 1859), 319-20.

B[roomhall]., B. 'In Memoriam—William Thomas Berger', *China's Millions* n.s. VII (Feb. 1899), 18-20.

Brown, David. 'The Blessed Hope', *The Christian* I (Nov. 10-Jan. 5, 1871), 513-p. 5 [sic], 8 parts, *passim*.

Bruton, Francis A. 'Pioneer Entomologist of Newfoundland', St. John's, Newfoundland *Evening Telegram* (16 Dec. 1927), 22.

————. 'Philip Henry Gosse's Entomology of Newfoundland', *Entomological News* XLI (Feb. 1930), 34-7.

Burkhart, Charles. 'George Moore and *Father and Son*', *Nineteenth-Century Fiction* (Sept. 1960), 71-8.

C[arrington]., J. T. 'Obituary. Philip Henry Gosse, F.R.S.', *Entomologist* XXI (Oct. 1888), 264.

Caws, Peter. 'Evidence and Testimony: Philip Henry Gosse and the Omphalos Theory', in O. Harold & G. J. Worth (eds.), *Six Studies in 19th Century English Literature and Thought*. Lawrence, Kansas: University of Kansas, Publications III, 1962, 69-90.

Chester, Richard. 'Principles of Futurist Interpretation', *Rainbow* III (1 May 1866), 222-6.

————. 'Futurist Principles Defended', *Rainbow* III (1 Aug. 1866), 348–52.

————. 'Have the Apocalyptic Seals as Yet Been Opened?' *Rainbow* IV (1 Feb. 1867), 58-64.

————. 'Is the Coming of the Lord to be Delayed?' *Voice Upon the Mountains* III (Nov. 1, Dec. 1, 1869), 141-2, 166-7.

————. 'The Coming Kingdom', *The Christian* I (Sept. 8-Nov. 3, 1870), 403-502, 9 parts, *passim*.

Coad, F. Roy. 'Prophetic Developments, with Particular Reference to the Early Brethren Movement', *CBRF Occasional Paper No.2* (1966).

Cockerell, T. D. A. 'A Little Known Jamaican Naturalist, Dr Anthony Robinson', *American Naturalist* XXVIII (Sept. 1894), 775-80.

Code, Lorraine. '*Father and Son:* A Case Study in Epistemic Responsibility', *The Monist* 66 (April 1983), 268-82.

C[olville]., R[obert]. '"Father and Son". An Interview with Mr. Edmund Gosse, LL.D.', London *Great Thoughts from Master Minds*, ser. 6, IV (4 April 1908), 8-10.

————. 'Mr. Henry Austin Dobson, LL.D. A Chat with the Famous Poet and Writer on the Eighteenth Century', London *Great Thoughts from Master Minds*, ser. 6, IV (1908), 376-8.

Cook, G. C. 'George Busk FRS (1807-1886), Nineteenth-century Polymath: Surgeon, Parasitologist, Zoologist and Palaeontologist', *Journal of Medical Biography* V (1997), 88-101.

Creamer, Jamie. 'Engrossed in Gosse: Entomology Prof Preps to Pen Biography', *AG Illustrated* IV (Summer 2007), 1-2.

Crombie, Ronald I. 'Jamaica', in Brian I. Crother (ed.), *Caribbean Amphibians and Reptiles*. San Diego: Academic Press, 1999, 63-92.

Cundall, Frank. 'Richard Hill', *Journal of the Institute of Jamaica* II (July 1896), 223-30.

————. 'Richard Hill', *Journal of Negro History* V (Jan. 1920), 37-44.

————. 'A Supplementary Bibliography of Richard Hill', *American Book Collector* III (Jan. 1933), 46-8.

Dana, James D. 'Zoophytes', *United States Exploring Expedition during 1838, 1839, 1840, 1841, 1842* ... Philadelphia: Lea and Blanchard, vol. VIII, 1848 [=1846].

Dance, S. Peter. 'Hugh Cuming (1791-1865), Prince of Collectors', *Journal of the Society for the Bibliography of Natural History* IX (April 1980), 477-501.

Darwin, Charles. 'Fertilisation of Orchids', *Journal of Horticulture* n.s. IV (31 March 1863), 237.

Davenport, L. J. 'In the Footsteps of Gosse', *Alabama Heritage* Issue 98 (Fall 2010), 51-2.

————. 'From Cro-Magnon to Kral: A History of Botany in Alabama', *Journal of the Botanical Research Institute of Texas* IX (30 Nov. 2015), 397-431.

Davies, C. Maurice. 'The Plymouth Brethren', in C. M. Davies, *Unorthodox London: or Phases of Religious Life in the Metropolis*. London: Tinsley Brothers, 2nd edition, 1874, 175-82.

Davis, G. H. 'Tracts—Their Production and Distribution', *The Revival* V (5 Oct. 1861), 109-10.

DeArce, Miguel. '*The natural history review* (1854-1865)', *Archives of Natural History* 39 (2012), 253-69.

————. 'The Parallel Lives of Joseph Allen Galbraith (1818-90) and Samuel Haughton (1821-97): Religion, Friendship, Scholarship and Politics in Victorian Ireland', *Proceedings of the Royal Irish Academy: Archaeology, Culture, History, Literature* 112C (2012), 333-59.

de Beer, Gavin (ed.) *Darwin's Journal*, in *Bulletin of BM(NH)*, Historical Series II (1959), 1-21.

DePaolo, Charles. 'Frederic E. Mohs, MD, and the history of zinc chloride', *Clinics in Dermatology* 36 (2018), 568-575.

Desmond, Adrian. 'Redefining the X Axis: "Professionals", "Amateurs" and the Making of Mid-Victorian Biology: A Progress Report', *Journal of the History of Biology* 34 (Spring 2001), 3-50.

Dickson, Beth. 'To Encourage Historians of the Christian Brethren: A Meditation', in Neil T. R. Dickson and Tim Grass (eds.), *The Growth of the Brethren Movement: National and International Experiences. Essays in Honour of Harold H. Rowdon*. Bletchley, Milton Keynes: Paternoster, 2006, 28-32.

Dickson, Neil T. R. 'Brethren and Baptists in Scotland', *Baptist Quarterly* 33 (Oct. 1990), 372-87.

————. '"The Church Itself is God's Clergy": The Principles and Practices of the Brethren', in Deryck W. Lovegrove (ed.), *The Rise of the Laity in Evangelical Protestantism*. London: Routledge, 2002, 217-35.

————. 'A Darbyite Mystic: Frances Bevan (1827-1909)', in Neil Dickson and T. J. Marinello (eds.), *Bible and Theology in the Brethren* (Glasgow: BAHN, 2018), 215-247.

————. 'Hunter Beattie (1876-1951): A Conscientious Objector at the Margins', *Scottish Church History* 50 (2021), 145–63.

————. '"Exclusive" and "Open": A Footnote', *Brethren Historical Review* 19 (2023), 82-90.

Dickson, Neil T. R. and Sam McKinstry. 'Elusive Exclusive? John Murray Robertson (1844-1901), Architect, Dundee', *Brethren Historical Review* 18 (2022), 75-122.

Dixon, Henry H. 'Edward Perceval Wright', *Irish Naturalist* XIX (April 1910), 61-3.

Dolan, John R. 'Tuffen West FLS, FRMS (1823-1891): Artist of the Microscopic, Naturalist, and Populiser [*sic*] of Microscopy', *Arts et Sciences* V (2021), 1-22.

Duerden, J. E. 'Philip Henry Gosse, F.R.S.', *Journal of the Institute of Jamaica* II (1899), 574-81.

d'Urban, William Stewart. 'Description of a Canadian Butterfly, and Some Remarks on the Genus Papilio', *Canadian Naturalist and Geologist* III (Dec. 1858), 417-18.

Edmondson, W.T. 'Rotifer Study as a Way of Life', *Hydrobiologia* 186/187 (1989), 1-9. *See also* WARD, H. B. and G. C.WHIPPLE, *Fresh-water Biology*.

Ellegård, Alvar. 'The Darwinian Theory and the Argument from Design', *Lychnos: Lärdomshistoriska samfundets årsbok* [Annual of the Swedish History of Science Society] (1956), 173-92.

————. 'The Darwinian Theory and Nineteenth-Century Philosophies of Science', *Journal of the History of Ideas* XVIII (1957), 362-93.

————. 'Public Opinion and the Press: Reactions to Darwinism', *Journal of the History of Ideas* XIX (1958), 379-87.

————. 'The Darwinian Revolution: A Review Article', *Lychnos* (1960-1), 55-85.

Elliott, E. B. 'Counter-retrospect', *Christian Observer* LXVIII (Dec. 1868), 945-9.

Elwes, E. V. 'P. H. Gosse as a Naturalist', *Journal of the Torquay Natural History Society* I (1914), 259-66.

Embley, Peter L. 'The Early Development of the Plymouth Brethren', in Bryan R. Wilson, ed., *Patterns of Sectarianism*. London: Heinemann, 1967, 213-43.

Endersby, Jim. 'A Life More Ordinary: The Dull Life but Interesting Times of Joseph Dalton Hooker', *Journal of the History of Biology* 44 (Winter 2011), 611-31.

Essig, E. O. 'A Sketch History of Entomology', *Osiris* II (1936), 80-123.

Farrow, Ruth T. 'Odyssey of an American Cancer Specialist of a Hundred Years Ago', *Bulletin of the History of Medicine* 23 (May-June 1949), 236-52.

Feuerstein, Anna. 'Falling in Love with Seaweeds: Seaside Environments of George Eliot and G. H. Lewes', in Mazzeno, Laurence W. and Ronald D. Morrison (eds.), *Victorian Writers and the Environment*. London: Routledge, 2016, 188-204.

Fisher, Susan W. and Megan E. Meuti. 'Contributions of Entomology to Natural Theology from the Late 17th to the Early 19th Century', *American Entomologist* 64 (Winter 2018), 242-50.

Fontaneto, Diego and Willem H. De Smet. 'Rotifera', in Andreas Schmidt-Rhaesa (ed.), *Handbook of Zoology. Gastrotricha, Cycloneuralia and Gnathifera. Volume 3: Gastrotricha and Gnathifera*. Berlin: De Gruyter, 2015, 217-300.

Forrest, J. W. '"The Missionary Reporter"', *CBRF Journal*, No. 21 (1971), 24-42.

Foster, John Bellamy. 'E. Ray Lankester, Ecological Materialist', *Organization & Environment* 13 (June 2000), 233-5.

Freeman, R. B. and Douglas Wertheimer. 'Emily Gosse: A Bibliography', *Brethren Historical Review* 17 (2021), 25-78.

Fryckstedt, Monica Correa. 'Charlotte Elizabeth Tonna & *The Christian Lady's Magazine*', *Victorian Periodicals Review* XIV (Summer 1981), 42-51.

Fyfe, Aileen. 'Natural History and the Victorian Tourist: From Landscapes to Rock-Pools', in David N. Livingstone and Charles W. J. Withers (eds.), *Geographies of Nineteenth-Century Science*. Chicago: University of Chicago Press, 2011, 371-98.

Fyles, Thomas W. 'Philip Henry Gosse', *Nineteenth Annual Report of the Entomological Society of Ontario, 1888* (1889), 37.

———. 'A Visit to the Canadian Haunts of the Late Philip Henry Gosse', *Twenty-third Annual Report of the Entomological Society of Ontario* (1892), 22-9.

———. 'The Rise in Public Estimation of the Science of Entomology', *Forty-Third Annual Report of the Entomological Society of Ontario, 1912* (1913), 40-6.

Gall, Dolores M. 'Titian Ramsay Peale: An American Naturalist and Lithographer', *Yale University Art Gallery Bulletin* 38 (Winter 1983), 6-13.

Gaskin, L. J. P. 'On a Collection of Original Sketches and Drawings of British Sea-anemones and Corals by Philip Henry Gosse, and His Correspondents, 1839-1861, in the Library of the Horniman Museum', *Journal of the Society for the Bibliography of Natural History* I (July 1937), 65-7.

Going, William T. 'Philip Henry Gosse on the Old Southwest Frontier', *Georgia Review* 21 (Spring 1967), 25-38.

Golden, Catherine. 'Beatrix Potter: Naturalist Artist', *Woman's Art Journal* 11 (Spring-Summer 1990), 16-20.

Goodman, Martin. 'Nature Vs Naturalist: Paths Diverging and Converging in Edmund Gosse's *Father and Son*', *Life Writing* XI (2014), 85-101.

G[oodrich]., E[dwin]. S. 'Edwin Ray Lankester—1847-1929', *Proceedings of the Royal Society of London. Series B* 106 (5 Aug. 1930), x-xv.

Goodrich, Edwin S. 'The Scientific Work of Edwin Ray Lankester', *Quarterly Journal of Microscopical Science* ser. 2 (1931), 363-381.

Gosse, Edmund W. 'The Lofoden Islands', *Fraser's Magazine* n.s. IV (Nov. 1871), 563-74.

[———]. 'George Cruikshank', *Spectator* 44 (2 Dec. 1871), 1465-6.

[———]. 'Ibsen's New Poems', *Spectator* 45 (3 March 1872), 344-5.

[———]. 'A Norwegian Drama [*Peer Gynt*]', *Spectator* 45 (7 July 1872), 922-3.

———. 'Norwegian Poetry Since 1814', *Fraser's Magazine* n. s. VI (1 Oct. 1872), 435-49.

———. 'Ibsen, the Norwegian Satirist', *Fortnightly Review* XIII (1 Jan. 1873), 74-88.

[———]. 'Frederik Paludan-Müller', *Spectator* 46 (1 Feb. 1873), 142-3.

———. 'The Present Condition of Norway', *Fraser's Magazine* n.s. IX (Feb. 1874), 174-85.

———. 'The Ethical Condition of the Early Scandinavian Peoples', *Journal of the Transactions of the Victoria Institute* IX (1875), 84-100.

[———]. 'Mr. Tennyson's Drama [*Queen Mary*]', *Examiner* (26 June 1875), 717-719.

———. 'Frederik Paludan-Müller', *Academy* 11 (6 Jan. 1877), 9.

———. 'Frederik Paludan-Müller', *Athenaeum* (6 Jan. 1877), 18.

———. 'Bishop Martensen', *The Expositor*, ser. 3, vol. I (Jan. 1885), 59-68.

[———]. 'The Unequal Yoke', *English Illustrated Magazine* (April-June 1886), 500-12, 562-76, 604-15.

———. 'The Late Mr. P. H. Gosse and Geology', *Spectator* (25 Oct. 1890), 559.

———. 'Bishop Fog', *Athenaeum* (7 March 1896), 314-15 (signed 'E.G.').

———. 'Fragments of the Autobiography of Thomas Gosse', *Burlington Magazine* XXVII (July 1915), 141-50.

Gosse, Emily. *All of the 40 contributions to periodicals by Emily Gosse, listed in* FREEMAN & WERTHEIMER-EG *have been consulted. For the complete list of these contributions, see that work.*

Gosse, P. H. *All of the 229 contributions to periodicals by P. H. Gosse, listed in* FREEMAN & WERTHEIMER-PHG *have been consulted. For the complete list of these contributions, see that work.*

The following articles were not listed in FREEMAN & WERTHEIMER-PHG. *The four items from the* London Quarterly Review *were first identified in the* Wellesley Index IV (1987).

Gosse, P.H. 'The Diseased Wheat', *Worcester Journal* (17 Oct. 1850) as reprinted in London *Standard* (18 Oct. 1850), 6 (PHG letter dated 12 Oct. 1850).

[———]. 'The marine aquarium: sea anemones', *London Quarterly Review* VIII (April 1857), 76-92.

[———]. 'The *Aquarian Naturalist*', *London Quarterly Review* XII (April 1859), 177-93.

[———]. 'The sea', *London Quarterly Review* XVI (April 1861), 63-92.

[———]. 'Worms', *London Quarterly Review* XXIII (Jan. 1865), 390-416.

———. ['On the botanical features of the district' of St. Marychurch and Torquay], letter PHG-[Revd R. H. Barnes], 6 Oct. 1864, published in 'History of St. Mary Church', Supplement to the *Exeter and Plymouth Gazette* (2 Nov. 1866), 10.

———. 'Emphasis in reading Scripture', *The Christian* (7 March 1872), 12.

———. 'Rhynchospermum jasminoides', *Gardeners' Chronicle* (4 Sept. 1875), 298.

———. [Waterfalls, St. David's, Jamaica], *Gardeners' Chronicle* (2 Oct. 1875), 428; letter dated Sept. 15.

———. 'Aristotelia Maqui', *Gardeners' Chronicle* (25 Dec. 1875), 812.

———. 'Orchids in July', *Gardeners' Chronicle* (18 Aug. 1877), 214.

———. [West Indian Seals], letter PHG-[Joel Asaph Allen], in J.A. Allen, *History of North American Pinnipeds: A Monograph of the Walruses, Sea-lions, Sea-bears and Seals of North America* (Washington, D.C.: Government Printing Office, 1880), 720. The letter as printed is dated Jan. 18, 1880, but according to PHG's *Corr. Bk.*, it was written on Jan. 8 in response to a letter from Allen of Jan. 7.

———. 'Philesia buxifolia', *Gardeners' Chronicle* (6 Aug. 1881), 183.

———. 'Dendrobium Breviflorum, *Lindl.*', *Gardeners' Chronicle* ser. 2, 26 (7 Aug. 1886), 181.

Gracie, William J., Jr. 'Truth of Form in Edmund Gosse's *Father and Son*', *Journal of Narrative Technique* IV (Sept. 1974), 176-87.

Granata, Silvia. '"Let us hasten to the beach": Victorian Tourism and Seaside Collecting', *LIT: Literature Interpretation Theory* 27 (2016), 91-110.

———. 'At once pet, ornament, and "subject for dissection": The Unstable Status of Marine Animals in Victorian Aquaria', *Cahiers victoriens et édouardiens* 88 (Fall 2018), 1-15.

Gray, Nicolette. 'The Nineteenth Century Chromo-Lithograph', *Architectural Review* 84 (Oct. 1938), 177-178, 187.

Greene, J. Reay. 'Observations on the Distribution of [Irish] Actinoida', *Natural History Review* V (1858), 35-7.

Greene, John C. 'American Science Comes of Age, 1780-1820', *Journal of American History* 55 (June 1968), 22-41.

Griffey, William A. 'A Bibliography of Richard Hill: Negro, Scholar, Scientist. Native of Spanish Town, Jamaica', *American Book Collector* II (Oct. 1932), 220-24.

Haddon, Alfred Cort. 'A Revision of the British Actiniae', Part 1, *Scientific Transactions of the Royal Dublin Soc.*, ser. 2, vol. IV (1889), 297-361.

Hadjiafxendi, Kyriaki and John Plunkett. 'Science at the Seaside: Pleasure Hunts in Victorian Devon', in Nicholas Allen, Nick Groom and Jos Smith (eds.). *Coastal Works: Cultures of the Atlantic Edge.* Oxford: Oxford University Press, 2017, 181-203.

Hall, Mrs S. C. [Anna Maria Hall]. 'A New Pleasure. The Marine Aquarium', *Art-Journal* n.s. II (1 May 1856), 145-7.

Hamlin, Christopher. 'Robert Warington and the Moral Economy of the Aquarium', *Journal of the History of Biology* 19 (Spring 1986), 131-153.

Hanawalt, Mary Wheat. 'Charles Kingsley and Science', *Studies in Philology* XXXIV (Oct. 1937), 589-611.

Harring, Harry K. 'Synopsis of the Rotatoria', *Bulletin of the United States National Museum* LXXXI (1913), 1-226.

Harring, Harry K. and Frank J. Myers. 'The Rotifer Fauna of Wisconsin', *Trans. Wisconsin Academy of Science, Arts, and Letters*, vol. XX-XXV (1921-30), *passim.*

Harris, C. S. 'On the Marine Vivarium', *AMNH* ser. 2, XV (Feb. 1855), 131-4.

Hasler, Charles. 'Mid-nineteenth-century colour printing', *Penrose Annual* 45 (1951), 66-8.

Hedgpeth, Joel W. 'A Century at the Seashore', *Scientific Monthly* LXI (Sept. 1945), 194-8.

———. 'Fishers of the Murex', *Isis* XXXVII (May 1947), 26–32.

———. 'De mirabili maris: Thoughts on the Flowering of Seashore Books', *Proc. Royal Society of Edinburgh*, Sect. 8, vol. LXXII (1972), 107-14.

Helmstadter, Richard J. 'The Nonconformist Conscience', in Peter Marsh (ed.), *The Conscience of the Victorian State.* Syracuse: Syracuse University Press, 1979, 135-72.

Heron-Allen, Edward. 'On Beauty, Design, and Purpose in the Foraminifera', *Nature* 95 (5 Aug. 1915), 634.

Hertwig, Richard. 'Report On the Actiniaria Dredged by H.M.S. Challenger During the Years 1873-1876', *Report of the Scientific Results of the Voyage of H.M.S. Challenger, Zoology*, vol. VI. London: H. M. Stationery Office, 1882, 1-136.

Hewlett, R. Tanner. 'One Hundred Years of Microscopy: The Royal Microscopical Society', *Nature* 144 (18 Nov. 1939), 850-2.

Hill, A.V. 'Age of Election to the Royal Society', *Notes and Records of the Royal Society of London* II (April 1939), 71-3.

———. 'Age of Election to the Royal Society', *Notes and Records of the Royal Society of London* XI (Jan. 1954), 14-16.

———. 'Age of Election to the Royal Society', *Notes and Records of the Royal Society of London* XVI (Nov. 1961), 151-53.

Hillhouse, W[illiam]. 'Thomas Bolton, F.R.M.S.', *Midland Naturalist* X (1887), 297-301.

H[itchcock]., H. C. 'A Little of our History', *Brook St. Chapel, Tottenham Magazine* no. 4 (Nov.-Dec. 1962), 7-10.

Hodges, John P. 'Mode of address of the nineteenth-century naturalist P. H. Gosse', *Annals of Natural History* 38 (April 2011), 172-4.

Holdsworth, E. W. H. 'Descriptions of a New Sea Anemone', *Proc. Zoological Society* (1855), 85-6.

———. 'Description of a New Species of Actinia from the Devonshire Coast', *Proc. Zoological Society* (1855), 172.

———. 'Description of Two New Species of Actinia, from the South Coast of Devon', *Proc. Zoological Society* (1855), 235-7.

Holland, Richard. 'Notes on Newfoundland butterflies', *Journal of The Lepidopterists' Society* 23 (1969), 33-42.

Hollowday, E. 'Introduction to the Study of Rotifera', *Microscope* V-VII (1945-50), 17 parts.

Howell, W. '1867', *Voice Upon the Mountains* I (Feb. 1867), 21-2.

Huber, Florian. 'Spiegelbilder vom Meeresgrund. Leopold Blaschkas marine Aquarien' ['Reflections from the Ocean Floor. Leopold Blaschka's marine Aquaria'], *Berichte zur Wissenschaftsgeschichte* 36 (June 2013), 172-86.

Hudson, Charles Thomas. 'On a New Rotifer', *Monthly Microscopical Journal* VI (1 Sept. 1871), 121-4.

———. 'On Pedalion Mira', *Quarterly Journal of Microscopical Science* n.s. XII (Oct. 1872), 333-8.

———. 'Is Pedalion a Rotifera?' *Monthly Microscopical Journal* VIII (1 Nov. 1872), 209-16.

———. 'On the Classification and Affinities of the Rotifera', paper delivered 26 Aug. 1875 summarized in *Report of the Forty-fifth Meeting of the British Association ... Bristol*. London: John Murray, 1876, 161-2.

———. 'An Attempt to Re-classify the Rotifers', *Quarterly Journal of Microscopical Science* n.s. XXIV (July 1884), 335-56.

———. 'The President's Address', *Journal of the Royal Microscopical Society* (April 1889), 169-79.

———. 'The President's Address on some Needless Difficulties in the Study of Natural History', *Journal of the Royal Microscopical Society* (April 1890), 129-41.

———. 'The President's Address on some Doubtful Points in the Natural History of the Rotifera', *Journal of the Royal Microscopical Society* (1891), 6-18.

H[ughes]., W. R. 'Philip Henry Gosse. F.R.S.', *Midland Naturalist* XI (1888), 297-302.

Hunt, Arthur Roope. 'Some Personal Reminiscences of the [Torquay Natural History] Society', *Torquay Directory* (31 Oct. 1894), 6.

———. 'Mr. P. H. Gosse and Mr. Edmund Gosse', *Torquay Directory* (15 July 1908), 6.

Hussey, Charles G. 'An Historical Survey of the Collection and Study of Rotifers in Britain', *Hydrobiologia* 73 (1980), 237-40.

Huxley, Thomas Henry. '*Lacinularia socialis*. A Contribution to the Anatomy and Physiology of the Rotifera', *Trans. Microscopical Society* n.s. I (1853), 1-19.

Ineichen, Bernard. 'Losing the Rapture: Escaping from Fundamentalist Christian Belief', *Mental Health, Religion & Culture* 22 (Sept. 2019), 661-73.

Ingle, Ray. 'Who Was ... William Alford Lloyd?' *Biologist: Journal of the Institute of Biology* 60 (Feb./Mar. 2013), 24-7.

Ingram, K.E. 'W. Osburn, Naturalist—His Journal & His Letters', *Jamaican Historical Review* 2 (1978), 33-7.

Inkster, Ian. 'A Note on Itinerant Science Lecturers, 1790-1850', *Annals of Science* 28 (April 1972), 235-6.

———. 'The Public Lecture as an Instrument of Science Education for Adults—The Case of Great Britain, c. 1750-1850', in Ian Inkster, *Scientific Culture and Urbanisation in Industrialising Britain*. Brookfield, Vermont: Ashgate, 1997, 80-107.

Innis, Mary Quayle. 'Philip Henry Gosse in Canada', *Dalhousie Review* XVII (1937), 55-60.

Irmscher, Christoph. 'Nature Laughs at Our Systems: Philip Henry Gosse's *The Canadian Naturalist*', *Canadian Literature* No. 170-1 (Autumn/Winter 2001), 58-86.

Ishida, Juro. 'Digestive Enzymes of *Actinia mesembryanthemum*', *Annotationes Zoologicae Japonenses* XV (20 June 1936), 285-305.

Jackson, Christine E. 'M. & N. Hanhart: printers of natural history plates, 1830-1903', *Archives of Natural History* 26 (1999), 287-92.

Jeffrey-Smith, May. 'Gosse's Observations on Jamaican Birds—Some Further Observations on Warblers', *Natural History Notes of the Natural History Society of Jamaica* IV (Jan. 1951), 207.

Jensen, J. Vernon. 'The X Club: Fraternity of Victorian Scientists', *British Journal for the History of Science* V (June 1970), 63-72.

———. 'Interrelationships within the Victorian "X Club"', *Dalhousie Review* 51 (1972), 539-52.

Johnson, Howard. 'Edward Long, Historian of Jamaica', in Edward Long, *The History of Jamaica, or, General Survey of the antient and modern state of the island: with reflections on its situation, settlements, inhabitants, climate, products, commerce, laws, and government.* Montreal: McGill-Queen's, 2002, I: i-xxv.

Johnson, James Yate. 'Notes on the Sea-anemones of Madeira, with Descriptions of New Species', *Proc. Zoological Society* (1861), 298-306.

Johnston, J. Charteris. '"Literary" Torquay', *Report and Trans. of the Devonshire Association* L (1918), 293-327.

Jones, W. P. 'The Vogue of Natural History in England, 1750-1770', *Annals of Science* II (15 July 1937), 345-52.

Julian, Mrs Hester F. 'The Scientific Correspondence of Charles Kingsley and William Pengelly', *Journal of the Torquay Natural History* II (1920), 361-73.

King, Amy M. 'Reorienting the Scientific Frontier: Victorian Tide Pools and Literary Realism', *Victorian Studies* 47 (Winter 2005), 153-63.

———. 'Tide Pools', *Victorian Review* 36 (Fall 2010), 40-5.

Kjærgaard, Peter C. '"Within the bounds of Science": Redirecting Controversies to *Nature*', in Louise Henson, et. al., *Culture and Science in the Nineteenth-Century Media* (London: Routledge, 2004), 211-221.

———. 'The Missing Link and Human Origins: Understanding an Evolutionary Icon', in Kris Rutten, Stefaan Blancke, and Ronald Soetaert (eds.), *Perspectives on Science and Culture*. West Lafayette, Indiana: Purdue University Press, 2018, 89-105.

Kochav, Sarah. שיבתם של היהודים לארץ-ישראל והתנועה האוונגלית באנגליה' ('The Evangelical Movement in England and the Restoration of the Jews to Eretz Israel'), *Cathedra: For the History of Eretz Israel and Its Yishuv* (Dec. 1991), 18-36 [Hebrew].

Koste, Walter and Eric D. Holloway. 'A Short History of Western European Rotifer Research', *Hydrobiologia* vol. 255/256 (April 1993), 557-72.

Kritsky, Gene. 'Entomological Reactions to Darwin's Theory in the Nineteenth Century', *Annual Review of Entomology* 53 (2008), 345-60.

[Lankester, Edwin]. 'Zoological Gardens, Regent's Park', *Athenaeum* (22 Jan., 28 May, 15 Oct. 1853), 110-1, 647, 1228-9.

Lankester, E. Ray. 'Remarks on Pedalion', *Quarterly Journal of Microscopical Science* n.s. XII (Oct. 1872), 338-42.

———. 'Limulus an Arachnid', *Quarterly Journal of Microscopical Science* n.s. XXI (July and Oct 1881), 504-48; 609-49.

Lapage, Geoffrey. 'Draughtsmanship in Zoological Work', *Endeavour* VIII (April 1949), 70-79.

Larsen, Timothy. 'Bishop Colenso and his Critics: The Strange Emergence of Biblical Criticism in Victorian Britain', *Scottish Journal of Theology* 50 (Nov. 1997), 433-58.

———. '"Living by faith": A short history of Brethren practice', *BAHNR* 1 (1997-8), 67-102.

Levy, Catherine. 'History of Ornithology in the Caribbean', *Ornithologia Neotropical* 19, Supplement (2008), 415-26.

———. 'Gosse's Sojourn in "Glorious Jamaica"', *BirdLife Jamaica Broadsheet* no. 92 (Sept. 2010), 10-16.

Lewis, W. J. 'Gospel Narrative Tracts', *The Revival* VIII (26 March 1863), 155.

Lightman, Bernard. '"The Voices of Nature": Popularizing Victorian Science', in Bernard Lightman (ed.), *Victorian Science in Context*. Chicago: University of Chicago Press, 1997, 187-211.

———. 'The Visual Theology of Victorian Popularizers of Science: From Reverent Eye to Chemical Retina', *Isis* 91 (Dec. 2000), 651-80.

———. '*Knowledge* Confronts *Nature*: Richard Proctor and Popular Science Periodicals', in Louise Henson, et. al., *Culture and Science in the Nineteenth-Century Century Media*. London: Routledge, 2004, 199-210.

Lingard, Ann Lackie. 'Seaside Pleasures: Philip Henry Gosse and the Bathing Women', *The Linnean* 19 (Oct. 2003), 27-30.

Linyard, Fred. 'The Moravians in Jamaica from the Beginning to Emancipation, 1754-1838', *Jamaica Journal* III (March 1969), 7-11.

Lister, Raymond. 'William Gosse's Botanical Miniatures', *Gardeners' Chronicle* (26 April 1952), 140 ff.

———. 'Thomas Gosse: Miniaturist and Diarist', *The Connoisseur* CXXXII (Dec. 1953), 158-61.

Little, J. I. 'The Naturalist's Landscape: Philip Henry Gosse in the Eastern Townships, 1835-38', *Journal of Eastern Townships Studies* 20 (Spring 2002), 56-69.

Lloyd, William Alford. [Letter to (Thomas) Bolton on artificial salt water, 26 Sept. 1854], in *Athenaeum* (15 Nov. 1854), 1401.

———. 'The Aquarium', *Popular Recreator* (1873) –Vol. I:57-61; 126-8; 187-90; 245-7; 309-10; 373-8; Vol. II: 87-9; 113-15; 170-1; 270-2; 332-3.

———. 'Aquaria: Their Present, Past, and Future', *Popular Science Review* XV (1876), 253-65.

———. 'Aquaria', *Journal of the Society for Arts* XXIV (24 Mar. 1876), 427-32 (letter to the editor, with addition, 7 April 1876, 483).

Lynn, W. Gardner, and Chapman Grant. 'The Herpetology of Jamaica', *Bulletin of the Institute of Jamaica*, Science Series no.1 (1940), 1-148.

MacLeod, Roy M. 'The X-Club: A Social Network of Science in Late-Victorian England', *Notes and Records of the Royal Society of London* 24 (April 1970), 305-22.

———. 'The Royal Society and the Government Grant: Notes on the Administration of Scientific Research, 1849-1914', *Historical Journal* 14 (June 1971), 323-58.

M'Cullagh, Thomas. 'Memoir of the Rev. John Haigh, Sometime Missionary in Newfoundland', *Wesleyan-Methodist Magazine* ser. 5, VII (April 1861), 294-304.

McDonnell, R. 'On the Electrical Nature of the Power Exercised by the Actiniae of our Shores', *Proc. Royal Society* (1858), 103-7.

Malles, H. M. 'The Microscope During the Last Hundred Years', *Microscope* X (Jan.-Feb. 1955), 113-21.

Mattheisen, Paul F. 'Gosse's Candid "Snapshots"', *Victorian Studies* VIII (June 1965), 329-54.

Meechan, Chris. 'A Glass Menagerie: The work of Leopold and Rudolph Blaschka', *The Glass Cone* #39 (Spring 1995), 4-5.

Michael, Michaelis. 'Philip Henry Gosse and the Geological Knot', in idem, *Evolution by Natural Selection: Confidence, Evidence and the Gap* (Boca Raton, FL: CRC Press, 2016), 97-106.

Millhauser, Milton. 'The Scriptural Geologists. An Episode in the History of Opinion', *Osiris* XI (1954), 65-86.

Mills, Eric L. 'Amphipods and Equipoise: A Study of T. R. R. Stebbing', *Trans. Connecticut Academy of Arts & Science* XLIV (Dec. 1972), 239-56.

Milner, Richard. 'Huxley's Bulldog: The Battles of E. Ray Lankester (1946-1929)', *Anatomical Record* 257 (15 June 1999), 90-95.

Moore, James. 'Deconstructing Darwinism: The Politics of Evolution in the 1860s', *Journal of the History of Biology* XXIV (Autumn 1991), 353-408.

Moore, LeRoy, Jr. 'Another Look at Fundamentalism: A Response to Ernest R. Sandeen', *Church History* 37 (June 1968), 195-202.

Moore, P. G. 'Popularizing marine natural history in eighteenth- and nineteenth-century Britain', *Archives of Natural History* 41 (April 2014), 45-62.

Nelson, E. Charles. 'Patrick Browne's *The civil and natural history of Jamaica* (1756, 1789)', *Archives of Natural History* 24 (1997), 327-36.

———. 'Additions to Philip Henry Gosse's Bibliography: Letters to Newspapers and Horticultural Periodicals 1864-1879', *Archives of Natural History* 41 (April 2014), 172-5.

———. 'Philip Henry Gosse: More Additions, Mainly Horticultural, to his Bibliography', *Archives of Natural History* 49 (April 2022), 207-10.

Nelson, E. Charles and R. B. Williams. 'An Unrecorded Publication on Tree-ferns by P.H. Gosse', *Archives of Natural History* 20 (1993), 425-6.

Nicol, Adam. 'The Ecology of Science and Slavery in Philip Henry Gosse's *Letters from Alabama*', *Prose Studies* 35 (2013), 189-201.

North, J.E. 'God Knows Best: the "Separated" Life of Anna Shipton', Knighton, Powys *Gospel Magazine* n.s. 1663 (Nov.-Dec. 2008), 201-4.

O'Brien, Charles F. '*Eozoön Canadense*, "The Dawn Animal of Canada"', *Isis* 61 (Summer 1970), 206-23.

[Oliphant, Margaret]. 'Modern Light Literature—Science', *Blackwood's Magazine* LXXVIII (Aug. 1855), 215-30.

Paden, W. D. 'Arthur O'Shaughnessy in the British Museum; or, the Case of the Misplaced Fusees and the Reluctant Zoologist', *Victorian Studies* VIII (Sept. 1964), 7-30.

———. 'A Neglected Victorian Poet: Theo. Marzials', *Notes and Queries* 210 (Feb. 1965), 60-2.

Parker, W. M. 'A Modern Tour to the Hebrides. The Criticisms of Edmund Gosse', *Scots Magazine* XXIV (Jan.-Feb. 1941), 263-72, 341-50.

Peacock, A. D. 'John Hood of Dundee. Working-man Naturalist', *Scots Magazine* (1939), 409-18.

Pengelly, William. 'On the Devonian Age of the World', *Geologist* IV (Aug. 1861), 334.

Peters, Robert L. 'Edmund Gosse's Two Whitmans', *Walt Whitman Review* XI (March 1965), 19-21.

Pfeiffer, Louis. 'Descriptions ... of New Species of Land-shells from Jamaica, Collected by Mr. Gosse', *Proc. Zoological Society* Part 13 (1845), 137-8.

Pointon, Marcia. 'The Representation of Time in Painting: A study of William Dyce's *Pegwell Bay: A Recollection of October 5th, 1858*', *Art History* 1 (March 1978), 99-104.

Provancher, Léon A. 'Naturalistes Canadiens', *Le Naturaliste Canadien* V (Feb. 1873), 130.

Rack, Henry D. 'Evangelical Endings: Death-Beds in Evangelical Biography', *Bulletin of the John Rylands University Library* 74 (1992), 39-56.

Raymond, W. O. 'Philip Henry Gosse and *The Canadian Naturalist*', *Trans. Royal Society of Canada*, ser. 3, vol. 45, sect. II (June 1951), 43-58 (repr. by Edgar Andrew Collard, 'All Our Yesterdays', Montreal *Gazette*, June 14-July 5, 1952).

Rees, Kathy. 'Life Writing by the Gosse Family: Family Portraits in Scientific, Evangelical and Auto/biographical Discourses', *Life Writing* 14 (2017), 199-215.

Rehbock, Philip F. 'Huxley, Haeckel, and the Oceanographers: The Case of Bathybius haeckelii', *Isis* 66 (Dec. 1975), 504-33.
———. 'The Victorian Aquarium in Ecological and Social Perspective', in Mary Sears and Daniel Merriman (eds.), *Oceanography: The Past* (New York: Springer-Verlag, 1980), 522-39.
Reiling, Henri. 'The Blaschkas' Glass Animal Models: Origins of Design', *Journal of Glass Studies* 40 (1998), 105-26.
Ribner, Jonathan P. 'John Ruskin, Philip Henry Gosse, William Dyce, and the Contemplation of Time at Mid-century', *British Art Journal* XVIII (Winter 2017/2018), 70-7.
Richter, Virginia. 'The Best Story of the World: Theology, Geology, and Philip Henry Gosse's Omphalos', in Rens Bod, Jaap Maat and Thijs Weststeijn (eds.), *The Making of the Humanities. Volume III: The Modern Humanities*. Amsterdam: Amsterdam University Press, 2014, 65-77.
Ritvo, Harriet. 'Zoological Nomenclature and the Empire of Victorian Science', in Bernard Lightman (ed.), *Victorian Science in Context*. Chicago: University of Chicago Press, 1997, 187-211.
Robinson, J. K. 'Austin Dobson and the Rondeliers', *Modern Language Quarterly* XIV (1953), 31-42.
———. 'A Neglected Phase of the Aesthetic Movement: English Parnassianism', *Publications of the Modern Language Association* LXVIII (Sept. 1953), 733-54.
Rompkey, Ronald, 'Philip Henry Gosse's account of his years in Newfoundland, 1827-35', *Newfoundland Studies* 6 (1990), 210-66.
Roos, David A. 'The "Aims and Intentions of *Nature*"', *Annals of the New York Academy of Sciences* 360 (April 1981), 159-80.
Ross, Frederic R. 'Philip Gosse's *Omphalos*, Edmund Gosse's *Father and Son*, and Darwin's Theory of Natural Selection', *Isis* 68 (March 1977), 85-96.
Rossmässler, E. A. 'Der See im Glase', *Die Gartenlaube* IV (1856), 252-6.
Rothstein, Edward. 'What Art Has Made of Nature', *The Wall Street Journal*, 25 Aug. 2016.
Rouster, Lorella. 'Father and Son: The Tragedy of Edmund Gosse', *Creation Social Science and Humanities Quarterly* II (Spring 1980), 10-12.
Ruse, Michael. 'The Relationship between Science and Religion in Britain, 1830-1870', *Church History* 44 (Dec. 1975), 505-22.
Sandeen, Ernest R. 'Towards a Historical Interpretation of the Origins of Fundamentalism', *Church History* XXVI (March 1967), 66-83.
———. 'Fundamentalism and American Identity', *Annals of the American Academy of Political and Social Science* 387 (Jan. 1970), 56-65.
———. 'The Distinctiveness of American Denominationalism: A Case Study of the 1846 Evangelical Alliance', *Church History* 45 (June 1976), 222-234.
Schuler, Monica. 'Coloured Civil Servants in Post-Emancipation Jamaica: Two Case Studies', *Caribbean Quarterly* 30 (Sept.-Dec. 1984), 85-98.
Sclater, P. L. 'Revised List of the Birds of Jamaica', in *Handbook of Jamaica for 1910*. Kingston: Institute of Jamaica, 1910.
Scudder, Samuel H. 'English Names for Butterflies', *Psyche* I (May 1874-March 1875), 6 parts.
———. 'Gosse's Observations on the Butterflies of North America', *Psyche* III (July-Sept. 1881), 245-7.
———. 'The Male Genital Armature of Lepidoptera', *Science* II (6 July 1883), 22.
Senior, Emily. '"Glimpses of the Wonderful": The Jamaican origins of the aquarium', *Atlantic Studies* (2021), 1-25.
Sessions, Emily. 'Anti-Picturesque Landscapes, Entangled Fauna, and Interracial Collaboration in Post-Emancipation Jamaica in the Work of Philip Henry Gosse and Richard Hill', *Terrae Incognitae* 53 (2021), 26-47.
Sheets-Pyenson, Susan. '"Pearls before Swine": Sir William Dawson's Bakerian Lecture of 1870', *Notes and Records of the Royal Society of London* 45 (July 1991), 177-91.
Sherlock, Philip. 'Jamaica in 1858', *Jamaican Historical Review* I (1945), 83-91.
Shick, J. Malcolm. 'Toward an Aesthetic Marine Biology', *Art Journal* 67 (Winter 2008), 62-86.
Smith, Jonathan. 'Darwin's Barnacles, Dickens's *Little Dorrit*, and the Social Uses of Victorian Seaside Studies', *Literature, Interpretation, Theory (LIT)* 10 (1999), 327-47.
———. 'Philip Gosse and the Varieties of Natural Theology', in Linda Woodhead (ed.), *Reinventing Christianity: 19th Century Contexts* (London: Routledge, 2001, 2019), 251-62.
Stather, W. C. '1866', *The Rainbow* III (1 Jan. 1866), 37-40.
Rupke, Nicolaas A. 'Neither Creation nor Evolution: The Third Way in Mid-nineteenth Century thinking about the Origin of Species', *Annals of the History and Philosophy of Biology* 10 (2005), 143-72 (the title of the journal is given incorrectly as *Annals of the History and Theory of Biology* in Rupke, *Richard Owen*, 327).
Stedman, Edmund C. 'Some London Poets', *Harper's New Monthly Magazine* LXIV (May 1882), 874-92.
Stephenson, T. A. 'On the Nematocysts of Sea Anemones', *Journal of the Marine Biological Association* XVI (May 1929), 173-200.

Stewart, D. B. 'Philip Henry Gosse', *Gosse Bird Club Broadsheet* Nos. 11-12 (Sept. 1968-March 1969), 2-5, 2-6.

———. 'An Eighteenth Century Bird Club (Dr Anthony Robinson and his Friends)', *Gosse Bird Club, Broadsheet* No. 13 (Sept. 1969), 8-10.

Strick, James. 'Darwinism and the Origin of Life: The Role of H.C. Bastian in the British Spontaneous Generation Debates, 1868-1873', *Journal of the History of Biology* 32 (Spring 1999), 51-92.

Stunt, Timothy C. F. 'The Victoria Institute: The First Hundred Years', *Faith and Thought: Journal of the Victoria Institute* 94 (1965), 162-181.

———. 'James Van Sommer, an Undenominational Christian and Man of Prayer', *Journal of CBRF* No. 16 (Aug. 1967), 2-8.

———. 'Early Brethren and the Society of Friends', *CBRF Occasional Paper* no.3 (1970), 5-27.

———. 'Homoeopathy and Brethren', *The Witness* 103 (April 1973), 127-8.

———. 'Thomas Barnardo: The Man and the Myth', *The Harvester* (Oct. 1979), 279-82.

———. 'Leonard Strong: the Motives and Experiences of Early Missionary Work in British Guiana', *Christian Brethren Review* (1983), 95-105.

———. 'Brethren or Philistine?' *Brethren Archivists and Historians Network Review* 2 (2000), 13-16.

———. 'Elitist Leadership and Congregational Participation Among Early Plymouth Brethren', in Kate Cooper and Jeremy Gregory (eds.), *Elite and Popular Religion*. Woodbridge, England: Boydell Press, 2006, 327-36.

———. 'An Early Account of the Brethren in 1838 With Some Explanation of its Origins and Context', *Brethren Historical Review* VIII (2012), 1-9.

———. 'Trinity College, John Darby and the Powerscourt Milieu', in Joshua Searle, Kenneth G.C. Newport (eds.), *Beyond the End: The Future of Millennial Studies*. Sheffield: Sheffield Phoenix Press, 2012, 47-74.

———. 'From Wandsworth to British Guiana: The Strong Family Saga', in T.C.F. Stunt, *The Elusive Quest of the Spiritual Malcontent. Some Early Nineteenth-Century Ecclesiastical Mavericks*. Eugene, Oregon: Wipf & Stock, 2015, 175-95.

———. 'Robert Nelson (1798-1895): Administrator, Judge, and Plymouth Brother', *Brethren Historical Review* XIV (2018), 1-15.

———. 'New Source Materials for the Open Brethren in the 1850s', *Brethren Historical Review* XVIII (2022), 64-74.

Stunt, W. T. 'James Van Sommer: Missionary Enthusiast', *Echoes Quarterly Review* IX (Oct.-Dec. 1957), 18-23.

Swabey, C. 'The Study of Natural History in Jamaica', *Natural History Notes of the Natural History Society of Jamaica* I (April 1941), 2-3.

Swan, R. G. 'Naturalists and Beachcombers: The Victorian Mania for the Seashore', *Country Life* CXLIII (2 May 1968), 1157-60.

Taylor, R. G. 'Gosse's Observation[s] on Jamaican Birds', *Natural History Notes of the Natural History Society of Jamaica* IV (Nov. 1950), 178-82.

Theberge, Elaine. 'The Untrodden Earth: Early Nature Writing in Canada', *Nature Canada* III (April-June 1974), 30-6.

Thomas, Oldfield. 'On Indigenous Muridae in the West Indies; with the Description of a New Mexican Oryzomys', *AMNH* ser. 7, I (Feb. 1898), 176-80.

Thompson, W. 'Remarks on the British Actiniadae, and Rearrangement of the Genera', *Proc. Zoological Society* (1858), 145-9.

[Tugwell, George]. 'Science by the Sea-side', *Fraser's Magazine* LIV (Sept. 1856), 253-60.

Turner, Frank M. 'The Victorian Conflict between Science and Religion: A Professional Dimension', *Isis* 69 (Sept. 1978), 356-76.

Turner, G. L'E. 'Special Invited Review: Microscopical communication', *Journal of Microscopy* 100 (Jan. 1974), 3-20.

Twyman, Michael. 'Charles Joseph Hullmandel: Lithographic Printer Extraordinary', in Pat Gilmour (ed.), *Lasting Impressions*. Canberra: National Gallery of Australia, 1988, 42-90, 362-7.

Underwood, Garth. 'Notes on a Hitherto Unpublished Gosse Illustration of Jamaican Herpetology', *Natural History Notes of the Natural History Society of Jamaica* IV (March 1949), 46-8.

Vartanian, Aram. 'Trembley's Polyp, La Mettrie, and Eighteenth-Century French Materialism', *Journal of the History of Ideas* XI (June 1950), 259-86.

Vega, Fernando E. 'A recently discovered manuscript by William Alford Lloyd on the growth of seaweeds in aquaria', *Archives of Natural History* 39 (2012), 349-51.

Vennen, Mareike. 'Wissen unter Wasser. Registrieren und Regulieren in der Aquarienpraxis des 19. Jahrhunderts', in I. Bolinski and S. Rieger (eds.), *Das verdatete Tier: Zum Animal Turn in den Kultur- und Medienwissenschaften* (Stuttgart: J.B. Metzler, 2019), 13-33.

Waller, Augustus. 'On the Means by Which the Actiniae Kill Their Prey', *Proc. Royal Society* (1859), 722-4.

Waller, John O. 'Christ's Second Coming: Christina Rossetti and the Premillennialist William Dodsworth', *Bulletin of the New York Public Library* 73 (Sept. 1969), 465-82.

Warington, Robert. 'Notice of Observations on the Adjustment of the Relations Between the Animal and Vegetable Kingdoms, by which the Vital Functions of Both are Permanently Maintained', *Quarterly Journal of the Chemical Society of London* III (1851), 52-4.

———. 'The Aquatic Plant Case, or Parlour Aquarium', *Gardeners' Magazine of Botany* n.s. Part I (Jan. 1852), 5-7.

———. 'Observations on the Natural History of the Water-Snail and Fish Kept in a Confined and Limited Portion of Water', *AMNH* ser. 2, X (Oct. 1852), 273-80.

———. 'On Preserving the Balance Between Vegetable and Animal Organisms in Sea Water', *Report of the Twenty-third Meeting of the British Association*. London: John Murray, 1854, 72.

———. 'On the Aquarium', *Notices of the Proceedings at the Meetings of the Members of the Royal Institution* II (Nov. 1856-July 1857), 403-8.

Weber, E. F. 'Faune Rotatorienne du Bassin du Léman', *Revue Suisse de Zoologie* V (1898).

Wertheimer, Douglas. 'T. W. Fyles on P. H. Gosse', *Canadian Notes and Queries* no. 11 (June 1973), 5-6; no. 13 (June 1974), 6-7.

———. 'Some Hardy Notes on Dorset Words and Customs', *Notes and Queries* n.s. 21 (Jan. 1974), 26.

———. 'The Identification of Some Characters and Incidents in Gosse's "Father and Son"', *Notes and Queries* n.s. 23 (Jan. 1976), 4-11.

———. 'Gosse's Corrections to "Father and Son", 1907-1928', *Notes and Queries* n.s. 25 (Aug. 1978), 327-32.

———. 'Gosse, Philip Henry', *Dictionary of Canadian Biography*. Toronto: University of Toronto Press, 1982, XI: 363-4.

———. 'Gosse, Philip Henry', *Canadian Encyclopedia*. Edmonton: Hurtig Publishers, 1ed. 1985, I: 753; (2ed., 1988), II: 913.

———. 'A Son and His Father: Edmund Gosse's Comments and Portraits, 1875-1910', *Nineteenth-Century Prose* 48 (Spring/Fall 2021), 45-92.

———. 'The Truth About 1843, and Why It's Important: Gosse, Brethren, Jamaica and the Scorpion', *Brethren Historical Review* 18 (2022), 15-63.

———. 'Deciphering a Wigram Letter to Darby', *Brethren Historical Review* 20 (2024), 189-99.

Wertheimer, Douglas and R. B. Freeman. 'Emily Gosse: A Bibliography', *Brethren Historical Review* 17 (2021), 25-78.

Wesenberg-Lund, Carl. 'Contributions to the Biology of the Rotifera', *Mémoires de l'Académie Royales des Sciences et des Lettres de Danemark, Section des Sciences*, ser. 8, IV (1923).

West, Gerald. 'The Early Development of Brethren Assemblies in London', *Christian Brethren Review* no. 41 (1990), 67-76.

Wheeler, Harry Edgar. 'Timothy Abbott Conrad, with Particular Reference to His Work in Alabama One Hundred Years Ago', *Bulletins of American Paleontology* XXIII (2 Sept. 1935), 1-157.

White, Paul. 'Cross-cultural Encounters: The Co-production of Science and Literature in Mid-Victorian Periodicals', in Roger Luckhurst and Josephine McDonagh (eds.), *Transactions and Encounters: Science and Culture in the 19th Century*. Manchester: Manchester University Press, 2002, 75-95.

White, William. 'Sir Edmund Gosse on Walt Whitman', *Victorian Studies* I (1957), 180-2.

Williams, Ernest E. 'Over 300 Years of Collecting in the Caribbean', in Brian I. Crother (ed.), *Caribbean Amphibians and Reptiles*. San Diego: Academic Press, 1999, 1-30.

Williams, L. Pearce. 'Michael Faraday's Education in Science', *Isis* 51 (Dec. 1960), 515-30.

Williams, R. B. 'P. H. Gosse (1810-1888)—Beware of the Ghosts', *Society for the History of Natural History Newsletter* No. 13 (1982), 8-9.

———. 'Three Posthumously Published Illustrations by P.H. Gosse (1810-1888)', *Society for the History of Natural History Newsletter* No. 20 (1983), 5-6.

———. 'More Fragments on Gosse Illustrations', *Society for the History of Natural History Newsletter* No. 23 (1984), 7-8.

———. 'Yet More on Gosse Illustrations', *Society for the History of Natural History Newsletter* No. 24 (1985), 7-8.

———. 'John Van Voorst: Patron Publisher of Victorian Natural History', *The Private Library* ser. 4, vol. I (Spring 1988), 5-12.

———. 'Gosse's Devonshire Coast', *Society for the History of Natural History Newsletter* No. 34 (1989), 7-8.

———. 'Original Paintings for Gosse's Birds of Jamaica', *Society for the History of Natural History Newsletter* No. 42 (1991), 4-5.

———. 'Three Unrecorded Publications by Philip Henry Gosse', *Archives of Natural History* 32 (2005), 34-40.

———. 'Supplementary Note on Articles by P.H. Gosse Printed on Wrappers of Issues of *The Zoologist*', *Archives of Natural History* 34 (2007), 199.

———. 'Philip Henry Gosse at Mobile, Alabama: His Unique Record of a Sea Shanty', *Archives of Natural History* 35 (2008), 360-363.

———. 'Another Published Letter by Philip Henry Gosse: A Beluga in the English Channel', *Archives of Natural History* 41 (April 2014), 170-2.

———. 'Bibliographical Notes on Variant Cloth-cases and Issues of Philip Henry Gosse's *The Aquarium*', *Archives of Natural History* 45 (April 2018), 162-5.

———. 'Philip Henry Gosse and the Microscopical Society of London, with additions to Gosse's Bibliography', *Archives of Natural History* 48 (Oct. 2021), 399-402.

See also NELSON, E. CHARLES

Williamson, George C. 'Edmund Gosse as a Boy: A Reminiscence', *London Mercury* XVIII (1928), 633-5.

Willson, Beckles. 'Newfoundland', *Encyclopaedia Britannica* (11th ed., 1910-11), XIX, 482.

Wilson, G. 'On the Artificial Preparation of Sea-water for Marine Vivaria', *Report of the Twenty-fourth Meeting of the British Association.* London: John Murray, 1855, 76.

———. 'On the Artificial Preparation of Sea Water for the Aquarium', *Edinburgh New Philosophical Journal* n.s. I (Jan. 1855), 129-32.

Wolf, Howard R. 'British Fathers and Sons, 1773-1913: From Filial Submissiveness to Creativity', *Psychoanalytic Review* LII (Summer 1965), 197-214.

Wright, E. Perceval. 'Notes on Irish Actinidae', *Natural History Review* VI (1859), 113-25.

Wright, H. G. S. 'Philip Henry Gosse's Microscope', *The Microscope* IX (Jan.-Feb. 1953), 113-5.

Wright, Thomas (preface and annotations), *The Autobiography of John Payne.* Olney, near Bedford: Thomas Wright, 1926.

Wright, T. S. 'On Two New Actinias from Arran', *Proc. of the Physical Society of Edinburgh* I (1856), 70-2.

Yonge, C. M. 'Thomas Alan Stephenson 1898-1961', *Biographical Memoirs of Fellows of the Royal Society* VIII (1962), 137-48.

———. 'John Graham Dalyell and Some Predecessors in Scottish Marine Biology', *Proc. Royal Society of Edinburgh*, Section 8, vol. 72 (1972), 89-97.

———. 'Victorians by the Sea Shore', *History Today* XXV (Sept. 1975), 602-9.

C. NEWSPAPERS AND PERIODICALS

In my research, I physically examined 104 titles of mainly British newspapers, weekly, fortnightly and quarterly reviews, and monthly magazines, which were seen at the British Library Newspapers (then known as the British Library: Newspaper Library at Colindale) or Cambridge University Library (those publications are listed in D. L. Wertheimer, 'Philip Henry Gosse', 591-6). Other serials cited here in footnotes (and not included in this total) were searched through Newspapers.com, Hathi Trust Digital Library, the British Library Newspapers' digital collection, and Readex America's Historical Newspapers.

Acknowledgments

Over the years, scores of individuals have assisted me by replying to letters, lending me privately held materials, and extending other courtesies. I wish here to record my special thanks to those to whom I am deeply indebted for their advice, guidance, and concern.

During my studies at the University of Toronto, Richard J. Helmstadter (d. 2012) was a wonderful role model as an historian. Michael Millgate, the distinguished Thomas Hardy scholar whom I knew at Toronto, early on took an unexpected interest in my work. He continued to show concern for my scholarly career even after it had formally concluded, a memory I treasure to this day. It was appropriate that the Toronto antiquarian bookseller Hugh Anson-Cartwright would be the one to suggest in 1972 contacting Richard Broke Freeman (1915-1986), University Reader in Taxonomy in the Department of Zoology, University College London, to learn more about his work on Gosse. It turned out that our separate interests in this imposing Victorian made advisable a collaboration on a Gosse bibliography, which Richard proposed. An unpretentious and meticulous scholar with a massive storehouse of knowledge and a well-honed wit, he never let on that he was the 'eminent zoologist and Darwinian scholar'[1] who was one of England's 'leading taxonomists.'[2]

The Gosse Family Collection of books, manuscripts, and drawings— even her residence near Reading, which my wife and I once house-sat—was put at my disposal by Jennifer S. Gosse, the lovely great-granddaughter of P. H. Gosse. This work would have been far poorer had she not so generously provided that access. M. J. Rowlands (1918-1995), the Librarian at what was then known as the British Museum (Natural History), graciously provided me with special facilities at that great institution. I was happy to exchange information about Gosse with the late Robert Boyd, an independent Brethren researcher from Fort William in Inverness-shire, Scotland, who went on to author the only biography of Emily Gosse. I benefitted from the generous help of my friends Dr N. Merrill Distad and Steve Beckow.

1. Obituary, 'Mr Richard Freeman', London *Times* (10 Sept. 1986), 18.
2. P.B. Medawar, 'Illustrated Taxonomy', *Nature* 244 (31 Aug. 1973), 582.

One of the unexpected pleasures in preparing this book has been my interactions with two exceptional historians. In November 2020, I contacted out of the blue Dr Neil T. R. Dickson, editor of the *Brethren Historical Review* to ask if he would consider publishing a bibliography of Emily Gosse. That launched a correspondence which quickly turned warm and open, touching on many topics of common interest as if we had been old friends. I am grateful to him for sharing his encyclopedic knowledge of Brethren history, helping me avoid errors and missteps concerning Brethren matters, cheerfully responding to my queries and guiding me towards helpful resources. I had initially contacted another remarkable scholar, Dr Timothy C. F. Stunt, in 1972 concerning my proposed Gosse dissertation. I did not then realize that his typed, four-page response to my inquiry was typical not only of his profound knowledge of virtually everything Brethren, but of his generosity in helping others. I treasure their friendship. I am also deeply indebted to them for their careful reading of the manuscript for this biography, which improved it and saved me from numerous errors. In the end, of course, I alone am responsible for all errors of commission or omission.

This book has benefitted from the care, graphics expertise, and untiring patience and good humour provided by Paul Lewis and Angela Lewis, of LUZ Design. But this work could not have reached its present form had I not had access to needed historical materials. I am deeply indebted to my wonderful friend Shoshanah Seidman—ever helpful, ever generous, and ever delighted in what I was doing. Dr Neil Summerton, CB, the highly-esteemed historian, was indispensable in seeing the book through its final stages.

My wife Gila has always been my first reader, critic, research assistant, and supporter. We first met half-a-dozen years before I started my Gosse studies, and she has accompanied me, and persevered, on this journey. Though set in a different context, an ancient liturgical poem captures my feelings for her. My gratitude and love

> could not be laid out in words,
> even were all the skies parchment, and all the forest reeds;
> if all the seas were ink, and all the lakes,
> and all the people, scribes and clerks.[3]

3. 'Akdamut' [Aramaic for 'Introduction'], *The Koren Shavuot Mahzor*, with introduction, translation and commentary by Jonathan Sacks (Jerusalem: Koren Publishers, 2016), 392.

Illustration sources

*Reproduced illustrations between pages 244 and 245 are either in the public domain or used with the kind permission of the owners. Abbreviations:*AW (Aaron Wertheimer photography); BHL (Biodiversity Heritage Library); CMN (Canadian Museum of Nature); DWC (Douglas Wertheimer Collection).

Illustration 1: EWG, *Father and Son*, Booklover's Edition (1912), frontispiece, DWC; AW;

Illustration 2: The Christian (21 Sept. 1888), 1, DWC;

Illustration 3: EWG, *Father and Son*, Booklover's Edition, DWC; PHG, *Memorial*, 66, DWC; AW;

Illustration 4: EWG, *Father and Son*, Booklover's Edition, DWC, AW;

Illustration 5: PHG, *Entomologia Terrae Novae (*CMN/BHL*);*Bruton, *Entomological News*, 37;

Illustration 6: PHG, *Entomologia Terrae Novae* (CMN/BHL);

Illustration 7: PHG, *Illustrations of the Birds of Jamaica* ([April 1848], book form 1849), 97, coloured lithograph Plate XIX: *Trochilus polytmus* Linnaeus, 1758 (BHL);

Illustration 8: PHG, *Naturalist's Sojourn in Jamaica (1851),* Plate IV, drawn by PHG; BHL; Freeman & Wertheimer-PHG s.v. Reptiles (index);

Illustration 9: PHG, 'Referenda for Jamaica' (Smithsonian Libraries and Archives, Washington, D.C. via BHL);

Illustration 10: PHG, *Tenby* (1856), plate XXI; 356; DWC; AW;

Illustration 11: PHG, *Aquarium* (1854), DWC; *Journal of the Society of Arts* VI, 13 Aug. 1858, 592; AW; 'Wie er= und behält man den Ocean auf dem Tische, oder das Marine=Aquarium', *Die Gartenlaube: illustriertes familienblatt* III (1855), 504;

Illustration 12: PHG, *Evenings at the Microscope* ([1859], New York, 1860), 396 (BHL);

Illustration 13: PHG, *Aquarium* (1854), DWC; AW;

*Illustrations 14-15:*PHG, *Actinologia Britannica*, Plates IX (left) and VI; DWC; AW;

Illustration 16: PHG, *Aquarium* (1854), Plate V, DWC; AW.

Index

Arrangement of the entries is alphabetical, letter by letter. Main citations only. Unless otherwise indicated, the scientific nomenclature reflects the scheme(s) current in PHG's time.

Abney Park Cemetery (Hackney):
Brethren purchase a section of, 273; EG, and other Brethren, buried at, 273 fn.195.

Abraham and his Children (1855), by EG:
lessons during a child's infancy, 175; characteristics of children, 175; role of wife and mother, 172 and fn.60; 252; greatest human responsibility guiding the child 'born for immortality', 439; 474; favourably reviewed, 256 fn.80.

Academy (weekly):
in 1871, EWG meets Appleton, founder and editor of, and Hueffer, assistant editor of, 506; meets W.B. Scott, staff member of, 506 fn.127; in 1872, PHG speaks with pride of EWG writing for, 511; support for Higher Criticism of Bible, 511; advertisement in 1874 for EWG's Victoria Institute paper, 524 fn.193; covers Victoria Institute talk, 524 fn.196; information on EWG's *On Viol and Flute*, in, 525 fn.200; and review, 525 fn.202; obituary notice of PHG in, 539 fn.11; 607;
CONTRIBUTORS TO: EWG, 505; 481 fns.24, 26; 504 fns.114, 118-19; 515 fn.173; 552 fn.94; Huxley, 511 fn.145; Lankester, 552 and fn.94; Lubbock, 299 fn.163; Westwood, 228 fn.389.

Achill Missionary Herald (monthly):
founded, edited by Edward Nangle, 429; anti-Catholic and anti-Darby, 429 and fn.183; favourably reviews PHG's *Geology or God*, 316 fn.247; and PHG's *Revelation*, 410; 411 fn.87, 416 fn.111, 429 fn.183; frowns on PHG's 'Brethrenism', 411 fn.87; 429 fn.183; Nangle corresponds with PHG, 429 and fn.183; cited 9 fn.10.

Acontia: *see* Sea anemones.

Actiniadae: see 'Researches on the Poison-apparatus'; Sea anemones.

Actinologia Britannica ([1858]–1860), by PHG:
one of PHG's most important scientific works, 360; he considered it the one by which he would be known, 539; research 'of the highest order', 348; the first detailed investigation of British sea anemones and corals, intended for the naturalist and amateur, 347-8; xviii; end of aquarium movement in Britain framed by, 241; sends copy to Bates, 585; the next single-volume treatment of this group appeared 120 years later, 350;
ILLUSTRATIONS IN: xix; coloured lithographs from PHG's watercolours gain consistent praise, 350; PHG 'stands alone and unrivalled' in 'difficult art of drawing objects of zoology', 350-1; xix; engraved by Dickes, 342; Blaschka's glass models based on, 351;
PUBLICATION RECORD: initially serialised in 12 bi-monthly parts from 1858, with one colour lithograph, inexpensively priced, 220 fn.337; 342; parts issue announced, 360; in book form, published in 1860, 585 fn.315; on author's-risk basis, PHG may only have broken even, 222; 4,000 copies printed, 296; advertised: 226 fn.374;
RESEARCH FOR: in 1852, PHG begins study of, 339; by 1856, PHG announces proposed work on, 340; enlists aid of volunteers 'from the Channel Isles to the Shetlands', 238; 340; 342-3; unlike his field work in Newfoundland, Canada, Alabama and Jamaica, 340; research while lecturing or travelling around Britain, 343-4; 343 fn.69; text completed in June 1859, 347;
SCIENTIFIC REPUTATION: PHG was '*il riverito autore*' ('the revered author'), 348; xviii; the 'first adequate monographer' of the subject, xviii; 348-9; the first to convey 'he understands what he is writing about', 349; xix; well-received in press, 350; critics vied in extolling its excellence, 347–350; develops nomenclature for, 349; 352 fn.132; 353 fn.140; questions about species multiplication, 351–3; 341 fn.57; research unsuccessfully contested by Lewes, 353–6; PHG's description of the teliferous system, q.v., 355; unclear evolutionary history of Anthozoa, 352; need for morphological investigations, 352-3; cited: 203 fn.239; 238 fn.452; 305; 307; 377; 440 and fn.8; 410.

Adam's Federal Headship: *see* 'Federal Headship'.

Agassiz, Alexander, marine zoologist:
(son of Louis Agassiz), sends greetings via EWG to PHG, 307; an evolution opponent, 307 fn.207; Assoc. Member, Victoria Institute, 326 fn.300; cited: 353 fn.138.

Agassiz, Louis, zoologist:
(father of Alexander Agassiz), his co-authored *Zoology* sells well, 224 fn.365; properly interprets sea anemone 'lasso-cells' or thread-capsules, 356 and fns.152-3, described as anticipating PHG on teliferous system, 357 and fn.161; Lewes claims his work on lasso-cells is inadequate, 366.

Alabama:
CHRONOLOGY: in 1838, PHG lived seven-and-a-half months in Alabama, 71; PHG's low view of 'Yankee' character, 70-1; 79-80; originally intends to go to Georgia or South Carolina, but in Philadelphia, PHG meets palaeontologist T. A. Conrad, who recommends he go there, 84; 78; reaches Mobile by boat from Philadelphia on 14 May 1838, 84; then

on a steamer to Claiborne, PHG meets R. Saffold, who persuades PHG to serve as a school-master in Pleasant Hill, Dallas County, 85; teaches some dozen students, 86; as an Englishman, PHG is suspect, 88 and fn.312; at end of November, his teaching position not renewed, 91; at end of Dec. 1838 inexplicably decides to return to England, 94; on 6 Jan. 1839, departs Mobile for Liverpool, 94; begins to visit British Museum after return from, in 1839, 11; cited: 125; 135;
ENTOMOLOGIA ALABAMENSIS: PHG keeps a graphic record of insects in, *see separate entry*;
LETTERS FROM ALABAMA (1859): 'an Alabama classic', xviii; 90; 'full of original observations' on entomology, 76 fn.240; 89; the 'most complete contribution to natural history', 90; also 'an authority' on social customs, language, 89-90; *see separate entry*;
RELIGIOUS LIFE: little formal support for PHG's religion at Pleasant Hill, turns to nature, 90-1; in Sept. 1838, PHG undergoes spiritual revival 'like a new conversion', 91; 101; strives for 'perfect sanctification', 91; 466; American Methodism tended towards traditional practices, and in Dec. 1838, contemplates serving as Methodist minister in Alabama, 92; where there was opportunity, 92-3; PHG attends Quarterly Meeting of Methodist Society in Selma, 93-4; confident he could become Wesleyan travelling preacher in England, 92; 97; cited: 126; 466;
SCIENTIFIC WORK: PHG first experienced naturalist in Alabama, xviii; 89; his most intensively studied subject there is entomology, 86; articles for *Zoologist* on Alabama, 122; 85 fn.292; 86 fn.295; Alabama lacking in support institutions for entomology, 86; his collecting is small in comparison to what he later did in Jamaica, 89; at Pleasant Hill, entomologizes in morning and evening, during afternoons writes, paints, arranges, 86;
SLAVERY IN: PHG's first view of the 'domestic institution', 87; 80; comparison to other British visitors to antebellum American South, 87-8; PHG apparently unaware of 'Trail of Tears', 96; terms slavery 'so enormous an evil', 91; predicts its doom, 88-9; may have influenced his leaving Alabama, 91.

Anderson, John, nurseryman: experiments on tropical orchids, writes Darwin, PHG, 375.

Andres, Angelo, Italian zoologist:
his landmark work on sea anemones cites PHG as 'the revered author', xviii fn.17; 348; corresponds with PHG, 348 fn.109; identifies most important aspect of *Actinologia Britannica*, 349 fn.114; PHG classificatory family virtually disappears in work of, 350 fn.117.

Andrews, Sarah, governess:
in May 1857, becomes governess for Gosses at Marychurch, 281; 439; 441; makes copies of letters for PHG, 304 fn.194; with PHG and EWG, in Sept. 1857 they go to Brethren Room at Marychurch for first time, 333 and fn.5; 534; knows how to discipline EWG, 441; PHG correspondence, 343 fn.73; 368 fn.214; 441 fn.11; present in Dec. 1860 when Eliza, the new Mrs Gosse, first comes to

Sandhurst, 370; appears in *Father and Son* as 'Miss Marks', 281 fn.42.

Appleton, Charles Edward, founder, editor of *The Academy*: in 1871, EWG meets, 506.

Apsey, George, Newfoundland counting-house clerk:
a clerk in Newfoundland from his teenage years, 41; his dissolute life, 41-2; a religious conversion over time, 42; Apsey becomes 'first-born child' of religious revival among Methodists in Carbonear, 1830-2, 41-2; 43; his remarkable life transformation celebrated among Methodists, 41; and clerks at Elson's, 42; he serves as the role model, 47-8; 61 and fn.165-6; rejoices over PHG's religious commitment, 46; 53 and fn.124; characteristics of his conversion, 46-7; and fn.88; PHG joins Methodist class of, 56; a popular Local Preacher and Class-leader, 59 and fn.153; remains a Methodist to his death, 61 fn.166; PHG sent a newspaper clipping about, 95 fn.365; PHG draws strength from, 507.

Aquarium:
invention of aquarium revolutionises popular view of marine fauna, 191; PHG 'Father of the Aquarium', xviii; 194; his role acknowledged in Britain, France, Germany, America, 208-9;
ETYMOLOGY: incomplete entry in *OED*, 208 fn.264; PHG first to use word in its present sense, xvi; 208 and fn.264; rationale for adoption of word explained, 208 fn.264; 'aquavivarium', 'marine vivarium', 'vivarium', all yield to 'aquarium', 208 fn.264; slowly, 212 fn.287;
EXPERIMENTERS WITH: Susan Bell claimed as 'first person to preserve invertebrate animals alive in aquaria of sea-water', 194 fn.182; and her son, Thomas Bell, in the 1820s, 194 fn.182; E. Lankester undertakes experiments, 192 fn.173;
FABRICATION OF: boosted by repeal of 'window tax', 193; Regent's Park, 198; manufacturers and suppliers, especially Lloyd, 226-7;
FORMULA FOR: PHG's sea-water analysis, 201-2; challenged but confirmed, 201 fns.230-1;
NATIONAL PUBLIC AQUARIA: in Britain in 1853, first in world, 198; 241 fn.472; America (1856), 210-11; France (1861), 211 and fn.279; Germany (1863), 211;
PHG'S AQUARIA: his large, rectangular one claimed as first-ever private one, 485 fn.41; in 1862, builds new sea-water tank, 368; in 1876 repairs his 2 tanks, 539 fn.12; in 1893, fell to pieces, 485 fn.41.

Aquarium (1854, 1856), by PHG:
BOOK BACKGROUND: in Dec. 1853, PHG works on 'The Aquarium: a Biography of Marine Animals', 180; it appears by June 1854, and is possibly the best of his seashore volumes, 203; letter-press and 6 chromolithographs praised in press, 203-7; and by later zoologists, 207; but expensive, 220; 221; 3,500 copies of 2 eds printed, 223; 243; 2ed reviewed in USA, 220 fn.336; PHG's profit on 2 editions of, 221; in 1856, 2nd eds appear of *Aquarium, Handbook*, 214; they sell slowly, 223; but are advertised, 226 fns.371-4; and imitated, 227-30; comparison to works by Kingsley, Lewes, 230-3;
ILLUSTRATIONS: with its chromolithographs of seashore creatures *in situ*, a landmark publication,

205-6; 350; incorrect claim that submarine land-scapes in, were done by EG, 203 fn.239; INFLUENCE OF: With *Naturalist's Rambles on the Devonshire Coast* (1853), frames beginning of aquaromania, 208; 241 and fn.472; Gosse's role credited in France, 208-9; 210; Germany, 209 and fn.269; Britain, 194–7; America, 209; aquarium is 'most effective aid' in study of marine natural history, 242; connection with oceanography and marine biological stations, 242 fn.477; RELIGIOUS LESSON OF: 'no scientific way to heaven', 239-40; 240 fn.461; Adam's 'Federal Headship', 314 and fn.236; danger of failing to praise the Creator, 322 and fn.269; 123; REPUTATION OF: 2nd most reviewed PHG book, 199 fn.214; 211; 217; 296 fn.137; listed among quali-fications for election to Royal Society, 251 fn.47; widely reviewed, inexpensive *Handbook to the Marine Aquarium* (1855) excerpts last chapter of *Aquarium*, 213-14 and 213 fn.292; SCIENTIFIC RESEARCH IN: PHG repeats account of teliferous system, 356 and fn.155; 358 fn.162.

Aquaromania:
movement dates to 1853–60, bookended by PHG's *Naturalist's Rambles* (1853), 199; *Aquarium* (1854), 208; and *Actinologia Britannica* (1860), 241–5; Lloyd gives slightly different years, 241 fn.472; Newman divides aquarium movement into 3 periods, 241 fn.472; compared to other 'manias', 208; 372 fn.239; idea of establishing 'a miniature sea' was 'utterly wild and visionary' until PHG 'loosed the Gordian knot', 194-5; PHG a phenomenon as a natural history populariser, 215-16; expansion of railway as factor in, questioned, 190 fn.162; incorrect characterisation of, in USA, 211 fn.277; popularisers, 227–30; response to of artists, q.v., verse, song, 212; from 1860–1914, only 2 guides to British seashore published, 242; AFTERMATH: an indispensable tool, 198; scientific attention transfers from littoral to deep-sea fauna, 242; 379; in 1870s, a marine biological station at Naples, in 1888, at Plymouth, 242; 242 fn.477; also Torbay, 545 fn.49.

Aquavivarium (aquarium):
incomplete entry in *OED*, 208 fn.264; neologism of Charles Knight (1791–1873) dates to June 1853, 208 fn.264; 'aquavivarium', 'marine vivarium', 'vivarium', all yield to 'aquarium', 208 fn.264; E. Lankester's *Aquavivarium* (1856), 192 fn.173; 228.

Archdeacon of Exeter: *see* Freeman, Philip.

Archives du Christianisme au dix-neuvième Siècle, leading French evangelical journal of Frédéric Monod: publishes EG tracts, 263; reports on 'Week of Prayer' in London, 402 fn.53.

Artists:
British artistic community reflects new appreci-ation of seashore, 217-18; Cruickshank, 'Tail of the Comet of 1853', 212; *Punch* (1856), 314-15; (1858), 217 fn.315.

Assyria (1852), by PHG: on the world's first empire, this is the 4th of PHG's books on biblical lands and peoples, 186; varying opinions on, 186 fn.142; advertised by SPCK, 215 fn.303; 225 fns.367–9; cited: 221 fn.342.

Author's-risk book publication:
PHG publishes 9 books on the risky approach of, beginning with *Illustrations of the Birds of Jamaica* ([1848]-1849), 149; which sold at a loss, 149; sale of copyright more common in 1850s Britain, 220; COMPARISON OF SELLING PRICE: PHG's books, with their coloured plates, were expensive, compared with those of Kingsley, Wood, 221; COMPARISON OF AUTHOR INCOME EARNED: PHG receives about 57% of retail price, a high percentage, max-imizing his income, 221; figures show lower earn-ings by Kingsley, Lewes, Wood, 222; COMPARISON OF NUMBER OF COPIES PRINTED: PHG's books sold in respectable quantities compared to Darwin, Kirby, or Lewes, but were overshadowed by Kingsley, Wood, 223-4; COMPARISON OF NEWSPAPER REVIEWS: PHG's works praised by reviewers, 225; comparison of number of reviews of *Omphalos* to Miller's *Testimony of the Rocks* (1857), Darwin's *Origin* gained more than either, 296 fns.136-7.

Baird, Spencer F., zoologist:
in 1884-5, meets EWG in America and sends greetings to PHG, 307 and fn.207.

Baird, William, zoologist:
staff member at British Museum, 10; 121; adheres to natural theology tradition, 12; Baird, A. White, and PHG, qq.v., contribute to *Excelsior*, a pop-ular evangelical serial, 12 fn.33; Baird is among those proposing PHG as Associate of Linnean Soc., 173 fn.68; shortly before his death, PHG suggests EWG could replace him at the Museum, 506; cited: 228; 507.

Baker, Mary Ann, annuitant living in Tottenham:
unmarried, Brethren, lives in 1866 with Anne Buckham, servant Mary Daniels, and boarder EWG, 451; notice on, 451 fn.72; frowns on Beddows's family, Brethren with whose daughter, Emma, EWG associates, 476; reports in confidence to PHG on EWG's literary activities, 501; suggests EWG not talk about Ibsen ('Mr. Gibson') so much, 503; EWG translates Danish sermon of Dean Fog for, 511; EWG reads his papers on Ibsen, Paludan-Müller, to, 516.

Baptism:
Open Brethren view of, 441-2; historic accounts of, in newspapers: 443 fn.22; and elsewhere, 442 fn.16; in 1807, EG baptized in London, 610; CHILD BAPTISM: in 1872, Bewes, q.v., members of PHG's St. Marychurch assembly, seek simultane-ous baptism of their 4 children, 512–14; episode sparks PHG, EWG disagreement on understanding of sacrament, 441–3; EWG's claim that his, in 1859, was 'remarkable', 443 and fn.23; 444 fn.24; 514 fn.166; but not beneficial, 442 and fn.16; 515; PHG ON: preaching, 336 fn.29; writing, 442 fn.20; 443 fn.21; baptising of Tydeman in Jamaica, 134; 152 fn.332; cited: 586.

Baptists:
PHG encounters Baptist minister in Compton, 79; 'breaking of bread', q.v., a term occasionally used by, 119 fn.106; in 1846, PHG likely encountered

Hume, q.v., earliest missionary of, in Jamaica, who later affiliated with Brethren, 134 and fn.202; in early 1840s, Baptist tract societies founded, 258; PHG apologizes for affront to a Baptist minister staying with him, 427 fn.169; PHG misinterprets use by butterfly collector of printed papers of Baptist missionaries, 586;
SEE ALSO: Brethren.

Barbour, Margaret Fraser (known as 'Mrs. Barbour of Bonskeid'), Scottish author and poet:
one of 2 notable mid-Victorian female religious tract writers, 262; some of her books and tracts named, 262.

Barnardo, Thomas J., philanthropist:
around 1868, EWG involved with, 461 and fn.136; 462 and fn.138; once aligned with Open Brethren, 461-2; 461 fn.136; PHG corresponds with, 338 fn.37; 426 fn.164; cited: 425 fn.162.

Barnum, P.T., showman:
works with D.W. Mitchell to bring first aquarium to America, in 1856, 210-11.

Basire, James, engraver:
engraves PHG's illustrations to 'Dioecious Character of the Rotifera', 559 and fn.137.

Bastian, Henry Charlton, neurologist:
an evolutionist who fell out of favour with the X Club, 362-3; 560 fn.142; in 1867, endorsed by Busk and Huxley for Royal Society fellowship, 362; his papers rejected by Royal Society in a case resembling that of PHG, 362; referee reports of Busk and Huxley on, 560 fn.142; his *Beginnings of Life* a search for origins in tune with Darwin's work, 567 fn.186; he proposes that the living emerged from the non-living, 568; cited, 364 fn.200.

Barnard, Frederick, microscopist:
in 1884, meets EWG and sends greetings to PHG, 307 and fn.207.

Batchelour, William, surgeon and cancer curer:
in 1856 claimed his cancer cure 'immediately relieved' pain, 249 and fns.36–8.

Bate, C. Spence, zoologist:
member of Plymouth Institution, 380 and fn.276; at British Association, 1869, cites PHG, 387-8.

Bateman, John B., printer and publisher:
from 1843, PHG knew, among Brethren, 120; 338 fn. 37; books published by, 132 fn.187; 335 fn.18.

Bates, Henry Walter, naturalist:
BIOGRAPHY: a Unitarian and agnostic, 585 fn.318; Stevens was agent for collecting by, 141; paying 25% commission, 141 fn.248; passed over for job at British Museum, 481;
EVOLUTION AND: his research is one of the earliest confirmations of Darwin's theory, 586, 549; influenced by opportunity to study effects of geographical isolation on species, 320; describes 'transition forms' of tropical butterflies, 567; PHG unaware that Bates presented his ideas on butterfly mimicry to Linnean Society in 1861, 586; opposed at Entomological Society by Westwood, 547 fn.56; PHG AND: shares with PHG interest in diurnal Lepidoptera and Coleoptera, 585 fn.316; comparison of natural history collecting of Bates, PHG, Wallace, 147-8; PHG corresponds with Bates, 371; 585; sends him a copy of *Actinologia*

Britannica, 585; PHG reads his *Naturalist on the River Amazons* (1863), 586 and fn.320, and sends him a copy of his *Naturalist's Sojourn in Jamaica*, 586 and fn.323; cited: 321 fn.266.

Bathybius haeckelii (named by Huxley):
supposed primitive protoplasm lining the ocean floor from which life had emerged, 311, 568; Huxley later recognizes it as 'little more than sulphate of lime', 568 fn.189; 311.

Baxter, Michael Paget, prophetic speculator:
editor, publisher, writer, known as 'Prophet Baxter', periodically predicted end of the world, an historicist, mid-tribulational rapturist, 590 fn.348; PHG calls his work 'odd', 590 fn.348; cites PHG's *6000 Years*, 415 fn.107; prints excerpts of PHG's *Mysteries of God*, 592 fn.367; Boyce writes for, 590; Chester writes for, 408;
PUBLICATIONS EDITED: *Christian Herald and Signs of Our Times*, 398 fn.31; 408; 415 fn.107; 589 fn.341; 590 fn.348; 592 fn.367; *Prophetic News*, 590 and fn.348; 592 fn.367.

Baxter, Nadir, evangelical organizational leader:
anti-Catholic premillennialist, supporter of A.R.C. Dallas, q.v., connected for a time with Clapham Sect, 112 and fn.71; in 1843, in contact with PHG through M. Habershon, 112; corresponds with PHG, 3 fn.1; 109 fn.52; 112 fn.72; 120 fn.110.

Beale, Lionel, microscopist:
his *Microscope* (1854), a technical treatment, 346; contains a chromolithograph, 205; book is illustrated by T. West, 526 fn.155; member of Victoria Institute, 326 fn.300.

Beddows, Emma, EWG friend:
in 1868, family is active in Tottenham Brethren circle, 476; at home of, EWG talks for 3 hours on 'perfect sanctification', 466; Mesd. Buckham, Baker, frown on Beddows family, 476; romance falters and ends, 476; unknown if she features in 'Tristram Jones', 476 fn.4; cited, 507.

Bell, Francis Jeffrey, zoologist:
editor of a rev. ed. of PHG's *Evenings at the Microscope* (1895), 425 fn.158;
ATHENAEUM REVIEWS: Wood's *J.G. Wood*, 228 fn.392; EWG's *Life*, 540 fn.18; 581 fn.288.

Bell, Susan *née* Gosse (PHG aunt):
first of Gosse children to succumb to Revival spirit, 17; gave her brother Thomas drawing lessons, 17; in 1812, brother Thomas joins her in Poole, 20; PHG's association with, a factor in his interest in natural history, 23; shows PHG how to keep sea anemones alive in a dish of sea-water, 23 fn.29.

Bell, Thomas (son of Susan Bell):
professor of zoology, president of the Linnean Society, 1st cousin to PHG, 98; author of *History of British Quadrupeds* and *History of British Reptiles*, 98; in 1839, PHG shows him MS of *Canadian Naturalist*, he recommends it to publisher Van Voorst, 98; PHG dedicates *Canadian Naturalist* (1840) to, 98 and fn.8; finds a bank job for PHG, 99; influential in getting SPCK to pay PHG to write an introduction to zoology (1844), 120-1; purchases from PHG crustacea specimens from Jamaica, 147 fn.296; in 1847, under Bell's supervision, PHG commences 5 guides to

British Museum natural history collection, 165 and fn.25; in 1849, PHG consults with Bell on SPCK-proposed *Text-book of Zoology for Schools*, 173 and fn.66; in 1849, among those who propose PHG for Associate membership in Linnean Society, 173 fn.68; in 1856, among those who propose PHG for Fellow of the Royal Society, 251; in 1858, dismisses evolutionary theories of Darwin and Wallace, 302 fn.183; signator to *Declaration of Students*, q.v., 383 fn.286; in 1878, shows to EWG a collection of tropical insects given him by PHG which were actually 'mimics in cardboard', 582; edits White's *Natural History of Selborne* (1878), 582 fn.291; ATHENAEUM REVIEWS, BY: Bishop's *Management of the Aquarium*, 194 fn.184; Lankester's *Aquavivarium*, 228 fn.384; Tugwell's *Manual of the Sea-anemones*, 341 fn.56; PHG's books: *Marine Aquarium*, 213 fn.292; *Tenby*, 215 fn.304; cited: 228.

Bell, Thomas George, clergyman:
editor, *Voice Upon the Mountains*; 'connected with Brethren', lectures on prophecy at Torquay, 403 fn.61;

Bemister, John, clerk:
a Carbonear native, clerk at Gosse, Pack, & Fryer, 59 fn.154: friends with PHG, 47 fn.86; 59 fn.154; later became Newfoundland's Receiver General, 59 fn.154; correspondence with PHG, cited, 47 fn.86; 95 fns.364-5; 603 fn.7.

Bennet, William Henry, editor:
leading Open Brother, 592 and fn.362; 338 fn.37; editor, *Golden Lamp*, 592; in views on Jesus' humanity expressed in *Mysteries of God*, says PHG may have 'unintentionally dishonour[ed] Him', 592; PHG's response to, 593; R.C. Morgan's response to, 593-4; corresponds with PHG, 338 fn.37; 426 fn.164; 592 fns.365-6.

Bennett, Edwin H. (1847–1903), businessman:
Open Brethren leader, corresponds with PHG, 338 fn.37.

Bennett, John J., secretary of Linnean Society:
knows PHG, 173 fn.67; supports his election to Linnean Society, 173 fn.68.

Berger, Ann *née* Cathcart, author:
wife of Samuel Berger, Jr., 113 and fns.74-5; seeks PHG's assistance in publishing, 113.

Berger, Capel Berrow, cashier:
cousin of William Thomas Berger, in 1843, attends Hackney Scripture reading, 6; biographical details of, 6 fn.12; 113; 119 fns.100, 102; 383 fn.286; around 1853, helps form Evangelical Tract Association, 257.

Berger, Capel Henry, in family business:
son of Capel Berrow Berger, and biography, 6 fn.12; 383 fn.286; signs *Declaration of Students*, q.v., 383 fn.286.

Berger, Jenny (2nd Mrs W.T. Berger): 5 fn.7.

Berger, Mary *née* Van Sommer (1st Mrs W.T. Berger): in 1843,
married to Berger, 5; sister of James Van Sommer, q.v., 5; biographical details of, 5 fn.8; 119 fns.100; both present in 1843 at Hackney Scripture Reading meeting at W.T. Berger's, 5-6; while PHG is in Jamaica, corresponds with, 118 fn.96.

Berger, Samuel, Jr., manufacturer:
brother of William Thomas and Thomas B., 4; 5 fn.7; on religious development, 5 fn.7; married to Ann, 113 and fn.74; influential member of Hackney Methodist Society, 113 and fn.73; in 1843, introduces PHG to brother William Thomas, and through him to Brethren, 8; 112–14; PHG takes specimens of Rotifera from pond at residence of, 181.

Berger, Samuel (the Younger), businessman:
father of W.T. Berger and Samuel Berger, Jr., 4.

Berger, William Thomas, businessman:
CHRONOLOGY: son of Samuel Berger (the Younger), brother of Samuel Berger, Jr., 4; biographical details of, 5 fn.7; 119 fn.100; description of personality by PHG, 113; in 1899, dies in Cannes, 4 fn.4; BRETHREN AND: unlike Brethren in other assemblies, Berger was wealthy, 119; raised as an Anglican, 4; 113; conversion experience of, 4; in 1843, marries Mary Van Sommer, 5 and fn.8; and is introduced to PHG by brother Samuel Jr., 113; from Methodism to Brethren, 113; in 1843, holds Brethren Scripture reading meeting at his Hackney home, attended by PHG, 4; 118; by 1846, in contact with B.W. Newton, 118; from at least 1848, knew EG, 254; while PHG is in Jamaica (and after leaving there), corresponds with him, 118 fn.96; 129 and fn.160; 537; Berger-Pearse-Gosse Brethren circle *vs.* Darby-Wigram circle in Jamaica, 153; 161; in 1856, purchases lease of Providence Chapel, Paragon Road, Hackney, 254; in 1857, PHG says goodbye to, before moving to St. Marychurch, 286; EVANGELICAL ACTIVITIES: around 1853, helps form Evangelical Tract Association, 257; 6; 'nursing Father' of the China Inland Mission, 5; acquaintance with J. Hudson Taylor, 462 fn.139; involved in East End Training Institute, 425 fn.162; EWG AND: in 1867, visits 'Saint Hill' in East Grinstead, Sussex, W.T. Berger country home, 5; 452 and fn.79.

Bevan, Frances, Brethren hymn-writer:
the most prolific nineteenth-century Brethren female writer, 262; role in Christian prophetic conferences, 401; aligned with Darby faction, 401 fn.48.

Bewes, Mary *née* Soltau:
niece of H.W. Soltau, in 1855 married to Bewes, 513; in 1872, they wanted 4 of their many children baptized, 512–14; 512 fn.150.

Bewes, Wyndham Edmund, colonel:
in 1855, married Mary Soltau, 513 fn.156; member of PHG's St. Marychurch assembly, in 1872 wants 4 children to be baptized by PHG, 512–15; 512 fn. 152; involvement of L. Strong, 514; PHG miffed, 514; issue of local autonomy, 514; 422 fn.144; PHG, EWG disagree on episode, 515; cited: 442 fn.16.

Bewley, Henry, publisher:
founder of Dublin Tract Society, distributed 500 million religous tracts, 260; 'to some extent a "Plymouth Brother" by conviction', 260 fn.113.

Bible: *see* Scripture.

Bible and Christian defence groups: *see* Christian

Evidence Society; Society of Biblical Archaeology; Victoria Institute.
Biblical criticism:
gains a foothold in Britain, 324; R. Hill's pamphlet on, 145; Harwood introduces work of Strauss to Britain, 503 fn.106;
COLENSO AND: _Pentateuch and the Book of Joshua_ is first 'indigenous attempt' at, in Britain, 325; PHG's 1871 paper for Victoria Institute on, 325–30; PHG's tactic in answering, 310; 331; EWG rejects PHG's conclusion, 520-1; cited: 320; 331.
Birds:
in 1834, PHG bought Wilson and Bonaparte's _American Ornithology_, 60 fn.161; 81; in Philadelphia in 1838, met American ornithologists Nuttall, Peale, familiar with work of Bartram, Wilson, 81; 82; later Audubon, 124 fn.132; prior to 1847, studies of, in Jamaica, 'not worth mentioning', 138; PHG is 'Father of Jamaican Ornithology', 149; in 1845 in Jamaica, turns attention to, 142; RESEARCH APPROACH: in studying birds, PHG's 'industry was amazing', 150; observations on culinary qualities of birds, xxi fn.35; on bird songs, 82 fn.275; to study birds, PHG preferred to strangle them than club them to death, also used a rifle, 142; 140; binoculars not then common for bird-watching, 142 fn.252; PHG failed to bring live humming-birds to England, 139; collectors purchase his specimens, 147 fn.294;
WORKS BY PHG: _see separate entries for Birds of Jamaica; Birds of Jamaica, Illustrations; Natural History: Mammalia (Birds); Popular British Ornithology_; cited: 307 fn.207.
Birds of Jamaica (1847), by PHG:
first of trilogy of books on Jamaica, 149;
BOOK RESEARCH: in Sept. 1845, contemplates writing book on Jamaican birds, 142 fn.252; in Oct. 1845, corresponds with Richard Hill, 143; meets Hill, March 1846, who provides much information on local birds, 144-5; Hill and PHG complete revised list of Jamaican birds, 145; PHG lauds ornithological drawings of A. Robinson, 145; in Sept. 1846, begins to revise field notes, 161-2;
REPUTATION: Jamaican ornithological works prior to, not worth mentioning, 138; _Birds_ was 'far ahead of its time' and for decades 'one of the best bird books on any part of the world', 150; PHG is 'Father of Jamaican Ornithology', xviii; _Birds_ is one of PHG's most significant scientific works, 'perhaps the most enduring', 152; the 'ornithological classic of the English-speaking Caribbean', 151; listed among qualifications for election to Linnean Society, 173 fn.68; Royal Society, 252 fn.47; praised in Victorian press, 134; 163 fn.13; and by naturalists, 162 fn.11.
SEE ALSO: _Birds of Jamaica, Illustrations; Naturalist's Sojourn in Jamaica._
Birds of Jamaica, Illustrations ([1848]-1849), by PHG:
2nd of trilogy of books on Jamaica, 149;
DESCRIPTION: 52 lithographs drawn on stone and coloured by PHG, 149; 162 fn.10; uses Robinson's drawings in, 147 fn.288; colour quality 'high throughout', 149 fn.312;

PUBLICATION RECORD: first of 9 books published on author's-risk basis, 149; perhaps 3 dozen copies issued, 149; every copy sold at a loss, 219-20; advertised, but not reviewed, 149 fn.312; 2 birds in, are separately described in _AMNH_, 162 fn.9; 174 fn.70; cited: 139 fn.236; 207 fn.259.
Blaikie, John, poet:
friendship with EWG develops, 474; provides encouragement for EWG's poetry, 473; 479; PHG requires he pay half of cost to print _Madrigals_, and vets his poems, 491; an annoyance to, 492 and fn.55; book appears in 1870, 499; mixed reviews, 500 fn.85.
Blaschka, Leopold, glassworker:
in 1863, commissioned to make glass models of marine animals, uses PHG's _Actinologia Britannica_, 351; relied on PHG's work until 1880, 351 fn.127; cited: 82 fn.270.
Bluefields, Jamaica:
at the foot of the Blue Mountains, close to the seashore, 133; John and Anna Coleman moved to, from Parker's Bay, 129; significance of move, 129–31; PHG breaks bread at, 133; site of Great House, PHG's scientific base in Jamaica, 133; in 1890, marine laboratory established at, 151 fn.325; in 1970s, a vacation property, 133 fn.195.
Bohannon [also Bohanan], Buddy (of Alabama):
PHG stays in Pleasant Hill at home of, 88 and fn.309.
Bonar, Horatius, editor, _Quarterly Journal of Prophecy_:
PHG corresponds with, 429 fn.184; PHG sends him two pamphlets, 429 fn.184; PHG subscribes to, and publishes an article in, his _Quarterly Journal of Prophecy_, 429 and fn.186.
Books by PHG: _see_ Author's-risk book publication; separate book titles.
Bosanquet, James Whatman, author:
Historicist writer on prophecy, 399 fn.37; cites Bishop Ussher's chronology, 407 fn.70; Treasurer, Society of Biblical Archaeology, PHG apparently corresponds with, 428 and fn.179; cited: 426 fn.164.
Bowerbank, James S., naturalist:
a knowledgeable microscopist, 176; natural history lecturer, 234 and fn.426; inherited wealth, 218; after contact with Ward, q.v., keeps an aquarium which influences D.W. Mitchell, q.v., in setting up one at the Zoological Gardens, q.v., 198; among signators to _Declaration of Students_, q.v., 383 fn.286; PHG AND: from at least early 1840s, PHG acquainted with, 121; 122 fn.121; 176 fn.80; purchases sponges from PHG in Jamaica, 147 fn.296; 233 fn.414; supports PHG's membership in Microscopical Soc., 173; PHG's referee report for Royal Society recommends publication of a paper on sponges by, 360 fn.171.
Bowes, Arthur (2nd brother of Emily Gosse):
born in North Wales, 167; in 1841, lives with parents and EG in London, 171; attends wedding of EG, 172; some think infant EWG looks like, 174; in 1854, lost money in Castle Dinas investment, 186 fn.145; PHG says goodbye to, before moving to St. Marychurch, 286.

Bowes, Edmund Elford (1st brother of Emily Gosse): born in North Wales, 167; in 1841, Cambridge BA, 171; in 1848, attends wedding of EG, 172; in 1849, sends samples of rotifers to PHG, 181; PHG names one after him, 181 fn.109; in 1854, lost money in Castle Dinas investment, 186 fn.145; in 1855, suffers a stroke, 256; PHG says goodbye to, before moving to St. Marychurch, 286.

Bowes, Emily (1st Mrs PHG): *see* Gosse, Emily.

Bowler, Peter J. historian of science: cited, 301 fn.182; 313 fn.232; 552 fn.98.

Boyce, Frederick, missionary: author of pamphlet on prophecy, in 1881 corresponds with PHG, 590.

Boyce, George Price, watercolour painter: 'Babbacombe Bay, Devon' inspired by PHG's *Naturalist's Rambles on the Devonshire Coast*, 217-18.

'Breaking of Bread': Brethren term a synonym for communion service, 119 and fn.106; 127 and fn.150; *OED* not include this usage, 119 fn.106; PHG breaks bread in Savannah-le-Mar, 134; of his St. Marychurch assembly, PHG writes 'We break bread and own no sectarian or distinctive name', 422; PHG on attitude to EWG and, 499.

Brethren (Evangelical movement): from the 1820s and 1830s, Brethren called for a return to the 'simplicity of Christian union', 114-15; ill-defined genesis of, 3 fn.2; Summerton's founding date overview, 114 fn.80; some chief characteristics of, 116-17; Brethren and PHG: in 1843, introduced to Hackney Brethren, 3–9; 112-13; 118; aligned with what was known in his lifetime as 'Open Brethren', xvii; summary of PHG's engagement with (1843–57), 337–9; Brethren with whom PHG was associated: 119-20; 254; 338 fn.37; 447; 451; 452-3; Assemblies with which PHG was associated: *Britain:* Brook Street (Tottenham): *see separate entry;* Collier Street: 254 and fn.73; Hackney: *see separate entry;* Henrietta Street, 254; Rawstorne St. (Camden Town), 120; Ilfracombe (1852): 337 fn.33; Tenby: 1856 and possibly 1854, 277 fn.12; 337 fn.33; *Jamaica: see separate entry;* Brethren (Exclusive): usage of term, 413 fn.94; PHG incorrectly assumed to be aligned with, 413 fn.95; differences of PHG with: interpretation of prophecy and open ministry, 421-2; 422 fn.144; 339; and congregational independency or autonomy, 422 fn.144; critique of dispensationalism, 411–14; differences between Open Brethren, and: 419 fn.137; Brethren (Open): usage of term, 465 fn.148; Müller and Craik the de facto founders of, 161; PHG a prominent figure among, xvii; from 1843, devoted to, 337–9; Brethren (Plymouth): a misnomer, xvii; 9 fn.10; 116 fn.86; 132 fn.184; 305 fn.198; as a synonym for Exclusive (Darbyite) Brethren, 464-5; PHG pejoratively referred to as, 300; 337; 411; 592 fn.367; EWG uses term incorrectly, 338 fn.39; 413; 452 fn.79; Brethren and Baptists: Theological gap between two groups not insurmountable and frequently overcome, 465 fns.147-8; PHG content that EWG should consider himself a Baptist, 465; the 'great gulf' is 'not between Baptist & Friend' but 'dead in sins & alive to God' (PHG), 338; 586-7; Brethren and Quakers: in early years, Brethren had come from Established Church, Dissent, and Quakers, 117; English Quaker examples: H. Abbott (1st wife of B.W. Newton), 171 fn.55; Eliza Brightwen (2nd Mrs PHG), 369 and fn.221; J.E. Howard, 118; 254 fn.67; M. Stacey, 245; James Ireland Wright, 254 fn.70; in Jamaica, E.O. Tregelles met Brethren De Leon, Lewin, 136 fn.212; (and Coleman); Hill, 136 fn.213; 145 fn.270; Brethren (Schism of): 1845–9, the 'Holy War between the two sections', 161; 422-3; issues in contention, 419 and fn.137; 422 fn.144; Brethren (terminology of): 119 and fn.106; 126-7; 126 fn.144; 127 fns.148–51; Individuals allegedly, or briefly, involved with: Barnardo; T. Gosse (brother); H.G. Guinness; R.C. Morgan, T.W. Saunders, qq.v.; See also: Baptism; Baptists; W. Bewes; Darby; Jamaica; Liberty of ministry; B.W. Newton; Moravian Brethren; Prophecy.

Brightwen, Eliza (2nd Mrs PHG): *see* Gosse, Eliza.

Brightwen, Eliza *née* Elder, naturalist: sister-in-law to PHG, married to George Brightwen, 325 fn.295; visits Lloyd's office at Crystal Palace Aquarium, 196 and fn.192; EWG visits her at The Grove, near Stanmore, 530; 595-6.

Brightwen, George, businessman: husband of Eliza *née* Elder, 295 fn.297; member, Victoria Institute, 325 fn.295; in 1875, attends EWG's wedding, 532; EWG visits at his residence, The Grove, near Stanmore, 530; 595-6.

Brightwen, John, banker: with Gurneys, Birkbeck, and Brightwens, 241 fn.469; on his death in 1864, leaves legacy of £400 p.a. to Eliza Gosse (his niece), 241 fns.469-70; 379 fn.271.

British Association (founded 1831): during 1860s, public interest in is partly due to discussions of Darwin's theory, 385; Exeter meeting (1869), 385–8; anti-Darwin faction at, 386; PHG invited by Dyer to speak at, but explains that he protests Association by ignoring it, 385–8; PHG referenced at, 387; in 1870, Dawson chastises Huxley for remarks, 364; cited: 183 fn.127; 193 fn.175; 201 fn.230; 358 fn.164; 386 fn.297.

Brown, David, clergyman: 'champion of postmillennialism', 433; prophecy series in *Christian*, 433, derived from previously published work, 433 fn.220.

British Messenger (monthly): Peter Drummond, proprietor, 263; reviews EG's *Abraham and his Children* (1855), 256 fn.80; on religious tract distribution, 258 fn.96; publishes EG tracts, 263; publishes Barbour tracts, 262 fn.124; in her last days, EG distributes, 272; obituary of, 273 fn.193; reviews PHG's *Omphalos*, 298; 296 fn. 136; 297 fns.141, 144; circulation of, 298 fn.148; positive view of PHG, 297 fn.141; favours Hugh Miller's day-period schema for Genesis, 298 and fn.149; hesitates to speculate on unfulfilled prophecy, 428; PHG sends to William Gosse, 456 fn.103; cited: 260 fn.111.

Broderip, William J., naturalist:
PHG admires his biographical approach to nature, 143; and follows it, 163; PHG's research attracts attention of, 162; 199 fn.213.

Brook Street:
Brethren assembly in Tottenham founded by J.E. Howard, 118; in 1849, caught up in Bethesda Chapel controversy, they align with Open Brethren, 452;
EWG AND: in 1868 formally joins, 452 fn.75; in early 1867, EWG thinks of leading Sunday School classes at, which he does, and enjoys, 459; lessons taught at, 459; by 1870, becomes Superintendent at, 498; after Theodore Howard succeeds him as Superintendent, he continues teaching at, 511; attends Scripture readings at, 459; leads Young Men's Prayer Meetings at, 460; people at, know he is a poet, 521; in 1874, severs his connection with, 529;
PEOPLE ASSOCIATED WITH: J. Hudson Taylor, 462 fn.139; Stacey, q.v., a member of, 245; Barnardo, q.v., baptised at, 461 fn.136; in 1848, PHG-EG married at, 172; EWG meets Theodore Howard at, 460-1; 511.

Brown, F. Martin, Lepidopterist:
co-author, *Jamaica and its Butterflies*; on PHG's butterfly collecting, 148 fn.301; CORRESPONDENCE WITH; 55 fn.134.

Brown, Ford Madox, Pre-Raphaelite painter:
rationalist friend of EWG, 507; O'Shaughnessy knew, 481; in 1871 EWG attends party hosted by, 506; PHG references in letter to EWG, 508.

Browning, Robert, poet:
in 1868, EWG admires his work, 473; is said to have praised a poem in EWG's *On Viol and Flute* (1873), 526; EWG places him among 3 greatest living poets, 485 fn.40; cited: 473 fn.178.

Buckham, Anne, affiliated with Brethren:
PHG arranges in 1866 for EWG to board with, in Tottenham, 451; 507; member, Committee of Ladies' Chinese Assoc., 452; disagreement with PHG on B.W. Newton, 466; frowns on EWG's friendship with Beddows, 476; PHG wonders if EWG talked to her about Mary Johnson, 477; after Johnson's death, she recommends to PHG a trip abroad for EWG, 496-7; 501; suggests EWG not dwell so much on Ibsen, 503; EWG translates Danish sermons for, 511; EWG reads essays on Scandinavian writers to, 516; attends EWG's 1875 London wedding, 532.

Busk, George, naturalist:
recommends PHG for Fellowship in Royal Society, 251 fn.49; friend of Huxley, promoters of Darwinism, 360; 360 fn.176; 560 fn.142; difference of approach from Huxley, 560 fn.142; among the top 14 most frequent referees for Royal Society,

360; provides Royal Society referee's report for PHG's 'Researches on the Poison-apparatus', 360; 357; from 1864, Busk and Huxley were part of the X Club, 360-1; turns against PHG, 361; comparison with Bastian, 362-3; comparison with Dawson, 363-5.

Butterflies: *see* Lepidoptera.

Campbell, Alexander Thomas, early Brethren figure:
Eliza Gosse stayed with in Exeter, 370.

Campbell, Samuel ('Sam'), of Jamaica:
a 'negro lad', 136 and fn.210; PHG hires the 17-year-old as a full-time, paid natural history assistant, 1 Jan. 1845, 138 and fn.230; 139 fn.231; captures 3 hummingbirds, 139; tries to capture a single bird, 140.

Canada, PHG's experience in:
Canadian Naturalist: see separate entry;
CHRONOLOGY: PHG determines to leave Newfoundland, largely impelled by 'dread' of 'papist Irish', low income, economic depression, friendship with Jaques, entomological interests, 62–4; original goal is Upper Canada, 65; 66; 3 reasons why PHG didn't return to England or go to the United States, 66-7; PHG and Jacqueses set out in June 1835, but in Quebec City they are told Lower Canada is better, and they end up in Compton, Eastern Townships, 68; description of in 1835, when on 7 August they purchase for £150 a 110 acre farm, 69 and fn.208; PHG's low view of 'Yankee' character, 70; 1835-7, PHG gets winter jobs as a teacher, 70; 72; 78; by winter of 1835-6 they realize they had been misled by glowing accounts, 71; arduous, demanding, unproductive labour, 71; but PHG hides truth from family members in England, 72; in 1837, PHG's brother Tom comes from Poole to help, but it is a disappointment and he leaves, 73; PHG recognizes failure, contemplates a return home but there are no jobs, 73; Rebellions of 1837 in Canada turn his attention to Georgia or South Carolina, and in March 1838 he heads that way via Philadelphia, 77-8; Jaqueses head for Cowansville, 78; PHG looks back favourably on years there, maintains friendships from, 95 and fn.365; compares Upper and Lower Canada, 71 fn.217; obituaries in Canada of, mentioned, 611; RELIGIOUS LIFE: assumes a secondary importance for PHG, 78–80; encounters with Wesleyan and Congregational clergymen, 79-80;
SCIENTIFIC WORK: Natural history of Canada, PHG's contribution to, xvii-xviii; 11; mid-1835, visits Literary and Historical Society of Quebec (LHSQ), 70; winter of 1835-6 composes his first book, 'The Entomology of Newfoundland', 70; in 1836, PHG elected a Corresponding Member of LHSQ and the Natural History Society of Montreal, and sends papers to both, 72 and fn.220; 82; in May 1837, comes up with idea to write what becomes the *Canadian Naturalist*, 74; entomologically, PHG was 'a pioneer in the wilderness', 76; sells insects to Melly, and other items, 95; his field experience, 123.

The Canadian Naturalist (1840), by PHG:
ASPECTS OF: in May 1837, comes up with idea to

write what becomes the *Canadian Naturalist*, PHG's first published book, 74; in 1839, completes MS for, on return voyage to England, 95; in 1839, shows T. Bell MS for, 98; Van Voorst pays £105 for text and illustrations, 98; 219;
PUBLICATION: it appears in 1840 and is well-received, 100 and fn. 16; 330; Van Voorst sends copies for press review, 162; for sale in 1858 in New York, 380 fn.277; in 1862 in Canada, 77; possibility of a new Canadian ed. of, in 1867, 380 fn.277; sells slowly, still available in 1911, 151 fn.318;
REPUTATION: the first work devoted solely to Canadian natural history, 77 and fn.244; work is 'full of original observations' on butterflies, 76 and fn.238; 'excellent' figures and observations in (*Naturaliste Canadien*), 76 fn.240; 'the most authoritative work' on the flora and fauna of the area, 77.

Cancer:
CANCER 'CURERS': *see* Batchelour; Fell; Pattison;
CANCER PHYSICIANS: *see* Laseron; Paget; Salter;
CANCER TREATMENT: cancer is known in mid-1850s England as 'dreadful in its character fatal in its results', 244; 248-9; sham cancer 'curers' surface, 249; Paget is 'first authority on cancer', 247; opiates used during, 268 fn.166; but general anaesthesia not common in 1856, with mastectomies performed in unsanitary environments, 248; 1852 study of breast cancer surgeries finds 60% die during, or not long afterwards—treatment was 'considerably worse than the disease', 248;
SEE ALSO: Gosse, Emily.

Carlisle, Seventh Earl of (George William Frederick Howard), politician, writer:
Review of *Remarks on the Eighth Chapter of Daniel* [=*The Second Vision of Daniel: A Paraphrase in Verse*, 1858] in *The Times*, 1859, 396 fn.25.

Carpenter, William Benjamin, physiologist:
Unitarian, part of scientific establishment, 294; his report (1856) recommends PHG's 'Manducatory organs' paper for Royal Society publication, 184-5; 185 fn.138; PHG said to consult with, in 1857, to reject Darwin's theory, 293; doubtfulness of this scenario explained, 294; his *Microscope* a 'classic work', 346 and fn.89.

Carrington, John T., entomologist:
helps PHG plan Sandhurst aquarium, 540 fn.14; corresponds with PHG, 540 fn.14.

Castle Dinas (Cornwall) mining scandal:
in 1852, 1854, PHG, EG lose £2,500 investing in non-existent gold mine, 186 fn.145; 594; William Gosse blames brother Tom, the 'Bath shareholder', 603-4 and 604 fn.17; EWG wonders why William Gosse is so antagonistic towards, 604 fn.20.

Catholics:
prejudice against, by Protestants, evangelicals, Brethren, students of prophecy, 101-2; 101 fn.23; anti-Catholic bias of *Achill Missionary Herald*, 429 fn.183; and Bateman, 335 fn.18; Baxter, 112; Croly, 107; Dallas, 112; Elizabeth, 111 and fn.66; Green, 493 fn.59; Habershon, 103; 108; 112; Kennedy, 24; Kingsley, 231; I. Newton, 101 fn.23; Tonna, 243;

PHG AND: issue defined, 62 fn.173; in *Tenby*, 101 fn.23; his connection of, to anti-Semitism, 24 fn.35; in Newfoundland, 37; 61-3; 65; to historicism, 399; 416-17; 432; 105-6; *Rambler* on, 242 fn.478.

Cats: *see* 'Fairy: A Recollection'.
Charlotte Elizabeth: *see* Tonna, Charlotte.
Chester, Richard, clergyman:
veteran Irish writer for prophetic journals, initially an historicist, 408 and fn.77; in 1866, presents futurist argument against PHG in *Rainbow*, 408-10; 433; futurists are literalists, 410; argues futurism more democratic than historicism, 421; critiques PHG's *Revelation*, 416 fn.111, and E.B. Elliott's 'Counter-retrospect', 431 fn.200; in 1870, 9-part series in *Christian* gives futurist position, 433; cited: 414 fn.102.

Christian Annotator (weekly):
edited by L.H.J. Tonna, 111 fn.66; an 'ultra protestant', 243; married to Charlotte, 111 fn.66; PHG writes for, 243; 153 fn.335; 392 fn.6; reviews EG's *Abraham and his Children*, 256 fn.80; criticism of, by J.N. Darby, 243 fn.483; in 1857, circulation of, 243 fn.483; closes with Tonna's death, 243 fn.483.

Christian Evidence Society (London):
evangelical defence group launched in 1870, 388-9; 388 fn.308; PHG financial support for, 389.

Christian Lady's Magazine (monthly):
edited by Charlotte Tonna for middle-class female readership, 111; PHG praises focus on end days, in, 111; PHG article on prophecy in, 111; 431; epigraph to article, 390 fn.1; review of *Horae Apocalypticae* in, 429 fn.187.

Christian Defence Groups: *see* Bible and Christian Defence Groups.

Christian Perfection: *see* Perfect Sanctification.

Chromolithography:
commercial colour printing dates in Britain to 1830s, popularly to 1850s, 204-5; as works containing chromolithographs of seashore creatures, *Naturalist's Rambles* (12, by Hullmandel and Walton) and *Aquarium* (6, by Hanhart) are landmark publications, 205; press acclaim for *Aquarium* plates, 206-7; but commenting on *Tenby* (20 coloured lithographs), there was disappointment at the high cost of PHG books, 220-1; 220 fn.337.

Clarke, William (Liverpool):
brother-in-law of Ann Jaques, q.v., in 1839 PHG stays with, he tries to get him work, 97-8.

'Clasping-organs ancillary to generation in certain groups of the Lepidoptera', by PHG:
the collecting of tropical insects c.1878 leads PHG to examine them under the microscope, 546; the resulting study is a 'classical' contribution 'beautifully illustrated', more recently PHG's techniques have been severely criticized, 555 fn.116; 556 fn.117; an example of PHG's frank treatment of sex, 202 fn.234;
GOAL OF: PHG believes he has evidence to scientifically question, if not disprove, Darwin's theory, rooted in definition of 'species', 546-7; 556; possible encouragement of R. Lankester to pursue this research, 547 fn.58; 552 fn.93;

ILLUSTRATIONS FOR: PHG's accompanying illustrations are 'very beautiful', 554; 560 fns.138-9; his concern for consistent tone of the microscopic lithographic drawings, 559;
ROYAL SOCIETY CONTROVERSY: though submitted in 1881 on note paper by PHG for publication in the *Philosophical Transactions*, 550 fn.83; and recommended by 2 referees, it is rejected and instead appears in abstract in the *Proceedings* (under the title 'Prehensores of Male Butterflies of the Genera *Ornithoptera* and *Papilio*', 551 fn.90), 554–61; PHG apparently attends 1882 meeting at which his paper is read, 559 fn.135; boycott of this work by scientific naturalists of the X Club, 555; objections to PHG's comments on evolution reference *Omphalos*, 556-7; 581; 307;
SUBSEQUENT RESOLUTION: complete version ultimately published in the Linnean Society *Transactions* (1883), 557–9, except for PHG's pages rejecting Darwin's theory, 560-1; PHG relents, 560-1; 561 fn.143; publication is paid for in part by a £25 subvention from PHG, 559; PHG discusses illustrations for his paper in *Transactions* of, 559-60; PHG probably realises this challenge to Darwin is unsuccessful, 561.

Clinton, Henry Fynes, chronologist:
his *Fasti Hellenici* is oft-quoted by writers on prophecy because it favours world's history ending about 1867, 396; an MP, he was not a student of prophecy, 396 and fns.22-3; PHG familiar with his writing, 399 fn.37; cited, 398 fn.29.

Code, Lorraine, philosopher:
critique of PHG's belief system, 308 and fn.209; 311; 319; cited: 295 fn.132.

Coleman, Anna Elizabeth, missionary:
wife of John Coleman, Moravian missionary in Jamaica, 129 and fn.167; founds New Hope station near Parker's Bay, 130-1; leaves Jamaica for England (1852), 132.

Coleman, John, Moravian missionary:
first-ever Brethren member in Jamaica, 124; 131-2; BIOGRAPHY: 129–32 and 130 fn.174; 131 fns.178-9; moved from Parker's Bay, 129; to Bluefields with wife Anna, and near death when PHG arrives in 1844, 129; significance of move, 124 fn.133; 129–32; 130 fn.168; Coleman recovers after PHG's arrival and 'breaks bread' with him, 119 fn.106; PHG rents 2 rooms at Bluefield's House, an excellent headquarters for the naturalist, 129; 133; previously a plantation, 133; PHG and Coleman maintain proper relations, 133; introduces PHG to Tydeman, whom PHG baptizes, 134; PHG says goodbye to 'dear Colemans' in 1846 before returning to England, 145; Colemans leave Jamaica for England (1852), 132;
BRETHREN AND: between 1841–8, Coleman aligns with Brethren, 131-2; 601 fn.421; in 1838, establishes New Hope station near Parker's Bay, before leaving Moravian church for Brethren, 130-1; has 50-60 members in his church, 'mostly negroes', 132 fn.190;
DARBY, WIGRAM AND: from at least 1842, Wigram and Darby correspond with, 131 fn.179; Wigram-Darby

not pleased with Coleman and other Brethren in Jamaica, including PHG, 132 fn.188; Coleman accused of teaching the 'non-eternity system', 132 fn.188;
WORKS BY, CITED: Coleman's *Prophecy Unfolded* (1861) expresses dispensationalist, pre-tribulationist, futurist premillennialist views identical to Darby's but opposed to PHG's, 132; a 2nd ed. entitled *"Time of the End"* (1862), 130 fns.168, 174; 601 fn.421.

Colenso, J.W.: *see* Biblical criticism.

Compton, Village of: *see* Canada.

Congregationalists: *see* Independents.

Conrad, Timothy Abbott, palaeontologist:
a Quaker, 83 fn.277; PHG meets, in Philadelphia, 83, 81; who recommends he go to Alabama and provides letter of introduction, 83-4, 85.

Conversion, evangelical:
morphology of, 18; 47 and fn.87; EG tracts on conversion, 265-6; EG's tracts result in five conversions, 266 and 266 fn.151; deathbed conversions, 272 fns.187, 190; 282 fn.47; value of, 261; from 1830–2, 'Great Awakening' at Carbonear leads to conversions, 41–8; analysis of conversion experience of PHG's fellow clerks, 46-7;
EXAMPLES OF: Apsey (conversion spans 1828–30), 41–3; 47-8; C.B. Berger (conversion in c. 1835), 6; W.T. Berger (1833), 4; 5 fn.7; EWG: recalls no moment of conversion, 442; 458; public confession at Brethren's Warren Road Room in Torquay, 443-4, apparently in 1859 (444 fn.24); EG, unknown if she had one, 168; realises that in children may be imitative, 175; PHG, on, 9; 29-30; 308; 443; his description of his: in Newfoundland (1832), 44–7; 308; in Alabama (1838), 91; 101; Thomas Gosse (father) (1790), 18; 443; his description of his, 17-18; Lush (1834), 47; 48; 61 fn.166; Newell (post-1835), 47 and fn.90; 61 fn.166; Raine, Wesleyan missionary, 79 fn.254; Sprague (1834), 47; 48; St. John (1834), 47; 61; 61 fn.166; Tocque (?1830), 47; 61 fn.166.

Craik, Henry, early Brethren leader:
with Müller the de facto founder of Open Brethren, 161; format of Scripture reading meetings, 8 fn.5; with Müller, condemned by Darby for advocating independency in church organization, 161; in 1830s, had visited Torquay with Müller, 334.

Creation (alternate title for *Omphalos*):
title apparently used to boost sales of *Omphalos*, 317; this title described, 317 fn.251.

Cremation: significance of EWG's preference for, 609; growth of movement in England, includes Hardy, James, R. Lankester, 609-10; Christian reaction to, PHG's words on, 610; EWG's cremation, Golders Green, 611.

Cruikshank, George, graphic artist:
'Tail of the Comet of 1853' shows Regent's Park 'vivarium', 212.

Cuming, Hugh, natural history dealer:
PHG introduced to, by Doubleday, 121-2; 141; PHG prepares Jamaican consignment to, 139; Jamaican insects sent by PHG to, sell well, 142 fn.251; Cuming, 'though upright was a churl', 141

and fn.248; PHG regrets choosing him as agent, rather than Samuel Stevens, 141; 543; PHG paid to, 12.5% commission, 141 fn.248.

Cumming, John, clergyman:
premillennial historicist writer on prophecy, 395 fn.18; featured writer, *Weekly Visitor*, 243 fn.482; undissuaded by failed predictions, 394 fn.14; ridiculed in periodical press, 395 fn.18; in 1859, lectures on prophecy in Manchester, Liverpool, 395 fn.18; 398 fn.31; review of his *Great Tribulation* in *The Times*, 395 fn.25; anonymous article in *The Times* attributed to, 397 fn.27; PHG sends EWG his *When Shall These Things Be?*, 417; cited: 398 fn.31.

Dallas, Alexander Robert Charles, clergyman:
historic premillennialist, EG once met as a young girl, 112 fn.70; his press in Ireland supported by N. Baxter, 112 fn.70.

Dallas, Eneas Sweetland, journalist:
possible anonymous author of *The Times* article, 'School of the Prophets', 397 fn.27.

Dallas, William Sweetland, writer:
early Darwin supporter, 299 fn.163; translates *Facts and Arguments for Darwin*, 299 fn.163; editor, *Popular Science Review*, contributor to *Westminster Review*, 214 fn.297; 217 fn.312; 291 fn.141; 299; 300 fn.164;
REVIEWS PHG BOOKS: *Manual of Marine Zoology*, 214 fn.297; *Omphalos*, 297 fn.141; 299-300; *Actinologia Britannica*, 350 fn.122; *Year at the Shore* in, 378 fn.270.

Dames, Mansell L.:
student with EWG at Menneer's school, 473-4; son of drawing master there, 445 fn.33; 474; appeared 'unsaved' to PHG, 474; 507; accompanies EWG on trip to Scotland, 497.

Daniels, Mary: servant at Baker-Buckham, qq.v. Tottenham residence, 451.

Darby, John Nelson, early Brethren leader:
joins embryonic movement in Ireland, 116; his itinerant ministry in Britain and overseas gives cohesion to the movement, 117 and fn.88; 153-4; 'Holy War' of 1845-8 divides Brethren into 'Exclusive' (Darby's followers) and 'Open' factions, 422-3; 452; Darby attacks Newton, Müller, Craik, Howard brothers, 161; opposes Wesleyan Christian perfectionism, 466 fn.152; does not care for *Christian Annotator*, 243 fn.483;
DARBY AND PHG: they met, perhaps at Rawstorne St., 120; EG annotated his work, 412; PHG considered Darby's views 'almost always valuable', but he generally rejected them, 412-13; and said Exclusives 'please not God', 464-5; 338; 3 areas of difference are prophetic interpretation, 421-2; 422 and fn.144; 'liberty of ministry', and congregational autonomy, 422 and fn.144; Darby's dispensationalist system, 411-12; PHG's critique of Darbyite dispensationalist Kelly, 109 fn.54; 309 fn.213; PHG's eclectic approach to the Darby-Newton duel, 412-14; dissatisfaction of Darby, Wigram, with PHG, 132 fn.188;
DARBY AND JAMAICA: from at least 1842, Darby connected with J. Coleman, first Brethren figure in

Jamaica, 153 and fn.338; 154; Darby and Coleman have identical prophetic views, 132; expresses dissatisfaction with Coleman and Jamaica Brethren, including PHG, 132 fn.188; gives financial support to Tydeman, 134;
DARBY AND B.W. NEWTON: difference on prophecy emerges at Powerscourt Conferences, 117 and fn.92; both premillennial futurists; 412; their disputes are many, 412; ecclesiastical difference: 'liberty of ministry', 419-20; Darby's criticism of Hargrove, 119-120;
GEOLOGY AND: appears to have favoured Chalmers' 'interval' or 'restitution' theory of earth's antiquity, 288 fn.89;
PROPHECY AND: Darby a futurist, 117; 339 fn.44; and a premillennialist, the latter inhibited his involvement in secular world, 117; criticised at prophetic gathering, 403; PHG's critique of, in *The Revelation*, 410 fn.86; 411-12; *Rainbow* favoured Darbyite futurism, 406 fn.67; 408; views on pre-Tribulation rapture explained, 411-12; 432 fn.205.

Darwin, Charles, naturalist:
BACKGROUND: is among naturalists advancing beyond Linnaeus' catalogue in first part of 19th Century with his 1851 barnacle study, 189; inherited wealth allows him to pursue scientific studies, 218; in 1854, elected Fellow, Linnean Society, 212 fn.284; in 1858, natural selection theories of Darwin, Wallace, presented at Linnean Society, 301-2; opposition to, of Victoria Institute, 326; 383; CD's linkage of short chronology and species evolution, 294-5; press response to *Essays and Reviews* exceeded *Origin*, 325; reviews of *Origin* by Dawson, 363 fn.194; Leifchild, 347 fn.94 (also *Descent of Man*); in 1861, few entomologists favour his theory, 549;
DARWIN AND PHG: (1) newspaper sets PHG near Darwin and 'some of the greatest minds the world has produced', 197; PHG's scientific work attracts attention of, 162; including PHG's *Birds of Jamaica* and *Naturalist's Sojourn in Jamaica*, 162 fn.11; 321 fn.266; quotes from *Letters from Alabama*, 321 fn.266; Darwin-PHG correspondence, 1856-64, 306 and fn.203; in 1856, Darwin asks PHG for a contact in Jamaica to assist in a study of pigeons, refers him to R. Hill, 538 fn.3; asks PHG to do experiment on molluscs, 280; unlike PHG, he was neither a lecturer nor an illustrator, 236; (2) Books: comparison of print run of *Origin* with PHG's books, 199 fn.214; 224 and fn.362; comparison of number of serials reviewing *Origin* by PHG's *Naturalist's Rambles*, 199 fn.214; 296 fn.137; (3) Meeting: in 1855, may have met PHG for first and only time at Linnean Society, 212 and fn.284; in 1857, CD and Hooker said to sound out PHG for his view of evolution, analysed, 292-3; 293 fn.116; 361 fn.180;
DARWIN'S VIEW OF PHG: impressed with PHG's aquarium work, 211-12; CD says he is tempted to set up an aquarium, 212; 'not reasoning enough' in *Naturalist's Sojourn*, 321 fn.266; critique of *Omphalos*, 303;
PHG'S VIEW OF DARWIN: praise for *Cirripedia*, 321

fn.267; 'a monument of research and acumen', 321 fn.267; a 'dependable' naturalist who does 'admirable' research, 321 and fn.266; PHG reads Darwin's *Voyage of the Beagle*, 321 fn.266; in 1857, PHG lectures on Darwin's theory of coral reef formation, 280; quotes from *Origin*, 321; appearance of *Origin* as possible reason why PHG ceased lecturing, 240; rejection of evolution theory, 12; 240-1; 320-4; in 1884, evolution called the 'lying science of the day', 538; EWG compares PHG unfavourably to Darwin, Huxley, 523 fn.187; SCIENTIFIC CHALLENGES TO, BY PHG: 331; 546-7; 556; reasons for PHG to think CD's theory might be short-lived, 311; (1) Orchid research: in early 1860s, PHG turns to collecting orchids, 539; PHG owns CD's book on orchids, 321 fn.266; 374 and fn.251; purpose of *Various Contrivances by which British and Foreign Orchids are Fertilised*, 373-5; book is praised by J.D. Hooker in 2 anonymous reviews, 376 fns.260-1; PHG letter to CD, on orchid fertilisation, 371 fn.231; 375 and fn.256; PHG fails to scientifically overturn Darwin's theory, 374-7; (2) Lepidoptera research: microscopic, morphological study of butterfly armature leads PHG to believe he can scientifically challenge Darwin's theory, rooted in definition of 'species', 546; 548; in 1881, presents his findings on 'Clasping-organs' to Royal Society, 550-61; position of McLachlan, 557;
SEE ALSO: Evolution; Non-Darwinian science; Orchids; X Club.
Dawson, John William, geologist:
DARWIN'S THEORY AND: Dawson an evolution opponent, 363 and fn.194; his *Archaia* (1860) a reconciliation of science and geology, 302; review of cited, 309 fn.212 and lauded, 363 fn.194; Victoria Institute member, 326 fn.300; like PHG, adopts year-day interpretation of biblical verses, 415 fn.109; critique of *Omphalos*, 297 fn.144; 302 and fn.187;
EOZOÖN CANADENSE: discovered in 1858 in Canada, said to be the 'greatest discovery in geology for half a century', 567; from 1864 promoted by Dawson, as refuting Darwin, 363 fn.194;
ROYAL SOCIETY EXPERIENCE: elected a fellow, 1862, by 'imperial royalty' of geology, 363 and fn.188; receives rough treatment from X Club's J.D. Hooker at Royal Society, Dawson's 1870 Bakerian lecture is rejected for *Philosophical Transactions*, 364 and fn.200; 365 fn.202; in 1877, Dawson's request for a grant from, is rejected, 364; chastises T.H. Huxley, 364; experience at Royal Society compared to PHG's, 557 fn.124.
Day, interpretation of biblical:
SCRIPTURAL GEOLOGISTS: 'interval' or 'restitution' theory of T. Chalmers asserts Bible did not establish earth's antiquity, 288-9; accepted by Darby, 288 fn.89; accepted by Thomas Gosse (father), 15 fn.7; rejected by PHG, 289; 308-9; *Omphalos* meant to solve 'geological argument', 289; 382; Hugh Miller interprets 'day' as a long period, 289 and fn.90; J.W. Dawson translates Hebrew word *yom* [day] in Bible as 'eon', 415 fn.109;
STUDENTS OF PROPHECY: disagreement on a 'literal'

or 'symbolic' meaning concerning unfulfilled prophecy, 105.
Dealers, natural history:
Bang-Haas, 542; Cuming, 141; Lloyd, 227; 226; Marsden, 542; Saunders, 147 fn.295; Stevens, 141; Staudinger, 542; Wailly and Watkins, 540.
De Beauchamp, Paul Marais, zoologist:
among the 'greatest rotiferologists' of the 20th century, 577; commends PHG's 'Manducatory Organs', q.v., memoir, 185; commends Hudson & Gosse, 577; finds Rotifera classification by Hudson 'unnatural', 575 fn.249; challenges significance of *Pedalion*, q.v., discovery, 569 fn.201.
Declaration of Students of the Natural and Physical Sciences (1865):
717 sign document challenging 'scientific truth in our own times' which casts doubt on 'Truth and Authenticity' of Bible, 383; PHG among signators, 382; others known to PHG, named, 383 fn.286.
De Leon, Aaron, merchant:
BIOGRAPHY: married to Helen De Leon, 134; PHG mainly wrote the surname as 'Deleon', a Jew in Jamaica converted to Christianity and a 'free coloured', 129 fn.161; Sephardic Jewish descent conjectured, 136 fn.211; PHG not comment on his race, 135-6; or Jewish background, 136 fn.212;
BRETHREN AND: PHG first meets in Dec. 1844 on landing in Jamaica, he is among Brethren active with Coleman in gospel work, 129; 132; seemingly aligned with Darby, Wigram, 153; though accused of 'heresy' by them, 154; PHG spends time with, at his Phoenix Park home, 133-4; PHG worships with, in Savannah-le-Mar, 134;
NATURAL HISTORY AND: brings specimens for PHG's collecting, 139; likely a connection to Richard Hill, 143; PHG bids him goodbye on leaving Jamaica, 145.
Descent of Man (1871), by Darwin:
anonymously reviewed by J.R. Leifchild, 347 fn.94; the most popularly sought link after the publication of, 567.
Design, argument from: *see* Natural theology.
Dickes, William, engraver:
in 1857, PHG gives his illustrations to, for colour printing of 2 plates for part I of *Actinologia Britannica*, 342; PHG wants him to see living sea anemones of Lloyd before beginning engravings, 342.
Dickson, Neil T.R., historian:
CORRESPONDENCE WITH: 9 fn.24; 18 fn.11; 114 fn.81; 132 fn.188; 262 fn.127; 277 fn.12; 422 fn.146; 664.
Die Gartenlaube (The Gazebo), weekly:
Leipzig magazine for middle-class, 210; founder of, 210 fn.272; in 1855 articles on aquarium in, 209 fn.269; 210 fn.272; 209 fn.270.
Dispensationalism:
history is divided into eras (dispensations) each with a distinctive activity of God, with Darby adding unique features concerning Jews and a 2-stage Second Advent, 411; PHG's critique of futurism and Darby's system of, 411–14; PHG expected sudden restoration of Jews to their homeland coincidental with the rapture of the church, unlike Darby, 432 fn.205; relationship of PHG's

critique of dispensationalism to Darby, Newton, 413-14; Coleman's dispensationalist futurism, 132; Kelly's dispensationalism, 109 fn.54; 309 fn.213; methodology of Bible study of American, Brethren dispensationalists, 404; by around mid-1840s, literalism in prophetic interpretation associated with, 409 fn.78.

'A Dollar's Worth' ([1859]), religious tract by PHG: expresses the thought (also stated in a PHG letter) that 'God loves me!', 539 and fn.8.

Doncaster, Arthur, natural history supplier: of Watkins and Doncaster, London, 586; letter from PHG, on his religious outlook, 338; enlisted help from, in identifying Lepidoptera, 542; misinterprets religious outlook of, 586-7.

Doubleday, Edward, entomologist: spent 2 years collecting in America, 11; a Quaker, arranges British Museum's butterfly collection for first time, 11; PHG meets at British Museum, entomologizes with, 121; PHG apparently visited home of, in Epping, 11 fn.16; in 1844, suggests PHG go collecting in the Tropics, ultimately Jamaica, 124; recommends PHG use Cuming as dealer for natural history collections in Jamaica, 141; purchases Jamaican ornithological specimens from PHG, 147 fn.294; thanks in part to, elected to Linnean Society, 173 and fn.68; signator to *Declaration of Students*, q.v., 383 fn.286.

Drummond, Peter, publisher: his Stirling Tract Enterprise circulates over 46 million religious tracts, 260 and fn.111; issues tracts of Mrs Barbour of Bonskeid, 262 fn.124; his *British Messenger* issues tracts of EG, 263.

Dublin Tract Society: issues 500 million religious tracts, 260.

Durant, Thomas, clergyman: PHG attends Independent meeting of, in Poole, with his father, 30; sermon left an impact on PHG, 30-1; a life filled with tragedy, 282 fn.47; while PHG is in Poole in 1832, disappointed he didn't inquire of his inner life, 53; biography of his son, William Friend, 282 fn.47.

Dyer, Henry, early Brethren leader: occasionally ministers at Providence Chapel, Paragon Road, Hackney, 254; PHG knows, 338 fn.37; among Open Brethren, 385; approaches PHG to speak at 1869 meeting of British Association in Exeter, 385–88; PHG on 'apostasy of science', in letter to, 379 fn.273; 387; PHG gives permission to, to circulate letter, 388.

Dyster, Frederic D., physician: in 1854, elected Fellow, Linnean Soc., 244 fn.489; Huxley, PHG on 'infusoria' discovered by, 185 fn.140; 182 fn.119; 184 fn.134; PHG friend, goes dredging with PHG at Tenby, 244, and supplies PHG with specimens, 343; inquires about health of EG, 244 and fns. 489, 491.

Eccles, Dorset: EWG co-worker at British Museum, 467; spends time at home of, a 'professed infidel', 467; uninterested in poetry, 473 and fns.180-1; cited: 529

Edgelow, Thomas, school proprietor: with his wife, operates boarding school at Thorn

Park, Coombe Vale, Teignmouth, 446; aligned with Brethren, 447; probably in 1863, EWG withdrawn from Montvidere school to enroll at Thorn Park, remaining for 3 years, 447; 2 of L. Strong's sons there, 447; EWG annually improves in local exams, 448; in Oct. 1865, PHG finds a position for EWG at British Museum, for which he needs language skills, 450; at the end of 1866, leaves school for London, 451.

Edwards, William Henry, entomologist: in 1883, provides introduction to PHG's Newfoundland journals (1832–5) on Lepidoptera, 55 fn.132; PHG seeks help from, in identifying butterflies, 57 fn.144; 542 fn.31; Edwards' entomological research supports Darwin's theory, 549; PHG sends a copy of his Royal Society *Proceedings* article on 'Prehensores of Male Butterflies', to, 553; correspondence with PHG: 11 fn.18; 55 fn.132; 56 fn.137; 57 fn.144; 540 fn.17.

Ehrenberg, Christian Gottfried, naturalist: in 1838, Prussian savant publishes his monumental Rotifera work, *Die Infusionsthierchen*, 178–80; improbable translation by EG, 180 fn.106; PHG's high opinion of, 179 fn.98; 183 fn.124; 189; the standard work until Hudson & Gosse, 179; 573; PHG finds classification system of, 'artificial', 183 and fn.124; Hudson modifies, 575; Ehrenberg argues that even single-cell creatures are 'complete animals', 178; Lewes contests findings of, 36.

Elliott, Edward Bishop, clergyman: PHG AND: PHG reads works of, 399 fn.37; PHG corresponds with, 429-30; 317 fn.249; 385; EG an enthusiast for writings of, 412; PROPHETIC VIEWS OF: *Horae Apocalypticae*, q.v., written to refute futurism, 106 fn.38; moves Second Advent to 1941, becomes a 'continuationist', 431-2; PHG rejection of, 588-9; WORKS OF: his *Horae Apocalypticae* (1844) 'the high point of the historicist tradition in British Evangelicalism', 429; *Warburtonian Lectures* of, read to EG, 271 and fn.183; PHG praise for, 430; *Last Prophecy* (1884), 430 and fn.195; 431 and fn.197, 199; 601 fn.421; cited: 400 fn.42.

Elliott, Harriette Emily *née* Steele, author: in 1835, married to E.B. Elliott (2nd wife and widow of), 430 fn.195; anonymous author of *Last Prophecy* (1884), 430 fns.194-5.

Elson, John, merchant: a partner in Slade, Elson and Co., one of largest Carbonear, Newfoundland, outfitters, 36; a Unitarian, 37; 65; president, Carbonear book club, 38; in 1830, permits closing of firm for Candlemas Day, 42; in 1832, allows PHG to return to Poole to visit sick sister, 46; PHG fond of daughter of, 38; Sprague, a PHG friend, 46; was a nephew of, 45; PHG collects insects with Andrew, son of, 57; 60; in 1835, uninterested when PHG leaves firm, 65.

Elson's: *see* Slade, Elson and Co.

Entomologia Alabamensis, by PHG: a graphic record of insects in Alabama from 1838, published some 175 years later, 87 and fn.304; filled with 'superb illustrations', 87.

Entomologia Terrae Novae, by PHG: in summer, 1833, PHG begins to illustrate insects

of Newfoundland, 57; 'excellent coloured figures',
57 fn.144; PHG considered them 'in no wise inferior' to others he did, 57; intended as companion
to PHG's *Entomology of Newfoundland*, 70; some
allusions to, in *Canadian Naturalist*, in 1883
excerpts from, in *Canadian Entomologist*, 55
fn.132; 57 fn.144; cited: 70 fn.213;
See also: 'Entomology of Newfoundland'.
Entomological Society of London:
    PHG elected member of, 1 Oct. 1879, 541; 196;
    paper published by, 541 fn.21; 551 fn.91; PHG
    knows Bowerbank, president of, 121; borrows
    books from, 544; 547; correspondence with: 184
    fn.128; 542 fn.31; 545.
Entomologist (monthly), edited by E. Newman:
    in 1841, PHG's first publication in, 72 fn.220; 100
    and fn.17; review of *Canadian Naturalist* in, 100
    and fn.16; in 1879, PHG's article on Great Atlas
    moth in, 541; other early 1880s articles in, 541
    fn.22; 583 fn.299.
Entomologists:
    in 1859 when *Origin* appeared, Darwin believes
    entomologists are his leading critics, 548–50; he
    incorrectly attributes *Athenaeum's* negative review
    of *Origin* to Westwood, 547; in 1861, few favour
    his theory among, 549; by 1880s, their research
    supports evolution, 548-9;
    Darwin and: opponents of evolution, 548-9; pro-
    ponents of, 549;
    Collectors for PHG: 541–4; Argentina, Paraguay:
    Perrens family, q.v.; Brazil: Fanstone, 542; British
    Guiana: Man, 542; Celebes (Sulawesi): Mesman,
    542; Honduras: Jackson, 542; Jamaica: Mais
    family, q.v.; Malacca (Malaysia): Biggs; Mexico:
    Pascoe, q.v.
Entomology:
    a shift in the study of, since mid-1700s; Europe
    and Britain compared, 50; *Introduction to
    Entomology*, q.v., boosts prestige of, 52; in 1832,
    PHG's purchase of *Essays on the Microscope*,
    q.v., focuses him on, 48; PHG's pioneer status
    in Newfoundland, in study of, xvii; 55; in Canada,
    'a pioneer in the wilderness', 76; 78; in Alabama,
    intently studies, 86; his articles for *Zoologist* on
    Alabama, 122; 85 fn.292; 86 fn.295; compiles
    'Insects of Jamaica', 87 fn.301; 138; 195; relevance
    to Darwin's evolution theory, 548-9.
'Entomology of Newfoundland', by PHG:
    his first book, composed while in Canada, current
    location unknown, 70; in 1871, excerpts from, 60
    fn.161.
Eozoön Canadense, the 'dawn animal of Canada':
    'the greatest discovery in geology' for 50 years,
    it was viewed by some in 1858 as a missing link
    confirming Darwin, 363 fn.194; or refuting him,
    as Dawson believed, 363 fn.194, 567.
Epps, Ellen: *see* Gosse, Nellie.
Epps, George Napoleon, surgeon:
    father of Nellie Gosse, step-brother of John Epps,
    528.
Epps, John, homoeopathic physician:
    treats EG in last days, 270; 528 and fn.216; is step-
    brother of G.N. Epps and knows Wigram, 528.
Essays and Reviews (1860):

quantitatively, received greater press attention
than Darwin's *Origin*, 324-5; Darby's comment
on, 288 fn.89; PHG's criticism of, 315; 328;
See also: Biblical criticism.
Essays on the Microscope, by George Adams, jr:
    in 1832 in Carbonear, PHG purchases a sec-
    ond-hand copy of 1798 Kanmacher ed. of, 48;
    propels his entomological study, 49; description
    of, 49-50; largely derivative, but well-received, 51;
    comparison with Kirby and Spence's *Introduction
    to Entomology*, 51-2; 'Animalcula Infusoria' the
    subject of chap. 8 in, 180; inquiry into nature
    confirms its divine origin, 238; engraved plates
    of, not drawn 'direct from the microscope', as in
    the case of PHG's *Evenings at the Microscope*,
    345; cited: 176; 177.
Evangelical Tract Association:
    Brethren group in Hackney, founded c.1853, 257;
    committee members, 6 and fn.12; 7 and fn.17;
    257; goal of, 257; in March 1854, publishes *The
    Railway Tract*, EG's first tract, 257, 263.
Evenings at the Microscope (1859), by PHG:
    Background: by 1859, microscope recognized as
    'indispensable' to the naturalist, 345; proposed to
    SPCK in 1858, 345; preceded by several technical
    and popular works by others, 346;
    Editions: 4 eds in UK, 345; comparison of 1859
    and 1874 ed. of, 321 fn.267; 425 fn.158; 1874 ed.
    favourably reviewed, 425 fn.158; comparison of
    1859 and 1884 ed., 562 fn.151; rev. ed., 1895, 425
    fn.158; in USA, eds by 3 publishers, 345; in USA,
    2nd most reviewed of PHG's books, 211 fn.277;
    345;
    Reviews: a contribution to science, 307; positive
    reviews, 346-7; in 1890, considered one of 7 best
    books on subject, 345;
    Science: almost all illustrations drawn by PHG
    'direct from the microscope', 345; repeats poi-
    son-apparatus findings, an example of Divine
    ingenuity, 365; comment on Darwin in, 321 fn.267;
    374 fn.251; advertised: 225 fn.370.
Evolution, Darwin's theory of:
    in 1858, natural selection theories of Darwin,
    Wallace, presented at Linnean Society, 301-2;
    'dynamic' understanding of species, 550; during
    1860s increasing public interest in British
    Association due to Darwin's theory of, 385-6;
    Missing Links: importance of, as support for
    Darwin's theory, 566–70; though lacking hard
    evidence, Darwin insisted that transitional forms
    existed, 566 and fn.180;
    Natural selection: provides a mechanism to dis-
    place natural theology's teleological explanation,
    52; supernatural vs. naturalistic at the heart of the
    public debate over, 240; PHG's belief in a perfect
    creation obviates need for, 405; transitional stages
    (or links), 566; PHG stands out among opponents
    of, 581;
    PHG and: PHG never favoured Darwin's theory,
    161; 320–4; in *Mysteries of God*, PHG's last book,
    evolution is the 'lying science of the day', 538;
    381; friends at British Museum also opposed,
    12; Milne-Edwards an anti-evolutionist, 341;
    in 1857, according to EWG, 305; Darwin and

Hooker reveal evolution theory to PHG, who consults with Carpenter, 292-3; difficulties in the scenario, 293-4; Carpenter not favour fixity of species, 294; PHG's scientific challenges to, xx: (1) orchid study, 370–77; (2) Lepidoptera, 545–61; PHG's studies of Rotifera, sea anemones, escape evolutionary picture, 183; 352; PHG was never in position to study effects of geographical isolation, 320; in 1858, not compelling reason for a botanist to believe in evolution, 373; Darwin's theory promotes infidelity, 379; THEORY OPPONENTS (SCIENTISTS): A. Agassiz, 307 fn.207; Barnard, 307 fn.207; Dawson, 363 and fn.194; PHG; Hibberd, 300 and fn.170; Stokes, 385-6; Westwood, 546-7; in 1859, anti-Darwinian activity at British Association, Exeter, 385-6; THEORY PROPONENTS (SCIENTISTS): Baird, 307 fn.207; Bastian, 362; 560 fn.142; Bates, 586; Busk, 560 fn.142; Carpenter, 294; Dallas, 299; Dohrn, 565; Duncan, 364 fns.200, 196; A. Gray, 307 fn.207; Haddon, 597; Haeckel, 311; 511; 565; 567; G. Henslow, 326 fn.298; J.D. Hooker, 294 and fn.121; Huxley, 511 and fn.145; 555; 560 fn.142; Jukes, 313; R. Lankester, 552; 568-9; Leidy, 307 fn.207; Lubbock, 386; Mackie, 302; C.S. Minot, 579; F. Müller, 299 fn.163; Pengelly, 303; Romanes, 558 fn.128; Weismann, 579; SEE ALSO: 'Clasping-organs'; Darwin; Entomologists; Non-Darwinian science; *Omphalos*; Orchids; species; *Vestiges*.

Examiner (London weekly): in 1874, EWG writes for, 527-8; W.R. Nicoll writes for, 528; reviews Blaikie and Gosse, *Madrigals*, 500 fn.85; reviews EWG's *On Viol and Flute*, 525 fn.202; reviews Tugwell's *Manual of the Sea-anemones*, 341 fn.55.

Excelsior (London monthly): evangelical periodical for which Baird, White and PHG, qq.v., wrote, 12 fn.33; from 1853-6, PHG's *Life in its lower, intermediate and higher forms* serialized in, 201 fn.224; *Tenby* reviewed in, 213 fn.295; 340 fn.53.

Exclusive Brethren: *see* Brethren.

'Fairy: A Recollection' [1877], PHG manuscript: about a beloved family pet cat, shows PHG's literary style, descriptive powers, emotional side, 617; compared to *Memorial* of EG, 281 fn.43; 615-16; his view of cats contrasts with other naturalists, 616; in 1871, Fairy, whose 'very meek & gentle face' indicated her disposition, was born, 621; 'she showed her love to me, thus', 623; musings on the saying 'Man is the God of the dog', 625, and on the possibility of a hereafter for 'the inferior creatures', 625; PHG makes a house for, 627 and fn.24; in 1877, death of, 618-19; possible cause, 629; PHG's efforts at intervention, 618-19; autopsy reveals death inevitable, 619; at burial of, 'I laid her, & covered her, &, having restrained my emotions before my servant, I came into the parlour & wept', 619; acquires cats, Daisy and Brue, 629-33.

Farre, Arthur, Pres. Microscopical Society: referee's report for Royal Society on PHG paper, 182 fn.116; 184 fn.135.

Father and Son (1907), by EWG: memoir of 'becoming', xxii; unreliability of: xxii and fn.44; 3 fn.1; falsification of chronology, 489 fns.49-50; uses PHG's *Memorial* without attribution, 282 fn.49; an archetypal struggle, 532-3; which has resonated with many readers, 533; among books shaping modern world, xxii; 'Five Best' column in *Wall Street Journal*, 532 fn.241; lacking a *Son and Father*, we have 4 words from PHG, 533; explanation of epigraph to, 607 fn.46; EWG's thoughts after appearance of, 608-9; Hunt's comments on, 540 fn.13; 'Septima', author of *Peculiar People*, a reply to *Father and Son*, 426 fn.164.

'Federal Headship', theological concept: explained, 314 and fn.236; allusion to, in *Glimpses of the Wonderful*, 123; PHG supplements *Omphalos* with argument of, 313; in PHG's rejoinder in *Natural History Review*, 314 fns.236-7; and subsequently *Geology or God: Which?*, 316 fn.246; PHG repeats in correspondence, 317 fn.254; criticism of argument, 315.

Fell, Jesse Weldon, cancer quack: an American claiming non-surgical, painless method of curing cancer, 247; using a 'secret medicament', 250; EG contacts for treatment, 247–50; recommended by Hyde Salter, q.v., 250; called 'Docteur Noir', 269-70; question about treatment, 270; continued publishing by, 274.

Fenn, Albert R., missionary: PHG letter to, 422 fn.149; dies at Marychurch, 605 fn.34.

Fertilisation of Orchids: see *On the Various Contrivances by Which British and Foreign Orchids are Fertilised by Insects*, by Darwin.

Fleure, Herbert John, zoologist: quoted on *Actinologia Britannica*, xviii fn.16; 348 fn.102; 349 fn.111; on Haddon, 597 fn.393.

Forbes, Edward, zoologist: mainly institution-based naturalist, 189; difficulty earning a living, 463 fn.143; aware of trends in geological science, 373; praises PHG's *Naturalist Sojourn in Jamaica*, 151; 162 fn.11; PHG's research attracts attention of, 162; 176 fn.80; PHG takes books of, to the seashore, 187; PHG correspondence, 195.

Fowler, George Herbert, zoologist: one-time assistant to Ray Lankester, 565 fn.174; 580; his questions about affinity claims for *Pedalion* rotifer, 565 fn.174; anonymous review of Hudson & Gosse, 580; 574 fn.239; signed review of work on Weismann, 579 fn.279.

Franco-Prussian War: to PHG, hostilities a signal 'advent was at hand', 428; 492; outbreak in 1870 disrupts EWG's travel plans, 497; 502.

Freeman, Philip, Archdeacon of Exeter: lecture opposing Darwin at British Association, 386; member, Victoria Institute, 386 fn.302.

Freeman, Richard Broke, zoologist: with D. Wertheimer, author of *Philip Henry Gosse: A Bibliography*, xxiii; 681; errors in, or additions to: 86 fn.295; 122 fn.125; 166 fn.32; 172 fn.61; 222 fn.346; 277 fn.10; 316 fn.246;

333 fn.3; 342 fn.65; 354 fn.148; 372 fn.237; 377 fn.264; 415 fns.105, 107; 416 fn.113; 582 fn.290; 583 fn.294; 585 fn.315; 590 fn.352; *Entomologia Alabamensis*, 87 fn.304;
CORRESPONDENCE WITH, COLLECTION OF: 25 fn.36; 180 fn.100; 181 fn.110; 244 fns.489, 491; 321 fn.266; 323 fn.276; 571 fns.212, 214; 587 fn.326.
French Revolution:
impact on believers, 50; and students of prophecy, 105–7; 392; in *Christian*, PHG traces signs of the times from, 431; called 'insane & atheistic effort to change & forget' the past, 431 fn.203.
Futurism: *see* Prophecy.

Garnett, Richard, writer:
EWG friend at British Museum, reviewer for *Athenaeum*, 500 fn.89; and *Illustrated London News*, 526 fn.204; critique of *On Viol and Flute* (1873), 526; critique of Payne, 482 fn.31; 483 fn.35.
Gastraea theory: Haeckel claims to trace all life to amoeboid blobs of jelly, 568.
Gates, Barbara T., academic:
confused claims of, concerning Emily Bowes, xxi fn.32; 203 fn.239.
Geology or God: Which? A Supplement to "Omphalos" (1866), by PHG:
PHG's letter in the *Natural History Review* in pamphlet form, though thought to remain unpublished, 316 and fn.246; contains new argument concerning Adam's 'Federal Headship', 314; PHG's logical strategy of *Omphalos* also apparent in, 310; denies Prochronism makes God a '*Deus quidam deceptor*', 291 fn.106; PHG would include a copy of, in correspondence, 317 and fns.249, 254; 429 fn.190; 434 fn.221;
REVIEWS OF: largely ignored by reviewers in Britain and in U.S.A., most reviews unfavourable, 306 fn.205; 316 and fns.247-8.
Gillispie, Charles Coulston, historian of science:
PHG a 'mediocre naturalist', xx; no plans for PHG entry in *DSB*, xx fn.29; different roles of science, religion, 311.
Gladstone, John Eddowes, clergyman:
'a zealous preacher', 336 fn.30; and PHG friend, who gave Bible reading classes at the Room and Sandhurst, 369; in 1861, left St. Marychurch, 369 fn.220; a son at Menneer's school, 444 and fn.30.
Gladstone, John Hall, chemist:
member, Victoria Institute, 325 fns.295; 326 fn.300; 548 fn.63; PHG consults with on entomological subject, 548; cited: 422 fn.150.
Glimpses of the Wonderful (1845), by PHG:
formally anonymous, but advertised as by PHG, 122 fn.125; natural theology in, 12; 123; allusion to 'Federal Headship' in, 314 fn.237; favourable reviews of, 123 fn.126; cited: 128 fn.153.
Gnoll College, South Wales:
in 1857, PHG allegedly offered resident professorship in natural history at, 282 and fn.50; at £500 p.a., 283; Gnoll, a science and technical school open to Dissenters, aimed to fill a lacuna in British education, 283–5; ultimately fails due to funder issue, 285.

Godman, Frederick DuCane, entomologist:
co-author with Salvin of *Biologia Centrali-Americana*, 548; on Salvin, 555 fn.111; PHG corresponds with, 547 and fn.58; 548 fn.61; research supports Darwin's theory, 549.
Golden Lamp (monthly), edited by W.H. Bennet:
Open Brethren publication, 592; cited, 532 fns. 364, 366.
Good Words (monthly), edited by Norman Macleod:
in 1864, serialises PHG's *Year at the Shore*, 383; comparison of concluding words in serial and book form, 383-4; hidden message in, 389; other PHG articles in: on Jamaica, 125 fn.139; 139 fn.236; marine zoology: 405 fn.64; scholars misdate PHG statement on depletion of marine fauna, unaware of its original publication, 368 fn.212; PHG submits EWG poem to, 468 fn.159.
Gosse, Edmund William (PHG's son):
the flawed source of dominant attitude to PHG, xxii–xxiii; characterization of PHG as 'hodman of science' examined, xx fn.30; inaccurate claim that PHG first associated in 1843 with Brethren, 3 fn.1; 124 fn.133; false narrative about *Omphalos*, 291–307; 312;
BACKGROUND: in 1849, born in London, they prayed 'that he may be the Lord's', 174; 252; 253; on her deathbed, EG refers to 'Willy', 272 and fn.190; after her death, EWG stays with cousin while PHG lectures, 277–80; moving to St. Marychurch, in 1857 they go to Brethren's Room, 333; produces juvenile natural history works, 439-40; goes dredging with PHG, 343; 440; Kent's Cavern with Pengelly, 439-40; beneficial effect of Eliza Gosse on, 370; before turning 8, is writing poetry, 441; in 1859, baptized; 443-4; 444 fn.24; differs with PHG on significance of, 441–4; attends Menneer's Montvidere school, q.v.; transfers to Edgelows' Thorn Park school, q.v.; around 1863, teaches in Sunday school at Marychurch, 445; at end of 1866, goes to London to work at British Museum, lives in Tottenham, 451; comparison of EWG's life in London in 1867 with PHG's in 1843, 451–4; 1867-8, writes poetry, 468–74; 496-7; EWG friends with poets at British Museum, 478-9; and outside, 479–85; they are all freethinkers and rationalists: *see* Brown; Dames; Garnett; Marston; Marzials; Morris; Payne; Rossetti; Scott; Swinburne; Tennyson; also Norwegian, Scandinavian writers: Andersen; Bjørnson; Daa; Ibsen; Løkke; Paludan-Müller; what troubled PHG was not his son, it was his son's circle of friends, 507; in 1870, M. Johnson, q.v., dies, 478; trip to Scotland, 497-8; PHG offers to oversee publication of poems, *Madrigals, Songs and Sonnets*: *see below*; EWG writing for *Academy, Athenaeum, Fraser's, Spectator*, 505; *Examiner*, 527; in 1872, why PHG tries to move him to a new job, 506–7; Scandinavian writings, 523; around 1874, acquaintance with Ellen (Nellie) Epps, q.v., 528; in 1875, marries Epps, 532; drops 'W.' middle initial, 606; 'My Joy & Crown', 532–4; helps PHG with Lepidoptera research, 548; 552; Clark Lecturer, 606; 591; 599; asks PHG to compose a prayer, 596; last views of PHG, 596; 598-9; 600 fn.417; 606–8; significance of cremation of, 609–11;

Brethren and: EWG felt a 'deep consciousness' that PHG tried to bring him up 'for God', 522; Thorn Park school attended by EWG run by Edgelows, who are Brethren, 447; lives in Tottenham with Buckham, Baker, associated with Brethren, 451-2; attends Brook Street chapel, 452; 511; EWG in contact with PHG's Brethren friends, 452-3; 460-1; in 1867, EWG leads class at Brook Street Sunday school, 458; 459; 511; in 1870, Superintendent, 498; attends Scripture reading meetings, 459; 476; Young Men's Prayer meetings, 460; visits Howards, 460; briefly involved with Barnardo, 461; also encounters non-Brethren, 459; 461; 465; 467; 473; EWG questions PHG on views, 412-13; 417; 464-5; enamoured with Emma Beddows, Brethren friend, 476; in 1870, remains associated with Brethren, 498; in 1872, aligns with Anglicans, 511; in 1874, leaves Brook Street, 529;
Correspondence with PHG: from St. Marychurch, 279 and fn.26; 441 fn.10; in 1866, EWG moves to London, 454-7; letters described, 454-6; statistics concerning, 456-7; 485-6; key issues in, 462; 486; 498-9; problem of 'separation from the world', 464-8; 493-4; watching for Second Advent, 417; 434-5; 497; 498; PHG's accusation of *hominum volitare per ora*, 470 and fns.168-9; 354 fn.148; 484; 500; 502; 527; 606 and fn.40; in 1870, no break in relationship, 485-6; critique of PHG by, 509-10; disagreement over baptism, Bewes episode, q.v., 512-15; analysis of March 1873 letter, 519-23; by 1874, correspondence, relationship cool, 530; 594-6;
Serial writing of: 1872, introduces Ibsen in Britain, 502-3; 'Ethical Condition of the Early Scandinavian Peoples' (1873), 524 and fn.197; in prestigious serials, *Academy*, *Athenaeum*, *Fraser's*, *Spectator*, 505;
Works by: *Madrigals, Songs and Sonnets* (1870), by EWG and J. Blaikie: in 1868, EWG asks PHG to pay for a volume of his poems, 470–4; PHG oversees, 491-2; in 1870, published at author's expense, 497 and fn.68; 499-500; mixed reviews, 500 fn.85; but apparent praise from Rossetti, Swinburne, 500; only 12 copies sold, 500 and fn.86;
On Viol and Flute (1873): inspired by Parnassians, 483; 484 fn.36; also Rossetti, Swinburne, Whitman, 524-5; poems are published, without consulting PHG, 525 fn.200; mixed reviews, 525 and fn.201; 526-7;
New Poems (1879): PHG's negative reaction to, 595;
Studies in the Literature of Northern Europe (1879): sends copy to PHG, 595 fn.377;
Life of William Congreve (1888): working on, during PHG's last illness, 599 and fn.409;
Life of Philip Henry Gosse (1890): *see separate entry*;
Father and Son (1907): *see separate entry*.
Gosse, Eliza *née* Brightwen (2nd Mrs PHG):
confused with 1st Mrs PHG, 203 fn.239; not to be confused with naturalist Eliza Brightwen *née* Elder, sister-in-law to PHG, 325 fn.295; 196 fn.192;
Background: apparently raised as an Anglican,

later a Quaker, she was familiar with Brethren personalities before meeting PHG, 369 and fn.221; distant cousin of the Hookers of Kew, 371;
Encountering PHG: in Feb. 1860, visiting St. Marychurch, attends Scripture reading meetings at Sandhurst, 368-9; 499 fn.83; in 1860, PHG proposes, they are married by Independent minister, 370;
Legacy for: in 1864, left a legacy of £400 p.a. by an uncle, John Brightwen, 186 fn.145; 241 fns.469-70; 379 fns.271-2; 463;
Life with PHG: PHG calls her 'a true yoke-fellow' on the same level as 'my sainted Emily', 605; 419 fn.134; in marrying PHG, agrees to being baptized as a believer, 370; her religious views (and influence on EWG), 370; 1861-2, takes EWG on summer break trips, 445; at end of 1860s, in correspondence PHG refers to her as 'your Mamma', 455; she reads poetry recommended by EWG, 469; 471; follows EWG's correspondence with PHG, 490; 509; and writes to EWG, 524 fn.190; 530 fn.229; recalls PHG's interest in orchids, 371 fn.231; in 1868, joins Dorcas Society, 418; in wake of controversy at the Room, with PHG visits Cornwall, 424; writes to NG, 307 fn.208; 529 fn.220; prior to EWG's marriage, describes Sandhurst lifestyle to NG, 528-9; neither she nor PHG attend EWG's wedding, 532; description of PHG's study area, 544-5; description of PHG's personality, 594; 538; her incorrect claims about PHG's *Mysteries of God*, 592 fn.367; enjoys gazing through the telescope with PHG, 597; her fondness for cats, 616; 620-1; 625; 628–33 *passim*; in 1888, NG is at Sandhurst to assist her caring for PHG, 599; reports PHG's last words, 600 fn.417; Life after PHG: NG is at Sandhurst after PHG's death, 602; EWG consults, on *Life* of PHG, 605; her last years, 605-6; leaves £50 to Marychurch Brethren, 605-6; NG is with her when she dies, 605 and fn.35.
Gosse, Elizabeth (PHG's sister):
born in Poole, 20; in 1832, seriously ill, PHG visits her, 45; she recovers, 52; marries James Green, 493; in 1837, PHG writes to, about possible job openings, 73; 78; 99; in 1840, dies in Sherborne, 99 fn.9.
Gosse, Ellen: *see* Gosse, Nellie.
Gosse, Emily *née* Bowes (1st Mrs PHG):
Early Years: confused with the 2nd Mrs PHG, 203 fn.239; born in London, raised in Anglican family to American-born parents, siblings Edmund and Arthur, 167; 169 fn.43; possible relation to Loddiges, 120 fn.113; father lost his property, they were reduced to poverty, 167; attended school at Exmouth, taught Sunday school, 168; not known if she underwent a conversionary moment, 168; early acquired a knowledge of French, German (180 and fn.106), Latin, Greek, 169; age 17, becomes governess, Berkshire, where she is for 14 years, 169; in 1838, becomes governess in Brighton, returning in 1841 to Brook Street, Upper Clapton, London, 171; in that year, associates with Brethren, 167; 171; 338 fn.37; at about that time, knows Hannah Newton, wife of

B.W. Newton, 171; her familiarity with works of Newton, Darby, 171; 412; enthusiasm for Elliott's *Horae*, 412; meets PHG at Hackney in 1843, 167, 171 and fn.58; 120; 507;

MARRIED LIFE: in 1848 they marry, 172; 452; PHG's *Popular British Ornithology* finished before marriage to, 166-7; only child, Edmund William, born in 1849, 174; evangelical child-rearing, 175; children 'born for immortality', 439; in 1850, receives portion of an inheritance, 186; devotes her time to son and husband, 252–5; nurtures spiritual life of EWG, 252-3; close spiritual bond to PHG, and assists him in his scientific work, 253-4; love letters from PHG, 255; 276; in fellowship with Brethren, 254; in 1853 corresponds with George Müller, 256; in 1852, 1854 PHG, EG lose £2,500 investing in non-existent Castle Dinas gold mine, 186 fn.145; they fail to get a portrait of EG, 275; 602 fn.6; her cancer (see below); buried at Abney Park, 273; 610; mourning for, 275-6; PHG returns to lecturing, 277; postponed from Feb. to March, 277; assessment of PHG's *Memorial of the Last Days*, 281-2; 528 fn.216; 544; 607; 615; EWG attributes publication of *Omphalos* to PHG's 'morbid' state after EG's death, 292; 305;

PUBLICATIONS: Next to Bevan, q.v., the most prolific of Victorian Brethren female writers, 262; *Hymns and Sacred Poems* (2 series, 1832, 1834), 169; 479; a chapter, with PHG, of *Seaside Pleasures* (1853), 201; in 1852, writes series with PHG for *Weekly Visitor*, 256-7; 1853-4, authors articles on education, 256; *Abraham and His Children* (1855) well-received, 256;

RELIGIOUS WORK: 'habitually walked with an exercised conscience', 255; in 1851, EG begins work for Irish Society, 256; in 1853, begins distributing tracts of others, next year writes her own, 257; 266; 269; PHG's 'sainted Emily', 605;

TRACTS: EG's true *métier* is as religious tract writer, her first appears in 1854, 257; EWG underestimates circulation of EG tracts, 259; EG author of 63 tracts, 263; printed in French, 263; and in evangelical periodicals, 263; leaflet and book format of: 266-7; style of: 262-3; subject of: salvation of souls, particularly the poor, 263; texts of: 6 often-quoted by EG, 264-5; publishers of: 263; distribution of: 257, 271; numbers of: 266; 400; in Britain, Canada, USA, 267; reception of: 265; constant demand for: 266; conversions from: 265–6; enclosed in letters of PHG, 258 fn.98; on deathbed of EG, 272;

TRACTS BY, CITED: 'Bathing Woman and her Visitor', 264 fn.140; 'Christian Soldier', 264 fn.137; 'Consumptive Deathbed', 127 fn.149; 265 fn.148; 'Cure for Cholera', 127 fn.149; 265 fn.148; 'Eleventh Hour', 266; 'Faithful Nurse', 264 fn.144; 'Is Christ Willing?' 127 fn.149; 265 fn.148; 'Dying Postman', 127 fn.149; 'King and the Prince', 264 fn.137; 'King's Daughter', 264 fn.140; 'Old Soldier's Widow', 264 fn.145; 'Pass Ticket', 264 fn.138; 'Pilgrim to St. Patrick's Well', 127 fn.149; 264 fn.136; 'Power of the Word', 265 fn.147; 'Railway Ticket', 264 fn.139; 'Scattered Tracts', 264 fn.141; 'Suicide', 264 fn.143; 'Thomas

Winter's Stray Sheep', 266; 'Two Maniacs', 264 fn.141; 265 fn.146; 'Young Guardsman of the Alma', 127 fn.149; 259; 265 fn.148;

TREATMENT OF CANCER: in 1856, diagnosed with breast cancer, 245; 244; 267; Gosses consult with physicians Laseron, Salter, Paget, Fell, 246–50; Fell is selected, on 12 May treatment begins, 250; in Sept. 1856, Fell encourages Gosses to make trip to Tenby, 250; in Oct. 1856, when family trip ends, they tell Brethren in Tenby of cancer, 244; extractive process continues, 250; 267–9; in Dec., Fell says cancer "'tis in your blood'", 269; Fell assessed: 269-70; reaction of Gosses, 270; 478; they review their married life, 272; they pray, 270; treatment by Epps, q.v., 270; 528; EG reads Elliott's Warburton Lectures, 271; to earn money, PHG commits to lecturing, 272; EG's last days, 272-3; nursed by Ann Morgan, 277-8; PHG's hope EG will be spared death, 399.

Gosse, Fanny *née* Parker:
2nd wife of Thomas Gosse, PHG's brother, they marry in 1869, 603 and fn.14; PHG corresponds with, 604 fn.21; after her death, 8 of their children move to New Zealand, 604-5.

Gosse, Hannah *née* Best (wife of Thomas Gosse; mother of PHG):
a domestic servant, she meets Thomas Gosse, a portrait painter, in Worcester in 1807, and is married then, 19; Thomas' sisters disapprove, 21; PHG's description of an unhappy marriage, 21-2; their first child, William, born in Bristol, 19; then PHG, in Worcester, 19; Elizabeth and Thomas, in Poole; Thomas travels for work, rarely returning, sends back little money, family is of 'reputable subgentility', 21; impact of 'shame of poverty' on PHG, 21; PHG encouraged by, learns chapters of Bible by heart, 24; PHG given religious works by, 25; attends Independent meeting in Poole, 30; tells PHG to read Bible daily in Newfoundland, 36; in 1839, she is living with son Thomas in Wimborne, 98; in 1842, she is in Hackney, 101; 120; in Jamaica, PHG corresponds with, 119 fn.106; 129 fn.166; 133 fns.194, 196; 138-9; 139 fn.231; 141 fn.245; sends her £25, 148; 141; on return from Jamaica, lives with, in Dalston, 160; 146; in 1848, living in Kingsland with PHG, 172; in 1849, not happy living with PHG family, moves out of Trafalgar Terrace, 175; 173; in 1858, moves to Sandhurst, 368 fn.214; requests William communicate with brother Thomas, 604; in 1860 dies at Sandhurst, 368; PHG buried near, in Torquay cemetery, 601.

Gosse, Jennifer Sarah (great-granddaughter of PHG):
assistance acknowledged, 681; *Entomologia Alabamensis*, 87 fn.304; *Fairy: A Recollection*, 615 fn.1.

Gosse, Nellie *née* Ellen Epps, artist (wife of EWG):
MARRIED LIFE OF: encounters EWG at Pre-Raphaelite meeting, 528; in 1874, EWG writes to PHG about, 528; Eliza Gosse describes Sandhurst lifestyle to, 529; hears Moody and Sankey, 531; for her wedding, PHG sends rare orchids to, 531; in Aug. 1875, marries EWG, 532; NG and EWG

visit Sandhurst for their honeymoon, 594; their moderately religious life, 595; accompanies EWG to USA, 307; in 1888, at Sandhurst with 3 children for 4 months to help care for PHG, 599; present at PHG's death, 602; William Gosse a visitor at home of, 603; present at Eliza Gosse's death, 605 and fn.35; married to EWG for 53 years, dies in 1929, 606.

Gosse, Pack & Fryer, Newfoundland mercantile trade outfitting business:
formerly the Kemp firm, 42; also known as Pack, Gosse and Fryer, and in England as Fryer, Gosse and Pack, 25 fn.37; 26 fn.38; size comparative to other mercantile firms, 36 and fn.21; in 1822, William Gosse becomes a clerk at, 25; 64; other clerks at: Bemister, 59; Apsey, 42; 'God's grace' not evident at, 45; 48.

Gosse, Philip Henry, early Brethren leader, naturalist:
career summary of PHG in religion and science, xvii–xx; versus prevailing view of, xx–xxii;
Chronology overview:
EARLY YEARS 1810–27: family background, 14–20; father Thomas, q.v., and mother Hannah, q.v.; on 6 April 1810, PHG born in Worcester, 19; in Poole, juvenile education and Sells' day-school, 23; from age 7, a 'love for natural history', 23 and fn.29; bookish tastes and avid reader, knows Scripture by heart, 23-4; 28; in 1822, brother William leaves for Carbonear, Newfoundland, clerkship 25; PHG moves to Hosier's school, then Jan. 1823, a classical education in Blandford at Lance's school, includes Latin, Greek, English grammar, Euclid, 26-7; PHG also later reads French and German, 180 and fns.102–6; expelled, he returns to Hosier's until 1825, when (at age 15) his formal education ends, 28; obtains junior clerk position at Poole counting-house, 28; 1826 a copied piece is published in *Youth's Magazine*, q.v.; always believed he was 'by nature fit for heaven' and must experience a conversion, q.v., 29-30; in 1827, gets clerkship at Carbonear, Newfoundland, counting-house, leaves home just before turning 17, 32; NEWFOUNDLAND 1827–35: *see separate entry;*
CANADA 1835–8: *see separate entry;*
ALABAMA 1838-9: *see separate entry;*
ENGLAND 1839–44: in 1839, returns to Liverpool from Alabama, 96; undecided about his future, around Sept. 1840 PHG takes over an Academy with 3 students in Hackney, 101; in 1842, there are 15 students, 101; among his students are Edward and Theodore Habershon, 103; in 1842, reads (and is influenced by) *Dissertation on the Prophetic Scriptures*, by Habershon, q.v., 103; 109; in summer 1843, introduced to Brethren, q.v., in Hackney, q.v., 3–9; 112–20; meets EG at, 167; 109 fn.53; 171; simultaneously pursues natural history studies at British Museum, 10–12; 120–2; in 1843, only 6 students at his school, 122; having in 1840 published his first book, *The Canadian Naturalist*, q.v., 100; and with other natural history works in progress, 122-3; in Dec. 1843, closes school and determines to 'look to literature for a livelihood', 122; in 1844, Doubleday, q.v., suggests he become

a natural history collector, he sets off for Jamaica, 124; to connect as well with the first Brethren member on the island, Coleman, q.v., 124; JAMAICA 1844–6: *see separate entry;*
ENGLAND 1846–88: upon his return, PHG resumes natural history writing, with 25 titles published from 1846–57, 159; 161–7; 173; Nov. 1848 marries EG, 172; in 1849, EWG born, q.v., 174; in 1849, buys a microscope and begins study of Rotifera, 176; income never exceeds £160 from 1846–51, 186; in 1852, an explorer at the seashore, 186–9; the aquarium marks the dawn of a new engagement with the seashore, 191–4; PHG's celebrated seashore trilogy, *Devonshire Coast, Aquarium, Tenby*, qq.v., 199; chromolithographed plates featured in, an early instance of colour printing and the first of its type, 203–6; aquaromania seizes Britain and the world, 208–15; 241-2; PHG becomes a phenomenon as a natural history populariser, 215–41; EG believes EWG 'was indeed a child of God', 253; close relationship of EG, PHG, 253–5; 19th century was the 'Tract Century', 257–62; among Brethren, EG (with her tracts, books, and serial contributions) is the second-most prolific of female writers, 262; EG struggles with, and eventually succumbs to, breast cancer, 245–74; in 1857, PHG apparently offered teaching opportunity at Gnoll College, 282–6; later that year, moves to St. Marychurch, Devon, 286; PHG publishes *Omphalos*, q.v., his response to uniformitarian geology, 286–91; X Club reaction against, *see entry on Omphalos;* myths surrounding its timing, subject, reception, and goal described and corrected, 291–320; PHG and Darwin's evolution theory, 320–4; in St. Marychurch, q.v., from 1857–88 the pastor of a 'simple Church of God', 333 fn.5; 337; 422; in 1860, PHG marries Eliza Brightwen, 368–70; focus on sea anemone research, culminating in *Actinologia Britannica*, q.v., 339–56; 'Poison-apparatus' of sea anemones research paper, q.v., is boycotted by X Club, q.v., 356–65; PHG's scientific challenge to evolution: (1) orchids, 370–7; (2) Lepidoptera 'clasping-organs', q.v., 545–61; PHG's protest against the 'lying science of the day', 377–89; 538; drives him to withdraw from scientific activity, 389; long engaged in the study of unfulfilled prophecy, PHG calculates the arrival of the Second Advent, q.v., 399; promotes his premillennialist, historicist prophetic view in 1864 lectures, 402-3; and in pamphlets, periodicals, and a book, critiquing futurist prophetic outlook, 400–19; 425–35; impact of PHG's prophetic views on his relationship with EWG, 435; EWG 'born for immortality', is guided by PHG after EG's 1857 death, 439; at age 10, EWG's baptism, 443-4; 512–15; EWG felt a 'deep consciousness' that PHG tried to raise him up 'for God', 522; PHG removes EWG from Menneer's school, q.v., to that of the Edgelows', q.v., the latter were Brethren, 445–7; having moved to London to earn a living, PHG associates EWG with Brethren acquaintants, 451–3; an initially warm father-son correspondence, 454–9; turns

tense, 462–8; 485–96; 505–23; EWG's turn to poetry, 468–74; Parnassianism, q.v., and the Pre-Raphaelite circle, q.v.; EWG's co-authored *Madrigals, Songs and Sonnets* (1870), 499-500; followed by a Scandinavian focus and promotion of Ibsen in Britain, 502–5; EWG's circle of friends troubling to PHG, 507; in 1873, a fraught relationship, 515–23; PHG's 1871 Victoria Institute paper on biblical criticism, 324–30; PHG's two attempts to scientifically challenge Darwin's theory, *see entry* on Evolution, Darwin's theory of; *The Rotifera*, by Hudson & Gosse, ushers in a new period in the study of these microscopic animals, and is published to world acclaim, 573–80; PHG again falls victim to the X Club boycott, 580; PHG dies on 27 Aug. 1888, 601; EWG's body is cremated, 609–11; wealth at death: PHG: 601; Eliza Gosse, 605; EWG, 611.

Subjects:

BRETHREN: *see separate entry;*

CHARACTER TRAITS OF PHG: self-described introspective personality, 23; bookish tastes from an early age, 23-4; personal optimism: 66; *nil desperandum* ('Do not despair!'), 270; 'a happy man', 538-9; uplift from engagement with nature, 71; 78; 85; metaphor of analysing 'as with a microscope', 518; 523 fn.187; 591 and fn.355; 345; descriptions by Eliza Gosse: PHG's personality, 594; 538; Sandhurst lifestyle, 528-9;

ILLUSTRATIONS, DESIGNED OR DRAWN BY PHG: *see separate entry;*

OCCUPATIONS OF PHG: Clergy: in Newfoundland, a local Wesleyan preacher, 58; in Alabama, contemplates serving as Methodist minister, 92; in London, a Wesleyan Methodist Class-Leader, 100; at St. Marychurch, a pastor of 'a little flock of believers', 422; Teacher: in Canada, 3 winter-only jobs, 70; 72; 78; did not enjoy the teaching, and said not to be good at it, 74 and fn.226; in Alabama, school-master for one season, 85; in London in 1840, takes over an existing 'Classical and Commercial School' in Hackney with 3 students, 101; in 1843, closes the school, 122; Author: from 1843, 122;

PROPHECY (UNFULFILLED): *see separate entry;*

RELIGIOUS ASSOCIATIONS OF: during all his early years in Poole, family was associated with Independents, q.v., 30; 27; in North America, PHG mainly turns from Independents, Anglicans to Methodism, 102; in 1832, PHG's conversion experience in Newfoundland, 44–6; upon return to England, continued his association with Methodism, 97-8; until in 1843 he encountered the newly-emerging Brethren, 3–9; 112–20; and severed his connection with Methodists, 120 and fn.114; in Jamaica, he plans to connect with Coleman, q.v., first-ever Brethren member on the island, 124; and remains in contact with Hackney Brethren, 118 fn.96; 1857–88, leader of 'Church of God' in St. Marychurch, q.v.;

SCIENTIFIC ACHIEVEMENTS OF: 'Father of the Aquarium', xviii; 194; 'Father of Jamaican Ornithology', xviii; 149; 'Father of Jamaican Herpetology', xviii; 149; Father of many other

aspects of Jamaican biology', xviii; 149; in the study of sea anemones, '*Il capo di tutti per merito e carattere*' ('the leader of all by merit and character'), xviii; 348; in the study of Rotifera, '*facile princeps*' (in a class by himself), xix; 574; for PHG's contributions to entomology, orchidology, marine zoology, natural history, scientific illustration, seashore, qq.v.; for PHG's philosophical, scientific approach to evolution, *see Omphalos;* Evolution, Darwin's theory of;

SCIENTIFIC SOCIETY MEMBERSHIPS OF: for UK, *see* Entomological; Linnean; Microscopical; Royal societies; for Canada, *see* Literary and Historical Society of Quebec; Natural History Society of Montreal;

WORKS BY: summary of number of religious works, xvii; summary of number of scientific works, xix; *see separate titles;*

WORKS PUBLISHED ON AUTHOR'S-RISK BASIS: *see separate entry.*

Gosse, Susan: *see* Bell, Susan.

Gosse's *Narrative* or *Gospel Tracts*: grant received to distribute, 266 fn.157; individual titles, *see* Gosse, Emily; Gosse, P.H.; book form, *see Narrative Tracts.*

Gosse, Teresa (Tessa), PHG granddaughter: at birth of Emily Teresa, EWG publishes poem on, PHG provides religious advice, 595; EWG asks PHG to compose prayer for, and teach to, 596; PHG names new rotifer after, 597 and fn.388; PHG letter to, cited, 597 fn.394; diary of, cited, 595 fn.380.

Gosse, Thomas, miniaturist (PHG's father): BIOGRAPHY: in 1765, born in Ringwood, Hampshire, 15; Henry, brother of, was like PHG a clerk in Newfoundland, lived in West Indies, 14; PHG recollections of, 21-2; PHG has similar traits, 23; books PHG read from library of, 24 fn.31; 25; studied mezzotinting, pursued engraving and for some 40 years, an itinerant miniature portrait painter, 15; output compared to son William, 603 fn.7; PHG inspired by miniaturist style of, 26; teaches PHG Latin, 27; inveterate (but unsuccessful) writer, 15-16; 29; in 1807, marries Hannah Best, q.v., 19; travels to earn a living, rarely returns home to 3 children, 21; 53; PHG's description of an unhappy marriage, 21-2; plans to start family magazine, 64; in 1844 with wife at 37, The Oval, Hackney Rd., 125; dies in 1844, while PHG is in Jamaica, 139 fn.231;

RELIGIOUS LIFE: in 1790, evangelical conversion of, 17-18; 29; 443; attends ministry of J. Newton, 18; Independent meeting, 30; 53; Brethren assembly at Rawstorne Street, 120; 'Why Am I a Christian?' rejected by Religious Tract Society, 18 fns.12-13.

Gosse, Thomas, grocer, sharebroker (PHG's younger brother): BIOGRAPHY: black sheep of family, 186 fn.145; PHG loses £2,500 in Castle Dinas shares, 186 fn.145; 594; born in Poole, 20; in 1823, works as grocer there, 26; his visit to PHG's Canadian farm a failure, 603; PHG lives with, in Wimborne, 98; in 1840, TG marries Emma Budden (1st wife), they have 3 children, 603 and fn.13; in 1869, marries

Fanny Parker, q.v., has total of 17 children, 603; or more, 603 fn.14; for a time, affiliated with Brethren, 434; EWG wonders why William Gosse is so antagonistic towards, 604 and fn.20; in 1898, dies in Bath, 604 fn.27;
PHG AND: in 1832, PHG entomologizes with, during a brief visit from Newfoundland, 52-3; sends PHG insect specimens, 60; PHG writes to, about his religious conversion, 60; in 1834, PHG invites him to come to Canada, 63-4; which he does, in 1837, but it is a failure and he returns to Poole, 73; 603; in 1839, after his return from Alabama, PHG is reunited with, in Wimborne, 98; worships at Methodist chapel with PHG, 98; PHG dedicates *Introduction to Zoology* (1844) to, 604 fn.21; from 1844, writes to PHG in Jamaica, 129; for a time, associated with Brethren, 434; in 1880, PHG writes to, about advent expectation, 434; towards end of his life, corresponds with PHG, and PHG helps support, 594.
Gosse, William, painter (PHG's older brother):
EARLY YEARS: born in Worcester, 19; attends Sells' day-school there with PHG, 23; sings in the Poole Congregation church, 30;
NEWFOUNDLAND: in 1822, at age 14, leaves England for clerkship in Newfoundland mercantile trade at his uncle John Gosse's firm (Gosse, Pack, & Fryer), 25; 26; 32; 64; stays for 14 years, 602; in Carbonear debating society, 44; on PHG's arrival at Carbonear in 1827, gives him a code of etiquette, 36 and fn.18; 457; plays violin in Carbonear church choir, 58; briefly returns to England, 37; and for six weeks in 1832, WG reunited with other family members in Poole, 53; in 1835, sent to Bay Roberts branch, 64; Thomas (father) invites WG, PHG to return to England to work to start a family magazine, 64;
PAINTER: *c.*1830, composes an illustrated volume of 'Wild Flowers and Fruits of Newfoundland from Nature', 54; 'a brilliant book of *trompe l'oeil* water-colour studies', 54 fn.131; compared to Thomas Gosse, father, 603 fn.7; in St. John's (1836–42), WG is the 'most successful' of painters living in the colony in first half of 19th Century, 602; in 1841, draws portrait of W.C. St. John, 37 fn.27; careers of PHG, WG confused, 54 fn.131;
RELATIONSHIP TO FAMILY: from 1844, writes to PHG in Jamaica, 129; in Nov. 1856, PHG informs him of EG's cancer, 250; complains of PHG's 'meddling officiousness', 456 and fn.103; visits EWG at Morgans, shows EWG his 'Wild Flowers' of Newfoundland, 54 fn.131; 279; in 1857, notes what would have been his parents' 50th anniversary, 19 fn.15; in 1860, WG's mother Hannah dies at St. Marychurch, 368 and fn.214; in 1871, WG is 'hale & hearty', 95 fn.365; PHG writes then that WG 'has accepted Jesus as his own Saviour', 501; WG's admiration for PHG is enormous, 603; displeased with brother Tom, 603-4; annoyed at PHG, 456; WG and PHG regularly correspond, PHG helps to support him, 603; dies on same day as PHG, five years later, 602; life-long bachelor, 603;
WORK: returns to England in 1842, works at Maull & Co. and then as a miniature painter of photographs in London, 602-3; in 1857, PHG sends WG photos of EG to serve as the basis of a portrait, 275; WG completes work by early April, 276;
WORKS OF PHG: in 1857 at the railway station, as PHG heads for St. Marychurch, WG learns of *Omphalos*, 286; 292 fn. 110; books PHG sent to WG include *Glimpses of the Wonderful*, 122 fn.125; *Memorial* of EG, 281 fn.43; *Omphalos*, 286 fn.81.
Gould, Stephen Jay, biologist:
analysis of *Omphalos* by, examined, 305-6.
Gray, Asa, botanist:
summer of 1857, informed of Darwin's evolution theory, 293 fn.117; in 1884, meets EWG and sends greetings to PHG, 307 and fn.207.
Great Atlas Moth (1879), by PHG:
serial title, '*Attacus Atlas*', 541 fn.19; PHG acquired a specimen of this moth in 1839, 541.
The Great Tribulation (1868), by PHG:
bibliography of, 415 fn.105; PHG believes events of, have been continuously unfolding since the 1st century AD, 408; 414 fn.99; in 1866, PHG writes on, 408 fn.74; PHG's 1868 pamphlet on, 415; though PHG believes most of Tribulation had been endured, he seems to waver on rapture of the Saints, 414 fn.99; EWG discussion of, 417 and fn.119; PHG sends copy of, to Elliott, 430 fn.190; and to others, 434 fn.221; advertised, 416 fn.112.
SEE ALSO: Cumming, John.
Green, James (husband of Elizabeth *née* Gosse):
schoolmate of PHG, 492-3; dedicates his *Shadow & Sunshine* (2ed., [1871]) to PHG, 493; anti-Catholic views of, 493 fn.59; PHG calls him 'fellow-heir of the grace of life', 493; in 1871, PHG tells him that all of his close family have been 'redeemed with the Blood of the Lamb', 501.
Grimley, E.:
Brethren figure in Jamaica, 132; associate of Coleman, 133; takes PHG to meetings at Shrewsbury, 134 fn.198; from at least 1845, Darby and Wigram in contact with, 153; he tells them of alleged heretical teachings of Coleman, implicates PHG, 153-4.
Guinness, Fanny Emma *née* Fitzgerald, writer:
1st wife of H. Grattan Guinness, 426 fn.165; PHG sends a copy of *Omphalos* to, 317 fn.254; corresponds with PHG, 426 fn.164; including on prophecy, 588 fns.336-7; PHG sends donation to, 426 fn.165; author (with H. Grattan Guinness) of *Light for the Last Days*, cited: 588 fn.337; 589 fn.344.
Guinness, H. Grattan, evangelist, writer on prophecy:
BIOGRAPHY: married first to, and co-author with, Fanny, 426 fn.165; denied having joined Brethren, 588 fn.336; founder (1873), East End Training Institute, 425 fn.162; founder (1881), North African Mission, 7 fn.3;
PROPHETIC STUDY: leading premillennial historicist, 410; 588; PHG familiar with work of, 399 fn.37; says literalists must be Futurists, 410; Historicists follow unfolding of divine plan in history, 413-14; terms PHG's *Revelation* 'admirable', 416;
WORKS: PHG reads proofs of *Approaching End*

of the Age (1878) by, 588; and corresponds with, on, 588 fn.336; but PHG is unconvinced by continuationism of, 588; 17,000 copies sold by 10ed. (1886), 588 fn.336; cited: 410 fn.83; 414 fn.98; 416 fn.110; 429 fn.180; *Light for the Last Days,* written jointly with wife Fanny, 588 fn.337; PHG commends prophetic studies of, 589 and fn.344.

Gwatkin, Richard, clergyman:
 in 1865; lectures on prophecy at Torquay, 403 fn.61.

Gwyther, James T., Congregationalist clergyman:
 when PHG is ill, preaches in his stead, 583 fn.297; member, Victoria Institute, 325 fn.295.

Habershon, Edward: son of Matthew Habershon, a student at PHG's Academy, tells PHG of his father's works, 103.

Habershon, Matthew, architect:
 BACKGROUND: Historicist premillennialist writer on prophecy, 29; part of a circle of premillennialist anti-Catholics, 107; 111-12; his sons Edward and Theodore attend PHG's Academy, 103; in June 1842, he sends PHG his *Dissertation on the Prophetic Scriptures,* 103;
 BRETHREN ASSOCIATION: Habershon aligned with Brethren in Hackney in 1843, where PHG knew him, 109 and fn.53; 109 fn.53; buried in 1852 in Abney Park Cemetery, 273 fn.195;
 INFLUENCE: impact of, on PHG, 29; 107; 118; 152; 428; Duke of Wellington allegedly is influenced by his writing, 395 and fn.21;
 PALESTINE JOURNEY: in Nov. 1842 he is sent to Palestine to reverse plan to build a Catholic church in Jerusalem, 108; his prophetic studies, architectural work are intertwined in their concern for restoration of Jews to their homeland and anti-Catholicism, 107-8; the two converge to point to end of days in 1843-4, 108-9; 111 fn.61; unable to achieve his goal, he returns from Jerusalem and meets PHG no later than July 1843, 3 fn.1; 109 and fn.52.

Habershon, Theodore, son of Matthew Habershon:
 student at PHG's Academy in Hackney, 103; later 'lost his footing', 103 fn.30; claims Duke of Wellington corresponded with his father after studying his prophetic works, 395 fn.21.

Hackney (London area):
 in 1839, PHG moves to, where air is 'salubrious and healthy', 99; in 1840, PHG takes over school in, 101; in 1844, settles parents in, 125; Habershon lives near, 107; S. Berger, Jr., lives in, 112; 181; PHG knew Loddiges orchid nursery in, 371; EG buried in, 271;
 BRETHREN AND: in 1841, Brethren assemblies spread to, 8; 113-14; 118; 132; 171; early member includes EG, 171; in 1843, Scripture reading attended at, by PHG, is his introduction to, 3–9; 113; 337; profile of attendees, 118-19; PHG acquainted with 'open ministry' at, 420; activities of, 257; in 1843, EG, PHG meet at, 109 fn.53; 120; 167; 171 and fn.58; Habershon attends with PHG, 109; 120; during Brethren schism, W.T. Berger aligns with Open group, 161; in 1849, EG takes EWG to Room at, 174; 254; Room transferred to St. Thomas'

Rooms, then to Paragon Road, 254; in Jamaica, PHG remains in contact with Berger, Pearse, from Hackney, 124; 128; 129; 161; 337; lasting influence on PHG of friendships among, 507.

Haddon, Alfred Cort, zoologist:
 in 1880, sets up marine biological station at Torbay, 545 fn.49; early influenced by evolution, 597; in 1887, PHG lends sea anemone material to, 597; his *Revision* of sea anemones the first after PHG, 353; corresponds with PHG, 597 fn.391.

Haeckel, Ernst, biologist:
 Darwin's 'bulldog' in Germany, 511; 567; maintains original belief *Bathybius haeckelii* is living slime, even after Huxley changes his mind, 311, 568 fn.189; PHG surprised to be told that, like EWG, he writes for the 'heretical' *Academy*, 511 and fn.145; R. Lankester knows him, 565; in 1866, believes he found link between primates, humans, 567; in 1872, his Gastraea theory traces all life to amoeboid blobs of jelly, 568.

Haigh, John, clergyman:
 from the age of 21, Wesleyan minister in Newfoundland, 42; witness to 'Great Awakening' in Carbonear, 41-2; Apsey 'found peace' in his mission house, 43; PHG attends chapel of, 45.

Hake, William, early Brethren figure:
 associated with Soltau and Chapman, perhaps knew PHG, 212 and fn.289.

Hall, Anna Maria *née* Fielding, novelist:
 known as Mrs S.C. Hall, apparently attends PHG's marine natural history class at Ilfracombe, 233 fn.415; 234 fn.416.

Hall, Newman, preacher:
 in 1867, EWG attends speech of, 461.

Handbook to the Marine Aquarium (1855, 1856), by PHG:
 expansion of last chapter of *Aquarium,* an inexpensive guide, 213; 2eds, 3,000 copies, 223 and fn.357; well-received, 213 fn.292; PHG earned a profit of at least £189, 221; sold slowly, 223; advertised: 226 fns.372, 374; 238 fn.452.

Hannaford, Anne H. (sister of Mary Grace):
 member of Brethren Room in St. Marychurch prior to PHG's arrival there, 334; referred to in *Father and Son* under the pseudonym 'Burmington', 334 fn.7.

Hannaford, Mary Grace (sister of Anne):
 member of PHG assembly in Marychurch, writes to PHG, 370.

Hargrove, Charles Frearson, early Brethren leader:
 joined Brethren in 1835, 119; 'one of earliest I [PHG] knew among "brethren"', 119 fn.107; 338 fn.37; support for 'liberty of ministry' opposed by Darby, 119-20; in 1863, attends Trent Park meeting on prophecy, 401-2; in 1864, programme on the 'Sure Word of Prophecy', 403 fn.59; from 1868, connected with Tottenham Brethren, 453; EWG attends Scripture readings with, 459; dies at Robert Howard's home, 453 fn.81.

Harris, James Lampen, early Brethren leader:
 initially a follower of Darby, later with Open Brethren, 126 fn.143; on way to Jamaica, PHG reads his *On Worship,* 126; with PHG in 1865, a speaker on prophecy in London, 126 fn.143; 403; corresponds with PHG, 426 fn.164.

Harrison, Andrew John, historian:
PhD dissertation on Royal Society cited, 358; 360 fn.175; 361-2; 551 fn.89; 553 fn.104; 555; 558 fn.127; 559 fns.131-2.

Harrison, Samuel, of Poole:
in 1832 in Poole, promises to exchange insect specimens with PHG, 53; 60; PHG writes to from Newfoundland, about his conversion, 60.

Harrison, Slade & Co. (Poole):
in 1827, PHG sets off to Newfoundland counting-house of, paid £20 per annum, 31; in Carbonear, also known as Slade, Elson, & Co., q.v., 37 fn.21.

Haughton, Samuel, geologist:
in 1859, as president of Geological Society of Dublin, calls *Omphalos* a 'remarkable book which has given rise to much discussion', 301; though unconvinced by it, 302; rejects 'speculation of Messrs. Darwin and Wallace' as delivered at Linnean Soc. in 1858, 301-2.

Heap, George, Methodist preacher:
brother of Ann Jaques, q.v., took PHG to Wesleyan chapels in Liverpool, 97.

Hearn, Ebenezer, Alabama Methodist preacher:
first itinerant Methodist preacher in Pleasant Hill, may have persuaded PHG to serve as minister, 93-4; 93 fn.352.

Heath, Henry, early Brethren figure:
PHG knows in Hackney, 254; 453; around 1853, helps form Evangelical Tract Association, 257; 6 fn.12; EWG attends Scripture readings with, 459.

Heron-Allen, Edward (1861–1943), zoologist, polymath: xix fn.18.

Herpetology (amphibians and reptiles):
PHG 'Father of Jamaican Herpetology', xviii; 149; for a century, PHG recognized as a standout collector and investigator, 148; before PHG, herpetological studies in Jamaica were of little value, 138; Jamaican illustration by PHG published posthumously, 149 fn.310.

Hewitson, William C., entomologist:
purchases insects collected by PHG in Jamaica, 147 fn.295; PHG owns a copy of his *Exotic Butterflies*, 544 fn.42; opposed Darwin's theory, 548; PHG inquires of Van Voorst if Hewitson was 'a real *Christian*', 587 and fn.326.

Hibberd, Shirley, journalist and editor:
experiments with aquarium, 192 fn.173; in 1856, authors books on marine, fresh-water aquariums, 228; his *Rustic Adornments* is important for cultural historians, 230; an anti-Darwinian, 300 and fn.170; believed species divinely derived and immutable, 287 fn.86; recognizes PHG's scientific work, 297 fn.141; reviews *Omphalos*, 300.

'High Numbers of the Pentateuch' (1871), by PHG:
Victoria Institute paper deals with biblical criticism, 325 and fn.293; counters Thornton's paper, 327-8; pre-publication drama, 327; conflict within Institute on, 327-8; *Omphalos* and strategy of, 328; 310 and fn.216; argument of: 327-9; reception of: 329-30; off-prints of: 325 fn.293; sent to correspondents, 434 fn.221; 453 fn.82; in 1873 letter, EWG disagrees with conclusions of, 521.

Hill, Richard, naturalist:

Jamaica's first resident naturalist and ornithologist, 142; 137 fn.223; 142 fn.254; suggests derivation of 'Jamaica', 125 fn.136;
BIOGRAPHY: 142-3; 142 fn.255; active from at least 1833, 143; opinions on racial traits of, 136 fns.213–16; PHG not comment on, 136; last meeting of, with PHG, 146 and fn.281; after leaving Jamaica, PHG asks him to send orchids, 154 fn.340; 371; Darwin asks PHG for contact in West Indies to help with study of pigeons, is given name of, 538 fn.3; PHG AND: PHG's high opinion of, 143; 145; in Oct. 1845, PHG first corresponds with, 143; they meet in March 1846, 144; in Kingston, shows PHG scientific sites, 145; different scientific style from PHG, 143-4; the two complete a revised list of Jamaican birds, 145; 147; title pages of PHG's *Birds of Jamaica* and *Naturalist's Sojourn in Jamaica* state 'Assisted by Richard Hill', xxi fn.35; 573; PHG possibly shared views on prophecy with, 145 and fn.277; 399 fn.36; correspondence with PHG, 138 fn.228; 143 fns.260–2; 144 fns.263–5; PHG loses touch with, 537–8 and fn.3.

Historicism: *see* Prophecy.

History of Jamaica (1774), by Edward Long:
PHG reads before Jamaica trip, 124 fn.132; the 3vol. work includes a justification of slavery, 135 and fns. 208-9; it draws, without acknowledgement, from previous naturalists in Jamaica, 137 fn.222.

History of the Jews (1851), by PHG:
in 1846, PHG proposes that SPCK publish a work on, 165 and fn.24; in light of 'sure word of prophecy', 165; full version of book cited, 432 fn.205; PHG expected a sudden restoration of Jews to their homeland, in contrast to Darby's view, 432 fn.205; PHG associates Catholicism with anti-Semitism, 24 fn.35; 399; advertised, 215 fn.303; 225 fns.367–9.

'Hodman of science': Alleged description of PHG by Huxley, xx and fn. 30.

Home Friend (weekly, later monthly):
SPCK publication serialises PHG works: *Seaside Pleasures* (1852), 257 fn.86; *Letters from Alabama* (1855), 89; 243; quoted, 85; comparison of serial and book versions of, 95 fn.366; and *Wanderings through the Conservatories at Kew* (1855-6), 243.

Homoeopathists: *see* Batchelour; John Epps; Laseron; Tydeman.

Hooker, Joseph Dalton, botanist:
son of W.J. Hooker, 371; succeeds his father as director of Kew, 449 fn.60; possible source of expression 'an honest hodman of science', xx fn.30; DARWIN AND: in 1857 at the Royal Society, he and Darwin are said to have told PHG about Darwin's theory–an unlikely scenario, 292–4; 361 fn.180; Darwin views Hooker as key to gaining support among botanists, 376; but he does not commit to Darwin's theory until autumn 1858 (end of Sept. 1858, 294 fn.121), 294; 376 and fn.258; 449 fn.61; remaining publicly opposed to it until after 1859, 294; 373; writes 2 positive (and anonymous) reviews of Darwin's *Fertilisation of Orchids*, 376 and fn.261; in 1868 at British Association, addresses his known support for Darwin, 385;

DAWSON AND: Hooker a member of X Club, lead critic at Royal Society of Dawson, 364 and fn.198; 364 fn.200; 365 fn.202;
PHG AND: in 1857, corresponds with PHG, 280; warns PHG on difficulties of growing orchids in a hothouse, 371; in 1861, invites PHG to advance his status at Linnean Society by becoming a Fellow, 173 fn.68; 380 and fn.275; speculation on whether PHG knew his views on evolution, 449; 376 and fn.260; in 1865, PHG writes to, inquiring about a position for EWG at Kew, 449; in 1867, PHG contacts, thinking his research on embryology of orchids may challenge Darwin's theory, 377; at various times, PHG seeks expert advice of, 542 fn.31; 572 fn.219.

Hooker, William Jackson, Director of Kew Gardens: father of J.D. Hooker and distant cousin of PHG, 371; PHG introduced to, by Doubleday, 122; in 1862, visits PHG at Sandhurst, 371; his son succeeds him as director at Kew, 449 fn.60.

Horae Apocalypticae (1844), by E.B. Elliott: an 'instant classic' the 'high point of the historicist tradition', 429; written to refute futurism, 106 fn.38; identification of Rome with Antichrist, 271; PHG calls *Horae* 'beyond all praise as a guide to prophetic interpretation', 429; PHG owns copy of, 430 fn.191; EG an enthusiast for, 412; it was her penultimate book read, 271; in 1870, PHG corresponds with, 429-30; in 1884, abridged as *The Last Prophecy*, 430 and fn.195;
CRITIQUE OF: 1859 review of, in *The Times*, 396 fn.25; 397; undemocratic, 421; cited: 104 fn.35.

Howard, John Eliot, manufacturing chemist: older brother of Robert, 452; ex-Quaker, 118; 452; in 1833, founded Brethren meeting which he transferred to Brook Street, Tottenham, 118; in 1841, baptism officiant, 443 fn.22; in 1843, PHG knew among Brethren, 120; Pearse and, 7 fn.3; in 1849, excommunicated by Darby, 161; associates with Open Brethren, 338 fn.37; but denies it, 339 fn.42; PHG preferred him to brother Robert, 458; among signators to *Declaration of Students*, q.v., 383 fn.286; Vice-President, Victoria Institute, 308 fn.211; 326 fns.297; 300; at end of 1866, PHG introduces EWG to, 507; EWG attends Brook Street chapel of, 452; PHG content with EWG's being 'under the teaching' of Messrs. Howard, 465; PHG corresponds with, 308 fn.211; 426 fn.164.

Howard, Robert, businessman: younger brother of John Eliot, 452; in 1843, PHG knew among Brethren, 120; excommunicated by Darby, 161; associates with Open Brethren, 338 fn.37; 403 fn.59; in 1848, PHG, EG, married by, 172; 452; PHG preferred John Eliot to, 458; among signators to *Declaration of Students*, 383 fn.286; speaker at 'Sure Word of Prophecy' event, 403 fn.59; at end of 1866, PHG introduced EWG to, 507; in 1867-8, EWG visits home of, knows Theodore, son of, and attends Scripture readings with, 459-60; PHG content with EWG's being 'under the teaching' of Messrs. Howard, 465; in 1869, Hargrove dies at home of, 453 fn.81; buried at Abney Park Cemetery, 273 fn.195.

Howard, Theodore, missionary official:

son of Robert, EWG knew at Brook Street chapel, 460-1; Home Director, China Inland Mission, 461 and fn.129; superintendent, Brook Street Sunday school, 511; in 1851, J. Hudson Taylor meets, 462 fn.139.

Hubbert, James, botanist: in 1867, contacts PHG about bringing out Canadian ed. of *Canadian Naturalist*, 380 and fn.277; cited: 223 fn.358.

Hudson, Charles Thomas, microscopist:
BIOGRAPHY: nearly 3 decades as headmaster, 563; 1888, president, Royal Microscopical Society, in 1889 elected FRS, 573; 599;
PEDALION ROTIFER: in 1871, his scientific reputation as an 'able researcher' in Darwinian era, is linked to his discovery of 'remarkable' *Pedalion mirum* rotifer, q.v., a sensation, 563-70;
PHG AND: similarity in scientific approach to, 570-1; at least from 1870, they correspond, 570; about 1879, borrows PHG's Rotifera MSS, drawings, 570; in 1881, Hudson projects monograph on, 570; ROTIFERA MONOGRAPH: in 1854, Hudson first studies Rotifera, 563; in 1867, first publishes on, 563; in 1885, progress of monograph gains attention, 572; in 1886, appears in 6 parts and then 2 vols. + *Supplement* (1889), 573; 591; known as 'Hudson & Gosse', 573; appreciation of Ehrenberg, 179; the 'classic monograph', 180; PHG is assistant, 573; PHG's contribution, 573-4; calls PHG '*facile princeps*' among rotiferists, xix; 574;
SEE ALSO: Hudson & Gosse, *The Rotifera*.

Hudson & Gosse, *The Rotifera* (2 vols + supplement, 1886-9):
'classic monograph', 180; ushers in a new era in rotiferan studies, 573; worldwide praise for, 574-5; 576-9; 580; 'the rotiferist's "Bible"', 575; limitations of, 575-6; attitude of British scientific naturalists to, 578; the *Omphalos* factor, 307; explanation of their boycott of, 578-81.

Hueffer, Francis, assist. editor, *Academy*: in 1871, EWG meets, 506.

Humanity of the Son of God (1886), by PHG: pamphlet, PHG's last religious work, is a response to Bennet's attack on *Mysteries of God*, 593; rhetorical outlook of, 308.

Hume, William, missionary: in 1841, the earliest Baptist missionary in Jamaica, 134; affiliates with Brethren in 1846, almost certainly meets PHG then, 134; in contact from at least 1850s with Darby and Wigram, 153; Grimley accuses him of 'spirit of heresy', 154.

Hummingbirds: PHG plans to collect in Jamaica, 124; tries to domesticate them, 139; 140; admires *Trochilus polytmus*, 139.

Hunt, Arthur Roope, barrister: president, Torquay Natural History Soc., 584 fn.306; knew PHG for 30 years, 584; occasionally went dredging with him, 539-40 and fn.13; 584; in 1880, works to set-up marine biological station at Torbay, 545 fn.49; in 1882, PHG invites him to Scripture Reading meeting, but he declines, 584; after PHG's death, member of Victoria Institute, 584 fn.311; cited: 303 fn.188.

Huxley, Thomas Henry, man of science:
CAREER: 'Darwin's bulldog', a scientific institution-based naturalist, 189; agnostic, 552; newspaper sets him among 'the greatest minds the world
has produced', 197; the 'harsh truth' about earning
a living as a man of science, 219; by end of 1854,
earning £700 a year, in 1871, £1000, 463 fn.143;
writes for *Academy*, 511 and fn.145;
DAWSON AND: recommends Dawson for Royal
Society fellowship, 363; Dawson chastises British
Association address of, at Liverpool, 364;
PHG AND: EWG said he called PHG an 'honest hodman of science', xx and fn.30; EWG compares PHG
unfavourably to, 523 fn.187; THH praises PHG's
'Manducatory Organs' memoir, PHG praises his
research, 184 and fn.134; Rotifera are 'permanent
forms of Echinoderm larvae' with no connection to
radiates, 185; later open to PHG's view on Rotifers,
568; recommends PHG for Royal Society fellowship, 251; anonymous referee's report on PHG's
'Researches on the Poison-apparatus', q.v., states
it is 'hardly admissible into the [Royal Society's]
Philosophical Transactions', 358; explanation of
boycott of PHG's work, 360–2; in 1881, PHG asks
Huxley to 'bestow a brief glance' on his submission
to Royal Society on 'Clasping-organs', q.v., 550;
reason why Huxley may have favoured publication
in *Proceedings*, 551; unusual instance of rejection
of two referees' recommendations, 554; boycott
of PHG by Huxleyite scientific naturalists, 555;
HUXLEY AND HIS CONTEMPORARIES: critical of
Ehrenberg's research, 179 fn.98; disparages
Lewes, 232; Kingsley associates with, 304 and
fn.197; testy exchange with anti-Darwinian Morris,
386 fn.301;
ROYAL SOCIETY REFEREE'S REPORTS: on PHG (1858),
360; Bastian (1866), 362; 560 and fn.142;
SCIENCE ACTIVITY: in 1846, buys a microscope, 176;
in 1852, begins Royal Institution lectures, 234 and
fn.424; they include his own illustrations, 236 and
fn.438; praised as lecturer, 236; convinced origin
of life can be explained without a Creator, 311;
568 fn.189; his search for transitional forms, 567
and fn.185; believed life spontaneously arose from
inorganic matter he calls *Bathybius haeckelii*, 578;
human species evolved from state of barbarism,
315; importance of *Philosophical Transactions*,
357; appoints advocates of Darwin's theory to help
edit *Natural History Review*, 360 fn.176;
SEE ALSO: Busk; X Club.

Ibsen, Henrik, Norwegian poet and playwright:
EWG DISCOVERY OF: in 1871, EWG discovers *Digte*
(*Poems*) of, though he cannot read it, 502; EWG
brushes up on Dano-Norwegian, reviews *Digte* in
1872 for *Spectator*, first appearance of name of, in
Britain, 503; EWG has difficulty publishing further
articles on him, 503; 523 fn.188; Miss Buckham
suggests EWG not dwell so much on 'Mr. Gibson',
503; in Jan. 1873, another EWG paper on, appears
in the *Fortnightly Review*, 515;
PHG ATTITUDE TO: PHG explains his view on, in
letters to EWG, 516–19; rationalist outlook of
Ibsen, and others, opposed by PHG, 507; Ibsen

'an open unbeliever in Christianity', 516; EWG
continues writing on, 523, including a poem dedicated to, 525.

Ilfracombe (north coast of Devon):
for six months from April 1852 Gosse family is at,
and in communion with Brethren, 188; 277 fn.12;
337 fn.33; in Nov. 1852, returns to London from,
198; in Dec. 1852, transfers zoophytes to 'Fish
House' in Regent's Park, 198; PHG's love letters to
EG while he is at, 255; working at, George Robert
Lewis is among artists reflecting in their work the
new appreciation for the seashore, 218; Lewes'
Sea-side Studies at Ilfracombe, q.v., 231; Tugwell
of, publishes book on sea anemones, 340–1;
MARINE NATURAL HISTORY CLASSES AT: from July–
Sept. 1855, PHG holds first marine natural history
classes at, 213; 233–4; 233 fn.415; description of
classes, 235 fn.434; A.M. Hall attends, 233 and
fn.415; Shipton attends, 266.

Illustrations, designed or drawn by PHG:
his zoological colour illustrations 'among the finest of their kind ever produced', 207; he 'stands
alone and unrivalled in the extremely difficult art
of drawing objects of zoology so as to satisfy the
requirements of science', 351; 'to draw like Gosse
is no longer given to mortal man', 270;
BACKGROUND: T. Gosse (father) a miniature portrait painter, 15; at age 13, PHG's first attempt at
painting inspired by his father's miniaturist style,
26; PHG never studied art, 602; at age 17 before
reaching Newfoundland, 'found the power of stippling' (creating a half-tone affect), 36; at age 23 in
Newfoundland, draws insects, 57; around age 30,
contemplates trying to teach flower painting, 99;
around age 34, paints natural history objects on
way to, and in, Jamaica, also scenery, 149 fn.307;
BIRD ILLUSTRATIONS: *see* Birds; *Illustrations of the
Birds of Jamaica*, ([1848]-1849);
COLOUR (ZOOLOGICAL) ILLUSTRATIONS: *Devonshire
Coast* plates 'constitute in themselves a beautiful work of art', 199; *Aquarium* lithographs are
'exquisite', 206; 'the most beautiful applications of
chromolithography to natural history illustration
that we have seen', 206; *Tenby*: 'exquisite pictorial illustrations', 220; PHG drew the original art
directly on the stone for his coloured lithographed
works: *Illustrations of the Birds of Jamaica*,
149; *Naturalist's Sojourn*, 205; 220; works
using his original watercolours are *Aquarium*,
205-6; *Actinologia Britannica*, 350-1; 343 fn.72;
Devonshire Coast, 199; uses his coloured diagrams
at his lectures, 344;
ENTOMOLOGICAL ILLUSTRATIONS: drawings in
Entomologia Alabamensis ([1838]) 'remain
unmatched as the finest scientific illustrations of
invertebrates in the nineteenth century', 87 fn.304;
PHG considered his illustrations for *Entomologia
Terrae Novae* [?1836] 'in no wise inferior' to any
he later drew, 57; mimic tropical insects for Bell,
582; in 1880, prepares *Instructions* for butterfly
collectors, 'a sort of coup d'oeil of the arrangement
of Butterflies' for 9,500 species, 543 fn.35;
MICROSCOPIC ILLUSTRATIONS: 'The extreme minuteness, accuracy, and beauty of the drawings [of

Rotifera] have never been equalled in this particular department, and never exceeded in any line
of investigation', 574; Hudson & Gosse: *'le bel
ouvrage'*, 579; one of the 'beautifully illustrated
works' of the 19th century, 578; PHG's drawings
for 'Clasping-organs' called [c.1881] 'very beautiful', 554; also in 1979, 202 fn.234; illustrations for
Evenings at the Microscope drawn on the wood
'direct from the microscope', 345; at the end of his
life, 'his hand and eye were as perfect' in drawing
Rotifera as they had been years earlier, 574;
ORCHID ILLUSTRATIONS: contemplated 'large illus-
trated work' on Jamaican, 371 and fn.230; 372
fns.236–8; in 1865, declines invitation by Reeve
to author work on, 381;
SEE ALSO: Gosse, William.
Illustrations of the Birds of Jamaica: see *Birds of
Jamaica, Illustrations*.
Illustrators: *see* Basire; Dickes; Eliza Gosse; PHG;
Ray Lankester; Sowerby; West; Westwood;
Whymper.
Imperial Bible-Dictionary (1864–6), edited by
Patrick Fairbairn: PHG's 104 entries in, xvii; 416.
Independents (religious dissenters):
PHG raised as, 101; in Poole, Gosse family attends
T. Durant's meeting, 30; 21; at Blandford school,
PHG attends meeting of, 27; PHG reads Isaac
Watts in Newfoundland, 25; 40; briefly in Poole
in 1832, attends Durant meeting, 53; during years
in North America, PHG largely turns away from,
102; in 1839 in Liverpool, PHG fills in at local
meeting of, 98; in tradition of, reads in unfulfilled
prophecy, 102; married to Eliza in chapel of, 370;
in 1868, EWG attends church of, 465;
CONGREGATIONALISTS: often a synonym for, 30;
101 and fn.22; in 1835 in Newfoundland, editor
Winton attacked by Catholic gang, 65; PHG met
Congregationalist minister in Compton, Lower
Canada, 79; in USA, known for their educated
clergy, 94 fn.356; Leask, *Rainbow* editor, 408;
EWG hears preacher N. Hall, 461; Gwyther occa-
sionally preaches in PHG's place, 583 and fn.297;
Congregational Magazine praises *Canadian
Naturalist*, 100 fn.16; tract society of, 258.
Infusoria: *see* Rotifera.
Ingelow, Jean, poet:
EWG influenced by poetry of, 473; EWG received
encouragement from, 479; PHG and Eliza Gosse
read and admire poems of, 469; an imitation of
Pollak, q.v.; in 1869, EWG attends London garden
party of, 479; EWG later moves on from, 480.
Insects: *see* Entomology.
Introduction to Entomology (1815–26), by William
Kirby and William Spence:
'seminal' Victorian entomological text described,
51-2; reviewed, 50 fn.108; 51 fn.117; print run of,
224; compared to *Essays on the Microscope*, by
Adams, 52.

Jamaica:
during 1844–6, PHG is in Jamaica for 18 months,
129; 146; PHG known as 'Father of Ornithology',
'Father of Herpetology', Father of 'many other
aspects of Jamaica biology', xviii; 149; is 2nd

Brethren figure in Jamaica, 152–4; PHG sees
country as a hint of what the 'new earth' would
be like, 155;
CHRONOLOGY: in early 1844, Doubleday at British
Museum suggests PHG would benefit by becoming
a natural history collector, Jamaica is chosen, 124;
little then known about natural history of, 124;
136; PHG also on a spiritual mission to spread
Brethren ideas across the globe, 124; EWG's claim
that PHG did not associate with Brethren until
1847, refuted, 3 fn.1; 124 and fn.133; PHG leaves
for Jamaica in Oct. 1844, 125; on voyage to, PHG
communicates Brethren ideas, 126–7; uses latest
marine biology tools, 128; Dec. 1844, at Bluefields
Harbour, makes contact with Jamaica Brethren
De Leon and Forrest, 128-9; rents 2 rooms from
Coleman, q.v., at Bluefields, 129; and begins natural history collecting—entomology, herpetology,
fish, mammals, botany, ornithology, landshells,
etc., 138–42; meets R. Hill in March 1846, 144;
the 2 complete a revised list of Jamaican birds,
145; PHG returns to London in Aug. 1846, with
20 live birds, 146; 160;
RELIGIOUS LIFE IN: PHG spreads Brethren teaching across the world, extending his ties with the
movement from London, communing, evangelizing, teaching, preaching, baptizing, watching,
152–4; 337; in 1844 on reaching Jamaica, PHG
associates with Brethren in, 3 fn.1; corresponds
with W.T. Berger, Mary Berger, Pearse (Brethren
from London), qq.v., 118 fn.96; 452; on landing in
Jamaica, finds Jamaica Brethren leader Coleman,
q.v., not at Parker's Bay but Bluefields, where he
is seriously ill, 129; description of Coleman's
Brethren community, 132-3; PHG speaks to, 132;
PHG's religious activities centred at Content cottage and Phoenix Park, 133-4; in 1846, PHG meets
Tydeman, Hume, 134; encounters 'open ministry'
420; Darby, Wigram suspicious of PHG's theology, 132 fn.188; 412; PHG may have experienced
Brethren discord in, 161; 153–4;
SCIENTIFIC WORK: PHG's contribution to natural
history of, xviii; before leaving for Jamaica as free-
lance collector, 125 fn.141; 543; agrees to send
articles to *Entomologist, Zoologist*, 125; PHG
expects to find beautiful living objects, 136; 139;
considered generally, previous natural history
research there was random, problematic, unreliable, 136-7; botany and conchology were exceptions, 138; PHG's scientific activities centred in
Bluefields House, 133; PHG hires Sam Campbell,
17-year-old 'negro lad' as full-time paid assistant,
124-5; 340; PHG's first consignment is of orchids,
plants, seashore objects, 139; he contemplates an
illustrated work on orchids, 139; tries to domesticate hummingbirds, 139; PHG describes songs
of birds in, 82 fn.275; his collecting techniques
described, 139–41; 147; 150; becomes proficient
in using a gun, 142 and fn.253; from Aug. 1845,
focuses his collecting on ornithology, 142; PHG
bemoans selecting Cuming as London agent, 141;
meets Richard Hill, island's first resident naturalist and ornithologist, 144; 543; collects more
specimens in Jamaica than in Alabama, 147, 89;

PHG's collecting compared with Bates, Wallace, 147; PHG's income compared with Bates, 148; sells specimens, 161; British Museum selects Jamaican butterflies they want, and pays him 1*s*.6*d*. each, 543 fn.36; PHG's 'industry was amazing', 150; his work in Jamaica 'a scientific triumph', 148-9; 188; after leaving, maintains scientific interest in others' work there, 154 fn.340; in 1846, contemplates collecting trip to the Azores, 165; after return from, Doubleday, White, arrange for PHG to become Associate, Linnean Society, 173 fn.68; cited: 195; 238; 330;
WORKS: PHG's classic Jamaican studies, 146; 149-50; articles based on field studies in, 162; *Birds of Jamaica*: see separate entry; *Illustrations of the Birds of Jamaica*: see *Birds of Jamaica, Illustrations*; *Naturalist's Sojourn in Jamaica*: see separate entry.
SLAVERY IN: a slave country until 1838, when slavery was abolished in the British colonies, 135; Long's *History of Jamaica*, which PHG read, was a justification of slavery, 135; in Newfoundland in 1832, PHG aware of situation in Jamaica, 44; 135; PHG otherwise not known to have commented on the subject, or on the racial traits of those he knew, 135-6; cited: xxi and fn.35.

James, Henry, novelist:
like EWG, cremated at Golders Green, 609 and fns.56, 60.

Jaques, Ann *née* Heap (wife of G.E. Jaques):
married to Jaques in 1833, 47 fn.88; farms with PHG and husband in Compton, Eastern Townships, Lower Canada (Quebec), 67 and fns.200-1; daughter Alice born there, 67 fn.201; a difficult time for Ann, 71; after 1838, they leave Compton for nearby Cowansville, where in 1891 she dies, 67 fn.200; 78; in 1839 in Liverpool, brother George Heap and brother-in-law William Clarke help PHG, 97; S.R. Briggs (1839-87), a relative, publishes Toronto ed. of PHG's *Mysteries of God* (1884), 592 fn.367; remains long in touch with PHG, 78 fn.252.

Jaques, George Edward, businessman:
BACKGROUND: at end of 1832, dissolves Carbonear business partnership and starts mercantile business, 63 fn.178; PHG's Wesleyan friend, married in 1833, 47 fn.88; 58; part of PHG's religious circle, 47; PHG draws strength from, 507; around 1833, PHG joins the Methodist class in Carbonear, of, 58; 59; in 1834, as business is failing, 66 fn.190; Jaques hears 'very flaming accounts' of fertility of Lake Huron area, 63; discusses plans with PHG to move to Upper Canada, 65;
CANADA: with PHG, purchases farm near Compton village, they live in log house, 69; 67 fn.199; PHG rents a room from, 69 fn.210; depressed by unproductive, arduous, labour, 71; in Sept. 1836, divides common property with PHG, 72; Jaqueses not like Tom Gosse, who in 1837 comes to help, 73; with PHG, preached at Compton chapel (Methodist), 79; in March 1838, drives PHG to Burlington, Vermont, as PHG moves to USA, 78; they later leave Compton and move to Cowansville, 78; in

later years, remains in touch with PHG, 78 fn.252; 95 fn.365; 537; cited: 47 fn.86; 58 fn.149.

Jarman, G., engraver:
for PHG's *Lar sabellarum*, 560; for R. McLachlan's *Monographic Revision ... of Trichoptera*, 560 fn.138.

Jeffreys, J. Gwyn (1809-85), marine zoologist:
recommends PHG for Fellowship in Royal Society, 251 fn.49; PHG article on, cited: 367 fn.210; correspondence with, 367 fn.210.

Jews, Jewish:
ANTI-SEMITISM: PHG associates Catholicism with, 24 fn.35; 399;
CONVERTS TO CHRISTIANITY, 136 fn.212; Aaron De Leon, 129 fn.161; 136 fn.212; Laseron, 136 fn.212; 245-6; Lewin, 136 fn.212; 143 fn.259; Saphir, 459.
JEWISH-CHRISTIAN LINKS: in 1844, PHG reads Harris *On Worship*, 126; PHG seeks out Rabbi Nathan in St. Thomas, 146; Macaulay on Jewish civil rights, and prophecy, 393;
PROPHECY, JEWISH RETURN: Historicists see inextricable link of premillennial advent, return of Jews to their homeland, 106; only 6,000-years of human activity, 361-2 and 362 fn.75; Habershon's views on, related to architectural ideas, 108-9; influences PHG, 109; Croly's influence, 103; Baxter leaves MSS to Habershon on, 112 and fns.69, 71; PHG's *History of Jews* in light of 'sure word of prophecy', 165; PHG's view on, 432 fn.205; difference of PHG and Darby, 432 fn.205; dispensationalism and 'Jewish interpretation' of New Testament, 411, 414.
SEE ALSO: *History of the Jews.*

Johnson, Mary:
in 1868, EWG intends to become engaged to, 476-7; PHG counsels against acting 'rashly', 477; she becomes ill, 477; dies in 1870, 478; PHG consolation, 478; unknown if she figures in EWG's 'Tristram Jones', 476 fn.4; following the loss, Buckham suggests EWG needs a trip abroad, 496; it's funded by PHG, 497; cited: 491; 492; 496; 507.

Johnston, George, naturalist:
PHG calls him 'the father of our marine invertebrate zoology', 192; 187; 189; PHG names marine species after, 192 fn.174; PHG's comment on his *British Zoophytes*, 352 fn.130; PHG says he was first to achieve marine aquarium, 193 fn.178; 192; though he never wrote separately on subject, 197; as a lecturer, 234 and fn.423; illustrations for his work were by his wife, 236.

Jones, Thomas Rymer (1810-80), zoologist:
PHG uses his *General Outline of the Animal Kingdom*, 187; *Saturday Review* article on rise of aquarium movement by, 194-5; 213 fn.291; his *Aquarian Naturalist* (1858) successful, 230; it is illustrated by T. West, 562 fn.155; natural history lecturer, 234; uses the word 'aquariist', 277 fn.10; signator to *Declaration of Students*, q.v., 383 fn.286;
REVIEWS OF PHG BOOKS: lauds *Handbook to the Marine Aquarium*, 194-5 fn.185; 213fn.291; and *Manual of Marine Zoology*, 214.

'Jones, Tristram' (*c*.1872-3), by EWG:
unpublished autobiographical novel, 475 and fn.1;

Tristram a pseudonym for EWG, 475; the two compared, 476; observations from, likely autobiographical, 477-8; 479 fn.15; 487; 505.

Jukes, Joseph Beete, geologist:
a supporter of evolution, opposes praise for *Omphalos* in *Natural History Review*, 313, 315; like PHG, spent time in Newfoundland, 313 fn.3.

Kelly, William, prophetic writer and biblical commentator:
a Darbyite dispensationalist, PHG's critique of, 109 fn.54; 309 fn.213.

Kemp family:
relatives of PHG, 18; 20; George & James Kemp & Co. fishery merchants in Brigus and Carbonear, 34; 41; Apsey works at, 41; 43 fn.67; in 1837, counting-house closes, 34 fn.7; later Pack, Gosse, and Fryer, q.v., 42.

Kew, Royal Gardens:
PHG introduced to W.J. Hooker, Director of, by Doubleday, 122; J.D. Hooker, previously Assistant Director, succeeds his father, W.J. Hooker, 449 fn.60.
SEE ALSO: *Wanderings through the Conservatories at Kew.*

Kingsley, Charles, writer, clergyman:
BACKGROUND: interest in natural history dates to 1845, 230; in 1853, writes PHG and offers to collect marine specimens for him, 201; 230; in 1854, meets PHG at Linnean Society 212 fn.284; dredging with PHG, 343; gives natural history lessons to one of the Prince Consort's sons, 278 fn.18; by 1870, briefly loses contact with PHG, 538; *GLAUCUS*: CK writes, after reviewing in 1854 PHG seashore books, 211; theme of, 230-1; sends PHG a copy of, 231 fn.405; promotes PHG's marine natural history classes in, 213 fn.290; illustration in, compared to PHG's, 221; income from 5 eds of, compared to PHG's, 222 and fn.346; print run for, compared to PHG's books, 224;
OMPHALOS: expresses private disappointment to PHG on, 303-4; commits not to review, but notes his opinion in *Glaucus*, 304; aligns with 'young guard of science', 304;
PHG, EWG, AND: in 1865, PHG seeks his help to find EWG a job, 448-9; CK introduces EWG to British Museum librarian, 450; introduces EWG to Macmillan publisher, 497 fn.68; in 1872, PHG seeks his help to find EWG a job, 506-7; in 1874, EWG seeks CK's help in finding a job, 529; CK's poetry influences EWG, 450; PHG's criticism of CK's writing, 468 and fn.157.

Kinns, Samuel, author:
in a reply to an advance copy of *Moses and Geology* (1882), PHG writes him about Federal Headship, sends him *Geology or God*, 317 fn.254; in *Harmony of the Bible with Science*, he prints names of *Declaration of Students*, q.v., 382 fn.284.

Kirby, William, entomologist:
early entomological study of Canada, 75; co-author of *Introduction to Entomology*, q.v., which boosted prestige of entomology, 52.

Knowledge (weekly), edited by R. Proctor, q.v.:
London rival to *Nature*, 578; PHG sends correspondents copies of, though it's 'tainted with the godlessness of all science', 578 fn.268; favourably reviews Hudson & Gosse, 574 fns.235, 239; 575 fn.241; 4 notices of, 578.

Land and Sea (1865), by PHG:
collection of 1853–63 PHG articles, 378; mostly favourable reviews, 378 fn.270; advertised, 581 fn.286; unfamiliarity with bibliographic history of, leads to misdating of Devon shore devastation, 368 fn.212; cited: 378.

Lankester, Edwin, naturalist:
father of R. Lankester, co-editor of *Quarterly Journal of Microscopical Science*, 565 fn.168; in late 1840s, PHG attracts attention of, 162; PHG visits home of, 552; comment on Ehrenberg's research, 179 fn.96; in 1857, most naturalists viewed species as divinely derived, 287; favours earth's long chronology, 289 fn.90;
AQUARIUM RESEARCH: in 1849, undertakes experiments with aquarium, 192 fn.173, but credits N.B. Ward as fresh and marine aquarium introducer, 193 fn.179;
BOOKS BY: *Aquavivarium* (1856) highly regarded, 228; 192 fn.173; confusion about authorship of *Half-Hours with the Microscope* (1859), 346 and fn.90; its sales, 346 fn.90; illustrated by T. West, 346 fn.90; 562 fn.155;
LECTURES BY: an early natural history lecturer, 234, his talks were illustrated, 236 fn.438, and he received 5 guineas per lecture, 235; 1855 Birmingham lecture by, 159 fn.96; 234 fn.425;
PRESS ACTIVITY: writes for *Athenaeum*, 198 fn.211; 199 fn.213; 208 fn.264; 227 fn.381; 287 fn.86; favourably reviews Miller's *Testimony of the Rocks*, 296 fn.136;
REVIEWS OF PHG BOOKS: favourably reviews PHG's *Naturalist's Sojourn*, 162 fn.11; *Naturalist's Rambles*, 199 fn.213; *Aquarium*, 206 fn.255; unfavourably reviews *Omphalos*, 296 fn.136; 299 and fn.159.

Lankester, Ray, zoologist:
born Edwin Ray, called 'Ray', son of Edwin Lankester; 'best-known proponent' of Darwin in post-Huxley era, 'the greatest morphologist' of his day, 552; an accomplished scientific illustrator, 207;
GOSSE CONNECTION: PHG calls him 'one of our ablest zootomists', 552; met PHG as a child, 552; was unusual as a Darwinian for his outspoken public admiration for him, 552 and fn.99; calls PHG 'a great naturalist', 552 fn.99; EWG dedicates *Life of Philip Henry Gosse* to him, 552 fn.93; said to visit PHG in 1881, 547 fn.58, and to have encouraged PHG to undertake 'Clasping-organs' research, 547 fn.58; 552 fn.93; PHG hopes Lankester will be referee for 'Clasping-organs' submission to Royal Society, enlists EWG's help, 552; he recommends PHG's paper for *Philosophical Transactions*, 553; urges excision of PHG's reference to theological issues, 556, to which PHG reputedly agrees, 561 and fn.143; admires PHG's illustrations and uses ones from PHG's *Aquarium*, 207, and *Manual*

of Marine Zoology, 214 fn.302; attends EWG's funeral, 552 fn.99; Lankester's remains cremated, 609-10;

MISSING LINKS: hails Hudson's discovery of the 'astonishing' rotifer, *Pedalion*, 565; 568; which seemed to provide a missing link in the animal kingdom, 566–8, meaning support for Darwin's theory, 566; morphological significance of *Pedalion* exaggerated, 569 fn.201; conviction of, that the lower jawbone of a creature found in 1915 at Piltdown is 'a real "missing link"' between apes, humans, 570;

PERIODICAL ACTIVITY: co-editor, *Quarterly Journal of Microscopical Science*, 565 and fn.168; writes for *Academy*, 552; *Nature*, 562 fn.150;

SCIENTIFIC CAREER: an effort to establish a 'tree of evolutionary relationships', 569; in that regard, he creates the phylum Appendiculata, 569.

Lar sabellarum, Gosse (microscopic aquatic animal):
PHG's Linnean Soc. paper is 'one of his most enchanting', though its accuracy is viewed with 'polite suspicion' for 15 years, 359 and fn.167; PHG calls Jarman's engraved figures 'very nice', 560 and fn.138.

Laseron, Michael M.A.H., physician:
confused with Edward Laseron, 245 fn.6; examined EG's cancer, 246; Jewish convert to Christianity, 136 fn.212; 246; associated with Open Brethren, 338 fn.37; compared to Müller, 245 fn.6; buried at Abney Park cemetery, 273 fn.195.

Lavers, William, solicitor:
president, Torquay District Gardeners' Association; in 1887, delivers exotic tropical plant to PHG, 584-5.

Leask, William, clergyman:
Congregationalist, founder, editor of *The Rainbow*, 401; attends Trent Park Conference (1863) on prophecy, 401; supports Darby's prophetic views, 408.

Lectures, Public:
BACKGROUND: reason why public lecturing became respectable in 1850s Britain, 234-5; 233 fn.414; around 1850, voluntary movement to improve adult education in Britain, 235; innovations in shorthand provide newspaper summaries, 238; PHG not alone as public natural history lecturer, 234; comparatively low pay for science lecturing, 234-5; competition from Thackeray, Lola Montez, 237 and fn.447; appeal of lecturing to PHG: economic, 238; scientific (field research), 238; ideological (promote design argument), 239; MARINE ZOOLOGY: PHG's lecturing skills unusual, though not unique, 234; PHG's experience as educator, 233; his artistic skills and knowledge of marine zoology, 236; 278; 344; from July 1855-Feb. 1861, PHG delivers at least 28 public natural history lectures at 19 venues in England, Scotland, Wales, 236-7; 233 fn.414; 277-80; 343 and fn.73; 344 fn.74; speaks at mechanics' institute, literary and philosophical societies, on marine zoology and aquarium, 237; well-received, 237; 278-9; 344; unanswered questions about, 277 fn.12; 1857 whirlwind tour by PHG, 280; his lecture themes,

238-40; 381-2; explanation for PHG's brief career, 237-8; 240-1; claim that PHG gave private lessons to Royal children, 278 fn.18;

PROPHECY: in 1856, PHG lectures on, in: Tenby, 399 fn.36; 1864: London, 'Week of Prayer', 402-3; 'Sure Word of Prophecy', 403; 315; 382; 1870: Teignmouth, 418 and fn.1267; lectures by others, 403 fn.61;

RELIGION: PHG lectures on, in 1865: Torquay, 399 fn.36; 1869: St. Marychurch-area, 418; SEE ALSO: Marine Natural History Classes.

Leeuwenhoek, Antoni van, microscopist:
in 1676, pathbreaking work on Rotifera, 177 and fn.89; 573; assigned a role in the invention of the aquarium, 209.

Leidy, Joseph, palaeontologist:
in 1885, meets EWG and sends greetings to PHG, 307 and fn.207.

Leifchild, John Roby, clergyman:
reviewer of science books for *Athenaeum:*
REVIEWS OF DARWIN: *Origin of Species*, 547 and fn.56; *Descent of Man*, 347 fn.94;
REVIEWS OF PHG (generally unfavourable): *Aquarium*, 351 fn.124; *Letters from Alabama*, 347 fn.94; *Romance of Natural History*, 378 fn.266; 2nd series, 324 fn.283; *Year at the Shore*, 378 fn.270.

Lepidoptera (butterflies):
NEWFOUNDLAND: from Newfoundland days, butterflies were PHG's 'first love' in natural history, 11; in 1832, inspired to collect 'the more handsome' ones, 49; 57 fn.141; black swallowtail his first 'cabinet' specimen, 60; PHG's is first record of island's, 55; not published until 1883, 55 fn.132; carries specimens to Canada, 65;

CANADA: PHG attracted by 'profusion of fine butterflies' at Compton farm, 69; submits paper on, to Natural History Society of Montreal, 72 fn.220; in 1840, 26 described in PHG's *Canadian Naturalist*, 76 (index to, by Scudder, 76 fns.238, 240); in 1841, *Entomologist* article on, 72 fn.220; 100 and fn.17;

ALABAMA: *Letters from Alabama* full of 'original observations' on butterflies, 76 fn.240; *Entomologia Alabamensis* includes illustrations of, 87 and fns.301–4;

JAMAICA: before leaving for, PHG reads up on, 124; expects to find forests filled with beautiful butterflies, 136; 139; PHG is third of island's collectors of, but he had 'superb powers of observation', 148; British Museum buys from him only ones it wanted, 543 fn.36; urchin's offer of 'bats', 140; 'unparalleled' description of flight patterns of various butterfly species in, 148; 55; first to describe larva, 541 fn.21;

BRITAIN: in 1832, at Poole, PHG collects, 52-3; in 1843, he sees Table Cases at British Museum with numerous species of, 10;

ST. MARYCHURCH: in 1860, EWG's work on, 440; from 1879, PHG absorbed with research on, 541; from early 1880s, PHG buys specimens from around the world, 541-2; publishes on, 541 fn.22; focuses on 'Clasping-organs' of males, q.v., 546; 556-7;

ILLUSTRATIONS BY: 13 butterflies depicted in PHG's

Entomologia Terrae Novae, 57 and fn.144; 38 Lepidoptera depicted in *Entomologia Alabamensis*, 87 fn.303; 'mimics in cardboard', 582; 543 fn.35; SEE ALSO: Bates; 'Clasping-organs'; '*Papilio homerus*'.

Letters from Alabama (1859), by PHG:
INFLUENCE OF: work is 'unparalleled in its detailed evocations of the natural history and cultural conditions' of the state, 89-90; 'an Alabama classic', xviii; 90; Alabamian social customs, language, described in, 87 and fn.306; 89; ethno-musical record in, 94;
PUBLICATION RECORD: at end of 1854, book offered to SPCK but rejected, 89; then serialised in 1855 in SPCK's *Home Friend*, 89; 85 fn.289; 243; in 1859, published by Morgan and Chase, 89; serial and published versions compared, 95 fn.366;
REVIEWS, ADVERTISING, OF: favourably reviewed in Britain, 347 and fn.94; 88 fn.314; barely noticed or advertised in USA, 347 fn.95; advertised, 226 fn.373; 238 fn.452;
SCIENTIFIC RESEARCH IN: full of 'original observations' on butterflies, 76 fn.240; and insects, 89; some research published in *Zoologist*, 86 fn.295; nature description in, 89-90; PHG's natural history collecting enumerated, 89; Darwin had copy of, probably a gift from PHG, 321 fn.266;
SLAVERY: comparison of comments on, in serial and book form, 95 fn.366; *Literary Gazette* says PHG showed 'sound discretion' in not writing extensively on, in *Letters from Alabama*, 88 fn.314;
SEE ALSO: Alabama (slavery); Slavery.

Lewes, George Henry, philosopher, writer:
in 1856, first uses microscope, 366 fn.208; disparaged by Huxley as a mere 'book scientist', 232; GHL commends Lloyd's aquarium business, 197 fn.201;
PRESS REVIEWS BY: in *Blackwood's Magazine* (PHG, *Actinologia Britannica*, 350 fn.121; PHG, *Romance* 2ed., 324 fn.283; 378 fn.266); *Leader* (Tugwell, *Manual*, 341 fn.55); *Saturday Review* (Tugwell, *Manual*, 341 fn.55);
SEE ALSO: *Sea-Side Studies*.

Lewin, J. L., of Jamaica:
PHG apparently unaware of religious background of, 136 fn.212; Lewin a Jewish convert to Christianity, 143 fn.259; and acquaintance of R. Hill, 143 and fns.259-60.

'Liberty of ministry':
or 'open' ministry (at the communion table), a source of contention for Brethren, 419-20; Brethren reject ordained ministry and rally around 'open communion and liberty of ministry', 126 and fn.144; PHG questioned its validity, 420; asserts deduction from 1 Cor. xiv is 'utterly worthless', 423; rejects 'undemocratic' claim, 421; in 1857 move to St. Marychurch, PHG assumes leadership at 'Church of God', 422; in 1868, PHG's role is challenged, 423-4;
SEE ALSO: Darby; Hargrove; B.W. Newton.

Life in its Lower, Intermediate and Higher Forms (1857), by PHG:
PHG's 4th and last general natural history survey, 201; 3rd most-reviewed PHG book in USA, 211 fn.277; serialized in *Excelsior* (1853-6), q.v., 201

fn.224; book appeared in Jan. 1857, 278 fn.18; just before EG died, and just as he was beginning to lecture, 278; percent devoted to Rotifera and other radiates in, compared with other PHG books, 186; favourable reviews of, 278 fn.18; 346 fn.86; cats described in, 616fn.4; 622 fn.18.

Life of Philip Henry Gosse (1890), by EWG:
conventional Victorian biography, xxii; but unreliable, xxii and fn.44; EWG lacks sympathy for PHG's religious views, acquaintance with his scientific studies, 545 fn.51; EWG contradicts PHG's claim that he first associated with Brethren in 1843, 3 fn.1; 124 fn.133; adds new detail on *Omphalos* in, 292; title change in 1896 re-issue reflects EWG's memory of, 606 fn.45; cited: *passim*.

Lindroth, Carl H., entomologist:
on Newfoundland entomology, xvii fn.6; 55 fn.133.

Linnaeus, Carol, botanist, taxonomist:
in Newfoundland, PHG uses his *Systema Naturae*, 55; 10th ed. (1758) of, lists only 10 microscopic animals, 189; PHG follows definition of species as 'distinct forms', 287; PHG critical of Linnean nomenclature, 349 fn.115; places Ehrenberg alongside of, 179 fn.98.

Linnean Society of London:
Thomas Bell, president of, is PHG cousin, 98; 582; in 1849, PHG elected Associate of, at initiative of White and Doubleday, 173 and fn.68; his additional supporters, 173 fns.67-8; 196; in 1850, PHG's Rotifera drawings shown at meeting of, 185 fn.139; Kingsley meets PHG at 1854 meeting of, 212 fn.284; PHG reads paper on *Peachia hastata* at 1855 meeting of, 212 fn.284; in 1858, Darwin-Wallace presentation at, 293 fn.119; 294 fn.121; 301-2; in 1861, PHG declines J.D. Hooker's invitation to become a Fellow, 173 fn.68; 380 and fn.275; paper by Bastian published by, after being rejected by Royal Society, 362; Bates's ideas on butterfly mimicry presented at, 586 and fn.321;
'CLASPING-ORGANS' OF LEPIDOPTERA: *see separate entry*;
TRANSACTIONS: PHG's 3 articles in: 'Description of *Peachia hastata*' (1855), 352 fn.131; 356 fn.156; 'On a new form of corynoid polypes [*Lar sabellarum*, q.v.] (1857), 359; 'Clasping-organs', q.v. (1883), 202 fn.234; 546 and fn.54; 557-9; offprints of still available in PHG's library at his death, 559 fn.133.

Literary and Historical Society of Quebec:
founded 1824, 72; in mid-1835, PHG visits, 69; meets members of, sends them duplicate insects collected, 70; in 1836, elected Corr. Member of, sends papers to, 72 and fn.220; PHG uses designation, 99.

Literary Gazette (weekly):
in 1855, suggests cheap excursion trains will aid attendance at PHG's marine natural history classes, 190 fn.162; on PHG's marine natural history classes, 213 fn.290; 234 fn.416; on aquaromania, 226-7; on proliferation of aquarium books, 227; ads for PHG books, 226 fn.371; on Gnoll College, 283 fn.60; 284 fn.60; on species multiplication, 351-2;

REVIEWS IN, BY PHG: for a time, PHG writes for, 344 and fn.79; analysis of 1858 review by PHG of *Sea-Side Studies*, 354 fn.148;

REVIEWS OF PHG WORKS, IN: *Canadian Naturalist*, 100 fn.16; *Glimpses of the Wonderful*, 123 fn.126; *Birds of Jamaica*, 163 fn.13; *Popular British Ornithology*, 166 fn.31; *Naturalist's Sojourn in Jamaica*, 151 fn.324; 163 fns.11, 13; *Text-book of Zoology*, 166; *Naturalist's Rambles on the Devonshire Coast*, 199 fns.213–15; *Manual of Marine Zoology*, 214 fn.297; *Life in its Lower, Intermediate, and Higher Forms*, 278 fn.20; *Omphalos*, 296 fn.136; 297 fn.144; 299; *Letters from Alabama*, 88 fn.314; 347 fn.94; *Actinologia Britannica*, xix fn.20; 350-1; 350 fn.122; 351 fn.124; 360 fn.172; *Evenings at the Microscope*, 345 fn.80; 346-7; 347 fn.93; *Romance of Natural History* (2nd series), 306 fn.200; 324 fn.283.

Lloyd, William Alford, aquarium entrepreneur: conflicting biographical details, 227 fn.378; AQUARIUM BUSINESS: best known of aquarium dealers, PHG provided stock for, 227; 344; he twice needs to expand his premises, 344; had not seen the sea before he became interested in aquarium, 197; his first marine specimen collecting, in 1876, was with PHG, 197; Warehouse, 227; 344; AQUARIUM MOVEMENT: gives span as 1853–62, high-water mark of aquaromania 1854–60, 241 fn.472; 242; in 1853, carried out aquarium experiments, 192 fn.173; credits Ward and Thynne as 2 earliest aquarium researchers, 193 fn.179; in 1863, under guidance of, world's largest aquarium built in Germany, 211; LLOYD AND PHG: calls PHG 'Father of the Aquarium', xviii; 194 fn.183; in 1871, hangs PHG's portrait in his office at Crystal Palace Aquarium, 196; privately, was critical of PHG's ability to maintain an aquarium, 196 fn.192; however confirms PHG's sea-water formula, 201 fn.231; affirms PHG's priority in use of word 'aquarium', 208 fn.264; PHG asks permission of, for engraver Dickes to study sea anemones in his aquaria, 342; in 1876, assists PHG at Sandhurst in constructing 49-gallon aquarium, 540; corresponds with PHG, 227; 280; 333 fn.4; 342 fns.62, 64; 344 fn.78; 367 fn.211; 540 fn.14; WORKS BY, CITED: *Guide Book to the Marine Aquarium* (1872), 200 fn.221; 241 fn.472; *List ... of Whatever Relates to Aquaria* (1858), 227; *Official Handbook to the Royal Aquarium*, 192 fn.173.

Lockyer, Norman, founder, editor of *Nature*: Kingsley a friend of, 304 and fn.197; amongst 'elite of the Victorian scientific world', their goal was to establish 'agnostic naturalism', 580-1.

Loddiges, George, nurseryman: PHG introduces himself to, a fellow Wesleyan, 99 and fn.12; 99; PHG present at a 'nocturnal soiree' of a tropical orchid at store of, 100 fn.14; apparently a relative of EG, 120; purchases from PHG Jamaica consignments, 147 fn.293.

London Quarterly Review: in 1858, name changed to *London Review*, 298 fn.146; PHG transformed 'almost universally neglected' field of marine zoology, xviii fn.14;

examination of articles attributed to PHG, in, 277 fn.10; articles attributed to PHG cited: 223 fn.354; 227 fn.380 and 230 fn.399.

London Review: see *London Quarterly Review*.

Long, Edward: *see History of Jamaica*.

Lower Canada (Quebec): *see* Canada.

Lubbock, John, naturalist: referee's report by PHG for Royal Society, 360 fn.171; X Club member, raised possibility of human species evolving, 315; 386; his *Pre-Historic Times* is target of anti-Darwinians, 386 and fns.297-8; 386 fn.302; cited: 299 fn.163.

Lush, William F., counting-house clerk: aged 18, PHG convinces him to 'yield to God', 47; but he later 'relapsed', 48; 61 fn.166; in Canada, PHG hears of his positive religious life, 79-80; by 1838, moves to Philadelphia, 67 and fn.198; PHG writes to, about opportunities there, 78; works as clerk at American Colonization Society, 80 and fn.260; PHG stays with, passing through Philadelphia, 80; significance of his speech defect, 80 fn.260; with PHG, attends Dutch Reformed Church, 81; PHG draws strength from, 507.

Lyell, Charles, geologist: uniformitarian geology of, leads to conclusion that earth is more than 6,000 years old, 288; 294; 323; geologists were most receptive to generalizing theory concerning historical causes, 373; among greatest minds, 197; EWG claims that in the summer of 1857, at the suggestion of, select naturalists (including PHG) were given preview of Darwin's theory, 293 and fn.117; Lyell among those who raised possibility that humans evolved, 315; PHG claims 'not a tittle of proof' supports uniformitarian view, 323; 386 fn.297; visiting antebellum South, Lyell did not find slavery objectionable, 88 and fn.308; visits aquarium at Regent's Park Zoo, 211; in 1862, among those who propose J.W. Dawson as Fellow of Royal Society, 363; cited: 365 fn.202.

Macaulay, Thomas Babington, politician: in speech and writing, cites Christian belief in second coming, 393 and fns.8–10; photographic portrait of, by Maull and Polyblank, 275.

Macfadyen, James, Glasgow-born botanist: early researcher in Jamaica, 137 fn.223; PHG reads his *Flora of Jamaica*, 124 fn.132; in 1846, PHG meets in Jamaica, 144.

Mais, J. Leslie, clergyman: Anglican minister, 2 sons collect insects for PHG in Jamaica in 1880, 541-2; 542 fn.26; PHG sends observations on insects by, for publication by Entomological Society of London, 490 and fn.91.

'Manducatory Organs in the Class Rotifera', by PHG: PHG memoir published in Royal Society *Philosophical Transactions*, 184; the first to examine the biting apparatus of Rotifera, it is illustrated by his own drawings and considered among his best scientific studies, 184; 250; 359-60; he argues for the affinity of Rotifera to insects, 183-4; praised by Carpenter, 184-5; de Beauchamp, 185, 360; Huxley, 184, 360.

Manual of Marine Zoology (2 parts, 1855-6), by PHG:

a groundbreaking list of British marine animals, illustrated by the author, 213-14; published on an author's-risk basis, 2,000 copies printed, 223; at cost of £318, 296 fn.135; yields £251 profit, 221; sells slowly, 223; positive reviews of, 214 and fn.297; 213 fn.293; 300; advertised in the press: 226 fns.371-2, 374; woodcuts reprinted by R. Lankester, 214 fn.302; marine natural history classes advertised in, 243 fn.484.

Marine Natural History Classes:
novelty of marine classes, 234; PHG's *Manual of Marine Zoology* (1855-6) 'indispensable to the sea-side visitor', 214; claimed facilitation of, by railways, 190 fn.162; complaint about cost of, 235 fn.434;
ILFRACOMBE: in July 1855, PHG began lecture career with out-of-doors marine natural history classes for men and women at, 233; 213; general description of, 235 fn.434; advertising and promotion for, 213 fn.290; 234 fn.416; Kingsley's effort, 213 fn.290; praised by Mrs Hall, 233 fn.415; Shipton and 2 women attend, 234 fn.416;
TENBY: 2nd classes in Sept. 1856, at Tenby, 234 and fn.418; 216; 243; lectures described, 234 and fn.416; *Tenby Observer* remarks on 'enthusiastic' attendees, 197; on PHG as the 'hero' who drew 'a circle of admirers of nature's charms', 243-4; 196-7; classes well-publicized, 234 fn.416; 243 fn.484; PHG's books advertised for sale during, 238 and fn.451.

Marine zoology:
BACKGROUND: in 1852, zoophytes just beginning to gain attention among naturalists, 339; PHG praises Bowerbank for expertise in, 121;
PHG'S ROLE: PHG transformed 'almost universally neglected field of', into 'the most popular', xviii; other factors promoting, 189-90; invention of the aquarium, 191; PHG's knowledge of, unequalled, 213; 200; 'no keener observer of marine organisms ever lived', xix; 233; 196; 'in acquaintance with marine animals he is excelled by no one', 203; his colour illustrations 'among the finest of their kind ever produced', 207; 'to draw like Gosse is no longer given to mortal man', 270; PHG's *Manual of Marine Zoology* a groundbreaking, comprehensive work, 213; 296 fn.135; in 1856, PHG recognized for his contributions to microscopic zoology, 251; 1855-61, PHG lectures on, in London, provinces, Scotland, 160; 280; though popular, are no match for Thackeray or Lola Montez, 237; SEE ALSO: Lectures, Public.

Marston, Philip Bourke, poet:
minor Pre-Raphaelite poet, EWG meets, 506; sister marries O'Shaughnessy, 506; objects to religious funeral rites and is buried in 'unconsecrated ground', 609 fn.60; 507.

Marzials, Théophile-Jules-Henri, poet:
biography, 482 and fn.27; 483; friend of EWG, works at British Museum, 481; attached to Parnassianism, 482; alleged homosexual relationship with EWG, 481-2; 482 fns.27, 29; a freethinker, 507; author of *Passionate Dowsabella* and *Gallery of Pigeons* (both 1873), 483 and fns. 34-5.

Mayhew, Henry, investigative journalist:
on tract distribution, 261, 259; his *London Labour and the London Poor*, cited: 257 fn.90; 259 fn.99; 289 fn. 116.

Max Müller, Friedrich, Orientalist:
PHG writes to, about Rig-Veda, 426-7; views of, and communications from, occasionally aired at Victoria Institute, 427 fn.168; other correspondence: 405; cited: 405 fn.63.

McCann, James, clergyman:
at British Association, objections to Darwin, 386; member, Victoria Institute, 386 fn.302.

McLachlan, Robert, entomologist:
'among the most prominent' of London entomologists of the time, 554; supporter of evolutionary theory, 549; 557; elected Fellow of the Royal Society, 1877, 553;
PHG AND: PHG corresponds with, 552 fn.93; 553; 560; selected as referee for PHG's 'Clasping-organs' paper, q.v., 553; he recommends publication in Royal Society's *Philosophical Transactions*, calling PHG's drawings 'very beautiful', 554; suggests Salvin as a 3rd referee, 554; keeps PHG informed of deliberations, 558; 560; urges excision of PHG's remarks on Darwin's theory, 556-7.

Meldola, Raphael, entomologist:
Darwin's 'entomological bulldog', 549 and fn.73; as Entomological Soc. secretary, corresponds with PHG, 551 fn.91.

Melly, Andrew, insect collector:
in 1839, PHG shows *Entomologia Terrae Novae* to, 57 fn.144; and sells him his insect collection, 95; PHG sells him entomological specimens from Jamaica, 147 fn.295.

Memorial of the Last Days on Earth of Emily Gosse (1857), by PHG:
'a harrowing narrative of useless torture', 269; rarest of all PHG's books, 281 and fn.43; used in Shipton's *'Tell Jesus.'* and without attribution in EWG's *Father and Son*, 282 fn.49; when written, 281; 292 fn.110; its literary character, 281-2; purpose of, 282; comparison of, to PHG's 'Fairy', 615-16; EWG familiar with *Memorial*, 528 fn.216; PHG occasionally sends copy of, to correspondents, 544.

Melicerta ringens, a Rotifer:
PHG's first Rotifera article, read Jan. 1850 (published Mar. 1851), 176 and fn.83; he is the first to describe how it builds its surrounding tube, not given in greater detail for 100 years, 182-3; today called *Floscularia ringens* (Linnaeus, 1758).

Menneer, Nicholas T., school proprietor:
operates Montvidere day school in St. Marychurch, 444-5; in 1860, EWG enrolled in, 444; PHG's high opinion of, 445-6; critique of, 446; referred to in *Father and Son* as 'Mr. M.', 444 fn.26; name frequently misspelled 'Meneer', 398 fn.26.

Methodism, Methodists:
at the heart and backbone of Evangelical movement, 102; Thomas Gosse (father) attends Whitefield's chapel, 17; different characteristics of, in Newfoundland, Canada, Alabama, 92; 68; in North America, PHG mainly turned from Independents, Anglicans to, 102;
NEWFOUNDLAND: from 1830-2, a 'Great Awakening'

in Carbonear, 41; from nominal church-attending to 'experience and passion', 42; Apsey, a counting-house clerk, ignites the revival, 41; 1830, PHG's religious outlook confused, not inclined to Methodism but contemplates the ministry, 40; Tocque belongs, 47 fn.84; in 1838, Sprague, 47 fn.89; who is 'a passionate Methodist', 61 and fn.165; PHG joins Methodist class of Apsey, 56-7; CANADA: in Compton, occasional Sunday services, 79 and fn.253;
ALABAMA: in 1838, PHG apparently considers serving as a minister in, 92–4; attends Fourth Quarterly Meeting at Selma, 93-4; confident of a position in England as travelling preacher, 92; ENGLAND: in 1839 in Liverpool, PHG aided by Heap, preacher, 97; mourns over 'degeneracy of Methodism', 97; worships at Methodist chapel, serves as a local preacher, but too old for regular Methodist ministry, 98; but serves as a Class-Leader, 100; 'my crude theology', 100 fn.15; in 1843 at Hackney, acquainted with Samuel Berger, Jr., a Class-leader, 8; 112-13; he introduces PHG to his brother, W.T. Berger, aligned with Brethren, 113; experiencing Brethren, PHG shortly afterwards terminates Methodist connection, 120 and fn.114;
REVIEWS OF PHG's BOOKS: publications of, oppose uniformitarian geology, 288; commend PHG's *Omphalos*, 298; critical of *Mysteries of God*, 592-3.
Michell, W. D., self-described archaeologist: argues against antiquity of man at British Association meeting, 386 and fn.297; spoke at Victoria Institute, 386 fn.302.
Microscope: c.1608, invented, 177; draws attention in 18th century to smaller invertebrates, 188; microscopy gaining attention by early 1830s, 176; 51; in 1832, PHG purchases *Essays on the Microscope*, 48–51; 177; 180; 239; 345; Ehrenberg's monumental work, 178-9; his outmoded microscope, 179 and fn.96; in 1846, Huxley purchases one, 176; in 1849, PHG, 176; in 1856, Lewes, 366; in early 1850s, they go down in price and up in quality, 189 and fn.159; other microscopists whom PHG knew: Bowerbank, 121; Dallinger, 326 fn.300; Hudson, 563; Loddiges, 100 fn.14; Newman, 176; Quekett, 173 fn.67; Barnard in USA an admirer, 307; Agassiz's use of, 356; Hudson puts *Pedalion* under, 564; Lankester follows, 565;
ILLUSTRATIONS FROM, BY PHG: in 1857, creates drawings from, for his lectures, 278; PHG's *Evenings at the Microscope*, 345; Rotifera series in *Popular Science Review*, engraved by West, 562 and fn.155; in 1882, PHG's concern with quality of lithographic rendition of his microscopic illustrations of 'Clasping-organs', q.v., 559-60; 560 fn.139; 561; 'so careful an observer', 576; PHG's 'hand and eye' remained perfect to the end, 573-4; PHG's MICROSCOPE: PHG short-sighted in one eye, his microscope described, 576 and fns.253-4; in 1881, buys new equipment for, 547; in 1903, PHG's microscope displayed at meeting of Microscopical Society, 254;

PHG's USE OF: PHG's familiarity with, in Newfoundland, 48; 176; use of, in Jamaica, 140; London, 176; 181; 366 fn.208; an 1849 purchase, 176; to study Rotifera, 176-7; 181-2; 186; to the Marychurch seashore in 1852, PHG takes compound microscope, 187; 188; 333; 368; and uses it in his Marine Natural History classes, 235 fn.434; significance of *mundus invisibilis*, 239; PHG's microscopic contributions recognized, 251; in 1859, PHG's *Evenings at the Microscope* for a popular audience, 345; in 1874, lightly rev. ed., 425; in 1884, reissued, 562; in Britain, numerous books on, 346; PHG uses to study sea anemone thread-capsules, 355-6; with improved microscope, 356; to study tropical orchids, 371; 375; to study tropical insects, 546; to study Rotifera, in mid-1880s, 571; having turned 78, continues use of, 598 and fn.402; at 5 a.m., begins daily research with, 550; metaphor of investigating 'as with a microscope', 518; 523 fn.187; 591 and fn.355.
Microscopical Society of London: PHG elected member of (1849), 173; Member of Council (1851) and Hon. Fellow (1887), 173 fn.69; 196; in 1850, PHG reads his first paper on Rotifera before, followed by 2 others, 176; Hudson's research on *Pedalion mirum* appears in *Journal*, and meeting, of, 564; in 1888, Hudson elected president of, 565-6; 573; 581; when nearly 78, Society was 'proud' to have 3 studies on Rotifera by PHG, 573; Hudson & Gosse commended in *Journal* of, 574; in 1903, PHG's microscope displayed at meeting of, 254.
Mildmay Conferences : devoted to Second Advent and other topics, founded by William Pennefather, 401; PHG had been invited to, but did not attend, 401 fn.50; criticism of, 402 fn.51; in 1868, EWG attends, 461; Pascoe speaks at, 542 fn.29.
Millar, Thomas (of Lurgan), tract writer, distributor: impact of 'Tracts for Ireland' series and appeal for support, 260 and fns.107–109; EG tract published by, 263.
Millenarianism: usage here defined, 102 and fn.25; not a major concern to PHG prior to reading Habershon in 1842, 102; 104; at the time, increased interest in, 104; early millenarians were literalists, later only futurists were, 409 fn.78; includes belief in inerrant Bible, 410; Darby's dispensationalism adopted by many believers in, 411; Barnardo, 461-2;
SEE ALSO: Second Advent.
Miller, Hugh, geologist: leading geology populariser, 330; his *Testimony of the Rocks* favourably reviewed, 296 and fn.136; 299 fn.153; reviewed in same publications as *Omphalos*, 296 fn.136; same number of reviews as *Omphalos*, fewer than Darwin's *Origin*, 296 fn.137; interprets biblical 'day' metaphorically, 289; compared to PHG, 298; skill as lecturer, 236.
Milne-Edwards, Henri, zoologist: encouraged focus on marine life, 189; 339; his *Histoire Naturelle des Coralliaires* (1857) improved classificatory system for sea anemones, 341; not impressed with PHG's work, 341; PHG

considered his work 'full of manifest error to one personally familiar with the animals in a living state', 341-2; 342 fn.61; 350; anti-evolutionist, 341; work of, improved by morphological studies of Hertwig brothers, 353.

Missing links:
though lacking hard evidence, Darwin insists that transitional forms exist, 566; hunt for, to support evolution theory, 189, 566–70; Piltdown man, 570; SEE ALSO: Bastian; *Bathybius haeckelii; Eozoön Canadense*; Gastraea theory; Huxley; R. Lankester; *Pedalion mirum.*

Mitchell, David W., naturalist:
secretary of the Zoological Gardens in Regent's Park, 198; in early 1840s, PHG acquainted with, 121; corresponds with PHG in Jamaica, 122 fn.121; ornithological purchases from PHG in Jamaica, 147 fn.294;
AQUARIUM: in 1852, plans to build an aquarium, 198; PHG collects for 'Fish House', 198; in 1853, first public aquarium in world is constructed at Zoological Gardens, 198; *Punch* notes popularity of 'vivarium', 217; quarrel with PHG, resulting in his no longer supplying marine animals to, 200; works with P.T. Barnum to bring first aquarium to America in 1856, 210-11.

Montez, Lola, actress:
stage name, 237 fn.447; far greater turnout to see her than attend PHG lecture, 237.

Montvidere House, preparatory school:
mistranscribed by Charteris as 'Mt. Veden', 445 fn.31; school of Menneer located in St. Marychurch, EWG attends c.Aug. 1860–Jan. 1863, 444-5; subjects studied, 445; EWG's creditable achievement on public exams, 445; EWG apparently meets dramatist J.S. Knowles on walk to, 445; PHG's high opinion of Menneer, 445-6; PHG explains reason for transfer of EWG to Edgelow's school in Thorn Park, 446; EWG's classmate Mansell Dames appeared 'unsaved', 473-4.

Monuments of Ancient Egypt (1847), by PHG:
first of PHG's books on Bible lands, 165 and fn.24; copy inscribed by author to EG, 172 and fn.63.

Moody and Sankey, revivalists:
in 1875, EWG, NG hear them speak in London, 531 and fn.234; Dwight L. Moody involved in East End Training Institute, 426 fn.162.

Moore, James, historian of science:
cited, 88 fn.308; 136 fn.213; 145 fn.276; 361 fn.177; 538 fn.3.

Moravian Brethren (Protestant church):
Church of the United Brethren (known as Moravian Brethren), 126-7; comparison of Moravian, Brethren views, 126-7; 133 fn.193; in 1754, first Protestant missionaries in Jamaica, 130; at beginning of 1800s, the most successful missionaries in the world, 130; on way to Jamaica, PHG meets Plessing, 126; PHG visits, on island of St. Thomas, 146;
COLEMAN AND: in 1829 Coleman starts off with, but in 1841 leaves, for Brethren, 130, 132; unknown how Coleman came to Brethren, 131-2; in 1848, Coleman rejoins Moravian Brethren, 132.

More, Hannah, writer:
launches modern tract era with Cheap Repository Tracts, 257; tamping down revolutionary enthusiasm, 260; sets an example for women tract writers, 261.

Morgan, Ann *née* Gosse (b.1811):
also spelled 'Anne', a cousin married to John Morgan, 277 fn.14; in 1848, attends PHG, EG wedding, 172; in 1857 in London, nurses EG during her last days, and while PHG is lecturing, EWG stays with, in Clifton, 277; 'eternity only can repay' her actions, 278; William Gosse visits EWG at, 279-80.

Morgan, Ann *née* Morgan (1841–1907):
married to Alex Waugh, 277 fn.14; 279 fn.23.

Morgan, Richard Cope, publisher:
founder, editor of *The Revival*, 265; 402; later *The Christian*, 13; 433; and *Bible-Reader's Journal*, 393-4; associated for a time with Open Brethren, 338 fn.37; 'sympathetic' to G. Pearse, 7 fn.3; Barnardo seeks advice from, 461 fn.136; involved in East End Training Institute, 426; member, Victoria Institute, 325 fn.295; embraces 'perfect sanctification', 466 fn.151;
PHG AND: between 1850-4, Morgan met at St. Thomas' Rooms, Hackney, 254; Morgan corresponds with, 426 fn.164; 537; solicits series on prophecy for *Christian*, from, 431 and fn.202; Morgan pleased with series, responds to critics, 433; obituary of PHG cited, 13; 132 fn.190; 416 fn.111; 607 fn.49; Morgan defends, 593-4;
PUBLISHER: under Morgan and Chase imprint, publishes PHG's *Omphalos*, 291 fn.106; *Letters from Alabama*, 89; *Narrative Tracts*, 96 fn.367; 266 and fn.151; *6000 Years of the World's History*, 407 fn.69; *The Revelation*, 106 fn.39; and Shipton, *'Tell Jesus.'*, 169 fn.44; 282 fn.49.

Morris, Francis Orpen, clergyman, naturalist:
author of 'Difficulties of Darwinism', speaks at British Association, 386; testy correspondence with Huxley, 386 fn.301; cited: 385 fn.294.

Morris, William, poet, graphic artist:
c.1868, EWG reads *Defence of Guenevere* by, 473; EWG's purchase of *Defence* leads to his bibliomania, 473 fn.179; O'Shaughnessy knew, 481; French influence on, 483; on 13 Jan. 1872, EWG meets, 506; the Pre-Raphaelite is among freethinkers, rationalists known to EWG, 507.

Mother's Friend (monthly), edited by Ann Jane:
in 1853-4, EG publishes articles on education in, 256; reviews EG's *Abraham and his Children*, 256 fn.80; PHG's *Memorial*, 282 fn.48.

Mrs Barbour of Bonskeid: *see* Barbour, Margaret F.

Müller, George, early Brethren leader:
format of Scripture reading meetings, 8 fn.5; with Craik the 'de facto' founder of Open Brethren, Summerton argues, 161; with Craik, condemned by Darby for advocating independency in church organization, 161; Laseron's reliance on 'living by faith' compared to Müller's, 245 fn.6; in 1830s with Craik, visited Torquay, 334;
GOSSES AND: in early 1853, EG corresponds with, and later reads his *Narrative*, 256; PHG corresponds with, 338 fn.37; 426 fn.164; Eliza Gosse attends his church and Orphanage in Bristol, 369-70.

Murie, James, Linnean Society librarian:
compiles index to PHG's 'Clasping-organs', 559;
PHG corresponds with, 559-60.
Mysteries of God (1884), by PHG:
CONTENT OF: from PHG's Sunday sermons, 590
and fn.352; prochronic theory of *Omphalos*
repeated in, 319 and fns.257-8; PHG claims in, his
Revelation has resisted all attacks, 410; indecision
about rapture of the Saints, 414 fn.99; analysis
of baptism in, 442 fn.20; 443 fn.21; 515 fn.171;
opposition to evolution, 538; musings over colonization of the planets, 597; 591 fn.355;
REVIEWS OF: mainly unfavourable, contrary to Eliza
Gosse's claim, 591 and fns.354-5; 592 fns.367-
8; 593; 296 fn.138; stinging criticism by Bennet
in *Golden Lamp*, 592; Toronto printing of, 592
fn.367;
SEE ALSO: 'Humanity of the Son of God'.

Nangle, Edward, editor:
founder and editor of *Achill Missionary Herald*,
429; an historicist, anti-Catholic polemicist, 429;
unsympathetic to PHG's Brethren affiliation, 429
fn.183; but recommends PHG's *Revelation*, 429
fn.183; corresponds with PHG, 429 and fn.182.
Narrative Tracts ([1864]), book by PHG and EG:
BACKGROUND: in 1864, 4-page tracts by EG, PHG,
collected into book form, 400;
CIRCULATION: circulated in Britain (until at least
1882), Canada, and the US, 267; PHG occasionally
sends copy of, to correspondents, 544;
IMPACT: this work 'blessed to the conversion of
many persons', 266 fn.151;
PURPOSE: an evangelical narrative tract emphasizes
'the application of truth *to the heart*', 257;
TOPICS: statement on importance of good works
in, 127 fn.148; comment on slavery in, 96 fn.367;
comment of EWG cited, in, 253 fn.57; notes 'God
has loved me', in, 539 fn.8; comment on a hereafter for animals in, 625 and fn.22.
SEE ALSO: *Gosse's Narrative or Gospel Tracts*.
Natural History Classes: *see* Marine Natural History
Classes.
Natural History: Mammalia (1848); *Birds* (1849);
Reptiles (1850); *Fishes* (1851); *Mollusca* (1854),
by PHG:
intended as guides to British Museum natural
history collections, with PHG's woodcuts, 165-
6; published by SPCK, 166; all were derivative,
except *Mollusca*, 166; advertised: 215 fn.303;
225 fns.367-70.
Natural History Museum, London *previously known
as* British Museum (Natural History), q.v.
Natural History Society of Montreal:
founded in 1827; in 1836, PHG elected Corr.
Member of, sends paper to, 72 and fn.220; PHG
uses designation, 99.
Naturalist's Rambles on the Devonshire Coast
(1853), by PHG:
ASPECTS OF: first of PHG's seashore books based
entirely on his observations, 221; most frequently
reviewed of all PHG books, 19 fn.214; 296 fn.137;
experiments with aquarium, 192 fn.175; 198
fn.208; eating sea anemones, 188 and fn.153;

increases public awareness of Regent's Park
aquarium, 199; word 'aquarium' appears twice
in its modern sense in, 208 fn.264; comments
on 'Federal Headship' concept in, 314 fn.236;
Lewes errors on sea anemones, 354-5; he fails to
give priority to PHG, 354 fn.148; PHG describes
researches on *acontia*, q.v., 356 and fn.154; 386
fn.162;
PUBLICATION RECORD: date of appearance of, 199 and
fn.212; includes 12 chromolithographed plates,
printed by Hullmandel and Walton, drawn on
the stone by PHG, a landmark publication, 205;
expensive, 220; published on an author's-risk
basis, PHG receives 57% in division of profits,
221; 1,500 copies printed, 199 fn.214; 296 fn.135;
PHG's cost to print, 296 fn.135; £592 profit over
16 years, 221; advertised, 226 fns.371-4;
REPUTATION: a new genre in marine natural history writings initiated, 199; outbreak of aquaromania dates to appearance of, 185; 208; 241;
listed among qualifications for election to Royal
Society, 251 fn.47; healthy moral tone of, 199;
Catholic *Rambler* complains of 'bitter spirit of
Protestantism' in, 242 fn.478.
Naturalist's Sojourn in Jamaica (1851), by PHG:
ASPECTS OF: on title-page, book 'Assisted by
Richard Hill', 573; PHG's statement of proper
way to study nature, 163-5; he expected to find
in Jamaica hordes of butterflies, humming-birds,
orchids, 136; 139; in 1845, hires 'negro lad' Samuel
Campbell as paid assistant, 138; work routine,
138-9; 1845 consignment to Cuming, 139; first
to describe methods of commercial fishing, 148;
comments on songs of birds, 82 fn.275; knowledge
of orchids, 372 and fn.234; PHG and assistants
collect 21,200 specimens during time in Jamaica,
147 and fn.289; 148; high regard for Hill, 144-5;
inscribes copy to EG, 172 and fn.63; sends copy
to H.W. Bates, 586 fn.323;
PUBLICATION RECORD: in 1848, rejected by SPCK,
151 fn.323; 1,000 copies printed by Longman on
author's-risk basis, in print until 1865, 220; 8
plates in book drawn on stone by PHG, with tinted
lithographs by M. & N. Hanhart, 205; advertised,
226 fn.373;
REPUTATION: part of Jamaica trilogy which
accounts for his reputation as 'Father of Jamaican
Ornithology, Herpetology', 149; one of PHG's finest books, shows his powers as field naturalist, still
of value today, 151-2; listed among qualifications
for election to Royal Society, 251 fn.27; positive
press reviews, 151 fn.324; 162 and fns.11; 163 and
fn.13; praise from Forbes, E. Lankester, Owen,
Darwin annotates his copy of book, 162 fn.11; 195;
but for Darwin, not enough theorizing, 321 fn.268.
Natural selection: *see* Evolution.
*Natural Theology: or Evidences of the Existence
and Attributes of the Deity, Collected from the
Appearances of Nature* (1802), by William Paley:
argument from design in nature points to a wise
and powerful Designer, 238–40; 287; two comple-
mentary guides from the Creator, Book of Nature
and Book of Scripture, 101; PHG believes a perfect Creator created a perfect creation as-is, and

evidence of design in nature affirms that, 240; by around age 17, PHG reads Paley, 29; a common text, 30; never deviates from that outlook, 52; 240 fn.461; 287; 538; popular works by Adams, and Kirby and Spence, reflect its dominance, 50; 52; naturalist's at British Museum adhere to the tradition, 12; 121; while natural theology is valuable, it is unable to answer how to be saved, 56 and fn.139; a point PHG made in books and lectures, 238; 240 and fn.461;

DARWIN AND: Darwin's natural selection theory dispensed with teleological explanation and the need for a creator, 52; his *Various Contrivances* book on orchids intended to understand nature without relying on design argument, 376; Lewes not a proponent of, 232; cited: 232.

Nature *see* Science.

Nature (weekly), founder, editor N. Lockyer: Britain's premier scientific serial, 566; 578; Kingsley a friend of Lockyer, 304 and fn.197; in 1869, reviews PHG's *Romance of Natural History*, 377 fn.265; remarks on Dawson, 363; 364 fn.197; praises Hudson's discovery of *Pedalion*, 566; omits any comment on Hudson & Gosse's *Rotifera*, though a landmark publication, 578 and fn.264; explanation, 578–81; *Nature* acts as the 'mouthpiece' of 'agnostic naturalism' (X Club members and others) excluding opponents, 580–1.

'The Negro Slave' (gospel tract [1860]), by PHG: 96 fn.367.

Newell, Thomas, bookkeeper: in Carbonear, encouraged to convert by Apsey, 47; married c.1824, 47 fn.88; converted after 1835, 47 fn.89; 61 fn.166; PHG draws strength from, 507.

Newfoundland:

CHRONOLOGY: Henry Gosse, a PHG uncle, previously worked in a Newfoundland counting-house and went to West Indies, 14; in 1822, PHG's brother William leaves for Carbonear firm of Gosse, Pack, & Fryer, 25; in 1827, PHG leaves for Carbonear firm of Harrison, Slade & Co. for five or six years of service, 32; description of Newfoundland, 36–9; on arrival at Carbonear, William gives him a code of etiquette, 36; 457; becomes friends with William C. St. John, 37; in July 1832, PHG returns to Poole to visit sick sister, Elizabeth, 45; she recovers, he entomologizes, 52-3; PHG family reunited in Poole, 53; in 1832, tension mounts in colony between Irish Catholics and English Protestants, 61-2; 35 fn.11; in spring, 1833, PHG's indenture at counting-house ends, he decides to stay on, 57; around the end of 1834, PHG decides, with the Jaqueses, to leave Newfoundland for Upper Canada, 64-5; on 25 June 1835, they head there, 65; but detour to the Eastern Townships of Quebec, Lower Canada, 68;

ENTOMOLOGIA TERRAE NOVAE: PHG's illustrations of insects in: *see separate entry*;

'ENTOMOLOGY OF NEWFOUNDLAND': PHG's first book (unpublished), *see separate entry*;

RELIGIOUS LIFE: in 1830, PHG's religious outlook was confused, not inclined to Methodism but he contemplates the ministry, 40; the religious revival of Methodism of 1830-2, the 'Great Awakening'

in Carbonear, 41; example of George Apsey, 'firstborn child of the revival', 41-3; the model for the religious 'regeneration' of PHG and others, 1832 is PHG's *annus mirabilis*, 44-8; conversion experience comparison, 46-7; after return from Poole at end of 1832, PHG joins Methodist Society in Carbonear, entering Apsey's class, 56; around 1833, he switches to the class of G.E. Jaques, and becomes a local Wesleyan preacher, 58; Sprague acknowledges PHG as the source of his commitment to Methodism, 60-1;

SCIENTIFIC WORK: PHG the first to systematically investigate and record entomology of Newfoundland, xvii; 55; his investigations on Lepidoptera of Newfoundland not published until 1883, 55 fn.132; in 1832, begins in Newfoundland study of entomology, 11; which he later calls 'a cold barren unproductive region', 64; in 1832, purchases *Essays on the Microscope*, by Adams, q.v., 48; it propels his entomological study, 49; description of the book, 49–51; comparison with Kirby and Spence's *Introduction to Entomology*, q.v., 51-2; his friend St. John shares his enthusiasm, 49; 1832–5, PHG publishes meteorological record of Carbonear, 54; in 1832 in Newfoundland, PHG becomes 'a *scientific naturalist*', 56; limitation of study of nature from religious viewpoint, 56; in 1834, PHG acquires first insect cabinet, 60.

Newman, Edward, naturalist, editor: editor, *Zoologist*, 122; and *Entomologist* and other publications, 121 and fn.119; 125; Quaker naturalist, Darwin critic, 322; 548; a knowledgeable microscopist, 176; PHG agrees to send articles to, while in Jamaica, 125; publishes in *Zoologist* 4 articles by PHG on entomology of Alabama, 122;

AQUARIUM MOVEMENT: periodization of aquarium movement, 241 fn.472; writes on W.A. Lloyd, 227 fn.378;

REVIEWS OF BOOKS: PHG, *Canadian Naturalist*, 100 fn.16; 121; PHG, *Actinologia Britannica*, 349 fn.113; PHG, *Romance of Natural History*, 2nd series, 324 fn.283; Kirby & Spence, *Entomology*, 51 fn.117; Darwin, *Origin of Species*, 322 and fn.273.

Newton, Benjamin Wills, early Brethren leader: helps make Plymouth a Brethren focal point, 116; ideas on prophecy promoted by *Voice Upon the Mountains*, 406 fn.67; ; by 1846, appears to know W.T. Berger, q.v., 118;

DARBY AND: primary source of contention is interpretation of prophecy, 117 fn.92; 419; similarities and differences with, 412; difference with Darby on prophecy emerges at Powerscourt Conferences, 117 and fn.92; 161; both are premillennial futurists, 412; they disagree on dispensationalism, 412; Darby attacks him over ideas on 'liberty of ministry', 161; 419-20; humanity of Christ, 161; 592; GOSSES AND: EG initially 'enthralled' by his teaching, 171; and annotated his works, 412; PHG familiar with work of, 427 fn.37; PHG opposes Newton in 'Psalm's heresy', views his *Thoughts on the Apocalypse* as 'most erroneous', 413 and fn.96; PHG's eclectic approach to the Darby-Newton duel, 412–14; like Newton, PHG not involved in social reform, 400; EWG confused about view of PHG, on 'perfect sanctification', 466; PHG critical of Newton on 'perfect sanctification', 466; 92 fn.343.

Newton, Hannah *née* Abbott:
1st wife of B.W. Newton, 171 fn.55; 412; EG knew her in early 1840s, and was initially enthralled by her husband's teaching, 171.

Newton, Isaac, mathematician:
as prophetic expositor, an historic pre-millennialist, 102; but warns again foretelling 'times and things', 427; prejudice against Catholics, 102; PHG familiar with prophetic work of, 399 fn.37; *Observations on the Prophecies* by, cited, 427 fn.170; in France, a substitute for Newtonian world-machine, 50; cited: 197; 399 fn.38.

Non-Darwinian science:
defined, 305; PHG practitioner of, xx; Carpenter explains importance of, 184-5; PHG's biographical and ecological bent, 195; 84; 140; 165; 349; 278; writing R. Hill, PHG calls it 'my humbler path', 143-4; similar approach of Hudson, 571; irrelevancy of evolution theory to PHG's sea anemone, Rotifera researches, 320; USA scientists admire PHG, 307;
SEE ALSO: Science.

Norman, Alfred Merle, zoologist and clergyman:
PHG sends his Rotifera drawings to, 370-1.

Ocean (1845), by PHG:
in 1844, proposal for, submitted to SPCK, 122; 128 fn.153; publication of, in 1845, gains PHG £120 and modest scientific attention, 122, 128; the only book on the subject at the time, 190; it was largely derivative, but was one of PHG's most successful, 123; new 'ed.', 1860, 238 fn.452; still in print in USA in 1874, and UK in 1902, 123 fn.128; reviewed in USA, 211 fn.277; advertised in UK, 215 fn.303; 225 fns.368–70; 226 fn.371.

Omphalos (1857), by PHG:
omphalos is Greek word for navel, 290;
ARGUMENT OF: 289-91; among attempts to resolve age of earth question, 288 fn.87; based on 'grand physical law, hitherto unrecognized', 290; i.e., Law of Prochronism in Creation, explained, 290-1; PHG calls prochronism argument 'logically impregnable', 318; why PHG clung to the omphalotic argument, 405-6; PHG's unwavering commitment to prochronism in later years, 317-18; 323-4; 591; 'prochronism', 'brachychronology', 'diachronic', 'macrochronology' are neologisms used in, 289 fns. 94-5; 290 fn.103;
INFLUENCE OF: on British art, 218; on PHG's reputation, 291; and X Club reaction against, in 1858: 360-1; 305–7; in 1880s: 556-7; 581; 20th century assessments of, 319; revival of support for, 319-20;
MYTHS ABOUT: xxiii; 296; (1) why it was written in 1857, 291–4; (2) what influenced PHG to write on uniformitarian geology, 294-5; Darwin's theory unappealing, 321–4; (3) reception of: EWG's universally-accepted account of ridicule for, xxi; 295; refuted by evidence from reviews, 295–301; and comments by geologists, 301–4; (4) PHG's goal in writing said to be to 'defend his science on religious grounds', 305; resulting in PHG being 'outside the pale of science', refuted, 305–7; PHG's goal in writing, explained, 307–11; EWG's claim that PHG became 'angry with God' not aligned with facts, 312–19; response to Canadian correspondent's questions concerning religion and science, 318;
PUBLICATION RECORD: its large print run reflects high hopes for, 296; consideration of cost of printing, 296 fn.135; PHG may have broken even on publication of, 222; advertised, 226 fns.372–4; a slow seller, title change to *Creation*, q.v., 317; not noticed in USA press, 306 and fn.205;
REVIEWS OF: third most-reviewed of PHG's books, 199 fn.214; 296; 296-301; most unfavourably-reviewed of PHG's books, 296; analysis of, in *Natural History Review*, 312-15; Kingsley's critiques: private, 303-4; public, 304;
SUPPLEMENT TO: *Geology or God: Which?* 316-17; 416; adds argument of 'Adam's Federal Headship', q.v., 313-15.

On the Various Contrivances by Which British and Foreign Orchids are Fertilised by Insects (1862), by Darwin:
supports findings of *Origin of Species*, but initially arouses little debate, 373-4; PHG owns a copy of, 321 fn.266; PHG reads it, and unsuccessfully sets out to show Darwin's conclusions are scientifically untenable, 374-5; 2 anonymous reviews praising book are actually written by J.D. Hooker, 376; unaware of Hooker's conversion to Darwinism, in 1867 PHG seeks his advice on his research, 377.

Open Brethren: *see* Brethren.

'Open' ministry': *see* 'Liberty of ministry'.

Orchids:
DARWIN'S *ON THE VARIOUS CONTRIVANCES* (1862): PHG reads, and sets out to show his conclusions are scientifically untenable, 374-7; Hooker's anonymous reviews of *Orchids*, 373-4; their author and purpose, 376; PHG writes Darwin, 375; 371 fn.231, and J.D. Hooker, 377;
PHG'S GROWING AND COLLECTING: from around 1839, PHG acquainted with Loddiges nursey in Hackney, 99; 100 fn.14; 371; he collected in Jamaica, and projected illustrated work on orchids of, 139; 371-2; PHG's later interest in, precedes the mania for, 371 fn.231; 372 and fn.239; in 1861, PHG begins collecting, with Sandhurst hothouse well-stocked, 371 and fn.231; 582 and fn.290; seeks help from H.W. Bates finding orchid dealers, 371; seeks identification help from *Gardeners' Chronicle* orchid growers, 372; in 1862, gets orchids from R. Hill in Jamaica, 371; Sandhurst visit by W.J. Hooker, 371; had orchids flowering only for a day, some for a whole year, 371 fn.231; in 1865, publisher Reeve, q.v., asks him to write book on, 381; in 1875, sends NG orchids prior to wedding, 531; in 1884, grows a prize-winning orchid, 539 and fn.11; at his death, reputedly has one of the finest private collections in the area, 539.

Origin of Species (1859), by Darwin:
PHG AND: appearance of, may have influenced PHG's lecturing, 240; critique of *Omphalos* in, 303; PHG's comments on, 321–4; 321 fn.266;

PHG's cryptic 'measure of truth', 322; print run of PHG's books compares favourably to, 199 fn.214; 224;
REVIEWS OF: in periodical press, greater attention given to Essays and Reviews (1860), 325; negative review in Athenaeum, by Leifchild, 547 fn.56 (incorrectly attributed by Darwin to Westwood, 547); Darwin's erroneous view of entomologists' opposition, 548; review by J.W. Dawson, 363 fn.194; by Edward Newman, 322; by Popular Science Review (4th ed.), 379; number of reviews of PHG's Naturalist's Rambles compares favourably to, 199 fn.214; 296 fn.137;
SCIENCE OF: connection of denial of species evolution to short chronology for earth, 294; Darwin's critique of common idea on cause of species extinction, 323 fn.279; though transitional links were not visible, Darwin believed in them, 566; human-ape missing links, 566-7; cited: 288; 302; 304; 386.
Ornithology: see Birds.
O'Shaughnessy, Arthur W.E., herpetologist and poet:
works in Zoology Department, British Museum, 481; visited France, familiar with later Pre-Raphaelites, his poetry espouses Parnassianism, 481; 483; in 1870, apparently meets EWG, not particularly close, 481; married to sister of P.B. Marston, 506.
Oxford English Dictionary (OED):
PHG ranked among top 1,000 sources, xix;
COINAGES BY PHG APPEARING IN: malleus, manubrium, mastax, 184 fn.132; diachronic, prochronic, 290 fn.103; teliferous, teliferous system 353 fn.140; 349;
COINAGES BY PHG APPEARING IN, FOR WHICH HE IS NOT GIVEN PRIORITY: cinclides, cnida, craspedum, 349 fn.115; incus, trophi, 184 fn.132;
COINAGES BY PHG NOT MENTIONED IN: acontia, 352 fn.132; ecthoreum, peribola, pterygia, strebla, 349 fn.115;
DEFICIENT ENTRIES APPEARING IN: 'aquarium', 'aquavivarium', 208 fn.264; aquariist, 277 fn.10; breaking bread, 119 fn.106; 'Open Brethren', 465 fn.147;
EARLIEST USE OF SOME TERMS APPEARING IN: Darbyite, Darbyism, 9 fn.10; Plymouth Brethren, 8 fn.10; 413 fn.94;
RARE WORDS USED BY PHG APPEARING IN: scient, 83 fn.282; synchronology, 111 fn.60; zootomist, 552 fn.92;
TERMS DEFINED IN: bionomics, ecology, ethology, 165 fn.20; pteridomania, 208 fn.265.

Pack, Gosse & Fryer: see Gosse, Pack & Fryer.
Paget, James, surgeon:
the 'first authority on cancer in London', in May 1856, EG gets an appointment with, who recommends tumour excision, 246-7; his cancer investigation findings for women, 247-8; in 1868, PHG refers EWG to, 247 fn.14.
Palestine Exploration Fund: PHG support of, 426.
'Papilio homerus, its ovum and larva' (1880):
PHG communicated research containing observations by Mais, q.v., to the Entomological Society of London, where it appeared in its Proceedings,

551 fn.91; the first printed record of the larva of Jamaican swallow-tail butterfly, 541 fn.21.
Parnassianism, French poetic movement:
influential in Victorian England; Morris' Defence of Guenevere, 473 fn.179; emerges from the French l'art pour l'art movement, 480; British practitioners include EWG, Marzials, O'Shaughnessy, and Payne, 481-3; Tennyson opposes, 483; called 'incoherent ineffectual ecstasy', 483-4; EWG inspired by, 525; PHG frowns on, 484.
Pascoe, James, missionary:
PHG donates to Mexican Evangelical Mission, founded by, 542 fn.29; corresponds with PHG, 109 fn.56; PHG sends him works of Proctor, 544 fn.39;
INSECT COLLECTION: collects for PHG, 542; PHG persuades him of value of collecting, 543; 544 fn.38; amount paid per specimen, 543 fn.36;
PROPHETIC VIEWS: they share prophetic positions, 542 fn.29; 588 fn.335; 600 fn.413; 544 fn.41.
Pattison, John, physician:
claimed to be from Scotland, 249; a quack cancer curer confused with Fell, 247 fn.18; claimed effective treatment of cancer without 'the knife', 249; in 1852, denied access to Middlesex Hospital, 249.
Payne, John, solicitor:
Parnassian poet, friend of O'Shaughnessy, 482; 483; among EWG's freethinker friends, 507.
Pearse, Charlotte, missionary:
1st wife of George, 7 and fn.3; EG friend, 254.
Pearse, George, stockbroker, missionary:
BIOGRAPHY: of the London Stock Exchange, 6; associated with Open Brethren, 338 fn.37; member of Evangelical Tract Association, supports missionary causes, 6 and fn.12; 7; 119 fns.100, 102; 257; a founder of Illustrated Missionary News, possible editor of Gleaner in the Missionary Field, and other serials, later missionary in France, India and Algeria, 7 and fn.3; at home of, J.H. Taylor forms China Inland Mission, 7; introduces W.T. Berger to Taylor, 5 fn.7; knows EG (from at least 1848), 254; and Mary Stacey (from 1851), 245;
PHG AND: long-time friendship with PHG, 426 fn.164; 507; 537; participant with PHG in Scripture reading of Hackney Brethren, 6; 119 fns.100,102; 254; with PHG and Berger, may have formed a circle of Open Brethren influence in Jamaica, 153-4; writes to PHG in: Jamaica, 118 fn.96; 129 and fn.160; St. Marychurch: 334 fn.6; 419 fns.135-6; 422 fn.150; 424 fns.154, 156; 583 fn.300; 587 fn.328; 588 fn.332; 605 fn.30;
PROPHETIC VIEWS: discusses with PHG, 410 fn.85; 434 fns.222, 224; 589; 590 fn.348.
Pedalion mirum, a Rotifer:
C.T. Hudson's 1871 discovery of, hailed by Ray Lankester and others as 'remarkable', 563-6; 563 fn. 162; 569; perhaps a missing link, 566-8, and support for Darwin's theory, 570; 581; Lankester creates phylum Appendiculata, 569; morphological significance of, exaggerated, 569 fn.201.
Pengelly, William, geologist:
early convert to Darwin's theory, 303; critiques Law of Prochronism, 303; journal and newspaper versions of critique compared, 303 fn.189; in 1859, visits Kent's Cavern with PHG, 439.

Perfect Sanctification (Wesleyan doctrine):
also known as 'Christian perfection', 'sinless sanctification' or 'perfect love', 92; doctrine of John Wesley, 92; in 1838, PHG experiences spiritual revival in Alabama and strives for, 91 and fn.330; in 1868, EWG encounters advocates for, in East End of London, 466; some embrace idea, 466 fn.151; Darby opposed to, 466 fn.152.

Perrens, Fanny:
sister to Richard and Thomas, niece of W.K., corresponds with PHG, 544 fn.40.

Perrens, Richard:
of Paraguay and Argentina, nephew of William K., brother to Thomas and Fanny, collects insects for PHG, 542; PHG prepares butterfly identification book for, 543 fn.35; PHG donates for tracts, 426 fn.163; PHG asks about religious views, 544 fn.41; PHG sends *Knowledge* to, 578 fn.268.

Perrens, Thomas, of Paraguay and Argentina:
nephew of William K., collects insects for PHG, 542.

Perrens, William King, missionary:
of Paraguay and Argentina, uncle to Fanny, Richard, and Thomas, collects insects for PHG, 542; when PHG was ill at Sandhurst, filled religious duties, 583 and fn.297; PHG names Argentinian butterfly after, 583 fn.299; in Florence, 583 fn.299; after 2nd marriage, PHG welcomes them to 'Table of the Lord', 583 fn.299; witness to PHG's will, 583 fn.299; corresponds with PHG, 583 fn.300; 572 fn.218; 588 fn.333; 589 fn.342.

Petrie, Francis W.H. (d.1900), official:
Secretary, Victoria Institute, 327 fn.302; PHG's letters to, 327 fns.302; PHG threatens to quit Institute, 326 fn.303.

Phoenix Park, Westmoreland, Jamaica:
home of the De Leons, 134 and fn.198; not a good natural history collection site, 144 fn.268.

Philosophical Transactions of the Royal Society:
see Royal Society.

Plessing, Gustavus Henry, clergyman:
German Moravian Brethren missionary, 126; PHG discusses theological issues with, on way to Jamaica, 126-7; PHG learns German, perhaps to talk with, 180 fn.102.

Plymouth Brethren: see Brethren.

'POISON-APPARATUS': *see* 'Researches on the Poison-apparatus in the *Actiniadae*'.

Pollok, Robert, poet:
in his best-selling *Course of Time*, combined a standard historicist interpretation 102; 107; with a 'warped & distorted' postmillennial view, 28-9; 28 fns.59-60; Ingelow poem an imitation of *Course*, 469.

Popular British Ornithology (1849), by PHG:
well-received in press, 166 fn.31; 242 fn.478; advertised, 226 fns.371, 373; in 1853, 2nd ed., 242 fn.478; 320 letterpress pages written in 10 weeks, 166; 292 fn.110; when completed, 172 fn.61; includes observations on bird songs, 82 fn.275.

Popular natural history (PHG and):
PHG stands 'absolutely companionless among those who have popularized scientific objects', 216; 'the most voluminous writer on Natural History among the present generation', 215; he 'has done more to diffuse a taste for his favourite studies than all the writers who preceded him', 330; 'to draw like Gosse is no longer given to mortal man', 270;
AQUARIUM: *see separate entry*;
AQUAROMANIA: *see separate entry*;
ILLUSTRATOR: *see separate entry*;
LECTURES, PUBLIC: *see separate entry*;
MARINE NATURAL HISTORY CLASSES: *see separate entry*;
MARINE ZOOLOGY: *see separate entry*;
PHILOSOPHY OF: 163–5; *see* Science;
SEASHORE: *see separate entry*;
SEASHORE BOOK TRILOGY: *see Naturalist's Rambles on the Devonshire Coast*; *Aquarium*; *Tenby*;
WORKS BY PHG: *see separate entries*.

Poulton, Edward Bagnall, entomologist:
research supports Darwin's theory, 494.

'Prehensores of Male Butterflies': *see* 'Clasping-organs'.

Pre-Raphaelites, Victorian artistic movement:
the 'fleshly school' of poetry, 526; difficult to define, 480 and fn.22; O'Shaughnessy an intimate of later Pre-Raphaelites, 481; EWG wedges himself into their circle, meeting (besides O'Shaughnessy) C. Rossetti, W.B. Scott, Swinburne, 484; D.G. Rossetti, 484; 506; F.M. Brown and Marston, 506; in mid-1871, EWG attends fortnightly meetings, 501; a *bêtise* (act of foolishness) in EWG's *Viol and Flute*, 526; at meeting of, encounters artist Ellen (Nellie) Epps, whom EWG marries, 528; cited, 609 fn.60.

Preterism: see Prophecy.

Prochronism, Law of:
announced in PHG's *Omphalos*, 286; 'prochronic' a PHG neologism, 290 and fn.103; explained, 290-1; 290 fn.104; meaning of, to PHG, 310–12; press critique of, 299-300; 303; *Natural History Review* calls its laws 'fairly deduced', 312; Kingsley calls it dangerous, 304; PHG never stopped supporting, contrary to EWG, 312; PHG defended it in *Romance of Natural History*, 201 fn.201; 315; 323-4; in 1864 lecture, 316; in *Mysteries of God*, 319 fns.257-8; in published and private letters, 317-18; its modern revival, 319-20; cited: 320.

Proctor, Richard, astronomer:
a freethinker, PHG enjoyed sending correspondents his books, 544 fn.39; editor, *Knowledge*, q.v., 578 fn.268.

Profit-sharing book publication: see Author's-risk book publication.

Prophecy (unfulfilled):
upheaval of the French Revolution and reactionary movements in 19th century Europe encouraged a new Christian focus on, 390–8; one-third of Bible said to consist of prophecy, 104 and fn.34; PHG influenced by reading Habershon, q.v., to become a historicist premillennialist, 152; 118; 428; study of unfulfilled prophecy an important stimulus for the progress of the Brethren movement, 117; premillennialist perspective had a pessimistic political, social impact on many Brethren,117; 400; FUTURISM: in the earliest period of prophetic interpretation, the futurist school (prophetic

predictions have a future literal realization at end times) was visible, 104; literalism associated with futurism, dispensationalism, q.v., 409 fn.78; 110 fn.59; after mid-1860s, dominant in England, 406; HISTORICISM: the historicist school arose during the Protestant Reformation, interpreting past and contemporary events as having occurred and still occurring, as foretold, 104-5; during first-half of 19th century, a revived historicist determination to align history with prophecy, 105-6; 390–2; 'Continuationism' responded to past failed predictions of historicists and moved the timing of the Second Advent to beyond their lifetime, 431; PRETERISM: the preterist school interpreted prophecies as having occurred during early years of Christian era, 105; its popularity fades by at least 1866, 106 fn.39; R. Chester frames his futurist principles in opposition to, 408 fn.77; SECOND ADVENT TIMING: opinions on the timing of the Second Advent divided between premillennialists (occurring before the millennium) and postmillennialists (after the millennium), 105; PHG AND: before 1842, millenarianism not a major concern to, 102; his prior reading, 102-3; then Habershon, 107; PHG scrutinizes Scripture 'as with a microscope', 591 and fn.355; PHG's *Revelation* a critique of futurism, dispensationalism, 411; futurists whose writings PHG read: 399 fn.37; also Chester, q.v.; historicists whose writings PHG read: 399 fn.37; also Habershon, Pollok, qq.v.; PHG-Chester exchange reveals central differences between futurism, historicism, 408–10; PROPHETIC ACTIVITY: Societies devoted to, conferences on: including Trent Park (1863); Week of Prayer (1864); 'Sure Word of Prophecy' (1864), 401–4; lecturers on: T.G. Bell; Cumming; Elliott; PHG; Gwatkin; Strong; qq.v.; periodicals: *Rainbow* favoured Darbyite futurism; Newtonian futurism favoured by *Voice Upon the Mountains*, *Quarterly Journal of Prophecy*, qq.v., 406 fn.67.
Prophetic Times (1871), by PHG:
PHG's last published work on prophecy, 434; often enclosed a copy of, in correspondence, 434; on the prophetic periods of Daniel and Revelation, 415; 1877 seen as important date in, 434.
Provancher, Léon, entomologist:
'father of French-Canadian entomology', editor of *Naturaliste Canadien*, 548; opposed to *le darwinisme*, 548 and fn.69; comments on PHG's *Canadian Naturalist*, 76 fn.240.
Purdon, Robert A., clergyman:
of Torquay, editor, *The Last Vials*, historicist prophetic journal, 403 fn.61.

Quakers (Society of Friends):
PHG: the 'great gulf' is 'not between Baptist & Friend' but 'dead in sins & alive to God', 338; NATURALISTS: in 1838, PHG visits Philadelphia, the 'Quaker City', 80; where Quaker faith was long dominant among scientists like Bartram, Conrad, Say, 82-3; 83 and fn.277; English examples: Doubleday, 11; J.E. Howard, 118; 452; E. Newman, 322.

SEE ALSO: Brethren.
Quarterly Journal of Microscopical Science:
editors include E. and R. Lankester, 565 fn.168; one of the leading zoological publications, 564-5; in 1872, Hudson describes *Pedalion* rotifer in, 564; reviews Hudson & Gosse, 578; PHG articles in, 182 fns.118-19; 184 fn.134; 185 fn.140.
Quarterly Journal of Prophecy (monthly):
edited by Horatius Bonar, 429; favours futurism of B.W. Newton, 406 fn.67; PHG corresponds with Bonar, 429; PHG article published in, 394 fn.16; PHG owns volumes of, 429 fn.185; notices PHG's *6000 Years*, 407 fn.71; reviews PHG's *Revelation*, 416 fn.111.
Quebec (Lower Canada): *see* Canada.
Quekett, John Thomas, microscopist:
PHG knew, corresponds with, 173 fn.67; 176 fn.80; his *Practical treatise on* microscope, cited, 346.
Quekett Microscopical Club, Journal:
3 reviews of Hudson & Gosse, 578; 574 fn.239; 575 fn.245.

The Railway Lamp (1854), tract by EG:
her first evangelistic tract, issued by Evangelical Tract Association, q.v., 257.
Rainbow (monthly):
journal of prophecy, W. Leask, editor, founder, 401; favours Darbyite futurism, 406 fn.67; importance of year 1866 in, 398 fn.31; 1866 PHG articles in, 406; 408; 414 fn.99; 1866 articles by R. Chester in, 408–410; 433; L. Strong articles in, 335 fn.18; 4 vols. in PHG's library, 399 fn.37; REVIEWS OF PHG WORKS: *6000 Years*, 407 fn.71; *Revelation*, 416 fn.111.
Rawstorne Street (Brethren assembly in Camden Town): *see* Brethren.
Reddie, James (1820–71), civil servant:
founded Victoria Institute (1865), 325-6; dim view of British Association, 385; speaks on John Lubbock, 386 fn.302.
Reeve, Lovell, publisher:
in 1849, PHG's *Popular British Ornithology*, 166 fn.31; in 1857, advertises it, 226 fn.371; in 1865, approaches PHG to publish book on orchids, 381.
Regent's Park Zoological Gardens: *see* Zoological Gardens, Regent's Park.
Reichenbach, Heinrich Gustav, orchidologist:
PHG corresponds with, and sends orchids to, 372 fn.238.
Reichenbach, Ludwig, museum director:
commissioned Blaschka, q.v., to create glass models of marine invertebrates, based on *Actinologia Britannica*, 351.
Religious conversion: *see* Conversion, evangelical.
Religious Tract Society:
successful early non-denominational tract publisher, 257; 258 fn.92; rejects for publication tract of Thomas Gosse (father), 18 and fn.12; publishes EG tract, 263; publishing data, 260 fn.112.
'Researches on the Poison-apparatus in the Actiniadae' (1858), by PHG:
research summarized PHG's knowledge of teliferous system thread-capsules, q.v., 356-7; anonymous referees' reports (by Busk, Huxley, 360)

conclude that the paper is 'hardly admissible' to Royal Society's *Philosophical Transactions*, 357-8; it is published in the *Proceedings*, 361-2; intimating that after PHG's *Omphalos* (1857), X Club members Busk, Huxley, boycotted his work, 361-2; comparison to Royal Society treatment of Bastian, Dawson, supports that view, 362-5; whether PHG knew of X Club influence, he later reprinted his original findings as a 'wonderful example' of Divine contrivances, 365; 367; Lewes questions PHG's claim of a stinging function of the thread-capsules, 365-6; significance of dispute, 366-7.

The Revelation: How is it to be Interpreted? (1866), by PHG:
PHG claimed its arguments incontrovertible, 410; 431; he would likely have placed it alongside *Actinologia Britannica*, 410; a critique of Darbyite dispensationalism, 410–15; PHG commended as able defender of historicism, 415-16; by H.G. Guinness, 416; 588 fn.336; by R.C. Morgan, 416 fn.111; reviews mainly favourable, 416 fn.111; 429 fn.183;
LETTER ENCLOSURE: is 3rd most frequently included pamphlet by PHG in his correspondence, 434 fn.221; 317 fn.249; 429 fn.190.

Rix, Herbert, Royal Society clerk:
writes PHG, 550 fn.86; seeks advice from Michael Foster on marking submissions 'safe' for publication prior to referee assessment, 551 fn.89.

Robinson, Anthony, naturalist:
wrote on all Jamaican natural history fields, 137; PHG studies ornithological and botanical MSS of, 145–7; and uses them, 147 fn.288; praises them, 145; 146; 138 and fn.225.

Romance of Natural History (2 series, 1860, 1861), by PHG:
work shows 'poetic conception and romantic love of nature', 377 and fn.265; *Romance* 1st series was among PHG's most popular in UK and USA, 378; in USA, by far the most-reviewed of all PHG's books, 211 fn.277; 378 fn.269; PHG's earliest allusion to Darwin's theory in 1st series, 321-2; 322 fn.270; 2nd series obliquely criticised it, 322; and supported Law of Prochronism, 315; it received several negative reviews, 296 fn.138; 306 fn.202; 324 fn.283; 378.

Romanes, George John, Sec. of Linnean Society:
one of Darwin's 'strongest supporters', 558 fn.128; correspondence on PHG's 'Clasping-organs' memoir, 557-8; supports publication of, but plates are too expensive and seeks subsidy for, 558; 559 and fn.133; funding approved, memoir printed by Linnean, 559.

Rossetti, Christina, poet:
Pre-Raphaelite, sister of D.G. Rossetti, her work influenced by sermons of Dodsworth, a futurist premillennialist, 395; in 1870-1, EWG meets, 484; 506.

Rossetti, Dante Gabriel, poet, illustrator:
founder of Pre-Raphaelite Brotherhood, brother of C. Rossetti; French literary influence on, 483; friend of W.B. Scott, 484 fn.39; in 1871, EWG meets, 505; 507; influences EWG, 525; said to refer to EWG as 'Our youngest poet', 501; said to have praised EWG poem in *Madrigals, Songs and Sonnets*, 500; and another in *On Viol and Flute*, 526 and fn.203; writes for *Athenaeum*, 500 fn.89.

Rossmässler, Emil Adolf, zoologist:
influenced by PHG's *Aquarium*, 209; founder, aquarium movement in Germany, 210; author, *Das Süsswasser-Aquarium* (1857), 209 and fn.270; critical review of, 210 and fn.271; credits invention of aquarium to Europeans, 209-10; wrote for *Die Gartenlaube*, q.v., 210 fn. 272.

Rotifera (microscopic aquatic animals):
BACKGROUND: absence of paleontological record for, 320; subject of research from 1676, 177–80; Ehrenberg's 'monumental' 1838 work marks 2nd period of research into, 178; PHG finds classification system of, 'artificial', 183 and fn.124; majority views them as having affinity with Annelida but PHG sees them allied to Arthropoda, 183-4; 183 fn.127; 568; Hudson & Gosse marks 3rd period, 573; Hudson modifies Ehrenberg's system, 575; PHG AND: PHG's 'own special delight' in all of the animate world, 562; at end of his life, PHG considered '*facile princeps*' among Rotifera researchers, xix; in 1849, PHG first turns his attention to, after buying a microscope, 176-7; in Jan. 1850, reads first paper on, 176; others follow, 176-7; his significant studies, 180–6; PHG's focus transitions to microscopic world, 186; paper on 'Manducatory organs in the Class Rotifera', q.v., noted in his election as FRS, 250-1; between 1861–6, PHG publishes on, 371; 379; apparently thinks of popularizing Rotifera, but after 1866, stops writing on, 562-3; PHG's 1884 issue of *Evenings at the Microscope* same as 1859 ed., 562; around winter 1884, PHG resumes studies of, 571-2; in spring 1888, PHG resumes study of after ill health, 598 fn.402; 599;
PHG AND HUDSON: *see* Hudson.
PHG'S ILLUSTRATIONS OF: xix; shown at 1850 meeting of Linnean Society, 185 fn.139; in 1860, sends drawings to A.M. Norman, 371; in Hudson & Gosse, lauded, 574–7; PHG's 'hand and eye' remained perfect to the end, 573-4;
SEE ALSO: Ehrenberg; Hudson; Hudson & Gosse; 'Manducatory Organs'; *Pedalion mirum*.

Rotifera; or Wheel-Animalcules, by C.T. Hudson: *see* Hudson & Gosse, *Rotifera*.

Royal Botanical Gardens: *see* Kew, Royal Gardens.

Royal children:
in 1860, 1861, Owen, Kingsley gave lessons to, 278 fn.18; evidence lacking that PHG gave natural history lessons to, 278 fn.18.

Royal Microscopical Society: *see* Microscopical Society of London.

Royal Society of London:
Victorian Britain's premier scientific body, 358; in 1856, PHG elected to, 250-1; 160; 246; in 1857, alleged meeting of PHG and Darwin at, likely did not occur, 292-3; 293 fn.116; 361 fn.180; PHG borrows books for research, from, 544; comparison of treatment at, of PHG, Bastin, 362; Dawson, 557 fn.124;
PHILOSOPHICAL TRANSACTIONS: the difference between

Philosophical Transactions and *Proceedings*, 357; PHG's 2 articles in: 'Manducatory Organs', q.v. (read, 1855), 184; 359-60; 'Dioecious Character of the Rotifera' (read, 1856), 182 and fns.115-16; referees reject PHG's 1858 paper on 'Poison-apparatus', q.v., intended for, 356–60; X Club role, 360–5; referee reports by Lankester and McLachlan recommend PHG's 1881 'Clasping-organs', q.v., for the *Philosophical Transactions*, 553; a 3rd referee (Salvin) is added, who rejects it, 554-5; X Club role, 555; PHG kept in the dark, 558-9; a search for another scientific group to publish PHG's paper ends with Linnean Society *Transactions* (1883), 561;

PROCEEDINGS: abstract of PHG's 1858 paper on 'Poison-apparatus ', q.v., printed in, 356–62; abstract of PHG's 1881 paper on 'Prehensores of Male Butterflies' [='Clasping-organs', q.v.] printed in, 551 and fn.90;

REFEREE'S reports for: by Busk, 360; 560 fn.142; Carpenter, 184-5; Carruthers, 364 fn.196; Duncan, 364 fn.196; Farre, 182 fn.116; 184; PHG, 360 and fn.171; 238 fn.455; Hooker, 364 and fns.196, 200; Huxley, 360-1; 560 fn.142; Lankester, 552-3; 556; McLachlan, 550 fn.83; 553; 556; Salvin, 554-5; 559 fn.134; referee selection promotes scientific naturalist agenda, 361-2; 555; 560 fn.142; custom of only 2 referees, 554; submissions frequently marked 'safe' for publication, 551 fn.89; reports on Dawson's Bakerian Lecture, 364 fn.196; SEE ALSO: X Club.

Russell, Bertrand, philosopher: on *Omphalos*, 319.

Ryle, John Charles, bishop: 'Prince of Tract-Writers', published over 200 tracts, including *Living or Dead?*, with 12 million in circulation by 1897, 259; cited, 267.

Sacks, Jonathan, rabbi: cited: xxv; xxvii; 457 fn.106; 537; 608 fn.53.

Sacred Streams (1850), by PHG: among his most successful works, 186; USA ed., 186 fn.141; in 1854, the 2nd ed. is titled *Ancient and Modern History of the Rivers of the Bible*, 242 fn.479; reason for title change, 242 fn.479; prophetic views expressed in, 399 fn.36; 427 fn.172; 428 fn.177; meaning of baptism explained in, 443 fn.21; 336 fn.29; religious discourses sometimes based on, 583; REVIEWS OF: well-received in press, 583 fn.302; by Spurgeon for 1877 ed. of, 584; 583; 1883 issue, 584 fn.304.

Saffold, Reuben, Chief Justice: in 1838, meets PHG on Alabama River steamer, convinces him to be schoolmaster in Pleasant Hill, 85 and fn.293; PHG's contract not renewed, 91; says goodbye to, prior to leaving Alabama, 94.

'Saint Hill' (East Grinstead, Sussex): in 1867, EWG visits the country home of W.T. Berger, q.v., 5; 452 and fns.79-80.

Salter, Henry Hyde, physician: a relative of PHG, 246 fn.12; in 1856, elected FRS at same meeting as PHG, 246; in 1857, PHG seeks advice of, on EG's cancer, 246; gets EG an appointment with Paget, 246-7; proposes consultation with Fell, 247; 249-50; and recommends Fell, 250.

Salter, Thomas Bell, botanist: PHG cousin, helped arouse his love of natural history, 23 and fn.29; in 1832, PHG on botanical hikes in Poole with, 53 and fn.125; cited, 60.

Salvin, Osbert, entomologist: known for his 'generally sound' scientific advice, 554; research supports Darwin's theory, 549; 555; co-author with Godman of *Biologia Centrali-Americana*, 548; in a highly irregular move, a 3rd referee's report is sought from, for PHG's 1881 paper on 'Clasping-organs', q.v., and he declines to recommend it for the Royal Society's *Philosophical Transactions*, 554-5; proposes instead the Linnean Society, 555; his report analysed, 555; 556 fn.118; late date of his report, 559 fn.134.

Sanctification, Perfect: *see* Perfect Sanctification.

Sandhurst (St. Marychurch, Devon): in 1857, PHG leaving London, sets out to find new home at St. Marychurch, q.v., 285-6; 'Sandhurst', 286 and fn.77; unpersuasive explanation for 'Flight to Devonshire', 286 fn.76; EWG's friend, Benny, lives near, 439; Walker, q.v., visits EWG at, 459 fn.118; in 1860, PHG's mother Hannah dies at, 368; description of PHG's library at, 544-5; his study at, 368; Eliza Brightwen attends Scripture readings at, 369; in 1861, PHG builds orchid house at, 371; PHG's watercolours of orchids at, 372 fn.238; prize-winning orchid named after, 539 fns.10-11; in 1877, 79 orchids in flower, 582; in 1862, W.J. Hooker visits, 371; in 1868, 1869 EWG visits, 485 and fn.42; 487; in 1873, 522 fn.185; 523 and fn.186; 530; 531; 596; in 1879, 541; in 1888, 599; in 1890, 605; Eliza Gosse describes their lifestyle to NG, 528-9; constructs 49-gallon aquarium at, 540 and fn.14; death of their cat, Fairy, 615-633; in 1896, Fenn, a missionary, dies at, 605 fn.34. SEE ALSO: St. Marychurch.

Saunders, Trelawney William, geographer: at one time, associated with Brethren, 283; proposes Gnoll College, 283; chagrin at failure of Gnoll, 285 fn.69; delivers paper before Victoria Institute, 283 fn.53.

Saunders, William Wilson, entomologist: former president of Entomological Society; PHG knew, 121; 122 fn.121; purchases Jamaican insects collected by PHG, 147 fn.295.

Savannah-le-Mar (Jamaica): variously spelled, 128-9; 129 fn.158; on reaching Jamaica, PHG disembarks at, 128; PHG broke bread with H. De Leon at, 134; rarely left region, 144.

Say, Thomas, entomologist: 'Father of American Entomology', 75; PHG familiar with work of, 75 fn.233; 82 fn.271; which he found useful for Canada, not Alabama, 81 and fn.268; 86; a field collector, identifier, classifier, 83; benefitted from a patron, 83 fn.280; a Quaker, 83 fn.277.

Schooling, C.W., archivist:

CORRESPONDENCE WITH: 130 fn.174; 131 fn.178.

'School of the Prophets', article in *The Times*: anonymous 1859 analysis in, of prophetic works, 396; widespread attention given to, 396–8; reprinted as a pamphlet, 40,000 circulation in 2 years, 398; article attributed to John Cumming or Samuel Lucas or Eneas S. Dallas, 397 fn.27.

Schopenhauer, Arthur, German philosopher: pessimism of, 392; explanation of his aphorism used as epigraph to *Father and Son*, 607 fn.46.

Science, PHG's attitude to: purpose of study of nature is to find '*God appearing in the creatures ... without Him they are very nothings*', 155; studying the *mundus invisibilis* helps us understand Creator's plan, 239; the result is 'a fund of intellectual delight that would never satiate', 216; proper study of nature focuses on biography of living things, 163-5; 202; their organization and habits, 188; PHG's credo: approach nature with an 'open eye', 216-17; study of nature reveals that which is apparently simple can hide marvellous complexity (*e.g.*, teliferous system of sea anemones), 405; PHG's illustrations of birds, insects, sea anemones, Rotifera (frequently) locate them *in situ*, adding to their value, 148-9; 205; the harmonious nature of religious and scientific thought, 405-6;
DEVELOPMENT OF: in Newfoundland, PHG becomes 'not merely a collector ... but a *scientific naturalist*', 56; in Jamaica, more than a collector, 'a keen observer' of birds, 150;
'FALSELY SO CALLED': PHG has 'no quarrel' with science, only 'Science falsely so called' which makes 'bold assertions & deductions which trample under foot his authority', 388; danger of giving up faith 'to the conclusions of man', instead 'trust my God with a difficulty', 316; science undermines trust in, belief in, Second Advent, 546; Victoria Institute, q.v., established to counter 'the opposition of Science, falsely so called', 325.
SEE ALSO: Evolution, Darwin's theory of; Natural theology; Non-Darwinian science.

Sclater, Philip Lutley, zoologist: comment of, on PHG's *Birds of Jamaica*, 149; secretary, Zoological Society, correspondence on PHG's 'Clasping-organs', q.v., 557; addresses problem of backlog of papers at, 558 fn.126.

Scott, Thomas, clergyman: his Bible *Commentary* the 'most popular' among early 19th Century works, 102 fn.26; influence on PHG, 24-5; 29; 46; 102; 428; PHG learns historicist positions, 107; learns to expect Second Advent to begin in 1866, 31; Scott a postmillennialist, 107.

Scripture Help (1816), by Edward Bickersteth: in 1827, PHG brings popular evangelical work with him to Newfoundland, 32; 35; 126; teaching of, 46.

Scripture readings: also known as 'conversational' (or Bible) readings, in 1843 Hackney meeting is attended for first time by PHG, 3; EWG's contradiction of PHG's chronology, 3 fn.1; format of, 9; subject of, 4; influence of, on PHG, 8, 13; profile of attendees, 118-19; they exemplified Brethren methodological approach to

Scripture, 'the most influential' approach to Bible study in Victorian era, 9; 8 fn.5; deep impact of, on J. Van Sommer, 6; in 1860, 1867-8 in London, EWG's participation in, 460; 476; 511; with other Brethren, 459; PHG's meetings at Sandhurst, 418; 584-5; Eliza Gosse attends weekly readings at Sandhurst, 369; in 1870, important letter from EWG arrives on morning of, 490; in 1882, PHG invites A.R. Hunt to, but he declines, 584; some dissatisfied with PHG's leadership at, 424 fn.156.

Scudder, Samuel Hubbard, entomologist: 'first great paleoentomologist', 549 fn.75; until about 1870, opposed Darwin, 548; when he accepted the theory, 494 fn.75; 549 and fn.75; indexes PHG's notes on butterflies in *Canadian Naturalist*, 76 fn.238; PHG's observations there, and in *Letters from Alabama*, are 'full of original observations', 76 fn.240; lauds PHG's 'Clasping organs', q.v., 556 fn.117.

Sea Anemones (invertebrate marine animals related to corals): as a young boy, aunt Susan Bell shows PHG how to keep them alive in a dish of sea-water, 23 fn.29; 194 fn.182; around 1830, Ehrenberg challenges view they are not complex creatures, 178; factors increasing interest in, 349-50; evolutionary history of, remains to this day controversial, 320;
PHG STUDY OF: in 1852, PHG commences study of, at St. Marychurch, 187; 333; 339; including eating sea anemones, 188 and fn.153; in 1854, begins gathering materials for a monograph on, 201; while lecturing, searches for, and seeks help in finding, on British shores, 238; 541; in 1856, announcement in *Tenby* of 'Proposed Work on British Sea-Anemones', 340; 360 and fn.172; PHG's work preceded by 2 others, 340-1; early 1858, 1st of 12 bi-monthly parts appears of *Actinologia Britannica*, 342; in 1887, lends sea anemone material to A.C. Haddon, 597;
TELIFEROUS ('dart bearing') SYSTEM: 1853–9, PHG publishes on offensive and defensive apparatus in sea anemones, beginning in *Devonshire Coast*, 199; 355-6; also talks of 'thread capsules' in lectures, 239; 'acontia' is his coinage in *Actinologia Britannica*, 352 and fn.132; capsules originally thought to be spermatozoa, 356; description of 'masterpieces of ingenious contrivance and wonderously elaborate mechanism', 355-6; PHG apparently the first to use them as a classificatory tool, 352 fn.132; in 1858, submits paper on, to Royal Society; why it was published in *Proceedings*, 356–65; PHG repeats his findings in 2 subsequent works, 365; Lewes challenges PHG's view on, 365-6; significance of dispute, 366-7.
SEE ALSO: *Actinologia Britannica*; Andres; Haddon; Illustrations; 'Researches on the Poison-apparatus'; Stephenson.

Seashore: PHG's work marks a new era in history of, 191–216; his 'open eye' philosophy, 216-17; 190-1;
BACKGROUND: at Bluefields, Jamaica, PHG is a few hundred yards from, he rises at daylight to start his work, 133; orchids, plants, seashore objects,

139; in Devon, PHG an explorer in darkest Africa, 188; railway apparently not a factor in bringing people to, until after heyday of aquarium, 190 fn.162; the word 'vacation', 190;
PHG AND: the PHG phenomenon analysed, 219–43; the artistic community reflects, 217-18; tract disseminators turn to, 256; 259; by 1861, the results of the invasion of, 367-8; 368 fn.212; 340; seashore audience fades, 379; EWG's juvenile writings on, 439-440;
SEE ALSO: Marine Natural History Classes; Marine zoology.
Sea-Side Studies at Ilfracombe, Tenby, the Scilly Isles, & Jersey (1858), by G.H. Lewes:
the philosophical treatment of 'the complex facts of life', 231; approach varies from PHG, 366-7; PHG's review of, in *Literary Gazette*, 354 fn.148; PUBLICATION RECORD: first serialised in *Blackwood's Magazine*, 232; publishing figures compared to PHG: print-run of, 224; income from, 222; analysed, 232-3; PHG owns copy of, 232 fn.406; SCIENTIFIC ASPECT: contests PHG's scientific findings, 353-5; 365-6; PHG refers to 'foolish hypothesis' of, 354.
Second Advent:
a core concern for Brethren, 153 and fn.336; in mid-Victorian Britain, thousands of Christians lived in expectation of, 392; 1860 poll shows American preachers agree age is 'near ending', 394; premillennial or postmillennial, 105; in Darby's futurist hermeneutic, will occur in 2 stages, 411-12; Newton sees single stage, 412; ANTICIPATED DATES OF HISTORICISTS, FOR:
    1843–47, 1848: 111; 392 and fn.7; 399; 108; 111 and fn.61; Brethren leader P.F. Hall predicts it will occur 19 Mar. 1844, 111 fn.61; 399;
    1855-6: 392; 399;
    1864–72: 398;
    1866-7: 392; 398 and fn.31; 407; 415 fn.107; 428; 430;
    1870-1: 428; 434; 492;
    1872: 415;
    1877: 588; 434;
    1880-1: 588-9;
    1923: 588; 392 fn.7;
    1934: 588;
    1941: 431 ('Continuationist');
PHG's POSITION ON: PHG a premillennialist, 107; learns from historicist Habershon it is imminent, 108; 107; PHG believes its arrival can be predicted and watches for, xvii; xxiii; 427-8; 434-5; 492; 538; in 1870, EWG not persuaded of imminence of, 494; but changes his mind, 497; PHG thinks miraculous events not to precede, 406; science undermines trust in belief in, 546; not persuaded by sensationalist claims of Boyce, 589-90; PHG not persuaded by continuationist calculations of Elliott, 588; 432-3.
Secret rapture:
at Second Advent, doctrine that Jesus would first come for the church at any moment, which would be raptured; supported by Darby, a pretribulationist, futurist premillennialist, 411-12; disagreement with Newton, 412; pessimistic political,

social impact, 117; 400; PHG's view on, 414-15; 415 fn.104.
Sex:
NATURAL HISTORY STUDIES: Ehrenberg claims even single-celled animals have sexual organs, 178; denied by Lewes, 354; affirmed by PHG, 'Dioecious Character of the Rotifera', 354 fn.142; after 1859, Darwin proposes to show that orchids had sexual structures adapted to cross-fertilization by insects, 376; Weismann's view concerning asexual reproduction in Rotifera cited, 579; French naturalists who disapproved of sexual habits of cats, 616; EWG: alleged homosexual relationship of, with Marzials, 482 and fn.27;
PHG: assertion he was a misogynist, xxi and fn.32; his *Actinologia Britannica* said to contain 'more than a hint of forbidden sexual pleasures', xxi-xxii; in PHG's observations on marine animals, he handled sex in nature for descriptive purposes and as a morphological tool, writing about sex characteristics of Rotifera and Lepidoptera, 202 fn.234.
Shipton, Anna, writer:
EG AND: around 1853, EG passes along to, copy of *Narrative of ... George Müller*, 256; in summer 1855 at Ilfracombe, accompanies 2 women to Marine Natural History class, 234 fn.416; after encountering EG, she accepts 'Jesus as her personal Saviour', 266; in 1856, EG writes her that EWG is 'indeed a child of God', 253; in 1857, EG writes to, about breast cancer, 247; her assessment of cancer prognosis, 270;
TELL JESUS.' ([1863]): uses PHG's *Memorial* in writing, 282 and fn.49; bibliography of, 282 fn.49; incorrect date for EG's death given in, 273 fn.193.
Sinless Sanctity: *see* Perfect Sanctification.
6000 Years of the World's History Now Closing (1866), by PHG:
sees world's end possibly in 1866, 407; 415 fn.107; references tenets of historicist position, 415 fn.109; basis for PHG's chronology, 406 and fn.68; 407 fn.70; lauds Elliott, 429 fn.; most reviews notice, do not endorse, PHG's views, 407 fn.71; 2nd ed. (1867) sees termination of 6000 years about 1872: 415 and fns.106-7; sends Elliott copy of, 429 fn.190; epigraph to, 601 fn.420; cited: 396 fn.22; 407 fns.69-70; 415.
Skrine, Clarmont, clergyman:
in 1863, convenes Trent Park prophecy conference, 401 and fn.49; among the speakers (including PHG) at a prophecy conference at Freemasons' Hall, 403 fn.59.
Slade, Elson, and Company, merchant trading firm (counting-house) in Newfoundland:
known under different names, 36 fn.21; in 1827, PHG begins working at, starting at £20 per annum, 28; 32; 63 and fn.177; comparative size of, 36; John Elson, a Unitarian, is resident partner, 37; in 1828, PHG sent to a branch of, in St. Mary's, 39; 65 fn.184; in 1830, Apsey astonishes clerks at, about his conversion, 42; Apsey's influence on Slade clerks, 43; 47-8; in 1833 PHG completes terms of indenture at, but stays on, 57; towards end of 1834, PHG decides to leave the colony, 63; his salary is then £50, 63; John Elson is unfazed

by the decision, 65; in 1835, PHG heads towards Upper Canada, 65; in 1835, P. Tocque works at, 58 fn.147; 59 fn.153; and St. Mary's branch destroyed, 65 fn.184.

SEE ALSO: Harrison, Slade & Co. (Poole).

Slavery:
T. Gosse (father) attends ministry of John Newton, former African slave-trader, 18-19; Lyell on, 88 and fn.308; E. Long on, 135; Darwin on, 136 fn.213; R. Hill on, 142-3; L. Strong on, 334; 335 fn.22;
PHG ON: in Newfoundland, debates West Indian slave compensation, 44; 135; arrives in Jamaica after emancipation, 125; 135; not comment on Jamaican, 135; in Alabama, sees 'domestic institution' for first time, 87; 'so enormous an evil', 91; 80; 96; it is doomed, 88-9; locals suspect him, 88; PHG's position compared to that of antebellum British travellers to American South, 87-8; PHG's views of, not aired fully until 1859, 95 and fn.366; sets within his prophetic system, 432.

Slim, Benjamin T., early Brethren leader:
in Jamaica, 152 fn.331; promoter of Darby, Brethren in West Indies, known there as 'Slimites', 9 fn.10.

Sloane, Hans, physician and natural history collector:
spent 15 months in Jamaica, 137-9, first of island's butterfly collectors, 137; PHG writes that natural history notes of, were 'full of confusion and error', 137-8; PHG first to advance ornithological studies in Jamaica since Sloane, 149.

Smiles, Samuel, author:
popular lecturer, 234; PHG echoes *Self-Help* (1859) advice of, 463.

Society for Promoting Christian Knowledge (SPCK):
did not send out review copies of its books, 150; 162 fn.12; but did advertise them, 225; 214-15;
PHG BOOKS PUBLISHED BY: *Introduction to Zoology*, 81 fn.267; 122; *Ocean*, 122; 123 fn.128; 128 fn.153; *Monuments of Ancient Egypt*, 165; 5 volumes on natural history planned as manuals to British Museum collection, 12 fn.24; 166; *Text-book of Zoology for Schools*, 166; 173; *History of the Jews*, 165; *Assyria*, 221 fn.342; *Seaside Pleasures*, 217 fn.311; *Wanderings Through the Conservatories at Kew*, 100 fn.14; *Evenings at the Microscope*, 345; 425 fn.158;
PHG WORK PUBLISHED IN SPCK SERIAL: *Letters from Alabama*, 89; 95 fn.366; 243; *Wanderings Through the Conservatories at Kew*, 243;
PHG BOOKS REJECTED BY: *Letters from Alabama* 89; *Naturalist's Sojourn in Jamaica*, 151;
PHG PAYMENT RECEIVED FOR BOOKS: 219; 173; 221 and fn.342.

Society of Biblical Archaeology (London):
founded 1870, 389 fn.313; aims to show that 'Biblical science' corroborates the Bible, 389; PHG a member of, from its inaugural meeting, 389 and fn.311; cited: 428.

Soltau, Henrietta Eliza, early Brethren figure:
daughter of H.W. Soltau, prominent among Open Brethren, 513; biography of, cited: 212 fn.289.

Soltau, Henry William, early Brethren figure:

among Open Brethren, 403 fn.59; 513; mythology about being disowned by family, 513 and fn.157; EWG may have met daughters of, 212; PHG associated with, 338 fn.37; and reads works of, 399 fn.37; Chapman and Hake associates of, 212 fn.289; in 1864, among speakers (with PHG) at 'Week of Prayer', 403; corresponds with PHG, 426 fn.164; 3 daughters of, baptized as teenagers, 442 fn.16; niece married Bewes, q.v., 513 and fn.156.

Sowerby, George Brettingham (1812–84), illustrator:
illustrated Wood's *Common Objects of the Sea Shore* (1857), 228; his *Popular History of the Aquarium* (1857) called 'good-for-nothing', 228.

SPCK: *see* Society for Promoting Christian Knowledge.

Species, definition of:
SPECIAL CREATION: Linnaeus, Cuvier, believe species 'distinct forms' created by God, 287; Lamarckian (transmutationist) view considered 'unphilosophical', 287; the *Introduction to Entomology* (1815 *et. seq.*) of Kirby and Spence follows dominant natural theology view of fixity of species to explain design, 52; in 1857, common view of naturalists was that animate world was divinely derived, immutable, 287; 297; Tugwell expresses that view, 341 fn.57; botanist J.D. Hooker then unconvinced species had evolved, 293-4; Westwood maintains distinct created species until his death in 1893, 547 fn.56; PHG's argument for immutability of, 323; 352; 561;
EVOLUTION OF: in 1856-7, Darwin writes PHG on species variation and distribution, 306; in 1858, neither special creation nor evolution appeared to satisfactorily account for diversity of orchid species, 373-4; 376-7; in 1859, Darwin's theory substitutes unchanging species for explanation of their dynamic origin, 550; Darwin relates species definition to assumption of earth's short duration, 294-5; Darwin insists on, but initially has no evidence of, transitional forms between species, 566; contribution of Bates, 567; PHG's, Darwin's different explanations for extinction of, 323 and fn.279; morphological, microscopic, study of butterfly armature leads PHG to believe he may have discovered a scientific challenge to Darwin's theory, rooted in definition of 'species', 546-7.

Spencer, Edward:
present at 1843 Hackney Scripture reading, 7; lack of information on, 7 fn.4; around 1853, helps form Evangelical Tract Association, q.v., 6; 257.

Sprague, Samuel W., counting house clerk:
nephew of John Elson, at the age of 13 he became a clerk in Carbonear, Newfoundland, 45; comment on Apsey's conversion, 43; 20 years old at conversion of, 47; PHG responsible for conversion of, 48; 60; 61 and fn.165; influenced by Apsey, 61 fn.165; joins Carbonear Wesleyan choir, 58; in 1838, becomes a local, then regular, Wesleyan minister, 47 fn. 89; 48; 59 fn.153; 61 and fn.166; corresponds with PHG, 79; 95 fn.365; PHG draws strength from, 507.

Spurgeon, Charles Haddon, preacher:
commends PHG's 'profound reverence for the Word', xvii; massive turnout to hear him speak at

1864 'Week of Prayer' in London, 402-3; involved in East End Training Institute, 425 fn.162; corresponds with PHG, 426 fn.164;
REVIEWS OF PHG BOOKS: in *Sword and the Trowel*, 592 fn.360; unimpressed with argument of *Omphalos*, 319 fn.258; praises *Sacred Streams*, 584; takes the high road in reviewing *Mysteries of God*, 592.

Stacey, Mary, early Brethren figure:
raised a Quaker, 245; later among Open Brethren, 245 fn.5; 338 fn.37; from 1838, member, Brook Street assembly, 245; from 1856, knew PHG, EG, 452; member, Ladies' Chinese Association, 452; suggests EG have physician examine lump in breast, 245; accompanies her to Laseron, 246; in 1857, PHG says goodbye to, before moving to St. Marychurch, 286; in 1868, EWG attends Scripture readings with, 459; 452; dines at home of, 461.

Stephenson, Thomas Alan, marine biologist:
his *British Sea Anemones* (1928, 1935) displaces *Actinologia Britannica*, 353; controversial evolutionary history of, 320; favourable comments on PHG's sea anemone studies, 348; 349; 352 fn.132; acontia, q.v., as a classificatory tool, 352 fn.132.

Stevens, Samuel, natural history agent:
agent for collecting of Bates and Wallace, PHG bemoans not using him in Jamaica, 141; commission charged by, 141 fn.248; insect specimens collected by Wallace, 147 fn.292.

Stirling Tract Enterprise (Scotland):
of Peter Drummond, 260; founded 1848, 258; circulates over 46 million tracts, 260 and fn.111; including EG tracts, 263.

St. John, William Charles, publisher, writer:
BIOGRAPHY: 37 fn.26-7; 67 fns.196-7; the 'Newfoundland Poet' and 'Philosopher of Newfoundland', born in Harbour Grace, 37; confused with his son, Charles Henry, 40 fn.38; PHG's description of, 37-8; portrait of, by William Gosse, 602 fn.5; founder, *Conception Bay Herald*, 37 fn.27; in 1830, marries Elizabeth Susanna Comer, sister of William S. Comer, editor, *Conception Bay Mercury*, 40; in 1831, leaves Carbonear for Harbour Grace to open a wine-importing business, 40; 66; following Apsey's evangelical conversion in 1830, St. John undergoes a rebirth, 61 fn.166; 43; 47; winter 1830, part of a debating society, 44; 135 fn.207; in 1835, authors *Catechism of the History of Newfoundland*, 33 fns.1-2; 34 fn.8; 44 fn.74; in 1854, moves to Boston, becomes a journalist, 67;
PHG AND: in 1827, a clerk at Slade, Elson & Co., 45; friendship with PHG, 37; in 1834, PHG prays for him as he nearly succumbs to scarlet fever, 61; shares PHG's natural history enthusiasm, 49; promotes PHG's *Canadian Naturalist*, 77 and fn.242; sporadic correspondence with PHG, 67 fn.196; 95 fn.365; 77; 537; cited: 60.

St. Marychurch (Devon):
in 1852, PHG family leaves London to spend 3 months in, 187; 255; brings natural history books, microscope to the seashore, 187; 333; in 1857, moving to, he tells William Gosse at train station of plans for *Omphalos*, 286; description of village,

332-3; 587; EWG attends Menneer's school in, 444; searches tide-pools for sea anemones, 342; 368; at death, PHG known mainly in circle of his friends, 601;

CHURCH OF GOD: history of Brethren in St. Marychurch-Torquay area, 334 and fn.8; in 1857, PHG attends Brethren's Room in, for first time, 333-4; 277 fn.12; 534; 583; PHG soon 'sole pastor and conductor' of all meetings at Brethren Room, 336; 422; which he sometimes calls 'Church of God', 422; in 1860, Eliza Brightwen attends meeting at, 368; converts won, 400; it grows in size, moving in 1860 to a new chapel on Fore Street, 337; 444 fn.24; 1867 expansion plans, 418; description of membership, 418; they accept PHG's prophetic views, 419; in 1868, dispute over open ministry, 419–24; in 1872, disagreement with Bewes, q.v., a member of PHG's assembly, over believer's baptism, 512-15; dissatisfaction with Scripture readings, 424 fn.156; W.K. Perrens attends, 583 fn.299; membership increase means Room might no longer be large enough, 587-8; Babbacombe Gospel Hall, an offshoot of, 588 fn.333; cited: 417; 444 fn.24;
SEE ALSO: Sandhurst.

St. Thomas' Rooms (Brethren assembly on St. Thomas's Road, Hackney), 254 and fn.69.

Stokes, George Gabriel, physicist:
president, British Association, 385; anti-Darwinian, counters Darwinians at British Assoc., Exeter (1869), 385-6; president, Victoria Institute, 386 fn.302; 326 fn.300; secretary, Royal Society, 553 fn.106; claims PHG's 'Clasping-organs' paper is 'too limited' for *Philosophical Transactions*, recommends Linnean Society, 557 and fns.124-5; comparison of PHG, Dawson at Royal Society, 557 fn.124.

Strong, Leonard, early Brethren leader:
a missionary in Demerara 'amongst blacks and slaves', 334-5; 335 fn.22; among Open Brethren, 334; Brethren presence in Torquay from 1830s, but in 1848-9, with arrival of, assembly increases, 334; in 1854, opens 'unostentatious building' seating 500, does weekly open-air preaching, 336; in 1859, officiates at baptism of EWG, 443-4; sons Robert and James attend school of Edgelows, with EWG, 447; in 1860, officiates at funeral of Hannah, PHG's mother, 368; in 1864, speaks (with PHG and others) at meeting on 'Sure Word of Prophecy', 403; in 1872, after first trying PHG, Bewes contacts, concerning simultaneous believer's baptism of their 4 children, 512-515; baptism by, on 25 Dec., 514; while PHG does not approve the process, he accepts the action, 514; an example of congregational autonomy among Brethren, 422 fn.144.

Stunt, Timothy C.F., historian:
CORRESPONDENCE WITH: 664; 212 fn.289; 400 fn.40; 403 fn.59; 426 fn.164; 512 fn.152; 513 fn.157; 517 fn.178.

Sturridge, Mrs (of Jamaica):
she went with PHG into Savannah-le-Mar, where she worshipped at Wesleyan chapel, 134; in 1880, corresponds with PHG, 134 fn.199; she knew Mais,

an Anglican minister who collected insects for PHG in Jamaica, 542 fn.26.

Surrey Zoological Gardens, Crystal Palace: PHG collects for short-lived aquarium, 200 and fn.221.

Sweet, Mrs (of Jamaica): PHG and others break bread at, 134.

Swinburne, Algernon Charles, poet: in 1867, EWG sends writing sample to, 469; 479; O'Shaughnessy friendly with, 481; Parnassian influence on, 483; in 1870 meets EWG, 484; 485 fn.40; said to have praised EWG poem in *Madrigals, Songs and Sonnets*, 500; EWG is friendly with, and inspired by, 525; 507; EWG's high opinion of, 485 fn.40; 'amatory paganism' of, 527; cited: 473.

Talmon, Jacob L., historian: on political messianism, 391 and fn.2.

Taylor, Peter, MP: proprietor, London *Examiner*, in 1874, EWG meets at home of, 527-8.

Taylor, H. Wilbraham, preacher: Brethren co-convener of two 1864 religious meetings in London, 402; involved in a fund to which PHG donates, 422 fn.151.

Teleological argument: see Design, argument from.

Teliferous ('dart bearing') system: see Sea anemones.

Tenby (Wales): 1854: for 2 summer months, PHG family staying at, 212; 283 fn.57; result is *Tenby*, the first work on the 'special features' of the seaside town, 215; 1856: in Sept., 2nd marine natural history classes at, 234 and fn.418; 243; Fell encourages EG to go with family to, 250; they tell Brethren at, of EG's breast cancer, 244; in Oct. 1856, leave Tenby, 244; RELIGIOUS ACTIVITY: in 1856 (and possibly 1854) Gosses break bread with Brethren at, 244; 277 fn.12; 337 fn.33; in Sept. 1856, 4 lectures on prophecy at, 399 fn.36; SCIENTIFIC ACTIVITY: PHG's marine natural history classes in 1856 at, promoted, 213 fn.290; described, 234 and fn.416; area depleted of sea anemones, 327 fns.211-12; dredging with Dyster at, 244 and fn.489; Lewes's research at, 232; SEE ALSO: *Sea-side Studies* (Lewes).

Tenby: a sea-side holiday (1856), by PHG: ASPECTS OF: final volume in PHG's seashore trilogy, based on 1854 summer holiday at, 215; the first work on 'special features' of that seaside town, 215 and fn.308; in describing jellyfish, interjects comment on 'Papal cruelty', 101 fn.23; PHG praises Darwin's *Cirripedia* in, 321 fn.267; announces 'Proposed Work on the British Sea-Anemones', 340; PHG wonders at cause of depletion of sea anemones there, 327 fns.211-12; PHG explains depletion, in a remark misdated by scholars, 368 and fn.212; PUBLICATION RECORD: 20 colour, 4 plain lithographs, nearly all by PHG, 221; published on author's-risk basis, PHG receives 57% of profits, 221; 1,500 copies printed, 223; at least £360 profit by 1869, 221; reviewers bemoan high cost of book, 220-1; book sells slowly, 223; advertised: 226 fns.371-4;

REPUTATION: 4th most reviewed of PHG books, 199 fn.214; hailed in press, 215; 214 fn.299; part of local lore, 215 and fn.308; Kingsley on, 230-1.

Tenby Observer (weekly): comments on enthusiasm of PHG's students, 197; 243-4; PHG books advertised in, 238 fn.451.

Tennyson, Alfred, poet: around 1871, EWG meets, 500; who had apparently read some of his verse, 501; opposition of, to English Parnassians, 483; EWG receives from, introduction to Norwegian writer, 504; regarded by EWG as one of 3 greatest living poets, 485 fn.40; EWG reviews work by, 528 fn.214; cited: 479; 497.

'Testimony of Prophecy', by PHG: a manuscript book into which PHG pasted scriptural passages on unfulfilled prophecy, 109-10; includes letters and memoranda; table of contents listed, 110 fn.57; 638; *passim*.

Text-book of Zoology for Schools (1851), by PHG: largely unoriginal, resembling Patterson's *Introduction to Zoology for the Use of Schools* (1849), 166; British government *vs.* independent publishers, 166; SPCK pays PHG £100 for, 173; 18% of, devoted to rotifera and other radiates, 186; reason for lack of reviews of, 162 fn.12; advertising of, by SPCK, 225 fns.367-8, 370.

Thackeray, William M., novelist: comparison of lecturing income of, to science lecturing, 234-5; 237; priority given to, over science lectures, 237 fn.446; 277 fn.13; criticism of lectures by, 235 fn.430.

Thompson, D'Arcy Wentworth, zoologist: on PHG's artistic talent, xix; 207 fn.263; on *Manual of Marine Zoology*, 214; xv fn.23.

Thornton, Robinson, clergyman: paper on 'Numerical system of the Old Testament' at Victoria Institute, 327 fn.305; opposed in 2 papers, one by PHG, 328-9; PHG apologizes for perceived insult, receives no reply, 330.

Thread-capsules: see Sea anemones; 'Researches on the Poison-apparatus'.

Three Days' Meetings of Prayer, and Addresses on the 'Sure Word of Prophecy': held in May 1864 at Freemasons' Hall, 403; 316 fn.245; 335 fn.22; 382; characterization of speakers at, 403 and fn.59; quotations from PHG at, 315-16; 382 fn.282.

Thynne, Anna, naturalist: claimed priority as aquarium inventor, 192 fn.173; 193 and fns.179, 181; not use the word 'aquarium', 208 fn.264.

The Times of London, daily newspaper: known as 'The Thunderer', 396; advertisement for *Omphalos*, 286; assessment of PHG's *Memorial*, 282 fn.46; PHG testimonial for telescope in, 597; PHG reads, for prophetic developments, 428; 589 fn.342; EWG's *Life* published, 605 fn.32; OBITUARIES: Bjørnson (attributed to EWG), 505 fn.120; C.T. Hudson, 566; Eliza Gosse, 605 fn.35; EWG, 610 fn.69; 611; 'SCHOOL OF THE PROPHETS': letter by C.J. Fynes Clinton states his brother, H.F. Clinton, q.v., was not a student of prophecy, notwithstanding his conclusions in *Fasti Hellenici*, 396; *Times* publishes anonymous 4,100 word analysis in 1859 on, 396–8; which is reprinted as a pamphlet, 398; conjectures about authorship, 397 fn.27.

Tocque, Philip, clergyman, writer:
a Carbonear native, 59; and an Anglican, 59 fn.153; 'Newfoundland's first man of letters', 67 fn.195; in 1830, at age 16, he joins Carbonear Methodist Society, 47 fn.84; 56 fn.140; as a local preacher, 59 fn.153; characterization of Methodism, 58; his conversion experience, 46–7; in 1835, a clerk at Slade, Elson and Co., 58 fn.147; 59 fns.153-4; in 1840, denied membership in Methodist Missionary Society in London, 59 fn.153; in 1849, moves to Boston to become an Anglican minister and writer, 66–7; 61 fn.166; corresponds with PHG, 95 fn.365.

Tonna, Charlotte *née* Browne (1st wife of L.H.J. Tonna):
editor, *Christian Lady's Magazine*, 111 and fn.66; part of a circle of Protestant, premillennialist anti-Catholics, 111-12; PHG writes to, 111 fn.65; and publishes article in *Magazine*, 111 fn.64.

'Tracts for Ireland', religious tract series:
series started, and paid for, by Millar, q.v., 260; appeal in USA for funds to continue, 260; EG tract published by, 263.

Tracts (religious):
19th century called 'the Tract Century', 258; DISTRIBUTION OF: widespread, 258 and fn.96; venues: 259; numbers: 259-60; modes and means: 258-9; 261; in 1853, EG distributes tracts of others, 257; and then her own, 266; and as she travels by rail, 271 fn.181; on deathbed, 272; PHG, on return from Jamaica, 146; in correspondence, 258 fn.98; funding for, 425-6; Pearse, in Algeria, 7 fn.3; IMPACT OF: 261; 263; 265-6;
LANGUAGES OF: 259, 260; 266;
PURPOSE OF: 'directing the sinner to the Saviour', 258; 260-1; 263–5;
PUBLISHERS OF: 257-8; 266; *see* Dublin Tract Society; Evangelical Tract Association; Religious Tract Society; Stirling Tract Enterprise; Tracts for Ireland; Weekly Tract Society;
TYPES OF: 258;
WRITERS OF: 261–3; women *see* Barbour; EG; More; men *see* PHG ('The Negro Slave', 96 fn.367; Dollar's Worth', 539 fn.8); Millar; Richmond; Ryle.
SEE ALSO: *under Gosse's Narrative* or *Gospel Tracts* (leaflets); *Narrative Tracts* (book); and individual titles.

Transitional forms: *see* Missing links.

Tregelles, Samuel Prideaux, Bible scholar:
nephew of E.O. Tregelles, in prophetic outlook, a futurist premillennialist, 399 fn.37; 400 and fn.40; PHG familiar with work of, 399 fn.37; critique of Mildmay Conferences, 402 fn.51.

Tydeman, William W., homoeopathic physician:
about 1846, Coleman introduces the Englishman in Jamaica to PHG, who baptizes him, 134; 152 fn.332; his activities after leaving Jamaica, including financial support from Darby-Wigram, and living in Knoxville, Tennessee, 134 and fn.200; under the influence of Darby-Wigram, 153; 154; later corresponds with PHG, 134 fn.200; abandons

Brethren for 'Universalism' (funeral held at a Knoxville Episcopal church), 154.

'Unequal Yoke', by EWG:
anonymous 1886 novellette by EWG, 476 fn.4; unknown if portrayal is relevant to Emma Beddows or Mary Johnson, 476 fn.4.
Upper Canada (Ontario): *see* Canada.

Van Sommer, James, law student:
brother of Mary Berger, q.v., in 1843, attends Brethren Scripture reading in Hackney, 5-6; 6 fn.10; 119 fn.100; supporter of missionary activity, editor, author, 6; signator to *Declaration of Students*, q.v., 383 fn.286; cited: 4 fn.3.

Van Voorst, John, natural history publisher:
in 1839, T. Bell shows him MS for PHG's *Canadian Naturalist*, which he publishes, 98 and fn.8; 100; 219; 223; sends copies of his books for press review, 162; beginning with *Illustrations of the Birds of Jamaica*, publishes PHG books on an author's-risk basis, 219-20; in 1859, he is advertising 8 PHG titles at once, 226 and fns.371-2, 374; *Omphalos* sells slowly, 317; and *Canadian Naturalist*, 380; offers to sell copyright to Hubbert for new ed., 380 fn.277; PHG hopes he knows 'the happiness of reconciliation to God', 587.

Various Contrivances: see *On the Various Contrivances by Which British and Foreign Orchids are Fertilised by Insects.*

Vestiges of the Natural History of Creation (1844), by Richard Chambers:
though condemned by men of science and theologians, crude espousal of evolution is a sensation, 160-1; but never gains traction, 311; PHG derides, 287; praised by Carpenter, who was asked to revise it, 294.

Victoria Institute, Bible-defence group:
in 1865, founded by James Reddie, 325; 385; anti-Darwinian, 326; members oppose British Association, 385-6;
EWG AND: in 1873, EWG becomes member of, and reads paper at, 524 and fns.196-7; EWG's critique of members, 524; EWG ends membership in, 530;
PHG AND: PHG a founding Vice President, 325 and fn.294; 383; and contributor to their library, 326 fn.296; membership in, is part of PHG's public opposition to science as practiced, 383; owns a run of their *Journal of the Transactions*, 326 fn.296; PHG family relations and friends belonging to, 325 fn.295; 584 fn.311; Brethren belonging to, 326 fn.297; 308 fn.211; men of science belonging to, 326 and fn.300; PHG referees a paper for, 308; PHG paper for: 'High Numbers of the Pentateuch', *see separate entry*;
SEE ALSO: Bible and Christian Defence Groups.

Voice Upon the Mountains (monthly), edited by T.G. Bell:
favours futurism of B.W. Newton, 406 fn.67; PHG's *Revelation* criticized, 416 fn.111; contributors to: Chester, 408; 431 fn.200; L. Strong, 335 fn.18.

Walker, Charles A. L.:

EWG friend at British Museum, in 1868 they attend talk by Saphir, 458-9; Walker later visits Sandhurst, corresponds with PHG, 459 fns.117-18; opposed to poetry, 473.

Wallace, Alfred Russel, entomologist: research by, supports evolution theory, 549; Darwin's *'little'* disappointment in *Travels on the Amazon* by, 321 fn.266; in 1858, natural selection theory of, presented at Linnean Society, 301; Haughton's low estimation of it, 301-2; 302 fn.183; compares it to *Omphalos*, 302; PHG AND: Wallace studies geographical isolation of species, compared to PHG, 320; collection of 110,000 insect specimens by, compared to PHG, 147 and fn.292; Stevens acts as his collection agent, 141; corresponds with PHG, 317 fn.254; PHG contacts Mesman, known to, 542; PHG owns copy of *Malay Archipelago*, by, 542 fn.27.

Wanderings through the Conservatories at Kew ([1856]), by PHG: serialised, 243 and fn.481.

Warburtonian Lectures (1856), by E.B. Elliott: eds. published, 271 fns.182-3; PHG reads to EG, 271; 430.

Ward, Nathaniel Bagshaw, botanist: in 1830s, realised that ferns could survive in closed glass containers ('Wardian cases'), builds early freshwater aquarium, 192; in Jamaica, PHG familiar with Wardian cases, 140; 195; several consider Ward 'true inventor of the aquarium', 193 and fn.179; did not author a separate work on it, 197; in contact with, Bowerbank has an aquarium, 198.

Warington, George, chemist: son of Robert Warington, chemist, 325 fn.295; member, Victoria Institute, 326 fn.300.

Warington, Robert, chemist: candidate for inventor of aquarium, in 1849, does experiments on, 192 fn.175; 193 fn.180; 'ignorant' about natural history, 197; significance of misspelled name, 192 fn.175; 277 fn.10; father of George Warington, 325 fn.295; PHG AND: in 1852, publishes on sea-water aquarium, at the same time as PHG, 193 fn.180; 208 fn.264; corresponds with PHG, 193 fn.180; PHG supplies sea animals to, 198; PHG cites him in *Naturalist's Rambles*, 208 fn.264; denounces PHG's sea-water formula, 201 fn.230; jealous of attention to PHG, 201 fn.230.

Weekly Tract Society, for labouring classes: publishing record, 258; 260; issues EG tracts, 263; PHG speaks before, 263.

Wellington, 1st Duke of (Arthur Wellesley), soldier and statesman: said to correspond with Habershon after studying his prophetic works, 395 and fn.21.

Wellesley Index: anonymous *London Quarterly Review* articles by PHG identified in, 667-8; attributions examined, 277 fn.10; CORRESPONDENCE WITH: 162 fn.11.

Wells, T. Spencer, surgeon: author, *Cancer Cures and Cancer Curers*, 269 fn.172; characterization of Pattison, 249; of PHG's *Memorial of the Last Days*, 269; of Fell, 270 fn.173; excerpts from *Memorial*, 281 fn.45.

Wertheimer, Gila, 682; quoted, 532 fn.240; [vii].

Wesenberg-Lund, Carl, zoologist: commends Hudson & Gosse, 577; 579; but considers its classification 'unnatural', 575 fn.249.

Wesleyans: *see* Methodists.

West, Tuffen, engraver and lithographer: illustrates PHG's series on Rotifera, 562; and natural history works by Beale, Jones, Lankester, Wood, qq.v., 562 fn.155; confusion about the authorship of Lankester's *Half-Hours with the Microscope*, 346 fn.90.

Westwood, John Obadiah, entomologist: 'pre-eminent' entomological systematist, 546 and fn.55; PHG meets at British Museum, 10 fn.14; 11; 82 fn.270; 121; 507; critic of Darwin, 12 and fn.23; 547 fns.56-7; 548; Darwin incorrectly attributes the *Athenaeum's* negative review of *Origin* to, 547 and fn.56; admires work of T.R. Peale, 82 fn.270; PHG owns books by, 544 fn.42; PHG writes about his research to, 546–8; writes for *Academy*, 228 fn.389; insect artistry of, compared to PHG, 582; correspondence with PHG: 10 fn.14; 11 fn.17.

Weymouth: in 1853 (Apr.–Dec.), PHG dredging and trawling for marine animals at, 200; using notes from, begins what becomes *Aquarium* (1854), 202; in 1855 (Mar.-May), at, 212-13; Kingsley mistakenly thinks Marine Natural History classes will be located at, 213 fn.290.

White, Adam, naturalist: from 1839, PHG knows, 12; in 1843, PHG visits at Insect Room, British Museum, 11; 12 fn.21; 99; 121; adherent to natural theology tradition, 12; plenary inspiration of Scripture, 12 and fn.21; opposes Darwin, 12 and fn.23; writes for *Excelsior* (monthly), 12 fn.20; on initiative of (with Doubleday), in 1849 PHG is elected A.L.S., 173 and fn.68; exhibits PHG's drawings at Linnean, 185 fn.139; cited: 453.

White, Gilbert, naturalist: PHG reproduces his motto in *Canadian Naturalist*, 75; reviewers compare that book, and *Birds of Jamaica*, to White's classic *Natural History of Selborne*, 100 fn.16; 151; 163; ed. of *Selborne* by T. Bell, q.v., reviewed by EWG, 582 fn.291.

Whymper, Josiah Wood, wood-engraver: spelled 'Whimper' before 1840, illustrations by, appear in PHG's early books (such as *Ocean*; *Glimpses of the Wonderful*), 121; corresponds with PHG while in Jamaica, 122 fn.121.

Wigram, George Vicesimus, early Brethren leader: Darby stalwart, helps early meeting at Plymouth prosper, 116; mocked, 9 fn.10; apparently initiates Brethren meeting at Rawstorne Street around 1833, 117; 118 fn.95; apparently meets PHG at Rawstorne St. in 1843, 120; 338 fn.37; connected with Coleman of Jamaica, 130 fn.168; sends him money from at least 1842, 131 fn.179; dissatisfaction with Coleman and Jamaica Brethren, including PHG, at least in part over 'non-eternity system', 132 and fn.188; 153-4; sends money to Tydeman, 134; in Jamaica in 1840s, competing Brethren outlooks of Darby-Wigram *vs.* Berger-Pearse-PHG, 153; 161; an acquaintance of Epps, 270.

Winn, James Michell, physician:
  critic of British Association, 385; paper read at
  Victoria Institute, 385 fn.294.
Wollaston, Thomas Vernon, entomologist:
  critic of Darwin, 548; member, Victoria Institute,
  326 fn.300.
Wood, John George, clergyman naturalist:
  popular natural history writer, 222; said to have
  authored over 70 books (not all scientific), 222
  and fn.348; exaggerated natural history claims for,
  228-9; 229 fns.395-6; member, Victoria Institute,
  326 fn.300; dies destitute, 222 and fn.352;
  ILLUSTRATIONS: modest talent as an illustrator, 236
  and fn.443; his Common Objects of the Sea Shore
  (1857) illustrated by Sowerby, 228; his Common
  Objects of the Microscope (1861) illustrated by T.
  West, 562 fn.155; 346;
  LECTURING: said to have lectured widely, 236; in
  1856, lectures on insects, 234 fn.427; in 1879, low
  pay as a lecturer, 235 and fn.432;
  PHG AND: comparison of UK selling price of PHG
  books, to books by, 221; comparison of USA selling price of PHG book, to book by, 220 fn.336;
  comparison of PHG book income, to book income
  of, 222; comparison of print run of PHG books, to
  book by, 224 and fn.365; exaggerated print run
  claims for, 224 fn.365.
Wright, Edward Perceval, zoologist:
  founder, editor, Natural History Review, 300;
  312 fn.224; zoology lecturer, 312 fn.224; in 1860,
  solicits support of Huxley to expand NHR, 360
  fn.176; a friend, correspondent of PHG, 312 and
  fns.224-5; 456; EPW's research on sea anemones, 340 fns.51-2; NHR review of Omphalos may
  have been written by, 312; commends Actinologia
  Britannica, 348; critique of EWG's Life, 545 fn.51;
  differs with EWG on PHG's letter writing, 456.

X Club:
  'a sort of masonic Darwinian lodge' of 9 men at
  the Royal Society, founded in 1864 to promote
  Darwinism, prevents hearing for opponents, 358;
  361; 555; in control of Royal Society after 1870,
  358; in 1883, at the height of their influence, 555;
  'inordinate influence' of Huxley, Busk, 360-1;
  PHG AND: X Club obsession with Omphalos, 307;
  581; in 1858, action against PHG's 'Researches on
  the Poison-apparatus', 356-60; in 1880s: action
  against PHG's 'Clasping-organs', 555-7; snub of
  Hudson & Gosse, 581; other examples of X Club
  exclusionary influence similar to PHG: Bastian,
  362-3; 560 fn.142; Dawson, 363-5; Hudson, 580-
  1; members of, cited: Busk; J.D. Hooker; Huxley;
  Lubbock, qq.v.

Year at the Shore (1865), by PHG:
  initially serialised in Good Words (1864), 383;
  date when book published, 383 fn.288; coloured

plates in book of poor quality, 378; favourable
reviews of, 378 fn.270; reviewers' disappointment at concluding words in, 384 fn.290; hidden
meaning of, 404; comparison of concluding protest against science in magazine and book forms,
383-5; 384; comments on Darwin in, 321 and
fn.268; poison-apparatus in sea anemones exemplifies Divine ingenuity, 365; misinterpretation of
EWG's statement about Eliza Gosse's contribution
to, 203 fn.239; cited: 367 fn.210.
The Young Guardsman of the Alma ([<Feb. 1855]),
EG tract:
  publication date, estimated circulation, of, 259
  and fn.100; message of 'free gift', in, 127 fn.149;
  265 fn.148.
Youth's Magazine (monthly):
  evangelical miscellany, 29; in 1826, PHG's
  first publication (under pseudonym Φιλιπ
  [Greek=Philip]), 29 and fn.64.

Zoological Gardens, Regent's Park:
  in 1852, D.W. Mitchell apparently plans 'Fish
  House' (i.e., aquarium) at, 198; PHG promotes
  it, 199 and fn.213; he is hired to collect marine
  animals for, 198; dredging at Weymouth, PHG
  sends 4,000 marine animals to, 200; collecting
  terminated by dispute with Mitchell, 200; in May
  1853, site of world's first public aquarium, 198 and
  fn.211; 241; advertised, 200 fn.221; popularity
  of, 226; in 1853, George Cruikshank's illustration, 212; in 1854, visitors increase, aquarium is
  most 'attractive spot' at, 211; terminology used
  in 1853 in describing aquarium at, 208 fn.264;
  in 1856, Barnum works with Mitchell at, to bring
  aquarium to USA, 210-11; Lloyd situates Aquarium
  Warehouse near, 227; in 1857, EWG visits, 279.
Zoologist (monthly), edited by E. Newman:
  on leaving for Jamaica, PHG agrees to send articles to, 125; PHG forwards letters by W. Osburn
  to, for publication in, 154 fn.340; critique of
  Darwin's Origin in, echoes that of PHG, 322;
  view of Lepidopterists on Darwin's theory, 548
  and fn.68; 549 and fn.70; PHG cites Bates' articles
  in, 585; EWG's use of, 440 fn.8; obituary notice
  of PHG in, 389 fn.315;
  PHG ARTICLES IN: on Alabama: 85 and fn.292; 86
  fn.295; 122; Jamaica: 128 fns.153-4; 163 fn.13;
  Britain: 367 fn.210; 369 fn.215;
  REVIEWS OF PHG WORKS IN: PHG 'the most voluminous writer on Natural History', 215; Naturalist's
  Sojourn in Jamaica, 163 fn.13; Handbook to the
  Marine Aquarium, 213 fn.292; Manual of Marine
  Zoology (Part I and Part II), 214 fns.297, 301;
  Tenby, 215 and fn.305; Actinologia Britannica,
  349 and fn.113; 351 fn.124; Romance of Natural
  History: 1st series, 378 fn.266; 2nd series, 324
  fn.283; 378.

BAHN Publications

Series Editors

NEIL DICKSON
Editor, *Brethren Historical Review*

T. J. MARINELLO
Professor of Systematic and
Historical Theology,
Tyndale Theological Seminary,
the Netherlands

TIM GRASS
Senior Research Fellow,
Spurgeon's College, London

MARK STEVENSON
Professor of Bible and Theology,
Emmaus Bible College,
Dubuque, Iowa

Studies in Brethren History

Tim Grass, *Gathering to His Name: The Story of the Open Brethren in Britain and Ireland* (2012)

Tim Grass (ed.), *Witness in Many Lands: Leadership and Outreach among the Brethren* (2013)

Neil T. R. Dickson and T. J. Marinello (eds.), *The Brethren and Mission: Essays in Honour of Timothy C. F. Stunt* (2016)

Neil Dickson and T. J. Marinello (eds.), *Bible and Theology in the Brethren* (2018)

Neil Dickson and T. J. Marinello (eds.), *The Brethren and the Church* (2020)

Tim Grass, *Brethren and their Buildings* (2021)

Tim Grass and T. J. Marinello (eds.), *Brethren and the Last Things* (forthcoming)

Studies in Brethren History *subsidia*

Pauline Summerton, *Fishers of Men: The missionary influence of an extended family in Central Africa* (2003)

Óli Jacobsen, *Daniel J. Danielsen: Missionary Campaigns and Atrocity Photographs* (2014)

Gerald T. West, *From Friends to Brethren: The Howards of Tottenham— Quakers, Brethren, and Evangelicals* (2016)

Ian Burness, *From Glasgow to Garenganze: Frederick Stanley Arnot and Nineteenth-Century African Mission* (2017)

Tim Grass, *Ernest and May Trenchard: Evangelical Mission in Franco's Spain* (2019)

Neil Summerton, *Charisma and Organization: Unresolved Tensions in the Brethren* (2021)

Ken Newton, *'I will build my Church': The Kollegal Mission 1886–1995* (2021)

Neil Summerton, *'I thanked the Lord, and asked for more': George Müller's Life and Work* (2022)

Douglas Wertheimer, *Philip Henry Gosse: A Biography* (2024)